Dare To Prepare!
4th Edition

Researched and Written by

Holly Drennan Deyo

Pre-Press and Cover by

Stan Deyo

Publishers: Deyo Enterprises LLC

Pueblo West, Colorado, The United States of America

Dare To Prepare!

Copyright © Holly Deyo and Stan Deyo 2011
Fourth Edition 2011

ISBN: 978-0-9727688-9-4

Publishers: Deyo Enterprises LLC
P.O. Box 7711, Pueblo West, Colorado, USA 81007

Web Sites:
http://standeyo.com/
http://daretoprepare.com/
http://standeyo.com/News_Files/Hollys.html

Published Works:
Dare To Prepare (4th Edition)
Prudent Places USA 3rd Edition (CD)
Garden Gold: Growing Maximum Veggies With Minimum Effort
The Cosmic Conspiracy – Final Edition 2010
The Vindicator Scrolls
UFOs Are Here (DVD)
The Gemstone Scrolls (parts 1 and 2)

Email Addresses:
holly@standeyo.com   standeyo@standeyo.com

Disclaimer:
No remuneration in any form has been received regarding products or companies cited in this book.

Reproduction Notice:
All rights reserved. No part of this book may be reprinted or reproduced or utilized in any form or by any electronic, mechanical or other means, now known or hereafter invented, including photocopying and recording, or in any information storage or retrieval system, without the permission in writing from the copyright-holder, excepting brief quotes used in connection with reviews written specially for inclusion in a magazine or newspaper.

-Thank you.

Acknowledgments

> **Dedicated in loving memory to Vera and Leo Drennan**
> **...who taught by example and loved unconditionally...**

Rarely do we accomplish a task without the help of those around us. With appreciation to:

Karen Ashcraft: Coordinator, Department of Emergency Management, Pueblo, Colorado
Australian Bureau of Meteorology
Australian Geological Survey Organization
Australian SAS
David Bassett, US Department of Energy
Robert Byrnes
Peter Caffell
Jerry Christensen
Danise Codekas
Al and Karen Collier
Dr. Jim Cummings, US Naval FNMOC
Al Durtschi, Walton Feed
EMA, Emergency Management of Australia
Erik (weapons expert)
FEMA (Federal Emergency Management Agency)
Lilian Gilmour
Alan Hagan
Keith Hendricks
Ian (law enforcement, Perth, Australia)
Julie King
Byron Kirkwood, B & A Products
Jeff Lewis
Karen Lyster
Dave Martin, Martronics
Kathy Moore
Merle Norman Cosmetics
John and Katie Miller
National Oceanic and Atmospheric Administration
National Weather Service
Turner Patton
Steve Quayle
Richard (weapons expert)
Alan Schroeder, US Dept. of Energy
Doug Smith
Frugal Squirrel
Ralph Swisher; FEMA, Community & Family Preparedness Program Manager, State Emergency Services
Lisa Thiesse
USGS, United States Geological Survey
Terry (New Zealand)
Ton Verbant, and Diggers
United States Bureau of Meteorology

Special Thanks To Stan Deyo, Husband And Partner In Life.
Zeh Dodi v'Zeh Rei

Table of Contents

- ACKNOWLEDGMENTS ... 3
- TABLE OF CONTENTS ... 4
- PREFACE ... 19
- **INTRODUCTION: WHY PREPARE?** ... 28
  - THOSE WHO DO ... AND THE REST OF THE PLANET ... 28
  - THIS ISN'T YOUR MAMA'S WORLD ... 28
  - ALL DISASTERS GREAT AND SMALL ... 29
  - CHANGE – THE ONE CONSTANT ... 31
- **CHAPTER 1: GETTING STARTED** ... 32
  - WHY DID THE PREP BUG BITE? ... 32
  - HOW TO PLAN FOR AN EMERGENCY ... 32
    - *ASSESSING YOUR OPTIONS* ... 32
    - *THINGS TO CONSIDER:* ... 33
    - *IF YOU PLAN TO LEAVE THE CITY* ... 33
    - *IF YOU PLAN TO STAY WHERE YOU ARE* ... 34
  - MAIN PACKS OR EMERGENCY PACKS ... 34
    - *CHOOSING THE RIGHT PACK* ... 35
    - *CLOTHING* ... 35
    - *MISCELLANEOUS CLOTHING ITEMS* ... 35
    - *EATING UTENSILS, PLATE AND BOWL* ... 36
  - BEDDING, SLEEPING BAGS OR SWAGS ... 36
  - THE MEDICINE KIT OR FIRST AID KIT ... 37
    - *COMMUNICATON* ... 38
    - *MONEY* ... 38
  - KITCHEN ... 38
    - *WATER* ... 39
    - *FOOD* ... 40
  - TOOL BELT ... 41
  - ADDITIONAL ITEMS TO CONSIDER ... 41
    - *CARRY CART* ... 41
    - *ROPE* ... 41
    - *HAMMOCK OR CAMP BED* ... 42
    - *TENTS* ... 42
    - *RAFT AND/OR BOAT* ... 42
  - LITTLE THINGS HELP ... 42
  - COMMON SENSE ... 42
- **CHAPTER 2: URBAN SURVIVAL – ARE YOU READY?** ... 43
  - TEST YOUR PREPAREDNESS ... 43
- **CHAPTER 3: STORING SHORT TERM** ... 46
  - 72-HOUR PREPAREDNESS ... 46
  - GETTING DOWN TO THE NUTS AND BOLTS – LISTS OF EVERYTHING ... 46
  - TIPS FOR ALL OF THE ABOVE ... 51
  - BEFORE YOU SAY, "TOO HARD"... ... 52
  - MONEY SAVERS ... 52
- **CHAPTER 4: EMERGENCY WATER TREATMENT** ... 53
  - LIQUID GOLD ... 53
  - MAKING WATER POTABLE (DRINKABLE) ... 53
  - WATER PURIFICATION – BOILING ... 53
  - WATER PURIFICATION – CHEMICAL TREATMENT ... 53
    - *1. CHLORINE* ... 53
    - *2. IODINE* ... 54
    - *3. PURIFICATION TABLETS* ... 56
    - *4. MICROPUR MP1 (CHLORINE DIOXIDE)* ... 56
    - *5. STABILIZED OXYGEN* ... 56
    - *6. HYDROGEN PEROXIDE* ... 57
  - WATER PURIFICATION – MECHANICAL FILTRATION ... 57
    - *WATER PURIFIERS AND WATER FILTERS – WHAT'S THE DIF?* ... 57
    - *WHICH ONE?* ... 57
  - BLACK BERKEY PURIFYING ELEMENTS ... 60
    - *SHELF LIFE* ... 60
    - *CLEANING YOUR BLACK BERKEYS* ... 61
    - *BUILD YOUR OWN MICROFILTER* ... 62
  - ALTERNATE PURIFYING METHODS ... 62
    - *SILVER* ... 62

WINE-TREATED WATER 62

CHAPTER 5: WATER TREATMENT ON A BIG SCALE 64
- *CHLORINE-WATER TERMINOLOGY* 64
- *WHAT ARE FREE RESIDUALS?* 64
- *CHLORINE TEST KITS* 64
- *PH TEST KITS* 64

TYPES OF CHLORINE 64
- *LIQUID (HOUSEHOLD BLEACH)* 64
- *DRY CHLORINE* 65

CHLORINATING WATER OUTSIDE 65
- *RAIN TANKS* 65
- *WELLS* 65
- *DISINFECTING BORED OR DUG WELLS* 65
- *DISINFECTING DRILLED WELLS* 66

SLOW SAND FILTERS 67
- *CONSTRUCTION* 67

ACTIVATED CHARCOAL FILTER 67

REVERSE OSMOSIS 68
- *HOW IT WORKS* 68
- *PROS AND CONS* 68

TREATMENTS REQUIRING ELECTRICITY 69
- *OZONE* 69
- *UV LIGHT* 69

DISTILLATION 71
- *SOLAR STILLS* 71

POTASSIUM PERMANGANATE 72

WHAT ARE WE DOING? 72
- *RAIN WATER* 72

TEST YOUR WATER 72

CHAPTER 6: WATER COLLECTION AND STORAGE 73

STORING WATER 73
- *DRUMS* 73
- *FOUR AND FIVE GALLON CONTAINERS* 73
- *SOFT DRINK BOTTLES* 73

CONTAINER SOURCES 74
- *REMOVING STUBBORN SCENTS* 74

HOW LONG WILL STORED WATER KEEP? 74

FINDING HIDDEN WATER IN YOUR HOME 74
- *PLUMBING* 74

WATER COLLECTION 75
- *WELLS* 75
- *SPRINGS* 75
- *SURFACE WATER* 75
- *DAMS AND RESERVOIRS* 75
- *RAIN WATER CATCHMENT (FREE WATER!)* 77
- *WHAT WOULD I NEED?* 79
- *ACCESSING CISTERN WATER* 81
- *WATER TREATMENT* 81
- *HOW MUCH RAIN CAN I CATCH?* 82
- *HOW MUCH WATER DO YOU USE?* 83
- *OUTSIDE WATER REQUIREMENTS* 84

SWIMMING POOL WATER 84

CHAPTER 7: FINDING SURVIVAL WATER 85
- *TERRAIN* 86
- *VEGETATION* 86

DESERT WATER 86
- *DESERT TRAVEL HINTS* 88

WHERE TO FIND WATER IN ROCKY SOIL 88
- *LAVA, SANDSTONE, GRANITE* 88
- *IN SOFT SOIL* 88
- *ON MOUNTAINS* 88
- *OTHER SOURCES OF SUPPLY* 88

INSECTS, BIRDS AND ANIMALS AS WATER INDICATORS 89
- *INSECTS* 89
- *BIRDS* 89
- *ANIMALS* 89

VEGETABLE SOURCES 89
- *POISONOUS PLANTS* 90
- *ARID AREAS* 90
- *DEW* 90

ON THE SEA COAST 90

- *BEACH OR SAND WELLS* 91
- *MOISTURE FROM FISH* 91
- *CONDENSING SALT WATER* 91
- MOISTURE CONDENSATION IN ARID AREAS 91
  - *METHOD 1: BUSH STILL* 91
  - *METHOD 2: WATER* 92
  - *TRANSPIRATION BAG* 92
- OTHER WAYS TO FIND WATER 92

CHAPTER 8: FOOD – WHAT AND HOW MUCH TO STORE 94
- SIX REASONS TO HAVE A FOOD STORAGE PROGRAM 94
- HOW DO I PLAN MY FOOD SUPPLIES? 95
  - *NUTRTIONAL GUIDELINES* 95
- NEW FOOD PYRAMID SPECIFICS 96
- DEYO FOOD STORAGE PLANNER 98
  - *HOW TO USE THE DEYO FOOD STORAGE PLANNER* 98
  - *EXPIRATION DATE* 99
- YOUR FOOD STORAGE PLANNER 100
- MAKING GOOD CHOICES 114
- OTHER FOOD STORAGE PROGRAMS 114
  - *FREEZE-DRIED AND DEHYDRATED FOODS* 116
  - *MORMON FOOD GUIDELINES* 116
- WHICH PROGRAM SHOULD I PICK? 119
- FOOD STORAGE – HOW WE DID IT 119
  - *SPECIFICS* 120
- MAKE WHOLE MILK FROM POWDERED MILK 120
- MAKING YEAST 121
  - *EVERLASTING YEAST* 121
  - *SOURDOUGH STARTER #1* 121
  - *SOURDOUGH STARTER #2* 121
  - *DRIED HOPS YEAST* 121
  - *YEAST NOTES* 121

CHAPTER 9: PREPARING THE PANTRY AND SAVING $$ 122
- ORGANIZATION 122
- ABOUT THAT FOOD STORAGE ROOM... 123
  - *HANTAVIRUS WARNING* 123
- TIPS TO SAVE MONEY 124
  - *COUPONS* 124
  - *SALES* 124
  - *SHAREHOLDER CARDS* 125
  - *PREFERRED CUSTOMER CARDS* 125
  - *AT THE STORE – DESIGNED TO DELAY* 125
  - *BULK WAREHOUSE* 125
  - *CO-OP PURCHASING* 125

CHAPTER 10: TAKING CARE OF YOUR INVESTMENT 126
- SIX EASY STEPS 126
  - *TIME – IT KEEPS ON TICKIN'* 126
  - *TEMPERATURE: OR TOO HOT TO HANDLE* 126
  - *HUMIDITY: YOU'RE ALL WET* 127
  - *OXYGEN? KISS IT GOODBYE!* 127
  - *LIGHT: TURN IT OFF!* 127
  - *PESTS: WHAT'S WIGGLING?* 128
  - *SHAKE, RATTLE AND ROLL* 129
  - *HOT HEADS* 129
  - *COLD SHOULDERS* 129
  - *GETTING EARTHY* 129
- FOOD STORAGE CONTAINERS 130
  - *CONTAINER SIZE* 130
- USING MYLAR BAGS 130
- HOW TO PACK CONTAINERS 131
  - *VACUUM PACK METHOD* 131
  - *DRY ICE METHOD* 131
  - *NITROGEN FLUSH METHOD* 132
  - *OXYGEN ABSORBERS – GETTING RID OF AIR* 133
- DESICCANTS – GETTING RID OF MOISTURE 134
  - *HOW DO THEY WORK?* 134
  - *TO USE DESICCANTS* 135
  - *HOW TO REGENERATE OLD DESICCANTS* 135
  - *PACKING WITH ASH* 136
- NO SPACE? BE CREATIVE! 137
  - *WHAT IF I DON'T WANT ALL THIS HASSLE – CAN I STILL PREPARE?* 137

CHAPTER 11: SHELF LIVES 138
TIPS 138
CUPBOARD STORAGE CHARTS 139
REFRIGERATOR STORAGE CHARTS 144
FREEZER STORAGE CHARTS 148

CHAPTER 12: UNRAVELING DATING CODES 152
DATING REQUIREMENTS 152
TYPES OF FOOD DATING 152
    SNEAKY DATING VS OPEN DATING 152
    NEW NEWS IS OLD NEWS 153
    INFORMATION FORT KNOX 153
    MOVE IT OR LOSE IT 153
UNDERSTANDING DATING METHODS 153
COMPANY AND PRODUCT "SECRETS" 154

CHAPTER 13: GENERAL SUPPLIES 182
SPECIFIC LISTS 182
    CAMPING GEAR 182
    CARRYING ITEMS 183
    CLOTHING 183
    COMMUNICATION ITEMS 183
    FUEL AND LIGHTING 184
    PERSONAL HYGIENE 184
    COOKING ITEMS 185
    INFANT SUPPLIES 186
    SENIOR CARE 186
    PERSONAL HYGIENE 186
    LATRINE AND GENERAL HYGIENE 187
    MISCELLANEOUS 187
    TOOLS AND REPAIR ITEMS 188
    VEHICLE REPAIR 189
    GARDEN ITEMS 190

CHAPTER 14: FIRST AID SUPPLIES 191
    CAR KIT CASE 192
    ANTIBIOTICS 192
SPECIFIC LISTS 192
    FIRST AID SUPPLIES 192
    FIRST AID MEDICATIONS 194

CHAPTER 15: THE REAL SHELF LIFE OF MEDICATIONS 196
    FEED THE PIG 196
    THE TRUTH ABOUT SHELF LIVES 196
    HERE'S THE RUB 199

CHAPTER 16: SHELF LIVES OF NON-FOODS 200
CLEANING PRODUCTS 200
HANDYMAN ITEMS 201
MEDICATIONS/HEALTH ITEMS 202
MISCELLANEOUS 202
PERSONAL CARE PRODUCTS 203
    ADDITIONAL NOTES: 204
PET SUPPLIES 205

CHAPTER 17: BUILD BASIC UNDERGROUND STORAGE 206
U.S. INSTRUCTIONS 207
    U.S. MATERIALS LIST 207
METRIC INSTRUCTIONS 207
    MATERIALS LIST – AUSTRALIA 208

CHAPTER 18: BUILD A HAND PUMP 209
    PUMP ASSEMBLY NOTES AND INSTRUCTIONS 209
    DEPTH USE 210
    HAND PUMP PARTS LIST 211

CHAPTER 19: MAKING COLLOIDAL SILVER 212
MAKING YOUR OWN GENERATOR 212
    OPTION 1 212
    MAKING COLLOIDAL SILVER USING OPTION 1 212
    OPTION 2 213
BUYING COLLOIDAL SILVER PRODUCTS 214
    SOME C.S. IS B.S. 214
    BUYING COLLOIDAL SILVER 215

CHAPTER 20: SOAPMAKING 216
SOAPMAKING 216
    SOAP VS DETERGENTS 216

- SAFETY MEASURES FOR USING LYE ... 217
- SUPPLIES LIST ... 217
- SOAPMAKING INSTRUCTIONS ... 218
- ADDITIVES ... 219
  - *CHOICES FOR VEGETABLE OILS* ... 220
  - *CHOICES FOR FATS* ... 220
  - *RENDERING 5 POUNDS (2.27 KG) BEEF FAT* ... 221
- SLICING SOAP INTO BARS ... 221
- MAKING YOUR OWN RECIPES ... 221
  - *SODIUM HYDROXIDE (NAOH)* ... 222
  - *USING THE SODIUM HYDROXIDE (NAOH) SAP CHART* ... 223
  - *POTASSIUM HYDROXIDE (KOH)* ... 224
  - *USING THE POTASSIUM HYDROXIDE (KOH) SAP CHART* ... 225
- LUXURIOUS HAND-MILLED SOAP ... 226
  - *FINAL TIPS* ... 226
- WHAT ELSE CAN I ADD? ... 227
  - *SAFETY PRECAUTIONS FOR USING ESSENTIAL OILS AND FRAGRANCE OILS* ... 227
  - *WITHSTANDING THE TEST OF HEAT AND TIME!* ... 228
  - *OTHER TRADITIONAL SOAP FRAGRANCES* ... 228
- FIXATIVES, WHEN TO USE THEM ... 228
  - *ADDITIVES AND THEIR BENEFITS* ... 228
  - *WHEN ARE ESSENTIAL OILS ADDED?* ... 228
  - *HOW MUCH SCENT IS NEEDED?* ... 229
- COLORING YOUR SOAP ... 229
- MOLDS ... 230
- MAKING SOAP IN A BLENDER ... 232
- SOAP RECIPES ... 232
  - *GENERAL PURPOSE SOAP* ... 234
  - *GOAT MILK SOAP* ... 234
  - *LAUNDRY SOAP* ... 235
  - *LIQUID SOAP* ... 236
  - *SOAP BALLS* ... 236
  - *SHAMPOO* ... 236
- HOW TO MAKE "LYE WATER" ... 237
  - *INGREDIENTS* ... 237
  - *BAKING SODA TEST* ... 237
  - *MAKING "LYE WATER"* ... 237
  - *SOAPMAKING – TIPS AND TROUBLESHOOTING* ... 238

CHAPTER 21: CANDLEMAKING ... 240
- EQUIPMENT ... 240
- SAFETY TIPS ... 240
  - *RECORDKEEPING* ... 241
- WAX ... 241
  - *PARAFFIN* ... 241
  - *BEESWAX* ... 241
  - *HOW MUCH?* ... 241
- WICKS ... 242
  - *PICKING THE WICK TYPE* ... 242
  - *PICKING THE WICK SIZE* ... 242
- ADDITIVES ... 243
  - *STEARIC ACID (STEARINE)* ... 243
  - *LUSTER AND TRANSLUCENT CRYSTALS* ... 243
  - *VYBAR* ... 243
  - *COLORANTS* ... 243
  - *SCENT* ... 244
  - *MOLDS* ... 245
- HOW TO MAKE CANDLES ... 246
  - *CLEAN UP* ... 246
  - *MEASURING ADDITIVES* ... 247
- BASIC RECIPES ... 247
  - *VOTIVE CANDLES* ... 247
  - *SCENTED CANDLES* ... 247
  - *WATER BALLOON CANDLES* ... 247
- TIPS AND TROUBLESHOOTING ... 248
  - *BURNING TIPS* ... 248

CHAPTER 22: FIRE BUILDING ... 251
- FUELS ... 252
  - *BURNABLES* ... 252
  - *BURNING QUALITIES OF DIFFERENT WOODS* ... 252
- TEEPEE FIRE ... 253
- PYRAMID FIRE ... 253

- FIRE STARTING ERRORS 254
- CAMPFIRE TIPS 254
- FIRESTARTERS 254
  - *COMMERCIAL PRODUCTS* 254
  - *SINGLE-HAND FIRESTARTERS* 255
  - *MATCH OVERVIEW* 256
- MAKING YOUR OWN FIRESTARTERS 257
  - *WOOD KNOTS* 257
  - *LINT-FILLED CONTAINERS* 257
  - *PINE CONES WITH PARAFFIN – VERSION 1* 257
  - *PINE CONES WITH PARAFFIN – VERSION 2* 257
  - *CANDLE CUPS – VERSION 1* 258
  - *CANDLE CUPS – VERSION 2* 258
  - *CARDBOARD AND SCRAP WOOD* 258
  - *IT'S IN THE BAG!* 258
  - *CANDLE KISSES* 258
  - *COTTON "GOO" BALLS* 259
  - *LOOKING UP* 259
  - *OLD NEWS* 259
  - *CLOSE SHAVE* 259
- STARTING FIRE WITH A BATTERY 259

CHAPTER 23: MAKING CHARCOAL 260
- METHOD 1 260
- METHOD 2 260
- METHOD 3 261
- ACTIVATED CHARCOAL 261

CHAPTER 24: MAKING BIODIESEL FUEL 262
- BIODIESEL 262
- VEGETABLE OIL / KEROSENE MIX 262
- VEGETABLE OIL 262
- FUEL COMPARISON 263
  - *COMPARISON OF DIFFERENT VEGETABLE OIL FUEL METHODS* 263
- HOW TO MAKE BIODIESEL 263
  - *NEW VEGETABLE OIL* 263
  - *USED VEGETABLE OIL* 263

CHAPTER 25: KEEPING FOOD SAFE IN AN EMERGENCY 265
- WHAT TO KEEP AND WHAT TO TOSS – REFRIGERATOR FOODS 267
- WHAT TO KEEP AND WHAT TO TOSS – FROZEN FOODS 268

CHAPTER 26: COMPOSTING 269
- COMPOSTING BASICS 270
  - *WHAT GOES INTO COMPOST* 270
- 5 EASY STEPS FOR COMPOSTING 271
- NO BROWNS? – NO WORRIES, GO WITH WORMS 271
  - *FIVE EASY STEPS TO WORM COMPOSTING* 271
  - *BE A GRACIOUS HOST* 272
  - *COLLECTING THE REWARDS* 272
  - *USING WORM COMPOST* 272
  - *PREVENTING UNINVITED 4-LEGGED GUESTS* 272
  - *GIVING PESTS THE HEAVE-HO!* 273
  - *PREVENTING UNINVITED WINGED GUESTS* 273
  - *COMPOSTING "RECIPES"* 273
  - *TAKE ITS TEMPERATURE* 273
- IS IT COMPOST YET? 274
  - *WHERE TO USE COMPOST* 274

CHAPTER 27: GROWING FOOD 275
- GARDEN OPTIONS 275
  - *IN THE BEGINNING, THERE WAS…THE SEED* 275
  - *GETTING TO THE ROOT OF IT* 275
- WHAT'S AN HEIRLOOM SEED? 275
  - *THE TERMINATOR* 276
- THE ART OF SEED SAVING 276
  - *FIRST FRUITS* 276
  - *WHEN TO COLLECT SEEDS* 276
  - *CLEANING* 277
  - *DRYING* 277
- STORING SEEDS 277
- HOW LONG WILL SEEDS STAY VIABLE? 277
  - *SHELF LIFE OF STORED VEGETABLE SEEDS* 278
  - *SHELF LIFE OF STORED HERB SEEDS* 280

CHAPTER 28: DEHYDRATING FOODS 281

DEHYDRATING METHODS COMPARED 281
   DRYING *281*
WHAT TO LOOK FOR IN A DEHYDRATOR 282
NATURE'S CANDY – FRUIT 282
   PREPARING THE FRUIT.. *282*
   AFTER DEHYDRATING *285*
FRUIT LEATHER 285
   LEATHERS FROM FRESH FRUIT *286*
   LEATHERS FROM CANNED OR FROZEN FRUIT *286*
   READY, AIM, POUR!.. *286*
   ADDING PIZZAZ!... *286*
DRYING VEGETABLES 287
   PREPARING THE VEGETABLES *287*
HANG 'EM! HANG 'EM HIGH – CHILIES THAT IS 289
   MAKE YOUR OWN RISTRA *289*
   OTHER DRYING METHODS *291*
MAKING JERKY 292
   PREPARING MINCED MEAT JERKY IN A PRESS *292*
   PREPARING MINCED MEAT FOR JERKY WORKS *292*
   PREPARING MINCED MEAT JERKY WITH A ROLLING PIN *293*
   USING MEAT STRIPS FOR JERKY... *293*
   PREPARING MEAT STRIPS FOR JERKY *294*
JERKY RECIPES 294
IS IT DRY YET? 296
   PERCENT SOLIDS IN RAW FRUIT AND VEGETABLES *296*
STORING DRIED FOODS 297
   DRYING SEEDS, POPCORN AND NUTS *297*
USING DRIED FRUITS 297
   REHYDRATING DRIED FOOD.. *298*
USING DRIED VEGETABLES 298
   VEGETABLE CHIPS.. *298*
   VEGETABLES FLAKES AND POWDERS *298*
   DRYING VEGETABLE LEATHERS *299*

CHAPTER 29: GENERATORS...**300**
   LIGHTS OUT... *301*
   A MATTER OF MONEY AND RISK *302*
WHEN THE UNTHINKABLE HAPPENS: POWER GRID COLLAPSE 304
   2003 BLACKOUT NOT A FIRST... *304*
WHAT'S FOR DINNER 304
DIESEL, GAS (PETROL) OR TRIFUEL? 305
FIGURING WHAT SIZE GENERATOR TO BUY 306
   POWER METER... *306*
   GENERATOR WATTAGE REQUIREMENTS – HOUSEHOLD... *307*
   (AMPS X VOLTS = WATTS) *307*
   GENERATOR WATTAGE REQUIREMENTS – TOOLS... *308*
   GENERATOR WATTAGE REQUIREMENTS – FARM... *309*
   GENERATOR WATTAGE REQUIREMENTS – INDUSTRIAL MOTORS *309*
RUNNING A COMPUTER FROM A GENERATOR 310
RUNNING A MOTOR FROM A GENERATOR... 310
   RUNNING MOTORS FROM A GENERATOR *310*
ONCE YOU GET THE GENERATOR HOME... 310
   TIPS... *310*
CONNECTING IT: TRANSFER SWITCH 311
   MANUAL VS. AUTOMATIC.. *311*
PLAN B: CONNECTING IT WITH EXTENSION CORDS 312
   WHICH GAUGE EXTENTION CORD TO USE *312*
CARE AND MAINTENANCE 313
   GAS (PETROL)... *313*
   DIESEL.. *313*
   FOR BOTH... *313*
FEATURES TO CONSIDER 314
THEFT PREVENTION 314

CHAPTER 30: FUEL **316**
WHY SHOULD WE STORE FUEL?... 316
   KEEP IT CLEAN *316*
STORING FUEL 316
   STORING FUEL UNDERGROUND *317*
CONTAINERS 317
   FUEL STORAGE LOCATIONS... *317*
FUEL DRUMS... 318

  DRUM SOURCES *318*
INDISPENSABLE HELPERS 318
BUILD A DRUM DOLLY 319
  MATERIALS NEEDED FOR A DRUM DOLLY *319*
GETTING THE FUEL OUT 320
KEEPING FUEL FROM DEGRADING 321
  FUEL STABILIZERS *321*

CHAPTER 31: COOKING WITHOUT POWER 322

THE BURNING QUESTION...FUELS 322
  FUEL CHOICES *322*
CHOICES FOR COOKING 325
INDOOR COOKING 325
  FONDUE POT AND CHAFFING DISHES *325*
STOVES 326
  PORTA-CHEF STOVE *326*
  ALPACA KEROSENE COOKER *326*
  GAS TABLE STOVES – KEROSENE 1, 2 & 3 BURNERS *326*
  PYROMID *327*
BACKPACK STOVES 327
  MSR DRAGONFLY *328*
  PRIMUS OMNI FUEL *328*
  OPTIMUS NOVA MULTI-FUEL STOVE *329*
  COLEMAN EXPONENT XPEDITION *329*
  BRITELYT – PETROMAX *329*
  TRANGIA *330*
CAMP STOVES 330
  PROPANE TANKS AND ACCESSORIES *331*
  EXTENSION POLES *332*
MARINE BBQ GRILLS 332
CAMP OVENS 333
  COLEMAN INSTASTART CAMP OVEN *333*
BBQ GRILLS 334
  CHARCOAL CHIMNEY *334*
  OPEN FIRE HELPERS *334*
DUTCH OR CAMP OVENS 336
  WHAT TO LOOK FOR IN A DUTCH OVEN *337*
  WHAT SIZE TO BUY? *337*
  SEASONING THE DUTCH OVEN *337*
  NO-SEASON DUTCH OVENS *338*
  CARE AND CLEANING DUTCH OVENS *338*
  BUYING A USED DUTCH OVEN *339*
  DUTCH OVEN COOKING ESSENTIALS *339*
  USING CHARCOAL *339*
  DUTCH OVEN RECIPES *340*
THE VOLCANO! 343
COBB GRILL 344

CHAPTER 32: SOLAR COOKING 345

BOX OVEN COOKING 345
  1. OPEN TOP BOX OVEN *345*
  2. COPY PAPER BOX OVEN *345*
  3. BOX OVEN *345*
SOLAR BOX COOKING 346
  OVEN SIZE *346*
  REFLECTOR *346*
  LID *346*
  TRAY *346*
  INSULATION *347*
  POTS *347*
  COOKING STRATEGY *347*
SOLAR COOKER #1 347
SOLAR COOKER #2: REFLECTIVE OPEN BOX 348
SOLAR COOKER #3: 349
THE "EASY LID" COOKER 349
  IMPROVING EFFICIENCY *351*
COMMERCIAL SOLAR OVENS 351
SOLAR COOKBOOKS 351
  GENERAL COOKING TIMES *352*

CHAPTER 33: COMMUNICATIONS 353

CONVENTIONAL PHONES 353
VOIP 353

- CELL PHONES 353
  - *CELL PHONES PLUSES* *353*
  - *DRAWBACKS* *354*
- SATELLITE PHONES 354
- TWO-WAY RADIOS 354
  - *TWO-WAY RADIOS PLUSES* *354*
  - *THEIR DRAWBACKS* *355*
  - *CHANNELS* *355*
  - *DECIDING WHAT TO GET* *355*
  - *POWER* *355*
  - *DISPLAY* *358*
  - *WEATHER AND WATERPROOFING* *358*
  - *"TOYS" WITH BENEFITS* *358*
- SHORTWAVE – HAM – AMATEUR – HIGH FREQUENCY (HF) RADIO 358
  - *HURRICANE KATRINA* *358*
  - *HAYMAN FIRE* *359*
  - *WHAT IS REQUIRED?* *360*
  - *GETTING STARTED* *360*
  - *BANDS* *360*
  - *FINDING STATIONS* *360*
  - *RECEPTION TIPS* *361*
- ANTENNAS 361
- STANDING WAVES AND SWR METERS 361
  - *HALF-WAVE RESONANT DIPOLE ANTENNA* *363*
  - *BUDDIPOLE ANTENNA* *363*
  - *EXPEDIENT ANTENNAS* *364*
  - *VERTICAL WIRE ANTENNA* *364*
  - *LONG WIRE DIRECTIONAL* *365*
  - *SLOPING V-ANTENNA* *365*
  - *VERTICAL HALF-RHOMBIC ANTENNA* *366*
  - *HANGING "SKYWIRES"* *366*
  - *ANTENNAS FOR APARTMENT RESIDENTS* *368*
  - *EMERGENCY REPAIR OF WHIP ANTENNAS* *368*
  - *POWER SUPPLIES* *368*
  - *STARTING OUT* *368*
- AUTO TUNERS 370
- EMERGENCY BROADCASTS 370
- EMERGENCY HURRICANE NETS 370

CHAPTER 34: THE WONDER OF CLOROX **373**
- GENERAL GUIDELINES 373
- FOOD APPLICATIONS 373
  - *FRUIT & VEGETABLE WASHING* *373*
  - *EGGS* *373*
  - *MEAT AND POULTRY PROCESSING WATER* *374*
- DISINFECTION AFTER DISASTER 374
  - *DROUGHTS* *374*
  - *FIRES* *375*
  - *FLOODS* *375*
  - *WATER MAIN BREAKS* *375*
- DISEASE PREVENTION 375
  - *HIV ON SURFACES* *375*
  - *BACTERIA* *375*
  - *TUBERCULOSIS* *376*
  - *VIRUSES* *376*
  - *FUNGUS* *377*
  - *CANDIDA* *377*
- LIVESTOCK AND ANIMALS 377
  - *POULTRY CARE* *377*
  - *LIVESTOCK, HORSES, PETS* *378*
  - *SWINE* *378*
- CLOROX BLEACH DILUTION TABLE 379

CHAPTER 35: MAKING CLEANING SUPPLIES **380**
- LIQUID CLEANER 380
- ALL-PURPOSE CLEANSER 380
- TOILET BOWL CLEANER 380
- TUB AND TILE CLEANER 380
- WINDOW AND GLASS CLEANER 381
- OVEN CLEANERS 381
- LAUNDRY PRODUCTS 381
- DISINFECTANTS 382
- POLISH 382

DRAIN CLEANERS AND DRAIN OPENERS	382
MOLD KILLER	383
MOLD PREVENTION	383
CHAPTER 36: SHOWER WITHOUT POWER	**384**
SINGING IN THE SHOWERLESS SHOWER	384
CAMP SHOWERS AND ALTERNATIVES	384
STEARNS AIR POWER SUNSHOWER	*384*
SOLAR HEATED WATER BAGS	*385*
STOVE-TOP WATER HEATER	*385*
ZODI HOT TAP CAMP SHOWER SYSTEM	*385*
ZODI HOTMAN EXTREME SC	*385*
COLEMAN HOT WATER ON DEMAND	*386*
SHOWER ENCLOSURES	386
CHAPTER 37: TRASHY TALK	**388**
SERVICE DISRUPTION: DISPOSING OF GARBAGE	388
FOOD	*388*
BURNABLES	*388*
NON-BURNABLES	*388*
PLAN AHEAD	*388*
TOILET TOPICS	389
USING EXISTING TOILETS	*389*
FOLDING TOILETS	*389*
BUCKETS	*389*
TOILET BUCKET ALTERNATIVES	391
RELIANCE HASSOCK TOILET	*391*
LIQUID WASTE COLLECTORS	392
LITTLE JOHN, LADY J	*392*
FRESHETTE	*392*
CHEMICAL TOILETS AND PORTA POTTIES	392
COMPOSTING TOILETS	393
COMPOST TOILET CONSIDERATIONS	*393*
BUILD A COMPOSTING TOILET	393
COMPOST DO'S AND DON'TS	*394*
PIT PRIVY OR YE OLE DUNNY	395
CHAPTER 38: PET PREPAREDNESS	**396**
PLACES FOR PETS TO STAY	396
LOST PET	*396*
EMERGENCY SUPPLIES	397
PET FIRST AID KIT	397
CONTAINMENT	*398*
IF YOU MUST LEAVE ANIMALS BEHIND. . .	400
EMERGENCY HELP FOR YOUR PET	402
BURNS	*403*
CHOKING	*403*
EAR MITES	*403*
FLEAS	*403*
FRACTURE	*403*
HEAT STROKE	*403*
INSECT STING	*403*
MOTION SICKNESS	*403*
OBJECT IN EYE	*403*
OVEREXPOSURE TO COLD	*404*
POISONING	*404*
SHOCK	*404*
SKUNK SPRAY	*404*
SNAKE BITE	*404*
TICKS AND LYME DISEASE	*404*
MINOR WOUND	*404*
SERIOUS WOUND	*404*
WARNING ON RAWHIDE CHEWS	404
DAY ONE	*405*
DAY TWO	*405*
DAY THREE	*405*
DAY FOUR	*405*
DAY EIGHT	*405*
THE CURE	*405*
DAY TEN	*406*
WHAT'S IN THE RAWHIDE (BESIDES HIDE)?	406
HIDDEN DANGERS	*406*
RAWHIDES, COW HOOVES AND PIGS' EARS	*406*
WHAT YOU CAN DO	407

CHAPTER 39: FIREARMS ... 408
PRIMER ON PERSONAL SECURITY ... 408
FIREARMS ORGANIZATIONS ... 411

CHAPTER 40: TERRORISM – VENTURING INTO THE UNTHINKABLE ... 412
THE WAKE-UP – WORLD TRADE CENTER 1993 ... 412
STRIKING THE HEARTLAND ... 413
U.S. EMBASSIES ... 413
USS COLE ... 413
911 ... 414
POST 911 ... 415
WHAT MIGHT WE EXPECT? ... 416

CHAPTER 41: BUYING A GAS MASK AND FILTERS ... 417
SO WHAT DO I BUY? – ADULTS ... 417
BE A WISE SHOPPER ... 418
NON-AMERICAN MASKS ... 418
CHILDREN AND INFANTS MASKS ... 418
PROPER FIT OF MASKS ... 419
MASK TIPS ... 419
GAS MASKS – TO BUY OR NOT TO BUY ... 419
    GAS MASK BUYING GUIDE ... *420*
GAS MASK BUYING GUIDE ... 421
MASKS AND FILTERS TO AVOID ... 422
"MASKS" FOR PETS ... 422
FILTERS ... 423
    GAS MASK-SPECIFIC FILTER CANISTERS ... *423*
    FILTER CANISTER COMPARISON ... *424*
    FILTER TIPS ... *424*
BEEF UP YOUR IMMUNE SYSTEM ... 424
IN CASE OF AN ATTACK ... 425
MASK AND FILTER SOURCES ... 425
PRICE GOUGING ... 425

CHAPTER 42: BIO-WARFARE DECONTAMINATION ... 426
MAKING DECONTAMINATION SOLUTION ... 426
    FURTHER DECONTAMINATION ... *426*
DECONTAMINATION, ASSUMING NO SEVERE EXPOSURE ... 427
    PROCEDURE IF WEARING FULL PROTECTIVE CLOTHING, HAT, GLOVES AND MASK ... *427*
BUILD A DECONTAMINATION SHOWER ... 427
    OVERVIEW ... *427*
DECONTAMINATING YOUR BODY ... 428
    SKIN ... *428*
    BATHING ... *428*
    HAIR ... *428*
    CLOTHING ... *428*
DECONTAMINATING EQUIPMENT ... 429
    USING HEAT AND RADIATION ... *429*
WATER PURIFICATION ... 429
    REVERSE OSMOSIS ... *430*
    ULTRAVIOLET ... *430*
    OZONATION ... *430*
FOOD ... 432
DECONTAMINATION FOR MOST LIKELY USED BW AGENTS ... 432
    ANTHRAX ... *432*
    BOTULISM – (TOXIN) ... *432*
    BRUCELLOSIS ... *432*
    CHOLERA ... *433*
    GLANDERS AND MELIOIDOSIS ... *433*
    PLAGUE ... *433*
    Q FEVER ... *433*
    RICIN – (TOXIN) ... *433*
    SMALLPOX ... *434*
    STAPHYLOCOCCAL ENTEROTOXIN B – (TOXIN) ... *434*
    TRICOTHECENE MYCOTOXICOSIS [T-2 MYCOTOXINS] – (TOXIN) ... *434*
    TULAREMIA ... *434*
    VENEZUELAN EQUINE ENCEPHALITIS ... *435*
    VIRAL HEMORRHAGIC FEVERS ... *435*

CHAPTER 43: SHELTERING IN PLACE ... 436
SEPARATING FACT FROM FICTION ... 436
DO IT SAFELY ... 437
MAKING THE SHELTER ... 437

LOOKING FOR LEAKS IN ALL THE RIGHT PLACES ... 438
A BREATH OF FRESH AIR ... 439
HOW MUCH OXYGEN DO WE NEED? ... 439
   HOW FILTERS WORK ... 440
HYGIENE ... 440
4-LEGGED KIDS ... 441
THE REST OF THE HOUSE ... 441
COMMERICAL SAFE ROOM ... 442
   RAINBOW TENT ... 442
   LAST THOUGHTS ... 443

CHAPTER 44: NUCLEAR EMERGENCIES – WHAT TO EXPECT ... **444**
CUBAN MISSILE CRISIS REVISITED ... 444
   AND NOW A WORD FROM OUR PRESIDENT ... 444
PRESENT DAY ... 445
   THE NEED TO PROTECT YOURSELF ... 445
   JUST WALK AROUND THE CORNER ... 446
   GONE IN SECONDS ... 446
FIRST, THE GOOD NEWS ... 446
WHAT IS THE EFFECT OF A NUCLEAR DETONATION? ... 447
WHAT TO EXPECT ... 448
   EFFECTS ... 448
FALLOUT MAPS ... 449
HOW BIG? ... 450
   BLAST FORCE ... 451
RADIATION TERMS: RADS, REMS, REINS AND ROENTGENS ... 452
RADIATION EXPOSURE: KEEP IT AS LOW AS POSSIBLE ... 452
   EFFECTS OF SHORT-TERM RADIATION EXPOSURE ... 452
ESCAPING THE RADIATION ... 453
   TRACKING FALLOUT ... 453
GETTING OUT OF DODGE ... 454

CHAPTER 45: SHELTER DURING NUCLEAR EMERGENCIES ... **455**
EXPEDIENT SHELTERING ... 455
   BE CREATIVE ... 456
   VENTILATION ... 456
   STOCKING THE SHELTER ... 456
SAMPLE EXPEDIENT SHELTER ... 458
WHERE HAVE ALL THE SHELTERS GONE? ... 458
LOCATING EXISTING SHELTER ... 459
   POSSIBLE FALLOUT SHELTERING SITES * ... 459
BUYING A FALLOUT SHELTER ... 460
BUILDING A FALLOUT SHELTER ... 460
SHELTER CONSTRUCTION PLANS ... 461
FEMA FALLOUT AND TORNADO SHELTER ... 462
   PLANS FOR THE SHELTER ... 462
   BUILDING THE SHELTER ... 462
   MODIFICATION OF PLANS ... 464
BURYING SHIPPING CONTAINERS ... 474
   SHIPPING CONTAINER HOUSE PLANS ... 477

CHAPTER 46: NUCLEAR AND RADIOLOGICAL ATTACK ... **481**
DIRTY BOMB ATTACK 'ALL BUT INEVITABLE' ... 481
   WHAT MIGHT HAPPEN ... 481
CESIUM-137 (CS-137) SCENARIO ... 482
COBALT-60 ... 483
PROTECTION ... 484
NUCLEAR POWER PLANTS ... 485
   TEMPTING TO TERRORISTS ... 485
WHAT TO DO BEFORE A NUCLEAR OR RADIOLOGICAL ATTACK ... 485
WHAT TO DO DURING A NUCLEAR OR RADIOLOGICAL ATTACK ... 486
WHAT TO DO AFTER A NUCLEAR OR RADIOLOGICAL ATTACK ... 486
   RETURNING TO YOUR HOME ... 487

CHAPTER 47: WATER AND FOOD IN NUCLEAR EMERGENCIES ... **488**
WATER ... 488
   LIGHT FALLOUT REMOVAL ... 488
   HEAVY FALLOUT REMOVAL ... 488
   SOURCES OF WATER IN FALLOUT AREAS ... 488
   WATER FROM WELLS ... 489
REMOVING FALLOUT AND DISSOLVED RADIOACTIVE MATERIAL ... 489
   POST-FALLOUT REPLENISHMENT OF STORED WATER ... 490

FOOD DURING AND IMMEDIATELY AFTER A NUCLEAR ATTACK 490
   FOOD PREPARATION AND MEAL PLANNING FOR SHELTERING *490*
EXPEDIENT COOK STOVE 491
REPLENISHING FOOD SUPPLIES 492
EMERGENCY FOOD FOR BABIES 492
   MAINTAINING A BALANCED GRAIN DIET *493*
   MEETING VITAMIN AND FAT REQUIREMENTS *493*
GARDENING AND FARMING AFTER A NUCLEAR ATTACK 494
   WORST CASE GROWING SCENARIO *494*

CHAPTER 48: FIRST AID IN NUCLEAR EMERGENCIES 495
RADIATION SICKNESS 495
POTASSIUM IODIDE AND IODATE 495
   WHAT IS THE DAILY DOSAGE REQUIRED? *496*
PSYCHOLOGICAL FIRST AID 496
   HELPING VICTIMS *496*
DEALING WITH DEATH 497

CHAPTER 49: ELECTROMAGNETIC PULSE – EMP 498
ELECTROMAGNETIC PULSE 498
WHAT WOULD HAPPEN IF AN EMP DETONATED? 500
SHIELDING 502

CHAPTER 50: PREPARING FOR CHALLENGES 503
TIME TO PREPARE 503
THREE DAYS IS NOT ENOUGH 503
HURRICANE FRANCES – A VALUABLE LESSON FOR ALL 503

CHAPTER 51: PREPARING FOR EARTHQUAKES 506
WHAT TO DO BEFORE AN EARTHQUAKE 506
WHAT TO DO DURING AN EARTHQUAKE 507
WHAT TO DO AFTER AN EARTHQUAKE 508
LIVING IN EARTHQUAKE COUNTRY 509
MOBILE HOMES 510
WOOD FRAME HOMES 510

CHAPTER 52: PREPARING FOR DROUGHT AND WATER SHORTAGE 514
EMERGENCY WATER SHORTAGE 514
WATER WARS 514
   LAKE POWELL *514*
MORE THAN DROUGHT 515
WATER CONSERVATION 515

CHAPTER 53: PREPARING FOR HEAT WAVES AND HEAT EMERGENCIES 517
OUR MERCURIAL STAR 517
THE NEW "BIG BANG" 517
HOPI PROPHECY 518
HOT SHOTS 518
WHAT TO DO BEFORE AN EXTREME HEAT EMERGENCY 518
WHAT TO DO DURING EXTREME HEAT OR A HEAT WAVE EMERGENCY 519
FIRST-AID FOR HEAT-INDUCED ILLNESSES 519
   SUNBURN *519*
   HEAT CRAMPS *519*
   HEAT EXHAUSTION *519*
   HEAT STROKE (SUN STROKE) *519*

CHAPTER 54: PREPARING FOR FIRES 520
WHAT TO DO BEFORE FIRE STRIKES 520
WHAT TO DO DURING A FIRE 522
WHAT TO DO AFTER A FIRE 522
WILDFIRES 523

CHAPTER 55: PREPARING FOR FLOODS 525
THE BIG WET 525
WHAT TO DO BEFORE A FLOOD 526
WHAT TO DO DURING A FLOOD 526
WHAT TO DO AFTER A FLOOD 527

CHAPTER 56: SANITATION AFTER A FLOOD 528
LIVING IN SOGGYVILLE 528
SANITATION AND FLOODS 528
FUN FOR KIDS, MISERY FOR ADULTS 529
NOTHING IS WORTH THE RISK 529
   AFTER A FLOOD... DISCARD *529*
CANNED FOODS 530

Dare To Prepare: Table of Contents

FROZEN / REFRIGERATED FOODS AND POWER OUTAGES 530
   REFRIGERATED FOOD – WHAT TO KEEP, WHAT TO TOSS *530*
KITCHEN CLEANUP 530
GENERAL CLEANUP 531
STANDING WATER 531
   WATER QUALITY *532*
WATER FOR DRINKING AND COOKING 532

CHAPTER 57: PREPARING FOR HURRICANES 533
INLAND / FRESHWATER FLOODING FROM HURRICANES 534
WHAT TO DO BEFORE A HURRICANE 534
WHAT TO DO DURING A HURRICANE THREAT 536
WHAT TO DO AFTER A HURRICANE 537
UTILITIES AND SERVICES 537
   DEBRIS *538*
   GARBAGE *538*
ADDITIONAL GUIDES AND INFORMATION 538
WINDOW / DOOR PROTECTION OPTIONS 539

CHAPTER 58: PREPARING FOR METEOR AND ASTEROID STRIKES 542
METEOR CRATER 542
TUNGUSKA, JUNE 30, 1908 542
ARE THESE ISOLATED EVENTS? 543
   WATCH OUT! *544*
DEEP IMPACT: FACT OR FANTASY? 544
WHAT'S BEING DONE – AND NOT? 545
   NEW "EYES" *545*
   NEW MISSIONS *546*
WHAT'S BEEN FOUND SO FAR 546
PREPAREDNESS 546

CHAPTER 59: PREPARING FOR TORNADOES 547
TORNADO FACTS 547
WHAT TO DO BEFORE TORNADOES THREATEN 548
WHAT TO DO DURING A TORNADO WATCH 548
WHAT TO DO DURING A TORNADO WARNING 549
WHAT TO DO AFTER A TORNADO 549
SAFE ROOM AND SHELTER 549
   AVERAGE COST TO BUILD A SAFE ROOM IN EXISTING HOME *550*
   FREE FEMA TORNADO SHELTER PLANS *551*

CHAPTER 60: PREPARING FOR TSUNAMIS 552
THE BIG WAVE 552
   THE REAL DEAL *552*
WHAT TO DO BEFORE A TSUNAMI 553
WHAT TO DO DURING A TSUNAMI 553
WHAT TO DO AFTER A TSUNAMI 554

CHAPTER 61: PREPARING FOR VOLCANIC ERUPTIONS 555
MOUNT ST. HELENS 555
WHAT TO DO BEFORE AN ERUPTION 556
WHAT TO DO DURING AN ERUPTION 556
WHAT TO DO AFTER THE ERUPTION 556

CHAPTER 62: PREPARING FOR WINTER STORMS, EXTREME COLD 557
WHAT TO DO BEFORE A WINTER STORM THREATENS 557
WHAT TO DO DURING A WINTER STORM 558
WINTER DRIVING (SEE CHAPTER 63 ON PREPARING YOUR VEHICLE) 558

CHAPTER 63: PREPARING YOUR VEHICLE 560
NORMAL MAINTENANCE 560
WINTER DRIVING 561
   COMMON SENSE *561*
   TRAPPED IN A STORM OR SNOW BANK *561*
   WHAT TO DO IF YOUR CAR GETS STUCK IN THE SNOW *562*
   ICE AND SLEET *562*
   ON "SKID" ROW *562*
WHO WOULD HAVE THOUGHT THIS COULD HAPPEN? 563
GO OR STAY... THE DILEMMA 564
STAYING 564
I'M OUTTA HERE! 565
   CAR PREPAREDNESS (MAKE SEASONAL CHANGES) *565*

CHAPTER 64: STAYING WARM WITHOUT POWER 567
STOVES 567

KEROSENE HEATERS 568
   KEROSENE SAFETY *568*
PROPANE HEATERS 569
   HOUSEWARMER *569*
   MR. HEATER *569*
REFILLING PROPANE TANKS 570
   PROPANE CYLINDERS *570*
IF YOU GET CAUGHT COMPLETELY BY SURPRISE… 571
SETTING UP WITHOUT HEAT 571
CLOTHING 572

CHAPTER 65: PREPARING FOR A PANDEMIC 573
THE NEXT PANDEMIC 573
NATURAL RESERVOIRS 574
BIRD FLU'S ENTRANCE 574
   NORTH AMERICA *574*
GRIM NUMBERS 574
PANDEMIC IMPACTS 575
   SIGNIFICANT DISRUPTION OF: *575*
THE KATRINA OF MEDICINE 576
   20TH CENTURY PANDEMICS *576*
   PANDEMIC SEVERITY INDEX *577*
   BIRD FLU DESCRIPTION *577*
PREVENTION – THE BEST CURE 577
   HOW LONG CAN AVIAN FLU SURVIVE ON SURFACES? *578*
   HAND-WASHING: MEDICAL MARVEL *578*
MASKS 578
   NIOSH-APPROVED N95, N99 AND N100 RESPIRATORS *578*
   SIZE MATTERS *579*
   THE SNEEZE FACTOR *580*
   EXHALATION VALVES *580*
DISPOSABLE OR REUSABLE? 581
   3M HALF FACEPIECE RESPIRATOR *581*
   SURGICAL MASKS *581*
   NANOMASKS *582*
HOW MANY DISPOSABLE MASKS DO I NEED? 582
MASK OF LAST RESORT 583
   TO MAKE *584*
   TO WEAR *584*
PPE (PERSONAL PROTECTIVE EQUIPMENT) 584
DISINFECTING MASKS AND PPE CLOTHING 584
   REUSABLE 3M MASKS *584*
   NANOMASK MASKS *585*
   CLOTHING *585*
DON'T WAIT TILL THE BOAT SINKS TO START BAILING 585
FOOD SUPPLIES: JUST-IN-TIME SEVERELY IMPAIRED 585
WATER SUPPLIES 586
ENERGY 586
PREPPING FOR PANDEMIC 587

CHAPTER 66: PREPARING FOR FINANCIAL MELTDOWN 588
THE COMING CRASH 588
PRACTICAL MONEY 589

CHAPTER 67: STAYING IN A SHELTER 591
REALITY CHECK 591
TIPS 592
   WHAT TO TAKE TO A SHELTER *592*

CHAPTER 68: DEALING WITH STRESS 594
COPING WITH DISASTER 594
HELPING CHILDREN COPE WITH DISASTER 595
HELPING OTHERS 595

CHAPTER 69: HOPE AND ENCOURAGEMENT 596
WHAT'S IN A NAME? 596
YOU'RE NEVER ALONE 596
   A MESSAGE TO CHRISTIANS *596*
TAKING PERSONAL RESPONSIBILITY 597

APPENDICES 598
U.S. AND METRIC CONVERSION CHARTS 598

INDEX 603

ENDNOTES 627

Preface

I
San Jose
October 16, 1989

"C'mon Erik, hustle," his dad called out. "You're going to miss the bus." Seconds later six-year-old Erik Davorin hurtled downstairs. Steve bent his 6'3" frame and scooped his son into the air. "How's my little man this morning?" Steve marveled again at the miracle he held in his arms.

Amanda padded downstairs freshly showered in shorts and matching halter, raven hair still damp. Her turquoise eyes sparkled with happiness.

Erik wriggled free to bury his face in Amanda's stomach, arms tightly wrapped around her waist. Kissing the top of his chestnut hair, Amanda enveloped him in a perfumed hug.

"OK, you two, breakfast."

"Yes, ma'am, Captain, ma'am!" Both men snapped to attention, saluting smartly. Her heart swelled seeing the two people she loved more than life.

Amanda hauled turkey bacon, eggs, milk and juice from the fridge. Steve automatically pulled glasses and an electric skillet from the cupboard. Soon the aroma of French vanilla coffee permeated the kitchen.

"I wanna help," Erik piped up.

"OK, honey, how about if you set the table?"

Not wanting to be left out, Erik bounded to the pantry and returned with gaily colored turquoise and cream striped placemats. Standing on a stool, he carefully selected three dinner plates. "Hey sport, let me hold those for you."

Climbing off his perch, Erik eagerly held up his hands for his contribution. "Be careful," his dad reminded him gently.

Erik smiled acknowledgment and scurried off to fulfill his part of the breakfast ritual.

Their banter continued as Amanda busied herself at the stove. Bacon sizzled crisply as she squeezed fresh orange juice and popped bread in the toaster. Steve appreciated his wife's constant care for their small family down to the smallest detail.

Sniffing bacon, Scruffy, the family mutt, tore around the corner, toenails laying tracks in his eagerness to join the clan. Seeing Mom was the bacon keeper, Scruffy made a dash for her feet. "Scruf, you get leftovers, my boy, not first pick," she scolded him.

Ears wilting, Scruffy promptly removed himself to his favorite location under the kitchen table. It offered him the best position for 'clean-up duty'.

"What's on your agenda today Manda?" Steve asked, slathering butter on golden toast.

"First, hit the club for a workout and then off to look for wallpaper. The Stapletons want two rooms done ASAP. I've got to find those swatches. Knowing 'Murphy', they'll want a paper that's not in stock."

"Honey, you know you don't have to do this," Steve smiled indulgently.

"Yes, I do know that, but I like having something of my own, plus it makes a few dollars in the process. You want a Christmas present don't you?" She teased.

Steve eased his classic Corvette down the driveway and headed for Future Flight, Inc. Azure eyes scoped the road for traffic. *How unpredictable life is* Steve thought, remembering Future Flight's shaky start. Three talented yuppies pooled their dreams over Coronas their last year at CSU. Unknown to them, the careers of Steve Davorin, Troy Davids and Damon Freeman had targeted an exhilarating path. The 'Big Three' dreamed of becoming rocket jockeys, flying their own missions and view that extraordinary sapphire marble from above. They also knew technology must improve radically to see real progress.

Steve paused his thoughts, checked the road and headed for Future Flight's R & D department. Research and development may have been dull and tedious to some, but Steve knew its importance and thrived on discoveries.

Coming from a middle class family, Steve had seized the American dream and run with it almost unconsciously. He loved aerospace and marveled at making a comfortable living when he would gladly do the work for free. The future looked challenging, filled with possibilities.

ii
San Jose
October 17, 1989, 6:00 a.m.

"Hey baby," Amanda rolled over spoon fashion behind her husband. "It's time to get up sleepyhead. This is Erik's big day. Don't forget to give him lunch money."

Steve snuggled sleepily against his wife's soft skin. "Where's he going again?"

"Since a lot of parents are taking their kids to the World Series, Mrs. Roberts planned a special day trip for the rest. They start with a personalized tour of the Naval Reserve Shipyard, then off to Fisherman's Wharf for lunch and time at the beach. The bus brings them back home and Debbie will be here to baby-sit. She knows where the key is."

"Erik likes Debbie and she's conscientious. Sounds good. Ready for a play day Mrs. Davorin?" Steve queried, rolling over to give Amanda a morning hug.

"Sure, what'd you have in mind?" Amanda inquired innocently, tossing her dark head.

Steve turned to give her a horrified look. "Have you forgotten the Wor—" Steve broke off seeing her smirking face. "You ought to be ashamed of yourself." Steve scolded in mock anger. "I should have known you were pulling my leg. It's not fair to mess with an unarmed soldier you know. I haven't had my coffee yet." Grinning groggily, he looking handsome despite serious bed head.

"Tell me dear, did you work at this hairstyle?" Amanda teased ruffling his untamed cowlicks. "Or get hit by a tornado?"

"Boy, you're in rare form this morning!" Steve observed wryly as his wife bounced out of bed.

Around the breakfast table, Erik could barely contain his excitement. "Dad we're going to see the big boats today! The Navy's giving us a special toot."

"I think you mean 'tour' honey," Steve corrected, hiding a smile behind his napkin.

Undeterred Erik continued happily. "Then we're going to Fisher's Warp for lunch."

Amanda's dimples played around the corners of her mouth.

"Boy I wish I were going with you little guy." Steve enthused watching their son in pleasure.

"Aw, no you don't Dad," with six-year-old wisdom. "I know, you and Mom are going to the ball game. Wish I were going with *you*." Erik said wistfully.

"Son, you're going to have a terrific time today! Davy will be going too won't he?" Erik nodded still downcast. "Tell you what. We'll drive down to the San Diego Zoo this weekend."

Erik bounced up and down excitedly. "Can Davy come too?" Steve looked over at Amanda who nodded silently. Catching the exchange, Erik's small face broke out in happy grins.

"Gotta go Mommy. Bus is here." Erik advised them already sliding off his chair.

"Woops, not so fast. Come here and give me a hug first. I love you son. Have a good time today."

"I love you too Dad." Steve inhaled his son's fresh clean scent, reveling in his innocence.

Erik trotted over to give Amanda a hug. She felt strangely emotional and gave Erik an extra big squeeze. "I love you sweetheart."

Amanda held him close until he wriggled free. "Mind the teachers and stay with the other kids. OK honey? We'll see you tonight. Debbie will be here when you get home."

"OK Mommy. Love you too."

Taking Amanda's hand, Steve said, "And now lovely lady, I thought we'd make a day of it. Before the game we'll run into the city for a little shopping, then down to Lou's Village for some Dungeness crab. OK, you can have your Maine lobster," Steve corrected grinning. "One of these days I fully expect your arms to sport pinchers and claws." Steve tweaked her on the rump.

"That'd be fine as long as I don't have their beady little eyes."

"Agreed. I love the ones you've got," kissing her eyelids tenderly.

Excitement crackled throughout The Stick. Game 3 of the World Series between the Oakland A's and the San Francisco Giants was about to kick off. This was the first-ever all-Bay area Series. Baseball fever shot to an all-time high and the title already looked good for the A's. With the first two games under the A's belt, Steve knew the Giants had better get busy. The next two were away games, which made the tension even higher today for Oakland fans.

"Gee, your dad must have had tickets a long time to snag these seats." Amanda observed. Sitting in section 18 of the lower box offered a tremendous view of the game.

"This is going to be great, honey!" Steve beamed in anticipation. "Beer here!" Steve hollered to the passing vendor. "Com'on honey, gotta have an icy brew. It's tradition!"

Amanda busily scanned the field picking out players. Excitedly she pointed out, "Oh, there's Lansford, number 4."

Jose Canseco and Mark McGwire, 'the Bash Brothers' trotted out and exchanged a fisted high-five.

"Yeah, well Canseco and McGwire better have an off-night," Steve commented soberly. "Garrelts and Mitchell need to look good, real good! They've already lost two games and on home turf too! Let's hope the A's luck continues—all bad!" Steve joked, but under the humor Amanda knew Steve was serious. After all, baseball was serious business.

Steve glanced at his gold and stainless Rolex, tapping his heel up and down. "It's nearly 5:00. They're getting ready to announce the lineups."

"Steven, you're one big kid under that 6'3" hunky—" Amanda broke off mid-sentence as the hair raised on the back of her neck. "What was *that*?" Amanda squealed.

"Oh, my God! We're having an earthquake!" cried the woman next to her.

"Steve!" Amanda gripped his arm in alarm. Candlestick Park shook to its very core. The field rolled and undulated as though propelled by ocean waves.

"Relax honey, it'll be over in a second." Steve hugged his wife reassuringly but the shaking didn't stop. Terror lit Amanda's turquoise eyes as she joined the screaming. Steve looked around and saw the press box swaying eerily. Everyone vibrated like Mexican jumping beans.

Fifteen seconds of tremendous shaking stretched into eternity before deafening thunder-like chaos overtook the airwaves. While the press box danced, seats banged shut as people streamed onto the field. Power to The Stick went dead.

People stared in horror as slabs above the upper deck separated several feet and slid back together. Light stanchions snapped 15 feet left and right of center. It was a sight to behold.

"Steeeven!" Amanda screamed a second time. "Oh, my God!"

As Steve and Amanda waited for what would come next, a shrieking, sobbing woman flung herself into catcher Terry Steinbach's arms. That one picture captured the panic at Candlestick and it played time and again around the world. Terry and Mary Steinbach had left their two-year-old daughter, Jill, with a babysitter in Alameda. With no news and miles away, for all they knew, their home might be flattened. The riveting, touching portrayal immortalized that day's terror.

Panicked players and fans alike streamed onto the field and huddled under doorways, anything to feel safe.

Beer soaked Steve and Amanda as the sloshing continued. Programs fluttered to the ground like oversized confetti. Cushions shimmied off seats. Popcorn, hotdogs and binoculars flew from hands.

Amazingly the stadium held together. People throughout the ballpark cried in fear thinking they were living through The Big One. Steve looked at his watch. It was 5:04pm when "the good life" disappeared.

Stunned and dazed, Amanda cried softly. Steve witnessed people pulled to their feet and small children comforted. Many others wept besides Amanda, but no one seemed seriously injured.

"Ladies and gentleman," announced Commissioner Fay Vincent. "Ladies and gentleman, please, let me have your attention. Quiet everyone, please. The game has been called."

The crowd's milling and mumbling ceased in hopes of good news.

"The game has been called," repeated Vincent. "We will not have power back on anytime soon. I repeat, no game today. Please leave the stadium in an orderly manner. We want everyone evacuated before dark."

Fans who brought Walkmans and TVs to the game frantically searched for information. Devastating news filtered in from KFOX, but it didn't seem real. What had seemed so vital just minutes ago, the winning and the losing, became meaningless.

Snippets of information were passed along like hotdogs to the inside bleachers.

"Folks, they're saying we've just had a 6.9 earthquake. The epicenter was somewhere in the Santa Cruz Mountains. I'm sorry to say the upper deck of the Bay Bridge has collapsed," stated the radio announcer. "Reports are coming in of considerable bridge and highway damage."

As soon as Amanda heard the words 'Bay Bridge', she thought her heart would stop. Steve and Amanda shared the same horrifying thought: "ERIK!" They cried.

Dimly in the background, people began to joke saying the "big one" hadn't been so bad. They had experienced worse shaking under the sheets, bragged some of the men. But they were still within the protected bowl of Candlestick. They had no clue what lay outside.

iii

San Jose
October 17, 1989, 6:00 p.m.

"Steve, our baby, our baby," Amanda whimpered as they ran to the car. "What are we going to do? The school bus would be taking Erik on that same route! Dear Lord, what if they were on the Bridge? I just can't bear it!" She moaned.

"Amanda, get a hold of yourself! This isn't helping," Steve spoke to her sternly in hopes of snapping her back to sanity. "Stop it!" He ordered.

Amanda jerked at his harsh words, but in her mind she knew he was trying to help. Her wrenching tears subsided to sniffles.

"It will be at least an hour before we get out of here," Steve observed looking at the gridlocked cars.

"Turn up the radio," Amanda pleaded.

Steve was reluctant in case they heard more bad news sending Amanda into another tailspin, but he knew information was imperative. At this point, Steve had no idea what roads and highways were open. As he feared, the news became worse every minute.

Steve punched in another station. ". . . Hardest hit were Watsonville, Los Gatos, Hollister and Santa Cruz. There's major damage to both downtown and residential areas. Substantial damage is also being reported in Oakland, Gilroy, San Jose, San Martin and Salinas."

Steve and Amanda exchanged worried looks before the broadcaster continued.

"For Frisco, the worst impacted area remains the Marina district around Jefferson and Divisadero. The district was built mostly in the '20s and these old wooden homes and apartment buildings are burning like tinder! Fires are completely out of control. Four story buildings are pancaking! Police ask that you stay away and let emergency vehicles through."

"Steve, that's only blocks from Fisherman's Wharf," Amanda voice crept toward hysteria.

"Honey, the kids wouldn't have been anywhere near the area that late in the day. Most likely they were already home by 5:00. We'll have worried for nothing." Steve squeezed her shoulder reassuringly. "Erik is probably stuffing his face with nachos right now." Steve grinned to hide his own fear.

"We've got to drive over there and see. We've got to!"

Steve took Amanda by the shoulders and peered into frantic turquoise eyes. "Look baby, I know you're frightened. I'm half outta my mind too, but we've got to look at this reasonably. Cops will have all those roads barricaded. They won't let anyone pass. Even if we could get through, the roads are torn up. It's best to make our way home and see if he's there.

"Call Debbie and check with the sitter. Now aren't you glad I insisted we buy one of those things when you said mobile phones were still too new?" Steve inserted his car keys.

Amanda nodded absently, grabbed the cell phone and punched in the number. "All circuits are busy. Please try your call again later." Amanda looked at Steve disheartened.

"Keeping trying, honey. I'll see how to get us home. Buckle up. We might be playing bumper cars tonight," he warned.

Steve scanned the streets noting dead traffic lights. Police directed traffic at every corner. Steve inched onto the 101 praying it was still open all the way home.

KFOX's broadcaster broke in with the information Steve needed.

"If travel is not imperative, please stay home. Do not attempt to sightsee. Emergency equipment is being shuffled all over San Francisco and Oakland as far south as the Santa Cruz Mountains. They need clear access.

"The following bridges and roads are closed from what has been dubbed "the Loma Prieta quake": Martinez-Benicia Bridge closed to trucks in both directions, I-80 and I-880 closed between Berkeley and I-980 in Oakland, Bay Bridge and Embarcadero Freeway, closed. I-280 is closed from U.S. 101 to downtown San Fran. The 101 is closed to northbound traffic at the Highway 92 overpass. Highway 9, closed at the San Lorenzo River Bridge. Highway 17, closed from Scotts Valley to Highway 9. Highway 1 north, closed at Struve Slough Bridge. Highway 129, closed at Aromas Road, and Highway 25 is closed from the 101 to 15 miles south of Hollister. Repeat, do not attempt travel on any of these roads. If possible, stay home and keep phone lines clear for those trying to locate family and friends."

Steve breathed a sigh of relief. It looked like the 101 would get them home unless the unthinkable happened—a large aftershock.

Death tolls started to roll in. Power was on and off targeting areas at random. More reports of uncontrolled fires in the Marina District poured in. Tongues of flame illuminated San Francisco's skyline in an eerie glow. The broadcaster broke in with another update.

"At least fifteen bodies have already been found with the collapse of buildings in the Marina District. Broken power mains are flooding streets and hampering firefighters. Homes and businesses are without water. Folks, this is amazing footage. I will try to describe it for those listening on radio.

"Flames are shooting seventy-five feet into the air as people desperately try to evacuate apartments and homes. Since these wood structures date back fifty, sixty years, flames are swallowing buildings whole. Parents frantic to save their children are tossing them to safety below into makeshift nets. Others are leaping from third and fourth story windows praying they will survive the fall with only broken bones. As more firefighting equipment is desperately needed, for some, jumping may be their only hope.

Photo: San Francisco, CA, October 1989. Fire ravaged the Marina District of San Francisco in the wake of the Loma Prieta earthquake. (FEMA News Photo)

"In the background you can hear heart-ripping screams of people unable to escape the sheets of fire. Burning rubber permeates everything. The only light visible in San Francisco tonight, friends, is from this inferno."

By 6:45, the fireboat *Phoenix* docked in Marina Lagoon and brought 5,000 feet of hose and aerial ladders. Firefighters worked quickly against the soaring flames jabbing the night sky. With homes so tightly packed, the entire neighborhood threatened to ignite. The devil put on a mighty show that night.

"Steve, can't we go any faster?" Amanda asked pointlessly.

"Honey, the Embarcadero is closed as is I-280 and the Bay Bridge. More traffic than ever is funneling onto the 101. At least we're moving. Even if it's going way out of our way, the road is nearly intact. We have to be patient sweetheart. Don't worry, we'll get there. Keep trying the phone."

An hour and a half later Amanda finally got through to Debbie, two and a half hours after their world split apart.

"Debbie! Thank God! How's Erik? How are you? Do you have power? Is everything OK?" Amanda rushed on in a torrent of questions.

"He's fine, Mrs. Davorin, —"

"Oh, thank God!"

Steve saw the relief in his wife's face and that was all the confirmation he needed.

"But your house needs help," Debbie continued. "A lot of help. It's really messed up."

"Oh, I don't care! That you two are safe is all we need to hear!"

"Everything's a disaster zone Mrs. D. Bookcases turned over. Dishes and lamps broke. There's no lights. Your fireplace looks weird, too; it's sort of leaning funny. The fridge came open and it looks like someone had a major food fight. I tried to clean up the glass but there's too much and that really cool crystal dolphin, that Stubeen —"

"Steuben", Amanda corrected absently. "Debbie don't worry about it. We'll take care of it later. You guys matter, not the things!"

Amanda sighed thinking of the mess to clean, but so grateful the kids were OK.

KFOX broke in with more news.

"This just in, Highway 17 into the Santa Cruz mountains received extensive damage and is expected to be closed for several months. Besides huge ruptures and holes, aftershocks are rolling in by the score and triggered massive landslides in the mountains. More slides are anticipated as heavy rain is expected for the next several days. Folks we realize as many as 30,000 of you commute to the Frisco-Oakland area daily, but unless you use the torturous back roads, you are in effect, cut off."

Steve looked at Amanda's white face. *This is a nightmare!* At least their son was alive.

iv
San Jose
October 17, 1989, 9:00 p.m.

"We take you now to the Bay Bridge for live coverage. Let me describe this unbelievable scene."

He painted an all-too-real picture of a crushed Ford Escort dangling over a cavern on the Bay Bridge. Two people were skewered together in the little car. A young woman bled from seemingly all over while the man next to her sobbed, unable to move.

"Apparently the Ford Escort, now in this precarious position, along with some fifty other vehicles, was on the lower deck of the San Francisco-Oakland Bay Bridge. When the earthquake ripped through the area, traffic froze. Though emergency workers directed cars to safety motioning them toward Oakland, in a massive wave, they panicked and climbed onto the top deck. None of them knew about the fifty foot gap in the road ahead." News reporter Ron Browne paused for the information to sink in.

"All of the cars managed to stop except the Escort which hit the breach at a 40mph wallop. It bounced off the fallen section and slammed into the side across from that hole. For those of you still with power, you can see the Escort now hangs by just its front end. This is simply an astounding event!"

His mike caught ambulances and rescue equipment screaming in the background. Before the pinned people could get emergency care, the Escort had to be hauled to safety. Through masterful efforts of a well-drilled team, freeing the car took only 30 minutes. But in those precious intervening moments, the young woman bled to death. Photos later revealed the agonized face of her brother, the man with grotesquely mangled legs.

No one could have prepared onlookers for the hell that tore their eyes. Steve and Amanda locked looks of disbelieving horror. Steve swallowed bile rising in his throat and Amanda began to whimper. Chopper reporter 'Skye' Adams explained what viewers saw.

Photo: Crushed cars near the intersection of Fifth and Townsend Streets, South of Market. (C.E. Meyer, USGS)

Photo: One of the most spectacular effects of the Northridge earthquake was the collapse of several freeway overpasses. Pictured here is the collapse at the Antelope Valley (SR14) – Golden State Freeway (I-5) interchange – the primary traffic artery between northern and southern California. Two sections of highway fell in this earthquake, and there were displacements of a number of inches between span sections that remained standing. I-5 then under construction, also collapsed in the San Fernando earthquake of 1971. It was later rebuilt using the same specifications. A policeman was killed when he ran his motorcycle off the edge of the freeway. Northridge earthquake, California; January 17, 1994. (J. Dewey, USGS)

"Down below us is a brown wavy ribbon that used to be the Cypress viaduct. The middle section has completely dropped some twenty-five feet below. You can see numerous support columns that gave way under the earthquake's stress. They appear to have shattered like so much hard candy."

Massive columns cracked and twisted right down to the reinforcing steel bars. Concrete had peeled away like banana skins leaving re-bar exposed. It resembled giant handfuls of overcooked spaghetti. Dust clouds billowed heavenward as the freeway continued to lurch and settle. Skye continued her report shouting over the helicopter racket.

"In between those two layers of highway are numerous vehicles and their unfortunate passengers—"

Ron Browne broke in. "Skye, does there appear to be any survivors?"

Steve and Amanda pulled into the driveway. The children flew out the front door and were quickly enveloped in welcoming arms.

"Erik, darling, are you and Debbie OK?" Amanda held her son at arm's length inspecting him for her own peace of mind.

"Yeah Mommy, we're fine. Just some cuts and bruises."

"You're hurt? What happened?" Instantly alarmed rang in Amanda's voice. "What happened?" She repeated, trying for calm.

"Me and Debbie, we were watching TV when everything started to shake. You know those really nice plates you told me not to touch? Well, they started to wiggle right off the shelves just before the whole thing fell over. And I thought, 'Boy, is Mom gonna be mad!' Erik flashed her a worried look. He knew his mother treasured her custom Steuben collection.

"It's OK honey, tell us happened? How'd you get hurt?"

"Debbie said maybe we should get out of the room with all these windows. You know, in case they started to wiggle again. That's when the big light fell down."

Sighing, Amanda mentally canvassed her great room visualizing the shattered crystal chandelier. Erik picked up his tale.

"We were going when it just fell out of the ceiling and banged Deb."

"Let me look at that arm and then I'll take you home. Thanks for staying till we got here." Steve's suntanned face lifted in a grateful smile.

Steve knew Amanda had been after him to secure her china cabinet to the wall... just in case. *Oh boy, there'll be hell to pay now.* Pause. *My computer! Can't worry about that now. At least we're alive; 67 other people weren't so lucky.*

"To tell you the truth Mr. Davorin, I was too scared to leave."

Steve's attention swiveled back to the teenager who desperately needed reassurance. A flicker of fear crossed Debbie's face.

"Listening on the radio, well, it's getting pretty weird out there. Gas and water lines are broken. Water is shooting everywhere. They warned people about the power lines. Trees have fallen on a lot of them and they look like electric snakes! I know that's not good with all the flooding!" Deb tried for a tremulous smile.

Steve visualized the live lines writhing and crackling across the pavement.

"People are starting to panic," Deb continued. "They said grocery stores are picked clean, at least those in this area. You can't get gas because the pumps aren't working and no store is taking anything but cash. Gee, even the ATMs quit!" Debbie frowned trying to absorb what she'd just said.

"No, ATMs, how is that possible? I thought they *always* worked!" Deb's eyes got rounder as the magnitude of what she'd heard kicked in. She continued.

"Many of the roads are blocked so we can't get into the city. What are we going to do, Mr. D.? We've only got food for three days at home..." Debbie whispered.

Steve's face registered shock. He hadn't contemplated anything beyond finding his son. His mind raced over their situation – food, water.

Wait a minute! Hadn't Amanda stashed a bunch of stuff like a two-legged squirrel? He turned crimson thinking of the ribbing he'd given her for being such a worrywart. When he got home, he'd have to see how he could rig up some light. If only we had a generator...[1]

Introduction: Why Prepare?

THOSE WHO DO . . . AND THE REST OF THE PLANET

Two kinds of people make up our world – those who know massive change is bearing down on us and the rest who remain totally oblivious.

Unfortunately, the latter is the majority. They charge forth blindly pursuing "life" like a missile clamped to its target. 'What if' is not part of their thought process and who can blame them.

Change rules the day. It's harder to cope. Yet we are asked to absorb change with the ease of tying a shoe, ramp up our stress load and keep going. Denial is easier.

Within the first crew – those who know this isn't their mama's world – are two camps. One group sees no threat from these changes. Mankind's ingenuity will save them from global shifts and lurches. They do nothing 'cause she'll be right mate!

The other group acknowledges potential threats and realizes man's technology can't always protect it. They accept *personal responsibility* and prepare for life's speed bumps.

The "awake" bunch has come to their understanding by various means. Some looked to Bible prophecy. Some followed futurists like Edgar Cayce, Nostradamus, Lori Toye or Gordon-Michael Scallion. Native American teachings were scoured for hints of things to come. Others have simply observed weather and world events over time and saw things weren't as stabile as they used to be. Maybe they can't exactly put their finger on it, but something seems amiss. They have an uneasy feeling, an urging to *do something*.

If you have experienced any of these promptings, take heed. Keep extra food, water, first aid and general supplies on hand. It is for you *Dare to Prepare* was written.

Acknowledging change is underway and that you need to act is the first step—and the biggest. Congratulations! You're taking action!

If you've not given much thought *how* to prepare your household, maybe you're already asking, "Where do I start? *How* do I prepare? How much do I need, and what? Then what do I *do* with it? Arrrrgh! Make me crazy!"

The task may seem overwhelming, but don't panic. It's truly very doable. *Dare to Prepare* will show you how-to without mistakes and hassle, and *why* we need to set aside provisions in the first place. This is especially helpful if you "get it", but family or friends need convincing. *Dare To Prepare* gives you all the ammunition necessary to convince even the most blind that we're on a serious and deadly path of global change.

It's unfortunate that some people who want to stock up meet resistance. Presenting family with concrete evidence of these increasing challenges may make them more receptive. Practically speaking, you SAVE MONEY purchasing products in bulk and have fewer opportunities for impulse buying. You SAVE TIME (and gas) going to the store less often. You SAVE SANITY in the event illness or unemployment when income doesn't stretch as far as the bills. You SAVE STRESS if unexpected company shows up at the dinner table and there's no need to dash to the store because you have a well-stocked pantry!

If you've already begun, then *Dare* will be an invaluable reference guide. Use it and share it with others around you.

Dare to Prepare is also your bridge to those past and near-forgotten skills which modern society foolishly gave the boot. You'll be able to learn many of these lost skills and techniques with a minimum of effort. And they're fun for the whole family!

THIS ISN'T YOUR MAMA'S WORLD

Countless events are manifesting geophysically, astronomically, meteorologically, politically, economically and prophetically that give reasons to prepare. There is absolutely NO DOUBT disruptive events are increasing globally in scope, frequency and economic impact. That is fact. Add to this equation, terrorism and worldwide unrest. 'Weird' and 'devastating' are the new norms.

Hopefully this reality has already caught your attention and now you want to prepare for the unexpected. Life's challenges are never as intimidating when you have a degree of control. That's what prep is all about! It gives you the edge to calmly sail through disruptions.

Most of us can remember a disaster here and there but we forget the particulars. Because each day is packed with so much information, details fade as we survive one disaster only to be engulfed by another. The more disasters we experience or watch on television, the more we feel invincible.

ALL DISASTERS GREAT AND SMALL

Insurance companies and relief organizations keep disaster statistics two ways, either as great catastrophes or as general natural disasters. If a distinction isn't made, information can seem out of kilter. Munich Re, the world's top reinsurer (a company who insures insurance companies), defines *great catastrophes* as those that require aid from other regions or even international help. This is usually the case when thousands of people die, hundreds of thousands are made homeless, or when a country suffers massive economic losses. The January 12, 2010 Haitian and the February 27, 2010 Chile earthquakes and tsunamis were two such events.

At nearly 5pm local time, a 7.0 shaker devastated Port-au-Prince and its suburbs. The quake left nearly 300,000 dead; 300,000 injured and over 300,000 homes destroyed or damaged. More than 3.5 million people were affected. The resulting tsunami, which was smaller than anticipated, washed many people out to sea never to be found. Those who endured the staggering 8.8 Chile quake fared better since the country was more prepared. These events started 2010 off with a horrific death and dollar toll.

By definition Great Catastrophes occur less often than natural disasters and are shown in the following chart.[2]

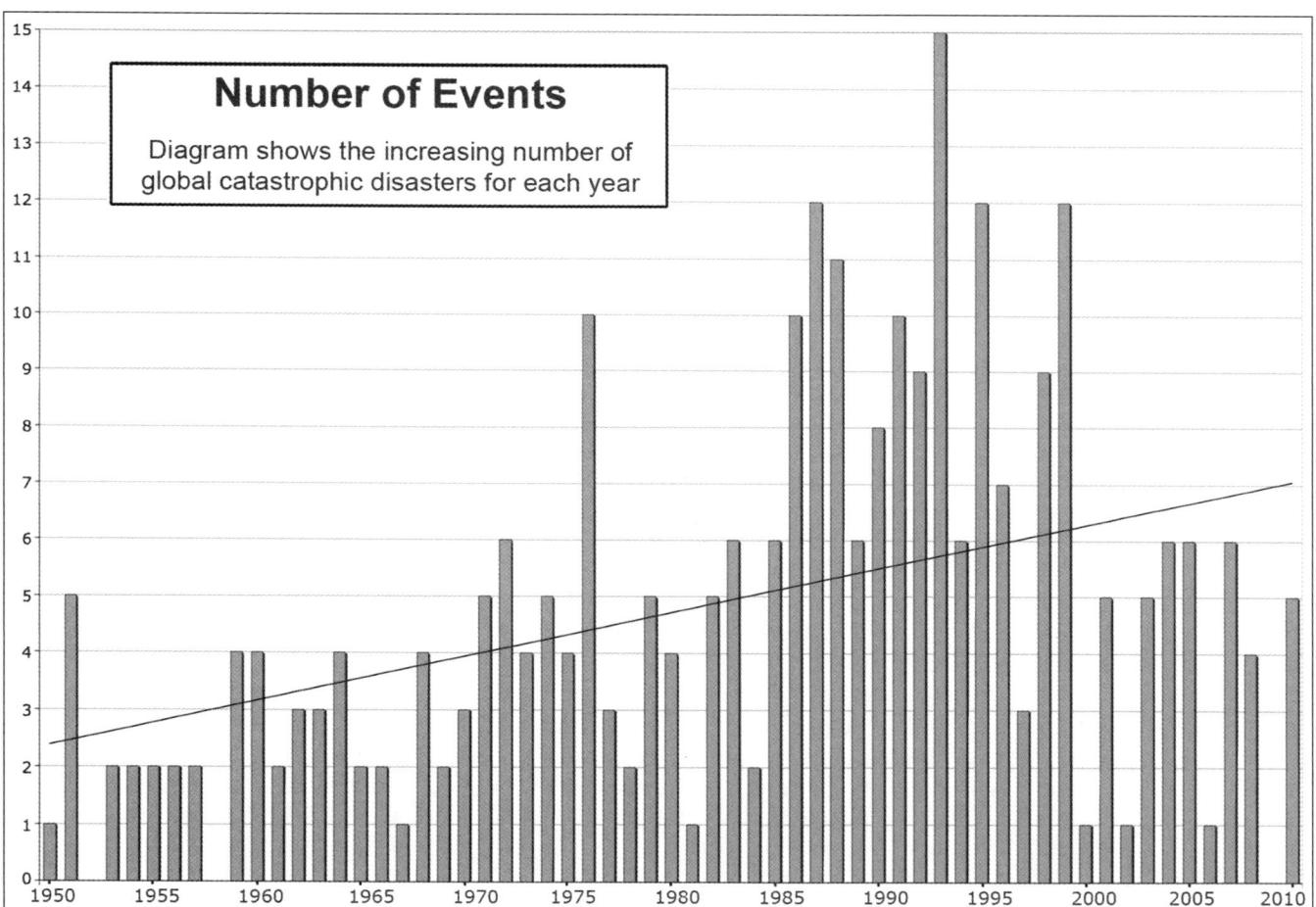

Since 1950, the number of GREAT natural catastrophes worldwide increased 400%, while economic losses from these events, after adjusting for inflation, rose by an astonishing 1400%.

Natural disasters on the other hand, aren't as large in scope. These upheavals are loosely described as killing 10 or more people and/or affecting at least 100 folks to the point where they need food, water, shelter, sanitation and immediate medical aid. A state of emergency is declared. Losses from these events, especially when viewed over a year, climb to very significant numbers both in dollars and in human costs.

Over the past 31 years, America has been pummeled by 99 weather disasters that exceeded $1 billion <u>each</u>. Ninety of these events hit between 1988 and 2010 – approaching *three-quarters of a trillion dollars*. Nine catastrophes hit in 2008 alone – the most for any year during this time. By far, the worst was 2005 – The Year of the Hurricane. Four monster storms – Wilma, Rita, Katrina and Dennis killed over 2,000 people and created $193 billion (2010) in damages.[3] Today Katrina would cost $142 billion. It's just too much for the brain to conceive.

"Natural disasters kill one million people around the world each decade, and leave millions more homeless each year."[4] Over the last 30 years the number of people killed by disasters stays around 80,000 per year. However, the number of affected people tripled to around 250 million every year.

Economic losses from disasters rose in the 1990s to an average of US$63 billion a year. That's five times as much compared to the 1970s! Some estimates project disasters related to climate change could soon cost over $300 billion every year.[5] This graph shows how natural disasters have escalated globally over the past 60 years.[6]

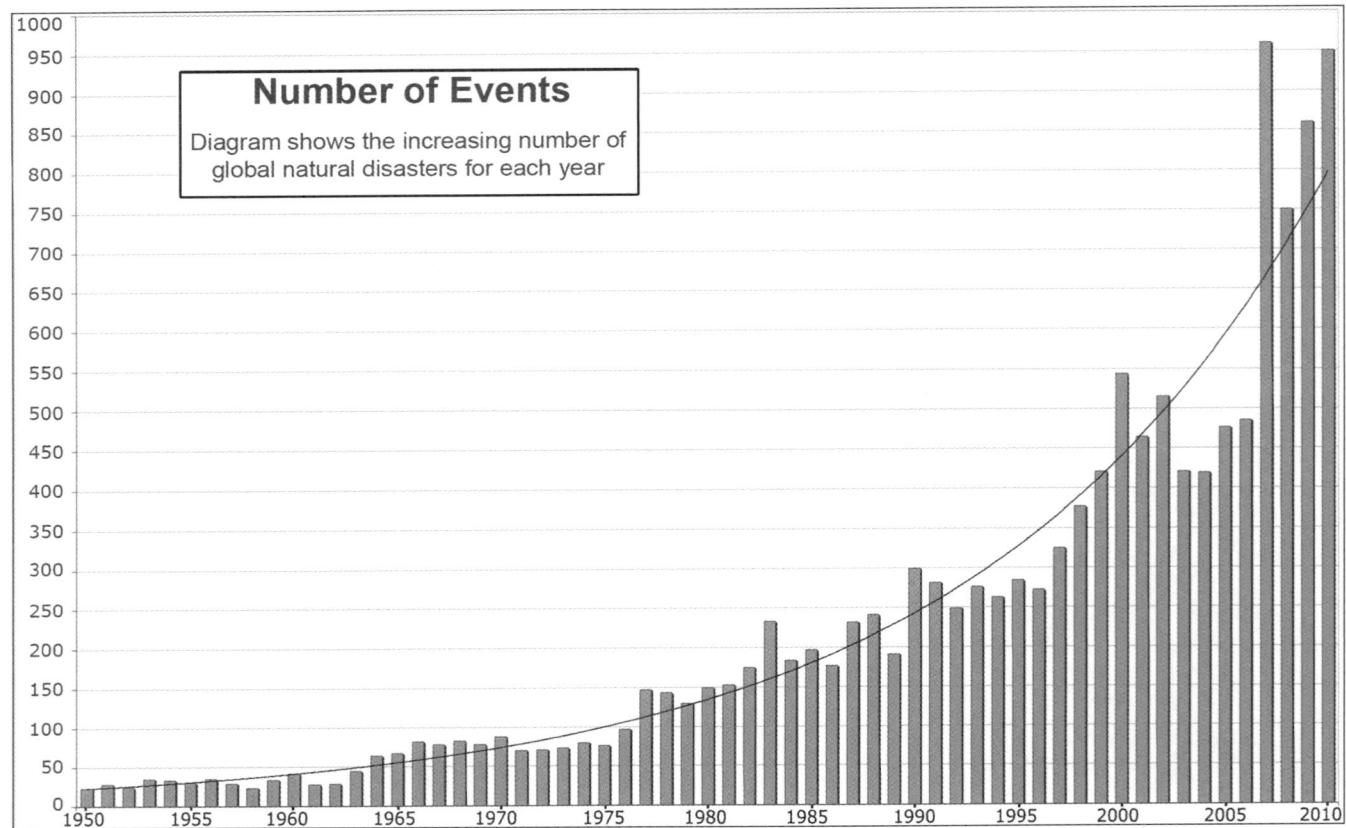

Number of Events
Diagram shows the increasing number of global natural disasters for each year

The 2004 International Strategy for Disaster Reduction report stated that "more than 254 million people were affected natural hazards last year, **a near three-fold jump from 1990**. Hazards ranging from storms, earthquakes and volcanoes to wildfires, droughts and landslides killed some 83,000 people in 2003 compared with about 53,000 deaths 13 years earlier, it noted. Not only is the world globally facing more potential disasters, but increasing numbers of people are becoming vulnerable to hazards."[7] Enter 2010. Natural disasters claimed 295,000 lives in another huge jump and the second highest number of events in 60 years. The report continued, "the intensity and frequency of disasters are very likely to increase due to climate change". Earth is set for massive challenges.

No matter how we look at it, either by great catastrophes or general natural disasters, upheavals are gaining momentum. Governments and insurance companies can't keep bailing us out of escalating disasters. They have their hands FULL! Federal disaster funds are stretched to the limit and so is the government manpower pool.

FEMA's relief aid alone for the '94 Northridge quake pegged $6.98 billion. In 2011 dollars, this is nearly $10.5 billion. This figure doesn't include funding from other federal agencies or costs to insurance companies and individuals.[8] But that's nothing compared to Hurricane Andrew ('92). When those damages were tallied, costs rang a $27 billion bell. Today, that's a whopping $43 billion!

Charities, too, feel the pinch. June 2003 saw Red Cross funds nearly depleted with only $1.5 million in its coffers. That was their lowest balance since 1992, when it ran completely dry.

Ditto for 2004. After hurricanes Charley and Frances hit, the Red Cross had to borrow $10 million. And two more hurricanes were just around the corner.

Insurers are even more highly impacted. Hurricanes Charley and Frances struck just days apart with combined damages of $30 billion. Right on their heels, Ivan pegged over $16 billion (2010). Unbelievably, more was to come. In a 1-2-3-4 punch, Jeanne pummeled Florida days later. Another $8 billion (2010) lost. Incredibly, Ivan doubled back and gave Southeastern states a second wallop! These four storms took at least 160 lives. Florida is the first state to be pounded by four hurricanes in one season since Texas received that same distinction in 1886.

Swiss Re, the world's second largest re-insurer, released a March 2004 report revealing how climate change is rising on corporate agendas. When businesses lose dollars to due disaster, they rapidly look to prevention.

Swiss Re stated that economic costs from these events threaten to *double* to $150 billion annually within a decade. That is now about 5 years away. Insurers will struggle with multiple $30-40 billion claims annually, each the equivalent of one Sept. 11 attack.[9] They simply cannot withstand these continual cash payouts.

You might think, *not a drama, that's the insurance companies' problem.* But it's *our* problem because their costs trickle down to us. We ultimately pay their increased expenses in higher premiums. What happens when their money runs out?

Due to increased risk, major insurers have already cancelled some disaster coverage in certain areas like earthquake and hurricane. Others companies balk on payment and the insured have to press lawsuits for claims.

CHANGE – THE ONE CONSTANT

From changes we've experienced geophysically and now terrorism, we know to expect more challenges. Drought or floods have wiped out wheat, corn, soy, rice and cotton crops. Global grain and foods stores are down.

Places that don't need rain see too much, other locations are dying for moisture. What we considered to be "freak storms" are now not so unusual, just violent.

Animals are good barometers of earth in flux. Fish, frogs and micro-organisms are sick and/or mutating. Whales and dolphins are beaching themselves more frequently. Massive numbers of honeybees, which pollinate over one-third of our crops, are dying yearly. Entire species are disappearing daily at an astonishing rate.

Birds are off-kilter too. Their mating songs can be heard in winter, not just in spring, when it's normal to lay eggs. Can hatchlings survive winter's rebound? During El Niño and La Niña, plants that should be dormant attempt to flower. Their growing cycles are confused.

More than 50 diseases have surfaced or re-emerged in the last 25 years. Some aren't treatable while others grow antibiotic resistant.

Global temperatures are rising and causing horrific storms over the entire planet.

Polar ice is diminishing and this continuous melt-off will lead to massive coastal flooding. Islands are already being swallowed by watery intrusion. Mount Kilimanjaro's glacier is crumbling, the Swiss Alps are melting and Alaska's permafrost is mushy. This is not good news for anyone living coastally or on low-lying islands.

Earthquakes, which can trigger tsunamis, landslides, mudslides, flooding, fires and volcanic eruptions are more active. The 2010 Icelandic volcano eruption grounded flights and cost airlines over $200 million a day.

The Sun, that taken-for-granted 'constant,' is shooting flares so large they can't be measured. As of 1991, the Sun began emitting two new spectral frequencies.

Scientists released information in June 1999 showing the Sun is more "energetic" than ever – saying its interplanetary magnetic field had increased 40% since 1964 and **doubled** since 1901! We are blasted with more radiation and have less protection. Solar flares and CMEs bombard our lives with great regularity. In 1998, the number of CMEs had increased by over 400% compared to 1997.

When giant sunspot 720 erupted on January 20, 2005, it unleashed a powerful X7 flare. This solar belch hurled a CME into space sparking the strongest radiation storm since October 1989. Though extremely strong that was small compared to events on November 4, 2003. The Sun unleashed its largest recorded solar flare, capping 10 days of unprecedented activity. When the Sun blasted off a never-before-seen X45 megaflare, NASA stated the Sun had "gone haywire".

This increased energy output directly affects everything weather-related. Trickle down effects show up in disease, disaster, agriculture and ultimately, the economy. Unlike greenhouse emissions, which could be reduced, the Sun's output is a much larger problem and one over which we have no control.

Plus. PLUS! **PLUS!** Whew!

Add to these geophysical, astronomical and meteorological concerns, an overblown unstable financial market, a burst housing bubble and anxiety over terrorism. 2000 and 2008 saw the birth of recessions. The 2000 event coupled with 2001 terrorist attacks and Enron-style "creative accounting", tanked the U.S. economy. It resulted in three million lost jobs. Families struggled to stave off bankruptcy and keep their homes and retirement. Financial worries were eased for those who could rely on their stored foods and other necessities.

More than a dozen years ago, FEMA's Director James Lee Witt, warned people they must take preparedness into their own hands and be *personally* responsible. He reiterated this warning on January 6, 2000, after the millennial rollover, and urged people to keep up their Y2K preparedness. Some listened. Others let this good start fall in a heap. Increasingly, this is a time when "personal responsibility" is more than a catchy comment. It should be a way of life.

Holly Drennan Deyo

Chapter 1: Getting Started

WHY DID THE PREP BUG BITE?

Growing up, my mother always kept a large stash of canned goods, staples, peanut butter, toilet paper, disinfectant, (of course chocolate!) and other useable items in the crawl space under our house. Foods were neatly lined on makeshift shelves, rotated into meals toward expiration and replaced after consumption. When asked why she stored things, Mom never really pinned it down. Her parents had owned a small-town mercantile and maybe it was the security of always having goods on hand. It might have been still vivid memories of the Depression or an underlying sense of unease most people feel now. Whatever the reason, she unknowingly passed on the baton of emergency preparedness.

We were fortunate not to have endured destructive hurricanes, earthquakes, unemployment or civil unrest, but we Missourians certainly experienced power outages from thunderstorms as well as tornadoes, hailstorms, blizzards, ice storms and flooding. On several occasions we were very glad Mom had squirreled away plenty of food, candles and extra blankets. I suspect these occurrences are only a whiff of what's in store for planet Earth.

With that in mind, we encourage each of you to do several things. First and foremost, have a daily chat with the Lord. He will point you in the right direction and help with hard decisions. Times ahead will be very unnerving and it helps to know He is on our side.

Next, take positive steps to organize your household with the following pages as guidelines. Amend the lists to suit personal preferences. This information has been researched and cross-referenced through many organizations such as FEMA, EMA, EPA, American Red Cross, USGS and SAS as well as countless other disaster preparation agencies and survival specialists. Our direct personal experiences and methods of choice have been included. Hopefully we've made all the errors so you don't have to! These suggestions are simple and specific, yet flexible enough to cover many situations.

HOW TO PLAN FOR AN EMERGENCY

One of the first reactions people have when they realize how ill prepared they are is fear. This often morphs into feeling totally overwhelmed. Getting started is often only a matter of breaking down preparedness into manageable bites. It does require planning and assessing your particular situation to decide what will work best – either relocating or "digging in" in your present location.

The original "Plan For An Emergency" was written by a friend and it is recognized in preparedness circles as an excellent organizational primer. Over the years, this document has morphed to meet changing times, though its core material remains.

It's packed with information and common sense guidelines. There's something of value for experienced planners as well as people new to the job. For this reason "Plan For An Emergency" is included with Lisa's blessings. It covers "bare essentials" for emergency planning especially if you end up temporarily relocating by foot. The rest of *Dare To Prepare* covers in detail food, water, first aid and general supplies. "Dare" provides extended list suggestions, recommended quantities and specific preparedness for virtually every natural and manmade disaster.

ASSESSING YOUR OPTIONS

First and foremost you need to know what you want to do and assess your circumstances. Where is your safe place(s)? Where is your 'dig in' site? What is your particular situation? Do you live in an apartment? In the city? In a small town? On a farm? Is anyone in the family disabled or very ill? Do you have children/pets? Do you care for anyone outside your immediate household; i.e. elderly parent, children with previous spouse? All of these considerations will be important for YOUR personalized plan. Even the ages of children will make a difference in what you plan, how you pack, what you need for supplies.

Will your plan mean moving out of the immediate area? That is a personal decision. So start by organizing your group on paper.

Dare To Prepare: Chapter 1: Getting Started

THINGS TO CONSIDER:

Generally, in the case of a major earthquake or other catastrophic happening, plan on three to five days before help arrives. This is a good rule of thumb.

What type of emergency might you expect in your locale? Storm, bad earthquake, impending hurricane, fire? Will this involve extended periods without power, access to safe places? If you plan to stay, be prepared with at least:
- Food
- Water
- Medicine kit
- Flashlight and lots of batteries
- Portable radio and batteries or solar/crank powered
- Candles (emergency candles burn a long time)
- Cash
- Clothes
- Other items which should go in your MAIN PACKS

Specifics will be addressed later for all of the above. If you live in the city and a catastrophic event occurs, you may need to evacuate, especially if power is out for extended periods or major damage is sustained.

IF YOU PLAN TO LEAVE THE CITY

1. Locate as many routes out as possible – your route of choice may be inaccessible. Plan several places to go. For a family, a designated meeting place is a must. You may need several locations:
   - One just outside your home (as in case of a house fire)
   - One in your neighborhood
   - One outside your neighborhood (in case of major destruction)
   - One in a well-known place just inside your city
   - One outside your city

2. Decide where you will go. Your safe place can be a cabin, a campsite, a relative's home or another home you own or lease.

3. Routes need to be accessible using different modes of transportation. Can't drive your car because roads are out? Ride a bike or horse. Can't ride? Walk. Consider whether any of your planned routes have bridges. They may be vulnerable to collapse during earthquakes, mud- or landslides and floods, or clogged from gridlock. If they are impassable, is there another way? Should you have to ride a bike or walk, think ahead what and how much you can carry and what makes good carrying carts or packs.

4. Have routes laid out to safe places and shelters if you plan to stay. People with small children may have fewer choices in an emergency.

5. If you have school children, map routes for them in case they're cut off from you during the day and/or they need to walk/ride home – or to the prearranged places.

6. Safety tips and common sense:

The fewer people around you, the safer you will be. You may be required to walk all the way to your destination and people outside your group might want what you have. People can become unhinged during disasters and do things they wouldn't ordinarily consider. Your provisions may make those who didn't prepare angry and they may hassle your group or try to take your supplies. When at all possible, stay away from other people. Keep the following in mind as you plan your routes.
- The more supplies and routes you have, the more choices you'll have on short notice.
- The more first aid, basic and secondary treatments you know the better.
- The more you practice, the easier it is to make decisions in emotional scenarios.
- Know how far you are willing to go. Will you carry a weapon for self-defense or hunting food? Not a pleasant thought but necessary.
- Know the capabilities of those who will travel with you. How far can they walk or ride and what skills do they have? Someone with medical knowledge is a great benefit, as is someone with hunting skills, plant and other food gathering experience, or map reading expertise. Plan on each person in your group learn some of these skills, even young children can take part. Think of it as Girl or Boy Scout training in action. Make it a family project and practice while camping or hiking.
- Don't forget your pets. Plan extra water for them. Most pets can eat what humans eat so don't burden yourself trying to carry dog or cat food. Pet birds can ride on your shoulder. Don't ever leave pets in cages, tied up or penned in rooms. This surely would be a slow and painfully cruel death and it happens way

too often during floods. Your animals can also carry items. Big dogs can carry packs or be trained to pull small wagons. Horses, and other larger animals can also be useful, but that goes without saying.

IF YOU PLAN TO STAY WHERE YOU ARE

The following pages will take care of your needs for a short-term emergency. You have the luxury of not worrying about how much weight you can carry. Plus, you may not need emergency rations for as many days. Stock all or as many of the items as possible listed on the next pages. Plan as though you won't have outside help, electricity or medical aid, or be able to purchase necessities for two weeks. Any assistance arriving earlier is a boon.

Photo: Many people camped in their yards after the Loma Prieta quake. (J.K. Nakata, USGS)

You must have at least one gallon of water per person per day in storage. This covers <u>drinking</u> needs only, not hygiene, doing dishes or flushing commodes. (Water purification and storage will be discussed later.) You may not be able to sleep in your home and have to camp out in the yard or in one of your town's shelters. Keep these emergency items out of your home along with your main packs so they can be retrieved if your residence is unsafe to enter.

TIPS: Use an old refrigerator or large container for storage of these items. Bury the container in the backyard, without the lid, halfway or mostly underground. Make a waterproof cover over the top of the chest. Plant flowers around it or decorate with yard statues or any other means of concealment. If you live in a flood-prone area, choose an outside location other than in-ground.

Inside the container, store waterproofed packs and sleeping bags, medical kit and other items. Properly protected, there should be little worry of water, insect or vermin damage.

A shed or other small building could be ideal for storage. Use LARGE, heavy weight plastic garbage cans with locking lids as your storage bins. They are almost completely waterproof, but wrap tarps and plastic bags around packs and clothing. Other options are to keep these supplies in RVs, fifth wheels, trailers or barns.

MAIN PACKS OR EMERGENCY PACKS

If you have looked into assembling packs, you've probably suffered sticker shock from the price of emergency foods and supplies. You don't have to spend a fortune to meet family needs, but there are a few tricks.

Consider those in your household. If you are single or have a small family, you might want to combine with another small family or with very close friends. Does anyone have health concerns? Need medicines? Glasses? These items need to be duplicated and put into your Main Packs.

Main Packs should be placed outside the home in a storage shed, waterproofed container or other major building. Main Packs will contain the most important items whether you stay or leave your home. Each member of your family or group should have a Main Pack including the littlest baby.

Along with these packs, keep copies of family records and personal identification. Doubly protect these documents from moisture, as well as any necessary books, and your medical kit. The First Aid kit will be in a pack by itself and marked as such. Each person should keep medications they take in his own pack along with eyeglasses and other personal items.

CHOOSING THE RIGHT PACK

Invest in a good heavy-duty backpack for each member of your family or group. Take time to find a pack big enough to carry your Main Pack items (and possibly some of the children's things), but not so large you can't carry it comfortably. Make sure the pack's contents are well balanced. Do a trial run by packing it and going on a hike to find the best balance. The pack should be waterproof and be made of a material that won't wear out fast or invite insects or animals. (Can it be sprayed with insect and water repellents?)

It's important to not have a pack filled with just clothes or just dishes. If that pack became lost or destroyed along the way, *everyone* would be without. You will need to carry in your individual Main Pack: Clothing, Personal Items and Eating Utensils.

CLOTHING

Clothing can be expensive, so be smart. Go to discount stores and purchase plain, ordinary sweat pants and shirts in various sizes and colors when they're on sale. **Always buy them larger than you normally wear** to allow for shrinkage and layering.

WHY SWEATS?
- Sweats are easy to wash. You may be doing your washing by hand and drying them on a line.
- They dry quicker than jeans or other clothing, and without a mildew smell.
- They can be worn by anyone. (Even children can wear adult sizes if need be. They can push up legs and sleeves, and pull the drawstring tighter.)
- Sweats are warm when it's cold, and cool when it's hot because they "breathe".
- Sweats can be layered without restricting movement.
- They roll up compactly and take little pack space, and are lightweight to carry.

Now don't you just love them! T-shirts are great too, because they can go as an under layer or as a lightweight shirt in hotter weather. They also roll up tightly and are inexpensive. Don't forget sweat shorts!

The one negative about sweats is that they are very absorbent which makes them less clever in the rain. Wrap each set in a garbage bag and place them in your pack. The garbage bag then makes an inexpensive rain poncho. Just cut a hole for your head and arms and continue to march. If you get too wet – change into another pair of sweats, wrap them back up in the garbage bag, and use the new garbage bag from the new sweats as a raincoat. The next time you stop or do laundry, pull the wet sweats out of the bag, wash, dry and pack in a new garbage bag.

OTHER CLOTHING ITEMS
Socks. Two kinds are recommended, cotton tube and 100% wool. Wool, though itchy, keeps you warm even when wet. Pack several good pairs for each family member.

Shoes. Pack at least two good pairs. Sneakers are practical and cheap if you don't buy name brands. When wet, they won't fall apart. Consider two pairs of sneakers and one good pair of knee high rubber boots, like the farm type "muck" boots or sturdy gumboots. These roll up pretty small, aren't any heavier than a good hiking boot and reasonably priced. If you live in or anticipate walking through rough terrain, substitute one pair of tennis shoes with a pair of <u>well broken in</u> hiking boots. New boots will make your feet tired and leave painful blisters. Do not scrimp on socks and shoes. Your feet are your friends and take you everywhere you need to go!

Jacket and Coat. Wool will keep you warm even when wet. Purchase a good wool insulated hunting shirt large enough so you can double- or triple-layer sweats underneath. Also purchase a lightweight jacket, preferably with Thinsulate. Ski jackets are lightweight and warm. Buy them off-season on sale. Again, allow plenty of room for easy movement and layering.

Bandannas. Purchase a bunch. They can cover the head for warmth, tie back long hair, be used as a sweatband, be soaked in water and worn around the neck as a cooler, be used for private stops, and substitute as a hankie. They take up little space, are cheap and extremely light. (Women, they can be used as sanitary napkins when triple folded. You can even use moss or other clean vegetation as an absorbent pad, but watch for poison ivy! Place the bandanna around the absorbent material and have at least two layers next to your skin.) They wash easily and cleanly, and dry quickly.

MISCELLANEOUS CLOTHING ITEMS
- Undergarments
- Gloves
- Stocking hat and/or rain hat

Clothing needs to be easy to wash, dry, carry and pack without being too heavy or bulky. Be sure to remove everything from boxes, and wrap in plastic for waterproofing.

\multicolumn{3}{c}{MAIN PACK ITEMS}		
QTY. PER PERSON	**CLOTHING ITEMS**	**COMMENT**
2 sets	Sweat suits	Oversized
2 sets	Sweat shorts and T-shirts	Oversized
4 pair	Socks	2 cotton, 2 all wool
4 sets	Undergarments	100% cotton is recommended over silk or nylon for durability and washability
2	Support bras for women	Choose good quality
2	Jock straps for men	Choose good quality
6-8	Bandannas	Many uses
1 roll	Garbage bags, leaf-size	Use as rain gear, waterproofing packed clothing or place under sleeping bags when on the ground
1-2 pair	Sneakers	
1 pair	Boots, black rubber, gum boots or hiking boots	Boots can be strung on a bungee strap and hung from the pack
1	Jacket	Good quality ski jacket
1	Wool hunting shirt	Insulated and oversized
2 pair	Gloves	1 lightweight and 1 heavyweight
2	Hats	1 stocking cap and 1 rain hat.
5 days	Emergency rations	Purchase good quality that you've tried and appeal to your tastes. More later. These can be carried in other packs. Two more days' rations should be carried in another pack with the kitchen items.
2	Toothbrushes	
1	Toothpaste	
1	Deodorant	Unscented
As needed	Tampons or pads	Tampons take up less room, but pads can substitute for bandages.
As needed	Personal medicines	
1	Eyeglasses	
\multicolumn{3}{c}{**NOTE: THIS IS AN OVERVIEW LIST ONLY** \newline Later we will get very specific about quantities and additional items}		

EATING UTENSILS, PLATE AND BOWL

You will benefit by purchasing military type kits – *a good strong* set for each family or group member. It should have a plate/bowl with full assortment of utensils that fold up in the middle of the plate and bowl. Purchase a strong metal cup that can be tied to the outside of each pack and used for drinking along the way. Try to have one extra set for every 4 persons if one becomes damaged or lost. Everyone carries and is responsible for his own eating and drinking set. It is best to color code packs for each person.

You can even opt to color code or tag clothing, sleeping bags, mats, tents and all other items. This is especially helpful with younger children – and for us confused adults too!

BEDDING, SLEEPING BAGS OR SWAGS

It's a good idea to purchase the best *warm* sleeping bag or swag your budget will allow. Look for lightweight, heavy duty, warm sleepers that roll up compactly. Small camping pillows that roll up inside the sleeping bag are a clever addition. Roll the sleeping bag into a small plastic tarp for further waterproofing and use bungee straps to wrap and secure to your pack. The tarp can be spread under the sleeping bag for extra moisture protection and another layer of warmth. It can also provide quick shelter and immediate cover. Purchase a good thermal blanket and roll it with your sleeping bag for times when you need that extra "something". These are generally very inexpensive, lightweight and worth the small amount of room they require.

Consider sleeping bags that zip together. Sharing body heat will help on cold nights. Another good purchase is a dense sleeping mat or closed-cell foam pad that rolls up small. They are light and will be a welcome barrier between you and the hard cold ground. Attach your sleeping bag by bungee or rope to the top of your Main Pack.

Dare To Prepare: Chapter 1: Getting Started

You might think that a small pillow and mat aren't necessary, but if you're over 30 or have a bad back, the ground can be mighty cruel. The last thing you want during a disaster is to need a chiropractic adjustment if no "bone breaker" is handy.

With a pillow and a blanket tucked at the center, roll the sleeping bag or swag inside a tarp. Secure this roll to the frame of your Main Pack with straps. Tie the rolled mat to the top of the Main Pack.

BEDDING ITEMS		
QTY/PERSON	ITEM	COMMENT
1	Sleeping Bag or Swag	Purchase warmest and best quality within your budget
1	Tarp, small	
1	Camp Pillow, small	
1	Thermal Blanket	
1	Sleeping Mat	
2-3	Bungee or "Okie" Straps	
1	Hammock, optional	Keep you off the ground, makes you less vulnerable to insects, snakes and moisture. Roll up inside or outside the sleeping bag.

THE MEDICINE KIT OR FIRST AID KIT

It's easy to spend a lot of money setting up a good first aid kit. Using common sense, it doesn't have to be expensive. Items like hydrogen peroxide and anti-bacterial ointments are a must. Some of the other items 'they' say are a must, can be substituted for less expensive alternatives.

GENERAL FIRST AID ITEMS FOR THE BUDGET-MINDED	
ITEM	COMMENT
Bandages	Can be made from white cotton sheets. Wash; then boil. Dry and cut into desired sizes. Roll and put into Ziplocs to keep dry.
Gauze	Purchase in bulk. Separate gauze into different first aid kits throughout the house and your Main Pack kits.
Cotton Balls	Work great, are cheap, have multiple uses. Buy in the plastic bags.
White Tape	Important but again, don't spend a fortune.
Cloth Bandages	Split at each end several inches so they make their own tie. Cloth bandages can be boiled and used again.
Syrup of Ipecac	In 2003, discussion arose among doctors that Ipecac isn't the best way to rid the body of poison – vomiting alone may not remove all poisons from the stomach. If possible, call 1-800-222-1222 to reach a local poison-control center, or 911 if symptoms are severe. If this isn't an option, Ipecac may serve.
Diarrhea Medicine	Tablets
Surgical Gloves	Buy bulk and cheap
Scissors, Tweezers, Needles	Include several curved needles. Don't skimp quality here!
Thread or fine fishing line	Purchase white thread for sewing stitches. Make sure it's new stock and not subject to breakage and fits through your needles.
Safety Pins	Assorted sizes
Splints	One 6-8" (15-20cm) and one 12" (30cm) sanded boards will serve as light splits.
Packs	Chemical heat and cold packs are handy for initial kit needs and aren't too heavy.
Rubbing Alcohol	
Iodine	
Anti-Bee Sting Ointment	
Itch Cream	
Snake Bite Kit	
Insect Repellent	
Sun Block	

Bandages, aspirin, multi-vitamins, and a 5-day supply of everyone's personal prescription medications should be kept in this group First Aid Kit. The rest of their medications will be kept in their Main Pack.

This kit should be easy to carry. It will be readily available and complete enough to handle most emergencies. This won't be a kit to cover everything, but it will be handy and useful for those most common injuries. (In-depth information on First Aid Kits is covered in Chapter 14.)

Two books covering common medical procedures and basic surgical procedures should be included. Keep them small and lightweight, and stored in the first aid pack. Another book to consider would cover herbs and other natural remedies.

If you're staying in one place, you can have a more comprehensive medical kit. Waterproof everything as much as possible. Buy in bulk and on sale, use sheets for bandages, and practice other common sense approaches. Check First Aid Kits every six months for expired dates.

COMMUNICATON

Purchase phone cards for members in your group. Cell phones may or may not work depending on how widespread the disaster is and how many people clog the lines. Walkie talkies are a simple, inexpensive solution if family members expect to be separated only short distances. (See Chapter 32 for details and solutions.)

MONEY

In the event of power outages, stores can and do stop giving change, accepting checks or running credits cards because they can't be verified. Additionally, banks may be closed, so cash is a must.

At home, keep at least $250 per person, more if you can afford it. No bills should be larger than $20's. Tens, $5s and $1s are best. Hide funds in an unusual place that's not easily accessible. Forget the freezer or the toilet tank. Every thief on the planet checks those spots. Have change, but keep most of it in quarters or twenty-cent pieces.

If you're buying things during a disaster, carry small bills or risk losing any change due you. Have a secret pocket or other place to hide it. People under stress or in civil unrest are more prone helping themselves to what others have. In case of robbery, don't fight them for it. If you get off with only losing money, count yourself lucky.

Should you run out of food while on the road, vending machines may be your only source if everyone else didn't have the same idea. Many machines ran out of stock very early on during Hurricane Katrina. Empty film canisters or prescription vials are good coin keepers.

TIP: Opt for a higher amount of cash and store it in several places, some in your Main Pack, some on your body. If you're robbed, perhaps one or the other location will be overlooked. How much cash you keep at home should depend on how well stocked you are or how much you plan to carry if you relocate. Common sense needs to be the guideline. This concludes the Main Packs.

KITCHEN

A portable "kitchen" is optional but it's good planning to have one assembled should it be needed. If you carry emergency rations like MREs (Meals Ready to Eat), HeaterMeals or similar products in your Main Packs, you may not need the items listed below. MREs and such are easier, but if you have special dietary needs or salt restrictions, these foods may pose a problem. If you travel by vehicle or have health considerations, you may want to opt for a mini-kitchen.

The portable kitchen will not be as difficult as some might think. These items can be distributed among the packs and pans can hang from packs. Make a special carrier for the knives and other utensils. Or, make another pack to be carried on poles between people.

These same poles can be used for shelter and lean-tos, protection from sun or rain and in sleeping areas. They can also be used to make a travois on which you could load kitchen and other items to be pulled. Store smaller items inside larger ones.

Plan on using a lot of vinegar, dish soap and bleach (buy bulk, inexpensive house brands). Carrying these items will be heavy, so it will be up to you to decide what you'll need.

If you remember that a little bit goes a long way, you can get by with less. Practice using these items for washing dishes and clothes by hand and for washing your body and hair. Determine how much was used in that week, and then multiply by the number of people in your group. Keep in mind that all of these items are very useful, but balance that against the weight must be carried. If you can use a travois, cart or wagon that can be pulled, it would make it easier.

Dare To Prepare: Chapter 1: Getting Started

\multicolumn{3}{c}{PORTABLE KITCHEN (AMOUNTS ARE PER FAMILY UNIT)}		
AMOUNT	**ITEM**	**COMMENT**
2	Frying Pans	One large, one medium. An iron pan provides some iron in the diet.
3	Pots	1 large, 1 medium, 1 small
1	Coffee Pot	Percolator type
2	Spatulas	Metal
2	Large Spoons	Metal
4	Hot Pads	
2	Cutting Boards	
2	Sharp Knives	
1	Ladles	Metal
2	Wire Racks	
1	Measuring Spoons	Metal, plastic is subject to melting and breaking
2	Cooking Forks	Metal
1	Tongs	Metal
1	Sm. Portable Grill	Propane or charcoal
1	Measuring Cups	Metal, plastic is subject to melting and breaking
1	Knife Sharpener	
2	Hunting Knives	
1 roll	Garbage Bags	Leaf size, heavy duty
1 gallon	Bleach	Use for wiping down and sterilizing cutting boards, knives and other cooking surfaces after cutting meats, and to purifying water.
1 box	Steel Pads	Use for cleaning. Buy the scratchy type pads instead of the S.O.S., Brillo or Steelo type
2 jugs	Liquid Soap	For washing hands: Mix dish soap and vinegar – equal parts – makes a great, inexpensive anti-bacterial soap and keeps hands soft. It also works well for washing your clothes. Use 1 part dish soap to 3 parts vinegar to keep clothes clean and odor free. Too much soap requires more rinsing. A little goes a long way. It also can be your shampoo using the handwashing recipe. Experiment and find out what is best for you. Hair will benefit from the vinegar. Keep 1 soap container by the kitchen, the other by the area used for the bathroom.
1 gallon	Vinegar	
TIP: Washing your hands after you use the toilet, and before cooking or eating, will cut way down on colds, flu and other illness. The last thing anybody needs is to get sick especially if traveling. Stress weakens the body, and when in emergency situations, you will be UNDER STRESS! Strengthen it, both mentally and physically, by being prepared and as sanitary as possible.		

WATER

This is the most important and necessary item. Plan 1 gallon (4L) per person per day. This won't cover anything besides drinking water. (More is required in the heat, and slightly less in the cold.) Learn and watch for the signs of dehydration. Too little water in hot weather leads to heat stroke; too little in cold temps encourages frostbite and cracked skin. The latter invites infections and disease.

Water adds a lot of weight and bulk – 8 lbs/gal, 3.6kg/4 L. Plan for water refill spots when you lay out your routes. Lakes, rivers, streams, melted snow and man-made water sources must all be hoped for, but not counted on. Refill water supplies at **every** stop. (See Chapter 7 for Finding Survival Water.)

Purchase and carry a portable water purifier in a designated person's pack. *This can't be stressed strongly enough.* If water supplies aren't replenished through purchase or rain catchment, it **must be** purified – even if it looks OK. This is no time to come down with gastro-intestinal problems – or worse. (For Water Purification see Chapter 4.)

During floods, be extra careful of polluted water sources especially in the city and lowland areas. Higher ground streams and rivers are safer, but should never be assumed pure even if they look crystal clear. Rainwater can't be beat!

Water tanks holding 3-5 gallons (12-20L) are inexpensive and useable. However, if the water must be carried, packing an extra 40 pounds (18kg) might be too difficult. One gallon (4L) is certainly doable, in addition to a canteen or camelbak. Everyone should have a canteen to carry on his/her belt along with a knife, whistle, and other items, which will be discussed later. In the case of a camelbak, it replaces a canteen and more evenly distributes weight across the body. For people with back or neck problems, this is a better alternative than a canteen. If you're carrying a backpack, consider getting just the camelbak reservoir and stashing it in your backpack.

DO NOT DRINK STRAIGHT FROM YOUR CANTEEN. Pour small amounts into your cup, which should be hanging from your Main Pack and then drink. This will help keep your canteen bacteria-free and cut down on colds and other disease.

FOOD

What and how much depends on your circumstances. Plan for 5 days' emergency rations per person. Canned foods add a lot of weight. HeaterMeals **www.heatermeals.com** (1.800.503.4483) and MREs are clever especially if water supplies are an issue and they eliminate many portable kitchen items. Dehydrated and freeze-dried foods keep well, but require water for reconstituting and should be heated for best taste and hastening rehydration.

Five days' food may be more than is needed, but since these are light and compact; it's better to have too much than too little. Military surplus stores, camping and outdoor shops as well as numerous Internet resources supply these shelf stable foods. MREs have been around a long time and have considerably improved flavor. They're lightweight, taste good, have a long shelf life, don't require outside heating (heaters included with HeaterMeals and Inferno Meals) and are durable when traveling.

HeaterMeals debuted in 1994 and the company now offers 30 selections. The original was an entrée-only product with a shelf life of 3 years from date of packaging. The EX line is also an entrée-only product, but has a shelf life of up to 5 years.

Their Meal *Kits* include snacks and a beverage and are divided into two groups. HeaterMeals Plus are for hungry people offering 6 snacks and a canned drink. Due to the shorter viability of crackers and cookies, these meals have a shelf life for up to 1 year. HeaterMeals 3 have a shelf life of up to 3 years since their snacks are M&Ms and fruit, plus a powdered beverage. All HeaterMeal shelf lives are based on storing products at 80°F (27°C) or less.

For the health conscious, HeaterMeals have at least 25% less sodium and less cholesterol compared to MREs, and no trans fats.

To heat, open the food heater bag and place the food try inside, film side down. Pour in the supplied water and close with the sticky tab. Set it on top of the HeaterMeal box and watch the water bubble. Your meal is ready just 10 minutes. Entrées run around $4.50 and Meal Kits about $5.50. **When ordering online, make sure to ask what is the Date of Production or Use By Date stamped on the box.** Tray foods' shelf life is 2 years, pouches last up to 5 years, pancakes are 1 year.

Purchase in bulk or by the case to save money. You might want to include dried foods like pasta, rice, beans and beef jerky, though many dried foods require water and heat before they're ready to eat.

Powdered milk is ideal and a can or two of milk could be an asset. Frozen items are unrealistic in warm weather, but could be used in the first day or two and on the third day in very cold weather. Carrying ice chests is unrealistic unless driving or having a cart/travois and good ground for traveling. Always keep in mind how far you will be going and by what method: foot, bike or vehicle.

PORTABLE KITCHEN "MUST HAVES"

Carry these items in sacks that can be waterproofed by double wrapping them in plastic bags. Anything else is luxury. Your portable kitchen might include:

- Chocolate Bars, Candy items or Marshmallows (morale and energy are closely related).
- Coffee, Tea and Hot Chocolate Mix
- Dehydrated Fruits
- Dried Beans
- Flour
- Garlic, cloves and/or powder
- Grains
- Onions, bulbs or powder
- Salt and Pepper
- Sugar
- Vinegar

TOOL BELT

The military and some survivalist type groups sell a good wide belt that can carry many items. On this belt you may want to carry:

TOOL BELT ITEMS			
QTY/PERSON	ITEM	QTY/PERSON	ITEM
1	Canteen and cup	1	Whistle
1	Machete or Small Hatchet in strong, protective carrying case	1	Pocket or Hunting Knife
1	Holster, Handgun and Ammo Pouch	1	30 yds. (30 m) Rope

Whistles are a good safety measure in case of separation. Organize a code. A certain sound like two short blasts might mean "all come now"; three blasts may signify "danger". Each child should have his own whistle and learn how to respond individually by tone or by group to a different tone. This is an important tool to keep everyone together and to forage more safely if separated.

A hunting or pocket knife should be age appropriate; however, most everyone can carry one or the other. A pocket knife can be extremely helpful when hiking or camping and even more useful on a survival mission. The hunting knife can be used the same way but will make skinning and gutting animals much easier.

The ammo pouch and handgun are optional. You must register a weapon in most states, and for concealed a permit is required. In Australia, which has been largely disarmed, regulations are stringent and vary greatly from state to state. See Chapter 38 for whom to contact on firearms information.

A handgun or a rifle can mean life or death for either attacker or defendant. If you carry one, KNOW HOW TO USE AND CARE FOR IT. The same applies for a bow and arrow. Instructional classes are a great idea. Don't ever point a weapon at anybody unless you are prepared to use it.

If you will be hunting, know how to use the weapon effectively so the animal isn't wounded unnecessarily or caused undue pain. Be compassionate. Take time to get an accurate shot so it drops in the first attempt. You may not have the luxury of following a wounded animal.

Buy the best shot, not the cheapest, to avoid misfires. Carry the cleaning kit needed for that weapon and several hundred rounds per weapon.

ADDITIONAL ITEMS TO CONSIDER

These suggestions are very dependent on how and under what conditions you are traveling. If you will be crossing a river, a boat is necessary for supplies. While you might be able to swim across it, keeping food items bedding and medical supplies dry is essential.

CARRY CART

As your "stuff to carry" starts to grow, you might want to consider a game cart. For $130, the cart pictured right will carry up to 300 pounds. Larger load bearing carts are available. They're constructed of tough welded steel with durable, 16" puncture-proof tires. It has a special zero-weight-on-the-handle design and low-profile axle for non-tip stability plus to take weight off the transporter. Hauling your supplies over rough terrain is a cinch if you avoid this one snag. Debris can get caught in the spokes. Consider welding on wheel discs to cover the spokes. Check for these carts at Cabela's **www.cabelas.com** or 1.800.237.4444.

ROPE

Good strong nylon and natural fiber rope. KNOW HOW TO MAKE KNOTS. Carry more than you think you will need. If you select nylon rope, be sure to carry extra matches. When nylon rope is cut, the ends need to be burned to prevent fraying.

HAMMOCK OR CAMP BED

Hammocks get you off the ground, are lightweight and can be adjusted. If you're traveling in the plains or desert, trees may be scarce. Camp beds, while they don't fold up small like hammocks, are very comfortable; get sleeping bags off the ground and away from moisture and insects. In Australia, many campers and hikers use swags. They are excellent choices providing mosquito netting and a totally enclosed environment without a tent.

TENTS

Two-person tents that pop into place work great. You may not have the time, the weight capacity or the room for carrying a tent, but depending on time of year and weather, they may be a necessity. Keep them small and lightweight. For every tent, bring a tarp big enough to put under it. Tarps are great waterproofers. Wet tents or sleeping bags make people miserable and you won't have time to dry them out while traveling.

RAFT AND/OR BOAT

Depending on the circumstances, these items may be essential. Looking at televised flooding accounts, people often motor around in their little fishing boats and rubber rafts. Sometimes boats or rafts are a must. It may also need to carried or used in your travels so plan several rubber rafts to carry your group. Think carefully of all your routes to travel. Pre-planning and anticipation of possible complications can't be stressed enough.

LITTLE THINGS HELP

1. Always refill your gas/petrol tank before or when the fuel gauge reaches the halfway mark. Keeping a tank topped up will be a plus if you are on the go and no gas/petrol or diesel is available. It's also good practice to keep gas tanks full to avoid running out of fuel if you get caught in a snowstorm, mudslide, extended traffic jam, earthquake or other unforeseen disaster.
2. Anchor items at home so they are stable in case of an earthquake. It's a good practice wherever you live.
3. Know how to turn off the power, water and gas to the house. Children should learn this as well.
4. Know how to access the water in your hot water heater in case it is needed. This is simple to do, but if you don't know how, it doesn't matter how easy it is.
5. Purchase a generator or split the cost with a neighbor and purchase one large unit together. It can keep the freezer working and afford a bit of comfort. Remember to store fuel for it. Proper fuel storage and purchasing a generator is discussed in Chapters 28 and 29.
6. Keep an emergency pack for every vehicle. Store an extra blanket, emergency candle and matches with each one.
7. Keep as physically fit as possible. The healthier and better shape you're in, the less your body will weaken during an emergency. This goes for Spiritual fitness as well; fellowship is good for you!
8. Purchase USGS or AGSO maps for the area where you live and travel, and a good quality magnifying glass. It can be used for starting fires, map reading or looking for slivers.
9. Practice fire drills.
10. Walk and drive your evacuation routes as often as possible until you can do so in your sleep.

COMMON SENSE

God gave us this gift as a reasoning tool. USE IT. If you feel you should move elsewhere, do so. To help you decide where's best for you, look at *Prudent Places USA* by Holly Deyo.

Don't move because someone tells you to. If you're thinking about it, make your decision and plan from there. Going round and round only delays progress and puts one further behind.

If you plan to stay where you are, 'dig in', equip your home and family. Don't feel pressured to go elsewhere, but be prepared in case you must.

Once you've made your plans and have prepared as much as possible, relax and enjoy your life and loved ones. All of this may never be needed for an emergency so keep rotating stored goods into your daily foods and medical needs. Make "rotation" a part of normal living. It's a great way to save money because you always have a well-stocked pantry. Having food reserves allows you to shop only when goods are on sale. It frees more of your time not having to run to the store as often. It also prepares you for unexpected company, illness or unplanned job loss.

Last and most important, whatever your personal spiritual route, be in touch with God. Pray daily and keep your Bible with you and your family/group wherever you go. The best-prepared person is the one who balances their spiritual, physical and emotional lives.[10]

Chapter 2: Urban Survival – Are You Ready?

Plan For An Emergency gave you the basics and an overview of what's needed to prepare, especially if you expect to be mobile. Think you're ready? If many survival solutions for your home involve electricity or gas, how would you change these plans if power weren't available?

In 1986, my husband and I underwent a 4-day test. One lovely April day in Colorful Colorado, just when everyone was eager for spring flowers, Old Man Winter made an unexpected ugly return. At the time, we lived in a newly developed rural setting; the subdivision had not yet buried its utilities. Power lines were looped precariously over makeshift poles. A sinking feeling hit our stomachs as snow and ice piled on trees and wires, bending everything into dangerous positions. Heavy, wet snow knocked out all power in a matter of hours and it remained off for four long, cold days. In the meantime, the white stuff continued to multiply.

Unless you owned a 4-wheel drive or heavy pick-up, no one came in or out of our housing area, not even snow plows. They had their hands full digging out people and businesses in town. In this subdivision there were only five families scattered throughout and everyone worked as a team. Neighbor checked with neighbor to see if children had enough milk and food. Did everyone have candles, flashlights and firewood? Families forged groups to dig out one household at a time. It spawned a real feeling of community, of pulling together.

Besides electrics, our home had one wood-burning fireplace in the great room (games room for Aussies) and it was not heat-efficient. Most of the warmth went up the chimney instead of heating the house. Icy showers and a cold bed wore thin by the third day. It took hours for my waist-length thick hair to dry. From layering lots of clothing, we looked more like polar bears than people. Ski pants, jackets and snow boots felt nice and warm.

Without electricity, the freezer and fridge items became a concern. Everything was removed from both and buried outside in snow drifts. Though the FDA doesn't recommend this, it worked great! You just have to monitor the situation and be sure everything stays snow-covered. If you're worried, it's not cold enough, check temps a thermometer. Fortunately a BBQ grill with full propane tanks was just outside the kitchen door.

Meals cooked quite nicely on the grill. Left over from the early 70s, I had an old fondue pot heated by Sterno. Many times I had threatened to give it a toss in favor of an electric model. Cans of soup, beans and other vegetables were heated in this ancient pot for meals. After that experience, I vowed never to throw it away and today, it's still among our survival gear.

Even though we had plenty of food, water, firewood and candles in our home, it became very obvious some preparedness areas definitely needed help. That was over 20 years ago and many things have changed. I'm grateful it was only a *small* test and just a snowstorm!

TEST YOUR PREPAREDNESS

Suppose conditions are extreme and you aren't able to return home for a while. Shelter, communication, clothing, tools and possibly cooking items will be needed. If your home remains intact, but power is out, alternate sources for warmth and cooking have to be found. Many supplies you'll already have on hand and don't need to be duplicated. The best way to prepare for an "in-home camping trip" is to take this test:

Assume there is no electricity or power for the purpose of effective planning.

How must you alter your routine? What would you need to get through each day's activities? Do you have the proper equipment? Are your appliances all electric? Do they depend on gas? If, after the initial crisis has passed – maybe in a week to 10 days, the power returns. Great! But what if it hasn't... This is not being pessimistic, only prepared. While we lived in Australia, there was a mighty gas explosion in Melbourne, Victoria. Thousands of gas customers were without fuel for as long as 3 weeks, some even longer. It was hugely inconvenient for most people.

For example, if you purchase an electric grain grinder, make certain it can be converted to manual operation. If there is no power and only microwaveable dinners are in the freezer, dinner is already shot in the foot. Without power, foods thaw and spoil in approximately 3 days. Should half of your stored foods be canned goods and you don't have a manual can opener, getting to the food will be tough.

Do a mental walk-through for a typical day. Imagine waking to the clock radio. Does it run on batteries?

You're showered, groomed and ready for the day. Did you use an electric razor, curling iron or blow dryer? Did you need a lighted make-up mirror or drink a steamy cup of brewed coffee? Did you use a space heater to ward off the morning chill or a heat lamp? Don't forget to factor in time to heat bath water!

For breakfast, did you warm pastries in the toaster? Boil tea water on the stove? Electrically juice vegetables? Perhaps you flipped on the stereo to catch the morning news. Are you stocked up on batteries? Do you have a solar, battery-powered or crank radio?

Next on the day's agenda is a little house cleaning. Do you have adequate disinfectant? Germs rampage with broken sewer mains. The vacuum cleaner won't run; do you have a decent broom, mop and pail? How will you wash laundry? If the sewer lines are broken, how will you go to the toilet? Do you know proper sanitation measures? Practice composting. It makes one less reliant on the garbage disposal or landfills and feeds a sprouting garden.

Will you survive without the Internet? Did you make a hard copy of every important file on your hard disk? Let's hope the only copy of your address book is NOT kept in cyberspace. Don't plan on calling Aunt Nell with your cell phone. Your regular phone, should it be working, may be jammed with emergency calls. A visit to Aunt Nell is probably not feasible either due to inoperable traffic lights.

As we've already seen during tornado disasters in Arkansas January 1999, martial law and curfews were imposed. A similar situation took place after Hurricane Katrina. While technically not martial law, it was the closest thing to it. President Bush dispatched 7,200 active-duty ground troops to Louisiana and Mississippi in addition to 10,000 National Guard troops sent by the Pentagon. This brought the total Guard contingent to about 40,000. With curfews strictly enforced and businesses closed, how long will your gasoline/petrol or diesel last? This is an excellent reason to have a dependable bicycle, spare tires and repair parts.

Photo: Bourbon Street in New Orleans' famous French Quarter, paratroopers from Bravo Company, 2nd Battalion, 505th Parachute Infantry Regiment, 82nd Airborne Division, patrol nearly deserted streets. (Daren Reehl)

This scenario is enough to set your imagination in motion. Continue visualizing the rest of your day and cooking the evening meal. Have you ever cooked over an open fire? It requires some practice. After dinner, what do you do for entertainment? In winter, daylight may be gone by 5 PM. Activities will need to be something other than watching TV or playing video games. Remember the good old days of books, talking with your neighbor and playing Monopoly? It's time to turn the clock back, at least for a little while!

Did you see from this exercise where there might be some holes in your preparedness? Fill in the blanks with the necessary items and try again.

Now are you ready?

At this point, have a "practice" weekend with your family or by yourself, especially if you've not spent a lot of time camping. Pick a weekend and shut off the electricity. No cheating. OK? No one is grading you except yourself and it's a terrific way to see what areas need boosting. This is one of those instances where nothing can take the place of actual experience!

If you found more "holes" in your planning than you liked, the next chapters will help you plan smoothly for emergencies. The information is specific and detailed, yet flexible to allow for any changes you wish to make.

Print off a copy of this quiz for each family member. It will help you assess your family's emergency readiness. It's also a good way to discuss preparedness in a non-threatening manner with children and make them feel like an active part of the planning. In the safety of their home, children can see you in an unfrazzled mode, handling everything calmly. <grin> Ready to test your family's preparedness?

1. Has your family rehearsed fire escape routes from your home in the last year?
___YES ___NO   What are they?
_____
_____
2. Where are the upper story escape ladder(s) located? Are they in good repair?
_____ ___YES ___NO
3. Does your family know what to do before, during, and after an emergency?
___YES ___NO   Give a brief outline _____
_____
4. Where would the family meet if a disaster occurs while some members are away from home?
_____
5. If heavy objects hang over beds that could fall during an earthquake, have they been secured?
___YES ___NO
6. Is there a flashlight in every bedroom? (candles shouldn't be used until you're sure there are no gas leaks)
___YES ___NO   Checked the batteries lately? ___YES ___NO
7. Are shoes near your bed to protect your feet against broken glass? ___YES ___NO
8. If a water line ruptured during an earthquake, do you know how to shut off the water main?
___YES ___NO   Where is it located?_____
9. Can this water valve be turned off by hand without the use of a tool? Do you have a tool if one is needed?
___YES ___NO
10. Where the main gas shutoff valve to your house is located?
_____
11. If you smell gas, how would you shut off this valve?
_____
12. Gas valves usually can't be turned off by hand. Is there a shutoff tool near the valve?
___YES ___NO
13. Would you be able to safely restart your furnace when gas is available? ___YES ___NO
14. Are smoke alarms in each bedroom and living area? ___YES ___NO
Checked the batteries lately? ___YES ___NO
15. Do you have and know how to operate a fire extinguisher? (The fire department will test it for free.)
___YES ___NO   Checked the expiration date? ___YES ___NO
16. Are duplicate keys and copies of important papers stored outside your home? ___YES ___NO
17. Do you have a battery or solar powered emergency radio? ___YES ___NO
Checked the batteries lately? ___YES ___NO

FOR A THREE DAY EMERGENCY, WOULD YOU. . .
18. Have sufficient food? ___YES ___NO
19. Have the means to cook without power? ___YES ___NO
20. Have sufficient water for drinking, cooking, pets, spillage and sanitary needs? ___YES ___NO
21. Have you made 72 hour evacuation kits for each family member? ___YES ___NO
22. If made last year, have you checked all expiration dates and replenished supplies? ___YES ___NO
23. Can you carry or transport these kits? ___YES ___NO
24. Who are your out-of-state contacts? _____
_____
25. Do you have first aid kits in the home and in each car? ___YES ___NO
Checked the expiration dates lately? ___YES ___NO
26. Do you have work gloves and tools for minor rescue and clean up? ___YES ___NO
27. Do you have emergency, small currency cash on hand? (During disasters, banks and ATM machines may close; checks and credit cards can't be verified.) ___YES ___NO
28. Without power, could you heat at least part of your house? ___YES ___NO
29. If you take medications, do you have a month's supply? ___YES ___NO
30. Do you have alternate toilet facilities if there is an extended water shortage? ___YES ___NO

How'd you do?

Chapter 3: Storing Short Term

72-HOUR PREPAREDNESS

Good emergency preparedness requires two types of planning: short term and long term. Both need common sense and assessment of your particular situation. Many people talk about "72-hour" kits, but this is an arbitrary time frame though an accepted one in preparedness circles. **If you want to extend this for another few days, it is strongly recommended, but supplies for less than 72 hours is not worth the effort.** Most emergency and rescue teams take at least three days to make their rounds. Sometimes emergency supplies don't arrive until the fourth day. Under extreme conditions, it may be even longer.

This list includes essentials for three days' survival plus a few "extras" to cover most scenarios. It takes the "budget" kit in *Plan For An Emergency* and includes some necessary extras. Many other items would be nice, but for those watching $$, plan your gear around these core products. Include additional supplies to suit personal taste and finances. Where quantities aren't noted, assume only one is needed. **Suggested amounts are for one person only**, especially for water. The exception to this rule is the First Aid Kit. These medical items are planned for a small family. They can be divided between the adults or maintained in one central kit.

Keep you 72-hour survival kits in your car with a light source at the top of each pack. If disaster strikes while you're home, chances are you can get to your vehicle. If a crisis occurs while traveling, even to the grocery store, your survival supplies are already on board.

Each family member should carry an identical pack in his/her car making changes to each kit to suit personal needs. If you live in a particularly vulnerable area, one that is prone to natural disasters or is a high-risk terrorism area, make sure your pack is on board. Include provisions for children and pets if they are accompanying you. If children aren't of driving age or don't have a car, keep their supplies in your vehicle. Many items for small children need not be duplicated like a compass, tools or much of the camping gear, but each person must have the daily-recommended amount of water and food.

Since the early 1980's, every winter Denver meteorologist Ed Greene reminded people to keep water, candles, matches, chocolate, extra blankets, energy bars and peanut butter in the car. Planning for the unexpected became embedded in our brains. In just minutes a heavy, wet "white-out" (blinding snow) could drop from the mountains and strand motorists. Preparation was merely common sense. This is much the same theory with a few embellishments!

GETTING DOWN TO THE NUTS AND BOLTS – LISTS OF EVERYTHING

For food selections, pick any combination for three days' supply. No items are listed that require cooking so forget pots and pans. This 72-hour kit is designed to meet needs if you are stuck away from home and have just your vehicle and supplies. If you're at home when the emergency occurs, you should have access to cookware. Since most people have BBQ grills, you can still cook and heat food if power is out. Should power be off for more than five days, this type of emergency preparedness falls into "long term" plans.

When planning for extended power outages, you'll want to know alternate methods of cooking without power. This is discussed in detail in Chapter 30, but for short-term emergencies, suggestions are kept simple eliminating the need to cook meals. If you are exhausted from stress or stuck in a blizzard or severe storm, few would want to venture outside their dry vehicle to heat a can of beans!

KITCHEN ITEMS – 72 HOUR	
QTY/PERSON	ITEM
1	Manual Can Opener
3-9 sets	Paper plates, plastic eating utensils, disposable cups. One set per meal plus extra cups – quantity depends on foods selected
5	Plastic sealable bags like Ziploc or Click Zip Freezer, 1 gal/4 lt. or large
5	Plastic sealable bags like Ziploc or Click Zip Freezer, 1 qt/1 lt. or medium

FOOD AND WATER – 72 HOUR	
ITEM	COMMENT
Water, three gallons or 12 liters	One gallon per person per day will supply drinking water only -- not hygiene or cooking needs water, don't forget pets
Canned Fruit Juices	Need can opener if cans don't have pull tabs
Canned Meats, Vegetables and Fruits	May need can opener
Canned Soup, ready-to-eat variety	May need can opener
Canned Tea and Soda Pop	Need can opener if cans don't have pull tabs
Cookies	
Dehydrated Food Packages	These will need water and preferably, a method of heating
Dried Fruit	
Granola, Trail Mix and Power Bars	
Hard Candy and Chewing Gum	Helps keep moisture in your mouth
Snack Puddings	
Peanut Butter and Crackers	
Jerky	Very salty
Instant Coffee / Tea Bags / Hot Cocoa Mix	Pick something easily dissolvable if water heating isn't available
Creamer/Whitener and Sugar	Small restaurant-style packets
MREs (Meals Ready to Eat)	MREs aren't high on nutritional charts, but they are convenient, lightweight, have a long shelf life, need no refrigeration or any special preparation. They do have a high sodium count so if you are on a salt-restricted diet, these might not be the best choice. Again though, we are only looking at three days.
HeaterMeals	These are non-refrigerated emergency meals with a built in heating element. They run approximately US$6-8. each
Inferno Meals	

TIP: In freezing temperatures, stored water may need to be brought into the house. Depending on the container, it may freeze and break. Leave room at the top of the container for freezing expansion. Canned goods should not be allowed to freeze either. Be sure to ROTATE food and water supplies in your 72-Hour Kits!

GENERAL SUPPLIES – 72 HOUR	
QTY/PERSON	ITEM
4	Candles, enough for 36 hours use
1	Safe Candle Holder or Base (can be an empty tuna or small soup can)
1	First Aid Kit (see list)
3	Light sticks (12 hour)
1	Lighter
1	Pillow, small
1	Plastic Sheeting
1	Sleeping Bag, Bedroll, Swag or Wool Blankets
1	Space Blanket (reflects up to 90% of your body heat and only weighs 20 oz)
3	Trash Bags, extra (heaviest and largest available for numerous uses)
2 boxes	Waterproof Matches
1	Tube Tent

TIP: Always have at least two ways to start a fire.

CARRYING ITEMS – 72 HOUR	
QTY/PERSON	ITEM
1	Backpack for carrying supplies
1	Water Canteen with strap
1	Five Gallon Pail (20 liter)* with tight sealing lid, (store part of your supplies in here)

*TIP: Can be used as an emergency toilet if lined with a trash bag. Can be used to haul water, bail water and hold and keep other survival items dry. Invert for a handy seat. These pails are invaluable!

CLOTHING – 72 HOUR	
QTY/PERSON	ITEM
1 set	Clothing, complete change
1 pair	Eyeglasses (if needed)
2 sets	Underwear
3 each	Dust Masks, especially in volcano country
1 set	Rain Poncho or Rubberized Parka & Rain Pants, oversized to allow for layering
1 pair	Boots, sturdy, hiking
2 pair	Socks, heavy
1 pair	Sunglasses
1 pair	Tennis shoes, gives your feet a "break" from the heavier hiking boots
1 pair	Work Gloves, heavy duty

TIP: Most people will need to consider weather changes. Every season, update your stored change of clothes. Make sure they're appropriate for current weather conditions. For winter, include coat, hat, gloves, thermal underwear, snow boots and clothes for layering. Check kids' sizes to be sure they still fit.

COMMUNICATIONS – 72 HOUR	
QTY/PERSON	ITEM
$100	Cash and change, small bills and phone cards for calls (during times of disaster, charge cards and checks will not be honored)
1	Compass of good quality (these are expensive but necessary)
1	Map of your local area
1	Mirror, can be used as signal
1	Notepad
1	Pencil, Pen
1	Phone numbers and addresses of friends / family
5	Pre-addressed, stamped postcards of friends and family out-of-state (if a disaster is widespread, you'll want to contact someone out of the area)
1	Radio, small, battery or crank powered
3	Signal Flares (these are not legal in Australia)
1	Whistle

TIP: Money is always hard to tuck away and leave alone, but in this case, it is a must. One can't assume that credit cards will be usable during a crisis. Whenever you make a credit purchase, it is always verified. If power is out and authorization is not possible, chances are your purchase won't be allowed.

SANITATION AND GENERAL HYGIENE – 72 HOUR

QTY/PERSON	ITEM
1 bottle	Disinfectant, small
1 bottle	Liquid Soap, small for personal washing
1 roll	Paper Towel, flattened
1 each	Sponge
3 pair	Surgical Gloves, very inexpensive and obtained at discount and grocery stores
1 roll	Toilet Paper, flattened
1 box	Towelettes, pre-moistened
3 each	Trash Bags and Ties, for human waste and miscellaneous rubbish

TIP: During an emergency is no time to fool around with germs. If water and sewer mains or septics back up, bacteria will be rampant. Be sure to wash hands often especially after using the toilet and before preparing food.

PERSONAL HYGIENE – 72 HOUR

QTY/PERSON	ITEM
1 tube	Body/Hand Lotion
1	Comb and Brush
1	Dental Floss, lots of uses
1	Deodorant
1	Shampoo
2 boxes	Tampons/Sanitary napkins
1	Toothbrush
1	Toothpaste
1	Tweezers, pointed
1	Wash Cloth & Towel

TIP: Many items can be found in 'travel' or trial sizes. If not available in your area, fill small plastic bottles and label each with the contents/date of filling. (See Shelf Life Charts for Non-Food Items.)

MISCELLANEOUS – 72 HOUR

QTY/PERSON	ITEM
1	Bible
1	Book for pleasure reading

1 set	Certified copies of important documents*: (have these items with you if traveling)
	    Bank Account Numbers
	    Births, Deaths and Marriage Certificates
	    Charge Card Account Numbers and their "lost or stolen" notification numbers
	    Driver's License
	    House and Life Insurance Policies, Insurance Claim Form
	    Medical Records
	    Passports
	    Social Security Numbers/Tax File Numbers
	    Stocks, Bonds, Investments
	    Wills

1	Firearm for Protection (personal choice item) and ammunition
1	Magnifying Glass
1	Paper Clips
1	Playing Cards
1	Rubber Bands, assorted sizes
1	Safety Pins, assorted sizes
1	Survival Manual

TOOLS & HANDYMAN ITEMS – 72 HOUR

QTY/PERSON	ITEM
2 roll	Duct Tape (this has innumerable uses)
1	Flashlight or Torch (extra batteries, spare bulb)
1	Folding Shovel
1	Hatchet
1	Multi-Purpose Tool with knife, pliers, screwdrivers
1	Needle Nose Pliers
1	Needles and Thread, select several needles with large and regular-sized eyes
100' or 30m	Nylon Rope (100' or 30 meters)
1	Swiss Army Knife
100' or 30m	Twine/String
1	Vise Grips

INFANT SUPPLIES (if applicable) – 72 HOUR

QTY/PERSON	ITEM
Blanket, spare	Lotion
Bottles, spare	Teething Ring
Diapers, disposable	Toys
Powder	Formula

SENIOR CARE (if applicable) – 72 HOUR

QTY/PERSON	ITEM
Denture Care Items	Prescriptions
Eyeglasses	Special Dietary Items
Heart or Blood Pressure Medication	Warmer Clothing (elderly can have trouble with poor circulation and do get cold easier).

PET CARE (if applicable) – 72 HOUR

QTY/ANIMAL	ITEM
1	Food and Food Bowl
1	Leash and Collar
1	Muzzle
1 set	Toys or Chew Bone:
1	Water Bowl
1 gallon	Water, per day. A cat needs about 1 pint. (Even if you have a small animal, plan on the unexpected. Somebody will undoubtedly spill his or her day's ration. Use the pet's water in an emergency.)

FIRST AID ITEMS (GENERAL PRODUCTS) – 72 HOUR

QTY/PERSON	ITEM
1	Basic First Aid Book, in plain language
1	Bandages (Ace) elastic, 4" (10cm)
2	Bandages, gauze, 2" x 2" (5cmx5cm)
2	Bandages, gauze, 4" x 4" (10cmx10cm)
10	Band-Aids in assorted sizes, flexible and moisture resistant best
2 Tbsp	Bicarbonate of Soda
5	Butterfly sutures or Leukostrips
20	Cotton Swabs
1 box	Dental Floss

FIRST AID ITEMS (GENERAL PRODUCTS) – 72 HOUR

QTY/PERSON	ITEM
1	Eyedropper
1 roll	First Aid Tape, ½" (2cm) x 10 yards (meters)
1 tube / can	Insect Repellent
1 bottle	Isopropyl Alcohol
1	Nail Clipper
1	Prescription of current medications
2	Razor Blades, single edge
10	Safety Pins, assorted sizes
1	Scissors, Surgical pointed
1 bottle	Soap, liquid, antibacterial
2	Tongue Depressors
1	Tweezers

FIRST AID ITEMS (SPECIFIC PRODUCTS) – 72 HOUR

QTY/PERSON	TREATMENT	PRODUCT BRANDS
1 tube	Analgesic Cream	Camphophenique, Paraderm Plus
1 box	Antacid	Mylanta, Tums, Pepto-Bismol
1 box	Anti-Diarrheal	Imodium, Diasorb, Lomotil
1 box	Antihistamine	Benadryl, Claratyne, Demazin, Sudafed, Actifed
1 tube	Antiseptic Ointment	Neosporin, Dettol, Betadine
1 bottle	Bandage, liquid	New Skin
1 tube	Burn Relief	Hydrocortisone, Derm-Aid
1 box	Cold/Flu Tablets	Nyquil, Repetabs, Codral
1 box	Constipation	Ex-Lax, Dulcolax, Durolax
1 box	Decongestant	Actifed, Sudafed, Repetabs
1 bottle	Eye Drops	Visine, Murine
1 box	Hemorrhoid relief, suppositories	Preparation H, Anusol
1 box	Ibuprofen	Advil, Motrin, Nurofen, Paracetamol
1 tube	Itch Relief	Lanacane, Dibucaine, Paraderm
1 tube	Lip Balm	ChapStick, Blistex
1 bottle	Nasal Decongestant	Sinex, Ornex
1 box	Nausea, Motion Sickness	Dramamine, Kwells, Travacalm, Meclizine
1 box	Non-Aspirin Pain Reliever	Tylenol, Panamax
1	Prescriptions	A supply of any you are taking
1 sm. jar	Petroleum Jelly	Vaseline
1 can	Sunburn Relief	Solarcaine, Paxyl
1 bottle	Sunscreen	SPF 50, at least

TIPS FOR ALL OF THE ABOVE

1. Common sense also plays a role here. All of the suggested items will not fit in a backpack, but are things you should keep in your vehicle or safe room. Tools, for example, can be kept in either a cardboard box or regular tool kit in the car's trunk or boot. Many SUV's have under-the seat storage as well as side-panel space. First Aid items may be kept in their own pack or container. It goes without saying; don't give firearms to a child. Balance food choices so everything is not in cans. While convenient, they add weight and take up space.
2. Personalize your kits. Make sure you fill the needs of each family member. If you smoke, you'll want to include cigarettes. When under stress, there's no need to make yourself tenser by omitting items you normally use.
3. For contact lens wearers, don't forget cleaner, saline solution and lens case.
4. Be sure to check 72-Hour Kits twice a year. Make sure nothing leaks or is past the expiration date. Check food, water and first aid supplies to be sure they are intact.

BEFORE YOU SAY, "TOO HARD"...

Many items can be obtained at discount stores like Target, Wal-Mart, K-Mart and buying clubs. Other supply sources are second-hand stores, Salvation Army, Army Surplus, Army Disposal stores and garage sales. This doesn't have to be "designer" gear, only functional. This is for SURVIVAL!

If your first inclination is to say, *I can't afford this!* think realistically where you can cut waste from the weekly budget. If your family goes to the movies, why not rent a video and "rat-hole" those $$ spent for the show? If nothing else, bring your refreshments from home – expensive candy bars, soft drinks and popcorn CAN cut into the wallet. Put those extra dollars toward emergency supplies. A few less nights of fast food pays for your 72-hour survival food.

In the area of Personal Hygiene, discount stores offer travel sizes which can reduce not only the carrying weight of your backpack, but space required and $$ spent. Many areas of Australia do not offer travel size products but small plastic containers are readily available. Make your own "travel size" containers of shampoo, etc. and label each little bottle.

Empty film canisters (if you can still find them) and prescription vials with label removed are great small containers for mini-sewing kits, corralling coins, keeping matches dry or holding an assortment of safety pins, even lotions, medicines and vitamins. Make sure each canister is clearly labeled and dated if the item has a shelf life.

Stored water doesn't have to be an expensive name brand. Treated tap water stored in empty 2-liter soft drink bottles suffice nicely. In fact, mineral water only makes a person thirstier.

TIP: Before bottled water was readily available, my mother kept a large-sized prescription vial filled with water in her purse. If she were away from home without water, she could take her allergy pills with this "travel water". These containers are small, water-tight and hold up to ½ cup of water.

The most expensive item on this list is a compass. Some hand-held compasses range from US$50 – $250, but a decent Silva compass can be purchased for $30 to $50. If you're completely lost, no dollar value can be placed on this item. It's not cheap, but money saving tips are listed in the next section.

For those short of time and want to purchase preassembled kits, numerous companies offer a wide selection. They do vary in price and product, so compare their offerings.

MONEY SAVERS

1. Talk to other folks of like mind. Put together a group purchase or co-op to bring down individual cost. Try this approach with Army surplus stores. Many companies are interested in turning a larger amount of product and might agree to further lower prices for a "group" sale.

2. If you have a Sam's Club, Costco, BJ's, Big Lots, Campbell's Cash & Carry or other bulk food warehouse in your area, ask them about supplying some of the desired items for large purchases.

3. In America, make use of food coupons. Those dollars and cents add up.

4. Online coupons are huge. Before you shop, take 10 minutes to check for these savings. When you're at a company website, if you don't see the coupon area right away, do a search. Or, Google for "the brand name" + coupon or "the brand name" + "special offer". Depending on company, they might have as many as 20 coupons available. All you have to do is print them out. Most manufacturers have different WEEKLY specials so check often. If you're not taking advantage of these dollars-off deals, you're missing out!

Along this same line, just Google "grocery coupon". This takes you to websites that specialize in online coupon savings like **www.coupons.com** or **www.thegrocerygame.com**. Sometimes a fee is charged for the service, but depending on how much you shop, it can be an advantage.

5. For Australians, purchase a few shares of Coles-Myer stock. This grants you a shareholder's card, which automatically discounts food purchases 5% over and above any sale price. Other stores that honor the Coles-Myer card are: Bi-Lo, Bi-Lo Mega Fresh, Coles Express, Coles Supermarkets, Fosseys, Grace Bros, Katies, K-Mart, Liquorland, Myer, Myer Direct, Newmart, Officeworks, Pick n Pay Hypermarket, Red Rooster, Target, Tyremaster, Vintage Cellars. Watch for weekly sales in addition to using a Coles-Myer discount card where prices are dropped anywhere from 20%-30%. Apply this strategy to the First Aid Kit and General Supplies as well as the Food Items.

6. Look in the Yellow Pages for co-ops. They are a great source for bulk purchases.

Check **Tips to Save Money** at the end of Chapter 9.

Some of the most practical reasons to keep a private storehouse have already been listed. If you've completed and survived the 72-Hour List, it's time to broaden your preparedness again. What? You have a life? You don't need any more challenges? Come on, you stop learning, you stop growing!

Chapter 4: Emergency Water Treatment

LIQUID GOLD
Water is *the* most important factor in staying alive. It's essential that every person has *enough* and it is safe to drink.

> Calculate 1 gallon (4 liters) DRINKING water per person, per day, as a rule of thumb.

Needs differ according to age, physical condition, activity and environment. This does not include water for cooking, bathing, flushing toilets, washing clothes or pet needs. If you have a medium-size dog, for example, plan at least another 1 gallon of water for each dog per day, 1 pint per day for each cat.

If you run out of stored water, you will need to locate an alternate source. **Especially in times of disaster, assume any water not stored or purchased is contaminated.** You might find a crystal clear stream and it could still be polluted.

MAKING WATER POTABLE (DRINKABLE)
This is a two-step process: removing particles (filtration) and disinfection (purification).

For filtering there are numerous products on the market where water is either pumped or gravity fed through a filter to remove particles. Then the water must be disinfected to remove bacteria and any other organic material.

If the water is brackish, first strain the debris through a paper towel, clean cloth or coffee filter before running it through your filter. This will remove the major "chunks" and extend the life of your filter. Then treat by one of the following methods: *Boiling, Chemical Treatment, Mechanical Filtration*.

WATER PURIFICATION – BOILING
This process is recognized as the safest treatment method. Bring water to a rolling boil for a *minimum* of 10 minutes. Cover the pot to shorten the time it takes to boil. For every 1000 feet (305m) above sea level, add one more minute to the boiling time.

TIP: Use a pressure cooker to minimize water lost in boil off.

If fuel is scarce, boiling is an "expensive" method of treatment. However, if your home is wood-heated, many free-standing fireplaces have built in cooking surfaces. African aid agencies estimate it takes a little over 2 pounds (1kg) of wood to boil 1 quart (1L) of water. Hardwoods and efficient stoves require less fuel.[11]

Boiling water removes all chlorine as well as the bacteria. If you don't plan on drinking this water right away, add 4 drops or 1/16 teaspoon chlorine. Make sure the household bleach contains NO detergents, scent, phosphates or any other additive. The label should state in the ingredients either 5.25% or 6% sodium hypochlorite.

While the boiled water cools, airborne bacteria can contaminate it. Anything that is not sterile (like possibly the water storage container) may have bacteria in it. Even though you've boiled the water, using no other additional treatment such as chlorine, won't kill the germs if it comes in contact with bacteria.

WATER PURIFICATION – CHEMICAL TREATMENT
There are quite a few chemical methods available so we'll look at these individually starting with ordinary laundry bleach, which is definitely a preferred method.

1. CHLORINE
Liquid chlorine bleach **must have 5.25% or 6% sodium hypochlorite and contain no soap, scent or phosphates**. Be sure to read the label. If bleach is more than one year old, it loses approximately half of its strength. Full strength starts to diminish after 6 months and degrades more quickly depending on how it's stored. In this case, double the amount of bleach if the bleach is not replaceable. After treating with chlorine, mix well and allow water to stand 30 minutes before using. If you measure the bleach with an eyedropper, label it and don't use it for anything else. If the bleach is not dated, note the date of purchase on the container with a permanent marker.

55 GALLON DRUMS

Quick calculation: Treat the barrel with 1¼ ounces (35ml) of fresh liquid bleach. Use a test kit to ensure levels of chlorine free residuals are between 2 and 5 ppm. (1 gal = 128 oz = 3785ml)

AMOUNT HOUSEHOLD BLEACH TO ADD (5.25%-6% sodium hypochlorite)		
WATER	**CHLORINE – CLEAR WATER**	**CHLORINE – CLOUDY WATER**
1 quart (.95L)	2 drops	4 drops
1 gallon (3.78L)	8 drops (⅛ tsp / 0.5ml)	16 drops (¼ tsp / 1.25ml)
5 gallons (19L)	½ tsp (2.5ml)	1 tsp (5ml)
50 gallons (190L)	1 Tbsp (3 tsp / 5ml)	2 Tbsp (30ml)
100 gallons (378L)	1 oz (2 Tbsp / 30ml)	2 oz (60ml)
500 gallons (1893L)	2 oz (¼ cup / 60ml)	4 oz (120ml)
1,000 gallons (3785L)	4 oz (½ cup / 120ml)	8 oz (240ml)
5,000 gallons (18,927L)	16 oz (2 cups / 475ml)	32 oz (946ml)
10,000 gallons (38,800L)	32 oz (1 qt. / 946ml)	60 oz (1774ml)

NOTE: If liquid pool chlorine (10-12% strength) is used, add half of the amounts shown on chart above.

2. IODINE

Iodine emerged as a water purifier after WW2, when the US military looked for a replacement for Halzone tablets. Iodine was found to be in many ways superior to chlorine in treating small batches of water. Iodine is less sensitive to the pH and organic content of water and is effective in lower doses.

Iodine is normally used in doses of 8 ppm to treat clear water for a 10 minute contact time. The effectiveness of this dose has been shown in numerous studies. Cloudy water needs twice as much iodine or twice as much contact time. In cold water (below 41°F or 5°C), double the dose or time. In any case, doubling the treatment time allows using half as much iodine.

If no instructions are provided on the container, use 12 drops per gallon of water. If the water is in question, double the amount of iodine. Mix well and allow the water to stand 30 minutes before using.

TIP: Iodine is light sensitive and must be stored in a dark bottle. It works best if the water is over 68°F (21°C).

IODINE PREPARATIONS		
PREPARATION	**IODINE**	**PER QUART / LITER**
Iodine Topical Solution	2%	8 drops
Iodine Tincture	2%	8 drops
Lugol's Solution	5%	4 drops
Povidone-Iodine (Betadine)	10%	4 drops
Tetraglycine hydroperiodide (Globaline, Potable Aqua, EDWGT)	8 mg	1 tablet
Kahn-Vassher Solution (Polar Pure)	9 mg	9 mg

DISINFECTING CONTACT TIMES		
	WATER TEMPERATURE	
WATER CLARITY	**41°F / 5°C**	**59°F / 15°C**
Clear	30 minutes	15 minutes
Cloudy	60 minutes	30 minutes

HOW DO I GET RID OF THE TASTE?

Water treated with iodine can have any objectionable taste removed by treating the water with ascorbic acid (vitamin C), AFTER the water has stood for the correct treatment time. Sodium thiosulfate can also be used to combine with free iodine, and either of these chemicals will help remove the taste of chlorine as well.

Usually iodine can't be tasted below 1 ppm, and below 2 ppm the taste isn't objectionable. Iodine ions have an even higher taste threshold of 5 ppm.

NOTE: Removing the iodine taste doesn't reduce the dose of iodine ingested by the body.

TIP: To improve the taste of any treated water, pour water from one clean container to another several times. This will help re-oxygenate the water and remove some of the flat taste noticed after treatment.

Powdered drinks like Kool-Aid, Tang, Crystal Light or teas help disguise any off-taste. Add these only after completing the specified standing time after treatment. These first two products are good sources of Vitamin C. Instead of using powdered drinks, add a pinch of salt per quart or lemon juice to improve treated water's flavor.

SOURCES OF IODINE

Tincture of Iodine
USP tincture of iodine contains 2% iodine and 2.4% sodium iodide dissolved in 50% ethyl alcohol. Sodium iodide has no water purifying effect, but contributes to the total iodine dose. Add 5 drops per quart when water is clear; 10 drops per quart when water is cloudy.

It's not a preferred source of iodine, but can be used if other sources aren't available. If the iodine tincture isn't compounded to USP specs, then you'll have to calculate an equivalent dose based on the iodine concentration.

Lugol's solution
Contains 5% iodine and 10% potassium iodide. For purification, add 3 drops per quart or liter of water.
NOTE: 3 times more iodine is consumed compared to sources without iodide.

Betadine (povidone iodine)
Some have recommended 8 drops of 10% povidone iodine per liter of water as a water treatment method, claiming that at low concentrations povidone iodine can be regarded as a solution of iodine. At 1:10,000 dilution (2 drops/liter), one study indicated 2 ppm of iodine were present, while another test showed conflicting results.

However, at 8 drops/liter, there is little doubt that it kills microbes. The manufacturer hasn't spent the money on testing this product against EPA standard tests, but in other countries it's sold for use in field water treatment.

Kahn-Vassher solution (Polar Pure)
Fill the Polar Pure bottle with water and shake. The solution will be ready for use in one hour. Add the number of capfuls (per quart of water treated) listed on the bottle, based on the temperature of the iodine solution. The particle trap prevents crystals from getting into the water being treated. It is important to note that you are using the iodine *solution* to treat the water, not the iodine crystals. *The concentration of iodine in a crystal is poisonous and can burn tissue or eyes.* Let the treated water stand for 30 minutes before drinking. In order to destroy *Giardia* cysts, the drinking water must be at least 68°F (20°C). Warm the water in the sun before treating or add hot water. Refill the treatment bottle after use so that the solution will be ready one hour later. Crystals in the bottle make enough solution to treat about 2,000 quarts. Discard the bottle when empty.

One criticism of this method is the chance of pouring iodine crystals into the water being treated. This isn't a problem as iodine is very weakly toxic and Polar Pure incorporates a collar on the neck of the bottle to help prevent this. Another objection to this method is that the saturated iodine solution must be kept in glass bottles, and is subject to freezing, but this is not an insurmountable problem. Freezing doesn't affect the crystals.

Tetraglycine hydroperiodide: (Potable Aqua)
This is the form of iodine used by the US military for field water treatment in canteen-sized batches. Usual dose is one tablet per quart of water to give a concentration of 8 mg/l. Two tablets are used in cloudy or cold water or contact time is doubled to 1 hour. The major downside of this product is that it rapidly loses its iodine when exposed to the air. According to the manufacturer, it has a near indefinite shelf life when sealed in the original bottle, but should be discarded within a few months of opening. The tablets change color from gunmetal gray to brown as they lose the iodine. You should see a brown tint to the water after treating.

Iodine Resin Filter
Some commercial microfilters incorporate an iodine resin stage to kill viruses and bacteria, which doesn't put as much iodine into the water compared to adding it directly to the raw water. A few products rely exclusively on an iodine resin stage and there are 3 disadvantages to these filters:
1. they are fragile
2. effectiveness depend on flow rate
3. it's hard to tell when they need to be discarded

If you're treating water likely contaminated with viruses, then use a well-known brand filter such as the Katadyne or Sweetwater ViralStop. More than one pass through the filter may be necessary in cold weather.

Resins do have the advantage of producing less iodine in the water for the same anti-microbial effect. For the most part, they only release iodine when contacting a microbe. The downside is that physical contact between the microbe and the resin is needed.[12]

IS IODINE SAFE?

Some individuals are allergic to iodine, and there is some question about its long-term use. The safety of long-term exposure to low levels of iodine was proven when inmates of three Florida prisons were given water disinfected with 0.5 to 1.0 ppm iodine for 15 years. There were no effects on either the health or thyroid function of previously healthy inmates. Of 101 infants born to prisoners drinking the water for 122-270 days, none showed detectable thyroid enlargement. However, individuals with pre-existing cases of hyperthyroidism became more symptomatic while drinking the water.

Nevertheless experts are reluctant to recommend iodine for long-term use. Average American iodine intake is estimated at 0.24 to 0.74 mg/day. After 2001 reevaluation, the RDA is .15mg/day for adult men and women, and adolescents. Recommend Daily Allowances during breastfeeding jumps to .295mg. Children 1-8 should keep consumption at .09mg[13] These doses are calculated to remove all pathogens (other than Cryptosporidia) from the water. Of these, Giardia cysts are the hardest to kill, and are what requires the high level of iodine. If the cysts are removed with a microfilter (any model will do since cysts are 6 microns), only 0.5 ppm is needed to treat the filtered water.

People who should not use iodine are those with iodine allergies (often those allergic to shellfish) or have thyroid problems or are on lithium, women over fifty, and possibly pregnant women. Expectant mothers should consult their physician prior to using iodine for purification.

3. PURIFICATION TABLETS

These tablets are either iodine or chlorine based. One or two tablets purifies one quart or one liter of water depending on contamination of water and length of time allowed for treated water to stand. Follow instructions on the package.

IMPORTANT NOTE: While economical and convenient, not every brand of purification tablet kills Giardia. It is really nasty, causing severe gastric troubles and it's particularly difficult to get rid of once you drink contaminated water. Chlorine doesn't remove viruses. It destroys them through an oxidation reaction, but Giardia and Cryptosporidium *are chlorine-resistant*.

Remove them with a 1 micron filter or super-chlorination followed by dechlorination with activated carbon. When living in Australia and using tank water, we opted for a 1 micron filter in conjunction with UV treatment, just to be safe. It eliminated super-chlorinating and running the water through charcoal.

Chlor-Floc, Aquatabs, Puritabs, Steritabs, LifeSystems usually can be purchased from drug and sporting goods stores. Directions are on the packages for disinfecting water. As a rule of thumb, use one tablet for each quart of water to be disinfected. Shelf life for chlorine tables is about two years in their original sealed containers.

Chlorine seems to be the overall best alternative. The few drawbacks are already known and there are easy ways around them.

4. MICROPUR MP1 (CHLORINE DIOXIDE)

This is not the same as chlorine and has a lot of advantages. Katadyn's Micropur MP1 uses soluble silver ions but the amount of silver consumed is less than when eating a salad using a silver fork. MP1 is registered with EPA as a "purifier" and currently the only product available effective against cysts, viruses, bacteria, protozoa, worm eggs, Crypto and Giardia. It destroys viruses and bacteria in 15 minutes, Giardia in 30 minutes and Cryptosporidia in 4 hours. Four hours is the maximum time needed to rid water of Crypto and this length of time is only necessary if water temperature is cold and very dirty. One table purifies one quart or liter of water.

Since this purification method doesn't require chemicals or boiling, the water tastes fresh taste and remains bacteria free for up to 6 months. Shelf life of product is 3 years from date of manufacture when tablets are sealed.

5. STABILIZED OXYGEN

People using this method feel it's better than iodine and chlorine. Both iodine and chlorine leave a taste, but this is easily filtered. The active ingredient in stabilized oxygen, sodium chloride, is neither harmful or leaves a taste. Conversely, manufacturers claim a number of health benefits.

For long-term water storage, treat 1 gallon of already-chlorinated water by adding 10 drops of stabilized oxygen. For one gallon non-chlorinated water, add 20 drops.

6. HYDROGEN PEROXIDE

Peroxide is a perfectly acceptable disinfectant for water, as it oxidizes like chlorine, but it's not a preferred method. Two factors make using peroxide different from chlorine. Peroxide degrades even more rapidly than chlorine and potency may be a problem if it's to be stored.

The other drawback to peroxide is it's more difficult to test for residual levels. Residuals need to be measured just like for chlorine to ensure complete disinfection.

Studies show 99% of poliovirus is killed in 6 hours with 0.3 percent hydrogen peroxide and a 99% of rhinovirus is eliminated with a 1.5% solution in 24 minutes. Hydrogen Peroxide is more effective against bacteria, though pure iron (Fe^{+2}) or copper (Cu^{+2}) needs to be present as a catalyst to get a reasonable concentration-time product.[14]

WHAT ARE "RESIDUALS?"

A "residual" is the peroxide or chlorine that remains in water from the original treatment dosage that wasn't used to kill contaminants. Example: if one cup of water has 20 parts per million (ppm) of 'bugs' in it, the disinfectant dose needs to be at least 20 ppm, but no more than 25 to prevent illness. A dosage of 23 ppm chlorine would have 3 ppm left over chlorine after the 20 ppm was used to kill off bacteria.

A quick calculation to use daily is the required dosage in parts per million, times the volume treated in gallons, divided by 120,000 (which is a constant). This calculates the number of pounds needed to give that dosage. Unfortunately there is no simple answer.[15]

WATER PURIFICATION – MECHANICAL FILTRATION

WATER PURIFIERS AND WATER FILTERS – WHAT'S THE DIF?

A water filter is not the same as a water purifier. Filters only screen out particles down to a certain size and they may remove some chemicals. Viruses are so small they can slip right through the filter element. That's when you need a water purification system. Stan and I use MSR's SweetWater with ViralStop, which is a chlorine-based liquid that does the actual purifying. The procedure is to filter the water first, add five drops of ViralStop per quart of water, then wait five minutes before drinking.

Devices identified as "purifiers" usually cause water to interact with iodine (often in the form of iodine resins) or chlorine, which renders viruses inactive. Another purifier uses a positive electrostatic charge in its filter medium to capture viruses.

If you don't have a purifier, but you still want to ensure against viral contamination, you can use any of the methods covered in this section. First, pre-treat the water with any accepted method outline above to kill the organisms, and then run the water through the filter to remove the chemical taste and odor, as well as most of the dead microbes. Alternatively, you may filter the water first, and then treat with the chemical purifiers. Or third, filter and then boil the water.

WATER PURIFYING UNITS

Before purchasing a purifier, there are several things to consider:

- Durability/reliability (will parts break down with heavy use?)
- How easy is the unit to pump? (if not gravity fed)
- How much treated water can you expect in a half hour?
- Will this particular unit filter Giardia and other viral and bacteria agents?
- Will it work in brackish water?
- Cost and availability of additional filters

WHICH ONE?

Water filters come in an assortment of sizes and styles, use various types of filtering mediums and produce different amounts of drinkable water. Which one you select will depend on how much water you need and how much you want to spend. Filter costs cover a wide spectrum running from $45 to more than $500. On the next two pages you'll find a comparison chart to help you decide. The chart does not cover every unit available, but gives a good idea of their differences and what to consider.

WATER FILTERS

Product	Unit Cost	Filter Replacement	Output	Ave. Filter Life Before Replacement / Cleaning	Filter And Pore Size
British Berkefeld Big Berkey	$250-$340	$99 for 2, can use 4	1 gal. (3.78L) per hour	up to 3,000 gallons (6,000 gallons per set of two)	0.2 micron silver infused ceramic / carbon core
Katadyn Base Camp Filter	$70	$60	1.3 gal. (5 L) per hour	up to 5,300 gallons, depending on water source	0.2 micron ceramic
Katadyn Combi Plus	$160	$75 - ceramic; $9 - activated carbon	1.2 qt. (1.1L) per minute	ceramic – up to 14,000 gallons, depending on water quality; change activated carbon every 2 fillings	0.2 micron ceramic / carbon / micro-strainer
Katadyn Expedition	$1200	$200	1 gal. (3.78L) per minute	up to 26,000 gallons, depending on water quality;	0.2 micron
Katadyn Gravidyn Drip Filter	$220	$50 each	13 gal. (49L) per day	up to 13,000 gallons, depending on water quality; change at 6 months	0.2 micron ceramic
Katadyn Vario	$90	$45 filter $10 / 2 pack carbon $26 cartridge	2 qt (2L) per minute	up to 500 gallons; carbon cartridge treats up to 106 gal; glass fiber up to 530 gal.	0.3 micron pleated glass fiber / carbon granulate ceramic pre-filter
Katadyn Hiker (was PUR)	$65	$45	1.6 qt. (1.5L) per minute	up to 200 gallons	0.3 micron pleated glass fiber /carbon core
Katadyn Hiker Pro	$80	$40	1 qt. (1L) per minute	up to 200 gallons	0.3 micron pleated glass fiber /carbon core
Katadyn Mini	$100	$50	.38 qt. (0.36L) per minute	up to 2,000 gallons	0.2 micron ceramic micro-strainer
Katadyn Pocket with Output Hose	$320	$155	.91 qt. (0.86L) per minute	up to 14,000 gallons	0.2 micron ceramic micro-strainer
MSR MiniWorks EX	$90	$38	1 qt. (0.83L) per minute	up to 500 gallons, depending on water quality	0.2 micron ceramic with carbon core
MSR Sweetwater Microfilter	$90	$40; $20 - Siltstopper (optional)	1+ qt. (1+ L) per minute	up to 200 gallons if cleaned regularly	0.2 micron labyrinth w/ carbon; Siltstopper 5 micron
MSR WaterWorks EX	$145	$40 filter; $60 PES membrane cartridge	0.9 qt. (0.85L) per minute	up to 500 gallons, depends on water quality; second-stage PES membrane delivers extra filtering	0.2 micron membrane / ceramic with carbon core
Sawyer Water Filter System 2L / Complete 2L	$100 / $132	N/A	1+ qt. (1+ L) per minute	Million gallon guarantee, no need for replacing. "Complete" system has storage vessel.	0.1 micron Innova hollow-fiber

WATER FILTERS				
Field cleanable	Wt.	Size	Pump force (lbs) / Strokes per liter	Removes
Yes	8 lbs	19¼ x 8 in.	gravity fed	giardia, e.coli, cryptosporidia, cholera, salmonella, dysenteria
Yes	1 lb 6 oz	Packed 12 x 4 in.	gravity fed	bacteria, protozoa
Yes, clean ceramic with abrasive pad	1 lb 5 oz	11 x 2.4 x 2.4 in.	unavailable	bacteria, protozoa, cryptosporidia, giardia, e.coli, chemicals
Yes, clean ceramic with abrasive pad	11.5 lbs	23 x 8 in.	gravity fed	bacteria, protozoa, cysts, algae, spores, sediments, viruses; reduces radioactive particles
Yes, clean ceramic with abrasive pad	6 lbs 14 oz	10 x 18 in.	gravity fed	bacteria, protozoa, giardia, crypto, cholera, salmonella, e.coli
Replaceable element	15 oz	7½ x 4 in.	6.2 lbs / 34	giardia, e.coli, cryptosporidia, cyclospora, salmonella, shigella
Pump only	11.7 oz	7½ x 4 x 2½ in.	8 lbs / 40	giardia, e.coli, cryptosporidia, cyclospora, salmonella, shigella
Yes	11 oz	6½ x 3 x 2.4 in.	48	giardia, e.coli, cryptosporidia, cyclospora, salmonella, shigella
Yes	8 oz	7 x 2¾ x 1¾ in.	5.3 lbs / 167	cryptosporidia, cyclospora, e.coli, giardia, shigella, salmonella, not viruses
Yes	1 lb 3 oz	10 x 2 in.	16½ lbs / 70	giardia, e.coli, cryptosporidia, cyclospora, salmonella, shigella
Filter: yes; membrane: no	1 lb, 1 oz	9 x 4 in.	11.7 lbs / 70	cryptosporidia, giardia, e.coli, salmonella, bacteria, chemicals
Yes	11 oz	7½ x 2 in.	1.6 lbs / 82	giardia, e.coli, cryptosporidia, polio, cyclospora, salmonella, shigella, chemicals, viruses inc. Hepatitis A
Yes	14.6 oz	8 x 4 in.	10.4 lbs / 72	giardia, e.coli, cryptosporidia, cyclospora, salmonella, shigella, chemicals
Yes	16 oz	17.5 x 7 in.	gravity fed	bacteria, protozoa, cysts including giardia, salmonella and cryptosporidia

WATER PURIFIERS

Product	Unit Cost*	Replacement Filter	Output	Ave. Filter Life Before Replacement / Cleaning
General Ecology First Need Base Camp	$692	$100	½ gal (1.9L) per minute	500 gallons, depending on water source
General Ecology First Need Deluxe Water	$112	$60	2 qt. (1.9L) per minute	up to 125 gallons in ideal conditions
General Ecology First Need Trav-L-Pure Water	$203	$46	1.4 qt. (1.37L) per minute	up to 100 gallons, depending on water source
Hydro Photon Steri-Pen Journey	$120	N/A	32 oz (.95L) per 90 seconds	2 lithium AA purify 2000 gal. (8000 treatments) over the life of UV bulb
Hydro Photon Steri-Pen Adventurer Opti	$100	N/A	32 oz (.95L) per 90 seconds	2 lithium AA purify 2,555 gal. over the life of UV bulb; solar charger available
Katadyn MyBottle; 24 oz capacity	$50	$25	2 qt. (2L) per minute	Replace 3-part Virustat cartridge after 26 gallons
MSR MIOX	$140	~$7, 3V lithium battery	53+ gal (200L) per battery life	Yes
MSR Sweetwater with ViralStop	$100	$45 cartridge $20 SiltStopper $10 ViralStop	1.3 qt. (1.25L) per minute	up to 200 gallons; 2 oz. ViralStop treats 80 gal. of water
New Millennium Concepts Sport Berkey	$35	$13	1 qt. (1L) per minute	160 refills
Sawyer Complete Water Purifier System - 4L	$210	N/A	½ gal (1.9L) per minute	Million gallon guarantee, no need for replacing

* Prices subject to change at discretion of manufacturer

MSR Sweetwater Filter

Kayadyn Gravity Fed Filter

Katadyn Camp Filter

Katadyn Expedition Group Filter

British Berkefeld Big Berkey Filter

BLACK BERKEY PURIFYING ELEMENTS

Black Berkey elements are the core feature of the Berkey line of gravity fed purifiers. Besides being specially designed for the Big Berkey, they can replace most other gravity fed elements.

SHELF LIFE

These elements have no shelf life, but if you purchase in quantity, store them in Ziplocs to prevent absorption of air-borne contaminants. If left unprotected, it could reduce their expected purifying capacity.

WATER PURIFIERS

Field cleanable	Material & Pore Size	Wt.	Size	Pump Force Strokes / liter	Removes / Destroys
Replaceable element	0.1 micron structured matrix	3 lbs. 12 oz	5½ x 9 in.	3 lbs / 12 oz	cryptosporidia, chemicals, giardia, bacteria, viruses, cysts
Replaceable canister	0.1 micron structured matrix micro-strainer	1 lb. 3 oz.	8 x 4 in.	5.6 lbs / 45	cryptosporidia, giardia, viruses, bacteria, cysts
Replaceable canister	0.1 micron structured matrix	1 lb 4 oz	6.6 x 4.4 x 3.3 in.	5.4 lbs / 44	giardia, cryptosporidia, chemicals, bacteria, viruses, cysts
Yes	N/A	6 oz with lithium	7¼ x 1½ x 1¼ in.	Stir with Steri-Pen 48 seconds	cryptosporidia, giardia, protozoa, bacteria, viruses
Yes	N/A	3.6 oz with lithium	6 x 1½ x 1 in.	Stir with Steri-Pen 48 seconds	cryptosporidia, giardia, protozoa, bacteria, viruses
Replaceable cartridge	glass fiber / penta-iodide resin / coconut carbon	9.7 oz	10.25 x 3.8 x 3 in.	No pumping; fill, squeeze, sip	cryptosporidia, giardia, protozoa, bacteria, viruses
Salt	N/A	3.5 oz pen only	7 x 1½ x 1 in. pen	No pumping	viruses, bacteria, giardia, cryptosporidia
Yes	labyrinth w/ ViralStop solution	14 oz	7½ x 2 in.	1.6 lbs / 81.6	viruses, giardia, cryptosporidia, bacteria
Replaceable element	Proprietary information	5.3 oz	11 x 3 x 3 in.	No pumping; fill, squeeze, sip	bacteria, viruses, cysts, chemicals, organic compounds
Yes	0.1 hollow fiber membrane filter	20 oz	20 x 10 in.	No pumping; gravity fed	cryptosporidia, giardia, bacteria, viruses, cysts

CLEANING YOUR BLACK BERKEYS

Unlike other filtration elements, Black Berkey purification elements are cleanable. What typically causes filters to drip slowly is sediment clogging the elements' pores. Simply remove them from your system, scrub the exterior of each element with a white Scotch-Brite pad or stiff toothbrush. Clean a portion of the filter until a bit of black appears on the white pad, and then move to the next section. It's simple to do and takes less than a minute. Then re-prime each element according to instructions and reinstall.

TESTING THE FILTER

If you're concerned that you've over-scrubbed the filters, you can perform a simple test. Remove the lid from your unit and add about 10 drops of dark food coloring. Properly working Big Berkey elements will remove every trace of color.

FILTER REPLACEMENT

Each element has an expected life of 3,000 gallons or 6,000 gallons for a set of two. The best way to gauge when to replace the filters is to do the following:

Step 1 Multiply the number of filters in your system by 3,000 gallons to get Total Gallons For All Filters within the system.
Step 2 Keep track of how many times you refill the upper chamber in one week.
Step 3 Multiply that figure times the capacity in gallons of your particular system. This determines Total Gallons Used Per Week.
Step 4 Divide the Total Gallons Used Per Week into the Total Gallons For All Filters and that tells you how many weeks before the filters should be replaced.

Step 5 Next calculate the future date for replacement (52 weeks per year) and write that date on a sticker and attach it to the bottom of your system for future reference.

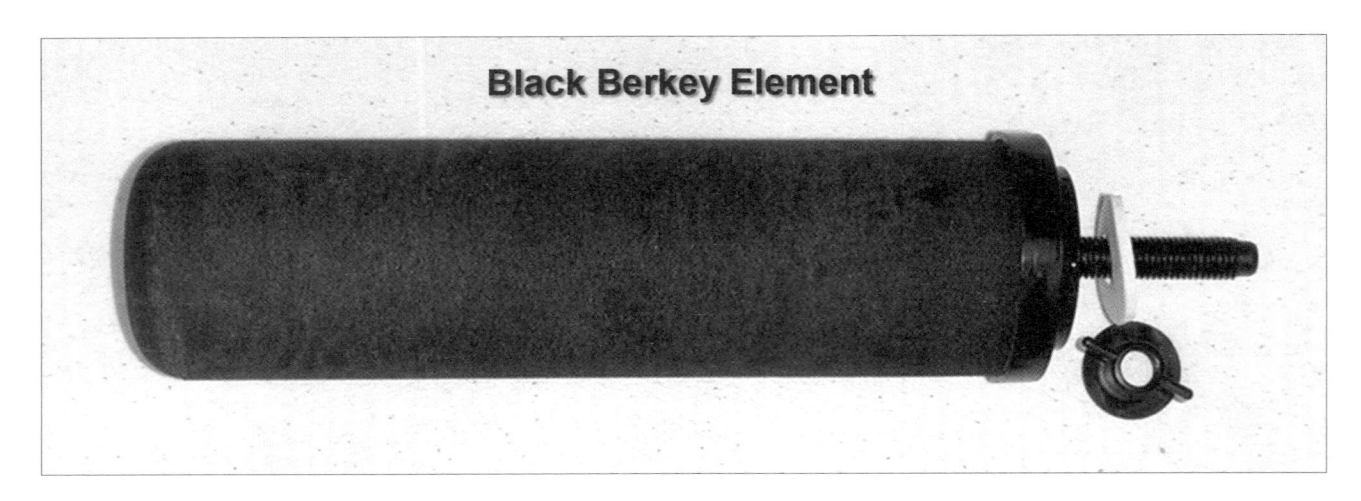

Black Berkey Element

BUILD YOUR OWN MICROFILTER

TIP: You can build your own microfilter using diatomaceous earth (DE), sold for swimming pool filters. Usually pressure is required to achieve a reasonable flow rate. A DE filter will remove turbidity (suspended solids) as well as pathogens larger than 1 μm.

ALTERNATE PURIFYING METHODS

SILVER

Silver has been suggested by some for water treatment and may still be available outside the U.S. However, in America, it's currently out of favor with the EPA establishing a 50 ppb (parts per billion) maximum limit for silver in drinking water. This limit is set to avoid argyrosis, a permanent cosmetic blue/gray staining of the skin, eyes, and mucous membranes.

As the disease requires a net accumulation of 1 gram of silver in the body, one expert calculated you could drink water treated at 50 ppb for 27 years before accumulating 1 gram. However, people who regularly use colloidal silver may accumulate this amount at a faster rate. Silver has only proved effective against bacteria and protozoan cysts, though it's quite likely also effective against viruses.

Silver can be used in the form of a silver salt, commonly known as silver nitrate; a colloidal suspension, or a bed of metallic silver. Electrolysis can also be used to add metallic silver to a solution.

Evidence shows that silver deposited on carbon block filters kill pathogens without adding as much silver to the water.[16]

WINE-TREATED WATER

From digesting many romance novels over the years, I remembered reading about watered wine. While thinking "watered" wine didn't sound terribly appealing to adults, it was also given to children. This made me wonder if there had been a water shortage in those times or if the water were just too awful to drink!

One night Stan and I were discussing the Bible's instruction to "hurt not the oil or the wine." This conversation evolved into a Net search on the history of both items which uncovered some interesting information.

Since ancient times in countries like Israel, Rome, and more recently France, water was too polluted to drink untreated. By mixing one part red wine to three parts water, they achieved sufficient purification. For killing bacteria in laboratory conditions, red wine ranked three to four times more effective than pure alcohol or tequila. The effective ingredient is believed to be phenol compounds enhanced from charred wood of the wine-aging casks. This is important because the phenol compounds appear to be related to sulfur drugs previously used in basic antibiotics.[17]

Dare To Prepare: Chapter 4: Emergency Water Treatment 63

First Need Base Camp Purifier

Katadyn MyBottle Purifier

MSR MIOX Purifier

Steri-Pen Purifier

Sweetwater Filter & Purifier

Katadyn Combi Plus Filter

Chapter 5: Water Treatment On a Big Scale

Once again, chlorine is usually the treatment of choice for purifying large amounts of water. For this reason, the subject is covered in-depth. Don't be intimidated by the amount of information. You may not require it now, especially if you live in the city or suburbs, but if you relocate to the country, the information is ready for you. Read the parts necessary for your situation now and don't worry about the rest.

CHLORINE-WATER TERMINOLOGY
When looking for information on chlorine treated water, you're bound to run across several terms repeatedly. Relax, there is no test, but sometimes it's just nice to know what "they" are talking about!

FIELD WATER – any water not certified as drinkable
POTABLE WATER – safe to drink
PPM – Parts Per Million measures how many "bugs" or chlorine is present in water
CHLORINE DEMAND – amount of chlorine required to disinfect water with no chlorine left over
REACTED CHLORINE – chlorine used to kill bacteria
UNREACTED CHLORINE – chlorine in water that has NOT been used to kill bacteria or neutralize organic matter
RESIDUAL OR FREE CHLORINE – any chlorine left over in water after killing the bacteria
TOTAL CHLORINE – the sum of residual and reacted chlorine

WHAT ARE FREE RESIDUALS?
Untreated water generally contains all sorts of bacteria. Water coming into your home via the public system has already been treated with chlorine to eliminate these problems. When tap water is to be stored for longer than 6 months, you need to treat it with additional chlorine. After adding this extra chlorine and it kills the nasties, you want to have 2-3 ppm or parts per million of free chlorine. How do you know when you have this amount? It's really easy!

CHLORINE TEST KITS
This is when a test kit is needed. These are readily available at swimming pool and spa supply stores. Many grocery stores and discount chains in areas where swimming pools are common like Los Angeles, Phoenix, Tucson and Perth carry these kits. They are inexpensive and simple to use.

After adding the right amount of chlorine for how much water you want to store, mix thoroughly and wait 30 minutes. The best chlorine test kits give readings for both Total Available Chlorine and Free Available Chlorine.

Insert one of the treated pieces of paper from the kit. Match the color on the test paper to the container and it shows you how many ppm chlorine is present. It is better to err on the low side of chlorine and add a little more than to add too much and have to wait for it to dissipate. Chlorine levels above 5 ppm tastes terrible and above 10 ppm causes diarrhea, so aim for the 2-3 range.

Shelf life of these kits is generally 2 years.

PH TEST KITS
For chlorine to work best, the pH level needs to be below 8. Somewhere in the range of 4 to 7 is optimal. These kits are also readily available at swimming pool and spa supply stores. While pH kits are really good to have, the Chlorine Test Kit is just as important as having the actual water. For a few dollars, it's great insurance!

TYPES OF CHLORINE

LIQUID (HOUSEHOLD BLEACH)
When purifying water with household bleach, check the label. It should read sodium hypochlorite (NaHOCl) 5.25% or 6%. Use only products that contain **no soap, no scent, and no phosphates**. If bleach is more than one

year old, it loses approximately 50% strength. Full strength starts to diminish after 6 months. In this case, double the amount of bleach if the bleach is not replaceable. A "smell" test isn't an accurate indicator of its current effectiveness.

Commercial liquid bleach contains twice the chlorine – 10-12.5% sodium hypochlorite. You can use this product for purification, too, but add only half the amount of chlorine.

DRY CHLORINE

This form, calcium hypochlorite, has the added benefit of extended shelf life over household bleach. Providing it's kept dry, cool and in an airtight container, dry chlorine may be stored up to 10 years with minimal degradation. If you want to keep chlorine in larger quantities, this is the item to store. It's available at swimming pool supply stores and many hardware and grocery stores. It also requires less storage space than its liquid counterpart. When purchasing calcium hypochlorite, make sure there are no other active ingredients in it.

Calcium hypochlorite is the solid form with 65%-70% strength and sodium hypochlorite is the liquid form.

CAUTIONS FOR DRY CHLORINE

Do not allow it to become warm and moist. It can explode and burn if dropped. Since it's very concentrated compared to liquid bleach, don't breath it or get it on your skin. Dry chlorine can cause burning and skin irritation, and its fumes are toxic. Inhaling concentrations of 30 ppm can lead to harsh coughing and concentrations of 1,000 ppm can be fatal in few breaths.[18]

Don't let these words of caution frighten you unnecessarily. Dry chlorine is what Stan and I store and use; we're careful but not concerned about the drawbacks. We keep it dry, don't breathe the fumes and add it to water wearing gloves. Using simple precautions makes it a very good choice.

CHLORINATING WATER OUTSIDE

RAIN TANKS

Western Australia Health Dept. regulations state for first time chlorination, add 7 grams dry (¼ ounce by weight) or 40 ml (1.35 ounces) liquid per 1000 liters (264 gallons) and let stand for 24 hours before drinking. To maintain adequate chlorination, **each week** add 1 gram dry (.035 ounce by weight) or 4 ml (.135 ounces) liquid per 1000 liters (264 gallons) of water. Let stand for two hours before drinking.

WELLS

Adequately chlorinating an existing well can be tricky. The bigger the well's diameter, the more difficult it becomes. Deep wells aren't easy to treat since chlorine wants to settle on the bottom and it's challenging to mix in evenly. It's also harder to ensure all of the tile surfaces come in contact with the chlorine.

When chlorine is added to a well, it reacts first with inorganic compounds. Once these compounds have been reduced, it still needs to be disinfected.

Next, the chlorine left over attacks the organics like algae, phenols and slime. This may eliminate some of the offensive odors and tastes, but it's still not safe to drink because of trihalomethanes, which can cause cancer.

The third step in disinfection forms chloramines. This results in long-lasting disinfection but it takes a long time for it to react, so additional chlorine is needed.

The last step of added chlorine destroys the chloramines and we end up with safe water with chlorine residuals.

DISINFECTING BORED OR DUG WELLS
1. Use the next table to calculate how much liquid or dry bleach to use.
2. To determine the exact amount needed, multiply the amount of disinfectant required (according to the diameter of the well) by the depth of the well. For example, a well 5 feet (1.5m) in diameter requires 4½ cups of bleach per foot or every 30.5cm of water. If the well is 30 feet deep, multiply 4½ by 30 to determine the total cups of bleach required (4.5x30 = 135 cups). There are 16 cups in each gallon of liquid bleach. For metric, If the well is 9.1 meters deep, multiply 4½ by 914cm to determine the total cups of bleach required (4.5x914 = 135 cups).
3. Add this total amount of disinfectant to about 10 gallons (38L) of water. Splash the mixture around the wall or lining of the well. Be certain the disinfectant solution contacts all parts of the well.
4. Seal the well top.

5. Open all faucets and pump water until a strong odor of bleach is noticeable at each faucet. Stop the pump and allow the solution to remain in the well overnight.
6. The next day, operate the pump by turning on all faucets, continuing until the chlorine odor disappears. Adjust the flow of water faucets or fixtures that discharge to septic systems to a low rate to avoid overloading disposal system.

BLEACH FOR A BORED OR DUG WELL[19]

Diameter of Well in		Amount of 5.25-6% chlorine laundry bleach per each 12" or 30.5cm water		Amount of 70% dry chlorine per each 12" or 30.5cm water	
Feet	Centimeters	Cups	Liters	Ounces	Grams
3	91	1½ cups	355 ml	1	28
4	122	3 cups	710 ml	2	57
5	152	4½ cups	1064 ml	3	85
6	183	6 cups	1.42 liters	4	113
7	213	9 cups	2.13 liters	6	170
8	245	12 cups	2.84 liters	8	227
10	305	18 cups	4.26 liters	12	340

Source: Illinois Dept. of Public Health. Recommendations may vary from state to state, country to country.

DISINFECTING DRILLED WELLS

1. Determine the amount of water in the well in U.S. (gallons are American) values by multiplying the gallons per foot by the depth of the well in feet. For example, a well with a 6" diameter contains 1.5 gallons of water per foot. If the well is 120 feet deep, multiply 1.5 by 120 (1.5 galx120 ft = 176 gal).

BLEACH FOR A DRILLED WELL (U.S.)[20]

WELL DIAMETER	3 in.	4 in.	5 in.	6 in.	8 in.	10 in.	12 in.
gallons/foot of water	0.4	0.7	1.0	1.5	2.6	4.1	5.9

Determine the amount of water in the well in **Metric** values by multiplying the liters per meter by the depth of the well in meters. For example, a well with a 15cm diameter contains 17.7 liters of water per meter. If the well is 37 meters deep, multiply 17.7 by 37 (17.7Lx37m= 655L).

BLEACH FOR A DRILLED WELL (METRIC)

WELL DIAMETER	8cm	10cm	13cm	15cm	20cm	25cm	30cm
liters/meter of water	5.0	7.9	13.3	17.7	31.4	49.1	70.7

2. For each 100 gallons (380L) of water in the well, use the amount of chlorine (liquid or granules) indicated in the table below. Mix the total amount of liquid or granules with about 10 gallons (38L) of water. If using liquid chlorine, make sure it contains no additives, no soaps or scents.

AMOUNT OF CHLORINE REQUIRED	PER 100 GALLONS	PER 100 LITERS
Laundry Bleach (5.25-6% Chlorine)	3 cups	188 ml
Dry Granules – Hypochloride (70% Chlorine)	2 ounces	15 g

3. Pour the solution into the top of the well before the seal is installed.
4. Connect a hose from a faucet on the discharge side of the pressure tank to the well casing top. Start the pump. Spray the water back into the well and wash the sides of the casing for at least 15 minutes.
5. Open every faucet in the system and let the water run until the smell of chlorine can be detected. Then close all the faucets and seal the top of the well.
6. Let stand for several hours, preferably overnight.
7. After you have let the water stand, operate the pump by turning on all faucets continuing until all chlorine odor leaves. Adjust water flow from faucets or fixtures that empty into septic tank systems to a low rate to avoid overloading the disposal system.

SLOW SAND FILTERS

Slow sand filters pass water slowly through a bed of sand. Pathogens and turbidity (suspended solids) are removed by natural die-off, biological action, and filtering. Typically the filter consists of 24 inches (61cm) of sand, then a gravel layer in which the drain pipe is embedded. The gravel doesn't touch the walls of the filter so that water can't run quickly down the wall of the filter and into the gravel. Building the walls with a rough surface also helps. A typical loading rate for the filter is 0.2 meters/hour (the same as .2 m^3/m^2 of surface area). The filter can be cleaned several times before the sand has to be replaced.

Slow sand filters should only be used for continuous water treatment. If a continuous supply of raw water can't be insured (say using a holding tank), then choose another method. It's important for the water to have as low turbidity as possible. Turbidity, or inorganic and organic compounds, can be reduced by changing the method of collection (for example, building an infiltration gallery, rather than taking water directly from a creek), allowing time for the material to settle out (using a raw water tank) or flocculation (adding a chemical such as alum to cause the suspended material to floc together.)

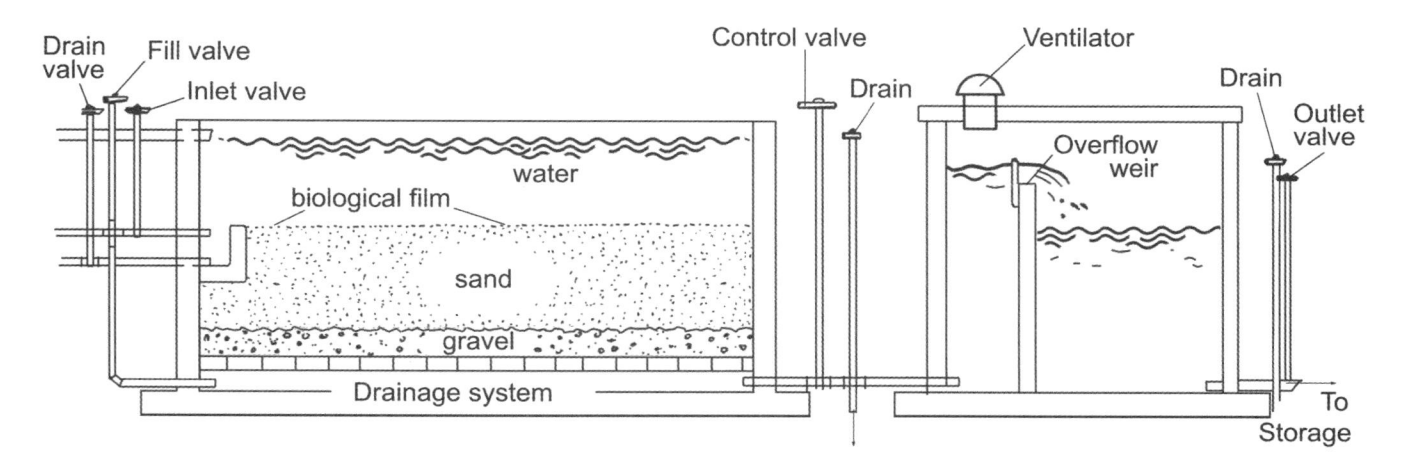

CONSTRUCTION

The SSF filter itself is a large box, at least 5 feet (1.5 m) high. Make the walls as rough as possible to reduce the tendency for water to run down the walls of the filter, bypassing the sand. The filter's bottom layer is a gravel bed in which a slotted pipe is placed to drain off filtered water. Its slots or the gravel should be no closer than 8 inches (20cm) to the walls, again to prevent water from bypassing the sand.

Sand for a SSF needs to be clean, uniform in size and the correct size – 0.1 to 3mm. The sand can be cleaned in clean running water, even if it's in a creek.

Sand is added at a minimum depth of 2 feet (0.6 m). Additional thickness allows more cleanings before the sand must be replaced. Twelve to 18 inches (.3 to .5 m) of extra sand allows the filter to work for 3-4 years. An improved design uses a geotextile layer on top of the sand further reducing the frequency of cleaning.

The outlet of a SSF must be above the sand level and below the water level. Keep the water at a constant level to insure an even flow rate throughout the filter. Increase the flow rate by lowering the outlet pipe or by increasing the water level.

ACTIVATED CHARCOAL FILTER

Activated charcoal filters water through adsorption chemicals and by attracting and attaching some of the heavy metals to the surface of the charcoal. Charcoal filters remove some pathogens though they'll quickly clog it. They can even contribute to contamination as the charcoal provides an excellent breeding ground for bacteria and algae. Some charcoal filters are impregnated with silver to prevent this, though current research concludes that the bacteria growing on the filter are harmless, even if the water wasn't disinfected before contacting the filter.

Activated charcoal can be used in conjunction with chemical treatment. Iodine or chlorine kills the pathogens, while the carbon filter removes the treatment chemicals. In this case, as the filter reaches capacity, there will be a distinctive chlorine or iodine taste.

You can make activated charcoal at home (see Chapter 22), though it will vary in quality compared to commercial products. Burning off the molecules adsorbed by the carbon can recycle either purchased or homemade charcoal. (They won't work with heavy metals.)

The more activated charcoal in a filter, the longer it lasts. Its carbon bed must be deep enough for adequate contact with the water. Most designs use granulated activated charcoal ranging in size from 0.6 to 0.9 mm for maximum flow rate. Home or field models can also use a compressed carbon block or powered activated charcoal (roughly <0.01 in size) to increase contact area. Powdered charcoal can be mixed with water and filtered out later. As far as life of the filter is concerned, carbon block filters last the longest for a given size, simply due to their greater mass of carbon. A pressure source is usually needed with carbon block filters to achieve a reasonable flow rate.[21]

REVERSE OSMOSIS

HOW IT WORKS

Reverse osmosis forces water, under pressure, through a semi-permeable membrane that blocks the transport of salts and other contaminants. Most reverse osmosis technology uses a process known as crossflow to allow the membrane to continually clean itself. As some of the fluid passes through the membrane the rest continues downstream, sweeping the filtered particles away from the membrane in wastewater.

Reverse osmosis is only one stage of a typical RO system. Sediment and carbon filtration is normally included with an RO system, with each stage of filtration contributing to the purification process.

1. The first stage of filtration is the sediment filter, which reduces suspended particles such as dirt, dust, and rust.
2. The second stage uses a thin film membrane carbon filter to reduce volatile organic chemicals, chlorine, and other taste and odor causing compounds.
3. The RO membrane is the heart of the system. It's responsible for rejecting up to 98% of the total dissolved solids in the water. This is where the purification takes place.

PROS AND CONS

RO is most commonly used aboard boats to produce fresh water from the ocean. The membrane is better at getting rid of salts than it is at barring weak acids, bases and organic matter less than 200 microns. RO also tends to leave in weak organic acids, amines, phenols, chlorinated hydrocarbons, some pesticides and low molecular weight alcohols. Larger organic molecules and all pathogens are stained out. It's possible to have an imperfection or blemish in the membrane that allows molecules or whole pathogens to pass through.

Using reverse osmosis to desalinate seawater requires considerable pressure (1000 psi) to operate. For a long time only electric models were available.

Recovery Engineering designed a model for the U.S. Navy that operates manually. It cleverly used wastewater to pressurize the backside of the piston. About 90% of the water ends up as wastewater, with only 10% passing through the filter. This design was later acquired by PUR, which is now owned by Katadyn.

RO requires a lot of water since it produces about 1 gallon of drinkable water for every 10 gallons used in the process. If you're in a marine setting, having plenty of water is not a problem. On the plus side, the wastewater can be used for things other than consumption.

While there is little question that desalinators work well, they require a lot of effort to operate manually. However, those who have actually used them on a life raft credit the availability of water from their Katadyn (reverse osmosis) watermaker for keeping them alive.

Katadyn manual desalinators are available in two models:

The Survivor 06 (pictured left) produces 1 quart of water every hour with 40 pump strokes a minute. This super light unit weighs only 2½ pounds and costs about $900. Since its output is relatively low, the Survivor 06 should be considered for emergency use only and supplying fresh water for only one or two persons.

The Survivor 35 ($2200) produces 1.2 gal/hr in about 30-pump strokes/minute. It's lightweight at 7 pounds and widely used by US and international military forces, voyagers, sea kayakers, and other adventurers.

The PowerSurvivor 40E ($3400) produces 1½ gallons of water every hour using just four amps of 12 VDC. This unit is extraordinarily compact weighing 25 pounds. The biggest plus of the 40E is its ability to convert to manual operation and it's the only power desalinator with this feature. Its rugged yet simple construction is so well thought out that the high-pressure pump can run for extended periods on AC power alone. Most components of the 40E have a 3-year warranty.

Katadyn recommends replacing the O rings after 1000-1200 hours and a kit is available for maintenance. Estimates for membrane life vary, but units designed for production use may last a year or more. Every precaution should be taken to prevent petroleum products from contacting the membrane as they will damage or destroy it. The pre-filter must also be changed regularly, and the membrane may need to be treated with a biocide occasionally.

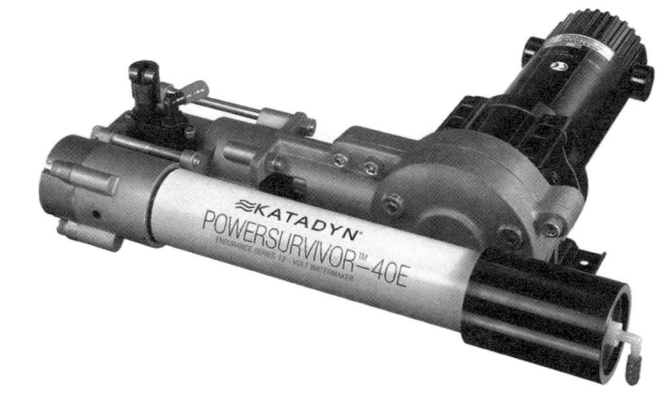

On the next page you'll find a chart that shows the relative size of various contaminants and what is required to remove them. Reverse osmosis filters are available that use normal municipal or private water pressure to remove water contaminates, as long as they aren't present at the levels found in seawater.

Water produced by reverse osmosis, like distilled water, will be close to pure H_2O. You may need to take mineral supplements to compensate for their loss during RO.

TREATMENTS REQUIRING ELECTRICITY

OZONE

Ozone, a molecule composed of 3 atoms of oxygen rather than two, is formed by exposing air or oxygen to a high voltage electric arc. It's much more effective than chlorine as a disinfectant, but no residual levels of disinfectant remain after ozone turns back into O_2. One source quotes a half-life of only 120 minutes in distilled water at 68°F (20°C).

However, ozone is used extensively in Europe to purify water and we'll likely see increased use in the US since it's a way to avoid producing trihalomethanes. While ozone breaks down organic molecules, sometimes this can be a disadvantage as ozone treatment can produce higher levels of smaller molecules. This provides "food" for microorganisms. If no residual disinfectant is present (as would happen if ozone were the only treatment method used), these microorganisms will cause water quality to deteriorate in storage.

UV LIGHT

Ultraviolet light has been known for a long time to kill pathogens. A low-pressure mercury bulb emits 30-90% of its energy at a wavelength of 253.7 nm, which is right in the middle of the UV band. When water is exposed to enough light, pathogens are killed. The problem is that some pathogens are hundreds of times less sensitive to UV light than others.

The most resistant pathogens to UV are protozoan cysts. Studies show many commercial UV treatment units can't destroy Giardia. Fortunately these are the easiest pathogens to remove with a mechanical filter.

The effectiveness of UV treatment is very dependent on particles suspended in the water. The more opaque the water is, the less light will be transmitted through it. Treatment units must be run at the designed flow rate to ensure sufficient exposure, as well as ensure turbulent flow rather than plug flow.

Another problem with UV treatment is that the damage done to the pathogens with UV light can be reversed if the water is exposed to visible light (specifically 330-500 nm) through a process known as photo-reactivation.

UV treatment, like ozone or mechanical filtering, leaves no disinfecting agents in the water to guarantee its continued safe use. Check any purchased UV filter to make sure it complies with the 1966 HEW standard of 16,000 µW.s/cm^2 with a maximum water depth of 7.5cm.

The US EPA explored UV light for small-scale water treatment plants and found it compared unfavorably with chlorine due to higher costs, lower reliability, and lack of disinfecting residuals.[22]

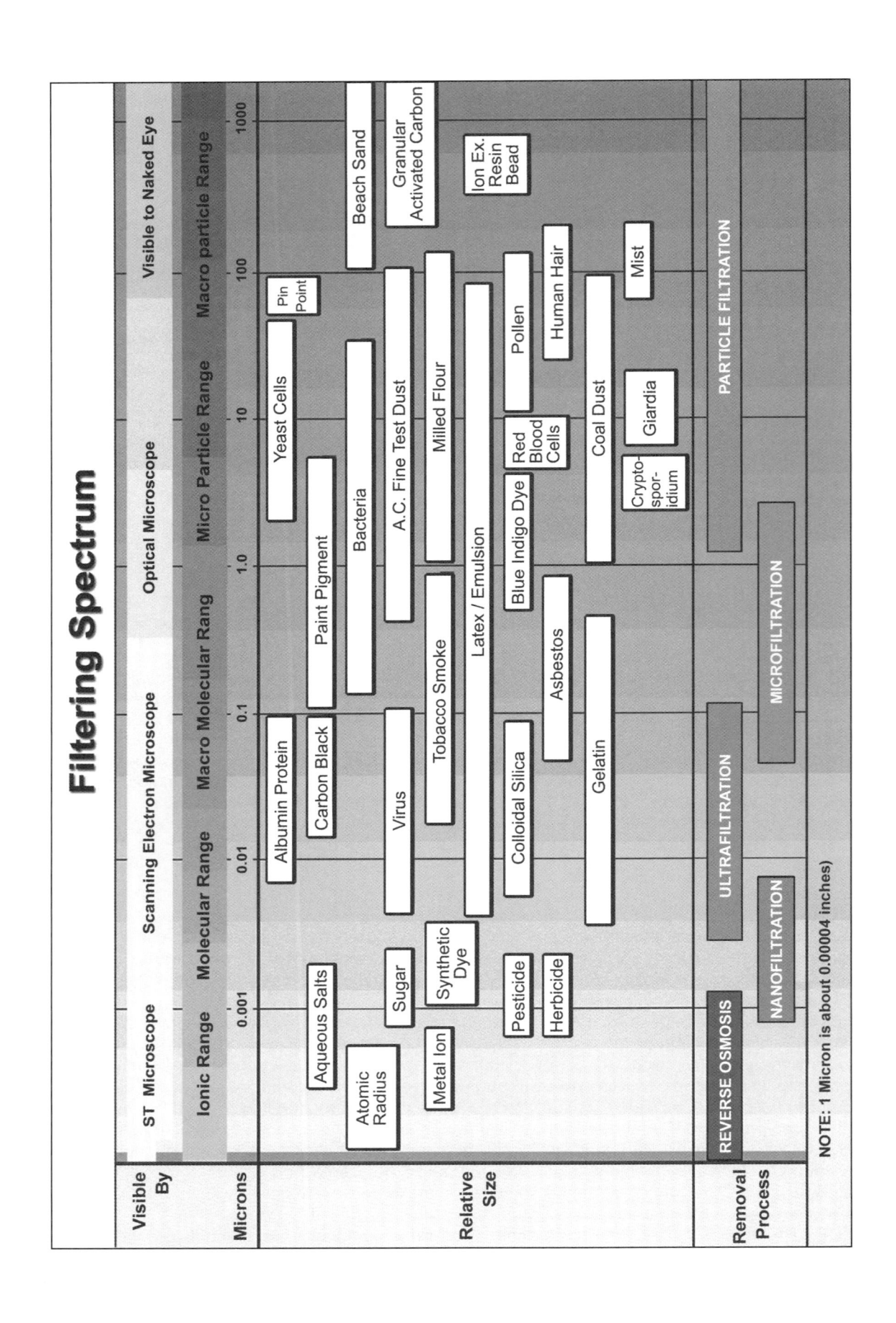

Filtering Spectrum

Visible By	ST Microscope	Scanning Electron Microscope	Optical Microscope		Visible to Naked Eye
	Ionic Range	Molecular Range	Macro Molecular Range	Micro Particle Range	Macro particle Range
Microns	0.001	0.01	0.1	1.0	10	100	1000

Relative Size (items shown across the spectrum):
- Aqueous Salts
- Atomic Radius
- Metal Ion
- Sugar
- Synthetic Dye
- Pesticide
- Herbicide
- Albumin Protein
- Carbon Black
- Virus
- Colloidal Silica
- Gelatin
- Tobacco Smoke
- Paint Pigment
- Latex / Emulsion
- Asbestos
- Bacteria
- Yeast Cells
- A.C. Fine Test Dust
- Milled Flour
- Blue Indigo Dye
- Red Blood Cells
- Coal Dust
- Cryptosporidium
- Pin Point
- Pollen
- Human Hair
- Giardia
- Mist
- Beach Sand
- Granular Activated Carbon
- Ion Ex. Resin Bead

Removal Process:
- REVERSE OSMOSIS
- NANOFILTRATION
- ULTRAFILTRATION
- MICROFILTRATION
- PARTICLE FILTRATION

NOTE: 1 Micron is about 0.00004 inches

DISTILLATION

Distillation is the evaporation and condensation of water to purify water. It's most commonly used to remove dissolved minerals and salts from water, but it has two disadvantages:
1) A large energy input is required
2) If simple distillation is used, chemical contaminants with boiling points below water will be condensed along with the water.

SOLAR STILLS

The simplest form of distillation is a solar still. It uses the sun's heat to evaporate water below the boiling point, and the cooler ambient air to condense the vapor. Water can be extracted from the soil, vegetation piled in the still, or contaminated water (such as radiator fluid or salt water) can be added to the still. (See Chapter 7 on Finding Survival Water.) Output is low but they are useful if water is in short supply. To help combat the slow output, multiple still could be used simultaneously.

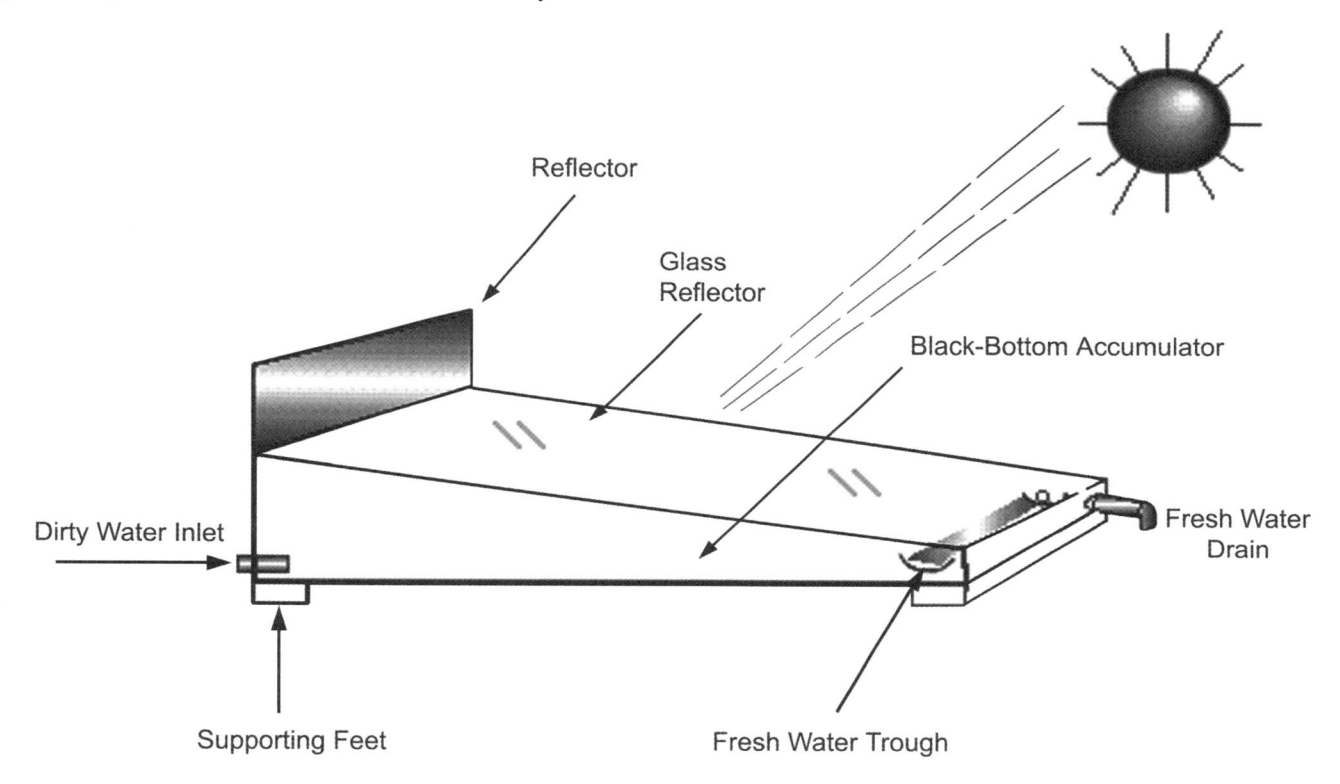

Other forms of distillation require a concentrated heat source to boil water, which is then condensed. Simple stills use a coil to return this heat to the environment. These can be improvised with a boiler and tight fitting lid and some copper tubing. Avoid using lead-soldered tubing if possible. In an emergency, use a hand towel to collect steam above a container of boiling water.

More efficient distillations plants use a vapor compression cycle where water is boiled off at atmospheric pressure. The steam is compressed and condensed above the boiling point of the water in the boiler, returning the heat of fusion to the boiling water.

Hot condensed water runs through a second heat exchanger, which heats up the water feeding into the boiler. These plants normally use an internal combustion engine to run the compressor. Waste heat from the engine, including the exhaust, is used to start the process and make up any heat loss. This is the method used in most commercial and military desalinization plants.

WATERCONE

One company took an old idea and turned it into a clever product. It uses a simple hardened plastic cone that sits over a dark plastic base. The cone can also float directly on a source like a pond or swamp and the Sun performs the magic. Clean, condensed water forms inside the clear plastic top, runs down its sides and collects in the lid's lip. While much sturdier than the Aquamate, it's also less costly at $150. **www.watercone.com**. Its main drawback is that it's not made for ocean use, calm waters only.

AQUAMATE
Inflatable solar stills are available from marine supply stores, but avoid the WW2 surplus models, as those who have used them saw an extremely high failure rate. Even newer inflatable solar stills like the Aquamate may only produce from 3 to 16 oz (89 to 473ml) under actual conditions, compared to a rating of 48 oz/day (roughly 1½ liters) under optimum conditions.[23] Aquamate sells for about US$200.
See: **www.landfallnavigation.com** and **www.aqua-mate.co.uk**.

POTASSIUM PERMANGANATE
Potassium Permanganate is no longer commonly used in the developed world to kill pathogens. It's much weaker than the alternatives, more expensive, and leaves an objectionable pink or brown color. If it must be used, 1 gram per liter would probably be sufficient against bacteria and viruses. There is no data on its effectiveness against protozoan cysts.[24]

WHAT ARE WE DOING?
Folks comment these options are great to know, thanks very much, but what are YOU doing? Several things determine what type water treatment you choose:
- What is your water source?
- How clean is your water?
- Are you looking for short term or long-term methods?
- How often will you be replacing stored water?
- Under what conditions do you plan to be treating water?
- Do you wanting to purify large quantities for the home environment or when you must be mobile?

While living in Australia, we chose several water treatment methods for different circumstances. For roof catchment water stored in large tanks, we treated it with chlorine, UV light and filtering units. This ensured 100% best quality even though rainwater is very pure. "Things" can and do get into water from the roof so purification is necessary. Stored are several MSR SweetWater purifiers (portable units) and replacement filters as well as a supply of Puritabs and Polar Pure in case we're mobile. At home, we use a Big Berkey. For larger disinfection needs, we store liquid and dry chlorine.

RAIN WATER
Then our main source of drinking and household water was rain roof catchment as are a lot of rural areas in Australia. This is a wonderful method if you're not around industrial areas where the water is likely contaminated with acid rain. The main drawback is that whatever is on your roof – leaves, bird droppings, insects or other undesirables – can end up in the drinking water. Before roof water ever entered the tanks, it went through a wire mesh to strain out unwanted particles.

Water then traveled through a pipe and deposited into two 10,000-gallon storage tanks. Before entering our water system, the water passed through a pre-filter, then a smaller filter to remove Giardia and Cryptosporidium and last, it was zapped by ultraviolet light. By then, the already very clean water was sparkling, but to ensure it remained that way, Stan dosed it with chlorine so any residual bacteria lurking in the tanks were killed.

TEST YOUR WATER
Prior to purchasing farm property in Australia, we took water samples from its bores to the local water department for testing. Since Ballarat, Victoria was an old mining town, it was highly likely our water was contaminated with arsenic or other poisons. We were fortunate that the results came back even purer than the town's water, but odds were against it. Know what's in your water.

Chapter 6: Water Collection and Storage

STORING WATER

After treating the water, it needs to be stored in good containers. Ideally they should block light and be small enough to move. If they're too heavy to lift, when it comes time to change the water, it will need to be siphoned out rather than dumped. Being able to roll a container on its side is much easier than siphoning and will encourage you to keep it changed. Plan to keep at least a portion of your stored water in containers you can carry should you need to become mobile. Each gallon of water weighs approximately 8 pounds or in comparable metric, 3.64 liters weighs 3.64 kg. A five-gallon jug translates into 40 lbs or 18 liters weighs 18 kg.

DRUMS

Fifty-five gallon drums can be purchased reasonably from area beverage dealers like Coke or Pepsi. Even though they are primarily white, you can cover them with an opaque drop cloth or black plastic sheeting.

Prior to filling, make sure you have thoroughly cleaned any syrup residue from the container. Over time the syrup may have leached into the plastic. When stored, these flavorings may reintroduce themselves to the water. They won't hurt you and repeated washings will help get rid of this taste.

A 55-gallon container is too large to be moved easily – unless you use a drum truck – (see Chapter 29), but it's good insurance against water shortages. On the drums we purchased, the entire top doesn't come off, but they have two 2½" (6.4cm) openings with re-closeable screw type caps.

Food grade containers are coded the bottom. They will be stamped with HDPE (High Density Polyethylene) and the symbol for recycle with a "2" inside. **NOTE:** HDPE plastics will melt or become soft at 266°F (130°C).

FOUR AND FIVE GALLON CONTAINERS

Also from the local beverage dealer, we purchased for next to nothing, 20-liter containers, in opaque dark blue, screw type tops with built-in handles. As the soft drink companies recycle these containers for their own use, phone first for availability.

SOFT DRINK BOTTLES

Save 2 liter soft drink bottles; they're ideal for water storage. Even though the container is clear and water purity will deteriorate more quickly, their small size makes changing water easy and they're easy to transport. They can be tucked into unused corners of your home, under beds and tables, suspended from ceiling rafters in basements. Two liter bottles are excellent to keep in cars.

To prolong its purity, store treated water in a dark room. As with any water storage container, make sure it is properly sterilized before filling with water.

TIP: When washing pop bottles for water storage, it's easier to rinse them thoroughly with a water-chlorine solution than using dishwashing soap. It takes forever to get the bubbles out – and a LOT of water.

Step 1 Rinse empty bottle.
Step 2 Wash cap thoroughly, paying special attention to the screw threads where bacteria easily get caught.
Step 3 Empty and refill about ¼ full with water and 1 teaspoon of chlorine (the amount isn't critical, but don't use less than the tsp.).
Step 4 Screw on top and swish thoroughly so the entire interior comes in contact with the chlorine.
Step 5 Empty and rinse.
Step 6 Refill completely and add 4 drops of unscented, no additives, 5.25 or 6% liquid bleach.
Step 7 Cap immediately and store.

CONTAINER SOURCES

Check area restaurants especially ones like Dairy Queen, Mexican restaurants, yogurt places and some coffee shops for containers. They buy ice cream, yogurt and assorted toppings in large, hard plastic pails with re-sealable plastic lids. These can be purchased for very little second hand.

Assorted sizes are periodically available at Sam's Club and Costco. However, they don't keep the same product lines continuously and are more costly than the used ones purchased through restaurants and delis.

Containers NOT to be used are ones retaining strong odors from previously stored food, ones that held toxic products or were made from biodegradable plastics for milk and distilled water. They will break down in 6 months and you'll have a leaky mess on your hands.

Some of the biodegradable plastics used for distilled water or "bottled" water are very misleading. These plastics are very flimsy and generally have a milky, translucent white appearance. We're not talking about the clear, hard plastics for soft drink bottles. These work fine, but some of these other containers have an expiration date of a year and a half or longer for the water. Possibly the water is OK for that length of time, but the container may not be! Someone didn't have his brain switched on that came up with this packaging. We've had numerous reports from folks complaining their bottles sprang leaks! Why would any company package "1½ year water" in "6 month" containers?

There are several options. One solution is to change containers when you get the water home. However, once the seal is broken on the container and the water is exposed to air, it's no longer bacteria-free and should be treated with chlorine or one of the other water purifying methods. It's simpler to use the water within 6 months than transfer it to a new container and having to treat it. And why pay for expensive store water? You'll be money and time ahead to store treated tap water in sterilized 2-liter soft drink bottles and adding four drops of chlorine.

REMOVING STUBBORN SCENTS

If you want to use food storage containers that still have a scent like pickles, the best way to clean them is wash thoroughly with soapy water and a little bleach. Let them sit with the lid off for a week, where direct sunlight can heat them. Wash again and wipe dry. Set them in the Sun upside down to drain any excess water droplets. Dry completely if you'll be storing "dry" items in them. The smell should be gone by this point.

HOW LONG WILL STORED WATER KEEP?

If your storage container is light permeable, change the contents every 6 months, even if you've treated it with additional chlorine. If you are using opaque airtight containers, bacteria-free tap water can be kept indefinitely if you have treated it with chlorine and test it to have 3-5 ppm residual free chlorine. They key question: is it bacteria-free? To be truly safe, treat with chlorine, iodine or stabilized oxygen, store in a dark area and check your water for taste every 6 months. Water stored under these conditions need not be replaced for several years.

FINDING HIDDEN WATER IN YOUR HOME

PLUMBING

There is quite a bit of water trapped in pipes of the average home. If the municipal water system was not contaminated before you shut the water off to your house, this water is still fit for consumption without treatment. To collect this water, open the lowest faucet in the system, and allow air into the system from a second faucet. Depending on the diameter of the pipe, you may want to open every other faucet, to make sure all of the water is drained. This procedure usually drains just the cold-water side. The hot water side will have to be drained from the hot water heater. Again, open all of the faucets to let air into the system, and be prepared to collect any water that comes out when the first faucet is opened. Toilet tanks (not the bowls) are another source of water.

Some people have plumbed old hot water heaters or other tanks in line with their cold water supply to add an always-rotated source of water.

Two cautions are in order. Make sure the tanks can handle the pressure (50 psi min.), and the tanks are in series with the house plumbing.

This method is susceptible to contamination from the municipal water supplies. The system can be fed off the water lines with a shutoff valve (and a second drain line), preventing the water from being contaminated as long as the valve was closed at the time of contamination.[25]

WATER COLLECTION

WELLS
Water can only be moved by suction for an equivalent head of about 20' (6 m). After this, the water boils off in tiny bubbles in the vacuum created by the pump rather than being <u>lifted</u> by the pump. At best, no water is pumped; at worst, the pump is destroyed. Pumps in wells deeper than this work on one of these principles:
1) The pump can be submerged in the well; this is usually the case for deep well pumps. Submersible pumps are available for depths up 1000 feet (305m).
2) The pump can be located at the well's surface with two pipes going into the well: one carries water down, and one returns it. A jet fixture, called an ejector, on the bottom of the two hoses causes well water to be lifted up the well with the returning pumped water. These pumps must have an efficient foot valve as there is no way for them to self-prime. These are commonly used in shallow wells, but can go as deep as 350 feet (107m). Some pumps use the annular space between one pipe and the well casing as the second pipe this requires a packer (seal) at the ejector and at the top of the casing.
3) The pump cylinder can be located in the well, and the power source located above the well. This is the method used by windmills and most hand pumps. A few hand pumps pump the water from very shallow wells using an aboveground pump and suction line.

A variety of primitive, but ingenious, pump designs also exist. One uses a chain with buckets to lift the water up. Another design uses a continuous loop rope dropped into the well and returning up a small diameter pipe. Sealing washers are located along the rope, so that water is pulled up the pipe with the rope. An ancient Chinese method used knots, but improved designs intended for African villages use rubber washers made from tires. These work at much greater depths.

Obviously a bucket can be lowered down the well if the well is big enough, but this won't work with a modern drilled well. A better idea for a drilled well is to use a 2' (60cm) length of galvanized pipe. Use end caps that fit in the well casing. The upper cap is drilled for a screw eye, and a small hole for ventilation. The lower end is drilled with a hole about half the diameter of the pipe, and on the inside a piece of rigid plastic or rubber is used as a flapper valve. This allows water to enter the pipe, but not exit it. The whole assembly is lowered in the well casing, the weight of the pipe will cause it to fill with water, and it can then be lifted to the surface. The top pipe cape is there mostly to prevent the pipe from catching as it is lifted.

SPRINGS
Springs or artesian wells are ideal sources of water. Like a conventional well, the water should be tested for pathogens and any other contaminants found in your area. If the source is a spring, it's very important to seal it in a spring box to prevent the water from becoming contaminated as it reaches the surface. It's equally important to divert surface runoff around the spring box. As with a well, you will want to periodically treat the spring box with chlorine, particularly if the spring is slow moving.

SURFACE WATER
Most US residents are served by municipal water systems supplied with surface water, and many residents of underdeveloped countries rely on surface water. While surface water will almost always need to be treated, a lot of the risk can be reduced by properly collecting the water.

Ideal sources of water are fast flowing creeks and rivers, which don't have large sources of pollution in their watershed. With the small amounts of water needed by a family or small group, the most practical way to collect the water is though an infiltration gallery or well. Either method reduces the turbidity of the collected water making it easy for later treatment.[26]

DAMS AND RESERVOIRS
Many rural families have dug one or more dams or reservoirs on their property. The previous owners of our farmlet dug a small dam in one of the paddocks for livestock. After living there a few months, Stan and I decided to dig a second dam closer to the house. It was one of those very challenging learning experiences!

We had purchased property in an old volcanic region. At one time Mt. Pisgah had blown scoria and lava over that area seen in the red clay soil. There is clay and then there is CLAY!

Stan spent a lot of time on that dam calculating the esthetics, vs. evaporation rate, cost vs. extra water storage and even designed a small island in the middle with a nice wooden bridge to cross to it. He worked out every last detail except the possibility of hitting a huge deposit of basalt, a rock commonly found around volcanic areas.

Unhappily a large vein ran right through the dam only 6 feet down. Even the excavators marveled at the unfortunate location and its jagged base.

The next decision was how to get rid of it or even if we could. It was too massive for the excavating buckets, too close to the house to dynamite. It was decided to use a 6" bit fitted to a huge "jack hammer" to break it out. That didn't work either. Instead, the successful shattering of the rock created a persistent, massive leak.

Photo: Partial view of the larger Deyo dam, Victoria, Australia, after the island had been removed. The pond's 500,000 gallon capacity was excellent drought and fire insurance as well as emergency water and home to 60 gold and silver perch. Seismo and Taco immediately took over the dam as their private playground swimming countless laps every day. When we first saw their deep paw prints all around its banks and into the water, we worried they had punched holes in the bentonite. Their antics turned out to be a huge blessing as all of the traffic further packed the clay and sealed the dam. When the dogs let us "borrow" some of their pool water, it was used to irrigate the garden and fill the steers' stock tanks. The tall trees in the background are eucalyptus.

Back to the drawing board... We removed the island thinking some of the leakage occurred there. Then we brought in several truckloads of bentonite from South Australia. Bentonite is fairly expensive in Australia, not like in Colorado where it's as common as sand at the beach.

When the bentonite arrived, it was mixed with soil and heavily pressed and rolled into the dam's base and up the sides. It looked pretty good for holding water. We held our breaths...

The next morning after refilling it, the dam still held. Our dogs, Seismo and Taco, thought they'd died and gone to dog Heaven. They played in it all day swimming laps and I could swear Seismo rolled on his back saying, "Ahhh Taco, it really *is* a dog's life!"

By the third day, no one was smiling. Massive amounts of water had disappeared – again.

Now most people would be very discouraged at this point, but Stan was determined not to let it beat him. After making countless phone calls, every dam builder had given up but one. This last dam expert brought different clay to waterproof the bottom and sides. The leak slowed but didn't stop. The old-timers, who had lived many years around dams, told us it had to "season" to hold water. Seasoning is a process of waiting for mud, clay and ooze to fill all remaining holes. Algae and plants grow on the bottom further sealing it. When it rains, more clay runs into the places it needs to seal. Dams are not built overnight unless conditions are perfect.

This water source, when it fully sealed, backed up water supplies used for the grounds, vegetable gardens and fruit trees, and for fighting bushfires. If it were used as drinking water, it would need filtering and chlorine treatment first.

The lesson learned from this exercise was that before you dig a dam in any location, be sure to take a ground core sample first. If we had, the big layer of basalt would have shown up and we could have relocated the dam saving time, money and aggravation!

Photo: Eight-foot waterfall about 50 feet away from the dam (to the right of photograph). Topmost part of image shows the bubbler that filled the top pond before water cascaded into an 8 foot holding pond. From the holding pond, water re-circulated out to the dam and aerated it for the fish. The waterfall served several purposes making a restful landscape addition and keeping the dam healthy. And yes, when the dogs were too lazy to trot out to the dam for a swim, they took frequent dips in the pond at the foot of the waterfall.

RAIN WATER CATCHMENT (FREE WATER!)

Another type of water collection and storage to consider, should your property permit it, is free standing above ground or in-ground tanks. These tanks are quite common in Australia and rural North, Central and South America where public/scheme/municipal water is not readily available. On the next page is a typical arrangement for rainwater catchment. Our system on the farm in Australia was the same concept but we ran our feed pipes underground from the house down to the barn where we kept the 10,000-gallon concrete tanks.

This system utilizes rainwater caught from rooftops of homes, barns and other outbuildings. It runs through pipe or gutters carrying rainwater from the roof collection area to the cistern. Cisterns (storage tanks) are made from a variety of materials including reinforced concrete, fiberglass, stainless steel, tin and even brick.

In most places, stainless steel tanks are the most expensive followed by concrete tanks. Ideally, concrete tanks are poured on-site to prevent cracking rather than be transported to the destination.

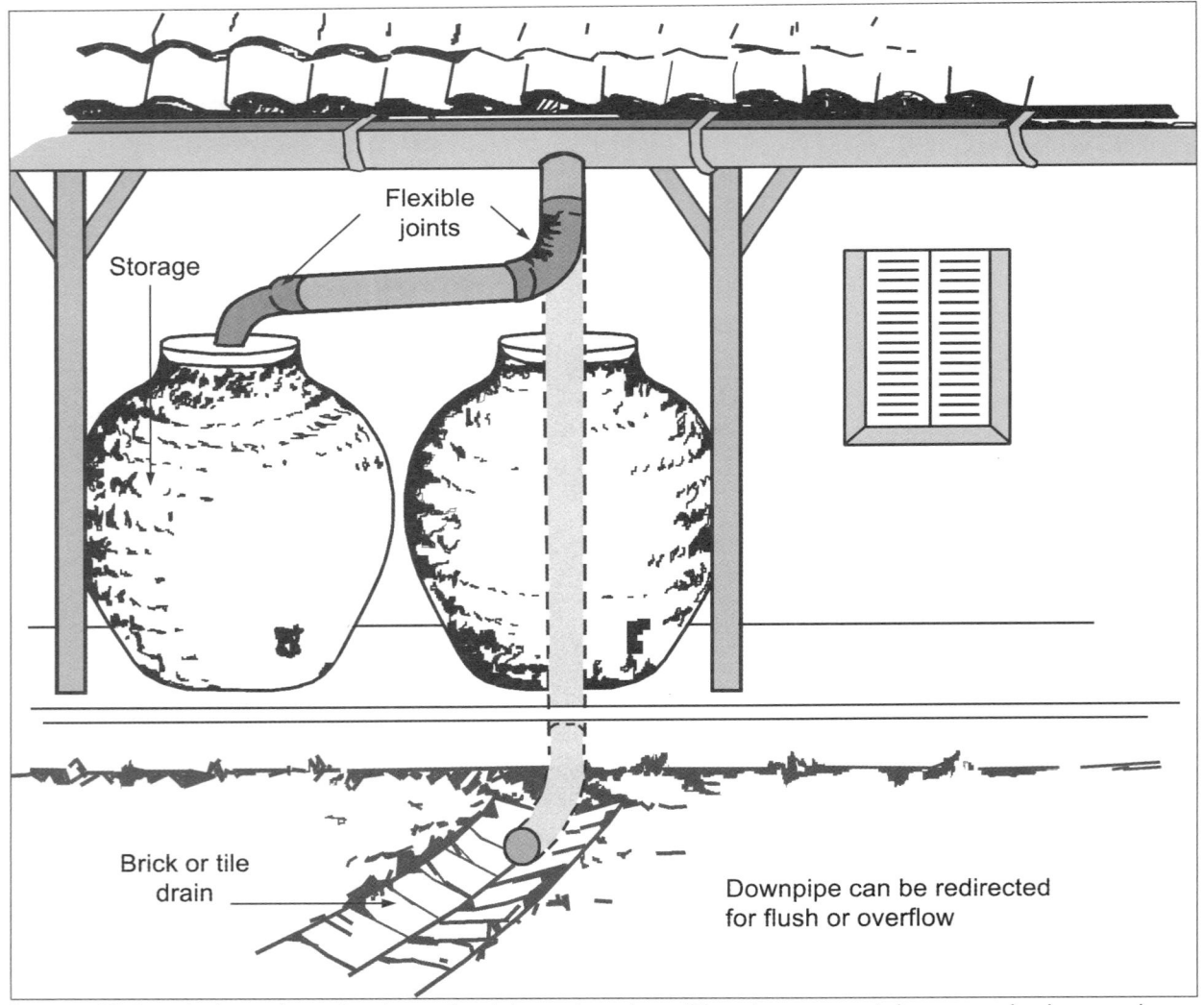

Image: Pictured above is a simple roof catchment system. The storage containers can be in any shape that fits your storage needs. During periods of no rain, dust, dead leaves and bird droppings will accumulate on the roof. These materials are washed off with the first rain and will enter the cistern if some basic steps are not taken. While roof catchment need not be as comprehensive as the illustration on the next page, debris filtering and water purification needs to be performed on *any* roof catchment system.

In order to select the right construction material for your area, you need to consider if it's earthquake-prone or extremely windy. If earthquakes are a problem, concrete or brick aren't the best choices since the tank could crack with shifting ground. Adding a plastic liner solves this potential problem.

While fiberglass tanks are less expensive, concrete is not subject to UV radiation damage. Over time, you can expect fiberglass tanks to become more brittle.

If you reside in a very windy area, fiberglass tanks are less desirable especially when first being filled or are nearly empty.

A school in Australia had an aboveground metal tank delivered to the property. Before it had time to fill, a windstorm "stole" the tank and it was seen rolling down a country road. This could easily happen to empty fiberglass tanks as well, but this situation can be avoided by securing these tanks when empty.

Stainless steel is very durable but expensive by comparison. With a tin tank, the plastic liner is a necessity to avoid a "tinned can" taste. Especially for water acquired through means other than the public systems, it is essential to have it tested for bacteria, insects and minerals. It is also prudent to have water tested if purchasing property with an existing tank water supply. People tend to take rainwater's purity for granted and get lax in draining and cleaning the holding tanks. Generally speaking, these tanks only need to be drained and cleaned every 5-10 years depending on the filtering system used, and much more frequently if the storage tanks are without lids.

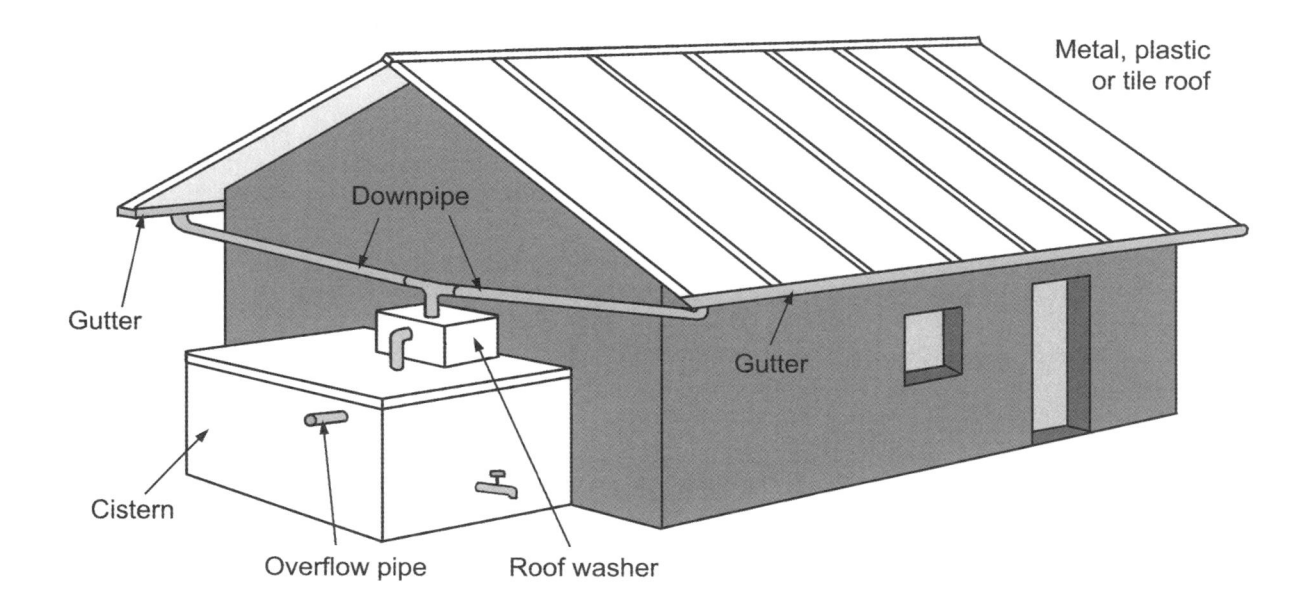

ADVANTAGES TO ROOF CATCHMENT SYSTEMS
1. They are easy and inexpensive to construct
2. Owner performs the maintenance
3. They are an essential backup water supply in times of emergency if you're on town water and the pipes break
4. Rainwater quality is likely to be higher than other sources
5. Rainwater provides an excellent freshwater supply where surface and groundwater are unavailable, scarce or contaminated
6. After the initial cost of the tank, the water supply is free

DISADVANTAGES MIGHT INCLUDE:
1. Water supply is rainfall dependent
2. Cost of constructing a home with a cistern is higher than one without
3. In areas near industrial sites, acid rain is common which could contaminate the rainfall supply

WHAT WOULD I NEED?
- Catchment area/roof, the surface upon which the rain falls;
- Gutters, downspouts and transport channels from catchment surface to storage;
- Leaf Screens and roofwashers, the systems that remove contaminants and debris;
- Cisterns or storage tanks, where collected rainwater is stored;
- Conveying, the delivery system for the treated rainwater, either by gravity or pump; and
- Water treatment, filters and equipment, and additives to settle, filter, and disinfect.

GUTTERS AND DOWNSPOUTS
These components catch the rain from the roof surface and transport it to the cistern. Standard shapes and sizes are easily obtained and maintained, although custom fabricated profiles are also available to maximize the total amount of harvested rainfall. Gutters and downspouts must be properly sized, sloped, and installed in order to maximize the quantity of harvested rain.

Gutter Materials And Sizes

The most common material for off-the-shelf gutters is seamless aluminum, with standard extrusions of 5 and 6-inch sections, in 50-foot lengths. A 3-inch downspout is used with a 5-inch gutter and a 4-inch downspout is used with a 6-inch gutter.

Galvanized steel is another commonly used metal. It can be bent to sections larger than 6 inches, and in 10 and 20-foot lengths. A seamless 6-inch extruded aluminum gutter with a 4-inch downspout can handle about 1,000 square feet of roof area and is recommended for most cistern installations. Downspouts are designed to handle 1¼ inches of rainfall during a 10-minute period.

For roof areas that exceed 1,000 square feet, larger sections of gutters and downspouts are commonly made from galvanized steel or the roof is divided into several guttered zones.

Copper and stainless steel are also used for gutters and downspouts but they are much more expensive than either aluminum or galvanized steel. Downspouts are typically the same material as the gutters but of a smaller cross section. The connection between the downspout to the cistern is generally constructed of Schedule 40 PVC pipe.

To keep leaves and other debris from entering the system, gutters need a continuous leaf screen, made of ¼ inch wire mesh in a metal frame, installed along their entire length, and a screen or wire basket at the top of the downspout.

Gutter hangers are generally placed every 3 feet. The outside face of the gutter should be lower than the inside face to encourage drainage away from the building wall. Where possible, the gutters should be placed about ¼ inch below the slope line so that debris can clear without knocking down the gutter.

As with the catchment surface, it's important that these conduits are lead-free and not come in contact with any other substance that could contaminate the water. If you are retrofitting onto older gutters and downspouts, make sure they don't contain lead solder or lead-based paint.

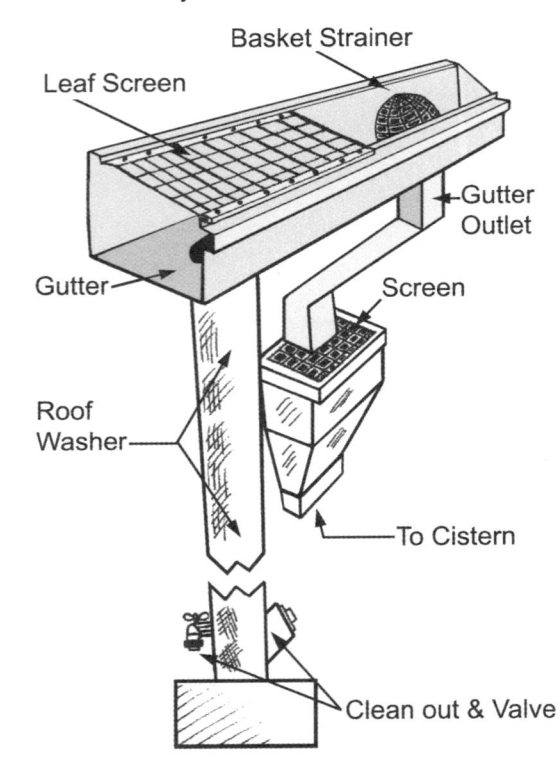

ROOF WASHERS

Roof washing, or the collection and disposal of the first flush of water, is really important if the collected rainwater is intended for human consumption. First flushes pick up most of the dirt, debris, and contaminants, such as bird droppings that have collected on the roof between rains. The simplest system consists of a standpipe and a gutter downspout located ahead of the downspout from the gutter to the cistern.

The pipe is usually made from 6 or 8-inch PVC with a valve and clean out at the bottom. Most of these roofwashers extend from the gutter to the ground where they are supported. The gutter downspout and top of the pipe are fitted and sealed so water won't flow out of the top. Once the pipe has filled, the rest of the water flows to the downspout connected to the cistern.

These systems should be designed so that at least 10 gallons of water are diverted for every 1000 square feet of collection area. Rather than wasting this water, the first flush can be used for lawn or garden irrigation. Several types of commercial roof washers also contain filter or strainer boxes. Trim any tree branches that overhang the roof. These branches are perches for birds and produce debris.

STORAGE TANK(S)

Tanks are available in a range of materials and sizes, new and used, large and small, to accommodate your system design and budget. For small installations, readily available new and used tanks, including whiskey barrels, 55-gallon drums, and horse troughs can be fashioned into supplemental do-it-yourself systems. If used tanks are selected, be sure that they did not contain any toxic substances that could affect water quality for many, many years. For large installations, many options exist for manufactured and site-built systems.

TANKS AND CISTERN TYPES			
	Material	Feature	Caution
PLASTIC	Garbage Cans (20-50 Gallon)	Commercially available, inexpensive	Use only new cans
	Fiberglass	Commercially available, alterable and moveable	Degradable, requires interior coating
	Polyethylene / Polypropylene	Commercially available, alterable and moveable	Degradable, requires interior coating
METAL	Steel Drums (55 Gallon)	Commercially available, alterable and moveable	Verify prior use for toxics, corrodes and rusts, small capacity
	Galvanized Steel Tanks	Commercially available, alterable and moveable	Possible corrosion and rust
CONCRETE and MASONRY	Ferrocement	Durable, immoveable	Potential to crack and fail
	Stone, Concrete Block	Durable, immoveable	Difficult to maintain
	Monolithic Poured In Place	Durable, immoveable	Potential to crack
WOOD	Redwood, Douglas Fir, Cypress	Attractive, durable	Expensive

TANKS AND CISTERN CAPACITY (gallons)[27]							
Diameter of Round Type							
DEPTH	6'	8'	10'	12'	14'	16'	18'
6'	1,266	2,256	3,522	5,076	6,906	9,018	11,412
8'	1,688	3,008	4,696	6,768	9,208	12,024	15,216
10'	2,110	3,760	5,870	8,460	11,510	15,030	19,020
12'	2,532	4,512	7,044	8,532	13,812	18,036	22,824
14'	2,954	5,264	8,218	11,844	16,114	21,042	26,628
Length of Sides of Square Type							
DEPTH	6'	8'	10'	12'	14'	16'	18'
6'	1,614	2,874	4,488	6,462	8,796	11,490	14,534
8'	2,152	3,832	5,984	8,616	11,728	15,320	19,378
10'	2,690	4,790	7,480	10,770	14,660	19,150	24,222
12'	3,228	5,748	8,976	12,924	17,592	22,980	29,068
14'	3,766	6,706	10,472	15,078	20,524	26,810	33,912

ACCESSING CISTERN WATER

Remember, water only flows downhill unless you pump it. Gravity flow works only if the tank is higher than the kitchen sink. Water pressure for a gravity system depends on the difference in elevation between the storage tank and the faucet. Water gains one pound per square inch of pressure for every 2.31 feet of rise or lift. Many plumbing fixtures and appliances require 20 psi for proper operation, while standard municipal water supply pressures are typically in the 40 to 60 psi range. To achieve comparable pressure, a cistern would have to be 92.4 feet (2.31 feet x 40 psi = 92.4 feet) above the home's highest plumbing fixture. That explains why pumps are frequently used, much in the way they are used to extract well water.

Pumps prefer to push water, not pull it. To approximate the water pressure from a municipal system, pressure tanks are often installed with the pump. They have a pressure switch with adjustable settings of 5 to 65 psi.

For example, to keep your in-house pressure at about 35 psi, set the switch to turn off the pump when the pressure reaches 40 psi and turn it on again when the pressure drops down to 30 psi.

WATER TREATMENT

Before making a decision about what type of water treatment method to use, have your water tested by an approved laboratory and determine whether your water will be used for potable or non-potable uses. The types of treatment discussed are filtration, disinfection, and buffering for pH control. Dirt, rust, scale, silt and other suspended particles, bird and rodent feces, airborne bacteria and cysts will inadvertently find their way into the cistern or storage tank even when design features such as roof washers, screens and tight-fitting lids are properly installed. Water can taste or look unappetizing without being unsafe; so filtration and disinfection is the minimum recommended treatment if the water is for human consumption (drinking, brushing teeth, or cooking). The most common treatment of rainwater systems is filters to remove sediment, in conjunction with either ultraviolet light or chemical disinfection.

FILTERS

Filtration can be as simple as the use of cartridge filters or those used for swimming pools and hot tubs. In all cases, proper filter operation and maintenance in accordance with the instruction manual for that specific filter must be followed to ensure safety. Once screens and roofwashers remove large debris, smaller filters are available which help improve rainwater quality. Keep in mind that most filters are designed to treat municipal water or well water. Therefore, filter selection requires careful consideration. Screening, sedimentation, and pre-filtering occur between catchment and storage or within the tank. A cartridge sediment filter that traps and removes particles five microns or larger is the most common filter size used for rainwater harvesting. Sediment filters used in series, referred to as multi-cartridge or in-line filters, sieve the particles from increasing to decreasing size.

These sediment filters are often used as a pre-filter for other treatment techniques such as ultraviolet light or reverse osmosis filters which can become clogged from large particles.

Unless you are adding something to your rainwater, there is no need to filter out something that is not present. When a disinfectant such as chlorine is added to rainwater, an activated carbon filter at the tap may be used to remove the chlorine prior to use. Remember that activated carbon filters are subject to becoming sites of bacterial growth. Chemical disinfectants such as chlorine or iodine must be added to the water **prior** to the activated carbon filter. If ultraviolet light or ozone is used for disinfection, the system should be placed **after** the activated carbon filter. Many water treatment standards require some type of disinfection after filtration with activated carbon. Ultraviolet light disinfection is often the method of choice. All filters must be replaced per recommended schedule rather than when they cease to work; failure to do so may result in the filter contributing to the water's contamination.

Performing the tasks to keep your system in tip-top share isn't difficult and it's important to keep your water safe and your family in good health. These responsibilities include regular inspections of all the previously discussed components, plus pruning branches that overhang catchment areas, keeping leaf screens clean, checking tank and pump, replacing filters, and testing the water. Keep a maintenance schedule and checklist to ensure proper performance.

HOW MUCH RAIN CAN I CATCH?

The amount of rainwater harvested depends on the total roof surface collection area, volume of storage, and the amount of rain. Newer storage tanks also use its top for additional catchment, equipping it with gutter that funnels rainwater directly into the tank.

ANNUAL CATCHMENT IN GALLONS, ROOF SIZES AND RAINFALL AMOUNTS[28]									
Roof Size	Rainfall In Inches								
sq. ft	20	24	28	32	36	40	44	48	52
1000	11,236	13,483	15,730	17,978	20,225	22,472	24,719	26,966	29,214
1100	12,360	14,832	17,303	19,775	22,247	24,719	27,191	29,663	32,135
1200	13,483	16,180	18,876	21,573	24,270	26,966	29,663	32,360	35,056
1300	14,607	17,528	20,450	23,371	26,292	29,214	32,135	35,056	37,978
1400	15,730	18,876	22,023	25,169	28,315	31,461	34,607	37,753	40,899
1500	16,854	20,225	23,596	26,966	30,337	33,708	37,079	40,450	43,820
1600	17,978	21,573	25,169	28,764	32,360	35,955	39,551	43,146	46,742
1700	19,101	22,921	26,742	30,562	34,382	38,202	42,023	45,843	49,663
1800	20,225	24,270	28,315	32,360	36,405	40,450	44,495	48,540	52,584
1900	21,348	25,618	29,888	34,157	38,427	42,697	46,966	51,236	55,506
2000	22,472	26,966	31,461	35,955	40,450	44,944	49,438	53,933	58,427
2100	23,596	28,315	33,034	37,753	42,472	47,191	51,910	56,629	61,349
2200	24,719	29,663	34,607	39,551	44,495	49,438	54,382	59,326	64,270
2300	25,843	31,011	36,180	41,348	46,517	51,686	56,854	62,023	67,191
2400	26,966	32,360	37,753	43,146	48,540	53,933	59,326	64,719	70,113

HOW MUCH WATER DO YOU USE?

Assessing your indoor and outdoor water needs will help determine the best use for the rainwater. If you are already connected to municipal water, then it may be most cost-effective to use collected rainwater for lawn and garden irrigation – unless your aim is to be off-grid or want control over additives like fluoride. If you have already invested in a well system, rainwater could augment it or sidestep having to drink mineralized well water, or provide back-up water when underground water sources are low.

Some people install a complete rainwater system designed to supply both their indoor and outdoor water needs. If you are considering this, it's imperative that you use best conservation practices to ensure a year round water supply. Three variables determine your ability to fulfill your household water demand: local precipitation, available catchment area, and your financial budget.

If you are accustomed to simply turning on a water tap and then paying a bill at the end of the month, switching to a rain catchment system will require adjustment.

HOUSEHOLD WATER BUDGET

An easy way to calculate your daily water consumption is to review previous water bills, if you presently use municipal water. Another method is to account for every water-using activity, including shower, bath, toilet flush, dishwashing run, washing machine load. A house with low-flow plumbing fixtures such as 1.6 gallon-per-flush toilets and 2.75 gallon-per-minute showerheads, might use 55 gallons or less of water per day per person. Very conservative minded households might be able to reduce water use to as low as 35 gallons per person per day.

However, for the purposes of designing a rainwater system, estimate 75 gallons per person per day for indoor use to ensure adequate year-round indoor supply – unless you are sure that all of your fixtures are the newer, more efficient ones and you plan to follow strict water conservation. Complete the Household Water Consumption Chart to see how your household's water consumption compares with the recommended design allowance.

While inside water use remains relatively level throughout the year, total water demand increases during the hot, dry summers due to increased lawn and garden watering, and decreases during the cool, wet winters when the garden is fallow and the lawn needs little attention. To determine your daily water budget, multiply the number of persons in the household times the average water consumption.

HOUSEHOLD WATER CONSUMPTION CHART					
Fixture	**Use**	**Flow rate**	**# users**	**Total**
Toilet	flushes/person/day	1.6 gal/flush (new toilet)*		
Shower	# minutes/person/day (5 minutes max.)	2.75 gallon/minute* (restricted flow head)		
Bath	# baths/person/day	50 gal/bath (average)		
Faucets	bathroom and kitchen sinks (excluding cleaning)	10 gallons per day	N/A	
Washing Machine	# loads per day	50 gallons (average)	N/A	
Dishwasher	# loads per day	9.5 gallons per load	N/A	
			Total	Gallons / day
			Multiply by 365	Gallons / year
Note: All flow rates are for newer fixtures. Older toilets – those manufactured prior to 1994 – use from 3½ to 7 gallons per flush. Older showerheads have flow rates as high as 10 gallons per minute.				

While inside water use remains relatively level throughout the year, total water demand increases during hot, dry summers due to increased lawn and garden watering, and decreases during the cool, wet winters when the garden is fallow and the lawn needs little attention. To determine your daily water budget, multiply the number of persons in the household times the average water consumption. Estimates of indoor household water use range from less than 55 gallons per person a day in a conservation minded household to well over 75 gallons per person a day in non-conserving households.

Another way to estimate how much stored tank water is needed for your family is based on this calculation:

ESTIMATED HOUSEHOLD WATER USAGE FOR 1 YEAR[29]				
WASTE SYSTEM USED	GALLONS		LITERS	
	Per Person	Family of 4	Per Person	Family of 4
House With Septics	17,200	68,700	68,700	260,000
House Without Septics	15,800	63,400	63,400	240,000

OUTSIDE WATER REQUIREMENTS

If you have to supplement rainfall to keep your lawn green, you'll need to complete the following chart to determine your lawn watering requirements in order to properly size your cistern.[30]

Multiply the water demand (inches per year) times your lawn size (square feet) and divide by 12. This will give you the cubic feet of water demand per year. _____ cu. ft.

Multiply the number cubic feet of water demand per year (line 1) times a conversion factor of 7.48. This gives you the number of required gallons of water per year. _____ gal.

Multiply the inches of natural rainfall for your area times your lawn size (square feet) and divide by 12. This gives you the cubic feet of water supplied by natural rainfall. _____ cu. ft.

Multiply the cubic feet of natural rainfall times a conversion factor of 7.48. This gives you the gallons of natural rainfall per year. _____ gal.

Subtract the gallons of natural rainfall from the required water demand for your grass type (line 2). This gives you the gallons required. _____ gal.

SWIMMING POOL WATER

Think of a pool as "backup" water and keep it treated. Maintaining free chlorine residuals at 3-5ppm prevents microorganisms from growing. To monitor this, you'll need a supply of chlorine testers. The problem with using swimming pool water is that organics can enter through dirt, sweat, body oils and the inevitable kiddie tinkle. This can form chloramines that can be harmful to drink. Imagine walking in and out of your drinking water a hundred times and then consuming it. Don't let clarity fool you. Some crystal clear mountain springs have tested out to be laced with cholera. In a survival situation it may be necessary, but steps can be taken to minimize this.

Partial and complete water changes should be done when feasible. Although it's impossible to make a general rule, change the pool water at least 1-2 times a year and do partial changes after a lot of use.

Keep dry chlorine on hand as it has a much longer shelf life than liquid. Additionally, when the need arises to convert a pool to potable water, it's too late to change the water; however, the residual should be elevated over 5 ppm free chlorine up to ten parts, then allowed to naturally dissipate. This should take a couple of days ensuring any of the more tenacious bacteria is destroyed. If other stored water isn't available, remove the necessary pool water and boil it or just treat with chlorine to the normal 5ppm. It's best to err on the side of caution.

When adding solid chlorine, dissolve the granules in a bucket first and then add to the pool water. Much better mixing will result. Also, without power, a clean paddle or an oar should be designated as a mixer. Thirty minutes' minimum contact time is needed before use, more if temperatures are cold or if mixing is poor.

For smaller amounts of water, if you still have power, boiling is a reliable treatment. However, boiling water is not an efficient use of fuel, if it's scarce. Bear in mind, while boiling pool water is fine, boiling alone won't prevent re-infection from airborne contamination. Once water is boiled, a lower chlorine residual of 3 ppm is OK.

Make sure to store an adequate supply of pH balancers and available chlorine testers if you intend on using pool water for consumption. Chlorine loses effectiveness above 7.5pH; that's why pH control is important. Bromine chemistry works in higher pH ranges, but it's not approved for potable water. Use bromine disinfection for washing dishing, laundry, clothes and people.

You might consider a filtration system that removes the chlorine taste. Activated carbon in any form removes chlorine, but remember, once you remove the free chlorine, your water doesn't have protection. It should be consumed immediately following chlorine removal.

In a pinch, filter highly chlorinated water through a cloth filled with ashes. Make sure the cloth allows only the water to pass through, not the ash.

Covering the pool at all times when not in use is a good idea. Try to keep the cover clean and wash the area you lay it on when removing it.[31]

Chapter 7: Finding Survival Water

Hopefully, you will never run out of water, but should you find yourself in desperate circumstances, this information may save your life. Before setting out on a camping trip or on some other adventure, especially in drier climates, purchase a USGS geodetic contour map. It should be a 7.5-minute Series (topographic) Map no larger than 1:24,000 scale. These invaluable tools locate old roads and water sources not found on road atlases, local or gazetteer-type maps. If you have a bug out location, it's clever to have maps for between the area where you live and your destination. These maps can help in your journey if you become stranded or lost, or need to find alternative routes during an evacuation.

If you end up on foot, they point out obscure trails and no longer used roads. Some water sites may still be viable or require only minimal effort to use. These maps also indicate water flows so if you plan to dig a well on your property, it can show where would be the best place to drill. Well digging can be an expensive venture since most drillers charge by the foot whether you end up with a dry hole or hit a bonanza.

The following table gives a water source overview depending on location.

\	\	WATER SOURCES SUMMARY	\
WHERE	**SOURCE**	**GETTING IT AND MAKING WATER POTABLE**	**REMARKS**
FRIGID AREAS	**Snow and ice**	Melt and purify.	**Do not** eat without melting! Eating snow or ice can reduce body temperature and lead to more dehydration. Snow or ice is no purer than the water from which they come. Milky or gray sea ice with sharp edges is salty. Do not drink without desalting it. Bluish or blackish sea ice that is crystalline with rounded corners and shatters easily has little salt in it.
AT SEA	**Sea**	Use desalinator.	**Do not** drink seawater without desalting.
	Rain	Catch rain in tarps or in other water-holding containers.	If tarp or water-holding material is coated with salt, wash it in the sea before using (very little salt will remain on it).
	Sea ice		See remarks for frigid areas.
BEACH	**Ground**	Dig hole deep enough to allow water to seep in. Find rocks, build fire and heat rocks. Drop hot rocks in water. Hold cloth over hole to absorb steam; wring water from cloth.	*Alternate method if a container or bark pot is available*: Fill container or pot with seawater. Build fire and boil water to produce steam. Hold cloth over container to absorb steam; wring water from cloth.
	Fresh	Dig behind first group of sand dunes for collection of fresh water.	
DESERT	**Ground** • In valleys and low areas • At foot of concave banks of dry rivers • At foot of cliffs or rock outcrops • At first depression behind first sand dune of dry lakes • Damp surface sand • Green vegetation	Dig holes deep enough to allow water to seep in.	In a sand dune belt, any available water will be found beneath the original valley floor at the edge of dunes.

Between the geodetic map and the following water clues, you should be able to relieve your thirst. Start out knowing **it usually doesn't pay to dig for water.** The energy used and the moisture lost in sweat digging a hole usually far exceeds the water found.

You will need 2 quarts (2 liters) a day, *minimum*, to maintain fluid level. In the desert, during periods of heavy activity or in illness, the amount required doubles. If you've been without water for a long while, once you find it, drink slowly and gradually. Consuming too much at once can cause nausea and vomiting.

If you're getting enough water, urine will be pale yellow.

Slowed bowel movements are natural when going without enough water and food. Your system will re-adjust when normal conditions resume. Don't take laxatives under such conditions as it further depletes the body of fluid.

TERRAIN

Try to discover the signs that indicate the presence of water. Since everything flows downhill, look for water at the base of hills, not at the top. The bottom of a valley, at the foot of a sharp slope, a corner of vegetation which has sheltered a spring during rainy season, a low forest and sea shores are among many places where the water level lies just under the surface.

Scan the landscape for greenest areas. They can indicate a water trail.

VEGETATION

Lush vegetation in arid terrain indicates water in one form or another. In arid country, cottonwoods serve much the same purpose as willows in wetter areas. A chain of cottonwood outlines a river bed. Whether that bed turns out to be wet or dry is another question. If it's dry, check the ground by one of the largest and oldest cottonwoods. On the inside bank of the river's curve, you will usually find a small pool of water. There should be enough ground moisture so if you really need water, you can dig down a foot or so and find seepage.

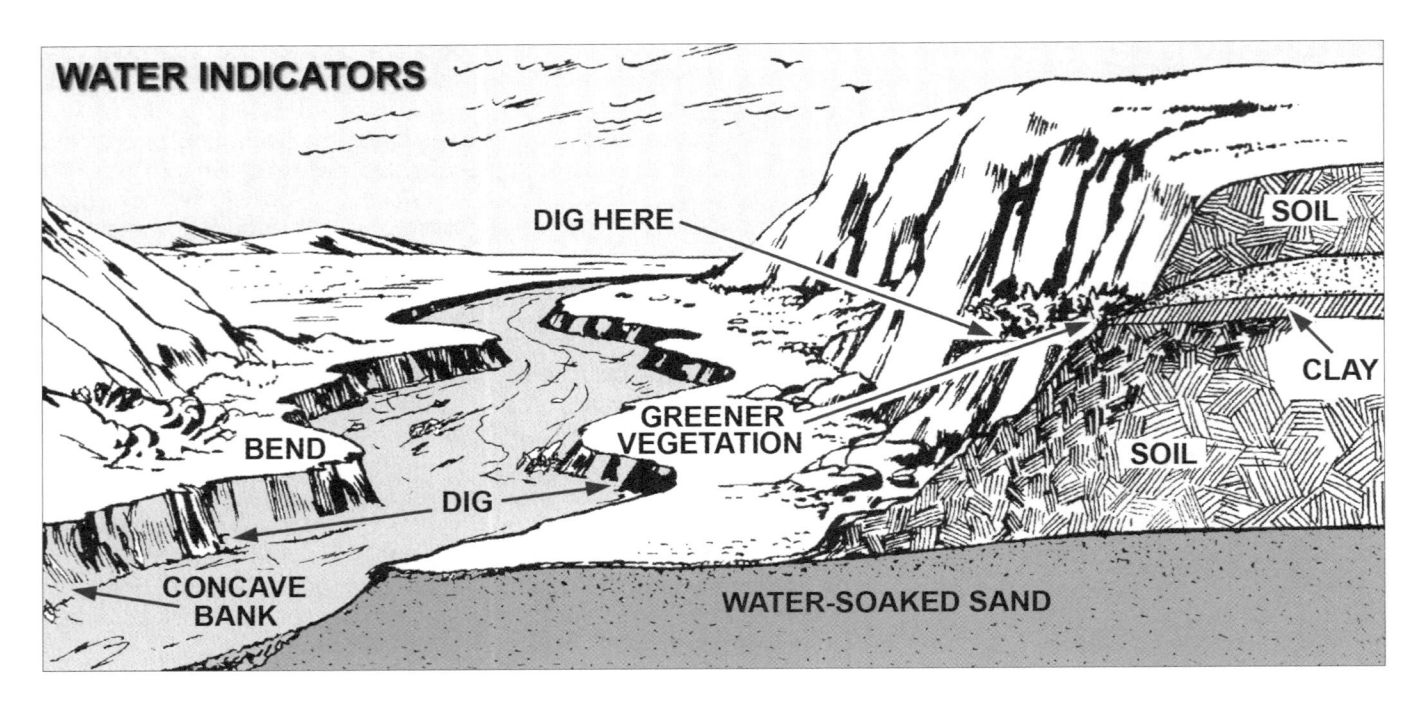

DESERT WATER

Water seeks the lowest level and in the desert, this may be underground. If you see hills, head toward them, since the likeliest place to find water is at their base.

Even though it's dry, water may lie beneath the surface of a thin, shallow stream bed or arroyo. Hunt for a low place in the bed and dig. The same applies to dry lake bottoms. The presence of any water will be indicated by damp sand.

Game trails in desert country usually lead to water. Follow them downhill if the land slopes. Otherwise scout around till you find the paths most used; this will be the way to go.

Grazing animals such as deer, are usually never far from water and generally drink at dawn and dusk. Meat eating animals aren't good water indicators as they usually get enough moisture from their food and can go without water for long periods.

Birds. Watch the flight of birds particularly at dawn and dusk. Birds glide and hover around marshes. Go there every day. Parrots and pigeons are rarely very far from it.

Trees. The following trees can also provide water:
- *Palms.* Water is usually found within several feet of a tree's base. The buri, coconut, sugar, rattan, and nips all contain a tasty sugary liquid. To get it, bruise a lower frond and pull it down so the tree releases its juice. For a larger supply of liquid, bend down a flowering stalk and cut off the tip. By cutting a thin slice off the stalk every 12 hours, the flow will renew, making it possible to collect up to a quart per day. Nipa palm shoots grow from the base that makes working at ground level possible. On other adult palms, you may have to climb the tree to reach a flowering stalk. **NOTE**: Coconut milk contains a large amount of water, but milk from ripe coconuts has a strong laxative effect. With a dose of "Montezuma's revenge" you might lose more fluid than you drink.
- *Traveler's tree.* Found in Madagascar, water collects in cup shaped sheaths at the base of its leaves.
- *Umbrella tree.* Growing in the West African tropics, water can be found in leaf bases and roots.
- *Baobab tree.* Found in the sandy plains of northern Australia and Africa, water collects in its bottle-like trunk during the wet season. Frequently, you can find clear, fresh water in these trees after weeks of dry weather.

Reed grass is also a sound sign that moisture is near.

Desert plants. It's often futile to search for water near desert plants since they've already taken it. Instead, dig, pull up and section off plant roots. Roots of some desert plants like the Australian Water Tree, the Desert Oak and the Blood Wood are found very near the surface soil. Remove these roots and cut them or better still, break them in 2-3 feet (61-91cm) lengths. Remove the skin and suck the water contained inside.

Cactus. Cut off the head and avoid the milk. The only danger comes from cacti's milky sap. Barrel Cacti are the exception. One misconception is that Barrels are full of water. Instead, they contain a slimy pulp. Once the top of an Echinocactus type Barrel is chopped off, mash the pulp and strain it through a cloth. The liquid is bitter and unpleasant but it has saved people in an emergency.

Photo: Even this seemingly dry stream bed could hold water along its inner banks and in the plants.

DEW

Dew that settles after cold nights in many stretches of deserts has also been a life saver. Survivors have mopped it from the metal of their wrecked plane or collected it in tarps.

Dew evaporates quickly and must be collected before sunrise. Heavy dew can give a little more than 1 quart of water/hour. Thirsty Bedouins sometimes dig up cool stones just before sunrise and wait till dew settles on them, then lick the stones dry.

TIPS
- Where you see damp soil, dig in surface.
- Look behind rocks, in trenches and small ditches, on canyon flanks or under sharp cliff edges to find natural reservoirs. Often in those places, the soil is made of solid rock or very hard, well packed soil that collects water.
- In the Gobi Desert, don't count on plants for water, but in the Sahara, Wild Gourd or Pumpkin can quench thirst.

DESERT TRAVEL HINTS
- Travel at night as much as possible.
- Cover yourself as much as possible. Clothing stops sweat evaporation and helps keep you cool. If you remove your shirt, you will feel more comfortable, but you'll also sweat much more besides risking sunburn. You will walk further if you don't sweat too much.
- Unless you have a lot of water, don't waste it washing.
- When drinking, don't swallow big gulps in one shot. Drink small quantities. If low in water, then only dampen your lips.
- Keep a few small pebbles or gum in your mouth to ease your thirst and encourage saliva.
- Breathe through the nose and don't talk.
- Absorb salt only with water and only if you have a lot of water.
- Drink as often and as much as you can. Saving water won't get you much further, but don't waste it.
- When extremely thirsty any liquid is tempting, but don't drink alcohol, urine or blood. Aside from its effects, alcohol only dehydrates the body and blood is salty and considered a food; therefore, requires additional body fluids to digest. Additionally, it may transmit disease.
- Smoking dehydrates your body and heightens the need to drink.

WHERE TO FIND WATER IN ROCKY SOIL
Water easily disintegrates limestone and digs caverns. This is where you'll find springs and water sweating.

LAVA, SANDSTONE, GRANITE
Because of its porous nature, lava retains a lot of water, so you'll find springs along valleys that cross old lava flows.

When a dry canyon cuts across a sandstone layer, water sweats on its walls.

In a region rich in granite, dig a hole in green grass and you'll discover water coming up.

IN SOFT SOIL
Water is ordinarily more abundant and easier to spot in soft than in rocky soils. Moisture below the normal water table often comes to surface in valleys and slopes.

Springs and sweating are found in the high level line of rivers after they have shrunk back.

There is no need to dig deeply in order to find water. Above the water table's normal level, there are small streams and ponds. However, those waters are often contaminated and dangerous even when far away from civilization. Example: Springs below towns. Don't drink this water under any circumstances without purifying it first.

ON MOUNTAINS
Dig in dry spring beds; water often hides under gravel. Mountain slopes usually hide springs at their base.

OTHER SOURCES OF SUPPLY
Creosote plants, Willows, Elder Berry, Salted Herbs grow only where water is near the surface.

At night, use a handkerchief to mop and gather up to 1 quart of water per hour from damp soils where you see flies.

INSECTS, BIRDS AND ANIMALS AS WATER INDICATORS

INSECTS
ANTS – Many ants need water, so if you see a steady column of small black ants climbing a tree trunk and disappearing into a hole in a crotch, it's highly probable you'll fill find a hidden reservoir of fresh. Dip a long straw or thin stick down the hole where the ants are going.

If it's wet, then water is there. To get the water, do not on any account chop into the tree. If the hole is very small, enlarge it with your knife-point at the top. Make a mop by tying grass or a rag to a stick. Dip the mop into the water and squeeze into a container.

Another method is to take a long hollow straw and suck the water you need from the reservoir. These natural tree reservoirs are very common in dry areas, and are often kept full by the dew. It condenses on the upper branches of the tree, trickles down into the crotch and slides into the tree's reservoir.

Water reservoirs are very common in the She-Oaks (casuarinas) and many species of Wattle, all Australian natives.

BEES – These insects are a sure water sign. Rarely will you find a hive of wild bees more than 3 or 4 miles from fresh water. A bee flies a mile in 12 minutes. So you can be sure if you see bees that you are not far from fresh water, but you will probably have to look for further indications before you find the water supply.

MASON FLIES – These large, hornet-like creatures are sure water indicators. If you see a mason fly building in an area, know that you are within a few hundred yards of a soak of wet earth.

Look carefully and you'll see the mason fly hover and then suddenly drop to the ground. If you examine where she landed, you'll find the soil is moist and that she is busy rolling a mud pellet for her building. By digging down a few inches or at most, a couple of feet, you should find a spring and clear, fresh, drinkable water.

BIRDS
CARNIVOROUS – Being flesh eaters, they get most of the moisture they need from the flesh of their prey thus not reliable water-drinkers. Nor should you regard the water living birds as indicators of fresh or drinkable water.

DOVES or BLACKBIRDS – Flocks on the ground and **QUAIL** in any quantity are signs of water nearby.

FINCHES – All finches are grain-eaters and water drinkers. In dry belts, if you see a finch colony, you can bet you are near water, probably a hidden spring or permanent soak.

GRAIN EATERS – All of the grain eaters and most of the ground feeders require water, so if you see their tracks on the ground, be fairly certain there is water within a few miles of your location. Parrots and cockatoos are an exception and aren't reliable water indicators.

PIGEONS – They are reliable water indicators. Being grain and seed eaters, they spend the day out on the plains feeding. When dusk approaches, pigeons make for a water hole, drink their fill and fly slowly back to their nest. Their manner of flying tells you the direction of their water supply.

If they are flying low and swift, they are flying *to* water but if their flight is from tree to tree and slow, they are *returning* from drinking their fill. Being heavy with water they are vulnerable to birds of prey.

ANIMALS
FROGS and SALAMANDERS – These animals always look for a damp place to rest. If you dig under them, there will be water signs, even springs.

MAMMALS – Nearly all mammals need water at regular intervals to keep alive. Even the flesh eaters MUST drink, but animals can travel long distances between drinks and therefore, unless there is a *regular* trail, you can't be sure of finding water where you see animal trails. This is a general rule.

However, certain animals never travel far from water. For example, a fresh track of wild pigs is one sign that there is water near. Look for fresh tracks of roosters and of most grazing animals, whose habit is to drink regularly at dawn or dusk. In general, water is found by following these trails downhill.

REPTILES – Most land-living reptiles are independent to a very large extent on water. They get what they need from dew and the flesh of their prey and thus, not an indicator of water.

VEGETABLE SOURCES
In general, water is more plentiful from plants in gullies than on ridges. Roots and branches of many trees contain enough fluid to relieve thirst. Collect it by *breaking* the roots or branches into 3-foot lengths and standing them in a trough of bark that serves as a container.

Some plants store a tremendous amount of water that gushes out when the plant is cut.
IMPORTANT NOTE: Don't keep water from plants more than 24 hours as the liquid can ferment.

POISONOUS PLANTS

If the fluid is milky, red or colored in any way, it must be considered dangerous, not only to drink, but also to the skin. Many milky saps contain latex, a natural rubber, and are extremely poisonous. Exceptions are the ficus (fig) family and the Barrel cactus in the US. (This explains why rabbits totally decimated our Barrel Cacti one winter and left the others alone.)

Milky sap of many weeds and succulents can poison the skin and form sores. If sap gets into the eyes, it can cause blindness and a lot of pain. With **all** vegetable sources, even though the water itself is clear, taste it first and if quite or almost tasteless, it should be safe to drink. Pig-face and Ice plant and Pig weed contain large proportions of drinkable moisture.

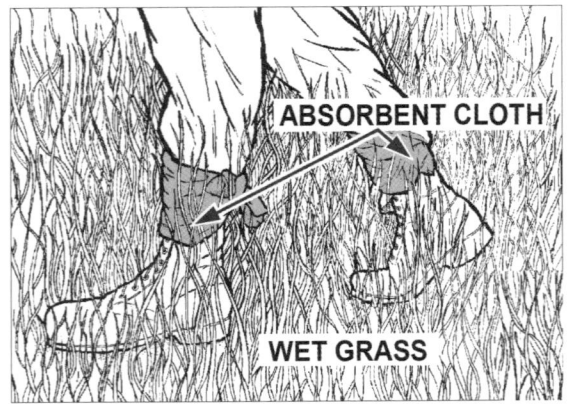

ARID AREAS

The most abundant volume of liquid is generally found in surface roots. If roots are close to the tree, you may be able to pull out 10-20 foot lengths. These MUST be broken into 3-4 feet lengths for draining. Unless these breaks – not cuts – are made, the fluid can't flow. Cutting tends to seal the water-containing veins. It's similar to pouring gas from a jerry can. To make the fuel flow better, open the vent.

DEW

In barren areas where there are no trees, it may be possible to collect enough moisture from dew on the grass to stay alive. One of the easiest ways is to tie cloth or tufts of fine grass around the ankles and walk through the blades before the sun burns off the moisture. Squeeze the dew collected by the cloth into a container.

ON THE SEA COAST

Fresh water can always be found along the sea by digging behind the wind blown sand hills that back most ocean beaches. These sand hills trap rain water that floats on top of the heavier ocean water. Sand hill wells must be just deep enough to uncover the top inch or two or water. If dug deeper, salt water will intrude and the water from the well will be undrinkable. You'll notice, too, that the water in those wells rises and falls slightly with the tides. These sand wells are completely reliable sources of water all over the world.

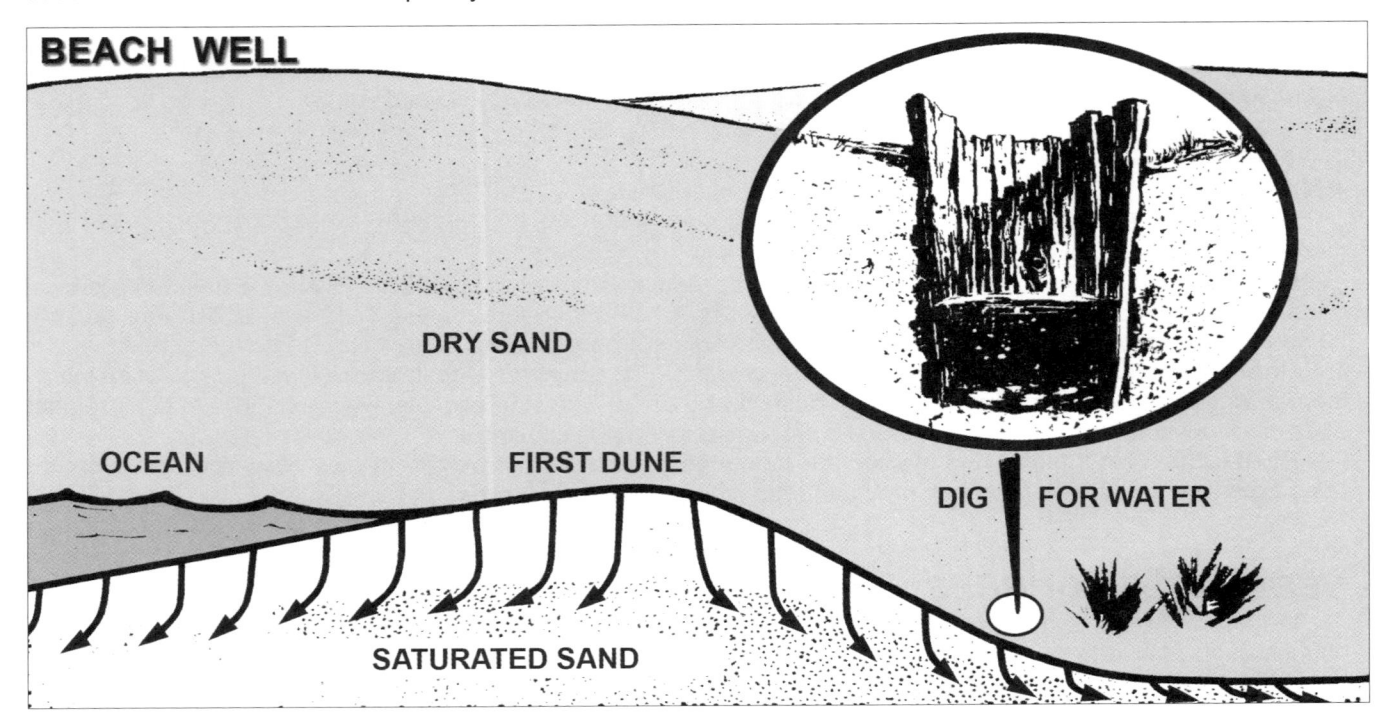

BEACH OR SAND WELLS

Where cliffs meet the sea, search along the lower edges for soaks and small springs. These generally follow cracks in the rocks indicated by a lush growth of ferns and moss.

Check near the cliff, at the bottom where fallen rocks meet the sand. You should find water about one foot down. This plentiful source of water should refill daily.

Be sure to shore up the sides so it doesn't refill because sand from the nearby hill will cover it fairly quickly. To protect it from animals, cover the hole with some planks or driftwood.

MOISTURE FROM FISH

Think fish when no fresh water is available. Dice and put them in a piece of cotton cloth and wring out the moisture. This has saved many people lost at sea.

CONDENSING SALT WATER

It's possible to condense sea water without equipment to get fresh water. Dig a hole in the ground, line the bottom and pour in salt water. Build a fire and heat stones or rocks. When hot, put them into the salty water. When it boils, soak up the water vapor with a cloth towel or thick mat. In time, the cloth will become saturated and can be wrung out, yielding a fair amount of fresh drinkable water. Once the cloth is cool, water vapor collection is fairly fast. For other similar water collection methods, see Chapter 5, Solar Stills.

MOISTURE CONDENSATION IN ARID AREAS

METHOD 1: BUSH STILL

You can make a simple still for condensing water in arid areas with a 4 foot (122cm) square piece of light plastic sheeting. A fully cut open, clean garbage bag works too.

Select a site in moist ground – a creek bed depression is ideal. Dig a hole in a sunny area 3 ft. wide by 1½ ft. deep. If vegetation is nearby, line the hole with it and pack it down. You may need to weigh it down with a few flat stones. In the center of the hole, set a cup or other container to catch the moisture.

Why the vegetation? Not only does it contain moisture, it provides more evaporative surface area thereby producing water more quickly.

Lay plastic sheet across and covering the hole. Hold it in place with some of the scooped out earth to lightly seal the edges. Place a stone on top of the plastic in its center directly over the container below.

Moisture in the soil and in the greenery placed in the hole will be drawn off by the Sun's heat and condense on the underside of the plastic. The condensed moisture will collect into droplets, coalesce and trickle down the underside to the lowest point where it drops off into the container.

If the underside of the plastic sheet is slightly roughened with fine sandpaper or similar fine abrasive like a piece of finely grained stone, the droplets will coalesce and run off more cleanly than if the underside is absolutely smooth.

Urine, brackish water, prickly pear cactus, waste food, moist tea leaves, etc. can be put into the hole. Only pure moisture will be condensed. This still produces about 50% more water between 8pm and 8am than during the day, but it still works day and night.

It takes about 24 hours to collect a cup of water. If the stay in the area will be more than a day or two, remove the top few inches of the hole and replace the green material with fresh foliage and the still will continue to work. After three days, a new still site may be necessary.

This is not a new concept. Though this water collection method is often credited to Arizona's Water Conservation Laboratory, Arabs used similar methods in the mid-1500s. The Australian Aborigines have secured water with a "bush still" for many years using animal skins. Plastic is certainly more efficient.

Drinking from the bottom bucket with a straw as shown in the next photo is the most efficient. While it doesn't interrupt the water collection by disturbing the condensation process, it leaves a lot to be desired for sanitation and sharing germs.

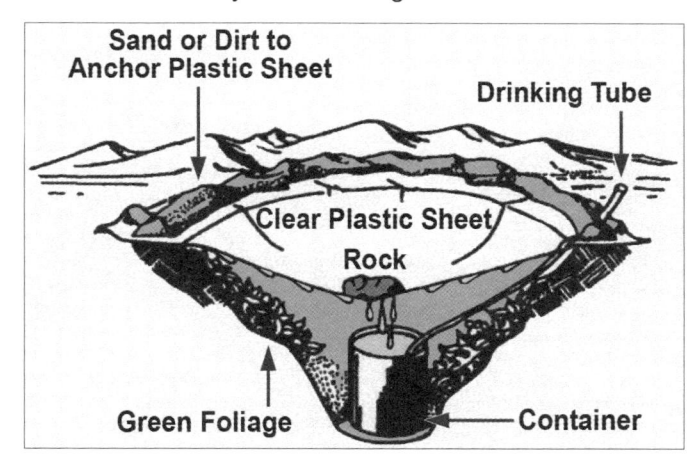

METHOD 2: WATER TRANSPIRATION BAG

This is even simpler and works better. Place a clear plastic bag over the ends of tree branches and leaves or even a nice-size shrub. Secure it with string or a shoe lace. Moisture will condense with the heat of the sun and collect in the bag.

Water will taste like the plant smells.

DO NOT use poisonous/toxic plants in transpiration bags.

OTHER WAYS TO FIND WATER

RAIN WATER

It's always safe to drink and easy to collect with any tarp, but unfortunately there are three exceptions. A chemical, atomic or bacteriological attack would render this water unsafe unless filtered and boiled. In a nuclear event, water itself doesn't become radioactive, but the fallout which floats overhead and lands everywhere is.

WATER IN COLD CLIMATE

Clean snow can be eaten any time you're thirsty. The only precaution is to treat it like ice cream and not consume too much at once when overheated or chilled. Instead, let it melt in your mouth *in small quantities*. It's better not to eat snow when extremely cold, since it has the tendency to dehydrate the body and cause chills.

One of the nicest desert desserts is ice cream made with snow. Pour milk into a container, add sugar and some flavoring such as chocolate. Stir in preferably fresh, light snow to taste and desired consistency.

Snow's main drawback is that it takes a considerable amount to equal a glass of water. Depending on the snow's moisture content, it takes about 10 inches of snow to produce one inch of water. For an 8 oz. glass of water, you'd need 2½ quarts of snow. Packed snow gives more water than "powder" and ice, even more.

When melting snow, be careful not to burn the pot. Melt the snow until the bottom of the pot is safely covered with several inches of water before adding more snow. Use any tool to pack the snow as it melts to avoid the bottom of your pot drying up and burning.

Surprisingly, you'll need a lot more water in cold weather than expected. The kidneys have to take over much of the elimination process otherwise done by the sweat glands.

ICE AND FRESH WATER

This is the water supply for many Arctic locations, though cutting and melting ice is inconvenient. It's usually easier just to chop or chisel holes in a lake or stream to get water. It's also the preferred method since it doesn't require fuel. Because of the higher water content in ice, you need twice the fuel to melt snow for the same quantity of water.

To break ice, it's better to use a pointed tool. First, hit a few light strokes to create a fracture, then strike a hard blow to break off a piece of ice. On a great lake or long river, cut toward an already existing split to avoid getting only small bits. Once made, these holes **must** be covered to discourage refreezing.

When making a hole in a lake or river ice, be careful to avoid splashing. Axe all around the hole making very sure not to puncture the ice down to the water. Do this only when the hole is deep and wide enough for your bucket.

Then and only then, once you are near water on all sides, give a sharp blow to completely break the ice. If you don't do this, water will seep into the hole and you'll get very wet while trying to enlarge it. This could be life threatening in winter if you don't have a change of dry clothes.

As far as purity is concerned, ice and the water obtained from melting it are no cleaner than the water originally frozen.

WATER FROM AN OLD HAND PUMP

Many of us have seen old water hand pumps but few of us *remember* or know how to make them work.

Before pumping yourself crazy and thinking there is no water, prime it first. Most pumps that aren't self-primers require this. The reason is simple. If you don't add water, you will pump air. Adding several cups of water creates the suction needed to pump water.

To prime a pump, water must be added to the upper cup at the base of the crank. Raise the handle all the way up, pour in the water and pump. In some cases, there is a spout. On these pumps, pore water in the spout, and cover with your hand to keep the water in place. Then start pumping. When it's primed, you'll have nice cold fresh water.

If you are at this location more than 24 hours, you might find that the pump needs to primed daily or after a couple days without use.

Chapter 8: FOOD – What and How Much to Store

In the land of plenty it's easy to become too dependent on our grocery stores. Have you ever noticed just before a storm or holiday how rapidly food and water disappear from stores? It's like an invisible vacuum descends and sucks everything off the shelves. We tend to think of stocking up immediately before a big snowstorm but quickly dismiss this precaution when it's warm and sunny.

Earthquakes, hurricanes, tornadoes, volcanoes, fires, tsunamis and terrorism don't tell time or consult us for convenience. Should an emergency occur and roads are impassable, how would delivery trucks bring fresh produce, milk and meat? How soon would our grocery stores be stripped of canned goods and bottled water? How long would meats and refrigerated items last with no electricity No longer than ours.

Since the average grocery only warehouses three days of food on-site, it's easy to see how quickly shelves could be picked clean.

SIX REASONS TO HAVE A FOOD STORAGE PROGRAM

1. Stop Wasting Money. Disasters aside, who likes wasting money? Does anyone *want* to pay $3.50 for taco sauce instead of $2.95? With enough supplies in your pantry, you pick and choose when to shop. If things aren't on sale and you already have a supply at home, forget the grocery store. Use the pantry items and restock when they're on sale again. Buying on sale doesn't make you cheap, it shows you're clever!

This is one example when a freezer will pay for itself in a manner of months. How often do your favorite cuts of meat go on sale? By stocking up when prices are slashed, you're keeping dollars in your wallet instead of paying for the butcher's vacation.

In the current gas crunch with fuel running around $4/gallon, every 32 mile round trip to the store costs about $8. Weekly trips add up to more than $400/year just for the privilege of grocery shopping. If you go to the store after work, three times a week "just to pick up a thing or two", it's even worse. Since we're on our way home, we'll chop off half of the driving expense just to be fair. But wouldn't you rather use that extra $600 for something fun?

2. Loss of Income. Who could have predicted it? Fred broke his arm and couldn't hang wallpaper for two months. Sandra lost her job in corporate downsizing. It took six months to replace her job – at lower pay. Additionally, businesses close their doors as competition closes in. During the recession that began in 2000, 3,000,000 U.S. jobs evaporated.

Any number of unforeseen circumstances can cause a sudden reduction in family income and these days that hurts! Food is one of the most expensive on-going costs in supporting a family. Many families, due to illness or loss of work, have relied on their stocked pantries to see them through lean times.

3. Unexpected Company. Has your spouse ever called at the last minute saying he or she is bringing home a client? It's easier on the nerves to walk into the pantry and bring out extra jars of pasta sauce and bags of spaghetti than dash to the store. (Plus, you show off your organizational and practical skills!)

4. Bulk Purchasing Power. It's a <u>lot</u> cheaper to buy in bulk and repackage foods when you get home. Even if you weren't planning on storing extra food, this reason alone may motivate you to purchase in bulk.

To give one example, when in Australia, we bought a 4.4 pound (2 kg) bag of jelly crystals (Jell-O) for $4.54. If we had purchased that same amount in individual packages, the price would have been $13.60 or 3 times the bulk price!

5. Less Temptation. Studies show that the more trips we make to grocery stores, the more we spend. Little things pop into our shopping basket when we aren't looking. (Those sneaky little gremlins!) Much as I love Stan's company, when he comes along, you can't believe all the "extras" that wind up in the shopping cart! We are all victims of impulse purchasing. One simple way to resist is make fewer trips to the store.

6. Time Saver. Making fewer trips to the store saves time. Sounds simple doesn't it? I try to plan all my chores on one day. Unlike a lot of people, I actually enjoy grocery shopping. It's fun to check out new products, plan menus, dawdle over gadgets, but this dawdling can be expensive. By the time a single grocery trip is finished, 2½ hours are blown.

Dare To Prepare: Chapter 8: FOOD — What and How Much to Store

How can that be?
- 15 minutes to find shoes, put on lipstick, collect purse and grocery list, grab cash and car keys, get the car out of the garage
- 20 minutes to drive to the store and park
- 2½ minutes to walk across the parking lot and into the store
- 45 minutes to shop
- 15 minutes to wait in line and check out
- 7½ minutes to walk back to the car and load it
- 20 minutes to drive home
- <u>20 minutes to put groceries away</u>

2 hours 25 minutes to take the entire grocery trip

For people living rurally, drive time can easily double. The time and dollars saved by using a food storage program really adds up!

HOW DO I PLAN MY FOOD SUPPLIES?

If your budget can withstand some initial stretching, setting up a food pantry is a great idea. There are numerous food storage programs to choose from though some people follow no particular pattern but set aside a little this and maybe too much "that"!

The simplest program is the Basic Four designed by the Church of Jesus Christ of Latter Day Saints. It's the backbone of numerous other emergency preparedness programs. The Mormon 4 was created by their church to provide one year of food at low cost with a very long shelf life. Part of the Mormon faith stipulates that all families should have at least one year's food supply stored.

MORMON TABLE OF FOUR – ONE PERSON						
Food	Lbs/per Person Average	Lbs/per Person Range	Kgs/per Person Average	Kgs/per Person Range	Shelf life	Comments
Wheat, Hard Red	300	200-365	136	91-166	Indefinite	Packed in nitrogen
Powdered Milk	85	60-100	39	27-45	Varies 1-5 yrs	—
Sugar or Honey	60	35-100	27	16-45	Indefinite	Keep sugar dry and pest free
Salt	6	1-12	3	.5-5.5	Indefinite	More is needed for preserving

These four foods will **not** make a good diet or a very interesting one, but it will keep you alive. Vitamins and mineral supplements are needed as well as a source of fat and oil.

Several other factors need to be considered:

1. Do you know how to prepare numerous wheat dishes?

2. Has this much wheat already been a part of your normal dining? If not, large amounts of wheat suddenly introduced to the diet can cause major bowel discomfort.

3. Studies show that people deal with stress much better if their diets are maintained as close as possible to normal times.

4. If you experience prolonged power outages with no backup power, cold wheat mush will get pretty boring. Make sure you **know how to prepare** the foods stored regardless of the food storage program you choose.

While this is a place to start, most people want more variety, more choices, but how much of what items is needed?

NUTRTIONAL GUIDELINES

The Deyo Food Storage Planner (DFSP) listings for what to stock in your pantry are based on U.S. Department of Health and Human Services and U.S. Department of Agriculture latest recommendations. They revamped this food pyramid by taking into account different age groups, gender and level of physical activity. Since it wouldn't be possible to list all the variations without reproducing their 84-page booklet, the DFSP v.2.1 is based on a 2,000 calorie for a moderately active person. You can download their booklet here: **standeyo.com/News_Files/Food/USDA_Guide_2005.pdf**. If you are sedentary or very active, adjust the amounts of stored food up or down to reflect your personal needs. That said, extra stored food never goes awry. When tough times hit, there will always be a neighbor, friend or relative who didn't prepare.

Personalized Food Pyramid

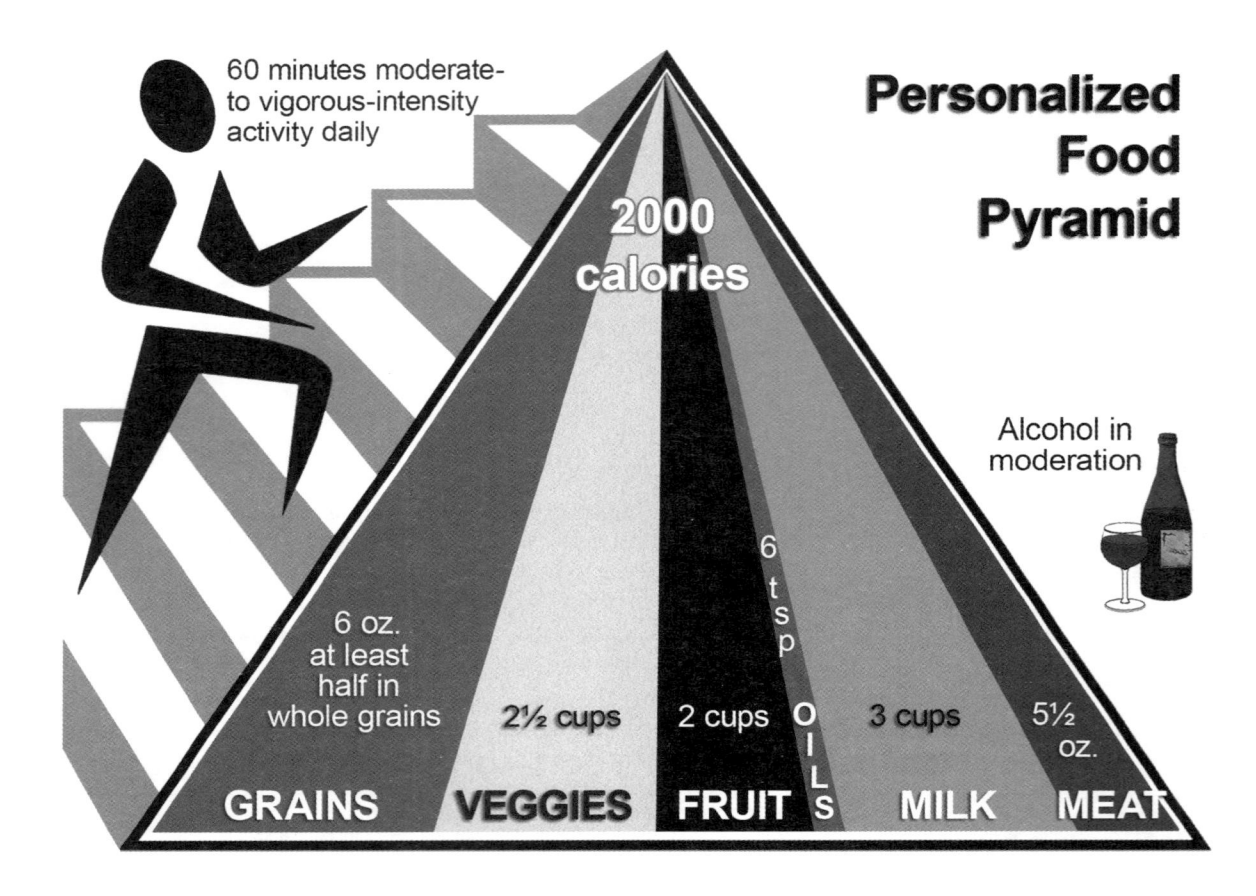

- 60 minutes moderate- to vigorous-intensity activity daily
- 2000 calories
- Alcohol in moderation
- GRAINS: 6 oz. at least half in whole grains
- VEGGIES: 2½ cups
- FRUIT: 2 cups
- OILS: 6 tsp
- MILK: 3 cups
- MEAT: 5½ oz.

This new pyramid also allows for Discretionary Calories. Based on the amounts listed for the 2000-calorie plan, it leaves about 267 calories up to you. This could be a Snickers bar, a couple of cookies, a glass of wine, a bowl of granola or a tub and a half of yogurt. It's your choice. If you have special health issues, let them guide your selections.

Sugar is strongly linked to ill health. Studies show consuming only a few tablespoons – less than in a soft drink – can suppress the immune system for up to 5 hours. (Most soft drinks have 4-6 tablespoons of sugar per can!) That lets your guard down to an array of germs and bacteria for those 5 hours. If you ate sugar several times throughout the day, your body would have few defenses. Especially during stressful times, your body needs all the help it can get fighting disease.

NEW FOOD PYRAMID SPECIFICS

WHOLE GRAINS – At least 3 oz. daily. 1 oz. is about 1 slice of bread, about 1 cup of ready-to-eat cereal, or ½ cup of cooked rice, cereal, or pasta. Any food made from wheat, rice, oats, cornmeal, barley or another cereal grain qualifies as a grain product like bread, pasta, oatmeal, breakfast cereals, tortillas, and grits.

Grains are divided into 2 groups, *whole grains* and *refined grains*. Whole grains keep the entire grain kernel – the bran and germ, which gives them that nice crunch. On food boxes you'll often see the word 'whole' in front of a grain listing like whole-wheat flour or whole cornmeal but sometimes it's missing like with bulgur (cracked wheat), brown rice and oatmeal.

Refined grains have been milled to remove the bran and germ. It gives them a finer texture and improves shelf life, but it also removes fiber, iron, and many B vitamins. Refined grain products are often 'white foods' like white flour, white bread, white rice and cornmeal.

Most refined grains are enriched indicating some B vitamins are added back after processing. Fiber is not. Check the ingredient list on refined grain products to make sure the word "enriched" is included in the grain name.

> INGREDIENTS: WHOLE OATS, WHOLE GRAIN WHEAT, SUGAR, CORN SYRUP, RICE, ALMONDS, MOLASSES, MODIFIED CORN STARCH, HIGH FRUCTOSE CORN SYRUP, PALM OIL, SALT, CINNAMON, NONFAT DRY MILK, NATURAL AND FLAVOR

Some foods are made from a mix of whole and refined grains. **TIP**: On food labels, ingredients are listed in order of concentration. For example the food label on the box of Low Fat Granola starts out healthy. This cereal's ingredients in largest quantity are whole oats and whole grain wheat. That's good. But the third ingredient in highest concentration is sugar and so is the 4th. In fact, out of the first nine ingredients, five are sugars. And then there's the Palm Oil. Uh-oh.

OILS AND FATS – Get most of your fat from fish, nuts and vegetable oil. Limit solid fats like butter, stick margarine, shortening and lard. Oil is just fat that becomes liquid at room temp. It's not very appetizing in that context, is it, except some fat is actually good and necessary. However, not all oils are created equal.

These days everyone is concerned about their cholesterol count or should be to ward off heart disease. When storing oils, keep the ones that are best for you. Generally speaking, bad fats are Saturated and Trans Fats. The better fats are Poly-unsaturated and Mono-unsaturated. Here's the quick breakdown in the table on the left.

The average American gets one third or more of his or her daily calories from fats, so placing them near the foundation of the pyramid makes sense. Good sources of healthy unsaturated fats include olive, canola, soy, corn, sunflower, peanut, and other vegetable oils, as well as fatty fish such as salmon. These healthy fats not only improve cholesterol levels (when eaten in place of highly processed carbohydrates) but can also protect the heart from sudden and potentially deadly rhythm problems.

Percent of Different Fats in Oils and Fats [32]				
OILS	**Saturated**	**Mono**	**Poly**	**Trans**
Effect	Raises both LDL and HDL	Lowers LDL; raises HDL	Lowers LDL; raises HDL	Raises LDL, Triglycerides; Lowers HDL
Canola	7	58	29	0
Safflower	9	12	74	0
Sunflower	10	20	66	0
Corn	13	24	60	0
Olive	13	72	8	0
Soybean	16	44	37	0
Peanut	17	49	32	0
Palm	50	37	10	0
Coconut	87	6	2	0
COOKING FATS				
Shortening	22	29	29	18
Lard	39	44	11	1
Butter	60	26	5	5
MARGARINE/SPREADS				
70% Soybean, Stick	18	2	29	23
67% Soybean & Corn Spread, Tub	16	27	44	11
48% Soybean Spread, Tub	17	24	49	8
60% Sunflower, Canola & Soy Spread, Tub	18	22	54	5
Mono = Mono-unsaturated; Poly = Poly-unsaturated				

VEGETABLES – Eat more dark green and orange veggies; more dry beans and peas. A diet rich in fruits and vegetables can decrease the chances of having a heart attack or stroke; protect against a variety of cancers; lower blood pressure; help avoid painful intestinal diverticulitis; guard against cataract and macular degeneration, the major cause of vision loss among people over age 65; and add variety to your diet and wake up your palate.

FRUIT – Eat a variety of fresh, frozen canned or dried, but go easy on fruit juices. Any fruit or 100% fruit juice counts as part of the fruit group.

MEAT & BEANS – Choose low-fat or lean meats and poultry served baked, broiled or grilled. All foods made from meat, poultry, fish, dry beans or peas, eggs, nuts, and seeds are considered part of this group. Dry beans and peas, also part of the vegetable group, are important sources of protein. A wealth of research suggests that eating fish can reduce the risk of heart disease. Chicken and turkey are full of protein and can be low in saturated fat. Eggs, which have long been demonized because they contain fairly high levels of cholesterol, aren't as bad as they're cracked up to be. In fact, an egg is a much better breakfast choice than a doughnut cooked in trans fats or a bagel made of refined flour.

MILK – Go low-fat or fat-free. If you don't or can't consume milk, choose lactose-free products or other calcium sources. Building bone and keeping it strong takes calcium, vitamin D, exercise using weights, and a whole lot more. Dairy products have traditionally been Americans' main source of calcium. But there are other healthy ways to get calcium than from milk and cheese, which can contain a lot of saturated fat. Three glasses of whole milk have as much saturated fat as 13 strips of cooked bacon.

MULTIPLE VITAMIN – Daily. A multivitamin, multimineral supplement offers a kind of nutritional backup. While it can't in any way replace healthy eating, or make up for unhealthy eating, it can fill in the nutrient holes that may sometimes affect even the most careful eaters. You don't need an expensive name brand or designer vitamin. A standard, store-brand, RDA-level one is fine. Look for one that meets the requirements of the USP (U.S. Pharmacopeia), an organization that sets standards for drugs and supplements.

ALCOHOL – In moderation. What's moderation? The FDA and Harvard Medical Center's definition is up to one drink per day for women and up to two drinks per day for men. A drink consists of: 12 fluid ounces of beer, 5 ounces of wine, or 1½ ounces of hard liquor.

More than 100 studies point to a healthful component of red wine: resveratrol found in red grape skins. Research indicates this antioxidant protects from obesity and diabetes, and boosts physical endurance. Red wine may also guard against cavities, gum disease, and tooth decay.

For the heart, resveratrol increases good cholesterol (HDL) and reduces LDL – the substance directly linked to clogged arteries. Scientists suspect it may help explain the "French paradox" – why French people have fewer heart attacks despite high-fat diets, and why eating a very low-calorie diet can extend our life span.

These liver- and heart-protective phenols aren't present in white wine or other alcohol, but are found in dark chocolate, apples and cranberries.

NOTE: Drinking more than moderate amounts of alcohol has just the opposite health effect of elevating blood pressure. It also leads to weight gain and cancer risks.[33]

DEYO FOOD STORAGE PLANNER

The Deyo Food Storage Planner is built around the USDA's (U.S. Dept. of Agriculture) food groups and the amounts needed for a balanced diet. Any quantity can be adjusted up or down to fit personal needs, budget or taste. These are suggestions only.

Stan designed our food storage planning software using Microsoft Excel. You may download a more detailed, computerized version of the DFSP free from our website. Instructions for how to use it are in the file.

If you would like U.S. measures, it can be downloaded from our website at:
www.millennium-ark.net/News_Files/FTP_Files/DFPlanImp2008.xls.zip
For our friends across the sea using Metric measures version, downloaded from our website at:
www.millennium-ark.net/News_Files/FTP_Files/DFPlanMet.zip

A "paper" version of the Deyo Food Storage Planner (DFSP) is on the following pages. It's a straightforward, easy-to-use program that will help you determine how much to store based on number of family members and for how long you want to store supplies.

HOW TO USE THE DEYO FOOD STORAGE PLANNER

Most of the items you might want to store have already been entered for you along with their **minimum** shelf life date. Extra lines are included so you can write in additional items.

The DFSP has these headings:

Item	Ounce (or Cup) Equivalent	Target Amount	Amount On Hand	Amount Needed	Shelf Life Minimum	Expire Date

Step 1   Start the worksheet on the next page by filling in how many family members you have for each **Age/Sex** group in the **# In Group,** first column on the left.

Step 2   Then determine how many weeks you want to store. Write that number on the bottom row where it reads **Weeks Storing**. The amount has been figured for each food group *for one week* (see **1 Wk** column) based on 2,000 calories daily. Use these figures to multiply by how many weeks you want to store. This gives you the total amount of cups or ounces you'll need. Fill that number in under **Need** column for each food group.

Step 3   Keep track of your purchases by entering them in **Amount On Hand**. Subtract out any foods you consume and don't replace.

Step 4   To see how close you are to your storage goals, subtract the amounts entered in **Amount On Hand** from the amounts listed **Target Amount** and enter this figure in **Amount Needed**.

Step 5 The last two columns pertain to food rotation – the absolute necessity of any good storage program. For every product purchased, write in the **Expire Date** from the package or can. If one isn't listed, enter the purchase date in that column AND on that food's package. By looking at the **Minimum Shelf Life** provided, you'll know when to rotate these stored foods if the expiration date is missing. You're done!

Use the following table to figure the number of adult shares in your family.

		WORKSHEET FOR HOW MUCH TO STORE											
GROUP		GRAIN		MEAT		VEGGIE		FRUIT		DAIRY		FAT & OIL	
Age, Sex	# in	Amount		Amount		Amount		Amount		Amount		Amount	
		1 Wk	Need	1 Wk	Need	1 Wk	Need	1 Wk	Need	1 Wk	Need	1 Wk	Need
Kids 2-3		28 oz		21 oz		11 cups		7 cups		14 cups		26 tsp	
Girls 4-8		35 oz		44 oz		14 cups		9 cups		18 cups		32 tsp	
Girls 9-13		42 oz		37 oz		18 cups		12 cups		21 cups		39 tsp	
Girls 14-18		46 oz		39 oz		18 cups		12 cups		21 cups		40 tsp	
Boys 4-8		39 oz		35 oz		14 cups		11 cups		21 cups		35 tsp	
Boys 9-13		51 oz		42 oz		21 cups		14 cups		21 cups		46 tsp	
Boys 14-18		63 oz		47 oz		25 cups		16 cups		21 cups		58 tsp	
Women 19-30		49 oz		42 oz		21 cups		14 cups		21 cups		44 tsp	
Women 31-50		44 oz		39 oz		19 cups		12 cups		21 cups		40 tsp	
Women 51+		42 oz		37 oz		18 cups		12 cups		21 cups		39 tsp	
Men 19-30		65 oz		47 oz		25 cups		16 cups		21 cups		58 tsp	
Men 31-50		61 oz		46 oz		25 cups		16 cups		21 cups		54 tsp	
Men 51+		56 oz		44 oz		21 cups		14 cups		21 cups		49 tsp	
Totals													
Weeks Storing													

EXPIRATION DATE

You'll want to rotate into your normal meals any foods nearing the expiration date. The shelf life dates listed in the DFSP are the **minimum** for each item. These are the dates that companies will stand by their product for **optimum nutritional value**, but most items can be consumed safely past these dates even if you do nothing else to lengthen their "life expectancy". Many foods can be kept much longer than this by using simple storage techniques we'll discuss in Extending Food Shelf Lives. By keeping stored goods away from the enemies of moisture, light, heat, air and pests, shelf lives will be greatly lengthened.

In Australia, if a product has a shelf life of more than two years, law doesn't require companies to date stamp their products. This can be misleading for the customer because even though a product might have a two-year expiration date, it doesn't tell us how long the product sits in a warehouse(s) or on the retailer's shelf. This law assumes products are distributed, purchased and consumed on a timely basis. Judging by some of the dusty cans and learning how to decode "mystery dated" cans, this isn't always the case. Later I'll show you how to interpret these secret dating codes.

YOUR FOOD STORAGE PLANNER

GRAINS GROUP: **FOODS MADE WITH GRAIN**						
Item	Ounce Equivalent	Target Amount	Amount On Hand	Amount Needed	Shelf Life Minimum	Expire Date
Bagel	1 mini				10-14 days	
Bisquick	1 oz				1 year	
Bread Mix	1 slice				2 yrs. w/o yeast	
Cake/Brownie Mix	1 oz				18 months	
Cornbread Mix	2½ x 1¼ x 1¼"				1 year	
Corn Chips	1 oz				2 months	
Crackers, Misc.	7				8 months	
Crackers, Ry Krisp or Ryvita	2				18 months	
Crackers, Saltines	7				8 months	
Muffin Mix	½ muffin				9 months	
Pancake Mix, buttermilk, plain	2 sm. (3" dia.)				15 months	
Popcorn, kernels					3 years	
Popcorn, microwave	3 cups, popped				18 months	
Pretzels	1 oz				6 months	
Stuffing Mix, dry	1 oz				2 years	
Taco Shells	1 small				6 months	
Tortillas, Corn	1 small – 6"				1 month	
Tortillas, Flour	1 small – 6"				1 month	
Waffle Mix	1 med. (4½" dia.)				15 months	

GRAINS GROUP: **GRAIN FOODS**						
Item	Ounce Equivalent	Target Amount	Amount On Hand	Amount Needed	Shelf Life Minimum	Expire Date
Cornmeal/Polenta	1 oz				1 year	
Rice, brown	½ C cooked				1 year	
Rice, flavored	½ C cooked				6 months	
Rice, jasmine	½ C cooked				8 months	
Rice Sides	½ C cooked				6 mos-indefinite	
Rice, white enriched	½ C cooked				2 years	
Rice, wild	½ C cooked				8 months	
Flour, White, enriched	½ cup				1 year	
Wheat, raw, whole	½ cup				25 years	

GRAINS GROUP: **PASTA**						
Item	Ounce Equivalent	Target Amount	Amount On Hand	Amount Needed	Shelf Life Minimum	Expire Date
Pasta, dry, lasagna	1 oz				2 yrs-indefinite	
Pasta, dry, manicotti	1 oz				2 yrs-indefinite	
Pasta, dry, penne	1 oz, ½ C cooked				2 yrs-indefinite	
Pasta, spaghetti	1 oz, ½ C cooked				2 yrs-indefinite	
Pasta Sides	½ C cooked				6 mos-indefinite	
Ramen Noodles, beef	½ C cooked				1 year	
Ramen Noodles, chicken	½ C cooked				1 year	
Spaghetti w/ sauce, canned	½ C cooked				2 years	
Suddenly Pasta Salad	½ C prepared				18 months	

Dare To Prepare: Chapter 8: FOOD — What and How Much to Store

GRAINS GROUP: **BREAKFAST**						
Item	Ounce Equivalent	Target Amount	Amount On Hand	Amount Needed	Shelf Life Minimum	Expire Date
Breakfast Bars	1				6-9 months	
Cereal, cooked	½ C cooked-1 pk				9 months	
Cereal, ready-to-eat	1 cup				9 months	
Corn Flakes	1 cup				9 months	
Cream of Wheat	½ C cooked-1 pk				1 year	
Granola	1 oz				1 year	
Mini-Wheats	½ C cooked-1 pk				1 year	
Oatmeal	½ C cooked-1 pk				18 months	
Toaster Pastry	1				6 months	

MEAT GROUP (PROTEIN): **MEAT, FISH & POULTRY**						
Item	Ounce Equivalent	Target Amount	Amount On Hand	Amount Needed	Shelf Life Minimum	Expire Date
Beef, Corned, canned, Hormel	1 oz				indef, seal intact	
Beef, Roast, canned, Hormel	1 oz				indef, seal intact	
Beef Stew, Dinty Moore	1 oz				indef, seal intact	
Chicken, canned, Hormel	1 oz				indef, seal intact	
Chicken, canned, Valley Fresh	1 oz				3 years	
Chicken, pouch, Valley Fresh	1 oz				2 years	
Chili, canned, Hormel or Stagg	1 oz				indef, seal intact	
Clams, canned	1 oz				1-2 years	
Crab, canned	1 oz				1-2 years	
Deviled, chicken, ham	1 oz				1-2 years	
Fish, canned	1 oz				5 years	
Ham, canned, Hormel	1 oz				indef, seal intact	
Hard Salami	1 oz				4-6 weeks	
Lunch Meat, pre-packaged	1 oz				2-6 weeks	
Leg Ham, canned, single srv.	1 oz				5 years	
Oysters, canned	1 oz				1-2 years	
Pork, canned	1 oz				5 years	
Sausage	1 oz				4-6 weeks	
Salmon, canned	1 oz				2-3 years	
Shrimp, canned	1 oz				1-2 years	
Spam	1 oz				indef, seal intact	
Tuna, canned	1 oz				5 years	
Turkey, canned, Hormel	1 oz				indef, seal intact	
Turkey, canned, Valley Fresh	1 oz				3 years	

MEAT GROUP (PROTEIN): **DRIED BEANS & PEAS**						
Item	Ounce Equivalent	Target Amount	Amount On Hand	Amount Needed	Shelf Life Minimum	Expire Date
Beans, baked	¼ C cooked				1 year	
Beans, Borlotti, dry	¼ C cooked				1 year	
Beans, Chick Peas, dry	¼ C cooked				1 year	
Beans, Kidney, dry	¼ C cooked				1 year	
Beans, Pinto or Pink, dry	¼ C cooked				1 year	
Beans, Refried (Old El Paso)	¼ C cooked				2 years	
Lentils, dry	¼ C cooked				1 year	
Peas, dry	¼ C cooked				1 year	
Soybean	¼ C cooked				1 year	
TVP-Textured Veggie Protein	¼ C cooked				2-3 years	

MEAT GROUP (PROTEIN): NUTS

Item	Ounce Equivalent	Target Amount	Amount On Hand	Amount Needed	Shelf Life Minimum	Expire Date
Almonds	½ oz				2 years	
Macadamia	½ oz				2 years	
Nuts in shell	½ oz				2 years	
Peanuts	½ oz				1 year	
Peanut Butter, Jif	1 Tbsp				2 years	
Pecans	½ oz				1 year	
Pistachio	½ oz				1 year	
Sunflower	½ oz				1 year	
Walnuts	½ oz				1 year	

MEAT GROUP (PROTEIN): EGGS

Item	Ounce Equivalent	Target Amount	Amount On Hand	Amount Needed	Shelf Life Minimum	Expire Date
Egg	1				3-5 weeks	
Egg, hard cooked	1				1 week	
Egg Replacer	1 tsp				2 years	
Eggs, Dehydrated	½ oz, dry				5 years	
Egg White, Powdered	2 tsp				5 years	
Egg Yolk, Powdered	1 tsp				18 months	

MEAT GROUP (PROTEIN): SOUPS, SOUP BASE & SOUP MIX

Item	Ounce Equivalent	Target Amount	Amount On Hand	Amount Needed	Shelf Life Minimum	Expire Date
Bouillon	½ C prepared				2 years	
Broth, Beef, powdered	½ C prepared				2 years	
Broth, Chicken, powdered	½ C prepared				2 years	
Dry Soup Mix	½ C prepared				1 year	
Dry Soup Mix, Bear Creek	½ C prepared				3 years	
Soup Base, Tone	½ C prepared				10 years	
Soup, condensed	½ C prepared				2 – 3 years	
Soup, ready to eat, bean	½ cup				2 – 3 years	

MEAT GROUP (PROTEIN): BOXED DINNERS

Item	Servings Equivalent	Target Amount	Amount On Hand	Amount Needed	Shelf Life Minimum	Expire Date
Chicken Helper (B Crocker)	box = 4 serves				1 year	
Compleats Microwave Meals	box = 1 serve				18-24 months	
Complete Meals (B Crocker)	box = 5 serves				1 year	
HeaterMeals, EX Entrees	box = 1 serve				3 years, 5 years	
Hamburger Helper (B Crocker)	box = 4 serves				1 year	
Homestyle Bakes	box = 4 serves				1 year	
Mac & Cheese, Easy Mac, Kraft	1 serve				1 year	
Mac & Cheese, Kraft	7.25 box = 3 serv.				1 year	
MREs	box = 1 serve				8½ years @70ºF	
Tuna Helper (Betty Crocker)	box = 4 serves				1 year	

VEGETABLE GROUP: **VEGETABLES**						
Item	Cup Equivalent	Target Amount	Amount On Hand	Amount Needed	Shelf Life Minimum	Expire Date
Artichoke Hearts	1 cup				3-4 years	
Asparagus	1 cup				2 years	
Bamboo Shoots	1 cup				3-4 years	
Beans, 4-Bean Mix	1 cup				2 years	
Bean Dip	1 cup				1 year	
Bean, Green	1 cup				2 years	
Beans, Corn, Peppers	1 cup				2 years	
Beans Lima	1 cup				4 years	
Beans, Mexe (Old El Paso)	1 cup				2 years	
Beans, Wax	1 cup				2 years	
Beets	1 cup				3+ years	
Brussel sprouts	1 cup				4 years	
Capers	1 cup				3-4 years	
Carrots	1 C or 2 med.				8 years	
Corn	1 C, 1 large ear				2 years	
Corn, creamed	1 cup				2 years	
Corn/Peas	1 cup				2 years	
Corn/Peppers (Mexicorn)	1 cup				2 years	
Hominy	1 cup				2 years	
Jalapenos, sliced	1 cup				2 years	
Mushrooms	1 cup				3-4 years	
Onions, Cocktail	1 cup				2 years	
Onions, French fried	1 cup				2 years	
Peas	1 cup				8 years	
Peas & Carrots	1 cup				8 years	
Potatoes, canned, Tiny Taters	4				2 years	
Potatoes, instant	1 cup				2 years	
Potatoes, white, fresh	1 med, 2½-3" dia.				2-3 weeks	
Pumpkin	1 C cooked mash				4 years	
Sauer Kraut	1 cup				3 years	
Spaghetti Sauce	bottle				2 years	
Spinach	1 C cook, 2C raw				2 years	
Tomatoes, Italian	1 cup				2 years	
Tomato Paste	can				2 years	
Tomatoes, peeled	1 cup				2 years	
Tofu	½ C cooked				3 weeks	
Water Chestnuts	1 cup				3-4 years	

VEGETABLE GROUP: **VEGETABLE JUICE**						
Item	Cup Equivalent	Target Amount	Amount On Hand	Amount Needed	Shelf Life Minimum	Expire Date
Mixed Vegetable (V8)	1 cup				2 years	
Tomato Juice	1 cup				2 years	

FRUIT GROUP: **FRUIT JUICE**						
Item	Cup Equivalent	Target Amount	Amount On Hand	Amount Needed	Shelf Life Minimum	Expire Date
Apple	1 cup				2 years	
Cranberry	1 cup				9 months	
Grape	1 cup				2 years	
Orange Juice (Tree Top)	1 cup				6 months	
Pineapple	1 cup				1-2 years	

FRUIT GROUP: FRUIT

Item	Cup Equivalent	Target Amount	Amount On Hand	Amount Needed	Shelf Life Minimum	Expire Date
Apple, fresh	½ lg, 1 C sliced				3 weeks	
Apple slices, canned	1 cup				2 years	
Applesauce	1 cup				3 years	
Apricot, dried	½ cup				6 months	
Banana, fresh	1 C sliced (1 sm)				7 days	
Banana, dried chips	½ cup				8 months	
Beets, canned	1 cup				3 years+	
Blackberry, canned	1 cup				1 year	
Blueberry, canned	1 cup				2 years	
Cantaloupe, uncut	1 C diced or balls				12-16 days	
Cherries, Bing or dark	1 cup				2 years	
Cherries, Maraschino	1 cup				2 years	
Cranberry	1 cup				2 years	
Dates	½ cup				6 months	
Dried Fruit	½ cup				6 months	
Fruit Cocktail	1 cup				2 years	
Fruit, frozen	1 cup				2 years	
Fruit Preservative, Fruit Fresh	N/A				3 years	
Grapefruit	1 med. (4" dia.)				10 days	
Grapefruit, canned	1 cup				3 years	
Grapes	1 cup				5 days	
Lychees, canned	1 cup				3-4 years	
Orange	1 cup				10 days	
Orange, Mandarin	1 cup				2 years	
Peach, slices, canned	1 cup				18 months	
Pear halves, canned	1 cup (2 halves)				3 years+	
Pineapple, Crushed	1 cup				3 years+	
Pineapple, Pieces	1 cup				18 months	
Pineapple, Slices	1 cup				2 years	
Plum	1 C sliced (2 lg)				5 days	
Raisins	½ cup				16 months	
Raspberry, canned	1 cup				2 years	
Rhubarb, canned	1 cup				1 year	
Strawberry, canned	1 cup				2 years	
Strawberry, fresh	1 cup (8 large)				2 days	
Watermelon	1 C diced or balls				6-8 days	

MILK GROUP: MILK

Item	Ounce Equivalent	Target Amount	Amount On Hand	Amount Needed	Shelf Life Minimum	Expire Date
Buttermilk, dry (Saco)	1 cup				indefinitely	
Evaporated Milk	½ cup				1 year	
Milk, fresh	1 cup				8-20 days	
Milk, Full Cream, dry (Nido)	1 cup				2 years	
Milk, Non-fat, dry	1 cup				2 years	
Milk, Rice	1 cup				1 year	
Milk, Shelf Stable	1 cup				6 months	
Milk, Soy	1 cup				1 year	
Sweetened Condensed	½ cup				1 year	
UHT Milk (shelf stable)	1 cup				6 months	

MILK GROUP: MILK-BASED DESSERT

Item	Cup Equivalent	Target Amount	Amount On Hand	Amount Needed	Shelf Life Minimum	Expire Date
Ice Cream	1½ cups				1-2 years	
Pudding, canned	1 cup				1-2 years	
Pudding, Vanilla/Chocolate	1 cup				1 year	

MILK GROUP: CHEESE

Item	Cup Equivalent	Target Amount	Amount On Hand	Amount Needed	Shelf Life Minimum	Expire Date
Cheese, Cheddar	1½ oz				6 months	
Cheese, cottage	2 cups				6 weeks	
Cheese, grated	⅓ cup				6 weeks	
Cheese, hard	1½ oz				6 months	
Cheese, Mozzarella	1½ oz				6 months	
Cheese, Parmesan	1½ oz				9 months	
Cheese, processed, American	2 oz				9 months	
Cheese, Ricotta	½ cup				2 weeks	
Cheese, Swiss	1½ oz				6 months	

MILK GROUP: YOGURT

Item	Cup Equivalent	Target Amount	Amount On Hand	Amount Needed	Shelf Life Minimum	Expire Date
Yogurt, flavored	1 cup				14 days	
Yogurt, frozen	1 cup				1 year	

MILK GROUP: CREAMER

Item	Ounce Equivalent	Target Amount	Amount On Hand	Amount Needed	Shelf Life Minimum	Expire Date
Coffee Mate, dry	1 oz				2 years	
Coffee Mate, liquid	1 oz				3 months	

FATS GROUP: FATS & OILS

Item	Tablespoon Equivalent	Target Amount	Amount On Hand	Amount Needed	Shelf Life Minimum	Expire Date
Butter, canned (Red Feather)	1 Tbsp				3 years	
Butter, dehydrated, reconstitute	1 Tbsp				5-8 years	
Butter, fresh	1 Tbsp				3 months	
Canola Oil	1 Tbsp				1 year	
Copha	1 Tbsp				1 year	
Corn Oil	1 Tbsp				2 years	
Crisco, solid, butter flavor	1 Tbsp				2 years	
Crisco, solid, plain	1 Tbsp				2 years	
Ghee	1 Tbsp				3 months	
Mayonnaise	1 Tbsp				6 months	
Olive Oil	1 Tbsp				6-9 months	
Vegetable Spray (Pam, Crisco)	N/A				2 years	
Salad Dressing	2 Tbsp				1 year	

FATS GROUP: SUGAR, SWEETENERS & SYRUPS

Item	Tablespoon Equivalent	Target Amount	Amount On Hand	Amount Needed	Shelf Life Minimum	Expire Date
Chocolate Syrup	1 oz				2 years	
Corn Syrup, dark	1 oz				1 year	
Corn Syrup, light	1 oz				1 year	
Fudge Topping	1 oz				18 months	
Honey	1 oz				1 year	
Maple Syrup	1 oz				2 years	
Molasses	1 oz				1 year	
Splenda	pkt				indefinitely	
Splenda, Flavors for Coffee	pkt				1 year	
Splenda, Brown Sugar Blend	½ oz				indefinitely	
Splenda, Sugar Blend, Baking	pkt				indefinitely	
Sugar, brown	1 oz				6 months	
Sugar, granulated	1 oz				indefinitely	
Sugar, powdered	1 oz				2 years	
Sugar, raw	1 oz				indefinitely	
Sweet 'N Low	pkt				10 years	

COMFORT / SNACK FOODS

Item	Amount	Target Amount	Amount On Hand	Amount Needed	Shelf Life Minimum	Expire Date
Chewing Gum	pkg				1 year	
Chocolate Bars	1 oz				1 year +/-	
Hard Candy	bag				2 years	

BAKING ITEMS – Select according to how much you bake

Item	Amount	Target Amount	Amount On Hand	Amount Needed	Shelf Life Minimum	Expire Date
Baking Chocolate	squares / packets				2 years	
Baking Cocoa	can				indefinitely	
Baking Soda	box				2 years	
Baking Powder	can				6 months	
Bread Improver	box = 15 loaves				18 months	
Chocolate Chips	pkg				2 years	
Chocolate Melts	pkg				18 months	
Coconut Flakes	bag				1 year	
Cornstarch	box				indefinite, if dry	
Fruit Preservative, Fruit Fresh	N/A				3 years	
Frosting, canned	can				10 months	
Frosting mixes	box				12 months	
Gelatin	box				3 years-indef.	
Malted Milk Powder, Carnation	bottle				12 months	
Marshmallows	bag				4 months	
Marshmallow Cream	jar				4 months	
Pectin	box				1 year	
Pie Crust Mix	box				12 months	
Pie Filling, Comstock	can				3 years	
Pie Filling, Wilderness	can				2 years	
Tapioca	box				1 year	
Yeast, Dry	packets				18 months	
Yeast, Dry, Breadmaker	jar = 16 loaves				18 months	

SPICES & FLAVORINGS – Select as needed, great barter item						
Item	Ounce Equivalent	Target Amount	Amount On Hand	Amount Needed	Shelf Life Minimum	Expire Date
Allspice	ounce				3 years	
Bacon Flavored Bits	ounce				2 years	
Basil Leaves (Sweet)	ounce				3 years	
Bay Leaf	ounce				4 years	
Caraway Seed	ounce				4 years	
Cardamom Seed	ounce				3 years	
Cayenne	ounce				3 years	
Celery Seed	ounce				3 years	
Chervil	ounce				2 years	
Chili Flakes, Red Pepper Crushed	ounce				2 years	
Chili Powder	ounce				2 years	
Chili Powder, Mexican	ounce				2 years	
Chilies, ground	ounce				2 years	
Chives	ounce				2 years	
Cilantro	ounce				2 years	
Cinnamon, ground	ounce				3 years	
Cinnamon Stick	ounce				4 years	
Cloves, ground	ounce				3 years	
Cloves, whole	ounce				3-4 years	
Coriander	ounce				3 years	
Cream of Tartar	ounce				indefinite	
Cumin, ground	ounce				3 years	
Cumin, whole	ounce				4 years	
Curry Powder	ounce				2 years	
Dill Seed	ounce				4 years	
Dill Weed	ounce				2 years	
Ginger	ounce				3 years	
Garlic Bread Seasoning	ounce				2 years	
Garlic, fresh, minced	ounce				2 years	
Garlic Powder	ounce				1 year	
Garlic, minced	ounce				3 years	
Italian Seasoning	ounce				2 years	
Lemon Peel	ounce				1 year	
Marjoram Leaves	ounce				3 years	
Meat Tenderizer	ounce				2 years	
Mexican Seasoning	ounce				2 years	
Mustard, dry	ounce				3 years	
Nutmeg	ounce				3 years	
Onion Powder	ounce				4 years	
Onion, chopped, dried	ounce				2 years	
Orange Peel	ounce				1 years	
Oregano, ground	ounce				3 years	
Oregano, leaves	ounce				3 years	
Paprika	ounce				2 years	
Parsley Leaves	ounce				1 year	
Pepper, garlic	ounce				2 years	
Pepper, ground	ounce				2 years	
Peppercorn, whole	ounce				4 years	
Pizza Seasoning	ounce				2 years	
Poppy Seeds	ounce				2 years	
Poultry Seasoning	ounce				2 years	
Pumpkin Pie Spice	ounce				2 years	
Rosemary	ounce				3 years	
Sage	ounce				3 years	

SPICES & FLAVORINGS – Select as needed, great barter item

Item	Ounce Equivalent	Target Amount	Amount On Hand	Amount Needed	Shelf Life Minimum	Expire Date
Savory	ounce				2 years	
Sesame Seed	ounce				2 years	
Shrimp & Crab Boil	ounce				2 years	
Spices, ground	ounce				2-3 years	
Spices, whole	ounce				3-4 years	
Taco Seasoning	ounce				2 years	
Tarragon	ounce				3 years	
Thyme	ounce				3 years	
Turmeric	ounce				3 years	

SALT & SALT SUBSTITUTE – Select as needed, great barter item

Item	Ounce Equivalent	Target Amount	Amount On Hand	Amount Needed	Shelf Life Minimum	Expire Date
Also Salt, butter	ounce				indefinite	
Also Salt, plain	ounce				indefinite	
Celery Salt	ounce				2 years	
Garlic Salt	ounce				2 years	
No Salt	ounce				indefinite	
Onion Salt	ounce				2 years	
Mrs. Dash (no salt)	ounce				2 years	
Salt, Sea, Mediterranean	ounce				4 years	
Salt Iodized, table – 2.5 lbs, per adult, for 6 months (less if not canning)	ounce				indefinite	
Salt, Sea	ounce				indefinite	
Seasoned Salt	ounce				2 years	

FLAVORINGS & EXTRACTS

Item	Ounce Equivalent	Target Amount	Amount On Hand	Amount Needed	Shelf Life Minimum	Expire Date
Almond, McCormick	ounce				4 years	
Lemon, McCormick	ounce				3 years	
Orange, McCormick	ounce				3 years	
Vanilla, McCormick	ounce				indefinite	

CONDIMENTS: MEXICAN

Item	Ounce Equivalent	Target Amount	Amount On Hand	Amount Needed	Shelf Life Minimum	Expire Date
Enchilada Sauce, Hatch	1 oz				2 years	
Fajita Sauce	1 oz				2 years	
Green Chile Sauce, Stokes	1 oz				3 years	
Picante, Pace	1 oz				1 year	
Red Chile Sauce, Stokes	1 oz				3 years	
Salsa, Ortega	1 oz				3 years	
Salsa, Pace	1 oz				1 year	
Taco Sauce, Old El Paso	1 oz				2 years	

CONDIMENTS – Select as Desired						
Item	Ounce Equivalent	Target Amount	Amount On Hand	Amount Needed	Shelf Life Minimum	Expire Date
BBQ Sauce	1 oz				2 years	
Butter Sprinkles, Butter Buds	1 tsp				3 years	
Butter Sprinkles, Molly McButter	1 tsp				2 years	
Cranberry Sauce, jellied	1 oz				18 months	
Chili Sauce	1 oz				2 years	
Gravy Mix	1 oz				6-12 months	
Hollandaise Sauce	1 oz				2 years	
Horseradish	1 oz				18 months	
Jam / Jelly	1 oz				18 months	
Ketchup	1 oz				2 years	
Lemon Juice	1 oz				1 year	
Lime Juice	1 oz				1 year	
Liquid Smoke	1 oz				2 years	
Mustard, American	1 oz				2 years	
Mustard, Dijon	1 oz				2 years	
Mustard, English	1 oz				2 years	
Olives, pitted	1 oz				2 years	
Olives, sliced	1 oz				2 years	
Pickle Relish	1 oz				2 years	
Pickles	1 oz				2 years	
Sauce Mix	1 oz				6-12 months	
Shake 'N Bake	1 pkg				2 years	
Sloppy Joe Sauce, Manwich	1 can				2 years	
Steak Sauce	1 oz				1 year	
Tabasco	1 oz				5 years	
Vinegar	1 oz				2 year	
Worcestershire Sauce	1 oz				indefinite	

WET YOUR WHISTLE: BEVERAGES – Daily, Select 2 servings minimum, per adult						
Item	Ounce Equivalent	Target Amount	Amount On Hand	Amount Needed	Shelf Life Minimum	Expire Date
Coffee, auto drip	pound				3 months	
Coffee, instant, decaf	ounce				2 years	
Coffee, instant, regular	ounce				2 years	
Crystal Lite	ounce				2 years	
Gator Aide/StaminAid	ounce				2 years	
Hot Cocoa	ounce				8 months	
Kool-Aid	ounce				2 years	
Ovaltine	ounce				18 months	
Powdered Drink/Kool-Aid	ounce				2 years	
Tang	ounce				2 years	
Tea, green	bags				6 months	
Tea, Bigelow	bags				3 years	
Tea, Celestial Seasonings	bags				2 years	
Tea, Lipton, Green, Mandarin Orange	bags				30 months	
Tea, Lipton, Iced & Cold Brew	bags				18 months	
Tea, Lipton, Powdered Iced Mix	ounce				1 year	
Tea, Lipton, most, Herbal, Black	bags				18 months	
Tea, Twinings	bags				3 years	

BOOZE – Select as desired						
Item	Ounce Equivalent	Target Amount	Amount On Hand	Amount Needed	Shelf Life Minimum	Expire Date
Sherry, cooking	bottle				7-10 years	
Wine, red	bottle				7-10 years	
Wine, red, cooking	bottle				7-10 years	
Wine, white	bottle				5-7 years	
Wine, white, cooking	bottle				5-7 years	

WATER – PER DAY: Store 1 gallon (4L) per person; 1 gallon per large dog; 1 pint (500ml) per cat*						
Item	Gallon Equivalents	Target Amount	Amount On Hand	Amount Needed	Shelf Life Minimum	Expire Date
Water, drinking (treated tap)	gallon				2 years	
Water, drinking (bottled)	gallon				9 months	

* Keep a **minimum** of 1 month's supply *drinking* water on hand for every person and pet. These amounts **do not** include water for bathing, cooking, washing clothes or dishes or extra water in case of spills.

PET FOOD: CAT						
Item	Ounce Equivalent	Target Amount	Amount On Hand	Amount Needed	Shelf Life Minimum	Expire Date
Cat Food, canned	ounces				18 months	
Cat Food, dry	ounces				18 months	
Cat Food, Foil Pouches	ounces				12 months	

PET FOOD: DOG						
Item	Cup Equivalent	Target Amount	Amount On Hand	Amount Needed	Shelf Life Minimum	Expire Date
Dog Food, canned	cups				18 months	
Dog Food, dry	cups				18 months	

HOUSEHOLD ITEMS: BATTERIES & LIGHT						
Item	Each	Target Amount	Amount On Hand	Amount Needed	Shelf Life Minimum	Expire Date
Batteries, 6 Volt Lantern	each				4 years	
Batteries, 9 Volt	each				4 years	
Batteries, AA	each				4 years	
Batteries, AAA	each				4 years	
Batteries, C	each				4 years	
Batteries, D	each				4 years	
Flashlight (one per person)	each				indefinite	
Flashlight Replacement Bulbs	each				indefinite	
Light (Glow) Sticks, all colors	each				4 years	
Light Bulbs, 75W	each				indefinite	
Light Bulbs, 60W	each				indefinite	
Light Bulbs, 60W Reflector	each				indefinite	
Light Bulbs, 100W	each				indefinite	

HOUSEHOLD ITEMS: PAPER, PLASTIC & ALUMINUM

Item	Amount	Target Amount	Amount On Hand	Amount Needed	Shelf Life Minimum	Expire Date
Aluminum Foil, long	each				indefinite	
Aluminum Foil, short	each				indefinite	
Baking Cups	each				indefinite	
Brown Paper Bags, lunch size	each				indefinite	
Coffee Filters	each				indefinite	
Kleenex	each				indefinite	
Oven Bags, large	each				indefinite	
Oven Bags, small	each				indefinite	
Paper Bowls	each				indefinite	
Paper Cups	each				indefinite	
Paper Napkins	each				indefinite	
Paper Plates	each				indefinite	
Paper Platters	each				indefinite	
Paper Towels	each				indefinite	
Plastic Forks, Knives & Spoons	each				indefinite	
Plastic Wrap	each				indefinite	
Styrofoam Cups	each				indefinite	
Toilet Paper	each				indefinite	
Toothpicks	each				indefinite	
Trash bags, clear	each				indefinite	
Trash bags, large	each				indefinite	
Trash bags, x-large	each				indefinite	
Wax Paper	each				indefinite	
Ziploc, 1 qt. (1L)	each				indefinite	
Ziploc, ½ gal. (2L)	each				indefinite	
Ziploc, gallon (4L)	each				indefinite	
Ziploc, sandwich size	each				indefinite	
Ziploc, snack size / pint	each				indefinite	

HOUSEHOLD ITEMS: FIRE STARTERS

Item	Amount	Target Amount	Amount On Hand	Amount Needed	Shelf Life Minimum	Expire Date
Bic Lighters	each				indefinite	
Firestarters (kerosene soaked)	each				indefinite	
Gas Match	each				indefinite	
Magnesium Starter	each				indefinite	
Matches	box				indefinite	

HOUSEHOLD ITEMS: PEST CONTROL

Item	Amount	Target Amount	Amount On Hand	Amount Needed	Shelf Life Minimum	Expire Date
Mouse Traps	each				indefinite	
OFF/Bug Repellent	each				5 years	
Raid House and Garden	each				3 years	
Raid/Black Flag Ant & Roach	each				3 years	
Ratsak	each				3 years	
Rat Traps	each				indefinite	

112 Dare To Prepare: Chapter 8: FOOD — What and How Much to Store

HOUSEHOLD ITEMS: **CLEANSERS**						
Item	Ounce Equivalent	Target Amount	Amount On Hand	Amount Needed	Shelf Life Minimum	Expire Date
409, Spray & Wipe	each				1 year	
Ammonia	each				1 year	
Bleach	each				9 months	
Cleanser (Comet)	each				18 months	
Dishwasher Soap	each				2 years	
Dishwashing Liquid	each				2 years	
Disinfectant (Pine Sol)	each				5 years	
Drain Clog Remover (Drano)	each				5 years	
Fabric Softener, dryer sheets	each				indefinite	
Fabric Softener, liquid refill	each				1 year	
Furniture Polish	each				3 years	
Laundry Soap, dry	each				indefinite	
Laundry Soap, liquid	each				indefinite	
Lysol, spray or Glen 20	each				2 years	
Mildew Remover (Exit Mold)	each				2 years	
Soap, bars	each				indefinite	
Soft Wash Liquid Soap Refill	each				indefinite	
Sponges	each				indefinite	
Steel Pads (Brillo, SOS, Steelo)	each				indefinite	
Windex	each				indefinite	

HEALTH & HYGIENE: **HYGIENE**						
Item	Amount	Target Amount	Amount On Hand	Amount Needed	Shelf Life Minimum	Expire Date
After Shave/Men's Cologne	each				5 years	
ChapStick	each				3 years	
Cosmetic Items (make own list)		See "Personal Care Products" in Chapter 15				
Cotton Balls	each				indefinite	
Cream Rinse/Conditioner	each				5 years	
Dental Floss	each				indefinite	
Denture Adhesive (Effergrip)	each				indefinite	
Denture Cleanser (Efferdent)	each				indefinite, in foil	
Deodorant	each				3 years	
Foot Exfoliating Cream	each				5 years	
Hair Color	each				3 years	
Hand Lotion	each				3 years	
Hand Sanitizer (Purell)	each				3 years	
Heel Softener	each				3 years	
Heel Stone	each				indefinite	
Mouthwash	each				2 years	
Panty Liners	each				indefinite	
Perfume	each				5 years	
Q-Tips	each				indefinite	
Razor Blades	each				indefinite	
Sanitary Pads	each				indefinite	
Shampoo	each				5 years	
Shave Cream	each				5 years	
Tampons	each				indefinite	
Toothbrush	each				indefinite	
Toothpaste	each				3 yrs. – indefinite	

HEALTH & HYGIENE: **MEDICATIONS & 1st AID**						
Item	Amount	Target Amount	Amount On Hand	Amount Needed	Shelf Life Minimum	Expire Date
Advil / Motrin (ibuprofen)	each				3 years	
Alka-Seltzer	each				2 years	
Antidiarrheal (Imodium caplet)	each				3 years	
Antidiarrheal (Imodium capsule)	each				4 years	
Antifungal (Lotrimin, Lamisil)	each				2 years	
Aspirin (Anacin, Bayer, Bufferin)	each				2 years	
Aspirin Extra Strength	each				2 years	
Band-Aids	each				indefinite	
Benadryl	each				2 years	
Betadine Spray	each				4 years	
Betadine Ointment	each				4 years	
Birth Control	each				2 years	
Chlor Trimeton	each				2 years	
Crepe Bandages	each				2 years	
DayQuil, Vicks	each				3 years	
Dust Masks	each				indefinite	
Epson Salts	each				4 years	
Eyedropper	each				indefinite	
Eye Drops (Visine)	each				18 months	
Hair Restorer (Rogaine)	each				3 years	
Lactaid	each				2 years	
Leukostrips/Butterfly bandages	each				indefinite	
Medihoney Antibacterial Gel	each				1 year unopened	
Medihoney Active	each				9 months	
Merthiolate	each				indefinite	
Moleskin	pkg.				indefinite	
Motion Sickness (Dramamine)	each				4 years	
Mylanta Tablets	each				2 years	
Neosporin	each				3 years	
NyQuil, Vicks	each				3 years	
Prilosec	each				2 years	
Pepto-Bismal	each				2 years	
Poison Ivy/Oak Relief	each				2 years	
Prep H, ointment	each				2 years	
Prep H, suppositories	each				2 years	
Robitussin	each				2 years	
Sinex	each				2 years	
Solarcaine	each				2 years	
Sudafed Severe Cold Caplets	each				2 years	
Sudafed Sinus/ Allergy Tablets	each				2 years	
Sudafed 12 hour Antihistamine	each				2 years	
Surgical Tape	each				indefinite	
Syrup of Ipecac	each				2 years	
Tea Tree Oil	each				4 years	
Throat Lozenges	each				2 years	
Tylenol	each				2 years	
Tylenol 3	each				2 years	
Vitamin, Echinacea	each				2 years	
Vitamin, Multi	each				2 years	
Yeast Infection (Monistat)	each				2 years	
Zantac	each				2 years	

MAKING GOOD CHOICES

JUST DO IT!
After returning from the grocery store, there's a room in our home where I park non-perishables, in their grocery sacks, until the expiration dates are logged. This way it gets done. Putting food in the cupboard only to haul it out again to log these dates is zero incentive to do it. However, seeing a mess in "that corner" is! It only takes a couple of minutes and the $$ saved by not letting foods run past their expiration date makes it worthwhile.

WHAT TYPES OF FOOD SHOULD I STORE?
One thing to remember is the water factor. Rather than keep all dried or dehydrated foods that require water for reconstituting or cooking, store a good amount of food in cans. Canned items should include meats, fruits, soups, juices and vegetables. Not only do canned items require little or no cooking or water, they'll provide a change in texture and taste, and supply the body with liquid.

Especially in prolonged disasters, it's important to keep food and beverage choices as near normal as possible. If your diet consists of lots of Italian food, stock up on stewed tomatoes, pasta, grated cheese and spices. This is not time for a lot of experimentation.

I BOUGHT IT, NOW WHAT DO I DO?
When purchasing items to store, **make sure you know how to prepare these foods**. It's clever to include unfamiliar foods in normal meals before disaster strikes. We won't need the added stress of fixing and digesting unfamiliar foods. If you store large quantities of legumes because it's convenient and economical, then later find out you can't look another bean in the face, it's best to find out now. Practice making entire meals with selections from only stored foods. You may find certain ingredients were accidentally omitted. You'll also be familiar with their cooking procedure if it's a new dish.

TRY IT, YOU'LL LIKE IT – MAYBE
When purchasing dehydrated foods, especially the pouch variety, before investing in a case of Chile con Carne from Company X, buy ONE and try the product. Not all of the same variety foods taste the same from different companies. Too, one manufacturer might have a terrific Chicken Tetrazzini but a lousy Hearty Beef.

Stan and I make a point to try ALL of our stored foods before purchasing in quantity. This saved us from one really bad mistake. We'd brought home a sample Lobster Bisque Soup. Sounded good on the package, but "on the tongue" it was another story. Maybe if we were starving it would have tasted like barbecued lobster basted in butter, sprinkled with lemon juice and herbs, but this stuff made our tongues curl.

BUT I GOTTA HAVE CHOCOLATE!
Be kind to yourself. If you are a big fan of Snickers, be sure to include these in your stored items. The key to any good storage plan is to purchase high quality foods, purchase foods you like and **always rotate** them. As foods near their expiration date, rotate them into your regular meals and replenish the supply.

Common sense goes a long way to help plan food choices. If you bananas, include dried banana chips. They're lightweight, a good source of potassium, sweet, and last longer than their fresh counterpart. Be good to yourself!

OTHER FOOD STORAGE PROGRAMS

Two other well-known food programs belong to Cresson H. Kearny and Esther Dickey. Books like Kearny's *Nuclear War Survival Skills* and Dickey's original *Passport to Survival* also gave techniques for sprouting, gluten making and growing wheat grass. These items supply vitamin C and a wide variety of dishes can be made from these four items. Though Esther Dickey's book was written more than 30 years ago, its practical information is timeless. Rita Bingham has updated this book.

Besides the Mormon 4, Dickey recommends 40 additional foods that can be rotated and have a shelf life of one to five years. The 40 + 4 yields a healthy diet of over 100 dishes that can be used for varied meals. Among the additional items Dickey recommends are peanut butter, tomato juice, canned and dried vegetables, dried legumes, molasses, yeast, dried fruit, vegetable oil, evaporated milk, grains and multi-vitamins.

The Kearny diet is basically the Mormon 4 plus cooking oil (about 23 pounds/10.5 kg) and beans (around 113 pounds/15 kg). This provides essential oils and a much better amino acid balance, but lacks in variety.

Changing spices can vary even simple dishes like beans and vegetables. Spices are an easy, economical way to make the same vegetables "put on a different face."

Kearny's *Nuclear War Survival Skills* updated and expanded 1987 edition can be downloaded free at: **standeyo.com/News_Files/NBC/nwss/**

KEARNY'S BASIC SURVIVAL FOR MULTI-YEAR STORAGE				
Food Ration	Ounces / Day	Grams / Day	Pound / Month	Kilos / Month
Whole-kernel Hard Wheat	16	454	30.00	13.6
Beans (use a variety)	5	142	9.00	4.3
Powered Milk	2	57	3.80	1.7
Vegetable Oil	1	28	1.90	0.9
Sugar	2	57	3.80	1.7
Iodized Salt	⅓	10	0.63	0.3
Multi-vitamins	1 per day			

The Mormon 4 is the basis of most long term food storage plans. The quantity and quality of various food storage plans depends on what problems the survivalist expects to encounter down the road. An economic survivalist who expects several months' turmoil might have a 60-day supply of canned goods that's continuously rotated. A social decline survivalist might keep a mix of grains, freeze dried, air-dried and canned goods, and seeds to supplement available food supplies. A nuclear war survivalist might store a five-year supply of the Mormon 4 and freeze dried foods, plus nitrogen packed seeds, commercial-grade water purifiers, and other supplies.

CORNELL BREAD

The ideal diet in terms of amino acid balance is meat. You can get the correct amino acid balance from grains the easiest by making "Cornell" bread.[34] Substitute this mixture in any bread recipe. For each cup of wheat flour replace with:

- 1 tablespoon of soy flour
- 1 tablespoon of nonfat dry milk
- 1 teaspoon of wheat germ
- Fill the balance of the cup with wheat flour.

Dr. Arthur Robinson developed a nutritious bread recipe using a ratio of 40-40-20: wheat, corn and soy. If a recipe calls for 3 cups of flour, use about 10 ounces each (1¼ cups) flour and corn, and 4 ounces (½ cup) of soy. Adjust the liquid to the consistency that you'd normally use for the bread recipe. Soy flour is pretty fine, but cornmeal is grainy. You might need a little extra liquid.

Another basic food plan alternative is the following: You can add to or alter to suit personal tastes. Many folks want guidelines of "how much". That is the intention of this plan.

A ONE YEAR SUPPLY TO FEED ONE ADULT		
Amount	Item	Comment
150 lbs	Beans	Obtain a variety to prevent boredom
160 lbs	Rice	Check oriental food stores for good buys
60 lbs	Wheat, Hard Red Winter	Check gluten level for 16%+
50 lbs	Corn	Whole, hard yellow corn (popcorn is best food value)
25 lbs	Soybeans [1]	Whole, NOT meal. KEEP COOL.
12 lbs	Dry Milk [2]	Non-fat and preferably non-instant
8 lbs	Baking Powder [2]	
8 lbs	Salt	Kept dry will last indefinitely
1 lbs	Vitamin C	Ascorbic acid, soluble fine crystals, NOT tablets
4 gals	Soybean Oil [3]	
3 gals	Honey [4]	Kept cool will last indefinitely
750 tabs	Calcium Oyster Shell, 500 mg	A necessary supplement when on a high grain diet.

[1] Soybeans have high oil content, check yearly and keep cool
[2] Should be replaced every 12 to 18 months
[3] Substitute Olive oil if preferred, check yearly
[4] Liquefy stored honey crystallize by placing the containing in hot water

FREEZE-DRIED AND DEHYDRATED FOODS

Freeze-dried and dehydrated foods are clever for people short on space. They require little preparation; just add water and heat. Of the two processes, freeze-dried is generally more expensive and considered by many to taste better. However, drying techniques have greatly improved thereby narrowing but not closing the yum factor.

Freeze-drying prepares either fresh or cooked foods and flash freezes them in a vacuum chamber that reaches -50°F (-45°C). Low heat is applied and the ice crystals evaporate without returning to liquid. This process removes about 98% of the moisture, which prevents spoilage and makes long-term storage possible. Dehydration uses high heat to bake out 97% of all moisture. Older techniques left up to 10% dampness in foods so they just weren't crisp. Additionally, dehydrated foods don't taste exactly like canned counterparts due to weaker flavor, but seasonings and butter improve flavor.

Mountain House claims at least a 25-year shelf life for foods packed in #10 cans. Foods in pouches have a 7-year shelf life as of 2006. **www.mountainhouse.com**. eFoodsDirect sells both dehydrated and freeze-dried products with these important differences. Their foods contain no MSG, no genetically modified ingredients, no hydrogenated oil in the Nutriversal line and dehydrated products use only #1 grade fresh raw foods. Product information states their foods store for 15 years although they can be safely consumed beyond this time. **www.efoodsdirect.com**. AlpineAire Gourmet Reserve foods have widely varying shelf lives of up to 10 years depending on the product. Pouches should last 5-7 years, based on ingredients. **www.aa-foods.com**. You'll find a complete selection of freeze-dried and dehydrated foods as well as other prep products at **freezedryguy.com**.

Unopened canned contents are protected until you're ready to use them. Mountain House advises on their website, that after opening #10 cans, food should be consumed within 1 week. AlpineAire claims their foods are OK to eat after opening for up to 90 days. Opened, dry contents should be resealed with the plastic lid provided and kept in a cool location or stored in the freezer in a Ziploc bag. Treat reconstituted leftovers like any fresh food.

BUY WITH EYES WIDE OPEN

When purchasing either freeze-dried or dehydrated products, make sure you know what you're getting. There is no set standard as to what constitutes a 'year's supply' nor what makes up a single serving. Make sure you're comparing apples to apples. Look at the quantity of cans and variety of foods offered. Are you just buying "stuff" in a panic or is it food you like and normally eat? Does it provide breakfast, lunch, and dinner and clearly indicate how much you'll get daily?

In addition to the specific foods provided, check the daily calorie allotment. The FDA states that the average adult male burns about 2500-3000 calories a day and females about 2200 calories per day. Your stored foods should match this. It's also important to pay attention to storable foods labels.

There's little point in saving yourself from disaster if you've "killed" yourself by eating unhealthy foods. Give your body foods that won't have consequences down the line. Be sure to compare nutritional information. Mountain House readily admits in their FAQ that their foods' sodium content is much too high and that they will be reformulating them at some point. Another supplier, Wise Foods, also shows a very high salt load besides using saturated fats in some of their products. Many prepared entrées are loaded with salt, hence the great taste.

If you purchase just the plain freeze-dried or dehydrated meats like chicken, beef or pork, you'll get only the animal protein without bad additives. However, it's up to the purchaser to add the zest. You can do this easily by adding freeze-dried, dehydrated or canned vegetables and spices. This requires little time and gives big rewards.

Two possible drawbacks come with either of these type foods. Both require water for reconstitution and a method of heating. A bigger concern is can size. Most of these products are packed in #10 cans, which is 10½ to 13 cups of reconstituted food depending on ingredients. To make these a good choice, you need a large family, several families to split a can among, be willing to eat the same thing for quite a while, or toss out the balance. All of these foods must be kept in a cool, dry environment.

MORMON FOOD GUIDELINES

Today, the LDS church encourages people to store a wider variety than the Basic 4. Items on the next two pages are the current Mormon Food Guidelines. Food quantities listed cover one year. **NOTE**: The amount of chlorine bleach needed is greatly understated. During disasters, sanitary conditions are at much greater risk especially since many bacteria are growing treatment-resistant. For this reason, plan for a **minimum** of 1 gallon (4 liters) of bleach per month, possibly more depending on your family's usage. For example, families with immune compromised members or infants might require great amounts.

More importantly, their amount of suggested water only covers 2 weeks. Since water is THE MOST IMPORTANT SURVIVAL ITEM, we encourage you to store a 3-month supply or longer. This does not include water for personal hygiene, washing, cooking or pets – only drinking.

MORMON FOOD GUIDES			
FEMALES TOTALS			
STORAGE ITEM	Ages 0-6	Ages 7-11	Ages 12+
Wheat	107 lbs/48.5 kg	139 lbs/63 kg	151 lbs/68.5 kg
Flour, white enriched	10 lbs/4.5 kg	12 lbs/5.5 kg	14 lbs/6 kg
Corn Meal	24 lbs/11 kg	31 lbs/14 kg	34 lbs/15.5 kg
Oats, rolled	24 lbs/11 kg	31 lbs/14 kg	34 lbs/15.5 kg
Rice, white enriched	48 lbs./22 kg	62 lbs/28 kg	67 lbs/31 kg
Pearled Barley	2 lbs/1 kg	2 lbs/1 kg	2 lbs/1 kg
Spaghetti and Macaroni	24 lbs/11 kg	31 lbs/14 kg	34 lbs/15.5 kg
TOTAL GRAINS GROUP	**239 lbs/109 kg**	**309 lbs/139.5 kg**	**337 lbs/153 kg**
Beans (dry)	25 lbs/11.5 kg	25 lbs/11.5 kg	25 lbs/11.5 kg
Beans, Lima (dry)	1 lb/.5 kg	1 lb/.5 kg	1 lb/.5 kg
Beans soy, (dry)	1 lb/.5 kg	1 lb/.5 kg	1 lb/.5 kg
Peas, split (dry)	1 lb/.5 kg	1 lb/.5 kg	1 lb/.5 kg
Lentils (dry)	1 lb/.5 kg	1 lb/.5 kg	1 lb/.5 kg
Dry Soup Mix	5 lb/2.5 kg	5 lb/2.5 kg	5 lb/2.5 kg
TOTAL LEGUMES GROUP	**34 lbs/16 kg**	**34 lbs/16 kg**	**34 lbs/16 kg**
Vegetable Oil	2 gal/4 L	2 gal/4 L	2 gal/4 L
Shortening	4 lbs/2 kg	4 lbs/2 kg	4 lbs/2 kg
Mayonnaise	2 qts/2 L	2 qts/2 L	2 qts/2 L
Salad Dressing-Mayo	1 qt/1 L	1 qt/1 L	1 qt/1 L
Peanut Butter	4 lbs/2 L	4 lbs/2 L	4 lbs/2 L
TOTAL FAT/OIL GROUP	**26 lbs/12 kg**	**26 lbs/12 kg**	**26 lbs/12 kg**
Milk, nonfat (dry)	14 lbs/6 kg	14 lbs/6 kg	14 lbs/6 kg
Evaporated Milk	12 cans	12 cans	12 cans
TOTAL MILK GROUP	**16 lbs/7 kg**	**16 lbs/7 kg**	**16 lbs/7 kg**
Sugar, white granulated	40 lbs/18 kg	40 lbs/18 kg	40 lbs/18 kg
Sugar, brown	3 lb/1.5 kg	3 lb/1.5 kg	3 lb/1.5 kg
Molasses	1 lb/.5 kg	1 lb/.5 kg	1 lb/.5 kg
Honey	3 lb/1.5 kg	3 lb/1.5 kg	3 lb/1.5 kg
Corn Syrup	3 lb/1.5 kg	3 lb/1.5 kg	3 lb/1.5 kg
Jams and Preserves	3 lb/1.5 kg	3 lb/1.5 kg	3 lb/1.5 kg
Fruit Drink, powdered	6 lb/3 kg	6 lb/3 kg	6 lb/3 kg
Flavored Gelatin	1 lb/.5 kg	1 lb/.5 kg	1 lb/.5 kg
TOTAL SUGARS GROUP	**60 lbs/28 kg**	**60 lbs/28 kg**	**60 lbs/28 kg**
Dry Yeast	½ lb/500 g	½ lb/500 g	½ lb/500 g
Soda	1 lb/1 kg	1 lb/1 kg	1 lb/1 kg
Baking Powder	1 lb/1 kg	1 lb/1 kg	1 lb/1 kg
Vinegar	½ gal/2 L	½ gal/2 L	½ gal/2 L
Salt, Iodized	8 lb/3.5 kg	8 lb/3.5 kg	8 lb/3.5 kg
TOTAL MISC.	**12 lbs/5.5 kg**	**12 lbs/5.5 kg**	**12 lbs/5.5 kg**
Chlorine Bleach	1 gallon/4 L per family		
Water	14 gallons/56 L per person for 2 week supply		

MORMON FOOD GUIDES

MALES TOTALS

STORAGE ITEM	Ages 0-6	Ages 7-11	Ages 12+
Wheat	107 lbs/48.5	176 lbs/80 kg	187 lbs/85 kg
Flour, white enriched	10 lbs/4.5 kg	16 lbs/7 kg	17 lbs/8 kg
Corn Meal	24 lbs/11 kg	39 lbs/18 kg	42 lbs/19 kg
Oats, rolled	24 lbs/11 kg	39 lbs/18 kg	42 lbs/19 kg
Rice, white enriched	48 lbs/22 kg	78 lbs/35 kg	84 lbs/38 kg
Pearled Barley	2 lbs/1 kg	2 lbs/1 kg	2 lbs/1 kg
Spaghetti and Macaroni	24 lbs/11 kg	39 lbs/18 kg	42 lbs/19 kg
TOTAL GRAINS GROUP	**239 lbs/108 kg**	**391 lbs/177 kg**	**420 lbs/190 kg**
Beans (dry)	25 lbs/11.5 kg	25 lbs/11.5 kg	25 lbs/11.5 kg
Beans, Lima (dry)	1 lb/.5 kg	1 lb/.5 kg	1 lb/.5 kg
Beans soy, (dry)	1 lb/.5 kg	1 lb/.5 kg	1 lb/.5 kg
Peas, split (dry)	1 lb/.5 kg	1 lb/.5 kg	1 lb/.5 kg
Lentils (dry)	1 lb/.5 kg	1 lb/.5 kg	1 lb/.5 kg
Dry Soup Mix	5 lb/2.5 kg	5 lb/2.5 kg	5 lb/2.5 kg
TOTAL LEGUMES GROUP	**34 lbs/16 kg**	**34 lbs/16 kg**	**34 lbs/16 kg**
Vegetable Oil	2 gal/2 L	2 gal/2 L	2 gal/2 L
Shortening	4 lbs/2 kg	4 lbs/2 kg	4 lbs/2 kg
Mayonnaise	2 qts/2 L	2 qts/2 L	2 qts/2 L
Salad Dressing-Mayo	1 qt/1 L	1 qt/1 L	1 qt/1 L
Peanut Butter	4 lbs/2 kg	4 lbs/2 kg	4 lbs/2 kg
TOTAL FAT/OIL GROUP	**26 lbs/12 kg**	**26 lbs/12 kg**	**26 lbs/12 kg**
Milk, nonfat (dry)	14 lbs/6 kg	14 lbs/6 kg	14 lbs/6 kg
Evaporated Milk	12 cans	12 cans	12 cans
TOTAL MILK GROUP	**16 lb/7 kg**	**16 lb/7 kg**	**16 lb/7 kg**
Sugar, white granulated	40 lbs/18 kg	40 lbs/18 kg	40 lbs/18 kg
Sugar, brown	3 lb/1.5 kg	3 lb/1.5 kg	3 lb/1.5 kg
Molasses	1 lb/.5 kg	1 lb/.5 kg	1 lb/.5 kg
Honey	3 lb/1.5 kg	3 lb/1.5 kg	3 lb/1.5 kg
Corn Syrup	3 lb/1.5 kg	3 lb/1.5 kg	3 lb/1.5 kg
Jams and Preserves	3 lb/1.5 kg	3 lb/1.5 kg	3 lb/1.5 kg
Fruit Drink, powdered	6 lb/3 kg	6 lb/3 kg	6 lb/3 kg
Flavored Gelatin	1 lb/.5 kg	1 lb/.5 kg	1 lb/.5 kg
TOTAL SUGARS GROUP	**60 lbs/28 kg**	**60 lbs/28 kg**	**60 lbs/28 kg**
Dry Yeast	½ lb/.25 kg	½ lb/.25 kg	½ lb/.25 kg
Soda	1 lb/.5 kg	1 lb/.5 kg	1 lb/.5 kg
Baking Powder	1 lb/.5 kg	1 lb/.5 kg	1 lb/.5 kg
Vinegar	½ gal/2 L	½ gal/2 L	½ gal/2 L
Salt, Iodized	8 lb/3.5 kg	8 lb/3.5 kg	8 lb/3.5 kg
TOTAL MISC.	**12 lbs/5.5 kg**	**12 lbs/5.5 kg**	**12 lbs/5.5 kg**
Chlorine Bleach	1 gallon/4 L per family		
Water	14 gallons/56 L per person for 2 week supply		

WHICH PROGRAM SHOULD I PICK?

The easiest program to store up front might not be the best program for you. For example, the "One Year Supply To Feed One Adult" is pretty straightforward for figuring which supplies to store and how much is needed, but it overlooks several key points.

- This program suggests storing several whole grains like corn kernels, whole soybeans and hard red winter wheat. It doesn't mention needing a grain grinder. If there's an extensive power outage and you purchased an electric grinder, it will have to be converted to manual power. In order words, you crank it.
- We've ground our own cornmeal, by hand and motorized. Electricity makes it go a lot faster and smoother. If you're super fit, your biceps and triceps will love you. If you're unfit, you'll have some nicely developing arm and shoulder muscles in short order!
- This program doesn't call for any fruits, vegetables or vitamins.
- Comfort foods are a recognized necessity during stressful times. This program provides none.
- Spices. One of the simplest ways to vary food is by adding spices. Different flavors transform the bland and the tasteless to interesting dishes. This program leaves out all of them except salt.
- There is no provision for sugar, only honey, which isn't recommended for children under the age of one. Why? Some honeys harbor minute traces of botulism. For adults and people with fully developed immune systems, there aren't enough of these bacteria to cause illness. However, in small children this might not be the case. Sugar keeps indefinitely as long as it's stored in dry conditions. Honey's shelf life is about one year before it begins to crystallize. It can still be used in this form but must be heated to re-liquefy. Honey does reach a point where it resembles granite and must be replaced.
- The last point to consider is that every meal from the foods listed must be prepared from "scratch". This program doesn't allow for any canned goods, prepackaged mixes, freeze-dried or dehydrated products.

On the plus side, the "One Year Supply To Feed One Adult" doesn't require much thinking and it's economical. The plan includes good quantities of beans and rice that are nutritionally excellent foods all by themselves.

Whatever program you choose, think about more than just the cost and how quickly you can get it assembled. Ask yourself, *do I really want to eat this stuff?*

That's why we designed the Deyo Food Storage Planner. It uses the USDA's recommended daily requirements for a good diet, there is a lot of flexibility, it consists of foods we normally eat and already know how to prepare, and on days when time is short, it allows for pre-packaged items and canned goods. Works for us!

FOOD STORAGE – HOW WE DID IT

The first thing we decided was what foods to store and to see what was available.

For emergencies, we have two cases of MREs, but they aren't the backbone of our stored supplies. We also have some pre-packaged, single-serve dehydrated meals purchased in camping and recreational stores. Entrées run anywhere from $4.50 – $8 per person per meal. That's pretty expensive so we've kept them to a minimum. They're an excellent choice if you're traveling and have access to heated water. One caution: try before you buy in quantity. Not all foods are palatable from the same company. We tried one company's chili that was fine, but not their lobster bisque soup. *Patoui!* Some freeze-dried foods are also in the pantry. However, more than half of our storables are canned goods and vacuum-packed foods.

After determining what foods were available, we built our supplies using the Deyo Food Storage Planner. It allowed us to meet nutritional guidelines, yet be flexible. This fall after garden harvests are in, home canned vegetables, fruits, meats and sauces will be added to our supplies.

Since our food storage program is ongoing, it's important to store foods normally eaten. We are storing a larger quantity of dried goods like beans, rice, whole corn kernels and flour than if we weren't preparing for tough times. In the proper environment, they will keep for a long time. More on this in the next chapter.

The next step was to add any other items to the Deyo Food Storage Planner that we use only occasionally. I penciled in these products after rummaging through our cupboards for ideas. Then we calculated our goals and made shopping lists. We buy things weekly and fill in the progress on the Deyo Food Storage Planner. Not many of us can afford to outfit an entire pantry in one trip. It's good to see supplies grow, plus, it's not such a huge undertaking to organize it bit by bit.

SPECIFICS

As previously stated, we store some freeze-dried and dehydrated goods, MREs and HeaterMeals, but concentrate primarily on canned goods and dry foods like a variety of beans, pastas, whole corn, rices, lentils, peas, flour, teas, coffee, sugars, honey and bread mixes. Canned and jar goods include fruits and fruit juices, vegetables, Mexican sauces, meats, fish, soups, condiments and flavorings. Packaged items cover muffin/cake mixes, cereals, baking products, drink mixes, potatoes flakes, flavored rices, pasta dishes, crackers and sauces. We also store lots of spices. Not only do they perk up meals, change and enhance flavors, they are a great bartering item. These are foods we normally eat so it's what we store.

Depending on the food, most canned items have a shelf life of 2 – 8 years with more items at the shorter end of the "life expectancy" chart. (See Chapter 11.) To help fill in any possible gaps in supplies, there are open pollinated, non-hybrid seeds. After growing your own vegetables, it's hard to look a tasteless store bought tomato in the face!

Dry foods like flour, rice, beans, legumes and dehydrated vegetables are packed in food grade buckets with a nitrogen flush, oxygen absorbers and desiccants. (See Chapter 10.)

One category not to overlook is comfort foods. Especially during times of stress a familiar treat can brighten the day. Hard candy keeps longer than chocolate treats containing high fat and oil. Even chocolate like Mars Almondettes and Snickers will store at least 9 months. By sticking to rotation, even short shelf life foods are never lost. (Somehow keeping chocolate for 9 months has never been an issue in the Deyo house!) Hot cocoa is another great food to have and even some ready-to-eat puddings like Hunt's brand lasts two years without refrigeration.

Canned (tinned) butter and cheese are added along with dehydrated eggs. Most of these products are easily found in western countries but require considerable searching in others. Some products aren't as readily available like most dehydrated long-term storable foods found easily in North America and on the Internet. While living abroad, due to very strict import laws, we had to "make do" or substitute in a number of areas.

Other items added are a supply of homemade jerky and home-canned goods.

Dog food (and cat food) lasts about 18 months from date of packing. With two large dogs, Taco at 45 pounds (20.5 kg) and Seismo at 55 (25kg), it means they require a *lot* of dog food. We've opted for a mixture of dry and canned. Dry food helps keep their teeth cleaner and sacks are burnable; and cans are impervious to pests. To keep mice away, dry dog food is stored in the original sack, and while stored, it's kept in heavy duty trash cans with lockable lids.

MAKE WHOLE MILK FROM POWDERED MILK

If you don't like the taste of fat-free powdered milk, you can recreate whole milk by adding the following:

Milk, whole 1 cup
1 cup reconstituted non-fat powdered milk   **OR**   ½ cup evaporated milk + ½ cup water
2½ Tbsp butter or margarine   **OR**   ¼ cup sifted powdered whole milk powder + ⅞ cup water

MAKING YEAST

EVERLASTING YEAST
1 qt. (960ml) warm potato water
½ yeast cake or ½ Tbsp (5g) dry yeast
2 cups (286g) white flour or (274g) whole wheat flour

2 Tbsp (25g) sugar
1 tsp (6g) salt

Stir ingredients together. Set mixture in a warm place to rise until ready to mix for baking. Leave a small amount of everlasting yeast for a "start" for next time. Between uses, keep in covered jar in refrigerator until a few hours before ready to use again.

Add same ingredients, except yeast, to the everlasting yeast start for the next baking. Maintaining the everlasting yeast start and remaking some each time, keeps yeast on hand indefinitely.

If you don't have electricity – keep in a cool place as our ancestors did.

SOURDOUGH STARTER #1
2 cups (286g) white flour or (274g) whole wheat flour
2 cups (480ml) warm water
2 tsp (10ml) honey or (8g) sugar

SOURDOUGH STARTER #2
2 cups (286g) flour
2 Tbsp sugar
1 tsp salt (5ml)
2 cups (480ml) warm water

Mix well. Place in a loosely covered bowl or crock. Allow mixture to ferment 3-5 days in a warm room. Stir mixture several times daily to aerate and activate it. The starter will smell yeasty, become spongy, and small bubbles will rise to the top when it's ready. After using some starter and to keep the starter active, you'll need to "feed" it weekly.

Feeding Starter #1: Replace the amount used in baking by adding equal parts flour and water or potato water.

Feeding Starter #2: Weekly or after each use, stir in 1 cup flour, 1 cup milk and ¼ cup sugar. In 24 hours, yeast will form and be ready for use.

Store unused portion of yeast in the refrigerator in a glass or crock with a tight fitting lid. Shake the container often. Activate the yeast before using by adding 2-3 Tbsp (18-27g) flour and the same amount (30-45ml) of water. Store. Homemade yeast can be used to replace all or part of the commercial variety.

Seasoned "starter" makers agree it's easiest to either get your initial starter from a friend or purchase it. Once you have a batch going, then add to the mixture to keep it active and replenished.

DRIED HOPS YEAST
Boil a handful of dried hops (locate at food co-op or brewers' supply) in 4 cups of water for half an hour. Strain off the hops. Mix in ½ cup whole wheat flour and let cool till lukewarm. Add 3 Tbsp dried yeast and mix well. Let rise until very light. Thicken with cornmeal until a stiff dough forms. Roll thin. Cut into 3" (7½cm) squares. Dry in oven with only the pilot light on or another safe location out of direct sun. Do not allow yeast to get hot or it will die. Turn often during drying. When dry, store in mesh bag in a cool, dry location. To use, soak each square in 2 cups warm water. You'll have to experiment with homemade yeast for correct strength.

YEAST NOTES
- Yeast requires warmth to grow. Growth slows above 95°F and dies at about 109°F (46°C). It goes dormant at 63°F (14°C) and works best between 80-95°F (24-35°C).
- It's fragile, easily contaminated and killed by bacteria. Keep all wooden or plastic spoons, and everything added to the pot as sterile as possible.
- Don't use metal containers or utensils with the yeast culture pot – ceramic, wood or plastic only.
- When at room temp, place only a loose fitting lid on top to allow the gases to escape.
- A clear liquid might rise to the top of the starter. This is OK; just stir it in. However, if a pink liquid appears, the starter has spoiled and must be discarded.
- It's possible for yeast to kill itself by the alcohol it produces. For bakers yeast, this happens at about 12% alcohol content. Watch the yeast for signs of this. When it stops frothing, it's either out of food or is near 'death'. Add more water and carbohydrates. If crock is full, empty 1 cup of the contents.
- Sourdough starter improves with age. It usually takes at least 2-3 feedings before your baked bread has that tangy taste associated with sourdough recipes.
- Don't expect your yeast culture to act like dried, high potency yeast. It may take several hours to rise.

Chapter 9: Preparing The Pantry and Saving $$

ORGANIZATION

Pantries are what and where you make them. In our Perth home, we had converted a bedroom to food storage. On the farmlet in Victoria, Australia, storage space was nearly nonexistent so we built a separate structure outside, described below. Back in Colorado, our pantry is in the cool basement. There is no one "right" way to do it, but there are wrong ones like in a hot garage, shed or attic. You have to look at your options and see what could work.

In Ballarat, Victoria, we built a windowless secured pantry out of a 20-foot diameter concrete water tank. Its double-reinforced walls (two 4-inch concrete walls with airspace between) and 4 inch concrete ceiling were designed to take earthquake shaking and other natural disasters, including extreme heat. We didn't want this tank to be an eyesore so it was incorporated into the landscape and no one ever knew it was there. This turned out to be a real blessing as the Earth-covered structure remained consistently cool which greatly helped shelf life.

Having a separate pantry is not nearly as convenient as one inside the house especially during bad weather. Because the entrance is exposed to the outside, mice can sneak in if you leave the door open "just to pick up a thing or two". After a round of Ratsak and disinfecting annoying "mouse tracks", we remembered to keep the door closed – always, and that ended the problem.

Photo: Getting started. While Stan completed assembling the shelving, I arranged stored goods from boxes, sacks and buckets. Later, as we became more organized, glass containers found their way to the bottom shelves and "sideboards" were added to keep goods from being knocked to the floor. In order to use space more efficiently, food groups of lesser quantity or bulk, like spices, were moved to the lower shelves and replaced by taller items. Shelves can be set at any height you need, but placing rows too closely together means a tougher time getting items out. To load newest goods to the rear, you need room to maneuver.

The interior was lined with shelving butted to the walls. It took Stan just a couple days to assemble all shelving using the clip-fit "gorilla" variety. No screws, no nails to lose.

Then we anchored them to the perimeter wall to prevent earthquake damage. Stan inserted masonry eye-bolts into the wall about 3 inches on either side of the shelving uprights. Through one eye he threaded heavy gauge wire, ran it around the uprights and through the eye-bolt on the other side tying it off securely. Each set of shelves was bolted to the next set and so on around the pantry.

The pantry was organized according to type: soups, dried beans, baking ingredients, spices, Mexican foods, canned meats, fruits, vegetables, condiments, medicine and survival. That way time spent locating things was cut to a minimum. Every can and jar was assigned its location by expiration date with the newest stuff to the rear.

Heaviest items lived on bottom shelves, as did breakables. To prevent goods from falling, we added "sideboards" along open shelf areas made from styrofoam sheets and heavy cardboard. "Case purchases" stayed in their original containers for extra protection with the expiration date clearly labeled on the box. Slippery-packaged items like dried soups, rices, pasta dishes, and dehydrated meals were lined "standing up" in cardboard boxes.

Boxes of foods were cut down to about 4 or 5 inches (10-12cm) and reinforced on the bottom with 2" wide packing tape. Boxed and stacked, they took up less room and weren't forever sliding onto the floor. Expiration dates were labeled on the front near the top in a wide-tip permanent marker so the "dead date" was easily seen. We could take down these cardboard boxes, flip through the packages, see the expiration date and choose a variety in one easy step.

Cardboard boxes were also cut down for other small breakables like spice bottles, extracts and other seasonings. Oftentimes when we've stacked several items on top of each other, some invariably got knocked off (like by Taco's happy tail or Seismo's huge feet!) Home canned foods were also protected in cardboard boxes.

Bulky items like toilet paper, paper towels, Kleenex were stored in very large cardboard boxes like wardrobe moving boxes to not waste shelf space. These cardboard boxes were set on 2x4s or pallets, off the concrete floor to guard against moisture.

By anticipating potential problems and doing things that encourage everyone to use food storage to its best advantage is time well spent. Stan is now very good about rotating and keeping track of things we add or subtract from supplies.

A current copy of our Deyo Food Planner stays in the pantry **with a pencil** so when things are removed, there's no "I'll remember to mark it off later". Who's gonna remember "later"? Make it a family project rather than leave it to one person so everyone has something invested. Plus, it teaches kids responsibility. It's fun and rewarding to see your supplies grow and know you are a clever shopper by beating the system.

ABOUT THAT FOOD STORAGE ROOM...

After completing and stocking the food storage area, we had several universal issues to tackle: rodents, temperature and moisture. Another area normally of concern is light but this room had no windows so that wasn't a problem.

I moved food to the new pantry area when Stan had little more than half of the shelving completed. Two days later mice moved into their new "condo" complete with party feast, and party they did! The first thing they ravaged was bags of flour and, of course, they hit only the newest ones! (Who knew mice could read expiration dates!) The freshest ones were stacked to the back and that's what they ate. Two bites from this bag, three nibbles from that one... and then proceeded to leave their calling card EVERYWHERE! Shelves were immediately disinfected. We determined they had shinnied down a ventilation pipe and wriggled through a drainage hole. We needed access to these openings so we couldn't use a permanent seal like cement. One pipe housed electrical wire, which made it tricky to seal.

These were exceptionally smart mice. We'd set traps that they managed to evade even when Stan hot-glued bait to the trap. This is a nasty, but clever trick he learned to help mice into "rodent heaven". Stan stuffed the hole with heavy styrofoam, which they chewed through like mashed potatoes! Next he plugged the holes with stainless steel wool and that stopped them cold – for about a week. Finally we squirted in foam caulk and they didn't chew through that.

HANTAVIRUS WARNING

If your pantry will be an area previously home to mice or other rodents, like a cellar, it needs to be thoroughly and carefully cleaned. A 1993 outbreak of Hantavirus in "The Four Corners" of America makes this precaution necessary. Colorado's Dept. of Health began tracking Hantavirus that year and they have documented 61 cases with 23 fatalities – about a 1-in-3 death rate.[35] So while Hanta is fairly rare and not contagious between people, it's something to avoid.

Transmission is through rodent droppings, urine and saliva. When people breathe in the virus, it can cause severe body aches, high fever, stomach flu-like symptoms, shortness of breath and death occurs when the lungs fill with fluid. That's why it's important not to sweep, vacuum or raise dust where these rodents have stayed. So far, these animals are identified hanta carriers in the U.S.: deer mice, cotton and rice rats (in the Southeast), and the white-footed mouse (in the Northeast). Hantavirus is also present in Canada, South America, Europe and Asia. The CDC advises the following clean-up measures:

HOW TO CLEAN A RODENT-INFESTED AREA
- Put on rubber, latex, vinyl or nitrile (synthetic latex) gloves.
- Don't stir up dust by vacuuming, sweeping, or any other means.
- Mix a solution of 1½ cups household bleach in 1 gallon of water. Soak for a few minutes.
- Thoroughly wet contaminated areas with a bleach solution or household disinfectant.
- Once everything is wet, take up contaminated materials with damp towel. Mop or sponge the area with bleach solution or household disinfectant.
- Spray dead rodents with disinfectant and then double-bag them along with all cleaning materials. Bury, burn, or throw out rodent in appropriate waste disposal system. (Contact your local or state health department for disposal methods.)
- Treat gloves with disinfectant or soap and water before taking them off.
- After removing the clean gloves, thoroughly wash hands with soap and water (or use a waterless alcohol-based hand rub when soap is not available)[36].

Next we had to deal with humidity and temperature control. Ballarat was a bit humid occasionally and since lichens even grew on asphalt that should tell you something. Because our food storage area was made of new concrete, it naturally contained water from the pour. That made moisture a double worry. To solve the problem, we bought a small ½ horsepower air conditioner. This knocked out two issues at once. It condensed water from the air and it kept the temperature at 66°F (19°C) or less.

In winter the pantry temperature dropped to around 54°F (12°C), so the air conditioner thermostat kept shutting it off, but the moisture kept coming. We solved this winter problem with a dehumidifier. Even a fairly small unit immediately took out a sizable amount of moisture.

The air conditioner didn't go to waste. Running it a couple hours every day during summer helped maintain the temp around 65°F (18°C) or less. Lower storing temperatures mean longer shelf life.

TIPS TO SAVE MONEY

COUPONS
Various countries have different and also similar ways to save $$. In the U.S. there are always coupons. Some people are fanatical about using them and rake in big savings. For others it's too much trouble. They are the equivalent of cash as long as you purchase the specified item before the expiration date. For special promotions, a grocery store may offer double or triple coupon days, but this is increasingly rare. Some stores will even accept competitor's coupons rather than lose the business.

ONLINE COUPONS
Online coupons are huge. Before you shop, take 10 minutes to check for these savings. When you're at a company website, if you don't see the coupon area right away, do a search. Or, Google for "the brand name" + coupon, "Betty Crocker" + coupon or "Betty Crocker" + "special offer". Depending on the company, they might have as many as 20 coupons available. All you have to do is print them out. Most manufacturers have different WEEKLY specials so check often. If you're not taking advantage of these dollars-off deals, you're missing out!

Along this same line, Google "grocery coupon". This takes you to websites that specialize in online savings like **www.coupons.com** or **www.thegrocerygame.com**. Sometimes a fee is charged for the service, but depending on how much you shop, it can be an advantage.

SALES
In Australia, on Dollar Days, prices might be cut on specified products as much as 25%. Sales are so often and advantageous, by purchasing supplies in bulk, you can almost buy products **only** when on sale.

SHAREHOLDER CARDS

Also in Australia, Coles-Myer has a little known benefit if you hold company shares. With every purchase you receive a 5% discount even on sale items. Major purchases like appliances garner a 10% discount. Coles, Myer, Tyremasters, K-Mart, Target, Liquorland, Officeworks, Bi-Lo and other stores also honor this card.

PREFERRED CUSTOMER CARDS

A store chain issues these cards that allows extra savings at their locations. Savings vary according to product featured and by store. Preferred customer cards often give gasoline savings, since many stores have filling stations. The trade-off with these cards is it allows stores to track every purchase – "Big Brother" at work.

AT THE STORE – DESIGNED TO DELAY

Shop during off-peak hours when it's least crowded or shortly before you have a scheduled appointment. The longer we stay, the more we buy. The longer you wait at check-out, the more "impulse items" – those lining shelves by the cash register – end up in your cart. Grocers intentionally place the most often-purchased items – milk, butter, and eggs – furthest away so you must walk past aisles of other items. Frequently purchased goods are moved around so you have to hunt for them. Retailers hope that while searching, you'll put more things in your cart. Music is intentionally lulling to keep you shopping at a slowed pace. Our newest upscale grocery is enhanced with soft lighting. Colors pop enticingly on fruits, vegetables and packaging against purposefully muted walls and hardwood floors. The ambiance is so enjoyable, you really *want* to stay longer. To counteract these marketing tools, make out a shopping list and stick to it!

THE SHELF HOOK

Stores often place the most expensive items at eye level, on middle shelves and the one right above. In the cereal and cookie aisles, the most expensive and sugar-laden foods might be a bit lower – right at children's head heights. Manufacturers pay top rates for these prime locations because they know they move product.

BULK BINS

Some stores have large containers filled with an assortment of beans, pet food, grain, candy, dried fruit and nuts. Though scoops are provided, I've seen people reach in with their hands for free samples. When bins aren't sealed, germs have easy access. While prices are cut for bulk bins, you have to weigh the savings against less sanitary conditions. Things to consider:
- Are they closed to the air?
- Can the food be washed before being consumed?
- Are they at the level where children are tempted to help themselves?

BULK WAREHOUSE

Most countries have warehouse stores like Sam's, Costco, BJ's, Big Lots or Campbell's Cash & Carry. They can give better prices due to one-time and large lot purchases, overstocked items and products near expiration.

Warehouses constantly rotate stock so you may not see the same products or same brands.

Most warehouses, besides discounted prices, offer even better case pricing. Though prices are marked clearly on the label in front of the product, make sure you know what you're buying. In one warehouse, the prices were clearly marked on the shelves at the <u>per</u> <u>each</u> price. If you bought a case, it looked like you were getting a terrific deal. In smaller "squint print" was case price. This isn't sneaky, just good marketing, so be smart.

Whenever going to bulk-buy warehouses, I take a copy of our Deyo Food Storage Planner. The DFSP makes a great grocery list and since prices are already logged, it's easy to see if a "sale" is really a SALE!

TIP: Purchasing a product in a larger size doesn't automatically mean the price-per-ounce is less. Check it.

CO-OP PURCHASING

Another way to save money is through a co-op. You can find them in nearly every developed country and they can produce great savings. To start a co-op all you need is:
1. A group of as little as five members and one person to keep track of who ordered what. Get a receipt book and give members a copy of their order.
2. One person collects the money up front and sends it to the mill or co-op company along with the order.
3. The shipped order is dropped off at one location and a date is set for everyone to sort out orders.
4. All orders should be for whole bags only. Trying to split bags can lead to messy problems.
5. The feed mill can give you an idea what the shipping per pound or kilo will be.
6. Collecting an additional $5.00 from every member should cover any unforeseen expenses. This form of co-op is very casual and doesn't require too much effort yet net good savings.

Chapter 10: Taking Care of Your Investment

As you stock the pantry, you'll want to protect these supplies and extend their shelf life as long as possible. It gives you more flexibility and saves time and money. Besides time itself, perishables have five common enemies to long shelf life: temperature, air, moisture, light, and pests with temperature being most important. It has been established many times over, if foods can be maintained at a constant temperature of 68°F (20°C) or lower, the expected shelf life is greatly improved.

Once your supplies start to build, the dollars invested add up. To encourage keeping track of expiration dates, think of these things as money in tangible form. Your stored goods are a hedge against tough times no matter what form they might take.

ROTATE! That's really all that needs to be said. If you plan to store foods in quantity, use these measures to ensure best quality and maximum shelf life.

SIX EASY STEPS

SIX things?! Don't panic, it's not hard at all and we'll walk through each item. Here's what needs to be considered and most are really, really simple:

1. Time
2. Temperature
3. Humidity
4. Oxygen
5. Light
6. Pests

TIME – IT KEEPS ON TICKIN'

Simply put, rotate foods before the expiration date. The key to successful food storage is easy – **ROTATE!** Use all foods, including pet food, medicines and perishable supplies before the expiration date. Nothing is wasted.

A few simple precautions will keep your stored goods considerably beyond traditional expiration dates. Packaged foods can normally be eaten past the printed "dead date", but the overall nutritional value may have degraded along with taste, color and texture. For instance, a can of green beans has a shelf life of about two years. However, if the can is completely intact, not rusted, there is no bulging and no mold inside, the food is probably OK to consume. In other words, it may be eaten safely, but the nutritional benefits could be lessened. Without question, the best way to insure getting the best out of your foods is to rotate these items into normal meals as they near expiration.

TIP 1: For products that have a dead date on the bottom of the can or back of the package, mark them on the front in a wide permanent marker so it's easy to see. This saves fumbling with stacked goods and allows you to select which to use more quickly.

TIP 2: Manufacturers use several types of dating. Some are "Best by" or "Use by". (See Chapter 12 for unraveling date codes.) Other makers indicate the date of manufacture (DOM), which doesn't tell you anything if you don't know its shelf life. (See Chapter 11.) If you are the only one accessing pantry items and already know exactly how long every product has for maximum freshness, then no extra marking is required. If a spouse or kids will be in the food storage area, chances are they'll understand a clearly marked dead date but not DOM. In the case of DOM coding, mark the foods on the front with the actual expiration date using the shelf life tables in the Deyo Food Planner. That way everyone is clear when foods need to be used.

TIP 3: Keep your Deyo Food Storage Planner in the pantry. If anyone takes supplies out of stock, make sure they know to mark it off the list. This is a good way to get family members in the habit of food rotation plus keep your records straight.

TEMPERATURE: OR TOO HOT TO HANDLE

Rule of thumb: for every 10°F (5.5°C) the temperature is lowered in the storage room, shelf life may double. For example, if foods were stored at 70°F (21°C), they should last twice as long as those stored at 80°F (27°C). Use the following table to compare foods' general shelf lives when stored at different temperatures. The chart on the following page is not for any particular food. It illustrates possible shelf lives one can expect – within reason.

Storing items at 68°F (20°C) sealed away from oxygen, light and moisture greatly extends most shelf lives. Controlling the temperature is the number one factor in storing foods long term.

STORAGE LIFE DEPENDING ON CONSTANT TEMPERATURES[37]		
Constant Storage Temperature in °F	Constant Storage Temperature in °C	Storage Life in years
40	4	40
50	10	30
60	16	20
70	21	10
80	27	5
90	32	2.5
100	38	1.25

This will be easier for some people than others. If you live in the desert or where climate continually climbs to 90°F (32°C) and above, chances are you have an air conditioner. This is an excellent way to both cool and remove humidity in the air. A swamp cooler, while it brings down temperature, adds moisture – something we don't want around food.

Some locations in the home are better suited for storage than others. Since heat rises, keeping supplies in an attic is a poor choice unless it's air-conditioned and rodent-proof.

Foods kept outside in poorly insulated tin sheds will cook in the Sun's heat and may not last even the shelf life printed on the package.

In Australia and New Zealand, the coolest side of the house is on the south. In the Northern Hemisphere, the coolest side is on the north. If you must store foods in any windowed room in your home, pick an area that receives the least sunlight, preferably none. An interior hall closet could be an excellent choice. A basement or underground location is usually best.

In additional to keeping temperatures cool, they need to be constant. Equally important as the actual temperature is the degree of variance and *how rapidly* the temperature changes. A slow temperature shift of ten degrees between winter and summer is not a big problem. Daily or weekly changes age food prematurely. However, strive for temperatures no warmer than a constant 68-70°F, (20-21°C).

HUMIDITY: YOU'RE ALL WET

Moisture is the third enemy of food storage promoting various mold and bacterial growth. Ideally foods should not be exposed to more than 15% humidity, but in many areas, this isn't possible except in the desert. To decrease humidity in a larger room, consider using either an air conditioner or a dehumidifier.

DampRid is another option designed for small, enclosed spaces where electrical dehumidifiers aren't practical. Product information suggests one DampRid unit per 100 square feet (9.3 sq. meters). They are simple to use; simply peel off the foil protective top and place in a room. As moisture is absorbed, the beads inside liquefy. Replace when the container is filled with water. DampRid works up to 8 weeks in sub-zero temperatures absorbing over 125% of its weight in moisture. If a lot of humidity is present, this product probably won't be effective enough, but they are ideal for small areas. They are available worldwide at hardware, grocery and drug stores.

Another technique especially clever for larger cans is to coat them with paraffin wax. To do this for every small can would be a tedious and time-consuming project, but if storing these foods long-term, it's a viable option.

Spraying cans with rust retardant paint like Rust-Oleum and Wattyl's Killrust also works well. If using a colored paint, label each can with the product and expiration date or you might open a lot of "surprises"!

Storing foods in sealable, moisture-proof containers is yet another option. Besides blocking moisture, buckets and containers help bar oxygen.

OXYGEN? KISS IT GOODBYE!

Another factor contributing to shortened shelf life is oxygen. "Air contains about 78% nitrogen and 21% oxygen, leaving about 1% for the other gasses. If oxygen is absorbed, what remains is 99% pure nitrogen in a partial vacuum."[38] One of the most popular ways to prepare food for long-term storage is nitro-packing. It's an excellent method of oxygen flushing, but requires some equipment. This technique is explained in a few pages.

LIGHT: TURN IT OFF!

Light does two nasties to food. It kills off desirable vitamins and promotes bacterial growth. That's why many vitamins are sold in dark brown glass or opaque plastic containers. While rows of brightly colored jar goods are attractive to the eye – especially home canned foods and spices – they'll be first to degrade when exposed to ultraviolet light. Keeping foods in a dark room is a better idea.

If this isn't possible, keep stored foods in cardboard boxes or other light barring containers. An alternative is to throw an opaque tarp over foods.

PESTS: WHAT'S WIGGLING?

Ugh! Nothing inspires disgust quite so quickly as seeing something wiggly around food. Another ugly discovery is mouse droppings. You can take several steps to keep the food storage environment pest free.

1. Before installing any foods in the pantry, thoroughly clean all surfaces. This means vacuuming first and then scrubbing with hot water and a good disinfectant. Mice have an excellent sense of smell and are attracted to the slightest invitation. If mice think a banquet is available, they are there with fork in hand. They also mark their previous routes with urine so mice are definitely unclean visitors.

2. Check for any holes giving access and plug them.

MICE SOLUTIONS

The best way to be rid of mice and other pests is to discourage them in the first place. Plug all holes with an expanding foam caulk for permanent solutions. In the meantime, if a hole even as small as ¼" (6.35mm) is spotted, fill it with steel wool. They hate this stuff and generally won't chew through it, however, a few of ours did. They must be related to "Jaws" in the James Bond movies!

Aromatherapy

If a mouse does sneak inside, try flushing them out with an aromatherapy mixture. Seal up the infested area and temporarily close all ventilation points. Remove pets and leave the room as soon as diffusion begins. Leave one small, easy-to-find exit hole. Diffuse a strong, heavy blast of Mouse Chaser:

5 parts Peppermint (Mentha piperata)
2-3 parts Thyme (Thymus vulgaris)
2-3 parts Lemon

Thirty to sixty minutes should do it. Pick a time when you know they'll be active. Precautions: Thyme oil is very strong. It's not for kids, and should not be breathed for more than 5-10 minutes at a time. Peppermint can cause sleeplessness if used to excess in the afternoon or evening.

Traps

When baiting a trap, cheese works fine, but dries out if mice are slow at taking a hint. The bait we found they like best is dry dog food.

One house we rented while waiting to move from Perth to Victoria was anything but mouse-proof. We tried a variety of baits and sometimes they managed to snatch the bait and evade the trap. The third time this happened, Stan fixed the clever rodents by hot gluing bait to the trap. This did the trick because when they jerked harder on the dog food, the trap snapped shut. Good-bye mice!

Poison Bait

One thing you don't want to use around the house, especially if you have pets or children is poisoned bait. We decided to take more active measures against the mouse challenge but on the first day we used it, we had a near-tragedy.

Around noon Stan had set out a container of Ratsak. The pellets were held in a cardboard container with a 1" (2½cm) hole cut in the top so rodents could feed. They'd eat the poison and later die from internal bleeding. This doesn't sound terribly humane, but in 1999 Victoria suffered from a huge infestation due to drought. Mice were so prolific it called for drastic measures. Minutes after Stan set three mousetraps they would immediately fill.

Mice didn't penetrate our home but they hit every one of the out buildings and the attic of our house. You could even hear them scurrying around in the ceiling. Let me explain.

In Australia, it's very common for roofs to be tiled instead of using shake or asphalt shingles. Instead of laying sheets of particle board over roof trusses, they tile directly over roof battens, which are strips of lumber about 1" wide spaced 6-12" apart. This allows rodents easy access to the ceiling since the tiles have lots of voids. For thieves to break into a home, they only have to move a few roof tiles and pop through the ceiling drywall. That's why it's common Downunder to get mice and possums under your roof but not necessarily in the house.

That same afternoon about 4:30, I remembered leaving some papers in the workshop and trotted out to retrieve them. Using the door off the office took me right by an area where Seismo and Taco left their treasures like a new bone. It was also the area where they deposited "paybacks" – retaliation for leaving them at home for instance, like a chewed up plastic flower pot. That day's offering was a shredded Ratsak container.

What a sinking feeling that brought! We had no idea which dog, or if both dogs, tore it up or if they had eaten any. Since it could have happened any time over the past four hours, every minute was crucial. We picked up every single remaining pellet and by weighing a new box, Stan determined 14 grams were missing. The vet wanted to see them immediately as the poison starts to work in as little as an hour.

Neither Seismo nor Taco "fessed up" and since both sets of ears went back when showed the shredded box, it was impossible to determine who did the deed. The vet gave both animals shots to induce vomiting. Poor doggies! Less than 10 minutes later, Taco lost it first and there was no trace of green pellets. We were thinking possibly the dogs had scattered the missing 14 grams in the backyard even though we had looked thoroughly.

No such luck. Seismo's deposit was riddled with telltale green! When there was nothing left but their toenails, Dr. Marlene gave each dog a shot of Vitamin K (potassium antidote) and Seismo was on daily Vitamin K for the next 2 weeks as an extra precaution.

Looking at the amount of poison ingested, the vet said Seismo would have died without treatment and probably without warning. We should have known it was Seismo since he is our 4-legged garbage bucket!

Maybe the dogs didn't put two and two together – that leaving poison where they could eat it was not clever, but their parents learned a valuable lesson! Use these products with extreme care. If you set poisoned bait around your home and they die inside the walls or ceiling, the odor is simply awful for at least a week.

INSECT SOLUTIONS

1. Keep the pantry spotless. Don't allow food to spill and attract pests. Ants adore honey and many have a sixth sense when it comes to this sticky delicacy.
2. Only purchase the freshest products.
3. Check all dried foods when purchased in bulk. If any bugs are present, return the package for a replacement.
4. Put a bay leaf in the flour canister. Bay leaves are natural insect repellents.

Sometimes after following all these precautions, insects still show up in dried foods. There are several methods to get rid of them:

SHAKE, RATTLE AND ROLL

If the insects are large enough, run foods through a sifter to remove them. Stretch screen mesh tightly over a wire frame and gently shake it back and forth. This lets the flour sift through but not any bugs.

HOT HEADS

Another technique is to bake grain at a low temperature for a short time. Pour the food onto a jelly roll or pizza pan – something with sides – no thicker than ½" (1¼cm) deep. Bake at 150°F (65°C).

COLD SHOULDERS

Freezing is the least effective but most used process because it's the easiest. Freezing for 72 hours kills live insects, but not the eggs. In order to kill insects hatched after the first freezing, a second treatment may be needed.

GETTING EARTHY

Adding Diatomaceous Earth sometimes referred to as DE, to dried foods like beans, pasta, peas and legumes, cereals, seeds, and whole grains works well.

You're probably wondering if this is really dirt and the answer is no. DE is the broken up shells and fossils of marine life known as diatoms. While safe for human and animal consumption, it's deadly to insects. Why? DE particles are sharp compared to an insect's skin and it cuts right through. These punctured areas cause the insect to dehydrate and die. It's not at all harmful to life with internal skeletons (that's us 2 and 4-legged creatures).

There are two forms of DE. One contains a high amount of silica, which is used in swimming pool filters. This kind is not acceptable for food storage. Instead, check garden centers and hardware stores for the right kind of DE, which contains no pesticides. An organic garden center should have the most desirable product. You can also order DE through Best Prices Storable Foods **www.internet-grocer.net** or phone: 903.356.6443

HOW DO I USE DE?

Nothing could be simpler. For every 5-gallon (20 liter) container, add 1¼ cups of DE. Snap on the lid and shake the container thoroughly making sure all of the food is thoroughly coated. DE has no shelf life and doesn't degrade, so if eggs are present and hatch, DE will kill all emerging insects.

Do not breathe the dust when applying it as DE can irritate the lungs. Other than that, it's a safe, inexpensive and thorough treatment for insects.

FOOD STORAGE CONTAINERS

Whether food containers are air and moisture-proof is the most important thing to consider. Food grade containers are labeled HDPE, which stands for High Density Polyethylene. Containers should also have the number "2" inside the recycle triangle on the bottom. If the buckets are white or natural in color they <u>should</u> be food grade. If purchasing yours directly from the manufacturer, ask. If you are obtaining second hand containers, make sure they have had nothing in them but food and that the lids still seal properly. Chemicals previously kept in these buckets can be absorbed by the plastic and leach back into your food.

To seal buckets with snap on lids, put something between the lid and the hammer to prevent damage to the lid, just like when you close a paint can. A 2x4 works great for this since it redistributes the blow evenly over the lid, forcing it down without denting it.

We've used these less expensive buckets lined with mylar bags for years. They work great and cost less.

To find food grade containers check bakeries, ice cream manufacturers and parlors, yogurt shops, restaurants, food processing plants, LDS canneries, emergency preparedness centers, rural produce and livestock supply centers. Look in the Yellow Pages under "Plastics".

Food containers like the one pictured uses a special screw-type lid most commonly sold as the Gamma Seal. The lid, which can be purchased separately from the pail, permanently transforms 12" diameter buckets into airtight/leak proof storage containers. Simply fasten the Gamma Seal to your bucket and access foods inside by un-screwing the inner portion of the lid. The outer portion contains a large O-Ring for an airtight fit and it stays on the bucket. The inner portion also contains an O-Ring unscrews for easy access. The Gamma Seal lid fits virtually any 3½ to 7-gallon bucket including 20 liter. Gamma Seal lids retail for about US$8 each.

CONTAINER SIZE

You can choose from numerous sizes and bigger is not always better. Before packing all your foods in 5-gallon containers, ask yourself:
- Is this a food we use in great quantity?
- Could we use it up before it goes bad?
- How many people in your family will consume this food?
- If using this food for bartering, do I want to exchange 5 gallons or 20 liters of wheat for a hair cut?

TIP: Pack some of each food in several different sized containers.

USING MYLAR BAGS

One of the best oxygen barriers is the mylar bag. Mylar is the silver-colored film wrapped around many foods like nuts, candies or MREs. Mylar, DuPont's brand name for this polyester film, was first manufactured for packaging Macadamia nuts but like Kleenex, it's become the name everyone uses, no matter who makes it.

As with anything, there are suitable varieties and ones to avoid. The best mylar for food packing is 4 – 4.5 mil thick and looks similar to very heavy aluminum foil, but is far more tear resistant.

Transparent varieties and lightweight products used for balloons aren't food storage quality. The point of using mylar is to keep oxygen away from food. Remember how quickly mylar balloons lose air? It only takes about a day for them to partially collapse. If air escapes this easily, it's just as easy for air to leak inside.

Using mylar bags isn't necessary when storing food in metal cans, but they are added protection for food grade plastic buckets. Buckets are <u>fairly</u> good oxygen barriers, especially ones with gasket-sealing lids. However, they are made of polyethylene, which allows small amounts of air to pass through.

Another problem arises when the wrong size or too many oxygen scavengers are used. When used incorrectly they can "overkill" as they absorb O_2. This causes the sides of the bucket to suck in loosening the sealed lid.

Mylars are a good precaution and should be used in conjunction with plastic buckets, but never in place of them. Even though mylar bags are good oxygen barriers on their own, they puncture easily. (Heavy-duty plastic freezer bags like Ziplocs and Click Zips can't be substituted for mylars; they leak air in and out.)

Sealing a mylar bag is easily done with an iron. Since all irons heat differently, begin at the "Wool" setting and adjust hotter or cooler as needed. The seal should be strong enough not to rip open when you try to pull it apart. Sometimes the bag looks sealed but isn't. Set the iron hotter. Test to make sure it doesn't pull apart. If the mylar starts to melt, move the temperature to a cooler setting.

An ironing board adjusted to just above bucket height allows you to move the bucket close to the ironing surface. You can also place a very smooth board (splinters can puncture the bag) across the edge of the bucket to use as the sealing surface. To seal, pop in the oxygen scavengers, apply whatever method chosen to extract extra air (see next page), lay the mylar smoothly across the ironing "board" and seal shut.

Another option for sealing is Smart Sealer found in most discount stores in North America and Australia. We've used the Smart Sealer and it worked great. Using these small portable sealers eliminates the need for an "ironing" surface.

TIP: Don't fill the mylar bag completely to the top. Allow a little extra room to make the sealing process more manageable.

HOW TO PACK CONTAINERS

There are four main ways to pull air from dry food storage containers before sealing: vacuuming, dry ice (CO_2), nitrogen flushing and oxygen absorbers or oxygen scavengers. Each has pros and cons:

METHOD	PROS	CONS
Vacuum	Easy. Sealers last many years.	Must have vacuum sealer.
Dry Ice	Inexpensive. Easy.	May have to special order. May form carbonic acid if too much moisture is present. Handle with gloves.
Nitrogen Flush	Very fool proof. Does not involve moisture that could promote mold.	Requires more equipment but it can be rented from welding suppliers.
Oxygen Absorbers	Convenient	More costly. Has a shelf life. Must know oxygen content of storage container for amount to use.

VACUUM PACK METHOD

If you already have a vacuum sealer like Tilia's FoodSaver line, this might be your best option. Vacuum sealers have many other uses so they're a good investment. It is the food storage method we use because it's efficient and easy, requires no extra equipment and is always ready to go!

HOW TO PACK USING A VACUUM SEALER
Step 1 Wash and dry the food buckets. Set bucket to be filled between two empty, overturned pails.
Step 2 Place the overturned pails on either side of the center bucket about 6 in. away and so they sit in front of it. Lay a 2x4 across the two overturned buckets.
Step 3 Fill a mylar-lined bucket with food. Leave several inches of bag unfilled for easy sealing.
Step 4 Add 1 or 2 oxygen absorbers. Press out excess air with your hands.
Step 5 Place the opened ends of the bag together across the 2x4. Seal the mylar closed with a medium-hot iron leaving a 2-inch opening in one corner.
Step 6 Insert the vacuum sealer hose into the opening. Keep nozzle away from food and vacuum out air.
Step 7 Immediately iron this opening shut. Snap on the lid. Label and date the food bucket. Done!

DRY ICE METHOD

Dry ice is relatively inexpensive and easy to use. From many years of boating on Lake Powell, we learned to keep foods frozen longer by using dry ice. This huge lake is nearly 200 miles long, idyllically set in the middle of the Utah-Arizona desert. Only six marinas dot the nearly 2000 miles of shoreline, so bringing your own food is necessary.

Interior boat space is normally limited for the average boater so refrigerators are small. Keeping foods cold always presents a problem, especially in 115°F (46°C) heat. Before embarking on a Powell vacation, all food is frozen at home including milk, cheese, butter, bread, meat and entrees. If nothing "dies" in frigid temps, it's frozen.

Just before leaving for Utah, slabs of dry ice are wrapped in brown paper sacks and newspaper, and secured with rubber bands. A layer of 1" thick, one foot square slabs cover the bottom of very large coolers or eskies. Next comes the food layered halfway up. Then two more paper-wrapped slabs of dry ice are inserted – one at each end of the cooler, and several on top of the food. The rest of the food is stacked in and the packing is finished with the last slabs of dry ice on top.

The cooler is immediately snapped shut. Duct-tape is wrapped around lid's opening sealing the coldness inside. By this time, the cooler is really heavy. It takes two of us to lift it. The finishing touches are completed when the entire cooler is wrapped in a thermal blanket and secured with more duct tape. Even wrapped this tightly and surrounded by frozen foods, dry ice will evaporate (turn into CO_2 gas) within 3 days. Dry ice greatly lengthens the frozen state and it does wonders for food storage.

Since dry ice melts quickly, or more correctly, changes into CO_2 gas, have everything ready before you pick it up. For the drive home, take along a container (not glass) to hold the dry ice and rubber gloves. A Rubber Maid or Tupperware type container and lid is ideal.

HOW TO PACK USING DRY ICE

Step 1 Wash and dry the food buckets and equipment. Line up the cleaned buckets to be filled.

Step 2 Put on gloves before handling dry ice. It is *very* cold, -110°F (-78.5C), and can "burn" the skin (actually it freezes flesh causing a burning sensation). Dry ice evaporates into carbon dioxide gas even in a household freezer since the average freezer temperature is only 0°F (-18°C). If frost forms on the dry ice, wipe it off.

Step 3 If the dry ice comes in a slab, use a flat screwdriver or chisel to chop off enough to fill ⅓ cup. If you buy the pellet or cube variety, measure about ⅓ cup. Approximately 2 ounces (57g) is the amount needed for a 5 or 6-gallon (20 or 24L) pail. For a 1-gallon (4L) pail, use 1 oz (28g) or about 1/6 cup of dry ice.

Step 4 Wrap dry ice in cut-down brown paper bags or lunch sacks, butcher paper or paper towels and place in the bottom of the food bucket. This prevents direct contact with food.

Step 5 Pour in the food and stop about ½" (1¼cm) from the top.

Step 6 Attach the lid loosely all the way around except for one small area. This allows the oxygen to escape. If no exit is left, your bucket could split or explode.

It should take about 45-60 minutes for the dry ice to evaporate. If some is still present after an hour, recheck the bucket every 10 minutes. You can tell if dry ice is present; there will be a very icy spot on the bottom of the bucket. Don't remove the lid to check or the buckets will refill with air. Recheck the dry ice often because as soon as the dry ice is gone, oxygen will sneak back into the container.

Step 7 When the dry ice is gone, snap on the lid. Label and date the food bucket. Done!

Depending where you live, dry ice is normally found in ice cream shops, grocery stores, dairy products wholesalers, ice supply companies, welding suppliers, and chemical and gas companies. In America there are many different phone books, but try first under "Dry Ice" in the Yellow Pages. In Australia, look under either "Gas--Industrial &/or Medical" or "Gas Suppliers". Air Liquide, an international company is also a good source to check.

NITROGEN FLUSH METHOD

This process is about as foolproof as it gets. It removes virtually all of the oxygen. There is no chance of introducing extra moisture as with dry ice and there is no shelf life like with oxygen absorbers. If you rent the equipment, the gas is inexpensive and when you're done, there's nothing to store. If you want to purchase the needed bits and pieces, it's the most expensive method of food packing. Rent or purchase the following equipment:

- Nitrogen Bottle
- Pressure Reducing Valve and Gauges
- Hose

- Wand (connect this rigid tubing to the hose and push to the bottom of the bucket)
- Hand held valve at the top of the wand

TO USE NITRO FLUSHING

Step 1 Assemble the above equipment. Wash and dry the food buckets. Line up the cleaned buckets and fill with food.

Step 2 Set output pressure to 60-70 PSI or 410-480 KPA.

Step 3 Place the lid on top of the bucket and off-set it just enough so the wand can be inserted down to the bottom of the pail.

Step 4 Hold a lighted match or cigarette lighter over the spot where the oxygen will be escaping. Like testing with canaries in the old mining tunnels, when there's no more oxygen, the flame will go out.

Step 5 Turn on the valve and start the nitrogen flowing. As soon as you begin the flush, time it with your watch till the flame goes out. After a few buckets, you'll have a good idea how long it takes to flush the oxygen and will no longer need the flame as a guide.

Step 6 If you're unsure you flushed all the oxygen, an oxygen absorber can be added but it's not necessary. DONE!

OXYGEN ABSORBERS – GETTING RID OF AIR

When you purchase oxygen scavengers, they will arrive in a sealed bag. Leave them sealed until ready to use. If you don't plan to use all of them, pull out the needed amount and immediately reseal the remainder in an airtight container. After the container or mylar bag-lined container has been filled with food, toss in the individual oxygen absorber(s), <u>unopened</u>, on top.

Some people have slam-dunked a couple oxygen absorbers into containers and called it good, but there's a little more to it. To determine the number of oxygen absorbers needed, you need to consider bucket size and your elevation.

Al Durtschi, formerly of Walton Feed, conducted extensive testing on the amount of air in containers filled with dry foods. His studies indicate that <u>as a rule of thumb</u>, whatever the dry product stored, the usual amount of oxygen in the container (along with the food) is about 37.5%.[39] If air-dense foods like macaroni are stored, the ratio of air to food might be even greater. Conversely, if storing powdered milk, the air volume will probably be less. However, considering the amount of oxygen in ratio to the amount allowed for the oxygen scavenger, there should be plenty to cover any fluctuation. Regardless, buckets filled with food still have about ⅓ of the space taken up by oxygen. It is the oxygen scavenger's job to get rid of it.

HOW MANY DO I USE?

The next chart shows how many oxygen absorbers to use depending on container size, elevation at packing location, and oxygen absorber size.

The elevation where you're packing the foods also has a role in how many oxygen absorbers are needed. The higher you are, the thinner the air, the less oxygen absorbers are required. There is roughly 17% less oxygen at 6000 feet than at sea level, so you can use fewer scavengers. The number has already been calculated for you based on two elevation categories: 0-4000 feet (0-1219m) and 4001-7000 feet (1219.5-2134m).

To determine how many scavengers you need, locate the size container you're packing. Read across the table to the oxygen absorber size used: 200, 500 or 750cc. Where the two intersect for your elevation shows the number of oxygen absorbers required.

\multicolumn{8}{c}{HOW MANY OXYGEN ABSORBERS TO USE}
Container Size	Oxygen in Container Based on 37.5% Air Space	Absorbers Needed Using 200 cc size		Absorbers Needed Using 500 cc size		Absorbers Needed Using 750 cc size	
		Elevation 0-4000'	Elevation 4001-7000'	Elevation 0-4000'	Elevation 4001-7000'	Elevation 0-4000'	Elevation 4001-7000'
1 quart	73	1	1	1	1	1	1
1 liter	78	1	1	1	1	1	1
#10 can	256	2	1	1	1	1	1
1 gallon	294	3	2	1	1	1	1
4 liters	310	3	2	1	1	1	1
5 gallons	1469	8	7	3	2	2	2
20 liters	1553	8	7	3	2	2	2
6 gallons	1763	9	8	4	3	3	3

To determine how many scavengers you need, locate the size container you're packing. Read across the table to the oxygen absorber size being used: 200, 500 or 750cc. Where the two intersect for your elevation shows the number of oxygen absorbers required.

SHELF LIFE OF OXYGEN ABSORBERS

There are two types of oxygen absorbers. One variety contains its own moisture, which is required for the driest of dry pack canning. Oxygen absorbers need moisture to activate. If the moisture content in food isn't sufficient, the absorbers provide the amount necessary to start working. This type scavenger has a shorter shelf life of about 6 months.

The second type of oxygen absorber is for moister foods like dried fruits. This variety works more slowly since it uses only the moisture in the food to activate. Expect a shelf life of one year.

Oxygen scavengers begin absorbing as soon as they come in contact with air. When packing food, remove only the amount of oxygen absorbers needed for that session and keep the remainder in an airtight container. Absorbers containing their own activating moisture will begin doing their thing immediately upon exposure to air and will have completed their job in about 20 minutes. Using this type means working quickly. Scavengers relying completely upon moisture in food take about 2 hours, start to finish, until their absorbing capacity has been met. These are a little easier to use since they absorb over a longer period of time, but working quickly means you'll have more absorbing power working for you.

HOW TO USE OXYGEN ABSORBERS
- **Step 1** Wash and dry the food buckets. Line up the cleaned buckets and fill.
- **Step 2** Pop the needed amount of oxygen absorbers (see preceding chart) on top of the food.
- **Step 3** Snap the lid closed and it's done!
- **Step 4** Label and date the contents.

DESICCANTS – GETTING RID OF MOISTURE

Another enemy of storage is moisture. Oxygen absorbers, nitrogen flushing and dry ice remove only oxygen and have nothing to do with removing moisture. Desiccants have been used for many years in food storage and particularly in vitamin bottles, medicines and high-end electronic equipment. When using desiccants, put the individual paper packet, unopened, into the food container.

There are three main types of desiccants: silica gel, clay and molecular sieve. Silica gel is the most common variety used for packing food containers.

HOW DO THEY WORK?

Typically silica gel desiccants contain deep blue crystals. While absorbing moisture, the crystals turn pink starting at 8% of capacity. Usually they can absorb up to 40% of their weight in moisture. At this point, they need to be changed.

TO USE DESICCANTS

Step 1 Wash and dry the food buckets. Line up the cleaned buckets and fill.
Step 2 Place the desiccant into the bottom of the empty container.
Step 3 Place the food into the container directly over the desiccant.
Step 4 Use any of the four methods of oxygen removal. If using an oxygen absorber, put it on top of the food. Desiccants and oxygen absorbers do not work well in close contact.
Step 5 Secure the lid. DONE!

This chart shows what size desiccant to use.

DESICCANT REFERENCE CHART

Desiccant	Container Size	Desiccant	Container Size
5 grams	1 gallon / 4 liter	66 grams	12 gallons / 45 liter
10 grams	2 gallons / 8 liter	132 grams	19 gallons / 72 liter
16 grams	3 gallons / 11 liter	264 grams	50 gallons / 189 liter
25 grams	5 gallons / 19 liter	528 grams	100 gallons / 378 liter
33 grams	6 gallons / 23 liter		

HOW TO REGENERATE OLD DESICCANTS

To Regenerate Desiccants In The Oven

Step 1 Arrange bags on a wire tray, single layer, to allow for adequate air flow around bags during the drying process. The oven's inside temperature should be room temperature (77-85°F or 25-29°C). Only a convection, circulating or forced air type oven is recommended as seal failures may occur if any other type of oven is used.
Step 2 Allow a minimum of 1½-2 inches (3.8-5cm) air space between the top of the bags and the next metal tray above the bags. If placed in a radiating exposed infrared element type oven, shield the bags from direct exposure to the heating element, giving the closest bags a minimum of 16 inches (41cm) clearance from the heat shield. Excessive temperature due to infrared radiation will cause the plastic material to melt and/or the seals to fail. Seal failure can occur if the temperature is allowed to increase rapidly. Temperature should not increase faster than ¼ to ½ degree per minute.
Step 3 Set the temperature of the oven to approximately 245°F (118°C) and allow the desiccant bags to reach that temperature. Tyvek has a melt temperature of 250°F (121°C). Activation or reactivation of both silica gel and Bentonite clay can be achieved at temperatures as low as 220°F (104°C).
Step 4 Desiccant bags should remain in the oven at the assigned temperature for 5 hours or until the crystals have turned blue again. When finished, the bags should be immediately removed and placed in an airtight container for cooling otherwise they may re-absorb moisture during handling.
Step 5 Store in airtight container until needed.

To Regenerate Desiccants In The Microwave

This method may cause the escaping moisture to fracture the desiccant material and is not recommended as it may also damage the microwave. Use this method in an old microwave is possible.

Step 1 Empty the saturated desiccant from the desiccant bag into a microwave-safe dish.
Step 2 Place the dish into the microwave and set on the highest level for 6-8 minutes (900watt microwave or greater). When finished, remove bags immediately and place in an airtight container for cooling otherwise they may re-absorb moisture during handling.
Step 3 After desiccant has been allowed to cool in the airtight desiccator, refill the Tyvek pouches, re-seal the pouch with a heat sealer and place in an airtight, moisture-proof container. Store in airtight container until needed.

NOTE: Microwaved desiccant gets very hot.

PACKING WITH ASH

When Stan and I visited the Hopi Indians in 1996 and 1997, they shared prophecies of the not-too-distant future. One particular prophecy tells of the Sun becoming very hot forcing The People to live underground in their kivas for a time. Inside the kivas, the Hopi store food and water. Their technique for storing rice, beans and corn is pouring the grain into the food storage container and mixing it with a coating of wood ash.

Any wood will suffice that makes good ash and has not been chemically treated. Phenols in the burned woods, especially pine, act as a bacteria-inhibitor. The Hopi told us they have used this method to preserve grains for over 40 years. Two things should be remembered if you're thinking of doing this: 1) living in the desert provides naturally low humidity and 2) underground storage keep grains as cool as possible for good shelf life.

We have no way of testing this method for spoilage. If, down the track, other food preservation methods aren't available, it's something to keep in mind.

TO USE WOOD ASH

- **Step 1** Wash and dry the food buckets.
- **Step 2** Line up the cleaned buckets and fill.
- **Step 3** If you have a fireplace, gather cooled ashes to use. If no fireplace is available, build a fire outside and cool the ashes complete before using. If using new ash, make sure it has cooled at least 24 hours and check for any signs of warmth.
- **Step 4** Fill the bucket half way with food, add half of the wood ash, then the second layer of grain and the last wood ash.
- **Step 5** Secure lid and shake thoroughly to distribute ash throughout the grains.

Using the methods outlined previously, there is no reason why foods stored can't retain good nutritional value for 10-15 years if stored at correct temperatures. The exception to this is brown rice because it contains a high amount of oil. The higher the oil content, the quicker foods become rancid.

The chart below gives expected shelves when stored under optimal conditions, which extends shelf life considerably over taking no extra precautions.

GENERAL SHELF LIVES WHEN STORED HERMETICALLY AT 70°F (21°C)[40]		
Category	**Examples**	**Shelf Life**
Beans, Dry	Adzuki, Borlotti, Black, Garbanzo, Lentils, Mung, Pink, Pinto, Red, Soy	8-10 years
Dairy Powders	Cheese, Butter/Margarine, Eggs, Milk	15 years
Flours	All-purpose, Bakers, Cornmeal, Gluten, Granola, Unbleached, White, Whole Wheat	5 years
Fruits, Dehydrated	All types	5 years
Grains, Hard	Buckwheat, Corn, Flax, Kamut, Millet, Spelt, Triticale, Hard & Soft Wheat	10-12 years
Grains, Soft	Oats, Barley, Groats, Quinoa, Rye	8 years
Honey	Types with water and sugar added	Indefinite
Pasta	All types	8 – 10 years
Peanut Butter	Powdered	4-5 years
Rice, Brown	All types	Not recommended
Rice, White	All types	8-10 years
Salt and Sugar	All types	Indefinite
Seeds		4 years
TVP	All flavors	15-20 years
Vegetables, Dehydrated	Broccoli, Cabbage, Carrot, Celery, Onion, Pepper, Potato	8-10 years
Yeast	Refrigerated	5 years

NOTE: All foods should keep longer if stored at temperatures lower than 70°F (21°C). See chart on "Storage Life Depending on Constant Temperatures" earlier in this chapter.

NO SPACE? BE CREATIVE!

People in apartments are more limited in their choices, but storing supplies is not impossible. One of the first things to do is get rid of extra junk. Start in closets you've been meaning to organize and rooms you've intended to sort. For any of these treasures you can part with, have a garage sale or do eBay and put these $$ toward shelving or storable goods. Can existing storage be arranged more efficiently? Are shelves only partly filled? Could they be extended out or up? For storage problems, the follow suggestions might give you some ideas:

1. Large garbage cans and large food and water containers can double as nightstands or coffee tables with a nifty little tablecloth over the top.
2. Store goods at a friend or family member's house that has extra space.
3. Some apartment complexes have a locked storage area for their tenants.
4. Is there room on closet floors? You can line the floor of your closet with five gallon buckets. By placing a board across the top, you have a handy shelf for shoes and boots. Look for closet space above clothing rods. If shelving doesn't exist here, this area can be converted to usable storage with a trip to the hardware store. Invest in commercial closet systems. They can create an abundance of storage area from wasted space.
5. Some kitchens have cupboards with space above them. Cupboards can be modified to use these open areas.
6. RVs, 5th wheels, campers, trailers or boats might provide space in the off-season for items not subject to heat concerns.
7. Root cellars and crawl spaces are good choices providing they are free of moisture and pests.
8. Stack food storage buckets along a wall of the living room and hang a curtain in front of it.
9. Check under beds, dressers and chests for using this dead space.
10. Suspend stored water in 2-liter pop bottles from ceilings in closets.
11. Most homes have enclosed staircases, which hide valuable space. These can often be opened to make closets, niches, or even shelf space. Enclose the underside of the staircase that leads to your basement to create a storage area.
12. If your home is built with studs and drywall, you can add cabinets or shallow shelves between the studs anywhere you need them. Because they are recessed and don't project into the wall, they won't take up any space. Though these shelves will be narrow in depth, they can be used as pantry space or a second medicine cabinet, or to hold books or towels. They can also free up space in the basement or garage.
13. Dehydrated and dried foods take up less room than canned goods. Consider putting a higher percentage of these foods than their hydrated counterparts.
14. Build a small storage shed if you have a balcony or patio. Keep it sun-shielded as much as possible. These outside areas should only be used for non-perishables.
15. Do you have unused areas in the attic? Since heat rises, the higher you go in a home, the hotter it will be. Store here only items that are unaffected by heat.
16. Install over-the-door racks.
17. Choose the shortest wall in a room and hanging a curtain rod from the ceiling 2 feet from the wall. Hang an opaque wall-to-wall fabric curtain that compliments your decor to conceal this space.
18. If you have any ground on your property, bury an old freezer, refrigerator or bathtub (fit with a water-tight cover) in the ground. This area can be landscaped to disguise it. If you bury food cans, make sure these items are freeze-dried to ensure long shelf life. It won't be convenient to continually excavate and rotate them. The deeper you bury them, the more heat protection they'll have. If buried storage is used, make sure it is water- and rodent-proof.
19. Find a remote location away from prying eyes, and bury extra food supplies. Make sure the containers are properly prepared as suggested in #14.
20. As a last resort, store supplies in a temperature-controlled public storage facility. However, in a power outage, access to these supplies might be difficult as many of the facilities now have electronic gates.

WHAT IF I DON'T WANT ALL THIS HASSLE – CAN I STILL PREPARE?

ABSOLUTELY! If you are planning to keep foods for whatever purpose and rotate them on a regular basis, you'll need to be very aware of shelf lives for the cupboard, refrigerator and freezer. The following charts will help you rotate effectively.

Chapter 11: Shelf Lives

Shelf lives of grocery products are based on the packing date if no expiration date is marked. It's important to know when a particular food was packaged so you can buy the freshest items and understand when they need to be consumed.

TIPS

- Buy fresh-looking packages. Dusty cans or torn labels may indicate old stock.
- Carefully check dented cans before buying. Don't purchase bulging or rusted cans.
- Check for products at the back of the shelves for best dating.
- Make sure a deal is a deal. At a club warehouse store, they had 4 cans of cleanser strapped together for a decent, though not exceptional price. In looking at the date code, the products were 1 YEAR out of date. Though still usable, the bleach they contained would strain to do a good job.
- Buy from high traffic stores. The more product they turn, the better the expiration date is likely to be.

When purchasing products for storage, make sure to buy from a store that regularly moves its goods. The grocery store closest to us is a national chain that prices their products way higher than other retailers. It has the reputation for being "a place to stop for just a loaf of bread". Few people do "big hauls" at this location. Even though I knew this, it came home most sharply when researching food date codes.

Due to time constraints that day, I purchased brands not usually in our pantry and didn't know their dating system. One pasta company who uses closed dating (date stamping in coded numbers rather than using a readable date) had products nearly a year past expiration. Another company's sauce mix was 9 months past peak. It's conceivable since this store has trouble attracting business; they chose to pass on these old goods to the customer, regardless. With date codes unraveled for you in Chapter 12, you won't make the same mistake.

CUPBOARD STORAGE CHARTS

STAPLES – CUPBOARD		
FOOD	**SHELF LIFE 70°F (21°C)**	**STORING TIPS**
Arrowroot	2 years	Store in airtight container
Baking Powder		
(unopened)	18 months	Store dry and covered
(opened)	6 months	
Baking Soda		
(unopened)	2 years	Store dry and covered
(opened)	6 months	
Bread Crumbs, dried	6 months	Store dry and covered
Brownie Mix	12 months	Store dry and covered
Bouillon, cubes or granules	2 years	Store dry and covered
Breakfast Mix, powdered drink	6 months	Stored in covered containers or original packages.
Cake Mix	12 months	Store dry and covered
Casserole Mix		Keep cool and dry. After preparation, store refrigerated or frozen.
complete or add meat	9-12 months	
Cereal		
ready-to-eat (unopened)	6-12 months	
ready-to-eat (opened)	2-3 months	Refold package tightly
cooked	6 months	
Cereal Bars	9 months	
Chocolate	1 year	
semi-sweet	2 years	Keep all cool
unsweetened	18 months	
Cocoa Mix	8 months	
Coconut (unopened)	1 year	Store in airtight container
Coffee cans		
ground (unopened)	2 years	
ground (opened)	2 weeks	Keep tightly closed
instant (unopened)	1-2 years	
instant (opened)	2 weeks	Keep tightly closed
Coffee Whiteners, dry		
(unopened)	1-2 years	
(opened)	6 months	Keep tightly closed
Cookies		
home baked	2-3 weeks	Product can be used past this date, but may not rise to desired height
mix, boxed	18 months	
mix with nuts, boxed	12 months	
packaged	3 months	
Cornmeal	1 year	Keep tightly closed
Cornstarch & Cornflour	indefinite, if dry	Store in airtight container
Couscous	2 year	Store in airtight container
Crackers	8 months	Keep tightly closed
Eggs		
whites, powdered	1 year	
yolks, powdered	1 year	

STAPLES – CUPBOARD		
FOOD	SHELF LIFE 70°F (21°C)	STORING TIPS
Flour		
white	1 year	Store in airtight container
whole wheat	6-8 months	Refrigerate
Frosting	1 year	
canned	3 months	
mix	8 months	
Fruit, dried	18 months	
Gelatin	18 months	Store in original container
Grits	4-6 months	Store in airtight container
Imitation Bacon	4 months	Keep tightly covered; refrigerate for longer storage.
Molasses		
(unopened)	1 year	
(opened)	6 months	
Marshmallow Cream (unopened)	3-4 months	Refrigerate. Serve at room temp.
Marshmallows	3 months	
Milk		
condensed or evaporated (unopened)	15 months	Invert cans every 2 months
condensed or evaporated (opened)	1 week	Refrigerate after opening
nonfat dry (unopened)	6-24 months	
nonfat dry (opened)	3 months	Store in airtight container
soy (unopened)	1 year	
UHT	6 months	
Muffin Mix	18 months	Product can be used past this date, but may not rise to desired height
with nuts	12 months	
Oil, Vegetable		After this time, color or flavor may be affected, but product is still generally safe to consume.
(opened)	2 years	
(unopened)	1 year	
Olive Oil	6-9 months	Store away from light
Pancake Mix	6-9 months	Store in airtight container
Pasta		
egg noodles	2 years	
garlic and herb products	2 years	Store in airtight container
oven ready	1 year	
spaghetti, macaroni, etc.	3 years	
vegetable-containing	18 months	
Peanut Butter	9 months	
Pectin		
dry (opened)	1 year	Refrigerate
dry (unopened)	1 year	Store in airtight container
liquid (opened)	1 month	Refrigerate
liquid (unopened)	1 year	Refrigerate
Peppers, canned or pickled	1 year	
Pickles	18 months	Refrigerate after opening
Piecrust Mix	8 months	Keep cool and dry
Popcorn		
popped	2-3 months	
unpopped	3 years	

STAPLES – CUPBOARD

FOOD	SHELF LIFE 70°F (21°C)	STORING TIPS
Potato Flakes	18 months	
Pudding Mix	1 year	Keep cool and dry
Rice		
white	2 years	
brown	1 year	Keep all tightly closed
flavored or herb	6 months	
Salt		
iodized, sea, rock, canning	Indefinitely	
seasoned	2 years	
Shortening, solid, Crisco		No refrigeration, even after opening, but keep cool and tightly covered. Crisco suggests that though its solid product has an indefinite shelf life, once opened, it's best when used within one year, but can be used longer with no odor or taste present.
original or butter (unopened)	2 years	
original or butter (opened)	1 year	
sticks (unopened)	2 years	
sticks (opened)	6 months	
Stuffing Mix	6 months	
Soft Drinks		
regular	9 months	
diet	3 months	
Soup Mix	1 year	Keep cool and dry
Sugar		
brown	4 months	Store in airtight container
confectioners or icing	18 months	Store in airtight container
granulated	2 years	Cover tightly
artificial sweeteners	2 years	Cover tightly
Tea		
bags	18 months	Store in airtight container
instant	3 years	Cover tightly
loose	2 years	Store in airtight container
Toaster Pastry	2-3 months	Store in airtight container
Vinegar		
apple cider	18 months	
distilled white	42 months	Keep tightly closed. Cloudy appearance doesn't affect quality.
malt	24 months	
salad	42 months	
tarragon	30 months	
wine	42 months	
Yeast, dry	2 years	Freeze to extend shelf life

SAUCES & CONDIMENTS (ROOM TEMP OR REFRIGERATED)

FOOD	SHELF LIFE 70°F (21°C)	STORING TIPS
BBQ Sauce		
Bull's-eye	1 year	
KC Masterpiece (opened)	9 months	Refrigerate all after opening
Fountain	2 years	
Chili Sauce	2 years	
Chocolate Syrup		
(unopened)	2 years	
(opened)	6 months	Refrigerate
Cocktail Sauce	18 months	
Gravy and Broth		
leftover	2 days	Keep covered in fridge.
mixes	18 months	

SAUCES & CONDIMENTS (ROOM TEMP OR REFRIGERATED)

FOOD	SHELF LIFE 70°F (21°C)	STORING TIPS
Honey	1 year	Cover tightly. If crystallized, warm jar in hot water.
Horseradish Sauce	1 year	
Jelly, Jam, Preserves		
(unopened)	18 months	
(opened)	6 months	Store refrigerated
Ketchup		After these times, color or flavor may be affected, but product is still generally safe to consume.
(unopened)	1 year	
(opened)	6 months	
Lemon Juice	1 year	Refrigerate after opening
Lime Juice	1 year	Refrigerate after opening
Molasses		
(unopened)	1 year	
(opened)	6 months	
Mayonnaise		
(unopened)	6 months	
(opened)	2 months	Refrigerate after opening
Marinades		
KC Masterpiece (opened)	5 months	
Mustard	2 years	
Relish	2 years	
Salad Dressing		
bottled (unopened)	10-12 months	Store on shelf
bottled (opened)	3 months	Refrigerate after opening
made from mix	2 weeks	Refrigerate, after mixing
Salad Oil		
(unopened)	1 year	Store on shelf
(opened)	1-3 months	Refrigerate, after opening
Sauce, packaged, dry	2 years	
Smoke Sauce	2 years	Due to low pH, product may be used up to 4 yrs
Soy sauce		
(unopened)	2 years	
(opened)	3 months	
Spaghetti Sauce	18 months	
Steak Sauce		
A-1	1 year	
Heinz 57	30 months	
Syrup		
Pure Maple	3 years	Refrigerate after opening
Pure Maple, sugar-free	1 year	
Taco Sauce	2 years	
Tartar Sauce	1 year	Refrigerate after opening
Tomato Sauce or Paste	2 years	
Worcestershire Sauce	indefinite	

FRUITS – FRESH (ROOM TEMP & REFRIGERATED)

FOOD	SHELF LIFE	STORING TIPS
Apples	1-3 weeks	Discard bruised or decayed fruit. Don't wash before storing – moisture encourages spoilage. Store in crisper or moisture resistant bag.
Avocadoes	2-3 days (after ripening)	Store unripened avocados at room temp; ripe avocados in the fridge.
Bananas	2-3 days (after ripening)	Best stored at room temp. When refrigerated, skins turn black but fruit isn't damaged.
Berries, Cherries	2-3 days	Discard bruised or decayed fruit. Don't wash before storing – moisture encourages spoilage. Store in crisper or moisture resistant bag.
Canned, opened	3-7 days	Store in airtight container, not in opened can.
Citrus Fruit	3 weeks	Discard bruised or decayed fruit. Don't wash before storing – moisture encourages spoilage. Store in crisper or moisture resistant bag.
Cranberries	3-4 weeks	Place in airtight bag or keep in original package. Clean just before use.
Grapefruit	2-3 weeks	Can be stored at room temp but will stay fresh longer stored in the fridge.
Grapes	1-2 weeks	Store in perforated bag or in a bowl. Extend storage time by placing in a sealed bag and keep in the salad crisper drawer of the fridge.
Juice, bottled or canned	1 week	Transfer canned juice to glass or plastic container if not used up in one day.
Kiwi Fruit	6-8 days / 2-3 days	Refrigerated / Room temperature
Lemons	2-5 weeks	Can be stored at room temp. Stays fresh longer stored uncovered in the fridge. Keep fruit from touching.
Limes	1-3 weeks	Put in plastic bag and refrigerated
Melons	1 week	Ripen at room temp, then refrigerate uncut fruit wrapped to prevent odor spreading to other foods.
Oranges	2-3 weeks	Can be stored at room temp, but stays fresh longer stored in the refrigerator. Place in a plastic bag and refrigerate.
Peaches	2-3 days	Ripen at room temp. To speed ripening, place in a loosely closed paper bag. They're ripe when they yield to slight pressure and have a sweet smell. Refrigerate when ripe.
Pears	10-14 days	Ripen at room temp, then store in coldest part of refrigerator.
Pineapple	3-5 days	Store at room temp, then refrigerate.
Plum	2-3 days	Store in fridge.
Rhubarb	1-2 weeks	Cut leaves from stalks and store in a plastic bag or wrapped in plastic.
Tangerine	1 week	Store in fridge.
Watermelon	6-8 days	Uncut watermelon can be stored at room temp for a few days. Store cut sections wrapped with plastic wrap in the refrigerator.

REFRIGERATOR STORAGE CHARTS

VEGETABLES – FRESH (REFRIGERATOR)		
FOOD	SHELF LIFE 37°F, 3°C	STORING TIPS
Asparagus	3-5 days	Don't wash, wrap in paper towel, place in plastic bag, or place upright in a jar or glass containing ½ inch cold water.
Beans, Green or Wax	1-2 days	Keep moist.
Beans, Lima	3-6 days	Shell and store in a perforated plastic bag
Beans, Snap	3-6 days	Leave beans whole, unwashed. Store in perforated plastic bag in warmest area of fridge.
Beets	1-2 weeks	Leave roots. Trim stems to 1-2. Don't wash. Allow to dry in shady area. Place in a plastic bag with a moist paper towel. Check weekly.
Broccoli	5-7 days	Store in perforated plastic bag.
Brussel Sprouts	2-3 weeks	Trim damaged leaves. Store in perforated bag.
Cabbage	4-8 weeks	Remove loose leaves from outer surface. Place cabbage head in plastic bag.
Carrots	1-3 months	Trim tops, leaving ½-1 inch. Clean dirt from roots. Wrap in paper towel. Place in plastic bag or perforated plastic bag.
Cauliflower	10-14 days	Don't wash and place in plastic bag.
Celery	1-2 weeks	Wrap in damp paper towel, then wrap all with aluminum foil.
Corn, Sweet	1-2 days	Refrigerate with husks on.
Cucumber	10-12 days	Wrap in plastic.
Endive	2-3 weeks	Wash thoroughly, shake to remove excess moisture. Gather leaves together and tie. Place tied head in a plastic bag. Discard outer leaves as they wilt but inner leaves will still be good and crisp.
Fennel	6-7 days	Store in plastic bag.
Kale	7-10 days	Remove as much moisture as possible by blotting with a paper towel. Store in a loosely sealed or perforated plastic bag
Kohlrabi	2-3 weeks	Trim roots and stems. Place in loosely sealed or perforated plastic bag.
Leeks		Remove excess moisture by blotting with a paper towel. Place in plastic bag or wrap with plastic.
Lettuce, Head (washed, thoroughly drained)	10-12 days	Store away from other vegetables and fruits to prevent russet spotting.
Lettuce, Leaf and Bibb	10-12 days	Wash leaves. Dry in salad spinner or by shaking off excess water. Layer leaves between paper towels and place in a plastic bag.
Mushrooms	2-3 days	Do not wash before storing. Place in single layer on plate. Cover loosely with a damp paper towel or in paper bag. Leaving bag open.
Okra	5-7 days	Store in plastic bag in warmest area of the refrigerator.
Onions	1-3 months	Be sure onions are dry. Store in mesh bag or basket; must have good air circulation.
Parsnips	1-2 months	Be sure leaves have been trimmed and store parsnips in perforated plastic bag.

VEGETABLES – FRESH (REFRIGERATOR)		
FOOD	SHELF LIFE 37°F, 3°C	STORING TIPS
Peas, unshelled	5-6 days	Store in perforated plastic bag. Shelled peas can be stored in a regular plastic bag.
Peppers	1-2 weeks	Don't wash. Wrap in paper towel. Don't use a plastic bag. Store in the vegetable compartment of the refrigerator.
Potatoes, Sweet	2-4 month	Place in well-ventilated basket. Store in cool (55°-60°F), moist area with good ventilation. Don't refrigerate. If potatoes are harvested from your garden, cure by setting in a warm, dark place for one week before storing them. This will toughen skins and sweeten potato.
Potatoes, White	2-4 month	Place in a well-ventilated box or basket and store in a dark, cool (40°F best), moist area with good ventilation. Don't refrigerate and don't store in plastic bags. If potatoes are harvested from your garden, they must cure in a warm, dark place for about one week before storing. This will help toughen the skins and store longer.
Radishes	2-3 weeks	Trim off leaves. Place in loosely plastic bag. Wash. Trim roots just before using.
Salad Greens	1-2 days	Keep in moisture resistant wrap or bag.
Shredded Cabbage	1-2 days	Keep in moisture resistant wrap or bag.
Spinach	3-5 days	Remove damaged leaves, wash thoroughly with cold water. Drain well. Wrap with paper towels and store in a plastic bag.
Squash, Summer	1 week	Store in perforated plastic bag. Don't wash until ready to use.
Squash, Winter	2-3 months	Store whole, in cool, dry place. Don't wash till ready to use. If cut, store wrapped in plastic. Refrigerate up to 1 week. If whole squash is properly cured in the sun (at 70°-80° F) for 10 days, it will extend storage time.
Swiss Chard	2-4 days	Store unwashed in an open or perforated plastic bag. If leaves are damp, pat dry with paper towel before placing in plastic bag.
Tomatoes, green	2-5 weeks	Wrap individually in newspaper. Store with stems down at room temperature. Can be placed in a deep box in 1-2 layers, unwrapped. Allow for adequate air circulation. Avoid exposure to temperatures below 50°F. Check weekly for ripeness.
Tomatoes, ripe	5-7 days	Ripen tomatoes at room temperature away from direct sunlight; then refrigerate.
Turnips	1-3 weeks	Leave unwashed and trim leaves off. Store in a perforated bag.
Vegetables, canned (opened)	2-3 days	Store in glass or plastic container. taste.

MEAT, FISH, AND POULTRY- FRESH, UNCOOKED (REFRIGERATOR)

FOOD	SHELF LIFE 37°F, 3°C	STORING TIPS
Beef, Lamb, Pork, Veal		*All meat, poultry, and fish – When bought in plastic wrappings (from self-serve counters), store in these packages. If not purchased from self-serve counters, remove from package and wrap loosely in waxed paper. This allows surface to dry; dry surface retards bacterial growth. (Reason for difference: Many shoppers have handled meat packages in self-serve counters. Opening these before storage provides opportunity for contamination, which more than offsets merits of "dry surface".)
chops	3-5 days	
ground meat	1-2 days	
roasts	2-4 days	
steaks	3-5 days	
stew meat	1-2 days	
variety meats (liver, heart, etc.)	1-2 days	
Chicken & Turkey		
whole, pieces or ground	2 days	
Duck & Goose		
whole and pieces	2 days	
Fish and Shellfish:		
cooked	3-4 days	See *All meat, poultry, and fish storing tip above
smoked	2 weeks	
steaks and fillets, fresh	1 day	
Giblets	2 days	
Sausage, Pork	1-2 days	
Seafood, shucked		See *All meat, poultry, and fish storing tip above
clams, oysters, scallops, shrimp	1-2 day	Store in coldest part of fridge.
Seafood, in shell		
clams, oysters, scallops, shrimp	2 days	See *All meat, poultry, and fish storing tip above.
Tofu	4-5 days	

CURED AND SMOKED MEATS (REFRIGERATOR)

FOOD	SHELF LIFE 37°F, 3°C	STORING TIPS
Bacon	7 days	
Bologna Loaves, Liverwurst	4-6 days	
Corned Beef	5-7 days	
Dried Beef	10-12 days	
Frankfurters		
(opened)	7 days	
(unopened)	14 days	
Ham		
whole	1 week	* Keep wrapped. Store in coldest part of refrigerator or in meat keeper.
canned (unopened)	6-9 months	
Liver Sausage	4-5 days	
Luncheon Meat		
(opened)	5 days	
(unopened)	14 days	
Pepperoni, sliced	2-3 weeks	
Sausages, dry and semi-dry (Salami, etc.)	2-3 weeks	
Sausage, fresh and smoked	7 days	
Summer sausage		
(opened)	3 weeks	
(unopened)	3 months	

DAIRY PRODUCTS (REFRIGERATOR)

FOOD	SHELF LIFE 37°F, 3°C	STORING TIPS
Butter or Margarine	2-3 months	Store in moisture-proof container or wrap.
Butter or Margarine, whipped	2-3 months	Do not freeze. Product will separate
Buttermilk	1-2 weeks	Check date on carton. Will keep several days after date.
Cheese		
cottage & ricotta	5-7 days	
soft: Camembert	3-4 days	
hard: Cheddar, Edam, Gouda, Swiss, Brick, Mozzarella	2-3 months	Keep all tightly wrapped
Parmesan & Romano (grated)	1 year	
processed (loaf, slices)	1 month	
Roquefort & Blue	2-3 weeks	
spread & dips	1-2 weeks	
Cream		
light, heavy, half-and-half	3 days	Heavy cream may not whip after thawing; use for cooking. Thaw in refrigerator.
whipped	1 days	
Dip, Sour Cream		
commercial	2 weeks	
homemade	3-4 days	
Eggs		
egg dish, cooked	3-4 days	
hard-boiled	2 weeks	Do not freeze. Store in covered container
in-shell	4-5 weeks	Do not freeze.
Eggs *		For sweet dishes, mix each cup yolks with 1 Tbsp corn syrup or sugar. For other cooking, substitute ½ tsp salt for sugar.
whites, raw	2-4 days	
yolks, raw	2-4 days	
Milk		
evaporated (opened)	3-5 days	
fluid whole or low-fat	1 week	
reconstituted, nonfat, dry	1 week	
sweetened condensed (opened)	3-5 days	
soy (opened)	7-10 days	
soy (unopened)	84 days	
Sour Cream	1 month	Do not freeze; it will separate.
Whipped Topping		
in aerosol can	3 weeks	
prepared from mix	3 days	
frozen carton (after thawing)	2 weeks	
Yogurt	3 weeks	

* NOTE: If the egg carton has an expiration date printed on it, such as "EXP May 1," be sure that the date has not passed when the eggs are purchased. That is the last day the store may sell the eggs as fresh.

On eggs that have a Federal grade mark, such as Grade AA, the date cannot be more than 30 days from the date the eggs were packed into the carton. As long as you purchase a carton of eggs before the date expires, you should be able to use all the eggs safely in three to five weeks after the date of purchase.

BAKED GOODS (REFRIGERATOR)

FOOD	SHELF LIFE 37°F, 3°C	STORING TIPS
Bread, baked	1 week	
Cake, baked, with cream filled, whipped topping or cream cheese frosting	3-4 days	
Cookies, home made containing cream cheese or cream filled	3-5 days	
dough	4-5 days	
Pie		
chiffon & pumpkin	2-3 days	
custard, cream & meringue	2-3 days	Do not freeze custard, cream or meringue pies. Keep refrigerated.
fruit, baked	3-4 days	
fruit, unbaked	1-2 days	
Puddings & Custards (opened)	1-2 days	Keep covered.
Refrigerated Biscuits, Rolls, Cookie Dough, Pastries	Expiration date on label.	Don't store in refrigerator door; temperature fluctuation and jarring lower quality.

FREEZER STORAGE CHARTS

FISH (FILETS AND STEAKS) – HOME FROZEN OR PURCHASED FROZEN		
FOOD	SHELF LIFE 0°F, -18°C	STORING TIPS
Bluefish, Mackerel, Salmon	2-3 months	
Clams	6 months	
Cooked Fish or Seafood	3 months	
Fillets		
Cod, Flounder, Haddock, Sole	4-6 months	
Mullet, Ocean Perch, Sea Perch, Sea Trout, Striped Bass	3 months	All Meats – Check for holes in trays and plastic wrap of fresh meat. If none, freeze in this wrap up to two weeks. For longer storage, overwrap with freezer wrap. Put two layers of waxed paper between individual hamburger patties. Keep purchased frozen fish in original wrapping; thaw; follow cooking directions on label.
Fish		
breaded	3 months	
smoked		
King Crab	10 months	
Lobster Tails	3 months	
Oysters	4 months	
Scallops	3 months	
Seafood		
in the shell	3-6 months	
shucked	3-4 months	
Shrimp, uncooked	12 months	

MEAT – HOME FROZEN

FOOD	SHELF LIFE 0°F, -18°C	STORING TIPS
Bacon	1-2 months	Freezing cured meats not recommended. Saltiness encourages rancidity.
Corned Beef	1 month	Freezing cured meats not recommended. Saltiness encourages rancidity.
Frankfurters (open or unopened)	1-2 months	Freeze with caution. Emulsion may be broken, and product will "weep".
Game Birds	8-12 months	
Ground Beef, Lamb, Veal	2-3 months	
Ground Pork	1-2 months	
Ham & Picnic Cured		
whole	1-2 months	
half or slices	1-2 months	Freeze with caution. Saltiness encourages rancidity.
canned, opened	1-2 months	
Luncheon Meat (open or unopened)	1-2 months	Freezing not recommended. Emulsion may be broken, and product will "weep".
Rabbit & Squirrel	12 months	
Roasts		
beef	6-12 months	
lamb	6-9 months	
pork	3-6 months	
veal	6-9 months	
Sausage, dry, smoked	1-2 months	Freezing alters flavor.
Sausage, fresh, unsalted	1-2 months	
Steaks & Chops		
beef	6-12 months	
lamb	6-9 months	
pork	3-6 months	
veal	6-9 months	
Tofu	6-8 weeks	
Venison	8-12 months	

All Meats – Check for holes in trays and plastic wrap of fresh meat. If none, freeze in this wrap up to two weeks. For longer storage, overwrap with suitable freezer wrap. Put two layers of waxed paper between individual hamburger patties.

POULTRY – HOME FROZEN OR PURCHASED FROZEN

FOOD	SHELF LIFE 0°F, -18°C	STORING TIPS
Chicken Livers	3 months	
Chicken & Turkey		
whole	1 year	All Meats – Check for holes in trays and plastic wrap of fresh meat. If none, freeze in this wrap up to two weeks. For longer storage, overwrap with suitable freezer wrap. Put two layers of waxed paper between individual hamburger patties.
cut-up	10 months	
Duck & Goose	6 months	
Giblets	3-4 months	
Ground Turkey	3-4 months	
Poultry pieces, cooked		
chicken nuggets	1-3 months	
fried	3-4 months	
pieces without broth	2-4 months	

MAIN DISHES – PURCHASED FROZEN

FOOD	SHELF LIFE 0°F, -18°C	STORING TIPS
Bread	3 months	*Packaged foods tightly in foil, moisture vapor-proof plastic wrap, freezer wrap or water-tight freezer containers. For casseroles, allow head room for expansion.
Cake	3 months	
Casseroles, Meat, Fish, Poultry	3 months	
Cookies, baked and dough	3 months	
Dinners & Entrees	3-4 months	Keep frozen till used
Nuts		
salted	6-8 months	*See Packaged food comment above
unsalted	9-12 months	
Pies, unbaked fruit	8 months	*See Packaged food comment above

BAKED GOODS – HOME FROZEN OR PURCHASED FROZEN

FOOD	SHELF LIFE 0°F, -18°C	STORING TIPS
Bread		
baked	3 months	
unbaked	1 month	
Cake, baked, frosted	1 month	
Cake, baked, unfrosted	2-4 months	
angel food	6-12 months	
chiffon, sponge	2-3 months	
cheese cake	2-3 months	
chocolate	4 months	
fruit cake	1 year	
yellow or pound	6 months	Freezing does not freshen baked goods. It can only maintain the quality and freshness the food had before freezing.
Cookies		
baked	8-12 months	
containing cream cheese or cream filled	3 months	
dough	2-3 months	
Muffins, baked	1 year	
Pie		
chiffon, pumpkin	2 months	
fruit, baked	6-8 months	
fruit, unbaked	2-4 months	
Quick Bread, baked	2-3 months	
Rolls, partially baked	2-3 months	
Waffles	1 month	
Yeast Bread & Rolls, baked	3-6 months	

VEGETABLES – HOME FROZEN OR PURCHASED FROZEN

FOOD	SHELF LIFE 0°F, -18°C	STORING TIPS
Home Frozen	10 months	Cabbage, celery, salad greens, and tomatoes do not freeze well.
Purchased Frozen cartons, plastic bags or boil-in-bags	8 months	Cabbage, celery, salad greens, and tomatoes do not freeze well.
Rice, cooked	2 months	Remove excess air from container to avoid freeze burn

FRUITS – HOME FROZEN OR PURCHASED FROZEN

FOOD	SHELF LIFE 0°F, -18°C	STORING TIPS
Berries, Cherries, Peaches, Pears, Pineapple, etc.	1 year	Freeze in moisture-proof container.
Citrus Fruit and Juice frozen at home	6 months	
Fruit Juice Concentrate	1 year	

DAIRY PRODUCTS – HOME FROZEN

FOOD	SHELF LIFE 0°F, -18°C	STORING TIPS
Butter	6-9 months	Store in moisture-proof container or wrap. Thaw in refrigerator.
Buttermilk	1 month	If frozen, may separate; shake thoroughly.
Cheese		
soft: Camembert	3 months	Thaw in refrigerator.
hard: Cheddar, Edam, Gouda, Swiss, Brick, etc.	6-8 weeks	Freeze in small pieces; If frozen, may show mottled color due to surface moisture.
processed: (loaf, slices)	4 months	Thaw in refrigerator.
Roquefort, Blue	3 months	Becomes crumbly after thawing; still good for salads and melting.
spread & dips	1 month	
wax-coated	6-8 months	
Cream		Heavy cream may not whip after thawing; use for cooking. Thaw in refrigerator.
light, heavy, half-and-half	2 months	
Cream, whipped	1 month	Make whipped cream dollops; freeze firm. Place in plastic bag or carton; seal; store in freezer. To thaw, place on top of dessert.

The preceding charts on food storage in various environments were adapted from Extension materials produced by Kansas State University, Michigan State University, and Ohio State University and Hormel Foods.

TRUE MILITARY MREs – (3 yr. shelf life according to the military)[41]

Temperature	Months	Temperature	Months	Temperature	Months	Temperature	Months
120°F (49°C)	1	100°F (38°C)	6	80°F (27°C)	36	60°F (32°C)	48
110°F (43°C)	2	90°F (32°C)	18	70°F (21°C)	40	<50°F (<10°C)	50

CIVILIAN MREs (3-5 yr. shelf life)[42]

Temperature	Months	Temperature	Months	Temperature	Months	Temperature	Months
120°F (49°C)	1	100°F (38°C)	18	80°F (27°C)	48	60°F (32°C)	84
110°F (43°C)	5	90°F (32°C)	30	70°F (21°C)	66	<50°F (<10°C)	96

For *maximum* nutrition, MREs have a shelf life of about 3 years when stored at less than 85°F. The U.S. government requires MREs to 'maintain high quality for a minimum of 3 years at 80°F and 6 months at 100°F'.[43]

MRE shelf lives above rely on *constant* temperatures. Effects of temperatures are cumulative so MREs stored at 100°F for just 9 months lose half of their shelf life. If these MREs are moved to a 70°F (21°C) environment they'd have 33 months remaining, not 66. MREs should not be stored at 25-30°F (-4 to -1°C) due to reduced quality and freezing isn't recommended. The Civilian MRE shelf life is 3-5 years. The extended shelf life in the table above represents 'acceptable taste' only, not highest nutrition.

Look for MREs under these names: APack (Ameriqual) **www.ameriqual.com**, EverSafe (Wornick) **wornick.com,** MRE Depot **www.mredepot.com**, MRE Star (International Meals Supply) **www.mre-meals.net** and Sure-Pak (Sopaco) **www.sopakco.com**.

Chapter 12: Unraveling Dating Codes

DATING REQUIREMENTS

Except for infant formula and some baby food, product dating is not required by Federal regulation in the U.S. However, if a calendar date is used, it must show both the month and day of the month (and the year, in the case of shelf-stable and frozen products). If a calendar date is given, immediately next to it must be a phrase explaining the meaning such as "sell by" or "use before."

There is no uniform or universally accepted system used for food dating in the U.S. Food freshness dating is required by more than 20 states, but other areas have almost none.[44]

Canada only requires dating for foods whose "durable life" is 90 days or less, which is generally expressed as a number of days. Fresh meat, fish and poultry, must be labeled with a "packaged on" date and durable life information or with a best before date. Fresh fruit and vegetables, donuts and some restaurant and vending machine products aren't required to carry either a best before date or durable life information.[45]

Australia, a country with some of the strictest import regulations, does not require date stamping if a product has a shelf life of at least two years.

These rules, or lack of laws, leave a LOT of gray area for the consumer to wonder about food freshness.

TYPES OF FOOD DATING

Sell-by or pull-by date: How long the product should remain on a seller's shelf. Buy items on or before this date and use fairly quickly, especially fresh meat. However, other items remain edible after this date.

Use-by date: A recommendation from the manufacturer; the product's peak quality is guaranteed up to that date. Pantry products with use-by dates may remain useable after this date.

Expiration date: The last date a product should be sold. Product may or may not be good for quite a while longer.

Best By date: Similar to an expiration date; indicates that product quality may decrease after that date. Product may be useable for much longer.

Manufacture or Production date: When the item was made or produced. This information is the product date code, which is stamped or embossed on the package. The code is a series of letters and/or numbers roughly based on Julian dating that indicate the day, month and/or year. Manufacturers use their own coding systems so it generally requires a call to the company or visit to their web sites to decipher.

Pack date: When the item was packaged. This information is the product date code based on the same format as for the Manufacture or Production date.

SNEAKY DATING VS OPEN DATING

OK, maybe it's not fair to think manufacturers are trying to pull one over on us, but it's hard to think of a nice rationale why freshness dating has to be secret. Not only does it protect the consumer, but also truly helps the manufacturer.

Think about this. Someone tries a product that's new to him but its peak freshness has passed by nine months. He doesn't become sick, but something's not quite right. Maybe the flavor is bland or the color is a little brownish or dull. With so many choices on our shelves, who has to settle for that? The consumer will remember his not-too-terrific experience and choose another brand next shopping trip.

There is a trend for manufacturers to convert to an Open Dating system, which stamps the date on a package in PLAIN ENGLISH. *Kudos to those companies!* Not only kudos, but also we support those companies with our purchases rather than companies that hold these dates tighter than bark on hickory. Whenever the occasion arises to phone a company, I make it a point to give them raves if

1) They use open dating;
2) *Willingly* share their date code information;
3) Upload this information in an FAQ (Frequently Asked Questions) file on their website;
4) Provide a toll-free number to obtain #2.

You'd be amazed how far a little praise goes. It certainly encourages them to continue being open with their customers.

NEW NEWS IS OLD NEWS

In addition to companies using indecipherable dating, they often change coding every few years to further confuse the consumer. Nothing's changed – more sneakiness. Most of the date codings found in the 1999 edition of *Dare To Prepare* are obsolete. It's important to keep on top of these changes or you may be purchasing old product.

INFORMATION FORT KNOX

When calling companies for date code deciphering, one food line that nearly skunked me was tuna. Understanding their codes was like cracking Chinese with one exception: Starkist. BIG kudos to Starkist for coming out of the closet and openly marking products with a "Best By" date.

Two fish companies were extremely cagey with their dating information. There was no way to take a stab at the date. It followed no known pattern. On one company's web site, it answered the question *How do you read the code on your products?* like this: "Each packer considers this information strictly confidential and, for this reason, we cannot share the code breakdown. Code information is available from our Consumer Affairs department."

Blarney! Tuna is tuna. They're not guarding a national treasure or sacred recipe.

I played the game and went to their Consumer Affairs department. (Mind you, there was not a telephone number anywhere on their web site – toll-free or otherwise.) Once in the Consumer area, I had to supply the following personal information:

- full name
- street address, city, state, zip code
- email (though they state the answer will likely arrive via snail mail)
- code number for size of the container
- product as described on label
- UPC / bar code number
- place of purchase

IF this company truly wanted to help, customer service only needed the indecipherable code. Period. All I received from Consumer Affairs was what the code meant, NOT how to understand it. I will no longer buy their tuna or salmon or any product this $400+ million company sells.

Another fish company, Bumble Bee, began converting their tuna and salmon coding to Open Dating in 2004. Thank you Bumble Bee! I called their customer service (which does have a 1.800 number) and thanked them profusely for this customer courtesy!

MOVE IT OR LOSE IT

Fish companies were the only difficult industry encountered. As a rule, larger companies more frequently date their products in plain English. This might be due to having more funds to invest in date stamping equipment. Or, it could be that large companies turn more stock and aren't worried they'll be left with old product. Imagine what it would do to a small company's bottom line if it couldn't sell foods before expiration and had to "eat" the losses.

If you purchase undated products, be sure to note on their labels when you bought them. Then refer to the shelf life charts in Chapter 11.

The drawback of having no manufacturer date is the "guess factor". There is no way to know how long the food sat in a distribution warehouse, or in *multiple* warehouses, or on the grocer's shelf before you purchased it.

UNDERSTANDING DATING METHODS

Companies who mark their products with a "Use By", "Best By" or an expiration date stamped in plain English make understanding "dead" dates much easier. Sill many manufacturers mysteriously code this most necessary information for reasons known only to them. Customers could be forgiven thinking this was to keep them intentionally in the dark so they could purchase outdated and nearly expired products.

To complicate matters, some countries and products do not require a date stamp if it meets certain government specifications. It is up to the public to know what those time frames are.

For example, in Australia, if a product has a shelf life of two years or longer, the manufacturer isn't required to include it on packaging. Additionally, manufacturers assume food will be consumed fairly shortly after purchase. They further assume it hasn't stayed in a distribution center or a grocer's shelf for a long time. That's a lot of assuming.

You'll find that on most medicines and first aid items, manufacturers don't play this game. If people became seriously ill after taking expired products, lawsuits might follow. However, with foods consequences aren't likely to be so extreme and there IS the corporate bottom line to consider! It's more obvious when meat has gone off, but pills, well, they just look like pills. The eye can't tell if they're still effective.

Manufacturers date or code products somewhere on the packaging. Many codes contain information not pertinent to shelf life like plant location, production line, time of labeling, batch number or contents.

Though deciphering freshness coding can be a real challenge, there are a few standard methods that are pretty easy to sort out. For that which remains "Greek", their secret coding is revealed on the following pages. Shelf lives unraveled below are for unopened products only.

As a general rule, canned goods are fresh at least two years after date of packing (DOP) unless otherwise specified. For specific food listings, see the Shelf Life Charts in Chapter 11 as individual foods can vary a great deal.

In spite of stated shelf life, many foods are still OK to consume after the stamped expiration date as long as the can is intact. This means the can must show no sign of rust or bulging, and there is no mold inside. However, using foods long after the expiration date means the nutritional value will have degraded and possibly the taste, color and texture. Generally speaking, tomato or other acid-based foods have a shorter shelf life. Since we eat food to fuel the body, there's no point in giving it "dead" nutrition.

In the following pages, food companies' phone number is noted where possible. Julian Date means the days of the year are numbered consecutively starting with January 1st = 001 on through December 31 which will either be 365 or 366. At the end of this chapter is a Conversion Calendar for your convenience.

COMPANY AND PRODUCT "SECRETS"

409 ALL PURPOSE CLEANER & 409 OXI MAGIC (see CLOROX)
SHELF LIFE: 1 year

ACCENT 1.973.401.6500
First five digits for date of production
Position 1 and 2: DAY
Position 3 and 4: MONTH
Position 5: YEAR
Position 6: plant info
Example: 15014 P (January 14, 2004)
SHELF LIFE: 5 years. Can be safely consumed thereafter, but flavor may be degraded.

ACT II POPCORN
Date of production
Position 1: ignore
Position 2: YEAR
Position 3-5: JULIAN DATE
Example: B8119 (April 29, 2004)
SHELF LIFE: 1 year

ADMIRAL 03.9764.3622 (Australia)
First six digits of second line for date of production
Position 1 and 2: YEAR
Position 3 and 4: MONTH
Position 5 and 6: DAY
Example: 040211 = February 11, 2004
SHELF LIFE: acidic (tomato based) and fruit products 2 years. Mushrooms, officially 2 years, but may be consumed for several years thereafter as long as can is intact.

AJAX 1.800.338.8388
First five digits of second line for date of manufacture
Position 1 and 2: YEAR
Position 3, 4 and 5: JULIAN DATE
Position 6-11: production information
Example: 06091US9214 (April 1, 2006)
SHELF LIFE: 3 years

AMERICAN BEAUTY 1.800.730.5957 **(See NEW WORLD PASTA)**
First four digits for date of production
American Beauty uses two dating systems, however, all products are being converted to the first example.
Method 1:
Position 1: YEAR
Position 2, 3 and 4: JULIAN DATE
Position 5, 6 and 7: production information
Example: 4022MA (January 22, 2004)

Method 2:
Position 1: YEAR
Position 2 and 3: MONTH
Position 4 and 5: DAY
Position 6, 7 and 8: production information
Example: 40122MA (January 22, 2004)
SHELF LIFE: 3 years for regular pasta, 2 years for egg noodle and 1 year for the oven-ready.

ARGO CORNSTARCH 1.866.373.2300
First four digits for date of production
Position 1, 2 and 3: JULIAN DATE
Position 4: plant location
Position 5: YEAR
Example: 345D3 (December 11, 2003)
SHELF LIFE: Indefinite if it's kept dry.

ARMOUR STAR 1.800.528.0849
Vienna Sausage, Stew, Chili, Spreads, Treet, Potted Meat, Slice Dried Beef, Soups, and Lunch Bucket
Method 1:
Position 1 and 2: "PP" is the Product Plant
Position 3: YEAR
Position 4: MONTH A=Jan, B=Feb, C=Mar, etc.
Position 5 and 6: DAY
Position 7, 8, 9 and 10: time of production in Military form
Example: PP6A0610:30 (January 6, 2006, at 10:30 AM)

Method 2 (Original Coding):
Position 1: MONTH A=Jan, B=Feb, C=Mar, D-April, etc.
Position 2 and 3: DAY
Position 4: YEAR
Example: D056C23 (April 5, 2006)   ignore the last 3 digits of the code
SHELF LIFE: At least 2 years, though Armour states on the website that as long as cans aren't bulging and the seal is intact, products store indefinitely and can be consumed though flavor may be a bit degraded.

AUNT NELLIE'S VEGETABLES 1.315.926.8100
First two digits are date of production
Position 1: YEAR
Position 2: MONTH   A=Jan, B=Feb, C=March, etc.
Ignore everything else
Example: 7A5D3 (January, 2007)

BLUE BOY VEGETABLES (See AUNT NELLIE'S)

B&G FOODS 1.973.401.6500
Baked Bean, Brown Bread, Green Olives, Pickles, Peppers and Relish
First five digits for date of production
Position 1 and 2: DAY
Position 3 and 4: MONTH
Position 5: YEAR
Position 6-10: plant info and time stamp (if present)
Example: 27084 P (August 27, 2004)

Black Olives
Position 1: plant
Position 2: YEAR
Position 3, 4 and 5: product description
Position 6, 7 and 8: JULIAN DATE
Position 9-13: shift and time stamp
Example: 1 4 WBP/030G 1355 (January 30, 2004) 1:55pm

Sauerkraut
Position 1: YEAR
Position 2 and 3: plant info
Position 4 and 5: MONTH
Position 6: DAY   A to Z (1–26) then changing to a number from 1 to 5 for days 27–31
Example: 544125 13:52 (January 25, 2005) at 1:52 pm

BAKER'S COCONUT and CHOCOLATE   1.800.431.1001
First four digits for Best By date
Position 1: YEAR
Position 2, 3 and 4: JULIAN DATE
Example: 5077F (March 18, 2006)

BARILLA   1.800.922.7455
Barilla uses two dating systems. One is a Best By date in plain English. The other uses the following for date of manufacture.
Position 1-3: ignore
Position 4-6: JULIAN DATE
Position 7 YEAR
Example: 0951145ZA (April 24, 2005)

BAXTERS   03.9547.3111 (Australia)
Position 1: product
Position 2: will be either 1, 2, 3, or 4 indicating which period of the day it was made
Position 3 and 4: DAY
Position 5: MONTH
Position 6: YEAR x= 2003, Y = 2004, Z = 2005
Position 9,10 11 and 12: time
Example: L1132Y 0902 (February 13, 2004)

BERNSTEIN'S (see BIRDS EYE)

BERTOLLI OIL   1.800.908.9789
Use By date
Position 1: lot
Position 2, 3 and 4: JULIAN DATE
Position 5: shift
Position 6: YEAR
Example: L 136 AR
SHELF LIFE: 20 months

BIGELOW TEAS   1.888.244.3569
Bigelow has begun printing a Best By date
Last two digits for date of production
Position 1-7: production info
Position 8: MONTH   A=Jan, B=Feb, C=Mar, etc.
Position 9: YEAR
Example: 37993DPL7   (December 2007)
SHELF LIFE: 3 years; can be consumed thereafter but flavor may have degraded

Dare To Prepare: Chapter 12: Unraveling Dating Codes 157

BIRDS EYE   1.800.563.1786
Date of production
Position 1: YEAR
Position 2 and 3: plant production info
Position 4: MONTH (January through September are 1-9, October is "O," November is "N", December is "D")
Position 5: DAY (A-Z corresponds to the 1st-26th and 1-5 indicates the 27th-31st)
Position 6 and 7: production info (if present)
Example: 8077B5 (July 2, 2008)

BLACK FLAG   1.800.729-9029
Date of production
Position 1: ignore
Position 2 and 3: YEAR
Position 4-6: JULIAN DATE
Position 7-12: ignore
Example: H07250011047 (September 7, 2007)
SHELF LIFE: 1 – 2 years

BLUE DIAMOND NUTS
New:
Position 1 and 2: YEAR
Position 3-5: JULIAN DATE
Position 6-10: ignore
Example: 08169D349S (June 18, 2008)

Old:
Position 1 and 2: plant information
Position 3-5: JULIAN DATE
Position 6: YEAR
Example: DD2439 (August 31, 1999)

BRER RABBIT MOLASSES   1.973.401.6500
Five digits for date of production
Position 1 and 2: DAY
Position 3 and 4: MONTH
Position 5: YEAR
Example: 24014 (January 24, 2004)

BROOKS (see BIRDS EYE)

BUSH'S BEST   1.800.590.3797
As of September 2004 products are stamped with a "Best By" date. Shelf life in a 5-digit code has expired.
Baked Beans, Pinto Beans, and Sauerkraut
Five digits
Position 1: MONTH   January through September 1-9, October "O," November "N", December "E"
Position 2 and 3: DAY
Position 4: YEAR   2 is 2002, 3 is 2003, 4 is 2004
Position 5: ignore last digit; it's plant information
Example: 1234x (January 23, 2004)

Green Beans, Cut Green & Shelly Beans or Dubon Petit Pois Peas
Seven digits
Position 1: MONTH – A-L for January-December
Position 2: YEAR (4 = 2004)
Position 3 and 4: plant info
Position 5 and 6: DAY (01, 02, 31)
Position 7: pack period (1 = 6am-6pm, 2 = 6pm-6am)
Example: L3SD232 (December 23, 2003)

Black Beans
Five digits
Position 1: pack period
Position 2: MONTH (1-9 for Jan-Sep, A-Oct, B-Nov, C-Dec)
Position 3 and 4: DAY (01, 02, 31)
Position 5: YEAR – 2 is 2002, 3 is 2003, 4 is 2004
Example: 1B143 (November 14, 2003)
SHELF LIFE: Chili Magic is 1-1½ years; 2-3 years all other products

CADBURY CONFECTIONERY   1800.250.260 (Australia)
No date code provided.
SHELF LIFE: 1+ years

CAMPBELL'S   1.800.257.8443 (U.S.)   1.800.663.366 (Australia)   1.800.448.504 (New Zealand)
Arnott's, Bla Band, Campbell's Soups, Erasco Soups, Franco-American, Liebig Soups, Pace, Pepperidge Farm, Prego, Royco Soups, Swanson, Touch of Taste Bouillon, V8

Most products are plainly marked with a "Best Used By" date. Date codes should read either FEB08 or FEB2008. Older soup cans may be stamped in code and should be tossed.
SHELF LIFE: 2 years

CAPRI SUN   1.800.227.7478   (owned by Kraft)
Capri Sun All Natural Sugar Sweetened Drink

Capri marks products with a "Best By" Julian date. Late January 2004, Capri began switching over to dating in plain English.
Example: 09JUL2005 (July 9, 2005). The second line is production information.
Older coding follows this for date of production:
Position 1: YEAR
Position 2, 3 and 4: JULIAN DATE
Position 5, 6 and 7 and remaining digits, plant and production info
Example: 3003GCE0808:53 (January 3, 2003)
SHELF LIFE: 18 months

CASCADE   (see PROCTOR & GAMBLE)   1.800.765.5516

CATELLI   (see NEW WORLD PASTA)

CLOROX   1.800.292.2200
409, Clorox, Liquid-Plumr, Pine-Sol, Tilex
Method 1:
Product uses date of manufacture
Position 1 and 2: plant info
Position 3: YEAR
Position 4, 5 and 6: JULIAN DATE
Positions 7-10: military time
Example: A5825609:01 (September 13, 2008)

Method 2:
Position 1 and 2: plant info
Position 3: YEAR
Position 4, 5 and 6: JULIAN DATE
Example: E63033 (February 2, 2003)

COLGIN   1.214.951.8687
Product uses date of production
Position 1: MONTH   (A = Jan, B = Feb, C = Mar, etc.)
Position 2 and 3: DAY
Position 4 and 5: YEAR
Example: G2406   (July 24, 2006)
SHELF LIFE: 2 years, for best flavor but usable for another 2 years due to low pH and antimicrobial properties

Dare To Prepare: Chapter 12: Unraveling Dating Codes

COMET 1.800.926.9441
  Product uses date of manufacture
  Position 1: YEAR
  Position 2, 3 and 4: JULIAN DATE
  Position 5-8: time stamp
  Example: 71271731 (May 7, 2007)
  SHELF LIFE: 1 year

COMSTOCK FRUIT PIE FILLING 1.800.270.2743
  Product uses date of production
  Position 1: YEAR
  Position 2 and 3: plant production info
  Position 4: MONTH (January through September are 1-9, October is "O," November is "N", December is "D")
  Position 5: DAY (A-Z corresponds to the 1st-26th and 1-5 indicates the 27th-31st)
  Position 6 and 7: production info (if present)
  Example: 7077B5 (July 2, 2007)
  SHELF LIFE: 3 years

CONAGRA FOODS
  ACT II, Andy Capp's, Banquet, Banquet Brown 'N Serve, Blue Bonnet, Chef Boyardee, Crunch 'N Munch, DAVID Seeds, Dennison's, Egg Beaters, Fleischmann's, Gulden's, Healthy Choice, Hebrew National, Hunt's, Jiffy Pop, Kid Cuisine, Knott's Berry Farm, La Choy, Libby's, Luck's, Manwich, Marie Callender's, Orville Redenbacher's, PAM, Parkay, Patio, Pemmican, Penrose, Peter Pan, Ranch Style, REAL, Reddi-Wip, RoTel, Rosarita, Slim Jim, Snack Pack, Swiss Miss, Van Camp's, Wesson, Wolf
  Conagra products are currently coded with two systems showing date of production, and some products have a "Best By date in plain English as of 2005.
  New:
  Position 1-4: plant
  Position 5: MONTH
  Position 3: YEAR
  Example: Q63C 8333 (November 29, 2008)
  SHELF LIFE: 2 years for product line

  Old:
  Position 1: plant
  Position 2: YEAR
  Position 3, 4 and 5: JULIAN DATE
  Position 6-12: ignore
  Example: L4351BP 1435A (December 17, 2004)

CONTADINA PRODUCTS 1.888.668.2847
  As of 2004, coding is being converted to a Use By date in plain English
  Product uses date of production
  Position 1: YEAR
  Position 2, 3 and 4: JULIAN DATE
  Position 5-8: plant
  Position 6-9: time stamp
  Example: 3225HFT1114:42 (August 13, 2003)

COUNTRY TIME 1.800.432.1002
  Beginning late January 2004, Country Time began using a Best By date stamped in plain English. You will also still see the following system in use:
  Date of production
  Position 1: YEAR
  Position 2, 3 and 4: JULIAN DATE
  Ignore everything to the right of the first four digits
  Example: 3300ME212:25 (October 28, 2003)
  SHELF LIFE: 1 year

CREAMETTE (see NEW WORLD PASTA)

CRYSTAL LIGHT 1.800.431.1002
First four digits for date of production. They also use a Best By date.
Position 1, 2 and 3: plant info
Position 4: YEAR
Position 5, 6 and 7: JULIAN DATE
Position 8: flavor
Position 9-12: time stamp
Example: XPP4012L1443 (January 12, 2004)
SHELF LIFE: 2 years

DARE FOODS 1.800.668.3273 (Canada)
Bear Paws, Breton, Econo, Grains First, Grissol Melba Toast, Juiced Up, Maxi Fruits, Normandie Me teo, RealFruit, Simple Pleasures, Traditions, Ultimate, Vinta, Viva Puffs, Wagon Wheels, Whippit
Product uses a "Best when used by" date
Position 1 and 2: YEAR
Position 3 and 4: MONTH
Position 5 and 6: DAY
Example: 071101 (November 1, 2007)

DAWN (see PROCTOR & GAMBLE) 1.800.725.3296

DEB-EL FOODS
Dry Egg Whites and Whole Eggs
Product uses date of manufacture
Position 1: ignore
Position 2: YEAR
Position 3-5: JULIAN DATE
Position 6-7: ignore
Example: G7182BL (July 1, 2007)
SHELF LIFE: powdered egg white – 5 years; whole eggs – 18 months

DEC A CAKE 1.800.247.5251
First two digits for date of production
Position 1: YEAR
Position 2: MONTH A=Jan, B=Feb, C=Mar, etc.
Other numbers and letters will follow, but the first two digits indicate when the product was packaged
Example: 8C (March 2008)
SHELF LIFE: 2 years for Sprinkles, 1 year for Icings and Gels

DEL MONTE 1.800.543.3090
As of 2004, coding is being converted to a Use By date in plain English
Four digits of first line for date of production, disregard all other digits
Position 1: YEAR
Position 2, 3 and 4: JULIAN DATE
Example: 5045A (February 14, 2005)

DRANO 1.800.494.4855 (US)   877.506.7352 (Canada)
Product uses date of manufacture
Position 1: YEAR W=2003, Y=2004, Z=2005
Position 2, 3 and 4: JULIAN DATE
Position 5: ignore
Example: Y3261 (November 22, 2004)
SHELF LIFE: 3-5 years

DROMEDARY (Moody Dunbar, Inc.) 1.800.251.8202
    Product uses date of production
    Position 1 and 2: variety
    Position 3: MONTH A=Jan, B=Feb, C=Mar, etc. skips letter "I"
    Position 4 and 5: DAY
    Position 6: YEAR J=2002, H=2003, G=2004, F=2005, E=2006, D=2007, C=2008, B=2009, A=2010
    Example: 24K17HKC (October 17, 2003)
    SHELF LIFE: 3 years guaranteed, but may be consumed safely for an additional 2 years

DURKEE 1.800.964.8663
    First four digits for date of production
    Position 1: YEAR
    Position 2: MONTH A=Jan, B=Feb, C=Mar, etc.
    Position 3 and 4: DAY
    Position 5-7: ignore
    Position 8-11: time stamp
    Other numbers and letters will follow, but the first four digits indicate when the product was packaged
    Example: 8C24 ARF 0850 (March 24, 2008)
    SHELF LIFE: 1 year

DYNASTY 1.800.633.1004
    First four digits for date of production
    Position 1: YEAR H=2003, I=2004, J=2005, K=2006
    Position 2, 3 and 4: JULIAN DATE
    Position 5: shift
    Example: H2241 (August 12, 2005)
    SHELF LIFE: 1 year

EMERALD NUT SNACKS and HARMONY (see BLUE DIAMOND NUTS)

EMERIL'S (B&G Foods) 1.973.401.6500
    First six digits for date of production
    Position 1 and 2: DAY
    Position 3 and 4: MONTH
    Position 5 and 6: YEAR
    Position 7-13: production info
    Example: 290905 VS2 10:27 (September 29, 2005)
    SHELF LIFE: 2+ years

FRENCH'S MUSTARD 1.800.247.5251 (US)   1.800.888.0192 (Canada)
    Product codes date of production
    Position 1: production info
    Position 2 and 3: YEAR
    Position 4, 5 and 6: JULIAN DATE
    Example: M08020 (January 20, 2008)
    SHELF LIFE: Mustard – 12 months – squeeze bottle; 18 months – glass; 6 months – packet
       French Fried Onions – 12 months; Worcestershire Sauce – indefinite

FRESHLIKE (see BIRDS EYE)

FURMANO'S FOODS 1.877.877.6032
    First four digits, second line for date of production; a Best By date is now used
    Position 1: YEAR
    Position 2, 3 and 4: JULIAN DATE
    Example: 5045 (February 14, 2005)
    SHELF LIFE: Beans – 42 months; Tomato products – 30 months; all Furmano Foods can be used past the expiration date if the can is intact and not rusted.

GENERAL FOODS INTERNATIONAL COFFEES 1.800.432.6333
Beginning 2003 General Foods International Coffees has moved to a Best By code date, but two dating systems are still on store shelves.

Date of Production:
First four digits
Position 1: YEAR
Position 2, 3 and 4: JULIAN DATE
Positions 5-9: plant and military time
Example: 4195J 1414 (July 14, 2004)

GENERAL MILLS 800.328.1144 (US); 800.479.8505 (Canada); 613.9239.8777 (Australia); 44.1895.201100 (UK)
Betty Crocker, Big G Cereals, Bisquick, Cascadian Farm, Cheerios, Chex, Columbo, Fruit Snacks, Gardetta's, Gold Metal, Green Giant, Haagen Dazs, Helper Dinner Mixes, Jenos, Lloyds Barbeque, Lucky Charms, Muir Glen Organic, Nature Valley, Old El Paso, Patak's Indian Food, Pillsbury, Pop Secret, Progresso, Totino's, Trix, Wheaties, Yoplait

First four digits for date of production
Position 1: MONTH
Position 2, 3 and 4: JULIAN DATE
Position 5: plant location
Example: A525D (June 25, 2005)

DATE CODE: Many products have the date written in plain English, but you'll find codes on some cereal boxes. For these products, everything but the last letter is the date code in order of MONTH, YEAR and day. The MONTH coded is as follows skipping the letter "I". A=June, B=July, C=Aug, D=Sept, E=Oct, F=Nov, G=Dec, H=Jan, J=Feb, K=Mar, L=Apr, M=May

GHIRARDELLI 1.800.877.9338
Look at the last 6 digits. There can be either 5 or 6 digits preceding these, which is production info.
Last 2 Positions : YEAR
3rd and 4th Position from the right: DAY
5th and 6th Position from the right: MONTH
Example: G3575 **071107** (July 11, 2007)
SHELF LIFE: 2 years: dark chocolate products without added ingredients, liquor wafers, solid mint products, cocoa, hot chocolates
18 months: frappes
12 months: dark chocolate with raspberries, milk chocolate goods without added ingredients, white chips, white chocolate products, mint filled squares/bars
10 months: white candy making and dipping bars
9 months: products containing nuts, boxed chocolates, filled squares and bars, double chocolate candy making and dipping bars, syrups

GLADE   (see SC JOHNSON)   1.800.494.4855 (US)   1.877.506.7352 (Canada)

GOLDEN CIRCLE 1.800.357.021 (Australia)
Changes their coding every 3 years. Call toll-free for dating questions.

GOODMAN'S (see NEW WORLD PASTA)

GREEN GIANT 1.800.998.9996
Product uses date of packaging
Position 1: MONTH
Position 2: YEAR
Ignore all remaining characters
Examples: H3BE08 K 1750   (August 2003) or   I3UK25 (September 2003)
SHELF LIFE: Beans, 2 years. Corn/peas, 3 years. Mushrooms, 4 years.

GREENWOOD (see BIRDS EYE)

HANOVER FOODS CORP.
Bickels Snacks, Wege Pretzels, Spring Glen Deli Specialties, Myers Entrees
First five digits for date of production
Position 1: ignore
Position 2: YEAR
Position 3, 4 and 5: JULIAN DATE
Example: 86125 = May 5, 2006
SHELF LIFE: 2 years minimum

HEALTHY CHOICE 1.800.323.9980
Products are coded showing date of production. Some products use open coding with a Best By date.
Position 1: plant
Position 2: YEAR
Position 3, 4 and 5: JULIAN DATE
Position 6-12: ignore
Example: L5040HG2131BP 1435A (February 9, 2005)
SHELF LIFE: 2 years for soups

HIDDEN VALLEY
Dressing and Dip Mixes
Date of production
Position 1 and 2: ignore
Position 3: YEAR
Position 4-6: JULIAN DATE
Example: G68101B = April 11, 2008
SHELF LIFE: 1 year

HEINZ   1.800.255.5750
Products are coded with either of two systems for date of production.
New:
Position 1 and 2: production location
Position 3: YEAR
Position 4: MONTH A=Jan, B=Feb, C=March
Position 5 and 6: DAY
Example: FR8E06 (January 6, 2008)

Old:
Position 1 and 2: production location
Position 3, 4 and 5: JULIAN DATE
Position 4: YEAR
Example: VF0401 (February 9, 2001)
SHELF LIFE: 12 Months: Ketchup (including Heinz Ketchup Kick'rs and EZ Squirt), Tartar Sauce, Horseradish Sauce.
18 Months: Gravy, Pickles, cocktail Sauce, Wine Vinegar, Apple Cider Vinegar, Jack Daniel's Grilling Sauce.
24 Months: Mustard, Chili Sauce, Relish, Malt Vinegar.
30 Months: 57 Sauce, Worcestershire Sauce, Beans, Tarragon Vinegar.
42 Months: Distilled White Vinegar, Salad Vinegar.

HIRZEL CANNING   1.800.837.1631
First line, four digits
Position 1: YEAR
Position 2, 3 and 4: JULIAN DATE
Example: 7195 (July 14, 2007 – July 14th is the 195th day of the YEAR)

HORMEL PRODUCTS   1.800.523.4635
Bacon Toppings, Chili, Dinty Moore, Herb-Ox Bouillon, Kids Kitchen, Mary Kitchen Hash, Spam, Stagg
Second through sixth digits. They also use a Best By date.
Position 1: ignore, plant location
Position 2 and 3: MONTH
Position 4 and 5: DAY
Position 6: YEAR
Example: S02058 (February 5, 2008)

HUNT'S MANWICH   (see CONAGRA)

IDAHOAN FOODS   1.800.635.6100
First four digits for date of production
Position 1: YEAR
Position 2, 3 and 4: JULIAN DATE
Position 5-8: internal use only
Example: 8047YDK1 (February 16, 2008)
SHELF LIFE: 1 year, but may be consumed thereafter. However, varieties with higher oil content will see a shorter shelf life after this one year guarantee.

JELL-O   1.800.543.5335
Gelatin, Pudding & No-Bake Desserts
First four digits for the Best By date
Position 1: YEAR 4=2004, 5=2005, 6=2006, etc.
Position 2, 3 and 4: JULIAN DATE
The remaining numbers and letters are plant and the time of packing.
Example: 8122D1 16:44   (May 2, 2008)
SHELF LIFE: 2 years

JIFFY MIXES   1.734.475.1361
Uses date of production
All products except Baking Mix and Pancake Mix
Position 1: production info
Position 2: YEAR 5=2005, 6=2006, 7=2007, 8=2008, etc.
Position 3: 4 and 5: JULIAN DATE
Position 6: production info
Example: L8188A (July 7, 2008)

Baking Mix and Pancake Mix
Position 1: YEAR 4=2004, 5=2005, 6=2006, etc
Position 2, 3 and 4: JULIAN DATE
Position 5: production info
Example: 8188A (July 7, 2008)
SHELF LIFE: 2 years

JIF PEANUT BUTTER   1.800.283.8915
First four digits for date of production
Position 1: YEAR 5=2005, 6=2006, 7=2007, 8=2008, etc.
Position 2, 3 and 4: JULIAN DATE
The remaining numbers and letters are plant codes.
Example: 8122Y320 (May 2, 2008)
SHELF LIFE: unopened 2 years, opened 3 months

JOAN OF ARC   1.973.401.6500
Date of production
Position 1: MONTH A=Jan, B=Feb, C=Mar, D=April, etc. on through L=Dec
Position 2: YEAR
Position 3: plant info
Position 4 and 5: DAY
Position 6-9: time stamp
Example: E4F25 1836 126B1 (May 25, 2004)

JOHN WEST 1.800.061.279 (Australia)
Uses three methods.
Method 1: Pressed into lid with 2 lines of print. The first line is the dating. Last number in the line is YEAR.
Example: 354TS, line two ignore. The first line is the dating with the last number or middle character indicating the year 354TS. The "4" would be 2004.

Method 2: Also pressed into the lid with 3 lines of print; line 3 is date.
Position 1: YEAR
Position 2 and 3: MONTH
Position 4 and 5: DAY
Example: 40429 (April 29, 2004)

Method 3: Stamped on the bottom. Last group of numbers is date.
Last 5 digits
Position 7: YEAR
Position 8 and 9: MONTH
Position 10 and 11: DAY
Example: 63 EX10 41212. (December 12, 2004)
SHELF LIFE: 2 years

KARO 1.866.430.5276
Date of production; two date codes are in use.
Method 1:
Position 1: MONTH (Jan=1, Feb=2, Mar=3 thru Sept.=9, Oct=A, Nov=B, Dec=C)
Position 2 and 3: DAY
Position 4: plant location
Position 5: YEAR
Example: C27A8 (December 27, 2008)
SHELF LIFE: indefinite

Method 12:
Position 1-3: JULIAN DATE
Position 4: plant location
Position 5: YEAR
Example: 256D8 (September 13, 2008)

KEEBLER 1.800.453.5837
Keebler coding uses an expiration date.
Method 1:
Position 1 and 2: MONTH
Position 3 and 4: DAY
Position 5: YEAR
Position 6 and 7: ignore the rest
Example: 01018CG (January 1, 2008)

Method 2:
Position 1: ignore
Position 2 and 3: MONTH
Position 4 and 5: DAY
Position 6: YEAR
Example: T01018 (January 1, 2008)

Method 3:
Position 1-3: MONTH
Position 4 and 5: DAY
Position 6 and 7: YEAR
Position 8 and 9: ignore
Example: JAN0108 PM (January 1, 2008)
SHELF LIFE: 6-8 months

KINGSFORD (see ARGO CORNSTARCH)

KNORR 1.800.457.7082
Several dating systems are in use by Knorr for date of production. One is Best By stamped in plain English.
Method 1 for Mixes – Soups, Cheese Sauce, Gravies, Dips, Pasta & Pasta Sauce, Entree:
Position 1-4: ignore
Position 5: YEAR 1=2003, 2=2004, 3=2005, 4=2006, 5=2007
Position 6: MONTH   A=JAN, B=Feb, C=Mar, D=Apr, E=May, F=Jun, G=Jul, H=Aug, X=Sept, J=Oct, K=Nov, L=Dec
Position 7 and 8: DAY
Example: 0645 5L04 (December 4, 2007)

Method 2 for Knorr-Lipton Sides: Fiesta, Cajun, Asian, Italian, Pasta, Rice, Whole Grain
Position 1: YEAR 1=2002, 2=2003, 3=2004, 4=2005, 5=2006, 6=2007, 7=2008
Position 2: MONTH   A=JAN, B=Feb, C=Mar, D=Apr, E=May, F=Jun, G=Jul, H=Aug, X=Sept, J=Oct, K=Nov, L=Dec
Position 3 and 4: DAY
Position 5-8: ignore
Example: 6L04 LB11 (December 4, 2007)

Method 3:
Position 1-4: Military time
Position 5: last digit of YEAR
Position 6: MONTH, (12 months – A=1, B=2, C=3, D=4, E=5, F=6, G=7, H=8, X=9, J=10, K=11, L=12)
Position 7 and 8: DAY
Example: 1300 7G11 = 1:00pm (July 11, 2007)
SHELF LIFE: 2 years. Though safe to consume thereafter, flavor may have degraded.

KNOX GELATINE 1.800.323.0768
First four digits for date of production
Position 1: YEAR
Position 2, 3 and 4: JULIAN DATE
Position 5-8: plant and production info
Example: 8252XLM1 (September 9, 2008)
SHELF LIFE: 3 years

KOOL-AID 1.800.367.9225
First four digits for date of production
Position 1: YEAR
Position 2, 3 and 4: JULIAN DATE
Position 5, 6 and 7 and remaining digits, plant and production info
Example: 4231A1 08:53 (August 19, 2004)
SHELF LIFE: 2 years

KRUSTEAZ 1.800.457.7744
Large boxes or bags are marked with a "Best By" date in plain English.
Other products code with date of production
Position 1 and 2: ignore
Position 3: YEAR
Position 4-6: JULIAN DATE
Example: DG8107G (April 17, 2008)
SHELF LIFE: 1 year – Dessert Mixes and Pie Crust Mix
     18 months – Bread and Muffin Mixes (Krusteaz, Classic Hearth and Eagle Mills)
     2 years – Pancake and Waffle Mixes

KUNER'S 1.877.331.1400
Kuner's uses at least two coding systems for date of production and also open coding
Method 1:
Position 1: MONTH A=Jan, B=Feb, C=Mar, D=April, E=May, F=June, etc.
Position 2: YEAR
Position 3-7: ignore
Example: I5AU222 (September 2005)

Method 2:
Position 1-4: ignore
Position 5: YEAR
Position 6-8: JULIAN DATE
Position 9 and 10: ignore
Example: 161F5 315B1 (November 11, 2005)

LA CHOY (see CONAGRA FOODS)

LAKESIDE FOODS   1.920.684.3356
Second line, second through fifth digits for date of production
Position 1: ignore this digit
Position 2: MONTH (Jan=1, Feb=2, Mar=3 thru Sept.=9, Oct=A, Nov=B, Dec=C)
Position 3 and 4: DATE
Position 5: YEAR
Example: 4A104 (October 10, 2004)

LANCIA (see RONZONI)

LE SUEUR PEAS owned by Green Giant   1.800.998.9996
Date of production
Position 1: MONTH   A=Jan, B=Feb, C=Mar, D=April, E=May, F=June, G =July, etc.
Position 2: YEAR
Position 3 and 4: plant
Position 5 and 6: DAY
Position 7-12: ignore
Ignore the second line of information
Example: G7CK192A 1940   (July 19, 2007)
          1177 PEAS
SHELF LIFE: 3 years from date of production

LIBBY'S VEGETABLES   1.315.926.8100
First two digits are date of production
Position 1: MONTH
Position 2: MONTH   A=Jan, B=Feb, C=March
Ignore everything else
Example: 8B5D3   (February, 2008)
SHELF LIFE: 2-3 years for most. Sauerkraut, 18 months

LIGHT N' FLUFFY (see NEW WORLD PASTA)

LIME AWAY   1.800.228.4722
First four digits are date of manufacture
Position 1: plant
Position 2: YEAR
Position 3, 4 and 5: JULIAN DATE
Position 6: ignore
Example: S8003 1623 (January 3, 2008)
SHELF LIFE: 2 years

LINDSAY OLIVES   1.800.252.3557
Second number indicates year of production, ignore everything else
Position 1: ignore
Position 2: YEAR
SHELF LIFE: 5 years unopened, 10 days opened

LIPTON SIDES (see KNORR)

LIPTON TEAS   1.888.697.8668 (U.S.)
Some products are stamped with a Best By date. When not stamped, four digits are production date.
Position 1: YEAR
Position 2: MONTH   A=Jan, B=Feb, C=March
Position 3 and 4: DAY
Example: 4j24 (October 24, 2004)
SHELF LIFE: 18-30 months

LOHMANN   1.315.926.8100
First two digits are date of production
Position 1: YEAR
Position 2: MONTH   A=Jan, B=Feb, C=March
Ignore everything else
Example: 8C5D3   (March, 2008)

LYSOL   1.800.228.4722
Date of manufacture
Position 1: plant
Position 2: YEAR
Position 3, 4 and 5: JULIAN DATE
Position 6, 7 and 8: ignore
Example: B7353-NJ2 (December 19, 2007)
SHELF LIFE: 2 years, spray or liquid

MARANATHA NUT BUTTERS
Two types of dating are used. In the US, it is a Use by Date.
In Canada:
Position 1 and 2: YEAR
Position 3-5: JULIAN DATE
Example: 08263 (September 20, 2008)

MARTHA WHITE   1.800.663.6317
Most products have a Best By date. If they don't, they are probably too old and won't rise properly. First 2 digits are production date.
Position 1: MONTH   A=Jan, B=Feb, C=March
Position 2: YEAR
Positions 3-10: time and plant info
Example: A3J 14 1302D (January 2003)
SHELF LIFE: 8 months – corn meal mixes (including self-rising)
12 months – quick and regular grits; all flour except whole wheat; hush puppy, pancake, pizza crust, pound cake mixes;
18 months – corn muffin mix; brownies; pouch muffins, except corn; shortening

MARUCHAN   1.949.789.2300
First 6 digits for expiration date
Position 1 and 2: DAY
Position 3 and 4: MONTH
Position 5 and 6: YEAR
Position 7-14: ignore
Example: 070209HH (February 7, 2009)
SHELF LIFE: 1 year for cup-a-soup, 18 months for square packages

MAXWELL HOUSE   1.800.323.0768
Instant, Ground and Roast Coffee
Two coding systems are in use. The Best By dated is noted in plain English.
Some products will have a date of production code:
Position 1: YEAR
Position 2, 3 and 4: JULIAN DATE
Position 5, 6 and 7: production info
Example: 5003J5A (January 3, 2005)
SHELF LIFE: 1 year unopened; 2 weeks opened for optimal freshness. Can be used thereafter but flavor may have degraded.

MAXIM (see MAXWELL HOUSE)

MCCORMICK HERBS AND SPICES 1.800.632.5847 (U.S.)
   Spice Blends and **Flavor Medleys** and **Dry Seasoning Mix**
   Package and bottle dates are "Best By"
   Example: MAR1501AH = Best by (March 15, 2001)

   Spice and Extract Packages
   Method 1: Many of McCormick's newest spices are open coded, written in plain English.
   Method 2: If it's in green-labeled bottled with Baltimore, MC on the back, the spice is at least 15 years old.
   Method 3: If it's in a square red and white metal box, the spice is at least 15 years old.
   Method 4: This is the most convoluted method for some of their spices. It goes as follows:
   Date of production
   4 digits
   Position 1: YEAR – To obtain the YEAR, add 5 to the first digit
   Position 2, 3 and 4: MONTH and DAY – divide the last three digits by 50
   Example: 6310AY (July 10, 2001)
   Assume the number is 6310AY. To obtain the year, add 5 to the first digit (6 + 5 = 11). The second digit (in this case, 1) is the year, meaning 2001, is the year of manufacture. For the month and the day, divide the last three digits by 50 (310 ÷ 50 = 6 with 10 remaining). The 6 indicates the number of complete months before the production month, i.e. January, February, March, April, May, and June. July is the month of production and the remaining 10 is the day of the month. Code 6310AY is the code for a product made on July 10, 2001.
   NOTE: If position 2-4 isn't divisible by 50, then use that number for the day of the month.
   Example 1: 5012BH (January 12, 2000)   **Example 2**: 3062BH (February 12, 1998)

   SHELF LIFE:
   4 years for extracts, except Vanilla, which has an indefinite shelf life
   3-4 years for whole spices and seeds
   2-3 years for ground spices
   1-3 years for leafy herbs
   1-2 years for seasoning blends

   Old Bay
   Date of production
   jars or bottles – **Example:** 11JAN01 12 (January 11, 2001)
   boxed dry seasoning mixes – **Example:** 11204CH (November 20, 2004)
   SHELF LIFE: 1 year

   Golden Dipt
   Date of production
   jars or bottles – **Example:** 07054 1326 (July 5, 2004)
   boxed fry mixes – **Example:** 05174BH (May 17, 2004)
   SHELF LIFE: 15 months – 2 years, depending on product

MCKENZIE'S (see BIRDS EYE)

MOTTS 1.800.426.4891
   Apple Juice & Applesauce
   Date of production. Motts also uses a Best By date.
   Position 1 and 2: first two letters are plant info
   Position 3: YEAR
   Position 4 and 5: MONTH
   Position 6 and 7: DAY
   Last 4 digits: Time of production (in military time)
   Example: WP30219 15:31 (February 19, 2003)
   SHELF LIFE: 1 year

MOUNTAIN HOUSE (same as Marine Cuisine geared to the boating industry)
Several date codes are in use depending on the age of the product. Foods use a Best Buy Julian date.
1989 and after:
Position 1 and 2: YEAR
Position 3-5: JULIAN DATE
Position 6-8: production operator's initials
Example: 99028 CIA (January 28, 1999)

Before 1989:
Position 1 and 2: YEAR (see table on right)
Position 3-5: JULIAN DATE
Position 6-8: internal tracking code
Example: T20394D (July 22, 1987)

A	1970	E	1974	I	1978	M	1982	S	1986
B	1971	F	1975	J	1979	N	1983	T	1987
C	1972	G	1976	K	1980	P	1984	U	1988
D	1973	H	1977	L	1981	R	1985		

SHELF LIFE: #10 Cans 25+ years; Pouches 7 years; organic fruit snacks and ice cream 2 years. After opening, foods should be consumed within 1 week for best results and taste. Treat leftovers like any fresh food.

MRS. WEISS (see NEW WORLD PASTA)

MUSSELMAN'S
Use the second set or second line of code for production date. Products may have Best By dates.
Position 1: YEAR
Position 2-4: JULIAN DATE
Position 5-11: ignore
Example: CASR6200 6254M11 14:18 (September 11, 2006)
SHELF LIFE: 2 years for peak quality and taste, but can be eaten thereafter if seal is still intact. Brownish color doesn't affect safety of product.

NALLEY (see BIRDS EYE)

NIDO (NESTLE)   1.800.258.6727
Powdered Whole Milk
First four digits, second line, for date of production. Nido also uses a Best By date.
Position 1: YEAR
Position 2, 3 and 4: JULIAN DATE
Position 5 and 6: ignore
Example: 5535
       5350LA (December 16, 2005)
SHELF LIFE: 2 years, unopened

NESTLE TOLL HOUSE   1.800.851.0512
First four digits for date of production. Products should have a Best By date.
Position 1: YEAR
Position 2, 3 and 4: JULIAN DATE
Position 5-10: ignore
Example: 7170BWB18G (June 19, 2007)
SHELF LIFE :
12 months for white morsels
15 months for white baking bars
16 months for milk chocolate morsels
18 months for butterscotch morsels
24 months for semi-sweet morsels, mini morsels and chunks, baking cocoa, choco bake, semi-sweet and unsweetened baking bars

NEW WORLD PASTA   1.800.730.5957
American Beauty, Creamette, Light 'n Fluffy, P&R, Mrs. Weiss, Prince, Ronzoni, San Giorgio, Skinner
This company uses both open dating as well as the following coding system for date of production.
First three digits for date of production
Position 1: YEAR (0 – 9)
Position 2 and 3: MONTH (01 – 12)
Example: 902MA (February 2009)

OCEAN SPRAY 1.800.662.3263
This company uses both open dating as well as the following coding system for date of production.
Position 1 and 2: DAY
Position 3 and 4: MONTH
Position 5 and 6: YEAR
Positions 7-11: ignore
Example: 071203 H 1658 (December 7, 2003)
SHELF LIFE: unopened – up to 12 months from date of manufacture, 2-3 weeks opened and refrigerated

OLD EL PASO 1.800.300.8664
First two digits for date of production. Most products have a Best By date.
Position 1: MONTH A=Jan, B=Feb, C=Mar
Position 2: YEAR
Example: B4HN01 (February 2004)
SHELF LIFE: 2 years sauce, salsa, seasoning and refried bean; 18 months chilies; 6 months taco shells

ORTEGA 1.973.401.6500
Chiles, Jalapenos, Taco Sauces, Taco and Tostada Shells
First four digits for date of production
Position 1: YEAR
Position 2, 3 and 4: JULIAN DATE
Position 5-10: production info
Example: 4235XW1A07 (August 23, 2004)

ORVILLE REDENBACHER'S 1.800.243.0303
Second four digits for date of production. Redenbacher's also uses a Best By date.
Position 1-4: plant info
Position 5: YEAR
Position 6, 7 and 8: JULIAN DATE
Position 9-10: ignore
Position 11-14: time stamp
Example: 2165 2340 12 01:06 (June 16, 2002)
SHELF LIFE: 12 months microwave popcorn
18 months – oil and popcorn in jars

OUST (see SC JOHNSON) 1.800.558.5252

OWENS 1.800.966.9367
Last four digits for date of production
Position 1-3: ignore
Position 5, 6 and 7: JULIAN DATE
Position: 8: YEAR
Example: 5200745 (March 14, 2005)
SHELF LIFE: 6 month frozen

PAM 1.800.726.4968
First four digits for date of manufacture; cans now have a Best By date.
Position 1: MONTH   A=Jan, B=Feb, C=March on through Dec. X is used in place of I for September
Position 2 and 3: DAY
Position: 4: YEAR
Example: B185 (February 18, 2005)
SHELF LIFE: 2 years

PEPPERIDGE FARM 1.888.737.7374
This company uses both open dating (meaning one is plain English) as well as the following coding system. Date is Sell By.
Position 1 and 2: MONTH
Position 3 and 4: DAY
Position 5 and 6: YEAR
Position 7, 8 and 9: plant location
Example: 113005 AK1 (November 30, 2005)
SHELF LIFE: 12 weeks after this date

PERKY'S   1.888.473.7597
   Position 1-3: JULIAN DATE
   Position 4: YEAR
   Position 5: shift
   Example: 180 93 (June 29, 2009)
   SHELF LIFE: 9 months for all cereals, 6 months for Nutty Flax

PLANTERS PEANUTS   1.800.622.4726
   Beginning 2003, all Planters products are being converted from an expiration date to a Best By date, so you may see either system.
   First four digits is expiration date
   Position 1: YEAR
   Position 2, 3 and 4: JULIAN DATE
   Position 5 and 6: production info
   Position 7, 8, 9 and 10: military time (if included)
   Example: 3030A20826   (January 30, 2003)

POLANER ALL FRUIT   1.973.401.6500
   First five digits for date of production
   Position 1 and 2: DAY
   Position 3 and 4: MONTH
   Position 5: YEAR
   Position 6-9: time stamp
   Example: 26014 1600 (January 26, 2004)
   SHELF LIFE: 2 years from date of manufacture. Although safe to consume after this time, taste can change, the appearance will darken, and the consistency may become watery.

PROGRESSO   1.800.200.9377
   Progresso uses both open dating and the following coding.
   Position 1: MONTH A=Jan, B=Feb, C=March on through L for Dec
   Position 2: YEAR
   Position 3 and 4: plant
   Position 5 and 6: DAY
   Ignore everything to the right of 6th position
   Example: H2NV31 NEC7-I 11:58
   SHELF LIFE: 2 years

PRINCE   (see AMERICAN BEAUTY)

PROCTOR & GAMBLE
   Bounce, Bounty, Cascade, Cheer, Dawn, Downy, Dreft, Era, Febreze, Gain, Ivory, Joy, Mr. Clean, Tide, Swiffer
   Position 1: YEAR
   Position 2, 3 and 4: JULIAN DATE
   Position 5 and after: ignore
   Example: 8036172703RV (February 5, 2008)
   SHELF LIFE: 1 – 2 years

RANCH STYLE   1.800.799.7300
   Date of production
   Second through fifth digits
   Position 1: plant location
   Position 2: YEAR
   Position 3, 4 and 5: JULIAN DATE
   Position 6 and 7: ignore
   Example: F7184 XE (July 3, 2007)
   SHELF LIFE: 2 years

REGINA 1.973.401.6500
> **Vinegars and Cooking Wines**
> First five digits for date of production
> Position 1 and 2: DAY
> Position 3 and 4: MONTH
> Position 5: YEAR
> Position 6-9: time stamp
> **Example:** 15014 1600 (January 15, 2004)
> SHELF LIFE: 2 years from date of manufacture. Although safe to consume after this time, quality may have degraded.

RID-X and RID-X ULTRA 2 in 1 1.800.228.4722
> First five digits for date of manufacture
> Position 1: plant
> Position 2: YEAR
> Position 3, 4 and 5: JULIAN DATE
> Ignore everything else
> **Example:** B61910B (July 10, 2006)
> SHELF LIFE: 2 years

RONZONI 1.800.730.5957 (U.S.) 1.888.293.1333 (Canada)
> Ronzoni uses two date coding systems, however, all products are being converted to the first example.
> **Method 1:** First four digits for date of production
> Position 1: YEAR
> Position 2, 3 and 4: JULIAN DATE
> Position 5, 6 and 7: production information
> **Example**: 8252MAU (September 9, 2008)
>
> **Method 2**: First five digits for date of production
> Position 1: YEAR
> Position 2 and 3: MONTH
> Position 4 and 5: DAY
> Position 6, 7 and 8: production information
> **Example:** 40122MA (January 22, 2004)

ROSARITA 1.877.528.0745
> Date of production. They now use open coding.
> Position 1: plant
> Position 2: YEAR
> Position 3, 4 and 5: JULIAN DATE
> Position 6-12: production information
> **Example**: A4112SB21:17L (April 21, 2004)
> SHELF LIFE: 2 years

RO*TEL 1.800.544.5680
> **New:** Date of production
> Position 1: plant
> Position 2: YEAR
> Position 3, 4 and 5: JULIAN DATE
> Position 6-12: production information
> **Example**: A4112SB21:17L (April 21, 2004)
>
> **Old:** First four digits for date of production
> Position 1: MONTH   A=Jan, B=Feb, C=March on through L for Dec. X is used for Sept.
> Position 2 and 3: DAY
> Position 4: YEAR
> Position 5-9: production information
> **Example**: H282XAHT2 (August 28, 2002)
> SHELF LIFE: 2 years

ROYAL & MY-T-FINE PUDDING   1.800.323.2592
   Flavor Aid, Hawaiian Punch, Hy-Vee, Mix Aid, Mondo, Sure Fine, Wyler's
   Date of production
   Position 1 and 2: plant info
   Position 3: YEAR
   Position 4-6: JULIAN DATE
   Position 7-11: shift and time
   Example: WC8323 1 07:45 (November 19, 2008)

S&W FINE FOODS   (see DEL MONTE)

SACO FOODS   1.800.373.7226
   Cultured Buttermilk Blend
   First four digits for date of manufacture
   Position 1: YEAR
   Position 2, 3 and 4: JULIAN DATE
   Example: 5286 (October 13, 2005)
   SHELF LIFE: indefinite if unopened and properly stored. After opening, if kept refrigerated, it will stay fresh for a minimum of one year, usually several years.

SAN GIORGIO   (see NEW WORLD PASTA)

SANKA (see MAXWELL HOUSE)

SC JOHNSON   1.800.494.4855 (US)   Canada (1.877.506.7352)
   Drano, Edge, Fantastik, Glade, Off, Oust, Pledge, Raid, Scrubbing Bubbles, Shout, Skintimate, Vanish, Windex
   Product uses date of manufacture
   Position 1: YEAR: Y=2004, Z=2005, A=2006, C=2007, D=2008
   Position 2, 3 and 4: JULIAN DATE
   Position 5-9: ignore
   Example: Example: D008 24075   (January 8, 2008)
   SHELF LIFE: Raid – 4 years; Off – 3 years; Oust – 2 years; cleaners 2-3 years

SENECA   1.315.926.8100
   Method 1: First two digits are date of production
   Position 1: MONTH
   Position 2: MONTH   A=Jan, B=Feb, C=March
   Ignore everything else
   Example: 8A5D3   (January, 2008)

   Method 1: Two digits on the first line for date of production
   Position 1: MONTH (Jan.=A, Feb.=B, Mar=C, etc.)
   Position 2: YEAR
   Example: L5 (December 2005)

SKINNER   (see NEW WORLD PASTA)

SMART ONES
   First four digits for expiration date
   Position 1, 2 and 3: JULIAN DATE
   Position 4: YEAR
   Ignore everything else to the right
   Example: 0624 3990 1826 G4   (March 3, 2004)

SMUCKERS 1.888.550.9555
Smuckers uses either a Best By date or date of production.
Second through fifth digits for date of production
Position 1: ignore, plant location
Position 2: YEAR
Position 3: MONTH   A=Jan, B=Feb, C=Mar, D=April, E=May, F=June, G=July, etc.
Position 4 and 5: DAY
Positions 6-9: time stamp
Example: 25G23 20:16 (July 23, 2005)
SHELF LIFE:
   2 years for fruit spreads and ice cream toppings
   9 months for peanut butter

SPAM   (see HORMEL) 1.800.523.4635
Second through sixth digits for date of production
Position 1: ignore, plant location
Position 2 and 3: MONTH
Position 4 and 5: DAY
Position 6: YEAR
Example: S02055 (February 5, 2005)

SPC LIMITED 1.800.805.168 (Australia)
Four digits for date of production
Position 1: The first letter = YEAR of manufacture, based on the company's name. S = 2002 P = 2003 C = 2004 L = 2005.
Position 2: MONTH A=Jan, B=Feb, C=March
Position 3 and 4: DAY
Example: PA25 (January 25, 2003)
SHELF LIFE: 3-4 years from date on can

SPRING TREE MAPLE PRODUCTS 1.802.254.8784
Uses a Best By date
Position 1 and 2: ignore
Position 3 and 4: MONTH
Position 5 and 6: DAY
Position 7-10: YEAR
Example: BBO8212005 (August 21, 2005)
SHELF LIFE: 3 years pure maple syrup, 1 year for sugar-free

SPICE ISLANDS 1.800.247.5251
First two digits for date of packaging. Spice Islands also uses a Best By date.
Position 1: YEAR
Position 2: MONTH A=Jan, B=Feb, C=Mar, etc.
Ignore everything to the right of the second position
Example: 5C (March 2005)
SHELF LIFE: 2 years

STAGG CHILI   (see HORMEL) 1.800.611.9778

STARKIST TUNA 1.800.252.1587
On many products, Starkist is using a Best By date in plain English
Second line:
Position: 1, ignore
Position 2, 3, and 4: JULIAN DAY
Position 5: YEAR, M=2004, N=2005, O=2006, P=2007, etc.
Example: X274M (October 1, 2004)
SHELF LIFE: 4-6 years

STOKES CHILE SAUCES (Ellis Foods) 1.303.292.4018
  First six digits for date of production
  Position 1 and 2: ignore
  Position 3: YEAR
  Position 4 and 5: MONTH
  Position 6 and 7: DAY
  Position 8: ignore
  Example: G580609B (June 9, 2008)
  SHELF LIFE: 2 years, but may be consumed "for many years" after that date according to the manufacturer

SWISS MISS 1.800.457.6649
  Four digits for date of production and a Best By date is used.
  Position 1: plant
  Position 2: YEAR
  Position 3, 4 and 5: JULIAN DATE
  Position 6: ignore
  Example: W4047M (February 16, 2005)
  SHELF LIFE: 2 years

TABASCO (McIlhenny Company) 1.800.634.9599
  First four digits for date of production
  Position 1, 2 an 3: JULIAN DATE
  Position 4: YEAR
  Position 5 and 6: production info
  Example: 08451A (March 25, 2005)
  SHELF LIFE: 5 years

TANG 1.800.431.1002
  Tang uses two dating systems. The first is a Best By open date. The other uses:
  First four digits for date of production
  Position 1: YEAR
  Position 2, 3 and 4: JULIAN DATE
  Position 5 and 6: plant info
  Position 6-9: time stamp
  Example: 5003D2 09:04 (January 3, 2005)
  SHELF LIFE: 2 years

TIDE (see PROCTOR & GAMBLE)

TILEX (see CLOROX)

TOMBSTONE PIZZA
  Product code is a Use By date
  Position 1: plant info
  Position 2: YEAR
  Position 3-5: JULIAN DATE
  Example: 08177 (June 26, 2008)

TONE'S 1.800.247.5251
  Date packaged
  Position 1: YEAR
  Position 2: MONTH A=Jan, B=Feb, C=Mar, etc.
  Other numbers and letters will follow, but the first two digits indicate when the product was packaged
  Example: 5C (March 2005)
  SHELF LIFE: At least 2 years for spices; 4-6 years for pure and imitation extracts

TOP JOB 1.800.479.6603
  Date of production
  Position 1 and 2: YEAR
  Position 3-5: JULIAN DATE
  Position 6-8: ignore
  Example: 07194BCW (July 13, 2007)
  SHELF LIFE: 18 months

Dare To Prepare: Chapter 12: Unraveling Dating Codes

TRADER'S CHOICE (see TONE'S)

TYSON CHICKEN BREAST (canned) 1.800.233.6332
First line, first four digits for date of production. Tyson also uses a Best By date.
Position 1: YEAR
Position 2, 3 and 4: JULIAN DATE
Position 5-12: ignore
Example: 1283 CRI2 11:54 (May 8, 2003)
SHELF LIFE: 3 years

TYSON (frozen foods)
First line, first four digits for date of production
Position 1: YEAR
Position 2, 3 and 4: JULIAN DATE
Position 5-7: plant
Position: 8-11: production info
Example: 7243PLA0114 (August 31, 2007)
SHELF LIFE: 1 year

UNCLE BEN'S 1.800.548.6253
First four digits for date of production or a Best By date is used.
Boxed items:
Position 1: YEAR
Position 2 and 3: WEEK 1-52
Position 4 and 5: plant and shift
Example: 423AB (June 1, 2004)

Frozen Products:
Position 1, 2 and 3: JULIAN DATE
Position 4: YEAR
Example: 3554 (December 30, 2004)
SHELF LIFE: 2 years

UNDERWOOD 1.973.401.6500
Deviled Ham, Chicken, Liverwurst and Roast Beef
First five digits for date of production
Position 1 and 2: DAY
Position 3 and 4: MONTH
Position 5: YEAR
Position 6-9: time stamp
Position 10 and 11: variety
Example: 15016 1600 HF (January 15, 2006)
SHELF LIFE: 2 years from date of manufacture. Although safe to consume after this time, quality may have degraded.

Underwood Sardines
Last four digits for date of production
Position 1-5: ignore
Position 6: YEAR
Position 7-9: JULIAN DATE
I – IFC (International Fish Canners)
K – Kosher
S – Sardines
O – Oil
L – Lot #
4 – the last digit of the YEAR 2004
The next three numbers indicate the day of the YEAR from 1 to 365.
Example: IKSOL5010 (January 10, 2005)
SHELF LIFE: 2 years. Although safe to consume after this time, quality may have degraded.

WELCHES   1.800.340-6870
  Juices, Jams, Jellies
  Product uses date packaged or a Best By date
  First five digits
  Position 1: YEAR
  Position 2: production plant
  Position 3: DAY
  Position 5: MONTH   A=Jan, B=Feb, C=Mar, etc.
  Ignore everything to the right of 5th position
  Example: 5N11A   (January 11, 2005)
  SHELF LIFE: 1 year

WILDERNESS FRUIT PIE FILLING   1.800.270.2743
  Product uses date of production
  Position 1: YEAR
  Position 2 and 3: plant production info
  Position 4: MONTH (January through September are 1-9, October is "O," November is "N", December is "D")
  Position 5: DAY of the MONTH (A-Z corresponds to the 1st-26th and 1-5 indicates the 27th-31st)
  Position 6 and 7: production info (if present)
  Example: 8077O5 (October 2, 2008)
  SHELF LIFE: 2 years

WINDEX   (see **SC JOHNSON**)   1.800.558.5252

WOLFGANG PUCK SOUP   1.800.665.9026
  Four coding systems are used for production date. All soup produced as of October 1, 2007 will have a Best Used By date.
  Method 1:
  Position 1, 2 and 3: variety
  Position 4: factory
  Position 5: YEAR
  Position 6-9: time stamp
  Second line:
  Position 1, 2 and 3: JULIAN DATE
  Position 4 and 5: production info
  The EST XXXXX represents the USDA Inspected Meat Products code of this particular factory. If a P had appeared before the number it would represent a USDA Inspected Poultry product.
  Example: 674C5 0716
  　　　　　 212B2 EST 18816   (January 2, 2005)

  Method 2:
  Position 1, 2 and 3: variety
  Position 4 and 5: factory line
  Position 6: YEAR   E=2003, F=2004, G=2005, H=2006, etc.
  Position 7-9: JULIAN DATE
  Position 10: shift
  Second line: USDA info
  Example: 965P8/G278B
  　　　　　 EST 6166   (October 5, 2005)

  Method 3:
  Position 1: MONTH   A=Jan, B=Feb, C=Mar, etc.
  Position 2: YEAR
  Position 3 and 4: plant
  Position 5 and 6: DAY
  Position 7: shift
  Position 8-11: time stamp
  Second line: ignore
  Example: H5ED061 13:45
  　　　　　 69668 P.6166 (August 6, 2005)
  SHELF LIFE: 3 years

WRIGLEY'S   1.800.974.4539 (U.S. and Canada)
  Method 1:
  Position 1 and 8-10: ignore
  Position 2 and 3: DAY
  Position 4 and 5: YEAR
  Position 6 and 7: MONTH
  Example: L 06 12 05 014   (December 6, 2005)

  Method 2 for Lifesavers: Example: 07APR 2006   Expires April 6, 2007
  SHELF LIFE: 6-12 Months: Hubba Bubba
  9 Months: Orbit, Extra, Lifesavers Bag, Crème Savers, Gummi Savers and Crystal Craze
  9-12 Months: Ouch, Bubble Beeper, Bubble Jug
  9-15 Months: Big League Chew
  10 Months: Wrigley's Spearmint, Doublemint, Juicy Fruit, Winterfresh, Big Red, Freedent, Orbit White
  12 months: Eclipse, Juicy Fruit Grapermelon and Strappleberry, Altoids Gum, Lifesavers Roll
  13 months: Delites
  18 months: Altoids Mints and Sours

YUBAN (see MAXWELL HOUSE)

CONVERT JULIAN DATING TO CALENDAR DAYS

Julian Day	Calendar Day	Julian Day	Calendar Day	Julian Day	Calendar Day	Julian Day	Calendar Day	Julian Day	Calendar Day
1	Jan. 01	74	Mar. 15	147	May 27	220	Aug. 08	293	Oct. 20
2	Jan. 02	75	Mar. 16	148	May 28	221	Aug. 09	294	Oct. 21
3	Jan. 03	76	Mar. 17	149	May 29	222	Aug. 10	295	Oct. 22
4	Jan. 04	77	Mar. 18	150	May 30	223	Aug. 11	296	Oct. 23
5	Jan. 05	78	Mar. 19	151	May 31	224	Aug. 12	297	Oct. 24
6	Jan. 06	79	Mar. 20	152	Jun. 01	225	Aug. 13	298	Oct. 25
7	Jan. 07	80	Mar. 21	153	Jun. 02	226	Aug. 14	299	Oct. 26
8	Jan. 08	81	Mar. 22	154	Jun. 03	227	Aug. 15	300	Oct. 27
9	Jan. 09	82	Mar. 23	155	Jun. 04	228	Aug. 16	301	Oct. 28
10	Jan. 10	83	Mar. 24	156	Jun. 05	229	Aug. 17	302	Oct. 29
11	Jan. 11	84	Mar. 25	157	Jun. 06	230	Aug. 18	303	Oct. 30
12	Jan. 12	85	Mar. 26	158	Jun. 07	231	Aug. 19	304	Oct. 31
13	Jan. 13	86	Mar. 27	159	Jun. 08	232	Aug. 20	305	Nov. 01
14	Jan. 14	87	Mar. 28	160	Jun. 09	233	Aug. 21	306	Nov. 02
15	Jan. 15	88	Mar. 29	161	Jun. 10	234	Aug. 22	307	Nov. 03
16	Jan. 16	89	Mar. 30	162	Jun. 11	235	Aug. 23	308	Nov. 04
17	Jan. 17	90	Mar. 31	163	Jun. 12	236	Aug. 24	309	Nov. 05
18	Jan. 18	91	Apr. 01	164	Jun. 13	237	Aug. 25	310	Nov. 06
19	Jan. 19	92	Apr. 02	165	Jun. 14	238	Aug. 26	311	Nov. 07
20	Jan. 20	93	Apr. 03	166	Jun. 15	239	Aug. 27	312	Nov. 08
21	Jan. 21	94	Apr. 04	167	Jun. 16	240	Aug. 28	313	Nov. 09
22	Jan. 22	95	Apr. 05	168	Jun. 17	241	Aug. 29	314	Nov. 10
23	Jan. 23	96	Apr. 06	169	Jun. 18	242	Aug. 30	315	Nov. 11
24	Jan. 24	97	Apr. 07	170	Jun. 19	243	Aug. 31	316	Nov. 12
25	Jan. 25	98	Apr. 08	171	Jun. 20	244	Sep. 01	317	Nov. 13
26	Jan. 26	99	Apr. 09	172	Jun. 21	245	Sep. 02	318	Nov. 14
27	Jan. 27	100	Apr. 10	173	Jun. 22	246	Sep. 03	319	Nov. 15
28	Jan. 28	101	Apr. 11	174	Jun. 23	247	Sep. 04	320	Nov. 16
29	Jan. 29	102	Apr. 12	175	Jun. 24	248	Sep. 05	321	Nov. 17
30	Jan. 30	103	Apr. 13	176	Jun. 25	249	Sep. 06	322	Nov. 18
31	Jan. 31	104	Apr. 14	177	Jun. 26	250	Sep. 07	323	Nov. 19
32	Feb. 01	105	Apr. 15	178	Jun. 27	251	Sep. 08	324	Nov. 20
33	Feb. 02	106	Apr. 16	179	Jun. 28	252	Sep. 09	325	Nov. 21
34	Feb. 03	107	Apr. 17	180	Jun. 29	253	Sep. 10	326	Nov. 22
35	Feb. 04	108	Apr. 18	181	Jun. 30	254	Sep. 11	327	Nov. 23
36	Feb. 05	109	Apr. 19	182	Jul. 01	255	Sep. 12	328	Nov. 24
37	Feb. 06	110	Apr. 20	183	Jul. 02	256	Sep. 13	329	Nov. 25
38	Feb. 07	111	Apr. 21	184	Jul. 03	257	Sep. 14	330	Nov. 26
39	Feb. 08	112	Apr. 22	185	Jul. 04	258	Sep. 15	331	Nov. 27
40	Feb. 09	113	Apr. 23	186	Jul. 05	259	Sep. 16	332	Nov. 28
41	Feb. 10	114	Apr. 24	187	Jul. 06	260	Sep. 17	333	Nov. 29
42	Feb. 11	115	Apr. 25	188	Jul. 07	261	Sep. 18	334	Nov. 30
43	Feb. 12	116	Apr. 26	189	Jul. 08	262	Sep. 19	335	Dec. 01
44	Feb. 13	117	Apr. 27	190	Jul. 09	263	Sep. 20	336	Dec. 02
45	Feb. 14	118	Apr. 28	191	Jul. 10	264	Sep. 21	337	Dec. 03
46	Feb. 15	119	Apr. 29	192	Jul. 11	265	Sep. 22	338	Dec. 04
47	Feb. 16	120	Apr. 30	193	Jul. 12	266	Sep. 23	339	Dec. 05
48	Feb. 17	121	May 01	194	Jul. 13	267	Sep. 24	340	Dec. 06
49	Feb. 18	122	May 02	195	Jul. 14	268	Sep. 25	341	Dec. 07

CONVERT JULIAN DATING TO CALENDAR DAYS

Julian Day	Calendar Day	Julian Day	Calendar Day	Julian Day	Calendar Day	Julian Day	Calendar Day	Julian Day	Calendar Day
50	Feb. 19	123	May 03	196	Jul. 15	269	Sep. 26	342	Dec. 08
51	Feb. 20	124	May 04	197	Jul. 16	270	Sep. 27	343	Dec. 09
52	Feb. 21	125	May 05	198	Jul. 17	271	Sep. 28	344	Dec. 10
53	Feb. 22	126	May 06	199	Jul. 18	272	Sep. 29	345	Dec. 11
54	Feb. 23	127	May 07	200	Jul. 19	273	Sep. 30	346	Dec. 12
55	Feb. 24	128	May 08	201	Jul. 20	274	Oct. 01	347	Dec. 13
56	Feb. 25	129	May 09	202	Jul. 21	275	Oct. 02	348	Dec. 14
57	Feb. 26	130	May 10	203	Jul. 22	276	Oct. 03	349	Dec. 15
58	Feb. 27	131	May 11	204	Jul. 23	277	Oct. 04	350	Dec. 16
59	Feb. 28	132	May 12	205	Jul. 24	278	Oct. 05	351	Dec. 17
60	Mar. 01	133	May 13	206	Jul. 25	279	Oct. 06	352	Dec. 18
61	Mar. 02	134	May 14	207	Jul. 26	280	Oct. 07	353	Dec. 19
62	Mar. 03	135	May 15	208	Jul. 27	281	Oct. 08	354	Dec. 20
63	Mar. 04	136	May 16	209	Jul. 28	282	Oct. 09	355	Dec. 21
64	Mar. 05	137	May 17	210	Jul. 29	283	Oct. 10	356	Dec. 22
65	Mar. 06	138	May 18	211	Jul. 30	284	Oct. 11	357	Dec. 23
66	Mar. 07	139	May 19	212	Jul. 31	285	Oct. 12	358	Dec. 24
67	Mar. 08	140	May 20	213	Aug. 01	286	Oct. 13	359	Dec. 25
68	Mar. 09	141	May 21	214	Aug. 02	287	Oct. 14	360	Dec. 26
69	Mar. 10	142	May 22	215	Aug. 03	288	Oct. 15	361	Dec. 27
70	Mar. 11	143	May 23	216	Aug. 04	289	Oct. 16	362	Dec. 28
71	Mar. 12	144	May 24	217	Aug. 05	290	Oct. 17	363	Dec. 29
72	Mar. 13	145	May 25	218	Aug. 06	291	Oct. 18	364	Dec. 30
73	Mar. 14	146	May 26	219	Aug. 07	292	Oct. 19	365	Dec. 31

WEEK NUMBER CONVERSIONS

Week	Includes	Week	Includes	Week	Includes	Week	Includes
1	Jan 1-7	14	Apr 1-7	27	Jul 1-7	40	Sep 30-Oct 6
2	Jan 8-14	15	Apr 8-14	28	Jul 8-14	41	Oct 7-13
3	Jan 15-21	16	Apr 15-21	29	Jul 15-21	42	Oct 14-20
4	Jan 22-28	17	Apr 22-28	30	Jul 22-28	43	Oct 21-27
5	Jan 29-Feb 4	18	Apr 29-May 5	31	Jul 29-Aug 4	44	Oct 28-Nov 3
6	Feb 5-11	19	May 6-12	32	Aug 5-11	45	Nov 4-10
7	Feb 12-18	20	May 13-19	33	Aug 12-18	46	Nov 11-17
8	Feb 19-25	21	May 20-26	34	Aug 19-25	47	Nov 18-24
9	Feb 26-Mar 3	22	May 27-Jun 2	35	Aug 26-Sep 1	48	Nov 25-Dec 1
10	Mar 4-10	23	Jun 3-9	36	Sep 2-8	49	Dec 2-8
11	Mar 11-17	24	Jun 10-16	37	Sep 9-15	50	Dec 9-15
12	Mar 18-24	25	Jun 17-23	38	Sep 16-22	51	Dec 16-22
13	Mar 25-31	26	Jun 24-30	39	Sep 23-29	52	Dec 23-29

Chapter 13: General Supplies

Now that the two most important areas – water and food – have been covered, let's see what it takes to complete the task. The following lists are based on a Family of Four for several months. Alter the quantities and products suggested to fit your needs and length of time for which you want to plan. They cover three possible scenarios:

- Staying at home during temporary power and service disruptions
- Longer term service disruptions
- Being mobile and taking along necessary supplies

If you feel you would like to store supplies for longer periods of time, use the Deyo Food Planner to keep track of your goals. Even though it's primarily a food planner, other things are listed like cleaning supplies, medications, health and personal hygiene items, as well as and products we may use frequently.

Saving money, shopping smarter and preparing for emergencies has two things in common. The items you eat, wear and use are ready when you need them and they were purchased at the best possible price. It's just a part of prudent, practical planning.

Some of the products listed below will be one-time purchases like fishing poles (our guys seem to have a hard time resisting the jigs, etc. – guess that's the <u>real</u> reason they're called "lures!" Purchases like sleeping bags, compasses and the like won't need to be replenished. Many other items you'll already have around your home, but make sure you always have a supply on hand. As with all *Dare To Prepare* lists, use them as guidelines and adjust them to fit your personal needs.

SPECIFIC LISTS

\multicolumn{3}{c}{CAMPING GEAR}		
AMOUNT	**UNIT**	**ITEM**
1	each	Clothes Line and Clothes Pins or Pegs
1	each	First Aid Kit (see list)
2	each	Fishing Poles and assorted lures
4	each	Foam Mattress Pads for under sleeping bags, swags, etc.
4	cans	Insect Repellent with Deet
4	each	Mosquito Netting for around cook site and individual sleeping bags
4	each	Pillow, small
4	each	Plastic Sheeting to go between the ground and sleeping bag
4	sets	Sheets
4	each	Sleeping Bag, Bedroll, Swag or Wool Blankets
1	each	Solar Shower
1	each	Snake Bite Kit
4	each	Space Blanket (reflects up to 90% of body heat and only weighs 20 oz)
12	each	Tarps (these have many uses)
2	each	Tent (2 person)
1	each	Wash Board
1	each	Wash Tub for laundry

* Purchase the heaviest and largest trash bags available. They have countless uses like extra tent, emergency wind/rain protection/keeping pack and contents dry.

Dare To Prepare: Chapter 13: General Supplies

CARRYING ITEMS

AMOUNT	UNIT	ITEM
4	each	Backpack for supplies
4	each	Fanny pack for short excursions
1	each	Five Gallon Pail with lid, these have many uses
4	each	Canteen or Hydration Reservoir like Camelbak, Nalgene Bore Tanker and MSR Dromedary Bags (reservoirs strapped to body or pack take strain off shoulders and neck compared to carrying canteen)

CLOTHING

AMOUNT	UNIT	ITEM
12	each	Bandannas (inexpensive face shield, head cover, wash cloth, bandage, sanitary pad)
4	each	Boots, Sturdy
12	sets	Complete Change of Clothing* (3 for each person)
2	each	Current prescription glasses
12	each	Dust Masks
1	each	Hat for Sun protection
4	each	Rain Poncho or Rubberized Parka & Rain Pants (oversized to layer clothing underneath – these items are preferable over the Rain Poncho – offers more protection)
8	pair	Socks for boots, heavy (2 for each person)
1	each	Sweatsuit set
4	each	Sunglasses
4	pair	Tennis Shoes, high top
12	each	Underwear (3 for each person)
1	each	Winter Clothing, jacket, gloves, hat
4	pair	Work Gloves, heavy duty

* Every season, make sure to update your stored change of clothes for appropriate weather conditions. In winter, include coats, hats, gloves, thermal underwear, snow boots and clothes for layering.

COMMUNICATION ITEMS

AMOUNT	UNIT	ITEM
1	set	$500. Cash in small bills and coins (during times of disaster charge cards and checks will not be honored)
2	each	Compass of good quality
2	each	Map of your local area
4	each	Mirror or old CD to use as signaler
6	each	Notepad
4	each	Pen
4	each	Pencil
1	set	Phone numbers and addresses of friends/family
20	each	Postage Stamps, extra
1	set	Pre-addressed, stamped postcards of friends and family out of state (if a disaster is widespread, you'll want to contact someone out of the area)
1	each	Radio (solar, hand cranked or battery powered)
8	each	Road Flares (these are not legal is Australia)
1	each	Shortwave Radio (plus extra batteries)
12	each	Signal Flares (these are not legal is Australia)
4	each	Whistle

TIP: Money is always hard to tuck away and pretend it isn't there, but this is a necessity. Assume in a crisis or power outage you can't put expenditures on credit cards. Think about it. Whenever you purchase something with a credit card, it is always verified and authorized. If phone lines are down, the purchase won't go through.

FUEL AND LIGHTING		
AMOUNT	UNIT	ITEM
40	each	Batteries, assorted sizes
6	bags	Briquettes, charcoal
4	each	Candle Holders
36	each	Candles
200	each	Fire Starters (jelly, ribbon, tablets, impregnated peat bricks, wax- coated pine cones, magnesium block, flint, kerosene or paraffin treated)
3	cord	Firewood
4	each	Flashlight/Torch (extra batteries, spare bulbs)
2	each	Fuel for Camp Stove
As needed	each	Fuel Refills (for each type needed propane, Sterno, diesel, gas)
2	each	Kerosene lanterns and fuel
12	each	Light Bulbs/Globes, assorted watts, long life
12	each	Lighter, cigarette, like Bic
40	each	Lightsticks, Cyalume (8 and 12 hour)
200	boxes	Matches, assorted, some wind and water proof
2	each	Propane Lanterns and Extension Poles
2	each	Propane Tank (20 lb or 9 kg)
4	each	Propane Wicks/Socks/Mantles
4	cans	Sterno

PERSONAL HYGIENE		
AMOUNT	UNIT	ITEM
1	bottle	After Shave/Men's Cologne
4 tube	bottles	Body/Hand Lotion
4	set	Comb and Brush
1	set	Cosmetics
4	pack	Dental Floss
4	each	Deodorant
40	each	Razor Blade Replacements
4	each	Razors, if applicable
8	bottles	Shampoo and Conditioner
2	cans	Shave Cream
8	bars	Soap
3	box	Tampons/Sanitary napkins
4	each	Toothbrush
4	tubes	Toothpaste
4	each	Tweezers, pointed
4	sets	Wash Cloth & Towel

Dare To Prepare: Chapter 13: General Supplies

COOKING ITEMS

AMOUNT	UNIT	ITEM
3	rolls	Aluminum Foil, heavy weight
2	each	Boning Knife
1	each	Bottle Opener
2	each	Bread Loaf Pan
2	each	Butcher Knife
4	each	Camp Fork, long-handled for toasting bread, hotdogs
1	each	Camp Stove
100	sets	Canning Jars and Lids
1	each	Can Opener, manual, heavy duty
2	each	Cheesecloth
1	each	Cookbook for food storage
1	each	Corkscrew
2	each	Cutting Boards
6	each	Dish Cloths
1	each	Dutch Oven, 14" with lid, cast iron best*, stainless steel OK
1	each	Dutch Oven, large with lid, cast iron best*, stainless steel OK
1	each	Egg Beater, manual
1	each	Flour Sifter
...		Food/Water Supplies (see Deyo Food Storage Planner)
1	each	Grain Grinder, manual or convertible to manual
1	each	Grater
2	each	Hot Pads
1	each	Iron Tripod for suspending pots over an open fire
1	each	Kettle, huge (at least lobster pot size) for boiling water and water bath canning
1	set	Measuring Cups and Spoons
6	each	Melamine Plates and Cups-aluminum gets too hot
1	each	Metal Coffee Maker or Billy Can
1	each	Mixing Bowl, Large
1	each	Mixing Bowl, Small
2	each	Pancake Turners, not plastic
2	each	Paring Knife
2	roll	Plastic Wrap
1	each	Pressure Canner/Pressure Cooker
2	each	Quart (2 liter) Containers with Lids (for purifying water, you need 2 so water can be poured back and forth to re-oxygenate)
1	each	Sauce Pan, large with lid, cast iron best*, stainless steel OK
1	each	Sauce Pan, small with lid, cast iron best*, stainless steel OK
1	each	Skillet, large with lid, cast iron best*, stainless steel OK
1	each	Spoons, Metal
2	each	Spoons, Wooden
2	each	Thermos Bottles
100	each	Twist Ties
2	each	Water Purification System, portable
5	pkgs.	Water Purifying Tablets (50 count)
1	roll	Waxed Paper
2	boxes	Ziploc or Click Zip Freezer Bags, gallon (3.5 liter)
2	boxes	Ziploc or Click Zip Freezer Bags, quart (2 liter)

*If cooking outside, you may need to cover food to guard against insects. Using lids will also expedite cooking times and boiling water, which reduces fuel consumption.

INFANT SUPPLIES		
AMOUNT	UNIT	ITEM
3	sets	Baby Clothes
2	bottles	Baby Powder
2	bottles	Baby Wash
2	each	Blankets
3	each	Bottles
52	boxes	Diapers, disposable (24 count)
1	bottle	Diaper Rash Ointment
	cans	Formula, depends on age
2	bottles	Lotion
1	each	Teething Ring
2	boxes	Towelettes, Pre-moistened
		Toys

SENIOR CARE		
AMOUNT	UNIT	ITEM
2	each	Batteries for wheelchairs and hearing aids
1	each	Crutches or Walkers, Tips and Pads
2	boxes	Denture Care Items
1	spare	Eyeglasses
6	months	Heart or Blood Pressure Medications
6	months	Prescriptions
		Special Dietary Items
3	sets	Warmer Clothing (Generally the elderly have trouble with poor blood circulation and get cold easier.)

PERSONAL HYGIENE		
AMOUNT	UNIT	ITEM
1	bottle	After Shave/Men's Cologne
4 tube	bottles	Body/Hand Lotion
4	set	Comb and Brush
1	set	Cosmetics
4	pack	Dental Floss
4	each	Deodorant
40	each	Razor Blade Replacements
4	each	Razors, if applicable
8	bottles	Shampoo and Conditioner
2	cans	Shave Cream
8	bars	Soap
3	box	Tampons/Sanitary napkins
4	each	Toothbrush
4	tubes	Toothpaste
4	each	Tweezers, pointed
4	sets	Wash Cloth & Towel

LATRINE AND GENERAL HYGIENE

AMOUNT	UNIT	ITEM
2	each	Bathroom Cleaner
4	gallons	Bleach, liquid and Eyedropper
2	each	Camping Potty and Deodorizer
4	bottles	Detergent, liquid for clothes and dishwashing
2	bottles	Disinfectant, Concentrate
2	cans	Disinfectant Spray like Lysol or Glen 20
2	bottles	Fabric Softener
2	each	Garbage Cans, metal
250	each	Paper Napkins
12	rolls	Paper Towels
2	boxes	Pre-Moistened Towelettes (in addition to ones for infants)
2	pair	Rubber Gloves
8	each	Sponges
2	boxes	Steel Wool Pads like Brillo or Steelo
12	pair	Surgical Gloves (these are costly & can be obtained in discount stores)
60	rolls	Toilet Paper, rolls flattened
60	each	Trash Bags, large (for human waste and misc. trash)
60	each	Trash Bags, medium
4	bottles	Vinegar
2	bottles	Windex

MISCELLANEOUS

AMOUNT	UNIT	ITEM
1	each	Bible
1	each	Board Games and Deck of Cards
8	each	Books for pleasure reading
1	set	Car and House Keys, Spare

1	set	Certified Copies of all Important Documents:*
		    Bank Account Numbers and Last Bank Statement
		    Births, Baptism, Marriage and Death Certificates
		    Charge Card Account Numbers and their "Lost or Stolen" phone numbers
		    Contracts
		    Driver's License
		    House and Life Insurance Policies
		    Medical Records
		    Notification Numbers
		    Passports and Visas
		    Photo and Written Inventory of Home and Contents
		    Social Security Number/Tax File Number
		    Stocks, Bonds and Investments
		    Wills

1	each	Clock, wind-up manually like Big Ben and Baby Ben
1	each	Dare To Prepare
2	each	Firearm and appropriate ammo, if desired
1	each	Hunting Knife
1	each	Magnifying Glass
1	box	Paper Clips, assorted
1	box	Rubber Bands, assorted sizes
1	box	Safety Pins, assorted sizes

*Keep these items in waterproof containers. Many survival and camping stores sell flat, water tight pouches. If you have a food vacuum sealer, this is another great use for it!

TOOLS AND REPAIR ITEMS

AMOUNT	UNIT	ITEM
2	each	ABC Fire Extinguisher (check for expiration date)
1	each	Axe
1	each	Broom and Mop
6	each	Bungee or Okie Straps (variety of lengths)
1	each	Bung Wrench
1	each	Bush or Tree Saw
1	each	Caulking Gun and Caulk
1	each	Crowbar
1	each	Drill, hand-operated
4	rolls	Duct tape
1	each	Furnace Filter
1	each	Generator, gas/petrol or diesel, preferably at least 5 KW
1	each	Glue Gun
1	each	Grease Gun and Grease
1	each	Hammer, medium weight
1	each	Hatchet
1	each	Knife Sharpener
As needed	each	Lumber, misc. widths and lengths for repair jobs
1	roll	Masking Tape (for labeling, etc.)
12	each	Mouse and Rat Traps
2	box	Nails, Screws, Nuts and Bolts, assorted sizes
33	yards/meters	Nylon Rope
1	each	Pliers, needle nose and regular
1	each	Pliers, regular
1 per window	sheet	Plywood, (in case of window damage)
1	each	Post Hole Digger, auger type
1	each	Siphon
1	each	Scissors
1	each	Screwdriver, Phillips, assorted sizes
1	each	Screwdriver, flat head, assorted sizes
1	box	Screws, assorted sized
1	each	Shovel, rounded V-shaped for digging
1	each	Sledgehammer
1	each	Staple Gun and Staples
1	each	Swiss Army type knife or other multi-tool
33	yards/meters	Twine or Heavy String
1	each	Vise Grips
1	each	Wheelbarrow
1	each	Wire Cutters
1	each	Wench and Cable, manual
2	each	Wire, assorted gauges
1	each	Wrench

| \multicolumn{3}{c}{**VEHICLE REPAIR**} |
AMOUNT	UNIT	ITEMS PER VEHCILE
2	each	Air Filter
1	each	Antennas
1	each	Battery cable cleaner/battery cleaner
1	set	Belts and Hoses, with clamps
1	gallon (4L)	Brake Fluid
6	each	Clean Rags
1	set	Distress Reflector Triangles
1	each	Empty, clean gas can (clean after each use) with spout
1	each	Fire Extinguisher
1	set	Fuses for every fuse in engine, on all fuse blocks
1	each	Heavy Duty Jack
1	each	Ice Scraper
1	each	Jumper Cables
1	set	Lights for all vehicle lights, interior and exterior
1	each	Locking Gas Cap
1	each	Lug Wrench
1	each	Magnetic Antenna Mount
3	each	Oil Filter
5	quarts (4L)	Oil
1	each	Plastic Funnel
1	quart/liter	Power Steering Fluid
1	gallon (4L)	Radiator Fluid, pre-mixed,
1	each	Radiator Sealer
3	each	Road flares (not legal in Australia)
2	each	Sand Bags
1	set	Spare Tire and Rim
1	set	Spark Plugs
1	set	Tires, Full size
1	each	Tire Pressure Gauge
1	can	Tire Sealer/Inflator
1	quart/liter	Transmission Fluid
1	gallon (4L)	Washer Fluid
1	each	Water Pump
1	can	WD-40 light oil lubricant spray
2	pair	Wiper Blades

GARDEN ITEMS		
AMOUNT	**UNIT**	**ITEM**
Per garden	feet/meters	Chicken Wire and Stakes
3	each	Compost Buckets
1	each	Digging Fork
Per garden	bags	Fertilizer
2	each	Garden Hose and Spray Nozzle
100	each	Garden Label Stakes
2	pair	Gloves
1	each	Hand Trowel
1	each	Hoe
3	each	Pesticides, assortment
1	each	Pitchfork
6	bags	Potting Soil
1	each	Pruning Shears
1	each	Rake, Fan
1	each	Rake, Straight Teeth
1	each	Rototiller, if garden is large enough
Per garden	each	Seed Starter Pots
3	years	Seeds, Open Pollinated, Heirloom, non-hybrid
1	each	Shovel, Round Head, easier for digging holes
1	each	Shovel, Square Head, for killing snakes
1	each	Spade
Per plant	each	Tomato, Bean and Pea Trellises
Per plant	each	Walls of Water (ground warmers for early planting)

Chapter 14: First Aid Supplies

Whether readying for accidents or preparing for possible disasters, having a well-stocked first aid kit is good medicine. While Stan and I moved into our Australian farm, Seismo and Taco were safely tucked into a boarding kennel. The day we brought them home, they ran huge circles around the pastures. In Perth, they'd only had a small backyard and this was true doggie joy – a place to roam. While we continued unpacking, Seismo and Taco explored their new digs. At 8:30 that night, I checked on the mutts in their fenced area. There was blood everywhere – **lots** of it and it kept coming. When Taco moved her foot, blood bubbled around her toes.

Stan raced outside with the first aid kit as I gathered clean towels and a basin of warm saline. While exploring, Taco stepped in a metal-edged hole we hadn't yet discovered, and severely sliced her toes.

After thoroughly cleaning the paw, we used antibacterial ointment and bandaged her foot. We knew she'd lost a lot of blood because she lay quietly allowing us to work on her. Stan wrapped her foot with a self-adhering compression bandage and further secured it with surgical tape. Having these things on hand got Taco through the night until her paw could be stitched together in the morning. We hadn't been in this home three days when the first aid kit came in handy.

Experience shows it's better to build your own first aid kit than purchasing ready-made unit. This way it contains exactly what your family needs, not what a company wants to sell. You control the size, quantity, brand and freshness of everything you choose. When you purchase them on-line or in stores where kits are security-sealed (which they should be), it's impossible to check all of the expiration dates. If you buy a kit with half of the products nearing expiration, you've lost money from the get-go.

The following First Aid lists are the backbone of any comprehensive kit. In the second column you'll see a heading labeled **C, H, B** indicating **Car, Home** or **Both**. These are suggested items to keep in either or both locations. A car kit should have fewer things than the home kit or it will be too cumbersome, but enough to cover most scenarios. Take into consideration your family's special needs and adjust accordingly. The **AMT** column shows the *smallest*

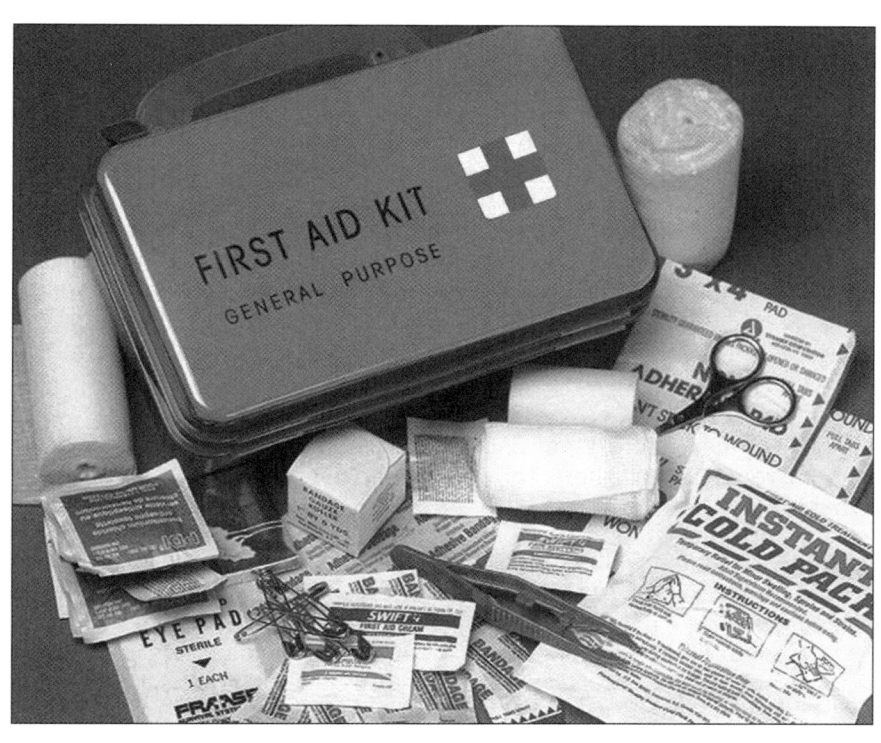

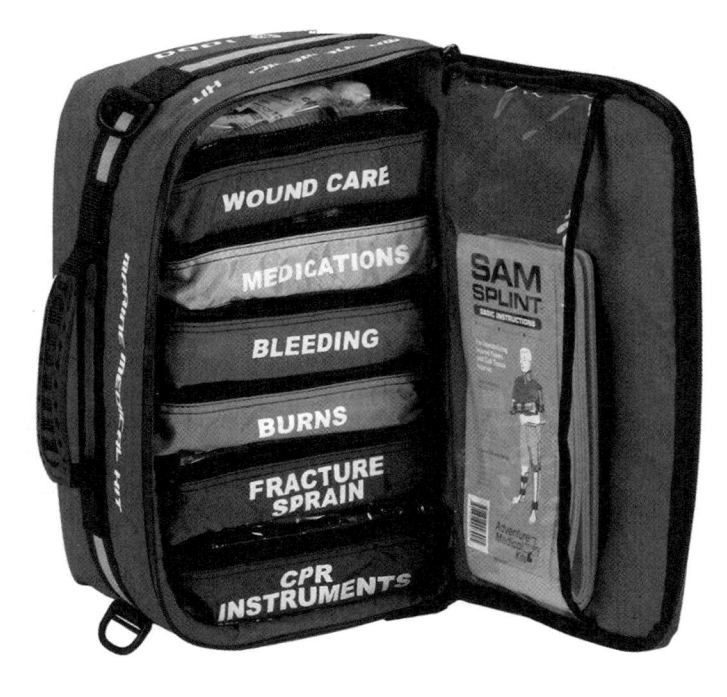

quantity to have. Some items designated with C only, assumes you already have plenty at home like Ziplocs or trash bags. For the Home Kit, you may want to double or triple certain items.

Be sure to check your kit periodically for expired medications and replacement of depleted supplies.

No home library is complete without a good first aid book. For emergencies information in plain English that cuts to the chase is crucial. Consider Dr. Kathleen A. Handal's *The American Red Cross First Aid & Safety Handbook*. Several other books to have on hand are *Pearson Nurse's Drug Guide* by Billie A. Wilson, Margaret T. Shannon, Kelly Shields; *Where There Is No Dentist* by Murray Dickson; *Where There Is No Doctor* by David Werner. All of these are available through Amazon if you can't find them locally. Having a nurse or doctor is the best scenario, but if an emergency becomes really dire, you may have to do the best you can on your own. Books and first aid supplies help.

CAR KIT CASE

A first aid carry case can be as simple as a tackle box. However, hardened plastic can't conform to either your body while carrying it or to nooks and crannies in your vehicle. Too, some tackle box compartments might be too small to be useful. You'll have to take a look. Tackle *bags* can be a good option as they're lightweight and pliable. Toolboxes have larger compartments and lift-out trays, which could be quite useful. Again, hardened plastic isn't the easiest to carry for any distance. Other options include a backpack or a professional-quality EMT bag made from urethane-coated DuPont Cordura. These packs strapped to the body free your hands. They also evenly distribute weight and won't stress the neck and shoulders. This is really important if you're walking for any length of time.

ANTIBIOTICS

If you can afford them and have access to these five antibiotics, they will heal illnesses and injuries when herbal remedies fall short. They won't help everyone and should never be taken by people with known allergies to them.

Zithromax: Urinary Tract Infection (UTI), Respiratory Tract Infection (RTI), STD's, Sepsis, Ear Infection
Ampicillin (Clindamycin is a good substitute**)**: Skin Infections, Gonorrhea, Sepsis, Ear Infections
Ciprofloxacin: Post-anthrax Exposure, UTI, Hospital-acquired Pneumonia, Infectious Diarrhea, Bone-Joint Infections
Doxycycline: Malaria, Rocky Mountain Spotted Fever, Diarrhea, E.Coli
Amoxacillin: Ear, Nose & Throat Infections, Tooth Abscess, Gonorrhea, Skin Infections
Additional meds worth considering: Clindamycin, Flagyl, Bactrim

SPECIFIC LISTS

		FIRST AID SUPPLIES
AMT.	C, H, B *	ITEM
1	H	Airways, Nasopharyngeal
1	H	Airways, Oropharyngeal
10	B	Alcohol wipes (prep pads)
5	B	Ammonia Inhalant (smelling salts), individually wrapped packets
1	H	Baby Powder/Talc (prevents chaffing)
2	B	Basic First Aid Book, in plain language
2	B	Bandage, 2", 4" and 6" Ace
2	B	Bandage, 2" elastic gauze (Flexicon) self-adheres but not to hair
2	B	Bandage, 3" elastic gauze (Co-Flex, Flex-Wrap)
2	B	Bandage, 4" and 6" elastic gauze (Flexicon)
5	B	Bandage, 3" x 4" non-adherent pad
30	20 H 10 C	Bandage, ⅞" plastic spot (Curad, Swift)
60	50 H 10 C	Bandage, 1" x 3"; flexible woven fabric (Swift, Tough-Strips, Elastoplast)
30	25 H 5 C	Bandage, fingertip #8; flexible woven fabric (Swift, Elastoplast)
30	25 H 5 C	Bandage, knuckle; flexible woven fabric (Swift, Tellus)
30	25 H 5 C	Band-Aids, 1" x 3" plastic character strips
1	H	Blood Pressure Cuff

FIRST AID SUPPLIES

AMT.	C, H, B *	ITEM
1	H	Brace, ankle, lace up
1	H	Brace, knee
1	H	Cold Pack, reusable
2	C	Cold Pack, single use – Instant Cold Pack (Lifeline, Kimberly-Clark, Jack Frost)
4	B	Cooler, neck (Cool Downz)
30	B	Cotton Swabs (Q-Tips)
2	B	CPR Mask, disposable, with one-way valve so you don't inhale their vomit
12	11 H 1 C	Dental Floss (stock lots at home)
1	H	Dental Mirror
1	H	Dental Pick
1	H	Dental Wax
2	B	Duct Tape
1 pr. ea	H	Ear Plugs, classic
4	C	Emergency Blanket
1	H	Epsom Salts
1	H	Eyedropper
1	H	Eye pad
2	B	Eye wash, 4 oz
2 ea.	B	First Aid Tape, ½", 2" and 4" silk, latex free (Dermicel)
2 ea.	B	First Aid Tape, 1" and 2" porous cloth (Johnson & Johnson, Zonas)
1	H	Flashlight, small to look down throats
1	H	Flu Mask, one mask for every family member plus extra filters (see Chapter 64)
20	16 H 4 C	Gauze Pad 4" x 4"
2	B	Gauze roll
1	H	Gas Mask with N95 filters, one mask for every family member (see Chapter 40)
200 H	6 C	Gloves, nitrile
50	H	Gunshot Wound Dressing 4" x 4 ¾" (Tegaderm)
1	C	Hand Sanitizer, 2 oz.
1	H	Hemostat 5"
1	H	Hot Water Bottle
1	H	Hydrogen Peroxide, 16 oz.
1	H	Ice Bag, large and small
2	H	Isopropyl Alcohol
1	C	Kleenex, travel size
10	B	Masks, Respiratory, surgical (like 3M's N95 particulate disposable respirators)
2 oz	H	Mastisol Liquid Adhesive secures dressings, non-water soluble, latex free
4	H	Moist Burn Pads, 3" x 3½" (Spenco 2nd Skin)
20	C	Moistened Towelettes
2	B	Moleskin, 4" x 12" (10 x 30.5cm) Dr. Scholl's, blister care when hiking
2	B	Nail Clipper
2	B	Needles, assorted sizes
1	C	QuikClot Travel
1	H	QuikClot Trauma Pack
2	B	Safety Pins, assorted sizes
4	H	Saline Solution (contact lenses, irrigate burns)
1	H	SAM Splint
2	C	Sanitary Maxi Pads (can be used as bandages)
1	H	Scalpel Blades (#10 size, can be clamped in the hemostat.)
2	B	Scissors, small, EMT
2	B	Snake bite kit
1	H	Soap, antibacterial
1	H	Splinter Removal Kit

FIRST AID SUPPLIES

AMT.	C, H, B*	ITEM
12 ea.	B	Steri-strips ¼" x 1½", ¼" x 3", ⅛" x 3"
1	H	Stethoscope, Littman Classic II S.E.
2	C	Tampons
6	B	Tongue Depressors
1	H	Thermometer, adult, + extra batteries
1	H	Thermometer, ear for babies, + extra batteries
4	C	Trash Bags, kitchen size
1	H	Triangular Bandage 40" x 40" x 56"
2	B	Tweezers
2	C	Vomit Bag / Urine Pouch, re-sealable, disposable (TravelJohn)
4	C	Ziplocs, gallon size for disposal of contaminated materials

* C = Car, H = Home, B = Both

FIRST AID MEDICATIONS

AMT.	C, H, B*	MEDICATION	EXAMPLES OF BRANDS / USE
1	H	Aloe Gel	Rocky Point, Johnson's, Vaseline
2	B	Analgesic Cream	Camphophenique, Paraderm Plus
1	H	Antibiotics	See list on page 192
2	B	Antacid	Mylanta, Tums, Pepto-Bismol
2	B	Anti-Diarrheal (Loperamide)	Imodium AD, Diasorb, Lomotil
2	B	Antihistamine, 25mg (Diphenhydramine)	Benadryl
1 oz.	H	Antiseptic Liquid	Betadyne
2	B	(Triple) Antibiotic Ointment	Neosporin
1	H	Artificial Tears	Tears Naturale, Artificial Tears, Nu-Tears
2	B	Aspirin, buffered	Anacin, Bufferin
1	H	Baby Powder	Johnson's, Gold Bond
2	B	Bandage, liquid	New Skin
1	H	Burning Urination with UTI	Azo
2	B	Burns	Hydrocortisone, Derm-Aid
1	H	Chaffing Relief	Boudreaux's Butt Paste
1	H	Clove Oil (tooth ache)	Nature's Alchemy, Now Foods
2	H	Cold/Flu Tablets	Nyquil, Repetabs
3	H	Condoms	Trojan, Durex
2	H	Constipation	Ex-Lax, Dulcolax, Durolax
40	30 H 10 C	Cough Drops	Hall's, Vick's
2	H	Cough Syrup	Robitussen, Dimetap
2	H	Decongestant (Pseudoephedrine)	Actifed, Claritin-D, Sudafed, Repetabs
1	H	Decongestant Rub	Vick's
32	C	Electrolyte Tablets	Nuun, Zym, CamelBak Elixir
1	H	Epsom Salts	Aaron Brands, Great Lakes Wholesale
2	B	Eye Drops	Murine, Visine
1	H	Foot Powder	Gold Bond
1	H	Ginger, ground spice	make into tea or paste for stomach upset
2	H	Hemorrhoid Relief	Preparation H, Anusol
2	B	Hydrocortisone 1%	Walgreen's, Pramosone
60	50 H 10 C	Ibuprofen, 200mg	Advil, Motrin, Nurofen, Paracetamol
1	H	Itch, feminine	Vagisil, Gyne-Lotrimin (Clotrimazole 1%)
1	H	Itch, foot	Lamisil, Fungi Cure, Gold Bond
2	H	Itch, insect/rash	Caladryl, Calamine

FIRST AID MEDICATIONS

AMT.	C, H, B*	MEDICATION	EXAMPLES OF BRANDS / USE
1	H	Itch, jock	Micatin, Lotrimin
9	8 H 1 C	Lip Balm	Blistex, ChapStick, Carmex
2	H	Lubricant, Water Soluble	K-Y Jelly
2	B	Mosquito Repellent	Repel 100, Deep Woods Off, Sawyer, Ultrathon
1	H	Mucus Relief (upper respiratory infection)	Mucinex (breaks up mucus, prevents pneumonia)
1	H	Mucus Relief DM	Robitussin, Walgreen's
1	B	Naproxen Sodium	Aleve, Anaprox, Naprelan, Naprosyn
2	B	Nasal Decongestant	Afrin, Sinex, Ornex (use for only 72 hrs straight)
1	H	Nasal Lubricant	Bacitracin (miracle relief for "Colorado nose")
1	H	Nasal Spray, saline	SalineX, Ocean Nasal Mist or NaSal
2	B	Nausea (also treats radiation poisoning)	Bonine, Dramamine, Meclizine, Kwells, Travacalm
2	B	Non-Aspirin Pain Relief (Acetaminophen)	Children's Liquid Tylenol
2	B	Non-Aspirin Pain Relief (Acetaminophen)	Excedrin, Tylenol
2 box	H	Non-adhering Pads 2" x 2", 4" x 4"	Telfa
2	H	Oil of Oregano	(Antiseptic, antifungal)
1	H	Prescription	A supply of any you are taking
1	B	Petroleum Jelly	Vaseline
1	H	Poison Ivy/Oak/Sumac	Ivarest or Zanfel
1 pkt	H	Poison Absorber	Activated Charcoal
2	H	Pregnancy Test	First Response, Clearblue Easy
1	H	Prescription	A supply of any you are taking
30	B	Stomach Soother	Pepto Bismol tablets, Tums
3	C	Sugar Packets (for diabetics)	
1	H	Sunburn Relief	Dermoplast, Solarcaine, Paxyl
1	H	Sunscreen	SPF 50
1	B	Tea Tree Oil (burns, insect bites)	Now Foods, Country Life, Jason Natural
		Vitamins:	Puritan's Pride, Nature Made, Equate
		B-12	Metabolism support, memory booster
		Super B-Complex	Energy, immunity
		C	Immunity
365 for each family member	H	Calcium	Bone health
		D3	Immunity, calcium metabolism
		E	Antioxidant, heart disease protection
		Fish Oil	Immunity
		Magnesium	Bone health & electrolyte loss in dehydration
		Melatonin	Sleep aid, hair growth in dogs
		Multi-Vitamins for seniors/mature	Have more B12 & chromium for metabolism
		Selenium	Immunity, wound healing,
		Zinc	Immunity, prostate cancer prevention, wounds
1	H	Vomit Inducer	Ipecac, Activated charcoal
1	H	Worms	Vermox, Food Grade Diatomaceous Earth
1	H	Yeast Infection Prevention	Azo Yeast
3	H	Yeast Infection Treatment	Monistat

* C = Car, H = Home, B = Both
Most medications are omitted from the car kit as high temperatures during warm months "kill" their effectiveness. If you need to include them, make sure to rotate these products regularly.

Chapter 15: The Real Shelf Life of Medications

This information will likely make you angry after considering the money we've wasted by tossing out perfectly good medications. According to Towers Perrin Health Cost Survey, prescription drugs in 2010 cost Americans $350 *billion*.[46] This doesn't include aspirin, Pepto-Bismol, Claritin-D or any other over-the-counter medication. Add in these figures and the waste skyrockets. Now take that vast pile of money and visualize setting a match to it and then replacing that stack every two years – the shelf life of most medications. Now burn it again.

To put this in perspective, think about how much is $1 billion. Most of us can grasp the magnitude of a million dollars, but how does a billion compare? If we paid $1 for every second of every day, it would take 31 years, 259 days, 1 hour, 46 minutes and 40 seconds. Now multiply this by 350. Payoff morphs into a mind-blinding 11,098 years; 93 days; 22 hours; 13 minutes and 20 seconds. This payout occurs every two years just in America. Now factor in the costs of every other country. Are you mad yet? Pharmaceutical companies are putting the screws to everyone.

Twenty-six years ago the military became similarly concerned and looked to see how they could cut medical costs. Since they stockpile enormous quantities of meds to treat chemical, biological, radiological and nuclear (CBRN) problems, plus drugs for diseases and injuries, the dollars ratcheted up. By 1986, they had amassed $1 billion in meds that would soon have to be torpedoed. In today's dollars that number doubles though the real cost is likely much higher. Today, military personnel have to prepare for even more nasties since hostile countries are more inclined to use unconventional weapons.

If military drugs couldn't be purchased at better prices, maybe they were looking in the wrong direction. Were they throwing away drugs unnecessarily? The Pentagon decided to find out. When the Air Force approached the FDA to evaluate viability of pharmaceuticals, the Shelf Life Extension Program (SLEP) was formed in 1986. If you go to their website, information is highly guarded, but over the years physicians, universities and researchers have looked at this same issue and some of SLEP's findings have been published. Now you will have access to them.

FEED THE PIG

Why is the secret guarded so tightly? Several reasons. It's very, very important that medications be stored just as carefully as food. Keep them in the original container and away from light, heat and humidity. Because it could not be assumed that people would follow careful storage guidelines, medications could only be guaranteed viable for several years. More importantly, it greatly benefits 'big pharma' for consumers to replace stock on a regular basis. On a side note, some of these same pharmaceutical conglomerates are in bed with seed companies that are gobbling up the world's non-hybrid seeds. These are detailed in my book *Garden Gold, Grow Maximum Veggies With Minimum Effort*.

Money is at the root of much of this waste. Former director of the SLEP testing program, Francis Flaherty nailed it, **"Manufacturers put expiration dates on for marketing, rather than scientific, reasons. It's not profitable for them to have products on a shelf for 10 years. They want turnover."** He went on to state, "We've cost the pharmaceutical companies hundreds of millions of dollars in sales of new stuff to the Department of Defense."[47]

THE TRUTH ABOUT SHELF LIVES

FDA test results were shocking. Instead of products "dying" at the accepted two to three year shelf life, most medications were viable *many* months beyond this – some as long as 15 years. Former FDA expiration-date compliance chief Joel Davis explains, "with a handful of exceptions - notably nitroglycerin, insulin and some liquid antibiotics - most drugs are probably as durable as those the agency (FDA) has tested for the military. 'Most drugs degrade very slowly,' he says. 'In all likelihood, you can take a product you have at home and keep it for many years, especially if it's in the refrigerator.'"[48]

Other products whose printed shelf lives should be strictly adhered to are water purification tables, vaccines, asthma inhalers like Albuterol, blood products and the malaria treatment drug mefloquine hydrochloride.

Further, Flaherty "notes that a drug manufacturer is required to prove only that a drug is still good on whatever expiration date the company chooses to set. The expiration date doesn't mean, or even suggest, that the drug will stop being effective after that, nor that it will become harmful."[49]

Rather than medications becoming harmful when used past the expected shelf life, they generally become too weak to do much good. There has only been one recorded instance of a person becoming ill from taking outdated medication. This occurred nearly 50 years ago when tetracycline likely caused liver damage. Since that time that component of the drug has been removed and there have been no further reports.

Why is the FDA compliant in this deception? Davis summarizes the FDA's attitude quite pointedly, "It's not the job of the FDA to be concerned about a consumer's economic interest."[50]

Regardless of what Joel Davis states that extended shelf lives could likely be applied across the board, with the listed caveats previously, you can take these medications in confidence based on the FDA's extensive testing.

THE REAL SHELF LIFE OF MEDICATIONS					
Drug (A)	Dosage Form (B)	Length of Original Dating in Years (C)	Extended *Range* in Months (D)	Median Extended Shelf Life in Years (E)	Total Shelf Life in Years (Col. C + E)
Acetylsalicylic acid (Bayer aspirin)	Tablets	2-3	12–24	-	4 *
Acetaminophen pseudophedrine (Tylenol)	Capsules	3	24–24	2	5
Aluminum acetate	Tablets	2	16–70	4	6
Amoxicillin sodium (Amoxil, Polymox)	Tablets	3	22–23	2	5
Ampicillin	Capsules	3	22–64	4	7
Ampicillin sodium	Injection-solution	2	29–87	5	7
Amyl nitrite	Inhalant	2	37–76	5	7
Atracurium besylate	Injection-solution	2	27–30	3	5
Atropine sulfate	Injection-solution	2-3	19–216	10	12-13
Atropine sulfate	Autoinjector	3	12–135	6	9
Atropine sulfate-pralidoxime chloride	Autoinjector	5	25–38	3	8
Benzonatate	Capsules	3	12–73	4	7
Bretylium tosylate	Injection-solution	3	15–71	4	7
Bupivacaine HCl	Injection-solution	3	79–95	7	10
Calcium chloride	Injection-solution	3	66–106	7	10
Calcium glucepate	Injection-solution	1	23–82	5	6
Cefazolin sodium	Powder	2	63–110	7	9
Cefoperazone sodium	Powder	2	25–57	4	6
Cefoxitin sodium	Powder	2	24–55	4	6
Ceftriaxone sodium	Powder	2	44–69	5	7
Cellulose, oxidized, regenerated	Dermal	2½	28–137	7	9½
Cephalexin	Capsules	3	28–135	7	10
Cephapirin sodium	Powder	3	50–114	7	10
Chloroquine HCl	Injection-solution	3	27–98	5	8
Chloroquine phosphate	Tablets	4	20–86	5	9
Chlorpromazine HCl	Tablets	5	23–78	4	9
Chlorpromazine HCl	Injection-solution	5	59–88	6	11
Cimetidine HCl	Tablets	3	59–75	6	9
Cimetidine HCl	Injection-solution	5	15–67	4	9
Ciprofloxacin	Tablets	5	12–142	7	12
Ciprofloxacin	Suspension	2	25–40	3	5
Clindamycin phosphate	Injection-solution	2	18–77	4	6
Codeine sulfate	Tablets	3	16–114	6	9
Dexamethasone sodium phosphate	Syringe-needle	2	24–93	5	7

THE REAL SHELF LIFE OF MEDICATIONS

Drug (A)	Dosage Form (B)	Length of Original Dating in Years (C)	Extended *Range* in Months (D)	Median Extended Shelf Life in Years (E)	Total Shelf Life in Years (Col. C + E)
Dextrose 5%	Injection-solution	3	13–128	6	9
Dextrose 10%	Injection-solution	2	23–29	2	4
Dextrose and sodium chloride	Injection-solution	2	51–73	5	7
Diazepam	Autoinjector	5	12–100	5	10
Diazepam	Syringe-needle	3	12–105	5	8
Diphenhydramine HCl	Syringe-needle	3	33–126	7	10
Dobutamine HCl	Injection-solution	3	29–79	5	8
Doxycycline hyclate	Capsules	3	37–66	5	8
Doxycycline hyclate	Powder	1	14–52	3	4
Doxycycline hyclate	Tablets	3	15–91	5	8
Edrophonium chloride (Tensilon, Reversol)	Injection-solution	5	33–114	6	11
Enalapril maleate	Tablets	3	27–42	3	6
Enflurane	Liquid	5	15–94	5	10
Ephedrine sulfate	Injection-solution	3	21–80	4	7
Epinephrine	Cartridge-needle	2½	17–24	2	4½
Erythromycin lactobionate	Powder	2	38–83	5	7
Fentanyl citrate	Injection-solution	3	70–96	7	10
Flurazepam HCl	Capsules	2	27–44	3	5
Furosemide	Injection-solution	5	31–90	5	10
Guaifenesin	ER Tablets	2	39–122	7	9
Halothane	Liquid	5	51–92	6	11
Heparin sodium	Injection-solution	3	22–82	5	8
Hetastarch in sodium chloride	Injection-solution	2	30–61	4	6
Hexachlorophene cleansing	Emulsion	3	58–106	7	10
Hydrocortisone sodium succinate	Injection-solution	5	37–56	4	9
Iothalamate meglumine	Injection-solution	2	20–78	4	6
Ketamine HCl	Injection-solution	5	42–87	6	11
Lidocaine HCl	Injection-solution	3	28–126	7	10
Mafenide acetate	Cream	2	56–63	5	7
Mannitol	Injection-solution	3	21–109	6	9
Mebendazole	Tablets	3	28–89	5	8
Meperidine HCl	Injection-solution	2	32–128	7	9
Mepivacaine HCl	Cartridge-needle	3	33–45	3	6
Metaraminol bitartrate	Syringe-needle	3	33–47	3	6
Methylprednisone acetate	Suspension	5	25–51	3	8
Morphine sulfate	Syringe-needle	2	35–119	7	9
Morphine sulfate	Autoinjector	2	29–37	3	5
Morphine sulfate	Injection-solution	3	21–115	6	9
Naloxone HCl	Injection-solution	2	60–95	7	9
Naproxen (Aleve, Anaprox)	Tablets	3	46–62	5	8
Neomycin & polymyxin B sulfates & bactracin	Ophthalmic ointment	2	12–40	2	4
Neostigmine methylsulfate	Injection-solution	2	31–78	5	7
Ophthalmic irrigating	Solution	3	19–77	4	7
Oxacillin sodium	Powder	5	28–116	6	11
Pancuronium bromide	Injection-solution	2	54–108	7	9
Penicillin G	Powder	1	22–95	5	6

THE REAL SHELF LIFE OF MEDICATIONS

Drug (A)	Dosage Form (B)	Length of Original Dating in Years (C)	Extended *Range* in Months (D)	Median Extended Shelf Life in Years (E)	Total Shelf Life in Years (Col. C + E)
Penicillin G benzathine	Suspension	4	61–84	6	10
Phenylephrine HCl	Injection-solution	3	53–78	6	9
Phenytoin sodium	Injection-solution	2½	29–100	4	6½
Potassium iodide	Granules	Indefinite	225–278	21	21
Potassium iodide (radiation tablets)	Tablets	7 - Iosat 6 - ThyroSafe	28–184	9	16, 15
Povidone-iodine	Ointment	3	35–134	7	10
Povidone-iodine	Solution	5	29–144	7	12
Pralidoxime chloride	Autoinjector	5	19–266	12	17
Pralidoxime chloride	Powder	5	23–186	9	14
Primaquine phosphate	Tablets	3	41–80	5	8
Prochloroperazine edisylate	Injection-solution	3	28–66	4	7
Promethazine HCl	Injection-solution	5	28–73	4	9
Protamine sulfate	Powder	3	57–77	6	9
Pyridostigmine bromide	Tablets	3	19–143	7	10
Ringer's, lactated and dextrose	Injection-solution	2	20–87	5	7
Ringer's, lactated	Injection-solution	2	23–125	6	8
Sodium bicarbonate	Injection-solution	5	14–101	5	10
Sodium chloride	Irrigation	2	40–108	6	8
Sodium chloride	Injection-solution	5	12–113	6	11
Sodium nitrite	Injection-solution	2	35–180	9	11
Sodium polystyrene sulfonate	Powder	5	45–74	5	10
Sodium thiosulfate	Injection-solution	3	24–151	8	11
Spectinomycin HCl	Suspension	3	55–109	7	10
Succinylcholine chloride	Powder	3	58–95	7	10
Sulfacetamide sodium	Ophthalmic ointment	2	35–44	3	5
Sulfadiazine silver	Cream	3	28–104	6	9
Sulfadoxine and pyrimethamine	Tablets	5	34–93	6	11
Sulfisoxazole	Tablets	3	45–68	5	8
Tetracycline HCl	Capsules	3	17–133	7	10
Thiopental sodium	Powder	4	23–96	5	9
Triamterene and hydroclorothiazide	Capsules	3	18–19	2	5
Tubocurarine chloride	Injection-solution	3	47–69	5	8
Undecylenic Acid and zinc salt	Powder	3	43–82	5	8

* Though Bayer AG uses a 2-3 year expiration date, it was tested at 4 years and found to be 100% effective. It was not tested beyond this date.[51]

HERE'S THE RUB

When you obtain prescription meds from your pharmacist, chances are he purchased them in a much larger batch than what you receive – sometimes as many as 99 bottles more than your single script. The extended shelf life relates to the *original* date from manufacturer, NOT the date you see on your label. Prescriptions from manufacturer to pharmacist must have at least one year of viability left, but there's no way for you to know the real date unless you have the pharmacist check the batch date. This is very important as it gives the pharmacist adequate leeway to move the product off his shelf in the accepted year to 18 month time frame and still be FDA-compliant.

Chapter 16: Shelf Lives of Non-Foods

Besides shelf lives of food, it's important to know the same information for household products, medications, cosmetics and handyman products. In order to have the longest shelf life, the great majority of these items prefer cool environments, just like food. The possible exception to this is paint. Stored too cool, it becomes unusable. As a rule of thumb, keep the following in cool locations, but not where they can freeze.

CLEANING PRODUCTS		
ITEM	**SHELF LIFE**	**COMMENTS**
Ammonia	3 years	Cloudiness does not harm effectiveness
Bleach, Liquid	9-12 months	Loses 50% strength after 1 year
Cleanser (Ajax)*	1½ years	Keep dry and air tight
Detergent (Surf, Fab, Tide)	Indefinite	Bleach variety may lose its strength
Dishwashing Soap, Liquid	2 years	Life may be extended with opaque bottles
Disinfectant, Household Spray* (Lysol, Glen 20)	5 years	Store in a cool place out of the sun
Disinfectant, Concentrated (Lysol, Glen 20)	2 years	Store in a cool place out of the sun
Disinfectant, Pine Cleaners (Pine Sol /Pine O Clean)	2 years	Do not mix with other chemicals or detergents
Fabric Softener	Indefinite	Softening agents may still work, but fragrance degrades
Laundry Pre-soak (Shout)	5 years	
Mould Remover (Tilex, Exit Mould)	2 years	Store in a cool place out of the sun
Paper Towels	Indefinite	
Soft Wash Liquid Soap	Indefinite	May gel if cold
Sponges	Indefinite	
Spray & Wipe	2 years	
Spray Starch	5 years	Store in a cool place out of the sun
Steel Wool Pads (Brillo, SOS)	Indefinite	
Toilet Bowl Cleaner, Bar Type (Flush Duck)	2 years	Can be used past expiration date, except product tends to dry out.
Toilet Bowl Cleaner, Drop-In Type (Clorox, Bloo)	Indefinite	
Toilet Paper	Indefinite	
Windex	2 years	

*ADDITIONAL NOTES: Products in aerosol cans tend to have a longer shelf life because they are in an opaque container and have minimal exposure to air. Cleansers containing bleach will degrade more quickly than those without.

HANDYMAN ITEMS		
ITEM	SHELF LIFE	COMMENTS
Acetone (Diggers)	Indefinite	Keep tightly capped
Brake Fluid	Indefinite	Keep tightly capped

Caulk/Sealant/Misc. Silicates
    Opened
    Unopened
	
	6 months
	2 years
		Opened tubes dry out and harden quickly.

Craft Glue (Elmer's, Selley's)	2 years	Keep tightly capped.
Diesel*	15 months	Keep water and sediments removed. See info under Fuel & Generators. Use PRI-D.
Duct Tape/Cloth Tape (3M)	2 years	Usable as long tape has not bubbled or glue residue does not come out along the sides.
Gasoline/Petrol	9 months	Extend life with PRI-G.
Glue Sticks	Indefinite	Keep from heat.

Grout, powdered (Selley's)
    Opened
    Unopened
	
	6 months
	2 years
		
		Keep dry and tightly sealed.

Gutter Sealant (Selley's)	1 year	

House Paint, Oil Based
    Stored on cold concrete floor
    Stored on shelving off floor
	
	2 years
	5 years
		Turn can over every 3-6 months. Keep tightly sealed, do not allow to freeze.

House Paint, Water Based	7-10 years	Turn can over every 3-6 months. Usable if no rust is present. Keep tightly sealed, don't allow to freeze.
Kerosene, Home Use (Record/Diggers)	Indefinite	Keep tightly capped
Lacquer Thinner (Record/Diggers)	Indefinite	Keep tightly capped
Linseed Oil (Diggers)	Indefinite	Keep tightly capped
Lubricants (WD-40, RP7)	5-6 years	Usable as long as propellants have not dispersed
Masking Tape (3M)	2 years	Exposure to heat will make it brittle
Methylated Spirits (Record/Diggers)	Indefinite	Keep tightly capped
Mineral Turps/Paint Thinner (Record & Diggers)	Indefinite	Keep tightly capped
Motor Oil, Unopened (BP)	5 years	Ideal storage under 20°C or 68°F
Power Steering Fluid	Indefinite	Keep tightly capped
Sandpaper	Indefinite	Keep dry
Spackling Compound	1½ years	Keep tightly sealed

Super Glue
    Opened
    Unopened
	
	3 months
	2 years
		
		Keep tightly sealed

Tent Repair Kit	Indefinite	
White/Wood Glue (3M, Selley's)	4 years	Keep tightly sealed

NOTE: Diesel must not be allowed to freeze or it will gel. Water and sediment coming out of the fuel mix should be removed or kept to a minimum. In winter to prevent wax solidifying in the fuel, diesel needs to be mixed with 40% kerosene.

MEDICATIONS/HEALTH ITEMS		
ITEM	SHELF LIFE (See Ch. 15)	COMMENTS
Antacid (Mylanta tablets)	1 year	Store below 30°C or 86°F
Anti-diarrheal (Imodium caplets)	3 years	Store at 15-30°C or 50-86°F
Anti-diarrheal (Imodium capsules)	4 years	Store at 15-30°C or 50-86°F
Anti-Itch Cream (Lanacane & Vagisil)	3 years	
Anti-Itch Powder (Lanacane)	Indefinite	
Antihistamine (Claratyne)	3 years	Store below 30°C or 86°F
Antiseptic Ointment	3-4 years	
Betadine	4 years	Store below 30°C or 86°F
Dettol	3 years	
Antiseptic Spray (Betadine)	4 years	Store below 30°C or 86°F
Aspirin	2 years	
300 mg, oral (Disprin Direct)		
500 mg (Bayer, Disprin Extra Strength)		
500 mg + 9.5 mg codeine (Disprin Forte)		
Birth Control-Condoms	3-4 years	Both latex and spermicide are at risk
Birth Control-Foam (VCF, Delfen)	3 years	Store below 30°C or 86°F
Birth Control-Pills	3-4 years	
Cold/Flu (Codral)	3 years	Store below 25°C or 77°F
Epsom Salts	4 years	
Eye Drops (Murine)	1½ years	
Hemorrhoid Cream (Preparation H)	2 years	
Ibuprophen (Motrin, Nurofen)	3 years	Store below 30°C or 86°F
Insect Repellent (Off, Aerogard)	3 years	
Ipecac Syrup	2 years	
Isopropyl or Rubbing Alcohol	Indefinite	
Mercurochrome/Merthiolate	3 years	Store below 30°C or 86°F
Mineral Oil	Indefinite	
Motion Sickness (Dramamine)	4 years	Store below 30°C or 86°F
Multi-Vitamins	2 years	Keep capped in a cool place, away from light
Paracetamol	2-2½ years	
Panamax	3 years	
Panadol	2 years	
Sinus	2-3 years	
Demazin 12 hour	1 year	Store below 30°C or 86°F
Panadol	2 years	Store below 30°C or 86°F
Sudafed Daytime/Nighttime	3 years	Store below 25°C or 77°F
Sudafed Plus	3 years	
Tea Tree Oil	4 years	
Throat Lozenges		
Difflan	2 years	Store below 30°C or 86°F
Strepsils	2 years	Store below 30°C or 86°F
Strepsils (sugar free)	3 years	Store below 30°C or 86°F
Vitamin B & C complex, water soluble	2 years	

MISCELLANEOUS		
ITEM	SHELF LIFE	COMMENTS
Batteries	3-4 years	
Buttons, assorted sizes	Indefinite	
Candles	Indefinite	Keep wax away from mice & heat, color and scent may fade
Cigarette Lighters (Bic)	Indefinite	
Fire Extinguisher	5 years	
Firestarters (Redheads)	1½ years	Store in a cool place away from flame
Gas Match	Indefinite	

MISCELLANEOUS

ITEM	SHELF LIFE	COMMENTS
Insect Killer (Raid, Mortein)	2-4 years	Store in a cool place out of the sun
Needles and Thread, assorted	Indefinite	
Matches	Indefinite	Keep dry
Needles, assorted sizes	Indefinite	
Pins	Indefinite	
Safety Pins, assorted sizes	Indefinite	

PERSONAL CARE PRODUCTS

ITEM	SHELF LIFE	COMMENTS
After Shave/Men's Cologne	2 years	Keep refrigerated to extend shelf life
Cosmetic Items	Variable	
Blush	3-5 years	
Clinique	5 years	
Estee Lauder	5 years	
Merle Norman	3-5 years	
Cleansers	2-3 years	
Clinique	2-3 years	
Estee Lauder	2-3 years	
Merle Norman	3 years	
Eye Shadow	3-5 years	
Clinique	5 years	
Estee Lauder	5 years	
Merle Norman	3-5 years	
Foundation	2-3 years	
Clinique	2-3 years	Keep refrigerated to extend shelf life
Estee Lauder	2-3 years	
Lipstick	3-5 years	
Clinique	5 years	Keep away from heat
Estee Lauder	3-5 years	
Merle Norman	3-5 years	
Mascara, Opened	3-6 months	
L'Oreal & Clinique	6 months	Do not share mascara; eye infections can occur. If too thick, discard; do not dilute with water
Merle Norman	3 months	
Mascara, Unopened	1-2 years	
L'Oreal & Clinique	2 years	
Merle Norman	1 year	
Moisturizers	2-3 years	
Clinique	2 years	
Estee Lauder	2 years	
Merle Norman	2-3 years	
Ponds	3 years	
Powder	3-5 years	
Clinique	5 years	
Estee Lauder	5 years	
Merle Norman	3-5 years	
Dental Floss	Indefinite	
Deodorant*	3 years	
Gillette	3 years	
Degree	3 years	
Revlon	3 years	
Dental Rinse, Prevident	30 months	
Exfoliating Cream	2-3 years	
Facial Scrub, Nivea	2 years	
Foot, Dr. Scholls	3 years	
Hair Color*	2-4 years	Shelf life may be extended if kept cool
Clairol	3 years	

PERSONAL CARE PRODUCTS

ITEM	SHELF LIFE	COMMENTS
L'Oreal	2 years	
Schwarzkopf	Indefinite	
Hair Conditioner	2-4 years	
Herbal Essence	3 years	
Nexxus	3 years	After shampoo, rinse out
Pantene	3-4 years	
Salon Selectives	3 years	
Schwarzkopf	2 years	
Sunsilk	3 years	
Hair Mousse	3-4 years	
Hair Spray	2-3 years	
Alberto Culver	3 years	
Salon Selectives	3 years	
Schwarzkopf	2 years	
Hand Lotion*	2-3 years	
Nivea	3 years	
Sally Hansen	3 years	
Swiss Formula	2 years	
Vaseline Intensive Care	3 years	
Lip Care	1½-2 years	Products with SPF additives degrade more quickly
ChapStick	2 years	
Lip-Eze	1½ years	
Mouthwash, Listerene & Listermint	2 years	
Nail Polish, Revlon & Sally Hansen	3-5 years	Thickens after 3 years but usable. Refrigerate.
Nail Polish Remover, Revlon	Indefinite	Keep tightly capped to avoid evaporation
Panty Liners	Indefinite	Adhesive strip may degrade
Perfume*	2-3 years	Keep refrigerated to extend shelf life
Petroleum Jelly, Vaseline	Indefinite	May liquefy if heated
Shampoo*	2-4 years	
Herbal Essence	2 years	
Nexxus	3 years	
Pantene	3-4 years	
Salon Selectives	3 years	
Schwarzkopf	2 years	
Sunsilk	3 years	
Shave Cream, Gillette & Skintimate	3 years	
Shower Gel, Gillette & Nivea	3 years	
Soap Bars*	2 years	
Cashmere Bouquet	2 years	
Lux	2 years	
Palmolive	2 years	
Sunscreen*	2-2½ years	Shelf life does not change with the SPF but do with additives like insect repellent
Banana Boat	2-2½ years	
Sundown	2 years	
Tampons/Sanitary Napkins	Indefinite	
Toothbrush	Indefinite	
Toothpaste*	2-3 years	May have date code on the crimped end of the tube
Aim	3 years	
Crest, Oral-B	2 years	

ADDITIONAL NOTES:

Hair Color – Nice N' Easy date codes their boxes. Look for the batch code that will read similar to "B 5 678". This product was made May 6, 1978 with the last two digits indicating the year; the first three are month and day.

Hand Lotion – Oils may separate if exposed to heat

Nail Polish – Use thinners if thickened. Can be used indefinitely until the color permanently separates.

Perfume – Of fragrances, perfume or parfum has the longest shelf life, then eau de toilette, then cologne. The more pure essence is diluted with alcohol, the shorter the shelf life. Heat quickly ruins the scent.

Sunscreen – shelf life does not seem to change with the SPF but does with additives like insect repellents. Sundown dates codes their products "<B> 706303." The "<B>" is for batch. "706" is for year and month. This product would have been made June, 1997. The last 3 numbers are the batch number, which can be ignored.

Toothpaste – some are products have the date code on the crimped end of the tube. Aim Toothpaste dates their products like 703412. The first digit "7" is the year in which it was made. Manufacturers also state toothpaste is OK to use 1 – 3 years past the expiration date but the flavor may have degraded.

PET SUPPLIES		
ITEM	SHELFLIFE	COMMENTS
Bird Seed	2 years	Keep dry and away from rodents
Bowls, Water and Food	Indefinite	
Cat Food, Canned	1½-2 yrs	
Cat Food, Dry	1½-2 yrs	Keep dry and away from rodents
Catnip Toys	1 year	
Collars	Indefinite	Allow for growth, if applicable
Dog Bones (rawhide)	Indefinite	* Keep dry and away from rodents. Moisture will induce mold.
Dog Chewies (rawhide)	Indefinite	* Keep dry and away from rodents. Moisture will induce mold.
Dog Food, Canned	1½-2 yrs	
Dog Food, Dry	1½-2 yrs	Keep dry and away from rodents
Fish Food, flakes	1½ yrs	Keep dry
Leashes	Indefinite	
Muzzles	Indefinite	
Kitty Litter, Plain	Indefinite	
Toys	Variable	

* NOTE: If you're going to give you dog rawhide chewies, only purchase products made in the U.S. Our dogs, Seismo and Taco suffered *severe* acute pancreatitis after eating chewies made in another country.

Salmonella bacteria are often present especially if the rawhide comes from outside the US. Another problem is arsenic being used as a preservative. This is, in essence, giving your pet poison!

Other dangerous additives can include antibiotics, lead and insecticides. Some countries like Thailand even include pieces of dog and cat skin in these products. Health problems from rawhide chews include fever, depression, dehydration, sore throat, choking, abdominal pain, loss of appetite and intestinal blockage as well as the profuse diarrhea Taco and Seismo experienced. You can read the details on the dangers of rawhide in Chapter 37 on Pet Preparedness.

Chapter 17: Build Basic Underground Storage

In preparing for what may come, we give consideration to a great many different potential problems and disasters:

- Flood
- Earthquake
- Fire
- Civil unrest
- Heating problems due to the sun
- Extra storage space
- Food shortages
- Need for temporary shelter
- Root cellar
- Volcano
- Disease
- Tornado

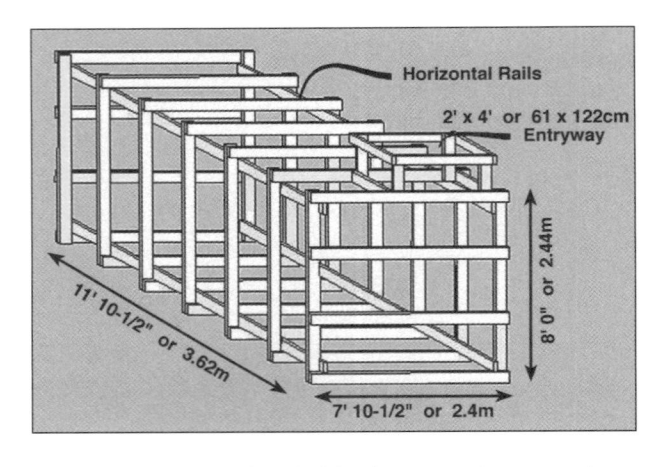

When food, water, general supplies and first aid items have been covered, one might begin to wonder where to store these reserves, especially if spare space is in short supply. A relatively inexpensive option is to construct underground shelter. Not only will it keep your goods handy for easy use, but also nature's insulator, the earth, will hold them at cooler temperatures. If civil unrest occurs, these supplies will be less obvious to intruders. It would also serve as temporary shelter from tornadoes.

Doug, a friend of ours, decided to store his items underground and he devised a simple plan to construct this shelter. It can be altered if different dimensions are desired. This plan is both relatively easy and an inexpensive method of storage.

Some folks choose geodesic domes; they are really nice but costly. Placed above ground, they don't offer privacy for storage. Used shipping containers cost around US$2000, which puts them out of range for some people. Other possibilities include area caves, but these are only available to the privileged few who have them close by. Most are now privately owned.

Doug's grandparents started to build a house in Connecticut in the late twenties, but as they progressed, money suddenly dried up and all they had built was the basement. They took the boards for framing what would have been the first floor and constructed a roof. Doug's mother grew up in that "underground" house, and while there, rode out the worst hurricane New England ever saw. While all of their neighbors' homes were literally destroyed by high winds, his grandparents and family were dry, safe and warm.

These are the plans for a simple box that can be put, or more accurately, built in a hole. Properly covered, it will withstand a great many adverse conditions. The construction plans were designed for the budget-minded and crafted as simply as possible. Construction directions also take into account that materials may not be purchased all at once. Once decent shelter is achieved, comforts can be added as materials are acquired.

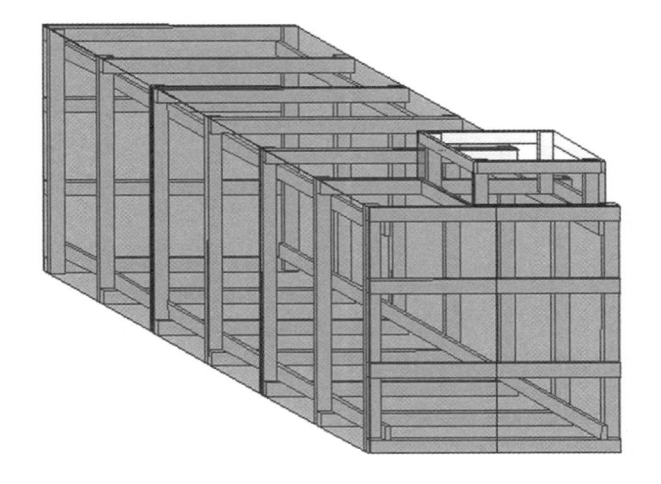

Most of us are physically able to dig a hole by hand with a shovel, pick and pry bar, but if you have access to a Bobcat or other similar small excavator, it would be worth it! Many rent-all stores have these available on day and half day rates. The hole should be twelve feet (4m) wide, by sixteen feet (5m) long. Depth is up to you. The deeper, the better as long as you don't mound too much dirt on top collapsing the structure. Save the dirt that comes out of the hole to cover the box.

NOTE: For Aussies, at this point, please skip down to: "Metric Instructions."

The box as shown here is made up of five ribs, and two ends. The simplest waterproofing is accomplished by using 10-mil plastic. Thicker is better since it resists tearing. First the entire box is wrapped in plastic, then the space between the box and the dirt wall is filled in with earth.

Last, the box is covered with earth, which is why deeper is better. Before putting the frame together, line the hole with plastic. Since the frame will be assembled over the plastic, be careful not to puncture it.

The box will be seven feet, ten and one half inches (240cm) wide, eight feet (244cm) tall, and eleven feet, ten and one half inches (362cm) long. The shaft for the entryway is two feet wide by four feet long by two feet high.

U.S. INSTRUCTIONS

To fasten this shelter together, if power is available, use 3" deck screws to join the 2x6's together and 2" deck screws to attach the wafer board to the frame.

If there is no power, then a good old hammer and nails will have to do. Use 10d cement coat box nails if possible, for everything.

The problem with hammer and nails is that with pounding, the boards may vibrate loose with this type frame. Have a good heavy brace on the other side of where you're nailing, like an 8-pound sledge hammer.

The horizontal members of the ribs and end pieces should be cut to seven feet, ten and one half inches long. All vertical members are to be eight feet. This allows for the overlap of the top panels over the side panels (image previous page).

Construct the ribs and ends, and using the horizontal rails, fasten the frame together. Everything must work in two feet increments, so the panels will match the frame. Be as meticulous as possible in making the frame square and it will make everything will fit better. The panels are four feet wide, and must butt together in the center of the rib.

Once the frame is complete, screw the panels to the frame. Do one end first, then the sides, working from one end to the other.

Before completing the remaining end and top, cut the floor panels to six feet, ten inches, place them inside, and fasten them down. Finish the remaining end.

You can now put the two whole top panels in place, and then cut the last panel to fit around the entryway. The last panel will cover the access entryway. This will keep debris from falling inside. Make the hatch cover 3 inches bigger than the outside of the entryway, and frame it with the last 2x6. It will cover the hatch, and fastened down with hook and eyes, will provide some security.

Chimney dimensions have been purposely omitted. Measure the biggest body that will be entering the shelter and cut to fit.

At this point, you will need a ladder inside for access, finish wrapping the plastic around everything. Backfill the dirt around the box and cover it with about a foot and a half on top. Pack it down as best you can so it won't blow away.

The inside can be finished with wood frame bunks for sleeping and storage. The exposed interior studs are easy to work with. Whatever framework is added inside, fasten it securely to the sides, top and bottom. This will serve to reinforce the entire structure.

Since the entire box is covered in plastic, it won't breath very well. A lot of bodies generate moisture. With nowhere to evaporate, this will eventually become a problem in moister climates. The hatch ventilation may or may not be sufficient.

U.S. MATERIALS LIST
- 40 – 2x6 – 8' studs
- 17 – 4'x8' particle board or wafer board if available
- 3" deck screws (option 10d cement coat box nails and hammer)
- 2" deck screws (option 10d cement coat box nails and hammer)
- 1 roll 20'x100' 6 mil black plastic
- 1 set hook and eye fastener

METRIC INSTRUCTIONS

The simplest waterproofing is accomplished by using 200μm plastic. Thicker is better since it resists tearing. This product is available only in smaller sizes so sections will need to be taped together with waterproof tape both on the inside and outside seams. Wrap the entire box in plastic, and then fill the space between the covered box and the dirt wall with earth.

Last, the box is covered with earth which is why deeper is better. Before putting the frame together, line the hole with plastic. Since the frame will be assembled over the plastic, be careful not to puncture it.

The box as shown above is made up of five ribs, and two ends. See first shelter picture. The box will be 245cm wide, 244cm tall, and 362cm long. The shaft for the entryway is 61cm by 122cm long by 61cm high.

As far as fastening this shelter together, if power is available, use 8cm deck screws to fasten the timber together and 5cm deck screws to attach the particle board to the frame. If there is no power, then a good old hammer and nails will have to do. Use titadeck nails, if possible, for everything.

The problem with hammer and nails is that with pounding, the boards tend to vibrate loose with this type frame. Have a good heavy brace on the other side of what you're nailing, like a 4kg sledge hammer.

The horizontal members of the ribs and end pieces should be cut to 2.40m long. All vertical members are to be 2.44m. This allows for the overlap of the top panels over the side panels. Construct the ribs and ends, and using the horizontal rails, fasten the frame together. Everything must work in 61cm increments, so the panels will match the frame. Being as meticulous as possible in making the frame square will make everything will fit better. The panels are 121.9cm wide, and must butt together in the center of the rib (see pictures on preceding page)

Once the frame is complete, screw the panels to the frame. Do one end first, then the sides, working from one end to the other.

Before completing the remaining end and top, cut the floor panels to 208.28cm long, place them inside, and fasten them down. Finish the remaining end.

You can now put the two whole top panels in place, and then cut the last panel to fit around the entryway. The last panel will cover the access entryway. This will keep debris from falling inside. Make the hatch cover 7.6cm bigger than the outside of the entryway, and frame it with the last 90 x 45 x 95cm stud. It will cover the hatch, and fastened down with hook and eyes, will provide some security.

Chimney dimensions have been purposely omitted. Measure the biggest body that will be entering the shelter and cut to fit.

At this point, you will need a ladder inside for access, finish wrapping the plastic around everything. Backfill the dirt around the box and cover it about 45cm on top. Pack it down as best you can so it won't blow away.

The inside can be finished with timber frame bunks for sleeping and storage. The exposed interior studs are easy to work with. Whatever framework is added inside, fasten it securely to the sides, top and bottom. This will serve to reinforce the entire structure.

Since the entire box is covered in plastic, it won't breath very well. A lot of bodies generate moisture. With nowhere to evaporate, this will eventually become a problem in moister climates. The hatch ventilation may or may not be sufficient.

MATERIALS LIST – AUSTRALIA
- 40 – 90 x 45 x 95cm – studs
- 17 – 2400 x 1200 x 95cm particle board
- 8cm deck or regular screws (option 75 mm titadeck nails and hammer)
- 5cm deck or regular screws (option 50 mm titadeck nails and hammer)
- rolls of 200µm polyethylene
- wide waterproof tape
- 1 set hook and eye fastener

Chapter 18: Build a Hand Pump

PUMP ASSEMBLY NOTES AND INSTRUCTIONS

Keith Hendricks, designer of this hand pump states he built it in 20 minutes for about US$20. It can be used in water wells that have no existing feed lines, wiring or submersible pumps in place, or in water wells with them in place by the addition of a 1½" (3.8cm) interior diameter PVC pipe as a pump guide sleeve. The 1½" (3.8cm) interior diameter PVC guide sleeve should have a cap glued on the bottom end and ½" (1.27cm) holes drilled through the bottom pipe section above the end cap. The holes allow water to flow freely into the 1½" (3.8cm) interior diameter sleeve when it's submerged into water.

The sleeve separates the hand pump from feed lines, wiring or submersible pumps so they don't rub during pumping. It also keeps the water clearer by keeping the hand pump off the bottom of the well. The guide sleeve can be bolted to the above ground well casing area with ½" (1.27cm) carriage bolts and nuts. Be sure to seal the bolt holes with rubber washers or caulking. The guide sleeve and pump should extend down below the water table.

As the foot valve of the pump is pushed down below the water table, the water flows up through the foot valve and into the pump shaft above it. The valve is open on the down stroke and closed on the up stroke. Repeated pumping motion shoves the water up the pipe and out the hose by a hydraulic ram effect. The water flows out the holes on the down stroke only.

Pump length is based on well depth and the water table height in it. The pump should be long enough to stay submerged in at least 3' – 5' (91.4 – 152.4cm) of water so the pump remains in the water during the pumping motion cycle. Remember that water tables may change with seasonal conditions.

If you plan to use a well has been abandoned, water samples should be tested. Stagnant or unused wells should be cleaned out with a power pump and disinfected. (See Chapter 5 for well purification.) Local health departments and well drillers maintain well records and can give information on well depths, testing and on keeping wells sanitary. Wells and water tables can also be established with a sanitized cord and plumb bob. When using untested well water, always water treat by boiling, bleach, iodine filters or other standard measures to protect from typhoid, dysentery, diarrhea, cholera, Giardia, Cryptosporidia and other diseases.

Disinfect hands before using the well. Keep all pump parts off the ground and disinfect them before placing them in the well. Ill persons must not have any contact with the well area, pump or water containers. Keep the area around the well sanitary and never drink from the hose or allow any waste water or animals near the well area.

Leaving the pump in the well and keeping the well cap on when not in use will help keep the well sanitary. If no sleeve is used in the well, the pump can be hung inside the casing by a cord with a Prusik knot around the pump shaft. Install a hook below the well cap area on the inside of the casing and hang the pump from it. If a pump sleeve is used, make the sleeve about 2" (5cm) shorter than the well casing top.

To tie a Prusik Knot (see photograph right), lay the loop over the rod (in this case, the pump shaft). Pass the tails behind the rod and through the loop to form the first turn. Wind the tail two or three more times through the loop. Pull on the tails as each turn is completed to shorten the loop. Pull on the tails to tighten loops after final turn.

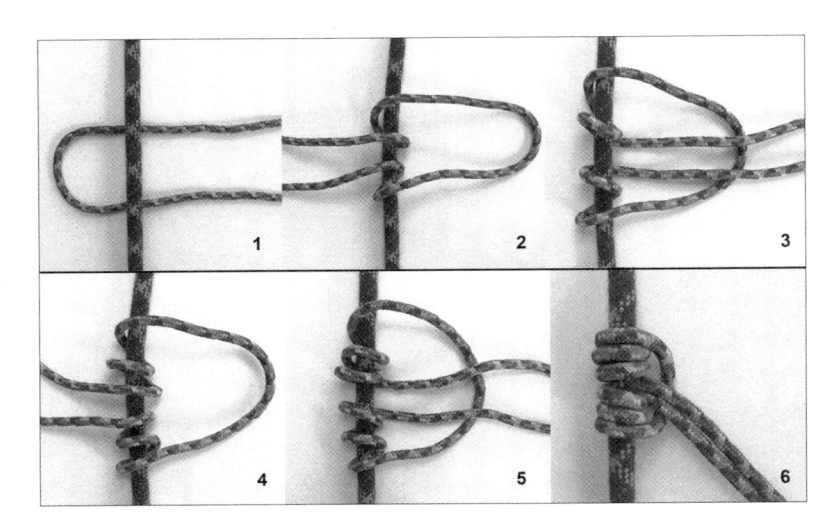

Make the pump long enough to stand above the sleeve but still be short enough for the well cap to be replaced over the well casing. A hook can also be wired to the top of the pump shaft and hung over the sleeve edge.

The pump can be made from copper and brass. It will cost more, be heavier and freeze easier in cold climates, but allows the pump to be used on fuels from storage tanks. Some makes and models of U.S. brass foot valves are: the Simmons model 1402, the Merril Series 810 model FV75, the Water Ace model RFV75 and the Brady model SFV75 (plastic).

A plunger action check valve can be used but you should put a ⅛" (.3cm) screen over the intake end and secure it with a ring clamp to help keep any well debris out of the valve. Foot and check valves have a closure spring which may need to be trimmed down or removed to get the best flow rate from pressures generated by hand pumping.

The weep hole is about ⅛" (.3cm) diameter. It should be drilled through one side of the pump shaft above the foot valve but a good distance below the frost line in your area. This allows the water in the pump shaft to slowly drain back down into the well when the pumping stops. This helps keep the well from freezing in cold weather.

DEPTH USE

This pump works great at depths of 0-20 feet (0-6m); good at 20-35 feet (6-10.7m); OK at 50 feet (15.2m) using the specifications previously given. It remains workable down to 75 feet (23m) for one person, but beyond that, it's too heavy for only one person to operate due to the increased water and pipe weight. It will work deeper and is limited only by the person's downward thrust with more energy than it takes to suspend the existing water column in the pipe.

If you need access to water at greater depths, make the following changes, which will increase working depth to about 150 feet (45.7m):

1. Substitute ½" (1.27cm) PVC pipe instead of ¾" (1.9cm) for the pump sections, collars and adapters.
2. Don't drill the ½" (1.27cm) holes in the 1½" (3.8cm) casing, keep the guide sleeve as a closed pipe except at the bottom.

Use a 1½ to ¾" (3.8 to 1.9cm) reducer as a replacement for part "S" (the end cap) and thread another ¾ foot valve into it, facing downward into the well.

The finished product should be a 1½" (3.8cm) guide sleeve with a foot valve at the bottom and the ½" (1.27cm) PVC pump with a foot valve on the bottom of it. The guide sleeve should be suspended into the water table at least 5 to ten feet.

When the pump is stroked up, it will suck the water in through the guide sleeve foot valve. On the down stroke, the guide sleeve foot valve closes and the pump pipe foot valve opens, shoving it up the ½" (1.27cm) pipe.

Flow rates of two to three gallons (7.5-11.3L) per minute are possible at this depth with a steady stroke. Mark your pipe lengths so you do not bottom out on your stroke when pumping. The reduction to ½" (1.27cm) PVC reduces the overall weight of the unit to allow for the greater depth.

The pump model shown is only one of an endless number of pump variations that can be built. Parts are becoming harder to find in quantity due to low inventory stocking practices at stores. Other pipe types, sizes, adapters and fittings can be readily made into pumps that will work with varying degrees of efficiency levels.

A functional pump only needs a foot valve, a weep hole for cold climates, a stiff hollow pipe shaft above the valve for the water to flow up in, and a hose or side pipe discharge to get the water away from the pump shaft and into a container.

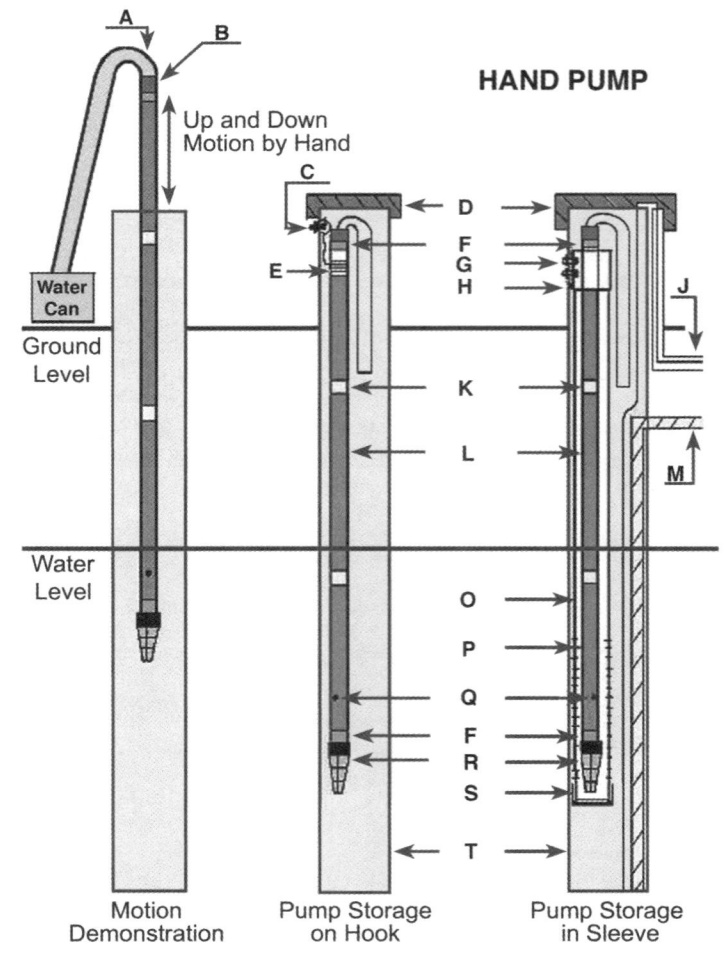

HAND PUMP

Motion Demonstration

Pump Storage on Hook

Pump Storage in Sleeve

Dare To Prepare: Chapter 18: Build a Hand Pump

HAND PUMP PARTS LIST

LEGEND FOR PUMP DRAWING:
- A. ⅝" (1.47cm) or larger garden hose (inside diameter)
- B. ¾" (1.9cm) NPT [National Pipe Thread standard] to garden hose adapter
- C. Open eye hook, washers and nuts
- D. Well cap
- E. ½" (1.27cm) thick nylon cord
- F. ¾" (1.9cm) PVC schedule 40 to ¾" (1.9cm) NPT adapter
- G. ½" (1.27cm) carriage bolts, washers and nuts
- H. 1½" (3.8cm) inside diameter PVC schedule 40 collar
- J. Electric power pump wiring
- K. ¾" (1.9cm) inside diameter PVC schedule 40 pipe collar
- L. ¾" (1.9cm) inside diameter PVC schedule 40 pipe section
- M. Electric power pump feed line
- O. 1½" (3.8cm) inside diameter PVC schedule 40 pipe
- P. ½" (1.27cm) holes in 1½" (3.8cm) PVC pipe sleeve
- Q. ⅛"(.3cm) diameter weep hole
- R. ¾" (1.9cm) foot valve
- S. 1½" (3.8cm) PVC schedule 40 pipe cap
- T. Metal well casing

NOTE: The letters above reference the drawing of the pump. For the pipe, adapters, etc. used, make sure all parts are made with the same thread count.

OTHER ITEMS NEEDED
- PVC solvent
- PVC glue
- Pipe tape or compound
- Sleeve bolt holes
- Pipe wrenches
- Drill and Drill bits for weep hole
- Eye hook hole
- Rags
- Crescent wrenches
- Allen wrench for well caps

These parts are for this model only. Parts and adapters can be varied. The only thing necessary for a working pump is a foot valve, a weep hole for cold climates, a stiff hollow shaft above the foot valve and a hose or side pipe discharge for the water as it comes out.

Parts are already scarce due to low inventory stock management practices in stores.

Chapter 19: Making Colloidal Silver

Over the last two decades, Colloidal Silver has enjoyed resurging interest. Silver was standard treatment for a long list of ailments dating back to Egypt. Ancient Romans recognized silver vessels, which stored food and drink, helped prevent some diseases. Before the invention of the icebox in America, it was common practice to place a silver dollar in the bottom of milk containers to keep it fresh.

People used to ingest small particles of silver with every meal when they dined from silver plates and drank from silver goblets. However, when modern medicine began implementing antibiotics, silver was gradually replaced. Additional incentives to promote sulfa drugs were purely economic. Prior to 1938, the cost of silver was US$100 an ounce. In today's market, that would translate to US$1,325 per ounce.

Second, drug companies couldn't patent silver, but they could patent sulfa drugs. These two factors greatly influenced the decision to promote prescribed antibiotics. While antibiotics certainly have their niche in healing, both improper use and over use have made stains of bacteria drug-resistant.

So once again, the pendulum shifts, not to replace antibiotics, but to again embrace silver's healing qualities. Colloidal Silver should not be used in place of a physician's treatment. If you have further questions about Colloidal Silver, consult your physician. While some people swear by its use, not everyone has the same response.

Here are several colloidal silver options:
1. Purchase the product bottled and ready to use
2. Purchase a colloidal silver generator and make your own silver solutions
3. Purchase the raw materials and make both your own generator and colloidal solutions

MAKING YOUR OWN GENERATOR

OPTION 1

Materials Needed
- 3 – 9V batteries (type MN1604 regular alkaline transistor radio batteries)
- 3 battery snap-on lead connectors
- 2 insulated alligator clips
- 1 "grain-of-wheat" 24V 40 mA sub-miniature incandescent bulb
- 1 foot (30.5cm) of 3/32" heat-shrink insulation tubing
- 10" (25.4cm) pure silver wire, 14 gauge is best (use .999 pure silver, not sterling silver which is only .925 pure)
- 1 foot (30.5cm) 2-conductor stranded insulated wire for clip-leads

The total cost is around US$20 and due to the difference in exchange rate, less than AU$30.

Assembly

To assemble the generator, solder the three snap-on clips in series, red to black. The three batteries will produce 27 volts. Next, connect the incandescent lamp in series with either the positive or negative output lead. Solder the red insulated alligator clip to the positive (anode) and the black insulated clip to the negative (cathode) 2-conductor lead wire. Heat shrink insulation over the soldered areas with a blow dryer. Cut the silver wire into 2 – 5" (12.7cm) lengths. Bend the top ends of the silver wires so they can clip onto the edge of a glass. Plastic may also be used but not metal.

MAKING COLLOIDAL SILVER USING OPTION 1

Step 1 Immerse the pure silver wires, attached to the alligator clips, in DISTILLED (not filtered or purified) water mixed with Sea Salt if the colloidal silver is to be ingested. (For household use, tap water may be used.) Make sure 75 – 80% of the wires is immersed.

Step 2 Never allow the submerged wires to touch. Spacing between the wires is not critical, but an allowance of 1½" (3.8cm) will produce a slightly higher ppm (parts per million). If the wires are allowed to touch, the process will stop. This small voltage can't shock you when submerging the wires so don't be afraid to touch them.

Step 3 The process starts immediately when the alligator clips are both attached to the submerged wires and stops when either or both clips are disconnected. During activation, the light bulb should remain very dim or even completely dark.

Step 4 A three-minute activation of 8 ounces (236 ml) properly conductive water at 70°F (21°C) will yield strength of approximately 3 ppm. Each additional one-minute of activation will increase the strength by 1ppm. Each 10% increase in temperature will double the ppm for a given length of time. A strength of 3 – 5 ppm is optimal. The conductivity of the water, surface of the electrodes, amount of current and the length of activation time will all vary the ppm of your colloidal silver.

Step 5 Disconnect the alligator clips and wipe the electrode wires clean after each use to remove silver oxide. Using a paper towel to wipe the electrodes while still damp should provide sufficient cleaning.

TIP: Use very little salt. One grain of Sea Salt per 8 ounces water should suffice. Mix with a non-metallic only stirrer or spoon. Too much salt will produce silver chloride, not colloidal silver, resulting in a gray, milky or dishwater color. Use only Sea Salt; table salt contains additives.

If the light bulb glows too brightly while making colloidal silver, too much salt has been added. This solution can be used for household cleaning. The bulb should remain off or glow only very slightly if the solution is to be ingested. Old batteries will also produce a very dimly glowing light bulb. Check your batteries by touching the two alligator clips together.

Each set of batteries should make at least 100,000 batches of colloidal silver before replacement becomes necessary. When making and storing colloidal silver, use non-conductive containers of dark brown glass or opaque plastic – never metal. Using non-pure silver containing nickel can be toxic. Use only .999 pure silver.

OPTION 2

MATERIALS NEEDED
A. 1 ounce fine (.999) silver
B. 1 – 9 volt battery adapter
C. 3 – 9 volt batteries
D. 1 – 40 milliamp, 28v bulb
E. 1 socket that fits the 28v bulb
F. 2 small alligator clips
G. 1 glass quart (liter) jar
H. 1 plastic lid that fit the jar opening
I. Distilled water

TOOLS NEEDED
1. Pliers
2. Wire stripper/cutter
3. Hacksaw
4. Electrical Tape
5. Scissors
6. Solder and Soldering Iron (optional)

ASSEMBLY
Step 1 Cut silver lengthwise with a hacksaw.
Step 2 Plug the 9v batteries into each other creating a 27-volt battery.
Step 3 Cut the 9-volt adapter in half by pulling the wire apart. Carefully cutting the plastic and cardboard between the positive and negative adapters. Patch newly created halves with electrical tape where needed.
Step 4 Strip the end of the 9-volt adapter halves. Crimp or solder the alligator clips to the stripped ends.
Step 5 Cut the wire to one of the adapter halves at its midpoint, strip the ends, and solder the wire ends to the bulb socket. Screw the bulb into the socket.
Step 6: Cut 2 holes an inch (2.54cm) apart in the plastic lid that will just allow the silver halves to pass through. The alligator clips should rest on the lid.
Step 7 Fill a sterilized glass jar with *distilled water*, and place the entire apparatus on the jar so the silver electrodes dip into the water ½ – 1" (1.27 – 2.54cm).

NOTE: The bulb should not light. The bulb will light under the following circumstances:
- Distilled water not used or had been contaminated

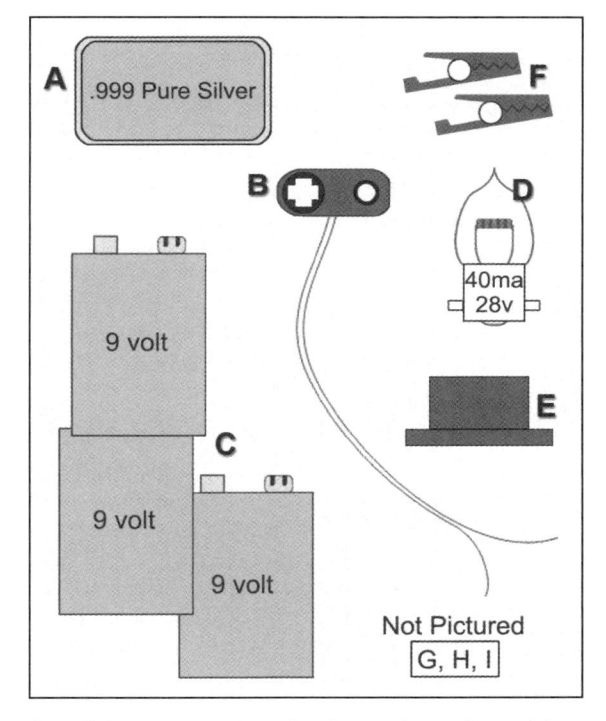

- Electrodes are left in the water too long
- Electrodes were touching in the water

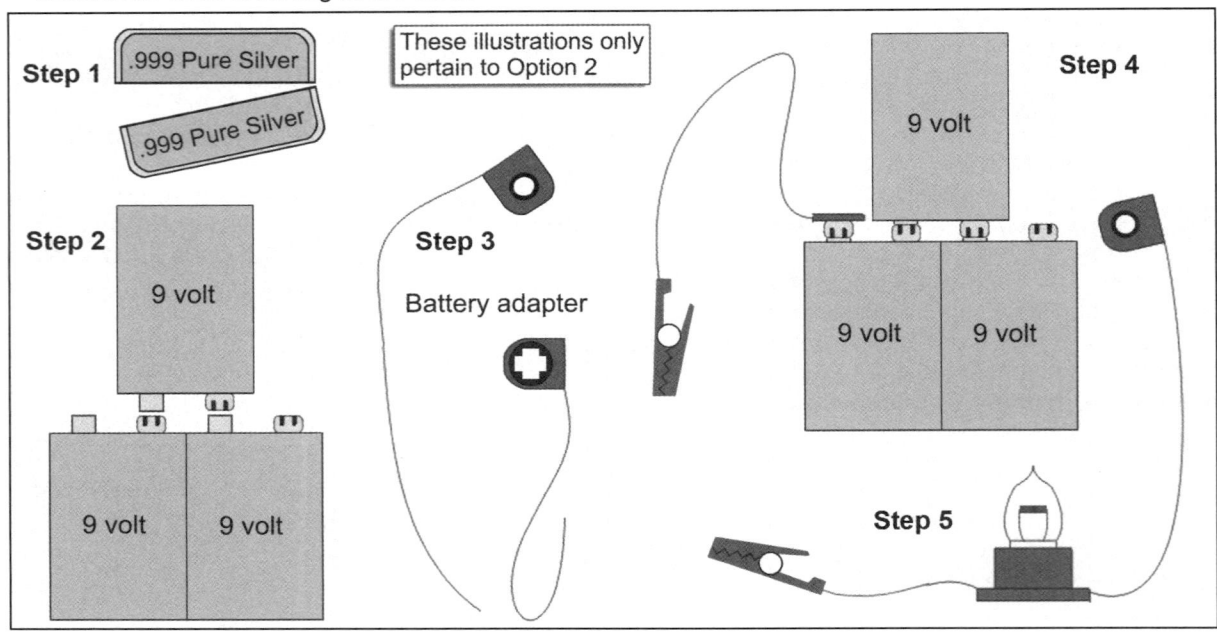

[Diagram: Steps 1–7 showing assembly of 9-volt batteries with .999 Pure Silver electrodes, battery adapter, clips, and a quart or liter jar. These illustrations only pertain to Option 2.]

An hour and a half should produce a quart or liter 75-ppm colloidal silver solution. After making the batch, clean the oxidation off the electrodes with a pot scrubbing type sponge.

STORAGE: Make and store the colloids in non-conductive containers of dark brown glass or opaque plastic – never metal.

DISCLAIMER: Holly Deyo and Stan Deyo specifically make no medical claims, or otherwise, for the treatment, prevention, cure, or mitigation of disease. If you have a medical condition, we recommend you see a health professional. The information found here is for educational use only and is not meant to be a prescription for any disease or illness.

BUYING COLLOIDAL SILVER PRODUCTS

For those who would rather purchase colloidal silver "ready-made", check area health food stores or order it through the Internet. There is a price spectrum ranging from $4.25 to $10/oz – and higher. Among many products names, colloidal silver is marketed under Silverkaire, Silver Ice, Nature's Rx, Ultra-Clear, WaterOZ and MesoSilver. Some of these are actually silver solutions or silver protein products, not colloidal silver. The rule of buyer beware applies.

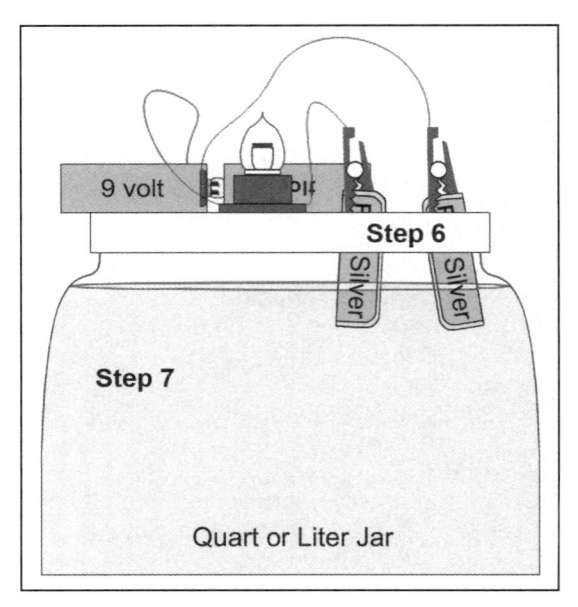

SOME C.S. IS B.S.

While some colloidal silver users report great benefits; others see nothing. How can that be? Maybe it's because they aren't using REAL colloidal silver.

The biggest difference in these marketed goods is the <u>total surface area</u> of the silver particles used in manufacturing. This directly relates to its effectiveness according to Dr. Ronald Gibbs of the University of Delaware, Center for Colloidal Science. He states that, "While the concentration of silver in colloidal silver samples is important, concentration alone is misleading without knowing the proportion of dissolved material to particulate material and without knowing the size distribution of the particles."[52]

The following information may account for widely varying results in colloidal silver usage. Available commercially are three types of products all marketed as Colloidal Silver:

1) Ionic silver solutions
2) Silver protein a.k.a. mild silver protein
3) True silver colloids

Confused? The following table highlights the important differences.

\multicolumn{6}{c}{THE COLOR OF SILVER}
Types of C.S.	Product Contents	Color	Silver Surface Area	Product Type Clues	Safe To Use?
True Silver Colloid	20-49% silver ions; 50%+ silver particles	colorless, but not clear	highest particle surface area relative to total silver content	never clear like water; most expensive	yes, won't cause argyria
Ionic Silver Solution* (most prevalent)	silver ions and silver particles	typically clear as water or has slight yellow tint	fairly low relative to total silver content	looks just like water	yes, when taken according to mfg. recommended dosage won't cause argyria
Silver Protein (second most prevalent)	metallic silver particles and protein binder like gelatin	light amber to almost black with higher silver content; concentration usually 30-10,000 ppm	very low particle surface area relative to total silver content	foams when shaken, high silver concentration, color	no, known to cause argyria; bacteria can grow in the gelatin

NOTES: * "Colloidal silver generators" sold to home hobbyists all produce ionic silver solutions.

BUYING COLLOIDAL SILVER

Below is a partial listing of other products marketed as Colloidal Silver. Again, some are, some aren't. According to Dr. Gibbs' research, avoid products that use gelatins and other proteins as binders. Look for colloids with more particle surface area. You'll reap a greater benefit while ingesting less silver. Pay particular attention to the 3rd column. Products are listed from most to least particle surface area and then cost (5th column) secondarily.

\multicolumn{7}{c}{COMPARISON OF "COLLOIDAL SILVER" PRODUCTS[53]}
Type	Product Name	Part. Surface Area cm^2/mL	Efficiency Index	Cents /mL	Cents Per cm^2 of Part. Surface	CM^2 Part. Surface Per $
C	MesoSilver 20	104.700	5235.00	11.970	0.1143	874.70
P	Innovative Natural Prod. 500	12.390	20.50	33.770	2.725	36.70
C	Utopia Advanced Col. Silver 20	12.200	924.00	12.240	1.003	99.70
P	Herbal Healer Col. Silver 500	2.513	3.81	30.430	12.11	8.25
C	Kelly Col. Silver 20	1.420	122.30	6.340	4.46	22.40
C	Source Naturals Col. Silver 30	0.881	24.30	13.940	15.83	6.32
I	Electra Clear Col. Sil. 10 ppm	0.662	25.10	3.16	4.77	20.90
P	Intl. Pharmacy Invive 50	0.621	0.44	7.608	12.25	8.16
P	Futurebiotics Adv. Col. Silver	0.591	6.00	28.65	48.00	2.00
I	ASAP 22	0.587	26.30	15.216	25.92	3.85
I	Argentyn 23 ppm	0.355	22.60	20.12	56.67	1.76
I	High Energy Lab Col. Sil. 15 ppm	0.319	15.10	4.22	13.22	328
C	Vitol Super Col. Silver 5 ppm	0.286	54.60	13.39	46.82	2.14
I	Ultra Pure Col. Silver 35	0.225	13.60	7.803	34.68	2.88
I	Sovereign Silver 10	0.217	22.30	25.36	116.9	0.86
I	ASAP 10	0.112	10.20	10.99	98.11	1.02
I	Wonder Water 10	0.096	9.60	4.666	48.60	2.06
I	Silver Wain Water 3	0.083	34.20	2.640	31.8	3.14
I	Daily Mfg. Col. Silver 20 ppm	0.080	3.77	10.100	126.3	0.79
I	Silver Lightning 5	0.078	17.00	1.05	13.44	7.44

Type: *Column 1* C=Colloid, I=Ionic, P=Protein.
Particle Surface Area: *Column 3* (cm^2/mL) is particle surface area in square cm per mL.
Efficiency Index: *Column 4* Relates how efficiently surface area is generated per unit of concentration (ppm).
Comparing Cost: *Column 5* is cost per mL. Column 6 (Cents/cm^2) is the price in cents per square cm of particle surface area. *Column 7* (cm^2/$) is square cm of particle surface area per dollar of cost.

Chapter 20: Soapmaking

Two very important things we can learn to become more self-sufficient are soap and candlemaking. Our family candlemaking days traced back to years in Girl Scouts and more of my mother's own self-sufficiency. We could have purchased these things, but she took pleasure and comfort knowing she could provide the family with these items if she had to. Actually, she just enjoyed creating and seeing faces light up when friends received these housewarming or "hope you're feeling better" gifts.

Soapmaking is a little more involved and just as rewarding. Not only can you make bar soap but laundry soap and shampoo as well by varying the ingredients. Supplies for both of these projects are readily available in most craft and hobby supply stores.

Just like having food and water tucked away, it's a good feeling to know you can easily provide these necessities for your family and friends.

SOAPMAKING

Why fuss making soap? Here are some good reasons:
- Home made soap can easily duplicate and surpass commercial products for considerably less price
- You can scent, color or make them all natural if that's your preference
- It's fun and creative
- It's a good barterable skill and a necessary item
- Makes a great home-based business
- Home made bars can last longer than their commercial counterparts depending on ingredients used

Benefits from knowing how to make soap don't stop there. Many of the same techniques are used in making shampoo, lip balm, lotions, bath salts and perfume. For some of these other products, the process is much simpler.

Like many skills, various legends surround soap's start. It's generally accepted that the origin traces back to early Roman days. One legend says soap was "discovered" after heavy rain saturated the slopes of Mount Sapo, an ancient site of animal sacrifice.

Left over animal fat and ash collected under ceremonial altars. This, mixed with rain, flowed into the Tiber River where women washed clothes. Miraculously their clothing cleaned easier and more quickly in water containing this substance! Voilà! The emergence of soap!

It's doubtful it really happened this way as there's a little more to the soapmaking process. With a bit of practice and experimentation, you'll be making your own fabulous creations!

SOAP VS DETERGENTS

There's some confusion between soap and cleansing items for shower and bath which really aren't soaps at all, but detergents.

Soap is made with just three things:
- Lye (a form of potash, sometimes called caustic soda or sodium hydroxide, NaOH)

- Animal fats and/or vegetable oils
- Water

Combining these ingredients to make soap is called "saponification", a term you'll hear frequently in this craft. Detergents differ from soap because they contain petroleum-based ingredients instead of fat or oil.

Before making your first batch, be sure to read "Safety Precautions for Lye." Lye is a caustic and needs to be handled carefully. A few simple but important guidelines will make soapmaking a fun, safe experience. The remaining topics will help you decide things like:

- What do I need to make soap
- Should I use fragrance oils or essential oils
- How can I color my soap
- What else can go in soap
- What type of molds are available
- Signs of problems and how to fix them
- And of course, recipes!

SAFETY MEASURES FOR USING LYE

The list is fairly short and mostly common sense. There's no way to make it interesting, but read through it anyway. Becoming familiar with these lye and lye/water safety precautions will make your soap projects rewarding, not painful. The object isn't to scare you away from soapmaking, only prevent injury. Don't be put off by the "list". People have made soap safely for many decades. Just anticipate any possible pitfalls.

1. Lye is caustic and poisonous so treat it with care.
2. Be careful not to inhale the dust and work in a well-ventilated area. Soapmaking is easiest if you have quick access to the stove and sink, making the kitchen the ideal work area. Use the exhaust hood when mixing lye or mix lye outside.
3. Have adequate space to work on. Protect all work surfaces. Lye can "redecorate" your kitchen!
4. Wear protective goggles and rubber gloves, long sleeve shirts and close fitting clothing; protect your feet, no sandals.
5. Lye corrodes metal so remove jewelry.
6. If you accidentally get lye on your skin, flush with ordinary vinegar and wash well with soap and water. (Lye will feel slippery on skin.)
7. Do not leave the area unattended. If you're tired or short of time, leave soapmaking for another day.
8. Keep containers, stirring spoons and molds just for soapmaking.
9. Do not attempt to heat lye in microwave or on the stove.
10. Keep children and pets away from the work area until all equipment has been cleaned and put away.
11. Let soap cure undisturbed away from children and pets.

SUPPLIES LIST

SAFETY ITEMS
Rubber or Plastic Gloves – for working with lye
Safety Goggles – use when mixing or pouring soap

EQUIPMENT FOR COOKING SOAP
Kitchen or Diet Scales – preferably digital in ounces and grams
Long Handled Wooden or Plastic Spoon – for stirring lye
Plastic (only) Pitcher – it should be:
- Dishwasher safe since lye temperatures will reach 200°F (93°C)
- ½ gallon or 2-liter capacity
- Equipped with a sturdy handle, pouring spout and lid that snaps or screws on securely

Sieve or Colander – (optional) when rendering fat or suet, you'll need to strain out debris
Soap Pot – unchipped enamel or stainless steel (lye will corrode most other types) 8 quart or 8 liter capacity
Stainless Steel Pots – smaller pots for making small batches. If too large a pot is used, the soap might scorch.

Two Kitchen Thermometers – these need to have clips to hook onto the side of the pot and be accurate within ½ degree and read as low as 100°F (38°C)

EQUIPMENT NEEDED TO COMPLETE SOAPMAKING

Freezer Paper – after slicing soap, it cures on this paper and does not absorb color

Large Clear Rectangular Plastic Container with Lid – this needs to hold at least 12 quarts or 12 liters. Clear plastic will help you spot soap that has not mixed properly. This shape is ideal for everyday bar soap that's to be cut in squares or rectangles.

Old Towels or Newspapers – insulates soap so it doesn't cool too quickly

Sharp Knife – cutting fats and finished bars of soap

Soap Molds – use candy or candle molds, sardine cans, individual tarts pans, aluminum gelatin molds, small cake pans, or any small semi-rigid container. Avoid straight sided, completely rigid molds, as soap will need to be pried loose. Molds must be able to withstand high heat and should have some inner detail to lend interest to finished soap.

Thin Cardboard – use for soap cutting templates

Thin Wire – cutting finished bars of soap

Wooden or Stainless Steel Ladle – to transfer soap to their molds

OPTIONAL EQUIPMENT

Blender – for making blender soap

Bowl – to hold grated soap

Grater – to make hand-milled soaps

SOAPMAKING INSTRUCTIONS

Step 1 Read Safety Precautions first!

Step 2 Lay out the ingredients and equipment in order of use so they are readily available.

Step 3 Familiarize yourself with the recipe and procedure so you'll only occasionally have to refer to the instructions. It beats fumbling around in critical moments and avoids mistakes. For your convenience, Metric and U.S. Conversion Charts for weights, temperature, length and volume are provided in the Appendices.

Step 4 Using diet or kitchen scales, measure the soft, rain or distilled water into any container. Make sure the water is very cold to avoid "boiling" when the lye is added. Set aside.

Step 5 Put on rubber gloves and goggles. Again using the scales, accurately weigh the lye and pour into the pitcher.

NOTE: You may want to cover the countertop or table area with newspapers – wherever you are mixing/stirring. Better yet, mix the lye and water outside. It saves on house "destruction" and offers good ventilation. Don't breathe the fumes.

Step 6 Carefully add lye to the water. Immediately stir the lye solution gently with a wooden spoon until completely dissolved. If the lye remains caked on the bottom, it's hard to dissolve without splashing. This should only take a minute or so to dissolve and the water will appear cloudy. Hook a thermometer over the edge. The lye will not need additional heating to raise the temperature; the chemical reaction will provide the heat. In fact, the lye/water will need to cool somewhat to reach the desired temperature. Monitor the lye's temperature while melting the fats.

Step 7 Weigh the fats/oils, place them in a non-corrosive pot and hook a thermometer over the edge of the pot. Make sure the thermometer doesn't touch bottom as it will give a false high reading. Place pot over low to medium heat and stir with a wooden spoon. Heat to just melted.

NOTE: Fat and lye need to be within 0-5°F (0-3°C) of each other, no further; and the closer the better. This is a delicate process that requires practice. It takes lye longer to change temperature than it will fats. Here's the easiest way to achieve the same temperature for each: when the lye is 5°F (3°C) above the target temp, begin heating the fats. To speed cooling of the fat, place container in a water bath in the sink. Stir fats to prevent resolidification and help them cool. If they solidify, re-melt fats in a hot water bath.

Don't be tempted to microwave the lye.

Step 8   When the lye and fats reach the same temperature, move the fats pot to the sink. Slowly pour lye in the designated pitcher and securely snap the lid in place. Stir fats gently while pouring lye in a thin, steady stream. If you see a considerable amount of lye floating on top of the fat, continue stirring. Don't pour in more lye until the floating portion has been absorbed. Resume pouring the remaining lye.

NOTE: "Saponification" is the chemical process that turns water, lye and fats into soap. It begins here:

Step 9   Continue stirring gently to avoid splashing. The fat/lye/water mixture should be kept in constant, smooth motion for 15 – 20 minutes to ensure total absorption of lye. As the mixture thickens, it will become opaque and a bit grainy. At this point, see if it traces or trails. "Tracing" or "trailing" refers to the soap's consistency or thickness. Several ways to check for tracing are:
   a. Slide a rubber scraper through the mixture. If it holds the line or indent for a few seconds, it's ready.
   b. Dribble a ribbon of soap on top of the mixture. If it holds for a few seconds, it's ready. The consistency should be similar to ripples across instant pudding.

NOTE: To reach tracing stage, it generally takes 15 minutes to one hour, sometimes longer. Test every 15 minutes. Before the soap reaches this stage, it can separate into layers of fat and lye. Sometimes soap has traced but due to the angle of looking at the soap or poor lighting, it can be difficult to see. Soaps containing higher amounts of liquid vegetable oil have tracings more difficult to see. Tallow based soaps are one of the best tracers.

Step 10   Once soap has reached the trace stage, you can add fragrance, more fats for (superfatting) and/or colorings or you can go on to Step 11. You only include these items AFTER the soap has reached this stage (unless otherwise directed by a specific recipe). Heat can alter color and fragrance.

Step 11   Gently pour or ladle the warm soap into prepared molds. Unless you are absolutely certain the soap on the sides of your pot has been thoroughly mixed, leave it. Adding unmixed soap can blow your whole batch causing it to separate. For additional ideas on shaping soap, see Molds.

Step 12   Immediately cover the filled soap molds with newspaper or whatever insulating material you have chosen. Don't disturb the insulated soap for at least 48 hours, allowing to cool slowly. Soap cooled too quickly may separate. After two days, gently uncover the molds. They should still be a bit warm and only touch your soap wearing gloves as they are still caustic. Examine the soap STILL IN THE MOLD for obvious problems like separation or curdling. If your finger leaves a dent in the soap, it's still too soft to unmold. Leave soap to dry for another 24 – 48 hours, **uncovered**.

Step 13   When the surface is hard, the soap is ready to unmold. Protect the surface where you are unmolding as there might be some remaining lye inside. Loosen the sides first and carefully turn upside down over the sink. If the soap refuses to budge, allow more drying time, but not till it becomes rock-hard. Cutting very hard soap produces splinters. Forty-eight hours drying time is usually sufficient.

Step 14   Unmold onto butcher paper or sheets of rigid plastic. Avoid using newspaper or cardboard; soap will absorb their color. If you poured the soap into individual molds, the process is nearly complete except for final curing. During the curing stage, you may see the soap "sweat" as moisture evaporates. This is normal. Expect the soap to shrink as it cures as well as some warping or irregularities. Hairline cracks may become visible, but these problems can be lessened. See Tips and Troubleshooting section.

Allow 2-6 weeks for complete curing, depending on the ingredients used. Soap should be placed on the butcher paper or rigid plastic, not touching. When hard to the touch, give it the skin test. Take a cured bar of soap and wash your hands.

If your skins stings, lye is still present and the soap is not ready. Allow to dry until stinging is no longer felt. Turn the bars once the tops sides have fully hardened so the resting side can equally cure.

Step 15   If you have chosen one large mold, decide if you want to slice it for individual bars or turn it into hand-milled soap. If you've opted for Hand-Milled Soap, go to that section. If you've decided to cut the block into finished bars, you can do this one of several ways. (This is explained several pages over.)

ADDITIVES

SUPERFATTING refers to fats/oils added over and above the amount called for in the recipe. These fats are added after the trace stage. The purpose is to make the soap richer and softer to the skin. Some of the best fats/oils for superfatting are avocado, sweet almond, castor and cocoa butter. If your recipe doesn't list a specific amount of oil for this process, use the rule of thumb measure: for every 16 oz (453.5g) of fat/oil, superfat with 1 oz. (28.3g) of additional fat/oil.

FRAGRANCES: There are three main types of fragrances: Essential Oils (EOs), Fragrance Oils (FOs) and Herbs. The latter is the least desirable overall due to weak scent, but it's personal taste. Essential and Fragrance Oils differ in several areas. For more information, see the Essential and Fragrance Oil section. As with perfume which is made of pure flower oils and no alcohol, you pay more for it than cologne or toilet water. Essential Oils are more expensive than Fragrance Oils due to higher quality. EOs used to be fairly difficult to find but are easily located in health food and department stores, bath and body shops, craft and hobby stores, and on the Internet.

COLORANTS: More fun! If there's anything that gives soap a nice touch (right behind fragrance), it's a lovely color. There are nearly as many color choices and sources as there are scents. If a soap is already tending toward a certain color, adding an opposite color will produce a muddy shade, unless you're using really strong colorants. By adding brighter hues you'll enhance natural tendencies and end up with a light or bright eye-pleasing color. Add Colorants at the same time as Fragrances and Other Additives, at the early soft-trace stage.

OTHER ADDITIVES: These ingredients are added when soap has been grated and re-melted to make Hand-Milled Soaps. Depending on the ingredients added, various soaps could be made. For example, adding oatmeal or juniper berry meal makes a good exfoliating soap; adding avocado makes it moisturizing. For a more complete listing of additives and their benefits, see Hand-Milled Soap Additives chart. Certain additives can impart their own coloring and scents. You might want to keep this in mind and use only complimentary fragrances and colorants. Unless otherwise directed, these substances are added immediately before the fragrances when the soap is just barely tracing. If you wait longer than this, it will be a race to get the additives thoroughly mixed in, not to mention the fragrances, before the soap is too hard to pour.

CHOICES FOR VEGETABLE OILS

Oils or fats will produce a soft, low lathering soap.

Apricot Kernel – used for centuries as skin softener.

Avocado – is more difficult to locate but can be found in food specialty stores. It will make soaps rich and especially emollient.

Castor – adds mildness and richness to soap. Find this medicinal oil at local pharmacies and in Australia in the grocery store.

Cocoa Butter – improves overall consistency of soap, making it both creamy and hard. Makes soap especially softening to the skin. Locate this oil at candy making suppliers.

Coconut – makes creamy lather and yields medium to hard soap, but tends to dry skin. Use it more sparingly in conjunction with other oils or fats.

Olive – many grades available and all are fine for soapmaking. Soaps from this oil are hard, brittle, mild, long-lasting, great latherers and considered very high quality.

Palm – is found in Asian specialty stores. It ranges in color from white to reddish. In soaps, this color will fade as the bars cure. This oil produces soap with long-lasting bubbles and is kind to skin; it makes an excellent facial soap. Since soaps with palm oil tend toward softness, mill quickly.

Peanut – readily available in local grocery store.

Safflower – readily obtained in grocery stores.

Sesame – generally available in grocery stores in Asian aisles.

Vegetable Oils – are about 10% olive oil and 90% either corn, soy or peanut, or a combination of these. It's an economical ingredient and yields a decent soap. It lathers well, but generally makes a softer soap than using all olive oil.

CHOICES FOR FATS

Beef – this fat is not as desirable as suet since it's more slippery to work with and doesn't yield as high quality tallow as suet. These soaps are softer and more difficult to work with. Keep fat refrigerated or frozen until used. Best used in laundry soap.

Mutton – produces a more brittle soap than beef tallow.

Lard – (pig fat) best used for making laundry soap. This soap is mild to the skin but doesn't lather well so combine it with other oils or fats. Keep fat refrigerated or frozen until used.

Rendered Kitchen Fats – (Rendering will be discussed later.) These are fats collected after frying foods and from skimming soup stocks. Since these fats can include a variety of sources; chicken, pig, cow, etc., soap results will vary. For this reason, it's not the best choice. Using too much chicken fat will produce too soft soap and quality will be limited. If using this fat, store collected fats in the refrigerator until desire quantity is obtained.

Suet – is the fat surrounding cow kidneys and once rendered, is the preferred fat of all tallows. Its hard tallow is easy to work with and produces a mild soap. Suet is easily obtained from a grocery butcher and should be white to off-white in color, not grey. Good suet is easily flaked and firm. Refrigerate or freeze until used.

Tallow – is the pure fat left after rendering suet or beef. Color is yellowish, soap will be mild and makes small creamy bubbles.

RENDERING 5 POUNDS (2.27 KG) BEEF FAT

Want to try your hand at making tallow? Place the fat in a large pot (stainless steel works best) and melt slowly to avoid burning, allowing about 30-60 minutes to heat. Stir melting fat occasionally with metal ladle. Cool slightly, then carefully run through a sieve to remove debris. To the cooled fat, add 50% more water. (If you end up with a quart or liter of melted fat, add 2 cups fresh water.) Return to the heat, covered, and slow boil 4 hours.

Cool again and strain through the sieve into a large ceramic or plastic bowl. Refrigerate over night. The cooked fat will settle into two or three layers. Invert fat and unmold unto a plate in the sink. On the inverted top will be gelatinous and grainy layers. Scrape this off leaving the pure tallow on the bottom. Wrap in plastic and store in refrigerator for use.

SLICING SOAP INTO BARS

Method One Take a short ruler and paring knife and lightly score the soap. When the lines are uniform, cut down through the soap using the ruler as a "backstop". Another tool that works well is a 4" (10cm) putty knife.

Method Two Make templates out of flexible cardboard. If a standard bar of soap is 2"x3½" (roughly 5x9cm), cut the templates ½" (1.27cm) bigger. This will allow for some shrinkage.

Take the longest template and place it length-wise against the edge of the pan. Score with a paring knife down the opposite edge of the template. Move the template over to the scored edge and make a second scoring next to the template. Continue sliding the template over until the entire block has been marked.

Then take the shorter template and lay it across the block's width. Use the same procedure until the entire block is marked into rectangles. Heat the knife in hot water, hold it exactly upright and cut through the soap. If the knife is allowed to lean, the soap will end up with sloped sides.

Method Three Wrap thin gauged wire around the ends of two wooden dowel rods or pencils. Wrap a length of wire approximately 12" (30.5cm) longer that the molded soap.

Example: If the longest side of soap is 13" (33cm) allow for a 19" (48cm) piece of wire stretching between the dowels and an extra 6" (15cm) to secure it around the dowels, totaling 25" (63.5cm) of wire. Make sure the wire is wound toward the bottom of the dowels or pencils to allow for the deepest cuts in the soap. Hold firmly onto each end of the dowel rods with the wire taut. Align the wire over the score marks and gently "saw" through the soap. Sometimes this method works better than the knife. Finish as per instructions in Steps 14 and 15.

NOTE: Be sure to keep all splinters and scraps for Soap Balls.

Until you get the hang of it, you might want to stick to proven recipes to eliminate most errors till you get your "soap wings"! If you want to switch fats/oils from any in the suggested recipes, use the following information to help you select alternatives.

MAKING YOUR OWN RECIPES

The preceding information is enough to get you started making soap. When you're ready to branch out, the following information and charts are useful, but master basic soapmaking first.

Ready to try your own ideas? You'll need to know the saponification values. They're different for many fats and oils. Oils are composed of fatty acids, which require a certain amount of lye to saponify them, or change them into soap. Use the chart below to find the saponification value of oils you want to use. Then fill-in the equation to see how much lye you need for your soap recipe. At the end of both the Sodium Hydroxide (NaOH) and Potassium Hydroxide (KOH) SAP Charts, you'll find the formula to determine how much lye and water are needed.

Both Sodium Hydroxide and Potassium Hydroxide can be used to make soap, but they react differently. However, Potassium Hydroxide tends to react more with the water and can cause splashing. For this reason, Sodium Hydroxide is preferred. As a rule of thumb, use Sodium Hydroxide (NaOH) for bar soaps and Potassium Hydroxide for liquid soaps. Make sure you are using the correct chart.

SODIUM HYDROXIDE (NAOH)

VEGETABLE FAT	\multicolumn{11}{c}{Desired Excess Fat In Finished Soap Based On Total Fat}
	0%	1%	2%	3%	4%	5%	6%	7%	8%	9%	10%
Almond Oil, Sweet	.136	.135	.134	.132	.131	.130	.129	.127	.126	.125	.124
Apricot Kernel Oil	.135	.134	.133	.131	.130	.129	.128	.126	.125	.124	.123
Arachis	.136	.135	.134	.132	.131	.130	.129	.127	.126	.125	.124
Avocado Oil	.133	.132	.131	.129	.128	.127	.126	.125	.123	.122	.121
Bayberry or Myrtle Wax	.069	.068	.068	.067	.066	.066	.065	.065	.064	.063	.063
Borage	.136	.135	.134	.132	.131	.130	.129	.127	.126	.125	.124
Brazil Nut, Babassu	.176	.174	.173	.171	.170	.168	.166	.165	.163	.162	.160
Carmellia Oil	.136	.135	.134	.132	.131	.130	.129	.127	.126	.125	.124
Canola Oil	.124	.123	.122	.121	.119	.118	.117	.116	.115	.114	.113
Caster Oil	.128	.127	.126	.125	.123	.122	.121	.120	.119	.118	.116
Chinese Bean	.135	.134	.133	.131	.130	.129	.128	.126	.125	.124	.123
Cocoa Butter	.137	.136	.135	.133	.132	.131	.130	.128	.127	.126	.125
Coconut Oil	.190	.188	.187	.185	.183	.181	.180	.178	.176	.174	.173
Cod-liver	.133	.131	.130	.129	.128	.127	.125	.124	.123	.122	.121
Coffee-seed	.130	.129	.128	.126	.125	.124	.123	.122	.121	.119	.118
Colza	.124	.123	.122	.121	.119	.118	.117	.116	.115	.114	.113
Corn Oil	.136	.135	.134	.132	.131	.130	.129	.127	.126	.125	.124
Cottonseed Oil	.138	.137	.135	.134	.133	.132	.130	.129	.128	.127	.125
Earthnut	.136	.135	.134	.132	.131	.130	.129	.127	.126	.125	.124
Evening Primrose Oil	.136	.135	.134	.132	.131	.130	.129	.127	.126	.125	.124
Flax Seed Oil	.135	.134	.133	.131	.130	.129	.128	.126	.125	.124	.123
Gigely Tree	.133	.132	.131	.129	.128	.127	.126	.125	.123	.122	.121
Grapeseed Oil	.127	.126	.125	.124	.122	.121	.120	.119	.118	.117	.115
Hazelnut Oil	.136	.135	.134	.132	.131	.130	.129	.127	.126	.125	.124
Hempseed Oil	.135	.134	.133	.131	.130	.129	.128	.126	.125	.124	.123
Jojoba Oil	.069	.068	.068	.067	.066	.066	.065	.065	.064	.063	.063
Kapok	.137	.136	.135	.133	.132	.131	.130	.128	.127	.126	.125
Katchung	.136	.135	.134	.132	.131	.130	.129	.127	.126	.125	.124
Kukui Nut Oil	.135	.134	.133	.131	.130	.129	.128	.126	.125	.124	.123
Linseed	.138	.137	.135	.134	.133	.132	.130	.129	.128	.127	.125
Loccu	.134	.133	.132	.130	.129	.128	.127	.125	.124	.123	.122
Macadamia Nut Oil	.139	.138	.136	.135	.134	.133	.131	.130	.129	.128	.126
Margarine	.136	.135	.134	.132	.131	.130	.129	.127	.126	.125	.124
Meadowform Oil	.139	.138	.136	.135	.134	.133	.131	.130	.129	.128	.126
Mink	.140	.139	.137	.136	.135	.134	.132	.131	.130	.129	.127
Mustard	.123	.122	.121	.120	.119	.117	.116	.115	.114	.113	.112
Neat's Foot	.136	.135	.133	.132	.131	.130	.128	.127	.126	.125	.124
Neem	.137	.136	.135	.133	.132	.131	.130	.128	.127	.126	.125
Niger-seed	.136	.134	.133	.132	.131	.129	.128	.127	.126	.124	.123
Nutmeg Butter	.117	.116	.115	.114	.113	.112	.111	.110	.108	.107	.106
Olium Olivate	.134	.133	.132	.130	.129	.128	.127	.125	.124	.123	.122
Olive Oil	.134	.133	.132	.130	.129	.128	.127	.125	.124	.123	.122
Palm Oil	.141	.140	.138	.137	.136	.135	.133	.132	.131	.129	.128
Palm Kernel, Palm Butter	.155	.154	.152	.151	.149	.148	.147	.145	.144	.142	.141
Peanut Oil	.136	.135	.134	.132	.131	.130	.129	.127	.126	.125	.124
Pecan Oil	.136	.135	.134	.132	.131	.130	.129	.127	.126	.125	.124
Perilla	.137	.136	.134	.133	.132	.131	.129	.128	.127	.126	.124
Pistachio Nut Oil	.135	.134	.133	.131	.130	.129	.128	.126	.125	.124	.123
Poppy Seed Oil	.138	.137	.135	.134	.133	.132	.130	.129	.128	.127	.125
Pumpkin Seed Oil	.135	.134	.133	.131	.130	.129	.128	.126	.125	.124	.123
Ramic	.124	.123	.122	.121	.119	.118	.117	.116	.115	.114	.113
Rapeseed Oil	.124	.123	.122	.121	.119	.118	.117	.116	.115	.114	.113
Rice Bran Oil	.128	.127	.126	.125	.123	.122	.121	.120	.119	.118	.116
Ricinus	.129	.127	.126	.125	.124	.123	.122	.120	.119	.118	.117
Safflower Oil	.136	.135	.134	.132	.131	.130	.129	.127	.126	.125	.124

SODIUM HYDROXIDE (NAOH)

VEGETABLE FAT	Desired Excess Fat In Finished Soap Based On Total Fat										
	0%	1%	2%	3%	4%	5%	6%	7%	8%	9%	10%
Sesame Seed Oil	.133	.132	.131	.129	.128	.127	.126	.125	.123	.122	.121
Shea Butter	.128	.127	.126	.125	.123	.122	.121	.120	.119	.118	.116
Shortening *	.136	.135	.134	.132	.131	.130	.129	.127	.126	.125	.124
Soybean Oil	.135	.134	.133	.131	.130	.129	.128	.126	.125	.124	.123
Stearic Acid	.145	.144	.142	.141	.140	.138	.137	.136	.134	.133	.132
Sunflower Oil	.134	.133	.132	.130	.129	.128	.127	.125	.124	.123	.122
Sweet Oil	.134	.133	.132	.130	.129	.128	.127	.125	.124	.123	.122
Theobroma	.137	.136	.135	.133	.132	.131	.130	.128	.127	.126	.125
Teel, Teal, Til Oil	.133	.132	.131	.129	.128	.127	.126	.125	.123	.122	.121
Tung Oil	.136	.135	.134	.132	.131	.130	.129	.127	.126	.125	.124
Walnut Oil	.136	.135	.134	.132	.131	.130	.129	.127	.126	.125	.124
Wheat Germ Oil	.131	.130	.129	.127	.126	.125	.124	.123	.121	.120	.119

ANIMAL FAT	DESIRED EXCESS FAT IN FINISHED SOAP BASED ON TOTAL FAT										
	0%	1%	2%	3%	4%	5%	6%	7%	8%	9%	10%
Beef Hoof	.141	.140	.138	.137	.136	.135	.133	.132	.131	.129	.128
Beeswax	.069	.068	.068	.067	.066	.066	.065	.065	.064	.063	.063
Butterfat, Cow	.162	.161	.159	.158	.156	.155	.153	.152	.150	.149	.147
Butterfat, Goat	.167	.165	.164	.162	.161	.159	.158	.156	.155	.153	.152
Chicken Fat	.138	.137	.135	.134	.133	.132	.130	.129	.128	.127	.125
Deer Fat	.138	.137	.135	.134	.133	.132	.130	.129	.128	.127	.125
Emu Oil	.135	.134	.133	.131	.130	.129	.128	.126	.125	.124	.123
Goat Fat	.138	.137	.135	.134	.133	.132	.130	.129	.128	.127	.125
Goose Fat	.136	.135	.134	.132	.131	.130	.129	.127	.126	.125	.124
Lanolin	.075	.074	.073	.072	.072	.071	.070	.070	.069	.068	.068
Lard	.138	.137	.135	.134	.133	.132	.130	.129	.128	.127	.125
Mink Oil	.140	.139	.137	.136	.135	.134	.132	.131	.130	.129	.127
Mutton Fat	.138	.137	.135	.134	.133	.132	.130	.129	.128	.127	.125
Neats Foot Oil	.141	.140	.138	.137	.136	.135	.133	.132	.131	.129	.128
Ostrich	.135	.134	.133	.131	.130	.129	.128	.126	.125	.124	.123
Sperm Whale Blubber	.092	.091	.090	.089	.089	.088	.087	.086	.085	.084	.084
Tallow	.138	.137	.135	.134	.133	.132	.130	.129	.128	.127	.125

The first 5 columns denote "proceed with caution."
The 5%-8% superfatted columns are most recommended and most often used.
The last 2 columns will create a softer soap due to its high fat content. It will also go rancid fastest for this same reason.

USING THE SODIUM HYDROXIDE (NAOH) SAP CHART

In the left column, find the fat or fats you want to use. Calculate the amount of lye needed, including any fat used for superfatting, by intersecting the listed fats in the left column with the desired percent of excess fat.

Example: Suppose the recipe calls for 16 oz. total fat, using 8 oz Lard and 8 oz. Olive Oil. You want to end up with 7% superfatted soap. In the left column, find Lard and Olive Oil. Intersect those rows with the column of 7%. You'll find .129 for Lard and .125 for Olive Oil. Multiply each of these numbers by 8 oz. ending of with 1.032 and 1.000. Add the numbers together for a total of 2.032 or rounded to 2 oz of lye. To convert to grams, multiply the 2 oz. by 28 for 56g of lye needed.

NOTE: To figure the amount of water needed, multiply the total amount of fat weight by .38.

POTASSIUM HYDROXIDE (KOH)

VEGETABLE FAT	DESIRED EXCESS FAT IN FINISHED SOAP BASED ON TOTAL FAT										
	0%	1%	2%	3%	4%	5%	6%	7%	8%	9%	10%
Almond Oil, Sweet	.190	.189	.187	.185	.183	.182	.180	.178	.177	.175	.173
Apricot Kernel Oil	.189	.187	.186	.184	.182	.180	.179	.177	.175	.174	.172
Arachis	.190	.189	.187	.185	.183	.182	.180	.178	.177	.175	.173
Avocado Oil	.186	.185	.183	.181	.179	.178	.176	.174	.173	.171	.169
Bayberry or Myrtle Wax	.097	.096	.095	.094	.093	.092	.091	.090	.090	.089	.088
Borage	.190	.189	.187	.185	.183	.182	.180	.178	.177	.175	.173
Brazil Nut	.246	.244	.242	.240	.237	.235	.233	.231	.228	.226	.224
Carmellia Oil	.190	.189	.187	.185	.183	.182	.180	.178	.177	.175	.173
Canola Oil	.174	.172	.170	.169	.167	.166	.164	.163	.161	.159	.158
Caster Oil	.179	.178	.176	.174	.173	.171	.169	.168	.166	.165	.163
Chinese Bean	.189	.187	.186	.184	.182	.180	.179	.177	.175	.174	.172
Cocoa Butter	.192	.190	.188	.187	.185	.183	.181	.180	.178	.176	.174
Coconut Oil	.266	.264	.261	.259	.256	.254	.251	.249	.247	.244	.242
Cod-liver	.186	.184	.182	.181	.179	.177	.175	.174	.172	.170	.169
Coffee-seed	.182	.180	.179	.177	.175	.174	.172	.170	.169	.167	.165
Colza	.174	.172	.170	.169	.167	.166	.164	.163	.161	.159	.158
Corn Oil	.190	.189	.187	.185	.183	.182	.180	.178	.177	.175	.173
Cottonseed Oil	.193	.191	.190	.188	.186	.184	.183	.181	.179	.177	.176
Earthnut	.190	.189	.187	.185	.183	.182	.180	.178	.177	.175	.173
Evening Primrose Oil	.190	.189	.187	.185	.183	.182	.180	.178	.177	.175	.173
Flax Seed Oil	.189	.187	.186	.184	.182	.180	.179	.177	.175	.174	.172
Gigely Tree	.186	.185	.183	.181	.179	.178	.176	.174	.173	.171	.169
Grapeseed Oil	.181	.179	.177	.176	.174	.172	.171	.169	.167	.166	.164
Hazelnut Oil	.190	.189	.187	.185	.183	.182	.180	.178	.177	.175	.173
Hempseed Oil	.189	.187	.186	.184	.182	.180	.179	.177	.175	.174	.172
Jojoba Oil	.097	.096	.095	.094	.093	.092	.091	.090	.090	.089	.088
Kapok	.192	.190	.188	.187	.185	.183	.181	.180	.178	.176	.174
Katchung	.190	.189	.187	.185	.183	.182	.180	.178	.177	.175	.173
Kukui Nut Oil	.189	.187	.186	.184	.182	.180	.179	.177	.175	.174	.172
Linseed	.190	.188	.186	.185	.183	.181	.180	.178	.176	.174	.173
Loccu	.188	.186	.184	.182	.181	.179	.177	.176	.174	.172	.171
Macadamia Nut Oil	.195	.193	.191	.189	.188	.186	.184	.182	.180	.179	.177
Margarine	.190	.189	.187	.185	.183	.182	.180	.178	.177	.175	.173
Meadowform Oil	.195	.193	.191	.189	.188	.186	.184	.182	.180	.179	.177
Mink	.195	.193	.191	.189	.188	.186	.184	.182	.180	.179	.177
Mustard Oil	.171	.169	.168	.166	.165	.163	.161	.160	.158	.157	.155
Neat's Foot	.190	.188	.187	.185	.183	.182	.180	.178	.176	.175	.173
Neem Oil	.192	.190	.188	.187	.185	.183	.181	.180	.178	.176	.174
Niger-seed	.190	.188	.186	.185	.183	.181	.179	.178	.176	.174	.172
Nutmeg Butter	.164	.162	.161	.159	.158	.156	.155	.153	.152	.150	.149
Olium Olivate	.188	.186	.184	.182	.181	.179	.177	.176	.174	.172	.171
Olive Oil	.188	.186	.184	.182	.181	.179	.177	.176	.174	.172	.171
Palm Oil	.197	.196	.194	.192	.190	.188	.187	.185	.183	.181	.179
Palm Kernel, Palm Butter	.217	.215	.213	.211	.209	.207	.205	.203	.201	.199	.197
Peanut Oil	.190	.189	.187	.185	.183	.182	.180	.178	.177	.175	.173
Pecan Oil	.190	.189	.187	.185	.183	.182	.180	.178	.177	.175	.173
Perilla	.192	.190	.188	.186	.185	.183	.181	.179	.178	.176	.174
Pistachio Nut Oil	.189	.187	.186	.184	.182	.180	.179	.177	.175	.174	.172
Poppy Seed Oil	.193	.191	.190	.188	.186	.184	.183	.181	.179	.177	.176
Pumpkin Seed Oil	.189	.187	.186	.184	.182	.180	.179	.177	.175	.174	.172
Ramic	.174	.172	.170	.169	.167	.166	.164	.163	.161	.159	.158
Rapeseed Oil	.174	.172	.170	.169	.167	.166	.164	.163	.161	.159	.158
Rice Bran Oil	.179	.178	.176	.174	.173	.171	.169	.168	.166	.165	.163
Ricinus	.180	.178	.177	.175	.173	.172	.170	.169	.167	.165	.164
Safflower Oil	.190	.189	.187	.185	.183	.182	.180	.178	.177	.175	.173

POTASSIUM HYDROXIDE (KOH)

VEGETABLE FAT	DESIRED EXCESS FAT IN FINISHED SOAP BASED ON TOTAL FAT										
	0%	1%	2%	3%	4%	5%	6%	7%	8%	9%	10%
Sesame Seed Oil	.186	.185	.183	.181	.179	.178	.176	.174	.173	.171	.169
Shea Butter	.179	.178	.176	.174	.173	.171	.169	.168	.166	.165	.163
Shortening	.190	.189	.187	.185	.183	.182	.180	.178	.177	.175	.173
Soybean Oil	.189	.187	.186	.184	.182	.180	.179	.177	.175	.174	.172
Stearic Acid	.203	.201	.199	.197	.196	.194	.192	.190	.188	.186	.185
Sunflower Oil	.188	.186	.184	.182	.181	.179	.177	.176	.174	.172	.171
Sweet Oil	.188	.186	.184	.182	.181	.179	.177	.176	.174	.172	.171
Theobroma	.192	.190	.188	.187	.185	.183	.181	.180	.178	.176	.174
Teel, Teal, Til Oil	.187	.185	.184	.182	.180	.179	.177	.175	.173	.172	.170
Tung Oil	.136	.135	.134	.132	.131	.130	.129	.127	.126	.125	.124
Walnut Oil	.190	.189	.187	.185	.183	.182	.180	.178	.177	.175	.173
Wheat Germ Oil	.183	.182	.180	.178	.177	.175	.173	.172	.170	.168	.167

ANIMAL FAT	DESIRED EXCESS FAT IN FINISHED SOAP BASED ON TOTAL FAT										
	0%	1%	2%	3%	4%	5%	6%	7%	8%	9%	10%
Beef Hoof	.197	.195	.193	.192	.190	.188	.186	.184	.183	.181	.179
Beeswax	.097	.096	.095	.094	.093	.092	.091	.090	.090	.089	.088
Butterfat, Cow	.227	.225	.223	.221	.219	.216	.214	.212	.210	.208	.206
Butterfat, Goat	.234	.232	.230	.227	.225	.223	.221	.219	.217	.215	.213
Chicken Fat	.193	.191	.190	.188	.186	.184	.183	.181	.179	.177	.176
Deer Fat	.195	.193	.191	.189	.188	.186	.184	.182	.180	.179	.177
Emu Oil	.189	.187	.186	.184	.182	.180	.179	.177	.175	.174	.172
Goat Fat	.193	.191	.190	.188	.186	.184	.183	.181	.179	.177	.176
Goose Fat	.190	.189	.187	.185	.183	.182	.180	.178	.177	.175	.173
Lanolin	.104	.103	.102	.101	.101	.100	.099	.098	.097	.096	.095
Lard	.193	.191	.190	.188	.186	.184	.183	.181	.179	.177	.176
Mink Oil	.196	.194	.192	.191	.189	.187	.185	.184	.182	.180	.178
Mutton Fat	.193	.191	.190	.188	.186	.184	.183	.181	.179	.177	.176
Neats Foot Oil	.197	.196	.194	.192	.190	.188	.187	.185	.183	.181	.179
Ostrich	.189	.187	.186	.184	.182	.180	.179	.177	.175	.174	.172
Sperm Whale Blubber	.129	.128	.126	.125	.124	.123	.122	.121	.119	.118	.117
Tallow	.193	.191	.190	.188	.186	.184	.183	.181	.179	.177	.176

The first 5 columns denote "proceed with caution."
The 5-8% superfatted columns are most recommended and most often used.
The last 2 columns create a softer soap due to its high fat content. It will also go rancid fastest for this same reason.

USING THE POTASSIUM HYDROXIDE (KOH) SAP CHART

In the left column, find the fat or fats you want to use. Calculate the amount of lye needed, including any fat used for superfatting, by intersecting the listed fats in the left column with the desired percent of excess fat.

Example: Suppose the recipe calls for 16 oz. total fat, using 8 oz Lard and 8 oz. Olive Oil. You want to end up with 7% superfatted soap. In the left column, find Lard and Olive Oil. Intersect those rows with the column of 7%. You'll find .181 for Lard and .176 for Olive Oil. Multiply each of these numbers by 8 oz. ending of with 1.448 and 1.408. Add the numbers together for a total of 2.816 or rounded to 3 oz of lye. To convert to grams, multiply the 3 oz. by 28 for 84g of lye needed.

NOTE: To figure the amount of water needed, multiply the total amount of fat weight by .38.

LUXURIOUS HAND-MILLED SOAP

Hand-Milling, Rebatching, Melt and Pour... these are all terms to describe hand-milled or French-milled soaps. This means the final soap has undergone a two part cooking processes.

Besides making lovely rich soaps, the rebatching process is a clever way to fix soapmaking's little disasters. If soap has separated in the curing process or if the bars have dried crooked for example, rebatching helps remedy most of these problems.

Here's how to do it. First, a basic batch of soap is made and at least partially cured. A good choice to use is the first one in the Recipes section, *Basic Soap*. It's virtually foolproof and works very well in hand-milled soaps.

Let's go through a hand-milled soap recipe together so you get a good feel for it. Assume we've already made the Basic Soap recipe and it's ready for milling. The *Basic Soap* recipe yields 12 oz (340g) of soap.

Step 1 Make a batch of *Basic Soap* using Steps 1-14 for soapmaking.

Step 2 If you have poured this into one large mold, break off chunks with a knife and run it through a vegetable grater. Some folks use their food processor, which is OK too. If you're grating soap that's still moist, wear rubber gloves since it still contains some lye. Grate soap over a protected surface, not newspaper or it will absorb the ink.

Step 3 When the soap is grated, place all of it and 7 ounces (198g) of water in the soap cooking pot. Melt soap and water together SLOWLY. If you turn the heat up high and rush the melting, it can end up an unusable mess. Stir melting soap and water together gently with a wooden spoon being careful not to make bubbles. If you see them forming, quit stirring for a bit. Make sure the soap doesn't stick to the pot's bottom. Melting takes 20 minutes to 1 hour depending on the recipe you use (if different from *Basic Soap*).

The recipe we've decided to use for our hand-milled soap is superfatted, extra rich and moisturizing. If you're allergic to lanolin, substitute a different animal fat. It calls for:

- 1 oz (28.3g) cocoa butter
- 1 oz (28.3g) lanolin
- 1 oz (28.3g) sweet almond oil
- 1 oz (28.3g) glycerin

Step 4 In a small saucepan, melt cocoa butter over low temperature. Add almond oil, lanolin and glycerin and mix together until soft.

Step 5 Add softened fats to the melted Basic Soap and water, and stir until slightly thickened. It is not necessary to do a temperature check on the milled soap mixture, but if you pour it into individual decorative molds when it is too hot, it will shrink away from the sides of the mold as it cools. A temperature of 150-160°F (66-71°C) is best. Pour into prepared molds.

Step 6 Fill molds full but not over the sides as it makes for a sloppy bar of soap and more difficult to remove from the mold. Use a rubber spatula to smooth the top of the soap.

Step 7 When the soap has a slight "skin" on the surface, place molds in freezer for 1-2 hours. Freezing will help soap release from molds.

Step 8 To unmold, you may need to give the mold a slight twist or a tap on the bottom. Handle them carefully as they will be quite soft.

Step 9 Turn soaps out onto white butcher's paper or needlepoint screen. Final curing, depending on ingredients used, will take 2-4 weeks. Soap will be ready for use when it's hard to the touch and your fingertips do not leave an impression on it.

Step 10 About one week into the final curing, you may see some warping and shrinking. It will be most noticeable in the longer rectangular bars. See Tips and Troubleshooting for ideas how to best fix this. Turn the bars of soap over once a week so all surfaces cure evenly.

FINAL TIPS

If you use more than 12 oz (340g) grated soap, follow these water guidelines unless otherwise specified (note the recipe above specifically calls for 7 oz (198g) of water):

SOAP – WATER GUIDELINE			
If using this amount Grated Soap	Use this amount Water	If using this amount Grated Soap	Use this amount Water
12 oz (340g)	9 oz (255g)	24 oz (680g)	18 oz (510g)
16 oz (453g)	12 oz (340g)	48 oz (1.4kg)	36 oz (1kg)
32 oz (907g)	24 oz (680g)		

WHAT ELSE CAN I ADD?

COLORANTS: Make sure soap is entirely melted before adding or soap will have white areas.

FRAGRANCES: Let your nose be your guide, but where to start? Because strengths differ between Essential Oils and Fragrance Oils, from scent to scent as well as from company to company, start with ½-1 oz (14.2-28.4g) oil per ¾ pound (340g) soap.

ADDITIVES: Heavier additives like oatmeal, bran, sand, etc. will sink to the bottom of the soap if they are added when the soap is very hot and thin. It may need to be stirred several times to redistribute these ingredients. Adding them just before pouring into the molds is best.

If you add liquefied vegetables or fruit, an equal amount of water needs to be <u>deducted</u> from the water added to the grated soap. If not, the soap will be runny and shrink in the molds.

ESSENTIAL OILS AND FRAGRANCES

Essential oils, absolute oils and resin oils are very concentrated, more expensive and somewhat stronger than fragrance oils. Essential oils are extracted from plants and fragrance oils are synthetically produced, hence the cost difference.

	ESSENTIAL OILS (Pure Plant Extract)	FRAGRANCE OILS (Synthetic Scents)
PROS	Stronger aroma, lasts longer in soap May contain beneficial plant proper-ties More stable reliable reactions in saponification Get more scent per ounce than fragrance oils	More scent varieties More widely available More economical Blended scents in larger variety
CONS	More expensive Must make most blended scents Evaporates with exposure to air	May contain extenders and alcohol More scents likely to cause soap to "seize" No therapeutic plant benefits. Scent doesn't last as long in finished product

NOTES: Many fragrance oils are very good for scenting soaps, but some can make soaps "seize" and turn it rock hard.

Though essential oils are more stable, they are generally made as single essences.

For folks who desire blends, especially the tempting Christmas scents, fragrance oils should be considered. If you prefer Essential Oils, you can make your own blends. Both are very strong and need to be handled carefully.

Especially in the case of Essential Oils, you get what you pay for. There are rarely any bargains unless you buy in bulk or from a wholesaler. Cheaper versions are created with extenders that tend to produce less-than-desirable results.

Avoid products containing alcohol. They can cause seizing and curdling, and these fragrances will dissipate more quickly.

SAFETY PRECAUTIONS FOR USING ESSENTIAL OILS AND FRAGRANCE OILS

Yes, there are safety tips for nearly everything, aren't there! If you follow a few guidelines for Essential Oils and Fragrance Oils, you should encounter no problems.

1. Keep them away from children.
2. Always read and follow all label warnings. They will be different depending on the oil.
3. Keep oils tightly closed, stored in a dark, cool area to preserve fragrance.
4. Never consume these oils unless specifically approved as a food.
5. Don't use undiluted oils on your skin. Dilute with vegetable oils (known as carrier oils); not water.
6. Skin-test oils before using. Dilute a small amount with vegetable oil and apply to the skin on your inner, upper arm. Your skin will look red or irritated within 8 hours if you have an allergy to certain oils.
7. When using these oils on your skin, avoid exposure to the sun or tanning beds.
8. Keep oils away from eyes and mucous membranes, use externally only. If contact is made with these areas, flush with water.
9. Do not use during pregnancy except with physician's approval.
10. Oils known to be irritating to **some** skin are: allspice, basil, bitter almond, cinnamon, love, fir needle, lemon, lemongrass, melissa, peppermint, sweet fennel, tea tree, wintergreen.
11. Epileptics should avoid these products.
12. People with high blood pressure should avoid hyssop, rosemary, sage and thyme.

WITHSTANDING THE TEST OF HEAT AND TIME!
The following scents are stronger and generally better at withstanding saponification:

Almond	Cloves	Jasmine	Orange	Pennyroyal	Sage
Cinnamon	Eucalyptus	Lemon	Patchouli	Peppermint	Vanilla
Citronella	Fr. Lavender	Musk	Peach	Rose	

OTHER TRADITIONAL SOAP FRAGRANCES

Apple	Geranium	Rose	Strawberry
Lilac	Pine	Sandalwood	Ylang Ylang

NOTE: A few drops of musk oil is enough to scent an entire batch of soap; less-potent fragrances such as a fruit oil might require 5-10ml. Soap scented with herbs is also popular; herbs like lemon, thyme, verbena or lavender work well. To scent with herbs, make an herbal oil by packing a 100-ml container with herbs and then filling it with a pleasant-smelling vegetable oil such as almond oil. Let this mixture sit for a few weeks, stirring it every day, then heat in a double boiler for 10 minutes, then cool and strain the oil.

FIXATIVES, WHEN TO USE THEM

If you anticipate making soap and not using it for a while, consider using a "fixative". These products will stabilize the scents in your hand-milled soap. However, using high grade Essential Oils generally makes it unnecessary.

Balsam of Peru	Cedarwood	Lemon Peel	Orange Peel	Sandalwood	Tangerine Peel
Benzoin powder	Cloves	Myrrh	Orris Root	Storax Oil	Vetivert

Fixatives are a little harder to find than the fragrances themselves, but can be located through soapmaking suppliers and hobby or craft stores.

As you become more adept at soapmaking, you'll want to add your own creative touches. A great way to do this is through scents and colorants. Due to the cost of EOs, it might be a good idea to add fragrance after perfecting soapmaking.

ADDITIVES AND THEIR BENEFITS					
Softens Moisturizes	**Unclogs Pores Mild Abrasive**	**Astringent Absorbs Skin Oil**	**Cleanser Anti-bacterial**	**Antiseptic Healing**	**Fragrance**
Almond Oil	Almond Meal	Almond Meal	Cucumber	Aloe Vera	Ginger
Apricot	Bran	Chamomile	Lemon	Cloves	Lavender
Avocado	Cinnamon	Clay	Milk	Kelp	Kelp
Buttermilk	Cornmeal	Cornmeal	Oatmeal	Oatmeal	Lemon
Calendula	Pumice	Cucumber	Sage	Tea Tree Oil	Nutmeg
Cocoa Butter	Sand	Rosemary			Peruvian Balsam
Glycerin	Wheat Germ	Sage			Rose Water
Honey		Witch Hazel			
Lanolin					
Rose Water					
Vitamin E					

WHEN ARE ESSENTIAL OILS ADDED?
Because heat can alter fragrances, save their addition until soap begins to trace. At this stage, soap drizzled from a spoon will leave a faint pattern on the surface of the soap before sinking back into the mass. This is the time to add your fragrances.*

Stir in the fragrances for only 20-30 seconds, but until completely mixed. More stirring encourages soap to streak and seize.

*****NOTE:** Just prior to the full trace stage is when all additives, colorants and scents are to be added unless otherwise directed by a specific recipe.

HOW MUCH SCENT IS NEEDED?

Scenting is very much governed by personal taste. It is difficult to have a hard and fast rule as Essential Oils and Fragrance Oils differ in strength, as do the individual oils. A good rule of thumb is for every ¾ pound (340g) of soap, use ½-1 ounce (14.2 – 28.4g) of scent. You want enough aroma to delight the senses, but using too much can cause skin irritations.

OTHER ADDITIVES

These ingredients are mixed in when a batch of basic soap is re-melted to make milled soap. (Note, however, that basic soaps may also be milled without adding extra ingredients.)

Additives are substances, which not only alter the overall look of soap but also lend their own special qualities to it. These substances range from honey, a wonderful skin softener, to oatmeal, whose gentle scrubbing quality enhances facial and body soaps.

Benzoin Powder – used as a fixative for fragrances in soaps and may curdle your soap.

Pectin keeps shampoos from separating.

Rosin helps bars of soap retain shape and produces large amounts of lather. Mix powder with any vegetable oil before adding to soap.

Strawberries contain acids that make them effective as skin tighteners and whiteners. Fresh strawberries are preferable; frozen berries will also work, but drain off liquid first.

COLORING YOUR SOAP

Coloring soap might be viewed as one of the more "fun" parts of the project. Since soapmaking involves a chemical reaction, there is always room for error along the way. For this reason, it is best to perfect soapmaking techniques before "muddying" the water with colors.

WHY ADD COLOR?

Adding color is another peg in soap sophistication. Besides eye appeal, it can enhance the overall effect you are striving for. A soap scented with lavender might be nicer if a lavender color carries out the theme.

A peach scented soap might be more effective in a peachy shade rather than green. Color is an easy way to tie in your soaps with bath or kitchen decor.

SUBTLE = NATURAL

A good rule of thumb is to keep the soap color subtle if you want to achieve a natural look. However, if you're trying to coordinate for special holidays like Christmas or Valentine's Day, brighter colors might be more fun. You'll know too much colorant has been added if the finished soap doesn't lather with white bubbles. Colored bubbles may stain your skin and towels.

NATURAL TENDENCIES

Depending on the ingredients used to make soap, the mixture will tend toward a certain color. For example, soap containing cinnamon, clove, vanilla or nutmeg will have brown tones. Cornmeal will give soap a pale yellow color while kiwi and rosemary will make green tones. Paprika will turn soap peach. Fats and oils will contribute their own characteristics too. Adding herbs, rose petals, bran or oatmeal will give the soap its own unique colorings as well as textures. Rather than swim upstream to change a color, it works best to enhance, brighten or deepen a soap's natural color.

If your plans are to market these soap products, you'll need to see what the law requires in your country for acceptable "cosmetic grade" products. Product labeling would also need to be investigated.

So many colors, so little time! There are as many opinions on color and coloring agents as there are on scents. If you want to maintain an "all natural" product, your best bet would be plant products, seasonings or natural pigments.

LIQUID DYES

Cheap and easy Rit is probably the best-known fabric dye in the industry. Liquid dyes come in a wide color selection and are readily available at grocery and discount stores. They don't need to be dissolved prior to adding to the soap mixture, are quite economical and allow for custom blending. A little of this dye goes a long way. To begin, use approximately ½ tsp (2.5ml) dye per ¾ pound (340g) soap. Curdling can result if too much is used due to the sodium content. If powdered dye is used, it must first be dissolved in hot water.

CANDLE DYES

These are easily obtained from craft and hobby shops and some discount stores that sell craft items. Candle dye is concentrated in small blocks of wax, which must first be melted. To use, melt one block of dye in two tablespoons (30ml) of vegetable oil. Any excess dye stores easily in a sealed container.

PIGMENTS

Pigments are natural colorants made from rocks ground into powder best known as coloring agents for artist's paints. Forty years ago, they made oil paints quite expensive, but are now very reasonable. Pigments vary widely in intensity from color to color so a set ratio of pigment to soap won't work.

Generally speaking, begin with 1 or 2 tsp (2-4g) for ¾ pound (340g) and increase as desired. Pigments work well because time doesn't alter their color, but color selection is limited and sometimes "what you see is not always what you get." Occasionally the color in powdered form varies what shows up in the soap; experimenting solves this problem.

UNUSUAL CHOICES: CRAYONS

Some methods of soap coloring fall into the unorthodox category, but have proven quite successful like crayons. They're inexpensive, come in a wide color assortment and are either already around the house or extremely easy to locate. For every one pound (454g) of fat, use 1 inch (2.54cm) from a ¼" (6.35cm) crayon. Prior melting before adding to the soap isn't necessary. The FDA hasn't approved crayons as soaps colorants, but they are perfectly acceptable for personal use. Like food dyes, crayon coloring can change over time. If you can live with this, it's a cheap source of soap colorant.

LAST RESORT: NATURAL DYES AND FOOD DYES

Natural Dyes are not a good choice because they require more work to obtain in the first place and the chemical reaction in soap can adversely affect their color. Food dyes are weak and require more dye to achieve stronger colors. When there are so many easier and less expensive choices, why make extra work for yourself?

COLORANTS – A BIG SUBJECT!

If one had the time, an entire book could be devoted to colorants, how they react with different fats and oils, how to extract plant dyes, which are best suited to soapmaking. Since there are so many variants, it will require experimentation since even altering the ratio of certain fats can change the soap's color. How long your color is in the soap before pouring into the mold will also affect color.

KEEP A RECORD

Even more important than when testing scent, it is a good idea to make notes regarding what and how much of a coloring agent you used and in what recipe. Also note if you were pleased with the outcome. Unfortunately, coloring will be a lot of trial and error, but it won't affect using the soap unless you end up with colored bubbles, which should be discarded.

MOLDS

A lot of the cute starfish and rosette shapes found in bath shops are professionally extruded soaps. To achieve the same 3-dimensional look and double-sided design, you need a two-part mold. It takes practice and basic soapmaking skills should be mastered first.

SIZE – TOO BIG?

When using candle molds, make sure they aren't gargantuan! Many two-part molds are too big for soap, measuring 7" tallx3" wide (17.8 x6cm) and larger. If the mold makes a figure, like a 6"x3" (15x6cm) rabbit for instance, it will be too big for a single bar of soap. Being non-uniform in shape means there wouldn't be a convenient place to divide it. This design would look pretty weird separated into a pair of bunny ears, fat tummy and cottontail. When selecting molds, choose them from a user's viewpoint; envision how the finished soap would look and feel in the hand.

SIZE – TOO SMALL?

Many candy molds are very small, some only an inch across, some only ¼" (.63cm) deep. This makes for nice bite-sized chocolates, but very small bars of soap. They are great for decorating, but not too practical at bath time. Also remember that as soaps cure, they shrink a bit, further reducing the finished size.

MOLDS TO AVOID

There's a quaint Midwestern saying about "not breeding a scab on the end of your nose." Loosely translated it means "don't court trouble." Courting trouble with molds is using anything out of tin, aluminum, zinc, china, untempered glass, flimsy plastic or colored molds. The first three will corrode; the middle two are prone to breakage; flimsy plastic can melt and the only color you want in your soap is that which occurs naturally or you add intentionally. These few no-nos will save grief in the long run!

SHAPES

In selecting a mold, consider the purpose of the soap. Is it decorative, guest soap or is it for practical, every day use? I bought cute bars of decorator soaps shaped like bears or lions, but when using them in the shower, try hanging onto a bear's ear or a lion's tail! Invariably they squirted onto the floor and then it became a game of "hunt the animal"! Maybe I'm just a klutz, but this was annoying.

MOLD FOR YIELDING LARGE BLOCKS

- Slab or Block Molds (yields one big piece of soap that needs to be cut into smaller bars):
- Tupperware or Rubber Maid type storage containers – 9"x13" (23x33cm) cake size
- Cardboard boxes that hold four 6 packs of beer or soda pop cans for shipping sometimes referred to as "flats"
- Cardboard shoeboxes
- Food containers:
  - Cardboard milk or juice containers
  - Soup, juice, vegetable and fruit cans
  - Microwave meals containers
  - Ice cream cartons
- PVC pipe 2¼" or 3" (5.7x7.6cm) diameter
- Window expanders of extruded vinyl plastic downspouts and guttering

INDIVIDUAL MOLDS

- Jell-O (jelly in Australia) molds
- Candle molds
- Cookie or muffin trays and tartlet molds
- Food containers like yogurt or pudding cartons, single serve size; plastic containers for cheese spreads and sauces
- Candy molds
- Plastic Easter egg containers
- Freezer popsicle molds

When I first looked for molds on the Internet and then later in local stores, they were the least readily available item on the soap supplies list. If you use any of these items for soap molds, then that's their permanent task in life. They shouldn't be used for anything else once exposed to lye.

PREPARING THE MOLD

Molds, like beauty, are in the eye of the beholder. They can be semi-rigid, heavy cardboard, sturdy plastic or wood. Here are a few suggestions to get you started. Preparing the mold has many different opinions.

Plastic Wrap Liners can wrinkle inside the mold and leave marks on the soap. If using plastic, be sure to smooth out all wrinkles before pouring the soap.

Garbage Bags can be cut to the appropriate size, which means enough to cover the insides and come over the outside walls of the container. Smooth out all wrinkles before pouring the soap.

Silicone Bakery Paper This is a Teflon-like paper used to line cake pans. It can be purchased through some bakeries but gets ruined after one soapmaking project. This method is a must for making the stickier milk-based soaps.

Greasing the Molds is marginally successful since it can be absorbed into the soap.

Vegetable Spray like Pam or Pure and Simple, vegetable shortening or Vaseline can also be used.

Generally soap will unmold with no problem, but using a slightly flexible mold helps get stubborn soap to release after receiving a gentle twist.

One sure trick to make soap release is to pop soap and mold into the freezer 2-4 hours before attempting to unmold it. If you use a huge slab or block mold, this could present some obvious space problems, but it does work. If you use the freezer method, unmold it quickly directly onto the surface you plan to dry the soap.

From being very cold or frozen, the soap will exude moisture almost immediately. The soap's wet surface will show fingerprints so work quickly and don't handle it a lot.

Whatever mold you choose, make sure it is white or clear. Soap loves to absorb color wherever it can get its molecules on it! One of the best things about soapmaking is all the creativity and flexibility this craft allows. Let your eyes roam and you'll spot heaps of soap mold candidates!

MAKING SOAP IN A BLENDER

Use a recipe that yields no more than a one-pound (.45kg) batch. Even using a blender, accuracy in measuring is still necessary, but exactness of temperatures for the lye and fat is not as critical.

Use cold, softened water or rain water to dissolve the lye. The lye is ready for mixing when it turns clear.

The fat should be just melted, at which point, everything including fragrances and colorants, goes together in the blender. Remember to carefully pour in the lye to avoid splashing. The blender shouldn't be much more than half full. Before turning on the blender and mixing at LOWEST speed, **make absolutely certain the lid is securely in place**. Mix at the lowest speed. Check often for tracing.

Before checking for trace, turn off the blender and allow to sit a few seconds before removing the lid in case the soap mixture "burps" and splashes. At the thin trace stage, stir soap gently to remove bubbles and pour into individual molds. If you wait until full trace, the air bubbles can't escape. While using a blender doesn't make big batches of soap, it has three distinct advantages:

1) Much shorter time to thin trace stage. Instead of 30-40 minutes, it may take only 30 seconds. Yes, *seconds*!
2) No thermometers are required.
3) The blender literally beats the lye water into the fats producing a much smoother mixture so the chances of separation are greatly reduced.

Using a blender is one way to achieve a floating bar of soap by deliberately whipping air into the mixture. This requires allowing the soap to mix to over-trace stage, which makes it trickier to pour. It might be easiest to first learn making soap the traditional way using thermometers and understanding what the trace stage looks like before attempting this method. Nothing is hard if you're familiar with it and familiarity only takes practice.

SOAP RECIPES

IMPORTANT NOTES: Make sure to use pure caustic soda. Old Red Devil metal cans held 12 ounces. Their later plastic containers held 18 ounces. Adjust soap recipes accordingly. Since it's increasingly difficult to locate Red Devil a substitution may be necessary. One option is Roebic Heavy Duty Crystal Drain Opener.

BASIC SOAP
32 oz (907g) blended vegetable or olive oil
74 oz (2,097g) tallow
14 oz (397g) lye (caustic soda)
 3 oz (85g) cocoa butter
41 oz (1,162g) cold water

Follow basic soapmaking directions to prepare lye solution and oils. Slowly pour lye solution into oils while stirring. Complete soap as per usual instructions. This soap is mild with long-lasting, creamy bubbles. It traces quickly, sets up and dries quickly. Good choice for hand milling as it can be milled either moist or dry and accepts additives readily. Soap is hard when cured.

PALM OIL CARMEL SOAP
1¼ cups milk (whole or 2%)
1 cup Palm Oil
¼ cup lye
1 cup either tallow, olive oil, Crisco, etc.

Use blender recipe instructions. One advantage with milk recipes is in having the milk chilled. The lye solution never gets very hot. This soap has a nice brown color and smells like caramelized sugar. Look for palm oil in 1 kg cans wherever you buy Indian or Middle Eastern groceries; also called "Vegetable Ghee." It's a comparatively inexpensive vegetable fat.

FACIAL SOAP
16 oz (454g) pure olive oil
6 oz (170g) water
2 oz (57g) lye

Place olive oil in an enamel pan to heat. While oil is heating, place the cold water into a glass bowl and pour lye into the water slowly and stir with a wooden spoon. Stir until water is clear and let cool. When the lye and olive oil are warm to the touch, pour the lye slowly into the olive oil while stirring. Olive oil soap will take at least an hour to trace so stir and check on it every 10 minutes and then stir again.

When you see trace, add whatever herbs are desired. Sage is a good choice which a nice scent and soft green color. Grease molds with a little olive oil and pour in the soap to set which usually takes about three days. Recipe yields one pound of soap.

CLEAR SOAP (FAUX NEUTROGENA)
1 cup tallow
1-1½ cup isopropyl alcohol
½ cup melted coconut oil or olive oil
4 Tbsp lye flakes
⅔ cup glycerin
yellow food coloring (optional)
¾ cup water

Melt tallow and coconut oil, as per general soapmaking instructions. Cool to lukewarm, by "floating" pan of oil in a tepid water bath. Stir lye into cold soft water. Cool to lukewarm. Pour lye into fat and stir. When creamy, add glycerin. Pour into molds greased with petroleum jelly.

After three days, grate soap into the top of a double boiler. Begin to heat over gently boiling water. Add alcohol and stir constantly. When the liquid is transparent, lift the spoon. If a ropy thread forms, remove from heat. If a skin forms immediately upon removing from heat, pour into molds.
Unmold after a few days and stack to air cure for 2 weeks.

FAUX IVORY SOAP
6 lbs grease (2.72kg), melted and clean OR 3 lbs (1.36kg) grease, PLUS 3 lbs (1.36kg) olive, coconut, or other rich oil
1 cup borax
½ cup water, boiled
2 Tbsp sugar

Optional:
1 Tbsp washing soda
2 oz (57g) glycerin
1 cup sudsy ammonia
2-4 Tbsp perfume
13 oz (370g) pure lye
2 cups oatmeal

Dissolve lye in 2 pints of water in a porcelain or enamel container. Set aside and let cool until the mixture is just warm. This may take hours.

Next, put the borax in a porcelain pan. Add ½ cup of boiled water, sugar and washing soda. Next, add the sudsy ammonia. Follow at once with lye (half solid fat and half liquid makes the best soap) and 2 pints of water. Check first to see that the lye water is just slightly warm. Hold your hand over it; don't stick your finger in it.

Add the melted grease, a third at a time. Stir constantly until it's the consistency of thick cream. (Both grease and lye need to be lukewarm to make good soap). If the goal is facial soap, when the mixture is thick as honey, add glycerin and perfume. Two cups powdered oatmeal can be added to create an interesting texture. When done, put the soap into paper boxes lined with freezer paper. When thickened, cut into bars. Place in the sun until it bleaches white. Store for use. One nice feature of this soap is that it floats!

FACE AND BODY SOAP

8.8 pounds (4kg) rendered suet, coconut or olive oil

12 oz (340g) lye

2 cups (500ml) lemon juice

3 cups (750ml) water

.25 oz (7.5ml) essential oil (optional)

This is a luxurious and gentle soap. Follow basic soapmaking instructions. Stir in lemon juice just before soap is to go into the molds. When the soap is firm but not yet hard, cut into bars with a knife. It should be hard in an hour or so; test lightly with your finger. Wrap in clean cotton rags and store in a cool, airy place for 3-6 months. Yield: 6 pounds soap.

The recipe works equally well with other animal fats to produce similar results. Coconut oil yields a softer, quick-lathering soap. Olive oil and other vegetable cooking oils yield very soft soap that never completely hardens. Since these oils are sensitive to air and light, soap made with these ingredients will spoil in a few weeks unless refrigerated. This soap works well with no fragrance. Finished soap will have a pH of about 9 which can be lowered by adding more lemon juice.

GENERAL PURPOSE SOAP

TONY'S NO FAIL (AND NO WEIGH) SOAP RECIPE

6 lbs (2.72kg) vegetable shortening

12 oz (340g) lye

2 cups water

Mix lye and water in an enamel pan and set aside to cool. Melt shortening and set aside to cool. When both are "hot to the touch" (on the outside of the pan), pour lye into shortening.

Stir until consistency is like mashed potatoes. Pour into prepared molds and let set 24 hours, covered. Uncover and touch to see if it's firm. If it is, turn soap out onto paper and cut it into bars. Allow to cure for 2-3 weeks, minimum. If soap is not firm, cover and let set for another 24 hours, then turn out and cut.

Tony's favorite mold is a cardboard box lined with a trash bag. He uses the boxes or "flats" for shipping soft drinks or beer as they're the perfect size for this recipe. Yield: approximately 24 bars.

GOAT MILK SOAP

BASIC GOAT MILK AND HONEY SOAP

13 cups (6.5 pounds or 2.95kg) lard or rendered fat

12 oz (340g) lye

4 cups goat milk

½ cup honey

1 cup hot water

In a large stainless steel or enamel container, dissolve honey in hot water. Add goat milk, stir to mix well and slowly add lye to the milk/honey mixture. This will get very hot. Let set until it cools down to 75°F (24°C) degrees.

This should take an hour or more. When the lye mixture reaches 75°F (24°C), warm the lard to 85°F (29.5°C) and pour it in a slow steady stream into the lye/milk mixture. Stir constantly until the mixture reaches the consistency of honey. This will take 20 or 30 minutes and pour into prepared molds. Allow to set for 24-48 hours. Unmold and cut into bars. Air-dry soap for 4-5 weeks to cure.

OATMEAL & HONEY GOAT MILK SOAP
  6 cups goat milk
  2 cups dry oatmeal (run through blender)
  4 cups (2 pounds or 907g) lard
  ½ cup honey
  8 oz (227g) lye

Carefully mix the milk and lye in a stainless container. Allow to cool to 85°F (29.5°C). Stir in refined oatmeal and honey. Mix well. Warm lard to 85°F (29.5°C) and slowly add to milk mixture. Mix for 15 minutes, let stand 5 minutes. Mix again for 5 minutes. Watch closely as soap traces suddenly. When thick like honey, pour into prepared molds. Let set 24-48 hours until set. Cut into bars and air cure for 3-4 weeks.

RHONDA'S GOAT MILK SOAP RECIPE
Here is a great recipe for goat milk soap... works every time!

  42 oz (1191g) olive oil
  28 oz (794g) coconut oil
  33 oz (936g) goat milk or buttermilk
  18 oz (510g) palm oil

  1 cup ground oatmeal
  12.7 oz (360g) lye
  4 Tbsp raw honey

Use general soapmaking making instructions bringing the fats and oil temperature to 92°F (33.3°C). Use the same temperature for the lye/milk. Soap should age 4-6 weeks. Even without adding fragrances, this soap still smells like honey and oatmeal 4 weeks later.

LAUNDRY SOAP

LAUNDRY SOAP #1
  16 oz (454g) coconut oil
  1 cup water (8 fluid ounces or 237ml)
  2.8 oz (79g) lye

Use general soapmaking making instructions bringing the fats and oil temperature to 120°F (49°C). Tracing time should be about 1½ hours with time in the molds approximately 48 hours. Aging time is 3 weeks.

LAUNDRY SOAP #2
Use Tony's No Fail (and no weigh) Soap Recipe on the preceding page. For Laundry Powder: Let it cure for a minimum of one month. Grate it up very finely and it's ready for use. Include a little dry bleach and borax to add whitening power and odor control.

GRANDMA HERALD'S LAUNDRY SOAP FLAKES
  1 quart cold water
  12 oz (340g) sodium hydroxide
  ½ cup borax
  1 cup sugar
  1 cup ammonia
  2 quarts washed, strained grease
  Scent

Pour water in earthenware jar. Pour in lye and stir with wooden stick. Let stand till cold which takes about an hour. Put sugar and borax into an earthenware or enamel vessel and stir well. Pour warm grease into borax mixture and stir well. Add ammonia and stir.

Add cooled lye solution to grease mixture. Stir until mixture thickens to fudge consistency. Pour into a simple mold like a paper box lined with waxed paper to set. Soap hardens in a few days. Grate soap finely for use. Favorite scents: Sassafras, wintergreen, pine.

LIQUID SOAP

LIQUID SOAP 1
    1 oz (28g) avocado oil
    3.1 oz (88g) lye
    4 oz (113g) coconut oil
    8 oz (227g) water
    11 oz (312g) soybean oil

Mix as usual per basic instructions. Combine water and lye, then add to melted fats. Stir until trace. Pour into mold and allow to sit for a few days until pH tests low. Grate soap, heat slowly and add 8 ounces of water slowly. Check consistency in a cool water bath. Correct thickness by adding water, thicken by adding more grated soap. Pour into container. Shake every few days to keep smooth.

LIQUID SOAP 2
    2 oz (56.7g) Basic Soap recipe, grated
    Scent or color as desired
    8 oz (227g) water

Slowly heat grated soap and water in saucepan. Stir gently until melted. Mix in any additives. Check consistency in a cool water bath. Correct thickness by adding water, thicken by adding more grated soap. Pour into container. Shake every few days to keep smooth.

SOAP BALLS

Soap balls are a nifty way to get rid of extra soap that won't fill an individual mold or use all those little scrap pieces left over from the shower. There are two easy ways to do this:

Method One – For Scraps: Gather like colors of soap or you'll end up with an ugly colored ball. Place scraps in a bowl. If they are very small – great, no further work needed. If not, either break them up with a knife or grate the pieces with a vegetable grater. Sprinkle pieces with warm water; let sit 15 minutes to soften. Gather a handful and squeeze into a ball shape. It will take from two days to two weeks to completely cure in a warm, dry area. Re-shape every two days to maintain roundness. Don't worry about irregularities; they will lend interest to your soap.

Method Two – Balls From New Soap: Select your favorite Hand-Milled Soap recipe, but instead of pouring it into individual molds, pour the soap into one large one mold. Place everything in the freezer until it can be cut into blocks that hold its shape.

Grate the blocks and allow to dry in a bowl up to a week. While still moist, gather a handful and squeeze into ball shapes. It will take from two days to two weeks to completely dry in a warm, dry area. Reshape every two days to maintain roundness. Again, irregularities will make your soap interesting.

SHAMPOO

SHAMPOO BAR
This soap does not wash away natural oils and eliminates the need for a conditioner. Squeeze the juice of a lemon into bottle for your final rinse.
    24 oz (680g) coconut oil
    12 oz (340g) lye
    28 oz (794g) olive oil
    32 oz (907g) water
    24 oz (680g) castor oil

Use general soapmaking making instructions bringing the fats/oil and the lye/water temperature to 95-98°F (35-37°C).

LIQUID SHAMPOO
    5 oz (142g) grated basic soap
    ½ tsp powdered pectin
    26 oz (737g) water

Mix all ingredients in a saucepan. Heat slowly until smooth and liquid. Add 3-6 drops of the oils of your choice. Suggested oils are rosemary, chamomile, pine, tea tree, lavender or cinnamon leaf. Pour into a plastic, shampoo type bottle. Keep tightly sealed. **NOTE**: Don't omit the powdered pectin or soap will severely separate.

HOW TO MAKE "LYE WATER"

In countries where lye (as known as caustic soda or sodium hydroxide) isn't readily available and before it became a commercial product, people used to make their own lye water for soap. All it requires is ash and soft water. Sounds easy but it can unnecessarily complicate soapmaking. If at all possible, stick to commercial caustic soda products. Make sure they are pure caustic soda. Red Devil's metal cans held 12 ounces. Their new plastic containers hold 18 ounces. Adjust soap recipes accordingly. When you make your own lye water, it can come out at varying strengths unhappily altering soap recipes.

It's a good idea to become proficient making at least one soap recipe with commercial lye so you're familiar with the procedure and know what to expect.

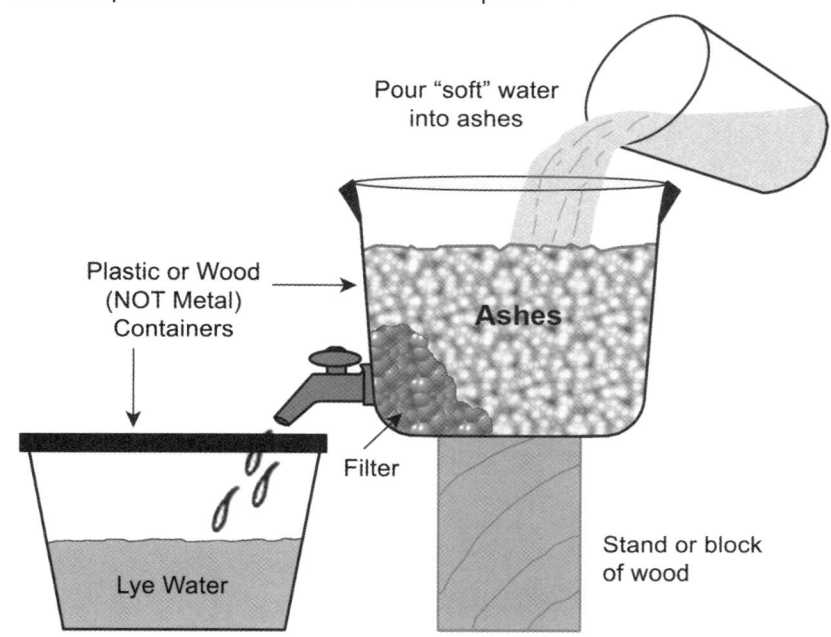

INGREDIENTS

To make lye water, burn wood in a very hot fire to end up with white ashes. Ordinary wood used in cooking fires will do in addition to dried palm branches, dried banana peels, cocoa pods, kapok tree wood or oak wood. For really white soap, apple tree wood makes the best lye ashes.

After the ashes are cold, store them in a covered plastic bucket, wooden barrel or stainless steel container.

The other ingredient required is soft water, which you can easily get by catching rainwater. You want water without metals or acids. Depending on the water, ordinary bore, well, or river water can be used for making soap, but you may have to add baking soda to it.

BAKING SODA TEST

If you use tap or some other possibly hard water, see if you can make soap bubble up or foam in it. If the soap lathers easily, the water is probably OK as it is. If not, add a little bit of baking soda at a time and mix thoroughly. Continue adding soda and mixing until the water lathers with the soap.

Be sure to keep track of how much total baking soda is added. Then add the same ratio of soda to "hard water" to achieve the same soft water as in your "test".

MAKING "LYE WATER"

If you are going to use a large barrel or drum to make the lye water in, and it has a tap or hole near the bottom, place some kind of filter on the inside of the barrel around the opening (as shown in the diagram). You don't want to be moving the lye water and risk splashing it on your skin.

Fill the barrel with white ashes to about four inches (10cm) below the top.

Boil half a bucket full of soft water and pour over the ashes. Slowly add more cold soft water until liquid drips through the tap into the lye water bucket. Close the tap or block the hole.

Add more ashes to top the barrel up again, and more soft water. Do not add so much water that the ashes swim. Let the water/ash mixture stand for four or more hours, preferably over night. Pour the brownish lye water into a plastic, wood or other "safe" container, but not any kind of metal.

Pour this back through the ashes again.

Let the lye water drip into "safe" containers. When the brown lye water stops coming out of the barrel, or ash container, then pour four to five pints (2½-3 liters) of soft water through the ashes. Collect the lye as comes out in a separate "safe" container, as this lye may be weaker than the first batch. Repeat using two to three pints (1-2 liters) of soft water until no more brown liquid comes out of the ashes.

Put the lye water into "safe" bottles or containers and keep tightly sealed, away from children, until ready to use. Dig the ashes into the vegetable garden.

LYE WATER STRENGTH

If an egg or potato floats just below half way, or a chicken feather starts to dissolve in it, then the lye water is the right strength. If the egg will not float, then the lye water could be boiled down if you wanted it to be stronger.

SOAPMAKING – TIPS AND TROUBLESHOOTING

PROBLEM	CAUSE	FIX
Soap won't trace	Not enough lye, too much water, wrong temperatures, stirring too slow	If measurements and temperatures are correct, continue stirring up to 4 hours or until trace. After 4 hours stirring, if it shows signs of thickening, pour into molds regardless of trace and hope for the best
Lye and fat separate in mold, pouring into mold	Cooking temp too high or too low, soap reaction to fragrance or essential oil, too much saturated fat used	Pour or scoop quickly into mold. Smooth as best as possible with spatula. More Fragrance Oils than Essential Oils cause seizing. Oils to avoid: cassia, clove, cucumber, grapefruit seed extract and rose. Avoid ANY oils containing alcohol.
As soap cools in the mold, a layer of oil rises to the top	Too much oil in recipe, incorrect measuring or poor ingredient substitutions	Fix as per first solution. Check soap in 2 – 3 weeks. If it doesn't lather well and is caustic, discard soap.
Soap curdles while making basic recipe or remelting for hand-milled soaps	Cooling basic recipe too fast, inaccuracy in measuring ingredients, adding dyes or additives with too much sodium, irregular stirring or not stirring briskly	If curdling comes from inaccurate measuring, try Fix as per first solution. If it's from too much sodium, try diluting it after remelting. Weigh out another batch of basic soap and water and add it to the hand-milled soap. Reheat and combine. If it curdles, discard soap.
When cutting up blocks for hand-milled soap, there is clear liquid present	Excessive amount of lye in recipe	These are lye pockets; put on gloves immediately. If pockets are large, throw it out. If small, cut the soap for hand-milling over the sink (wearing gloves), rinse off remaining lye and dry soap. Proceed with hand-milled recipe.
Free fat that hasn't combined with lye. It will smell rancid.	Too much fat or too little lye in recipe.	No remedy. Discard soap.
Soap in mold is grainy	Stirred too long or too fast	Does not affect soap usage, only its appearance
Soap in mold is streaky	Not enough lye, too much water	Does not affect soap usage, only its appearance
Air bubbles in cured soap	Stirred too long or too fast	Does not affect soap usage, only its appearance
Soap is too soft	Not enough lye, too much water	Try curing a couple more weeks to harden. Discard if it stays too soft or add more water to make liquid soap
Soap is too hard or brittle	Too much lye	No fix for this; discard soap
Mottled soap with shiny white spots – not streaks	Too much lye, stirring too slow	Shiny spots are pockets of lye – discard soap
Lots of white powder on curing soap	Hard water was used and lye didn't properly dissolve	Soap will be caustic, discard it.
Small amounts of white powder on curing soap	Excess sodium salts reacted with the air and formed sodium carbonate	Bars must be scraped before using. Check for caustic reaction. If present, discard soap
Cracks in soap	Too much lye, too much stirring, soap set up too quickly	If soap is not caustic, then it is OK to use. Does not affect soap usage, only its appearance
Irregularities in cured soap. Bar appears warped, bumpy	By-product of drying process or using misshaped molds.	Shaving with a vegetable peeler can lessen small irregularities and bumps. For very noticeable problems, try carving soap into shapes. For small problems, try lightly wetting soap and smoothing with your finger (watch out for fingerprints).

SAFETY NOTE: Be sure to wear gloves and protective eyewear when working with lye water. Should any touch your skin, treat with vinegar or lemon juice and rinse off.

Like many other skills, soapmaking is a craft that requires practice, but there is a lot of satisfaction in saying "I made it myself!" Besides being a good practical skill, everyone loves these soaps as gifts. Happy experimenting!

Chapter 21: Candlemaking

WHERE DID THEY COME FROM?

Mystery still surrounds the origins of the first candle, but similar lighting devices date to Biblical days of rushes and torches. Earlier evidence of candles was unearthed in Tutankamen's burial chambers dating to 3000 B.C. The Romans used candles and tapers dating back to 1st century A.D.

Until the 1400s, all candles were dipped when a Parisian inventor created the first wooden molds for tallow. This greatly speeded candle production over "dips" method. In 1834, Joseph Morgan invented continuous wicking and an automatic molded-candle injection system paving the way for today's machinery, which can produce up to 1500 candles per hour.

Besides Morgan's molds, three 19th-century additions greatly improved candlemaking: stearic acid; treated, braided wicking and paraffin.

In the last 150 years, candlemaking has not changed much and has enjoyed resurgence after their decline when electricity arrived. Today, candles have pizzazz and individuality with the addition of scent, color, wax carving, unique molds and agents to make waxes whiter, glossier and harder.

EQUIPMENT

Supplies are pretty easy to find and many things you might already have at home.
- Wax
- Wicking
- Double Boiler
- Candy or Wax Thermometer – a candle or candy thermometer that clips to the pot works fine.
- Large Can or Melting Pitcher
- Empty Soup Can, Soda Can, Stewed Tomato Can
- Wood Spoon (to stir wax)
- Newspaper and/or Wax Paper
- Popsicle Stick or Pencil – to suspend the wick
- Stearic Acid
- Potholders or Oven Mitts
- Mold
- Mold Release
- Scent (optional)
- Colorant (optional)

SAFETY TIPS

Before beginning, read the safety tips. Most are common sense just like for soapmaking.

1. Never leave melting wax unattended. Wax can ignite at 375°F (190°C) with no warning. If a wax fire occurs, turn off the heat and cover flames with a lid or use an ABC type fire extinguisher. Flour can be used to smother the flame, but don't throw water on a wax fire. Use a thermometer to check for getting too close to the flash point.

2. Do not "hurry" the melting process by using the microwave. Waxes are hydrocarbons and heating under microwave energy can cause explosions in the oven.

3. Use only the double boiler or water bath method; never place the wax container directly on the stove. A double boiler is a great choice since it keeps wax a couple inches away from the heat source and melting is very controlled. However, you may not want to use the wax-containing portion again for cooking. Alternately, take a large metal can like a 64 oz juice (2 liter) can and place it on a wire rack in the pan of water. Before using the can, pinch one edge to form a spout. This will make pouring hot wax a lot easier. If you find yourself making lots of candles, you may want to invest in a wax melting pot. An excellent alternative is an old metal camping coffee pot.

4. Keep a close watch on the water level, it evaporates quickly and must be replenished frequently but avoid getting water in the wax. It can cause the wax to sputter, splash, burn you and/or cause a fire hazard. Should you accidentally get water in your wax, remove the wax from the water bath and pour it into a heatproof dish and allow it to cool. When you remove the cooled wax from the dish, water will be left in the dish. Dry off the wax and remelt it.

5. Keep the stove area free from drips; wax drips are flammable too.

6. Use only scenting oils specifically approved for candlemaking. Some can catch fire and others may not mix properly with the wax and cause flaws.

If you want to use scented oil not specifically designed for candle use, test it for flammability first. Some oils can catch on fire. Test them by pouring a single candle using the quantity of scent you will routinely use. Burn this candle on a nonflammable surface with nothing flammable around it. Should the entire candle catch on fire, have a fire extinguisher handy. Don't use water. This doesn't happen often, but a little caution is OK.

RECORDKEEPING

In an effort to save a few minutes, sometimes I haven't written down certain color combinations or other options for a recipe thinking "**Of course,** I'll remember!" Wrong! Since there can be many variables, it's best to keep an on-going record of what has been tried. It saves repeating a mistake and captures THE perfect recipe! Recordkeeping is not only good for the beginner but also for the seasoned candlemaker. If you are considering marketing candles, it's essential. You'll want to keep track of type and quantity of wax, additives, colorants, scent, molds, wick size, pouring temperature, setting time and good/bad sources for supplies.

WAX

PARAFFIN

Before buying any wax, decide what type candle to make. Paraffin comes in three different melting points and each one is used for a specific type candle.

WHICH WAX DO I USE?			
CANDLE TYPE	MELT POINT	USE FOR	BURN TIME
Container	130°F (54°C) or lower	Candles that will remain in the container	Slowest Burning
Molded	139-143°F (59-62°C)	Dripless, freestanding candles that need to keep their shape like pillars	Moderate
Dipped	145°F (63°C)	Tapers because this wax easily sticks to itself, allowing for the building of layers, votives	Fast
Beeswax	146°F (63°C)	Rolled candles or combine with slow burning waxes for container candles	Fastest

BEESWAX

Beeswax is versatile and extremely easy to work with. It comes with its own unique scent and is slight sticky. This makes rolling sheets of honeycombed beeswax into candles easy since it sticks to itself. It also comes in easy-to-use beads. All you need for this type of candle is a container and a pre-stiffened wick. Pour the beads around the wick placed in the middle of the container and press them down. Voilá – done.

The last type of beeswax is in blocks – the most popular form. To use, chisel off the desired amount. One caution about all beeswax candles… With this wax's fast melt point, candles can burn a hollow straight down the wick leaving an outer shell of unburned wax. To counteract this problem, mix 1 part block beeswax to 3 parts of the slowest burning paraffin.

HOW MUCH?

One of the most common and easiest molds to work with is the pillar or round shape. Until you get a good feel for how much wax is need for different sized molds, the following table gives a reasonable estimate of how much wax is required for pillars.

HOW MUCH WAX TO USE FOR ROUND MOLDS

Candle Inches	Ounces Wax	Candle Inches	Ounces Wax	Candle Inches	Ounces Wax	Candle Inches	Ounces Wax
2x3	5	2½x3	7	3x3	11	4x3	19
2x4	6	2½x4	10	3x4	14	4x4	25
2x5	8	2½x5	12	3x5	18	4x5	32
2x6	10	2½x6	15	3x6	21	4x6	38
2x7	11	2½x7	17	3x7	25	4x7	44
2x8	13	2½x8	20	3x8	29	4x8	51
2x9	14	2½x9	22	3x9	32	4x9	57
2x10	16	2½x10	25	3x10	36	4x10	63
Tea light	1	Votive – square (1¾x2)	3.2	Votive – round	2		

WICKS

Wick size is determined by candle diameter. For every 2 inches (5cm) of candle width, use the next thicker wick. (Move from small to medium or from medium to large.) Make sure the wick is the right size in relation to the candle and use the correct wax for type of candle. This goes a long way toward making it burn longer, be dripless and smokeless.

TIP: Besides the wider candles, use a thicker wick for candles made from beeswax or wax containing hardening additives.

PICKING THE WICK TYPE

WICK TYPE	CANDLE USE	QUALITIES
Flat Braid	Versatile enough for most candles, especially good for tapers	Decorative, but tends to flop over into the burning wax
Square Braid	Molded, container dipped candles	
Metal Core	Votives, tea or floating lights, small container candles	Poor quality wicks can burn up leaving an un-burned candle
Paper Core	Votives, tea light, small container candles	May be smokier than the metal core wicks

TIP: When using a braided wick, make sure the "v" is pointing up or the candle may smoke and burn unevenly.

PICKING THE WICK SIZE

CANDLE SIZE		WICK SIZE	CANDLE SIZE		WICK SIZE
1"	2.5cm	Small	5"	12.5cm	Large
2"	5.0cm	Small	6"	15.0cm	Large
3"	7.5cm	Medium	Larger sizes		Use multiple wicks
4"	10.0cm	Medium			

INSERTING THE WICK

Some wicks have a small metal tab at one end, which is glued to the container before pouring the wax.

TIPS: Make your own metal tabs by cutting up aluminum cans and gluing or tying the wick to the tab. (Use only old scissors to cut the can!)

If you have unstiffened wicking, melt a little wax in a double boiler and run the wick through it. While drying, hold the wick taut at each end. When the wax has dried (only a few seconds), the wick will be easy to insert in a straight line. To help insert a wick properly, take a tongue depressor or popsicle stick and carefully slice it halfway through lengthwise. Insert the wick into the slice and it will be easy to pull the wick taut with the tongue depressor or stick braced against the top of the mold. If you don't have these flat sticks, tie the wick onto a pencil and use it the same way.

ADDITIVES

STEARIC ACID (STEARINE)
Add stearic acid to candle wax to make it harden and release more easily from the mold. Either animal or vegetable works well. Add 3 tablespoons per pound or ½kg of wax as the wax melts. Since container candles already use the slowest burning paraffin, you may not want to add a hardener. Container candles need to burn slowly so all the wax is consumed without burning a hole down the middle. Stearic acid lightens candle colors.

LUSTER AND TRANSLUCENT CRYSTALS
This additive hardens wax making it burn twice as long as paraffin-only candles. Wax colors come out opaque and vibrant. Since luster crystals melt at a much higher temperature than paraffin, melt wax and crystals separately, and then combine. The clear crystal variety, translucent, won't change the wax's opacity. Think of luster crystals as a transparent topcoat for nail polish, which forms a clear, hard, protective coating around the finished candle. Use about ½-2% per recipe or 1 teaspoon per 2 pounds of wax.

VYBAR
This product helps to reduce air bubbles and mottling while it enhances fragrances and color quality. However, it can cause increased shrinkage and rippling. Use Vybar 103 for melt points over 130°F and Vybar 260 for anything below 130°F. (54.4°C)

PROS AND CONS OF VYBAR		
Pros	**Cons**	**Comments**
More economical than Stearine	Difficult to find	Be sure to use the proper variety: one is for molded candles, the other is for container candles
Improves color	Makes candle color whiter	Makes colors softer, paler
Makes scent last longer	Candle may not release easily from mold	Using too much will cause the candle to not release the scent
Makes wax more resistant to mottling and flaws		Makes candles creamier
Binds up unwanted water		

Use 1-5% Vybar. Start at 1% and work from there. For every pound or .45 kilo of wax, use 1½ teaspoons of Vybar. Be sure to record amounts used, so you can vary future recipes if needed.

COLORANTS
Coloring and scenting a candle are my two favorite parts appealing to two very strong senses: sight and smell. Adding color ties your candles with room decor, enhances the motif of a dinner and carries out the theme of the candle. Imagine molding a luscious strawberry candle and scenting it with the same fragrance, but coloring the wax with a 'blah' tan. Kind of loses the appeal doesn't it.

Candlemaking colorants come in a variety of forms and there are plusses to each; however the dye buds get my vote. Crayons have been used in varying degrees of success, but they tend to make a color muddy. They can also give off an unpleasant odor and make candles sputter.

Dye Buds or Chips make coloring candles clean and simple. They are highly concentrated chips 1⅛" (3cm) in diameter which melt with the wax, giving rich color. Each bud colors about 1 pound (½kg) of wax. Use more chips for deeper color. They are the best choice if you're coloring less than 100 lbs. (45kg) of wax at a time. The most popular colors are Aquamarine, Bayberry Green, Black, Blue, Brown, Burgundy, Cranberry, Flame, Gold, Gray, Green, Ivory, Moss Green, Orange, Peach, Pink, Rust, Turquoise, Violet, White, and Yellow. There's no spilling and no measuring involved.

TWO DYE COLORS FROM THE SAME BOTTLE							
Use a Little For		**Use More For**		**Use a Little For**		**Use More For**	
Gray	.01%	Black	0.2%	Soft Yellow	.01%	Bright Yellow	0.1%
Sky	.01%	Blue	.05%	Violet	.005%	Purple	.01%
Caramel	.05%	Dark Brown	0.1%	Pink	.025%	Hot Pink	0.1%
Gold	.01%	Orange	.05%	Light Teal	.01%	Teal	.05%

TWO DYE COLORS FROM THE SAME BOTTLE							
Use a Little For		**Use More For**		**Use a Little For**		**Use More For**	
Mauve	.01%	Burgundy	.05%	Lime	.01%	Kelly	.05%
Country Blue	.01%	Navy	.05%	Dark Pink	.005%	Red	.05%
Moss	.01%	Hunter	.05%	Peach	.01%	Coral	.05%
Vanilla	.001%	Tan	.01%				

Powder Dyes are extremely concentrated. They are recommended only for batches over 100 lbs. (45kg) and require a scale accurate to within one gram.

Liquid Dyes now come in squeeze bottles and dripless dispensers, which makes these a viable choice. They also allow easy mixing and shading. Use the next chart for some color suggestions:

Dyes Flakes come in at least 36 colors. Because these are very lightweight and concentrated, use a digital scale to accurately weigh amounts.

Color Blocks work similarly to Dye Flakes, but first must be grated. Again, use a digital scale for accurate measurement. You can even mix you own colors if you have only a few basics. Remember the old color wheel from art class? If not, just use the following chart.

MIXING YOUR OWN COLORS							
This Color	+ This Color	= This Color	+ Stearine =	This Color	+ This Color	= This Color	+ Stearine =
Red	Blue	Violet	Lavender	Blue	--	--	Light Blue
Red	Yellow	Orange	Peach	Yellow	--	--	Lt. Yellow
Blue	Yellow	Green	Light Green	Red	Green	Brown	Tan
Blue	Green	Teal	Light Teal	Yellow	Violet	Brown	Tan
Red	--	--	Pink	Orange	Blue	Brown	Tan

For pure white candles, try Candle Whitener. Use 1 tsp per pound (½kg) of wax. It doesn't harden wax. Stearine's meltpoint is 165°F (74°C), so there is no need to melt it separately from the wax.

SCENT

Ahhh, lovely aromas... They set the mood, stimulate an appetite, stir up memories. As with dyes, make sure the essential oils are OK for candle use. If you're unsure, ask the manufacturer or supplier.

Some essential oils do not mix well with wax due to their carrier oils. They can leave oily residue on the candles or cause them to mottle and pit. Make sure no water or alcohol has been added to the fragrance.

If you're not certain, ask, but the label should list all ingredients, even water. Different essential oil manufacturers make their fragrances at varying strength. Ask the supplier what is recommended for candles though the next chart strength is standard.

HOW MUCH SCENT?				
CANDLE TYPE	WAX TYPE	VYBAR AMOUNT	SCENT	WICK
Container Candles	125-130°F (52-54°C) low melt point paraffin	¼-½ tsp Vybar per pound (½kg) of wax, melted with paraffin. Use Vybar only for container candles.	½ oz for 1 pound or 15 ml for ½kg wax	Depends on candle width. See Picking Your Wick Size
Pillars and Free-standing	138°F (59°C) moderate melt point paraffin	¼-½ tsp Vybar per pound (½ kg) of wax, melted with paraffin Use Vybar only for molded candles.	½ oz for 1 pound or 15 ml for ½kg wax	Depends on candle width. See Picking Your Wick Size

If using blended paraffin or a "one pour" wax, Vybar has already been added. In this case, omit any additional Vybar. Too much can have just the opposite desired effect by binding up the scent molecules and the candle will give off less fragrance.

Essential Oils are volatiles, which means they evaporate when exposed to air and heat. To minimize this, add the essential oils just before pouring the wax into the mold. Mix thoroughly. Happy sniffing!

MOLDS

Manufactured molds come in seven basic types with different sizes in each group. Many things around the home can be used for candle shaping as well – even sand!

Manufactured molds can be metal, two-piece plastic, hard or soft rubber, acrylic or Plexiglas, top up or flat. Of all molds, metal molds are the easiest to use.

\	SELECTING A MOLD		
MOLD TYPE	**PROS**	**CONS**	**TO USE**
Metal	One piece, easy to use. Multi-wick and no-seam varieties available	Limited shapes	Wick is drawn through hole in the base and secured with a screw. Seal hole on outside with putty. Insert wick as described above in Wicks and fill. Candle will have one seam to remove.
Two-Piece Plastic	Numerous innovative novelty designs.	More work than metal molds. Pigments can stain plastic. Too much scent or beeswax can damage mold.	Insert wick in one of the two halves and pour. Smooth edge where the two mold halves meet.
Soft Rubber	One piece and easier to use than two-piece rigid plastic. Come in many shapes and designs.	Beeswax can damage mold. Cooling wax in these molds can alter the mold over time.	Insert wick and pour.
Hard Rubber	Easy to use; make nice candles.	Shorter-term usage before mold needs to be replaced.	Insert wick and pour.
Acrylic and Plexiglas	Easy to use, more expensive	Easily scratched	Insert wick and pour.
Top Up	None	None	No wick hole. Wick is glue onto container bottom. Normally used for floating or votive candles.
Flat		Limited use – mostly for wax decorations	Used to make wax appliqués and hanging ornaments.

MOLDS AROUND HOME

Juice Cans – Many food cans are OK to use except ones with ridges like some brands of soup cans. Ridges make the candle too hard to remove from the mold. To use, coat the can with wax, make a hole in the bottom for the wick with a punch or ice pick. Seal with putty on the outside. When the candle has set, tear the can away. Coffee cans may also be used for larger candles but require more effort to remove from the mold.

Milk Containers – These come in a variety of sizes, heights and widths. Unmold as per juice cans. For the half-gallon or 2 liter size, try using multiple wicks.

Paper Cups – Paper cups work well especially with beeswax and one-pour waxes. Unmold as per juice cans.

Miscellaneous Food Containers – Pudding and yogurt containers, cottage cheese and sour cream cartons, plastic margarine containers, wax or foil lined cartons, hot chocolate mix and frozen juice cans. These come in a variety of sizes and shapes allowing for a nearly unlimited number of grouping combinations. Candles look particularly pretty when you have a variety of heights and widths grouped together in the same color and shape.

Mason/Canning, Bail Wire And Baby Food Jars – These jars are used to make container candles. Warm the jar before pouring the candle to reduce bubbles forming. It also encourages the wax to stick to the sides of the jar. Glue the wick tab to the bottom of the jar before pouring. One really nice feature about these jars is that they all come with lids. Putting lids in place after burning the candles will help retain more fragrance.

Galvanized Buckets – These are seen all around Australia in grocery and hardware stores usually holding "mozzy lights" – candles scented with citronella to ward off mosquitoes. Citronella candles are for outdoor use only.

Terra Cotta Pots And Bowls – These are one of my two "rustic" favorites. Stan and I have decorated our home in Southwestern teals and terra cotta. Candles in these containers fit in perfectly. Not only are they in abundance and inexpensive, but there are many bowls and decorative pieces in fun shapes like jalapenos, cacti, adobe houses, sombreros, boots and other southwestern motifs.

To use terra cotta, a barrier must go between the clay and the wax. There are several ways to do this:
1. Line the pot with aluminum foil
2. Spray the outside with non-flammable varnish; however, this does alter the terra cotta's matte finish.

Apothecary Jars – Many candlemaking companies use them. Sometimes these can be purchased cheaply at garage sales but check for defects. Adding hot wax to already weakened glass can cause the jar to break.

Sand – Time to be creative! Borrow sand from the beach, the little one's play box, leftovers from a construction site or buy it from your local hardware store. Line a heavy cardboard box with aluminum foil and fill with sand. Create the design of your choice in the dry sand and pour. Don't worry if some of the sand sticks to the wax. It will create and interesting texture to your candle. To ensure the sand stays in place on the finished candle, spray with a light coat of varnish or other sealant.

Logs And Stumps – This is a lovely way to create another rustic look. Any stump or log that has sufficient width in which to dig out a hole will work. Make sure the bottom is sawed off flat to prevent it from rolling over. Hollow out a wide enough wax area so the flame is nowhere close to the wood for a fire hazard. Insert a wick and pour the wax.

HOW TO MAKE CANDLES

Step 1 Decide what type candle to make and purchase the right wax.
Step 2 Cover the work surface with newspaper or old sheets.
Step 3 Line up the equipment and supplies to be used.
Step 4 Put the wax in the top of a double boiler or if using a metal pitcher for the wax, set the pitcher in a 2-3" (5-7.5cm) water bath. An old coffee or large juice can will work as the wax container. If you pinch a spout in one area, this will help in pouring.
Step 5 Prepare mold with candle release spray if making a freestanding candle.
Step 6 Suspend in place or glue to the container proper wicking.
Step 7 Melt wax or waxes separately if blending in beeswax. If using luster crystals, these will need to be melted separately too.
Step 8 When the wax reaches pouring temperature; pour in desired additives, colorants and/or scents. Mix in the colorants thoroughly first, and then the scent.
Step 9 Wearing gloves, carefully pour wax into the mold. Gently tap the sides of the mold and allow 45 seconds for the air bubbles to surface. Place the mold in the water bath.
Step 10 As the candles cools, the wax will shrink. Punch a couple holes along side of the wick with a narrow dowel rod. This will prevent air pockets forming along the wick. As the candle cools and shrinks, fill any voids and holes with extra wax.
Step 11 If making container candles, they are now finished. If using a mold, allow candle to fully harden before removing. If candle is stubborn and won't release, pop it into the freezer for 10 minutes. If it still won't budge, repeat, but don't pry it out or the mold will be ruined. As a last resort, reheat the wax, remove it, reapply mold release and try again.
Step 12 After unmolding, check the bottom for level seating. If unlevel, place candle in a baking pan and put both on top a pot of boiling water. Suspend the candle by the wick; allow it to lightly touch the pan until the base is flat and level.
Step 13 "Clean up" any seams by shaving them off and rubbing with a nylon stocking to blend this area with the rest of the candle.

CLEAN UP

Clean up is easy. For the wax-melting container, simply wipe out the melted wax with a paper towel. If old wax is left from previous pours, scents and dyes can clash. Don't pour any extra wax down the drain or it can clog. If you have a bigger-than-expected amount of left over wax, either make a smaller candle like a tea light or pour the wax in an old muffin tin to set up.

Use these scrapes in future candles or for firestarters. Be sure to label leftovers for wax formula, scent and dye used so they can be matched for the next batch. Store in a plastic bag.

The only other piece of equipment that needs extra care is the mold. Old wax residue can stain or pit future candles. Dry metal molds thoroughly to prevent rust. Most wax and stains wipe out. Should your mold have bits of wax, don't try to pry or scrape it off. Scratches will show up in the next candles. Set molds in the oven at 150°F (70°C) in a pan or cookie sheet lined with foil for 15 minutes. The wax should run out onto the foil.

If you find there is stubborn wax to remove, candle craft shops sell "Mold Cleaner". Pour it in the mold, swish it around and toss out. A properly cleaned mold shouldn't needed this very often.

MEASURING ADDITIVES

A number of recipes call for percentages for additives. Here are a few commonly used percentages:

% ADDITIVES DESIRED	FOR 1 LB. OUNCES	FOR ½ KG GRAMS	% ADDITIVES DESIRED	FOR 1 LB. OUNCES	FOR ½ KG GRAMS
1%	¼	4.5	8%	1¼ or 1.27	36
2%	⅓	9.5	9%	1½ or 1.44	41
3%	½	14	10%	1.6	45
4%	.64	18	15%	2½ or 2.4	68
5%	4/5 or .80	23	20%	3.2	91
6%	1	28	25%	4	113
7%	1.12	32	30%	4.8	136

BASIC RECIPES

VOTIVE CANDLES

90% paraffin melt point 131
2% micro 180 wax
6% stearic acid
2% luster crystals

Use a metal core wick and wick tabs. Pour wax when it reaches 190°F (88°C) unless the mold manufacturing instructions say differently.

SCENTED CANDLES

9 Tbsp paraffin wax
1 wick
1 Tbsp stearine (stearic acid)
1 wick rod, or pencil or toothpick
Candle dye
½ cup candle mold or yogurt container
3-4 drops essential oil

Melt wax in the top of a double boiler. Stir in stearine and dye to melt. Stir in fragrance oil just before pouring. Remove from heat and cool slightly.
Cut a piece of wick 3" (7.5cm) longer than the depth of the mold. Dip wick in melted wax and tie it close to one end, around the center of the wick rod. Lay the rod across the top of the mold and thread the other end of the wick through a hole in the center of the mold base. Stand the mold base upright.
Pour in as much wax as the mold will hold, taking care to keep the wick vertical. Tap the mold to release any trapped air and let the wax set slightly.
As it cools, a depression will form in the top. Gently reheat the remaining wax and pour it into the mold to level the surface. Let the candle cool completely in a waterbath.
Remove the wick rod. Peel off flexible molds, or tap rigid ones to release the candle. Trim the wick to ¼" (6cm) and polish the candle with a soft, dry cloth or nylon stocking.

WATER BALLOON CANDLES

Fill a balloon with water to the desired size. Dip the balloon in wax when it has cooled somewhat. Continue dipping balloon until a hard shell forms around it. Carefully pop the balloon at the top and empty out water. Pull the balloon out of the wax shell.
Pour a small amount of wax (a different color from the first) into the shell. Roll it around in the shell, making sure all areas are covered, until the wax is dry.
Continue doing this with different colors until the shell is almost filled. Insert the wick during the last fill. Once the candle is cool, use a vegetable peeler to shave the top of the candle, making it smooth and flat. These candles turn out to look something like a geode. They are time-consuming, but the result is really fun and pretty.

TIPS AND TROUBLESHOOTING

Once in a while the inevitable happens and there is the occasional "what happened to my candle?" May these questions be few! The following Troubleshooting chart should cover most dilemmas.

BURNING TIPS

1. Keep wick trimmed to ¼" (½cm).
2. Burning candles no longer than 3 to 4 hours at a time will increase total burn time.
3. Keep lit candles out of drafts to ensure even burning.
4. Container candles should be burned 1 hour for each inch of diameter. This allows the wax pool to cover the entire surface and extends the burning time.
5. Refrigerate candles wrapped in aluminum foil up to an hour to extend burn time.
6. Keep candles out of direct sunlight or color will fade. Rotate candles 90° occasionally to ensure any color fading will blend.
7. Always provide a base under the candle to prevent furniture damage.

TROUBLESHOOTING		
APPEARANCE	**CAUSE**	**FIX**
Mottling, White Patches	Too much oil in wax.	Use a higher melt point or harder wax. Use 1% Vybar, Micro or Poly to stop mottling.
	Essential oil's carrier oil may be incompatible with wax; EO may contain water	Check with supplier if EO is for candle use.
	Cooled too fast.	Cool slower.
	Too much mold release.	Wipe out extra release.
Bubbles	Cooled too fast.	Cool slower; adjust water bath
	Poured too cold.	Pour at a hotter temperature.
	Poured too fast.	Pour more slowly and carefully.
	Air didn't release.	Tap the mold to release air bubbles. Tilt mold while pouring wax. Add 1% Vybar to paraffin.
Scaly marks, white lines	Too much stearic acid.	Use less additive.
	Mold was too cold.	Warm mold and jars before pouring.
	Poured too cold.	Pour at a hotter temperature.
		Use a heat gun to reheat the outside of the jars to get rid of lines.
Candle shrinks from sides.	One-pour waxes are prone to shrinkage and some shrinkage is normal.	Try using 1 part beeswax to 3 parts paraffin or add some luster crystals to wax. Warm mold and jars before pouring.
Candle side caved in or is misshapen	Air pockets around wick.	Poke more holes around wick with long narrow dowel until candle is almost set and then fill in with wax.
Sink hole in center of candle	Natural shrinkage while cooling.	Warm the mold or container before pouring.
	Pouring wax at too hot a temp.	Poke holes around wick and refill while cooling. Repeat as needed.
Cracks in candle	Cooled too fast.	Cool at room temperature or in warm water bath, never in the refrigerator.
Small pit/pock marks	Too much mold release.	Wipe out mold and only leave light film of release.
	Poured too hot.	Lower pouring temperature.
	Dirty mold.	Use Mold Clean to thoroughly clean mold.
	Water in wax or scent.	Set wax aside to dry in separate bowl. Don't use essentials oils containing water.

TROUBLESHOOTING		
APPEARANCE	**CAUSE**	**FIX**
"Wet spots" in containers	Wax not adhering to jar in places.	Pre-heat jars before pouring wax. Add ¼ tsp per 1 lb or ½ kg of wax. Make sure your glass jars are clean before using. Use a heat gun to reheat the outside of the jars to get rid of the wet spots. Cool candles slowly, away from drafts.
Wax discoloration	Dirty wax	Keep molds clean.
Oil drops on candle surface	Too much oil in wax	Reduce amount of oil added to avoid oil leaking or seeping out.
Repour not blending	Second pour too late.	Repour when the candle is still warm.
CANDLE STUCK IN MOLD	**CAUSE**	**FIX**
Candle won't release from flexible mold	Left too long in mold	Place candle in hot water and unmold
Candle won't release from rigid mold	Didn't use mold release.	Spray mold with silicon or lightly wipe with vegetable oil before pouring.
	Second pour over fill line.	Do not pour over original fill line on repours. Put candle in freezer for a few minutes and many times it will pop right out.
	Pouring temp too hot. Cooled too slow. Too much Vybar.	Use less additive.
LAYERED CANDLES	**CAUSE**	**FIX**
Layers won't join	Next layer of wax poured too late or too cool.	Remelt
Loss of distinct layers in layered candle	Previously poured layer did not set long enough; it should feel rubbery	Not fixable, but candle is still usable.
Small line of bubbles around candle	Water bath mark. Water added after candle was already in water bath	Rub with nylon stocking to blend.
WICKS	**CAUSE**	**FIX**
Wick drowning out or not staying lit	Wick too small.	Try larger size wick.
	Wick getting clogged.	Do not use dyes that contain pigments, use those only for overdipping.
	Too much dye.	Use less.
Candle smokes when burned	Wick too large.	Try smaller wick size.
	Air pockets in candle.	Use higher pouring temperature and poke release holes and refill.
	"V" in braided wicking is pointing down.	No remedy for this candle. Make sure "v" opening is pointed up.
	Flame too high.	Keep the wick trimmed to ¼ inch
	High oil content.	Less oil will reduce smoke and soot.
Flame too large	Wick too large	Use smaller wick
Flame too small	Wick too small	Use larger wick.
Melt pool too small; leaves leftover wax on sides of container	Wax too hard/too high melt point.	Try a lower melt point/softer wax or additives such as petrolatum, hydrogenated vegetable oil, mineral oil, or beeswax.
	Wick too small.	Try larger wick size.
Flame flickers/sputters	Water trapped in wick from water bath.	Make sure wick hole is sealed completely on mold.
	Water in wax.	Be careful not to let any water drops from double boiler get into wax.

TROUBLESHOOTING		
APPEARANCE	CAUSE	FIX
Wick mushrooms	Wick is too large for the wax formula or candle diameter. Too much scent. Too much dye. Using vegetable oils or petroleum jelly.	Use Pick Your Wick Type chart to select correct size wick. Gradually reduce scent in formula to see if this is the cause. Wick clogging occurred, use less. Use alternative additives.
FRAGRANCE	CAUSE	FIX
Not enough fragrance when burning. No fragrance	Low quality fragrance. Not enough fragrance. Fragrance burned away before pouring. Fragrance not able to release into air.	Use a better quality essential oil. Make sure they are for candle use. Use higher percentage of fragrance in wax. Add fragrance last, just before pouring. Use a softer/lower melt point wax to produce a larger melt pool so fragrance can release. Used too much Vybar

Chapter 22: Fire Building

No gas? No electricity? How will you keep warm? Cook meals? Knowing how to make a fire under *any* circumstances can be a lifesaver. Following a few simple rules makes it a lot easier.

Two campfire methods are given. The Teepee Fire is a good "short term" option especially when cooking though it will last as long as fuel is added. Pyramid fires can last overnight without adding wood.

Photo: Loosely made Teepee Fire

If you want a fire to last through the night, start it during the daylight, unless fuel is very scarce. Both fires take a little practice to build with ease.

Burning is also a good way of to get rid of trash destined for landfills. While living in Australia, trash bin size was cut in half to force people into conservancy. This refocused our thinking on what could be recycled, burned or composted. These options are better for the environment than clogging landfills unless you live in a wildfire-prone or smog-filled area. Burning only exacerbates the latter problem.

Items not to burn include CCA treated wood (looks green after treatment), painted wood, and tires and rags containing toxic chemicals.

Should you build a fire in very cold weather, locate the site near large rocks or boulders if possible. Rocks reflect heat, conserve fuel, keep you warmer and speed food cooking time.

FUELS

Fires start easiest using three types of fuel: tinder, kindling and logs.

Tinder can be small twigs, dry grass or leaves, dry pine needles and bark, old cotton or linen cloth, dry lichen, fungi or moss, Birch bark, wood shavings, bird down, waxed paper, cotton lint, bird and mouse nests. Whatever the choice, it **must be dry**. Break or cut it into small pieces and make a small pile. Coat parts of tinder with Vaseline, ChapStick, or insect repellent to make it burn hotter once lit. When the tinder ignites, slowly add kindling.

Kindling – small dry twigs, a little larger than tinder and no larger than 1 inch (2.5cm) in diameter, heavy cardboard, small strips of wood removed from the inside of larger pieces.

Logs – 2-inch (10cm) diameter and larger.

BURNABLES	
FUEL CHOICES	**COMMENTS**
Hardwoods – Apple, Beech, Boxwood, Cherry, Cottonwood, Hickory, Mahogany, Mallee Roots, Maple, Oak, Pear, Red & Silver Gum, Walnut	Burns well, gives off good heat, coals last a long time, will keep a fire going through the night. Fruitwoods smell wonderful and burn cleanly leaving little chimney residue.
Soft Woods – Alder, Blue Gum, Cedar, Chestnut, Hemlock, Messmate Common, Pine, Spruce, Willow	Tends to burn too fast and give off sparks. Species with heavy sap burn too fast and can gum up chimneys.
Animal Droppings – Cow, Buffalo	Excellent fuel. Dry droppings thoroughly for a good smokeless fire. Can be mixed with grass, moss and leaves.
Peat or Peat Moss	Peat is soft and springy underfoot; used in gardens to enrich soil, break up clay. Exposed to air, it dries quickly and ready to burn. Peat needs good ventilation to burn.

BURNING QUALITIES OF DIFFERENT WOODS			
Species	Weight Per Cord (Lbs)	BTU's Per Cord (Millions)	Recoverable BTU's Per Cord (Millions)
Apple	4100	26.5	18.55
Aspen	2290	14.7	10.29
Balsam Fir	2236	14.3	10.01
Basswood	2108	13.5	9.45
Beech	3757	24	16.8
Black Ash	2992	19.1	13.37
Black Spruce	2482	15.9	11.13
Boxelder	2797	17.9	12.53
Cherry	3121	20	14
Cottonwood	2108	13.5	9.45
East. Hophornbeam	4267	27.3	19.11
Elm	3052	19.5	13.65
Hackberry	3247	20.8	14.56
Hemlock	2482	15.9	11.13
Hickory	4327	27.7	19.39
Jack Pine	2669	17.1	11.97
Norway Pine	2669	17.1	11.97
Paper Birch	3179	20.3	14.21
Ponderosa Pine	2380	15.2	10.64
Red Maple	2924	18.7	13.09
Red Oak	3757	24	16.8
Sugar Maple	3757	24	16.8
Tamarack	3247	20.8	14.56
White Ash	3689	23.6	16.52
White Oak	4012	25.7	17.99
White Pine	2236	14.3	10.01
Yellow Birch	3689	23.6	16.52

TEEPEE FIRE

Build a teepee fire when you need a concentrated light source, heat, or coals for cooking. This style works well with even wet wood. Place wetter pieces of wood toward the outside so they have time to dry out time while flames consume the inner, drier wood.

Step 1 Pick a place to build the fire away from the wind and protected from snow and rain. Clear away debris, leaves and twigs that could catch fire in an area 6 feet (2m) across. Make sure there are no branches overhead that can catch fire or tree roots underneath the designated campfire area.

Step 2 Gather tinder, kindling and wood that is already on the ground. Don't cut a live tree for a fire; it's too hard to burn.

Step 3 Find rocks to make a fire ring about 1 yard (1m) in diameter. The rocks will help retain heat, conserve fuel and keep the fire in an enclosed area. Avoid wet rocks; they can explode.

Step 4 Loosely pile the tinder in the middle of the ring. Take small twigs and stand them on end leaning them inward to meet at a 35°-angle "teepee" style over the tinder.

Step 5 For the outer layer of the teepee, lean the larger pieces of wood against each other forming a still larger teepee.

Step 6 Carefully reach in between the "teepee" sticks and ignite the tinder, adding a little more kindling as it begins to burn.

Step 7 When the fire is off to a good start, add larger pieces of wood. Be careful not to extinguish the fire by smothering it. Good air circulation is the key.

The teepee logs will eventually fall in on themselves, but by now the fire should be roaring and there is little concern it will smother at this point.

PYRAMID FIRE

A Pyramid Fire is a terrific choice for a longer lasting fire that doesn't need as much constant fueling. It's an excellent fire for drying wood and providing light, and it produces good coals for cooking. The Pyramid Fire generally burns overnight and fuels itself as the logs fall in on themselves. Layout is pretty straightforward.

Step 1 Pick a place to build the fire away from the wind and protected from snow and rain. Clear away any debris, leaves and twigs that could catch fire in an area 6 feet (2 meters) across. Make sure there are no branches overhead that can catch fire or tree roots underneath the designated campfire area.

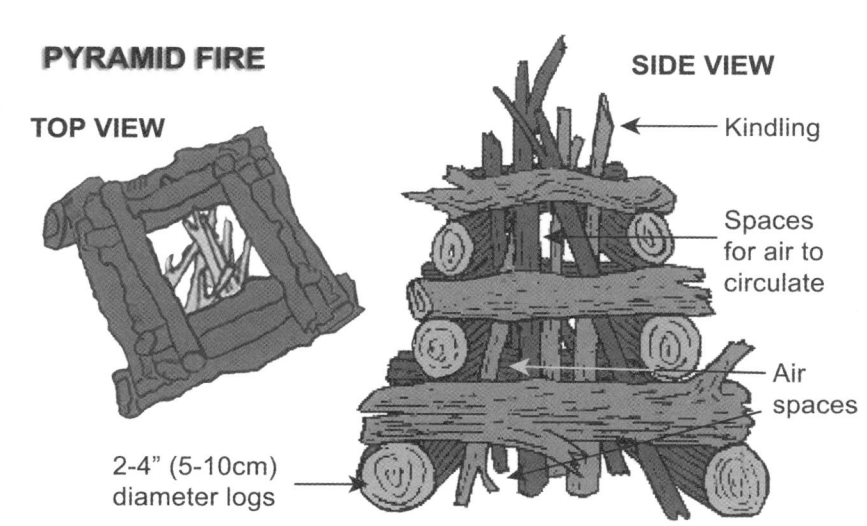

Step 2 Gather wood that is already on the ground. Don't cut a live tree for a fire; it's too hard to burn. You'll need three types of wood: tinder, kindling and 12 logs roughly 18" (46cm) in length, 4 each with 2", 3" and 4" (5, 7.6 and 10cm) diameters

Step 3 Arrange 4" (10cm) logs on the bottom in a square. One pair opposite each other will rest on top of the other pair. This arrangement will automatically build in gaps for air circulation. Build the same square out of the 3" logs on top of the first square. Complete the squares with the 2" (5cm) logs. When finished with this part, these 12 logs with look like a square pyramid. There should be a hole left in top.

Step 4 Gather kindling twigs and sticks about 18" (46cm) long of varying diameters from ¼" to 1" (.5 – 2.5cm) and poke these down the pyramid's hole.

Step 5 Place tinder on top of kindling and light.
Step 6 Add logs as needed.

Pyramid fires are especially good to use in adverse weather since they build a natural shelf around the tinder and kindling.

FIRE STARTING ERRORS

1. Choosing poor tinder and burning material.
2. Not protecting the match from the wind.
3. Lighting fire under wind instead of windward.
4. Smothering the fire by adding fuel too soon and choking the fire.
5. Not having dry matches or fire starters that work.

CAMPFIRE TIPS

1. If it is windy, dig a trench and build fire in it.
2. If the ground is wet or covered with snow, build a raised platform out of green logs and start the fire on this. You'll have a much better chance of it igniting away from moisture.
3. Should you want to cook over an open fire, allow the fire to burn down and use the coals only. Cooking food over a roaring fire may sound romantic, but generally results in a burned dinner.
4. When ready to extinguish a fire, break up the ashes and scatter them to cool. Dampen with water and stir with a stick. Continue this process until the ashes are cold to the touch.

FIRESTARTERS

Keeping firestarters with camping gear is a clever idea. There are about as many varieties as leaves on a tree and quite a few cost next to nothing to make. In areas where fireplaces are popular, firestarters are readily found in grocery and hardware stores with new varieties popping up on the market every fall. Camping, hiking and recreational stores and discount stores also carry these products.

COMMERCIAL PRODUCTS

KEROSENE SOAKED – The prime lighting ingredient is kerosene with a shelf life of 18 months. These starters are usually packaged individually with a foil covering to keep out air. They work fine but one variety resembles 1" waxy cubes. If dropped even gently on hard surfaces they break apart. Reasonably priced, yes, but because they are packaged in a divided container for each cube, they take up more space.

PARAFFIN SOAKED – These items may also be labeled "wax coated" firestarters. Paraffin starters have a variety of base items like recycled cardboard, wood chips and compressed pinewood sawdust. These required no individual packaging or will they shatter when dropped. The brick version is scored in 1" (2.5cm) intervals and they break off easily. Use one or two cubes per fire. Their shelf life is indefinite. Firelighting time is 20-30 minutes. We really like this type. They are about half the weight and size of the kerosene version with a long shelf life and no odor.

Wood shaving varieties generally come in individually packaged cellophane and the entire packet goes into the fire building area. They are convenient, but require more space to store.

Paper and cotton combined with household paraffin is another version of these firestarters. There are no toxic chemicals or additives. To use: fray the wick with your fingernail and light with a match. For stoves and fireplaces, position the firestarter at the base of a split edge and stack wood around and above the firestarter. For fires using small tinder, such as campfires, a half piece may be sufficient. The firestarter can be cut with a knife. Shelf life is indefinite.

ALL NATURAL

This category is not as plentiful and they are generally more costly. Super Cedar Firestarters are a 4"x1" disk made from cedar sawdust and highly refined wax. They leave no residues or toxic chemicals behind and even burn when soaked in water. Simply light the edge with a match and each starter will burn for 20-30 minutes. One piece is enough to start up to 4 fires.

Fatwood, sometimes called Fatlighter, is a terrific all-natural firestarter that we have used for years. Since they're made from high resin pine, they don't need added chemicals to light quickly and burn well. Their generous size, 8" by about 3/4" thick, makes them burn long enough to establish a roaring fire even for novices. They works equally well in fireplaces, pellet fuel stoves, barbecues, wood/coal stoves and campfires.

MAGNESIUM FLINT & STEEL

These are probably the best all around survival firestarters one could wish for but even these have a few drawbacks. They are reliable and have the reputation of lighting even wet wood since they put out such a hot spark! Flint and steel firestarters come in several widths and lengths but their design is fairly standard. Most start with a block of magnesium ranging from 2-4" (5-10cm) long with a strip of flint glued on top and a flint scraper attached to make the sparks. Some of the nicer versions have handles made out of wood or antlers.

In some cases, especially for shorter blocks of magnesium or if you have very large hands, it makes handling easier. They do take up more room and the cost reflects the fancy handles. While the flame from the magnesium shavings is extremely hot, it's also relatively short lived so have your shavings or tinder ready. If you're using the magnesium scraping/shavings, keep in mind that since they're so lightweight, they can easily blow away.

To use, hold the block with the flint side up, resting firmly on the wood/tinder. Press scraper or knife blade firmly against the flint at a 45° angle. Tinder should be very close to the end of the firestarter. The flint alone is hot enough to light any fine dry material such as moss, grass, wood shavings, pine needles, fine steel wool, cloth, paper.

For their relatively small size, magnesium flint and steel, can light a lot of fires. Generally speaking, the ⅜" (1cm) width provides 7000 strikes and the ½" (1.27cm) provides 10,000-25,000 strikes depending on length.

Think how many matches you'd need for the equivalent number of fires! As a guideline, the 25,000-strike unit will make about 500 fires. For the number of fires started, good spark output, rugged construction and relative low cost, they are a great addition to 72-hour packs as well as all other emergency preparedness supplies.

SINGLE-HAND FIRESTARTERS

SPARK-LITE

These are small 2¼x9/32x9/32" (58x7x7mm), and lightweight .02 oz. (5g) or about the size of a few matches, which makes them fit quite easily in any survival pack. The serrated wheel at the top rubs on a small flint that is encased in the plastic body. It operates much like a cigarette lighter, performs reliably and gives the user about 1,000 lights.

The sparks produced aren't as plentiful as those from the magnesium flint and steel units, but there are certainly enough to light tinder. Many Spark-Lite units include a small container of eight "Fire-Tab" tinders. Each waterproof Fire-Tab is a little over 1" (2.5cm) long made of cotton soaked with beeswax, petroleum and silicone, and burns about 2 minutes. Cost runs around US$6 – $7 including 8 Fire-Tabs.

To use, fan out the cotton so air can circulate between the fibers. Hold the Spark-Lite with a couple fingers and stroke the sparking wheel with the thumb or index much like operating an old style cigarette lighter.

BLASTMATCH

The BlastMatch is much larger 4x1⅜x⅞" (102x34x22mm), and heavier 2¾ oz. (78g) than the Spark-Lite. When the cap is removed, a 2" (5cm) flint rod springs out.

To use, hold the firestarter next to the tinder with the tip of the flint rod on a hard object such as a stone or piece of wood. While applying pressure to the side catch with your thumb, push down on the body, forcing the scraper inside the catch to scrape down the flint. This unit is aptly named as one strike puts out a **lot** of sparks! Because of its larger size, this unit can be operated wearing heavy gloves. Cost of this unit is US$20 with no tinder included. If weight and size are not a worry, this is an excellent unit.

MATCH OVERVIEW		
MATCH TYPE	**PROS**	**CONS**
Paper	Inexpensive. Easy to light. Readily available anywhere.	More likely to become crushed. Smallest match head. Not water or windproof. Difficult to waterproof with candle wax. Not as sturdy as wooden matches.
Wooden or Kitchen	Inexpensive. Easy to light. Readily available anywhere. Can waterproof by dipping match head in candle wax or clear nail polish. Sturdier than paper matches. Longer than paper matches so have more burn time per match.	Not water or windproof. Takes time to dip each match for waterproofing.
Waterproof only Coghlan's Waterproof Stansport Waterproof	Better than paper matches, but wooden matches can be waterproofed.	Available in sporting goods and discount stores like K-Mart, but not grocery stores. More expensive than paper or wooden matches. Prices vary widely. When the striker material gets wet, they are nearly impossible to light. Not as sturdy as wooden matches.
Wind & Waterproof NATO standard British product	Burns intensely for about 11 – 13 seconds and nearly impossible to put out, no matter how bad the weather. Match head 3-4 times the size of paper matches.	Not as readily available. More expensive. Harder to light without breaking. Striker material is on the outside of container, glued to the top. When it gets wet, it tends not to work. Not as sturdy as wooden matches.
Wind & Waterproof Hurricane match - Swiss product	Burns almost as intensely as the NATO matches Match head 3-4 times the size of paper matches.	Not as readily available. More expensive. Harder to light without breaking. When these get wet, they are harder to light than the NATO product. Not as sturdy as wooden matches.

MATCHES

These come in a variety from paper to wooden, waterproof and/or windproof. For matches, we've chosen a middle-of-the-road approach buying wooden kitchen variety by the bucket-load! Some of these matches we dipped in wax and store in film canisters for water protection. For strikers, that portion of the matchbox has been cut from the box and placed inside the film canister along with the matches.

TIP: Unless you have an over-abundance of matches and it's a perfectly still day, it might be a good idea to light a candle instead of lighting a fire directly with matches. At least the candle won't burn out as quickly, which will allow more time to get the fire started.

BUTANE LIGHTERS
These come in several sizes. Compact disposable lighters like Zippo are relatively inexpensive. Others have a long extension on the end and make lighting fireplaces or grills and getting into tight places easier. Most of these lighters now have childproof safety mechanisms, which makes lighting a little trickier.

Some lighters are refillable, but these units tend to evaporate fuel more readily. If you're storing butane lighters long term, the non-refillable variety are more dependable. As long as the butane remains intact, these lighters have an indefinite shelf life.

MAKING YOUR OWN FIRESTARTERS
This is a super opportunity to fulfill those creative urges and make something useful at the same time.

WOOD KNOTS
These require no construction, only a day in the woods. Search through rotted pine logs on the forest floor for preserved knots. They are rich in flammable resins which burn even when wet.

LINT-FILLED CONTAINERS
This is so easy it's ridiculous! Ever wonder what to do with all the dryer lint besides filing it in the trash bucket? Collect spools from empty toilet paper rolls and paper towels. If using paper towel spools, cut them in half. Fill these spools with laundry lint and use as you would any other firelighter.

Empty egg cartons work just as well. Each carton of 1 dozen yields three firestarters with four egg holders per starter. For the carton section that doesn't have one of those two 'puffed-out' type closures, secure with a little tape.

PINE CONES WITH PARAFFIN – VERSION 1
Using pinecones is my favorite method. Pinecones are plentiful in many parts of the world. They're a terrific way to use up extra candle wax and candle "stubs" and spend a great day picking up cones.

Melt wax in a double boiler or water bath just like for making candles. Dip the pinecone in melted wax thoroughly coating the cone. For a little pampering, add essential oil of your choice. Cinnamon and other scents used in your candles make them especially nice. They make attractive housewarming gifts arranged in a rustic basket.

PINE CONES WITH PARAFFIN – VERSION 2
If you feel even more creative, here's how to make those colorful pinecones sold in specialty stores for a fraction of the cost. (Who said preparedness couldn't be fun!)

COLORFUL BURNING PINE CONES
- 1½ gallons (6L) hot water
- ½ pounds (226g) Copper Sulfate or "Bluestone" (for green flame)
- ½ pounds (226g) Boric Acid (for red flame)
- ½ pounds (226g) Calcium Chloride (for yellow to yellow orange flame)
- 3 Containers, plastic or ceramic (one for each color)

PINE CONES
Step 1 Pour ½ gallon (2L) hot water into each of the three containers.
Step 2 Add one chemical to each container of hot water.
Step 3 Stir until chemicals are dissolved.
Step 4 Add pine cones and soak overnight.
Step 5 Allow pinecones to air dry thoroughly on newspaper for 2 days.

To use as firestarter: After the chemicals have dried, coat with wax as per Version 1. Add cones to fire two or three at a time. Colorful flames will only last a short time.

CANDLE CUPS – VERSION 1
Items needed:
- Paper (not foil) Muffin Cups
- Candle Wick
- Candle Wax
- Wood Shavings or Sawdust
- Potpourri
- Flower Petals – just before frost kills them

    Melt wax in a double boiler or water bath just like for making candles. Put muffin cups in a muffin tray to keep the wax shaped till hardened. While the wax is melting, suspend wicks tied to a dowel rod suspended over the muffin cups. This will work easiest if the wicks are stiffened with a little melted wax.

    Make sure the wicks are centered over each muffin cup and just touching bottom. (Balance the dowel rod on a couple of glasses at each end of the muffin tray so you don't have to hold it in place.) Pour melted wax into the muffin cups. Stir wood shavings/sawdust, potpourri, and flower petals into the melted wax.

    NOTE: You may need to re-center the wicks. Trim wicks to ¼" (½cm).

CANDLE CUPS – VERSION 2
    Instead of using muffin cups and muffin tray, for the base, substitute old peat pots.

CARDBOARD AND SCRAP WOOD
Step 1   Cut cardboard in ¾"x1½" (1.9x3.8cm) rectangles.
Step 2   Cut a 2x4 stud which is actually 1½" (3.8cm) finished into ¾" (1.9cm) sections. Using a wood chisel, split off thin sections to match the cardboard.
Step 3   Stack the cardboard and wood in alternating layers so that five pieces of cardboard and three pieces of pine are used.
Step 4   Tie each firestarter stack together with cotton string.
Step 5   Soak the firestarter in mineral spirits for about 15 minutes.
Step 6   While the material is soaking, melt the wax. Add fine sawdust until the wax has a grainy consistency. Carefully add the sawdust. It may temporarily foam a bit due to air trapped in the wax.
Step 7   Remove the firestarters from the mineral spirits and dry them for 15 minutes.
Step 8   Coat the firestarters with wax by dipping them repeatedly in the wax/sawdust mixture Allow the wax on the firestarter to cool between each dipping so that the wax eventually forms a layered coating. Coat each firestarter several times.
Step 9   After the final wax coating, pull out a section of the cotton string from each firestarter to use as a wick. These are a little more work, but they work great!

IT'S IN THE BAG!
Items Needed:
- Burlap
- Wax
- Wood Chips
- String
- Cinnamon Essential Oil (optional)

    Cut an old burlap sack into 8"x12" (20x30.5cm) rectangles. Fold each rectangle in half and stitch each side leaving the top open. Melt wax as per above and lightly coat the wax chips. Allow the chips to dry and fill each bag ¾ full. Sprinkle in a few drops of cinnamon essential oil for a nice holiday touch. Stitch top shut or tie off with string. Light under the kindling for an aromatic firestarter.

CANDLE KISSES
Items Needed:
- Candle stubs
- Waxed paper

    Save the stubs from your candles. Cut them into lengths about 1½-2" long. The longer the stub, the longer the firestarter will burn.

    Tear off strips of waxed paper. The strips should be several inches wider than the candle stub. Place one candle stub, centered on the narrow end of the strip. Roll the candle stub up in the waxed paper. Twist each end of the waxed paper several times so that they are secure.

To use, light the twisted end of the waxed paper. Children love to make these as they are quick. They also have the benefit of being very inexpensive and do not require the melting of any wax.

COTTON "GOO" BALLS
Items Needed:
- Cotton balls
- Vaseline

A good water-resistant firestarter is cotton balls heavily smeared in Vaseline. Purchase a bag of generic cotton balls, empty the bag and then smear each one with a healthy dollop of Vaseline. Store firestarters in the original bag, be careful to not shred the bag when you open it. The downside to these is that they can be very messy to make.

LOOKING UP
Items Needed:
- Ceiling tiles
- Paraffin

A very expensive firestarter is made from an old ceiling tile cut into 1" squares. Melt paraffin in a double boiler, dip on all sides and let dry.

OLD NEWS
Items Needed:
- Newspapers
- String
- Paraffin

Tired of rolling old newspapers into logs? Cut newspaper in two inch pieces, roll and tie with a piece of string tied around each bundle. Dip these in melted wax.

CLOSE SHAVE
Items Needed:
- Wood shavings, sawdust or small animal bedding
- "Dixie" cups
- Paraffin
- Spoon

Melt wax in a double boiler. If using old candle "stubs", it's not necessary to remove the wicks. Fill a second pot with the wood shavings, sawdust or pet bedding. Pour in melted wax and stir, allowing the shavings to soak up enough wax indicated by turning a darker shade. If needed, melt more wax, adding enough to achieve uniform color wood shavings.

Using the spoon, pack the wax coated wood shavings into the paper cups about half way full. As they cool, the wax will harden, adhering the wood shavings to each other and to the inside of the paper cup. To use, light the top of the cup. It will burn down to the firestarter.

STARTING FIRE WITH A BATTERY
Items Needed:
- Steel wool
- 9V battery
- Toilet paper

Step 1 Tuck a small piece of steel wool inside two sheets of toilet paper
Step 2 Expose several strands of steel wool to create sparks.
Step 3 Lightly touch the battery to the steel wool.
Step 4 Blow to encourage flame.
Step 5 Drop onto tinder pile.
Note: Steel wool will ignite even when wet.

Chapter 23: Making Charcoal

METHOD 1

YOU WILL NEED:
 1 55-gallon metal drum, cleaned, with the lid cut off
 Seasoned wood* to fill drum, chopped into 5x5" (12½x12½cm) pieces
 1 bag of sand
 4 bricks

 *The wood needs to have at least a couple of months to dry. The drier the wood, the faster the process completes.

TO CONSTRUCT:

Step 1 Cut 5 holes in the bottom of the drum, each measuring 2" square and keeping them towards the center.
Step 2 Place the drum on the bricks off the ground, careful not to cover the holes.
Step 3 Fill with wood and start a fire in the drum.
Step 4 When the fire is going well, put on the drum's top to maximize heat. Since the top was cut off roughly, it will allow in enough oxygen to keep the fire burning.
Step 5 Now turn the whole thing over onto its top and place drum back onto the bricks. Be careful the lid doesn't fall off. It will be heavy.

SMOKE SIGNALS

The smoke starts out white while the moisture burns out of the wood. Next, the smoke becomes blue/grey as the alcohols and phenols burn off. Then the smoke turns yellow, which is the tar burning off. Last, the smoke clears leaving only waves of heat.

Step 6 Carefully remove the bricks out from under the drum.
Step 7 Pour sand around the bottom of the drum and up the sides, sealing out all air from entering through the roughly cut lid.
Step 8 Cover the top with either a piece of sod or a large piece of metal.
Step 9 Use more sand to seal around the turf or metal on top so no air enters the drum being careful so no sand falls into the drum through the holes. If oxygen DOES enter the drum, the charcoal will just burn up.
Step 10 Allow the drum to cool 2-3 hours. Then turn the drum over, pry off the top and remove the charcoal.
 If a spark remains, the charcoal may reignite, and just douse it with water. The charcoal will still be hot enough to dry out. Repeat above process as necessary.
 When the process is complete, you'll have about 30-40 pounds of charcoal.

METHOD 2

YOU WILL NEED:
 1 55-gallon metal drum, cleaned, with the lid cut off
  Seasoned wood* to fill drum, chopped into 5x5" (12½x12½cm) pieces
  Dirt
 3 Bricks

Step 1 Prepare the drum by making five 2" (5cm) holes in one end with a chisel and completely remove the other end.
Step 2 Bend the cut edge of the open end to form a ledge. (Note, the lid will have to placed back on this ledge and made airtight).
Step 3 Position the drum, open end up, on three bricks to allow an air flow to the holes in the base.

Step 4 Place paper, kindling and brown ends (incompletely charred butts from the last burn) into the bottom of the drum and light.
Step 5 Once it's burning well, load branches at random to allow air spaces until the drum is completely full. Keep the pieces to a fairly even diameter but put any larger ones to the bottom where they will be subjected to a longer, more intense burn.
Step 6 When the fire is hot and clearly won't go out, restrict the air flow by placing earth around the base leaving one 4" (10cm) gap.
Step 7 Set the lid on top, leaving a *small* gap at one side for smoke to escape.
Step 8 Dense white smoke will exit during the charring process. When this visibly slows, bang the drum to settle the wood. This will create more white smoke.
Step 9 When the smoke turns from white to thin blue (charcoal starting to burn), stop the burn by closing off all air flow to the base by adding more earth, and secondly, by placing the lid firmly on its ledge. Make it airtight by the adding sod and soil as required. The burn will take 3-4 hours.
Step 10 After cooling for about 24 hours, the drum can be tipped over and the charcoal emptied out. Pack for later use.

METHOD 3
YOU WILL NEED:
  1 55-gallon oil drum with sealable lid
  2 pieces of rebar
  1 16-gallon steel drum (like for transmission fluid and gear grease)

Step 1 Cut the top from the 55-gallon (208L) drum. Keep the lid.
Step 2 Cut a 12"x10" or (30x25cm) hole cut in the lower side for maintaining the fire.
Step 3 Insert two iron rods or rebar through the sides of the larger drum, about 8" (20cm) from the bottom. These rods support the retort. (A retort is the container in which the wood burns turning it into charcoal.)
Step 4 Cut the top from the 16-gallon (60L) drum. Keep the lid.
Step 5 Cut six ⅜" (1.25cm) holes in the bottom of the retort with an acetylene torch or metal punch.
Step 6 Build a fire in the base of the large drum.
Step 7 Set the retort on top of the supporting bars and fill with seasoned wood cut into manageable chunks.
Step 8 Light fire in the large drum.
Step 9 After the fire is well established, place the top back on the 16 gallon drum to help hold the heat in yet allow a good draft.
Step 10 After the colored smoke clears indicating all gases have burned off, pull out the rods out of the drum allowing the retort to rest on the bottom of the larger drum. This seals the retort's base, blocking oxygen from entering and allows the retort to cool more quickly.
Step 11 Allow charcoal to cool completely. It's normal for the rebar to soften and bend during exposure to intense heat.

Making charcoal takes about 5 hours BUT time required is influenced by wind and temperature.

Expect to net about 35% charcoal, which is very good considering most direct burns result in a 20 -25% yield.

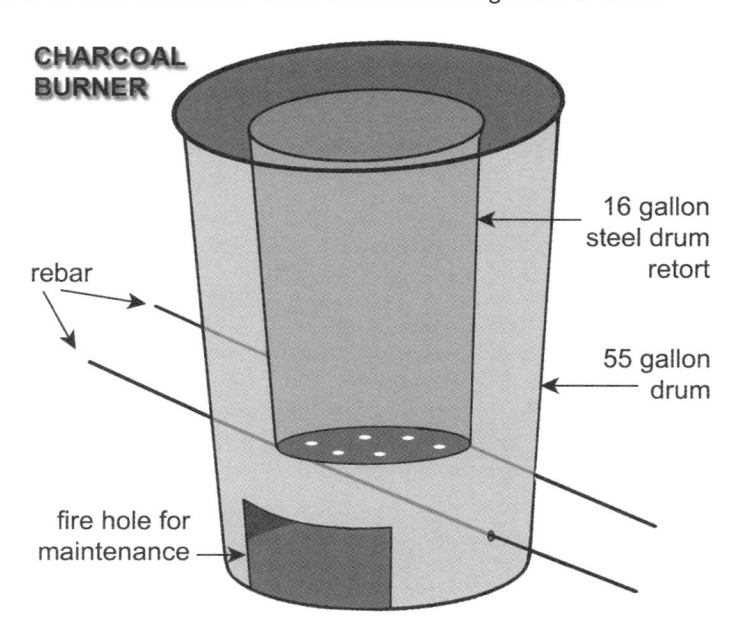

CHARCOAL BURNER
- 16 gallon steel drum retort
- rebar
- 55 gallon drum
- fire hole for maintenance

ACTIVATED CHARCOAL
This is the substance used in filters for aquariums and drinking water and air filters. To make your own, let the oxygen eat at the charcoal a bit before extinguishing the flame. It bores countless tiny holes into the surface. These holes are marvelous at trapping molecules of contaminants from the water or air passing through. Activated charcoal is just overcooked charcoal."[54]

Chapter 24: Making Biodiesel Fuel

Are fuel prices driving you nuts? Did you lose power and run out of diesel for your generator? Make your own biodiesel and easily solve the problem. In fact, some people run their vehicles exclusively from home made diesel. This process has caught on so well that finding used cooking oil in "standard supply centers" like fast food restaurants is becoming a challenge.

If you have rural property, you may want to devote and acre or two to fuel production. Crops suitable for fuels include coconut, soybean, canola (rapeseed), sunflower, safflower, corn, palm kernel, peanut, jatropha, and hundreds more. To learn which vegetable oil crop is best suited for your area, contact your state's office of agriculture, the agriculture department of a local university, or talk to local farmers. One of the crops with the highest yield of oil per acre is canola. From just one acre of canola, you can produce 100 gallons (379L) of vegetable oil. The most common oilseed crop in the U.S. is soybeans, which produces 50 gallons (189L) of vegetable oil per acre. Growing your own oilseed crop has an added bonus. The meal that's separated from the oil is an excellent source of protein. It can be used as animal feed or in breads, spreads, and other food products.[55]

This fuel is so engine friendly, you can use either pure vegetable oil or used cooking oil.

BIODIESEL

Recipes for biodiesel are quite simple:

Recipe 1
80-90% used vegetable oil
10-20% alcohol
0.35- 0.75% lye

Recipe 2
80 parts new vegetable oil
20 parts methanol
0.35 parts lye

Overview: Details are below. Mix ingredients for an hour then let settle for eight hours. Once this procedure is complete, you'll have two products: fuel and soap.

The biodiesel will be yellow to amber in color and flows like water. The soap will be brown and like gelatin. The heavier soap sinks to the bottom, allowing you to pump, siphon, or pour off the biodiesel.

VEGETABLE OIL / KEROSENE MIX

This ridiculously simple method is ideal in emergency situations and requires only two ingredients: kerosene and vegetable oil. To use, just mix the two ingredients in one of the following ratios:

Recipe 1
10% kerosene
90% vegetable oil

Recipe 2
40% kerosene
60% vegetable oil

Recipe 3
20% kerosene
80% vegetable oil

Veggie/Kero mixtures work best in heavy-duty engines and in warm temperatures. You can increase this fuel's reliability and effectiveness by starting and cooling down the engine on diesel fuel or biodiesel fuel first. To do so, you may want to install an extra fuel tank. This allows for easiest switching to the veggie/kero mix when the engine is warmed up.

VEGETABLE OIL

The third option is to run your diesel engine on straight vegetable oil but this method requires more mechanical know-how. As with veggie/kero, the engine must be started and cooled down on diesel or biodiesel. To use this method successfully, the vegetable oil needs to be heated to at least 160°F (71°C) at every stage – in the fuel tank, fuel hose, and fuel filter.

Most diesel engines have hoses that carry hot coolant. This coolant can be channeled to heat the vegetable oil hoses, tank, and filter. You can make simple modifications to the coolant hoses. These modifications combined with some extra fuel and oil hoses, an extra fuel tank, and an electrically operated switch will allow you to run your diesel engine on straight vegetable oil.

FUEL COMPARISON

The following chart shows you the pros and cons the three vegetable oil fuels. Biodiesel is a good substitute or diesel fuel "stretcher". Veggie/kero mix works great as an emergency fuel. Using straight vegetable oil is good if you can properly modify the engine's heating and fuel tank systems.

COMPARISON OF DIFFERENT VEGETABLE OIL FUEL METHODS			
Property	Biodiesel	Veggie-Kero Mix	Veggie Oil
Can be used as lubrication additive to diesel fuel	yes	no	no
Requires vehicle modification	no	yes	yes
Reliably cuts emissions in all diesel engines	yes	no	unknown *
Considered an alternative fuel under U.S. Energy Policy Act	yes	no	yes **
Simple way to run a vehicle in an emergency	yes	no	no
Stable fuel at room temperature	yes	no	no
Requires added chemicals to produce	yes	yes	no
Requires startup tank of biodiesel or diesel fuel	no	yes	yes
Good startup fuel	yes	no	no
Better lubrication than diesel fuel	yes	yes	yes
Gels in cold weather	yes	yes	yes
Covered by many engine warranties	yes	no	no
Can be made from used cooking oil	yes	yes	yes
Can be made from pure vegetable oil	yes	yes	yes
Safe to store and handle, biodegradable, won't spontaneously ignite, and non-toxic	yes	no	yes
Works in all diesel engines	yes	yes	yes
Can be reliably mixed in any proportion with diesel fuel without vehicle modification	yes	no	no
Approved by EPACT in 20% mix with 80% diesel fuel ***	yes	no	no
Engine life, power, torque, fuel mileage, and overall performance are relatively unaffected	yes	yes	yes
Can clog fuel injectors if used improperly	no	yes	yes
Requires heating for operation at any temperature	no	no	yes
Tested and documented by U.S. universities	yes	no	yes
Possible substitute for home heating oil in furnaces	yes	no	no
OK in Petromax and similar lanterns and stoves	yes	no	yes

*No recent U.S. University studies have been published on this.
** Under EPACT regulations, any biologically derived fuel is considered an alternative fuel.
*** EPACT law states that a fleet must use a minimum of 450 gallons (1703 l) of biodiesel per year.

HOW TO MAKE BIODIESEL

Before working with lye, read the lye precautions found in the soapmaking section. Be sure to protect any working surface, your eyes and skin. You can use the same blender that's used for soapmaking. When making large batches of biodiesel, you may want to build your own mixer.

If you don't have a measuring cup that measures in milliliters, buy one. It will be much more accurate than measuring in ounces and cups.

NEW VEGETABLE OIL
1 liter oil
200ml methanol
3.5 grams of lye

USED VEGETABLE OIL
100ml vegetable oil
20ml methanol
lye amount to be determined

When mixing new vegetable oil, the recipe is always the same. However, since used cooking oil isn't consistent, the amount of lye for each batch of biodiesel will be different. As a result, you'll need to make small test batches to determine the correct amount of lye. This is done in a blender. For the test batch, use 100ml vegetable oil to 20ml methanol.

Then add 0.45g lye to the Used Vegetable Oil. If two distinct layers form, the biodiesel and the glycerin, no more testing needs to be done for this particular used vegetable oil.

Make a larger batch using the exact same ratio of vegetable oil, methanol and lye.

If the layers didn't form, make a new test batch but increase the lye by .10 grams to .55. Continue increasing the lye by .10 grams in each new test batch until the distinct biodiesel and glycerin layers form.

Once this is achieved, you're ready to make biodiesel on a larger scale.

Step 1   Gather the vegetable oil whether new or used.
Step 2   Filter out food particles, if the oil was used for cooking.
Step 3   Buy methanol alcohol from a local racetrack or chemical supply store.
Step 4   Buy lye (pure caustic soda – sodium hydroxide [NaOH]) as used in soapmaking.
Step 5   Measure the amount of vegetable oil **in liters** you want to use and pour into the mixing vat.
Step 6   When the temperature is below 70°F (21°C), or when the vegetable oil is solid or lumpy, you'll need to heat the lye/oil/meth mixture before, during, and possibly after mixing. The ideal temperature to attain is 120°F (49°C). A fish tank heater will heat 10-30 gallons (40-120L) of lye/oil/meth.

For larger batches of biodiesel, mount a water heater element in a steel biodiesel mixing tank. Make sure that you follow the manufacturer's directions and safety precautions when adding any electrical device to the system. Be careful when heating vegetable oil in a plastic container. Polyethylene can't withstand temps above 140°F (60°C).

When making soap, use "dishwasher safe plastic" since it's made to withstand heat above 200°F (93°C). However, larger containers aren't likely to be this heat-durable since aren't made for dishwashers.

Alternate mixing containers include stainless steel pots and drums. Other metals are likely to corrode.

Step 7   Multiply the amount of vegetable oil **in liters** by 0.2. This is the amount of methanol **in liters** you'll need.
Step 8   To determine how much lye to add for new vegetable oil, multiply the amount of oil by 3.5 grams. For used cooking oil, use the number of grams of lye you determined from the small test batch. For example, if the "perfect" amount of lye in your test batch was 0.55 grams, multiply the amount of oil (in liters) by 5.5 grams of lye.
Step 9   Carefully pour the lye into the methanol. Stir until the lye is completely dissolved. Avoid breathing the fumes and work in a well-ventilated area.
Step 10   Immediately pour the lye/meth into the vegetable oil. Stir vigorously for one hour.
Step 11   Let set 8 hours.
Step 12   Pump the biodiesel from the top, or siphon it off with a hand siphon. If the container has a spigot, open the spigot and drain the glycerin. The glycerin will be much thicker and darker than the top layer of biodiesel. Keep glycerin for soapmaking. (See Chapter 19)
Step 13   Allow the glycerin to sit in the sun for a week while the trace methanol evaporates.
Step 14   Put the biodiesel through a 5-micron filter before fueling any diesel engine.

Chapter 25: Keeping Food Safe in an Emergency

August 15th, 2003 saw the largest blackout in North American history. At least 50 million people in the U.S. and Canada were without power, some as long as five sweltering days. Nine people died. Water supplies to millions of people became contaminated. Boil orders were issued and food spoilage was rampant. We can avoid foodborne illness at home by making sure it stays properly refrigerated during an outage.

Photo: Clean up commenced following devastating Midwest floods in June 1994. A total of 534 counties in nine states required federal disaster aid. Thousands were without power, many others lost their homes. In total, over 168,000 people registered for federal assistance. (FEMA News Photo)

Numerous other such power outages have occurred since then and more will follow. Hurricane Ivan shredded power lines in Alabama, Georgia, Florida, North and South Carolina leaving nearly 3 million people without power. Some were warned it might be as long as <u>two</u> <u>months</u> before their power was restored.

Former U.S. Energy Secretary Bill Richardson charged: "We're the world's greatest superpower, but we have a Third World electricity grid."[56] Today, the power grid is in no better shape and it's more heavily taxed than ever.

Power outages cause a ton of inconvenience and sometimes a world of hurt. This is especially true when people run generators indoors and are poisoned by carbon monoxide. The other common and sometimes deadly scenario arises when people unknowingly eat spoiled food. The following three questions were answered by the U.S. Department of Agriculture.

Q. A snowstorm knocked down the power lines, can I put the food from the refrigerator and freezer out in the snow?

A. No, frozen food can thaw if it is exposed to the sun's rays even when the temperature is very cold. Refrigerated food may become too warm and foodborne bacteria could grow. The outside temperature could vary hour by hour and the temperature outside will not protect refrigerated and frozen food. Additionally, perishable items could be exposed to unsanitary conditions or to animals. Animals may harbor bacteria or disease; never consume food that has come in contact with an animal.

Rather than putting the food outside, consider taking advantage of the cold temperatures by making ice. Fill buckets, empty milk cartons or cans with water and leave them outside to freeze. Then put the homemade ice in your refrigerator, freezer, or coolers.

HOLLY NOTE: This is the "official" response, but if it's *consistently* freezing and an overcast day, food will likely be safe to eat. I have done this successfully, but instead of just sinking the frozen food in the snow, it was thoroughly and deeply packed in a snowdrift. Watch your thermometer to see that temps don't get above freezing.

Q. Some of my food in the freezer started to thaw or had thawed when the power came back on. Is the food safe? How long will the food in the refrigerator be safe with the power off?

A. Never taste food to determine its safety! You will have to evaluate each item separately. If an appliance thermometer was kept in the freezer, read the temperature when the power comes back on. If the appliance thermometer stored in the freezer reads 40°F (4°C) or below, the food is safe and may be refrozen. If a thermometer has not been kept in the freezer, check each package of food to determine the safety. Remember you can't rely on appearance or odor. If the food still contains ice crystals or is 40°F or below, it's safe to refreeze.

Refrigerated food should be safe as long as power is out no more than 4 hours. Keep the door closed and food is safely cold for about 4 hours. Unopened full freezers hold the temperature for about 48 hours, 24 hours if it's half full. Discard perishable food (meat, poultry, fish, eggs, leftovers) that has been above 40°F for 2 hours.

Q. May I refreeze the food in the freezer if it is thawed or partially thawed?

A. Yes, the food may be safely refrozen if the food still contains ice crystals or is at 40°F (4°C) or below. You will have to evaluate each item separately. Be sure to discard any items in either the freezer or the refrigerator that have come into contact with raw meat juices. Partial thawing and refreezing may reduce the quality of some food, but the food will remain safe to eat. See the attached charts for specific recommendations.[57]

Photo: Hurricane Isabel struck seven states September 2003 and left 47 dead. More than 3.3 million residents were left without power for more than a week. This Category 2 hurricane – a relatively "small" storm – amassed over $4 billion in damages, mostly due to high wind and flooding. Poquoson, VA, pictured, was especially hard hit. (Andrea Booher / FEMA).

Dare To Prepare: Chapter 25: Keeping Food Safe in an Emergency

The US Department of Agriculture gives the following guidelines[58] for what to keep and what to through out under varying conditions after a power outage.

WHAT TO KEEP AND WHAT TO TOSS – REFRIGERATOR FOODS	
MEAT, POULTRY, SEAFOOD	**Held Above 40°F (4°C) for Over 2 Hrs.**
Raw or leftover cooked meat, poultry, fish, or seafood; soy meat substitutes	Discard
Thawing meat or poultry	Discard
Meat, tuna, shrimp, chicken, or egg salad	Discard
Gravy, stuffing, broth	Discard
Lunchmeats, hot dogs, bacon, sausage, dried beef	Discard
Pizza – with any topping	Discard
Canned hams labeled "Keep Refrigerated"	Discard
Canned meats and fish, opened	Discard
CHEESE	
Soft Cheeses: blue/bleu, Roquefort, Brie, Camembert, cottage, cream, Edam, Monterey Jack, ricotta, mozzarella, Muenster, Neufchatel, queso blanco, queso fresco	Discard
Hard Cheeses: Cheddar, Colby, Swiss, Parmesan, provolone, Romano	Safe
Processed Cheeses	Safe
Shredded Cheeses	Discard
Low-fat Cheeses	Discard
Grated: Parmesan, Romano, or combination (in can or jar)	Safe
DAIRY & EGGS	
Milk, cream, sour cream, buttermilk, evaporated milk, yogurt, eggnog, soy milk	Discard
Butter, margarine	Safe
Baby formula, opened	Discard
Fresh eggs, hard-cooked in shell, egg dishes, egg products	Discard
Custards and puddings	Discard
CASSEROLES, SOUPS, STEWS	Discard
FRUITS	
Fresh fruits, cut	Discard
Fruit juices, opened	Safe
Canned fruits, opened	Safe
Fresh fruits, coconut, raisins, dried fruits, candied fruits, dates	Safe
SAUCES, SPREADS, JAMS	**Held Above 50°F (10°C) Over 8 Hrs.**
Opened mayonnaise, tartar sauce, horseradish	Keep
Peanut butter	Safe
Jelly, relish, taco sauce, mustard, catsup, olives, pickles	Safe
Worcestershire, soy, barbecue, Hoisin sauces	Safe
Fish sauces (oyster sauce)	Discard
Opened vinegar-based dressings	Safe
Opened creamy-based dressings	Discard
Spaghetti sauce, opened jar	Discard
PIES, PASTRY	
Pastries, cream filled	Discard
Pies – custard, cheese filled, or chiffon; quiche	Discard
Pies, fruit	Safe
BREAD, CAKES, COOKIES, PASTA, GRAINS	
Bread, rolls, cakes, muffins, quick breads, tortillas	Safe
Refrigerator biscuits, rolls, cookie dough	Discard
Cooked pasta, rice, potatoes	Discard
Pasta salads with mayonnaise or vinaigrette	Discard

WHAT TO KEEP AND WHAT TO TOSS – REFRIGERATOR FOODS

MEAT, POULTRY, SEAFOOD	Held Above 40°F (4°C) for Over 2 Hrs.
Fresh pasta	Discard
Cheesecake	Discard
Breakfast foods –waffles, pancakes, bagels	Safe
VEGETABLES	
Fresh mushrooms, herbs, spices	Safe
Greens, pre cut, pre-washed, packaged	Discard
Vegetables, raw	Safe
Vegetables, cooked; tofu	Discard
Vegetable juice, opened	Discard
Baked potatoes	Discard
Commercial garlic in oil	Discard
Potato Salad	Discard

WHAT TO KEEP AND WHAT TO TOSS – FROZEN FOODS

MEAT POULTRY, SEAFOOD	Still Has Ice Crystals. Feels refrigerated	Thawed, Above 40°F (4°C) Over 2 Hours
Beef, Veal, Lamb, Pork, Poultry, Ground Meats	Refreeze	Discard
Poultry and ground poultry	Refreeze	Discard
Variety meats (liver, kidney, heart, chitterlings)	Refreeze	Discard
Casseroles, stews, soups	Refreeze	Discard
Fish, shellfish, breaded seafood products	Refreeze, expect texture, flavor loss.	Discard
DAIRY		
Milk	Refreeze	Discard
Eggs (out of shell) egg products	Refreeze	Discard
Ice Cream, frozen yogurt	Discard	Discard
Cheese (soft and semi soft)	Refreeze	Discard
Hard cheeses	Refreeze	Refreeze
Shredded cheeses	Refreeze	Discard
Casseroles containing milk, cream, eggs, soft cheeses	Refreeze	Discard
Cheesecake	Refreeze	Discard
FRUITS		
Juices	Refreeze	Refreeze. Discard if mold, yeasty smell or sliminess develops.
Home or commercially packaged	Refreeze. Will change texture and flavor.	Same as above.
BREADS, PASTRIES		
Breads, Muffins, Cakes, Rolls no custard fillings	Refreeze	Refreeze
Cakes, pies, pastries with custard or cheese filling	Refreeze	Discard
Pie crusts, commercial and homemade bread dough	Refreeze. Some quality loss may occur.	Refreeze. Quality loss is considerable.
OTHER		
Casseroles – pasta, rice based	Refreeze	Discard
Flour, cornmeal, nuts	Refreeze	Refreeze
Breakfast items –waffles, pancakes, bagels	Refreeze	Refreeze
Frozen meal, entree, specialty items (pizza, sausage and biscuit, meat pie, convenience foods)	Refreeze	Discard
VEGETABLES	Still Has Ice Crystals. Feels refrigerated	Above 40°F (4°C) Over 6 Hours
Juices	Refreeze	Discard
Vegetables, home or commercially packaged or blanched	Refreeze. May suffer texture and flavor loss.	Discard

Chapter 26: Composting

When Stan and I moved to rural Australia, we had a difficult time getting trash service. It took numerous conversations with the shire (county), to get a dumpster. After unpacking boxes for three weeks we had trash up to our ears. It was a relief when the long-awaited rubbish bin arrived.

You're joking; we thought when they delivered what resembled an overgrown wastebasket! Drastic measures were needed. We burned all paper and cardboard items; recycled cans, glass and plastic diligently, and organized compost bins outside. It was amazing how little was left for Monday trash pick up. Each week that little dumpster was lucky to be half full. However, scraps in the compost pail multiplied quickly, but what do you do with them – exactly?

Composting is nature's method of recycling. Added to gardens, it improves soil texture, aeration, and water retention. When mixed with compost, clay soils lighten up and sandy soils hold water better. It also helps control erosion, improves fertility, balances the pH, and stimulates healthy roots in plants. What a great way to turn fruit, vegetable and yard trimmings into an inexpensive soil conditioner. Besides getting rid of a lot of refuse, composting is fun and easy.

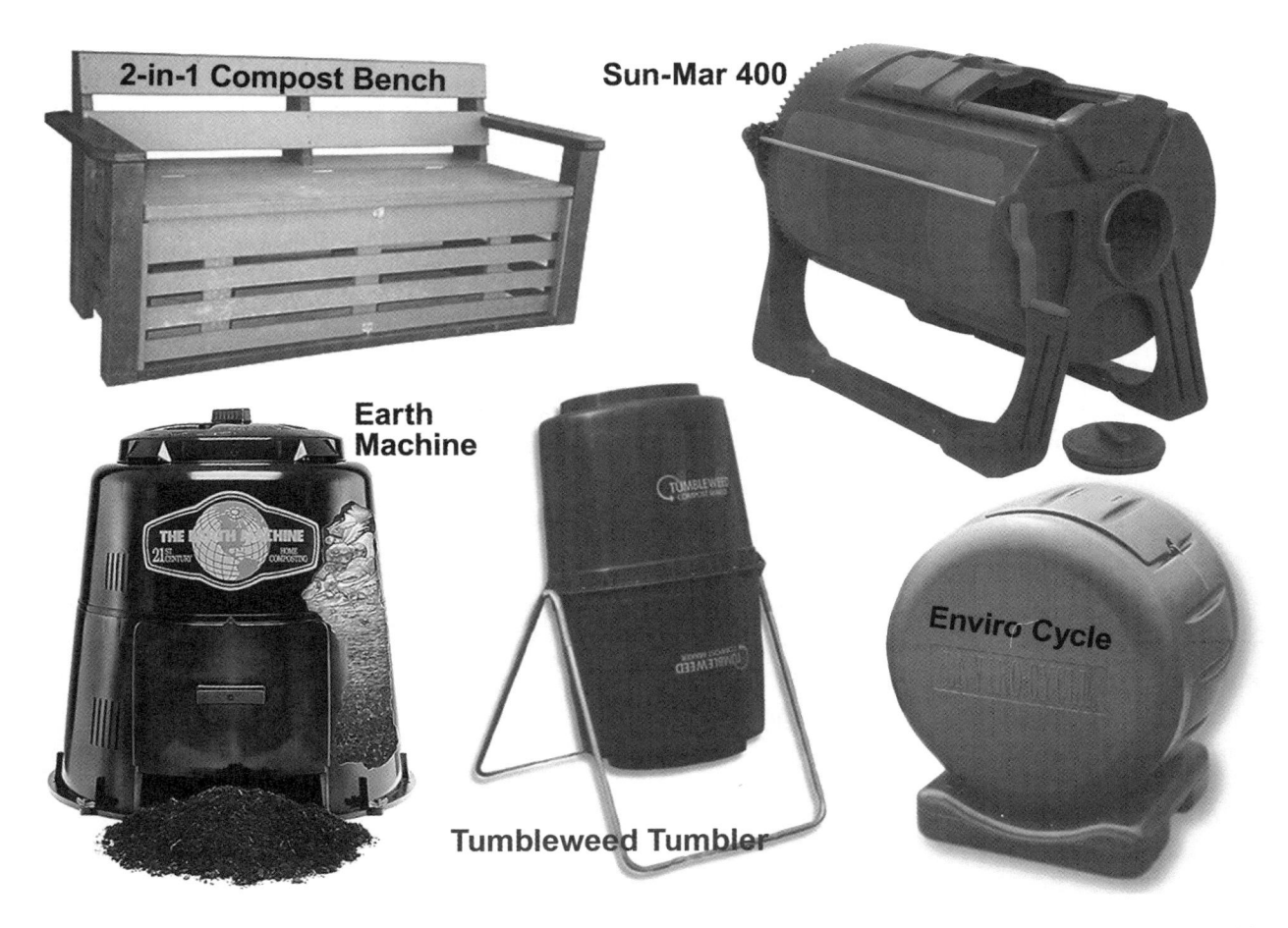

This is but a small selection of composters on the market. When purchasing a container, one that tumbles or rotates is nice, but price goes up significantly with this convenience. In addition to these units, there are slatted containers made with wood or PVC "boards", ones enclosed by wire mesh, models with no lids and others that expand by hooking more than one container together to form one large unit. Keep in mind that to make compost cook efficiently, it needs to be stirred regularly. If you purchase a unit that's too large, it may be difficult to reach all contents easily.

The 2-in-1 Compost Bench (pictured on previous page), while it has easy access with the front folding down and the seat folding up, keeping out rodents would be tough. Additionally, a clever do-it-yourselfer could whip out one of these benches in no time and save the $2400 retail cost.

Slatted, open mesh and lidless models present several problems. Too much ventilation lengthens "cooking time" and attracts unwanted visitors. It could invite ground squirrels, prairie dogs, skunks, coyotes, bear, mountain lions and snakes looking for mice. No thanks.

The visitors you do want are worms. Nature is amazing! When compost is cooking in the neighborhood, worms surprisingly find the stash. That's when you know you've got a tempting mix. They transform "kitchen trash" into wonderful garden mix. That is the biggest drawback to fully enclosed rotating composters. There is no way for worms to get inside and perform their magic.

In Australia, our unit most closely resembled the Earth Machine (pictured on previous page). It's open bottom invited worms by the dozens. A wide opening on top allowed compost to be turned easily. This is really important in the cooking stage, when compost is heavy due to moisture content and added water. You need plenty of room to stir the contents.

Models like this cone-shaped unit (pictured left) would make stirring the contents a nightmare. You could lift off the entire container, give the compost a good turn and then put the cone back in place. However, you'd likely end up having to shovel everything back in from the top. Worse, it would let valuable heat escape in the process.

It's easy to imagine banging the pitchfork or shovel against the composter's sides. With this shape, you'd nearly have to stand on top of the flared base to stir it. *Grrrr!* The stirrer would need to be inserted at a very sharp angle leaving little room to move the compost. To avoid aggravation give tall models with narrow openings a miss. They're not worth the cheapie cost. For a decent composter, expect to pay $80 and up.

COMPOSTING BASICS

There are four ingredients in good compost:

Browns – dry, dead material: fallen leaves, straw, sawdust, wood shavings, shredded newspaper
Greens – grass clippings, fruit and vegetable scraps, herbivore manure, coffee grounds and filter, tea bags
Air – the more frequently the pile is turned, the quicker it turns into usable compost
Moisture – keep the heap roughly as moist as a wrong-out sponge

WHAT GOES INTO COMPOST	
Compost Do's	**Compost Don'ts**
Citrus Rinds	Beans
Coffee Grounds and Filters	Bones
Eggshells, rinsed out and crushed	Bread
Fruit and Vegetable Trimmings	Dairy Products
Grass Clippings	Feces, Dog, Cat or Bird
Leaves, brown and dried	Fish
Manure from herbivores, only if certain it is free of poisonous residue	Grain
Newspaper, shredded	Grease
Paper Towels, no color and used	Meat
Plant Trimmings, soft and green	Sawdust from Plywood or Treated Wood
Straw	Woody Prunings (in closed-air systems, worm bins or underground)
Tea Bags	

TIP: Small twigs are OK, but they tend to inhibit contents from turning freely. If you have a tumbling unit, it's best to exclude them. If you're turning the compost with a pitchfork, twigs shouldn't present a problem.

5 EASY STEPS FOR COMPOSTING

1. BINS
A one cubic yard (cubic meter) bin is an excellent size as there is enough mass for microorganisms to do their job yet the pile is small enough to turn. If space allows, three bins work best. One bin is for a newly started compost pile, a second for "in-progress" and a third for compost ready to use.

2. WHERE?
Do you live rurally or in the suburbs? Rural locations present the most options for containers or no container at all. If urban, you'll need an enclosed bin set off concrete so fluids from decomposing material won't stain it. If on concrete, the benefit of worms, millipedes, snails, slugs and sow bugs visiting the pile is lost.

If rodents are a problem, an enclosed bin makes good sense especially if composting with food scraps. Compost piles work best in the shade or part sun, where they won't dry out from too much exposure to the Sun.

3. WHAT?
- Greens (indicating high nitrogen content) – 50%
- Browns – 50%
- Square-Headed Shovel for breaking items into smaller pieces
- Pitchfork for turning pile
- Hose or Large Watering Can

4. "SALAD" TIME
Build in air by layering larger twigs, prunings or corn stalks on the bottom. Keep prunings and twigs no longer than 6" (15cm). Alternate layers of browns and greens. Moisten each layer with water and mix with a pitchfork. Instead of tossing in a whole apple, cut it into quarters or eighths. The smaller the green items, the faster they will decompose. Continue layering and top off the "salad" with browns to keep away pests and for odor control.

5. YOU LITTLE ROTTER!
Properly balanced with greens and browns, the compost pile should begin to warm up within 24 hours. A "working" pile may reach temperatures of 150+°F (65+°C) and reduce in size by half within a couple of days. You can see evidence of it working when a steamy mist rises from your compost pile as you turn it or dig into it.

NO BROWNS? – NO WORRIES, GO WITH WORMS

If you live in an area absent of dried leaves and twigs, live in the city proper or for some other reason, choose only to use food scraps, you can still compost with the aid of worms. Another reason to consider worm composting is the resulting nitrogen-rich pile.

FIVE EASY STEPS TO WORM COMPOSTING

1. BINS
Buy or build one out of wood or plastic or use a shipping crate or barrel with a snug lid. The bin needs to measure 12"-18" (30.5 – 45.5cm) deep. Drill small holes no larger or smaller than ¼" (.50cm) in the bottom or sides of the container for ventilation. The rule of thumb for bin size is two square feet (1858 sq. cm) of surface area per person. An average two-person house would need a bin about 2'x2' = 4 square feet (3716 sq. cm), or two bins that are 1'x2' = 2 square feet (1858 sq. cm) each.

2. WHERE?
Place your bin away from direct sunlight where it won't freeze or overheat. Possible choices include a pantry, kitchen corner, laundry room, garage, basement, patio, deck or garden.

3. MAKE A WORM HOME
Worms like to burrow under moist paper or leaves. It keeps them cool and moist, gives them fiber to eat and prevents fruit flies from getting to their food. To make their worm home, tear black and white newspapers into one-inch strips, fluff them up and moisten them like a wrung-out sponge. Fill the bin ¾ full with this moist material. Shredded, corrugated cardboard, leaves, compost, sawdust and straw can also be added. Sprinkle bedding with a few handfuls of soil. Don't use glossy or colored paper or magazines.

4. ADOPT-A-WORM
Compost worms are often called Red Worms or Red Wigglers. You can find Red Worms in an established compost pile or buy them from worm farms. Start with one to two pounds or two big handfuls.

5. LOVE AT FIRST BITE
Start your worms off with 4 cups of fruit and vegetable scraps. Then let them alone for two weeks while they adjust to their new home.

BE A GRACIOUS HOST
1. Feed your worms about a quart (one pound) or 1 liter of food scraps (Worm Food) per square foot (929 sq. cm) of surface area in your bin per week. To avoid fruit flies and odors, always bury food under the bedding and don't overfeed them. If the bin starts to smell or food isn't breaking down quickly, give them less food. Worms have lots of babies, so they should be able to eat all your food if there's enough space and you increase the amount of food gradually.

2. Change their "sheets" by adding fresh newspaper shreds, etc. as needed, at least once a month. Always keep a 4"-6" (10-15cm) layer over the worms and their food.

3. A good host provides adequate moisture. Keep their bedding damp like a wrung-out sponge. Plastic bins may require less moisture or even the addition of dry bedding to absorb excess moisture. Wooden bins may require additional water occasionally.

4. Collect worm castings (excrement) periodically. On the average, small bins may need it every 3-6 months. Larger bins will need it every 6-12 months. You can start harvesting as early as 2-3 months after setting up your bin. This can be done several ways.

COLLECTING THE REWARDS
Down and Dirty: Scoop out the brown, crumbly compost, worms and all.

Enticement: Carefully move everything in the bin to one side. Place fresh bedding and a small handful of soil in the empty space. Bury new food scraps. In a month or two, the worms will have moved to the other side leaving harvestable compost.

Sluicing: Pour ALL the contents of your worm bin into a strainer over a 5-gallon bucket. (This may take several sessions unless you have a very large strainer.) Gently pour room temperature water through the strainer. The compost will wash through. Return remaining food scraps, worms and their bedding to the bin.

Persuasive: Spread a tarp out in a bright area out of direct sun. Take the bin contents and create small mounds over the entire tarp. After a few minutes, worms will wriggle away from the sun to the bottom of the piles. Scrape off the top layer of castings and return uneaten food scraps, worms and bedding to the bin.

USING WORM COMPOST
Worm castings or compost will help plants thrive by adding nitrogen-rich nutrients and humus to the soil. Sprinkle a ¼"-1" (0.5-2.5cm) layer at the base of indoor or outdoor plants or blend no more than 20% worm compost into potting mix or garden soil. Too much can "burn" plant roots. Digging worm compost into garden beds is another great way to use worm compost, particularly if you're adding woody compost at the same time.

PREVENTING UNINVITED 4-LEGGED GUESTS

WHAT GOES INTO COMPOST	
Dining Delights	**Menu No-No's**
Citrus Rinds	Beans
Coffee Grounds and Filters	Bread
Eggshells, Rinsed out and crushed	Dairy Products
Fruit and Vegetable Scraps	Feces, Dog, Cat or Bird
Paper Towels, used (unless used to clean with chemicals)	Grains
Plant Trimmings, soft and green	Grease
Tea Bags	Meat, Bones or Fish
	Sawdust from Plywood or Treated Wood
	Woody Prunings

Dare To Prepare: Chapter 26: Composting

1. Do not compost: meats, fish, bones, oils, fatty foods or pet manure. Animals will be attracted by the smell and the decomposition process will slow as these materials take longer to break down.

2. Place less appetizing materials like dry leaves, twigs or dead plants on the bottom of the pile and along the inside walls of your compost bin. This will provide good airflow, drainage and odor control. A well-managed bin will not attract as many pests.

3. Always cover food scraps with a layer of dry leaves or a 1" (2.5cm) layer of soil and bury food waste into the center of the pile. This will reduce smells that may attract pests and generate heat, which also repels them. Heating the pile speeds up the composting process.

4. Harvest finished compost at the bottom of the bin every 3-6 months. This discourages some pests from nesting in the warm finished compost.

5. Pick a location for your bin that has good drainage and partial sunlight. This improves the efficiency of your pile. Placing the bin 8"-12" (20-30cm) from fences, decks and buildings discourages pests, improves airflow, which decreases decomposing time.

6. Pests will be less likely to discover your compost pile if you don't hang out the welcome sign. They will take it as a gesture of hospitality seeing a ready-made bed (yard waste) next to the compost pile or smell "breakfast" cooking next to the compost pot. Keep your trash cans away from the composting area. To a rodent, the aromas are too tempting to resist.

GIVING PESTS THE HEAVE-HO!

If you already have "visitors", pest-proof the bin by preventing tunneling up through the bottom and climbing up the sides or top.

1. For mice, use 16 gauge, small mesh wire ¼" (0.5cm) sometimes called hardware cloth to line the bottom and outside walls of the bin. For larger pests, use 20 gauge.

2. Get a tight fitting lid or modify your existing lid by adding hinges and a latch. A bungie cord or chain can be stretched across the lid and fastened to the sides of the bin. Just as effective is a heavy brick or rock placed on the lid.

3. Pile rocks or bricks around the outside bottom of your bin as a good temporary measure against some burrowing animals. Mice can flatten their bodies and squeeze into a space the size of a dime or about ½" (1.25cm) in diameter so the rocks or bricks will have to be tightly butted together.

PREVENTING UNINVITED WINGED GUESTS

Flies, fruit flies, wasps, hornets and bees are discouraged from compost bins by covering food scraps with a 1" (2.5cm) layer of soil and browns. Turn the pile frequently adding air and keep it moist. These three things will cause the pile to heat up killing fly larvae and discourage bees, wasps and hornets from nesting.

COMPOSTING "RECIPES"

If you are in a hurry, here are two good recipes for moving things along. Ingredients – mix together and serve to your composter.

GETTING THE MIX RIGHT			
RATIO	HOT RECIPE	RATIO	COLD RECIPE
2 parts	Dry Leaves	3 parts	Dry Grass Clippings or Leaves
2 parts	Straw, Wood Chips or Sawdust	3 parts Combine with fresh grass clippings, not more than 3 parts total	Fresh Grass Clippings
1 part	Manure, herbivore only		Food Scraps, optional
1 part 1 part	Fresh Garden Weeds or Lawn Clippings Food Scraps		Mix and dump in composter

TAKE ITS TEMPERATURE

Hotter contents turns into useable compost faster. Monitor the temperature with a composter thermometer and aim for these ranges depending on how fast the material is needed:

Slow and Steady: 80-100ºF (27-38ºC) **Active**: 100-130ºF (38-54ºC) **Hot**: 130-160ºF (54-71ºC).

IS IT COMPOST YET?
Depending on how soon the compost is needed, there are 3 ways to approach your pile:

1. I Need It Yesterday! – Turn pile every 1 – 3 days, adding water as needed. Be diligent about the 50-50 ratios of greens and browns. The pile should get hot again quickly after each turning. After building the heap, do not add new materials. The high temperatures should kill most weed seeds. You can also add compost starters found in local garden supply centers to accelerate the initial process. Compost ready time: 3 – 8 weeks.

2. The Sooner the Better – Turn at least weekly. Add new materials as you generate them. If greens are added, especially food scraps, bury them in the center of the pile and cover with a layer of browns. Pile will heat several times, but eventually cool down. The initial heat will kill many weed seeds. There will be lots of worms in the bottom and middle of the pile at that point. Compost ready time: 3 – 6 months.

3. No Worries Mate – Whenever... – After building a pile, let it sit without turning. Water the pile occasionally maintaining moisture levels. Add new material in layers, keeping up 50/50 ratio of browns to greens. Compost ready time: 12 – 18 months.

YOU KNOW IT'S READY WHEN
It smells sweet and the texture is fine and crumbly. If there are large pieces of browns remaining, sift them out with a 1" screen and put them into a new pile. If the pile was not consistently hot, age the compost by letting it sit for 2-4 weeks. If remaining seeds sprout, turn them over and put it back into the pile until there are no more sprouts. NOW, it's ready!

WHERE TO USE COMPOST

Gardens – Before planting, mix a 4"-8" (10-20cm) layer of compost into new gardens or ones with poor soil. For existing gardens, mix in a ½-3" (1.25-7.5cm) layer at least yearly.

Yards – Spread a 1-6" (2.5-15cm) layer of compost on soil as a mulch, or spread a ½" (1.25cm) layer on top of turf. This can be done any time of year to improve soil fertility and reduce watering needs.

House Plants – Sprinkle a thin layer of compost over houseplant soil to provide nutrients. Make your own potting soil by mixing one part compost to two parts sand and/or soil.

TROUBLESHOOTING		
PROBLEM	**CAUSE**	**FIX**
Worms are dying	Food and bedding are all eaten	Harvest compost, add fresh bedding and food
	Too dry	Add water till wrung-out sponge consistency
	Extreme temperatures	Move bin into the sun so temperature reaches 50-80°F (10-26.5°C)
Bin attracts flies and/or has a bad odor	Food exposed or overfeeding	Add 4"-6" (10-15cm) layer of bedding and stop feed for 2-3 weeks
	"Composting Don'ts" have been included	Remove meat, pet feces, fatty foods, etc.
Sow bugs, snails, slugs, millipedes, worm in bin	Nothing wrong – these guys are desirables!	Remove meat, pet feces, fatty foods. Reinforce bin with wire mesh, brick and/or rock.
Mice and other rodents in bins	"Composting Don'ts" have been included	Start new bin or don't add any more no-no's
Pile won't heat	Pile is too small.	Add more composting ingredients.
	Contents are too dry.	Adjust water to resemble a wrung out towel.
	Needs more "greens" or nitrogen.	Add more grass clippings or a commercial compost activator or compost starter.

Chapter 27: Growing Food

Does anything smell and taste better than a REAL homegrown tomato? There's good reason. Most commercial tomatoes are picked when they're very green and haven't had time to develop. Even "vine-ripened" doesn't mean they were picked when they turned a rich red. It simply means they were left on the vine a *tad* longer, just long enough to show a minute change at the blossom end from green to a blush of color. If you're paying more for vine-ripened fruit, you're not getting much better than those picked when fully green.

Another hint about buying commercial tomatoes is the trick of stem scent. A lot of a tomato's heady scent is found in the attached vine, not the fruit itself. Unscrupulous vendors can also enhance the scent with a little tomato spray.

Hydroponic tomatoes may look beautiful and perfect to the eye, but they lack flavor and contain less vitamin C. Since hydropons are grown in greenhouses they don't get the full benefit of the Sun, nor do they pull flavor from natural soil. The best solution is to grow your own.

GARDEN OPTIONS

Don't live in a house? Even apartment, condo and mobile home dwellers can have container-grown veggies. Many species have "container" and dwarf varieties that take up less space. Some apartment and condos may have flat rooftop space that could hold pots, in addition to balconies. Ask apartment complex owners if they would allow you to "borrow" a bit of their land for gardening in exchange for some produce. Depending on the size you have in mind and space available, you may want to go in with a couple neighbors and create a joint garden.

If your neighborhood has a vacant lot, contact the owner and ask if you could use the space until he either sells or builds on it. In fact, if he were trying to unload it, a garden would attract attention plus improve the soil in the bargain. It's a win-win for everybody..... There are always options.

IN THE BEGINNING, THERE WAS...THE SEED

Just as important as nutritious soil in a bountiful garden is the essential seed. There is much discussion in the news about seeds being genetically altered and companies promoting mostly hybrids. Using hybrid seeds forces the gardener and farmer to purchase new seed every year unless we do at least one of two things.

One, purchase open-pollinated, non-hybrid seeds. Plant these and save the best seeds for future crops.

Two, purchase large quantities of hybrid seeds and store some for future use. The latter choice is a dead-end as seeds, like all food, have a shelf life. Once hybrid seeds are used up, there will be no viable seeds for planting.

GETTING TO THE ROOT OF IT

More people are electing to grow their own vegetables to further self-sufficiency, improve their food quality, produce extra income and relax. It allows the grower to choose what chemicals, if any, are added to the plants, grow exactly what the family likes to eat and cut the overall cost of food. In order to maximize savings, eat more healthfully and be less dependent on grocery stores, there is mounting interest in open-pollinated, non-hybrid or heirloom varieties of seed.

WHAT'S AN HEIRLOOM SEED?

To grasp this concept, it's easiest to understand "hybrid" first. To produce a hybrid, two very different parent plants are crossed. Hopefully the best of each parent is passed onto the resulting plant. In a rose for instance, of the two parent plants, one might have sweeter scent but smaller petals. The other rose might produce larger flowers but lack fragrance. When these two plants are grafted together, the aim is to produce a richer smelling, larger flower than either of the parents. In vegetables, the goal is much the same – to produce stronger, higher yielding, healthier, uniform, "predictable" crops.

WHAT'S WRONG WITH THIS?

Generally hybrids are grown to require larger amounts of fertilizers and accept larger amounts of herbicides, which we, in turn, ingest. These chemicals also get into our air and waterways and contaminant wildlife.

In terms of self-sufficiency, hybrids present another problem. The seed from hybrids was never intended to grow more crops. It's not that you can't grow anything from their seed, but the results are unpredictable. Some may produce fruit at differing times, sugar levels are inconsistent and in worst instances, plants grown from hybrids revert back to one of the parent plants.

So back to the original question, what is an heirloom seed? It's any non-hybrid seed that has been grown in a family and passed on generationally from seed to plant to seed, many times over.

THE TERMINATOR

Move over Arnold! There is another reason why people are returning to non-hybrids. Consider the following information from Geri Guidetti, founder of the Ark Institute. She is a biologist, science writer and educator with advanced degrees, and researcher/teacher of microbiology and plant/yeast molecular biology.

"On March 3, 1998, the U. S. Department of Agriculture (USDA) and the Delta and Pine Land Company, a Mississippi firm and the largest cotton seed company in the world, announced that they had jointly developed and received a patent (US patent number 5,723,765) on a new, agricultural biotechnology.

> Benignly titled, "Control of Plant Gene Expression", the new patent will permit its owners and licensees to **create sterile seed** by cleverly and selectively programming a plant's DNA to kill its own embryos. The patent applies to plants and seeds of all species. The result? If saved at harvest for future crops, the seed produced by these plants will not grow. Pea pods, tomatoes, peppers, heads of wheat and ears of corn will essentially become seed morgues. In one broad, brazen stroke of his hand, man will have irretrievably broken the plant – to – seed – to – plant – to – seed – cycle, THE cycle that supports most life on the planet. No seed, no food unless you buy more seed. This is obviously good for seed companies."[59]

What Geri describes above has been dubbed "The Terminator Seed".

Generally seed sold in discount stores, nurseries, hardware and grocery stores will be hybrids. If a store sells hybrids, in order for the customer to produce a good crop the following year, he must come back for more seed rather than using seed saved from the plants he grew last season.

That's one reason why non-hybrids are a little more costly; next year's plants are built in! For storing seed for the future, you must have non-hybrids. Call your local university Agriculture Department and they can supply the name of local sellers of non-hybrids. There are also many Internet dealers as well.

THE ART OF SEED SAVING

Like gardening, experience is the best teacher and a few seed saving guidelines help. Seed is generally harvested from annual and biennial plants. Perennials (ones that come back every year) are usually propagated through division or cuttings.

Plants that aren't self-pollinating are susceptible to cross-pollination. In other words, if two varieties of carrot bloom near each other, their seed is likely to be a cross between the two. Planting a taller crop between them like tomatoes, corn or climbing crops hooked on trellises **if** the garden is large enough and provides enough distance. Knowing which plants are not self-pollinating helps, but it's not a guarantee the variety will remain pure. Thwart cross-pollination by planting varieties that flower at different times. If you're only saving a small amount of seed, place a brown paper bag over the fruit until it has set.

FIRST FRUITS

When crops first begin to produce, it's very exciting and you'll be tempted to dine on the first harvests. However, saving seed from the first harvests ensures early-producers in next year's crops. The harvests you'll be most tempted to eat are the ones best saved for seed. **Save seed from the healthiest plants that have survived severe weather and insect attacks and are early bearers.**

For crops that produce numerous harvestable crops like tomatoes, beans or peas, don't wait to the end of the season when the plant is depleted of nutrients to save seeds. For plants that send up seed stalks at the end of the edible period or bolt in heat, save seed that has the longest production time before this stalk shows up. Mark any plants as seed savers so you don't accidentally eat these.

WHEN TO COLLECT SEEDS

The best seeds to save are from mature fruits, generally one to two weeks after they are prime for table serving. Collect seed just after the morning dew has dried. Pay attention to wet, windy weather if seed is to be saved from plants that drop it like carrots, onion and lettuce. Even a gentle pounding can send seed into the dirt.

CLEANING

Before storing, seeds should be cleaned from insects and chaff. For wet seeds (squash, tomatoes or cucumbers), run water over them and rub till the bits of flesh are removed.

For dry seeds like beans, corn, carrots, onions or lettuce, they can be dried on the bush and then gently crushed to remove seeds from their pods. To remove the chaff, lay the seed and chaff on a screen and shake the seeds through the mesh. Repeat the process with a smaller gauge screen mesh to remove further debris.

DRYING

Drying is necessary before storing to prevent mildew and rot. Simple ways of drying are:
1. Lay the seed on a windowsill out of the sun and turn occasionally.
2. Dry on newspaper or on screening out of the sun and turn occasionally. Keep seeds separate to prevent them sticking together and ensure thorough drying.
3. Hang larger quantities in paper bags or gunny sack (burlap or hessian bag) to finish drying. This is best accomplished with thin bags hung in breezy areas for larger seeds like bean and squash.

For humid or wet climates, place seed on racks near a heater. Do not allow seeds to be exposed to temperatures greater than 110°F (43°C).

STORING SEEDS

Next to saving the best seeds, proper storing is the most important factor. Successful seed storing depends on the same considerations as for food storage: temperature, moisture, oxygen, light, their container and pest control. Prior to storing, be sure to label each seed packet with the variety and the date when it was packed. After storing the seed, avoid opening the packages until you're ready to plant.

Temperature: 41°F (5°C) is ideal for storing seed, which makes refrigerators a good choice and freezers even better. Temperature is constant and it's a cool, dark environment except for brief periods when the door is opened. If you have a root cellar or underground storage, these are good options too. Alternative choices include the coolest rooms in your home. Avoid areas like the kitchen, garage and storage shed as they get very hot. Each 10°F (5.6°C) drop in temperature doubles the storage life of the seeds.

Moisture: Most seeds keep best at 4-10% humidity. Excess moisture causes rot so they must be dried before storing. To further ensure success, store seeds on dry days. Tape around the jar lid to seal out moisture.

Oxygen: Unlike storing food, there is still a lot of debate over which method is best for storing seeds; e.g. nitro-pak, vacuum packing, carbon dioxide or argon. However, the most respected wisdom comes from the National Center for Genetic Resources Preservation (NCGRP), which is part of Colorado State University in Fort Collins.

From decades of research on the topic, they have determined there is "no measurable difference in seed/grain viability whether stored in air, CO_2, N_2, or vacuum. If sufficiently dried, all of these seeds are effectively dormant to the point that the surrounding gas mix, or lack thereof, is insignificant to storage." So, keep the temperature low and humidity to a minimum.

Light: Like food and water, seeds' shelf light is lengthened when kept out of light. Store seeds in labeled paper bags, inside dark colored jars and place these inside cupboards.

Containers: Here is another use for old vitamin bottles and film canisters. They tend to be very airtight and opaque. Avoid glass jars that rely on cardboard and foil for a good seal like those found on beverage containers unless the lid is sealed to the jar with tape.

Insects and Rodents: To give stored seed the best possible chance, insect control is important. A simple trick to get rid of weevils and their eggs is to freeze seeds inside paper bags placed inside the sealed jars or film canisters. Leave them in the freezer for two days and only open the containers, if you must, after they have returned to normal room temperature. Opening them prematurely can cause moisture to collect inside. Make sure the seed storage containers are **mouse and rat proof**! These nasty little rascals, when it comes to seeds and food, have radar and their teeth can chew through things that would amaze the novice food storer!

HOW LONG WILL SEEDS STAY VIABLE?

According to NCGRP, "Seed longevity depends on storage conditions and seed quality. We expect most undamaged seeds that are properly dried to survive about a hundred years in conventional storage 0°F (-18°C) and about a thousand years under cryogenic (liquid nitrogen) conditions."[60]

Properly stored seed will be usable for varying lengths of time depending on the type of seed. Consult the chart below for shelf life information when not stored in the fridge or freezer.

SHELF LIFE OF STORED VEGETABLE SEEDS				
VEGETABLE	1 = Easiest Seed To Save 4 = Hardest	Annual, Biennial or Perennial	Shelf Life in Years for Stored Seed	Seeds per Gram
Artichoke	2	A,P	5	30
Asparagus	2	P	3-5	50
Basella (Malabar Spinach)	2	A,P	5	50
Bean	1	A	3	5-10
Beetroot	3	B	5	50
Bitter Gourd	2	A	5	12
Borage	2	A	5	65
Broad Bean	1	A	4	1
Broccoli	2	A,B	5	300
Brussel Sprouts	4	B	4	270
Butternut Squash (Gramma)	2	A	3-8	5
Cabbage	3	B	4	250
Cantaloupe (Rockmelon)	3	A	5	30
Cape Gooseberry (Jam Fruit)	2	A,P	3	400
Cardoon	3	P	4	25
Carrot	2	B	3	1,000
Cassava	3	P	N/A	N/A
Cauliflower	3	B	4	500
Celeriac	3	B	5	2,000
Celery	2	B	5	2,000
Celtuce (Chinese Lettuce)	2	A	5	1,000
Chicory (Endive)	2	B	8	600
Chilacayote	1	P	5	5-8
Bok Choy (Chinese Cabbage)	2	A	5	350
Chives	2	P	1	600
Choko (Chayote, Christophene)	1	A,P	N/A	N/A
Collard	3	B	4	200
Corn	4	A	2-10	3-8
Corn Salad	3	A	4	700
Cowpea (Kaffir Bean)	2	A	5	50
Cucumber	3	A	4-10	40
Dandelion	2	P	2	1,000
Eggplant	3	P	5	200
Endive	3	A	5	900
Garland Chrysanthemum	3	A	3	300
Garlic	1	A	N/A	N/A
Garlic Chives	1	P	1	250
Gourd	2	A	5	30
Green Onion (Spring Onion)	2	A,P	2	250
Guada Bean (Guada Gourd)	3	A	2	6
Hibiscus Spinach	2	P	3	70
Hyacinth Bean	2	P	4	4
Jerusalem Artichoke	2	P	N/A	N/A

SHELF LIFE OF STORED VEGETABLE SEEDS				
VEGETABLE	1 = Easiest Seed To Save 4 = Hardest	Annual, Biennial or Perennial	Shelf Life in Years for Stored Seed	Seeds per Gram
Kale	3	B	4	250
Kohlrabi	3	B	4	250
Korila (Achoa)	3	A	3	30
Leek	2	B,P	3	400
Lettuce	1	A	5	1,000
Lima Beans	1	P	3	1
Luffa	2	A	5	20
Mizuna (Japanese Cabbage)	2	A	2	600
Mustard	3	A	3-7	600
Mustard Greens	3	A	4	600
Nasturtium	1	A	3	30
New Zealand Spinach	2	P	6	20
Oca (New Zealand Yam)	3	P	N/A	N/A
Okra	2	A	3-5	N/A
Onion	3	B	2	250
Orach (Mountain Spinach)	3	A	5	250
Oriental Cooking Melon	2	A	5	70
Pansy	2	A	1	2000
Parsnip	3	B	1	200
Pea (Snow Pea)	1	A	3	5
Peanut	2	P	1	12
Peppers (Capsicum & Chili)	2	A,P	5	150
Peruvian Parsnip	2	P	N/A	N/A
Poppy	2	A	2	10,000
Potato	2	P	N/A	N/A
Pumpkin	2	A	3-10	4
Queensland Arrowroot	2	P	N/A	N/A
Radish	3	A,B	4	100
Rhubarb	2	P	1	250
Rocket (Arugula, Roquette)	2	A	2	500
Rosella (Red Sorrel)	2	A	3	70
Runner Bean	2	P	3	1
Salad Burnet	1	P	3	150
Salsify (Oyster Plant)	2	B	3-5	100
Shallot	1	A	2	250
Silver Beet (Swiss Chard)	3	B	10	60-90
Snake Bean (Asparagus Bean)	1	A	3-8	5
Sorrel	2	P	2	1,000
Soya Bean	2	A	3	5-10
Spinach	3	A	5	70
Squash	2	A	3-10	6-8
Sunflower	2	A	5	10-20
Sweet Potato (Yam)	1	P	N/A	N/A

SHELF LIFE OF STORED VEGETABLE SEEDS

VEGETABLE	1 = Easiest Seed To Save 4 = Hardest	Annual, Biennial or Perennial	Shelf Life in Years for Stored Seed	Seeds per Gram
Taro	2	P	N/A	N/A
Tomato	1	A	4	400
Tree Onion (Topset Onion)	2	P	N/A	N/A
Turnip	4	B	5	300
Violet	2	A	1 week	1000
Water Chestnut	3	P	N/A	N/A
Water Spinach	3	A	3	150
Watercress	1	P	5	4,000
Watermelon	2	A	5	6
Wax Gourd	2	A	3	10
Winged Bean	2	A,P	2	18
Yam Bean	2	P	5	5

SHELF LIFE OF STORED HERB SEEDS

HERB	1 = Easiest Seed To Save 4 = Hardest	Annual, Biennial Or Perennial	Shelf Life In Years For Stored Seed	Seeds Per Gram
Amaranth	2	A	5	800
Basil	1	A,P	5	600
Calendula (Pot Marigold)	2	A	2	100
Chervil	1	A	1	450
Coriander (Cilantro)	1	A	3	90
Dill	1	A	3	900
Fennel	1	A	4	500
Ginger	2	P	N/A	N/A
Lemongrass	1	P	N/A	N/A
Marigold	1	A	3	300
Marjoram	2	A,P	5	12,000
Mint	2	V,C	1	40,000
Mitsuba (Japanese Parsley)	2	A	3	500
Parsley	2	B	3	200
Rosemary	2	P	1	900
Sage	1	P	3	250
Tarragon	3	P	N/A	N/A
Thyme	2	P	5	6,000
Tumeric	2	P	N/A	N/A

For complete gardening information, see **Garden Gold: Grow Maximum Veggies With Minimum Effort**. *Garden Gold* equips you with the knowledge for a superior space-saving garden wherever there's sunshine. You'll grow more fruits and veggies with less time and effort spent, yet with more taste and nutrition than you ever thought possible. It will spoil you having to eat commercial produce again! **standeyo.com**.

Chapter 28: Dehydrating Foods

Once you have a dynamite garden, besides enjoying these lovely foods right from the stem or canning them, dehydration is another option. Dehydrated foods take up less space, they're lightweight and require no refrigeration, which makes them excellent for camping and storing. Drying your own is a lot more economical than purchasing these treats from health food and grocery stores. Plus, it smells wonderful when drying jerky aromas float through the air!

DEHYDRATING METHODS COMPARED

METHOD	PROS	CONS	COMMENTS
Commercial Dryer (CD)	Faster Maintains even heating Not dependent on sun or weather conditions Readily available	More costly Small units have limited capacity	Safest, most dependable method Expandable versions available
Oven	If you have an oven, you have a dehydrator Not dependent on sun or weather conditions In winter, will help heat your kitchen	Takes twice as long as CD Capacity more limited than CD In summer, may add unwanted warmth Not energy efficient May need oven for cooking Not for vegetables or meat	Can oven be set as low as 140° (60°C)? Fan-forced ovens dry foods faster than ovens without fans Must leave oven door propped open 2-6" (5-15cm) Improve air circulation by setting a fan outside oven door
Sun Drying	Inexpensive Works well for fruit	Does not work as well in cloudy locations Dependent on weather Takes several days Lay second screen or cheesecloth on top to protect fruits from birds, bugs	Ideal conditions: Humidity below 60% with temps at least 85°F (29.5°C) and a constant breeze. Fruit must be brought inside at night to protect against dew and lower temperatures. Don't use galvanized screens coated cadmium or zinc, aluminum or copper
Solar Drying	Can be made at home Better than sun drying Inexpensive	Not as efficient as CD Requires sun and low humidity	Adding foil or glass raises temperature 20-30°F (11-17°C). May require turning so all areas get enough sun
Room Drying	No equipment needed Least expensive method Works well in the desert	Least efficient method Foods open to dust, insects In humid areas, may not be possible to achieve dryness Needs well-ventilated room	Works best for chilies and herbs
Vine Drying	Works without power No equipment No space used in the home	Susceptible to weather Takes longer methods Mostly for beans and peas	

DRYING

Removing moisture from food – a basic principal for long-term storage – inhibits bacteria growth. The best temperature to accomplish this is a constant 140°F (60°C), which is why having a temperature control on a dehydrator is a good idea. Heat above this setting cooks foods on the outside instead of removing the moisture, making it more likely to mold.

Removing humidity around food makes it dehydrate faster. This is done by increasing the airflow around the food like using a fan, not turning up the heat. This only cooks the food.

Most foods can be dried indoors using dehydrators, counter-top convection ovens or conventional ovens. Microwaves are only recommended for drying herbs, because there is no way to create enough airflow in them. Herbs are also easily air-dried.

Depending on finances, without question, an expandable tray commercial unit is a great choice. Having used several different brands with various features and factoring in cost, this is truly an instance where you get what you pay for. When we lived in Perth and Colorado, a solar unit performed great, but in Ballarat, eastern Australia, it was too moist and cloudy to work well.

The first dehydrator we bought was a very inexpensive unit, which didn't expand or have a thermostat or fan. Drying took half of forever with uneven results.

In 1994, we bought a Nesco American Harvest Gardenmaster. It's well worth the dollars and still works perfectly today. Gardenmaster can expand to 30 trays, which allows for a lot of dehydrating at once. This same unit sells in Australia under the brand of Fowlers Vacola. There are other good products available and here are some key features to consider.

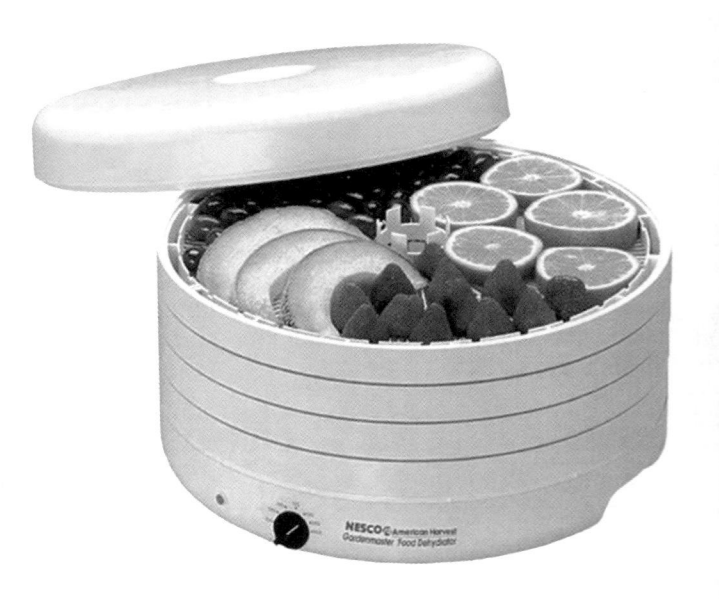

WHAT TO LOOK FOR IN A DEHYDRATOR

- Double-wall construction of metal or high grade plastic. Wood poses a fire hazard and is difficult to clean. Cheap plastic has been known to warp.
- Enclosed heating elements.
- Counter top design; make sure the unit will not burn countertops or be a fire hazard.
- Thermostat from 85°-160°F (30-71°C)
- Fan or blower; this will speed up dehydrating time.
- Four to 10 open mesh trays made of sturdy lightweight plastic for easy washing.
- UL seal of approval.
- A timer. Nice, but optional. Often the completed drying time may occur during the night and a timer can turn the dehydrator off and prevent scorching. However, depending on the day's humidity and moisture content of a particular batch of food, charts times for drying are only a guide. Food needs to checked for proper dryness

NATURE'S CANDY – FRUIT

PREPARING THE FRUIT

Wash and core fruit if needed. Cut fruit in half, slice or leave whole. Check the Fruits Drying Table for specific directions for preparing each fruit.

Uniform pieces work best so all slices are ready at the same time. Thinner, peeled slices dry faster than thicker pieces with their skin on. If skins are left on, boil fruit first for two minutes and then place in cold water. This is called checking and is done before dehydrating.

Coat the drying trays with non-stick cooking spray so the fruit lifts off easily. One to two hours into drying, turn the pieces over.

E. COLI PREVENTION

New recommendations include heating fresh fruits to 160°F (71°C) prior to drying to ensure adequate destruction of E. coli O157:H7, if it's present. Pre-heating also stops the maturing action of enzymes in the fruit, helps preserve the fruit's natural color and speeds the drying process. If you're using canned fruit, skip this step.[61]

PRE-TREATING METHODS

Light-colored fruits like bananas and apples darken when exposed to air if they aren't pre-treated. Using a sulfite dip or sulfuring agent gives the best results if you plan to store fruits long-term. This doesn't mean it's the best over-all treatment. Do not use sulfur if you are asthmatic without running a small test batch first. If you're not affected by it, then this gives you another option.

PRETREATMENT

METHOD	PROS	CONS	COMMENTS
Sulfuring	Keeps fruits from darkening the longest. Reduces loss of vitamins A and C.	Dehydration needs to be completed outside. Can be harmful or irritating to lungs. Not to be used by asthmatics.	Burn 1 Tbsp Sulfur Dioxide in a dish under the dehydrator for 4 hours
Sulfite Dip	Keeps fruits from darkening very well. Reduces loss of vitamins A and C. Easier to use than sulfuring. Can be dehydrated indoors or out.	Not as easy to locate. Check drug store, hobby shops and winemaking suppliers. Needs to make a new solution each batch.	Use ½-1½ tsp sodium bisulfite OR 1½-3 tsp sodium sulfite OR 1-2 Tbsp sodium meta-bisulfite (food grade) or Reagent grade (pure) to 1 qt. or liter water. Soak slices 5 minutes and halves for 15 minutes. Remove fruit and rinse in cold water.
Ascorbic Acid	Easy to use and readily available wherever vitamins are sold.	Protection isn't as long as sulfuring or sulfiting. After solution is used twice, add more ascorbic acid.	Mix 1 tsp powdered ascorbic acid (or 3000mg ascorbic acid tablets, crushed) in 2 cups water. Soak fruit 3-5 minutes. Drain well and place on dryer trays.
Ascorbic Acid Mixtures	Easy to use and readily available in canning sections of grocery stores.	More expensive and not as effective as using pure ascorbic acid	Mix 1½ Tbsp with 1 qt. or 1 liter of water. Soak fruit 3-5 minutes. Drain well and place on dryer trays.
Fruit Juice Dip	Flexible, Any juice with high vitamin C content is OK to use Inexpensive. Juice can be consumed after fruit soaking.	Not as effective as pure ascorbic acid. After this solution is used twice, replace.	Choose from orange, lemon, pineapple, grape or cranberry. Soak fruit 3-5 minutes. Drain well and place on dryer trays.
Honey Dip	Ingredients readily available Inexpensive.	Adds a lot of calories. Alters taste of fruits.	Mix ½ cup sugar with 1½ cups boiling water. Cool to lukewarm, add ½ cup honey. Soak fruit 3-5 min. Drain well; place on dryer trays.
Syrup Blanching	Helps fruit retain color. Inexpensive. Ingredients readily available at grocery store.	Works only with apples, figs, apricots, nectarines, peaches, pears, plums and prunes.	Combine 1 cup sugar, 1 cup light corn syrup and 2 cups water in a pot. Boil. Add 1 pound (.5 kg) of prepared fruit and simmer 10 minutes. Remove from heat and let fruit stand in hot syrup for 30 minutes. Remove fruit from syrup, rinse lightly in cold water, drain on paper towels and place on dryer trays.
Steam Blanching	Helps fruit retain color. Slow oxidation.	Changes flavor and texture.	In a steamer with boiling water, add fruit only 2" (5cm) deep. Cover, begin timing according to chart. Stir partway through for even blanching. Remove, blot moisture with paper towel, place on dryer trays.

From the Fruits Drying Table, select the fruit, pretreatment method and method of drying. When choosing fruit, pick fully ripe fruit so they have the highest sugar content. Avoid pieces that are bruised or "over-the-hill". Drying time will be affected by where you live, whether it is cold and/or how much humidity is in the air. Use these time frames only as a guideline and check the Indicators or Dryness column to see if the fruit is ready.

FRUITS DRYING TABLE

FRUIT	PREPARATION	PREFERRED PRE-TREATMENT	DRYING TIME	INDICATORS OF DRYNESS
Apples	Wash and core; peel if desired. Cut in ⅛" (3mm) slices or rings. Coat with ascorbic acid solution to prevent darkening during prep. Use 2½ tsp ascorbic acid solution to 1 cup water.	Sulfur time 45-60 min. OR Sodium sulfite 5 min. OR Steam 3 to 5 min. OR Ascorbic acid 2-3 minutes	Dehydrator 6-12 hours Sun 3-4 days	Soft and pliable; no moisture in center when cut.
Apricots	Cut in half or slice, remove pit, don't peel. Coat with ascorbic acid solution to prevent darkening during preparation. Use 1 tsp per cup.	Sulfur time 2 hours for halves; 1 hour for slices OR Sodium sulfite 5 min. OR Steam 3 to 5 minutes.	Dehydrator 16-36 hours halves; 7-10 hours slices Sun 2-3 days	Soft and pliable; no moisture in center when cut.
Bananas	Peel and cut into ⅛" (3mm) slices	Ascorbic acid 2-3 minutes OR Fruit juice dip 3-5 min. OR Honey dip 3-5 minutes	Dehydrator 8-16 hours; Sun 2-3 days	Leathery but still chewy. (longer drying will make banana chips – NOT pliable)
Blueberries; Cranberries	Halve or leave whole	No sulfuring, but can dip in boiling water 15 to 30 seconds to crack skins. OR Steam blanch 30 – 60 seconds.	Dehydrator 8-12 hours Sun 2-4 days	Leathery but still chewy
Cherries Sour Cherries	Pit, halve and remove stems	No sulfuring but can dip whole cherries in boiling water 15 to 30 seconds to crack skins. OR Syrup blanch 10 min.	Dehydrator 18-30 hours Sun 1-2 days	Leathery but still chewy and a little sticky
Citrus peel (thick-skinned with no signs of mold or decay and no color added)	Wash. Thinly peel outer 1/16-⅛" (1.5-3mm) of the peel; avoid white bitter part.	None needed.	Dehydrator 1-2 hours	Arrange in single layers on trays. Dry at 130°F (54°C) 1-2 hours; then at 120°F (49°C) until crisp.
Figs	Peel & Quarter	No sulfuring but can crack skins of whole figs in boiling water 15-30 seconds.	Dehydrator 10-12 hours Sun 4-5 days	Pliable; slightly sticky but not wet.
Grapes and Black Currants (seedless varieties)	Halve or leave whole; seed if desired	No sulfuring but can crack skins of whole in boiling water 15-30 seconds OR Steam 1 minute.	Dehydrator 24-48 hours Sun 3-5 days	Raisin like texture pliable; chewy.
Melons (mature, firm heavy for size; cantaloupe is better than watermelon)	Wash. Remove outer skin, any fibrous tissue and seeds. Slice ¼-½" (6-12mm) thick.	None needed.	Dehydrator 1½ days	Arrange in single layer on trays. Dry until leathery and pliable with no pockets of moisture.
Peaches or	Peel if desired. Halve or	Sulfur time 2-3 hours	Dehydrator	Arrange in single

FRUITS DRYING TABLE

FRUIT	PREPARATION	PREFERRED PRE-TREATMENT	DRYING TIME	INDICATORS OF DRYNESS
Nectarines	cut in ¼" (6mm) slices, remove pit. Coat with ascorbic acid solution to prevent darkening during preparation. Use 1 tsp ascorbic acid per cup water.	halves or slices OR Sodium sulfite 5-15 minutes. OR Steam halves 8-10 min. 2-3 minutes for slices OR Ascorbic acid 3-5 min. OR Fruit juice dip 3-5 min.	24-36 hours halves; 8-12 hours slices Sun 3-5 days halves or slices	layer on trays pit side up. Turn halves over when visible juice disappears. Dry until leathery and somewhat pliable.
Pears	Halve and core, or core and cut in ⅛-¼" (3-6mm) slices. Coat with ascorbic acid solution to prevent darkening during preparation (1 tsp/cup).	Sulfur time 5 hours halves or slices OR Soak 5 to 15 minutes in sodium sulfite OR Steam blanch 5-7 min. OR Ascorbic acid 3-5 min. OR Fruit juice dip 3-5 min.	Dehydrator 24-36 hours halves; 10-14 hours slices Sun 5 days halves or slices	Arrange in single layer on trays pit side up. Dry until springy and suede-like with no pockets of moisture.
Persimmons	For Fuyu variety, select firm fruit; for Hachiya variety, let fruit ripen until soft. Peel and cut in ½" (1.27cm) slices.	None needed, but may syrup blanch	Dehydrator 14-18 hours Sun 5-6 days	Light to medium brown; tender but not sticky.
Pineapple	Peel, core and cut crosswise into ½"(1.27cm) slices. Dry slices whole or cut them in wedges.	None needed.	Dehydrator 24-36 hours-slices; 18-24 hrs-wedges Sun 4-5 days slices; 3-4 days wedges	Chewy and dry to center.
Plums and Prunes	Halve or cut in ½" (1.27cm) slices, removing pit.	Sulfur time 1 hr OR Steam halves, slices 5-7 minutes OR Crack skins in boiling water 1-2 min.	Dehydrator 18-24 hours Sun 4-5 days- halves; 8-10 hours- slices	Fairly leathery and hard but still chewy. Pit should not slip when squeezed if prune not cut.
Rhubarb	Cut in ½" (1.27cm) slices.	None needed.	Dehydrator 18-20 hours Sun: 2-3 days	Hard to crisp
Strawberries	Halve or cut in ¼" slices.	None needed.	Dehydrator 20 hours- halves; 12-16 hours- slices Sun 1-2 days	Leathery but still pliable.

AFTER DEHYDRATING

Not all fruit was created equal nor will it all dry the same. Depending on the actual pieces of fruit and where they were placed in the dehydrator, some may finish with more moisture than others. Once dried, fruit should have only 20% moisture or it may mold. To make sure all pieces end up with approximately the same moisture, pack the dried and cooled fruit loosely in a glass jar with snug lid or Tupperware type container. Let the fruit stay here for the next week and shake it daily to redistribute moisture evenly. At the end of a week, pack the dried fruit for storage (providing it makes it that long!) Nibbling is permitted!

FRUIT LEATHER

Why pay grocery store prices for fruit roll-ups when you can easily make your own? Many commercial products are loaded with sugar and color additives. When you make yours at home, only the ingredients that you want will go in!

LEATHERS FROM FRESH FRUIT
Step 1 Select ripe or slightly overripe fruit.
Step 2 Wash fresh fruit or berries in cool water.
Step 3 Remove peel, seeds and stem. Cut fruit into chunks.
Step 4 Use 2 cups of fruit for each 13x15" (33x38cm) fruit leather tray. Puree fruit in a blender or food processor until smooth.
Step 5 Add 2 tsp lemon juice or ⅛ tsp (375mg) ascorbic acid for each 2 cups of light colored fruit to prevent darkening.
Step 6 Optional: To sweeten, add corn syrup, honey or sugar. Corn syrup or honey is best for longer storage because it prevents crystals. Sugar is fine for immediate use or short storage. Use ¼-½ cup sugar, corn syrup or honey for each 2 cups of fruit. Splenda, Sweet 'N Low and other saccharin products can be used successfully, but steer away from aspartame.

LEATHERS FROM CANNED OR FROZEN FRUIT
Step 1 Drain fruit, save liquid.
Step 2 Use 1 pint (2 cups) fruit for each 13x15" (33x38cm) leather.
Step 3 Puree fruit in a blender or food processor until smooth. If too thick, add reserved liquid. It should be pouring consistency.
Step 4 Add 2 tsp lemon juice or ⅛ tsp ascorbic acid (375 mg) for each 2 cups of light colored fruit to prevent darkening.

TIP: Applesauce can be dried alone or added to any fresh fruit puree as an extender. It decreases tartness and makes the leather smoother and more pliable.

READY, AIM, POUR!
Leathers are a little easier because the fruit doesn't need to be uniformly cut before drying. Fruit leathers will keep about 1 month unrefrigerated and 1 year in the freezer.

Step 1 If using a dehydrator, most come with liners for the fruit trays to do the leathers. Instead of a woven surface, it has a solid sheet with a hole in the center that fits inside the fruit tray. If drying in the oven, use a 13"x15" (33x38cm) cookie sheet with sides, sometimes called a jelly roll pan. A flat cookie sheet won't work for leathers. Line this pan with plastic wrap, not wax paper or aluminum foil.
Step 2 Spread puree evenly ⅛" thick onto the plastic.
Step 3 Allow to dry at 140°F (60°C) 6-8 hours in a dehydrator or 18 hours in an oven and 1-2 days in the sun.
Step 4 It's done when the center of the leather shows no indent.
Step 5 While still warm, peel from plastic and roll.
Step 6 Cool before wrapping in plastic.

ADDING PIZZAZ!
If you're tired of the same old leather, get creative and add your favorite spices and flavorings.

FRUIT LEATHER FLAVORINGS			
SPICES ⅛ tsp per 2 cups puree	**EXTRACTS & JUICES** ⅛-¼ tsp per 2 cups puree	**TASTY INDULGENCES**	**FILLINGS**
Allspice	Almond	Shredded Coconut	Melted Chocolate
Cinnamon	Lemon Juice	Chopped Dates	Cream Cheese
Cloves	Lemon Peel	Dried Chopped Fruits	Cheese Spreads
Coriander	Lime Juice	Granola	Jam/Preserves
Ginger	Lime Peel	Mini-Marshmallows	Marmalade
Mace	Orange Extract	Chopped Nuts	Marshmallow Cream
Mint	Orange Juice	Chopped Raisins	Peanut Butter
Nutmeg	Orange Peel	Poppy Seeds	
Pumpkin Pie Spice	Vanilla Extract	Sesame Seeds	
		Sunflower Seeds	

If using items from the last two columns, spread them on after the leather has dried and then roll. Store in the refrigerator. If you're watching calories and still want extra flavor, use the first two columns. And, speaking of healthy,... vegetables are next!

DRYING VEGETABLES

Soups, stews, entrees, Tex/Mex and vegetarian dishes are just a few areas where dehydrated vegetables come in handy. While fruits have about 20% moisture after dehydration, vegetables have about 10%. Fortunately bacteria can't grow with this little water content. Dry time is very important with vegetables. If dried too long, the taste and nutrition fall off greatly.

PREPARING THE VEGETABLES

Wash them in cool water to clean. Follow directions for each vegetable for cutting and trimming. Cut out bruised or woody sections. As with fruit, keep pieces uniform for even drying.

PRE-TREATING METHODS

There are a lot fewer choices for pre-treating vegetables. Some fruit pretreatments are more for esthetics, but for vegetables it's necessary to:
- Shorten drying time
- Stop color and flavor loss
- Shorten rehydration time

WATER BLANCHING

Not all vegetables require blanching. Onions, green peppers and mushrooms can be dried without blanching. For those that do, fill a large pot two-thirds full of water, cover and bring to a rolling boil. Place vegetables in a wire basket or a colander and submerge. Cover and blanch for time specified in the Vegetables Drying Table.

TIP: If it takes longer than one minute for water to come back to a boil, too many vegetables are in the pot.

STEAM BLANCHING

Use a deep pot with a close-fitting lid and a wire basket insert so the steam circulates freely around the vegetables. Fill with water and bring to a rolling boil. Place vegetables loosely in the basket no more than 2" (5cm) deep. Set the basket of vegetables in the pot **above the water**, not touching it. Cover and steam according to the directions for each vegetable in Vegetables Drying Table.

AFTER THE BLANCH...

Step 1 After blanching, run the vegetables briefly in cold water. They should still feel slightly hot, 120°F (49°C), not room temperature.
Step 2 Drain the vegetables and put them immediately on the drying tray in a single layer. Pop them quickly into the dehydrator or oven.
Step 3 Monitor the vegetables toward the end of drying as they will finish quickly and could burn.
Step 4 Vegetables are dry when they're brittle and crisp. Unlike fruit, there is no moisture redistribution step after dehydrating so store immediately.

NOTE: For green beans only, after blanching, place them single-layer in the freezer 30-40 minutes.

TIP: Dry very pungent veggies outside. People might think you're trying to ward off Dracula! Like cigarette smoke, onion and garlic odors can penetrate fabrics, draperies and carpets.

VEGETABLES DRYING TABLE

VEGETABLE	PREPARATION	BLANCHING METHOD	BLANCHING TIME IN MINUTES	DRYING TIME HOURS	DRYING DESIRED DRYNESS
Artichokes	Cut hearts into ⅛" (3mm) strips. Heat in boiling solution of ½ cup water and 1 Tbsp lemon juice.	Steam Water	-- 6-8	D 2-3 S 10-12	Leathery to Brittle
Asparagus*	Cut into ½" (1.27cm) pieces. Cut large tips in half.	Steam Water	4-6 4-5	D 103 S 8-10	Leathery to Brittle
Beans, Green	Cut in short pieces or lengthwise	Steam Water	2-2½ 2	D 2½-4 S 8	Brittle
Beets	Cook as usual; cool; peel, cut in ⅛" (3mm) slices.	None	N/A	D 2-3 S 8-10	Brittle, dark red

VEGETABLES DRYING TABLE

VEGETABLE	PREPARATION	BLANCHING METHOD	TIME IN MINUTES	DRYING TIME HOURS	DESIRED DRYNESS
Broccoli*	Trim; slice stalks lengthwise no more than ½" (1.27cm) thick	Steam Water	3-3½ 2	D 2-4 S 8-10	Brittle; crisp
Brussel Sprouts	Cut in half lengthwise steam	Steam Water	7-8 5-6	D 2-3 S 9-11	Hard to Brittle
Cabbage	Remove outer leaves; quarter and core. Cut in ⅛" (3cm) slices.	Steam Water	3 2	D 1-2 S 6-7	Tough to Brittle
Carrots	Cut off roots and tops. Peel; cut in ⅛" (3cm) slices.	Steam Water	3½	D 2½-4 S 8	Tough to Brittle
Cauliflower*	Break into tiny flowerettes.	Steam Water	4	D 2-3 S 8-11	Tough to Brittle
Celery	Trim stalks and cut in ½" (1.27cm) slices	Steam Water	2	D 2-3 S 8	Crisp; Brittle
Chili Peppers, green	Wash. To loosen skins, cut slit in skin, then rotate over flame 6-8 minutes or scald in boiling water. Peel and split pods. Remove seeds and stem. (Wear gloves.)	None	N/A		Crisp, brittle, medium green
Chili Peppers, red	Wash. String whole pods together with needle and cord or hang in bunches, root side up in area with good air circulation. See instructions.	None	N/A		Shrunken, dark red pods, flexible
Corn on the cob	Husk, trim, blanch until milk in corn is set.	Steam Water	3-5 3	D 4 S 8	Brittle
Corn, cut	Prepare as for corn on the cob, except cut the kernels from the cob after blanching.	Steam Water	3-5 3	D 1-2 S 6	Brittle; crunchy
Eggplant	Trim and cut into ¼" (6cm) slices	Steam Water	3-4 3-4	D 2½ S 6-8	Leathery to Brittle
Horseradish	Wash, remove small rootlets and stubs. Peel or scrape roots. Grate.	None	N/A	D 1-2 S 7-10	Brittle; powdery
Mushrooms**	Remove any tough and woody stems. Trim ⅛" off stems. Slice.	None	N/A	D 3½ S 6-8	Dry and leathery
Okra	Trim and slice crosswise in ⅛-¼" (3-6mm) slices.	None	N/A	D 2-3 S 8-11	Tough to brittle
Onions	Remove outer skin, top, and root end. In ⅛-¼" (3-6mm) slices.	None	N/A	D 1-3 S 8-11	Brittle and papery
Parsley and Other Herbs	Wash thoroughly. Separate clusters. Discard long or tough stems. Dry on trays or hang in bundles in area with good circulation.	None	N/A	D 1-2 S 6-8	Flaky
Peas	Shell	Steam Water	3	D 3 S 6-8	Wrinkled and hard
Peppers, Green, Red, Bell, Pimento	Stem and core. Cut crosswise into in ¼" (3mm) circles or ½" (1.27cm) strips.	None	N/A	D 3½ S 6-8	Flexible; dry to the touch
Parsnips	Cut off roots and tops. Peel; cut in ⅛" (3mm) slices.	Steam Water	3½	18	Tough to Brittle
Potatoes	Peel. Cut in ⅛" (3mm) slices or ¼" (6mm) strips	Steam Water	7	D 2-4 S 8-11	Brittle

VEGETABLES DRYING TABLE

VEGETABLE	PREPARATION	BLANCHING		DRYING	
		METHOD	TIME IN MINUTES	TIME HOURS	DESIRED DRYNESS
Spinach, Collard Greens	Trim	Steam Water	24	D 2½ S 6-8	Brittle
Squash, Banana	Wash, peel, slice in strips about ¼" (6mm) thick	Steam Water	2½-3 1	D 2-4 S 6-8	Brittle
Squash, Hubbard	Cut or break into pieces. Remove seeds and cavity pulp. Cut into 1" wide strips. Peel rind. Cut strips crosswise into piece about ¼" thick	Steam Water	2½-3 1	D 2-4 S 6-8	Brittle
Squash, Summer	Trim and cut into ¼" (6mm) slices	Steam Water	2	D 2½-3 S 6-8	Brittle
Squash, Winter	Peel and cut into 2-4" (5-10cm) pieces ¼" (6mm) thick	Steam Water	2	18	Crisp; hard
Tomatoes	Steam or dip in boiling water to loosen skins. Chill in cold water. Peel. Slice ½" (12mm) thick or cut in ¾" sections.	None	N/A	26	Crisp

NOTES: Blanching times are for 3,000 to 5,000 feet. Times will be slightly longer at higher altitudes or for large quantities of vegetables. S=Sun, D=Dehydrator   *Does not rehydrate well

WARNING: The toxins of poisonous varieties of mushrooms are **not destroyed by drying or by cooking. Only an expert can differentiate between poisonous and edible varieties.

HANG 'EM! HANG 'EM HIGH – CHILIES THAT IS
MAKE YOUR OWN RISTRA

Nothing smells quite like the aroma of roasting chilies and every year we look forward to the local Fall Chili Festival.

New Mexicans traditionally harvest and tie red chili into colorful strings called *ristras*. Chili is allowed to dry in New Mexico's warm sun, then stored – still on the ristra string – for use in various tantalizing dishes during winter. They're nice to string for home decor or hang to dry for later use. Now their popularity has spread countrywide.

Chilies are a meatier vegetable and have higher water content so drying is best done where air can circulate all around them.

When making chili ristras, select freshly picked, mature, red chili pods. If the chili still has a slight green color, put it in a cool, dark, but-well ventilated place for two or three days. This will finish ripening turning it a bright red.

Green chili is not acceptable for making ristras. Because it hasn't reached maturity, green chili will only shrivel and turn a dull orange color as it dries.

Let red chili pods sit for two or three days after picking. This allows the stems to lose some moisture. In the ristra tying process, stems often break if they're too fresh. Good ventilation is important in the final drying. If fresh chili is bought in closed containers or plastic bags, take the chili out of the container or bag to avoid spoiling.

You can also dry peppers in the sun by placing washed and seeded peppers on trays. Cover the trays with cheesecloth and place in the sun. Bring peppers inside at night to prevent moisture absorption. When medium in color and brittle, place in jars and store in refrigerator. De Arbol, Anaheim, Chimayo, Fresno, NuMex, Big Jim, Sandia, Cayenne and Poblano peppers make the best ristras.

MATERIALS NEEDED:
¾ – 1 bushel (27-35 liters) red chilies,... Lightweight cotton string (package string),....Twine

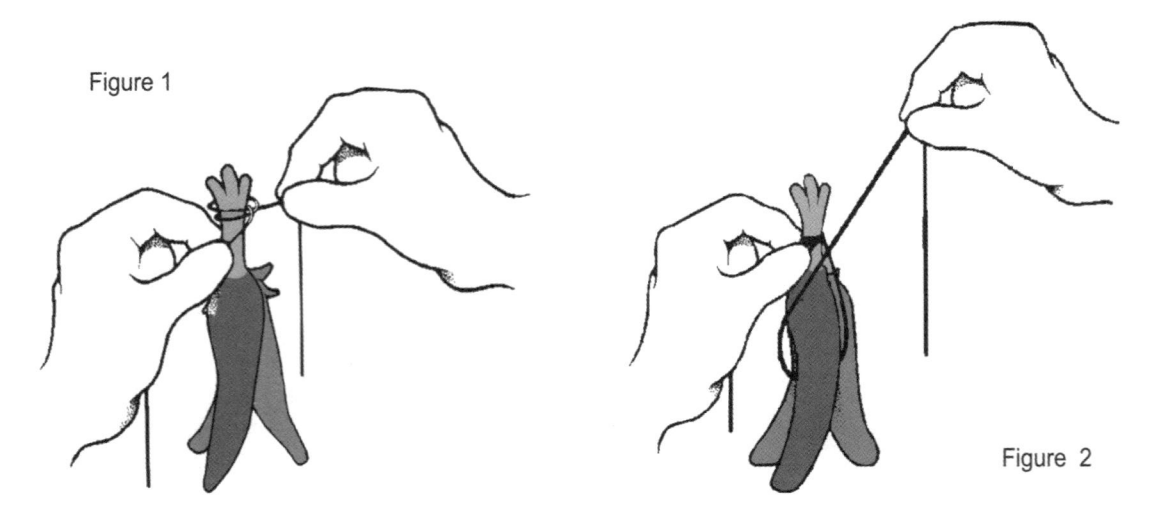

Fig. 1. Wrap the string around the stems of three chilies.

Begin by tying clusters of three chili pods on the lightweight string. To tie clusters, hold three chilies by their stems, wrap the string around the stems twice (fig. 1), bring the string up between two of the chilies, and pull tight (figure 2).

Fig. 2. Pull string uprightly between two of the chilies.

Make a half hitch with the string and drop it over all three stems; pull the string tight (fig. 3). Pick up three more chili pods, and, in the same manner, tie another cluster about three inches above the first cluster. Continue until there are several clusters of three chilies, or until the weight makes it hard to handle. Break the string and start again; continue tying until all the chili has been used.

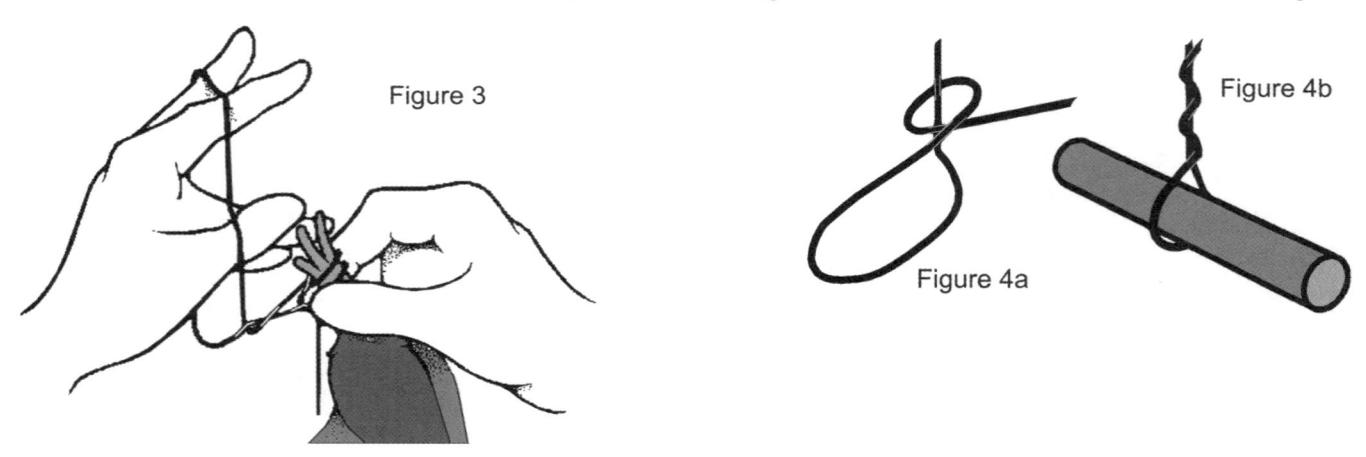

Fig. 3. Make a half hitch over the three stems.

Suspend the twine from a nail in a rafter or from a doorknob. Make a loop in the loose end of the twine to keep chili clusters from slipping off (fig. 4a). Some people like to use a wooden peg or dowel at the end of the wire or twine to keep chilies in place (fig. 4b). Beginning with the first three chili pods (one cluster) tied to the package string, braid the chilies around the twine.)

Fig. 4. Make a loop at the end of the wire (4a) or fasten it to a peg or dowel (4b).

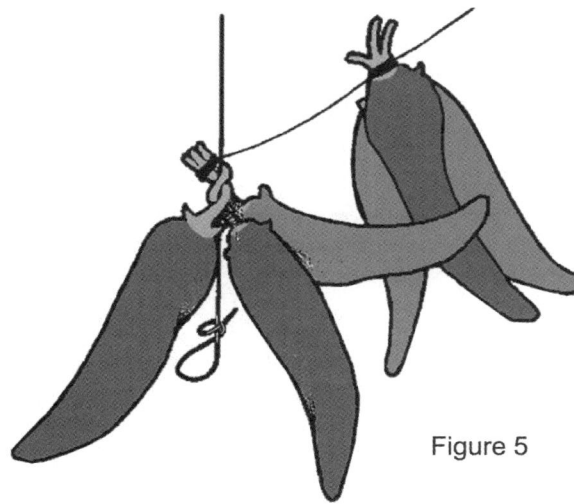

Fig. 5. Braid the clusters of chili around wire.
The process is like braiding hair. The wire serves as one strand and stems of two chilies in the cluster are the other two strands (fig. 5). As the chili is braided, push down in the center to make sure of a tight wrap. Position the chilies to protrude in different directions. If this is not done, empty spaces can develop along one side of the ristra. Continue braiding until all the chili clusters are used.

Hang the completed ristra in full sun, either on a clothesline or from outdoor rafters where there is good ventilation. The chili can turn moldy and rot without proper air circulation for final drying. This causes discoloration, which detracts from the ristra's natural beauty and prevents using the chili as food.[62]

Figure 5

OTHER DRYING METHODS
MICROWAVE
Microwave ovens are also a good way to dry herbs in small quantities. When using the microwave, place clean stems or leaves on a paper plate or towel and set the control on high for 1 to 3 minutes. Turn the stems over or mix the leaves every 30 seconds. Check the cookbook that came with your microwave for herb drying directions since ovens differ in energy output. This could change drying times.

CONVENTIONAL OVEN
Place the leaves or stems on a cookie sheet or shallow pan and warm at no more than 180°F (82°C) for 3 to 4 hours. Keep oven door open.

DESICCANTS
Silica Sand Drying is the same process commonly used to dry flowers. Silica sand draws the moisture out of the plant tissues and leaves them in their original shapes. Any container will do, as long as it is big enough to allow all of the plant materials to be covered with sand. The leaves should be clean and dry. Place a shallow layer of silica sand in the bottom of the container, then arrange herbs on top so they don't overlap. Cover with more silica sand and place container in a warm room. Dry time: 2-4 weeks. Store in glass jars.

HOW MUCH TO EXPECT
When starting with fresh vegetables, these are the weights you can expect for the dehydrated version, which helps to plans requirements and storage space.

\	DRYING HERBS	\
Herb	**Drying Method**	**Hardiness**
Basil	Hang a small bunch of herbs inside a paper bag to dry. Punch holes in the sides of the bag for ventilation. Close with a rubber band.	Tender, high moisture content. Dry quickly to prevent mold.
Bay Leaf	Remove best leaves from stem. Lay spaced separately on a paper towel. Cover with another paper towel and more leaves, up to 5 layers. Dry by oven light heat or pilot light only. Leaves are ready when they crumble in the fingers. Store in airtight container in dark room.	
Lemon Balm	Hang a small bunch of herbs inside a paper bag to dry. Punch holes in sides of bag for ventilation. Close with a rubber band.	Tender, high moisture content. Dry quickly to prevent mold.
Mint	Hang a small bunch of herbs inside a paper bag to dry. Punch holes in the sides of the bag for ventilation. Close with a rubber band OR dry as per instruction for Bay Leaf	Tender, high moisture content. Dry quickly to prevent mold.
Parsley	Air dry outdoor, better color and flavor retention drying indoors	Hardier
Sage	Air dry outdoor, better color and flavor retention drying indoors OR Remove best leaves from stem. Lay spaced separately on paper towel. Cover with another paper towel up to 5 layers. Dry by oven light heat or pilot light only. Leaves are ready when they crumble in the fingers. Store in airtight container in dark room.	Hardier

DRYING HERBS		
Herb	**Drying Method**	**Hardiness**
Summer Savory	Air dry outdoor, better color and flavor retention drying indoors	Hardier
Tarragon	Hang a small bunch of herb inside paper bag to dry. Punch holes in the sides of the bag for ventilation. Close with rubber band	Tender, high moisture content. Dry quickly to prevent mold.
Thyme	Air dry outdoor, better color and flavor retention drying indoors	Hardier

YIELD OF DRIED VEGETABLES[63]				
Produce	Fresh Produce (Lbs.)	Dried Produce (Lbs.)	Dried Produce (Pints)	Fresh Produce (kilos)	Dried Produce (Grams)
Beans, lima	7	1¼	2	3.2	567 g
Beans, snap	6	½	½	2.75	500 g
Beets	15	1½	3-5	6.8	680 g
Broccoli	12	1⅜	3-5	5.5	626 g
Carrots	15	1¼	2 to 4	6.8	567 g
Celery	12	¾	3½-4	5.5	340 g
Greens	3	¼	5½	1.3	113 g
Onions	12	1½	4½	5.5	680 g
Peas	8	¾	1	3.5	340 g
Pumpkin	11	¾	3½	5	340 g
Squash	10	¾	5	4.5	340 g
Tomatoes	14	½	2½-3	6.3	500 g

MAKING JERKY

Um hmm! Who doesn't love jerky and it's so easy to make! It's a favorite around our house that rarely makes it into the cupboard. It's great for snacks, camping and just plain munching as long as sodium isn't a major concern.

Jerky is a versatile dried meat and with poultry ground meat/minces, you can easily replace higher calorie hamburger with chicken or turkey. Since jerky is normally pretty heavily spiced, it's hard to tell poultry from beef.

Jerky can be made from any lean meat like round, flank, chuck, rump roast, brisket and cross rib.

If venison is used, the trichinella parasite must be killed before slicing and marinating. To do this, freeze pork in sections 6" (15cm) or less thick at 5°F (15°C) or lower, for 20 days. The best choices are beef or game meat, rather than pork or lamb. Freeze game meat at least 60 days before processing.

NOTE: About 4 pounds (1.8kg) of lean, boneless meat yields about 1 pound (½kg) of jerky.

PREPARING MINCED MEAT JERKY IN A PRESS

When we purchased the dehydrator, somehow a Jerky Works made by Nesco American Harvest (imported by Fowlers Vacola in Australia) made its way into the shopping cart too! We found using this caulking gun type dispenser makes jerky quickly and uniformly. You can make it with chicken, turkey or hamburger; buy only extra lean. The more fat contained in the meat, the quicker it will go rancid and it increases drying time.

Jerky Works

PREPARING MINCED MEAT FOR JERKY WORKS

Step 1 Break up the mince and mix in the seasoning thoroughly.

Step 2 Follow any additional directions on packaging if using a different brand.
Step 3 Select the desired jerky shape, insert tip and squirt the jerky onto the dehydrating tray.
Step 4 Dry jerky at 140°F (60°C). Drying time: 6-10 hours.

PREPARING MINCED MEAT JERKY WITH A ROLLING PIN
Step 1 Break up the mince and mix in the seasoning thoroughly.
Step 2 Roll the meat to ⅛" (3mm) thick between two pieces of waxed paper.
Step 3 Place the meat on the solid plastic trays used for fruit leathers.
Step 4 Dry two hours till meat can be handled and not fall apart.
Step 5 Blot moisture and fat with a paper towel.
Step 6 Cut the meat into 1" (2.5cm) strips and transfer it to the regular drying trays.
Step 7 Complete drying and blot off additional fat as it oozes from the jerky.
Step 8 Store in an airtight container.

If you want to make your own spices, this recipe works well but does not contain any preservatives. Minced or ground poultry can easily be substituted for hamburger or beef mince.

HAMBURGER BEEF JERKY I
2 pounds or 1 kg extra lean ground beef
1 tsp ground black pepper
1 Tbsp salt
½ tsp coarse ground black pepper
1 tsp garlic
1 tsp liquid smoke
    Optional ingredients: cayenne pepper, jalapeño powder, Worcestershire sauce, soy sauce and Tabasco

HAMBURGER BEEF JERKY II
1½ pounds (.68 kg) extra lean ground beef
¼ cup soy sauce
½ cup Teriyaki sauce
½ tsp garlic salt
½ tsp pepper

Mix all ingredients together well. Using a Jerky Works gun, make strips on dehydrator racks or foil lined oven racks. Follow the manufacturer's instructions for drying if using a dehydrator. If using the oven, set the temperature to 140-150°F (60-66°C). Jerky is done when dry, but not brittle. When the strips are done, blot with a paper towel, allow to cool, and store in the refrigerator in an airtight container. They will keep at room temperature for several days. Drying Time: 6-10 hours.

USING MEAT STRIPS FOR JERKY

PREPARATION
Remove any visible fat, connective tissue and gristle from meat. For easiest cutting, freeze meat in moisture-proof wrap until firm but not solid. Slice slightly frozen meat into strips ¼" thick, 1-1½" wide, and 4-10" long. Flatten strips with a rolling pin so they're uniform in thickness.

Cut with (not across) the grain. Small muscles, one or two inches (2.5-5cm) in diameter, are often separated and made into jerky without being cut into strips. These thicker pieces of meat take longer to absorb the salt and seasonings and longer to dry, but with these exceptions, no changes in the jerky recipes need be made.

Strip jerky is usually marinated in a solution of spices for 2 to 12 hours to enhance flavor; seasonings are "kneaded" into ground meat jerky then mixture is allowed to stand for 1 hour for flavors to mix. Strips may be dried either on a rack or tray or hung over the rungs of the oven rack with a pan below to catch drippings.

Some recipes call for drying jerky in the sun. Drying in the sun not recommended because of the inability to ensure steady heat and the potential for contamination by animals, insects, bacteria and dust. However, if sun drying is used, jerky should be cut into strips ¼" (6mm) thick or less.

Color of finished jerky ranges from a light brown to black. Color variations depend on the recipe used, species and age of the animal.

Store cooled jerky in airtight containers in the refrigerator.

Always wash cutting board, utensils, cutting boards or counter with hot, soapy water and sanitize with a solution of 1 teaspoon of chlorine bleach per quart of water before and after contact with meat or juices.

E. COLI

Colorado State University Cooperative Extension analyzed bacteria research and have developed new processing recommendations to assure E.coli destruction. Concern arose when an outbreak of Escherichia coli O157:H7 infection was traced to home-prepared deer jerky. Follow-up studies showed that E. coli O157:H7 bacteria survive traditional drying processes used for meat and fruit.

Drying food may be an old practice, but bacteria today are different. You can continue to use a favorite blend of secret spices, but adapt your recipe to include the following.[64]

E.Coli Vinegar Treatment
2 pounds of lean meat slices
Pre-treatment dip: 2 cups vinegar

Place vinegar dip in 9x11 inch cake pan or plastic container. Add meat strips, making sure they are immersed in vinegar. Soak for 10 minutes, stir occasionally. Follow with your favorite marinade and dry as described in the next pages.

PREPARING MEAT STRIPS FOR JERKY

Step 1 Slice meat into long, thin strips and trim off all fat. (Partially freezing meat before cutting makes it easier to slice.) Slice with the grain for chewy jerky, across the grain for tender jerky, cutting uniform strips ¼ inch (6mm) thick.
Step 2 Season with meat tenderizer and let stand as per instructions on tenderizer.
Step 3 Follow the marinade instructions per recipes. They will both season and tenderize the meat.

DRYING THE MEAT

Remove meat strips from the marinade, drain on absorbent toweling and arrange on dehydrator trays or cake racks placed on baking sheets. Place slices close together but do not overlap. Place racks in a drying oven preheated at 140°F (60°C). Dry until a test piece cracks but does not break when it is bent (10 to 24 hours). Pat off any beads of oil with paper towels and cool. Remove strips from the racks and package in glass jars or heavy plastic bags.

STORING THE JERKY

Properly prepared jerky will keep at room temperature 2 to 3 months in a sealed container. To increase the shelf life and maintain the flavor, refrigerate or freeze.

JERKY RECIPES

Meat is marinated for both flavor and tenderness. Ingredients for marinades generally include oil, salt and an acid such as vinegar, lemon juice, teriyaki, soy sauce or wine. Experiment with your taste buds!

Basic Marinade
½ tsp pepper
1 tsp hickory smoke-flavored salt
½ tsp garlic powder
½ cup soy sauce
½ tsp onion powder
1 Tbsp Worcestershire sauce
1½-2 lbs. (¾-1kg) of lean meat

Combine all ingredients. Place strips of meat in a shallow pan and cover with marinade. Cover and refrigerate 1-2 hours, better overnight. Remove strips from the marinade, drain on absorbent toweling and arrange on dehydrator trays or oven racks. Place slices close together but don't overlap. Place the racks in a drying oven at 150°F (66°C). Dry until a test piece cracks but does not break when bent (10-24 hours). Pat off any beads of oil with paper toweling and cool.

Teriyaki Marinade
¼ cup soy sauce
1 teaspoon freshly grated ginger root or ½ teaspoon ground ginger
2 teaspoons sugar
1 teaspoon salt
2 lbs (1kg) of lean meat

Combine seasoning, pour over meat strips in a large bowl and mix gently. Cover and refrigerate for at least 2 hours or overnight. Dry as for Basic Marinade.

Strip Jerky
1½ lbs. (.68kg) lean meat
1 Tbsp pepper or seasoned pepper
1 tsp garlic salt
2 Tbsp Worcestershire sauce
½ cup soy sauce
Liquid smoke (if desired)

Remove all visible fat, slice meat ⅛-¼" (3-6mm) thick with the grain. Mix soy sauce, Worcestershire, salt and pepper. Marinate meat 2 to 12 hours. Lay strips over oven rack rungs or on cookie sheets. Brush with liquid smoke. Dry 5 to 12 hours at 140-150°F (60-66°C) until meat is hard and brittle. Pat off any oil beads with paper towel. Store refrigerated in an airtight container.

Blue Ribbon Jerky
½ cup dark soy sauce
½ tsp garlic powder
2 Tbsp Worcestershire sauce
¼ tsp powdered ginger
1 tsp monosodium glutamate (optional)
¼ tsp Chinese Five-Spice Powder
3 lbs. (1.3kg) lean beef brisket, eye-of-round or flank steak

Trim completely all fat and cut across grain into slices ⅛" (3mm) thick.

Blend all ingredients except meat in small bowl. Dip each piece of meat into marinade, coating well. Place in shallow dish. Pour remaining marinade over top, cover and refrigerate overnight.

Oven method: Preheat oven to lowest setting, preferably 110°F (43°C). Place several layers of paper towels on baking sheets. Arrange meat in single layer on prepared sheets and cover with additional toweling. Flatten meat with rolling pin. Discard towels and set meat directly on oven racks. Let dry 8 to 12 hours (depending on temperature of oven).

Dehydrator method: Arrange meat on trays in single layer and dehydrate 10 to 12 hours, depending on thickness. Store jerky in plastic bags or in tightly covered containers in cool, dry area.

Paul's Spicy Beef Jerky
4 oz. (118ml) Teriyaki with Pineapple Juice – 30 Minute Marinade for Chicken, Meat & Fish
2 Tbsp A-1 Bold & Spicy Steak Sauce
4 Tbsp brown sugar
1 Tbsp Cajun seasoning
3 Tbsp pepper
1 Tbsp salt
1 tsp crushed chili pepper, optional
2 pounds (1kg) extra lean Round Steak, cut into ⅛-¼" (3-6mm) thick slices

Marinate for 30 minutes or longer. Dehydrate 4+ hours.

IS IT DRY YET?

You can determine dryness by feel or by calculating the amount of water remaining in the food.

By Feel

Fruits should be leathery, not hard. Drying time ranges considerably so refer to the Fruit Drying Chart for specifics. Fruit always feels softer and less dry when warm in the dryer. To check, remove a piece from the dryer and let cool before testing. The sample will show no moisture when cut and pressed. When a few pieces are squeezed together, they fall apart when the pressure is released. They have a leathery or suede-like feel. High sugar fruits, like figs, pineapple and cherries, will feel slightly sticky. Fruit leather can be peeled from the plastic wrap. Vegetables are generally brittle or tough when they are dry enough. If there is a question as to whether vegetables are dry enough, reduce the temperature and dry them a little longer, using a low temperature toward the end of the drying period. There is little danger of damage being done by this extra drying time.

By Calculation

For optimum plumpness of produce while maintaining safety, calculate the percent solids in the dried product to determine if the product is adequately dry.

Step 1 Weigh the tray that will be used for drying. (Tray Wt.)
Step 2 Weigh the raw food in the container (Food and Tray Wt.)
Step 3 Calculate Raw Food Weight. (Raw Wt.):

    Product & Tray Wt.
    <u>- Tray Wt.</u>
    Raw Wt.

Step 4 Calculate desired final weight of dried food using the following formula:

$$\frac{(Raw\ Wt.) \times (Solids\ \%)}{90\%^*} = Desired\ Dry\ Wt.$$ (* 90% solids is a good value to use for vegetables.)

Fruits are moister if 80% is used for calculation purposes. Do not use a lower percent value for solids. For example: We want to dry cherries to 80% solids (20% water). Solids in raw cherries from Table 3, next page = 14%

    Container = 5 oz.
    Container + cherries = 45 oz.
    Wt. of raw cherries = 40 oz.
    $\frac{40\ oz. \times 14\%}{80\%}$ = 7 oz. final dry weight

The final weight of the cherries should be 7 oz. Since it will be weighted in a 5 oz. container, the weight will be 7+5=12 oz. If you adjusted scales so that container weight = 0, the final weight is 7 oz. If fruit is dried to an 80% solids level, it will be safe from microbial spoilage with the exception of mold growth. To control mold growth, vacuum pack the dried fruit or freeze the product.[65]

PERCENT SOLIDS IN RAW FRUIT AND VEGETABLES			
Fruits	**Percent Solids**	**Vegetables**	**Percent Solids**
Apples	16	Beans	10
Apricots	14	Beets	13
Bananas	26	Broccoli	11
Blue Berries	16	Cabbage	8
Coconut	49	Carrots	12
Cherries, Sour	14	Cauliflower	8
Cherries Sweet	20	Celery	5
Figs	21	Corn	24
Grapes	19	Eggplant	8
Nectarines	14	Mushrooms	9
Peaches	12	Onion	9
Pears	16	Parsley	12
Pineapple	14	Peas in pod	12
Plums	14	Peppers, bell	7
Raspberries	14	Potato	21
Rhubarb	5	Spinach	9
Strawberries	9	Squash	6
		Tomatoes	6
		Turnip	7

STORING DRIED FOODS

Storing foods we dry at home is no different that packing foods from the grocery long term. Keep them away from insects, moisture, oxygen and light. Every time spices and foods are opened, they are further exposed to elements that cause deterioration. If you have dried large quantities, repackage them into smaller containers.

Sulfured fruit should not touch metal. Place fruit in a plastic bag before storing it in a metal can. Sulfur fumes will react with the metal and cause color changes in the fruit.

Recommended storage times for dried foods range from 4 months to 1 year, and dried fruits from 1 year at 60°F (15°C) to 6 months at 80°F (27°C). Fruit leather keeps for one year in the freezer, several months in the refrigerator, or 1-2 months at room temperature – 70°F (21°C).

Vegetables have about half the shelf life of fruits UNLESS long-term storage measures previously discussed are used.

When cooled, put jerky in an airtight container, store in dry, dark cool place for 2 weeks, 3-6 months in refrigerator or up to a year in freezer. Check occasionally to be sure no mold is forming.

Glass containers are excellent for storage because any moisture that collects on the inside can be seen easily. Discard moldy foods.

DRYING SEEDS, POPCORN AND NUTS

Food	Prep Work	Dry Method	Temp °F	Temp °C	Dry Time & Doneness
Pumpkin Seeds	Wash seeds to remove fibers. Stir often to avoid scorching.	Sun	--	--	10-15 minutes
		Dehydrator	115-120°F	46-49°C	1-2 hours
		Oven	Slow	Slow	3-4 hours
		To Roast – toss with oil and/or salt	250°F	121°C	10-15 minutes
Popcorn – Japanese Hullless, Hybrid S. American, Mushroom Creme Puff Hybrid, White Cloud Dynamite	No pretreatment necessary. Leave ears of corn on stalk till kernels are well dried. When dry, remove from ears and package.	Sun	--	--	Dried corn will appear shriveled. Pop a few kernels to test. Popcorn will dry down to about 10% moisture.
		Oven	below 130°F	below 54°C	
Sunflower	Wrap flower in cheesecloth so birds don't eat seeds.	Sun	--	--	
		Dehydrator	100°F	38°C	
		To Roast	300°F	149°C	10-15 minutes
Peanuts	Dry unshelled or shelled. Spread in single layer.	To Roast – Unshelled	300°F	149°C	30-40 min. Peanuts are dry when shells are brittle. Nut meats are tender, not shriveled.
		Shelled	300°F	149°C	20-25 min. Stir frequently.

USING DRIED FRUITS

Dried fruit is delicious eaten as is or it can be reconstituted. Soaking too long in water will make the fruit soggy and tasteless. For reconstituting, start with the water amounts and time to soak listed in the Redhydrating Dried Food table below. If more than 1-2 hours soaking time is needed, do it in the refrigerator.

To cook reconstituted fruit, simmer, covered, in the soak water to keep the highest nutrition. For more flavor, if a recipe calls for added liquid, use the fruit soaking water. This fruit may taste sweeter if the starch has changed to sugar during drying. Less sugar may be needed for recipes. Add sugar at the end of cooking so it doesn't interfere with the fruit's water absorption. A dash of salt will also bring out sweetness. Add just before serving.

REHYDRATING DRIED FOOD		
Food	Cups of Water to Add to 1 Cup Dried Food	Minimum Soaking Time (Hours)
FRUIT- Water is at room temperature		
Apples	1½	½
Peaches	2	1½
Pears	1½	1½
VEGETABLE – Water is boiling		
Asparagus	2½	1½
Beans, lima	2½	1½
Beans, green snap	2½	1
Beets	2½	1½
Carrots	2½	1
Cabbage	3	1
Corn	2½	½
Okra	3	½
Onions	2	½
Peas	2½	½
Pumpkin	3	1
Squash	1½	1
Spinach	1	½
Sweet Potatoes	1½	½
Turnip greens and other greens	1	½

USING DRIED VEGETABLES

Vegetables can be reconstituted three ways:
- soaked in cold water
- added to boiling water (see previous Rehydrating Dried Food table)
- added the dried vegetable to another food with lots of liquid, such as soup.

Whichever rehydration method is chosen, vegetables will return to their original shape. For extra flavor, if a recipe calls for more liquid, use the vegetable soaking water and/or soak them in bouillon or vegetable juice. Like with fruit, if more than 2 hours is needed for soaking, do it in the refrigerator.

Adding dried vegetables directly to soups and stews is the simplest way to rehydrate vegetables. Also, leafy vegetables, cabbage and tomatoes do not need to be soaked. Add sufficient water to keep them covered and simmer until tender.

VEGETABLE CHIPS

Dehydrated, thinly sliced vegetables or vegetable chips are a nutritious low-calorie snack. They can be served with a favorite dip. Slice thinly zucchini, tomato, squash, parsnip, turnip, cucumber, beet or carrots in a food processor, vegetable slicer or with a sharp knife before drying.

VEGETABLES FLAKES AND POWDERS

Make flakes by crushing dehydrated vegetables or vegetable leather using a wooden mallet, rolling pin or your hand.

Powders are finer than flakes and are made by using a food mill, food processor or blender. The most common powders are celery, chili, garlic, onion and tomato.

DRIED VEGETABLE EQUIVALENTS	
FRESH PRODUCE	DRY EQUIVALENTS
1 onion	1½ tablespoons onion powder, ½ cup dried minced onions
1 green pepper	½ cup green pepper flakes
1 cup carrots	4 tablespoons powdered carrots, ½ cup (heaped) dried carrots
1 cup spinach	2-3 tablespoons powdered spinach
1 medium tomato	1 tablespoon powdered tomato
½ cup tomato puree	1 tablespoon powdered tomato
20 pounds tomatoes	18 ounces dried sliced tomatoes

Dare To Prepare: Chapter 28: Dehydrating Foods

DRYING VEGETABLE LEATHERS

Vegetable leathers are made similar to fruit leathers. Common vegetable leathers are pumpkin, mixed vegetable and tomato. Puree cooked vegetables and strain. Spices can be added for flavoring.

MIXED VEGETABLE LEATHER

2 cups cored, cut-up tomatoes
1 small onion, chopped
¼ cup chopped celery
Salt to taste

Cook over low heat in a covered saucepan 15 to 20 minutes. Puree or force through a sieve or colander. Cook until thickened. Spread on a cookie sheet or tray lined with plastic wrap. Dry at 140°F (60°C).

PUMPKIN LEATHER

½ cup honey
⅛ teaspoon nutmeg
¼ teaspoon cinnamon
⅛ teaspoon powdered cloves
2 cups canned pumpkin or 2 cups fresh pumpkin, cooked and pureed

Blend ingredients well. Spread on tray or cookie sheet lined with plastic wrap. Dry at 140°F (60°C).

TOMATO LEATHER

Core ripe tomatoes and cut into quarters. Cook over low heat in a covered saucepan, 15 to 20 minutes. Puree and pour into electric fry pan or shallow pan. Add salt to taste and cook over low heat until thickened. Spread on a cookie sheet or tray lined with plastic wrap. Dry at 140°F (60°C).

REMEDIES FOR DRYING PROBLEMS

PROBLEM	CAUSE	PREVENTION
Moisture in Jar or Container	1. Incomplete drying. 2. Food cut unevenly, thus incomplete drying. 3. Dried food left at room temperature too long after cooling and moisture re-entered the food.	1. Test several pieces for dryness 2. Cut food evenly. 3. Cool quickly and package.
Mold on Food	1. Incomplete drying. 2. Food not checked for moisture within a week. 3. Container not air tight. 4. Storage temperature too warm plus moisture in food. 5. Case hardening. Food Dried at too high a temperature and food cooked on outside before the inside dried.	1. Test several pieces for dryness. 2. Check container within one week for moisture in container. Re-dry food at 140°F (60°C) until dry. 3. Use airtight container. 4. Store foods in coolest are of home below 70°F (21°C). 5. Dry food at 140°F (60°C).
Brown Spots on Vegetables	1. Too high drying temperature used. 2. Vegetables over-dried.	1. Dry vegetables at 140°F (60°C). 2. Check periodically for dryness.
Insects in Jars	1. Lids do not completely fit jar. 2. Food dried out-of-doors but not pasteurized.	1. Use new canning lid. 2. Pasteurize food in oven at 160°F (71°C) for 30 minutes, or in freezer for 48 hours.
Holes in Plastic Bags	1. Insects or rodents ear through plastic bags.	1. Avoid use of plastic bags except when food can be stored in refrigerator or freezer. 2. Store food in glass jars, rigid freezer containers or clean metal cans.

Chapter 29: Generators

Onan 6kW Gas

Honda 7.25kW Gas

Yamaha 1kW Gas

Honda 4.5kW Gas

Yamaha 6.5kW Diesel

Yamaha 5kvA Gas

Yanmar 3.3 kW Diesel

ENERGY is power

Many of us have tucked the 2003 Blackout behind us like a bad dream and we cross our fingers hoping it will be the last. This is doubtful. Besides increasing natural disasters and antiquated, overused and overtaxed equipment, bird flu could have a serious impact on electrical generation. (See Chapter 64.) It could be much greater than the 2003 blackout. Additionally, in 2007 it came apparent that hackers are making serious inroads toward bringing down the U.S. grid. This cybersecurity weakness is quietly receiving huge attention from the government. It behooves us to remember how ugly a prolonged power outage can be and to do what we can to prepare. Private back-up power is a must.

LIGHTS OUT

Shortly after noon, in sweltering August heat, an Eastlake, Ohio power plant couldn't handle the high demand and collapsed under the load. Extra power coursed through FirstEnergy's Hanna-Juniper lines, heated the wires and caused them to sag into a tree and trip. More Ohio plants winked offline.

At 4 pm, transmission problems were still contained in Ohio but had spread across the state. By 4:09 central Michigan's Kinder Morgan plant went down and then all bets were off. Literally, in the next minute, a massive blackout shot throughout the U.S. Northeast and southeastern Canada.

AUGUST 14, 2003, 4:13 PM

For 50 million people in Canada and the U.S., it was a painful and frustrating lesson. When 256 power plants succumbed to cascading grid failure, it brought on the largest blackout in North American history. The blackout encompassed over parts of Ontario, Michigan, Ohio, New York, Pennsylvania, Vermont, Massachusetts, Connecticut and New Jersey. Households were severely inconvenienced and businesses were crippled or shut down entirely.

Consequences from a brutal outage became more apparent when at least 12 people died. The blackout impacted everything from water availability and transportation to business and communication. In just six days, this is what happened:

Water:
- Cleveland, Ohio's water service completely stopped to its 1.5 million users because electric pumps supplied the city and backup power was available only on a minimal basis.
- Others areas lost pressure because pumps didn't have power. Water supplies became contaminated.
- Four million Detroit, Michigan customers were placed under boil advisories.
- Macomb County, Michigan ordered all 2,300 restaurants closed until they were decontaminated after the boil advisory was lifted.
- Kingston, Ontario lost power to sewage pumps. This caused raw waste to be dumped into the Cataraqui River.
- 20 people living on the St. Clair River became sick after bathing in the river during the blackout.

Transportation
- All New York area airports and rail lines were shut down and people were trapped in New York subways.
- All trains running in and out of New York City were stopped, initially including the Long Island Rail Road and the Metro-North Railroad.
- Amtrak's Northeast Corridor railroad service stopped north of Philadelphia.
- Subway and streetcars shut down in Toronto
- Tunnels and bridges between Windsor, Ontario and Detroit, Michigan closed.
- Flights were canceled all over.
- Passenger screenings at affected airports ceased shutting down regional airports.
- Traffic lights, having no backup power, were all knocked out.
- Gas stations were unable to pump fuel.
- Many oil refineries shut down on the East Coast.

Industry:
- Wall Street and the United Nations were completely shut down.
- The Toronto Stock Exchange shut down.
- Large numbers of factories closed.
- Businesses including the auto industry did not return to full production until August 22nd.
- A 7-hour wait developed for trucks crossing the Ambassador Bridge between Detroit and Windsor due to the lack of electronic border check systems.
- Freeway congestion affected the "just-in-time" supply system.
- 140 miners were marooned underground in the Falconbridge mine in Sudbury, Ontario.

Communication:
- Cell phone services were disrupted.
- Verizon's emergency generators failed several times, leaving the emergency 911 number out of service for several 15-minute periods.
- Cable television systems were disabled.
- CBS, NBC, ABC, FOX, and some cable TV Networks like HBO, MTV, and Nickelodeon were mostly unable to broadcast.
- Toronto's CBC studios shut down.

Emergencies:
- 60 serious blazes burned in New York City.
- 11 burglaries recorded in New York City.
- 80,000 were placed calls to 911 – more than double the average.
- A record 5,000 emergency medical service calls were made.
- 800 people trapped in elevators required rescue.
- At least 12 fatalities: 3 were from carbon monoxide poisoning, 3 from fires, 3 were vehicular accidents, 1 heart attack, 1 due to falling off the roof during a burglary and 1 unspecified cause.

President Bush summarized the 2003 blackout as "a wake-up call". While all fired up, he admitted, "The grid needs to be modernized, the delivery systems need to be modernized. We've got an antiquated system." [66]

New Mexico Gov. Bill Richardson, the energy secretary under President Clinton, blamed the blackout on the country's "Third World electricity grid."[67] That says it as plainly as possible without the politician-speak.

A MATTER OF MONEY AND RISK

Hope for a grid fix reawakened in December 2007 when President Bush signed the Energy Independence and Security Act. The name sounds pretty reassuring doesn't it.

However, it's only a partial fix and a very costly one at that. This policy would upgrade the existing (ancient) equipment with advanced communications and embed sensors to make it a "Smart Grid". Supposedly these measures would help avoid future power outages by moving electricity around the system as needed. But first it must be implemented and tested.

Smart Grid's other key selling point is "Time of Day" or TOD pricing. Once a "smart meter" is installed on a residence or business, it allows the customer to monitor peak energy and use their appliances accordingly. This seems like an incredible expense when most people already know that most appliances are run from 4pm into the evening.

Before this can happen utility companies have to adopt this new technology and nobody wants to be first. According to energy industry consultant Alison Silverstein, "the utilities all want someone else to make the mistakes and take the risk for 5 or 10 years. And regulators are not willing to get out of their way and let them take those risks. It will require a transformation."[68]

It's understandable in the midst of a recession, few companies want to step up to the plate. However, Xcel Energy announced they are making Boulder, Colorado the nation's first Smart Grid city. Boulder is a well-heeled college town with 100,000 green-minded residents. It's the right place for this type of technology to take off. Just to implement Boulder's Smart Grid, Xcel expects to spend $100 million.[69] Multiply those "zeroes" times every city in the country and it adds up to extraordinary dollars.

SMART GRID, STUPID ANSWER

At the core, this Smart Grid still doesn't replace the antiquated system we've used since the 50s.

Currently 150,000 miles of transmission lines send power across the nation. As cities grow and spread, demand for electricity rises. Electrical requirements increase 2-3% every year and in some markets, it's considerably more.

In addition to basic energy needs, each season more "toys" are launched, whether it's hi-def TV, bigger computers, or new gadgets, they all gobble power. Another strain comes with more frequent heat waves and the corresponding demand for air conditioning. As a result, over the last decade we've repeatedly experienced rolling brownouts and black-blackouts.

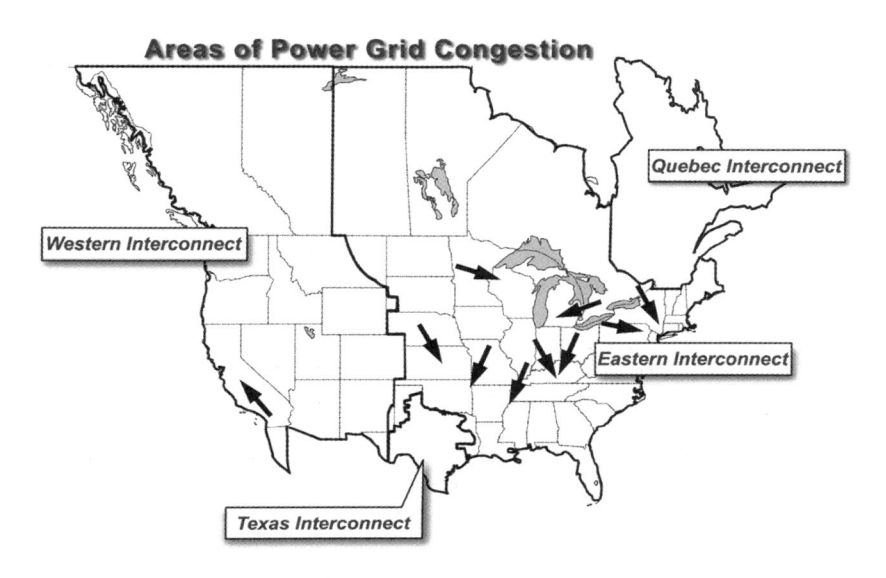

Areas of Power Grid Congestion

Understandably, no one wants transmission lines in their backyard for esthetics and health issues, but we're in a no-win game here. Regardless of the crisis a major grid failure can bring, government has not addressed the real issue.

The grid desperately needs more lines just to keep pace with use. Yet no more infrastructure has been built. This places enormous pressure on overburdened lines. In the image above, arrows point to locations where the grid is experiencing congestion.

RISKY BUSINESS

As the need grew, so did the incompatibility factor. Supplying power to the country is 140 control centers and 3,000 utility companies. Overall they've done a good job integrating the West, East and Texas interconnects which are essentially three different power grids. The East Interconnect must also be compatible with the Quebec Interconnect. Complicating matters, the Western and Texas Interconnects crossbreed into Mexico.

However, during this massive undertaking, widely varying levels of equipment and data systems were used. Even personnel's training isn't uniform. "The grid, as it was established, was never designed to absorb the transmission of high voltage across the country without the comparable and upgraded systems in place."[70] We're expecting 20th century technology to handle 21st century needs.

Equally alarming, since 2005, any foreign country or foreign government is open to buy U.S. utilities. This Energy Policy Act also removes review by FERC (Federal Energy Regulatory Commission). As of May 2008, no fix is even on the drawing board.

WHEN THE UNTHINKABLE HAPPENS: POWER GRID COLLAPSE

In prior outages, power was brought back on line with help from other areas of the grid and small generators kept on site. However, if a large portion or the whole thing goes black, it gets tricky because it takes power to make power.

To reinstate electricity, a "black start" would be used where small diesel generators start larger generators, which in turn fire up the main power station generators. Power from these now-operational plants would be used to "cold start" other locations.

Often this job falls to hydroelectric power plants. By comparison, hydroelectric stations need very little initial power to start. They require enough "juice" to open the intake gates, which manually, can take 300 turns each. Even with this best-case scenario, when HydroQuebec suffered a blackout in 1989, it took nine hours to restore 90% of its power. Other plants could take days to get back on line.

Just like with a generator, when an extensive blackout hits, extra power is required to restart beyond what is needed to operate under normal conditions. For example, appliances you want to run at home might require 5000 total watts. However, to start them, they might require three times this amount for "surge" power.

In the event of a severe event like a very large solar storm, the power grid can collapse and transformers can be damaged. Transformers aren't kept as "spare parts" since they can cost up to $10 million each and ordering one made can take a year.

2003 BLACKOUT NOT A FIRST

It is unthinkable that we could experience power outages for extended periods, but we have seen them before. Blackouts around the world hit fairly frequently, but most only last either minutes or days. However, with increasingly wicked storms combined with an infrastructure whose lifespan is already six decades, these outages will likely become more frequent and of longer duration. Factor in a threat as massive as avian flu and it's anybody's guess how well it will or won't hold up.

- November 1996 brought a severe ice storm to the U.S. Northwest. Power lines snapped under the weight of the ice. People around Spokane, Washington, and Coeur d'Alene, Idaho were left in the dark for two weeks.
- January 6, 1998 saw the worst ice storm in Canada's history. Its massive weight destroyed transmission towers plunging over 3.5 million customers into darkness. The outage hit residents hardest in Quebec, eastern Ontario and New Brunswick. Brutal cold claimed at least 25 lives, many elderly, who died from hypothermia. Most areas had electricity within a week, but south of Montreal and in communities west of Ottawa, people were without power for a hellish two weeks.
- After Hurricane Ivan in 2004, it took Alabama Power eight days to bring all customers back online.
- Hurricanes brought more ugly lessons the next year. In August during Katrina, Florida lost power for up to a week. Ditto for millions more in Louisiana, Mississippi and Alabama. Besides leaving people in the dark, blackouts can disrupt oil and natural gas distribution. Pipelines depend on pumps to keep petroleum flowing. With Katrina, this scenario was one more burden to bear. For some people, days turned into weeks of no power. It was simply too big of a mess to fix quickly.
- Two months later, Hurricane Wilma plunged more than 3 million Floridians into darkness. Power wasn't fully restored for nearly 3 weeks.
- In December 2007, a miserable ice storm cut power to over 1 million homes and businesses. People from Oklahoma to Nebraska were in the dark for 5 frigid days.

These are just some of the bigger events. If an outage doesn't personally affect us, we tend to forget the impact.

These blackouts, horrible as they were to endure, resulted from known factors. They were regional and caused by something that didn't inspire panic. How will the grid fare when faced with something worse?

If the power grid fails in greater measure or completely, we're all in trouble. This isn't a total stretch since we're depending on an antiquated system that's more often on life support. In addition to its own fragility, there's the possibility of a pandemic, EMP or cyber attack, which bring more problems along with harsher grid consequences.

If you live in an area conducive to sunshine and can afford an alternate system, solar panels would be wonderful back-up power. If not, at the least, portable generators are a doable, temporary solution.

WHAT'S FOR DINNER

No power, no dinner? It doesn't have to be that way. There are numerous ways to prepare foods that don't involve traditional cooking. First, let's look at generators – an excellent source of back-up power. Unlike solar or wind power, they work regardless of cloudy or dead calm days. They enable you to use regular household appliances, have lights, live life normally, comfortably. Depending on how large a generator is purchased, you may be able to use numerous appliances simultaneously.

Being novices 15 years ago, we began an extensive search for the perfect generator – one we could afford.

To keep you out of suspense, after sorting through tons of literature and having many conversations with manufacturers, we decided on two: Yanmar and Lombardini. Both are diesel 5.5 kW units. Now we have an additional unit. Possibly a gas/petrol generator would work better for you, but we'll share our reasoning why we chose diesel. Reading our discoveries and factoring in your own particular situation, you'll find a generator just right for you.

We looked at worst-case scenarios. Suppose there were an extended power outage and we needed the generator for a month, maybe two or three. How heavy a unit would we need to run 8 hours a day for several months? Which unit, diesel or gas or tri-fuel, would stand up to this type use? What could we afford? How large of a fuel tank should we get? The big catch was fuel storage.

Just as important as the generator itself was the issue of fuel. When we bought the first generator, both of our vehicles were diesels. If we wanted to store fuel for the truck and SUV, did we want to store two separate fuels? Would the gas or diesel store indefinitely? How safe were they? We have owned both gas/petrol and diesel generators and for the following reasons, diesel has our vote even though the family vehicles use gas.

DIESEL, GAS (PETROL) OR TRIFUEL?

If you anticipate relying on a generator minimally, where you think utilities will be back in a few days or a couple of weeks, gas/petrol models are fine. Over longer periods, fuel gets expensive. If there could be an extended outage and this is your only source of power, you have to go with diesel. After Hurricanes Frances and Charley, some Floridians were without power for two months! Diesel generators take the lead for reliability, being nearly maintenance-free and most cost effective to run. Their main drawback is the up front cost. For continuous use, 1800 rpm diesel units are the overall best recommendation. Higher rpm generators wear out faster.

DIESEL	GAS TYPE			CHARACTERISTICS
	GASOLINE PETROL	PROPANE (LPG)	NAT'L. GAS	
X	X	-	-	Smelly / greasy
-	-	-	X	Fuel *not* storable
15 mos.	9 mos.	Indefinite	N/A	Fuel storage life
X	X	-	-	Fuel must be treated for storage *
X	-	X	-	Fuel stores easily in large quantity
X	X	-	-	Widest fuel availability / refills easily
Best	Better	Lower	Lowest	Fuel efficiency **
-	X	-	-	Possible insurance problem for fuel stored in quantity
-	X	X	X	Explosive on leak
X	X	-	-	Fuel easily portable / transferable
X	X	X	-	Multiple appliance use
-	-	X	X	Burns clean
X	-	-	-	Highest upfront cost
-	-	X	X	Fuel system = higher install costs, conversion kit ~$400.
Best	-	-	-	Easy maintenance; no carburetor, spark plugs or ignition system
20,000	10,000	10,000	10,000	Hours till first overhaul
Best	OK	Good	Good	Engine life best
X	X	Mostly	No	Suitable in earthquake areas
Best	Acceptable	see note***	-	Stable rpm's
X	X	-	-	Wide selection of models

* Fuel must be protected from extreme cold or warmed up to 37°F (3°C) to melt wax.
** Propane lowers generator output by 10%. Natural Gas lowers generator output by 20%.
*** If capacity to demand is sufficiently over-rated, you should be OK.

For impartial input, skip talking to retailers that sell only one type – their aim is to sell generators. Period. Do pick the brains of suppliers who offer both gas/petrol and diesel models. Naturally they want to sell the more expensive unit – diesel, but they'll be better versed on both sides of the issue. Talk to independent service people; ask for their assessment of each. They should be able to outline a good comparison of maintenance and reliability issues.

FIGURING WHAT SIZE GENERATOR TO BUY

To determine what size kW generator to buy, first decide what appliances you'll need to run off the generator. Add up the wattage for each appliance you want to run at the same time, **plus** the start-up wattage of the largest motor and any others that will be started simultaneously.

Most electrical products have a tag on them indicating the watts (sometimes abbreviated as W or kW). Other appliances will only list the amps (sometimes abbreviated as A) which is not the same thing. **TIP:** To figure watts when amps is given, multiply the amps by the volts. In America volts is 120; in Australia volts is 240.

For motorless appliances like TVs, toasters, electric blankets and skillets, radios or stoves, their power usage is pretty constant even at start up, within a few watts. These are resistive loads.

Appliances like vacuum cleaners, blow dryers, air conditioners, washers and dryers are all examples of reactive loads. When these appliances are first started, they may require as much as three times the amount of power compared to running power. When selecting a generator based on size needed, allow up to 3 times the amount of wattage for running appliances with motors, (appliances with reactive loads), plus a little breathing room for power surges.

If the appliance has an electric motor, multiply by 3 to figure the load factor which is another way of saying how much power is required at start-up. If your appliance doesn't have a motor, the formula is just amps x volts.

Appliance **With Motor**:   amps x volts x 3 = watts or kW needed (Reactive Load)

Appliance **Without Motor**:   amps x volts = watts or kW needed (Resistive Load)

This is a general guideline; it's not chiseled in stone. We ran a number of tests and compared the tag on the appliance to what the power meter read. In some cases, there was significant difference. For example, the tag on the hot water pot said the unit required 2200 kW for continual run, but it really took 2300 kW. Our 4-slice toaster's tag said it needed 1550 kW, but the power meter read 1730 for continual use. For this reason, we bought a power meter from Brand Electronics.

POWER METER

When we lived in Australia, power meters weren't available Downunder. Stan phoned Brand Electronics and spoke the owner, Ethan Brand, to see if his product would work on Aussie appliances. It didn't, but he happily agreed to wire one of these meters for Australian appliances since the plugs are shaped differently down there. Talk about service!

Our meter, which retailed around $250, was money well spent. Overloading a generator can damage the unit and/or the appliance/tool/motor running on it. Generators are too expensive and necessary to ruin. Think of a power meter as cheap insurance.

They are super-simple to use. Even the mechanically impaired won't be challenged.

USING A POWER METER

Plug the power meter into the outlet and plug the appliance into the power meter. The digital readout tells how many kW are needed to run the appliance continuously as well as surge/peak/start-up kW requirements. The total cost to run an appliance can be displayed by entering the cost per kilowatt hour (look on your electric bill or call your utility company). You can also calculate the cost to run the appliance for one month (the most common billing period for electric bills.)

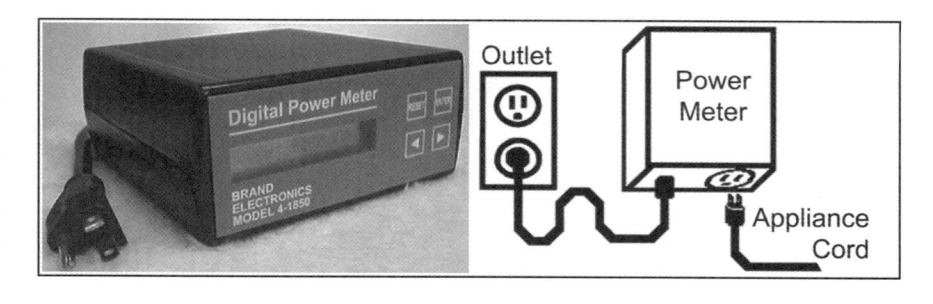

If you can't find a power meter in your area, contact Ethan Brand at Brand Electronics at: 801 2nd St, Kewaunee, WI 54216, Phone: 269-365-7744; **www.brandelectronics.com/**

Looking at the tags on the actual appliances and tools will give a clearer picture of how much power is required, but again, these aren't always accurate. It might be a good idea to make a chart of your different appliances and the load for each.

Then you can "mix and match" the different items without overloading the generator. The following chart gives you an idea of typical kW requirements to run appliances and tools. It doesn't matter if you're in America, Australia or Korea, a watt is a watt is a watt and one kW = 1000 watts.

GENERATOR WATTAGE REQUIREMENTS – HOUSEHOLD
(AMPS X VOLTS = WATTS)

APPLIANCE	RUNNING WATTS	START UP OR SURGE WATTS
Air Conditioner, Central		
10,000 BTU	1500	3750
20,000 BTU	2500	6250
24,000 BTU	3800	8750
32,000 BTU	5000	12500
40,000 BTU	6000	13000
Air Conditioner, Reverse Cycle	2700	6750
Blanket	400	400
Blender	200	3000
Blow Dryer, 1,600 watts		
High setting	1050	1055
Low setting	675	1055
Bread maker	550	550
Clothes Dryer		
Gas, convertible	700	1800
Electric	5750	1800
Coffee maker	1200-1750	1200-1750
Crock Pot	255	255
Deep Freezer	500	1500
Dehumidifier	650	800
Dishwasher		
Cool Dry	700	1400
Hot Dry	1450	1400
Fan		
Large, Floor model	200	00
Small, Table model	45	55
Floodlight	1000	1000
Furnace Fan/Blower (⅓ hp blower motor)	600	1800
Furnace Fan, gas or fuel oil		
⅛ hp	300	500
1/6 hp	500	750
¼ hp	600	1000
⅓ hp	700	1400
½ hp	875	2350
Garage Door Operator		
¼ hp	300	550
⅓ hp	725	1500
Hair Dryer	300-1200	300-1200
Hand-Held Mixer	135	170
Hot Plate (per burner)	1500	1500
Hot Water Pot	2300	2300
Iron	1200	1200
Juicer		
Small	170	330
Large	20	22
Knife	60	120
Light Bulb	as indicated on bulb	as indicated on bulb
Microwave Oven	625	800
	800	1200
Oven, Fan Forced		
Oven only	2200	2300
Grill only	2700	2800
Fan and Light	60	70
Popcorn Maker	1350	1450
Portable Heater (kerosene or diesel fuel)		
50,000 BTU	400	600

GENERATOR WATTAGE REQUIREMENTS – HOUSEHOLD
(AMPS X VOLTS = WATTS)

APPLIANCE	RUNNING WATTS	START UP OR SURGE WATTS
90,000 BTU	500	725
150,000 BTU	625	1000
Radio AM/FM	50-200	50-200
Radio, CB	50	50
Range, using one burner only		
6" (15cm) element	1250-1500	1250-1500
8" (20cm) element	2100	2100
Refrigerator/freezer	700-800	2200-2400
Skillet	1200-1300	1200-1300
Television, averages		
CRT	146	146
LCD, 40"	193	193
Plasma, 50" (127cm), post 2006 models	328	328
Rear-projection	208	208
Toaster, average		
2-slice	1050	1050
4-slice	1730	1800
Vacuum cleaner, canister type	1290	1670
Washing Machine	1150	2300
Water heater (storage type)	5000	5000

GENERATOR WATTAGE REQUIREMENTS – TOOLS

TOOLS	RUNNING WATTS	START UP OR SURGE WATTS
Air Compressor, average	2000	4000
½ hp	1000	2000
1 hp	1500	4500
1½ hp	2200	6000
2 hp	2800	7700
Battery Charger		
15 amp	380	380
60 amp with 250-amp boost	1500 / 5750	1500 / 5750
100 amp with 300-amp boost	2400 / 7800	2400 / 7800
Bench Grinder		
6" (15cm)	720	1000
8" (20cm)	1400	1400
10" (25cm)	1600	1600
Chain saw, average	1200	1200
12" (30.5cm), ½ hp	900	900
14" (35.5cm), 2 hp	1100	1100
Circular saw, average	1000-2500	2300-4600
6" (15.2cm)	800	1000
7¼" (18.5cm)	1400	2300
8¼" (21cm)	1800	3000
Concrete Cutter 12"	1500	3000
Drill		
¼" (.63cm)	350	350
⅜" (.95cm)	400	400
½" (1.27cm)	600-1000	600-1250
High Pressure Washer	1200	3600
Hedge Trimmer, 18" (46cm)	400	400
Line Trimmer / Whippersnipper		
Standard, 9" (23cm)	350	350
Heavy Duty, 12" (30.5cm)	500	500
Paint Sprayer	600	750

GENERATOR WATTAGE REQUIREMENTS – TOOLS

TOOLS	RUNNING WATTS	START UP OR SURGE WATTS
Pressure Washer		
⅝ Horsepower	900	2700
1 Horsepower	1200	3600
1½ Horsepower	1450	4300
3 Horsepower	3125	9300
Pumps		
Sump pump		
⅓ hp	800	1300
½ hp	1050	2150
Centrifugal, 900 gph (3407 lph)	400	400
Water Well pump (½ hp)	1000	3000
Well Pump		
⅓ hp	750	1400
½ hp	1000	2100
Submersible, 400 gph (1514 lph)	200	200
Router	1000	1000
Sander		
Belt	1000	1000
Disc	2000	4000
Saws, Misc.		
Worm Drive, 7¼" (18cm)	1800	2600
Band Saw, 14" (35.5cm)	1100	1400
Soldering Iron	200	200
Table Saws		
9" (23cm)	1500	3000
10" (25cm)	1800	4500
Miter Saw, 10 amp	1100	2000
Miter Saw, 15 amp	1650	3000
Welder		
200 amp AC	9000	9000
230 amp AC, at 100 amp	7800	7800
Wet/Dry Vac		
1.7 hp	900	900
2½ hp	1300	1300

GENERATOR WATTAGE REQUIREMENTS – FARM

FARM	RUNNING WATTS	START UP OR SURGE WATTS
Electric Fence, 25 miles	250	250
Milk Cooler	1100	1800
Milker (vacuum pump) 2 hp	1100	2300

GENERATOR WATTAGE REQUIREMENTS – INDUSTRIAL MOTORS

MOTORS	RUNNING WATTS	START UP OR SURGE WATTS
Split Phase		
¼ hp	600	1000
½ hp	1000	2000
Capacitor Start Induction Run		
⅓ hp	720	1300
1 hp	1600	4500
Capacitor Start Induction Run		
1½ hp	2000	6100
Fan Duty	650	1200

RUNNING A COMPUTER FROM A GENERATOR

Computers are delicate equipment and don't tolerate electrical spikes well. When looking for a generator, you may see the term "brush" and "brushless". These brushes take electricity out of the generator's coils. When in operation, they can cause small spikes or harmonic distortions. Brushes tend to rust and corrode unless the generator is kept in a dehumidified environment. To run a computer or any sensitive electronic equipment, it's best to either purchase a brushless generator or put on a smoothing filter.

Since so many computers are on the market today, it's nearly impossible to accurately plot their watts usage. Most monitors connect to the computer's USB port without having a separate wattage requirement. Factor in a wide selection of computer and monitor sizes, CRT or LCD, dual or single processors and what size, graphics cards plus an array of peripherals to consider. You'll need to check on your computer's specific requirements for an accurate assessment.

RUNNING A MOTOR FROM A GENERATOR

While these motors may not use a lot of watts during use (see Running Watts), they take a good deal more during the first several seconds of start-up time. These large start-up amounts must be factored in when buying a generator. Below are 4 types of motors and the start-up wattage required for each.

HP	RUNNING WATTS	APPROXIMATE STARTING WATTS			
		Universal Motors (small appliances)	Repulsion Induction Motors	Capacitor Motors	Split Phase Motor
1/8	275	400	600	850	1,200
1/4	400	500	850	1,050	1,700
1/3	450	600	975	1,350	1,950
1/2	600	750	1,300	1,800	2,600
3/4	850	1,000	1,900	2,600	x
1	1,000	1,250	2,300	3,000	x
1 1/2	1,600	1,750	3,200	4,200	x
2	2,000	2,350	3,900	5,100	x
3	3,000	x	5,200	6,800	x

x – Motors of higher horsepower aren't generally used. Some larger motors don't list the watt requirements. Instead, they are labeled with a letter.

ONCE YOU GET THE GENERATOR HOME...

The next decision is where to put it. Generators must never, **never ever** be run indoors. Period. During the extended Canadian/upper New England ice storm in January '98, several people died from carbon monoxide poisoning using their generator indoors. Sadly, more people perished in the same way during the massive power outage August 2003 in Canada and the U.S. northeast and again during Winter 2007-2008. Every year, just in the U.S. alone, carbon monoxide poisoning kills an average of 4,000 people. It's the #1 cause of poisoning deaths.

Don't use a generator indoors or in any room connecting to your home like a garage.

Carbon monoxide has a nasty way of seeping in around vents and ill-fitting doors and windows. Symptoms include nausea, headaches, general weakness and shortness of breath. At higher levels, people develop poor judgment, confusion and sometimes chest pain.

Protect the generator from weather to prevent corrosion. When under cover, it should not butt to walls. Leave at least 3 feet (1 meter) of room around all sides for air circulation and so nothing is burned by the exhaust pipe.

TIPS

Don't bolt the generator to the floor. They can vibrate creating even more noise than if left unbolted. Another tip is to rest the unit on polystyrene foam to further lessen vibration.

Unless the generator has a muffler, it's going to make noise. The bigger they are, the noisier they'll be. There's a fine line between locating it conveniently to everything it needs to power and how close is TOO close!

If the generator is in a semi-permanent location, install a light overhead. Murphy's law dictates that when a generator needs re-fueling, it will be at night.

CONNECTING IT: TRANSFER SWITCH

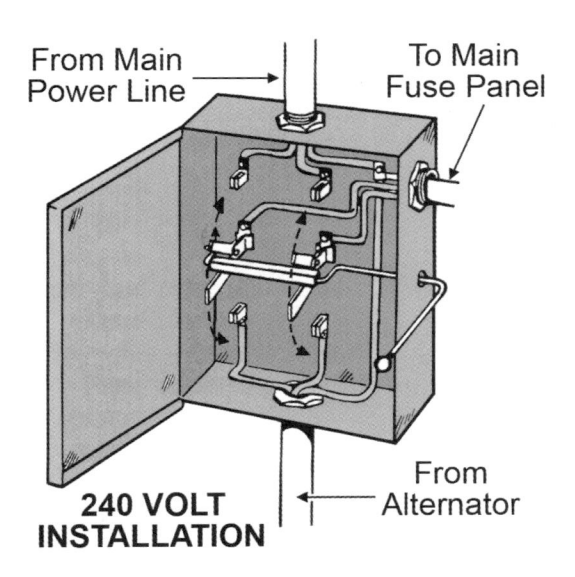

From Main Power Line → **To Main Fuse Panel** ← **From Alternator**

240 VOLT INSTALLATION

What's that? A transfer switch or Double Pole Double Throw (DPDT) safely links a backup generator to your home or business during a power outage. Properly installed, it isolates your generator from the utility company's power lines. Unless you are a licensed electrician, it's highly recommended the generator be professionally wired with a transfer switch.

By far, the transfer switch is the safest, cleanest way to hook up a generator. This switch is installed in your home's breaker box. For an electrician, it's fairly simple work. By having it installed professionally, there won't be incorrect wiring or nasty shocks – literally!

MANUAL VS. AUTOMATIC

With a manual transfer switch, when the power goes out, you need to start your generator, connect it to the transfer switch, then switch your house over to generator power. When the utility power is restored, switch your house back to utility power and turn off your generator.

With an automatic transfer switch, when the utility power goes out, the transfer switch signals your generator to start. Once the generator is running the transfer switch automatically connects your home or business to the generator. When power is restored, the transfer switch reconnects your home or business to the utility. It then turns off your generator and waits for the next power outage.

Photo: Power outages stem from a wide array of causes. Lightning is just one culprit. Pictured here is a thunderstorm at Pueblo Reservoir, Colorado. (Stephen Hodanish, Senior Meteorologist; National Weather Service, Pueblo, CO)

PLAN B: CONNECTING IT WITH EXTENSION CORDS

The alternative is to use heavy gauge (#10 and better) extension cords. This is less desirable than wiring the generator into the breaker box. Extension cords cause a small drop in usable power and they aren't quite as safe. Cords outside can become weathered and are subject to overloading in emergencies through hasty connections. Extension cords must never be run through puddles or standing water to reach the generator.

The easiest way to hook up a generator is with an extension cord. There are two important things to remember:

1. The maximum amount of current provided by an extension cord depends on the type of insulation used to make the cord and the number of conductors the cord has.

2. Because current is passed through resistance in the wire, plan for a drop in voltage. Keep this voltage drop under 2% to avoid damaging the appliance and keep it running efficiently. Using larger sized wire or removing some appliances from the generator can reduce this drop.

Although a 2% drop in current is safe, these charts are a little stricter so there's no danger of overloading the generator, damaging the appliance or seeing a power drop. Listings for 14 and 12-gauge extension cords are included, but they aren't encouraged due to safety issues. The general consensus is to stick to 10, 8 and 6 gauge extension cords.

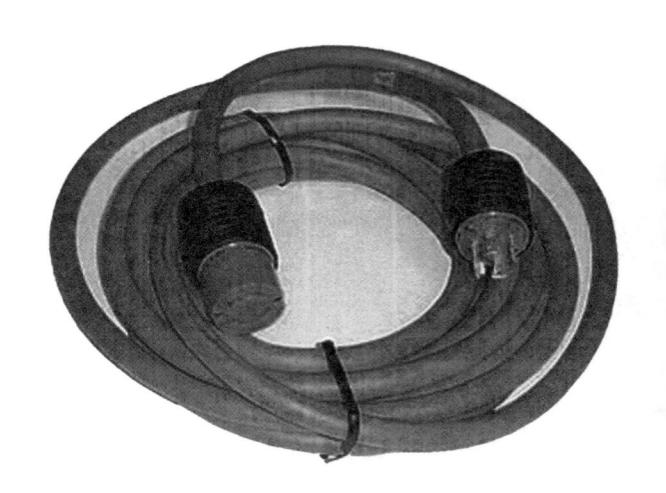

WHICH GAUGE EXTENTION CORD TO USE

To use this chart, if your generator is a 650 Honda, use the line for 600 watts and read across. It says for a #12 extension cord, the maximum length to use is 150' before there is a power drop.

If you wanted to use a #10 gauge cord, you could use up to a 225' extension cord. An #8 gauge will accept 380' of extension cord and a #6 gauge can take 600' of extension cord. In the spaces where it reads "DO NOT USE", the amount of voltage passing through these extension cords isn't safe and should never be used.

MAX. LENGTH EXTENSION CORD (FEET) AT 110V WITH 1% MAX. VOLTAGE Loss to Appliance/Tool – Using A.W.G. Safe Current Loadings						
110 VOLTS		MAX EXTENSION CORD LENGTH FOR GIVEN WIRE SIZE				
Amps	Watts	#14 AWG	#12 AWG	#10 AWG	#8 AWG	#6 AWG
1	120	470	750	1,120	1,900	3,000
5	600	95	150	225	380	600
10	1,200	DO NOT USE	75	110	190	300
15	1,800	DO NOT USE	DO NOT USE	75	125	200
20	2,400	DO NOT USE	DO NOT USE	DO NOT USE	95	150
25	3,000	DO NOT USE	DO NOT USE	DO NOT USE	*75	120
30	3,600	DO NOT USE	DO NOT USE	DO NOT USE	DO NOT USE	100
35	4200	DO NOT USE	DO NOT USE	DO NOT USE	DO NOT USE	85
40	4,800	DO NOT USE	DO NOT USE	DO NOT USE	DO NOT USE	*75

* These values are marginally safe; so if they have to be used, keep the wires well ventilated.

For Australia, the chart works the same way. Due to the higher voltage, the range is slightly different. If you have a 5 kW generator, use the last line, you'll see only the 3.3mm and 4.1mm extension cords are OK to use.

MAX. LENGTH EXTENSION CORD (METERS) AT 240V WITH 1% MAX. VOLTAGE
Loss to Appliance/Tool – Using A.W.G. Safe Current Loadings

240 VOLTS		MAX EXTENSION CORD LENGTH FOR GIVEN WIRE SIZE				
Amps	Watts	1.6mm	2.0mm	2.6mm	3.3mm	4.1mm
1.0	240	285	455	685	1,155	1,830
5.0	1,200	55	90	135	230	365
7.5	1,800	DO NOT USE	60	90	155	245
10.0	2,400	DO NOT USE	*45	70	115	185
12.5	3,000	DO NOT USE	DO NOT USE	55	90	145
15.0	3,600	DO NOT USE	DO NOT USE	*45	75	120
17.5	4,200	DO NOT USE	DO NOT USE	DO NOT USE	65	105
20.0	4,800	DO NOT USE	DO NOT USE	DO NOT USE	55	90

* These values are marginally safe; so if they have to be used, keep the wires well ventilated.

When using a smaller generator that has two outlets, the manufacturer may recommend splitting the power drawn from each outlet. If this is so, try to get each outlet divided as closely as possible. This is known as "balancing the load" and will make the generator run more efficiently.

CARE AND MAINTENANCE

GAS (PETROL)

A gas/petrol generator burns unleaded fuel. Be sure to keep extra spark plugs on hand. Regular maintenance includes oil changes, replacing the air-cleaner, spark plugs, ignition points, rotors, distributor caps and plug wires, and electronic ignition modules if used. Occasionally the carburetor will need adjustments and/or overhauls and a general tune-up.

DIESEL

Maintenance for a diesel model is pretty much just regular oil changes. It's very important to keep the fuel injectors clean and free of debris, which any good-quality fuel filter should do.

Be sure to use at least 40% of a diesel generator's capacity while running it. This ensures that the fuel burns completely and the system won't produce carbon.

Diesels work best when not started for short projects of 10 minutes or less. According to Skip Thomsen of Backwoods Home Magazine, the secret for long life in any engine is simple. For diesels "ideally, the generator should be started and allowed to reach normal operating temperature before any big loads are applied, and it should again be allowed to run at a light load for a few minutes before shut-down. The reason is to avoid rapid temperature fluctuations. One secret of long life (of any engine, actually) is to allow it to make its necessary temperature fluctuations gradually. Shutting down an engine after it's just been running at full load for a while means that it will cool more rapidly than is healthy for it."[71]

FOR BOTH

- Check the oil frequently if your generator doesn't have an automatic low-oil shut off. Many of your better generators have this feature built in. Unless something else is specified in your manual, use good quality 30w or 10w30 oil, which is recommended by most generator manufacturers.
- Wipe down the generator frequently. This will help you spot any oil leaks.
- Keep all the seals and engine parts lubricated by starting your generator monthly. Let it run 30 minutes to an hour. This will ensure that the battery remains charged which powers the electric start. For women, an electric starter is an especially nice feature!
- Store spare air and oil filter (if used) as well as motor oil.
- Generators can be tougher to start in the winter or if they have sat for a long time without start-up. It's also clever to keep starting fluid available.

- Make sure there is adequate room around your generator for easy servicing.
- Keep track of hours operated for service timing if your generator isn't equipped with an hour meter. Alternately, keep an "hours used" log by the breaker box, if the unit is wired in with a transfer switch. If not, keep your log with the generator.

FEATURES TO CONSIDER
- Brushless, to prevent power spiking
- Electric start, beats cranking!
- Low oil shut-off, to prevent engine from burning up
- Premium class-H insulation throughout
- Built-in battery charger
- Muffler
- Wheels for easier portability

One person can carry smaller units like 650's. Units in the 5 kW range require two people or a wheel kit. This is good idea if you plan on moving it around, but it also aids would-be thieves.

If you think you might need to use a generator for longer-term power sources, without question, diesel is the way to go. In the long run, they don't cost any more considering the fuel savings and the lack of repairs and maintenance work.

For longest life and quieter running in either diesel or gas/petrol models, purchase an 1800 rpm generator. They will run the best and have the longest life. Words like "consumer use" should tip you off that this generator is light duty only, even when specified "heavy duty". They wear out much faster. If you expect to use your generator for very light, intermittent duty, a gas unit works well and is less money up front. Does anyone have a crystal ball?

THEFT PREVENTION

After Hurricane Katrina generator theft was rampant. It is often the case after nearly every prolonged disaster. Imagine being without power for a week, then 6 weeks, then three months. It got *very* unpleasant, very quickly and people were brazen about stealing generators. Need overcame fear of getting caught.

Because generators can **never** be used indoors, they are vulnerable to theft outside. Don't be tempted to move it indoors under *any* circumstances. Carbon monoxide is completely odorless, colorless and tasteless. Every year people die because of improper use.

As this internal government report from 2006 stated, *"Based on the most recent CPSC staff analysis of the in-depth investigations (IDI) staff conducted on fatal incidents, the majority of reported CO [carbon monoxide] deaths associated with generators occurred during the winter months at a home location, including in a garage or shed at the residence. In the 146 deaths that occurred at home, the majority resulted when the generator was operated in the basement or crawlspace, garage enclosed carport or living space of the home. Fear of generator theft and concern about noise to neighbors were two of the most common reasons mentioned for using the generator indoors when a reason was given. At least five deaths occurred when the generator was operated outside the home near an open window, door, or vent that allowed CO to enter the home."*[72]

Outside, take measures to secure your unit. Below are measures to keep your generator from walking off. Some of these methods aren't "bullet-proof", but the resulting noise and inconvenience involved to steal a secured unit may delay them long enough for you to dissuade them by whatever means you choose.

1. Keep it in the garage and <u>properly</u> vent the exhaust outside. Correct venting is **critical**. If you aren't extremely knowledgeable in this area, have a professional do the job. Install a carbon monoxide detector to monitor any leaks.
2. Anchor the generator with hardened stainless steel security chains embedded in a concrete pad.
3. Weave the chain through wheels if possible, and attach to other heavy items that can't be easily loaded by hand onto a trailer. Use multiple locks like those in the ABUS Diskus series. Using recessed hasps discourage bolt-cutters. Additional recessed hasp locks can slow even a determined thief.
4. Better solution, secure the unit with a heavy, hardened chain like ABUS 14mm chain and a security lock like ABUS Granit Plus.
5. If you have the means, install the generator on a concrete block, bolted down, inside a heavily insulated shed. Install a muffler on the genny and any noise should be well disguised. A heavy-duty muffler goes a long way to disguise its

Hardened Steel Lock

presence.
6. You can also use galvanized anchor augers which you screw into the ground and then lock to the generator with chain or thick metal cables.
7. You can also install security lighting and motion detectors which are battery-powered with rechargeable batteries.

For sources of theft protection and other valuable accessories for your generator check these websites:

Lockitt: **www.lockitt.com**
Tulsa Chain: **www.tulsachain.com**
Xena Security: **www.xenasecurity.com**
Global Industrial: **www.globalindustrial.com**
Harbor Freight Tools: **www.harborfreight.com**

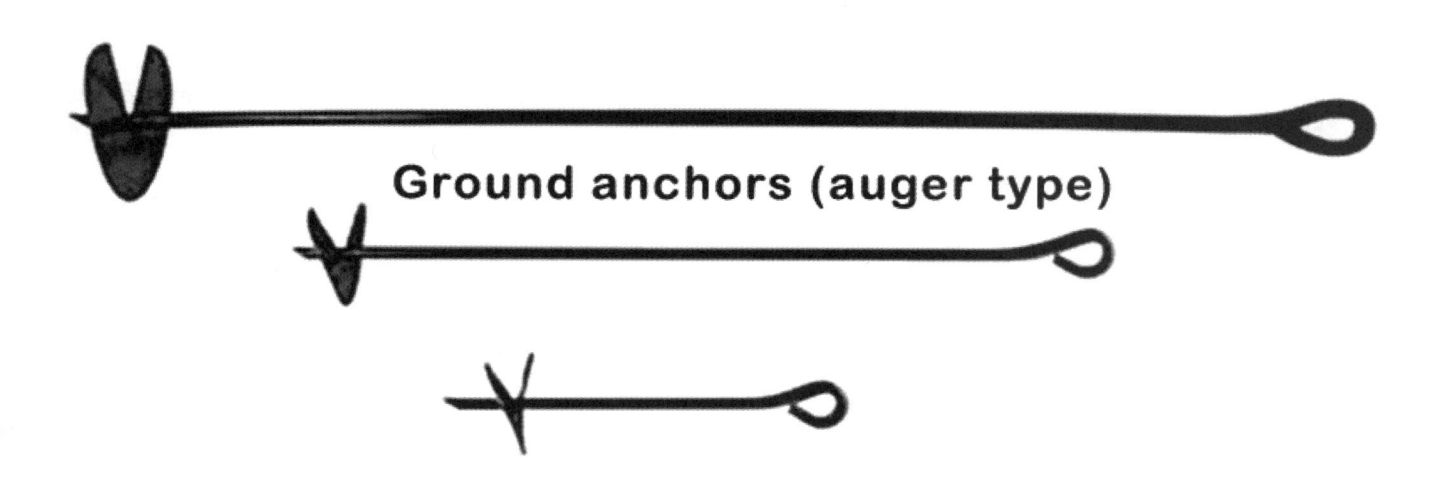

Ground anchors (auger type)

Chapter 30: Fuel

WHY SHOULD WE STORE FUEL?

Power outages and "feeding" your generator are just two reasons to keep fuel on hand. The image on the left greeted many Floridians when they were ordered to evacuate before Hurricane Frances. Evac routes that *should* have taken only two hours to cross were mired in 10-hour gridlock. While waiting for cars to inch forward, many ran out of gas. People who left too late, found no gas at service stations.

Photo: Fort Lauderdale, Florida, Sept. 2, 2004. Gas stations ran out of fuel as residents prepared for Hurricane Frances. (FEMA Photo / Mark Wolfe)

KEEP IT CLEAN

Having the best generator in the world won't help if your stored fuel isn't usable. Considering "70% of all back-up generator failures are fuel related,"[73] it's a concern. With the oxygenation of both diesel and gas, fuel is less stable, which makes it deteriorate faster. Today's fuel has an even shorter storage life. Gas/petrol keeps about 3 months, diesel about 1 year. Two simple things give you an edge:
1. Buy fuel from reputable companies. Don't buy off brands; they may sell lesser quality fuel.
2. Buy fuel from high-traffic service stations. Their supplies will be fresher with larger turnover.

STORING FUEL

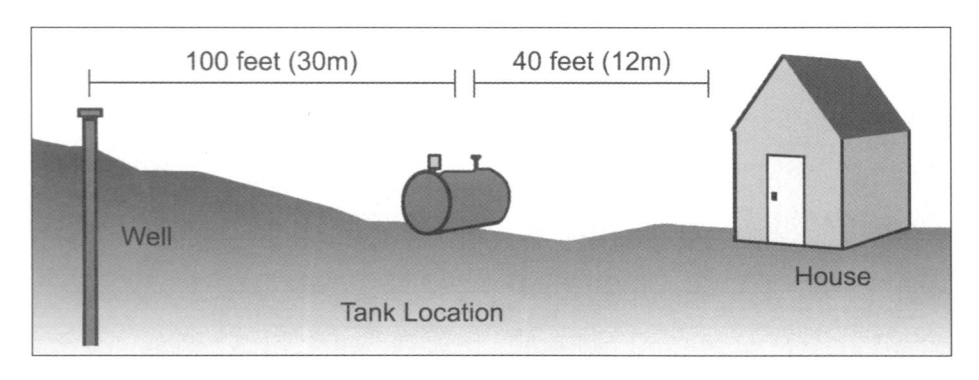

Where you live is the biggest factor in choosing your fuel storage. Gas/petrol is especially gas extremely flammable and should be stored at least 40' (12m) away from your home.[74]

Many regulations state fuel shouldn't be stored any closer than 100' (30.5m) to a water well on the downslope from the well. Check with your particular state or province for its requirements if storing large quantities of gas/petrol or diesel.

In Canada, if fuel tanks are within 500 meters (550 yards) of a water well or 200 meters (220 yards) from a surface water source, this is considered a Class A site and secondary containment is required. A pit liner must be installed or double-walled tanks and piping must be used.

FUEL STORAGE LOCATIONS

Factor	Underground	On-ground	Overhead
Purchase costs	medium	medium	low
Installation costs	high	medium	low
Fire hazard	lowest	medium	highest
Risk of accidental damage	lowest	medium	highest
Leak detection	difficult	vertical tanks – difficult / horizontal tanks – easy	easiest
Leak repair and cleanup	most difficult	difficult	least difficult
Risk of theft, vandalism	low	medium	high
Temperature variations, fuel degradation, evaporation and condensation	low	medium	high
Pumps and meters required?	yes	yes	no
Maintenance	pumps and meters	pumps and meters, painting cans	painting tanks and stamp
Record keeping	critical	vertical tanks – critical / horizontal tanks – important	recommended
Other	corrosion protection for steel tanks	dike recommended	dike recommended

STORING FUEL UNDERGROUND

Burying fuel tanks isn't easy or cheap. Environmental issues and lots of regulations govern underground storage. Gas leaks in buried tanks are harder to monitor and more difficult to clean up. The biggest concern for underground storage is that tanks will corrode and contaminate water tables. However, for gas/petrol, it's by far the safest form of storage due to volatility. Gas leaks are highly flammable and can explode.

Underground storage also keeps your fuel safer from intruders who might like to help themselves. Think it won't happen? It already has.

When gasoline hit $2 a gallon in 2004, "gas and dash" – filling up and not paying – jumped dramatically.[75] (In 2008, $2 gas would have been a gift!) Four years later when fuel prices doubled, "gas and dash" reappeared along with thefts where thieves tampered with the pumps.

In 2006, convenience stores lost $122 million due to gas theft. "The stuff is like liquid gold. Of course people are going to be stealing it more," Washington's King County Sheriff's Sgt. John Urquhart said.[76]

As times get tougher and especially in prolonged disasters, keeping your stored fuel from prying eyes will be very important.

CONTAINERS

So what are the options? Using a 5-gallon (20L) *metal* Jerry can is a better choice than plastic for gasoline due to volatility. The drawback for this size is the number of cans that's needed to store larger quantities of fuel.

Even storing fuel adequate for a generator adds up. Take for example the Honda EG2500XK1 2500 watt gas/petrol unit. This economy model uses one gallon (3.78L) of fuel every three hours. For three months, using it 8 hours a day is 730 hours. Every day, it would consume 2⅔ gallons (10L) of gas. In 3 months' time, you would need 243 gallons (920L) of fuel. To store this amount of gas requires 49 5-gallon or 47 20-liter Jerry cans. Because diesel generators consume roughly 50% less fuel, the number of Jerry cans needed is cut in half.

There is a huge difference in the price of these cans. Grade A plastic containers in Australia cost around $7 – a very good price! New ones is the U.S. range from $10 to $20. If you find a deal on metal Jerry cans, you might pay US$28. NATO-approved Jerry cans run US$49 and OSHA-approved gas cans sell for up to $78.

Price concerns aside, metal jerry cans are better due to safety issues and if you want to keep it transportable. On the downside, small containers are easier for people to steal. Plastic fuel cans are fine for diesel since combustibility isn't such an issue.

Be sure to leave a *little* space at the container's top for expansion during warm weather. If you see plastic containers bulge, "burp" them by opening and closing the vent. Make sure the vent points away from you to avoid splashing.

FUEL DRUMS

Besides Jerry cans, think about 30, 44 or 55-gallon drums. New drums have been quoted at US$50-80 and used drums around $20 for the 55- gallon size.

Diesel has a tendency to wax or gum up during cold temperatures. After talking with the chemical engineering departments of three leading fuel companies, all suggested storing diesel in an enclosed area that's heated during winter. To prevent fuel waxing, keep diesel stored above 32°F (0°C). Wrapping insulating foam around tanks helps in colder temperatures.

Drum Truck

DRUM SOURCES

Many commercial fuel suppliers like Mobile and BP sell new and used drums. New drums were quoted around $45 and used containers around $5 for the 55-gallon size. Occasionally you'll find drums and storage tanks for the right price at industrial equipment auctions. One excellent source for all types of containers – water, food and fuel – is Basco, which has six distribution centers throughout the U.S. The company president, Richard Rudy, underscored that no order is too small. In speaking with other container companies, they frankly didn't want to bother with small orders.

Contact Basco about products or order a catalog to peruse at your leisure at: Basco, 2595 Palmer Avenue, University Park, Illinois 60466; 1.800.776.3786, Fax 708.534.0902 **www.bascousa.com/.** Global Equipment Company also has a good selection. Contact information: PO Box 100090; Buford, GA 30515-9090; 1.888.978.7759, **www.globalindustrial.com**.

INDISPENSABLE HELPERS

A drum truck is essential is if you store fuel in large containers. When it's necessary to relocate fuel, the question is *how?* without draining it. Since 55 gallons (208L) of unleaded gas/petrol weighs 341 pounds (155kg) and diesel weighs about 396 pounds (180kg), moving it without help is impossible.

We purchased this Harper Drum Truck, model #9361. Other styles and brands are available, but when Stan talked with fuel *handlers* – not the retailers – this was their preferred choice over similar versions.

It loads easily onto two steel "toes" that slide under the drum. These toes are easier to maneuver than a full steel plate used on some models. A hook holds the drum in place, and slides up and down to accommodate different drum sizes. This is an important feature to keep the drum stable. Without the hook, once full drums start to tip, there's no stopping them. You need the toes and hook.

Most adjust for heights between 30" and 42". This particular model is rated to carry up to 800 pounds, which is more than enough grunt for fuel or water barrels. We keep the drum truck right by the fuel since the kickstand lets it stand up straight for out-of-the-way storage.

One style to avoid is the drum dolly. While priced less than the drum truck at $45-50, keep in mind that once you put the drum in place and fill it, the drum will end up "living" on the dolly. Due to fuel weight, you'd be unable to lift it off to move other drums. Even if you dedicate the dolly to one drum, it works best on flat surfaces only. Pushing it uphill or controlling it on a downward slope would be tricky if not impossible. If you purchase a drum dolly be sure to check its rated weight load. Several models look just the same but are rated differently.

BUILD A DRUM DOLLY

You can make your own drum dolly, but it has the same limitation. Still, they wouldn't cost $45, which seems to be the average price for this style pictured below. See instructions below.

This design project supports a 55-gallon metal drum, in a vertical position on four equally spaced casters. They make the drum mobile and easy to move on flat plane surfaces.

| MATERIALS NEEDED FOR A DRUM DOLLY ||||
Drawing No.	Name	Material	Qty.
1	Rolled Circle	Flat steel 2" x ¼" x 76"	1
2	Vertical diameter	Flat steel 2" x ¼" x 24"	1
3	Horizontal diameter	Flat steel 2" x ¼" x 11"	2
4	Caster Supports	Steel pipe 1" diameter x 3" long	4
5	Caster Support Covers	Steel rod 1" diameter x ⅛" thick	4
6	Colson casters	Self-locking wheels 3½" diameter	4

Step 1 Take a length of 2" x ¼" x 76" long flat steel and mechanically roll it into a 24" diameter circle.

Step 2 Where the ends meet, tack weld them together leaving a ⅛ gap, then make a full penetration butt weld, making the circle complete.

Step 3 Position circle on flat table with the ¼" side down.

Step 4 Lift up circle slightly and slide 2" x ¼ x 24" flat steel under circle, so that the circle is supported at top and bottom of its diameter. This flat steel should have the 2" side flat down on the table, thus raising the circle ¼".

Step 5 Slide 2" x ¼ x 11" length of flat steel from left to right to form half of the circle's horizontal diameter, (allow ⅛" gap at center for weld).

Step 6 Slide 2" x ¼" x 11" length of flat steel from right to left to form the other half of the horizontal diameter (allow ⅛ gap at center for weld).

Step 7 Use a small square and rule to equally space the vertical and horizontal diameter now created by the flat steel supports.

Step 8 Weld the vertical 2"x¼"x24" length of flat steel at both ends of the circle.

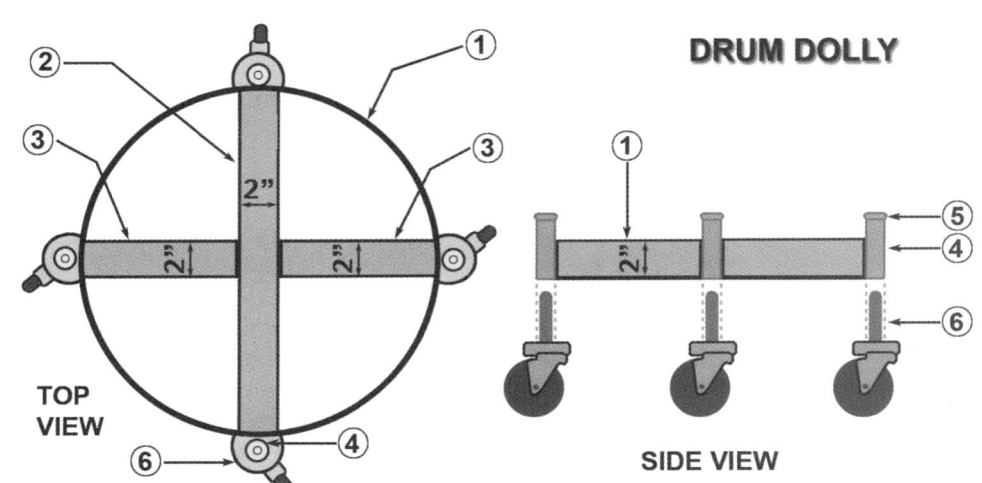

DRUM DOLLY

TOP VIEW

SIDE VIEW

Step 9 Weld the horizontal pieces of flat steel into position.
Step 10 Position the caster supports at the ends where the horizontal and vertical supports meet the outside of the circle. These pieces of pipe must be in a vertical position. Weld both sides of pipe at all four stations around circle.
Step 11 Cut four slices off a solid 1" diameter steel rod ⅛" wide and weld each on top of the four 3" pieces of pipe. These act as cosmetic covers for the wheel assembly, and are called caster support covers.
Step 12 Remove slag, grind and paint, insert Colson casters into 1" diameter pipe from the bottom. Casters are self-locking and will tighten into the 1" diameter. The design project is now completed.

GETTING THE FUEL OUT

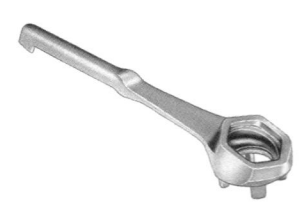

Two other important accessories are a bung wrench for unscrewing the drum caps and a manual drum pump. Not only do manual pumps bypass electricity, there's no chance of sparks causing an explosion. Since it's vital to access fuel, don't purchase a cheap plastic pump that may fail. These products are flimsy with only a plastic plunger to pump the fuel.

Pumping liquids out of storage drums is easy. Just turn the crank and liquids safely pull up the 1" suction tube and dispense from the outlet tube. The pump housing is both chemical- and rust-resistant. All models screw right into the bunghole on the drum's lid, which frees one hand while the other turns the crank.

These pumps work equally well with different liquids including oil, gasoline, kerosene, corrosive chemicals, juice, milk, wine and water. Some models are specifically NOT for use with fuels or corrosive liquids. Make sure it's fuel rated.

Among the materials to choose from are aluminum, cast iron, stainless steel and polypropylene. Any of these are sturdy enough and won't break the bank ranging from $50-$200. The models below run $80 for the polypropylene; $50 for cast iron; $60 for stainless steel and $70 for aluminum (not pictured).

Polypropylene Rotary Hand Pump

Cast Iron Rotary Hand Pump

Shaker Siphon

Stainless Manual Pump

One other nifty and inexpensive item is the Shaker Siphon or Jiggler as its marketed in Australia. For only $11, this handy little hose meets a multitude of needs. All you do is shake the hose to make it work! To use, place the small metal pump end in the liquid you wish to extract, jiggle the pump up and down, and the siphon does the rest. Yes, it's that easy! We purchased our first ones in Australia over a decade ago and they work very efficiently. After coming back to the States, Stan purchased replacements since the heavy plastic became brittle from exposure to fuel and normal aging. They're great for the workshop as well as filling a vehicle's gas tank with stored fuel. All pump models discussed can be used with 15, 30 and 55-gallon drums.

KEEPING FUEL FROM DEGRADING

Whether it's diesel or gas/petrol, keep fuel out of direct sunlight. Heat encourages condensation build up which collects in the bottom of the drum. Make sure the storage tank has a valve so this water can be drained easily. If your fuel is frequently rotated, it may not become a problem. Keeping fuel drums topped off also discourages water accumulation. Air and water both accelerate fuel degradation. You can prevent bacterial growth in diesel by adding a biocide.

FUEL STABILIZERS

Several products greatly help fuel storage, but without question, the best is PRI. Use PRI-D for diesel and kerosene and PRI-G for gas/petrol lets you keep fuel for a decade or more, simply by adding this product every 9-10 months. PRI has restored totally gummy, otherwise unusable fuel back to refinery specifications, even after 15 years. It prevents carbon build up, keeps fuel systems clean and at the same time, keeps tanks from corroding and collecting slime. You can read their test data results online: **www.priproducts.com**.

Originally developed for refiners, PRI's unique chemistry is an industrial-grade treatment. Their impressive client list includes nuclear power plants, major ISPs like AOL, telephone companies, boating and marines companies, hospitals and emergency services. They use PRI because they can't afford fuel failures. Lives may depend on it. They rely on PRI to keep back-up generators operating. The same industrial strength PRI-D used by these facilities is available but in smaller, containers. Currently it's the only commercial-grade product available to the public.

Stan and I first ordered PRI when we lived in Australia. We had it shipped Downunder since the product wasn't available locally and have used it ever since. In fact, we wouldn't be without it.

In the U.S. a 32oz. bottle runs $30-40. Shop around as retail prices vary widely. The best value may be found at Camping World **www.campingworld.com**. In US and Canada 1.888.626.7576. Other locations: 1.270.781.2718 or Survival Unlimited **www.survivalunlimited.com** 1.800.455.2201.

PRI FUEL STABILIZER			
BOTTLE SIZE		**1 BOTTLE TREATS**	
16 oz	473ml	256 gallons	969 liters
32 oz	907ml	512 gallons	1,938 liters
1 Gal	1. 78L	2,000 gallons	7,570 liters

The KEY to any storage program, whether it's food, fuel, water or medication, is rotation. When we can eliminate the need for constant vigilance to rotate goods, it's one thing off our minds. Fuel is so precious especially in times of crisis, and fuel and food supplies are the first things to be cut off. Anyone who lived through gas lines, sometimes taking half a day to *maybe* get fuel, will really appreciate this product.

Another product on the market is STA-BIL. It's readily available in the States at hardware and discount stores for about $12 for 32 oz. This size will treat up to 80 gallons. STA-BIL has the same goal as PRI but falls short of the mark for long-term storage. At best, it extends gas/petrol's shelf life to 9 months and diesel's to 15 months. For diesel, this is not much longer than its natural shelf life. Using this product is better than adding nothing, but if you can locate PRI, we highly recommend it.

FUELBIOCIDE FT-400 is sold by Fueltreat Australia but is a biocide only. PRI makes a similar product, PRI-OCIDE. While this is a good idea for keeping fuel clean and usable, it does nothing for shelf life. We did not find a product like PRI-D, PRI-G or STA-BIL in Australia. If you can't locate PRI products locally, you can reach their company at 713.490.1100.

Chapter 31: Cooking Without Power

Most of us rely on gas or electricity to cook meals, heat water, warm and cool our homes, and provide power for appliances. In short, they power nearly everything that makes our lives work. A variety of situations deliver power outages or interrupt services so it's a good idea to have alternate cooking methods available.

THE BURNING QUESTION...FUELS

The first consideration is fuel. Look through the comparison chart to see what works for you. If you live in an apartment or mobile home park, storing gas or petrol isn't an option. If you have a fireplace or a balcony or access to even a small outside area, your choices are broader.

According to Hearth, Patio, and Barbecue Association, 4 out of 5 households in America own a barbecue grill and more than half already cook on them year round.[77] With the nearly year-round good weather in Australia, grill owners must be close to if not exceeding that percentage. If you already own a grill, why re-invent the wheel? Your best option might be storing extra charcoal or propane. Propane camp stoves are also a practical choice as well as a Volcano stove.

There is a solution for everyone though some are more economical and space saving than others. Write down the options you must have for your particular situation and plan from there.

FUEL CHOICES
*Note: Fuels below within same color row are the same substance by other names.

FUELS AND ALTERNATE NAMES	PROS	CONS	OK TO USE
Butane Butane Blends Isobutane	Convenient Clean-burning Easy lighting, no priming or pumping Burns hot immediately Adjusts easily for simmering Can't spill Easy refilling – snap on new canister Works well in higher altitudes	More expensive Most fuel canisters aren't recyclable Performance decreases in temps below freezing. Blended alternatives like Butane-Propane and Isobutane work better in cold conditions.	Indoors or Outdoors
Kerosene Liquid Range Oil No. 1 Paraffin Kero Jet-A	Very Inexpensive Easy to find worldwide Burns easily High heat output Low volatility Can be used indoors Odorless except during lighting	Burns dirty Has an odor when igniting Priming required Can gum up stove parts Uses oxygen in a room; crack a window about ½" (1.27cm)	Indoors or Outdoors
White Gas Coleman Fuel, Shellite, Mobilite, Callite, Britolite, Pegasol, Fuelite, Washing Benzene, Lighter Fluid, Afta, Naptha, Blazo **NOTE**: This isn't gasoline	Inexpensive Easy to find Clean burning Easy to light Spilled fuel evaporates quickly Produces a lot of heat	More expensive in Australia Little harder to find outside of U.S. Volatile (spilled fuel can ignite quickly) Priming required Produces carbon monoxide Store outside, away from heaters Can evaporate like Sterno Highly flammable, use care	Outdoors
Denatured Alcohol Methylated Spirits Metho or Meths	Low volatility, safer to use Burns almost silently Renewable fuel resource Alcohol-burning stoves tend to have fewer moving parts than other	Cooking takes longer Requires more fuel Lower heat output Doesn't perform as well in colder conditions	Indoors or Outdoors

FUEL CHOICES
*Note: Fuels below within same color row are the same substance by other names.

FUELS AND ALTERNATE NAMES	PROS	CONS	OK TO USE
Ethynol Alcohol Stove Fuel	types, lowers chance of breakdown. Inexpensive Readily available most places		
Alcohol Gel Alco-Brite Sterno – methanol & acetone	Safe, no toxic fumes Easy to burn Lightweight Portable	Evaporates when exposed to air. Shelf life 2-3 years More expensive than other fuels Burn time – about ½ of Diethylene Glycol	Indoors or Outdoors
Diethylene Glycol & Isoparaffin Eco-Fuel, Heat it, Camp Heat, Dual Heat Burn time: 8 hours at 200°F (93°C) 4 hours at 450°F (232°C)	Unlimited shelf life Never evaporates, even left opened Non-flammable outside its container. No toxic fumes Odorless So safe to use it's allowed on airlines Even flame	24 cans generally around US$69 24 cans of fuel = 192 hours at moderate cooking intensity or 96 hours of high intensity cooking.	Indoors or Outdoors
Propane LPG Liquid Petroleum	Lights easily Relatively inexpensive Fair performance in colder temps Readily available Works well down to 0°F (-18°C) Stores indefinitely Can be used indoors Does not harm soil or water Puts out good heat	Ignition sources like water heaters and electrical sources can cause explosions. May need permit to store large quantities If used indoors, open a window Propane is heavier than air. Without ventilation can collect in low places like basements, pits, floors. Ignited, it will burn, explode. Steel cylinders are heavy, not good for camping unless attached to an RV (Recreational Vehicle)	Outdoors Indoors only with a window cracked open; it consumes oxygen.
Charcoal Briquettes	Can be "home made" Easy to locate Indefinite shelf life, store in airtight container Non-volatile Very inexpensive Heat is "predictable". Each briquette produces about 25°F (14°C) of heat.	Produces carbon monoxide Absorbs moisture readily so store in airtight container, not in the paper bags it is sold in Requires lighter fluid to ignite	Outdoors
Wood	Readily available in some areas. Can be free if you chop and haul your own. Smells nice burning. No toxic fumes	Scarce in some areas. Wood burning is banned in some cities during "no burn days" unless it is primary source of heat Requires ample storage space Should be protected from moisture Requires a year's seasoning before use. "Know your wood" or it's easy to select poor burning species	Indoors or Outdoors
Newspaper Logs	Good way to get rid of extra newspapers Inexpensive Logs roller available to make logs	Don't use colored sections; chemicals may be harmful Requires time and effort to "roll" logs compared to the amount of burn time	Indoors or Outdoors

FUEL CHOICES

*Note: Fuels below within same color row are the same substance by other names.

FUELS AND ALTERNATE NAMES	PROS	CONS	OK TO USE
	No toxic fumes if using black/white sections	expected	
Coal	Stores well in a dark, dry place	Dirty and sooty Store away from circulating air, light and moisture. Emits toxic fumes	Outdoors
Diesel	Easy to find worldwide Very inexpensive Burns well in some stoves Low volatility Diesel, treated, can be stored up to 10 years without degrading. "Poor or dirty" fuel can be reclaimed.	Can clog some stoves May need permit to store large quantities Emits toxic fumes Gels in cold conditions Must be protected from microbial growth & water condensing in fuel	Outdoors
Unleaded Gas Petrol	Easy to find worldwide Very inexpensive Burns well	Can lead to frequent stove clogs Extremely volatile Burns dirty/sooty Emits toxic fumes Highly volatile Needs priming Additives can be carcinogenic May need permit to store large quantities Oxygenated varieties don't store as well as non-oxygenated. Shelf life 15 months with fuel treatment; 3 mos., no treatment	Outdoors only
Wind	Good long-term choice Good in windy locations No odor No mess Quiet	Expensive to set up, upwards of $10K Won't work without wind Requires way to store and convert Not suitable for condo, apartment, duplex or city dwellers	Indoors or Outdoors
Manure Cow or Buffalo Chips	Inexpensive if you're on a farm Burns well	Needs to dry before using Need large on-going quantity Possible unpleasant odor	Indoors or Outdoors
Solar	Good long-term choice No damaging emissions into the air Good in sunny locations No odor No mess Quiet Life span of 20 years	Very expensive to set up Must have way to convert energy and store it Requires steady sunshine Not for mechanically inept to install Batteries may last only 2 years May not be suitable for apartments	Indoors or Outdoors
Generators	Small space required Apartment dweller could use this if a balcony is available Allows running multiple household appliances depending on unit size	Requires fuel storage Produces carbon monoxide Noisy Can be expensive depending on size/type purchased	Outdoors

After choosing what fuel works for you, the next thing to consider is the cooker itself.

CHOICES FOR COOKING

To find the right type cooking method for you, there are several criteria to help make that decision. Most importantly, will you be cooking inside or out? Some fuels can only be used outside which automatically pares down the selection. Since so many folks already have a BBQ grill, storing charcoal or propane is a good idea. However, it's clever to have a secondary cooking option available in case the first one runs out of fuel or breaks down. Should bad weather set in, have an indoor method of cooking as well. Not only does cooking time lengthen in cold weather, some fuels don't work as well in lower temps, plus it's no fun flipping burgers in a blizzard!

INDOOR COOKING

If you have a generator (see Chapter 28) large enough to power several appliances, this option opens up all appliances we use every day. If this isn't in the budget or circumstances where you live don't permit using one, there are still many alternatives.

The following suggestions assume there is no generator to power household appliances and the gas and electrics don't work. These methods are viable for everyone else, especially if weather is inclement.

In order to cook inside, one of the best means is a camp stove. Backpackers, campers, fishermen, sportsmen as well as emergency prepared folks use camp stove the world over. Lots of units are on the market, but for indoor use, make sure the only fuels used are kerosene, butane, mentholated spirits, denatured alcohol, gelled or pressurized canisters. Wood can be burned inside but requires a contained area like a fireplace or Volcano stove. More on this later.

Using propane indoors is questionable. Propane doesn't emit toxic fumes, but it does use the room's oxygen. For this reason, propane fueled grills work best outside.

Due to their toxic fumes, **under no circumstances** should these fuels be used indoors: diesel, gasoline/petrol, coal, charcoal and white gas.

Regardless of the method chosen, always keep a fire extinguisher handy. Even when regular household appliances are in operation, a fire extinguisher should always be within quick reach. If you've had yours for a while, check the expiration date; it's cheap insurance!

Next we'll look through a number of cooking options, for indoors and out. Keep in mind what fuels you can use. Each of these cooking choices details what fuel they burn. Some are suitable only for outside use but have been included here since they're appropriate for indoor use with the right fuel.

FONDUE POT AND CHAFFING DISHES

As supplemental heating/cooking, fondue sets work great. One April Spring day in Colorado when a wet, heavy snow broke power lines, we had to improvise cooking. Granted it was only a four-day "test", but we made some interesting rediscoveries.

In the late 60's and early 70's, nearly everyone had a fondue pot. When the fad passed, ours sat in the back of the cupboard till that snowy April in 1986. The electricity died, and out came the old fondue pot and Sterno, along with cans of beans, peas carrots, stews and soups. It even heated water for tea and coffee. Instead of pitching that useful little pot, it's kept with the rest of our prep gear.

Some fondue pots are made out of lightweight stainless steel or aluminum which makes them easier to transport. Others are made of pottery or copper. After moving to Australia, we purchased a little cast iron unit that uses methylated spirits since Sterno wasn't as readily available. Both fuels can be used indoors to heat liquids to boiling. Make sure the flame is adjustable on the fondue pot. Sometimes foods get too hot and the temperature must be turned down. Cost varies from US$29 up to $200, depending on serviceable vs. fancy dinner styles. If you're looking for a fondue that's useable anytime, make sure it is non-electric.

Recipe books are easily found in bookstores and on the Internet for many ideas other than heating canned foods. Recipes include appetizers to desserts and everything in between. Several "tried and true" cookbooks are:

The New International Fondue Cookbook; Ed Callahan; Bristol Publishing Enterprises, 1990; ISBN: 1558670084
The 125 Best Fondue Recipes, by Ilana Simon, 2001; ISBN: 0778800377
Fondues From Around the World; Eva and Ulrich Klever; Barron's Educational Services; 1992; ISBN: 0812013719
Fondue: The Essential Kitchen Series by Robert Carmack, 2001, ISBN: 9625939385
Fondue: Great Food to Dip, Dunk, Savor, and Swirl; Rick Rodgers, William Morrow, 1998, ISBN: 0688158668

STOVES

Fuel plays an important part in the decision, but there are other factors to consider:
- **Stability** – Will it tip over if slightly bumped? Will it hold my cookware and not wobble?
- **Ease of Starting** – Some units require more pumping and priming
- **Flame Adjustment** – Many units do not have this very necessary feature.
- **Fuel** – Is the kind your stove uses readily available?
- **Wind Shield** – How is the flame protected? Does it even have a shield? Many do not.
- **Size** – How many people will be fed from this unit? How many burners do you need?
- **Cost** – Camp Stoves range according to features and construction

PORTA-CHEF STOVE

This unit is self-igniting and puts out 7,000 BTUs of instant heat. It's compact measuring 13.3"x11.2"x3.4" (33.8x28.4x8.6cm) and weighing 4½ lbs (2kg). The cast aluminum burner head has a built-in windscreen with pot supports and accepts most 8 oz. (227g) butane cylinders. Changing fuel is easy and no priming or pumping is required. With any open flame unit, care needs to be taken, especially using around children. Price is approximately US$40 and fuel canisters are an additional US$9 for three or $30 for 12. Other companies manufacture this style product as well. Check **www.cabelas.com**.

ALPACA KEROSENE COOKER

Kerosene is one of the safest and most economical fuels for either heating or cooking. In many countries, especially in Indonesia, the Philippines, Australia and New Zealand, it is often the fuel of choice. This unit (pictured right) puts out 8,500 BTU's of heat and the fuel tank holds .9 gallon (3.4L). Each filling lasts 16 hours. These cook stoves run approximately US$90 and replacement wicks are around US$10 each. Check **www.lehmans.com**.

GAS TABLE STOVES – KEROSENE 1, 2 & 3 BURNERS

This three-burner kerosene stove burns 12.5 hours on one burner per full tank and is most efficient when using kerosene. A single burner produces about 7,000 BTUs of heat per hour when using kerosene. This is an extremely clean burning odorless kerosene stove due to its catalytic converter and it produces no smoke if properly used. The stove can be used with a kerosene oven by removing the second plate. It also works on diesel, methyl hydrate (alcohol) or lamp oil, etc. Non-pressure single wick gravity stove. Ideal kerosene stove for remote camping and emergency use. The Butterfly Oven works perfectly on this stove because the bottom of the oven is designed to fit over the steel burner frame to stabilize the oven. Very safe. Requires some assembly Box size: 39"x14"x8".

Singapore's Butterfly line, the best selling kero stove in Oceana, is one of the few offered in the U.S. and Canada. They have up to three burners (pictured), with or without stands. Prices are generally US$65 for 1-burner, $120 for 2-burner and $145 for 3-burner cookers.

They use a flat, woven fiberglass wick that lasts for years and replacements are inexpensive – about $6 for two. Stoves using wicks instead of being pressurized ensures silent operation. Portability, safety and reliability make Butterflies a good choice. Possible drawbacks are a bit of smoke and smell when first lit. Butterflies need to be used on a flat surface for proper operation. Check Harvest Outfitters **www.harvestoutfitters.com**, St. Paul Mercantile **www.stpaulmercantile.com** or 1-888-395-1164; and Survival Supply Canada **www.survivalpro.com** carries some stoves and spare parts.

TIP: The key to long wick life is to turn the fuel on and let the bowl fill before lighting the wick!

PYROMID

Pyromid's portable cooking system is a complete cooking system all in one. It's a grill, stove, oven, roaster and smoker. From baking bread to smoking fish to grilling steaks or vertically roasting poultry, the sky is the limit with a Pyromid.

It's currently available in a 12" size (30.5cm), which cooks a complete meal for 1 to 4 people. The proposed 15" model supplies food for up to 8 people.

Pyromids are all stainless steel, offer great flexibility and fold to only 1". They're one of the more efficient stoves because they use only 9 charcoal briquettes. Briquettes **cannot** be used indoors, but the Pyromid burns other solid fuels like twigs, wood chunks, pinecones, or gelled fuel like Sterno. Of these fuels, you might only have access to the Sterno type, which is very acceptable for use indoors.

However, if you take the Pyromid outside, line up the 9 briquettes as in the graphic. Be sure to protect whatever is underneath the Pyromid from getting too hot and burning the surface. Its perforated grill keeps small pieces of food from falling through.

The Pyromid allows baking with normal pans with an optional oven. It's easy to clean and dishwasher safe. Its vertical stainless steel chicken roaster also folds flat. Most families would be able to get by with the 12" oven which holds these size pans: 8½"x4½" (21.5x11.5cm), bread pan, 8½"x8½" (21.5x21.5cm) cake pan, 10"x7¾" (25.5x20cm)muffin pans. For a traditional 9x13" (23x33cm) cake pan, you'd need the 15" oven.

With the grill accessory you can stir-fry, sauté, or cook pancakes, bacon and eggs. The Smoker accessory lets you bake bread, steam vegetables and keep food warm for extended periods. Price for the 12" Pyromid is generally around US$130. The people at Pyromid plan for additional products. Visit their site at **www.pyromid.net/**.

BACKPACK STOVES

As an interim means of food preparation, backpack stoves are especially convenient when storage space is nearly nonexistent and you want to cook inside. The compact little stove is light and easily transportable and several models allow multi-fuels. Since some fuels work better than others at different altitudes and temperatures, its versatility is key.

The obvious downside is a single burner. It's hard to make a more elaborate dinner with limited cooking space. Backpack stoves work best for short-term use or for one person, one pot meals, but buying additional stoves is an option.

Before purchasing, there are a few things to consider since many models are on the market ranging from a modest $50 up to $150.

Look for a sturdy unit with curved pot supports. They create stability and help prevent the pot from sliding off.

Another important consideration is the boil time which can vary from 2½ to 5 minutes.

Ease of use is important too. Having a model that accepts a variety of fuels is a big plus if you plan to be in a variety of locations. They can be a bit more difficult to maintain.

For fuels, **Butane, Propane or Isobutane Blend Canisters** are great in warm to moderate weather, or cooking inside. They're easy to adjust and give few problems. If backpacking, they add a little extra weight to packs.

Kerosene is cheap and versatile though not as clean or easy to deal with as butane or white gas. It's readily found outside of the U.S.

White gas is a great overall performer in just about any weather. It's reliable, inexpensive and efficient.

Denatured alcohol takes longer to heat and output is overall lower, but it is environmentally friendly.

Unleaded gas is the least acceptable fuel choice. Though relatively cheap and plentiful, it's dirty. In winter, many parts of the U.S. sell oxygenated gasoline which should NEVER be used in backpack stoves unless instructions specifically state it's OK. This fuel destroys the stove's rubber parts and seals.

For more information on fuels, see Fuel Choices earlier in this chapter.

In relation to fuel, you'll also come across the term "Remote canister". This means the fuel is connected to the unit by a hose rather than attaching directly to the canister.

For backpack stoves, see Back Country Gear **www.backcountrygear.com**, REI **www.rei.com**, Campmor **www.campmor.com**, Backcountry **www.backcountry.com**, Cabela's **www.cabelas.com**, Gear Up for Outdoors **www.gear-up.com**, MSR Gear **www.msrgear.com**, Amazon **www.amazon.com**, Lakes Runner & Climber **www.lakesclimber.com**, Boots **www.bootscamping.com.au**, Eagle Eye Outfitters **www.eagleeyecanada.com**. Compare prices.

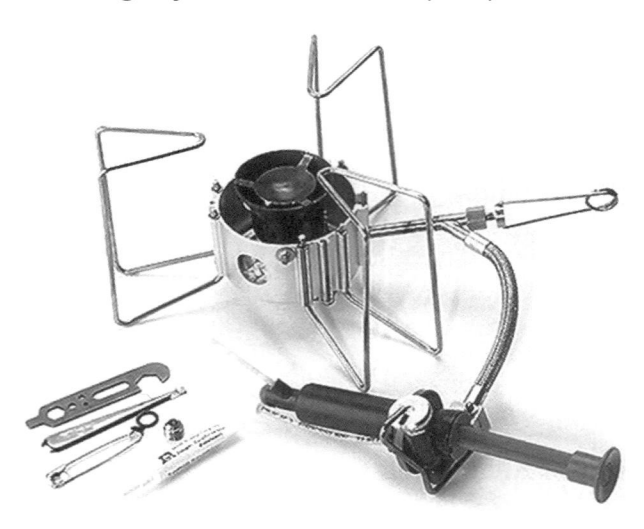

MSR DRAGONFLY

The Dragonfly, pictured left, debuted in 1998 and has received great reviews all around. It allows for excellent flame and cooking control. Besides kerosene, which can be used indoors, it also burns diesel #1, white gas, aviation (AV) gas, stoddard solvent, naphtha, and auto gas.

The Dragonfly is constructed of durable stainless steel, high quality aluminum, brass and copper yet weighs only 17 oz (482g). Its legs spring open for superior pot stability and fold in for compact storage. An aluminum windscreen and heat reflector greatly increase its cooking power and heat efficiency if used outside. Fuel capacity of 22 oz (624g) allows approximately 130 minutes of burn time and boils water in 3½ minutes. Average cost is around US$130 and users state it's well worth every penny.

PRIMUS OMNI FUEL

There are cheaper stoves, but you get what you pay for. Some stoves are so flimsy they end up as money wasted. The Primus unit is rated for unlimited usage year round and has no problem cooking at higher altitudes and lower temperatures.

The Primus Omni Fuel Stove burns virtually any fuel; gas canisters, cartridges with a butane-propane mix, white gas, auto gas, diesel, kerosene, paraffin and jet fuel. Its preheating system minimizes priming time. A built-in windshield allows the stove to function well even in very low temperatures and a pump for the fuel bottle is included. A fully adjustable flame allows you to simmer, boil, and everything in between. Simply turning the liquid fuel bottle upside down turns off the stove and bleeds the fuel line to prevent spills and flare-ups.

The Primus unit is also extremely lightweight, 19 oz (539g) and measures 6.6x4x3.8" (16.8x10x9.6cm). Small but mighty, it boils water in about 4 minutes. This Primus model, the OmniFuel runs around $190.

When looking at backpack stoves you'll see various fuel terminology. In the Primus Expedition line for instance, there is EasyFuel, VariFuel MultiFuel and OmniFuel. Here's the difference:

- **EasyFuel** – uses only LP gas
- **VariFuel** – uses liquid fuels such as gasoline/petrol, kerosene or diesel
- **MultiFuel** – uses LP gas, gasoline/petrol and kerosene
- **OmniFuel** – works with all types of fuel, LP gas, gasoline/petrol, diesel, kerosene and aviation fuel.
- **Dual Fuel** – usually indicates unleaded gasoline and Coleman Fuel, which is petroleum naphtha with a bit of rust inhibitor

OPTIMUS NOVA MULTI-FUEL STOVE

This backpack stove is similar to the Primus Omni Fuel in looks, cost and overall reviews. It has won a multitude of awards for performance, durability and easy use. Backpackers comment on its stability – even when boiling 8 quarts of water. This means it easily supported 16 pounds of water, plus the container. The Novi puts out a lot of heat and still simmers well. If you plan to use it outside, be sure to purchase a windscreen.

COLEMAN EXPONENT XPEDITION

Coleman's Exponent Xpedition is the first two-burner, true backpacking stove. It's extremely light 25 oz (709g) and measures only 15x11x4" (38x28x10cm) with a full 9" (23cm) burner spacing when open. This means it can service two 7½" (19cm) pots at the same time, yet folds down very flat for compact storage. Each burner operates independently with a full range of adjustability. It allows you to simmer on one side and boil on the other.

Butane/propane stoves have always been enticing because they're easy to use, but they didn't perform as well in cold weather. The Coleman Xpedition stove solves both these problems nicely. The innovative heat regulator ensures reliable performance even in sub-freezing temps and constant heat output. The Xpedition has received extremely good reviews in every category.

Propane/butane fuel works well in mildly cold weather situations and the flame controls adjust easily giving a good range of heat. The Xpedition boils water in just 3 minutes and costs about US$100 which is a very good price considering the two-burner feature.

BRITELYT – PETROMAX

Whenever a product has multiple uses, it really feels like you're getting your money's worth and then some! This Petromax heater / cooker / light is just such a product. In its 5th generation, BriteLyt is the newest model. The first lanterns developed named Petromax, were used by German armies before and during World War Two. The military significance of a lantern that would burn all liquid fuels from diesel oil to gasoline made it extremely useful. In time, heaters and stoves were developed for the individual soldier as well as for whole companies. These three features gave the German army the benefit of heat, light and a way to prepare food with the use of any of any liquid fuel available.

The original Petromax lanterns were used in the movie, "Kelly's Heroes" and are still used today by NATO forces, as well as various paramilitary groups around the world. The lantern's appearance and parts haven't changed since their development, and they are still constructed of solid brass and nickel plating.

BriteLyt is easy to repair since the stove has only two replaceable moving parts and it will last many years given a little TLC.

Petromax stoves are easy to start and run on a variety of fuels: kerosene, alcohol-based fuels, mineral spirits, citronella oil, gasoline, diesel oil and almost every flammable fuel available on the market. While some of these fuels can't be used indoors, this product gives lots of options. Its reservoir holds 1 quart of fuel which burns 3-4 hours.

Using 10,000 BTU's of heat, it boils water in minutes. The solid brass construction makes this a sturdy cooker and when not in use, it collapses to about 4" (10cm). Models range in cost from $60 to $450.00. There is something wonderful to be said for reliability and versatility! Call 727.856.9245 or check **www.britelyt.com**.

TRANGIA

Swedish Trangia stoves are lightweight and very portable. All components nest, which makes even the largest model convenient. Check **www.libertymountain.com**, **www.canadianoutdoorequipment.com**, **www.amg-group.co.uk**, **www.rucsacsupplies.com.au**, **online.ahm.co.nz** and **www.trangia.se/English**.

Their simple design eliminates moving parts, pistons, pressurized tanks, jets, tubes and pipes and valves. This cookware heats evenly, eliminates scorching and cleans up fast.

Trangia is phasing out their Titanium and Duossal ranges and replacing them with hardened anodized aluminum and ultralight aluminum. This makes them both stronger and more evenly heating. They've also done away with the Teflon surface that tended to flake with even a little use.

Original Trangia stoves burn denatured alcohol (methylated spirits). Though it takes the longest of any fuel to boil water, it's very safe to use indoors. Depending on which Trangia model is purchased, boiling 1 quart or liter of water takes 9½ to 14 minutes. That is slow. Newer models burn multi-fuels: white gas-kerosene-jet-auto-diesel, which heats quicker. Trangia now offers a line using a Primus gas burner. Stoves range US$85-130.

Stove 25 Series – for 3-4 people have two saucepans (1.75 and 1.5 L), an 8½" (22 cm) frying pan, kettle, windshields (upper and lower), a burner, a pan grip and a strap. Dimensions 8½" x 4" (22 x 10.5 cm)

Stove 27 Series – for 1-2 people have two 1L saucepans (1 graduated, 1 ungraduated), a 7" (18 cm) frying pan, kettle, windshields (upper and lower), burner, pan grip and a strap. Dimensions 7¼" x 4" (18.5 x 10 cm)

CAMP STOVES

These units are very similar to the Home and Camping Grillers and come in as many selections as calories in cheesecake. Major manufacturers include Coleman, Camp Chef and Century-Primus. Numerous other companies also sell house brands.

Portable gas ranges can be used indoors **with care**. When in operation, **always make sure a window is open**. While propane does not produce toxic fumes, it consumes oxygen. Whenever an open flame is involved, children should be away from the cooking area and keep a fire extinguisher within reach. These are just normal precautions. Unless cooking outside, make sure the range picked does not say "Dual-Fuel". This usually indicates unleaded gas/petrol or Coleman/white gas for the fuel. These fuels cannot be used indoors, but the ranges look very similar to the propane units. However the dual-fuels work well for outside cooking.

Ranges come in one-, two- or three-burner models with optional stands, wind screens, griddles and accessory racks. These portable gas units cook up a storm!

Stan and I use this Coleman 3-burner unit because it's compact but large enough to easily accommodate pans. When selecting a portable gas range, visualize, or better yet, bring along the exact dimensions of the pots and pans most likely used. The dimensions measure 18½" x 26" x 6" (47 x 66 x 15.25cm). With a little over two feet, it gives plenty of room to cook.

This Coleman Exponent InstaStart runs on propane though they have similar models that use dual-fuel. Taking into consideration our primary back-up fuel, propane made the most sense.

Additionally, we bought a bulk propane adapter. For extended power outages this $16 accessory lets you use less expensive bulk propane rather than chew through fuel in small cylinders.

The photo inset gives a close-up of the left and center burners. The middle 5,000 BTU burner provides even heat distribution and the outer two areas have the most grunt at 11,500 BTUs each. All three adjustable stainless steel burners work independently.

Both sides of the range have mini tables that fold up to double as windscreens.

Other nice features to look for are matchless starters or "piezo ignition". It eliminates using matches around open flames and reduces flare ups. Most better quality ranges have this feature. Their main drawback is simply wearing out. Appliances normally manage to fail *after* a particular model is no longer made or out of warranty though this unit has a 5-year guarantee. In a pinch, you can always ignite a camp stove with matches.

Also look for removable grates for easy cleanup. Gas ranges have a steady fuel output even in high winds or extreme cold and cooking power is adjustable. Better quality models like Coleman and Century-Primus can put out at least 10,000 BTU's cooking power for each burner. Some can be as low as 5500 BTU's, which makes a big difference in cooking time.

TYPICAL PROPANE TANK SIZES

PROPANE TANKS AND ACCESSORIES

Portable propane tanks come in a variety of sizes from 1½ to 40 pounds (¾ to 18kg) with either external or internal valves. The external valves already have the connection in place for BBQ grills and gas ranges.

A fuel indicator is a really good option to consider. For accurate readings, the best ones like the Gaslow's Gas Gauge (US$25 and $40) or Australia's Gasfuse (AU$40 Bunnings and K-Mart) attach right to the canister's fuel opening. These pressure activated gauges read as soon as the propane is turned on. Adhesive gauges that stick right onto the canister are inexpensive but don't give accurate readings. We ended up throwing these away.

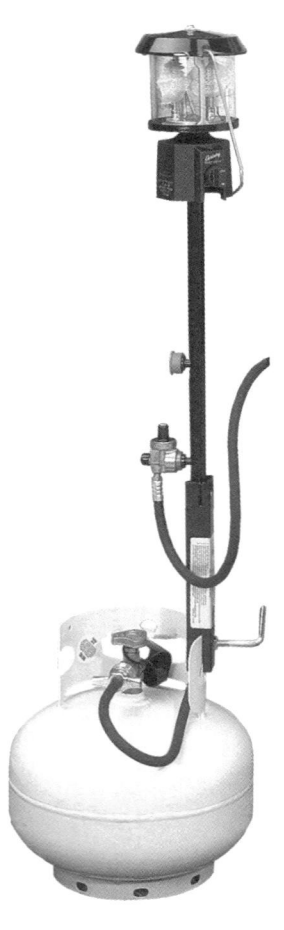

EXTENSION POLES

One of the best purchases we made was a lantern post. Sometimes they are referred to as "distribution trees" or "lantern posts". For emergency lighting, heating and cooking, they turn a propane tank into a multi-use tool. You just screw the pole onto a bulk propane cylinder and it allows up to three propane accessories to run at once.

Posts are usually 30" tall and some models break down into two parts so they can be used as a shorter 16" extension. The taller size places lanterns at optimum height for area lighting.

While in Perth one winter, we lost electricity for the evening and lit two propane lights. They were a bit noisy but provided excellent light.

Using an extension pole, as pictured, helps illuminate more area, but the steel light can connect directly to the fuel tank for a table lamp. They are windproof and have adjustable output up to 200 watts. Not only did they put out a great deal of light, but it exuded heat as well. If these are in your emergency supplies, don't forget extra mantles and socks. You can find lantern poles at Bass Pro Shops www.basspro.com, Cabelas www.cabelas.com and Campmor www.campmor.com.

MARINE BBQ GRILLS

As a last resort for the apartment dweller who has no outside, ground floor access for cooking, this is one option. Most boaters have cooked on Magna or marine kettle type barbecue grills. They come in two sizes, 14½" and 17" (36.8 and 43cm) and burn propane. These little BBQ grills allow you to heat water, grill or cook with a pan set on top of the rack. They cook quickly and efficiently.

Boats are notoriously cramped and designers get an A+ for using of every smidgen of spare space. To use these grills, companies designed different mounting brackets to accommodate various boat layouts. Besides standing alone (accessory table top legs can be purchased), grills can mount to 1" round railing, square railing or be wall mounted.

Mounting arms loosen to swivel inward or outward. If you have absolutely no other means to cook or heat water and live on the 15th floor of an apartment complex, consider placing one of these units outside your window or off your balcony. When it's time to cook, the arm can swing toward you for easy lighting and turning food.

Magma's round BBQ grill has a disk mounted on the lid's interior which hooks onto the edge of the cooker. This makes checking food or lighting the grill easy. So the lid doesn't go sailing down 15 floors or into the water, a wire "umbilical cord" keeps the lid attached to the grill at all times. This feature came in handy more times than I can say on choppy water.

Magma propane round grills are around $220 for the 15" and $270 for the 17". A charcoal version of the smaller model is available for $130.

The 17" round grill works well for two or three people. Depending on what you're BBQing, it might even stretch to cook for four persons. However, if feeding more than four people, consider the Catalina or Newport models (right). The Catalina and Newport look the same, but differ in dimension and heat output. Both models' lids slide back so there's no worry they will fall off.

Catalina's overall size is 22¼x14x14⅝ with heat output at 13,000 BTUs. Newport is slightly smaller at 22¼x11½x11⅝ with 11,500 BTU heat output. Though the larger Magmas start to become pricy, (Newport $300, Catalina at $370 and Monterey at $500) their unique mounting possibilities offer interesting options for people in apartments and high-rises. Even if there is no balcony, if you have at least a window, you can mount these outside on a swivel arm. Check for Magma's at www.westmarine.com and www.discountmarinesupplies.com.

If you haven't used marine grills, they work every bit as well as backyard patio BBQs. Magma, Force 10 and West Marine have these BBQs products.

CAMP OVENS

One accessory familiar to many outdoor enthusiasts is the camp oven. These ovens fit over one burner of an RV, gas or wood stove, electric range or the Pyromid. It lets you to bake biscuits, cornbread, pies, meatloaf, lasagna, fish, pizza, vegetables, casseroles, brownies, cookies, roast, bake chicken, breads, and much more.

Simply light whatever heating source you're using, center the oven over it and adjust the flame to reach baking temperature. Because these units are compact, they don't require a lot of heat. To prevent burning, start out with low heat, and increase it gradually to the desired temp.

Models with a removable middle shelf (the double oven) can accommodate larger items like a chicken roasted upright. Other features to consider are a temperature gauge and handles.

Camp ovens are made from rust resistant heavy aluminum, which bakes evenly. The double oven measures 10x10x9½" (25.4x25.4x24cm) and weighs only 4 lbs. 2 oz. (1.8kg).

Fox Hill makes a shorter version for US$50 – the single oven – which measures 10"x10"x6" and weighs only 2 lbs. 11 oz. (1.2kg). Their double oven retails for US$70. When we're considering saving space, generally we are interested in the width and depth and not as concerned for the height. If you go with the shorter unit, for only a few dollars less, you've greatly cut cooking options.

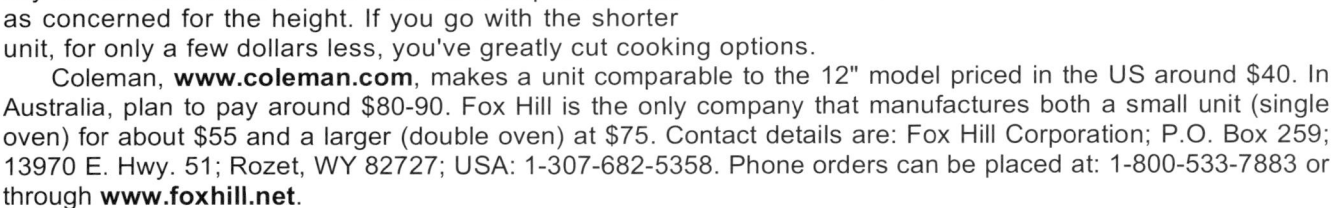

Coleman, www.coleman.com, makes a unit comparable to the 12" model priced in the US around $40. In Australia, plan to pay around $80-90. Fox Hill is the only company that manufactures both a small unit (single oven) for about $55 and a larger (double oven) at $75. Contact details are: Fox Hill Corporation; P.O. Box 259; 13970 E. Hwy. 51; Rozet, WY 82727; USA: 1-307-682-5358. Phone orders can be placed at: 1-800-533-7883 or through www.foxhill.net.

Lehman's, known since 1955 for its non-electric high-quality American made products, offers a portable oven for $35. It measures 11⅝"x11⅝"x12½" and features a door thermometer.

Lehman's offers such a variety of useful items, you should request a catalog online www.lehmans.com or through Lehman's, 289 Kurzen Road North; Dalton, Ohio 44618, US and Canada toll free: 1.888.438.5346; International: 1.330.828.8828 phone; 1.330.828.8270 fax.

Pyromid also makes a Smoker/Oven that smokes, bakes or roasts. To use, just set it on top of Pyromid stove or any other cooking source. These are slightly larger, available in 12" (30.5cm) or 15" (38cm) and priced around US$70 for the 12" and US$120 for the 15". All models fold flat to about 2½" (6.4cm).

COLEMAN INSTASTART CAMP OVEN

Coleman's InstaStart is an upscale version of the basic camp oven. Product description claims its 6,000 BTUs translate into 500°F, but users state it's closer to 450°F. The oven has 7 rack options and the top position toasts both sides of sliced bread. Some people remark that it's a bit large for camping, but it depends on

InstaStart Camp Oven

your conditions and mobility. However, in a power outage you may be very glad this camp oven accommodates even a full size 13 x 9 baking pan.

Owners say they were pleasantly surprised that everything from muffins to brisket to lasagna and cakes turned out perfectly without experimentation. It features a built-in top-mounted temperature gauge and viewing window. Like with breadmakers, the window may become too steamy for a good look-see. Outsides measurements: 12½"H x 15⅝"W x 23¼"D. Interior measurements: 12"D x 14"W x 5"H. Weighs 20 pounds $US80.

BBQ GRILLS

Besides the indoor methods of cooking, there are lots of options for preparing food outside. Without the worry of toxic fumes and burning down the house, choices expand considerably. Some are more cost effective, some are more reliable, but it's a matter of what you feel comfortable using and what will carry you through times of interrupted power.

The simplest, most familiar cooking method automatically cuts stress. It does little good to buy a lot of fancy equipment that you can't work. With the high percentage of BBQ grill owners, the best option might be to store EXTRA charcoal and/or propane.

While some people swear by propane's easy use, others can't be pried away from true charcoal flavor. Both store reliably.

Charcoal keeps indefinitely if it is away from moisture in airtight containers. For long-term storage, put them in plastic or metal containers or heavy-duty garbage sacks instead of just the original paper bags.

CHARCOAL CHIMNEY

One terrific way to get charcoal burning is a charcoal chimney or tower. Simply toss in a couple lit firestarters along with the coals. In short order they will be blazing and ready to put into your grill, Pyromid, Volcano stove or on the ground in a designated fire pit. Camp Chef, Weber, Grill Life, Lodge Manufacturing are among chimney charcoal starters. With a little hunting, you can find them for as little as $15.

With the popularity of BBQ's, nearly an infinite number of products are available. Many feature grill and griddle combinations, some have built in tables, racks and warmers. Others are purely functional like the small table top models. If cooking outside is an option for you, there is a BBQ for every price range. The ones pictured on the next page run from $38 to more than $9000.

Make sure to periodically clean the venturi tubes – those tube(s) leading from the temperature dial to the burner. Spiders love to spin webs inside which can cause flashback fires.

I have cooked on alcohol and camp stoves, and marine grills for several weeks at a time in cramped quarters. It is doable. Getting the rhythm down and understanding the general cook time compared to conventional cooking is the biggest deal. Like most things, familiarity overcomes a lot of pitfalls and it becomes very easy.

OPEN FIRE HELPERS

The oldest way to prepare food is over an open fire and it's still a viable method today. There's always something special about food cooked outside. The smell of wood burning, the aroma of simmering foods always sparks the appetite. (Hmmm, maybe this is a drawback!) A few tricks when cooking over open fire can prevent ruined dinners. The first tip is not to put pots directly in the flames. Food placed on a cooking grid with the fire under it has the same wonderful outdoor flavor without scorching.

Watch the fire to make sure it neither dies out nor blackens dinner if cooking over indirect flame.

Models like TexSport Open Fire Grill's frame are made of ¾" 16-gauge angle iron and the grill is 9-gauge expanded metal. Legs fold under for compact storage and transport. The TexSport Grill comes in three sizes: 16"x12", 24x16", 36"x18 priced at $25, $31 and $50. Check The Camping Store: **www.sleeping-bags-now.com**.

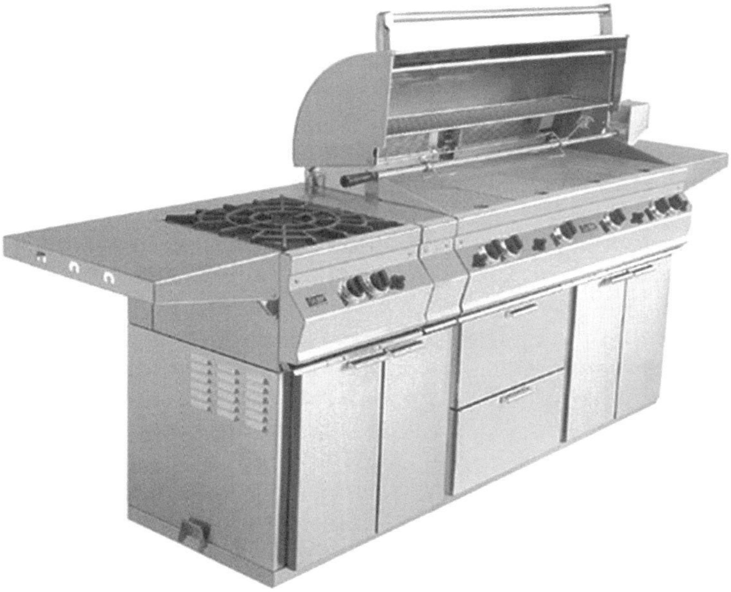
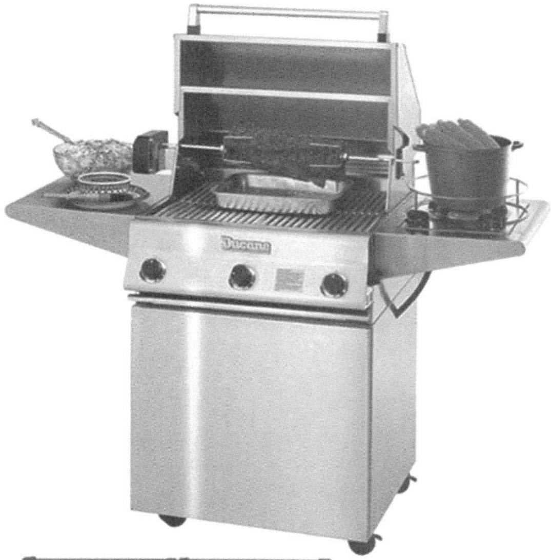
Ducane
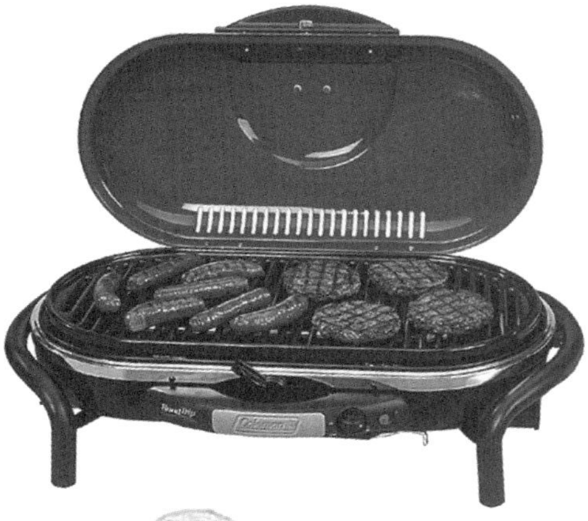
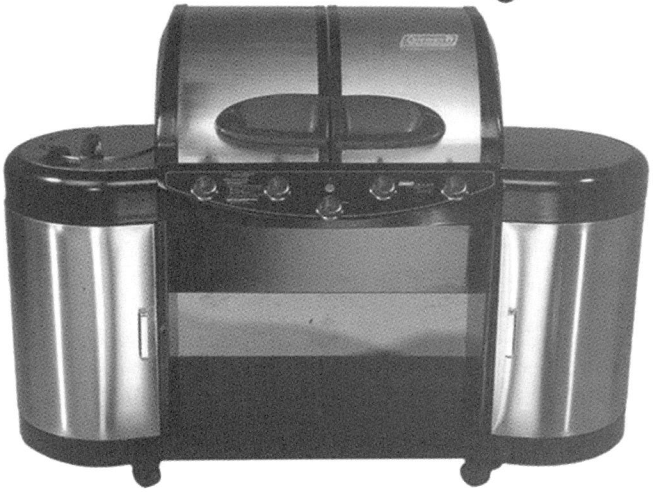
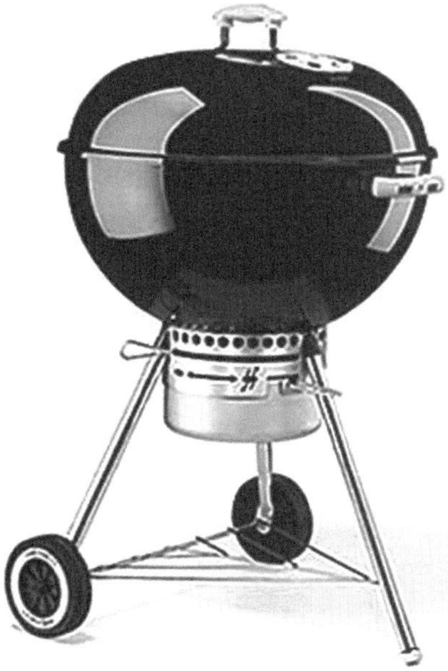
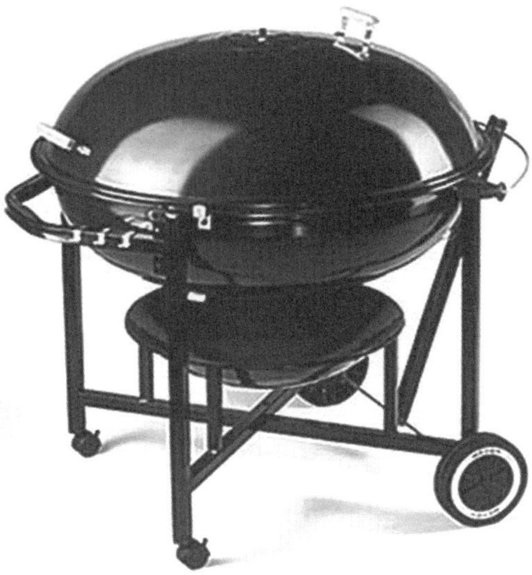
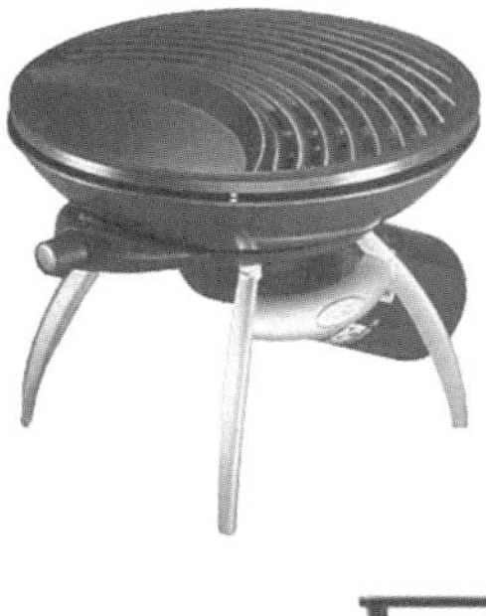
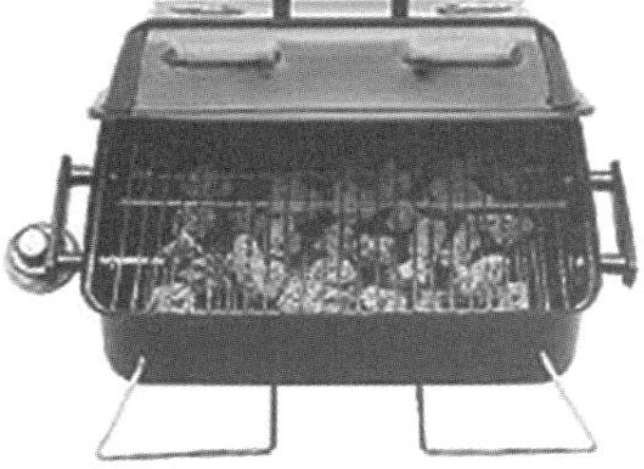

A popular alternative uses a tripod to suspend a pot over the fire. Tripods come in several heights and the center chain adjusts to hold pots at the right distance from the fire.

Other tripods suspend a circular grill, like the kind that comes with kettle BBQ's, and the pots rest on this surface.

This tripod is particularly good since it provides several options. Tripods can be purchased globally for around $15-20. Lodge , well known for their fine Dutch Ovens, makes tripods in two sizes. The smaller version has 43½" legs and a 24" chain for $44. The Tall Boy has 60" legs and 36" chain priced at $57. Generic models with grills can be had for US$18 while some tripods are hugely overpriced at US$70. Wisemen Trading and Supply carries a nice selection www.wisementrading.com or phone 1.888.891.8411.

To make your own, lash three 1½" (3.8cm) diameter tree limbs together to make a tripod. However, watch that the tripod doesn't catch on fire. Alternately, lashed together any three of the following: broomsticks, rebar, galvanized steel stakes or poles, T-posts (star pickets) or clothes closet poles. Splay the legs in a triangle.

DUTCH OR CAMP OVENS

These gems have been in use for hundreds of years. Supposedly they originated with Dutch traders, but other reports say this is a common misconception and that German immigrants (the "Deutch") were responsible for their beginnings. Over the years the name gradually morphed to "Dutch" and then "Pennsylvania Dutch" since these immigrants concentrated in this region of America. Since their highly prized iron cookware was manufactured there, the name stuck. Then the pots looked slightly different having no lip or flange around the lid and no legs.

Reportedly Napoleon groused when ash continually fell into his food. He demanded an improvement that supposedly resulted in the flanged lid. Paul Revere changed the Dutch Oven later to include three legs to straddle the fire and modified the size and the bale handle. Probably most of us associate Dutch Ovens with pioneering days, early settlers, cattle drives and gold miners.

In the Australian outback, Dutch Oven cooking is artwork in dining. People swear that after a week of cooking in a Dutch Oven, they're reluctant to eat food prepared the modern "good old fashion way".

In Australia, "camp oven" is the more common term and occasionally you'll hear "bush stove". Regardless, it usually means a cast iron pot with a flanged lid. It can be with feet or without, with or without bale wire handles.

While they've enjoyed a revival in America over the last three decades, Dutch Ovens is the primary way to cook in undeveloped Africa. This system has worked astonishingly well for over 200 years. In the photo left, "potjies" manufactured in Africa and are sold through small American retailers. This monster potjie is large enough to feed an entire neighborhood holding a whopping 33 gallons. There's a Dutch Oven for everyone.

African Potjie

In the U.S., a distinction is made between the foot and footless type. The ones without legs are referred to as "Bean Pots" or "Kitchen" Dutch Ovens since these are used primarily stove top. Oftentimes pots without feet have a highly domed lid with no lip. Why the feet? It allows air to circulate around and under the pot, which speeds up cooking.

In Australia, the legless distinction is rarely made. Even if their lid is somewhat domed, it still has a lip and coals are heaped on the lid with equal success.

Aluminum Dutch Ovens cost nearly much as cast iron. The plus side to aluminum is its lighter weight and it won't crack or warp. However, the thinner material can cause foods to burn more easily and if exposed continually to very high heat, it can damage the aluminum.

WHAT TO LOOK FOR IN A DUTCH OVEN

The two most important factors are a snug fitting lid and a smooth interior. For ease of handling and keeping the coals where they're supposed to be, we prefer the inverted lid, not the domed one. Handles are important too or you have to purchase or make lifting forks. Plus, no handles make hanging your Dutch Oven from a tripod much more difficult. A tripod with suspended grill then becomes a necessity.

Make sure the pot is a consistent thickness or uneven cooking will result. Some food will be raw when the rest is ready. Last, a flat bottom as opposed to a curved one is preferable. Food that sits on the curved parts is further from the coals, which makes cooking uneven. If you're making something like a soup or stew that can easily be stirred, it's not a big deal, but if you're making bread or a cake, stirring could be tricky!

WHAT SIZE TO BUY?

That depends on how large your family is. The most popular sizes are the 10" 12" and 14". The sizes below are commonly available at most dealers.

\multicolumn{5}{c	}{**WHAT SIZE DUTCH OVEN TO USE**}
Oven	**Size**	**Capacity**	**Food**	**Serves**
5"	12.7cm	1 pint	Small Serving Side Dishes	1-2
8"	20.3cm	2 quarts	Vegetables, Desserts	2-4
10"	25.4cm	4 quarts	Beans, Rolls, Cobblers, Good for Testing Recipes	4-7
12"	30.5cm	6 quarts	Main Dishes, Side Dishes, Rolls, Desserts	12-14
12" Deep	30.5cm	8 quarts	Turkeys, Hens, Hams, Standing Rib Roasts	16-20
14"	35.5cm	8 quarts	Main Dishes, Side Dishes, Rolls, Potatoes, Desserts	16-20
14" Deep	35.5cm	10 quarts	Turkeys, Hens, Hams, Standing Rib Roasts	22-28
16"	40.6cm	12 quarts	Big Turkeys, Soups and Stews, One Pot Dinners	22-28

SEASONING THE DUTCH OVEN

Before using your Camp Oven for the first time, it must be properly seasoned unless you're purchased pre-seasoned models. Most better quality Dutch Ovens have a protective waxy coating which needs to be removed before using. Washing in hot soapy water should get the job done. For stubborn labels, use steel wool to remove the sticky parts. Wash and rinse thoroughly, then season with a good grade shortening or olive oil inside and out, including the legs and lid. Crisco is the preferred seasoning since it doesn't "run" like vegetable oil. Steer clear of non-stick sprays; they don't provide the necessary protection. The other no-no is animal products like lard; they will go rancid.

After applying an even coating of shortening or olive oil, wipe with a paper towel and bake the new Dutch Oven for 15 minutes at 300°F (150°C). Repeat the process another three times, each time liberally coating the Dutch Oven with shortening. Don't be surprised if it smokes and puts out a bad smell. Place a foil lined cookie sheet on the rack below to catch shortening or oil run-off. The goal is to turn the pot's muted gray color into a black satin finish. This requires numerous bakings and seasonings to achieve, but this finish provides the non-stick quality.

NO-SEASON DUTCH OVENS

Not into seasoning your own? Logic Manufacturing, **www.lodgemfg.com** and Camp Chef **www.campchef.com** have DO cookware ready to use. When you first get it home, all that's required is a rinse with hot water (no soap) and dry thoroughly. Before cooking, prepare the surface by oiling or spraying with Pam. After cooking, clean utensil with a stiff brush and hot water. Again, soap is not recommended and harsh detergents should never be used. Towel dry immediately and apply a light coat of Pam or vegetable oil while it's still warm. Store in a cool, dry place. If the cookware has a lid, place a folded paper towel between the lid and the bottom to allow air to circulate. Cast iron cookware should NEVER go in the dishwasher. If your cookware develops a metallic smell or taste or shows signs of rust, wash with soap and hot water, scour off rust, and season using the instructions on the preceding page. For several lines see also Dutch Oven Pro **www.dutchovenpro.com** and Dutch Oven Cookware **www.dutchovencookware.com**.

CARE AND CLEANING DUTCH OVENS

When first using your Dutch Oven, avoid cooking acidic foods; they remove the seasoning. While cooking, use utensils kind to the interior. Nylon or wood is ideal; metal ones can scratch the surface. For clean up, use a green plastic scrubber or a natural fiber brush. Washing with soap is not a good idea as it removes the seasoning. When cleaning your Dutch Oven avoid:

- Strong detergents
- Dishwashers
- Steel wool pads
- Hard wire brushes

After removing the food from your Dutch Oven, it might seem perfectly natural to run cold water in the pot for easier handling. This is probably the biggest no-no of all. Cast iron is brittle and can crack if dropped or exposed to sudden extreme temperature changes.

Gently scrape the oven, fill it with 2" (5cm) of water and then boil for 15 or 20 minutes to steam out cooked on food. An alternate method is to mix 4 parts water to 1 part vinegar and clean with this solution while the pot is still hot.

Vinegar is a good disinfectant and tenderizes foods as well. After washing, dry thoroughly and coat lightly with vegetable oil or solid shortening.

If foods have baked on resembling concrete, here are two last resort measures:

Option 1. Soak pan in warm, sudsy water and then clean with steel wool pads and old-fashioned elbow grease.

Option 2. Spray with oven cleaner, wrap in a garbage bag for two days out of the reach of 2- and 4-legged kids, then remove and wash thoroughly. When removing the pot, be careful not to get the lye on your skin or clothes. It burns.

These two methods preserve **some** of the finish, but re-season with vegetable shortening.

For Australians, if you can't find Crisco, which is imported on a limited basis, use Copha or vegetable oil.

After washing, immediately dry thoroughly. Never allow your Dutch Oven to sit in water or let water sit on it no matter how well seasoned it is. Rust gravitates to these cast iron ovens. It's amazing how fast that nasty four-letter word R-U-S-T can appear! Lightly re-oil the entire Dutch Oven, inside and out. Place wadded up newspaper or paper towels inside the Dutch Oven to absorb any moisture from the cookware's pores. Store with the lid ajar in a warm, dry area.

Do not place an empty cast iron pan or oven over a hot fire. It's a sure invitation to cracking or warping.

BUYING A USED DUTCH OVEN

Finding a Dutch Oven at a garage sale is a good way to pick one up for less. Be sure to check for cracks, see that the lid fits snugly with no warping and that there are no pits. Since you don't know where it last lived, give that pot a thorough scrubbing! Use the hottest water you can stand and with a soapy steel wood pad, scrub it completely inside and out. Rinse thoroughly. Dry it in a 200°F (90°) oven for 45 minutes. Grease with solid shortening and bake in the oven for one hour at 350°F (175°C). Repeat the greasing and baking twice more.

DUTCH OVEN COOKING ESSENTIALS

Useful items to make Dutch Oven cooking easier
1. Charcoal, good quality only. If charcoal burns up too fast or won't stay lit, it screws up the cooking time, plus you have to stop cooking, re-light the coals and especially when baking, the results can be ugly!
2. Charcoal chimney or briquette starter.
3. Heavy-duty aluminum foil. In Australia, use at least 2 or 3 sheet sheets.
4. Heavy hot mitts
5. Leather gloves, insulated
6. Lid lifter, (pictured) a long one for removing the Dutch Oven from the heat, and a short one for removing the lid to serve the food.
7. Paper towels
8. Serving utensils
9. Shovel, a folding camp shovel is best for helping tend the fire or putting coals where you want them
10. Spatula, stainless steel
11. Steaming rack
12. Tin or Aluminum pie plates
13. Tongs, long pair to handle coals (check restaurant suppliers)
14. Whisk broom, for removing ashes from the Dutch Oven lid.
15. Dutch oven table

USING CHARCOAL

Before placing your pot on the coals, preheat briquettes for 30-45 minutes. Use the next chart for determining the approximate number of briquettes for the desired temperature. Arrange the charcoal under the Dutch Oven in a circle ½" from the outer edge. Set the coals on the lid in a checkerboard. If they are all piled in one place, hotspots can result. Second rule of thumb, every briquette adds 25°F (14°C). While cooking, **lift** the pot to prevent scratching and rotate the Dutch Oven ¼ turn every 15 minutes and rotate the lid ¼ turn in the opposite direction. This too helps prevent hotspots.

As a rule of thumb, use a 2 to 1 ratio of briquettes; put twice as many underneath the pot as on the lid for boiling, deep-frying, or stewing. Use the reverse ratio with the smaller number of briquettes on bottom for baking.

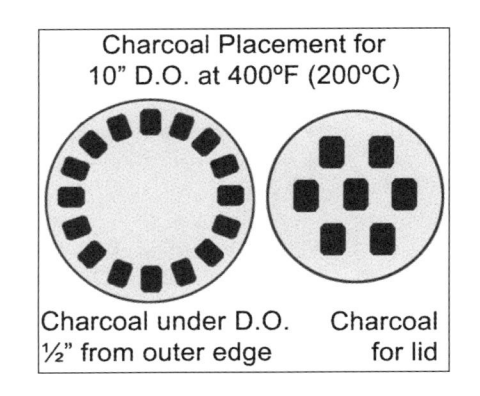

HOW MANY BRIQUETTES TO USE

TEMPERATURE		10" (25.4CM)		12" (30.5)		14" (35.5)	
°F	°C	TOP	BOTTOM	TOP	BOTTOM	TOP	BOTTOM
300	150	12	5	14	7	15	9
325	163	13	6	15	7	17	9
350	175	14	6	16	8	18	10
375	190	15	6	17	9	19	11
400	200	16	7	18	9	21	11
425	225	17	7	19	10	22	12
450	230	18	8	21	10	23	12
500	260	20	9	23	11	26	14

TEMPERATURE CONTROL
This is the one thing that worries most folks when they first begin Dutch Oven cooking. There's no thermometer, no dials to turn, making them think *Good grief! How does this WORK!* That's the beauty of it. You're learning how to function without the gadgets. Remembering a few simple rules makes it easier.
1. At higher altitudes, cooking slows. This is true whether using a conventional oven, the stove or Dutch Ovens.
2. Cold and/or cold, windy weather lengthens cooking time. So does high humidity.
3. Warm breezes and sunlight speed up cooking while shade slows cooking.
4. Don't forget to rotate the oven ¼ turn every 15 minutes but rotate the lid ¼ turn in the opposite direction to prevent hotspots.

How To Tell If You're At The Right Temp
1. LOOK! Remove the lid and take a peek. If your buns are still doughy after 30 minutes, increase the heat.
2. Until you get comfortable with Dutch Oven cooking, use a thermometer to test the temperature.
3. Flour Method. Place a teaspoon of flour in a pan inside a hot Dutch Oven and put the lid on. Leave it for 5 minutes. To "read" the flour: Not brown = less than 300°F (150°C). Light brown = ~350°F (175°C). Dark brown = ~450°F, (230°C). Dark brown in 3 minutes = too hot. Remove some coals.
4. Take the size of the oven and place that amount briquettes on the lid and that same number under the oven. Then remove 2-3 briquettes from the bottom and place them to the top also. This technique will maintain a temperature of 325-350°F (160-175°C). See "How Many Briquettes To Use" for Dutch Oven sizes. For every 2 briquettes added or subtracted to this amount will affect the temperature 25°F (14°C). Temperatures per amount of briquettes are for high altitude areas. If you live in another elevation, check these settings with an oven thermometer to make sure they are OK.

DUTCH OVEN RECIPES

DUTCH OVEN ENCHILADA PIE – DICK HILL
2 lbs. (907g) ground beef
1 cup water
1 onion chopped
9 – 8" (20cm) flour tortillas
1 tsp salt
2 cups grated cheddar or mozzarella cheese
10 oz. or (284g) condensed tomato soup
Green onions, chopped
20 oz. or (567g) enchilada sauce
Sour cream

Brown ground beef, salt, onion in Dutch oven. Drain off drippings. Add tomato soup, enchilada sauce and water. Simmer mixture 5 minutes. Spoon off into a medium bowl. Layer meat mixture, 3 tortillas and cheese. Repeat three times ending with cheese. Sprinkle with chopped green onions. Cook until cheese melts and tortillas soften about 7 to 10 minutes. Serve with sour cream.

GRAND JUNCTION OMELET – JEFF CURRIER
    20 Large Eggs
    ½ to 1 lb. (227-454g) Bacon, cut up in 1" (2.5cm) pieces
    1 lb. (454g) lean ham, cut into small cubes
    1 lb. (454g) grated cheese
    1 medium onion chopped
    1 bell pepper (red, yellow or green) chopped
    8 oz. (227g) mushrooms

Heat Dutch Oven to 400°F (200°C). Brown bacon until crisp but not burnt. Add ham, cover and bake 3 minutes. Beat eggs well. Add peppers and onion, cook until tender. Drain remaining grease and add eggs. Cover and cook approximately 3 minutes. Stir cooked part of eggs into middle of mixture. Cover and repeat 2 to 3 times. When egg has almost completely set, add mushrooms. Remove from bottom heat, and bake with top heat approximately 15 minutes until done. After 5 minutes sprinkle cheese on top. Serve with hot Soda Pop Biscuits and salsa.

SODA POP BISCUITS – JEFF CURRIER
    3 cups flour
    1 can soda pop (cream, peach, 7-Up, etc.)
    ⅜ cup Canola oil
    3 Tbsp baking powder

In a mixing bowl, pour in dry ingredients (omit baking powder if using self rising flour). Form a well in the middle of the bowl and pour in oil and soda pop. Mix into a nice sticky dough and roll out to about ½" (1.27cm) thickness. Cut into biscuits, place into oiled heated oven, and flip both sides into oil. Fill bottom of oven with biscuits, cover with lid. Cook using top and bottom heat until they are golden brown.

   TIP: When baking bread, rolls, or cake, remove the Dutch Oven from the **bottom** coals after ⅔ of the cooking time has elapsed. The top coals will finish the baking without burned bottoms.

OLD FASHIONED SOURDOUGH CINNAMON ROLLS – MIKE HENDRIKSEN
Dough:
1 cup starter
2 tsp salt
1⅛ cups
1 tsp lemon juice warm water
¼ cup oil
1 Tbsp yeast
¼ cup sugar
4 cups flour

Filling:
2 Tbsp ground Cinnamon mixed with 1 cup sugar
¼ cup melted butter or margarine
Topping:
⅛ cup milk
2 cups powdered sugar
1 Tbsp soft butter or margarine
1 tsp vanilla

Mix dough ingredients together and make a soft, slightly sticky dough, kneading for about 5 minutes. Let rest while the butter melts and mix the cinnamon and sugar for the filling. Punch down dough and roll out to a rectangle about 30"x12" (76x30.5cm). Spread the melted butter evenly across the surface of the dough. Sprinkle the cinnamon-sugar mixture over the buttered surface. Roll up from the long side. Cut into 1½" (3.8cm) pieces. Place in a warm, well oiled 14" Dutch oven and let rise 30 minutes, or until about double in bulk. Bake with approximately ⅔ of the heat on top and ⅓ on the bottom for 20-25 minutes. Mix the topping while baking and drizzle the topping over the cinnamon rolls while still very hot.

DUTCH OVEN POTATOES AU GRATIN
    Diced potatoes, enough to fill the Dutch oven
    1 lb. (484g) diced onions for every 5 lbs (2¼ kg) potatoes
    10½ oz (298g) cream of mushroom or cream of chicken soup, condensed
    16-24 oz. (484-680g) Sour Cream
    Salt and Pepper to taste

Cut the unpeeled potatoes into finger-sized pieces. Load them into the Dutch Oven, alternating layers with the onions. Add salt and pepper to taste for each layer. Fill the oven nearly to the top since it will cook down. Cook with top and bottom heat for about 1 hour, checking and stirring every 15 minutes so the potatoes do not stick to the bottom. When the potatoes are cooked, add the condensed cream soup and stir. Add sour cream. Continue to cook slowly for a few more minutes.

MONKEY BREAD – MARK & DEBRA MILES
    2 cups water (very warm)
    6 cups flour
    ½ cup sugar
    ¼ cup oil
    1 Tbsp salt
    2 large eggs (beaten)
    1 Tbsp yeast
    ¼ lb. (114g) butter

Mix water, sugar, salt and yeast. Let set until bubbly. Add eggs and 3 cups flour. Stir, do not beat.
Add oil and last 3 cups flour. Dough will be sticky. Cover and let raise until double in bulk. Roll dough out on a floured surface to ½" (1.27cm) thick. Cut into 2½" (6.35cm) circles.
Melt butter in a deep 14" (36cm) Dutch oven. Do not let butter get too hot. Dip circles of dough in butter, coating both sides. Lay circles of dough on inside edge of Dutch oven, overlapping approximately ⅓ (like shingles). Place the second layer of dough circles like shingles inside the first ring.
Cook with 11 briquettes on the bottom of each oven and 15-20 briquettes placed around the outer rim of each lid. Bake for about 25 minutes. Remove ovens from the bottom briquettes and finish cooking with top heat only for 10-15 minutes more. When finished, remove from Dutch oven and serve warm.
This recipe requires 2-14" (36cm) Dutch Ovens. Use 15 briquettes on the bottom and 15-20 on the top.

GARLIC PARMESAN MONKEY BREAD
Bread Follow above recipe adding ¼ teaspoon garlic power to the melted butter in the Dutch oven. After circles of dough are placed in the Dutch oven sprinkle the top with ½ cup Parmesan cheese.

SESAME SEED MONKEY BREAD
Follow the above recipe adding 1 tablespoon sesame seeds to melted butter in the Dutch Oven. After circles of dough are placed in the Dutch oven, sprinkle top with 1 tablespoon sesame seeds.

ENCHILADAS
    2 lbs. (907 g) hamburger or shredded beef
    1-2 cups salsa
    1 can or jar chopped black olives
    Grated cheese, as desired
    1 onion, chopped
    Flour tortillas
    1 large jar or can enchilada sauce

In a 12" (30.5cm) Dutch oven, cook the hamburger and onion. Remove from the Dutch Oven to a large bowl and mix in olives, enchilada sauce, and salsa. Layer in the Dutch Oven: tortilla, then meat mixture and, cheese, until you run out, topping with cheese. It should make about 4 layers. For coals, place 9 briquettes under and 15 briquettes top. Bake for about 35-45 min. Let cool. Slice and serve.

Dare To Prepare: Chapter 31: Cooking Without Power

ENCHILADA PIE SUPREME
2 lbs. (90g) lean ground beef
1 bunch green onions, chopped
1 large onion, diced
1 package large flour tortillas
1 teaspoon salt
2 cups shredded cheddar cheese
20¾ oz. (588g) cans tomato soup
2 cups shredded Monterey Jack cheese
28 oz. (828ml) cans enchilada sauce (mild)
1 large avocado sauce (mild)
16 oz. (473ml) cans tomato sauce
3 small tomatoes
1 cup sliced fresh mushrooms
1 can sliced black olives
1 large green pepper, diced

In a 12" (30.5cm) Dutch Oven, brown ground beef, salt, and ¾ of onion. Drain off excess fat. Move mixture into medium sized bowl. In another medium bowl, mix tomato soup, enchilada sauce, and tomato sauce together. In a third bowl, combine mushrooms, green pepper, green onions, and rest of large onion. Pour a small amount of sauce into Dutch Oven (just enough to cover the bottom). Use one tortilla and pieces of a second one to cover the bottom of the pan. Alternate meat, sauce, vegetables, cheese, and flour tortillas in layers. End with cheese on top. Put 8 coals under oven and 16 on top. Cook enchilada pie 45 minutes, turning oven and lid in opposite directions 45 degrees every 15 minutes. To garnish use avocado slices, olive slices, diced tomatoes, and parsley (optional) as follows: When pie is done and slightly cooled, place the avocado slices around the center in the shape of a pinwheel. Place a tomato rose in the center of the pinwheel. Scatter the chopped tomato around the outside. Scatter black olive slices over the top. Serves 18.

YUMMY BISCUITS
1 pint Whipping Cream
2 cups Self Rising Flour

Whip cream into nice peaks. Add approximately 2 cups of self rising flour. Adjust the flour until biscuits are the right consistency for drop or rolled biscuits. Both work fine. Bake at 425°F (225°C) for 10 minutes.

THE VOLCANO!

Introduced in 1993, the Volcano Stove crept into the product arena starting more or less as a hobby. It gained national attention in November 1998 after Hurricane Mitch killed more than 11,000 people and many were left without power or conventional means of cooking. The manufacturer sent over 2,000 Volcano Stoves to Honduras along with a shipment of charcoal and they proved to be extraordinarily efficient.

Because of the Volcano's design, it doesn't take a lot of fuel to create a great deal of heat. Product information indicates with 25 pounds (11.3 kg) of charcoal you can cook two meals a day for five people for up to three weeks. One Volcano and 300-400 lbs. (136-181 kg) of charcoal will last a family of 6 for about a year.

Fuel isn't limited to charcoal. Nearly anything works, however, if you want to use propane, you need to buy a conversion kit or purchase the propane model. Though designed for outdoor cooking, using a kerosene burner, wood or canned heat, the Volcano could even be used indoors.

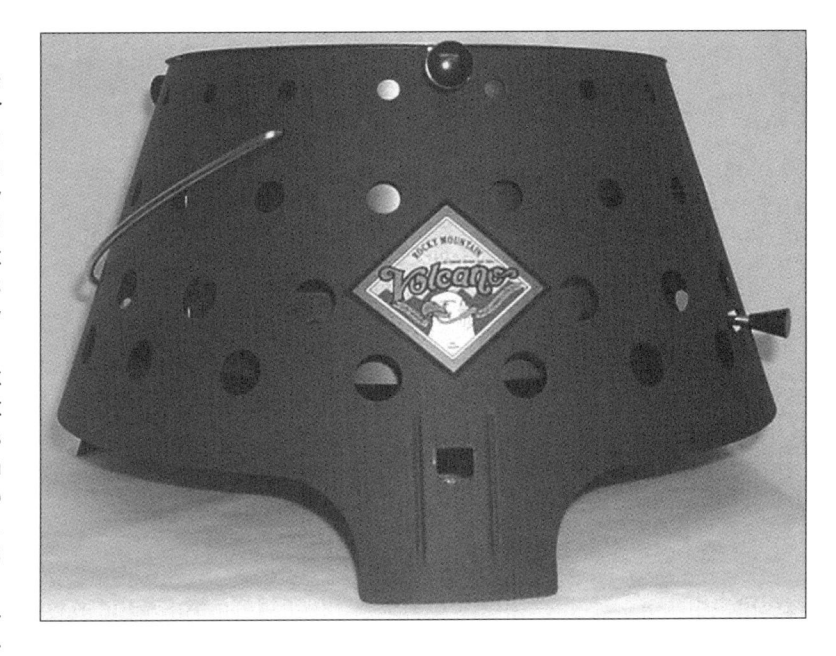

Volcanoes come fully assembled and are constructed of high quality 18-20 gauge cold-rolled steel. You can use them on a boat deck, patio, in the grass or even on a tabletop since the outer surface remains cool. Heat is funneled up, not down. Air enters through the holes on its side and a damper control near the bottom regulates temperature.

Its three-legged design, like that of some Dutch Ovens, provides a solid base to prevent tipping over. The fuel sits inside a cylinder similar to a charcoal chimney so it heats quickly. Nearly flush with the top of the Volcano is a grill for barbecuing. The neat thing about the Volcano Stove is this grill can be removed and replaced by a wok, an iron skillet or 12" Dutch Oven. You can use either aluminum or cast iron DOs, with or without legs. With the Dutch Oven on top, it makes frying, baking, simmering, stewing, steaming and roasting a breeze.

The Volcano measures 12" (30.5cm) high, 19 pounds (8.2kg) with a 12" (30.5cm) grill. The collapsible model folds to 5". Volcano stoves can be ordered through the following companies: Volcano Grills: **www.volcanogrills.com,** 888.320.2005 (US); In Case Of: **www.incaseof.ca/**, 888.901.3336 (Canada). For people outside of the U.S. and Canada, order the Volcano from various companies over the Internet or make inquiries to **info@volcanogrills.com**. Other resources: Dutch Oven Pro **www.dutchovenpro.com** and Amazon: **www.amazon.com**. Prices are around US$100 for the multi-fuel model and $150 for the propane unit.

COBB GRILL

An interesting alternative to the Volcano is a Cobb Grill. Its small size makes it ideal for those with limited space or for cooking on a balcony. Cobbs are restricted to charcoal only, but they make the best of this heat. Just 8 briquettes cook up to 3 hours. Especially in longer-duration emergencies this "coal-pinching" feature maximizes your charcoal supply. These little grills are so powerful; they are favorites of boaters, tailgaters and campers besides people who use them as their main outdoor BBQ. The Cobb has won multiple awards including *Time Magazine's* 2001 Invention of the Year and two prestigious VESTA awards at the Hearth, Patio & Barbecue Association Expo 2003.

Like the Volcano, Cobbs can bake, barbecue, boil, fry, grill or roast. Additionally, this one can smoke foods.

Cobbs come in two models: Premier and Pro. They are basically the same cooker except the Premier is totally made of stainless steel while the Pro's base is made in enamel-coated steel. Both weigh just 9 pounds (4kg) and measure 14"H x 12½" diameter (35 cm x 32 cm).

For fastest use, light coals in a chimney starter. This gets them ready in about 10 minutes though they can be ignited with a firestarter directly in the grill. Transfer the coals to the Cobb, replace the cooking surface and lid. Wait 5 minutes and then add food.

Cobbs cook like a convection oven reaching up to 500°F while staying cool on the outside. Because foods cook by heat swirling around them and don't have to be directly on the cooking surface, you can stack food on the grill.

Cobb's Pro Portable model starts around $100. The Premier starts at $140. Loaded with accessories – Wok, Skillet/Pan, Roasting Rack, Griddle, Smoker Pot, Thermometer, Cook Book, Cutting Board and Firestarters – adds about $200 to the base cost. Check Cobb Portable Grill **www.cobbq.com**, Amazon **www.amazon.com** and Orvis **www.orvis.com**.

Hmmm. . . .Maybe this is too easy. Do you want a new challenge? It could prove fun for the whole family.

Chapter 32: Solar Cooking

Are you feeling creative? How about making your own box oven? Remember each charcoal briquette puts out about 25°F (14°C) of heat. So plan how many coals you need on that average. Here's how to make a terrific little cooker, tested by many Boy Scouts!

BOX OVEN COOKING

Turn a cardboard box into an oven? You bet, and it works nearly as well as a house oven! Below are three variations of a cardboard box oven. These three variations all use charcoal briquettes as the fuel.

1. OPEN TOP BOX OVEN

Cut off the flaps that make the "top" so the box has four straight sides and a bottom. The bottom of the box will be the top of the oven.

Cover the box **inside completely** with aluminum foil, shiny side out. To use the oven, place the pan with food to be baked on a footed grill over the lit charcoal briquettes. The grill should be raised about 10" (25.5cm) above the charcoal. Set the cardboard oven over the food and charcoal. Prop up one end of the oven with a pebble to provide the air charcoal needs to burn or cut air vents along the lower edge of the oven.

2. COPY PAPER BOX OVEN

Use the cardboard boxes that hold 10 reams of 8½x11", 8½x14" or 21x29.5cm sized paper. Line the inside of the box and lid with aluminum foil, shiny side out. Dab some Elmer's or white glue around the inside and cover to hold the foil in place. Make several holes in the cover to let combustion gases out. Punch several holes around the sides near the bottom to let oxygen in.

Make a tray to hold the charcoal using one or two metal pie pans. Make feet for a single pie plate using nuts and bolts, or bolt two pie plates together bottom to bottom. Cut a couple coat hangers to make a rack to hold up the cooking pan. Poke the straight pieces of coat hanger through one side, and into the other. Two pieces will usually do fine.

Put several lit briquettes on the pie pan, place the cooking pan on the rack, and place the cover on top. The first time you use this box oven, check to make sure enough oxygen is getting in, and enough gases are escaping, to keep the charcoal burning.

HOW MANY BRIQUETTES TO USE					
Desired °F	Desired °C	Briquettes	Desired °F	Desired °C	Briquettes
250°F	120°C	6	375°F	190°C	9
300°F	150°C	8	400°F	200°C	10
350°F	175°C	9	450°F	230°C	12

NOTE: If it's windy or cold, add one or two extra briquettes.

3. BOX OVEN
Materials needed:
  1 large box (alcohol and wine boxes work great or any double corrugated box that will fit a cake pan or cookie sheet with about 1" (2.5cm) all around. Note: A lid or top is not necessary.
  Lots of long-length high quality, heavy duty, aluminum foil
  Four small TIN juice cans
  9x13" (23x33cm) cake/roasting pan or small cookie sheet
  1 #10 can, cut out both ends and vent bottom for charcoal chimney
  1 small stone to vent bottom

Cover the inside of box with two layers of foil. In Australia, aluminum foil is thinner; use four layers. Be sure no cardboard is showing anywhere. It can be taped on the outside. Place a large sheet of foil on a level, non-burnable, piece of ground. Place the charcoal chimney on the foil along with a firestarter and briquettes.

Light the chimney and wait about 20 minutes for charcoal to be ready. Pull off chimney and spread out charcoal to fit under pan used. Place four small juice cans to support cake pan and lower box oven over all. Vent on the side that's away from the wind with small stone propped under one edge. Cook for amount of time specified in recipe. If cooking for much more than 30 minutes replenish charcoal

SOLAR BOX COOKING

Solar cooking is not a new concept. A Swiss naturalist designed the first solar cooker in 1767. This technique is used in many countries including Australia, Canada, China, France, Germany, Great Britain, Greece, India, Italy, Kenya, Mexico, the Netherlands and United States. As long as you live in a sunny location, they work great and will work under less-than-sunny conditions though cooking time will lengthen. We have friends both in Perth and Phoenix using these simple solar boxes with great success. Possibly the key is that both cities have over 300 sunny days. Solar boxes cook well any time during the Summer months and when the sun is the strongest, between 10 AM and 2 PM during the rest of the year.

They could be a good option for folks living in apartments, condos or duplexes that don't have access to backyards, but do have a balcony or patio.

Still Skeptical? They work surprisingly efficiently. A single-reflector box cooker usually can reach 300°F (150°C). One misconception is that high temperatures are necessary for cooking food. Food will cook in solar boxes at temperatures of 200°F (90°C). The higher temperatures we use in conventional ovens are for cooking speed and browning. One really great thing about these cookers is that food can't burn so constant attention and stirring is not necessary. As a guideline, food takes about twice as long to cook.

Yes, believe it, cardboard will work just fine for your cooker. As long as you can count on at least 20 minutes of sun per hour, your solar box cooker will work. However, if you live in pretty windy areas or plan to leave it outside in the rain, you may want to make a solar box cooker out of more substantial materials like plywood. Some cardboard cookers have been in use for more than 10 years!

> *Solar Box Cookers can be made in many different dimensions to suit the size of your family and food needs. These general tips will help guide your construction.*

OVEN SIZE

If you are cooking for one, make the oven small. Family-sized units should have a glazed opening (glass area) approximately 18-24" (46-61cm). To help determine the size of oven to build, measure the pans you'll use and make the cooker 1" (2.5cm) deeper than your pots are high (including lid).

REFLECTOR

To get the most out of your oven, make the reflector as large as the whole lid, not just the glazed opening. Where sun is less strong or during the winter, this trick will maximize solar energy.

LID

Make sure the lid fits tightly against the cooker to seal in heat. When you cut the cardboard (or whatever you're making the solar box cooker from) be sure it is uniform in height.

TRAY

The bottom of the inside of the oven must be dark. Using dark cardboard will work, but a much better option would be metal. Look for aluminum flashing, galvanized tin or corrugated steel at your hardware store. Spray it flat black with a non-toxic paint used for BBQ's and wood stoves. Rust-Oleum and Krylon are just two brands that sell high heat paint, which can resist temperatures up to 1200°F (649°C).

Aerosols actually hold up to higher temps than the brush-on counterparts. Expect to pay around $5 per can. This paint is found in hardware and some BBQ supply stores.

If you raise this tray from direct contact with the box under it, cooking will improve since the heat isn't going out the bottom of the box. Do this by placing some additional cardboard under the tray.

INSULATION

Like the walls of your home, a little insulation keeps temperature constant. Filling the void between the inner and outer walls of your cooker improves cooking times. Real insulation is not a good idea due to fire hazards. Instead, cover several individual sheets of cardboard with foil and insert these between the inner and outer walls forming several extra "walls". By gluing ⅛" (3mm) pieces of wood or cardboard between the foil covered walls, it will naturally form additional air pockets. Other materials to insulate would be wool or feathers.

POTS

The best pots to use are made from non-reflective black metal. Baker's Secret has a line of cookware that is lightweight, dark, non-reflective and non-stick. Cast iron, while dark, is too thick which greatly slows or stops cooking. Look for shallower pans rather than deep ones. Pyrex also has a smoked-glass cookware line. Other ideas might include roughing up glass jars with sandpaper and painting them with the same non-toxic paint used on the tray. Another trick is to put shiny pots in a brown paper sack.

Figure A

One problem with solar cookers is using bowls or oven bags that don't allow easy access to the food. They retain moisture coming from the heated food and need periodic drying. This drawback can be avoided by putting the lower part of the cooking pot inside a glass bowl (Fig. A), instead of the whole pot with its lid. Place the dark pot into a glass dish whose diameter is slightly larger than that of the pot. The advantages of such a system are partially offset by extra heat loss from the uninsulated lid. By raising the pot off the ground a further gain is achieved.

COOKING STRATEGY

"The single biggest reason for failure in solar cooking is not putting in the food early enough in the day. Get it on early, and don't worry about overcooking!" [78]

It makes sense that foods cook fastest in a cloudless sky, during summer, near the equator. If you aren't cooking in these circumstances, it will still work well. In the absence of smog and haze, foods cook more quickly. There are two ways to cook in a solar oven. If you refocus the oven to follow the sun every 25 to 30 minutes, cooking times and methods will be more similar to cooking with a conventional stove or oven. The other way is to use it for slow cooking like a crock-pot. For this method, prepare your dinner, put it in the solar oven, and point the oven to where the sun will be approximately halfway through the cooking time.

If the recipe cooks food in less than 4 hours, there's no need to turn the box to follow the sun. If you're cooking beans or other foods that may require 8 hours, the box needs to be turned at least once.

TIPS: The cooker can be waterproofed with a coating of glue and candle wax. Cover the entire exterior of the solar box cooker with fabric dipped in white glue. Dry completely. Pour melted and partially cooled, but still pourable candle wax, coating all the fabric. Recoat until the box has all areas covered.

To remove condensation easily between double panes of glass (glazed area) in a wooden cooker, drill one or more holes into the airspace from the side. Plug these holes with corks during cooking. To clear condensation between the panes, remove the corks and allow the cooker to heat.

SOLAR COOKER #1

Step 1 Find two boxes, which fit one inside the other, leaving between 2-4" (5-10cm) of space between the inside box and outside box. Be sure this space is on the bottom as well.

Step 2 Place any type of insulation (newsprint, paper, Styrofoam, etc.) between the two boxes. Ensure the insulation does not protrude past the top of the inner box.

SOLAR COOKER #1

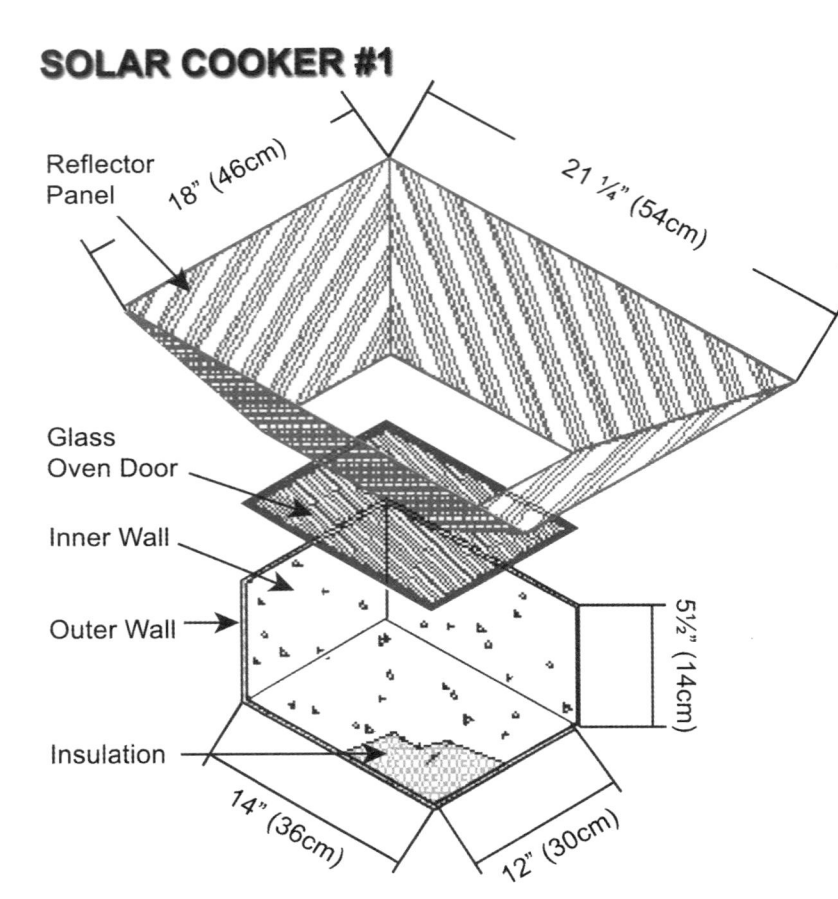

Reflector Panel — 18" (46cm), 21 ¼" (54cm)
Glass Oven Door
Inner Wall
Outer Wall
Insulation
14" (36cm), 12" (30cm), 5½" (14cm)

Step 3 Paint the inside of the smaller box with a mixture of non-toxic black paint and Elmer's or white glue.

Step 4 Reflectors are usually made out of cardboard or other stiff, durable material. Follow the diagram for pattern.

Step 5 Use glue to attach aluminum foil to one side of the reflector panel.

Step 6 Assemble the four reflectors according to the diagram using string or wire.

Step 7 Use care on this step. Cut a piece of window glass to the size of ½" (1.27cm) larger than the dimensions of the inner box top. The edges of the glass should be smoothed or covered.

Step 8 Use weather stripping or old bike tubing to seal the edges of the inner box with the glass cover. The better the seal, the more efficient the cooker will be.

Step 9 Before using the oven, let it heat up a few times, removing the glass top each time. This allows any noxious gasses to be burned off.

Step 10 Cook with Solar Power!

SOLAR COOKER #2: REFLECTIVE OPEN BOX

This is another easy solar oven designed by Roger Bernard who has made numerous original plans, each one improving upon the last. Mr. Bernard finds that the simpler the design, the more efficient overall is the unit – the KISS (Keep It Short 'n Simple) principal at work!

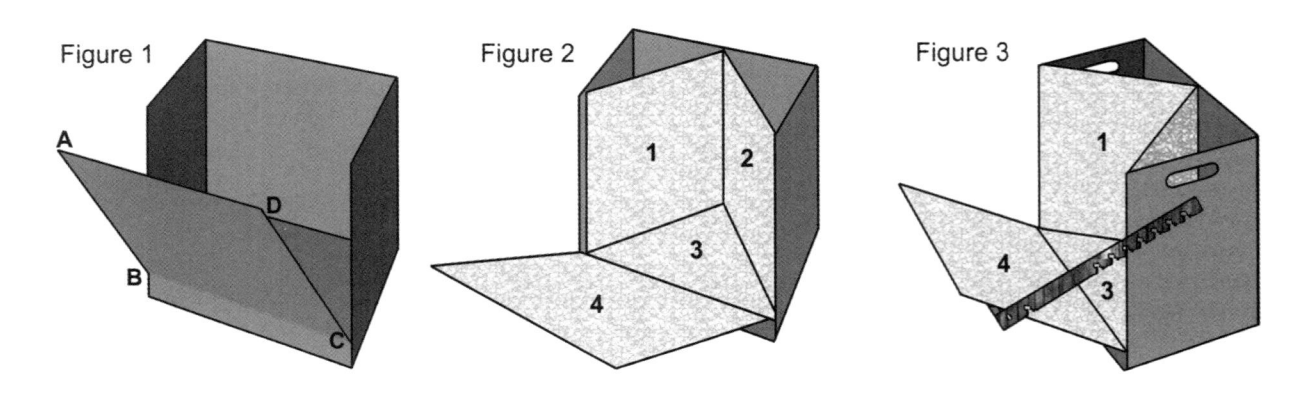

Figure 1
Figure 2
Figure 3

Step 1 To make this Reflective Open Box (ROB), start with a rectangular, tall cardboard box. On one of the broader sides, draw a horizontal line (BC) about 2 inches (5cm) above the bottom (Fig. 1) and cut the seams along AB (stop at B) and DC (stop at BC).

Step 2 Fold down the front panel ABCD using BC as a hinge.

Step 3 Stack a few rectangular pieces of cardboard in the bottom of the box, to raise the floor level up to the level of BC.

Step 4 Cut and fold another piece of cardboard so that it can be inserted into the box to form panels 1 and 2 in Figure 2.

The angle formed by these panels is adjustable during construction. Smaller angles concentrate the Sun more, but require more frequent adjusting to follow the Sun. A good compromise is 60-90°. Cover this piece with aluminum foil and glue or staple it in place. Apply aluminum foil to panels 3 and 4 as well.

These dimensions make a reflective area of about 775 sq. in. (5,000 sq. cm.), which is sufficient to cook for two persons.

Use a wooden prop to adjust the front panel (figure 3). The single notch near panel 4 is used to lock this panel in a closed position for storage. Rocks can be placed in the triangular chambers behind panels 1 and 2 to stabilize the cooker in windy conditions.

Photo: Finished Reflective Open Box Cooker with overall dimensions of: Length: 18" (46cm), Width: 12½" (32cm), and Height: 16½" (42cm). Designer Roger Bernard's contact info: A.L.E.D.E.S., Université de Lyon, 69 622 – Villeurbanne, France.

SOLAR COOKER #3:

THE "EASY LID" COOKER

Despite the simple design, in the right conditions, it can cook up a storm. One of the areas that presents the most difficulty in making solar cookers is fitting the lid properly. The Easy Lid Cooker, designed by Chao Tan and Tom Sponheim, eliminates this problem since a lid is formed automatically from the outer box.

NOTE: Illustrations for this cooker appear on the next page.

MAKING THE BASE

Step 1	Cut a large box it in half as shown in Fig. 1. Set one half aside for the lid and the other forms the base.
Step 2	Fold an extra cardboard piece so it forms a liner around the inside of the base (see Figure 2).
Step 3	Use the lid piece as shown in Figure 3 to mark a line around the liner.
Step 4	Cut along this line, leaving the four tabs as shown in Figure 4.
Step 5	Glue aluminum foil to the inside of the liner and to the bottom of the outer box inside.
Step 6	Set a smaller (inner) box into the opening formed by the liner until the flaps of the smaller box are horizontal and flush with the top of the liner (see Fig. 5). Place crumpled newspaper between the two boxes for support.
Step 7	Mark the underside of the flaps of the smaller box using the liner as a guide.
Step 8	Fold these flaps down to fit down around the top of the liner and tuck them into the space between the base and the liner (see Fig. 6).
Step 9	Fold the tabs over and tuck them under the flaps of the inner box so they obstruct the holes in the four corners (see Fig. 6).
Step 10	Now glue these pieces together in their present configuration.
Step 11	As the glue is drying, line the inside of the inner box with aluminum foil.

FINISHING THE LID

Step 1	Measure the width of the walls of the base and use these measurements to calculate where to make the cuts that form the reflector in Figure 7. Only cut on three sides. The reflector is folded up using the fourth side as a hinge.
Step 2	Glue plastic or glass in place on the underside of the lid. If using glass, sandwich the glass using extra strips of cardboard. Allow to dry.
Step 3	Bend the ends of the wire as shown in Figure 7 and insert these into the corrugations on the lid and on the reflector to prop open the latter.
Step 4	Paint the sheet metal (or cardboard) black and place it inside of the oven.

EASY LID SOLAR COOKER #3

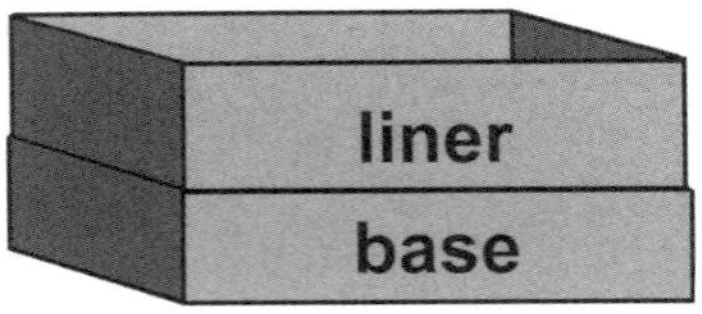

Figure 1

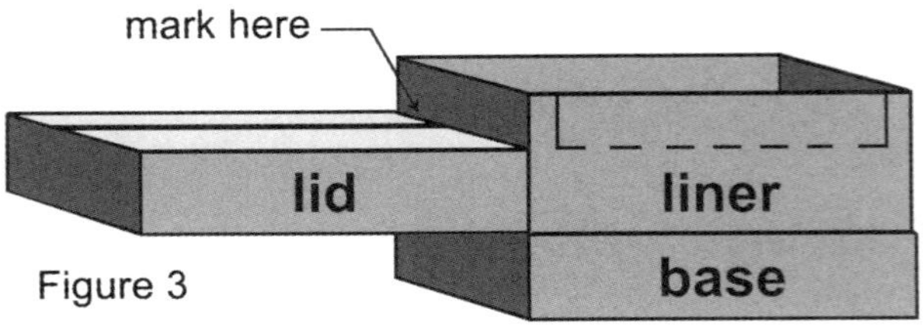

Figure 2

Figure 3
mark here

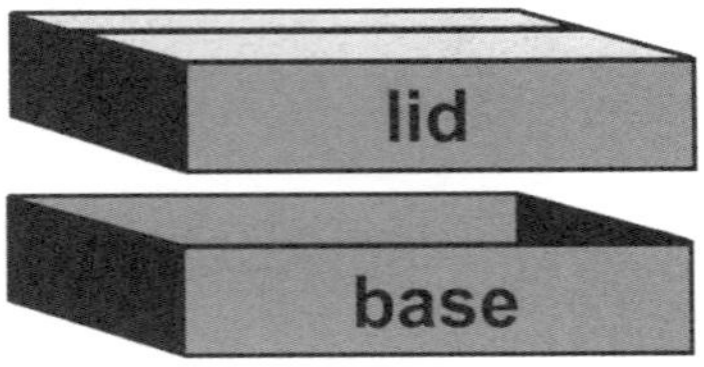

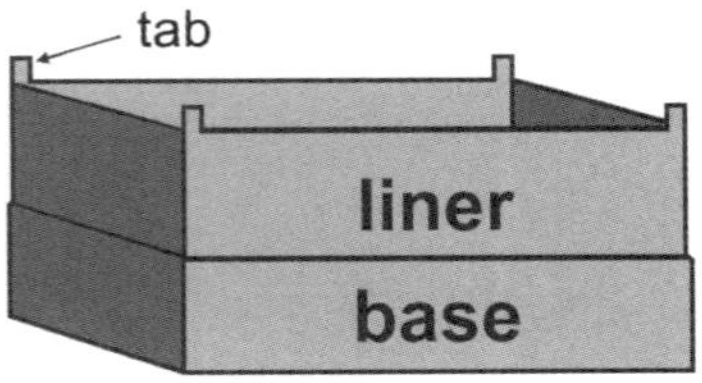

Figure 4
tab

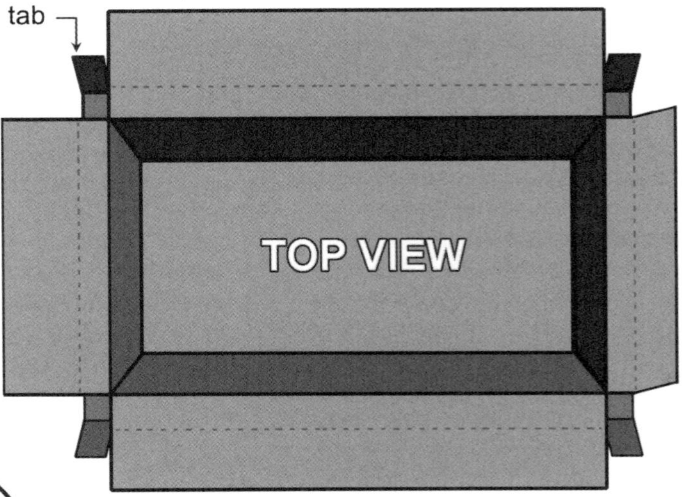

Figure 5
tab
TOP VIEW

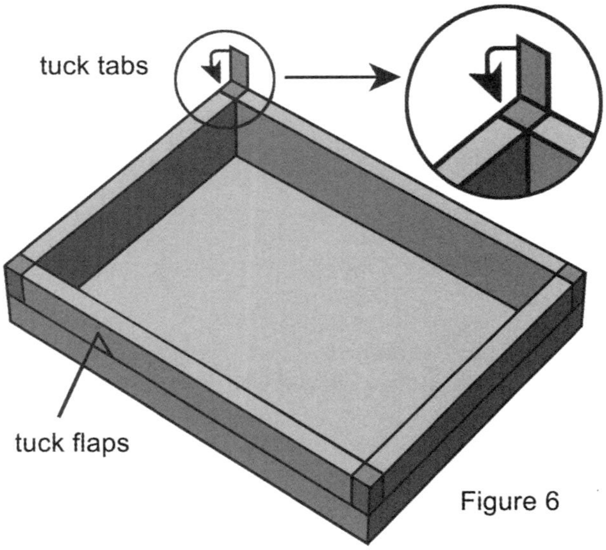

Figure 6
tuck tabs
tuck flaps

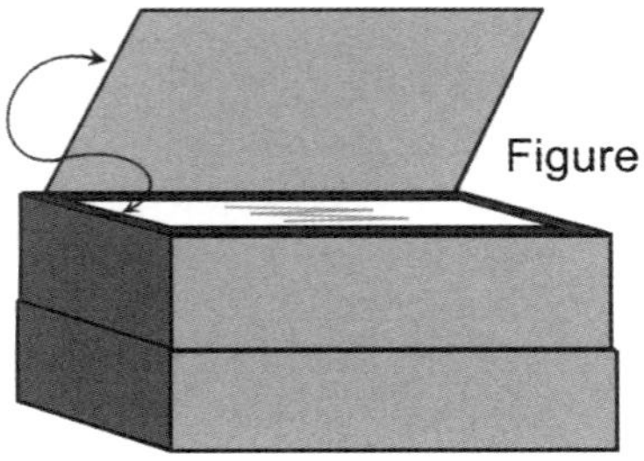

Figure 7

IMPROVING EFFICIENCY

Step 1 Glue thin strips of cardboard underneath the sheet metal (or cardboard) to elevate it off of the bottom of the oven slightly.

Step 2 Cut off the reflector and replace it with one that is as large as (or larger than) the entire lid. This reflects light into the oven more reliably.

Step 3 Turn the oven over and open the bottom flaps. Place a foiled cardboard panel into each airspace dividing it into two spaces. The foiled side should face the center of the oven.

Here's what your finished Easy Lid Solar Cooker will look like.

COMMERCIAL SOLAR OVENS

If you don't have time to make a solar cooker, a really nice commercial model, the Global Sun Oven, can be purchased starting at $225. Though it reaches temperatures of 360-400°F, food won't burn. Solar ovens are *very* forgiving. This is one of the few models with a built-in thermometer. It isn't necessary, but it's a nice amenity to help users judge cooking times till they get the hang of it. Because it's well-insulated cooking times are close those for a conventional oven.

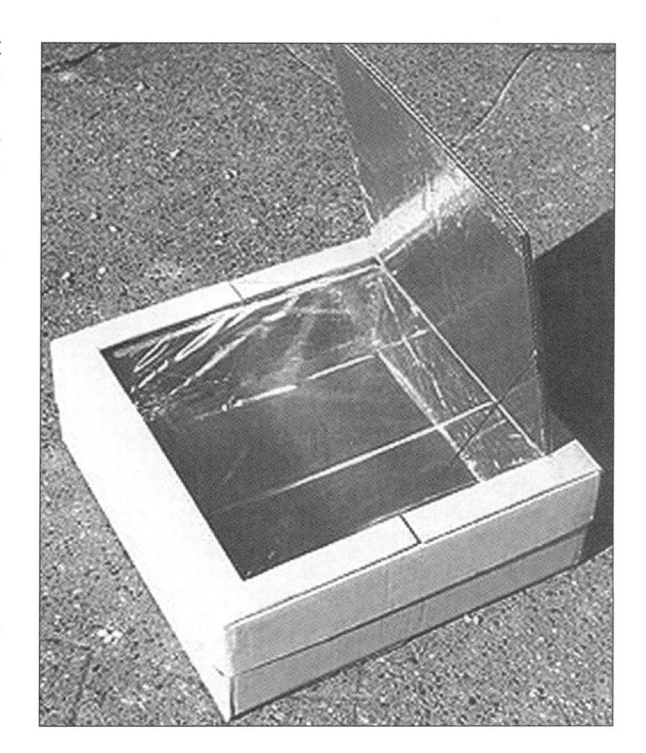

Suppliers include Sun Ovens **www.sunoven.com**, Solar Ovens and Sun Cookers **www.solarovens.net**, Bonza Buy **www.bonzabuy.com.au**, and Solar Chef Europe **www.solarchef.eu**.

The Sun Oven is portable weighing 21 pounds (9.5 kg). Cooking space might be its only drawback. Website information states its dimensions are 19"x19" (48x48 cm) with an average depth of 11". However, the actual cooking space measures roughly 14"x14" (35.5x35.5 cm) and about 7" (18 cm) deep at its shallowest. Using its "swinging shelf", drops the width down to 12" (30.5 cm).

If you are a solar cooking novice, you may want to purchase a cookbook as none comes with the Sun Oven and very little in the way of instructions.

SOLAR COOKBOOKS

Cooking With Sunshine, Complete Guide to Solar Cuisine with 150 Easy Sun-Cooked Recipes. Lorraine Anderson and Rick Palkovic, Da Capo Press, 224 pages, 2006, ISBN-13: 978-1569243008, **amazon.com**.

The Solar Chef, Southwestern Recipes for Solar Cooking. Rose Kern, 50 pages, 80 recipes, **www.sunoven.com**.

The Sunny Side of Cooking : Solar cooking and other ecologically friendly cooking methods for the 21st century. (vegetarian recipes) Lisa Rayner, 100+ recipes, 128 pages. P.O. Box 22324, Flagstaff, AZ 86002; **www.lisarayner.com**.

GENERAL COOKING TIMES		
FOOD	COOK TIME 4-5 SERVINGS	COMMENTS
CEREALS AND GRAINS Barley, Wheat Corn, Millet, Oats, Quinoa, Rice	2 hours	Start with usual amount of water. If sky conditions are less than ideal, preheat the water and grain separately, as suggested for pasta. This is especially helpful if the grain is either very slow to tenderize (brown rice, hulled but not pearled barley) or gets mushy easily (quinoa, millet).
VEGETABLES, Fresh	1½-2 hours	No Water
Artichokes	2½ hours	No water
Asparagus	1-1½ hours	No water
Beans, Dried	3-5 hours	Usual amount of water, can be soaked ahead of time
Beets, Carrots, Potatoes and other root vegetables	3 hours	No Water
Cabbage	1-1½ hours if cut up	No Water
Corn on the cob	1-1½ hours	No water; Cook with or without husk or even in a clean black sock.
Eggplant	1-1½ hours if cut up	No water. Eggplant turns brownish, like a cut apple, but flavor is good.
Squash, zucchini	1 hour	Will turn mushy if left longer
FRUIT	1-2 hours	
MEATS	1-8 hours	No water.
Chicken	2 hours cut up, 3 hours whole	No water. If cooked longer it just gets more tender.
Beef, Lamb, etc.	2 hours cut up, 3-5 hours for large pieces	No water. If cooked longer they just get more tender.
Fish	1-2 hours	No water. If cooked longer it just gets more tender.
Turkey, large, whole	All day	No water. If cooked longer it just gets more tender.
PASTA		Heat water in one pot and put dry pasta with small amount of cooking oil in another pot; heat until water is near boiling. Add hot pasta to hot water, stir, and cook about 10 minutes more.
BAKING	Best done 9 or 10 am to 2 or 3 pm)	May sprinkle cinnamon on top to darken surface & catch more sun.
Breads: Whole loaves	3 hours	Does not need to be covered.
Cakes	1-1½ hours	Does not need to be covered.
Cookies	1-1½ hours	Does not need to be covered.
Pies	1-1½ hours	Does not need to be covered. Avoid bottom crusts – they get soggy.
SAUCES AND GRAVIES Made With Flour or Starch	Minutes	Heat juices and flour separately, with or without a little cooking oil in the flour. Then combine and stir. It will be ready quickly.
SOUPS AND STEWS	5-8 hours	
NUTS, ROASTING		
Almonds	1 hour	Bake uncovered.
Peanuts	2 hours	Bake uncovered.
EGGS	2 hours for hard yolks	No Water. If cooked longer the whites turn brown, but the flavor is the same.

Chapter 33: Communications

Especially during emergencies, we all want to be in touch with loved ones and know what's going on. What happens when the power goes out, would your cell phone work? How about landlines? CBs? Two way radios? There isn't a one-size-fits-all solution, so maybe the best answer is multiple choice.

CONVENTIONAL PHONES

Corded landline phones – our conventional system – may work even when power is out to the rest of your home. It depends on what caused the failure and where it occurred. Standard phone lines receive electricity from a phone junction center, which often has power when the surrounding area doesn't. However, if the power failure struck at the junction box, then phones in that area won't work.

VOIP

The most at-risk phone system has to one that relies on broadband for connectivity – Voice over IP (VoIP). People tout much lower monthly bills, and if times were normal, this might be worth a second look. However, if your Internet connection goes down, so does this phone.

CELL PHONES

These phones are really just another form of radio like a walkie-talkie except they use two frequencies instead of one. This allows simultaneous conversations, a way to both speak and listen. With a CB or walkie-talkie, one person talks at a time.

Cell phones have greater transmitting capabilities than CBs with up to 1,664 channels. CBs are confined to 40 channels and walkie-talkies use just one. Federal regulations stipulate that there must be at least two service providers in an area to keep pricing competitive and they divide up the 1,664 channels. More channels mean less congestion – unless there's an emergency.

While 3G (third generation) – true multimedia electronics or smartphones – was supposed to unify mobile computing devices, they've hit snags. To integrate such globally diverse systems has proved challenging and they still have confusing sets of standards.

Without getting G3 problems fixed, technology has shifted to 4G, which offers true high-speed data rates. Entire movies download in minutes – 10 times faster than 3G. 3G phones operate in the 1920-1980MHz and 2110-2170MHz frequencies and may also find a home in the 700MHz band.

4G networks snagged the highly prized 700MHz band often referred to as "beachfront property". This band is coveted since its power comes from a much better signal than 2G and 3G's 1900MHz. It should give superior mobile broadband performance over greater distances and pioneering Verizon hopes for full U.S. coverage in 2013.

In case you're wondering, 1G technology was the analog system and 2G was digital capability. Kind of sounds like operating in the dark ages now.

CELL PHONES PLUSES

In emergencies, cell phones may work when other phones won't. Federal law requires that all cell phones – even ones not connected with a service plan or ones whose plan has expired or has been cancelled – be able to connect to 911. This means any cell phone with power and that can receive a signal is still capable of calling 911 even if you can't make other calls with it.

Some cell phones allow you to enter a short text message, which might get through if an emergency overloads voice circuits. Depending on your phone, you could preset a message like as "C U @ R spot" if you have a pre-arranged family meet-up location.

Most phones are automatically equipped with GPS which can aid in locate and rescue operations. It can also facilitate unwanted tracking even though it's illegal in the U.S. except when parents monitor their child.

Cell phones cover an incredible range and many carriers now offer free long distance. So if you need to contact family or friends around the country, it may cost next to nothing to stay in touch.

IMPORTANT: With so many people relying solely on cell phones and completely foregoing land lines, it puts them in an extremely vulnerable communication position.

DRAWBACKS

Since cell phones transmit calls by towers, if you are in a remote area, your cell may be out of range when it's needed. We've all experienced sudden drops during conversations or a frustrating "No Service" message.

Usually reliable cell phones may or may not work in power outages and cordless phones certainly won't since they require electricity. In extended outages, when landlines are useless, people often turn to cell phones. However, due to heavily increased traffic, it may be impossible to get through. If power is disrupted to the tower like with a lightning strike or damaged by some other event, cell phones are effectively neutered. Some towers have emergency generators or battery back-up systems, but this is only a short-term fix.

Something else that interferes with cell phones is solar activity. Now that Solar Cycle 24 is underway, chances of cell phone disruption increase due to solar storm activity. A 2002 study of 40 years' data showed solar energy bursts can drop calls across wide areas as often as twice a week. The problem stems from static overwhelming the signal when radio waves hit cell towers.[79] Since this energy from the Sun arrives in roughly 8 minutes, there's absolutely no warning. One minute you can be having a normal conversation, then dead air follows.

In prolonged power outages, you can simply lose cell phone use because the batteries haven't been charged.

A power outage doesn't have to occur to land you in cell phone strife. Pushing its buttons with damp fingers or using it in the rain can cause internal corrosion. If a cell phone gets wet, be sure it's totally dry before switching it on. Another problem is extreme heat, which can damage the battery or electronics. At the other end of the spectrum, extreme cold may cause the screen display to flicker.

SATELLITE PHONES

These mobile phones are more frequently used by overseas journalists, people involved in disaster response, and increasingly, by terrorists. Though similar in appearance to cell phones, their networks connect via satellite 22,000 miles (35,000 km) above earth instead of using land-based equipment.

Satphones are not deterred by equipment damage on earth, but they are subject to satellites remaining operational. More often news crops up about the weaponization of space. Despite treaties, China tried and failed to disable a U.S. satellite with lasers in 1996.[80] The following year, China succeeded in destroying a satellite via ballistic missile.[81] It would be a major coup for an enemy to take out a vital communications satellite. Loss of satphone would only be one of our worries.

In 1998, a massive satellite failure spontaneously occurred when Galaxy IV's on-board control system failed. Its loss wiped out pager traffic, halted credit card transactions and knocked TV and radio stations off the air.

Technology expert Lauren Weinstein stated on *Coast To Coast AM* late night talk radio that satellite phones aren't foolproof. They could be shut down much more readily than the Internet. They could be taken out of commission "with a few simple keystrokes" whether by hackers, a foreign agency or even our own government.

TWO-WAY RADIOS

What most of us grew up calling walkie-talkies now go by a variety of names: handheld transceivers (both transmits and receives), 2-way radios, walkie-talkies and handie-talkies. Occasionally a distinction is made saying there's a big gap between walkie-talkies and 2-way radios. There is, and it's kind of like the old joke of "what's the difference between *vase* (pronounced väz) and *vase*?" Answer: "About $300."

Despite some really nifty bells and whistles, they're still basically the same thing – gadgets that send and receive signals using a push-to-talk system.

Commercial 2-way radios are very much like consumer models but they're built to withstand more abuse. Some are waterproof, some aren't. Some have GPS, less expensive models don't. Some are like computers capable of text messaging. How they differ from cell phones is important in times of emergency. As with everything, there are pros and cons.

TWO-WAY RADIOS PLUSES

One of most important distinctions is that two-way radios don't rely on cell towers like cell phones. They are independent from any system or outside equipment operating radio to radio. In a serious crisis when even phone lines are down, they make communication possible. As long as you have charged batteries, you're good to go. Most radios using three or four AA batteries generally run 12-14 hours before they need replacing.

Communication is as fast as pressing a single button – PTT – press- (or push) to-talk technology. With cell phones, you have to enter the phone number or locate it in its address book and hope for a free line. Normally this isn't an is-sue, but in emergencies when landlines fail, people load up cell phone lines. Minutes can be critical.

If you want to communicate with family members or friends in close range, walkie-talkies can't be beat. Some radios can be set to the same frequency allowing "conference calls" or communication over larger distances. More expensive units also allow an individual to be singled out for private conversation while not sacrificing the "group" mode.

Beyond radio price and batteries, it costs you nothing to talk as much as you want unlike cell phone plans.

THEIR DRAWBACKS

Lack of range and blocked signals are walkie-talkies' biggest problems. With cell phones you can talk to people in other countries. The best walkie-talkies cover is about 18 miles.

Most FRS units operate at .5 watts output, some up to 5 miles or line of sight. This low wattage automatically limits communication to about one mile, sometimes two – providing no obstacles block transmission. Obstacles can be buildings, trees, vehicles, hills and mountains. Condition of the batteries can also lessen transmitting range as well as weather conditions and electromagnetic interference. Using 2-ways inside buildings or if one person is outdoors and the other is inside, also cuts talking distance. Higher wattage radios do give more range.

One way to boost transmission is a telescoping antenna for VHF models. This increases range over the radio's own short antenna. It's also possible to install an outside antenna which could increase communication to 5 miles if you aren't hampered by obstacles between points of communication. However, once you leave the vicinity of the antenna, you lose the boost and are back to square one.

Another option is a repeater. For this you need a specially built receiver with a repeater inside. This unit retransmits messages using a better antenna and more transmitting power. How much distance is gained depends on your location and the model. Ideally, if it's used on a mountaintop, range might jump to 100 miles.

CHANNELS

FRS (Family Radio Service) are 14 channels in the 462Mhz and 467MHz range used primarily by small groups like hunters, campers or families. Unlike the GMRS, no FCC license is required but it does have limitations. "Sport" radios using these channels have low power output from 0.2 to 0.5 watts. It's generally enough for their intended use – communication over short distances. They depend on line-of-site transmission and should reach about 2 miles under optimum conditions, providing nothing impedes the signal.

GMRS (General Mobile Radio Service) uses 10 channels in the 462MHz range. To communicate with other GMRS radios, you must have the same frequencies installed and the same programming for each channel. Since there are many programming variables, channel 5 on one radio may not be the same on another radio.

Like FRS, good, clear communication depends on terrain. These radios can cover up to 25 miles with their higher power of 2 to 5 watts. You must have an FCC license o operate GMRS radios. Only a small fee is charged. For details, phone 888-225-5322 or go online **wireless.fcc.gov/** to the FCC's Universal Licensing Sys-tem.

DECIDING WHAT TO GET

Before purchasing two-way radios, there are factors to consider. First, in what setting and how often will you likely use them? It would be easy to spend $500 on a single GPS/radio unit with 1½" color screen, barometric altimeter reading, electronic compass, USB port, lots of memory and other goodies. You have a spouse? Now you need two; that's $1000.

For about one-third the cost you can get still get a GPS mapping, waterproof radio with built in extras. One really useful feature is a memory chip that holds up to 500 trip markers and 20 different reversible routes. Being able to accurately backtrack your steps could be really important if you're in unfamiliar territory and chances of getting lost are high.

However, if satellites fail, GPS no longer works. Then you've spent a lot of money for technology that's unusable. However, if you go backpacking or off-roading frequently, it could be a worthwhile investment.

Sportsmen do well with less expensive models that can all tune to the same frequency. This makes communicating with each other easy over reasonably short distances. Models designed with camo exteriors are perfect for these settings. Waterproofing is another consideration unless you're a fair-weather fisherman. Sport units usually have animal call alerts as well as vibrate alert for silent communication.

POWER

Though higher wattage radios get better range, they drain batteries more quickly. To extend battery life, some models have the option of low, medium or high power settings. Most radios take two to four AA batteries with the option of either NiMH (nickel metal hydride) or lithium rechargeables. If you use walkie-talkies frequently, it's generally more cost effective to forego the AAs. When recharging isn't possible, AAs are good back-up power. Avoid radios using AAA batteries; operating life is too short.

Description/ (Radios per Pack)	Price	Size	Weight in Ounces	Screen Display	Power Watts	Max Range Miles	GMRS/ BRS Channels	FRS Channels
Cobra (2) LI 7000-2 WX silver/gray	$80	7 x 2 x ⅓	4.2	N/A	5	25	7	7 FRS
Cobra (2) LI 7020 WX-EVP Max-4 camo	$90	7 x 2 x 1⅓	4.2	N/A	2	25	8 GMRS	7 FRS; 7 FRS/ GMRS
Garmin (1) Rino 110 GPS Radio yellow/gray	$170	7 x 2¼ x 1¾	7.6 oz with batt. pack	1.4" x .4" 160 x 160 px, grayscale	½ FRS 1 GMRS	2 FRS 5 GMRS	8 GMRS	7 FRS; 7 FRS/ GMRS
Garmin (1) Rino 120 GPS Radio gray	$250	7 x 2½ x 1¾	7.6 oz with batt. pack	1.4" x .4" 160 x 160 px, grayscale	½ FRS 1 GMRS	2 FRS 5 GMRS	8 GMRS	7 FRS; 7 FRS/ GMRS
Garmin (1) Rino 130 GPS Radio gray	$350	7 x 2½ x 1¾	7.6 oz with batt. pack	1.4" x .4" 160 x 160 px, grayscale	½ FRS 1 GMRS	2 FRS 5 GMRS	15 GMRS	7 FRS; 7 FRS/ GMRS
Garmin (1) Rino 520HCX GMRS/FRS/GPS gray	$450	7½ x 2⅓ x 1¾	10.3 oz with battery pack	1.3" x 1.7" 176 x 220 px, 256 colors	5	2 FRS 14 GMRS	8 GMRS	7 FRS; 7 FRS/ GMRS
Garmin (1) gray Rino 530HCX GMRS/FRS/GPS	$500	7½ x 2⅓ x 1¾	10.3 oz with batt. pack	1.3" x 1.7", 176 x 220 px, 256 colors	½ FRS 2 GMRS	2 FRS 4 GMRS	8 GMRS	7 FRS; 7 FRS/ GMRS
Icom (1) IC-F21BR, FRS/GMRS black	$140	5 x 2 x 1½	10.6 oz with batt. pack	N/A	2	5	7 GMRS; 22 BRS	7 FRS
Icom (1) IC-F21GM, FRS/GMRS black	$160	5 x 2 x 1½	10.6 oz with batt. pack	N/A	4	5	7 GMRS	8 FRS
Icom (1) IC-F14S, BRS black	$190	4¾ x 2 x 1½	9.2 oz with batt. pack	N/A	5 – VHF 4 – UHF	6 mi. or 350,000 sq. ft.	16 BRS	0
Midland (2) GXT710 VP3 silver/black	$70	4¾ x 2½ x 1½	N/A	N/A	5	26	7 GMRS	7 FRS
Midland (2) GXT850VP4 GMRS camo	$100	8 x 2½ x 1¾	N/A	N/A	5	26	7 GMRS	7 FRS
Midland (2) GXT750VP3 GMRS camo	$80	7¾ x 2¼ x 1¾	1.8 lbs.	N/A	5	26	7 GMRS	7FRS
Motorola (2) FV750R camo FV700R blue	$60 $50	6¼ x 2⅜ x 1⅛	3.2 oz	1 x 1⅜	1	12	8 GMRS	7FRS; 7 FRS/ GMRS
Motorola (2) Talkabout T5000R silver	$40	6½ x 2⅜ x 1⅓	3.5 oz	¾ x ½	½ FRS; 1 GMRS; 1 FRS /GMRS	8	8 GMRS	7 FRS; 7 FRS/ GMRS
Motorola (2) T8500R orange T8550R camo	$70 $80	7¾ x 2⅜ x 1¼	6 oz	¾ x 1	½ FRS; 2 GMRS; 2 FRS/GMRS	18	8 GMRS	7 FRS; 7 FRS/ GMRS
Motorola (2) T9500 yellow T9550 camo	$80 $90	7¾ x 2½ x 1⅓	3.85 oz	¾ x 1	5	25	8 GMRS	7 FRS; 7 FRS/ GMRS
Motorola T9580 Talkabout (2) silver/black	$90	7¾ x 2½ x 1⅓	3.85 oz	¾ x 1	5	25	8 GMRS	7FRS; 7 FRS/ GMRS

NOAA Channel	Privacy Codes	Battery Type	VOX* or eVOX iVOIX	FCC License	Features
10	121	Lithium	Yes	Yes	2-port desktop charger, vibrate alert, 10-channel memory, scan function
10	22	Rechargeable Lithium Ion	Yes	Yes	2 rechargeable battery packs
N/A	38	3 AA 5-hours use	Yes	Yes	12-channel GPS mapping, accurate to 10 feet, 1 MB memory, holds 500 waypoints & 20 reversible routes, beams position 2 mi. to Rino users
N/A	38	3 AA	Yes	Yes	Same as Rino 110 with 8 MB memory, voice scrambler
7	38	3 AA	Yes	Yes	Same as Rino 110 plus voice scrambler, barometric altimeter, electronic compass, 24 MB memory, text messaging
None	38	Rechargeable Lithium Ion Pack	Yes	Yes	Charging eqpt., built-in basemap, vibrate alert, PC/USB interface, built-in basemap, color display, USB port, voice scrambler, vibrate mode, beam position to Rino users
Yes	38	Rechargeable Lith-ion pack, 14 hours	Yes	Yes	Same as Rino 520HCX plus NOAA weather, barometric altimeter, electronic compass, won Field & Stream Magazine 2006 Best of the Best Award
None	52	600mAh NiCD	available	Yes	Channels pre-programmed & user programmable, Mil spec, adjustable squelch, AC adapter, drop in charger, CTCSS signaling, "Frequency Find"
None	Yes	1650 mAh NiCD	available	Yes	Channels pre-programmed & user programmable, Mil spec, adjustable squelch, AC adapter, drop in charger, CTCSS signaling, "Frequency Find"
None	CTCSS /DCS	2000 mAh Li-Ion 14 hours use	available	Yes	2 channels pre-programmed & user programmable, Mil spec, adjustable squelch, AC adapter, drop in charger, simple operation, low battery alert
10	121	NiMH rechargeable pack or 4 AA	Yes	Yes	Charging eqpt. inc., NOAA weather alert, vibrate alert, silent function, 3 power levels, water resistant, silent op. auto squelch, auto scan, 5 call alerts
10	142	NiMH rechargeable pack or 4 AA	Yes	Yes	Charging eqpt. inc., waterproof-JIS4 spec, NOAA weather & vibrate, alerts, 5 animal call alerts direct call – talk with 1 person without notifying the rest.
10	121	4 AA	Yes	Yes	5 animal call alerts, vibrate alert, silent op., monitor, auto squelch, 3 power levels, auto squelch, channel scan
11	121	NiMH rechargeable or 3 AAA	Yes	Yes	Charging eqpt., battery life extender, low batt. alert & meter, AC wall adapter; digital signaling, backlit display, keypad lock, 10 call tones, priority scan
0	38	NiMH rechargeable or 3 AAA	Yes	Yes	Charging eqpt., 5 audible call alerts, time out timer, transmit LED, backlit display, noise filter, manual scan, low battery alert
11	121	Rechargeable pack or 3 AA	Yes	Yes	Charging equip. inc., vibrate alert, battery meter, low battery alert, keypad lock, 10 call tones, priority scan
11	121	Rechargeable or 3 AA	Yes	Yes	Same as T8500R with more range, NOAA weather alert, Camo model 9550 has 2 sets of push to talk microphones with earbuds, battery & power save
11	121	Rechargeable or 3 AA	Yes	Yes	Same as T9500 filters out distant weather info; local emergency & weather only

Some radios can be recharged at home with AC accessories and some can take 12-volt adapters for use in a car, boat or RV. Be sure you've included these extras.

DISPLAY
Is the screen is readable for *you?* The model on the right is only 4¼" high and 2½" wide. The left one is 6" tall and 2¼" wide, but the overall radio's screen is literally half the size. Most displays are backlit for easy night reading, but if you have trouble reading without glasses, think larger screen. If your glasses get broken in an emergency, you may have to rely on eyes only.

WEATHER AND WATERPROOFING
Depending on the circumstances, protecting your radio against the elements may be necessary. From years of boating on Lake Powell, we concluded VHF marine radios should be mandatory. Not only did they keep us informed of approaching bad weather, on a lake the size of Powell, it can be lifesaving. With literally hundreds of hidden canyons and "fingers", it's easy for novices to get lost. Only six marinas cover 1,900 miles of coastline, so it's a long time between gas and amenities. Depending on where you choose to explore, it may be several <u>days</u> before seeing another person. Occasionally we witnessed people stranded on the lake without radios, water or spare fuel – often with little kids aboard. Boaters with VHFs radioed for assistance for those ill equipped. Without proper radios, an unpleasant situation could become an emergency. It only takes one bad experience to wise up and come to the lake *fully* prepared.

When waves come over the bow in storm squalls, there's no other way to go except with waterproof radios. An IPX7 rating means your gear is waterproof for up to 30 minutes submerged in 3 feet of water. This allowance more than covers most situations. A JIS4 rating means the radio is suitable for light rain exposure for about 5 minutes.

No matter what brand or model you get, having access to NOAA weather alerts is a must. Particularly when traveling on water or off, it's important to know what storms may roll in. This is especially true since weather is more chaotic and unpredictable than it was 15 years ago.

Another feature to consider is S.A.M.E. (Specific Area Message Encoding) weather alert. With SAME programmed, your radio functions with county-specific severe weather warnings. This lets you weed out NOAA reports for areas outside your location and your radio isn't continually disrupting communications. To get your county's SAME code and coverage maps, visit **www.nws.noaa.gov/nwr/index.html**.

"TOYS" WITH BENEFITS
Something else to remember, more "extras" aren't necessarily desirable in emergencies. If you've only used your 2-way radio occasionally, it might be a challenge to remember how everything works. Lives could depend on quick communication. Reliable, clear connection with others is most important, not bells and whistles.

SHORTWAVE – HAM – AMATEUR – HIGH FREQUENCY (HF) RADIO
These are all names referring to the same thing. Ham radio operators are the backbone of emergency communication. When all other methods are down, it's always shortwave radio that comes though sending messages to emergency personnel and keeping people apprised on what's happening.

HURRICANE KATRINA
When the Red Cross asked for help during this massive hurricane, hams from 37 states and Canada poured in. Over 1,000 amateur radio operators set up and maintained communications across Alabama and Mississippi. They relayed messages to rescue agencies, to distressed people trying to get news of family members and enabled survival supplies to move in an otherwise stagnated rescue effort.

In such a monumental disaster where generators were scarce and electricity was non-existent, shortwave radio kept information, supplies and people flowing. Because many communication sites were completely obliterated, hams brought their own equipment and erected towers. Due to their technical skill and self-initiative, they eased the burdens of thousands.

When needed, amateurs provide many services in addition to communications. They work long hours, live in terrible conditions, contend with heat, bugs, ants, stench and in many cases, much worse. In addition to relaying communications, "amateurs repaired EMA repeaters, radios, antennas, generators, forklifts, telephone systems and a host of other electronic items."[82]

Photo: Amateur radio operator, Brice Phillips of Hancock County, Miss., broadcast locally throughout Hurricane Katrina on WQRZ-LP 103.5 FM. Pictured February 21, 2006, Phillips ponders the destruction of his home studio. Mr. Phillips received the 2006 Governor's Initiative for Volunteer Excellence (GIVE) Award for his continued dedication to keeping the community informed before, during and after the storm. (Mark Wolfe, FEMA)

Amateur radio led to the rescue of 15 people trapped by floodwaters on the roof of a New Orleans house. This is just one instance that was repeated throughout the aftermath of Hurricane Katrina. It's one of the finest testaments to their motto: When all else fails... Amateur Radio.

HAYMAN FIRE

Beginning in a campfire circle on the morning of June 8, 2002, the Hayman fire quickly raged out of control. Spurred by record drought and extreme weather, the Hayman fire burned nearly 138,000 acres in just three weeks. During that time, big thanks go to amateur radio operators who facilitated life-saving efforts and coordinated information. Nearly 200 amateur radio operators stationed themselves around the fire at two incident command posts, the Red Cross shelters and headquarters, Salvation Army headquarters and canteens, Sheriff's Offices in Douglas and Teller counties, the Woodland Park Police Department, the Metro 911 Center in Denver, and participated as part of the Jefferson County emergency response team.

HUMANITY IN PRACTICE

"Can you send a ham to the Westcreek Fire station please?"

The request came from Jim Leideritz, Director of Emergency Management for Teller County when the phones went dead at this fire station on the front lines of the burn area. Because Amateur Radio is fully integrated into his emergency response plan, he didn't have to waste time trying to figure out if ham radio could fill the void; he simply made the request to send someone in.

" 'All of Colorado is Burning'

"So declared Governor Bill Owens, much to the chagrin of the $6 billion Colorado tourist industry. "I was speaking metaphorically," he stated a couple of days later. He was, however, expressing the sympathies of most Coloradoans as more than eight major fires burned across the state. Amateur Radio support was involved with the ones that were closest to the more heavily populated areas. In May and June, these included the Schoonover Fire near Deckers, the Coal Seam Fire near Glenwood Springs and the previously mentioned Iron Mountain and Hayman fires.

"ARES (Amateur Radio Emergency Service) groups were involved because of their pre-planning and existing relationships. Without these relationships, Amateur Radio groups will generally not be asked to participate in emergencies. After an incident has started, it's too late to approach responding agencies with a sales pitch about how Amateur Radio can help them. They will be much too busy responding to worry about how to integrate an unknown group of volunteers into their agencies. Emergency Preparedness means up-front agreements and practical exercises. These two primary ingredients will go a long way toward ensuring that when needed, Amateur Radio will be at its finest."[83]

Photo: Castle Rock, Colorado June 18, 2002 -- Chris Krengel is a member of ARES, (Amateur Radio Emergency Service) helped provide communication around the Hayman fire just south of Denver. (Michael Rieger, FEMA News)

WHAT IS REQUIRED?

People have been intimidated not knowing how to jump into amateur radio. Since 2003, regulations and laws have relaxed and testing is simpler. Bringing American ham operators more in line with Canada and Europe, the FCC no longer requires learning Morse code. To listen, all you need is the right equipment. To talk, a license is required.

Licensing is earned in three classes: Technician, General, and Amateur Extra. Each level requires more knowledge, but you also get more privileges. Testing covers electronic theory plus FCC rules and regulations. In the U.S., Tech licenses consist of a 35-question written exam. This gets you talking with other hams. Go to the American Radio Relay League, www.arrl.org, to locate a testing location near you. They also have practice questions and sample exams. Once the test is passed, it normally takes about 2 weeks for a license to arrive in the mail.

If you're thinking about transmitting without a license, the Feds have triangulating technology to pinpoint your position. They won't hesitate to impose up to a $10,000 fine and possibly jail time, plus confiscate your equipment.

GETTING STARTED

If you're new to shortwave, listen only until you have a good handle on what's going on and understand proper protocol. Poor operators are referred to as *lids*. Nobody wants to talk to or be labeled a lid. It's the ultimate insult and gives you the equivalent of shortwave leprosy. Mark Twain said it best: *It's better to keep your mouth shut and appear stupid than to open it and remove all doubt.* Once you've got your feet on the ground, go for it. You'll find hams friendly and more than willing to help.

BANDS

In order to hear stations, you need to know where to tune in. Shortwave operates in "bands" which have specific frequencies assigned to them either shown in megahertz (MHz) or kilohertz (KHz). Shortwave bands have names like 20 meters or 40 meters, etc. which are often abbreviated as 20m or 40m. See the HF band chart on the next page.

FINDING STATIONS

Oops! Where'd it go? Keep in mind no SW frequency operates around the clock. If you tune to a certain frequency and there's nothing but dead air, it's just not being used right then. Complicating matters, while the country of origin is shown, many frequencies are relayed from elsewhere. This is especially true of China. Additionally, many of the strongest signals from strictly religious broadcasters in the US and other countries aren't shown.

Unlike TV, shortwave programs can move around the dial, but the bigger ones generally stay on the same frequency. You can usually count on the programs in this chart to have reliable locations. To save time and frustration, get a list of frequency locations like *Passport to World Band Radio*. For about $20, you can easily look up listening information country-by-country, channel-by-channel or hour-by-hour in this comprehensive book.

RECEPTION TIPS

Pulling in stations below 13 MHz is generally easier at night while frequencies above 10 MHz work well during the day. You might also find that stations come in better around sunrise and sunset. For line of sight communication, time of day doesn't matter. During lower sunspot activity, as is the case in 1995-96, higher frequencies are generally less useful than lower ones, and the range of frequencies used at any given time of day is generally shifted slightly downward.[84]

If you're trying to use a shortwave radio in a concrete, stucco or brick building, reception may be hampered. Wood allows signals to pass through more easily. Reception also can be impaired if you're in a building with one or more stories overhead.

Positioning your radio close to a window can improve reception considerably. Antennas certainly help, especially if you want to transmit.

STATIONS WITH CONSTANT FREQUENCIES		
Time (UTC)	Frequencies (MHz)	Program
1100-1700	15.220, 17.840	BBC, United Kingdom
2100-0400	5.975, 9.915, 12.095	
2330-0130	6.165, 9.845	Radio Netherlands, Holland
0100-0130	9.885, 9.905	Swiss Radio International (SRI)
0400-0500		
1100-1200	6.120	Radio Japan
0100-0200	11.705	
0100-0150	6.040, 6.085, 9.640	Deutsche Welle, Germany
0300-0350	6.085, 6.185, 9.615	
0500-0550	5.960, 6.045, 6.120	
1200-1300	9.640, 11.855	Radio Canada International
2200-2400	5.960, 9.755	
1600-1800	15.410, 15.445	Voice of America (VOA) U.S.A.
1800-2200	15.410, 15.580	
0000-0200	5.995, 7.405, 9.775	
0750-1200	9.580	Radio Australia
1200-1700	11.650	

ANTENNAS

Once your shortwave system is set up, an antenna will strengthen the signal. It's the first place to start to boost your tranceiver's effectiveness and it's the factor over which you have the most control. One golden rule: The higher the antenna, the better the reception. The bigger the antenna, the better the performance.

Entire books are dedicated to antennas so there is a lot to consider. If you get hooked on shortwave, you may want to look into more exotic antennas, but they're not necessary to make your gear work well.

You can buy all types of antenna, including many not mentioned here, but knowing how to erect one in an emergency is a good practical skill. Most are fairly simple and straightforward.

ANTENNA WIRE
Coated or Bare

When erecting antennas, coated (insulated) wire is generally easier to work with. To run properly, bare wire must be kept away from anything conductive or it becomes part of the antenna. This can ruin either the antenna's pattern or its ground. Without a working ground system, the antenna can short out or damage the radio with static discharge. Using insulated wire won't cause a drop in signal strength.

If a wire is to be left on the ground, insulation is a must. If an aerial wire is near to or touching anything conductive, use coated wire.

If a wire is on snow, it acts as the insulator.

For aerial wire away from anything conductive, either type is fine.

Thickness

Try to stay within the range of 16 to 24 gauge. If you live in a windy area or one that experiences ice storms, thicker wire of 16 or 18 gauge makes more sense. Thinner wire may be too fragile to withstand the onslaught. If you want to use thinner 22 or 24 gauge, consider using pairs for strength.

Copper vs. Everything Else

Copper works really well, but other wire is fine too. Keep it flexible yet strong and make sure it can be soldered. Price check wire for your area; this may help your decision.

STANDING WAVES AND SWR METERS

The goal is to bring your transceiver to its best performance without damaging equipment. One way to cause it grief is to construct an antenna that produces standing radio waves.

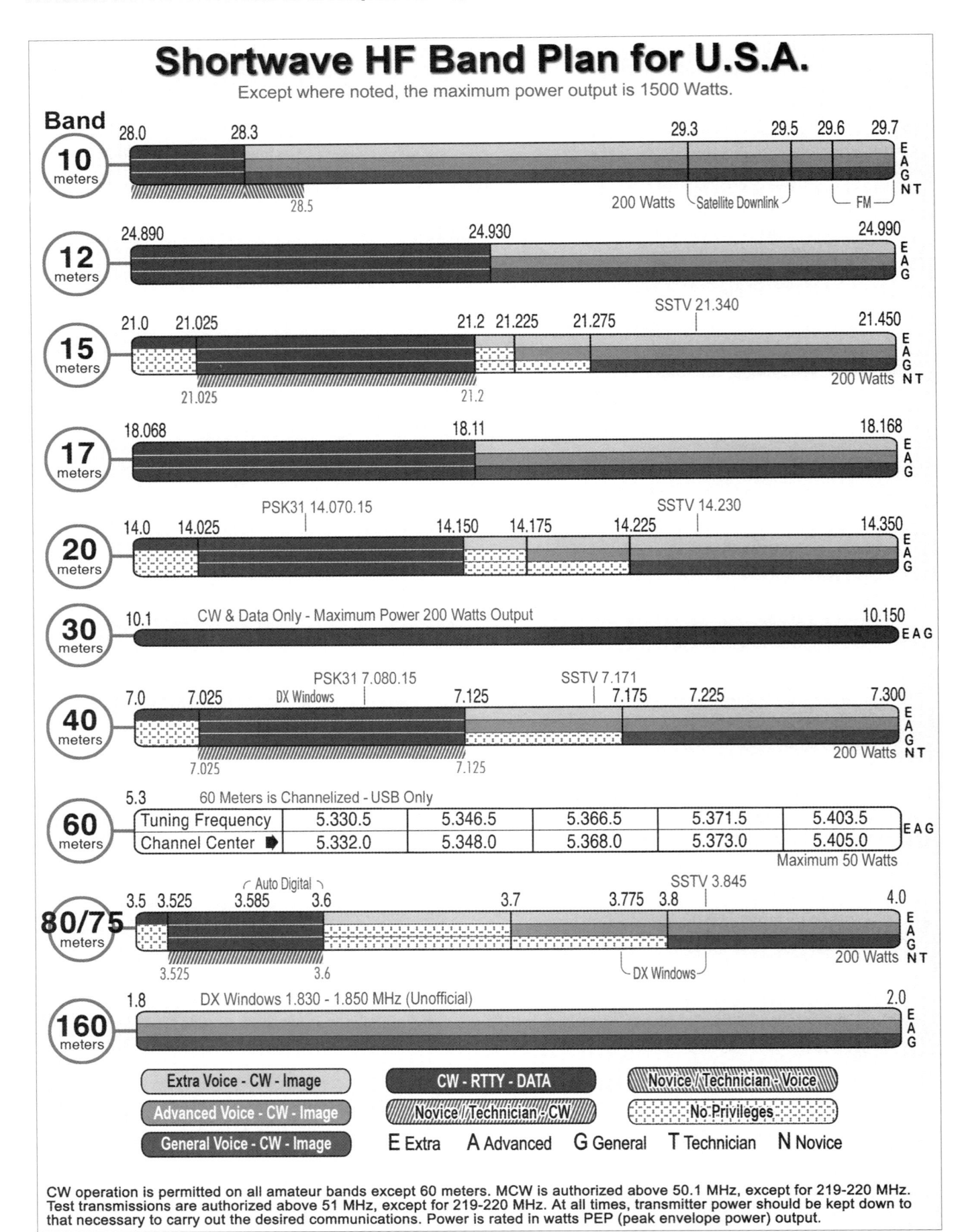

Shortwave HF Band Plan for U.S.A.

Except where noted, the maximum power output is 1500 Watts.

Band: 10 meters
- 28.0, 28.3, 29.3, 29.5, 29.6, 29.7
- 28.5
- 200 Watts, Satellite Downlink, FM
- E A G N T

Band: 12 meters
- 24.890, 24.930, 24.990
- E A G

Band: 15 meters
- 21.0, 21.025, 21.2, 21.225, 21.275, SSTV 21.340, 21.450
- 21.025, 21.2
- 200 Watts
- E A G N T

Band: 17 meters
- 18.068, 18.11, 18.168
- E A G

Band: 20 meters
- 14.0, 14.025, PSK31 14.070.15, 14.150, 14.175, 14.225, SSTV 14.230, 14.350
- E A G

Band: 30 meters
- 10.1, CW & Data Only - Maximum Power 200 Watts Output, 10.150
- E A G

Band: 40 meters
- 7.0, 7.025, DX Windows, PSK31 7.080.15, 7.125, SSTV 7.171, 7.175, 7.225, 7.300
- 7.025, 7.125
- 200 Watts
- E A G N T

Band: 60 meters
- 5.3 — 60 Meters is Channelized - USB Only

| Tuning Frequency | 5.330.5 | 5.346.5 | 5.366.5 | 5.371.5 | 5.403.5 |
| Channel Center ➡ | 5.332.0 | 5.348.0 | 5.368.0 | 5.373.0 | 5.405.0 |

- E A G
- Maximum 50 Watts

Band: 80/75 meters
- 3.5, 3.525, 3.585, Auto Digital, 3.6, 3.7, 3.775, 3.8, SSTV 3.845, 4.0
- 3.525, 3.6
- DX Windows
- 200 Watts
- E A G N T

Band: 160 meters
- 1.8, DX Windows 1.830 - 1.850 MHz (Unofficial), 2.0
- E A G

Legend:
- Extra Voice - CW - Image
- Advanced Voice - CW - Image
- General Voice - CW - Image
- CW - RTTY - DATA
- Novice/Technician - CW
- Novice/Technician - Voice
- No Privileges
- E Extra   A Advanced   G General   T Technician   N Novice

CW operation is permitted on all amateur bands except 60 meters. MCW is authorized above 50.1 MHz, except for 219-220 MHz. Test transmissions are authorized above 51 MHz, except for 219-220 MHz. At all times, transmitter power should be kept down to that necessary to carry out the desired communications. Power is rated in watts PEP (peak envelope power) output.

In the simplest terms, your receiver sends out radio waves that stack energy around the antenna. When that antenna's energy level becomes too high, it can fry your equipment. To avoid this, use a SWR or VSWR meter (voltage standing wave ratio). It measures how much power is coming out of the transceiver and how much is fed back from the antenna. Ideally, nothing is reflected back in untransmitted energy. In this case, the monitor would read 0 for the antenna and show 100% going out from the receiver. A reading of 1.9:1 indicates less than 10% of your power is reflected back from the antenna. Anything below 2:1 is fine.[85]

ANTENNA SAFETY
- It seems unnecessary to state that antennas shouldn't be installed when a storm is brewing. Then again, every year we hear of golfers hit by lightening on the greens. Standing in a backswing with a 9-iron is asking to be a human lightening rod. Ditto for antenna installation.
- Be sure no electrical wires or electrical equipment are so close that they could possibly come in contact with the antenna wire.
- Never install antenna wire over power lines.
- Do as much of the assembly on the ground.
- Take necessary precautions to protect yourself from falling, electrical shock, and other dangers.
- Make sure your antenna is in a safe place, high enough so people or pets won't walk into it by accident.
- For lighting protection, disconnect the antenna from the radio when not in use and connect the antenna lead to your outside ground wire when not in use. The other option is to install a good quality lightening arrestor.

OMNI – BI – UNI
Choosing your antenna(s) has a lot to do with what capabilities are needed. Each antenna has advantages and disadvantages. **Omni-directional antennas** like whips and Buddipoles enable communication in all directions.

Bi-directional antennas like dipoles, sometimes referred to as doublets, allow communications with two or more stations in opposite directions. These antennas must be parallel.

Long wire antennas, which transmit the furthest, are **unidirectional** – only transmit one way. Properly positioned it *may* be least open to interception. That said, if being monitored by sophisticated equipment, there is no escaping its all-seeing eye.

HALF-WAVE RESONANT DIPOLE ANTENNA
One of the most basic and easiest antennas to build is the half-wave dipole. This type antenna pulls in a relatively narrow band – generally bout 2% either side of the designed frequency. Most dipoles are constructed with two pieces of equal length wire, connected by an insulator in the middle and insulators at each far end. The antenna is held up by rope that connects the insulated ends of the antenna to two supports. To construct your own, decide what frequency you want and use this formula to determine its size:

length = 468 / frequency in MHz.

For example, if you want to monitor 10 MHz, divide 468 by 10. Each side would be about 23½ feet long (¼ wavelength) and you would erect the antenna about ¼ to ½ wavelength above ground level for long-range skywave. This is also applies to the inverted Vee and Sloping Vee antennas. For communication between 30 and 400 miles, (NVIS – Near Vertical Incidence Skywave), the antenna should be about ⅛ to ¼ wavelength above ground level. This is really useful when you're located in a hilly area and trying to connect with hams in closer proximity.

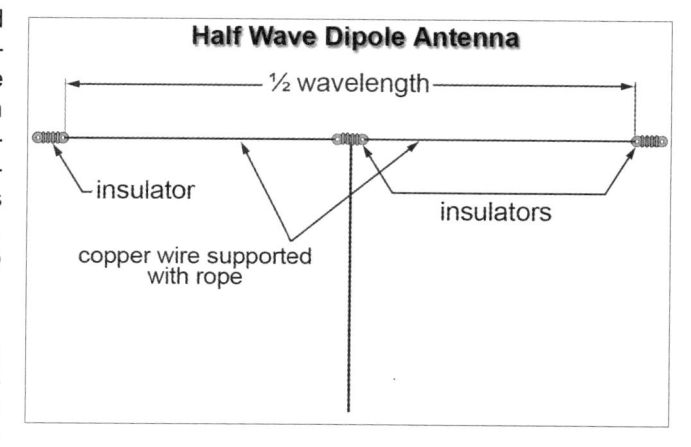

BUDDIPOLE ANTENNA
This type antenna works great in emergency scenarios, but reception can be hampered by its smaller size. A Buddipole basically takes two 8 ft. mobile whips (antennas on springs) to form a rotating antenna. They have great portability – especially important if you are traveling or camping. Most people find them easy to use in the

10-20 meter range and at 40 meters, a little more tuning is required. One way around this problem is to purchase an auto-tuner. The Buddipole is a good option for people in apartments who don't have room for a larger antenna.

Collapsed, it folds 16 feet to only 22 inches and weighs less than 2 pounds. Considering these antennas cover 7-54MHz continuous, plus 144-148MHz, they're good to have in your collection.

EXPEDIENT ANTENNAS

In most cases, your antennas will be stationary. However, if you are traveling, there may be instances where you need to erect a temporary antenna.

If you want to be discreet, use single strand insulated wire, preferably with neutral color insulation, depending on the terrain you will operate from. Army field manuals recommend WD-1 wire, which is one strand each of copper and steel. Steel is added for strength, but experience shows that WD-1 is generally a poor conductor of RF energy. It can be separated but why go to the extra work when single strand wire is readily available.

VERTICAL WIRE ANTENNA

Vertical antennas are omni-directional and can be made by using a metal pipe or rod held in place by guy wires. Insulate the lower end of the antenna from the ground by placing it on a large block of wood or other insulating material like polyethylene plastic.

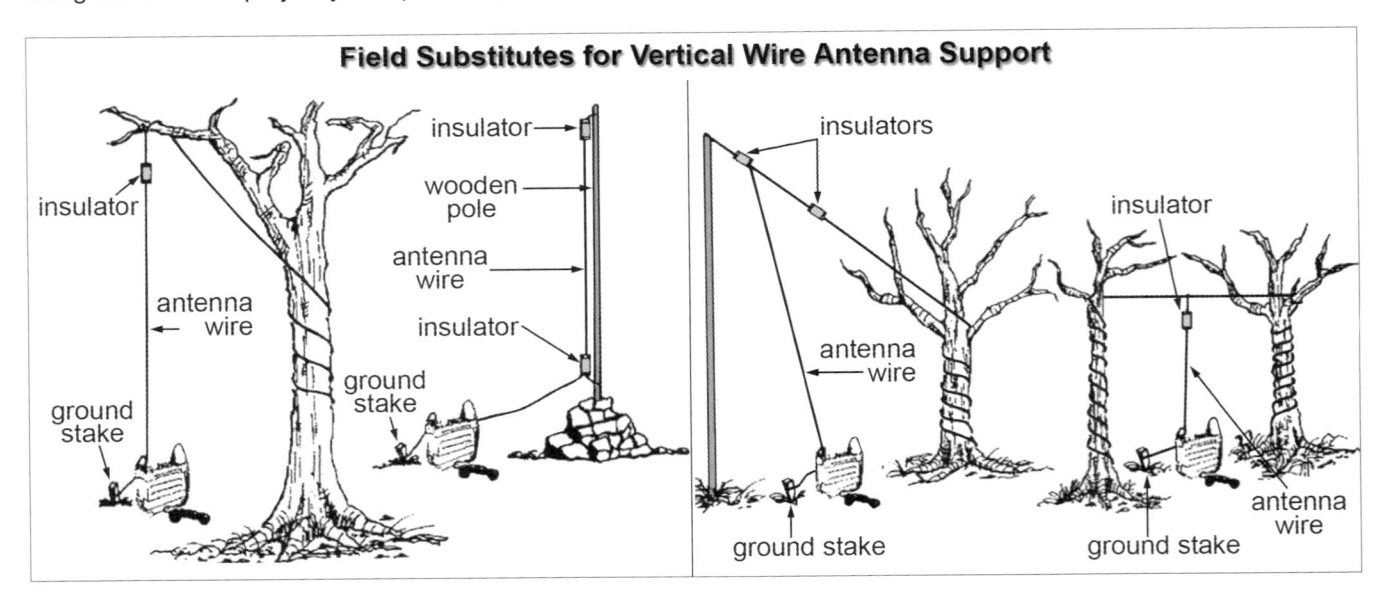

Field Substitutes for Vertical Wire Antenna Support

FOR ¼ WAVELENGTH

Operating Freq. in MHz	Wire Length
30	7' 10"
40	5' 10"
60	3' 11"
80	2' 11"

A vertical antenna can also be just a wire supported by a tree or a wooden pole as shown in the next image. Short vertical antennas may not even need pole supports if it's braced at the base with rocks or bricks.

If using insulated wire, be sure to loop the wire around the handle of the radio before attaching it to the antenna connector. If the antenna is made of bare wire, use a stake and insulator to prevent the antenna wire from pulling out of the antenna connector on the radio.

If you're replacing a regular whip antenna, use these steps to erect a quarter-wave vertical antenna:

Step 1 Use the quick-reference chart or the formula for a quarter-wave antenna to determine the length of the wire needed.

¼ **Wavelength Formula**: length = 234 / frequency in MHz

Step 2 Attach an insulator to one end of the wire and insert the other end (stripped) into the antenna connector on the radio.
Step 3 Tie a rope to the insulator end and throw the rope over a limb.
Step 4 Pull the rope until the wire is vertical.

LONG WIRE DIRECTIONAL

An expedient long wire directional antenna can be made out of readily available materials using a 500- to 600-ohm resistor at the far end of the wire.

Cut the antenna wire to between 2 and 5 full wavelengths of the operating frequency. Attach it to the long whip base of the radio and then run through the insulator as shown in the next image. Run the wire through insulator (2), down to the resistor (3), and ending at the ground stake (4). Attach another wire to the opposite end of the resistor. Run it back to the radio set and attach it to the radio set case, which is the ground. Transmission goes in the direction toward the end of the antenna with the resistor.

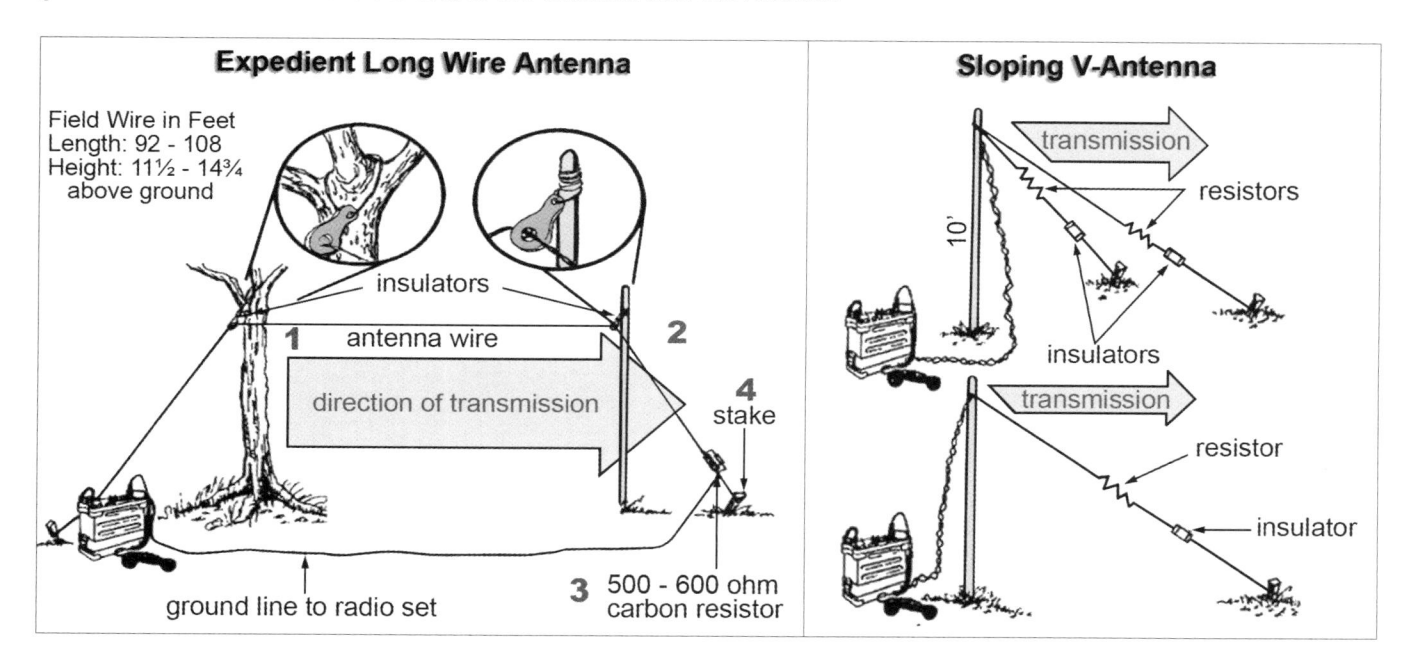

SLOPING V-ANTENNA

This field-expedient antenna can be either uni-directional or bi-directional. Its two wires forming the V point toward the desired direction of transmission. To make construction easier, slope the legs downward from the top of the V. The angle between the legs antenna varies with the length of the legs to get the greatest performance. Use this chart for a quick reference to determine the angle and the length of the legs.

When the antenna is used with more than one frequency of wavelength, an apex angle is used midway between the extreme angles determined by the chart. To make the antenna radiate in only one direction, add non-inductive terminating resistors from the end of each leg (not at the apex) to the ground. The resistors should be about 500 ohms and have a power rating of at least one-half that of the output power of the transmitter being used. Without the resistors, the antenna radiates bi-directionally, both front and back. A balanced transmission line must feed the antenna.

ANTENNA LENGTH (wavelength)	OPTIMUM APEX ANGLE (in degrees)
1	90
2	70
3	58
4	50
6	40
8	35
10	33

VERTICAL HALF-RHOMBIC ANTENNA

This is another easily constructed directional antenna. You'll get the best performance with the length of each leg measuring a minimum of one wavelength at the lowest frequency used. A typical military half-rhombic antenna has 100 feet of wire erected over a single 30-foot wood support with an 80-foot counterpoise laid about one foot above the ground. The 100 feet of wire should be erected on the support pole so that each leg is about 50 feet long. One leg of the antenna terminates at a 500-600 ohm resistor.

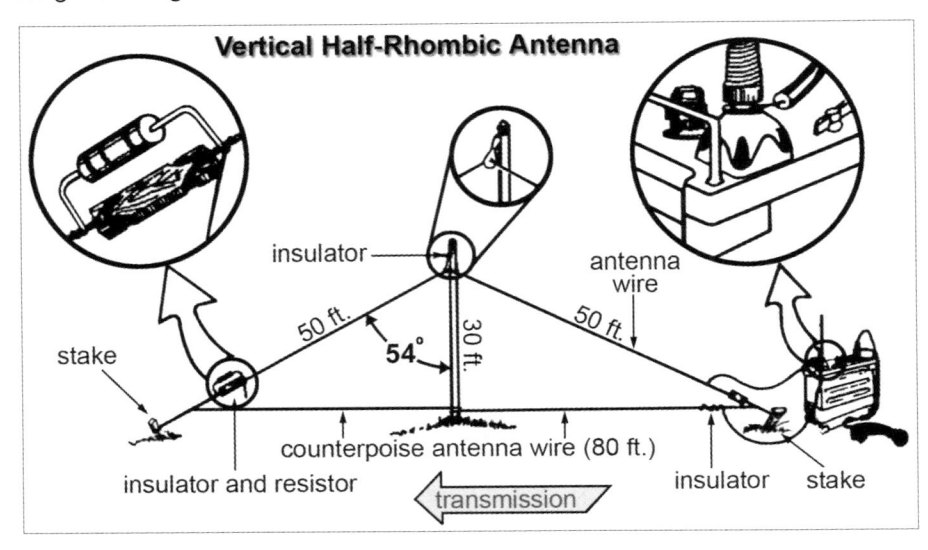

One end of the counterpoise also terminates at the resistor. A lead-in wire is attached between the other leg of the antenna and the radio. The other end of the counterpoise is grounded.

The supporting pole should be made from wood and anchored with rope.

Current will flow only from the transmitter toward the resistor. This resistor absorbs energy not radiated and it prevents any reflection along the antenna making it uni-directional. Direction of transmission is from the radio toward the resistor end of the antenna.

TO BUILD THE ANTENNA

Step 1 Cut 100 feet of wire for the antenna.
Step 2 Cut 80 feet of wire for a counterpoise. (This is a wire stretched across the bottom of the antenna. It acts as an artificial ground to help produce the required radiation pattern.)
Step 3 Connect an insulator to each of the antenna wires and one at the middle. Add a tie-down wire outside the insulators on each of the antenna wires.
Step 4 Connect the counterpoise to the insulators at the same point as the tie-down wire.
Step 5 Select or erect a middle support – a tree, pole, wire or rope suspended between two trees or structures. The midpoint must be at least 30 feet high.
Step 6 Stretch the counterpoise out in the direction of the target station with the middle of the counterpoise at the center support. Drive the stakes in by each tie-down wire, stretch the counterpoise tightly, and tie it down to the stake. Elevate the center of the antenna until it is right.
Step 7 Run the wire from the antenna terminal and connect it to the antenna above the insulator. Run a second wire from the head of the screw on the radio case to the bottom of the insulator.
Step 8 Place a 600-ohm, 2-watt carbon resistor at the end toward the desired station to make this antenna transmit only in that direction. Make sure the resistor is carbon and not wire-wound. A 2-watt resistor works only for a low-power radio. A resistor with wattage rating of half the power output is needed for a higher-power ratio.

NOTE: This antenna can be used without the counterpoise but it won't work as well.[86]

HANGING "SKYWIRES"

Since antennas generally function better in relation to their height, you might be wondering how to get the wire from here to "up there". Sad and funny tales have been multiplied over the years of how people got antenna wires to the perfect height. As you might guess, many of them involved falling off ladders, out of trees and off rooftops. In retrospect, they must have asked, *what was I thinking!* Here are several methods of getting that wire to impressive heights, each with varying degrees of success.

TOTALLY LOW-TECH FISHING POLE

This method involves fishing line, a sinker and orange paint. OK there's a little more to it. It's the least efficient and places the antenna at the lowest height. Here is what's needed:

- Fishing pole
- 1 dozen 1-2 oz. lead egg sinkers
- 1 Crossman or Wrist-Rocket slingshot
- Large spool trout line (4-5 pound weight)
- Large Nails
- Hammer
- Florescent orange or pink paint
- Fishing pole holder, if you can't find someone to help

BOW AND ARROW

Use the same method as above except launch the fishing line with a good bow and arrow like a 55-pound compound bow mounted with a large spinning reel. Arrows should be heavy; a solid fiberglass fishing type with points blunted. To improve arrow performance, try stacking washers at the tip with a machine screw threaded through them and into the standard removable point socket.

Again, this method requires practice for accuracy and also strength. Instead of lighter trout line, substitute 12 pound test line.

Pros: By using a bow and arrow you gain nearly double in height when launching the line. This method can easily shoot over 100' trees.

Cons: Falling weighted arrows are dangerous as well as expensive to lose if caught in a tree. The bow setup is large, fragile and fairly bulky to take to field.

PNEUMATIC ANTENNA LAUNCHER

For the serious antenna person (or those with chronically poor aim), there is an easier way to hurl wire over trees. This proves to be the most accurate, launches wire the highest and furthest, and is the easiest to use.

Overview. A smaller PVC tube holds a tennis ball with a fishing line reel attached at the end. The larger tank holds compressed air. Point the large end where you want the ball to go and squeeze he trigger. The tennis ball shoots out and the reel releases the line.

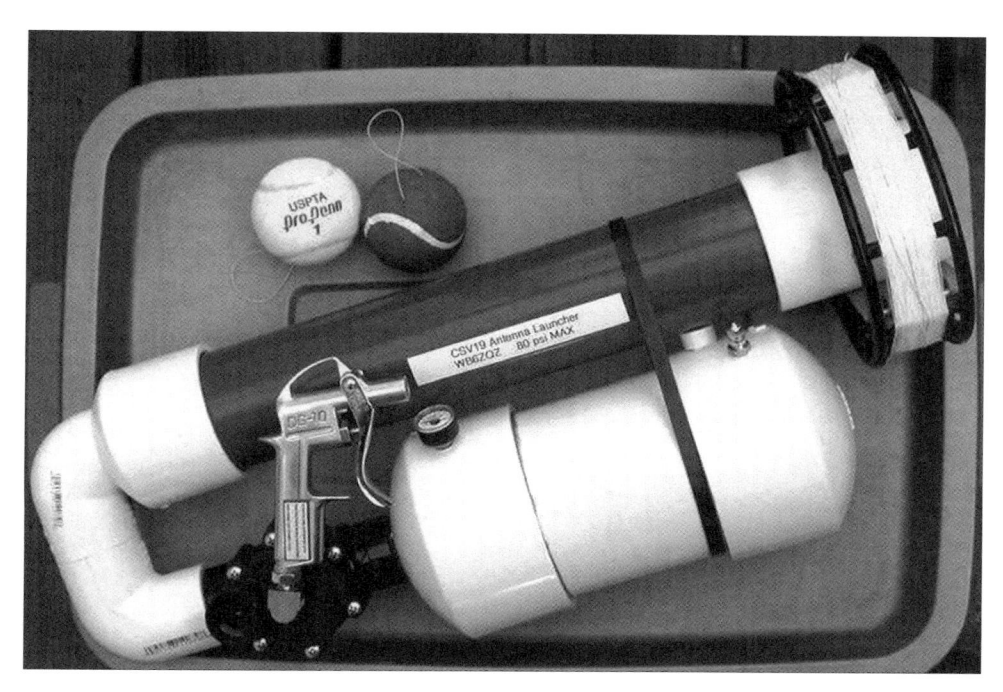

To operate, poke two small holes in the tennis ball about an inch apart and feed a wire between them with a needle. Bend the wire into a loop about 3" in diameter. Cut a slot in the ball, drop in 22 pennies to weight the ball and then seal the slot with a glue gun. Weight is added so the ball can pull the line down against friction from tree branches. The finished ball weighs about 4oz. and test findings show this weight performs the best.

Attach fishing line to the loop in the ball and insert the ball into the tube. Pump up the air chamber according to how high you want the tennis ball to fly. About 50psi shoots the ball nearly 200'.

Hold the launcher at arms length. Put the right hand on the trigger, and use the left hand to support the pressure chamber. Point the launcher slightly above the tree. Squeeze the trigger quickly without moving the launcher and the ball soars to the desired location.

Untie the ball from the line and tie on the mason twine or whatever you are using. Wind the launch line back on the reel and tow it over the tree. Untie the lines and attach the launch line to the antenna, or to heavier line and pull it up.

Tips: Launching too far can cause the line to get entangled in trees behind the target. Launching too high allows the breeze to move the line away from the desired location.

Standing closer to the target tree reduces the distance the tennis ball will go. Start about 20 feet from the tree (7 meters) and adjust as needed. To launch over a few trees at once, start about the tree height away from it. Adjust as needed.

Lines suggested by the manufacturer include:
- Monofilament 8 lb on up to perhaps 20 lb test
- Dacron Fishing Line (braided)
- Dacron Kite Line (twisted) 30 lb
- New Synthetics – Spectra 20-50 lb.

NOTE: Assembly is required and it takes time and patience. Their website **antennalaunchers.com** has detailed instructions. Pneumatic launchers run $100-$300 depending on model and degree of pre-assemblage.

ANTENNAS FOR APARTMENT RESIDENTS

Obviously, apartment dwellers will encounter more restrictions for radio antenna installation. If you plan to only communicate within your area, you can use VHF and UHF equipment. Most often a handheld model will suffice. Some apartment hams opt for using small beam antennas indoors. However, once you get hooked on shortwave or when emergencies strike, you'll want to contact people outside your area to find out what's going on.

To operate on shortwave bands, several options improve reception:

1. Install a wire antenna on the ceiling of your apartment and operate at lower power levels. This should avoid causing interference to neighbors from your antenna being close to their TV or stereo.
2. Install a dipole antenna on a balcony for the higher HF bands.
3. Using small gauge wire, string an "invisible" wire antenna from your apartment to a nearby support such as a tree.
4. Use a closed tuned loop antenna mounted on a balcony.
5. Set up a good mobile radio installation for HF bands and operate from your vehicle.
6. Check with management to see if they'd allow a single wire antenna to be strung on the building's roof.

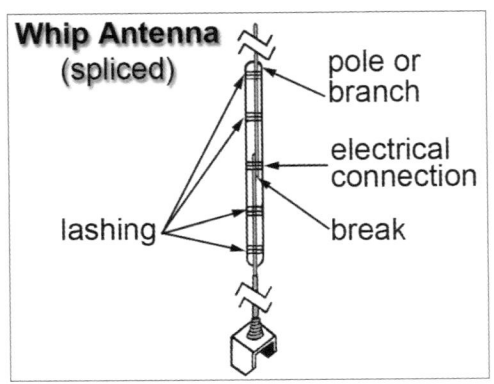

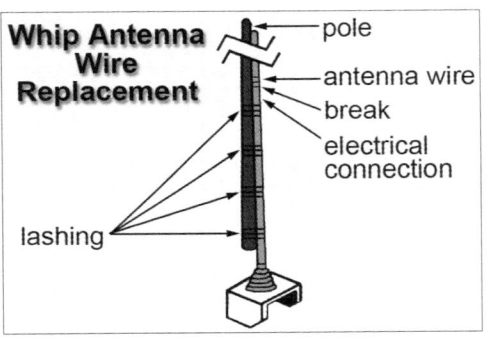

Whip Antenna (spliced) — pole or branch, electrical connection, lashing, break

Whip Antenna Wire Replacement — pole, antenna wire, break, electrical connection, lashing

EMERGENCY REPAIR OF WHIP ANTENNAS

Things happen and sometimes they strike at the most inopportune times. One of those inconveniences is a broken whip antenna. Though they're normally strong, high wind, vandalism or an accident can break them. When a spare isn't available, you may have to construct an emergency antenna.

An expedient splint is a quick way to repair a broken whip. Scrape any paint or coating 3 to 6 inches from each broken end. Clean the two antenna sections thoroughly to ensure good contact before connecting them to the pole support. If possible, solder the connections. If soldering isn't an option, overlap the cleaned ends and wrap them tightly together with about 1 foot of stripped copper wire. Sandwich the mended antenna between two sticks, poles, or sturdy branches, then lash them together with wire, rope or tape.

If the whip is broken at its base, wire can be used as an expedient replacement. Scrape the paint or coating off the top 2 inches of the whip's stub. Then strip 12 inches of insulation from one end of a 10-foot section of wire. Wrap the wire tightly around the stub, then over the top of the stub and join it into the hole with a wooden peg. Secure the wire to the stick with the peg and tape. Attach a 10-foot pole tightly to the antenna's base and stub. The remaining 9 feet of wire is attached along the pole with tape. Trim any excess. The total length of this repaired antenna shouldn't be more than 9 feet.[87]

POWER SUPPLIES

Your HF radio should have a DC battery pack, or operate from 12-volt mobile DC sources. A radio with AC-only power is very limiting and not much use except in a motor home with AC power. If your radio is a high-powered set, it will go through batteries much more quickly than low-power models.

Icom makes power supplies for HF radios. They're very nice products but cost more than others – in the neighborhood of $300 – $900. Another brand to consider is Jetstream's JTPS28M which is about $100. It takes up little space, performs well and runs quietly. Controlled Current Distribution (CCD) Antennas, another power supply source, has a good product reputation and is reasonably priced from $135 – $180. Contact information for CCD: **www.ccdantennas.com**. Dave Kelley, AI7R; 1605 W. Barrow Drive; Chandler, Arizona 85224; 480.612.2055.

STARTING OUT

Two of the best manufacturers are Icom and Yaesu. Both are Japanese makers and have reputations for product excellence and reliability. If you're new to amateur radio, one of the most frustrating aspects is getting gear too complex for beginners. Aim for equipment that takes you where you want to go without giving you a major headache. Reports from Icom 718 owners praise this unit for quality, price and ease of use. This model needs a power supply since it doesn't come standard with its own. New 718 models are about $600. Other Icoms HF radios peg $10,000 so there's a wide range – something for everyone.

One long-time shortwave radio user suggests that an ideal model for the survivalist and for emergency use is a low-power (up to 25 W PEP) portable transceiver. This transmitter should cover the 3-15MHz band (minimum) with CW and SSB (Single Side Band) capability. Both USB (Upper Side Band) and LSB Lower Side Band), are desirable for voice communications, but USB (or simple AM) would be the minimum requirement.

So many models exist with such a variety of features to consider it's counterproductive to chart even a portion of them. One would need a book dedicated just to shortwave equipment and many such catalogues are already available. You'll have to decide what are your needs and what your wallet will tolerate and go from there.

ASK THE EXPERT

When first looking to get Stan a shortwave radio, the many choices were overwhelming. After searching hours on the Internet, I turned to the expert, Art Bell, and asked for help.

For those unfamiliar with late night talk radio, Art is iconic in the truest sense. Bell got his ham license at age 13 and later, his Amateur Extra class. Over the course of his extensive career, including Air Force service, he worked both in front of and behind the mike as radio personality, board op and chief engineer. Though he's semi-retired from hosting the program he launched, *Coast to Coast AM*, Bell still owns Pahrump, Nevada-based FM radio station, KNYE 95.1 and is an active ham. In 2007, Bell received a Lifetime Achievement Award from Los Angeles' trade publication *Radio & Records*. Pinnacle recognition came in 2008 with Bell's induction into the National Radio Hall of Fame. If anyone knows shortwave, it is Art Bell.

For a decent, affordable unit that's just all around good, Art recommends the Icom IC706MKIIG. There are newer and more expensive models available, but this one has been around long enough to earn quality awards. For $1000, this transceiver is pretty easy to use and covers the spectrum.

SHORTWAVE RECEIVERS

If you want to *listen only* to shortwave, Sangean makes a very nice model – the ATS 909 – their flagship radio. It's fairly easy to use and coverage includes all long wave, medium wave, shortwave freqs. of 1.711-29.999MHz, AM and FM stereo. Tuning can be done manually, by directly entering the frequency, auto scanning or through memory presets. Among a lot of features, it includes single side band, RF gain control, signal and battery strength indicator and 3 timers. The digital clock can be set to local and world times and it has both an alarm and a sleep timer. Once you find a station, you can store it with 306 presets. The 909 also has a "priority" button so if there is a frequency you listen to often, you can program it and get there with the push of one button.

Two drawbacks come with the 909. It lacks is a NOAA weather alert system and it chews through batteries. Comparable radios like the Grundig's Yacht Boy 400PE or Sony's ICF-7600G last about 20-25 hours on AA alkalines. The Sony and Sangean both use 4 AAs; the Grundig requires 6 AAs. However, Sangean's battery life is noticeably shorter at 12-14 hours. Keep in mind that the Grundig has a 50% higher requirement. Depending on retailer, the ATS-909 range is $200-$275. All of these radios are well rated for the price.

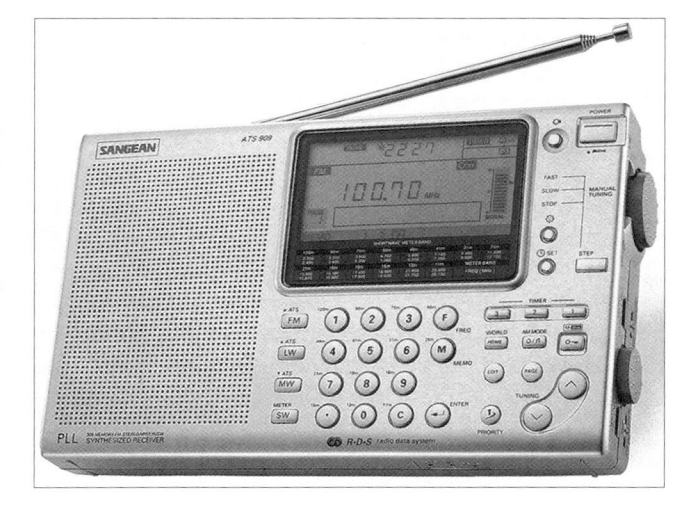

AUTO TUNERS

Another shortwave professional, David Martin, advises new hams to purchase radios *with* auto-tuners, especially if they aren't planning on taking classes. He knows the pitfalls that can beset new radio owners and states that auto-tuners help eliminate frustration when looking for stations. Dave earned his license nearly 50 years ago and holds an Amateur Extra class. During his career, Dave trained hundreds of people to obtain their licenses and has set up countless radio stations. Dave's experience includes teaching and providing communications for nuclear, chemical, and biological training, and working with RACES, ARES, and MARS. He has selflessly shared his expertise setting emergency communications for earthquakes, fires, floods and accidents, and during Hurricane Katrina. Ten years with the US Army Signal Corp. rounds out his extensive background. If you need assistance with emergency communications, Dave offers his services: **martronics.org**.

EMERGENCY BROADCASTS

During emergencies, the American Radio Relay League, W1AW, transmits special bulletins hourly by voice, teleprinter and CW (Morse code). These frequencies may change and can be checked for the most current information here: **www.arrl.org/w1aw.html**.

Transmission	AARL's Emergency Broadcast Frequencies (MHz)							
Voice (hh:00)	1.8550	3.9900	7.2900	14.2900	18.1600	21.3900	28.5900	147.555
Teleprinter (hh:15)	3.5975	7.095	14.095	18.1025	21.0950	28.0950	147.555	
CW (hh:30)	1.8175	3.5815	7.0475	14.0475	18.0975	21.0675	28.0675	147.555

You may also want to monitor Hurricane Frequencies. As stated previously, except for major broadcasters, times and frequencies are subject to frequent change. This list is current as of August 24, 2010. A column is on the right side of this table for you to log any updates.

DISASTER RECOVERY NETS[88]				
Frequency in MHz	Where	Who	Frequency Change	Notes
2.8024	USB	American Red Cross Disaster (F-91) **		
3.1714	USB	American Red Cross Disaster (F-92) **		
5.1364	USB	American Red Cross Disaster (F-93) **		
5.1414	USB	American Red Cross Disaster (F-94) **		
5.2110	USB	FEMA		
6.8595	USB	American Red Cross Disaster (F-95) **		
7.5070	USB	USN/USCG hurricane net (primary)		
7.5505	USB	American Red Cross Disaster (F-96 - primary) **		
7.6985	USB	American Red Cross Disaster (F-97) **		
9.3800	USB	USN/USCG hurricane net (secondary)		
10.4930	USB	FEMA		
14.3965	USB	SHARES Coordination Network (primary day)		
14.4550	USB	SHARES Coordination Network (alt day)		
EMERGENCY HURRICANE NETS				
1.9840	LSB	Virgin Islands (VI, Puerto Rico, Lesser Antilles)		
3.7100	LSB	Puerto Rico		
3.8080	LSB	Caribbean Wx (1030)		
3.8450	LSB	Gulf Coast West Hurricane		
3.8625	LSB	Mississippi Section Traffic		
3.8730	LSB	West Gulf ARES Emergency (night)		
3.8730	LSB	Central Gulf Coast Hurricane		
3.8730	LSB	Louisiana ARES Emergency (night)		
3.8730	LSB	Mississippi ARES Emergency		
3.9050	LSB	Pacific ARES (Hawaii)		
3.9050	LSB	Delaware Emergency		
3.9070	LSB	Carolina Coast Emergency		
3.9100	LSB	Central Texas Emergency		
3.9100	LSB	Mississippi ARES		
3.9100	LSB	Louisiana Traffic		

DISASTER RECOVERY NETS[88]				
Frequency in MHz	Where	Who	Frequency Change	Notes
3.9100	LSB	Virginia Emergency, Alpha (ARES/RACES)		
3.9130	LSB	New York State Emergency		
3.9150	LSB	South Carolina SSB NTS		
3.9150	LSB	Massachusetts/Rhode Island Emergency		
3.9150	LSB	Mississippi ARES		
3.9170	LSB	Eastern Pennsylvania Emergency		
3.9200	LSB	Maryland Emergency		
3.9230	LSB	Mississippi ARES		
3.9230	LSB	North Carolina ARES Emergency (Tarheel)		
3.9250	LSB	New York State Emergency		
3.9250	LSB	Central Gulf Coast Hurricane		
3.9250	LSB	Louisiana Emergency (alt.)		
3.9350	LSB	Central Gulf Coast Hurricane		
3.9350	LSB	Louisiana ARES (health and welfare)		
3.9350	LSB	Texas ARES (health and welfare)		
3.9350	LSB	Mississippi ARES (health and welfare)		
3.9350	LSB	Alabama Emergency		
3.9400	LSB	Southern Florida Emergency		
3.9500	LSB	Northern Florida Emergency		
3.9550	LSB	South Texas Emergency		
3.9650	LSB	Connecticut Emergency		
3.9670	LSB	Gulf Coast (outgoing traffic)		
3.9750	LSB	New Jersey ARES		
3.9935	LSB	Gulf Coast (health & welfare)		
3.9935	LSB	Kentucky ARES/RACES		
3.9935	LSB	South Carolina ARES/RACES Emergency		
3.9950	LSB	Gulf Coast Wx		
7.0700	USB	Manana (Baja California)		
7.0900	USB	Central America Emergency		
7.1100	USB	Cuba Emergency (day)		
7.1450	USB	Bermuda		
7.1650	USB	Antigua/Antilles Emergency and Weather		
7.1650	USB	Interisland 40-meter (continuous watch)		
7.2250	USB	Central Gulf Coast Hurricane		
7.2280	USB	Kentucky ARES/RACES		
7.2300	USB	New York State Emergency		
7.2300	USB	Southwest Traffic		
7.2320	USB	North Carolina ARES Emergency (Tarheel – alt.)		
7.2350	USB	Louisiana Emergency		
7.2350	USB	Baja California		
7.2350	USB	Central Gulf Coast Hurricane		
7.2350	USB	West Virginia		
7.2350	USB	Louisiana Emergency		
7.2400	USB	American Red Cross US Gulf Coast Disaster		
7.2400	USB	Texas Emergency		
7.2400	USB	Virginia Emergency, Bravo (health & welfare – alt.)		
7.2420	USB	Southern Florida ARES Emergency (alt.)		
7.2430	USB	Alabama Emergency		
7.2430	USB	South Carolina Emergency		
7.2450	USB	Southern Louisiana		
7.2450	USB	New York State RACES		
7.2475	USB	Northern Florida ARES Emergency (alt.)		
7.2480	USB	Texas RACES (primary)		
7.2500	USB	Belize		
7.2500	USB	Texas Emergency		
7.2540	USB	Northern Florida Emergency		

| DISASTER RECOVERY NETS[88] ||||||
Frequency in MHz	Where	Who	Frequency Change	Notes
7.2600	USB	Gulf Coast West Hurricane		
7.2600	USB	Virginia Emergency, Alpha (ARES/RACES alt.)		
7.2640	USB	Gulf Coast (health & welfare)		
7.2650	USB	Salvation Army Team Emerg. Rad.(SATERN – alt.)		
7.2680	USB	Bermuda		
7.2680	USB	Waterway		
7.2730	USB	Texas ARES (alt.)		
7.2750	USB	Georgia ARES		
7.2800	USB	NTS Region 5		
7.2800	USB	Louisiana Emergency (alt.)		
7.2830	USB	Gulf Coast (outgoing only)		
7.2850	USB	West Gulf ARES Emergency (day)		
7.2850	USB	Louisiana ARES Emergency (day)		
7.2850	USB	Mississippi ARES Emergency		
7.2850	USB	Texas ARES Emergency (day)		
7.2900	USB	Central Gulf Coast Hurricane		
7.2900	USB	Gulf Coast Wx		
7.2900	USB	Texas ARES (health & welfare)		
7.2900	USB	Louisiana ARES (health & welfare – day)		
7.2900	USB	Texas ARES (health & welfare)		
7.2900	USB	Mississippi ARES (health & welfare)		
7.2900	USB	Hawaii Emergency		
7.2900	USB	Traffic		
14.1850	USB	Caribbean Emergency		
14.2650	USB	Salvation Army Team Emergency Radio (h & w)		
14.2680	USB	Amateur Radio Readiness Group		
14.2750	USB	Bermuda		
14.2750	USB	International Amateur Radio		
14.2830	USB	Caribus (health & welfare)		
14.3000	USB	Intercontinental Traffic		
14.3000	USB	Maritime Mobile Service		
14.3030	USB	International Assistance & Traffic		
14.3130	USB	Intercontinental Traffic (alt.)		
14.3130	USB	Maritime Mobile Service (alt.)		
14.3160	USB	Health & Welfare		
14.3200	USB	Health & Welfare		
14.3250	USB	Hurricane Watch (Amateur-to-National Hurricane)		
14.3400	USB	Louisiana (1900)		
14.3400	USB	Manana (1900)		
14.3400	USB	California-Hawaii		
21.4000	USB	Transatlantic Maritime		
28.4500	USB	New Jersey ARES		

** Type-accepted equipment and an issued US FCC license are required to transmit on Red Cross frequencies

Amateur radio magazines like *QST*, *CQ*, and *World Radio* and websites like **www.qrz.com** or **www.qth.com** answer even the most obscure questions. Additionally, do a Net search for "Ham radio" or "amateur radio" for links to hundreds of advertisers. These magazine advertisers provide information of every type and equipment in every price range. In the U.S., books and information about radios of every description can be found and ordered ARRL, The American Radio Relay League; **www.arrl.org**. In Canada, check RAC – Radio Amateurs of Canada, **www.rac.ca/index.htm**. For Australians, see WIA – The Wireless Institute of Australia; **www.wia.org.au** and in Great Britain, go to RSGB – Radio Society of Great Britain; **www.rsgb.org**. For all other country listing, check the Internet at **www.ham.org**. For propagation conditions this site is really useful as well: **dx.qsl.net/propagation/index.html**.

Chapter 34: The Wonder of Clorox

It should have been named "miracle in a bottle" since liquid laundry bleach is to clean what penicillin was to health 60 years ago. There is practically no end to its use! Since many antibiotics are losing their effectiveness, good sanitation is more important than ever. After an emergency, especially when there has been heavy flooding, sewer failure, or widespread illness, etc. sanitizing is a <u>must</u>.

Clorox, a positive germicide, is a 6.0% sodium hypochlorite solution containing approximately 5.71% available chlorine by weight. In addition to being a highly effective laundry bleach and household cleaner, it's widely used for sanitizing poultry and livestock houses and equipment, dairies, creameries, restaurants and taverns. It's also an outstanding water purifier and swimming pool disinfectant.

In addition to the above suggestions, Stan and I chlorinate Seismo and Taco's summer "dunk pool" to keep mosquitoes out. In spite of West Nile's threat, with their heavy fur coats, the dogs need to cool off from the high desert heat.

I used to worry that Seismo's and Taco's black coats would turn blond, but bleach is always added when they won't be using their tub for a while. Within a few hours, the Sun "bake off" the chlorine.

We stir in chlorine thoroughly and then agitate it further with the spray nozzle when refilling this tub. Between splashing when they're getting in and out and Colorado's intense Sun causing evaporation, this little 25-gallon Rubbermaid tub needs about 3 inches of refill daily. We also regularly dose a recirculating fountain in the front yard. It keeps the water sparkling clear and the mozzies dead!

GENERAL GUIDELINES

- IMPORTANT: Always thoroughly mix with water as directed before using.
- Don't allow undiluted product to come in contact with any fabric. Clorox warns if it does, rinse out immediately with clear, cold water. But even then I found it was too late.
- Don't apply with natural sponge.
- Don't use on non-stainless steel, aluminum, silver, or chipped enamel.
- If used on metal, solution should be allowed to stand for no more than 5 minutes, and then rinse off thoroughly with clear water; otherwise, it may slightly discolor and eventually corrode the metal.
- If a metal sprayer is used to apply the solution, rinse sprayer thoroughly afterwards with clear water, and then oil the plunger.
- Septic systems are not affected by regular home and farm use of this product.

FOOD APPLICATIONS

FRUIT & VEGETABLE WASHING

Thoroughly clean all fruits and vegetables in a wash tank. Prepare a sanitizing solution of 25 ppm (parts per million) available chlorine. After draining the tank, submerge fruit or vegetables for 2 minutes in a second wash tank containing the recirculating sanitizing solution. Spray rinse vegetables with the sanitizing solution prior to packaging. Rinse fruit with potable water only prior to packaging.

EGGS

To sanitize food eggs: thoroughly clean all eggs. Prepare a 200 ppm available chlorine solution. The sanitizer temperature shouldn't exceed 130°F (54°C). Spray the solution so the eggs are completely wet. Allow the eggs to fully dry before casing or breaking. Do not apply a potable water rinse. The solution should not be reused to sanitize eggs.

MEAT AND POULTRY PROCESSING WATER

This product may be used in processing water of meat and poultry plants at concentrations up to 5 ppm calculated as available chlorine. Chlorine may be present in poultry chiller intake water, in water for reprocessing poultry carcasses internally contaminated with feces, and in red meat carcass final wash water at concentrations between 25 and 50 ppm available chlorine. Use Chlorine Test Strips to adjust to desired available chlorine level. Chlorine must be dispensed at a constant and uniform level. **NOTE:** Bleach to contain 6% sodium hypochlorite

CLEANING ACTION	LAUNDRY BLEACH	WATER	INSTRUCTIONS
TO SANITIZE			
Work Surfaces	1 Tbsp (½ oz.)	1 gallon	Wash, rinse, wipe surface area with bleach solution for at least 2 minutes. Let air dry.
Dishes, Glassware, Utensils	1 Tbsp (½ oz.)	1 gallon	Wash & rinse. After washing, soak for at least 2 minutes. In bleach solution. Let air dry.
Refrigerators and Freezers	1 Tbsp (½ oz.)	1 gallon	Wash, rinse, wipe surface area with bleach solution for at least 2 minutes. Let air dry.
Garbage Cans	¾ cup (6 oz.)	1 gallon	After washing & rinsing brush inside with bleach solution. Let drain.
Sponges, Dishcloths & Rags	¾ cup (6 oz.)	1 gallon	Pre-wash items then soak them in bleach solution for at least 5 minutes. Rinse well and air dry.
TO DISINFECT			
Floors and Walls	¾ cup (6 oz.)	1 gallon	Pre-wash surface, mop or wipe with bleach solution. Allow solution to contact surface for at least 5 minutes. Rinse well and air dry.
Bathtubs and Showers	¾ cup (6 oz.)	1 gallon	Pre-wash surface, mop or wipe with bleach solution. Allow solution to contact surface for at least 5 minutes. Rinse well and air dry.
Laundry	¾ cup (6 oz.)	Standard washer	Use 1¼ cups bleach for extra large washers. Use a detergent.
Toilet bowl	1 cup (8 oz.)	Toilet bowl	Flush toilet. Pour bleach into the bowl. Brush entire bowl including under rim. Let stand 10 minutes. before flushing again.
TO DEODORIZE			
Garbage Cans	¼ cup (2 oz.)	1 gallon	After washing and rinsing brush inside with bleach solution. Let drain.
Drains	1 cup (8 oz.)	--	Flush drains. Pour into drain. Flush with hot water.
TO BEACH & WHITEN			
Wooden Surfaces	¾ cup (6 oz.)	1 gallon	Apply for at least 2 minutes, rinse.
MOLD & MILDEW STAIN REMOVAL			
All Surfaces	¾ cup (6 oz.)	1 gallon	Add bleach to powdered detergent solution. Apply let stand 5-15 minutes. Wipe and rinse.

DISINFECTION AFTER DISASTER

DROUGHTS

Supplementary Water Supplies

Gravity or mechanical hypochlorite feeders should be set up on a supplementary line to dose the water to a minimum chlorine residual of 0.2 ppm after a 20-minute contact time. Use a chlorine test kit.

Water shipped in By Tanks, Tank Cars, Trucks, etc.

Thoroughly clean all containers and equipment. Spray a 500 ppm available chlorine solution and rinse with potable water after 5 minutes. During the filling of the containers, dose with sufficient amounts of this product to provide at least a 0.22 ppm chlorine residual. Use a chlorine test kit.

FIRES
Cross Connections or Emergency Connections

Hypochlorination or gravity feed equipment should be set up near the intake of the untreated water supply. Apply sufficient product to give a chlorine residual of at least 0.1 to 0.2 ppm at the point where the untreated supply enters the regular distribution system. Use a chlorine test kit.

FLOODS
Wells

Thoroughly flush contaminated casing with a 500 ppm available chlorine solution. Backwash the well to increase yield and reduce turbidity. Add enough chlorine solution to the backwash to produce a 10 ppm available chlorine residual. Use a chlorine test kit to determine the residuals. After the turbidity has been reduced and the casing has been treated, add enough chlorine solution to reach a residual level of 50 ppm available chlorine.

Agitate the well water for several hours and take a representative water sample. Re-treat well if water samples are biologically unacceptable. (See Chapter 5 for disinfecting water wells.)

WATER MAIN BREAKS
Mains

Before assembling the repaired section, flush out mud and soil. Keep the water flowing at a rate of 2½ feet per minute while injecting the disinfectant with a hypochlorinator. Stop the water flow when the chlorine residuals test 50 ppm at the low pressure end of the new main section after 24 hours retention time. When disinfection is completed, flush the system free of all heavily chlorinated water.

DISEASE PREVENTION

HIV ON SURFACES

This product kills HIV-1 (associated with AIDS) on pre-cleaned environmental surfaces/objects previously soiled with blood/body fluids in health care settings (e.g. hospitals, nursing homes) or other settings in which there is an expected likelihood of contaminating inanimate surfaces/objects with blood or body fluids.

Personal protection: When handling items soiled with blood or body fluids, use disposable latex gloves, gowns, masks, and eye coverings.

Cleaning procedure: Blood and other body fluids must be thoroughly cleaned from surfaces and other objects before applying this product.

Dilution and contact time: Prepare a 2400 ppm available chlorine solution and spray or flood surface; let stand 2 minutes.

Disposal of infectious materials: Use disposable latex gloves, gowns, masks, and eye coverings. Blood and other body fluids should be autoclaved and disposed of according to local regulations for infectious waste.

BACTERIA

Clorox when used as directed below, is effective against the following bacteria:

GRAM POSITIVE BACTERIA: (Have thicker cell walls – more susceptible to penicillin)

- Staph (Staphylococcus aureus)
- Strep (Streptococcus pyogenes)
- *Methicillin Resistant Staphylococcus aureus*

GRAM NEGATIVE BACTERIA: (Have thinner cell walls – often considered more dangerous because their presence is often obscured by slime)

- Salmonella (*Salmonella choleraesuis*)
- E. coli (*Escherichia serotype 0157:H7*)
- *Pseudomonas aeruginosa* which can cause infections of skin, bone, joints and urinary tract; blood poisoning, pneumonia and chronic lung infections, and persistent
- Dysentery (*Shigella dysenteriae*)
- *Legionella pneumophila*

Directions for use on Hard Non-porous Surfaces
To disinfect hard non-porous surfaces, first clean surface by removing gross filth (loose dirt, debris, food materials, etc.). Prepare a 2400 ppm available chlorine solution. Thoroughly wet surface with the solution and allow it to remain on the surface for 5 minutes. Rinse with clean water and dry.

To Sanitize Garbage Cans/Diaper Pails
Pre-clean garbage can/diaper pail with a cleaning product prior to sanitization. Rinse with water and drain. Pour in 2400 ppm available chlorine solution. Let stand at least 1 minute. Rinse and air dry.

Toilet Bowls
Flush toilet to remove gross filth. Add ¾ cup of bleach to the bowl and brush surfaces thoroughly, making sure to get under the rim. Let stand 2 minutes before flushing again.

TUBERCULOSIS
Clorox, when used as directed below, is effective against Mycobacterium bovis.

Directions for use on Hard Non-porous Surfaces
To disinfect hard non-porous surfaces, first clean surface by removing gross filth (loose dirt, debris, food materials, etc.). Prepare a 5000 ppm available chlorine solution. Thoroughly wet surface with the solution and allow it to remain in contact with the surface for 5 minutes. Rinse with clean water and dry.

VIRUSES
Clorox, when used as directed below, is effective against the following viruses on hard, nonporous, inanimate surfaces:

- Adenovirus Type 2
- Rotavirus
- Hepatitis A
- Cytomegalovirus
- Human Immunodeficiency Virus Type 1(HIV-1) *
- Influenza A2
- Respiratory syncytial virus
- Varicella zoster virus
- Herpes simplex virus 2
- Rhinovirus Type 17
- Rubella virus
- Canine parvovirus **
- Feline parvovirus **

Directions for use on Hard Non-porous Surfaces
To disinfect hard non-porous surfaces, first clean surface by removing gross filth (loose dirt, debris, food materials, etc.) Prepare a 2400 ppm available chlorine solution. Thoroughly wet surface with the solution and allow it to remain in contact with the surface for 5 minutes. Rinse with clean water and dry.

* See directions in the Clorox Service Bulletin entitled "Special Instructions for Using Clorox® Regular Bleach to Clean and Decontaminate Against HIV on Surfaces/Objects Soiled with Blood/Body Fluids"
** For Canine and Feline parvovirus use the same instructions as above but keep the solution in contact with the surface for 10 minutes.

To Sanitize Garbage Cans/Diaper Pails
Pre-clean garbage can/diaper pail with a cleaning product prior to sanitization. Rinse with water and drain. Pour in 2400 ppm available chlorine solution. Let stand [at least] 1 minute. Rinse and air dry.

Toilet Bowls
Flush toilet to remove gross filth. Add ¾ cup of bleach to the bowl and brush surfaces thoroughly, making sure to get under the rim. Let stand 2 minutes before flushing again.

FUNGUS

This product, when used as directed below, is effective against mold and Athlete's foot fungus (Trichophyton mentagrophytes).

Directions for use on Hard Non-porous Surfaces

To disinfect hard non-porous surfaces, first clean surface by removing gross filth (loose dirt, debris, food materials, etc.). Prepare a 2400 ppm available chlorine solution. Thoroughly wet surface with the solution and allow it to remain on the surface for 2 minutes. Rinse with clean water and dry.

To Sanitize Garbage Cans/Diaper Pails

Pre-clean garbage can/diaper pail with a cleaning product prior to sanitization. Rinse with water and drain. Pour in 2400 ppm available chlorine solution. Let stand at least 2 minutes. Rinse and air dry.

CANDIDA

Directions for use on Hard Non-porous Surfaces

To disinfect hard non-porous surfaces, first clean surface by removing gross filth (loose dirt, debris, food materials, etc.). Prepare a solution of 2400 ppm available chlorine solution. Thoroughly wet surface with the solution and allow it to remain in contact with the surface for 2 minutes. Rinse with clean water and dry.

To Sanitize Diaper Pails

Pre-clean diaper pails with a cleaning product prior to sanitization. Rinse with water and drain. Pour in 2400 pm available chlorine solution. Let stand at least 2 minutes. Rinse and air dry.

LIVESTOCK AND ANIMALS

POULTRY CARE

Keeping poultry healthy, productive and profitable is largely due to disease prevention. Treating disease is much more difficult and often less successful than preventing its spread to the flock. Regular use of chlorine bleach to sanitize and disinfect chicken houses, brooders, and other poultry equipment is an effective aid in preventing many bacterial and viral diseases.

To Sanitize Drinking Water

Prepare a 5ppm available chlorine solution using clear water. Let stand 1 minute. Use in glass, porcelain, stoneware or concrete containers. Clean containers daily; rinse.

For young chicks, prepare a 2 ppm available chlorine solution since baby chicks don't soil the water as rapidly as grown chickens, and the solution retains its effectiveness longer.

When cleaning drinking water containers, etc., a 1600 ppm available chlorine solution is effective in removing slime. DO NOT ALLOW BIRDS TO DRINK THIS SOLUTION.

To Clean And Disinfect Poultry Houses, Brooders, Hatcheries

Poultry houses should be cleaned and disinfected between cycles; hatcheries should be cleaned weekly or as necessary to keep sanitary. Metal surfaces can be satisfactorily disinfected. Wooden surfaces are difficult to sanitize by any method.

1. Remove all litter, loose dirt and debris.
2. Mix solution of 1 oz powdered detergent with per gallon of 2400 ppm available chlorine solution*.
3. Using this solution, scrub or pressure-spray all exposed areas, including floor, walls, ceiling posts and support beams. Let stand for 2 minutes.
4. Rinse with clean, clear, **cold** water.
5. Let dry thoroughly before introducing poultry.

Metal Incubators, Feeders, Water Containers, Other Poultry Equipment And Utensils

To clean and disinfect, remove loose dirt and debris. Scrub or pressure-spray with solution of 1 oz powdered detergent thoroughly mixed with each gallon of 1200 ppm available chlorine solution*. Let stand for 2 minutes. Rinse with clear, cold water. Let dry.

For continuous washers, prepare washing solution as above. Add an additional ½ oz of detergent per every 4 gallons of 50 ppm available chlorine solution every 30 minutes. Dump wash tank and recharge every 2 hours.

For manual method, soak eggs for only 1 to 2 minutes. Agitate basket. Make sure eggs are completely covered. Air-dry eggs as rapidly as possible. Store in cool (55°F) room. Maintain relative humidity of 60-80%.

NOTE: Keep egg-washing equipment sanitary. Frequent cleaning will aid in operation and produce more sanitary eggs. While equipment is idle, bacteria can multiply. This contamination can be reduced by thoroughly flushing all equipment immediately before use with a solution of 200 ppm available chlorine.

*Where this product/detergent solution is recommended for sanitizing poultry houses and equipment, use **hot** water (140°F or above) if available.

LIVESTOCK, HORSES, PETS

To Clean And Disinfect Barns, Stables, Hutches, Kennels

Remove all litter, loose dirt and debris. Mix 1 oz powdered detergent with each gallon of 2400 ppm available chlorine solution until detergent is dissolved*. Using the solution, thoroughly scrub or pressure-spray all exposed areas including floor, walls, ceiling posts and support beams. Let stand for [at least] 2 minutes. Rinse with clean, clear, cold water. Let area dry thoroughly before housing animals.

Loading And Hauling Equipment

Loading chutes, trucks, trailers and other equipment for transportation of animals should be cleaned and disinfected prior to use. Pressure-spray or scrub with solution prepared by thoroughly mixing 1 oz powdered detergent with each gallon of 2400 ppm available chlorine solution*. Let stand for [at least] 2 minutes. Rinse with clean, clear, cold water. Allow to dry before using.

Feeders And Drinking Water Containers – To Clean And Disinfect

Thoroughly scrub or pressure-spray with solution of 1 oz powdered detergent mixed with each gallon of 2400 ppm available chlorine solution*. Let stand for at least 5 minutes. Rinse thoroughly with clear, cold water; allow to drain dry. (A solution of 1600 ppm available chlorine is effective in removing slime, which sometimes forms on drinking water containers. DO NOT LET ANIMALS DRINK THIS SOLUTION.)

To Sanitize Animals' Drinking Water

Prepare a 5 ppm available chlorine solution using clear water. Use in glass, plastic, porcelain or concrete containers daily. (See directions above.)

SWINE

Hog Houses And Farrowing Houses – To Cleanse And Disinfect

1. Remove loose dirt, litter and debris. Dirty or coated surfaces cannot be disinfected.
2. Mix 1 oz powdered detergent with each gallon of 2400 ppm available chlorine solution until detergent is dissolved.* Let stand for [at least] 2 minutes.
3. Scrub or pressure-spray all surfaces with this solution. Rinse with clear, **cold** water.
4. Allow to dry before housing pigs.

Remove all animals, poultry, and feed from premises, vehicles, and enclosures. Remove all litter and manure from floors, walls and surfaces of barns, pens, stall chutes and other facilities occupied or traversed by animals. Empty all troughs, feeding and watering appliances. Thoroughly clean all surfaces with soap or detergents and rinse with water.

Ventilate buildings, cars, boats and other closed spaces. Do not house livestock, poultry or use equipment until chlorine has dissipated. All treated feed racks, manger, troughs, automatic feeders, fountains and waterers must be rinsed with potable water before reuse.

Clean And Disinfect Metal Watering Troughs And Feeders

Do this by pressure-spraying or scrubbing with solution prepared by thoroughly mixing 1 ounce powdered detergent and 2 ounces of this product with each gallon of 2400 ppm available chlorine solution*. Let stand for [at least] 2 minutes. Rinse thoroughly with clear, **cold** water; drain dry. (Drinking troughs and feeders should be cleaned and disinfected before housing pigs, and as often as necessary to keep sanitary.)

Dare To Prepare: Chapter 34: The Wonder of Clorox

To Sanitize Drinking Water
Prepare a 5ppm available chlorine solution using *clear* water. (Water containing debris is difficult to sanitize.)

NOTE: Clean metal surfaces can be sanitized using the above method. Wooden surfaces are difficult to sanitize by any method. Use chlorine test strips to adjust to desired available chlorine level.

To obtain a solution with an approximate available chlorine level (parts per million), thoroughly mix the indicated amounts of bleach and water.

*For bleach/detergent solution, use **hot** water if available.

CLOROX BLEACH DILUTION TABLE

APPROXIMATE PPM AVAILABLE CHLORINE	AMOUNT OF BLEACH	AMOUNT OF WATER
10,000	2 pints	9½ pints
5,000	3 oz.	1 quart
	1½ cups (12 oz.)	1 gallon
	7½ cups	5 gallons
2,400	1 part	23 parts
	4 tsp	1 pint
	2⅔ Tbsp	1 quart
	⅔ cups	1 gallon
	1⅓ cups	2 gallons
	cups (12 oz.)	
	2 cups	3 gallons
	3⅓ cups	5 gallons
1,600	7 Tbsp	1 gallon
	7 oz.	2 gallons
1,200	⅓ cup	1 gallon
	1 cup	3 gallons
800	4 tsp	1½ quarts
	3½ Tbsp	1 gallon
	7 oz.	4 gallons
400	2 tsp	1½ quarts
	1¾ Tbsp	1 gallon
	7 Tbsp	4 gallons
200	1 Tbsp	1 gallon
	2 Tbsp (1 oz.)	2 gallons
	5 Tbsp (2½ oz.)	5 gallons
	5 oz.	10 gallons
	1 quart (20 oz.)	100 gallons
	4 gallons	1,000 gallons
75	¼ tsp	1 quart
	1 tsp	1 gallon
	1 Tbsp (½ oz.)	3 gallons
50	16 drops	1 quart
	¾ tsp	1 gallon
	1 Tbsp (½ oz.)	4½ gallons
	2½ Tbsp	10 gallons
25	1 tsp	3 gallons
	2½ tsp	7½ gallons
	5 tsp (½ oz.)	15 gallons
10	16 drops	1 gallon
	¾ tsp	5 gallon
	1½ tsp	10 gallons
5	8 drops	1 gallon
	¾ tsp	10 gallons

Chapter 35: Making Cleaning Supplies

You can make your own cleaners if you run out of commercial cleaning products and have these ingredients. These recipes cost a lot less money because aren't paying for expensive packaging and advertising. Moreover, you aren't paying for the most "expensive" ingredient – water!

LIQUID CLEANER

2 qts. (liters) hot water
2 Tbsp cloudy ammonia
2 Tbsp white vinegar
½ cup baking soda (bicarbonate of soda)
Combine and shake till soda dissolves. For handy use, place in a spray bottle.

ALL-PURPOSE CLEANSER

2 tsp borax
2 tsp baking soda
1 quart water
Mix and pour into a spray bottle.

Baking Soda. Dissolve 4 Tbsp baking soda in 1 quart (liter) warm water for a general cleaner. Or use baking soda on a damp sponge. Baking soda will clean and deodorize all kitchen and bathroom surfaces.
Vinegar and Salt. Mix together for a good surface cleaner.

TOILET BOWL CLEANER

Bleach. Never mix bleach with vinegar, toilet bowl cleaner, or ammonia. The combination of bleach with any of these substances produces a toxic gas that can be hazardous.
Baking Soda and Vinegar. Sprinkle baking soda into the bowl, then drizzle with vinegar and scour with a toilet brush. This combination both cleans and deodorizes.
Borax and Lemon Juice. For removing stubborn stains, like toilet bowl ring, mix enough borax and lemon juice into a paste to cover the entire ring. Flush toilet to wet the sides, and then rub on paste. Let sit for 2 hours and scrub thoroughly. For less stubborn toilet bowl rings, sprinkle baking soda around the rim and scrub with a toilet brush. Borax can be toxic if ingested.

TUB AND TILE CLEANER

CERAMIC TILE

¼ cup vinegar
⅓ cup ammonia
½ cup baking soda
7 cups warm water
Mix and store solution in a spray bottle.

Baking Soda. Sprinkle baking soda like scouring powder. Rub with a damp sponge. Rinse thoroughly.
Vinegar and Baking Soda. To remove film buildup on bathtubs, apply vinegar full-strength to a sponge and wipe with vinegar first. Use baking soda like scouring powder. Rub with a damp sponge and rinse thoroughly with clean water.
Vinegar. Vinegar removes most dirt without scrubbing and doesn't leave a film.
Baking Soda. To clean grout, put 3 cups baking soda into a medium-sized bowl and add 1 cup warm water. Mix into a smooth paste and scrub into grout with a sponge or toothbrush. Rinse thoroughly and dispose of leftover paste when finished.

WINDOW AND GLASS CLEANER

WINDOW 1
½ cup ammonia
2 cups rubbing (isopropyl) alcohol
1 tsp Dawn liquid soap

Put all ingredients into a spray bottle, shake, and use as any commercial brand. **NOTE**: This is my personal favorite as Dawn cuts greasy film.

WINDOW 2
¼-½ tsp liquid detergent
3 Tbsp vinegar
2 cups water

Put all ingredients into a spray bottle, shake, and use as any commercial brand.

Vinegar. Wash windows or glass with a mixture of equal parts white vinegar and warm water. Dry with a soft cloth. Leaves windows and glass streakless. To remove stubborn hard water sprinkler spots and streaks, use undiluted vinegar.

Borax or Washing Soda. 2 Tbsp of borax or washing soda mixed into 3 cups water makes a good window cleaner. Apply to surface and wipe dry. Borax can be toxic if ingested.

Lemon Juice. Mix 1 Tbsp lemon juice in 1 quart (liter) water. Apply to surface and wipe dry.

Baking Soda. To clean cut glass, sprinkle baking soda on a damp rag and clean glass. Rinse with clean water and polish with a soft cloth.

Window washing tips:
- Wash windows when the sun isn't shining on them because they'll dry too leaving streaks.
- When polishing windows use up and down strokes on one side of the window and side to side strokes on the other to tell which side requires extra polishing.
- To polish windows or mirrors to a sparkling shine, try a natural linen towel or other soft cloth, a clean, damp chamois cloth, a squeegee, or crumpled newspaper. One word of warning about newspaper: while newspaper leaves glass lint-free with a dirt-resistant film, persons with sensitivities to fumes from newsprint may wish to avoid the use of newspaper as a cleaning tool.

OVEN CLEANERS

OVEN CLEANER 1
1 cup ammonia
4 cups water

Mix and place in oven in a shallow dish. Heat the oven on low for two hours. Turn off heat and allow to stand overnight. Rub vigorously the next day with an abrasive cloth.

OVEN CLEANER 2
½ cup baking soda (bicarbonate of soda)
¼ cup salt

Enough lemon juice to make a thick paste Apply to baked on areas. Allow to dry and rub of paste. Repeat as needed.

LAUNDRY PRODUCTS

Laundry Soap. (See Soapmaking Chapter)

White Vinegar. Eliminate soap residue by adding 1 cup white vinegar to the washer's final rinse. Vinegar is too mild to harm fabrics but strong enough to dissolve alkalis in soaps and detergents. Vinegar also breaks down uric acid; adding 1 cup vinegar to the rinse water is especially good for babies' clothes. To get wool and cotton blankets soft and fluffy, add 2 cups white vinegar to a full tub of rinse water. **Do not use vinegar if you add chlorine bleach to your rinse water. It will produce harmful vapors.**

Baking Soda. ¼-½ cup baking soda per wash load makes clothes feel soft and smell fresh.

Dry Bleach. Dry bleaches containing sodium perborate are of low toxicity (unless in strong solution, then they can be irritating to the skin). Use according to package directions.

Baking Soda. Cut the amount of chlorine bleach used in your wash by half by adding ½ cup baking soda to top loading machines or ¼ cup to front loaders.

Vinegar. To remove smoky odor from clothes, fill the bathtub with hot water. Add 1 cup white vinegar. Hang garments above the steaming bath water.

Cornstarch. For homemade laundry starch, dissolve 1 Tbsp cornstarch in 1 pint cold water. Place in a spray bottle. Shake before using. Clearly label the contents of the spray bottle.

DISINFECTANTS

Soap. Regular cleaning with plain soap and hot water will kill some bacteria. Keep things dry. Mold, mildew, and bacteria cannot live without moisture.

Borax has long been recognized for its disinfectant and deodorizing properties. Mix ½ cup Borax into 1 gallon hot water and clean with this solution. Borax can be toxic if ingested.

Isopropyl Alcohol. This is an excellent disinfectant. Sponge and allow to dry. (It must dry to do its job.) Use in a well-ventilated area and wear gloves. Be sure to wear gloves and work in a well-ventilated area.

POLISH

FURNITURE 1
½ tsp oil, such as olive (or jojoba, a liquid wax)
¼ cup vinegar or fresh lemon juice
Mix the ingredients in a glass jar. Dab a soft rag in the solution and wipe onto wood surfaces. Cover the glass jar and store indefinitely.

FURNITURE 2
1 teaspoon lemon oil
1 pint mineral oil
Mix and spray on the furniture. Wipe clean with a clean soft cloth.

BRASS AND COPPER CLEANER 1
2 Tbsp salt
1 Tbsp lemon juice
1 Tbsp vinegar
Rub with sponge and let dry. Then rinse with hot water, dry with a soft cloth.

BRASS AND COPPER CLEANER 2
1 pint of soap jelly
1 cup of whiting
1 tsp household ammonia
Make into a paste by adding whiting and ammonia to soap jelly before it congeals, and beat together. After using paste, wash articles in hot suds, rinse and dry thoroughly.

DRAIN CLEANERS AND DRAIN OPENERS
To avoid clogging drains:
- Use a drain strainer to trap food particles and hair
- Collect grease in cans rather than pouring it down the drain
- Pour a kettle of boiling water down the drain weekly to melt fat that may be building up in the drain;
- Pour vinegar and baking soda down your drain weekly to break down fat and keep your drain smelling fresh.

Plunger. A time-honored drain opener is the plunger. This inexpensive tool will usually break up the clog and allow it to float away. It may take more than a few plunges to unclog the drain. **Do not use this method after any commercial drain opener has been used or is still present in the standing water.**

Baking Soda and Vinegar. Pour ½ cup baking soda down the drain. Add ½ cup white vinegar and cover the drain if possible. Let set for a few minutes, then pour a kettle of boiling water down the drain to flush it. The combination of baking soda and vinegar can break down fatty acids into soap and glycerin, allowing the clog to wash down the drain. **Do not use this method after any commercial drain opener has been used or is still present in the standing water.**

Baking Soda and Salt. Pour ½ cup salt and ½ cup baking soda down the drain. Follow with 6 cups boiling water. Let sit overnight and then flush with water. The hot water should help dissolve the clog and the baking soda and salt serve as an abrasive to break through the clog.

Mechanical Snake (and Garden Hose). A flexible metal snake can be purchased at hardware stores or rented. It is threaded down the clogged drain and manually pushes the clog away. If used in conjunction with a running garden hose, it can even clear a blockage in the main drain to the street. First crank the snake and feed it into the pipe. Next withdraw the snake and flush the pipe by inserting a garden hose with the water turned on full. With some luck, it may save you the expense of a plumber.

MOLD KILLER
2 tsp tea tree oil
2 cups water

Combine in a spray bottle, shake to blend, and spray on problem areas. Do not rinse.
NOTE: tea tree oil scent is very strong, but will dissipate in a few days.

Heavy Build Up Formula
1¼ cups vinegar
¾ cup water
4 drops cinnamon essential oil
5 drops citrus seed oil
5 drops tea tree oil

Spray on area, let sit for a few hours, then rinse, reapply and let sit.

MOLD PREVENTION
2 cups water
10 drops citrus seed extract
5 drops juniper essential oil

Combine all ingredients in a spray bottle. Spray heavily onto areas, BUT do not rinse, let sit on spot indefinitely. If you already have a heavy build up of mold and mildew use this formula to remove it. Spray onto spots and let sit for a few hours, then reapply and let sit.

Chapter 36: Shower Without Power

SINGING IN THE SHOWERLESS SHOWER

None of us smells too pretty without regular bathing. Even people not breaking a sweat develop body odor from accumulated oils and daily life. Not only do we smell, but also our bodies become a germfest.

It's psychologically lifting to feel clean. Cleaner *is* nicer – period. Most people like to bathe at least daily, but what can we do during an emergency?

Besides the time-honored "spit bath", keep a supply of pre-moistened towelettes and "Baby Wipes" on hand. Water squirted on the body from a spray bottle helps conserve supplies.

Another alternative is "no water required" products. No-Rinse Laboratories' products have been around since 1948. They are biodegradable and contain no alcohol. To use the body wash, dilute with warm water, apply mildly foaming cleansing solution with a washcloth, and lightly towel dry. To shampoo, just apply, work into a lather, towel dry and style. The only thing left is a fresh scent and clean hair. This same company also makes pre-moistened towelettes, which can be microwaved for a warm "bath". These products are about $4 for 8 oz bottles.

NOTE: These products would be ideal for people severely injured or confined to their beds. The manufacturer's website **norinse.com** has a lengthy list of retailers for both the U.S., Canada and international purchases.

CAMP SHOWERS AND ALTERNATIVES

If water isn't running and your home is on septics, you can still use your own shower or tub area for an indoor bath. Heat water over your stove, oven or fireplace, in a reflective box or solar oven, campfire or BBQ outside.

For a makeshift shower, cut a small hole in the bottom of a 5 or 6 gallon plastic bucket and screw a showerhead into the hole. Detachable heads or watering can "roses" work great. To use, fill and hang from your showerhead or tree limb. Alternatively, there are numerous commercial shower bladders available.

STEARNS AIR POWER SUNSHOWER

The Air Power Sunshower really took my fancy because it can be used sitting on the ground without needing to be hung overhead for gravity feeding. It works anywhere, even in your own bathroom. Its foot pump pressurizes the bladder, which holds 5½ gallons (21L) of water. This is more than most portable shower bags and it has a 7' (2.13m) long hose. Thirty seconds pumping fully pressurizes the bag letting it run for 2 minutes without additional pumping. It's made from sturdy 600-denier polyester, which protects the double bladder. Mesh pockets keep accessories altogether. Check REI stores **www.rei.com** as well as most camping and outdoor shops. US$35-40.

SOLAR HEATED WATER BAGS

This is one of many versions of solar heated bags. To use, fill the bags with water, lay out flat with the clear side up. Product information says 3 hours heats the water, but this would depend on outside temperature, capacity and amount of sunshine. Typical sizes run in 0.6, 2½, 3½, 4, 5, 5½ and 8 gallon (2¼, 9½, 13¼, 15, 19, 21 and 30L) capacity. Companies manufacture these bags under SunShower, Solar Shower, H_2O Shower or Bush Bags. Expect to pay in the neighborhood of $20-$35. Solar showers are available at most camping, boating and outdoor sports stores.

STOVE-TOP WATER HEATER

Zodi Stove Top Shower (not pictured) is designed to deliver hot water and hot showers using the heat from your existing camp stove or even a wood-burning or pellet stove. To use, place the heater across stove burner, submerge the compact pump in water (requires 4 D cell batteries) and ignite stove burner.

Hot showers are ready in seconds! The padded gear bag doubles as a 4-gallon water container. Water temperature can be altered up to 100°F by adjusting the gas valve or through recirculation. The compact unit comes with an 8' hose and water saver showerhead for $150. Accessories to consider are a garden hose adapter for $10 and a shower pole for hands-free bathing for $35. Look for Hotman products at sport and camping stores. Check Powderfin **www.powderfin.com** or Cabela's **www.cabelas.com**.

ZODI HOT TAP CAMP SHOWER SYSTEM

Zodi also makes nifty Hot Taps in two models. They're very portable since all that's required is attaching one or two (depending on model) 16-oz. propane bottles to the burner and 4 D-cell batteries. A single propane tank is enough for 25 five-minute showers.

Fill the tank with water from any water source - a lake, river or tub - light the burner and in less than 1 minute, water will be 100°F (37.8°C). This unit heats over 60 gallons of HOT water between battery and propane refills. Like the Stove Top, water temperature can be adjusted. Most features are the same as the Stove Top model except that water is heated by propane. A two-canister model is also available. Lids for the cases of both models are removable to hold the propane cylinder(s) in the molded base to keep them from tipping. If you plan to be stationary, it would be more convenient and cost effective to buy the Bulk Propane Kit that gives up to 60 hours of use on a single fill. This step-up model is designed for heavier use with stainless steel burner construction.

Check Dosewallips **www.dosewallips.com** and Cabela's **cabelas.com**, and camping stores for available units. Choose the one-burner ($160) or super-fast heating two-burner ($260) model.

ZODI HOTMAN EXTREME SC

Zodi's other unit is the Hotman Extreme SC. Like the Camp Showers, this system let you enjoy long hot showers anywhere. The on/off showerhead allows for long bathing and the heavy-duty burner doubles as a cook stove. To use, attach a 16-ounce propane bottle to the burner, fill the tank with water and light the burner. Set up dimensions 32"Hx8"D (81x20cm). Expect to pay in the neighborhood of $160 and the stove accessories are about $70. See **zodi.com**. The optional Shower Pole ($35) lets you use your Hot Tap shower completely hands-free. Simply set up the pole and wrap the showerhead over the curved top. Pole height is 5' 6" and breaks down into seven pieces.

COLEMAN HOT WATER ON DEMAND

A really useful product is Coleman's hot water dispenser. Powered by a propane heater and a battery-operated water pump, the Hot Water on Demand heats water to 100°F (38°C) in only five seconds. Connect the heater to the 5-gallon water container and set your desired temperature. It heats up to 40 gallons of water on one 16.4-ounce propane cylinder and one charge of the rechargeable battery that is included. Hot Water on Demand's description states that it's for outside use only. Even so, water could be heated outside and used indoors. While pictured here with the faucet, a shower adapter with 48" hose and spray head can be purchased for $10. MSRP is $250 but it can be found at many sporting goods and camping supplies stores, often on sale. Check Cabelas **www.cabelas.com** and **www.amazon.com**.

SHOWER ENCLOSURES

Unless showering inside, you'll probably want to set up a privacy screen. They can also double as commode enclosures if you have a small portable facility. Large rolls of 6-mil thick black plastic do the trick. By the time you buy the plastic, some of the pre-made units cost nearly the same.

Tarps work even better than black plastic since they are tear-resistant and have reinforced eyelets ready for hanging. However, you'd need to improvise a closure. If you lack the time to deal with this detail, here's a sampling of ready-made portable shower enclosures.

The Bivouac Buddy (not pictured) comes with an 8 gallon (30L) capacity solar shower, which can also be filled with campfire-warmed water. It features an on/off gravity flow showerhead for up 12 minutes of continuous water flow. Roomy enough to double as a portable toilet enclosure, it measures 34"x6'2" (86x188cm) and folds to 9" tall. The Buddy shower even has a towel holder and storage pockets. This unit is available in camouflage, green or blue, retails around US$155-$250. Shop around as prices vary widely, but the best price is from the manufacturer. Bivouac Buddy **www.bivouacbuddy.com/**.

Paha Que manufactures The Tepee (picture next page), which provides a common-sense evolution in campsite restroom and shower facilities. This fully equipped portable outhouse/shower comes in either fiberglass or aluminum. The roomy ceiling peaks at 8 feet (244cm) with floor dimensions of 54" (137cm). The aluminum unit runs around US$200 and the fiberglass model at $US150. While this might be a little pricy to keep on hand just for emergencies, if camping is a part of your recreational life, it might be a good dual investment. For the best price, check Campmor: **www.campmor.com**. or Paha Que Wilderness **www.pahaque.com**. Fiberglass models are priced as much as US$60 higher at other retailers.

The Toilet/Shower Tent (not pictured) is nice compromise. It has good room for maneuverability measuring 35½x35½x90" (90x90x230cm). This enclosure is made from durable polyethylene fabric over a metal frame with a zipped doorway and vented roof. Look for this product online at Ray's Outdoors **raysoutdoors.com.au** priced at AU$150.

Stearns Shower Enclosure (picture next page), by the company who manufactures solar shower water bags, makes a very reasonably priced model. It measures 30"x30"x65" (76x76x165cm) and weighs less than 4 pounds (1.8kg). Expect to purchase this for US $30. Check Campbound for this item: **www.campbound.com**.

Restop (picture next page) sells a Privacy Tent for US$130. It has a zippered front, weighs only 7½ pounds (3.4 kg), collapses completely into a shoulder bag and is easily carried by one person. The Privacy Tent comes with ropes and tie down stakes should it get windy. This tent is especially good because it does not depend on overhead tree branches to hold it up. The gray fabric is water repellent and completely opaque even in direct sunlight for complete privacy. The Privacy Tent may have difficulty doubling as a shower tent unless a shower bladder is used that doesn't require overhead gravity feeding.

Dare To Prepare: Chapter 36: Shower Without Power

Paha Que   Stearns   Restop

The Privacy Tent was taken on the four-week 1998 Everest Expedition to an altitude of 21,300 feet (6,493m). According to product literature, it endured "freezing temperatures, driving wind and snow, sun radiation and even yak stampedes". How many tents can say this (especially the yak stampede)? If you're an avid camper, it would be a good investment. Restop products can be ordered on-line: **www.restop.com** or phone 888-924-6665 (toll-free in US)

Chapter 37: Trashy Talk

SERVICE DISRUPTION: DISPOSING OF GARBAGE

"Pee-yew!!" It doesn't have to be that bad! One thing easily overlooked in preparedness planning is the amount of garbage and rubbish the average household generates. If trash removal services weren't running for a few weeks or heaven forbid, a few months, most of us would drown in garbage. However, we can vastly cut down on refuse by composting leaves, twigs, grass clippings, scentless/colorless paper towels, tissues and many food scraps, and roll newspapers for "fireplace logs". (See Chapter 25 Composting) Recycling takes care of another portion of daily trash.

FOOD

Drain non-compostable foods of liquid (it takes up space and weight). If you're going through a short-term disaster, wrap food in several layers of newspaper and place in a container with a sealable lid. Odors will be negligible and flies, ants, bees and mice won't know "lunch" is lurking inside.

If electricity is still working and you have space, freeze food scraps. Wrap meat trimmings, etc. in heavy-duty Ziploc bags and place them in the freezer till trash pick up arrives.

Soft food items can be flushed down the toilet, but not bones. After all, that's what you're putting down there normally – just in different form.

If long-term interruption of trash removal is expected, pick an area in your yard to excavate a pit. Dig deep enough to allow for 2 feet (61cm) of dirt over the top. Coyotes, bears and rodents have extremely good sense of smell so it needs to be buried deeply.

Since digging "garbage pits" is no one's idea of fun, fill a large trash bucket with materials to bury and do it at one setting. Storing refuse in a bucket with a tight-fitting lid is an option for folks without access to a backyard. Then look for a vacant lot when you need to bury it or find a landfill.

BURNABLES

If you have a fireplace, many items can be incinerated easily and help heat your home at the same time. If no burning restrictions are in place, a campfire in the backyard is an alternative. If it's windy, use 55-gallon metal drum or dig a pit to contain the fire.

NON-BURNABLES

Used food cans are messy/smelly and can attract flies, ants, bees, mice and rats. In Colorado, it's common to see deer, coyotes, raccoons, possums, skunks and fox in our more rural area. Occasionally mountain lion tracks show up – or the remains of an unfortunate house pet. In cold weather when food is scarce, seeing bears is not out of the ordinary either. We don't need these visitors searching for dinner close to home. Once they find a good "diner", they mark it in their PDA and plan subsequent visits. Solve the canned food odor problem by placing tins in a campfire. The odor and food particles will burn out. When the fire is cold, remove cans and smash flat with a sledgehammer.

Instead of tossing garbage loosely in a trash sack, nest and stack rubbish to make best use of space. Crush anything when possible to save room.

Many locales have "burn bans" in effect during high fire (red flag), high pollution days. Check with your county or shire to see if there are special dispensations when trash pick up isn't available.

PLAN AHEAD

Search garages, attics and basements for anything you've "been meaning to throw away." When Stan and I moved across country May '98, there was no rubbish removal service in our little rural area. We began composting and burning what could be incinerated. This took care of a lot. There was still a mountain of Styrofoam "peanuts", bubble wrap and other assorted packing materials that couldn't be burned. This stuff was poured into several wardrobe boxes till we could make it to a landfill. When trash removal finally came to our area, we'd forgotten about the "peanuts". Going to the landfill never happened and since the peanut boxes were down in the barn, they weren't uppermost in our minds. Eventually we began adding a bit of this rubbish to each week's trash pick up and ended up peanut-free! Take a day to visit your neighborhood landfill for those hard-to-dispose-of "dead" appliances, bald tires and old junk.

Having a garage sale is a double benefit. It puts a few dollars in your pocket and frees yourself from clutter. You know what they say about one man's trash... The freed up space can be put to better use for storing necessities.

TOILET TOPICS

No one likes to think of using anything but the facilities we know and depend on. Anyone who has been on a "roughing it" camp out remembers the rude awakening each morning. Shivering on the long trek to the outhouse and plopping one's bottom on cold planking wasn't the day's peak moment. The smell was less than inviting and who knew when an irritable spider might show up. A necessary trip in freezing temperatures is even less appealing.

At some point, disposing of human waste may become an issue. What can I do with it? What's safe? Under no circumstances can it be left in a heap above ground. It exposes you and everyone else to the threat and spread of cholera, typhoid, infectious hepatitis, dysentery and diarrhea. "Although urine is usually considered a sterile waste product, it can carry, as it almost always does in developing countries, parasites such as schistosomes."[89]

To dispose of human waste, FEMA advises, "Bury human waste to avoid the spread of disease by rats and insects. Dig a pit 2 to 3 feet (61 to 91cm) deep and at least 50 feet (15 meters) downhill and away from any well, spring, or water supply."[90] Buck Tilton, who has worked in wilderness education for over 35 years and written 10 books on wilderness and safety, recommends even more distance from water sources.

He advises, "all human wastes should be at least two hundred feet (61 meters), or approximately 70 adult paces, from water, and placed where little chance of discovery exists."[91] The latter agrees with Paul Jackson of Health and Human Services, Victoria, Australia. A third source, Back Country Horsemen's Guidebook also recommends waste buried no closer than 200 feet (61m) from water sources.[92]

USING EXISTING TOILETS

If sewer lines break but the toilet bowl is usable, place a garbage bag inside the bowl. Using the existing toilet is an especially good idea for toddlers, elderly and handicapped persons. It keeps the familiar facility usable and eliminates having to construct a makeshift toilet. The possible drawback is if the garbage sack is punctured and waste falls into the bowl. This could create sanitation problems if flushing is not an option.

FOLDING TOILETS

These toilets are about as basic as one can get. Texsport makes a good unit with heavy-duty tubular steel legs and a durable white plastic seat.

Bags are held in place by a removable ring. This folding toilet comes with 6 replacements. Twelve replacement bags run less than $3.

Though economically priced under $10, I'd rather use a toilet bucket for several reasons:

> Esthetics
> Cleanliness
> Sealing off odors and germs
> No risk of punctured sacks

Emergency/camping toilets might be OK for outside, but better alternatives exist for indoor use, especially if the emergency lasts longer than a day or two.

BUCKETS

There are several variations of the bucket toilet are available. Some folks began using these in an emergency and ended up staying with them when it when the emergency was over. Why? Primarily water savings and production of usable, organic fertilizer. These toilets are excellent waste disposal ideas for apartment dwellers needing minimal fuss.

MAKE YOUR OWN

Building a makeshift toilet can be as simple as taking a "drywall mud" bucket, lining it with a garbage bag and placing a couple 2x4s on top for the seat. Five-gallon "mud buckets" are normally left at construction sites in trash piles or dumpsters after drywallers have completed taping and plastering. Since they're usually tossed out after this phase of construction, buckets are free. Be sure to grab the lid!

If several are available, ask for these too. Possibly your neighbor hasn't had the foresight to plan a temporary toilet. Drywall buckets also work great to hold garbage before disposal and as makeshift showers.

One area not often addressed is the proper height of makeshift toilets. For maximum comfort using a bucket toilet, it should be similar to the height of your normal toilet. If you're especially tall and the bucket is not at the right height, it can be a little uncomfortable. This is easily fixed by elevating the bucket with a couple of 2x4's or bricks.

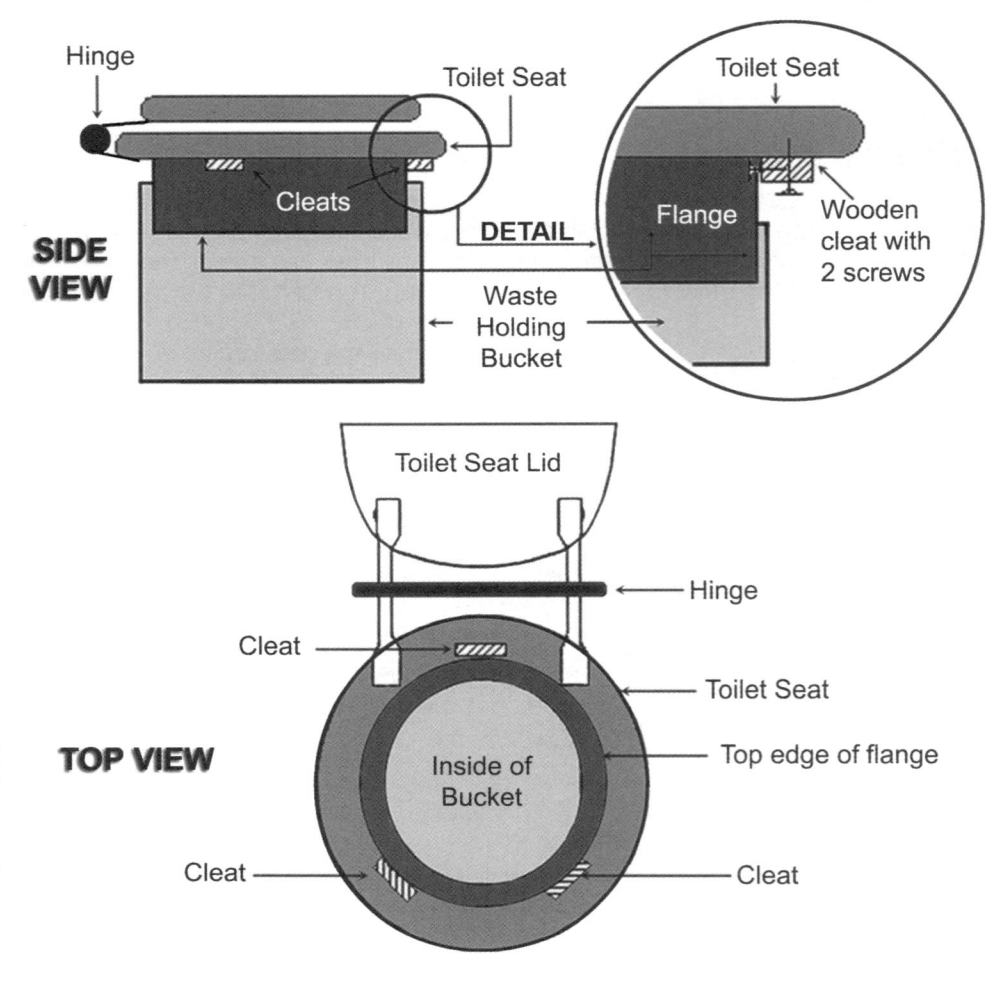

Other bucket toilets can be similarly constructed.

For a more solid or permanent bucket toilet, the diagram below shows how to make one for the cost of a toilet seat and a couple of screws.

MATERIALS:

3 drywall buckets or equivalent
6 wood screws
3 wood cleats, each cut 1x3x¾" (2.5x7.5x2cm)

CONSTRUCTION:

Step 1 To make the flange, cut the top 4-6" (10-15cm) from one bucket. A wood saw works well for this. The flange will slip inside the second bucket.

Step 2 Attach flange to the bottom of a toilet seat using two screws for each of three wood cleats. One screw attaches the cleat to the toilet seat; the second attaches the flange to the cleat. Remove and discard the original toilet seat spacers.

Step 3 The last bucket holds sawdust, chipped wood, chopped straw, or other absorbent carbon-rich organic matter. After each use, cover waste with several cups of this material. This handles most odors.

Step 4 When the toilet bucket is ⅔ full, transfer the flanged toilet seat to the now empty sawdust bucket, which then becomes the next toilet bucket.

Step 5 Empty the waste either into a humanure composting area and cover with a fresh layer of sawdust to prevent odors or bury and cover with a minimum of 2' (61cm) of soil. Clean the empty bucket and sanitize. The cleaned bucket will now hold the sawdust/wood chip/straw material. This simple toilet bucket costs under $10 to make.

KEEP IT CLEAN

After each elimination, use a layer of sawdust, chlorinated lime, kitty litter or peat moss to control odor. For disinfection, sprinkle on baking soda, alcohol, laundry detergent, Lysol, Pine-Sol/Pine O Clean or Glen 20 to control odor and germs. Some advisors suggest adding to the bottom of the bucket, one cup liquid chlorine bleach plus one-half gallon (2L) of water. However, if this solution should splash while seated, chorine could burn tender skin.

Chemicals for disinfecting boat and camper porta potties also work well and leave a pleasant odor. During many years of boating, we used both the powdered and liquid form. The liquid is usually a very intense blue and can stain skin temporarily.

The powdered form is lightweight and more compact, but either works well. Locate these items at RV and camping supply stores as well as in boating magazines and at marinas. They're usually marketed under Aqua-Chem, Bio-Blue, Dri-Kem, SeaLand, LectraSan and Headzyme Tablets.

NOTE: If you're saving the waste products for humanure, do not use disinfectants. Instead, use sawdust, wood shavings, etc. Never put disinfectants down a composting toilet. It kills the good bacteria.

TOILET BUCKET ALTERNATIVES

Restop has a novel twist to the toilet bucket. They provide a unit called the Commode Bucket if you purchase one of their higher end products.

The basis of this product line is a polymer, which when it comes in contact with urine or feces, it turns into a gel. The gel is self-sealing so it eliminates leaks. This allows for easy disposal of waste in the trash bin. While the gel is a good idea, if rubbish removal isn't running for long periods, the gel-filled pouches begin to pile up. For folks in apartments who don't have access to a yard for burial, this is a good alternative. While the gel does keep waste more manageable, it doesn't have disinfecting agents.

If you want to pass on the Commode Bucket itself, you can still purchase the waste bags and polymer. Their Restop Emergency Kit # RS2001 (US$39.95) provides enough polymer-filled bags for two people for one week. Kit includes 7 solid waste bags and 14 liquid waste bags. To use, empty your regular toilet bowl of water and line with one of the waste bags.

Product information indicates the polymer has a shelf life of at least 10 years with the powder working best in temperatures of 40-120°F (4.4-49°C). Restop products can be ordered on-line through: **www.restop.com/** or by phoning 888-924-6665 (toll-free in the US)

RELIANCE HASSOCK TOILET

This Hassock Toilet is made from lightweight, rugged plastic with a contoured seat. In the middle is a removable 4-gallon (15L) pail for easy cleaning. Its splash cover doubles as a toilet paper holder. Campmor **www.campmor.com** has the best retail price of US$30 and Dom's Outdoor Outfitters **domsoutdoor.com/** at US$44. Prices vary widely.

LIQUID WASTE COLLECTORS

Unlike solid waste, urine is (usually) sterile and can be disposed of outside without as much worry of spreading disease. When at all possible, keep urine in a container separate from feces. The two waste products decompose at much different rates. Feces contains toxic material, urine generally does not. This keeps your toilet bucket, porta potty or whatever receptacle you choose, usable for the longest time before emptying. Use one of the following products for urine collection. I promise you, either the Little John/Lady J or the Pipinette beats the socks off straddling a two-pound coffee can as in early camping days!

LITTLE JOHN, LADY J

Little John is a spill-proof, tip-proof, leak-proof plastic bottle that's great for containing life's little emergencies. Previously, women were often overlooked and had to be innovative. Now they can enjoy the same bathroom conveniences as men. Men use the Little John pictured on the right and women attach the Lady J adapter on the left. If you ever get stuck in your car away from facilities, this can be a little lifesaver. Little John and Lady J are priced very reasonably at US$$6-11 in most camping and/or boating supply houses or ordered on-line through the Internet from or Amazon **www.amazon.com**. For best prices check Campmor **www.campmor.com** and Cabela's **www.cabelas.com**.

FRESHETTE

Another product especially designed for women is this palm size portable restroom. For long car rides or for times when sanitary facilities are unavailable, relief is only seconds away. Easy to use while standing, the kit contains a discreet flesh tone unit, clear beveled extension, ready case, and 12 disposable bags. Everything stores in a zippered carry pouch. It's feather light, reusable and designed with a 6" retractable extension tube. Campmor sells this nifty little convenience for US$20. **www.campmor.com** and REI **www.rei.com**.

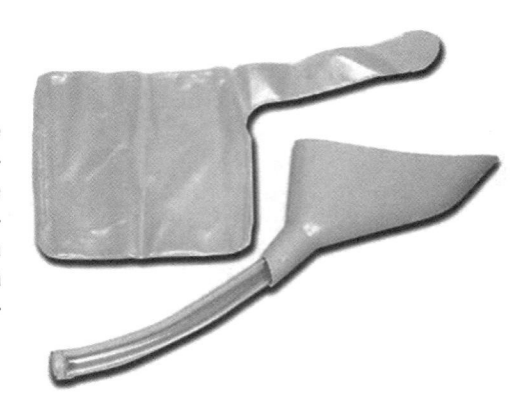

CHEMICAL TOILETS AND PORTA POTTIES

Chemical toilets are used mostly in boats and in recreational vehicles though some folks cart them along to campsites. They look like a squared off version of a conventional toilet. The first one we had in the early 80's was pretty primitive but functional. After completion of your business, a handle on the front of the porta potty pulls open a trap door and the contents fell into a holding tank. The top tank holds water to freshen the bowl. They're comfortable, practical and can be easily used indoors.

When full, the holding tank unlatches from the seat and water reservoir to be carried to the site of disposal. My husband always performed this task and I gather it was not terribly pleasant regardless of deodorant or disinfect being used.

To empty, the top portion disengages from the holding tank. Generally there is a screw cap that allows for easy disposal of contents.

TIP: Use biodegradable toilet paper. It takes up less room than conventional toilet paper as it dissolves.

Besides boating and RV stores, many camping and Army surplus outlets carrying porta potties as well as Wal-Mart and many discount stores. Depending on features, water capacity and waste holding tank, expect to pay from $100 to $350.

COMPOSTING TOILETS

With every flush, roughly 4 gallons or 13-15 liters of water are whisked down the toilet bowl! On average, each household member flushes at least five times daily. For a family of four, that's 80 gallons or 303 liters of drinkable water down the drain every day. With Stan and me working from home, I'd hate to think about the water waste if we didn't have water-saver commodes. During an emergency this would be unthinkable and many people believe it's a terrible waste of resources any time.

Composting toilets were formerly used only in parks and by remote homeowners, but now they are seen in conventional homes. Why?
- Tightening wastewater regulations
- Growing awareness of pollution sources
- Avoid skyrocketing sewer rates
- Avoid septic tank pumping costs
- Reduce the size of leaching beds

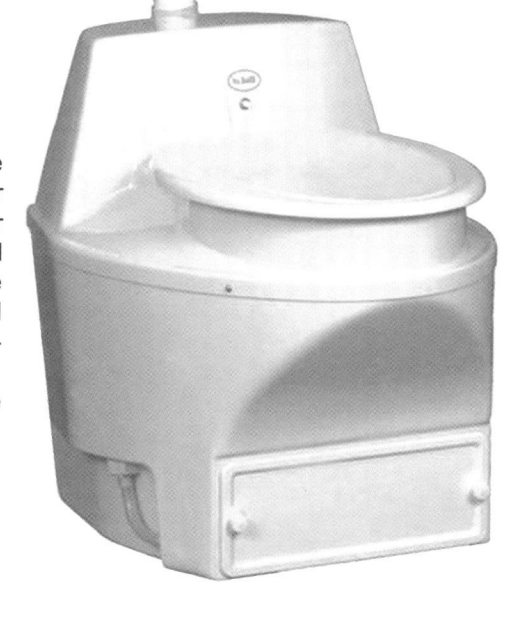

For short-term use and during emergencies, several waterless, self-contained units are available, but they are less "traditional" in appearance unlike the Sancor unit pictured here. BioLet's XL model sells for around $2,300. This model accommodates 4 people at full-time use or 6 part-time users. Other Biolets sell for $1500-2000. The Envirolet, manufactured by Sancor, has a moveable grate that can be manually pulled to break up, mix, and aerate the waste. Other excellent manufacturers in clued Phoenix, Sun-Mar and Clivus Multrum.

COMPOST TOILET CONSIDERATIONS

Before purchasing a compost toilet ask:
1. What are the durability, suitability and longevity of the materials used in manufacturing?
2. Will the size and shape of the composting toilet work in your home?
3. Does compost removal require a pumper truck or climbing into the tank?
4. Can you remove compost without also removing fresh waste?
5. What are the energy and ventilation requirements?
6. What are the long-term operating costs?
7. Would you personally be willing to perform the required maintenance?

BUILD A COMPOSTING TOILET

You can make your own composting toilet similar to the one on the next page. It's not a glam model like the one pictured right, just functional. Many commercial units sit a story above the composter. As waste falls down the chute it is aerated, a necessary factor in the process. These toilets are waterless; none is needed with ample liquid just from urine.

Several features are common to every homemade composting toilet:
1. Fly and rat-proof containers
2. Trap door(s) to access and remove compost
3. Aeration – generally a chute or drop from where the waste is deposited to where it lands
4. Drainage and vent for moisture to evaporate

5. Fan (optional)

Vaults can be constructed of reinforced concrete or bricks and mortar. The entire structure, including the vaults, rests on a concrete or brick base. Vaults measuring approximately one cubic yard should last 6-12 months before needing to be emptied. However long it takes, when the vault is ⅔ full, fill the last ⅓ with dirt, seal it off and

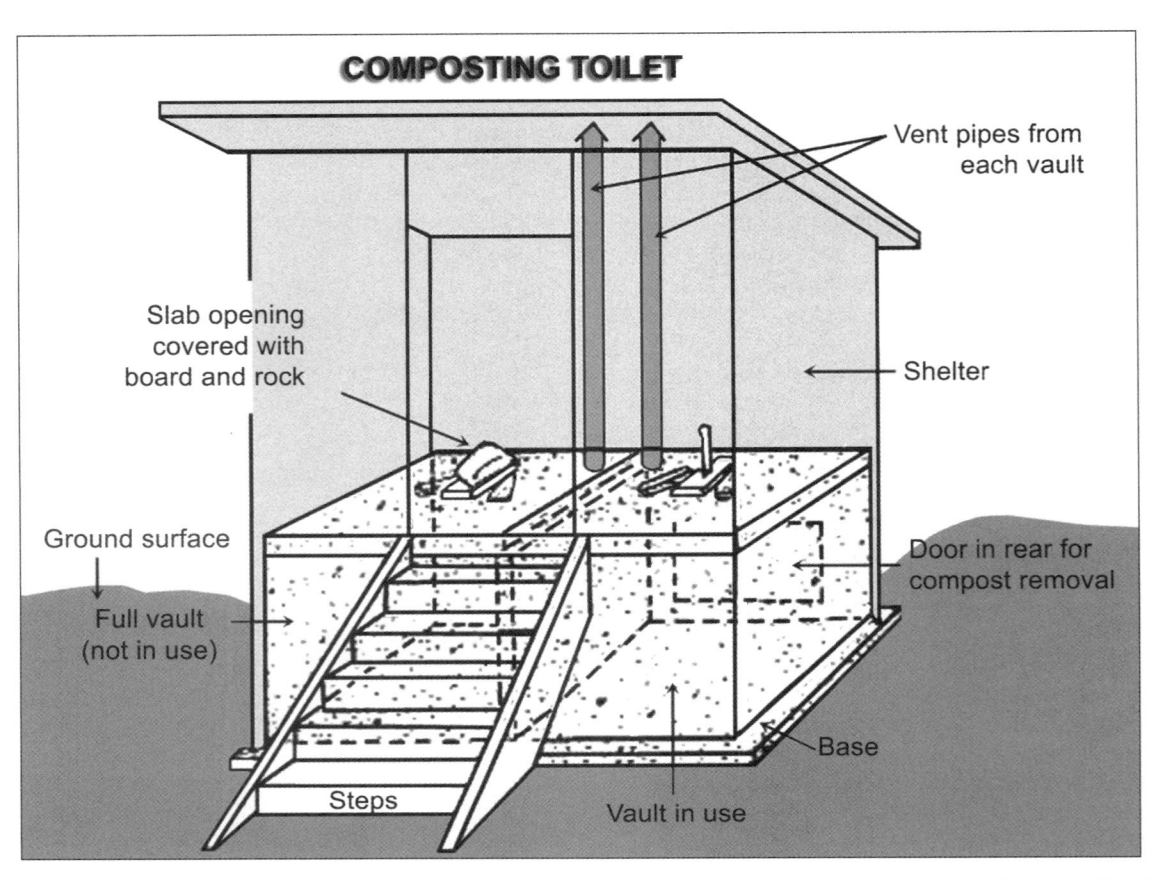

COMPOSTING TOILET

- Vent pipes from each vault
- Slab opening covered with board and rock
- Shelter
- Ground surface
- Full vault (not in use)
- Door in rear for compost removal
- Steps
- Base
- Vault in use

use the other side. When the second side has reached the ⅔ full mark, stop using that side. By now, the first vault should have completed the composing process.

Compost is excavated through the trap door in the rear and the cycle begins again, using the first vault.

Depending on the size of the holding vaults, they should last about 6 months to a year. Now before you wrinkle your nose in disgust, if the toilet is working properly, there should be nothing left but dry, odorless compost.

In talking with Collin Martin of Rota Loo, he shared that the average household generates 20 tons of waste yearly. This includes water usage. When folks switch to a compost toilet, the amount of waste per year is reduced to 44 pounds (20kg). That makes a composting toilet look even better!

COMPOST DO'S AND DON'TS

Check the list of items for those that are OK to put in the compost toilet. Add a thin layer of them daily, especially kitchen scraps. If you've had a party and lots of folks used your toilet for urinating, chances are you'll need to add extra bulking material like leaves to compensate.

WHAT CAN GO IN MY COMPOST TOILET?	
YES	NO
Tampons/sanitary pads	Diapers/nappies
Food scraps – ADD DAILY	Panty liners with plastic inserts
Hay and Grass clippings	Disinfectant – USE VINEGAR
Dog droppings	Fat, grease, oil
Corn stalks	Bottles and cans
Leaves	Antibiotics
Sawdust	Deodorizers, if it smells, it's not composting properly

PIT PRIVY OR YE OLE DUNNY

If you can't bear the thought of shoveling compost, tired of carting waste in a trash bag and don't want to spend the dollars on a commercial composter, consider the pit privy, unromantically tagged The Outhouse. These involve minimal cost and not much labor or construction. In general, pit privies last four to six years before a new hole needs to be dug. Like with the homemade composting toilet, you still have a slab and a shelter, but this type facility uses a pit.

Dig pits in moisture-permeable soil so the urine flows through. The bottom of the pit must be a **minimum** of three feet (1 meter) above the water table. The number of pits required depends on how many family members use the privy. To give an example, according to US Aid, a pit measuring a yard square by a yard and a half deep will last a family of five for six years. If you end up putting a lot of other refuse down the pit, it will last considerably less than six years.

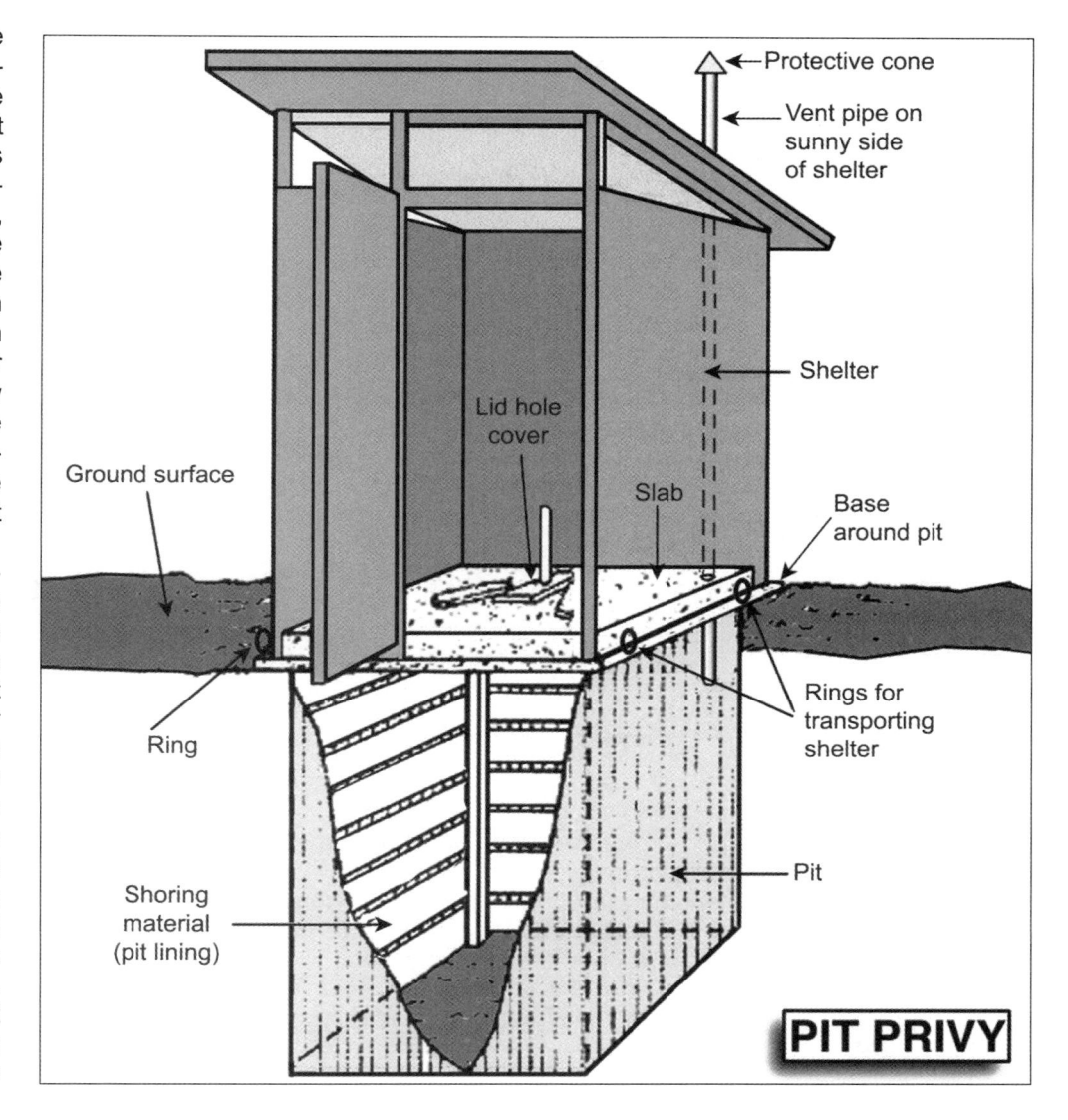

TIPS: Using biodegradable toilet paper like that made for boats and RVs helps. For any outside facility, be sure to keep the toilet paper enclosed in a container with a tight lid. No one wants to use soggy paper or paper covered in cobwebs.

Cover the pit with a "lid" made from precast concrete, which is also the slab base for the shelter. Shore up the pit with timber, brick or rocks. In this slab is a hole through which waste is deposited. You can leave it as a hole or add a seat for comfort.

Between uses, cover the hole in the slab with a board and rock or if you've used a wooden bench, make sure it has a snug fitting lid to keep out flies and rats.

You'll know it's time to dig a new hole when waste is a foot and a half below the slab. At this point, fill in the pit the rest of the way with dirt and dig a new location.

The main drawback is pit privy's honestly earned smelly reputation. However it is a viable solution for a large family or disasters extending for longer periods of time. During a long-term disaster, it might be very difficult to get a commercial composting toilet installed, but an outhouse requires a minimum of materials and could easily be constructed any time. Even though this may seem primitive to many people, not too long ago, this was in common use. It still is still seen dotting the countryside and in many remote camp areas. You'll also see it in areas of totally new construction where an enclosed dunny is a welcomed sight!

During all the preparation for ourselves, we can't forget our pets. Once we agree to have a pet, it's up to us, their caretakers/owners, to set aside provisions for them as well.

To many people, pets aren't "like" family members, they *are* family and so it is in the Deyo household. Preparing supplies for Seismo (right) and Taco (left) is just a matter of course.

During a full-scale disaster, much as our pets mean to *us*, they rank considerably lower to rescue workers when many people depend on their assistance. Pre-disaster planning greatly helps and could save your pet's life.

Could you say, *you'll have to stay behind* to these faces?

PLACES FOR PETS TO STAY

It's possible that you or your pet, or both, may need shelter at some time in a location other than your home. Prior to any emergencies, make a list of:

1. **Available boarding kennels and pet motels** in your area and in different parts of town. It is possible that some will have vacancies and may have escaped damage.

2. **Local humane societies, pet disaster, rescue agencies and animal shelters** – their names, addresses and phone numbers. Keep one copy in your address book and another copy with pet prep supplies.

3. **Area motels that accept pets** or at the very least, allow them to remain in vehicles in the parking lot. Pets Welcome **www.petswelcome.com** is a wonderful resource for U.S. and Canada listing pet-friendly lodging.

Ahead of disaster, see which motels accommodate pets. Ask if "no pet" policies could be waived in an emergency.

When Stan and I moved cross-country in Australia, it took 5½ days of pulling a loaded trailer to make the trip. We made reservations only at motels and caravan parks that allowed Seismo and Taco to be with us.

At first we were concerned they'd be cold at night, would bark a lot or make a mess in the back of the truck. We had fixed their bed with warm blankets and their favorite chew toys. After traveling in the truck all day, it soon became their "safe spot". They were quite content to sleep there and it helped in their transition to becoming outside doggies. (Yes, prior to this time, all 90 pounds [41 kg] of them were inside!)

4. **Friends and family**, addresses and phone numbers who could care for your pet if you have to stay in a shelter. Most facilities don't allow pets unless they are service animals that assist people with disabilities. Make sure these caregivers are folks your pet likes and vice versa. Chances are your pet will already be traumatized since an animal's sense of disaster is well honed.

If you must leave your pet in someone else's care, make sure they have a history of any pet allergies and their general medical background.

LOST PET

Should the unthinkable happen and your pet become lost, good planning includes an already made "pet poster". Make sure it has a current photograph of the animal, his or her name and your contact phone numbers. Keep a separate poster on each pet; provide detailed descriptions and any specific markings that will identify them. Photocopy shops can make numerous copies for only pennies and when it comes to our 4-legged, finned or feathered friends, it's little to invest. During emergencies, it can mean the difference in finding your pet. Statistics show that pets found sooner have a much better chance of survival.

EMERGENCY SUPPLIES

FOOD – Store food for whatever amount of time you choose and the brand/flavors your animal is used to eating. Like with people, during an emergency, is no time to change diets. Most companies stamp the date of manufacture right on the product. As a general rule, dry and canned pet food lasts 18 months from this date. We rotate Taco and Seismo's food just like we do our own.

We also incorporate table scraps into their diet so their tummies are used to broader tastes. (Yes, they've even had MREs!) This prepares their digestive tracts should pet food run out and they end up eating only people food. Since Stan and I love TexMex dishes, can you see the problem with dogs that aren't used to eating beans?

Be sure to keep all pet food dry, away from rodent and bug infestations. Mice LOVE dry dog food. In fact, that's the bait we've use on mousetraps. Keep pet food in metal or very heavy hardened rubber trash cans with tight-fitting lids for rodent proofing. We leave food in the original sacks for easy transport into the house or taking it in the car.

WATER – Have **at least** one week's worth of water stored for each pet. Medium to large dogs drink a gallon of water daily. Cats drink a pint. It's also wise to "plan a little extra" in case it gets knocked over. For fish aquariums, store enough water for at least one complete change. Depending how often you change fish water, you may wish to store more. For birds, a quart of water should cover most emergencies. As with people water, stored pet water should be treated and rotated in the exact same manner. (See Chapter 4)

TREATS AND TOYS – Like with people, familiar things are comforting during stressful times. Pets get bored easily especially if there is only one animal and his master is busy coping with an emergency. Toys and treats will take your pet's mind off the upheaval. Even if he doesn't play with it, the familiar scent gives a feeling of continuity.

SANITATION AND CLEANING SUPPLIES – For cats, include a supply of kitty litter, change of litter box liners and a pooper-scooper. Keep a scoop with doggy supplies too, unless you already have one stored for a cat. Keep a supply of plastic bags – ones from the grocery store are free and the right size. It's also a good idea to store newspapers wherever you might stay during a tornado or hurricane. Sometimes the extra tension pets pick up brings on diarrhea. Don't forget disinfectant and paper towels for life's little accidents.

For other animals, keep a supply of whatever goes in the bottom of the cages like wood shavings for gerbils for instance.

COLLAR, TAG, I.D., LEASH AND MUZZLE – Buy an extra collar, sturdy leash and/or harness and keep pet tags current even for "indoor" pets. For dogs, even if they would rather lick a thief to death than bite, buy a muzzle "just in case". Stress can bring on abnormal behavior in both 2-leggeds and 4-leggeds. If your pet is injured, a normal reaction is biting the hand that tries to help it; a muzzle helps pet and owner alike. Make sure birds are adequately leg-banded. Large animals should have identification on halters and neckbands. Additionally, horses and their owner should be photographed together from the front, both sides and rear. Have a legible board showing owner's name, address, phone and other pertinent information.

MEDICAL SUPPLIES – Keep a copy of your pet's veterinary records (including shots) in the disaster kit, stored in a waterproof bag. Don't forget to update the records. Store a month's supply of any medication your pet takes along with several rounds of worm, heartworm and flea medications. Just like people first aid, make sure to rotate all medications before expiration. In your own first aid kit or a separate pet version, include the following items:

PET FIRST AID KIT
(DOGS AND CATS)

1 roll -10 yards medical tape

2 jiffy wrap gauze bandages

2 pairs disposable latex gloves

2"x5 yards (5cmx5m) conforming self-adhering, gauze bandage

3"x5 yards (7.6cmx5m) conforming self-adhering, gauze bandage

4-2" (5cm) square sterile gauze pads

4-3" (7.6cm) square sterile pads

8-6" (15.25cm) Q-tips

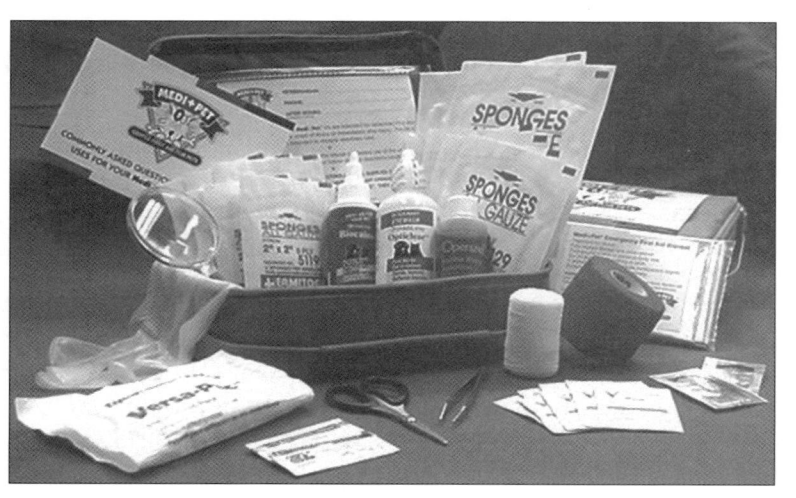

Bitter Apple Spray (keeps pets from chewing dressings)
Blanket
Buffered aspirin
Blunt tipped scissors (a must for cutting hair away from wounds)
Eyedropper
Eyewash
Flea/Tick/Mosquito Repellent
Hairball medicine (for cats)
Hemostat
Hydrocortisone 0.5% topical cream for external use only (not to be used in or near the eyes)
Hydrogen Peroxide
Kaopectate tablets (maximum strength)
Nail trimmer
Pet first aid book:
There are two pet first aid books we can highly recommend though there are plenty on the market. This series is easy to follow with good photographs and sound information to get you through most emergencies until you can see their vet.

First Aid for Dogs: The Essential Quick-Reference Guide, ISBN: 0876055463; and First Aid for Cats: The Essential Quick-Reference Guide; ISBN: 0876059078; both books are by Tim Hawcroft; April 1994, 96 pages.
Pepto Bismol tablets
Plastic flower pot large enough to go over their head
Plastic freezer bags like Ziplocs or Click Zips
Povidine iodine ointment for the treatment of minor wounds (not to be used in or near the eyes)
Rectal thermometer
Rubbing alcohol
Rubber bands
Self-adhesive elastic wrap bandages (Vetrap)
Straight blade pet grooming scissors
Syringe (plastic 20 ml)
Towels
Triple antibiotic ointment to help prevent infection in minor cuts (for external use only, don't use in or near eyes)
Tweezers
Water-soluble lubricating jelly

Now you're probably wondering about the plastic plant pot and baggies. When Taco sliced her paw severely, after bandaging her foot, the vet told us to keep the paw dry and bandaged for a week. That's a trick for an active, outside dog. In the morning before being released from their doggy enclosure, we wrapped the bandaged paw in two "freezer weight" plastic baggies (one inside the other) and secured them with wide rubber bands. If you try this, don't put rubber bands on so tightly they cut off circulation. She soon got used to her plastic "bootie" and trotted all over ignoring it for the most part.

Taco showed a big interest in removing the bandage, tape and stitches straight away. The vet suggested cutting a hole in the bottom of a plastic pot to slide it over her head like a large collar. The pot extended beyond her muzzle to prevent chewing. Holes punched in either side of the pot, close to the shoulders, allowed the pot to tie to the collar on both sides. This will not make their day, but it allows the bandage to stay put – unless Seismo chews it for her! (Photo by Dave Saville /FEMA)

CONTAINMENT

For all outside animals, if there are enclosures and fencing on your property, make sure they are solid and in good repair. When animals are frightened, they are apt to run right into fences collapsing weakened parts, injuring themselves and/or breaking through.

Dogs and Cats. If you are evacuating with your pet, a carrier cage is a very good idea especially for cats. Cats not used to car travel, can end up in a terrified ball attached to your head or clutching the metal structure under car seats. Walking a cat on a leash is a challenge for most people so a carry cage makes life easier for both you and puss 'n' boots. Whatever animals are transported, a separate cage for each is preferable. It's easier to find places for several smaller cages than one huge one. Carry cages keep accidents in one spot. A corkscrew type stake and tie-out chain for each dog also makes life easier.

Birds. Transport them in their regular cage. If it's cold, keep the interior warmer by wrapping a blanket over the cage. Birds tend to dry out in warm weather so give your feathered friends an occasional water squirt with a spray bottle.

While traveling, give your bird fresh fruit or vegetables with high water content to keep them hydrated. Putting water in their cage will only end up spilled. Birds are likely to dirty their cages if they become frightened so take extra cage liners. Make sure he is wearing an identifying leg band and until things are normal. Keep the bird caged. If they are allowed loose in unfamiliar surroundings, it's possible the bird will be gone for good.

Lizards. Treat the same as birds.

Snakes. Definitely need to be contained. If you are evacuating to a location with other people, many folks are wary of slithery pets and there's no point in adding to their anxiety. A secure cage will do much to alleviate this tension and keep your pet happy too. Pack a bowl large enough for a "snake bath" and a heating pad to keep him toasty.

Rodent Family. Animals like gerbils, hamsters, mice, etc. will need carriers, bedding, food and water. Running wheels and assorted toys will keep your pets occupied if you're busy elsewhere.

Livestock. This is one of those "easier said than done" situations, but when at all possible, large animals need to be evacuated as well. If you are warned of a severe storm, it might be possible to relocate with minimum hassle, but travel routes should be planned and tested well in advance of a crisis. Keep all trucks, trailers, and other vehicles suitable for transporting in good working order. During storms and other emergencies, animals will already be skittish so it's a good idea to familiarize the 4-leggeds with their transport with regular outings. It will help lessen tension for everyone, people and animals alike.

Photo: Midwest Floods, July 1993 — Many livestock and animals were rescued from high water levels. A total of 534 counties in nine states were declared for federal disaster aid. As a result of the floods, more than 168,000 people registered for federal assistance. (FEMA News Photo)

If evacuation isn't possible, a decision must be made whether to move large animals to available shelter or turn them outside. This decision should be based on the type of disaster and the structural soundness and location of their shelter. Turn large animals out, preferably in an area with a pond or ditch away from power lines. Fill all water troughs prior to a storm and anchor if possible, as well as filling any other large water holding receptacles.

All animals should have identifying markings or tags in case fences are knocked down and they become lost. In some states, a photograph of owner and livestock together is required for identification.

IF YOU MUST LEAVE ANIMALS BEHIND. . .

This is a decision that can drive many of us to grief, but sometimes there are no alternatives. It should be a solution of **last resort only**. They are many stories of miraculous survival but many, many more have sad endings. If there is any way possible to take your pet, don't hesitate.

1. Give your pets access to a safe, secure room, such as a bathroom or utility room with as few windows as possible, but with adequate ventilation. Line the floor with newspapers so they have some place they feel is OK to relieve themselves. They should revert to past housebreaking training. Additionally shredding newspaper is a good frustration release, especially for dogs.

2. Keep different types of animals separate: cats from dogs; and birds, hamsters and rabbits apart from cats and dogs. Stress-filled times can make normal buddies enemies.

3. Birds, rabbits, and hamsters should be in their individual cages. Secure bird cages so that they do not swing or fall, but high enough there is no chance of drowning. Cover the bird cages with a light sheet to provide a sense of security.

4. All cages should have plenty of water in self-waterers. Birds must eat daily to survive. Leave plenty of food in special feeders for them.

Photo: Some residents fled so quickly when Hurricane Katrina hit that pets were left behind on locked porches. Neighbors who did not evacuate tried to care for these animals. Roughly 600,000 pets were killed or were left without a home as a result of Katrina. Many pets lost their lives, some due to the weather, others because they couldn't be taken into public shelters and were left stranded. (Photo by Liz Roll on Sept. 8, 2005)

5. Make counters and other high places accessible to all pets in case of flooding in the house. Stack furniture so animals can climb to safety. Don't leave pets in a basement if there is any chance of flooding. **Under no circumstances should a pet be tie up**. If they are in a tornado, for instance, roaring wind will frighten them. Jumping and running about while tied can lead to injury. When well-meaning owners tied up pets during the 1999 Queensland flooding, people returned home to drowned pets. At least give them the chance of floating to safety.

6. Put away all vitamins, treats, cleaners or human products that may cause illness if eaten.

7. Place a large notice on your front door advising what pets are in your home and where they are located. The notice should include a telephone number where you can be reached. Don't forget to leave carriers and leashes in case an evacuation team needs to remove your pets.

8. Leave your pet in a utility or a bathroom where water is available. Leave the cold water faucet dripping into a container so there is a constant supply of water.

9. Leave dry food behind for them to eat, leave enough for many days. You may be told it will be for just a short time, but remember, this has happened in other emergencies. The short time turned into many days, and animals died because they were not adequately supplied with food, water and protection. Place cat food and water up on a counter and dog food and water off the floor but within easy reach for the dog. This prevents the food getting wet and spoiled. Pour water in no-spill containers.

For certain disasters, you can anticipate what problems your pet may face.

FLOODS AND STORMS – contribute to surges in flea, tick, and mosquito populations that may result in an increase of heartworm. Contaminated water, injury from floating or moving objects, and exhaustion can create other problems, drowning and lightning strikes.

EARTHQUAKES – cuts from glass, broken bones, injuries from falling objects, injury from being hit by a car, or dehydration.

HURRICANES AND TORNADOES – broken bones and severe injuries from being hit and cut open by flying objects.

FIRE – smoke inhalation, burns and injury from stampeding into fences.

Photo: September 23, 1999 – A Search and Rescue Team brought in dozens of stranded dogs from flooded Princeville, North Carolina. Rescuing stranded pets became a priority, as many towns along the Tar River were under water. (Photo By Dave Saville / FEMA News Photo)

If at all possible, evacuate your animals with you. When Stan and I adopt a new pet, it's with the understanding that their life is in our hands and we care for them as 4-legged children. They are not disposable creatures, where if things get a little difficult they can be put down for convenience sake. If dog is man's best friend, can we do any less for them?

Disaster could hit tomorrow. If you're prepared and have planned supplies for your pets, the experience will be less traumatic for all involved.

EMERGENCY HELP FOR YOUR PET

The following information is not offered as veterinary advice, but as suggestions for emergency first aid treatment until a veterinarian can be contacted. The author of this document is not licensed or qualified to give veterinary advice or assistance. Always contact a licensed veterinarian IMMEDIATELY in all matters concerning your pet's health.

Before you give anyone or any animal any medication, please consult your doctor or veterinarian about dosage and side effects. The medications and their dosages in the following list are only guidelines. Call your pet vet for your animal's dosages and put this list in your first aid kit. Dosages are for dogs only unless otherwise stated.

1. **Buffered (enteric coated) Aspirin** – 5mg per pound every 12 hours for pain relief; anti-inflammatory. [Maximum dosage – one 325mg tablet/33 lbs (max 2) every 12 hours – for small dogs you might want to use "Half Prin" which is an enteric coated aspirin with only 81mg. NOTE – acetaminophen is poisonous to most animals
2. **Pepto Bismol** – 1 tsp per 5 pounds every 6 hours for relief of vomiting, stomach gas or diarrhea
3. **Di Gel Liquid** – up to 4 Tbsp every 8 hours for antacid and anti-gas (feline dosage – up to 2 Tbsp every 8 hours)
4. **Kaopectate** – 1ml per pound every 2 hours for diarrhea (feline dosage – same as canine)
5. **Mineral Oil** – up to 4 Tbsp daily to eliminate constipation (feline dosage – up to 2 tsp. daily)
6. **Imodium AD** 2mg – 1 caplet per 30 lbs every 8 hours to relive diarrhea
7. **Benadryl** – up to mg per pound every 8 hours to treat allergies, itching, etc. Can also be used as a tranquilizer when the dosage is reduced. (feline dosage – same as canine dosage)
    Dogs under 30 lbs and Cats: 10 mg
    Dogs 30-50 lbs: 25 mg
    Dogs over 50 lbs: 50 mg
8. **Dramamine** – up to 50 mg every 8 hours to reduce motion sickness (felines – up to 10 mg every 8 hours)

Photo: Pets left to fend for themselves often end up injured – or worse. Even animals in the best of care can be hurt in disasters. Such was the case in Punta Gorda, FL, which took a direct hit from hurricane Charley. Charley, a category 4 storm, pounded the heavily populated Gulf Coast with 145 mph wind and towering storm surge. Storm shelters quickly filled as nearly 2 million people evacuated ahead of the strongest storm to hit Florida in a decade. Veterinarian Medical Assistance Team (VMAT, division of FEMA) member Lisa Dixon treats a puppy injured during that horrific hurricane. (Andrea Booher, FEMA, August 20, 2004)

BURNS

Symptoms: Pain, blistering, charring, discolor, odor of burning fur.

Treatment: Apply a cold compress to the burned area for at least five minutes. Do not use ointments. Then take the pet to a veterinarian.

CHOKING

Symptoms: Gagging, vomiting, pawing at mouth, crying in pain, excessive salivation, unconsciousness.

Treatment: Open the pet's mouth and pull his tongue forward. If an object is seen, and it is not string or a needle, use tweezers or your fingers to remove it. Calm the pet, and then take him to a veterinarian.

EAR MITES

Symptoms: Shaking or rubbing head on ground, carrying head to one side, scratching ears, dark red wax in ears. (Cats are more likely to get ear mites than dogs.)

Treatment: Call a veterinarian. Pets' ears are fragile and should be treated only by a professional.

FLEAS

Symptoms: Small red dots on skin, biting and/or scratching himself.

Treatment: Use only approved flea preparations. Vacuum your home thoroughly and then discard the vacuum bag. Use insecticides in your home and regularly wash and dry the pet's bedding on the hottest settings. Consult a veterinarian.

FRACTURE

Symptoms: Sudden lameness, limbs in an abnormal position, acute pain, swelling.

Treatment: Take the pet to a veterinarian. Keep him calm, wrap him in a towel, and place a splint on the limb if you can.

HEAT STROKE

Symptoms: Gasping, panting, very warm skin, dry tongue, blue-gray tongue, blue-gray gums, drooling, unconsciousness.

Treatment: If the condition is severe, take the pet to a veterinarian at once. If the condition is not severe, soak the pet in cool water or place a towel soaked in cold water on him.

INSECT STING

Symptoms: Stinger marks, weakness, pain, swelling, hives, refusal to walk on leg, heavy panting, breathing problems, vomiting.

Treatment: If the pet is weak, vomiting, or having trouble breathing, rush him to a veterinarian. If the stinger is visible, remove it by scraping it with a dull knife. Do not use tweezers. Apply an ice pack.

MOTION SICKNESS

Symptoms: Restlessness, panting, vomiting, diarrhea, excessive drooling or swallowing.

Treatment: Stop the car and provide the pet some fresh air. (Veterinarians can offer medication to administer before traveling.)

OBJECT IN EYE

Symptoms: Pain, swelling, redness, squinting, pawing at eye.

Treatment: Try to open the pet's eye. If object is visible and easily movable, try flushing with warm water. Take the pet to a veterinarian.

OVEREXPOSURE TO COLD

Symptoms: Very cold skin, ruffled fur, shivers, weakness, bloody stool, unconsciousness, gums and tongue pale pink-gray in color.

Treatment: If the condition is severe, immediately take the pet to a veterinarian, making sure to keep him warm on the way. If the condition is not severe, wrap the pet in a towel and apply a hot water bottle to him. Also try using a blow dryer on him. If the pet is conscious, offer him some warm broth.

POISONING

Symptoms: Heavy salivating, vomiting, weakness, twitching, collapse, strange breath, bluish gums and tongue.

Treatment: Immediately call a veterinarian or poison control center. Then take the pet and a sample of the poison to a veterinarian. Keep the pet warm, and be sure to prevent him from licking fur that has poison on it.

SHOCK

Symptoms: Rapid or feeble heartbeat, shallow, rapid breathing, pale pink or white gums and mouth, low body temperature, confusion, unconsciousness.

Treatment: Take the pet to a veterinarian. Loosen his collar, clear his mouth of all liquids, calm him, wrap him so that he is warm, and keep his head lower than his body.

SKUNK SPRAY

Symptoms: Offensive smell of skunk.

Treatment: Flush the pet's eyes with lukewarm water and then apply warm olive oil or over-the-counter artificial tears. Neutralize the smell by rubbing the pet's body thoroughly with tomato juice. Wear rubber gloves while doing so. Skunk spray is acid based and burns a pet's mucus passages. If the spraying is a direct hit, take the pet to the vet; he can neutralize the burning effects.

SNAKE BITE

Symptoms: Acute pain, swelling, refusal to walk on pained limb, heavy panting, fang marks with blood trickling from them, breathing problems, collapse.

Treatment: Keep the pet calm, wrap him in a towel or blanket, and take him to a veterinarian.

TICKS AND LYME DISEASE

Symptoms: Cats usually show no signs of ticks, but many kinds of ticks are visible on dogs, especially between their toes and behind their ears and front legs. Deer ticks, which transmit Lyme disease, often go undetected.

Treatment: Soak ticks in alcohol or small amounts of tick spray. Wait thirty minutes, and then carefully grasp the ticks with tweezers. Be sure to pull them straight out. After removal, apply antiseptic to the bites. Burn or flush the ticks, and thoroughly wash your hands.

MINOR WOUND

Symptoms: Small cut or puncture, with or without bleeding.

Treatment: Clean wound with hydrogen peroxide. If there is bleeding, use compression. If the bleeding continues, contact a veterinarian. (Deep wounds may require antibiotics.)

SERIOUS WOUND

Symptoms: Excessive bleeding, wound deeper or wider than a small puncture.

Treatment: If there is extensive bleeding, flap skin over or apply direct pressure to the wound with clean material. Then take the pet to a veterinarian.

WARNING ON RAWHIDE CHEWS

Stan and I made an unexpected trip to Colorado Springs for the day. Since we both work from home, we usually spend a great deal of time with our 4-leggeds. The thought of leaving them penned up for the day brought a few guilt pangs, especially when we found there were no marrow bones in the freezer. The only treat available was a couple of rawhide chewies neighbors gave them last Christmas. It was such a neat gift – four different types of rawhides, individually packaged by shape, tucked inside a clear plastic Santa sock and tied with a red bow.

We left them happily munching away on rawhides, with fresh water and kibble to tide them over. At 4:00 p.m. when we pulled into the drive, two black noses appeared over their gate and happy tails wagged. Everything seemed normal.

Though it was three hours past regular lunch time, no one complained. Food bowls filled with their favorite dinner were ignored and none of their dry food had been touched while we were away. Thinking it odd, especially for Seismo who eats anything not nailed down, Stan and I unpacked the car and worked through the evening.

DAY ONE

Seismo and Taco made their last pit stop around 10:00 p.m., which holds them quite comfortably till 6 a.m. Friday morning the garage floor was covered in enormous piles of barf, bile and diarrhea. The dogs didn't budge from their beds and ears flattened in shame. Sighing at the gross way for all to start the day, I promised them it was OK and scratched their cheeks and ears reassuringly. Normally this is the silent signal for Taco to receive her morning ritual chest scratch, but she remained motionless on her bed.

Seismo made a short rendezvous with a tree and flopped back into bed. All day they ate nothing and drank sparingly.

DAY TWO

The next day, the garage was a disaster zone again. What little had been in Seismo's system was now a chocolate puddle behind the car. Between the two of them, they had covered five of six throw rugs in bilious, yellow-colored vomit. Poor babies! Everything was washed and disinfected again.

That was Saturday. We agreed that if they weren't back to normal by Monday, they had to go to the vet.

The weekend was up and down. They drank plenty of water so there was no danger of dehydration. Taco, who is more selective about 'what's on the menu', ate only a cup of food but she couldn't keep much down.

DAY THREE

By Sunday, Seismo was looking more like his old self and thinking food might be clever. Using a bland diet, they both ate a mixture of equal parts boiled burger and rice. All fat was drained off with no seasoning added. Seismo ate about a cup and for a 65-pound pooch, that's not much. Taco ate half of that. For her dainty 52-pound frame, it was a mere snack considering they run all day.

They had resumed normal play but food was simply off-limits. That was it! In the morning – to the vet they went! What we found out was shocking!

DAY FOUR

When Stan and I described to the doctor what had transpired over the past four days, his face took on a knowing look. They had seen numerous cases of the same thing, but none as severe as Seismo and Taco. The primary problem was bacteria in rawhides, which can cause severe gastrointestinal upset. Seismo and Taco were diagnosed with acute pancreatitis and put on several antibiotics – Amoxicillin injections plus Gentocin and Baytril (antibiotics sent home with them) plus Reglan for nausea. After blood and stool tests were taken, they stayed overnight for observation. Though still not eating enough to keep a gnat alive, both were allowed to come home Tuesday – day 5 of this mess.

DAY EIGHT

Friday morning, the eighth day of sick dogs, there was a setback with more bile thrown up. Dr. Markway shared that their pancreases and intestines were still inflamed though there were no blockages.

No food for the next 24 hours and they were to take two 10mg Pepcid AC tablets twice daily.

THE CURE

Saturday they continued the Pepcid AC given ½ hour before small amounts of food were reintroduced. The vet sent home cans of Hills Prescription Diet I/D – a very, very bland mixture of tummy-friendly food. Each dog was given only ½ cup warmed I/D mixed with a little water. They were to have *absolutely no fat*. Small amounts of food or no food for 24-72 hours, depending of what your veterinarian prescribes, can't be emphasized enough. The pancreas must have time to rest in order to heal.

The first meal of Hills I/D served at 10:30am Seismo gobbled; Taco ate reluctantly. The next meal at 3:00pm was a happy surprise. Taco stood on the garage steps and *demanded* dinner (preceded by Pepcid AC). Boy was this a twist! Seismo wolfed his allotted ½ cup of food in a single snort and looked up hopefully for more. I was tempted, but after replaying both Dr. Markway's cautions and the horror of the past 10 days, we stuck strictly to the instructions.

At 7:30pm, Taco demanded – loudly – more food for both. (Now you know where Taco gets her name – she's a spicy-saucy woman! I tell Stan she just knows her mind.)

DAY TEN
Sunday morning the garage was immaculate and if dogs could smile, both grinned ear-to-ear. We bumped the size of their meals a little, preceded by the two Pepcid AC tablets. They continued on the Pepcid AC for two more days after they began to eat normally.

That was 2002. Taco and Seismo recovered nicely and just celebrated their 14th birthday.

WHAT'S IN THE RAWHIDE (BESIDES HIDE)?
The Internet provided a disgusting discovery. Dr. Markway was right on target with his diagnosis and comments. Salmonella is often present especially if the rawhide comes from outside the US. Another problem is arsenic used as a preservative. This is, in essence, giving your pet poison. Other dangerous additives can include antibiotics, lead and insecticides. Some countries like Thailand even include pieces of dog and cat skin in these products. Health problems from rawhide chews include sore throat, choking, intestinal blockage as well as the acute pancreatitis Taco and Seismo experienced.

Symptoms of acute pancreatitis can vary from mild gastrointestinal upset to collapse and death. Most animals with common gastrointestinal upset have any or all of the following:

- Vomiting
- Not eating
- Painful abdomen, hunched appearance (more common in dogs)
- Fever or below-normal body temperature
- Diarrhea
- Depression
- Dehydration (diagnosed by sunken eyes, drymouth and the skin "tents" when pinched)[93]

HIDDEN DANGERS
Dr. John Wedeking, an Iowa veterinarian, remembered hearing about rawhide in the news.

" 'Reports of arsenic contamination popped up in papers once," he says, but adds that it came from another country. Since rawhide is not regulated in any way, it could happen again. These foreign hides may also contain other detrimental things such as antibiotics, lead, or insecticides that could adversely affect your dog's health. Wedeking adds that dogs can easily choke on it when the original large rawhide object is chewed down to a smaller piece. 'Choking is a hazard, and rawhide can cause gastric irritation when dogs chew on it often," he says. Wedeking adds that gastric irritation can also cause vomiting and extreme discomfort in dogs."[94]

RAWHIDES, COW HOOVES AND PIGS' EARS
"These toys are favorites for many dogs and are popular with owners because they keep their pets occupied and supposedly out of trouble during holiday activities. There are definite risks associated with these treats, however. All three types are supposedly made of digestible animal products. However, they are digested quite slowly and, if consumed rapidly, can cause either vomiting or diarrhea from the many pieces still sitting undigested in the GI tract. If the treats are swallowed whole or in large chunks, there are additional dangers. Rawhide chews can lodge in the throat and cause choking, or a large piece may be swallowed, scraping and irritating the throat and esophagus on the way down. Once in the stomach or intestinal tract, a large piece of rawhide can also create a physical obstruction. An additional danger that is less widely known is the practice, in some countries, of using an arsenic-based preservative in the processing of rawhide toys. We recommend that, if you do purchase these products, stick to brands processed in the U.S. There has also been a recent FDA alert about the risk of Salmonella associated with dog chew products made from pork or beef-derived materials.

"**Cow hooves** are even more dangerous than rawhides. They are hard enough that a dog can actually break a tooth on one. They can also be chewed up into sharp fragments, which may cause a partial intestinal obstruction. Partial obstructions are often difficult to diagnose until the point at which the fragment is ready to perforate the wall of the bowel from pressure against the sharp edges. If perforation has occurred, the infection that ensues from leakage of intestinal contents can be fatal.

"**Pigs' ears**" can cause GI upset if overeaten, similar to the situation with rawhides, although obstructions are less common because the ears are not usually shaped into solid chunks. There is, however, a less widely known danger associated with pig ears: A recent FDA advisory published by the U.S. Dept. of Health and Human services on Oct.1, 1999, stated that there is "a nationwide public health warning alerting consumers about a number of recent cases in Canada of human illnesses apparently related to contact with dog chew products made from pork or beef-derived materials (e.g., pigs ears, beef jerky treats, smoked hooves, pigs skins, etc.)... FDA is urging pet owners... to handle them carefully. Anyone who comes in contact with these treats should wash their hands with hot water and soap. Initial reports of illnesses came from Canada and involved Canadian products, but subsequent examination of similar products produced in the U.S. indicate that all pet chew products of this type may pose a risk...."[95]

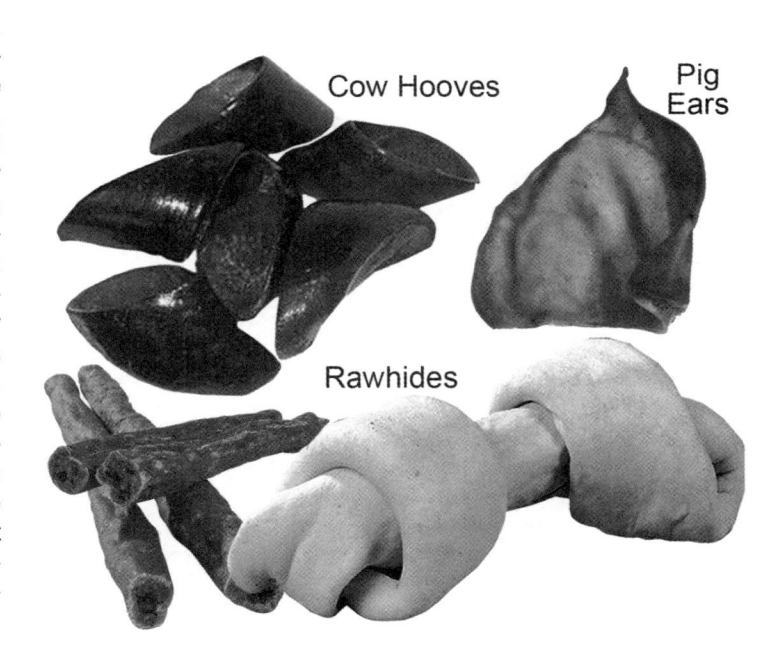

WHAT YOU CAN DO

If you must give your dog rawhide, offer it in limited quantity, under supervision, and throw away small chewed-down pieces. Always watch your dog carefully for any adverse reactions. Our veterinarian advises giving them a miss altogether. When we asked Dr. Markway why these products were still on the market, he too was mystified, but stated the public is largely unaware of rawhide dangers.

Choose only products made in the U.S. Numerous other dog chews are made from healthful ingredients. Some are vegetable based and infused with flavor. Hardened rubber versions that won't splinter are fine too.

Better yet, Markway recommends marrow bones as an excellent choice. After purchasing marrow bones from the grocery store, we throw them in the pressure-cooker for about 15 minutes.

Cool and freeze them until needed. That way your pet can avoid these tummy dramas and dogs adore the real deal!

Chapter 39: Firearms

Like many issues, the choice to have guns among your preparedness gear is up to the individual. Both Stan and I grew up in families that had and used firearms. My Dad was a Marksman in the Army and Stan was captain of his school small-bore rifle team. He beat the NRA National Champion in a match at the US Air Force Academy.

Many folks have written asking the weapons issue be addressed. As a self-professed gun illiterate, and since Stan's knowledge was limited to target rifles, we asked three of our friends to share their expertise. Only their first names have been used at their request.

RICHARD, a knowledgeable friend in law enforcement, contributed the basic informative primer and then two other law enforcement officers offered their expertise.

ERIK is a professional law enforcement officer and full-time firearms instructor. He's also a 16-year veteran of active and reserve military.

Our third contributor, **IAN**, is also a law enforcement officer in Western Australia with a total of 30 years to his credit. Ian spent six years with Australian Special Forces. He has also studied various martial arts including Judo, Jujitsu, Ti-Chi and Karate for over 40 years. Below you'll find valuable information regarding personal protection applicable for most countries. Overall, the three men have similar takes on guns, but it's always helpful to discuss some of the finer points.

PRIMER ON PERSONAL SECURITY

IAN: Firearms are merely a means to an end. First and foremost, it must be remembered that a firearm in the hands of an inexperienced person will do as much damage to him or his family as it will to the object they wish to shoot.

There are countless examples of children being seriously injured or killed because the weapons were not secured or the various parts, i.e. stock, bolt and ammunition etc. were not stored separately.

There are also many stories of persons having had their firearm taken from them and the offender turning the weapon on the owner.

There is no substitute for proper training. Remember, shooting is a skill that needs to be kept current as does first aid skills. If you are going to have firearms, learn how to deal with firearm-related injuries.

In relation to the type of firearm required, it is important to decide what the firearm is intended for, i.e. procurement of food or for personal protection. There are three basic types of firearms to consider and each has a particular killing zone. The killing zones are as follows:

1. Personal killing zone – distance to target 0 to 10 meters (0 to 33 feet)
2. Middle killing zone – distance to target 10 to 100 meters (33 to 328 feet)
3. Long range killing zone – distance to target 100 to 1000 meters (328 to 3280 feet)

A further point to consider is where am I going to carry the firearm. Special Forces training indelibly imprints on the mind of its members the three areas where survival gear is kept. They are:

A) **On the person**: These items are on you at all times, and include:
- Personal Survival
- Medical
- Protection Items (one "K-Bar" knife is recommended which is a Marine solid core, straight blade, survival knife.)

B) **On webbing**: These items are within arms reach all the time, and include:
- Emergency Water (1 liter)
- Shelter
- Warmth
- Food Items
- Personal Protection Items
- An Emergency Pack
- A handgun and Ammunition.

Dare To Prepare: Chapter 39: Firearms

C) **In pack**: These packs should be stored "ready to go" in an area that can be accessed very quickly, i.e. keep one in the house, one in your vehicle etc. and include:
- Liters of Water
- Small Tent
- Change of Clothing and Footwear
- Food for 5 days
- Personal Medical Supplies
- Fold Down Survival Weapon

One weapon will not satisfy all requirements so consider your choice carefully. For a handgun, Special Forces carry a revolver. Revolvers require less maintenance than pistols. Pistols have many moving parts and if you are unfamiliar with the weapon they are prone to jam. The United States Air Force has what I consider to be one of the ultimate survival handguns.

Their revolver has 3 barrels and 3 cylinders enabling a rapid change from a 22-Caliber, to a 38-Special to a 44-Magnum. The 22-Caliber is used for hunting small game; hollow point rounds are recommended. Sub-sonic rounds can be purchased to lessen the sound if noise is a consideration. "Stinger" ammunition (also 22 caliber) is recommended for larger game up to the size of a medium-sized dog. It has a higher velocity than the standard 22 round and with a pentagonal hole in the projectile rather than a "Hollow Point". The projectile fractures evenly on 5 points resulting in increased trauma to the game.

The 38-Special can be used for larger game as well as being a formidable caliber for personal protection. Finally, the 44-Magnum is capable of inflicting huge traumas to EVERYTHING it hits.

RICHARD: My recommendation for personal security in the home would be a 12-Gauge or 20-Gauge shotgun with an 18 or a 20-inch (46 – 51cm) barrel. The 20-Gauge has a lot less kick and performs almost as well as the 12-Gauge. Using "00 buckshot" ammo is the equivalent of firing a dozen rounds from a 9mm handgun all at once; and is the most deadly gun made. The short barrel is good for large game less than 100 yards (30 meters) with slug ammo, and with a longer barrel and different ammo you can hunt any kind of bird, rabbits, etc. Barrels are interchangeable. A Remington 12-Gauge with a 28-inch (72cm) barrel can be purchased in the US for about $210, new. A .410 shotgun is good for rabbits, but not for protection unless you can hit someone in the eyes with it.

ERIK: This is true, except for two points:
1. The recoil of a shotgun is so severe it would be difficult for most women, small men, or younger children to use. For these people, I recommend a pistol-caliber carbine, such as the US M1, Marlin Camp, or Ruger. These guns are available in America within the same price ranges as a shotgun.
2. The lethality of the shotgun is often overestimated. In many shotgun patterns, close to 50% of the pellets may miss or hit non-vital areas, even at close range. Follow-up shots are difficult because of the recoil. Accuracy is a **must**, so you have to practice with this or any other firearm.

For protection, a good semi-auto rifle in 7.62x39 or .223 (5.56mm) is, in my opinion, the best choice. It has low recoil, high capacity, and is very accurate, even up to 400 meters. It can also be used for hunting small game, or in the case of the heavier 7.62 round, even deer. Examples include the Ruger Mini-14, Colt AR-15, AK47 or MAK-90, SKS, or M1 Garand.

Lever-action rifles in .30-30 are also a good alternative to a semi-auto. Winchester Model 94 or Marlin 336 or 30AW.

RICHARD: For a personal protection handgun, the most deadly is the .357-Magnum revolver with a 125-grain hollow-point bullet. It far surpasses Clint Eastwood's movie .44-Magnum for one shot kills. However, the .44-Magnum with a 6-inch (15cm) barrel or longer is the best hunting handgun available without going to some of the more exotic calibers. A revolver is simple to use and trouble free. I recommend a Smith and Wesson .357 for ease of use and cleaning, or a Ruger .357 for durability -- if you are going to drag it through the desert, swamp, jungle, drop it from an airplane, etc. Tarus makes a very good and inexpensive gun too.

ERIK: I concur with this, except remember the .357 recoil is tough to get used to.

RICHARD: For a semi-automatic handgun, where I work, new Deputies are required to carry a Glock .40 caliber. It is the most efficient and deadly available and an excellent gun. It's one of the new "plastic guns".

ERIK: I don't have a quarrel with the Glock in a survival situation, but the .40 is not a good idea. 9mm is just as effective when shot accurately and is much easier to obtain in large quantities.

RICHARD: Everyone should have a .22 rifle. It is good for target practice and is more deadly than some of the larger caliber guns due to the high velocity of the bullet causing deep penetration. I know people who illegally shot an elk and a trophy deer at close range with a .22. I get a lot of disagreement from people, but if I had to choose one all-around gun to have it would be the .22.

ERIK: I agree wholeheartedly with this.

RICHARD: A .270 rifle or larger with a scope for hunting big game is best. Smaller calibers are used, but most hunting articles I have read say the 30-06 is the best hunting rifle for North American big game. I use a 30-06 but prefer my son's .270 since it has so much less kick. Shoot what you are comfortable with. For smaller game such as varmints, a 22-250 is very good.

ERIK: Your semi-auto 7.62x39 I mentioned earlier should be adequate for deer. The .30-06 and .270 are excellent calibers. I would suggest the .308 (7.62x51mm), because again, it's easy to obtain in large quantities.

IAN: There are many rifles to choose from. One can select from the 177 air rifle to the 50-caliber. With a 50-caliber Browning sniper rifle and telescopic mounts, a kill shoot in excess of 3000 meters (9,842 feet) is possible. The longest confirmed kill by a 7.62x59mm round was 2,800 meters (9186 feet).

My personal choice in rifles consists of two weapons. The first is known as an "over and under". What this means is that a 22-caliber rifle sits on top of a 12-gauge shot gun. Remember, in survival, everything needs to have more than one use.

My other choice is a 5.56mm (223) caliber rifle. This is a standard military round preferred by the United States and Australian Defense Forces. The temptation is to go for a weapon like the AR15, M16 or Styeir rifle. All of these rifles are military weapons capable of single shot, semi-automatic or fully automatic fire. Once the testosterone levels have subsided, a bolt action rifle should be your choice. Handled correctly, a bolt action is almost as fast as a semi-auto and there are fewer things to go wrong. Remember, the simpler it is, the better, in a survival situation.

ERIK: Remember to stockpile ammo; you need a lot of it. I recommend military calibers, because the surplus market allows you to buy in quantity.

Revolver: .38-Special Auto-Pistol: 9mm NATO (aka 9mm Parabellum) Rifle: 5.56mm, 7.62x39mm (Soviet), 7.62x51mm (NATO)

IAN: It would seem inappropriate to use a 7.62x59mm (standard NATO round) to hunt rabbit, but it may be very appropriate to hunt predators such as bear or man.

RICHARD: Eventually we would run out of ammo, so reloading (making your own ammunition) becomes a necessity. Reloading is expensive to get started in, but once the initial investment is made, the ammo is cheap to make.

IAN: I agree with a lot of what Erik and Richard have said, but in the end, it comes down to personal choice and reasons for purchase.

Stay with weapons that have a common caliber, have minimal moving parts and learn the associated skills that go with hunting. Those associated skills are tracking by sight and scent, snare construction, animal butchering, camouflage and concealment. In addition to these skills, you will need to know the animal's habits and movements.

Also, learn what defenses the animal possesses; nothing should come as a surprise in a survival situation – surprises kill.

If you intend to use modern methods to hunt at night such as Night Vision Goggles, infrared red or thermal imaging, sound or movement detectors, learn their capabilities and limitations.

For purchasing and licensing of firearms, it is recommended that you attend your local Police station to obtain your state's current legislative requirements. Some states require you to belong to a gun club before purchasing firearms. This is a common sense approach as it allows you to try several types, makes and models of firearms before purchasing your own. It also means you are trained correctly in the use, care and safety of you firearm.

Experience is the only true teacher.

RICHARD: Reloading supplies are normally easy to come by. However, when HCI (Handgun Control Inc.) and President Clinton attempted their gun grab several years ago, it was almost impossible to get primer caps (ignites the powder) at any price due to so many gun owners stocking up in case they were successful in their hair-brained scheme. Things are back to normal now, but shortages will occur again with the next gun grab attempt. Now is the time to get all you can get.

I am not an expert about guns and didn't own one until I was in my early 30's long before I became a Deputy Sheriff. As for a crash course in self-defense, the best defense is practice, practice, practice with the weapons you have. I have put 30,000 rounds through my S&W .357 and still practice. I have put 10,000 rounds through my .22 rifle just for fun since the ammo is cheap and easily available. I recommend a supply of 10,000 rounds be kept for when the crunch comes.

Practicing with a hunting rifle like a 30-06 is expensive so reloading is the only option. I recommend as much ammo for it as you can afford since this is going to put food on the table for a time, as well as for a "reach out and touch someone" defense at long range. Premium bullets run about $1 a round or a little more.

In America, joining the NRA or Gun Owners of America is critical if we want to keep our guns. I am a life member of NRA, and a member of GOA. Both have web sites. The NRA has more than 50,000 gun safety teachers.

This information does not cover everything there is to know about owning and operating a firearm, but it's a good place to start. When we are very new to a topic, it helps to understand the basics so we can at least ask intelligent questions.

Requirements for owning weapons are severely restricted in Australia. Their official gun recall for semi-automatics and pump action shotguns went into effect September 30, 1997. Only a few circumstances remain where citizens can own a weapon. The general law states you must belong to a gun club and have proof of actively practicing. In some states, you must attend at least twice each year, other states require monthly attendance and in still others, just being a member is enough. Another circumstance where having a weapon is permitted is if you own at least 100 acres and need the weapon for varmint control. A third option is if you hunt or target shoot on a farmer's property that has at least 100 acres. The farmer must write a letter stating this is your purpose, which is submitted with the application. Since laws vary from state to state, check the requirements for your area. For Americans taking firearms across the border, please checks Canada's laws: **panda.com/canadaguns**.

Good organizations to keep apprised of gun control legislation are:

FIREARMS ORGANIZATIONS	
USA	**CANADA**
National Rifle Association 11250 Waples Mill Rd. Fairfax, VA 22030 Phone: 1.877.NRA.2000 Fax: N/A www.nra.org/	**National Firearms Association** Box 52183 Edmonton, Alberta, T6G 2T5 Phone 780.439.1394 Fax: 780.439.4091 www.nfa.ca/
	NEW ZEALAND
Gun Owners of America 8001 Forbes Place, Suite 102 Springfield, VA 22151 Phone: 703.321.8585 Fax: 703.321.8408 www.gunowners.org/	**National Rifle Association of New Zealand Inc.** PO Box 47-036 Trentham, Upper Hutt, New Zealand Phone: 04.528.4843 Fax: 04.528.4198 www.nranz.com/
GREAT BRITAIN	**AUSTRALIA**
Sportsman's Association of Great Britain & Northern Ireland 2 Clockhouse Place London SW15 2EL Phone/Fax: 0208 7891211 www.sportsmansassociation.org.uk/	**Sporting Shooters Association of Australia Inc.** PO Box 906 Saint Marys, NSW 1790 Phone: 02. 8889.0480 Fax: 02.9623.5900 www.ssaa.org.au/
National Rifle Association of Great Britain Bisley, Brookwood Surrey GU24 0PB Phone: 01483 797777 Fax: 01483 797285 www.nra.org.uk/	**National Rifle Association of Australia Ltd.** 1485 Old Cleveland Rd. Belmont, QLD 4153 Phone: 07.3398.1228 Fax: 07.3398.3515 www.nraa.com.au/

Chapter 40: Terrorism – Venturing Into the Unthinkable

September 11, 2001 *forced* us to acknowledge terrorism is now a part of our lives. Prior warnings like the Oklahoma City bombing and the USS Cole slid into history and we toddled back to sleep. Swathed in a cocoon of invincibility, we were easy prey.

Whether we experience terrorism on such a magnificent scale again or not, it underscores the need for personal responsibility – and action. Much as we'd like to think Homeland Security and such will intercept every terrorist before an attack can be carried out is unlikely. They expect us to be hit and openly state this warning. It is a quiet call to steel our reserve.

Immediately after 911, we witnessed hundreds of rescue teams working themselves beyond exhaustion. Countless times we shed tears seeing heroic acts and selfless deeds, as well as from emotional strain and grinding sorrow. Unparalleled scenes of horror ravaged tired eyes, scraped raw nerves. Privately we thanked God "it" hadn't happened in our town. Yet, it did. September 11, 2001 touched the world.

THE WAKE-UP – WORLD TRADE CENTER 1993

In 1993 our safe womb of "invincibility" was ripped apart. No longer could we rest easy thinking, *it only happens over there*. A single event forced us to admit terrorism had trampled our homeland.

February 26, 1993. The New York World Trade Center's basement exploded when terrorists drove a 1200-pound (544kg) ammonium nitrate bomb into the garage.

Its detonation was supposed to topple one 110-foot tower into the other – like giant dominos. (Sound familiar?) People gaped in astonishment at the resulting 200-foot (61m) crater gouged five stories deep.

Amazingly this monumental explosion only took six lives and injured more than 1000. The ceiling of PATH, a commuter train that ran from New Jersey to Lower Manhattan, collapsed in the massive blast, and hurt another 50 people. Tough damages topped $550 million and it was a "good start" for the terrorists, casualties fell far short of their intentions.

This was America's first jab from Muslim extremists. Twenty-nine year old Ramzi Yousef masterminded the bombing and entered the country on a fake Iraqi passport concealing his Pakistani ties. Eyad Ismoil, 26, a Palestinian from Jordan, drove the explosives-filled van into place.

Egyptian fundamentalists Nidal Ayyad and Mahmud Abouhalima, and Palestinian Mohammed Salameh and Ahmad Ajaj who entered on a forged Swedish passport were all convicted of conspiracy in this bombing.

It's alarming and maddening that Nidal Ayyad received a 5-star education at Rutgers University in New Jersey. Afterwards he worked as a chemical engineer for Allied Signal, from which he used company stationery to order the bomb-making ingredients. Ayyad had also become a US citizen.[96]

All six are serving 240-year sentences – each without chance of parole.

Yousef had planned to kill 250,000 Americans, not six. To maximize death, they dispersed cyanide with the bomb, but didn't know the explosion's heat would vaporize the lethal gas.[97]

These terrorists were right under our noses living in New Jersey and New York. Though members of various extremist groups: Islamic Jihad, al-Qaeda, Hamas and Sudanese National Islamic Front, they united with one ambition – to inflict American suffering. For more information on Islamic Terrorist cells living in America, see *Prudent Places USA*.

STRIKING THE HEARTLAND

April 19, 1995. Who would have thought terrorism could touch America's heartland? It wasn't a major commerce site like Wall Street or the seat of Federal government. Tinker Air Force Base was only 15 miles away, but that wasn't the target either. Instead, Oklahoma City's Murrah Federal Building (pictured left) reaped the misery.

We didn't need another kick in the belly, but perhaps we needed another louder, stronger warning. It arrived just two years after the World Trade Center bombing.

Wednesday's workday was well under way by 9am. Spring's renewing freshness scented the air. But normal life shattered that bright morning at 9:02 when the front of the Federal Building blew out. The explosion took out every window in a two-block area. The unthinkable had happened again.

Until now, this bombing was the single most lethal act of terrorism in U.S. history stealing 168 lives. A well-placed bomb carved a massive 20-foot wide, 8-foot deep crater.

The Murrah Building's second floor housed a day care center. Its nearness to the blast cost 19 children their lives.

Fear, mixed with anger and sorrow, spread across America like oozing, sticky tar. We were no longer America The Beautiful. We had become America The Terrorized.[98] But we slipped back into slumber.

Photo: Oklahoma City, OK, April 26, 1995 — Search and Rescue crews work to save those trapped beneath the debris, following the Oklahoma City bombing.

U.S. EMBASSIES

August 7, 1998: Prodded again. Bombs exploded at U.S. embassies in Kenya and Tanzania, killing 259 people, including 12 Americans. Washington responded with cruise missile attacks on sites reportedly linked to Osama bin Laden. Back then public strikes on terrorists were rare. In the ensuing 24 months, 11 other U.S. embassies experienced terrorist threats in Malaysia, Albania, Zambia, Israel, Burundi, Tajikistan, Czech Republic, Sudan, Mali, Madagascar, Mozambique and Chad. Today the list is much longer.

July 2000: The State Department canceled two Independence Day celebrations, one in the Middle East and another in Europe, because of the threat of terrorism. Ditto for the U.S. Embassy in Amman, Jordan, and a street fair in Brussels, Belgium.

USS COLE

October 12, 2000. Two attackers on a small boat carrying 500 pounds (225kg) of high explosives rammed into the destroyer while it refueled in Aden port, Yemen. Seventeen U.S. sailors perished and at least 40 people were wounded in this homicide bombing. It was yet another terrorist act linked back to al-Qaeda.

The explosion ripped a 30 by 40 foot hole above the waterline to the keel port side of the vessel. Aden, one of the world's largest natural harbors, had been closed to U.S. Navy ships due to security risks. However, one year prior to the attack, Aden was opened as a refueling port. During that time, U.S. Navy had refueled there 12 times without incident. Then came the unlucky 13th.

At the occasion of his son, Mohammad's, wedding, Osama bin Laden recited *To Her Doom* honoring the attack on the USS Cole.

*"A destroyer: even the brave fear its might.
It inspires horror in the harbor and in the open sea.
She goes into the waves
flanked by arrogance, haughtiness and fake might.
To her doom she progresses slowly,
clothed in a huge illusion.
Awaiting her is a dinghy,
bobbing in the waves,
disappearing and reappearing in view."*[99]

At the poem's close, cheers erupted from hundreds of Arab militant supporters.

Photo: Port side view showing damage sustained by the Arleigh Burke class guided missile destroyer *USS Cole* on October 12, 2000, after a terrorist bomb exploded during a refueling operation in the port of Aden, Yemen. USS Cole is on a regular scheduled six-month deployment. (DoD Photo)

911

September 11, 2001. There probably isn't a Westerner alive who doesn't remember precisely what he or she was doing when THE NEWS hit the airwaves. It was the one event that left us truly speechless.

On the last leg home from Dallas, we stopped to fill up at Raton Pass, just south of the Colorado border. While I mulled what task to start first at home, Stan walked inside to pay for fuel and grab a snack. When he entered, instead of people paying for gas and goodies he noticed a crowd riveted to the counter TV. It took a few minutes for the news to penetrate. Then he raced outside, mumbled something unintelligible and dragged me to the TV. Ten pairs of eyes mesmerized with disbelief tried to absorb the images. It was 10:52am, MDT. More was to come. Our reaction was like much of the Nation's. Shock. Anger. Fear.

The remaining drive home seemed interminable. We wanted to pick up Seismo and Taco at the boarding kennel and get home to safety. Writing about terrorism and warning people as we had done in prior years, prepared us for this likelihood more than some people may have been, but not for the actuality. If felt like rape on a grand scale. Complete violation, a stripping of all protection. Raw exposure.

Photo: September 11, 2001, terrorists attack the Pentagon and World Trade Center. In multiple strikes, 2,976 people from 80 countries lost their lives.

The two best things that came out of Sept. 11 were finally getting the government to START to move on national security and disappointing bin Laden. Economic fallout in New York was estimated to be around $83 billion.[100] This number, while staggering, must have been deflating to UBL since he thought it would be nearer to $3 trillion.[101] Sad. That's small recompense for the 2,976 people who died.

With numerous terrorists' calling cards, the government warns us we need to prepare for yet another strike. Hard as it is to consider, Stan and I prepare for it as best as we can. We do it, don't dwell on it and get on with life. Like with any disaster, ignoring something does NOT make it go away. It only leaves you vulnerable.

If terrorists really want to inflict the most harm, they would release biological or chemical agents – or a bomb – when people are at work or school. Most people instinctively will want to get home and in that process may expose themselves to agents or radiation.

If you live in a high profile metropolitan city, the risk *is* higher, not just from an actual terrorist attack, but also from ensuing panic. If you're thinking to evacuate after a biological attack, it's probable roads will be gridlocked, and possibly officially closed. (Remember Stephen King's movie *The Stand*?) Residents of a targeted area may not be allowed to travel for fear the contaminants go with them. A viable option is to secure your home and rely on stored goods to see you through. Don't forget your pets. They need the same inside protection you do.

Conscientious folks living in metroplexes take extra precautions. They may choose to keep a gas mask at home in their nightstand, in a desk drawer at work and in the trunk of their car. For those on a budget, one mask would suffice providing you're willing to take it with you – home-car-office and back again. If you live in a rural community, odds are you won't be exposed to bio-chemical agents since terrorists want to instill fear and take the most lives. Though less likely, they may target smaller locations just to keep us off-balance. It can't be ruled out.

POST 911

Since then many more attempts have been thwarted. Groups have surfaced like 2002's Lackawanna 6 in New York and the Lodi, California cell in June 2005. In 2006, seven men were arrested in Miami and Atlanta for allegedly plotting to blow up the Sears Tower in Chicago, as well as the FBI offices and other buildings. Also in 2006, British police and intelligence agents stopped a terrorist plot to load 10 commercial airliners headed to

America and Canada with liquid explosives. Their targets included Chicago, Los Angeles, Miami, Orlando, Boston, Newark, New York City, San Francisco, Cleveland, Washington, D.C., and Montreal and Toronto in Canada. BBC security correspondent Gordon Corera said the plot involved a series of simultaneous attacks, targeting three planes each time. Approximately 24 people were arrested in the London area. The United Kingdom charged 16 of the 24 individuals, and trials began in April 2008.

In May 2007, six men were arrested in a plot against Fort Dix, a U.S. Army base in New Jersey. They planned to kill soldiers using assault rifles and grenades after training in the Poconos Mountains. In June 2007 four men plotted to blow up a jet fuel artery that ran through residential areas by New York City's JFK International Airport.

On July 17, 2008, 36-year-old neuroscientist, Aafia Siddiqui, was found and arrested in Afghanistan. She proclaimed she "wanted to kill Americans"[102]. *This MIT and Brandeis-educated* Afghani woman was arrested carrying information on chemical, biological and radioactive weapons. She also had documents detailing U.S. military assets and maps of New York City and its subway system, Times Square and the Statue of Liberty, as well as the nearby Plum Island Animal Disease Center, home to many lethal pathogens.

These are just a few of the recent, publicly known incidents. Terrorist scenarios are often not shared with us till a year or two after the fact. Many more are kept quiet due to national security.

It is just a matter of time till some terrorist, some mayhem-bound extremists break the barriers.

WHAT MIGHT WE EXPECT?

The most likely scenario is a dirty bomb though chemical and toxic agents could be used. For maximum effect, warheads deliver chemical weapons unless the target is a much smaller group. In 1995 when Aum Shinrikyo released sarin gas on a Japanese subway, they only managed to take 12 lives. I say "only" because terrorists have killed that many people with homicide bombers. That tactic has proved effective so why reinvent the wheel?

Chemical products can be mass-produced cheaply, but during an aerial dispersal it dilutes relatively quickly, and loses some toxicity. How fast it dissipates depends on climate conditions, wind and type of chemical used.

Chemicals can be blown away by the wind and are highly susceptible to air temperature. Colder temps allow chemicals to linger three to four times longer than in warm weather. For a variety of reasons, it makes less sense, other than the cost factor, for a terrorist to use this weapon.

Conversely, biological agents are easier to distribute and have higher impact. Infected people further spread the disease. Anthrax, for example, remains toxic for years and is resistant to destruction. For terrorists to use biologicals, it requires more skill for implementation plus the resources to obtain them.

During a high-risk illness, if you need to go outside for any reason, other precautions would need to be taken. One of these measures is a respirator mask. For more info on communicable disease protection, see Chapter 64 on Pandemics. For bio-chemical mask protection, turn the page.

Chapter 41: Buying a Gas Mask and Filters

SO WHAT DO I BUY? – ADULTS

Immediately following 911, reasonably priced gas masks were hard to find. Once initial panic buying subsided, gear became less expensive. People were in such a hurry to purchase masks and filters that they even snatched up old stock. Chances are that products now available will have optimum shelf life.

Here are guidelines to consider so you don't get ripped off.

You should be able to purchase a top-of-the-line US mask for $150-$270, depending on supplier. Acceptable gas masks sell for $75.

3M's M40 is a top-of-the-line American civilian mask. These can be purchased these for around $250. Communication is provided by two voicemitters. One is mounted in the front to allow face-to-face communication; the second is located in the cheek to permit the use of a radio telephone handset.

The drinking system, which is a very important feature, lets a user drink without removing the mask. It consists of internal and external drink tubes; the external tube has a quick-disconnect coupling that connects with the M1 canteen cap. A six-point, adjustable harness with elastic straps located at the forehead, temples, and cheeks comes together at a rectangular head pad for best fit. Optical inserts are provided for vision correction and outserts are available to reduce fogging and sun glare and to protect against scratching.

A very good alternative is the M95 US mask – normally available for $150-175. In appearance, it looks similar to the M40.

Due to extremely low breathing resistance, the M95 mask and filter are comfortable to wear even for long periods, without affecting user performance. Light in weight, the mask weighs around a pound. It has a small inner mask that reduces the dead-space to a minimum and the respirator is easy to take on and off.

Two other very fine products are made by MSA: the Millennium CBRN Mask and the Advantage.

Both masks are effective against a variety of chemical warfare and biological agents. They're made of super-soft Hycar™ rubber for superior comfort. Both have an elastic, six-point head harness that adjusts easily for the correct fit – and easy to put on and take off without pulling hair.

Each has a mechanical speaking diaphragm and dual-canister mount on the face piece.

Depending on which model is purchased, expect to pay between $160 and $350. Regardless of which one you purchase, make sure your mask is NATO or NIOSH rated.

BE A WISE SHOPPER

Israeli M15 Military 2002/2003

Though the Israeli M15 mask is the single most widely used model in the world, it's seen its share of controversy. These highly effective masks have an excellent reputation but there is an issue of age in product sold.

As long as you check the following three areas, you should end up with a terrific product.
- Make sure it's within its 20-year lifespan (many aren't)
- Thoroughly inspect the valves
- Purchase a new, current production filter

Developed by Shalon Chemical Industries in Israel, this adult sized mask is intended for the military and police, providing respiratory protection from NBC (nuclear, biological and chemical) agents in addition to CN, CS, (CN and CS are tear gas) and P100 particulates.

It's designed for excellent comfort and fit, causing minimal interference with the performance of duties, employment of weapons, and effective communication.

Key features include: an upgraded voicemitter for clear communication, optional canteen drinking system for safe drinking in contaminated environments, lightweight yet comfortable secure fit, durable construction and easy to don with a wide field of vision. This mask uses any standard 40mm NATO threaded filter. All features considered, it's an exceptional value for around $130. For this price, you'll need to shop around.

Before buying any mask, ask these three questions first:
- When was this mask factory tested?
- When was this filter manufactured and what is its expiration date?
- What will this filter protect against?

NON-AMERICAN MASKS

The British S-10 mask is also a very good choice. Its special adapter cap allows for drinking from a bottle without removing the mask.

Canada makes a terrific mask, the C4 IF you can find the real deal. They are reasonably priced and very comfortable but are <u>extremely</u> difficult to locate. You may need to contact a Canadian supplier to find this item.

Information from several sources state that "true" C4s have black facepieces and were manufactured by SNC Industrial Technologies in Quebec. Their production stopped around 1992 and since 1990, C4s have been manufactured by a different company using green facepieces. The first 30,000 of the green masks were defective and rejected by the Canadian military.

Several problems plagued the C4 production run. The most common defect involved the wrong adhesive used to assemble the voicemitters and valves. The adhesive dried too quickly and the mask, literally, fell apart.

Green-faced C4 masks are sold online to unsuspecting bidders. Buyer beware. In short, since the Canadian military is not releasing masks to the public, it's a good bet that any purchased online would be suspect. Too many choices remain open to take a chance on purchasing an inferior mask.

CHILDREN AND INFANTS MASKS

Youth masks are even scarcer than adult sizes and not all companies manufacturer children's sizes. Israeli and American masks do come in youth sizes.

Babies and toddlers can't use gas masks since it requires too much effort to breathe in. For them there is a special type hood that goes over the infant and snugs to their waist. It keeps their head and chest covered while still allowing diapers to be changed.

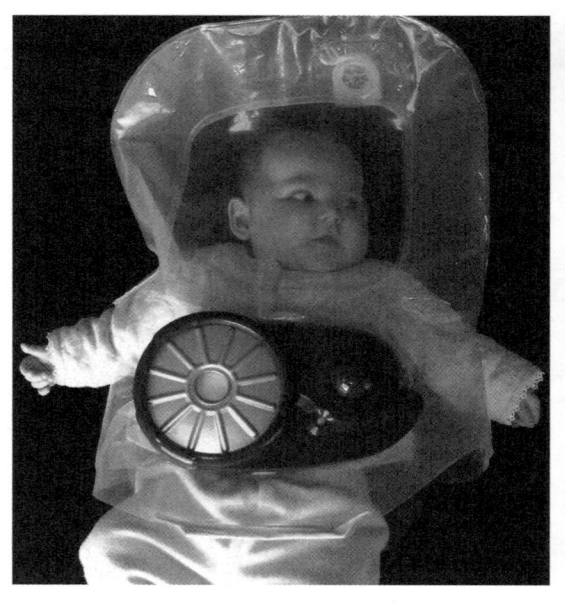

Generally these hoods are battery powered and have a pouch, tube and nipple inside for feeding. Be sure to find a unit that works through "positive pressure." They are generally noted as PAPR (Powered Air Purifying Respirator). On the Internet, you'll find wide price gaps from $400 – $800.

One thing to consider is that some retailers will try to sell you only their top-of-the-line product – ones suitable for military use. Keep in mind that troops would be exposed to much higher concentrations of chemical or biological agents and need only the strongest line of defense. This would be highly unlikely for the population at large.

PROPER FIT OF MASKS

Proper fit is vital for a mask to be effective. For example, you can't put an adult mask on a youth and expect it to do the job. Generally youth masks are for children ages 2-12, but correct fit depends on the child's head size.

It's best to try on a mask to see if it's comfortable. You may be required to wear it for a while and you want to make sure the edges seal well and that it doesn't pinch your face or pull hair.

Your eyes should be centered in the goggles and give you a wide field of vision. Make sure it doesn't fog up when you have it on.

To give it a test drive:

1. Loosen harness head straps.
2. Hold facepiece by straps and put chin in first.
3. Pull the mask up and over the face, back over the head.
4. Tighten lower straps first, by pulling end-tabs straight back, not out. Tighten side straps the same way.
5. Push headband pad towards neck and repeat step 4.
6. If necessary, tighten the top strap(s) for best visibility and fit.

MASK LEAK TEST

Check for leaks by placing one hand over the air hole on the filter. Breathe in and out. If the mask partially collapses and stays collapsed until you remove your hand, the seal is good.

Men with beards have an added challenge to get a good seal. Stubble can cause small leaks. In a pinch, it you have to don a mask quickly, apply Vaseline around the edge of the mask. The will help but a cleanly shaved face is best.

Some manufacturers of adult masks size their products Small, Medium or Large. Other makers use the one-size-fits-all approach, but this is harder to achieve.

How do you know which is right for you? Most retailers do not allow gas masks, filters, etc. to be returned. For this reason, and seeing firsthand that it isn't damaged, purchasing these items over the Internet might not be smart.

MASK TIPS

- If you need to economize, it's better to get a less expensive mask and the best filter.
- Make sure the mask and filter aren't damaged in any way. If they are, don't buy them. No discount is worth it.
- Important features to consider: anti-fogging nose cup and drinking capabilities.
- Escape hoods and pet protective devices with positive airflow (PAPR) require lithium batteries to operate. Spare batteries would be clever.
- Many face masks aren't made to accommodate eyeglasses. Some manufacturers offer a prescription spectacle kit for glasses that won't fit between the face and the face shield.
- Don't loan out your respirator. Doing so spreads germs. Speaking of those pesky things, be sure to disinfect the mask's interior surface.
- Last, keep your mask handy but away from moisture.

GAS MASKS – TO BUY OR NOT TO BUY

Purchasing a mask and several filters for every member of your family can add up to a lot of dollars. To provide masks and sufficient filters for a family of four, expect to spend around $1000 for a decent mask and 3 filters each.

GAS MASK BUYING GUIDE

Full Face Respirator Mask	NBC Effective	NIOSH Approvals	Police (P) Military (M) Use	Size	NATO 40mm Filter	Drink System
3M FR-M40 (mil spec)	X	X	P,M	S,M,L	X	X
3M FR-M40B (CBRN)	X	X	P,M	S,M,L	X	X
3M 6000 (DIN)	X	No	No	S,M,L	X	No
3M 7800 (DIN)	X	X	P	S,M,L	X	No
Kareta M Draeger	X	X	M	one size	X	X
Israeli M15 Mil. made 2003 & later	X	X	M	one size	X	X
Millennium MSA	X	X	P,M	S,M,L	X	X
1000 Advantage MSA	X	X	P	S,M,L	with adaptor	No
Millennium CBRN MSA	X	X	P,M	S,M,L	X	X
3100 Advantage MSA	X	X	No	S,M,L	X	No
3200 Advantage MSA	X	X	P	S,M,L	with adaptor	No
Phalanx Alpha MSA	X	X	P,M	S,M,L	No, Phalanx filters only	No
K-1 Military Kit	X	X	P,M	one size	X	X
MCU 2P MSA	X	X	M	S,M,L	X	X
North 54400	X	X	No	S,M	X	No
ProMask Scott	X	X	P	one size	X	No
M95 Military Scott	X	X	P,M	one size	X	X
SGE 1000 Tecnopro	X	No	M	S,M	X	X
SGE 400 Tecnopro	X	X	No	S,M	X	X
SGE 400/3 Tecnopro	X	X	P,M	S,M	X	X
SGE 400/3 Infinity Tecnopro	X	X	P,M	S,M	X	X
SGE 150 Tecnopro	with NBC filter	-	No	one size	X	X
Survivair Opti-Fit Tactical	riot gases only	X	P	S,M,L	X	No
Ultimate Protector Venus	X	X	-	one size	X	No

For every person who advises to purchase them, there is one saying it's a waste of money. Here's why. The key sticking points are
- knowing exactly when an attack would take place
- getting adequate warning

Dare To Prepare: Chapter 41: Buying a Gas Mask and Filters

GAS MASK BUYING GUIDE

Voicemitter	Field of Vision	Price Range	Ease to Breathe	Anti-Fog	Comfort Rate	Eyeglass Kit
X	Excellent	$450-470	negative pressure	X	X	X
X	Excellent	$530-$550	recently improved	X	X	X
No	Very Good	$140-160	X	X	X	X
No	Very Good	$245-265	X	X		No
	Good	$37	-	-	X	
	Good	$30-35	-	X	X	
X	Excellent	$375-390	negative pressure	X	X	X
X	Excellent	$200-250	negative pressure	X	X	X
X	Excellent	$375-400	X	X	X	X
No	Excellent	$160-190	low resistance	X	excellent	X
No	Excellent	$125-195	X	X	X	X
X	Excellent	$270-290	negative pressure	X	snug but OK	No
X	Excellent	$220	-	X	X	No
X	Excellent	$200-300	X	X	X	-
No	Excellent	$135-150	-	X	X	No
	Excellent	$150-170	X	X	X	X
threads to mask	Excellent	$170-240	very low resistance	X	X	X
No	Excellent	$160-215	X	X	X	X
No	Excellent	$120-200		X	X	X
No	Excellent	$140-175		X		
No	Excellent	$180-210				
No	Excellent	$150-170		X	X	X
No	Excellent	$160-190	-	X	X	Yes
X	Excellent	$195-290	low resistance	X	X	X

- was the attack even detected
- having the mask with you at the time of its occurrence
- having purchased a filter that removes the particular agent used
- chemical agents can also enter through the skin

Before buying, look at your budget and determine where your $$ are best spent. Do I need more food and water? Do we have adequate medical supplies and a generator? Do we have a way to keep warm in winter and toasty sleeping bags? These basics you'll use more frequently and they will be life sustaining.

Things to consider would include:
- Do you live in a vulnerable or target-rich area? (see *Prudent Places USA* by Holly Deyo)
- Do you work in a densely populated city?
- Do you use public transit like the subway to and from work?

Ultimately you must make your own decision. If you have plenty of spare $$, it can't hurt, but there are higher priority needs to meet first.

MASKS AND FILTERS TO AVOID

AVOID inferior quality or obsolete masks like the Russian M-10-M, M-41 Aardvark, Russian SMS Snorkel, M9 or M9A1, and GP-5 masks, Canadian M69 C3 and C4, and the East German masks. Other products to steer clear of are the French/Belgian ANP M51 and Hungarian civilian respirator.

Masks that were being sold literally 20 – 30 years ago and recycled products also should be avoided. Make sure the Israeli Military M15 mask is within its 20-year shelf life. Many on the market are not the newer model produced after 2002-03.

Recalled are over 27,000 Brookdale International Systems (British Columbia, Canada) Evac-U-8 Escape Hood, which were purchased for protection against tear gas or chemical warfare agents. These are for smoke inhalation.

Drawbacks on this Israeli Civilian gas mask include no option for a drink tube and low field of view.

These filters should also be avoided: West German models, American M-9 and American C2 models from, more than 10 years ago and C2A1.

Filters, like food, have a shelf life. Avoid ones that are nearly expired or already out of date.

Israeli Civilian

"MASKS" FOR PETS

Rather than try to keep a gas mask on an animal, IDL Cover solved the dilemma of how to protect your 4-legged family member. The Pet Shield, also marketed as Pet Safe and PetScape, protects against chemical, biological and nuclear poisons. It's positive pressure system is battery operated, which lasts for 6 hours.

It's hard to tell from this photo, but the Pet Shield is designed to enclose a pet's kennel so he feels safe in his normal environment. Simply place your pet inside his or her regular kennel, seal it up and activate the battery.

This solves several problems. We can't imagine Taco and Seismo letting anyone put something over their muzzle that blocks normal breathing. Gas masks for people offer a range of minimal-to-considerable breathing resistance. It would be extraordinarily difficult to explain to a dog, "Now Seis, even though it feels like you're getting NO AIR, just breathe normally, in and out." Right.

Additionally dogs and cats need to pant since it's a part of their internal air conditioning. Blocking this normal cooling mechanism would be very detrimental to their well being.

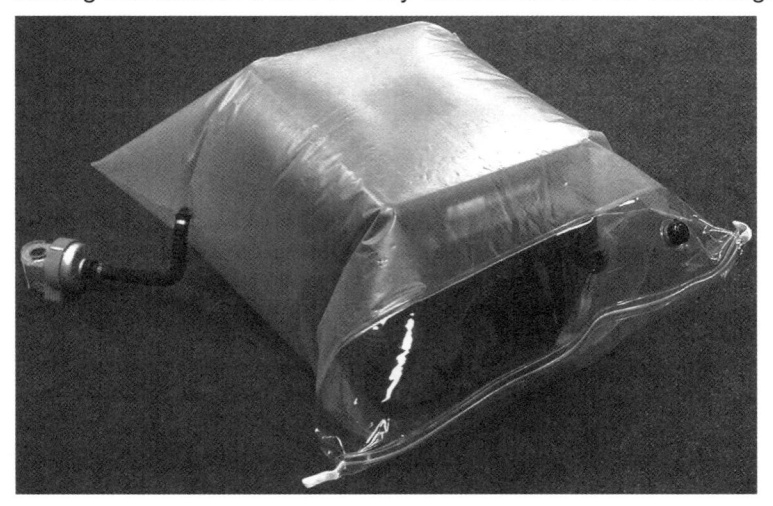

If you're worried that it will rip easily, it was manufactured with components and materials that meet the toughest military standards, developed in conjunction with veterinarians.

The manufacturer issues one very important warning. Don't leave your pet unattended especially as the batteries near their end. Unlike people, animals can't tell you they're suffocating.

Though designed for dogs and cats, it works with any standard cage. Pet Shield comes in three sizes:

Small (or Regular) (0-55 lbs) $324-348 fits cage size 19"Wx27"Lx19"H.

Medium (or Large) (55-100 lbs) $374-399 fits cage size 27"Wx40"Lx30"H.

Dare To Prepare: Chapter 41: Buying a Gas Mask and Filters

Large (or X-Large) (100+ lbs) $450-474 fits cage size 27"Wx40"Lx30"H. This model PetSafe is equipped with two blowers and two filters. This allows for proper airflow and oxygen levels for pets over 100 lbs. or for use in hot climates. Check Approved Gas Masks **www.approvedgasmasks**.com.

NOTE: Some retailers market the small as regular, the medium as large and the large as X-large. To eliminate confusion, it might be best to go by cage size.

FILTERS

Even more important than an expensive mask is a high quality filter. It would be better to by a less expensive mask – not a crummy one – and purchase high end American M-95 filters for about $30-$35 each. You should only need to purchase two or three filters per person.

Filters remove contaminants by absorbing them into pellets within the canister. Even unused, filters have a shelf life. Some expire in as little as three years, others five to seven and some as long as ten. Be sure to check the expiration date before purchasing.

An expired date doesn't render filters immediately ineffective, but over time they will absorb fewer contaminants. Besides soaking up smaller amounts of the bad stuff, they attract moisture making them less able to remove chemical and biological nasties. A severely degraded filter might only last 15 minutes instead of hours in heavy concentration of contaminants.

When filters reach their expiration date, you don't need to worry about changing the pellets. Each filter is permanently sealed. Simply replace the entire filter. Keep the old one to practice breathing with it.

Generally speaking, expect the filters to last 3-10 hours. Higher toxin concentrations shorten their effectiveness. When you purchase a mask, purchase a realistic supply of filters as well.

Gas canister and filters should be NBC, which give protection against chemical and biological agents and nuclear particles. That a filter is NBC rated is a major selling point for retailers and if it meets these standards, it will surely be posted. If you're buying online and unsure, email and ask first.

Most gas masks use the standard 40mm NATO threaded filters, except for MSA, which requires its own specialty filters.

M95 Filter

GAS MASK-SPECIFIC FILTER CANISTERS			
MODEL	**NIOSH APPROVAL**	**APPROXIMATE PRICE**	**SHELF LIFE**
3M FR-64 (for 3M FR-M40 or full facepiece 6000)	X	$50/each $190/4pk	5 years
Bardas / Shmartaf (for Escape Hoods)	No	$34.50/each	5 years
MSA Advantage 1000/3200 (use with corresponding mask)	X	$38/each $228/6pk	3 years
MSA Millennium (use with corresponding mask)	X	$44/each $250/6pk	3 years
MSA Phalanx (use with corresponding mask)	X	$44/each $250/6pk	3 years
MSA OptimAir PAPR	X	$90/pair	3 years
MSA ComfoFilter	X	$28/pair	3 years
Surplus Filters Buyer beware. No age, quality guarantee	No	$19/each $89/6pk	Indeterminate

FILTER CANISTER COMPARISON			
MODEL	NIOSH APPROVAL	APPROXIMATE PRICE	SHELF LIFE
NBC Gas Mask Filter for Most Masks (40mm NATO threaded)			
M-95 (most popular)	X	$44/each $127/3pk $246/6pk	10 years
Scott MPC Plus	Yes, except with a PAPR for organic vapors as of 2007	$45/each $90/3pk	5 years
Scott NTC-1 (2001 design)	No	$49/each	10 years
Scott NBC M95 Long Life	X	$42/each	10 years
MSA Optifilter GME-P100	X	$47/each $220/6pk	3 years
MSA CBRN*	with CBRN Millennium mask	$49/each $141/3pk $271/6pk $440/10k	3 years
North NBC-40	No	$34.50/each $179/6pk	8 years
Drager RA	X	$43/each	6 years
3M FR-57	X	$47/each $269/6pk	5 years
3M FR-64	X	$49/each $190/4pk	5 years
3M FR-15 CBRN	X	$49/each $190/4pk	5 years
3M FR C2A1	with FR-M40 mask only	$49/each $190/4pk	5 years
Type 80 NATO	No	$38/each	N/A
NP8000 NBC		$38/each	15 years
2200 Police CN/CS Gas	X	$39/each	10 years
NP1000K	X	$32/pair	15 years

*CBRN Chemical-Biological-Radiological-Nuclear   Shelf Life is for unopened, fully sealed filters.

FILTER TIPS

Make sure your filter is rated for NBC protection. These filters protect you from all known biological agents in addition to chemicals like sarin and other nerve gases, mustard gas, cyanogen, arsine, phosgene plus many organic and inorganic gases/vapors and inorganic acids.

Purchase new filters still sealed in the package. Once the seal is broken, filter degradation begins. Painter's respirators and ones used to prevent smoke inhalation don't work against biological and chemical agents.

Some websites sell dust or fiber masks as a line of defense against bio-chemicals. These simply won't do. They offer minimal protection and can't keep out chemical or biological agents. End of story.

Pass over M9 filters which have a different diameter thread. Stick with the NATO screw-on filters like the one pictured previously since they are interchangeable with a number of filters on the market.

BEEF UP YOUR IMMUNE SYSTEM

- As soon as you learn of a bio-chem attack (if you are not already doing so), limit your food intake so your body can devote more energy to the immune system rather than to digestion. Eat more raw foods, vegetables and juices.
- Load up on antioxidants – "C" is one of the best vitamins to take. Store plenty of the natural variety with rosehips and bioflavinoids. Some recommendations suggest as much as 1000 mg. of C every two hours, which requires fruit or juice intake so it doesn't make you sick.
- Antioxidants Vitamin E and B6 have reputations for boosting the immune system as does Vitamin A which helps ward off infections to the eyes, respiratory system and gastrointestinal tract.
- Eat organic foods as much as possible. No one needs pesticides in his system.
- Remove the "white" foods from the diet: white rice, white flour products and white (refined) sugar. Two cans of soft drink contain approximately 8 tablespoons of sugar – enough to suppress the immune system for five hours. If you're grazing all day on pop and sweets, what ammo does you body have to fight disease?

- People who are in tiptop shape – those who are physically active and haven't lived on junk food will have the best chance of fighting these poisons naturally. It's never too late to exercise! Not only does exercise rev up the immune system, it relieves stress – something that makes us more susceptible to disease.
- Give your body plenty of rest and water. Burning the candle at both ends depletes the body of disease-fighting capabilities.
- Grapeseed extract is a good idea as well as raw garlic. Raw garlic exits through the lungs, which is what the biological agents are most likely to attack. Raw garlic has both antibacterial and anti-viral aspects. Place raw garlic into a glass of tomato juice and add one small clove. Drink every six hours.
- Tea tree oil is reputed to be very good for treating bacterial infections of the skin. Apply to cuts, wounds and sores.
- Colloidal silver is also purported to have antibacterial, anti-viral effects as well. Again, check with your naturopath for the correct dosage as too much colloidal silver, over time, may cause a permanent graying of the skin – a condition known as argyria, depending on what type you're ingesting. (See Chapter 18 for more colloidal silver information) For shorter periods of time, use one dropper full of every six hours.
- Powerful blood cleansers include these three natural herbs: Echinacea, Goldenseal and olive leaf extract – all available in health food stores. Take at the first sign of illness.

NOTE: This information is NOT offered as medical advice, purely as food for thought.

IN CASE OF AN ATTACK

1. Put on your mask. Since the greatest harm comes from inhaling most biologicals, it's important to protect your face and lungs.
2. Remove the filter's seal just before use. It may have plugs or screw-on caps at both ends of the filter that must be removed before using.
3. If possible, leave the area immediately and with as much calm as you can muster. Head for an upwind rural area or home if that is your safe area. Remember, if your vehicle isn't equipped with a HEPA filter (and most aren't unless you've installed modifications) you'll need to wear your protective mask in your car or truck. Contaminants can enter through the air system.
4. If you are at home, lock your doors and go to your safe room. Where panic is flowing, people can act irrationally, do things they wouldn't under normal circumstances. You don't want to invite this into your home.
5. Since your safe room is already set up (hint, hint), you can live through the experience at calmer levels. All you need to do is turn on your radio to see what's happening – and wait it out.

MASK AND FILTER SOURCES

- Approved Gas Masks: **www.approvedgasmasks.com**. Box 9509, San Diego, CA 92169, 877.236.1010 (toll free), 301.931.6700, Fax 301.931.6655
- Safer America: **www.saferamerica**. 226 East 54th Street, Suite #502, New York, NY 10022; US 1.866.723.3799; International 1.212.374.4056
- Captain Dave's: **shop.captaindaves.com**. P.O. Box 72298; Durham, NC 27722; 1.877.413.2837
- ProKI: **www.proki.org**. PO Box 9119, San Diego, CA 92169 US 1.858.488.3300
- Dräger: **www.draeger.com**. US 1.800.922.5518; Canada 1.877.372.4371; Adelaide, Australia 1.800.67.7787; New Zealand 0.800.37.2437; UK 44.1670.35.2891
- Amazon: **www.amazon.com**.

PRICE GOUGING

Shopping around for the best price is crucial. In performing many, many comp checks, a huge retail price schism became very evident. Some vendors marked up identical masks as much as 200%. This was especially evident when it came to our soft zones – children and pets.

The next two chapters will give vital information on sheltering in place and decontamination.

Chapter 42: Bio-warfare Decontamination

Unless we have a crystal ball, chances are we won't know a bio-attack has occurred. It may only become evident when people fall ill *in a specific area* – all exhibiting symptoms of anthrax, plague or some other disease. Terrorists gave no warning, no notice, no demands prior to the day we will always remember – September 11, 2001. Why would they alter their M.O. now? Nothing has changed except we now understand we're clearly targeted.

If a biological or chemical attack has already occurred it makes purchasing a gas mask and/or protective over-garments moot. In order for them to be effective, though, one would have to live in this gear literally day and night. This is not living. Carrying on our lives as normally as possible IS.

Let's say this event transpires, what should you do? The following information is extracted from *The Medical Management of Biological Casualties Handbook*. You can download this manual from USAMRIID (U.S. Army Medical Research Institute of Infectious Diseases) in its entirety for FREE at:

standeyo.com/News_Files/NBC/USAMRIID_BlueBook_6ed.pdf

Their broad stroke bio-warfare decontamination is found in the box below. Detailed information follows.

> *Skin exposure from a suspected BW agent should be immediately treated by soap and water decontamination. "A 0.1% bleach solution reliably kills anthrax spores, the hardiest of biological agents."*[103]

"Dermal exposure to a suspected BW aerosol should be immediately treated by soap and water. Careful washing with soap and water removes nearly the entire agent from the skin surface. Hypochlorite solution (household bleach) or other disinfectants are reserved for gross contamination (i.e., after the spill of solid or liquid agent from a munition directly onto the skin). In the absence of chemical or gross biological contamination, these disinfectants will confer no additional benefit, may be caustic, and may predispose to colonization and resistant superinfection by reducing the normal kin flora. Grossly contaminated skin surfaces should be washed with a 0.5% sodium hypochlorite solution, if available with a contact time of 10-15 minutes."[104]

MAKING DECONTAMINATION SOLUTION

Make a 0.5% sodium hypochlorite solution by mixing one part Clorox or other household bleach containing 6% sodium hypochlorite with nine parts water. Keep in mind, swabbing your body with a Clorox wash is harsher treatment that what it's normally used to. However, when decorating cakes with seemingly "indelible" food coloring (and getting more pink or green on my fingers than in the frosting), I poured Clorox on those colorful digits, let it remain for a few minutes and lived to tell about it. The solution they prescribe above is MUCH weaker than this so you should be fine. Common sense says not to put any of this solution into open body cavities.

FURTHER DECONTAMINATION

(Excerpted from Medical Management of Biological Casualties Handbook)[105]

Contamination is the introduction of an infectious agent on a body surface, food or water, or other inanimate objects. Decontamination involves either disinfection or sterilization to reduce microorganisms to an acceptable level making them suitable for use. Disinfection is reducing of undesirable microbes to a level below that required for transmission. Sterilization is the killing of all organisms. Decontamination methods have always played an important role in the control of infectious diseases. However, we are often unable use the most efficient means of rendering microbes harmless (e.g., toxic chemical sterilization), as these methods may injure people and damage materials, which are to be decontaminated. BW agents can be decontaminated by mechanical, chemical and physical methods:

1) **Mechanical decontamination** involves measures to remove but not necessarily neutralize an agent. An example is the filtering of drinking water to remove certain waterborne pathogens (e.g. Dracunculus medinensis), or in a BW context, the use of an air filter to remove aerosolized anthrax spores, or water to wash agent from the skin.

2) **Chemical decontamination** renders BW agents harmless by the use of disinfectants that are usually in the form of a liquid, gas or aerosol. Some disinfectants are harmful to humans, animals, the environment, and materials.

3) **Physical means** (heat, radiation) are other methods that can be employed for decontamination of objects.

DECONTAMINATION, ASSUMING NO SEVERE EXPOSURE

Before entering your safe shelter, leaving behind all bacteria or chemical agents is essential. If there is even the remotest chance you've come in contact with bio-chemical agents, you must decontaminate yourself. Before entering your home, either outside, weather permitting, or in the garage, remove all clothing and shoes FIRST before going inside. Don't let modesty deter you. Peel down to the skin and seal everything in heavy plastic bags. Leave these bags outside and head immediately to the decontamination shower. You don't want to drag this stuff indoors.

Flush eyes with lots of water. Stand under a warm spray at least five minutes soaping your body thoroughly. Shampoo hair, beards and moustaches twice. If your pets have been exposed, take them into the shower with you and give them two shampoos as well. Change into clean clothing (item stored in drawers or closets are likely to be uncontaminated) and go to your safe shelter.

You can either purchase various decontamination showers or build one yourself. It doesn't have to be fancy.

PROCEDURE IF WEARING FULL PROTECTIVE CLOTHING, HAT, GLOVES AND MASK

Climb into the shower fully dressed. Make sure the shower curtain falls inside the wading pool or whatever wastewater catchment you've devised. While showering with the decontamination mixture, thoroughly scrub every part of your garments for at least 5 minutes. Decontaminate with a mixture of ¾ cup 6% Clorox to 1 gallon water.

After finishing, remove all protective gear except the mask and inner surgical gloves. Proceed inside and hang your suit inside where it can dry safely. You don't want to bleach flooring or furniture.

In the bathroom, remove all clothing except surgical gloves and place in a heavy garbage bag. Wash your face and the inside of your mask with a towel dipped in the same mixture solution used for decontamination. **DO NOT get this solution in your eyes.**

Remove surgical gloves and shower scrubbing with anti-bacterial soap.

Not using some sort of shower curtain would only be clever outside where the surfaces exposed to the agents could be thoroughly decontaminated.

BUILD A DECONTAMINATION SHOWER

You can build a decontamination shower easily with just 6 or 7 items:
- enough garden hose to reach the faucet
- kiddie wading pool with 5' or 6' diameter
- 10'x12' length of 4 mil plastic sheeting
- 15' rope
- garden tank sprayer
- 10' step ladder (optional)
- duct tape

OVERVIEW

The overall concept is to use the wading pool as a shower stall base with the sheeting as the curtain. For the shower curtain frame you could fold it over an erected clothes line or over a metal frame you've welded together or even 2x4's nailed together to form a structure measuring 9'Hx3'Lx3'W. This is your shower stall.

Your particular circumstances, what your garage looks like on the interior or if the decontamination shower is to be located outside, will determine how you'll suspend the sprayer.

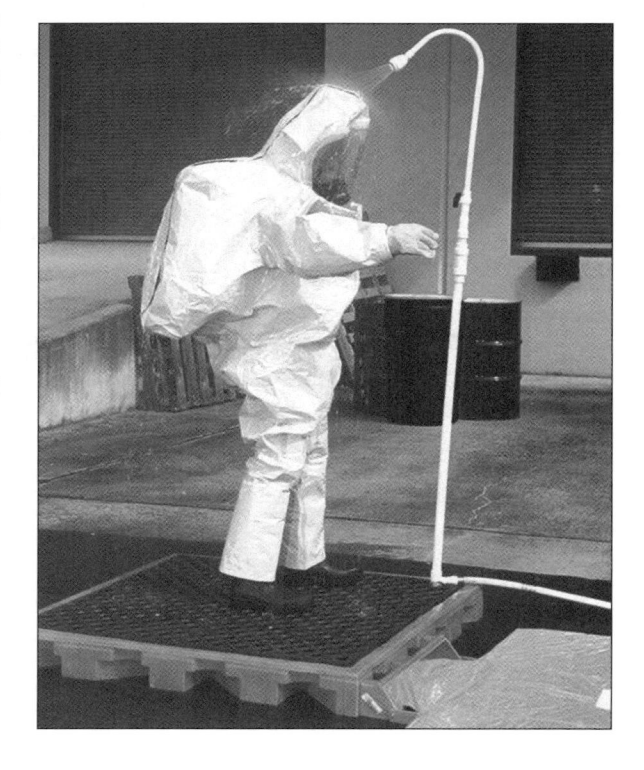

If your garage has open rafters or exposed ceiling joists, you can loop the garden hose with the tank sprayer attached through these and secure in place positioned over the shower.

Alternately, situate a 10-foot high stepladder next to the "shower". Duct tape the sprayer in place with the hose attached and secured to the ladder with duct tape. Secure the sprayer wand to the ladder's top platform. This leaves hands totally free.

The second option offers more control since the sprayer would be closer to the shower opening at the top resulting in less overspray. Also, parents could mount the ladder and make certain smaller family members are getting fully decontaminated.

Once the shower curtain is in place over whatever frame you choose, cut two doors in the plastic; one for entering and one for exiting. (After you've decontaminated, you don't want to walk through the "dirty" area.)

DECONTAMINATING YOUR BODY

SKIN

> *Dermal exposure to a suspected BW aerosol should be immediately treated by soap and water decontamination. Careful washing with soap and water removes nearly the entire agent from the skin's surface. A quick swish won't do. Wash hands thoroughly with at least 30 seconds of intentional scrubbing.*

Hypochlorite solution or other disinfectants are reserved for gross contamination (i.e. following the spill of solid or liquid agent from a munition directly onto the skin). In the absence of chemical or gross biological contamination, these will confer no additional benefit, may be caustic, and may predispose to colonization and resistant super-infection by reducing the normal skin flora. Grossly contaminated skin surfaces should be washed with a 0.5% sodium hypochlorite solution, if available, with a contact time of 10 to 15 minutes.

GROSS DECONTAMINATION SOLUTION	
To mix 0.5% sodium hypochlorite (Clorox) solution	To mix 5% sodium hypochlorite (Clorox) solution
3.2 oz (95ml) 5.25 or 6% bleach + 5 gal. (19L) water	32 oz (946ml) 5.25 or 6% bleach + 5 gal. (19L) water

These solutions evaporate quickly at high temperatures so if they are made in advance, store in closed containers. Also, the chlorine solutions should be placed in distinctly marked containers because it is very difficult to tell the difference between the 5% chlorine solution and the 0.5% solution.

To mix a 0.5% sodium hypochlorite solution, take one part Clorox and nine parts water (1:9) since standard stock Clorox is a 6% sodium hypochlorite solution. The solution is then applied with a cloth or swab. The solution should be made fresh daily with the pH in the alkaline range.

Chlorine solution must NOT be used in (1) open body cavity wounds, as it may lead to the formation of adhesions, or (2) brain and spinal cord injuries. However, this solution may be instilled into non-cavity wounds and then removed by suction to an appropriate disposal container. Within about 5 minutes, this contaminated solution will be neutralized and nonhazardous. Subsequent irrigation with saline or other surgical solutions should be performed. Prevent the chlorine solution from being sprayed into the eyes, as corneal opacities may result.

BATHING

A shower is always preferable to a tub bath and particularly so in for decontamination. Think about it. Whatever washes off your body, you are now sitting in it!

Were you just running around barefoot outside? Ugh! You don't want to think about it. This is particularly important for females at any time. If you miss the luxury of a bath, shower first, and then relax in the bubble bath. To decontaminate, shower with hot, soapy water.

HAIR

Don't forget this area! Shampoo twice and rinse thoroughly.

CLOTHING

To decontaminate clothing, use a 5-6% hypochlorite solution. Ordinary sunlight works miracles; use it after the "all-clear" has been announced. UV rays destroy many bacteria, viruses and fungi within 24-48 hours.

Optimum conditions require sunshine, a slight breeze and low humidity. Bulky clothes and dense fabrics make UV penetration much more difficult and increases the time clothes need to be outside.

If you're not terribly fond of the clothing, burning is a good way to get rid of the contamination. If they can withstand household bleach, mix ½ cup Clorox to a gallon of water and soak them for at least 30 minutes. Rinse thoroughly and dry them in the clothes dryer on the hottest setting.

Burying clothes is not a good idea due to ground contamination. Anthrax spores can survive in the soil 40 years – and longer.

DECONTAMINATING EQUIPMENT

To decontaminate equipment, use a 5% hypochlorite solution with contact time of 30 minutes prior to normal cleaning. This is corrosive to most metals and injurious to most fabrics, so rinse thoroughly and oil metal surfaces after completion.

USING HEAT AND RADIATION

BW agents can be made harmless through heat and radiation. To render agents completely harmless, sterilize with dry heat for two hours at 320°F (160°C). If autoclaving with steam at 250°F (121°C) and 1 atmosphere of overpressure (15 pounds per square inch), the time may be reduced to 20 minutes, depending on volume. Solar ultraviolet (UV) radiation has a disinfectant effect, often in combination with drying. This is effective in certain environmental conditions but hard to standardize for practical usage for decontamination purposes.

Health hazards from biological agents in the environment differ from those used in chemical weapons. Aerosolized particles in the 1-5 micron size range will remain suspended; but would be eventually inactivated by solar ultraviolet light, desiccation, and oxidation. Little, if any, environmental residues would occur. Possible exceptions include residuals near the dissemination line, or in the immediate area surrounding a point-source munition. BW agents deposited on the soil would be subject to degradation by environmental stressors, and competing soil microflora. Simulation studies at Dugway Proving Ground suggest that secondary reaerosolization would be difficult, and would probably not pose a human health hazard. Environmental decontamination of terrain is costly and difficult and should be avoided, if possible. If grossly contaminated terrain, streets, or roads must be passed, the use of dust-binding spray to minimize reaerosolization may be considered. If it is necessary to decontaminate these surfaces, chlorine-calcium or lye may be used. Otherwise, rely on the natural processes, which, especially outdoors, lead to the decontamination of agent by drying and solar UV radiation. Rooms in fixed spaces are best decontaminated with gases or liquids in aerosol form (e.g., formaldehyde). This is usually combined with surface disinfectants to ensure complete decontamination.

WATER PURIFICATION

Below are water purifying methods for some toxins. There is wide variance in what works and what doesn't.

Boiling water for 20 minutes is also an acceptable method of water purification, but this is only reasonable for smaller quantities of water. This can be a problem because the amount of water remaining at the end of 20 minutes' boiling will be considerably less compared to the original amount.

While the standard method of water purification was and is chlorine, sometimes this product simply won't kill everything, as evidenced by the table two pages over. This is the time for a filter.

Certain viral organisms are beyond minute, smaller than bacteria. The smallest bacteria are about the size of the largest virus. They range from 0.002 micron – 0.3 micron. The only things less in size are herbicides, pesticides, synthetic dyes, metals and salts. So viruses require correspondingly smaller filters. The drawback is that filters for extremely small particles clog quickly. To remove every type of virus, you would need one that could filter down to .005. (See Reverse Osmosis chart.) Replacing filters this size, as needed, can get very expensive.

In order to extend the life of the smaller filter, use a pre-filter – one that removes particles larger than bacteria. This puts the largest load on the less refined filter and allows the smaller one to tackle anything that slips through. Filters that remove bacteria automatically cover the size of giardia cysts and cryptosporidium.

Filters at .005 are not readily available since they fall into medical grade category. Locally, we could only find .5 filters, which is 1000 times too big to remove every virus.

Surface filtration-pleated cartridge filters are a good choice. "Pleated cartridge filters typically act as absolute particle filters, using a flat sheet media, either a membrane or specially treated non-woven material, to trap particles. The media is pleated to increase usable surface area. Pleated membrane filters serve well as sub-micron particle or bacteria filters in the 0.1 to 1.0 micron range. Newer cartridges also perform in the ultrafiltration range: 0.005 to 0.15 micron."[106]

MSR's Sweetwater Purifier System says it inactivates 99.99% of waterborne viruses; eliminates over 99.9999% of all waterborne bacteria and 99.9% of common protozoan parasites, such as giardia and cryptosporidium, as well as particulates, bad tastes, and odors. Even more high-end water units like Katadyn Combi Water Filter removes bacteria, protozoa, cysts and chemicals, but not all viruses.

We're not picking on either of these companies. Stan and I have portable Sweetwater units. Under normal circumstances these are excellent products, but we know they aren't effective against all viruses. If you're really concerned about water quality, it might be worth investing in reverse osmosis or ultraviolet systems.

REVERSE OSMOSIS

According to Osmonics, Inc. "RO can meet most water standards with a single-pass system and the highest standards with a double-pass system. RO rejects 99.9+% of viruses, bacteria and pathogens. Pressure, on the order of 200 to 1,000 psig (13.8 to 68.9 bar), is the driving force of the RO purification process. It is much more energy efficient compared to heat-driven purification (distillation) and more efficient than the strong chemicals required for ion exchange. No energy-intensive phase change is required."[107]

The downside to RO is that it uses a lot of water. They only net 5-15% of the water entering the system. The remainder is discharged as wastewater.[108]

ULTRAVIOLET

How UV purification works: Water enters the purifier's chamber. Once inside, it's exposed to UV light. The UV lamp used for germicidal disinfection produces light at a wavelength of 253.7 nanometers (2,537 Angstrom units). At this wavelength, UV light destroys up to 99.9% of all bacteria, protozoa, viruses, molds, algae and other microbes. This includes such waterborne diseases as: E.coli, hepatitis, cholera, dysentery, typhoid fever as well as many others.

UV purifiers work best when the water temperature is 35-110°F (17-43°C). Extreme cold or heat interferes with the purifier's performance. One must also look for situations that inhibit UV light from penetrating the water. Turbidity – cloudy water from having sediment stirred up – interferes with the transmission of UV. UV works on the following:

MICROORGANISM DESTRUCTION LEVELS[109]			
Ultraviolet energy at 253.7 nm wavelength required for 99.9% destruction of various microorganisms – in microwatts sec/cm squared			
MICROORGANISM	UV ENERGY REQUIRED	MICROORGANISM	UV ENERGY REQUIRED
Bacillus anthracis (anthrax virus)	8,700	Bacillus anthracia (anthrax spores)	4,200
Corynebacterium diphtheriae (Diphtheria)	6,500	Shigella dysentariae (dysentery)	4,200
Dysentery bacilli (diarrhea)	4,200	Shigella flexneri (dysentery)	3,400
Escherichia coli (E. Coli)	7,000	Staphylococcus epidermidis (staph)	5,800
Legionella pneumophilia (Legionnaires' Disease)	3,800	Streptococcus faecaelis (strep)	10,000
Mycobacterium tuberculosis (TB)	10,000	Vibro commo (cholera)	6,500
Pseudomonas aeruginosa	3,900	Bacteriophage	6,500
Salmonella (food poisoning)	10,000	Hepatitis	8,000
Salmonella paratyphi (enteric fever)	6,100	Influenza	6,600
Salmonella typhosa (typhoid fever)	7,000	Poliovirus (poliomyelitis)	7,000
Salmonella typhimurium (gastroenteritis)	15,200	Clostridium Tetani (Tetanus/Lockjaw)	23,000
Giardia Lamblia (giardia)	5,000-10,000	Cryptosporidium	5,000 - 10,000

OZONATION

This seems to be one of the most popular methods of water treatment. Look over this table of doses and reactions times for various.[110]

It seems no particular system gets rid of everything. The best solution is several methods in conjunction with each other, to ensure total purification.

For more in-depth information on Water Purification, see Chapters 4 and 5.

OZONATION	
TYPICAL DOSAGE	**REACTION TIMES**
Aspergillus Niger (black Mount)	Destroyed by 1.5 to 2 mg/1
Bacillus Bacteria	Destroyed by 0.2 mg/1 within 30 seconds
Bacillus Anthracis	Ozone susceptible
Clostridium Bacteria	Ozone susceptible
Clostridium Botulinum	0.4 to 0.5 mg/1
Diphtheria	Destroyed by 1.5 to 2 mg/1
Eberth Bacillus (Typhus abdominalis)	Destroyed by 1.5 to 2 mg/1
Echo Virus 29	After contact time of 1 minute at 1 mg/1 of ozone, 99.999% killed.
Escherichia Coli	Destroyed by 0.2 mg/1 within 30 seconds
Encephalomyocarditis Virus	Destroyed to zero level in less than 30 seconds with 0.1 to 0.8mg/1
Enterovirus Virus	Destroyed to zero level in less than 30 seconds with 0.1 to 0.8mg/1
GDVII Virus	Destroyed to zero level in less than 30 seconds with 0.1 to 0.8mg/1
Herpes Virus	Destroyed to zero level in less than 30 seconds with 0.1 to 0.8mg/1
Influenza	0.4 to 0.5 mg/1
Klebs-Loffler Virus	Destroyed by 1.5 to 2 mg/1
Poliomyelitis Virus	Kills 99.999% with 0.3 to 0.4 mg/1 in 3 to 4 minutes
Proteus Bacteria	Very Susceptible
Pseudomonal Bacteria	Very Susceptible
Rhabdovirus Virus	Destroyed to zero level in less than 30 seconds
Salmonella Bacteria	Very Susceptible
Staphylococci	Destroyed by 1.5 to 2 mg/1
Stomatitis Virus	Destroyed to zero level in less than 30 seconds with 0.1 to 0.8mg/1
Streptococcus Bacteria	Destroyed by 0.2 mg/1 within 30 seconds

WATER PURIFICATION METHODS EFFECTIVE AGAINST TOXINS[111]		
METHOD	**TOXIN (MW in d)**	**EFFECTIVENESS**
Reverse Osmosis	Ricin (64,000) Microcystin (1,000) T-2 mycotoxin (466) Saxitoxin (294) Botulinum toxins Staphylococcal Enterotoxin B (28,494)	Effective Effective Effective Effective * *
Coagulation/Flocculation	Ricin Microcystin T-2 mycotoxin Saxitoxin Botulinum toxins Staphylococcal Enterotoxin B	Not effective Not effective Not effective Not effective ** **
Household Chlorine 5mg/L (5ppm) for 30 min.	Ricin Microcystin T-2 mycotoxin Saxitoxin Botulinum toxins Staphylococcal Enterotoxin B	Not effective Not effective Not effective Not effective Destroys the toxins **
* not tested but expected to be effective **not tested but not expected to be effective		

FOOD

If there is ANY chance food has become exposed, toss it. It's not worth the risk. The exception to this is canned goods. They can be successfully decontaminated by soaking them a 0.5% sodium hypochlorite (Clorox) solution. Rinse thoroughly since this solution can corrode metal.

DECONTAMINATION FOR MOST LIKELY USED BW AGENTS

ANTHRAX

Isolation and Decontamination for Healthcare Workers: Standard precautions for healthcare workers. After an invasive procedure or autopsy is performed, the instruments and area used should be thoroughly disinfected with a sporicidal agent (hypochlorite).

Decontamination and Isolation: Drainage and secretion precautions should be practiced. Anthrax is not transmittable via the aerosol route from person to person. Following invasive procedures or autopsy, instruments and surfaces should be thoroughly disinfected with a sporicidal agent (high-level disinfectants such as iodine or 0.5% sodium hypochlorite). **In fact, 0.1% bleach solution reliably kills anthrax spores, the hardiest of biological agents.**

Outbreak Control: Although anthrax spores may survive in the environment for many years, secondary aerosolization of such spores (such as by pedestrian movement or vehicular traffic) generally presents no problem for humans. The carcasses of animals dying in such an environment should be burned, and animals subsequently introduced into such an environment should be vaccinated. Meat, hides, and carcasses of animals in affected areas should not be consumed or handled by untrained and/or unvaccinated personnel.

'Jeanne Guillemin is a medical anthropologist, and a Professor of Sociology and Senior Fellow at MIT's Security Studies Program. In 1992, she was part of a team that investigated a suspicious anthrax epidemic that took place in 1979 in the former USSR. She is an affiliate of the Harvard-Sussex Program, which is involved with the elimination of chemical and biological weapons' advises the following: "Sunshine destroys anthrax spores, but very little else does. Heat doesn't, radiation doesn't. It's resistant to explosives. That's precisely the reason why anthrax was developed as a weapon, because it's tough, whereas most bacteria and viruses are fragile."'[112]

BOTULISM – (TOXIN)

Isolation and Decontamination for Healthcare Workers: Standard Precautions for healthcare workers. Toxin is not dermally active and secondary aerosols are not a hazard from patients. Decon with soap and water. Botulinum toxin is inactivated by sunlight within 1-3 hours. Heat (176°F [80°C] for 30 min., 212°F [100°C] for several minutes) and chlorine (>99.7% inactivation by 3 mg/L FAC in 20 min.) also destroy the toxin.

Decontamination and Isolation: Decontamination of surfaces contaminated by toxin may be accomplished using soap and water, or 0.5% hypochlorite. Pressure-cooking foods to be canned best kills spores. Toxin is not dermally active (although spores may enter through skin wounds) and secondary aerosols from affected patients pose no risk of botulism transmission.

Outbreak Control: Intentionally-released aerosols of botulinum toxin probably pose little risk beyond the immediate period of release. In the event that food contamination is suspected, boiling for 10 minutes may destroy pre-formed toxins.

BRUCELLOSIS

Isolation and Decontamination for Healthcare Workers: Standard precautions are appropriate for healthcare workers. Person-to-person transmission has been reported via tissue transplantation and sexual contact. Environmental decontamination can be accomplished with a 0.5% hypochlorite solution.

Decontamination and Isolation: Drainage and secretion precautions should be practiced in patients who have open skin lesions; otherwise no evidence of person-to-person transmission of brucellosis exists. Animal remains should be handled utilizing universal precautions and disposed of properly. Surfaces contaminated with brucella aerosols may be decontaminated by standard means (0.5% hypochlorite).

Outbreak Control: In the event of an intentional release of brucella organisms, it is possible that livestock will become infected. Thus, animal products in such an environment should be pasteurized, boiled, or thoroughly cooked prior to consumption. Proper treatment of water, by boiling or iodination, would also be important in an area subjected to intentional contamination with brucella aerosols.

CHOLERA
Isolation and Decontamination for Healthcare Workers: Personal contact rarely causes infection; however, enteric precautions and careful hand-washing should be employed. Gloves should be used for patient contact and specimen handling. Bactericidal solutions, such as 0.5% hypochlorite, would provide adequate surface decontamination.

Outbreak Control: Strict attention must be paid to the avoidance of contaminated water in an outbreak area. Drinking water, as well as water used in bathing, washing utensils, and cooking, must be obtained from a safe source or must be boiled or chlorinated prior to use.

GLANDERS AND MELIOIDOSIS
Isolation and Decontamination: Standard Precautions for healthcare workers. Person-to-person airborne transmission is unlikely, although secondary cases may occur through improper handling of infected secretions. Contact precautions are indicated while caring for patients with skin involvement. Environmental decontamination using a 0.5% hypochlorite solution is effective.

PLAGUE
Isolation and Decontamination for Healthcare Workers: Use Standard Precautions for bubonic plague, and Respiratory Droplet Precautions for suspected pneumonic plague. *Y. pestis* can survive in the environment for varying periods, but is susceptible to heat, disinfectants, and exposure to sunlight. Soap and water is effective if decon is needed. Take measures to prevent local disease cycles if vectors (fleas) and reservoirs (rodents) are present.

Decontamination and Isolation: Use drainage and secretion precautions to manage patients with bubonic plague. Continue these precautions until the patient has received antibiotics for 48 hours and is responding to such therapy. Be careful when handling or aspirating buboes to avoid aerosolizing infectious material. Strict isolation is necessary for patients with pneumonic plague.

Outbreak Control: In the event of the intentional release of plague into an area, it is possible that local fleas and rodents could become infected, thereby initiating a cycle of enzootic and endemic disease. Such a possibility would appear more likely in the face of a breakdown in public health measures (such as vector and rodent control) which might accompany armed conflict. Treat with a suitable insecticide to rid patients and contacts of fleas. Use flea and rodent control measures where plague cases have been reported.

Q FEVER
Isolation and Decontamination for Healthcare Workers: Standard Precautions are recommended for healthcare workers. Person-to-person transmission is rare. Patients exposed to Q fever by aerosol do not present a risk for secondary contamination or re-aerosolization of the organism. Decontamination is accomplished with soap and water or a 0.5% chlorine solution on personnel. The M291 skin decontamination kit will not neutralize the organism.

Decontamination and Isolation: Patients exposed to Q fever by the aerosol route do not present a risk for secondary contamination or re-aerosolization of the organism. Decontamination is accomplished with soap and water or by the use of weak (0.5 percent) hypochlorite solutions.

Outbreak Control: Spore-like forms of Coxiella burnetii may withstand quite harsh conditions and thus persist in the environment for prolonged periods. Presumably, animals, especially sheep, in such areas would be at risk for acquiring infection, and contact with the products of pregnancy of such animals would represent a continuing hazard to humans. Little information exists to permit assessment of direct long-term hazards to humans entering an area contaminated by intentional release of aerosolized Q fever.

RICIN – (TOXIN)
Isolation and Decontamination for Healthcare Workers: Standard Precautions for healthcare workers. Ricin is non-volatile (does not evaporate into a gas), so it isn't a danger to caregivers. Decontaminate with soap and water. Hypochlorite solutions (0.1% sodium hypochlorite) can inactivate ricin.

Decontamination and Isolation: Ricin may be inactivated with 0.5% hypochlorite. Since it is not dermally active and is involatile, decontamination may not be as critical as with certain other biological and chemical agents.

Outbreak Control: Ricin does not, in general, pose a risk of secondary aerosolization.

SMALLPOX

Isolation and Decontamination for Healthcare Workers: Droplet and Airborne Precautions for a minimum of 17 days following exposure for all contacts. Patients should be considered infectious until all scabs separate and quarantined during this period. In the civilian setting strict quarantine of asymptomatic contacts may prove to be impractical and impossible to enforce. A reasonable alternative would be to require contacts to check their temperatures daily. Any fever above 101°F (38°C) during the 17-day period following exposure to a confirmed case would suggest the development of smallpox. The contact should then be isolated immediately, preferably at home, until smallpox is either confirmed or ruled out and remain in isolation until all scabs separate.

Decontamination: Given the extreme public health implications of smallpox reintroduction, patients should be placed in strict isolation pending review by national health authorities. All material used in patient care or in contact with smallpox patients should be autoclaved, boiled, or burned.

Outbreak Control: Smallpox has considerable potential for person-to-person spread. Thus, all contacts of infectious cases should be quarantined for 16-17 days following exposure, and given prophylaxis as indicated. Animals are not susceptible to smallpox.

STAPHYLOCOCCAL ENTEROTOXIN B – (TOXIN)

Isolation and Decontamination for Healthcare Workers: Standard Precautions for healthcare workers. SEB is not dermally active and secondary aerosols are not a hazard from patients. Decon with soap and water. Destroy any food that may have been contaminated.

Decontamination and Isolation: Decontamination of most surfaces may be accomplished with soap and water or with exposure to 0.5% hypochlorite solution. Food, which may have been contaminated, should be destroyed.

Outbreak Control: Prolonged environmental contamination would not be expected following release of aerosolized SEB.

TRICOTHECENE MYCOTOXICOSIS [T-2 MYCOTOXINS] – (TOXIN)

Isolation and Decontamination for Healthcare Workers: Outer clothing should be removed and exposed skin decontaminated with soap and water. Eye exposure should be treated with copious saline irrigation. Secondary aerosols are not a hazard; however, contact with contaminated skin and clothing can produce secondary dermal exposures. Contact Precautions are warranted until decontamination is accomplished. Then, Standard Precautions are recommended for healthcare workers. Environmental decontamination requires the use of a hypochlorite solution under alkaline conditions such as 1% sodium hypochlorite and 0.1M NaOH with 1 hour contact time.

Decontamination and Isolation: Clothing of T-2 victims should be removed and treated (exposed to 5% hypochlorite for 6-10 hours) or destroyed. Skin may be decontaminated with soap and water. Eye exposure should be managed with copious saline irrigation. Isolation is not required. Instruments and surfaces should be decontaminated by heating to 500°F (260°C) for 30 minutes or by brief exposure to 1N NaOH. Standard disinfectants effective against most other BW agents are often inadequate to inactivate the very stable mycotoxins.

Outbreak Control: Mycotoxin-induced disease is not contagious, but the stability of the toxins in the presence of heat and ultraviolet light make for the possibility of persistence in the environment following release.

TULAREMIA

Isolation and Decontamination for Healthcare Workers: Standard Precautions for healthcare workers. Organisms are relatively easy to render harmless by mild heat (131°F [55°C] for 10 minutes) and standard disinfectants.

Decontamination and Isolation: Tularemia is not transmitted person-to-person via the aerosol route, and infected persons should be managed with secretion and drainage precautions. Heat and common disinfectants (such as 0.5% hypochlorite) will readily kill F. tularensis organisms.

Outbreak Control: Following intentional release of F. tularensis in a given area, it is possible that local fauna, especially rabbits and squirrels, will acquire disease, setting up an enzootic mammal-arthropod cycle. Persons entering such an area should avoid skinning and eating meat from such animals. Water supplies and grain in such areas might likewise become contaminated, and should be boiled or cooked before consumption. Organisms contaminating soils are unlikely to survive for significant periods of time and present little hazard.

VENEZUELAN EQUINE ENCEPHALITIS

Isolation and Decontamination for Healthcare Workers: Patient isolation and quarantine is not required. Standard Precautions augmented with vector control while the patient is febrile. There is no evidence of direct human-to-human or horse-to-human transmission. The virus can be destroyed by heat (176°F [80°C] for 30 minutes) and standard disinfectants.

Decontamination and Isolation: Universal precautions should be practiced when dealing with VEE patients. Virus may be destroyed by heat (176°F [80°C] for 30 minutes) and by ordinary disinfectants (such as 0.5% hypochlorite).

Outbreak Control: Humans are infectious for mosquitoes for at least 72 hours after the onset of symptoms. Efforts at mosquito control thus become paramount to the prevention of secondary VEE cases following intentional or natural VEE outbreaks. In the event of intentional release of VEE virus by belligerents, the potential would be high for the development of an equine epizootic if the proper mosquito vector were present; veterinary vaccination would be useful in such circumstances.

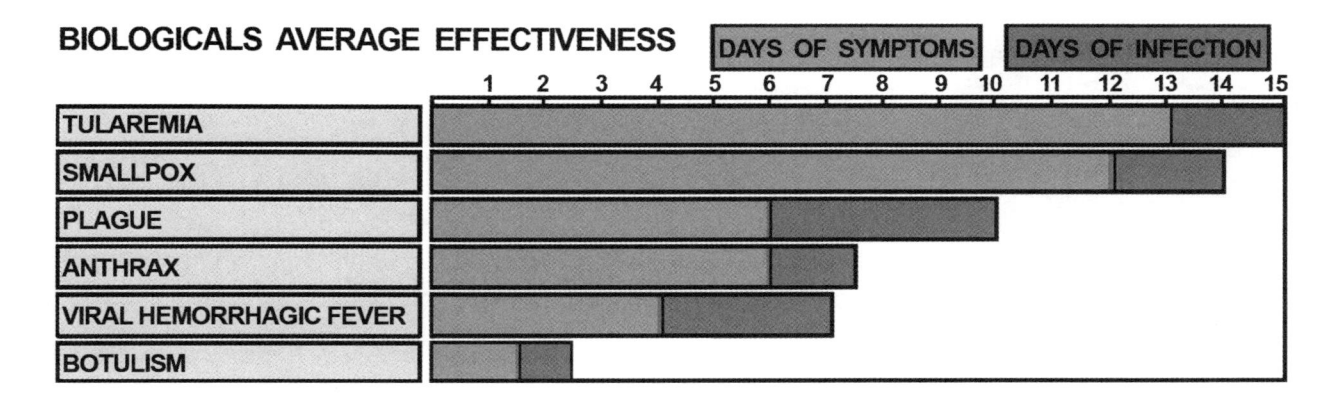

BIOLOGICALS AVERAGE EFFECTIVENESS

Disease	Days of Symptoms	Days of Infection
TULAREMIA	1–13	13–15
SMALLPOX	1–12	12–14
PLAGUE	1–6	6–10
ANTHRAX	1–5	5–7
VIRAL HEMORRHAGIC FEVER	1–3	3–5
BOTULISM	1	1–2

VIRAL HEMORRHAGIC FEVERS

Isolation and Decontamination: Contact isolation, with the addition of a surgical mask and eye protection for those coming within three feet of the patient, is indicated for suspected or proven Lassa fever, CCHF, or filovirus infections. Respiratory protection should be upgraded to airborne isolation, including the use of a fit-tested HEPA filtered respirator, a battery powered air purifying respirator, or a positive pressure supplied air respirator, if patients with the above conditions have prominent cough, vomiting, diarrhea, or hemorrhage. Decontamination is accomplished with hypochlorite or phenolic disinfectants.[113]

Chapter 43: Sheltering in Place

SEPARATING FACT FROM FICTION

Contrary to some information, you CAN make duct tape and plastic sheeting work for you with certain provisos. Studies performed at Oak Ridge National Laboratory conclude that "Duct tape and plastic sheeting (polyethylene) were chosen because of their ability to effectively reduce infiltration and for their resistance to permeation from chemical warfare agents."[114]

Three issues presented warning against constructing your own shelter have been put forth primarily by those selling commercial products. These three objections pointed to can be overcome:

OBJECTION 1) It's very difficult to create a perfectly sealed room using these materials, especially if the work is done hurriedly.
RESPONSE: Construct safe room in advance and check for leaks by the instructions provided. It is critical you make a full, tight seal with the duct tape, making certain all areas are completely pressed down.

OBJECTION 2) Normal plastic sheeting may not be resistant to certain gasses.
RESPONSE: Use the heaviest grades – 10 mil **or** 6 mil plastic sheeting *folded double*.

Tests of plastic sheeting permeability were conducted at the Chemical Defense Establishment in Porton Down, England in 1970; and more recently at Oak Ridge, TN., in the late 1980s and again at Edgewood, MD in the mid-1990's. Edgewood had a vested interest in reliable information since it housed a massive chemical weapons depot. It closed after successfully destroying the last of its stockpile in December 2006.

Tests involved single-family homes. Trials measured the air exchange for the whole house, the expedient room (mainly bathrooms) with a towel against the door, and the bathroom fully taped and sealed by a household member. Materials used included duct tape, flexible insulation cord, and plastic sheeting.

The data showed that at a thickness of 10 mil or greater, the plastic sheeting provided a good barrier for withstanding liquid (chemical) agent challenges.

Adding an air filtration system works by filtering out agents from piped in air at a rate faster than any gases can penetrate the sheeting. The plastic sheeting alone should keep out most gases, but this overpressure system blocks them from entering. This is same principle applied in commercial units.

OBJECTION 3) Even if a room could be thoroughly sealed, the air supply inside would be limited.
RESPONSE: No matter how you stack it, if you're going to build or buy a safe room, you *must* install a filtration system. If you don't, the choice is either carbon dioxide poisoning or be forced to step outside the safe room for air. Either option could lead to unpleasant results and defeats the point of building a safe room. This will be discussed later in detail.

Constructing your own safe room is the most cost-efficient method. A ballpark figure is about $1560 – $1400 filtration; $60 6mil sheeting, duct tape and foam sealant; $100 camping potty. The other items needed like food and water are things you would already be storing and not an additional cost.

DO IT SAFELY

Shelters and additional protective measures must be made *in advance* of an anticipated threat. Not only does it take a fair amount of time to construct properly, which will be explained below, but also fear and apprehension tend to make us clumsy and sloppy. If a person were rushed to build quickly, it would be easy to leave some areas unchecked for leaks and miss points of entry.

A means of adding oxygen to the room is A MUST while filtering out harmful agents.

This is the biggest area where Homeland Security and Ready.gov fell down in their instructions to the populace. Letting people think they have enough oxygen to survive for any length of time in an airtight plastic tent is both misleading and dangerous.

Furthermore, their initial vague instructions to purchase duct tape and plastic, as well as unspecified emergency supplies, was little help and it put people off.

Information supplied was just enough to further raise fear levels with no comfort in specifics. *What do I do with the duct tape and how do I do it? What and how much should go into emergency kits? How will I go to the toilet?* The only no-brainer information was "get a radio". Now they've gotten more specific on supplies, but still don't address the oxygen issue.

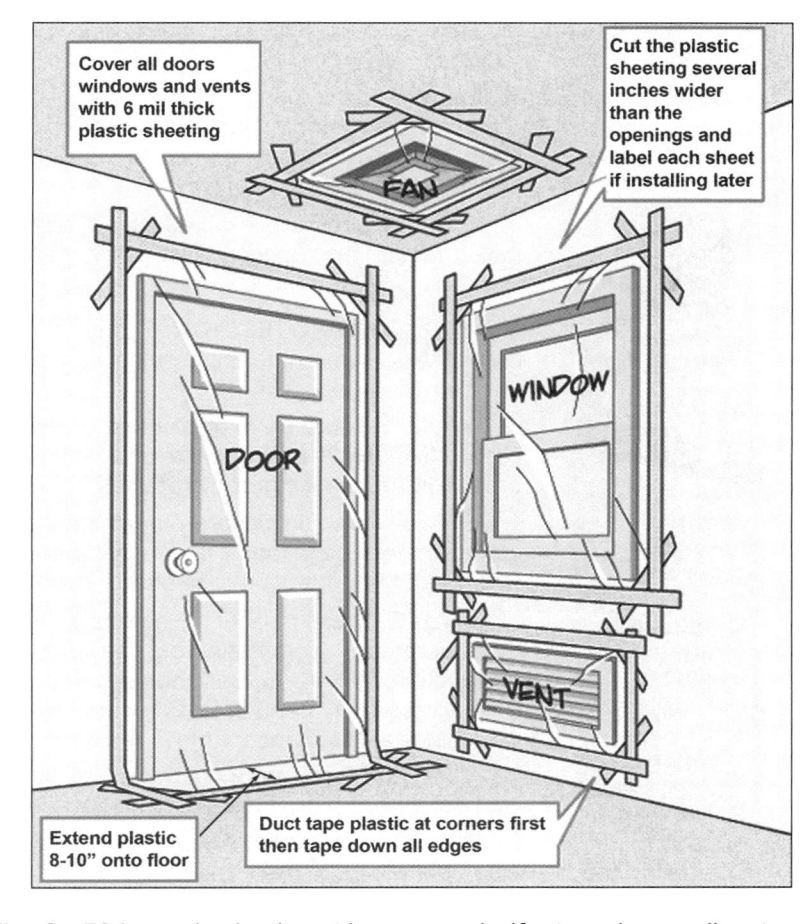

Additionally, asking folks to set aside supplies for 72 hours is simply not long enough. If a terrorism or disaster scenario is severe, stores, banks, utilities and services – in other words – normal life, may be on hold for several weeks. **Every household should have a *minimum* of 6 months provisions.** More is better up to a point.

This is not to indicate you will have to shelter in place that long, but services could be disrupted for extended periods.

What if smallpox comes to your neighborhood? Will you want to venture down to the local store? That's providing the stores even *have* food. Should an area become contaminated, no one is coming for a visit, not even dedicated truckers who bring fresh milk, produce and meat. (See Chapter 64 on Pandemics.)

With many commercial safety shelters costing $3000-$13,000 and more, here is a practical guide for sheltering in place. Please keep in mind this will NOT guarantee 100% safety, but it will considerably reduce the dangers of bio-chemical weapons and nuclear fallout. It will NOT protect you from nuclear radiation, just the blast particles.

It's unfortunate that a light duty, aboveground shelter like this simply won't work for all scenarios. However, if folks build or install a top shelf commercial blast shelter, it would certainly protect people from most challenges unless they are at ground zero.

MAKING THE SHELTER

PICK A ROOM with the least number of windows for your shelter area. Because chemical agents are generally heavier than air, choose a room *above ground level*, if possible, rather than a basement. This is exactly opposite in preparing for nuclear blasts and tornados.

CHECK FOR HOLES. Before beginning, make certain the chosen room doesn't have hidden pitfalls. You may need to the remove the carpet or other flooring to check for lurking holes. Examine the ceiling to make sure it isn't constructed with porous materials. Vinyl wallpaper and similar wall coverings may actually contribute to barrier protection.

SEAL EVERY OPENING. The idea is to completely seal ALL openings of your safe room – any place where air can leak inside, down to the last pin prick. Tape windows, door and other openings with duct tape, **every single crack and crevice**. Take time to fill all cracks and crevices with foam sealant. Pay special attention to door and window frames and vents.

Dap's newer latex foam sealant Daptex Plus meets American Architectural Manufacturers Association (AAMA) standards for windows and doors regarding resistance to air and water infiltration. Unlike polyurethane foam, this latex version is user-friendlier. It cleans easily from surfaces or skin with soap and water.

Seal crevices around wall switch plates and outlets. (Remember, these measures also lower heating and cooling bills, so it's a win-win!)

WINDOW PROTECTION. From inside your home, run 6-mil plastic sheeting* beyond the window frame extending onto the wall, and tape or staple it to the drywall. (See graphic on preceding page.)

While it would be nice to have a view outside, consider the likelihood a window could break. If there is any chance this could happen, nail plywood to the window's exterior. A breach in the plastic greatly reduces the effectiveness of these protective measures.

Plywood should be pre-cut with nails taped to the wood and ready to go up. Keep it stored in your safe room. It will only take a couple of minutes to install yet keep the window clear until the protection is needed.

*__NOTE__: Plastic sheeting comes in varying weights; 1, 2, 4 and 6-mil thicknesses are most common. 10-mil sheeting may have to be specially ordered. A 10'x100' roll of 4 mil generally runs $40-45, depending on supplier; a 10'x100' roll of 6 mil costs around $52-58. 6-mil is generally used in construction as a vapor barrier and offers the **best protection** and greatest tear-resistance. This is really important.

One- and 2-mil are too flimsy; 4-mil is too thin unless double or triple folded. Using these lightweight products runs the risk of chemicals permeating the material and they rip too easily. Stick to thicker sheeting.

Labeling the sheeting only needs to be done if the plastic is to be put up at a later date.

NOTE: When in your safe room, wear soft-soled shoes only

LOOKING FOR LEAKS IN ALL THE RIGHT PLACES

The rest of your home can serve as a "pre-filter" for your safe room. For maximum effectiveness, similarly seal off all windows, doors, garage and pet doors, fireplace dampers, attic fans, furnaces, swamp coolers, air conditioner units, dryer vents and switch plates to restrict all potential sources of infiltration. Replace ALL plain switch plates with foam-backed switch plates. This also adds to your home's insulation factor.

If you ever find mice or bugs in your home that didn't come from the grocery store (like in mesh potato sacks) or flew in through the door, you've got holes or cracks or leaks some place.

Before assuming tight seals have been achieved, check for leaks with a punk stick or stick of incense. Even a cigarette or cigar would work. You just need something that produces a steady stream of smoke. Place it next to all areas around doors, windows and electrical fixtures, outlet covers, light switches, ceiling and wall lamps and ceiling fans. Note the behavior and direction of the smoke stream to determine leaks. Seal with duct tape or sealing foam.

Having appropriate personal protective equipment, including a gas mask (see what to look for when buying a gas mask and filter, Gas Mask and Filter Comparison Charts) with a HEPA or NATO equivalent filter for each person in your safe shelter will help ensure your safety if you either have to temporarily leave your shelter, or if symptoms develop indicating possible infiltration of contaminants.

A BREATH OF FRESH AIR

Fresh filtered air is essential if you're required to stay in your safe place for more than a few hours.

Chemical agents dissipate more quickly during summer with strong sunlight. Other factors affecting their breakdown are wind, rainfall and time. The chart to the bottom right shows averages, but since variables can influence their "staying power", it's impossible to pinpoint how long one must shelter. You will be advised on your radio when it is safe.

If you are instructed to stay in your safe place for several days, there is the problem of bringing in needed oxygen. This is something Homeland Security did NOT discuss giving people a false picture that there's an easy "fix". The only reason we can see for this obvious oversight is that safe rooms with duct tape and plastic are presumed to leak air if not properly constructed. That's good if you need oxygen. However, leaking contaminated air could be deadly. So while it is vital you make your safe shelter positively airtight, another issue has been raised. We need air for life.

HOW MUCH OXYGEN DO WE NEED?

Since an average 7½x10x10 room would only be viable for a group of four adults under stress for 2½ hours – *tops* – one has to look at pumping fresh air into the room. When you breathe the same air in the room for too long it becomes toxic. Carbon dioxide gas builds up from your exhaled breath.

NASA, NOAA, the US Navy (submariner's manual) and the American Society of Heating, Refrigerating, and Air-Conditioning Engineers (ASHRAE) have made a number of studies. Data from these sources have been used to compile the next table, which shows how much filtered air and how much power you will need to provide that air for a given time (assuming you have no power except one fully charged car battery).

Studies conclude that the average, reasonably calm adult requires a minimum of 5 cubic feet of fresh air every minute. However, when people are under stress this demand can become as high as three times that much! This table is based upon these two extremes, assumes the sealed room measures 7½x10x10 feet (2.3x3x3m) and that the pump is ~$\frac{1}{5}$ hp or 135watt.

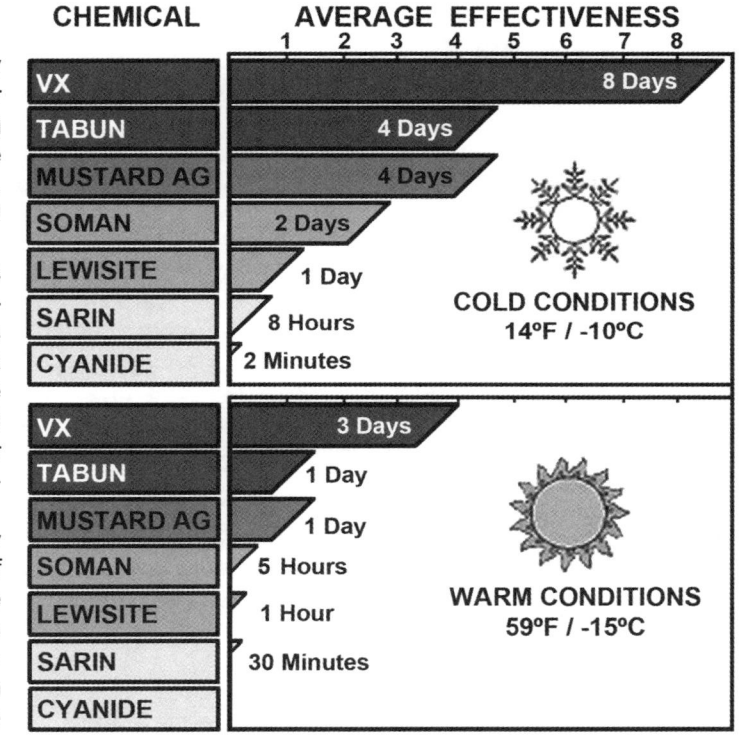

The bottom line shows the necessity of an air pump and HEPA filter if the safe room will be used for longer than a couple of hours. It's the same dilemma astronauts face when they are cooped up in that tiny spacecraft.

The following tables show how quickly you'd run out of oxygen in a 7½x10x10 room.

CHEMICAL — AVERAGE EFFECTIVENESS

COLD CONDITIONS — 14°F / -10°C

CHEMICAL	Effectiveness
VX	8 Days
TABUN	4 Days
MUSTARD AG	4 Days
SOMAN	2 Days
LEWISITE	1 Day
SARIN	8 Hours
CYANIDE	2 Minutes

WARM CONDITIONS — 59°F / -15°C

CHEMICAL	Effectiveness
VX	3 Days
TABUN	1 Day
MUSTARD AG	1 Day
SOMAN	5 Hours
LEWISITE	1 Hour
SARIN	30 Minutes
CYANIDE	

PEOPLE RESTING – BASED ON A 1/5HP OR 135WATT PUMP

Room Size in feet	Room Air Volume in cu. ft	Room Air Volume in m3	No. of People	Min. Air Volume Req.	12v 100, amp-hr battery continuous run, it will last	Running 12v, 100 amp-hr battery with On/Off cycle			No battery. Continual Hand Pumping Strokes/ min. for enough air
						On	Off	Bat. Life	
7½x10x10	750	21	4	10 cfm	7.00 hr	30min	75 min	27 hr	18
7½x10x10	750	21	2	5 cfm	7.00 hr	30min	2½ hr	46 hr	9
7½x10x10	750	21	1	2½ cfm	7.00 hr	30min	5 hr	85 hr	5

Room Size in feet	Room Air Volume in cu. ft.	Room Air Volume in m3	No. of People	Min. Air Volume Req.	12v 100, amp-hr battery continuous run, it will last	Running 12v, 100 amp-hr battery with On/Off cycle			No battery. Continual Hand Pumping Strokes/ min. for enough air
PEOPLE STRESSED – BASED ON A 1/5HP OR 135WATT PUMP									
						On	Off	Bat. Life	
7½x10x10	750	21	4	20 cfm	7.00 hr	30min	40 min	17 hr	35
7½x10x10	750	21	2	10 cfm	7.00 hr	30min	75 min	27 hr	18
7½x10x10	750	21	1	5 cfm	7.00 hr	30min	2½ hr	46 hr	9

HOW FILTERS WORK

A good way to ensure proper shelter ventilation is to install a HEPA air filter that is 99.97% efficient at .3 microns like those commonly available in air purifying equipment. These systems can't rely on natural airflows and require an over pressure system – one that pumps filtered air into a room faster than the air can escape.

The filtration unit draws in unfiltered air from outside your safe room through an intake vent.

The air passes through a bank of up to 6 filters certified for the collection of Nuclear, Biological, Chemical toxins or natural contaminants and allergens.

Then, the safe, breathable air is blown into your safe area with just the right force to produce a slight overpressure in the room. This overpressure keeps toxins from migrating into your safe room or bomb shelter from any other entry source. This is the same technology used by the US military to keep soldiers alive in a CBRN environment. To be clear, this does NOT keep out nuclear bombs' radiation; it would filter fallout dust particles.

Look for units that have a back-up power supply. The HEPA filter can be installed directly into your home heating system duct work. In installing the filter, be sure to follow the manufacturer's design velocity recommendations and ensure a good seal around the filter to avoid bypassing pollutants. Installation of a simple pre-filter will extend the life of your HEPA filter.

One source for these systems is American Safe Room, which range from $1370-1870. This is a good starting point, but we encourage you to make price and product comparisons. Even the smallest unit will supply enough filtered air for 8 adults in an 8x14½ x14½ room or approximately 1700 cu. ft.

You can choose an appropriate HEPA pumping system from this URL: **www.americansaferoom.com/** as well as numerous other dealers.

HYGIENE

Something that mustn't be overlooked is providing temporary toilet facilities. Don't be caught with the unhappy choice between exposing yourself to contaminants if using a bathroom outside your safe room and contending with a full bladder. It's one of Murphy's Laws. The more stressed you are, the more often you need to go.

One easy solution is using a 5-gallon bucket lined with a heavy duty trash sack – your basic toilet bucket. Place a toilet seat on top of the bucket during use. After use, remove the seat, sprinkle a little Clorox on the contents to keep down the germs and odor. Seal it with the pail's lid. This should keep odor to a minimum.

Another idea is a portable "camping" potty. This option might work better than a toilet bucket for families with elderly, handicapped or little children. Portable toilets are more solid than the bucket type toilet with a molded seat for maximum comfort. To control odor, add liquid or crystal deodorants.

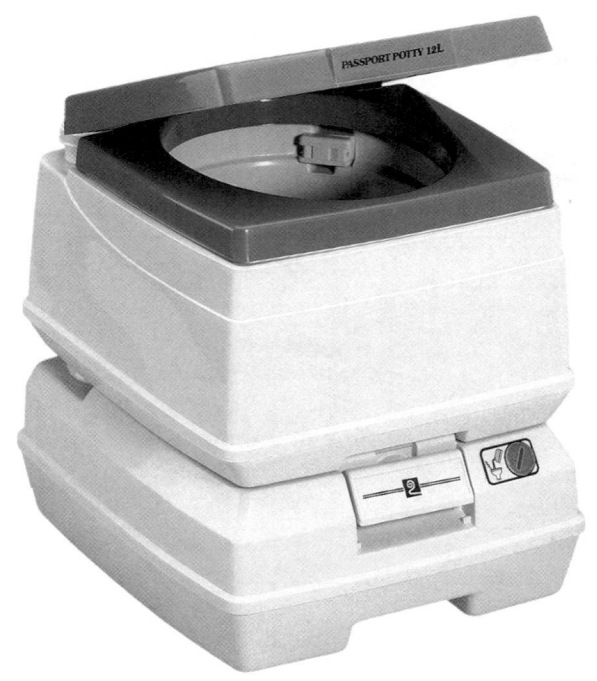

Camping toilets are constructed of high-density polyethylene, are completely self-contained and compact in size and easy to clean. Thetford offers four different sizes. The smallest unit #135 holds 2.6 gal. (10L) fresh water and 2.6 gal. (10L) waste while the largest, Campa Potti XG, holds 4 gal. (15L) fresh water and 5.5 gal. (21L) waste. The difference in cost is only about $10-20 per model, but size could be an important consideration. #135 measures 15-1/16"L x 13-9/16"W x 12⅛"H and the Campa XG measures 16½"L x 15"W x 16½"H.

Thetford manufactures two sizes in between these, and all but the smallest model hold 4 gallons of water. The major difference if the amount of waste storage. With more storage, size increases. Their fifth model, #465, is the same dimensions as the Campa XG, but it has a battery operated flush instead of using a bellows. Depending on how much you plan to use it, for the added $50 for a battery, the bellows work easily. Costs range from $70 - $200, depending on model and retailer. Check Cabela's **www.cabelas.com**, Amazon **www.amazon.com**, Camping World **www.campingworld.com** and Overton's **www.overtons.com**.

Another line worth considering is from Sanitation Equipment: the Visa 248 and Visa 268. Camping potties function pretty much the same and are built very similarly except this model claims an extra deep bowl, which the company labels as "added comfort". It could more accurately be described as 'better hygiene' since splash back is not desirable. The Visa 248 holds 3.7 gallons fresh water and 4.8 gallons of waste and the #268's holding tank stores 6.3 gallons. List price: for the #248 - $115 and #268 - $130. Sources include Amazon **www.amazon.com**, and Mobile Commode **mobilecommode.com**. For similar products in Australia, see Tentworld **www.tentworld.com.au** and BP Camping **www.bpcamping.com.au**.

For more suggestions on portable and makeshift toilets, see Chapter 36.

BASHFUL BODIES

If you simply can't make your bowels or bladder function without complete privacy, bring into your safe room an over-sized cardboard box. One that held a clothes dryer or washer is ideal. Another option is a mover's wardrobe box. Cut out one side for the "entrance" and turn the cut out portion toward the wall away from everyone else. Set the 5 gallon bucket or porta potty inside and pretend you're on a desert island! A can of Lysol is effective against cold/flu germs and odors, and is less oppressive than some sickeningly sweet air fresheners.

If infants are a part of the family, be sure to include a diaper pail for odor and germ control.

4-LEGGED KIDS

If pets are a close part of your family like Seismo and Taco, it's a given they go into the safe room too. They'll need food, water, their regular bed or blanket – something that gives them a sense of "OK" and a bathroom. Animals are quick to pick up on human stress and will follow suit. It's clever to provide them with toys or something to occupy their time.

Should you debate whether or not to include them, consider how much more stressed you'll be wondering how they're faring. Secondly, pets have positive, calming, therapeutic effects on their human counterparts and can help distract children. Third, it's the morally right thing to do.

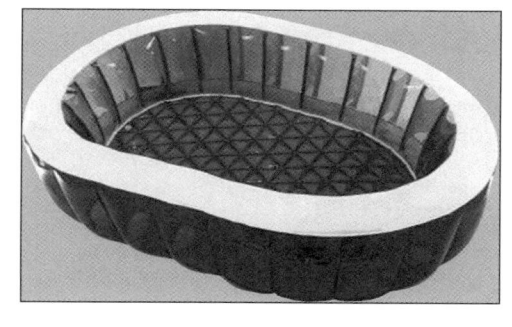

Make sure you provide animals with a litter box or newspaper, a place where they can relieve themselves. They have to know it's OK, given the circumstance.

One very tidy solution for corralling pet urine and far-flung litter is to set up a child's inflatable swimming pool. Place it into the safe shelter lined with newspaper, or set the litter box inside. (Make sure kitty doesn't claw holes in the pool.) After use, scoop up the soiled newspaper or litter and deposit into garbage bags. Be sure to praise your pet for using his new facility since this will undoubtedly be a new deal! Kiddie pools measuring 12x47" (30x119cm) can be purchased for as little as $12.

THE REST OF THE HOUSE

Next, seal off floor and wall openings such as laundry chutes and heating/cooling ducts, if they aren't part of a specially prepared HEPA ventilation system. If your safe room is the bathroom, seal the exhaust fan, sink drains (don't forget the overflow at the top rim on the side closest to you), the stopper and bathtub drains.

Doors are a special problem because it's harder to eliminate all air leaks. Especially here it would be a good idea to use 6 mil plastic sheeting, double folded. Check for leaks between the wood frame and drywall and fill with caulk. Seal off the space between the door, and its frame and hinges, with duct tape before covering with plastic sheeting.

Cover the door and framework with the double-folded plastic. Tape or staple onto the drywall above the door as suggested for windows. Before trimming the bottom, leave an extra 8-10" of plastic. You want this excess to extend below the door to cover the area just beneath the door and onto the floor. During an emergency, before entering, soak a towel with baking soda dissolved in water. Wring out the towel. When inside, force the wet towel into the space between bottom of the door and the floor. Make sure there are no gaps! Then roll the 8-10" of plastic down over the towel and secure to the floor in front of the door.

Alternatively, plastic sheeting can be used to completely line your safe area. If stapled in place, make sure the staple holes are securely taped.

COMMERICAL SAFE ROOM

One feature to consider in purchasing a safe room is the ability to see out. Some products use blue plastic and if anyone has the tendency toward claustrophobia, it will only enhance the stress factor.

This expandable Cabinet Shelter from Noah's Ark (pictured) is a clever concept. The best part is that it sets up in only two minutes by two people. (This does not take into account that once opened out; you'd need to stock your emergency supplies, potty, water, food, etc. inside.). When not in use, it folds shut into either a cherry, oak or pine-finished cabinet. Prices start at $8000 and vary according to size and cabinetry and finish options.

Four models accommodate 5 to 25 people. Product information states the Noah's Ark shelter provides an unmatched level of protection. Use this chart to determine what size unit fits your needs.

RAINBOW TENT

For the more economically minded, look at the Rainbow Tent or the Israeli Tent as it was originally named for its country of origin. This company has already sold over 1 million units.

The Rainbow 36A Protection System draws air in from outside the tent through a special filter that purifies the air and feeds it in to the interior. Its blower unit creates an overpressure environment, preventing the penetration of outside gases. This also relieves the occupants from wearing gas masks and protective clothing, enabling a safe and comfortable stay.

NOAH'S ARK EXPANDABLE CABINET				
Model	2023	2040	3540	3570
Max # persons	5	8	14	25
Cabinet width (ft)	7.5	7.5	12.5	12.5
Cabinet depth closed (ft)	2.1	2.1	3.0	3.0
Cabinet height (ft)	7.2	7.2	7.5	7.5
Cabinet depth open (ft)	9.7	15.3	16.1	25.9
Cabinet depth – door open (ft)	12.3	17.9	18.7	28.5
Filtered air supply cu. ft./min.	21	106	106	200

The specially designed Chemical, Biological and Nuclear particulate resistant tent is manufactured with 3 layers of polyethylene and polyamide laminates. Its resistance to gases exceeds military standards.

The Rainbow36A System is based upon over 20 years of developed technology and is built to the world's highest standards. The patented 3-stage filtration system features a pre-filter, a HEPA filter and an activated carbon filter exceeding NATO Standards. Over 1000 of these units are presently being sold every week and NATO Armed Forces are presently using it.

The Rainbow tent is portable and easily stored. It also can be set up and functioning in less than 5 minutes by one person.

The system operates from a standard AC power source (wall outlet) with an integrated battery back up in case of a power failure. The battery will run the system for up to 10 hours, recharging as soon as the system is reconnected to live AC power source. (It takes about 48 hours for the back-up battery to attain full charge.) The second back up is a Manual Blower that can be used alternatively or in cases of a discharged battery.

It's OSHA-approved, and the electrical system has been tested and approved to the UL Standards by TUV in the USA. Depending on the size Rainbow Tent you choose and where you buy it prices start at $3000.

TO USE

Step 1 Choose a suitable place for the tent. The tent's zippered entrance has to be accessible, and should be close to the door or to a ventilated area. Installation hooks must be mounted on the ceiling.

Step 2 Open the box of the tent in the place you want to build it up. Unfold the tent flat and stretch the tent so the four corners are exactly under the hooks mounted in the ceiling, and the opening of the tent (zipper) is on the accessible side.

Step 3 Hang the carabineer hooks at the ends of the ropes mounted in the ceiling. Tension the ropes by adjusting disc until the tent stands upright. Connect the power cord from the tent to the nearby receptacle.

Step 4 Connect the flexible hose 16.4' long (5m) to the plastic console (tub) from outside. The other end of the hose should reach out from the door to the next room.

Step 5 Take into the tent all components of the NBC-filtration-system (electrical blower, hand blower, filter and the short flexible hose). All persons to be protected should now enter the tent. All necessary items for prolonged stay should be brought into the tent.

Step 6 CLOSE THE ZIPPER Connect the NBC-filter to the plastic console. Connect filter and electrical blower together by means of the short flexible hose. Plug the cable of the blower in to the socket of the extension cord and switch on the system. Within 15 minutes the tent will be inflated with purified air.

LAST THOUGHTS

While waiting for the all-clear, the time spent in your safe room will pass more quickly if you have games, books, or something else that takes your mind off the circumstances. A Bible is also comforting.

For the remainder of the items to stock in your safe room, see 72-hour kit – at Home. Leave this assembled kit in your safe room. It's one less thing off your mind.

When supplying heat, cooling or light to your safe room, it should be battery-powered. Candles are not only a fire hazard, but they use precious oxygen.

Radios and shortwave will likely be your best source of information though a TV, loudspeakers on roving official vehicles or phones might provide valuable information. If there is doubt an all-clear has been sounded, stay in your shelter until you are positive it is safe.

Chapter 44: Nuclear Emergencies – What To Expect

CUBAN MISSILE CRISIS REVISITED

Isn't it extraordinary given the world's collective genius that we're still dealing with this same issue: *are we going to annihilate ourselves?* With a global list of great achievements and remarkable discoveries, humanity should have progressed beyond this point. However, considering the Book of Revelation refers to "war in the heavens", why should we think we could do better?

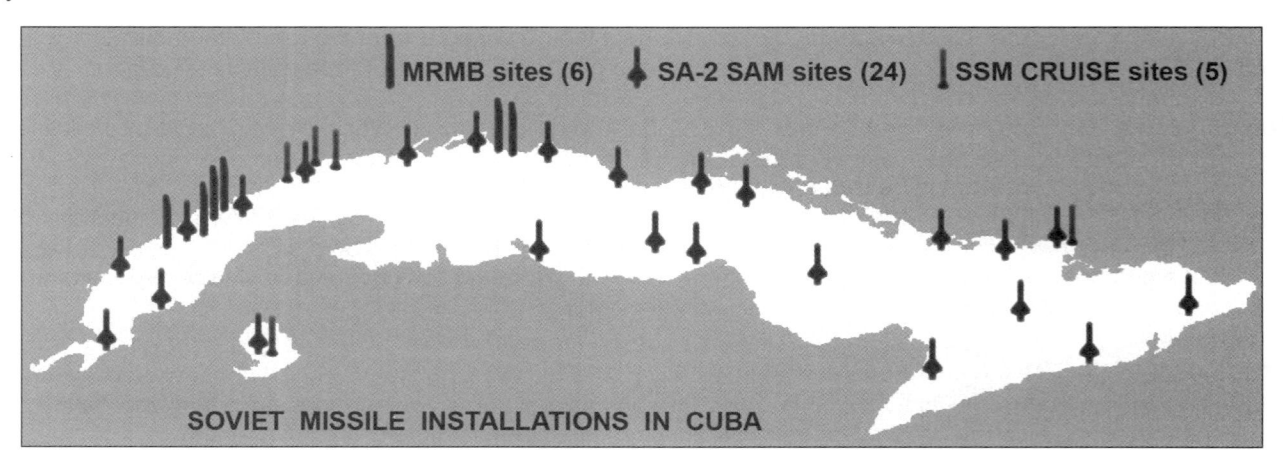

SOVIET MISSILE INSTALLATIONS IN CUBA
MRMB sites (6) · SA-2 SAM sites (24) · SSM CRUISE sites (5)

School kids from the 50s and 60s recall "duck and cover" drills. Once every few months this exercise was mandated. It beggars the imagination to think hiding under wooden desks would help. While the drill seemed like one more stupid school task, our minds tiptoed around an unnerving thought: *the Commies are going to nuke us.*

Fear coalesced during 14 days in 1962. The Cuban Missile Crisis nearly ignited nuclear war between the United States and Russia. Soviet troops had positioned nuclear missiles in Cuba, just 90 miles off Florida's coast. Some 35 missiles aimed to take a piece of prime real estate and we were just 5 minutes away from catastrophe. U.S. armed forces hovered at Defcon 2 – the highest state before imminent or an on-going attack. Nukes were officially authorized.

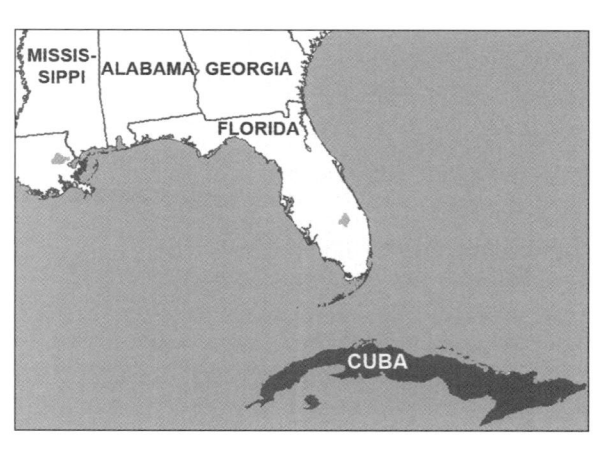

Soviet field commanders stationed in Cuba were likewise authorized to use tactical nukes if invaded by America. The fate of millions hinged on two men, President John F. Kennedy and Premier Nikita Khrushchev, reaching compromise.

On October 27, 1962, Kennedy sent Khrushchev a pivotal communiqué. It promised he would issue a statement that the U.S. would not invade Cuba IF Khrushchev removed the missiles from Cuba. The next day Khrushchev announced over Radio Moscow their agreement to comply ending the crisis.

However, "Nuclear catastrophe was hanging by a thread ... and we weren't counting days or hours, but minutes." — Soviet General and Army Chief of Operations, Anatoly Gribkov.[115]

AND NOW A WORD FROM OUR PRESIDENT

"My Fellow Americans:

"Nuclear weapons and the possibility of nuclear war are facts of life we cannot ignore today. I do not believe that war can solve any of the problems facing the world today. But the decision is not ours alone.

"The government is moving to improve the protection afforded you in your communities through civil defense. We have begun, and will be continuing throughout the next year and a half, a survey of all public buildings with fallout shelter potential, and the marking of those with adequate shelter for 50 persons or more. We are providing

fallout shelter in new and in some existing federal buildings. We are stocking these shelters with one week's food and medical supplies and two weeks' water supply for the shelter occupants. In addition, I have recommended to the Congress the establishment of food reserves in centers around the country where they might be needed following an attack. Finally, we are developing improved warning systems which will make it possible to sound attack warning on buzzers right in your homes and places of business.

"More comprehensive measures than these lie ahead, but they cannot be brought to completion in the immediate future. In the meantime there is much that you can do to protect yourself – and in doing so strengthen your nation.

"I urge you to read and consider seriously the contents in this issue of LIFE. The security of our country and the peace of the world are the objectives of our policy. But in these dangerous days when both these objectives are threatened we must prepare for all eventualities. The ability to survive coupled with the will to do so therefore are essential to our country."[116]

Sound familiar? Probably not. That was a message from President John F. Kennedy, September 7, 1961 printed in *Life* Magazine that same month. If we were adult enough to hear warnings then, why not now?

PRESENT DAY

It has taken us a little over four decades, but once again the world is in a precarious position. Since then the nuclear club has expanded considerably with countries periodically threatening to launch one of their bargaining chips. In the hands of unstable countries like North Korea or unpredictable nations like Iran, Pakistan, China and Russia, it's a frightening picture. Terrorists claim they, too, have weapons of mass destruction. Gone are the post-cold war days of relative security into a new, uncertain scenario.

With these growing threats in mind, Cham E. Dallas, director of the Institute for Health Management and Mass Destruction Defense at the University of Georgia, calls a nuclear attack against America "inevitable". He also stated after the Senate hearings where he testified on this present-day threat, "These people (nuke attack victims) are going to be on their own. There's no white horse to ride to the rescue."[117]

THE NEED TO PROTECT YOURSELF

Experience teaches us that when the government makes blatant warnings, it truly needs to be heeded. Officials are always reticent to issue warnings too loudly. Look how they tiptoed around terrorism for fear of causing panic and impair the recovering economy.

Simple yet strong warnings are given to the public to provide adequate shelter for themselves. This admonition is now openly stated for those looking for this type information. People who aren't inclined to prepare won't look into shelter until too late. No harm has been done keeping the waters still and peaceful. With just a "quiet" warning, those snoozing will continue to saw logs and those who want to protect their families have the knowledge to do so. Incidentally, this warning in FEMA's 2002 *Are You Ready Guide* was "sanitized" from the current edition. It must have been too controversial…

> *Learn how to build a Temporary fallout shelter to protect yourself from radioactive fallout even if you do not live near a potential nuclear target.* –
> FEMA's 2002 Are You Ready: A Guide to Citizen Preparedness, page 93.

Brochures published by FEMA and Ready.gov state pretty clearly that it's up to us to provide our own shelter protection, but specifics are missing. That's clearly worse than no warning since it instills fear without giving adequate solutions. Take for example Ready.gov's completely useless "safety information":

"*** Shielding**: If you have a thick shield between yourself and the radioactive materials more of the radiation will be absorbed, and you will be exposed to less. *How thick should the shield be? Made of what?*

* **Distance**: The farther away you are away from the blast and the fallout the lower your exposure. *No brainer.*

* **Time**: Minimizing time spent exposed will also reduce your risk. *Double duh.*"[118] (Italicized comments are the author's and not part of Ready.gov.)

JUST WALK AROUND THE CORNER

A piece in *The Washington Post* underscores this assessment quoting a physicist with the Federation of American Scientists:

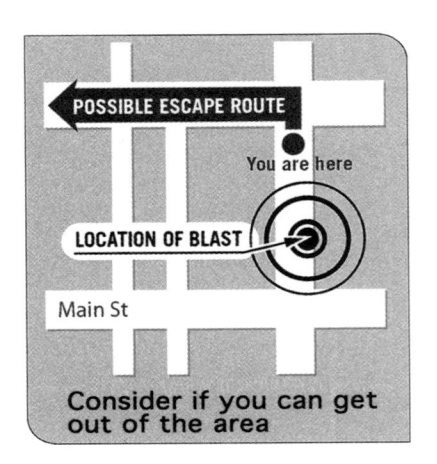

"Take, for example, a Ready.gov graphic showing that someone a city block from a nuclear blast could save his or her life by walking around the corner. The text reads, "Consider if you can get out of the area." Nuclear specialists say that advice is unhelpful because such a blast can destroy everything within a radius of as much as three-quarters of a mile.

"'Ready.gov treats a nuclear weapon in this case as if it were a big truck bomb, which it's not," said Ivan Oelrich, a physicist who studies nuclear weapons for the nonprofit Federation of American Scientists. **"There's no information in Ready.gov that would help your chances" of surviving a nuclear blast or the resulting mushroom cloud**, he said.'[119]

There's one big problem with Ready.gov's advice: you'd be dead.

A city block is usually considered to be about 300 feet. Even being generous and using the longest city block for New York City of 1,056 feet, at one fifth of a mile from ground zero, the result is the same. That person is toast. You wouldn't be walking anywhere and Ready.gov's suggestion to "walk around the block" is nonsense.

GONE IN SECONDS

Further illustrating the ridiculous nature of this "expert" advice are three Department of Energy photos. They detail what happens in an atomic blast *two thirds of a mile* from the detonation site. This house was obliterated in 7 seconds. "Walk around the corner" for safety? Right.

Photo: The atomic blast at Yucca Flat on March 17, 1953 completely destroyed this house 3,500 feet from ground zero. From first to third frame took just 7 seconds. To protect the camera against radiation, it was completely enclosed in a 2-inch lead sheath. The only light source for this photo was from the detonation. (Photo courtesy of National Nuclear Security Administration / Nevada Site Office.)

FIRST, THE GOOD NEWS

When we get past the first two weeks after a nuclear blast, the worst will be over. It's important to know and understand that a nuclear event is *VERY SURVIVABLE*. A horrible myth circulates today that a detonated nuke is the end of life. This is false unless you are at ground zero or very close to it. Most people will be around to share their "I survived the nuke attack" tales. This death-end rumor originated with pro-disarmament, anti-nuke groups and it's been perpetuated by academia, the entertainment industry and news media.

We have one side pushing that nukes equal total annihilation while the other – government prep agencies – pedal fluff solutions. Between these two extremes lies the truth. This is the good news:

> **Radiation's harmfulness decays very quickly. About 90% of the gamma radiation (the most deadly) is gone in 7 hours. Then 90% of the remaining 10% dissipates in 48 hours. After two weeks only 1/1000 (a 10th of 1%) remains. In most areas, after 2-3 days, it would be <u>relatively</u> <u>safe</u> to leave an expedient shelter.**

Dare To Prepare: Chapter 44: Nuclear Emergencies – What To Expect

Here is the same information said another way because it's very important you understand this:

In 7 hours, fallout is only 1/10 as deadly as it was in the first few minutes. After 24 hours, it's only 1/100 as dangerous. In 14 days, radiation is just 1/1000 as deadly as it was in the beginning. This is based on the standard rate of decay – the seven/ten rule. For every seven-fold increase in time, radioactivity decreases ten-fold.

FALLOUT DECAY RATE: RULE OF 7-10		
Hours After Detonation	Rate of Decrease	Level of Radiation
1	–	1,000 R/hr
7	1/10	100 R/hr
49 (2 days)	1/100	10 R/hr
343 (2 weeks)	1/1000	1 R/hr

Without question, it is BEST to **stay sheltered for the full 14 days or come out only briefly after 48 hours.** To know whether or not it's truly safe requires either an all-clear from official sources via the radio OR by using a dosimeter, an instrument that measures radiation. You can make the Kearny Fallout Meter by downloading this file online: **standeyo.com/News_Files/NBC/KFM.rad.meter.pdf.**

WHAT IS THE EFFECT OF A NUCLEAR DETONATION?

If you know what to expect, it takes away part of the angst. When a nuclear device explodes, a large fireball is created. Everything inside this fireball vaporizes, including soil and water, and it's carried upward. This creates the mushroom cloud that we associate with a nuclear explosion.

Radioactive particles mix with the vaporized material inside the mushroom cloud. As this vaporized radioactive material cools, it forms pieces that look like salt or rice or gritty dust. This is fallout.

Fallout can be carried long distances on the wind and end up hundreds of miles from the explosion. Fallout is radioactive and can contaminate anything it lands on, including food and water IF it's not covered. Here is another important piece of information:

Food and water do NOT become radioactive if fallout lands on them.
However, the fallout *particles* are deadly and need to be removed.

Photo: Surviving the unthinkable. . . what if it comes to this? Graphic illustration by Stan Deyo, 2004.

NOTE: This graphic utilizes an actual image of a 15-kiloton bomb named XX12 Grable. It was fired from a 200mm artillery gun – the only time a nuclear weapon was launched from an artillery weapon.[120]

This hypothetical bomb on NYC, with all of its horrific repercussions, was approximately the same size that hit Hiroshima. By today's standards, it's nothing fancy and relatively small. ICBMs today are between 70 and 1,000 times this size. Imagine what devastation they would create.

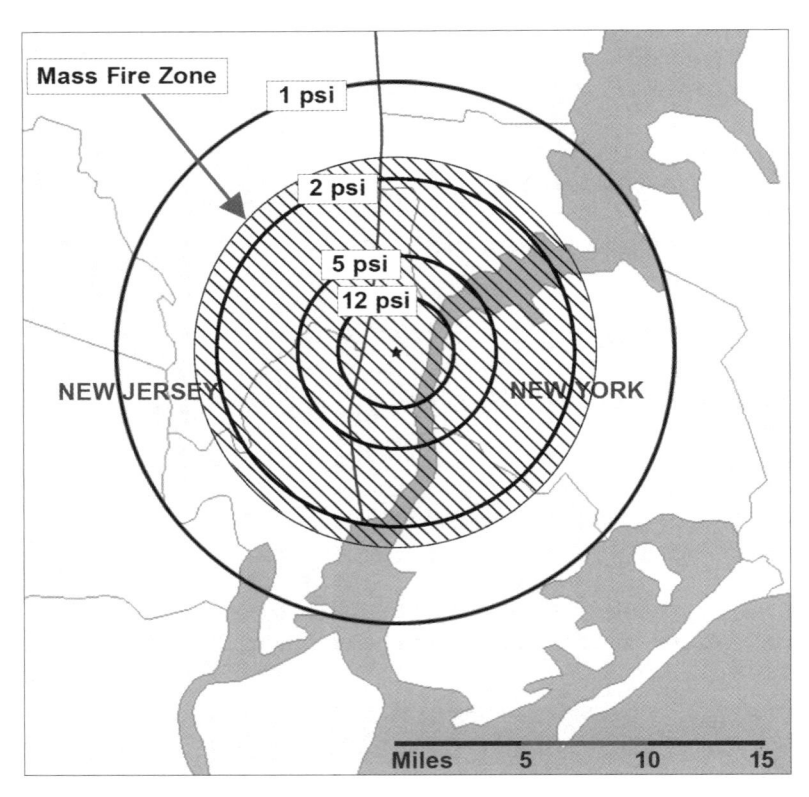

WHAT TO EXPECT

This image illustrates a 1 MT air burst detonated 2000 meters over Central Park in New York City. Shown in stripes is the zone of "superfires". The psi rings mark casualty zones from the blast effects alone based on the model in *The Effects of Nuclear War*.

In 2001 scientists from Natural Resources Defense Council calculated that such a blast would kill about 1.25 million people and injure another 2.65 million using this model.

MIT physicist Dr. Theodore Postol determined that much higher-yield weapons than those detonated at Nagasaki or Hiroshima would create "superfires". They would give birth to unimaginably high heat, noxious smoke and gases, and hurricane-force winds. These superfires would spur the death rate to nearly 100 percent in urban areas.

Dr. Postol's firestorm model means nearly 4½ million people would be killed – 3½ times as many fatalities as the NRDC.[121]

Either way, a direct hit would be grim. Odds are the majority of people wouldn't be in the line of fire. This means we have to know what to do to be safe.

EFFECTS

BLINDING FLASH OF LIGHT: At the moment of detonation, just for a fraction of a second, a blinding blue-white light appears. Don't be temped to watch; this flash can cause temporary blindness. At worst, it destroys the retina and vision is permanently lost. Those who regain their sight do so in about 40 minutes.[122]

In 2006 CBS aired a short-lived TV series on the nuclear threat. *Jericho's* storyline centered on residents in a small Kansas town after 23 nuclear strikes on major U.S. cities. The series opened with a visible nuclear detonation over Denver, Colorado and a young boy watching the rising mushroom cloud. It was worrisome to see this program show someone staring at a blast and suffer no blindness. Considering people sometimes assimilate TV entertainment as *fact*, the show should have gotten key information right.

AIR BLAST: A nuclear explosion produces two shock waves or air blast waves. The first wave carries the most energy as it travels away from the explosion. Depending on the size and distance of the bomb, the first shock wave arrives in about 30 seconds. If you were outside, you'd have just enough time to cover your eyes and drop into a ditch or culvert.

A second lighter, but still deadly wave sucks back over this same path.

The air blast creates horrific winds flattening structures and trees. (See the triple house photo two pages back.) In addition to the blast effects, falling debris and flying glass shards can injure people.

An air blast from a 1 KT detonation could cause 50% mortality from flying glass shards if people are within a 300-yard (275 m) radius. This radius increases to about ⅓ mile (590 m) for a 10 KT bomb.

FIREBALL: The second effect is extreme heat, a fireball, with temperatures into millions of degrees. This extreme heat is can burn material far from the fireball and its intense light can cause blindness. Heat from a 1 KT detonation could cause 50% mortality from burns for people within a half mile radius. For a 10 KT bomb, this radius increases to a little over a mile. Structures between people and the fireball will prevent or reduce heat effects.

INITIAL RADIATION: Radiation is produced in the first minute following detonation. This initial pulse is so intense from even a 1 KT device that its radiation would likely kill 50% of everyone within a ½ mile (790m) radius.

Dare To Prepare: Chapter 44: Nuclear Emergencies – What To Expect

This distance increases to ¾ mile (1200m) for a 10 KT bomb. Individuals in buildings, particularly in the basements, may receive a reduced exposure due to the additional shielding.

GROUND SHOCK: The detonation brings a shock equivalent to a large localized earthquake. It would likely damage buildings, roads, communications, utilities, and other portions of the infrastructure resulting in major disruptions.

FALLOUT: Radiation exposure from fallout would impact mostly downwind from the blast. Roughly 80% of fallout drops during the first 24 hours with the largest, heaviest particles landing closest to ground zero. However changing weather conditions can spread radioactivity and enlarge the area affected.

It's estimated that a 1 KT bomb would form a fallout plume 2½ to 3 miles long and maybe ¼-mile wide within an hour. Anyone exposed would get a lethal dose of radiation.

This distance increases to approximately 6 miles (9600m) for a 10 KT detonation. These distances can be greater or smaller, depending on wind and weather. Individuals in intervening buildings and building basements may get a lesser exposure due to the additional shielding.[123] Snow and rain, especially coming from considerable heights, will accelerate local fallout by forcing it to the ground. Predicting accurate fallout patterns is very difficult and extremely dependent on weather, terrain, bomb design and size.

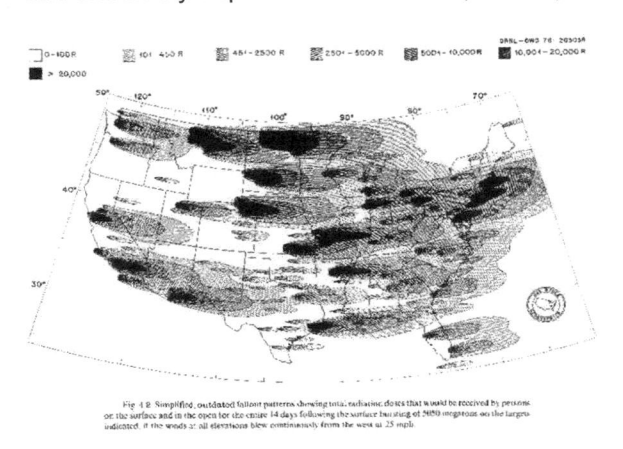

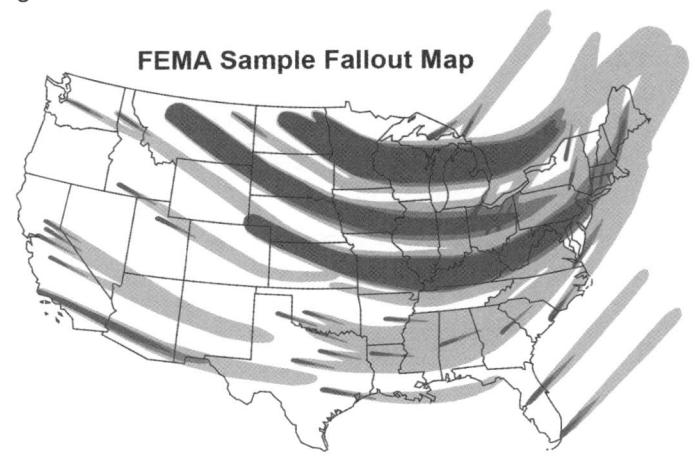

FALLOUT MAPS

Especially on the Internet, a common misconception has mushroomed (pardon the pun) that an "absolute" fallout pattern map exists. It doesn't. Most often passed around is the FEMA sample fallout map dating back to the 70s. It's just a sample, nothing more. Where fallout goes depends on the wind ON THE DAY and the following two weeks.

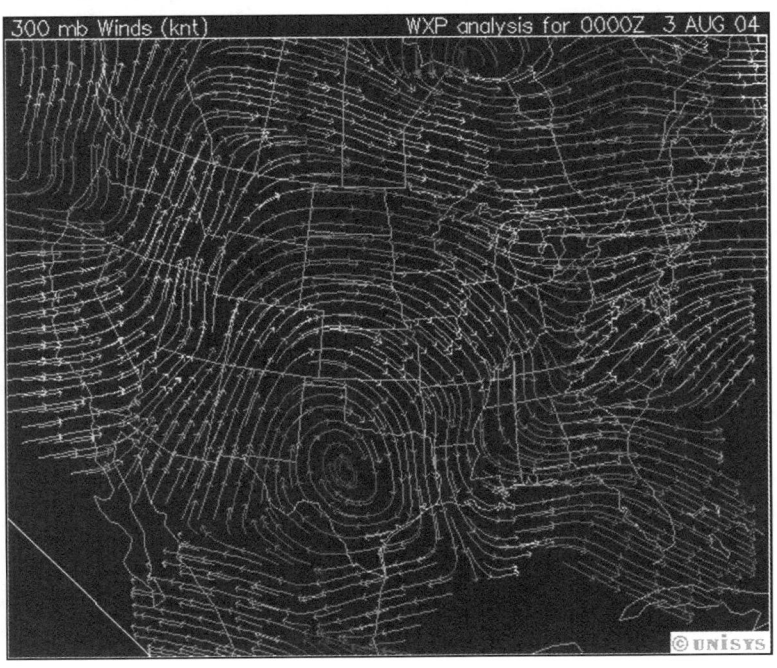

If people judged their safety looking at this map, everyone would move to the tip of Texas, anywhere in Oregon or the northern portions of California and Nevada.

Another map from Cresson H. Kearny's *Nuclear War Survival Skills*, passed the Internet as "gospel", even states in its own caption that it's outdated: "Fig. 4.2 Simplified, outdated fallout patterns showing total radiation ... " Unfortunately this caption has been deleted from many websites, giving a false sense of accuracy.

Date and time stamped maps should not to be relied on for constant wind patterns. Maps are marked with this data for a reason – to show it's valid for that time period.

As an example, where Stan and I live in southern Colorado, the wind blows from the north roughly 70% of the time and about 25% from the west. It's rarely still here.

Occasionally a storm back into us from the east or southwest, but it's infrequent. Because we're in a fairly breezy area, wind can and does shift frequently throughout the day.

Looking at the preceding map (picked at random), it appears that most of Colorado's wind comes from the southwest. Yes, it did, on August 2, 2004 at midnight.

It could be a deadly assumption thinking this is indicative of our prevailing winds, let alone what would occur during a nuclear incident. These maps are excellent when used for the purpose intended, but don't stake your life on them.

It would help to view your wind direction *at the time and after* a nuclear disaster, but chances are you're going to be occupied with other things than the Internet – providing it's still functioning. Doubtful.

TIP: A simple way to check wind direction is to drop a handful of dirt or leaves and see which way they move. This won't tell you what wind in the surrounding areas is doing, just your immediate area.

HOW BIG?

This graphic illustrates what a 25-megaton blast would do to the Denver area. Compare this detonation to the much smaller 1 megaton graphic. The most telling marker is to find the city of Littleton in each illustration and see where the blast rings are in each image.

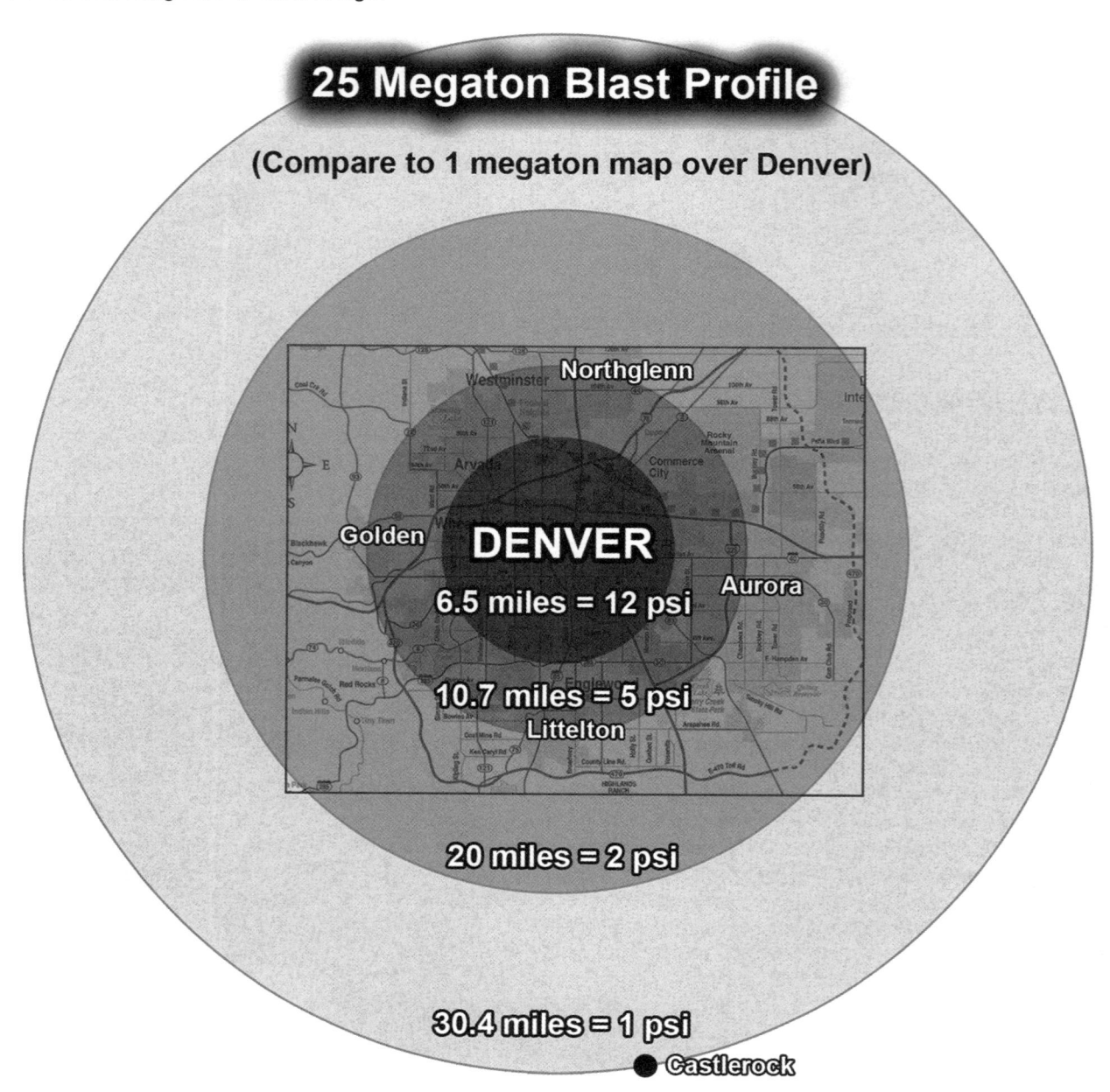

25 Megaton Blast Profile
(Compare to 1 megaton map over Denver)

- 6.5 miles = 12 psi
- 10.7 miles = 5 psi
- 20 miles = 2 psi
- 30.4 miles = 1 psi

● Castlerock

The effects would depend on the yield and success of the detonation. A "homemade" or poorly maintained bomb could be a dud, producing no explosive yield but spread radioactive material. Or, the device could "fizzle" and only partially detonate. However, even a fizzle device yielding 0.01 KT would have much greater impact than what was used in the 1995 Oklahoma City bombing. The A bomb detonated over Hiroshima was a 15 KT device; India's test on May 11, 1998 was 60 KT while most strategic weapons today are over 1 MT.

To put nuke sizes in perspective, 1 KT (kiloton) = 1,000 tons of TNT; 1 MT (megaton) = 1,000,000 tons of TNT.

1 MEGATON SURFACE BLAST: PRESSURE DAMAGE

The fission bomb detonated over Hiroshima had an explosive blast equal to 12,500 tons of TNT. A 1-megaton hydrogen bomb detonated on earth's surface has about 80 times the power of that 1945 explosion.

Graphic: The illustration pictured left shows that a 1- megaton detonation in Denver would have disastrous consequences for millions. (Graphic Stan Deyo, 2004)

BLAST FORCE

The blast force creates the initial damage and its strength is measured in psi – pounds per square inch. As the explosion blows outward, the damage lessens. Studies show that nuclear explosions produce somewhat identifiable "rings" of destruction. They assess blast damage only, not fallout. Weather and terrain would alter their shape.

Radius of destructive circle: 1.7 miles (2.7km)   12 psi

At the center is a crater 200 feet (61m) deep and 1000 feet (309m) wide. It's rimmed in highly radioactive soil and debris. Nothing is recognizable within 3,200 feet (0.6 mile, 975m) of the center except the remains of some building foundations. Only reinforced, poured concrete structures are still standing. Some 98% of the population is killed.

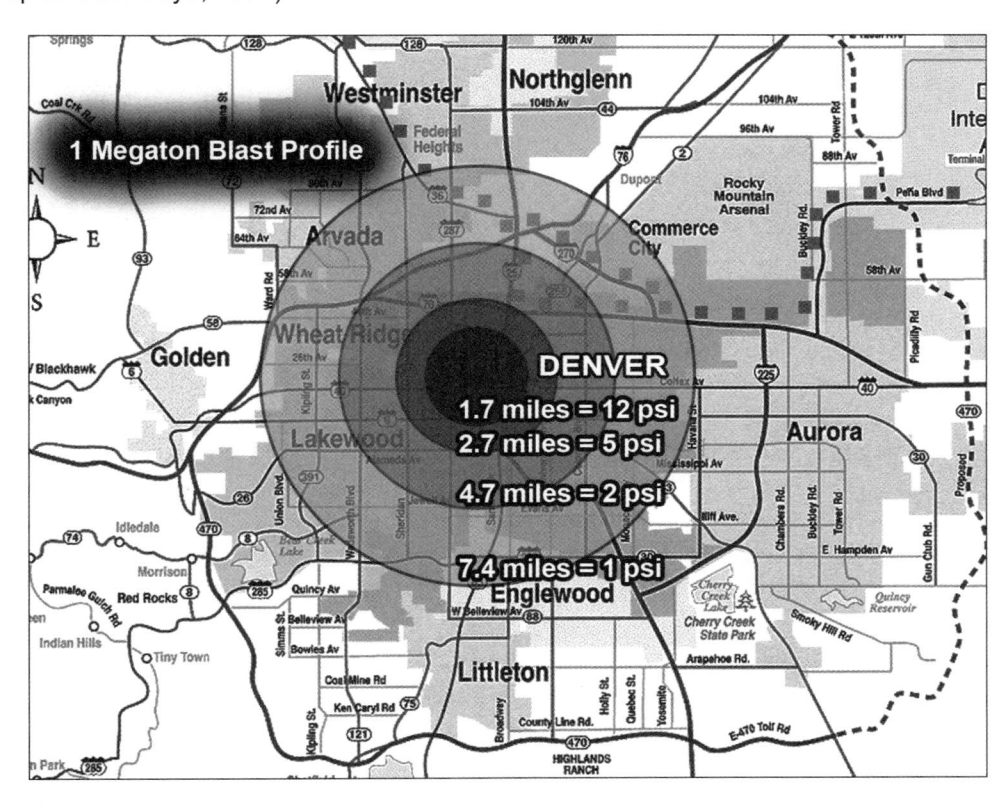

Radius of destructive circle: 2.7 miles (4.3km)   5 psi

Virtually everything is destroyed within the second ring. Walls of typical multi-story buildings, including apartments, have been completely blown out. Bare, structural skeletons of more and more buildings rise above the debris as you approach the 5 psi ring. Single-family residences have been completely blown away – only their foundations remain. Half of the population is dead; another 40% are injured.

Radius of destructive circle: 4.7 miles (7.6)   2 psi

Single-family residences not completely destroyed are heavily damaged. Office building windows are blown away as are some of the walls. Contents from the upper floors, including the people who were working there, are scattered on the street. A substantial amount of debris clutters the entire area. About 5% of the people in the 2 psi ring are dead; 45% are seriously injured.

Radius of destructive circle: 7.4 miles (11.9km)   1 psi

Residences are moderately damaged. Commercial buildings sustain minimal damage, mostly broken glass. No one is killed this far from the blast but 25% of the population is injured, mainly by flying glass and debris. Many others have been injured from thermal radiation – the heat generated by the blast.[124]

RADIATION TERMS: RADS, REMS, REINS AND ROENTGENS

When looking at radiation information, three words often crop up. They're all radiation measurements but address different things. For practical purposes, *roentgen, rad* and *rem* are essentially equivalent for gamma and beta rays, and can be used interchangeably.[125]

Put simply, here's what they refer to:

Roentgen (R) – pronounced like "renken" – measures radiation intensity. It describes an amount of gamma rays and X-rays in the air.

Rad (Radiation **A**bsorbed **D**ose**)** measures the amount of radiation absorbed. It's used for any type of radiation – gamma rays, x-ray, beta or alpha particles.

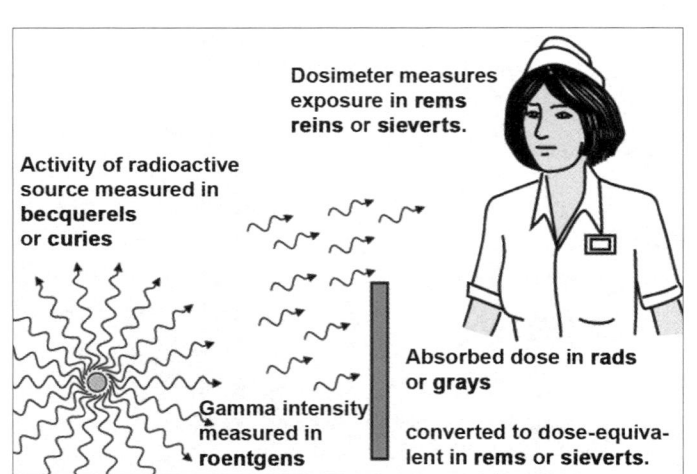

Rem (Roentgen **E**quivalent **M**an**)** measures doses absorbed by human tissue. Not all radiation has the same effect on the body, even for the same amount that's absorbed. (100 rems = 1 sievert)

Rein is the newer word for *rem* and used when estimating biological risk.

Sievert measures doses absorbed by human tissue. (1 sievert = 100 rems)

Activity of radioactive source measured in **becquerels** or **curies**

Dosimeter measures exposure in **rems reins** or **sieverts**.

Absorbed dose in **rads** or **grays**

Gamma intensity measured in **roentgens** converted to dose-equivalent in **rems** or **sieverts**.

RADIATION EXPOSURE: KEEP IT AS LOW AS POSSIBLE

Detonated nuclear weapons all release alpha, beta and gamma radiation. Alpha particles are the least dangerous and a plain sheet of paper is enough to stop them. Stronger beta particles can be blocked by ¼" of aluminum or ½" of plexiglass or PVC-type plastic. Anything that shields gamma rays – the most harmful – will shield betas. Shielding gamma rays is covered in the next chapter.

EFFECTS OF SHORT-TERM RADIATION EXPOSURE	
Roentgens	**Effect and Treatment**
0-25	No change in blood cells and no visible effects.
25-100	Loss of appetite and some nausea, blood changes noticeably. Recovery is about 1 week.
100-200	Definite changes in blood cells at low dose range. 50% have radiation sickness: weakness and fatigue, diarrhea, vomiting, fever and infection. In the higher R range there is hair loss, hemorrhaging and some will have heart failure. 25-100% are incapacitated, 25% die in 30-60 days. Recovery is about 40 days. Treat with rest, light diet, water and antibiotics for infections.
200-450	Serious radiation sickness for several days. Patients often experience 1-3 weeks of apparent recovery then lose hair. 100% are eventually incapacitated. 50% die in higher R range within 1-2 months. Treat as above. Watch for dehydration. Blood transfusions help survival rate.
50-600	Very serious radiation sickness but onset is earlier. Hemorrhaging common in mouth, throat and skin. Infections and pneumonia common. 50-75% die within 3-4 weeks. For survivors, recovery is months to years. Treat as above plus bone marrow transplant.
600-800	Extreme radiation sickness, vomiting immediate. Central nervous and circulatory systems malfunction. Treat as above; bone marrow transplant and life support required. 75-99% die in 2 weeks.
800+	Death within hours.

Dealing with the effects of nuclear gamma radiation is something no one wants to experience. From the following table you can see it's not an automatic death sentence, but the less exposure, the better. People respond to radiation differently, to a small degree, which is why some survive when others succumb.

Most important is the *accumulated* amount of radiation received over a short period of time. Keep your *total exposure* under 100 roentgens if at all possible.

ESCAPING THE RADIATION

You have two, possibly three, options to ensure your safety:
1. Leave the affected area
2. Shelter in place
3. Find a designated bomb shelter

If the nuclear blast is far enough away, relocating out of harm's way for several days may be the easiest solution. It will depend, too, if you live rurally or in a congested city. Suppose home is in a densely populated area with few evacuation routes. By jumping on the freeway you may be trapped in gridlock or end up playing demolition derby. Count on panicked people driving recklessly in an effort just to get away. Fear and ignorance will fuel the chaos. People operating with only with information gleaned from disaster movies won't realize that survival is within their grasp if they keep calm.

Florida, for instance, has a population of over 18 million. It has two main north-south interstates and only one road, Highway 1, connecting The Keys to the mainland. Despite modernization, this 127-mile highway is mostly two lanes. Key West, with its very dense population, lies clear at the outermost tip. Residents there would have to travel the entire 127 miles just to reach the mainland.

In a disaster, this highway would likely be converted to two additional outbound lanes. Still, funneling more than 90,000 panic-stricken people from The Keys onto one highway would very tough. Based on hurricane evacuation times, it requires up to 39 hours to vacate The Keys and Miami, and up to 60 hours for Ft. Myers residents.

Compounding matters, Florida has a high water table that makes taking refuge in basements impossible. Sheltering in place would require some serious advance planning.

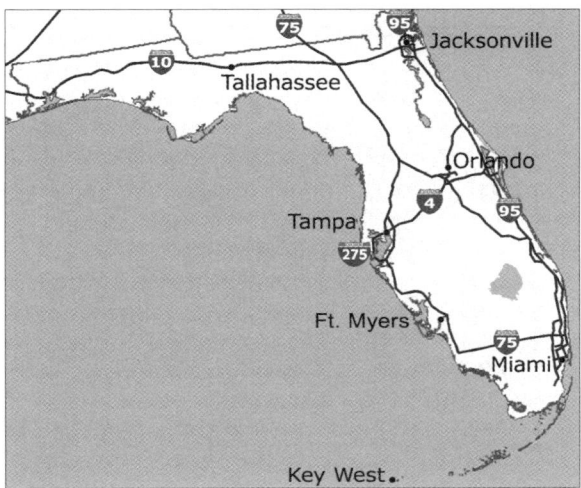

TRACKING FALLOUT

This image depicts the fallout cloud from a bomb detonated on March 1954. Within 36 hours, the plume had traveled about 200 miles from Bikini Atoll. After 36 hours, fallout had moved only 320 miles. The detonation took place on a very calm day since the cloud moved less than 1mph.

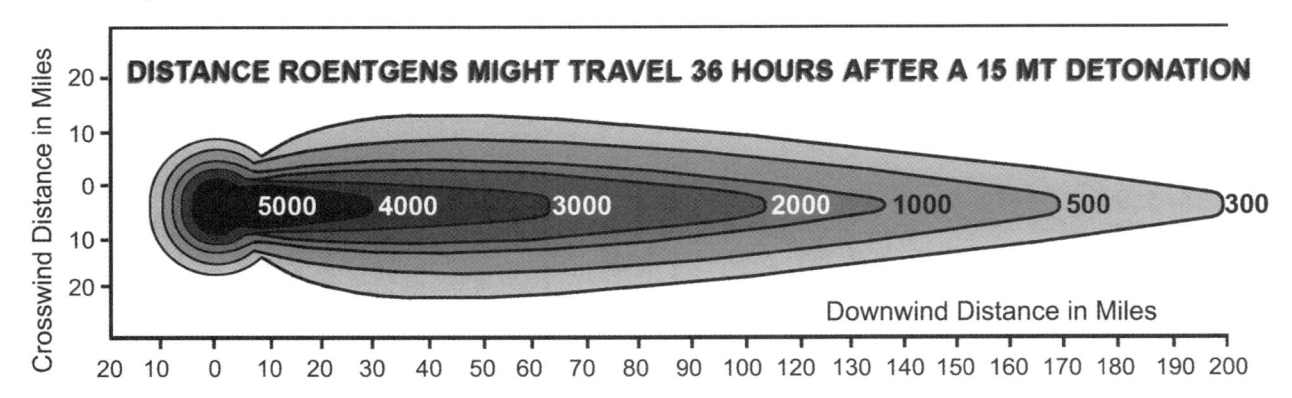

Most importantly, it illustrates that radiation doesn't necessarily contaminate "everything". Beyond a 40-mile wide swath, in this particular instance, the air was relatively "clean". Depending on terrain and wind conditions though, this picture could alter considerably.

WIND DIRECTION

After the initial mushroom cloud appears, the wind will usually shape it into an anvil, much like what we see with severe weather. The rounded "nose" points in the direction where the fallout cloud is moving.

Keep in mind the Bikini Atoll fallout and the relatively safe area on either side of its plume. Since the day of detonation was nearly windless, fallout stayed in a tidy pattern.

If you live in a very breezy area or a fallout cloud travels through windy conditions, it will change shape. Generally speaking, the higher the cloud rises, the more distortion it will experience.

If you know the location of the strike and how fast the wind is moving, you can calculate the time till fallout is overhead.

Anemometers, instruments that measure wind speed, would give you an immediate, more accurate answer. They can be purchased for $40-$200. Check hardware, boating and marine equipment suppliers, electronics and gadgets stores plus online locations like Cabela's. www.cabelas.com. They seem to stock everything.

Emergency announcements should broadcast that vital information providing they're still operational. If that's not an option, you can estimate wind speed with the next chart, but it would only be an educated guess.

Wind Speed		Indicators	Term Used by NWS
MPH	KmPH		
0-1	0-2	Calm; smoke rises vertically.	Calm
1-3	2-5	Shown by direction of wind smoke drift, but not by wind vanes.	Light
4-7	6-12	Wind felt on face, leaves rustle, ordinary vanes moved by wind.	Light
8-12	13-20	Leaves and small twigs in constant motion, wind extends light flag.	Gentle
13-18	21-29	Raises dust and loose paper, small branches are moved.	Moderate
19-24	30-39	Small trees in leaf begin to sway, crested wavelets form on inland waters.	Fresh
25-31	40-50	Large branches in motion, whistling heard in telephone wires, umbrellas used with difficulty.	Strong
32-38	51-61	Whole trees in motion, inconvenience felt walking against the wind.	Strong
39-46	62-74	Breaks twigs off trees, generally impedes progress.	Gale
47-54	75-87	Slight structural damage.	Gale
55-63	88-101	Seldom experienced inland, trees uprooted, considerable structural damage.	Whole gale
64-72	102-116	Very rarely experienced inland, accompanied by widespread damage.	Whole gale
73+	117+	Very rarely experienced, accompanied by widespread damage.	Hurricane

GETTING OUT OF DODGE

Once you establish wind direction and arrival time, you can just leave. Sounds simple doesn't it. By using one of the more extreme cases – a 15 MT bomb – you can see how doable this is.

Scenario: You live in Salt Lake City and a nuke targets Los Angeles. In order for it to be dangerous to you, the cloud must angle sharply northeast – a generally unnatural wind direction between these two locations – and it must pass right over top of you. By air, these cities are 580 miles apart.

Given a worst case scenario, this 40-mile wide fallout cloud comes directly overhead, traveling at 10mph. You are exactly in the middle beneath it. Getting away from fallout means traveling only 20 miles in either direction, *perpendicular to the cloud*.

If the cloud were still moving northeast, then the cleverest direction to go would be 20 miles southeast. With the wind moving at 10mph, you would have 58 hours to get out of harm's way. Again, in a worst case scenario if the freeway is gridlocked, you could do this on foot.

The average person walks about 3mph, which is a fairly slow pace. Even so, it would take just a little over 6½ hours to walk. Given the situation, adrenalin would probably kick in and you'd unconsciously pick up the pace.

If you have children, pets, senior citizens or disabled members in your group, driving might be your best choice. It *is* doable.

Chapter 45: Shelter During Nuclear Emergencies

"President Kennedy, speaking on July 25, 1961, put it this way, 'In the event of attack, the lives of those families which are not hit in the nuclear blast and fire can still be saved if they can be warned to take shelter and if that shelter is available. We owe that kind of insurance to our families and to our country.'"[126]

This forthrightness was obviously spoken in a time when government thought we were better able to handle crises. Now the public is often kept in the dark.

When President Kennedy spoke, about 50 million fallout spaces were earmarked for people. That covered about 25% of the population, but provisions have deteriorated drastically over the decades. Since many public fallout shelters have vanished, if you choose not to evacuate or are unable to, your best protection might be right under your feet.

Taking shelter during a nuclear attack is absolutely necessary. There are two kinds of shelters – blast and fallout. Blast shelters protect against the bomb's detonation pressure, initial radiation, heat and fire. Even a blast shelter, though, can't withstand a direct hit.

Fallout shelters don't need to be specially constructed for that purpose. They can be any protected space, provided the walls and roof are dense enough to absorb radiation. Most structures aren't sufficient all by themselves and need to be upgraded with additional materials.

Three factors are vital for an effective fallout shelter: *shielding*, *distance*, and *time*.

• *Shielding*. The more heavy, dense materials – thick walls, concrete, bricks, water, books and earth – between you and the fallout particles, the better.

• *Distance*. The further you are from the fallout particles, the better. An underground area such as a home or office building basement offers more protection than the first floor of a building. A floor near the middle of a high rise may be better, depending on what is nearby at that level where fallout particles would land. Flat roofs collect fallout particles, so the top floor is not a good choice, nor is a floor adjacent to a neighboring flat roof.

• *Time*. Fallout radiation loses its intensity fairly rapidly. In time, you will be able to leave the fallout shelter. Radioactive fallout poses the greatest threat to people during the first two weeks. By then it has declined to about one-tenth of 1% compared to its initial level. Any protection is better than none at all, but the more shielding, distance and time you can take advantage of, the better.

EXPEDIENT SHELTERING

The next table gives thickness of various materials that would keep radiation exposure to an acceptable and safe level. More importantly, it is *doable*. Most people may not be able to lead-line their home shelter due to cost or time considerations. Plus, it is something that would have to be done in advance. Since most people procrastinate on bigger projects, other materials listed are likely to be at home and readily available for an expedient shelter.

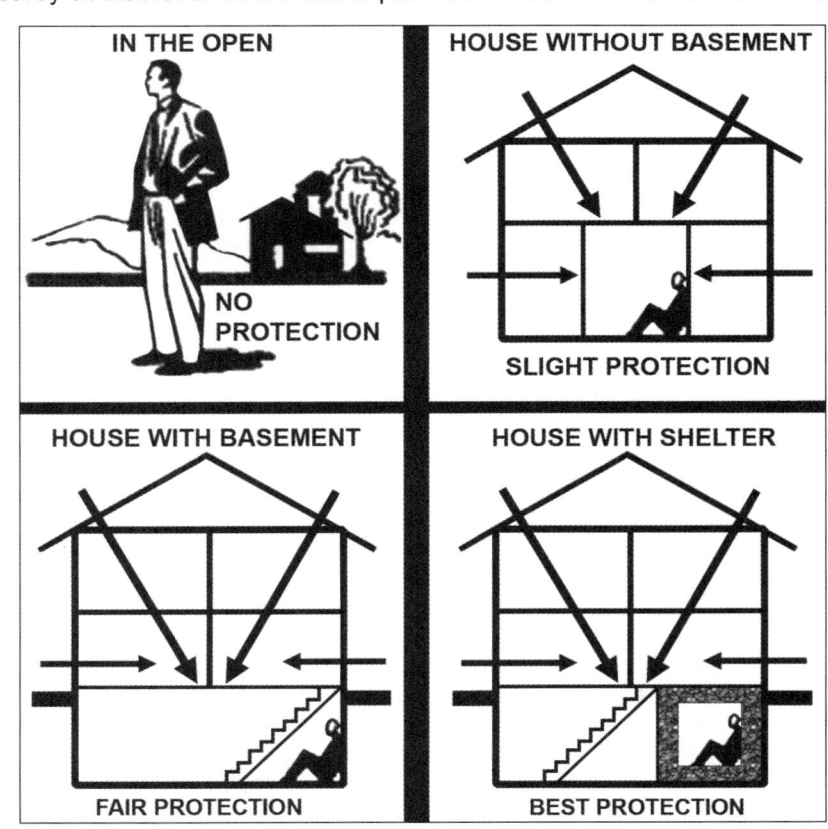

With an accumulated dose of 80 rads over a 2-week period, you may experience some nausea and loss of appetite, but there wouldn't be lasting damage or serious radiation sickness. With only 25 rads total exposure, side effects would be non-existent.

While we'd all like radiation exposure to be zero, it may not be possible if a shelter hasn't been erected beforehand. Considering the time required to move that much stuff into place and using what might be available, there has to be a balance between the tolerable and the practical.

Two scenarios are given for outside radiation strength: 500 R/Hr and 1000 R/Hr. To keep your total radiation exposure at no more than 80 roentgens or 25 roentgens over two weeks, use these material thicknesses:

MATERIAL	Minimum Thicknesses to Keep Radiation Accumulation Over 2 Weeks at			
	80 RAD TOTAL EXPOSURE		25 RAD TOTAL EXPOSURE	
	500 Rads/hr	1,000 Rads/hr	500 Rads/hr	1,000 Rads/hr
Lead	2½"	3¼"	3.8"	4.6"
Steel	3¾"	5"	5¾"	6.9"
Concrete	12"	16"	18½"	22½"
Earth or Solid Brick	17"	23"	26	31½"
Water	22"	29"	33¼"	40¼"
Magazines, slick paper	30"	40"	46¼"	56"
Drywall/Sheetrock	32"	43"	50"	60½"
Wood	36"	48"	56"	67¾"
Newspapers/Books	36"	47½"	55½"	67¼"
Plywood	60"	80"	92¾"	112"

BE CREATIVE

An effective shelter doesn't have to be made of all one substance. You can use several different materials in combination. Think of objects around your home that are made of these things like steel desks and file cabinets. A mini-portable refrigerator would be good for a number of reasons.
- Stored water and stacks of canned goods add to density.
- Fill pillowcases and cardboard boxes with sand or dirt.
- Take drawers out of dressers and fill them up with life-saving dirt.
- Use doors from upstairs closets and bedrooms as bases on which to stack items for overhead protection.
- Duffle, laundry and golf bags are workable "containers" too.

Should radiation exceed these rad/hr numbers, your best bet might be to leave the fallout area as described in the previous chapter or try to find an existing designated fallout shelter. If you haven't already scouted those available in your area, you might be in for some surprises.

VENTILATION

A small family sheltering in the basement would be able to survive on the available air. If you have a larger family, a door to the upstairs can be safely left ajar to bring in additional oxygen. Radiation won't "leak" downstairs and poison the air.

STOCKING THE SHELTER

FOOD Keep meals as simple as possible. If it's summer or there's the likelihood that shelter inhabitants would generate too much heat in close quarters, cooking will only add to the discomfort. This is one of those instances where MREs, shelf stable entrees and canned goods are the best choices. Don't forget a can opener and paper plates and plastic utensils. This is not the time for freeze dried or dehydrated foods since they require additional water to reconstitute and in most instances, heat for cooking.

WATER Under normal circumstances, people should drink 1 gallon of water per day. Aim for this amount. It's more important than food if space is at a premium. Stack it along the wall where radiation would be the strongest. It adds density to your shelter. Because sanitation is vital for health and morale, plan for a half-gallon per person per day for "bare necessities" cleanliness. More, if there's room.

Dare To Prepare: Chapter 45: Shelter During Nuclear Emergencies 457

SANITATION Toilet paper, paper towels, Ziplocs, garbage bags, toilet bucket (see Chapter 36), personal hygiene items, spray disinfectant.

Photo: Basement family fallout shelter that included a 14-day non-perishable food supply, battery-operated radio, auxiliary light sources, two-week water supply, first aid, sanitary items, and other miscellaneous supplies and equipment, ca. 1957. (U.S. National Archives and Records Administration)

PETS Store food and water for them too. They'll need a place to relieve themselves. See "4-Legged Kids" in Chapter 42.

LIGHT If you have access to electricity, great! However, there's no way to know how long it will stay on. Bring battery-powered lanterns and flashlights, and *lots* of batteries – enough to last the entire shelter stay using them full-time. Kerosene and propane lights and candles are not a good idea. They will add heat and fumes, and consume oxygen.

RADIO Be sure to have a battery-powered or crank radio to hear emergency broadcast announcements. This is especially important to know when it's safe to leave the shelter if you don't have a radiation monitor.

ACTIVITIES You can only sleep so much to pass the time. Bring books, games and cards – things that don't require much space or make a lot of noise. Toys with repetitive or annoying sounds are apt to grate on already frayed nerves.

BEDDING Foam mats will add cushioning if you're sleeping on the floor, sheets, pillows and blankets.

CLOTHES At least one change of exterior clothing and daily clean underwear.

FIRST AID KIT (See Chapter 14)

RADIATION MONITOR If you have spare cash, purchase a good quality radiation monitor at a fair price through Shane Connor's **www.ki4u.com** or make your own Kearny Fallout Meter – the KFM (see preceding chapter).

SAMPLE EXPEDIENT SHELTER

Canned food
Drinking water
2 Interior doors
Dresser drawers filled with dirt
Mattress, Blanket, Pillows, Toilet Bucket, etc.

Improvise an expedient shelter using furniture, doors, dressers, file cabinets or other sturdy objects. Remove doors from their hinges and place them over supports in the corner of your basement with the best protection. Supports for the table can be chests of drawers or anything that can take a heavy load. Use at two or three doors over each support to provide sufficient strength to hold the protective loads placed on them. Stack bricks, concrete blocks, earth- or sand-filled drawers, books, an inflatable swimming pool filled with water or bottled water over the doors to provide overhead shielding. Use anything with density that can be moved. Materials can be used in combination with each other to make up the necessary denseness. Check the **Minimum Thicknesses to Keep Radiation Accumulation Over 2 Weeks** chart in the chapter for how much your shelter need.

WHERE HAVE ALL THE SHELTERS GONE?

When was the last time you saw one of these fallout shelter signs on a building? This New York City Chinatown sign is an increasing rarity.

"In the words of Dr. Jane Orient, President of Doctors for Disaster Preparedness, 'If that soot raining down in Brooklyn [from the World Trade Center] had been radioactive, there would be many thousands, maybe millions of people dying slow, agonizing deaths from radiation sickness that could have been prevented had people had access to shelter.' But there are no shelters.

"After an early rush to protect Americans in the 1950s – from the construction of fallout shelters to the famous "duck and cover" drills in schools – civil defense was effectively killed by President Kennedy. It didn't fit with the spirit of MAD (mutual assured destruction); nor did it have big-ticket defense contractors to lobby for it. After a brief revival under Reagan, the program ended with the official close of the Cold War. Bill Clinton actually abolished the Office of Civil Defense, and sold off such emergency supplies as remained.[127]

LOCATING EXISTING SHELTER

People may choose to build their own protective shelters, but if you live in an apartment, condo, trailer park, or are on a limited budget, an alternate solution must be found. There *are* options.

First, contact your local Emergency Management center and Red Cross chapter. Phone the office nearest you as they'll likely have the most up-to-date, pertinent information. Ask what provisions have been made, if any, and where people would be instructed to go. If a shelter exists, locate it now and time how long it takes to get there. Can you get there on foot? Should shelters be minimally equipped, find out what you'd need to bring for a 2-week stay.

Also check for shelters with county and state officials. Shelters are increasingly difficult, if not impossible, to find in rural and suburban areas. Some smaller towns use their community center as shelter.

When speaking with the Director of our local Emergency Management Division, I asked where the community fallout shelters were located. She replied that in the mid-70s our town had 100 designated facilities. Today there are 0. Renovation struck down many replacing them with parking lots. Facilities evaporated as Cold War fears cooled. Other previously designated buildings have turned their shelter basements into storage rooms and they claim there's no going back. There'd be no place to put all the junk and not enough time to move it.

Local Emergency Management offices might seem an obvious choice. However, when I spoke to the EM Director here, she stated that during a disaster, their facility goes into complete lockdown. No one comes in without authorization. Other than that facility, our area has no designated fallout shelters. Many towns are likely in the same predicament so it pays to sniff out possibilities in advance.

TIP: It can't be stated strongly enough the importance of finding your shelter now. Have a Plan B location if your first choice has filled. Look for two locations: one close to work and one close to home. Remember, if you could see that blinding flash at detonation, you'd have approximately 20 minutes *at the outside* to get to shelter. Less, if you're in close proximity.

POSSIBLE FALLOUT SHELTERING SITES *

Airports – usually have massive underground areas with excellent concrete protection.
Apartment Building Basements
Banks – basement vault or safety deposit areas. Normally these would be off-limits to the public, but if an attack were expected, rules might be bent.
Boiler Rooms – in churches, school and other large buildings.
Buildings in General – below ground level in most buildings with more than 10 floors and interior rooms on middle floors of some tall buildings.
Caves* – stay well back from entrance.
Churches – many structures are made from thick stone and have sturdy basements.
City and County Buildings
Convention Centers – are normally multi-floored with numerous layers of concrete.
Culverts – look for long runs under highways. Watch for rats and water runoff.
Department Stores
Fire Departments
Gas Stations – grease pit areas.
Hospitals – usually have massive, well-built basements.
Libraries
Mines* – Use these as a last resort. Mines pose multiple hazards in the form of noxious gas, falling timber and rocks, or shafts. A sharp ground shock could make it a death trap.
Morgue – much of the embalming and such takes places in well-protected basements. This may be too gruesome for some to contemplate, but it may be a viable option.
Residential Homes – look for basements with maximum soil and concrete coverage.
Root Cellars – offers better fallout protection than blast protection.
Schools – most schools have pipe chases** and some have good basements.
Subways
Tunnels
Underpasses – offer good blast protection, up to 10 psi, but no radiation protection.
Underground Parking Garages – provide both blast and radiation protection. The drawback is whether the above floor(s) collapse leaving people trapped.

FOR ABOVE POTENTIAL SHELTER SITES :
   * Windows of the sheltered area must not view fallout-covered ground closer than 1 mile (1.5 km). Radiation travels in a line-of-sight.
   ** Chases are the fully or partially enclosed housing for pipes. Pipe runs are typically in the same location on each floor or above the ceiling near elevator shafts or restrooms.
   *** *Prudent Places USA 3rd Edition* by Holly Deyo addresses locations of caves, mines and abandoned mines in America.

BUYING A FALLOUT SHELTER

It's well established now that we need to provide some sort of shelter for ourselves whether it is in a community shelter or within the home or at a pre-stocked, separate location.

If you have plenty of cash, you can always purchase shelter protection. It can be quite expensive depending on what is chosen and options included. Various models are available from fairly swank shelters that offer comforts of regular housing to bare bones units. Pre-fabricated shelters offer expediency, but again, can be quite costly.

Typical of the "bare bones" category are corrugated steel cylinders generally measuring 4 feet across and 12 feet long. Unless only two people were inside, there would be no room to stretch your legs, let alone stand unless the person is a small child. It may save your life, but it would be exceptionally uncomfortable. If anyone has the slightest tendency toward claustrophobia, conditions might be unbearable. Stark units like these can be built for around $1500 not including ventilation or hygiene measures. They weigh upward of 1000 pounds so hiring help to move it plus excavation costs must be factored in. The nicest units fetch a hefty $68K with many choices in between.

BUILDING A FALLOUT SHELTER

If you have construction knowledge and experience, this is a project you may want to consider. To get started, some ideas have been included as a guide. Additionally, you can find no-longer-available FEMA fallout shelter plans in PDF (Portable Document Files) files on our website. Access this free information here: **standeyo.com/News_Files/menu.nuke.html.**

It would have been preferable to include them in *Dare To Prepare*, but by the time drawings fit onto paper, many are too small to read. PDF allows you to zoom text up to a much larger font and print them out. If you have access to a computer, please download these documents.

I was curious why the 2nd edition of FEMA's "Are You Ready" book urged people to build their own temporary fallout shelter, yet plans weren't readily available.

FEMA's Preparedness Division Director stated they'd gone pretty much the way of fallout shelters – no longer needed. He *personally* is not of that belief and hopes to remedy the situation. Though these documents aren't available on FEMA's website, he indicated they might be again – in time.

Not only does he have to go through channels and approvals, but he also stated that the material list needed to be updated.

When the director mentioned "update", I asked if the materials were still valid. The protection information itself is fine, but the material list needs adjusting. Some construction items are no longer available or referred to by a different name.

He seemed quite anxious to get this project moving – once higher-ups give it the go-ahead. As slowly as the government wheel turns, it could be a long wait. So in the interim, please feel free to grab this material off our website.

TIPS: If you're in a high-protection blast shelter and expecting an attack:
- Keep your head away from the ceiling. "Air slap" from the blast wave may push down the earth in an undamaged shelter much more rapidly than a person can move. If one's head were only a few inches from the ceiling, it could cause a skull fracture.
- Stay away from walls. They may move very rapidly, horizontally as well as vertically.
- It's safest to sit in a securely suspended, strong hammock or chair, or lay on a thick foam rubber mattress or on a pile of small branches. Ground shock may cause the whole shelter (including the floor) to rise very fast and injure persons sitting or standing on the floor.
- In dry areas or in a dry expedient shelter, ground shock may produce choking dust. Shelter occupants should be prepared to cover their faces with towels or other cloth, or put on a mask.

Dare To Prepare: Chapter 45: Shelter During Nuclear Emergencies

SHELTER CONSTRUCTION PLANS

As addressed earlier, several home shelter plans from FEMA are available in PDF files on our website **standeyo.com/News_Files/menu.nuke.html**. These FREE downloads show how to build your own shelter.

Several are for various basement shelters. Another plan details an above ground shelter for high water table areas. A second outside choice is an underground design for people without basements. Beyond these are still other construction choices including a blast shelter.

The following fallout and tornado shelter is a FEMA publication scanned word-for-word. The only difference is FEMA printed the brochure in two columns.

Plans include instructions, detailed drawings as well as the materials list. Though this document is dated 1987, FEMA's Preparedness Division Director assured that the information is still valid.

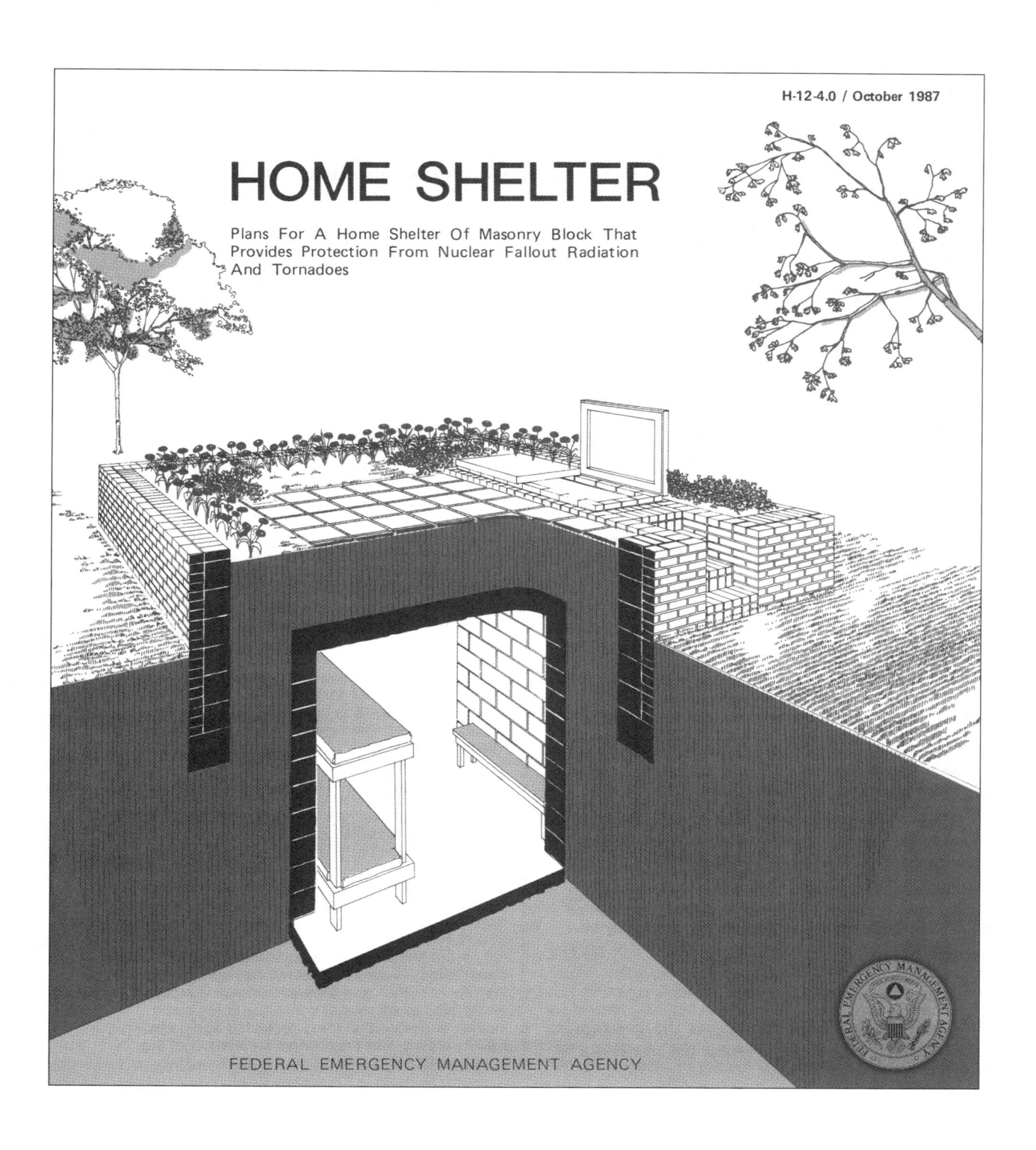

H-12-4.0 / October 1987

HOME SHELTER

Plans For A Home Shelter Of Masonry Block That Provides Protection From Nuclear Fallout Radiation And Tornadoes

FEDERAL EMERGENCY MANAGEMENT AGENCY

FEMA FALLOUT AND TORNADO SHELTER

This protective shelter is designed to serve as a family fallout shelter and is suitable for other utilitarian purposes as well-including use as a tornado shelter and everyday functions of the residence. The shelter is designed for placement in the yard and primarily is for houses without basements.

To function as a fallout shelter, it is designed to have a protection factor (PF) of at least 40, which is the minimum standard of protection for family and public shelters recommended by the Federal Emergency Management Agency. The belowground location of the shelter also will provide some protection against blast and fire effects of a nuclear explosion.

The facility also can serve as a storm in regions of the nation where tornadoes are common. The roof structure of the shelter is suitably strong to resist the most severe tornadoes, and the below ground location provides protection for occupants from wind-blown debris and even from possible collapse of nearby buildings.

The day-to-day use for the particular design illustrated is for housing residential swimming pool filtration equipment in a weather-protected location out of sight in the yard. Other utilitarian uses for the facility are possible that may be more suited to a particular homeowner's needs – such as use for yard equipment storage or use as a cellar for storage of perishable foods – or the facility may be used solely as a refuge from natural and man-made hazards.

An elevated brick planter placed atop the roof of the shelter creates a landscape feature in the yard and provides overhead protection against radioactive fallout and tornado forces. Attractive landscaping and enhanced protection are achieved with this arrangement without burying the shelter deeply into the ground.

PLANS FOR THE SHELTER

Plans illustrated in the Home Shelter accommodate up to six adults. The shelter has a reinforced concrete floor and roof slabs and reinforced masonry block walls. An elevated planting area, with brick-faced garden walls, retains a 2-ft. deep soil cover over the roof of the shelter. Access to the shelter is by a hatch and wood stair. A hand-operated centrifugal blower provides ventilation. Air intake and exhaust pipes extend above the ground level of the planter.

Dimensioned plans in this booklet provide sufficient information for a professional contractor to build the shelter. For the novice "do-it-yourself" builder, a companion booklet, H-12-4.1, is available from the Federal Emergency Management Agency that gives step-by-step instructions plus additional details for constructing the shelter.

A list of construction materials is provided after the drawings. It includes quantities for all materials needed to complete the construction except miscellaneous items such as stakes, nails, and other fasteners. The companion booklet, H-12-4.1, provides more detailed information on sizes and quantities of materials needed for each phase of the construction.

BUILDING THE SHELTER

Before commencing construction, verify that the plans conform to requirements of the local building department. A site plan showing where the shelter would be located in the yard relative to property lines and adjacent buildings may be required by the building department before a building permit will be issued.

If the shelter is to be constructed by a local contractor, check his reputation for doing quality work and get a written agreement with the contractor. The written agreement should be specific as to the work to be done, the quality of materials to be installed, the quality of workmanship, and cost for the work. Require the contractor to furnish proof of insurance protection against any liability or other claims (such as from materials suppliers) that might arise in the course of construction.

LAYOUT AND EXCAVATION

Initial layout of the shelter entails measuring and marking necessary to correctly locate the facility in the yard. Care should be exercised in this phase of the work to assure that the shelter will be built where it is intended and at the depth intended in relationship with yard elevations.

Side walls of the excavation should be sloped sufficiently so that soil will not slough off into the work area. Alternatively, the side walls can be shored if the soil is especially loose, deeper than the bottom level of the slab or drainage fill (if any) to assure that the bearing soil is not disturbed.

During the excavation phase, do not excavate deeper than the bottom of the slab or drainage fill (if any) to assure that the bearing soil is not disturbed.

FOOTINGS AND FLOOR

A combined footing and floor slab is designed for the shelter. By thickening the slab at its edges, support is provided for the block walls.

Underground utilities should be in place before the floor slab is poured – such as floor drain or sump, and water piping. A sump is provided for floor drainage of the shelter illustrated, but other drainage methods can be used provided that the drainage water has someplace to flow.

All concrete should have a minimum compressive strength of 2,500 psi (pounds per sq. inch). Locations and sizes of reinforcing steel (rebar) are indicated in the plans. All reinforcement indicated in the plans should be installed even though it might seem possible to omit some.

MASONRY BLOCK WALLS

The walls of the shelter are constructed of standard 8" thick masonry block. The block walls are reinforced both horizontally and vertically. Prefab trussed wire reinforcement is used in horizontal joints, placed continuously at every second bed course. Vertical reinforcement is No. 4 steel bars spaced at 8" on centers (one bar in each block cell). Every other vertical bar (one each block unit) is secured to dowels formed in the floor slab.

Cells of the block units are grouted to provide a bond between vertical reinforcement steel and block units. Grout lifts should not be greater than 4 feet for any one pour. Type S mortar is specified for block masonry joints and for grout.

ROOF SLAB

A reinforced concrete roof slab 8" thick is designed for the shelter. The roof slab is supported on the masonry block walls. Shoring and formwork for the roof slab are described in the companion booklet, H-12-4.1.

Sizes and locations of reinforcement steel for the roof slab are indicated in the plans shown in this booklet. Reinforcement consists of No. 4 bars spaced 8" O.C. running in the direction of the short dimension of the shelter (structural reinforcement) and No. 4 bars spaced at 16" in the long dimension (temperature reinforcement). Reinforcement around the hatchway opening, also No. 4 bars, is indicated in the plans.

DAMP PROOFING / WATERPROOFING

Protection of the underground facility from water and moisture penetration is recommended. If soil conditions are relatively dry and if there is good surface water drainage, then damp proofing should be sufficient. If ground water is observed in the excavation and if the excavation is likely to become a collector basin for water, then waterproofing probably will be necessary to achieve a dry shelter space. Damp proofing and waterproofing concepts and techniques are described in the companion booklet, H-12-4.1.

PLANTER WALLS

Walls of the surrounding planter are constructed after the basic shelter is completed and after backfill is placed up to a level of the footings for the planter walls. Concrete footings for the planter walls should be set below the frost line depth for the region where the shelter is built.

Planter walls consist of 4" standard face brick and 8" backup block. The planter walls are capped with brick. Type S mortar also is specified for this work.

These walls do not require grouting or vertical reinforcement bars unless the height of the walls above the surface of the yard is greater than about 3 feet. Horizontal joint reinforcement for a 12" wall should be used in alternate bed courses of the block. Brick steps leading to the hatchway are indicated in the plans for the shelter.

VENTILATION

The ventilation system for the shelter consists of a hand-operated centrifugal blower, air intake pipe with filter hood, and air discharge pipe with hood. Air intake and discharge pipes are placed on opposite or adjacent walls of the shelter space to provide optimum movement of ventilation air. Piping should be placed with outlets more or less at the heights above the floor level of the shelter as shown in the plans. Piping and fittings may be either galvanized steel or ABS (plastic).

The air intake pipe is fitted with a hood and screen filter so the blower won't pull radioactive particles into the shelter space. No filter is needed. The air exhaust pipe is hooded.

Centrifugal blowers can be purchased commercially. One such supplier is:
Spec Air, Inc., 13999 Goldmark Drive, Suite 401, Dallas, Texas 75240, Telephone – 214.644.6806

HOLLY NOTE: Spec Air is now defunct, but in an effort to keep this document identical to the original, it has been included. You will need to locate a local source for <u>manual</u> centrifugal blowers. Document resumes:

Electrical service for lighting and power equipment also may be added. Electrical service should be from a separate circuit and with a branch circuit breaker inside the shelter that has ground fault protection.

An electrically powered centrifugal blower may be substituted for the hand-operated blower. It should be recognized that electrical power to the shelter might be disrupted by a tornado or nuclear explosion.

Air intake filter and exhaust hood can be fabricated by a local sheet-metal shop in the homeowner's area in accordance with details included in the plans.

MODIFICATION OF PLANS

The shelter plans shown on this and subsequent pages may be modified within certain limitations as may be necessary to meet particular needs of the homeowner. To accommodate more than six occupants, increase the length of the shelter 2' 8" for each two additional occupants. The width of the shelter should not be increased unless the roof structure is redesigned. The roof structure of the shelter illustrated is designed to span in the short dimension, and new engineering analysis is needed for longer spans.

Other designs for an elevated planter and for access into the shelter are possible without changing the basic shelter. Each homeowner's preference for landscape character can be met in this phase of the work.

Piping for water may be added during construction such as for the swimming pool filter equipment that is illustrated.

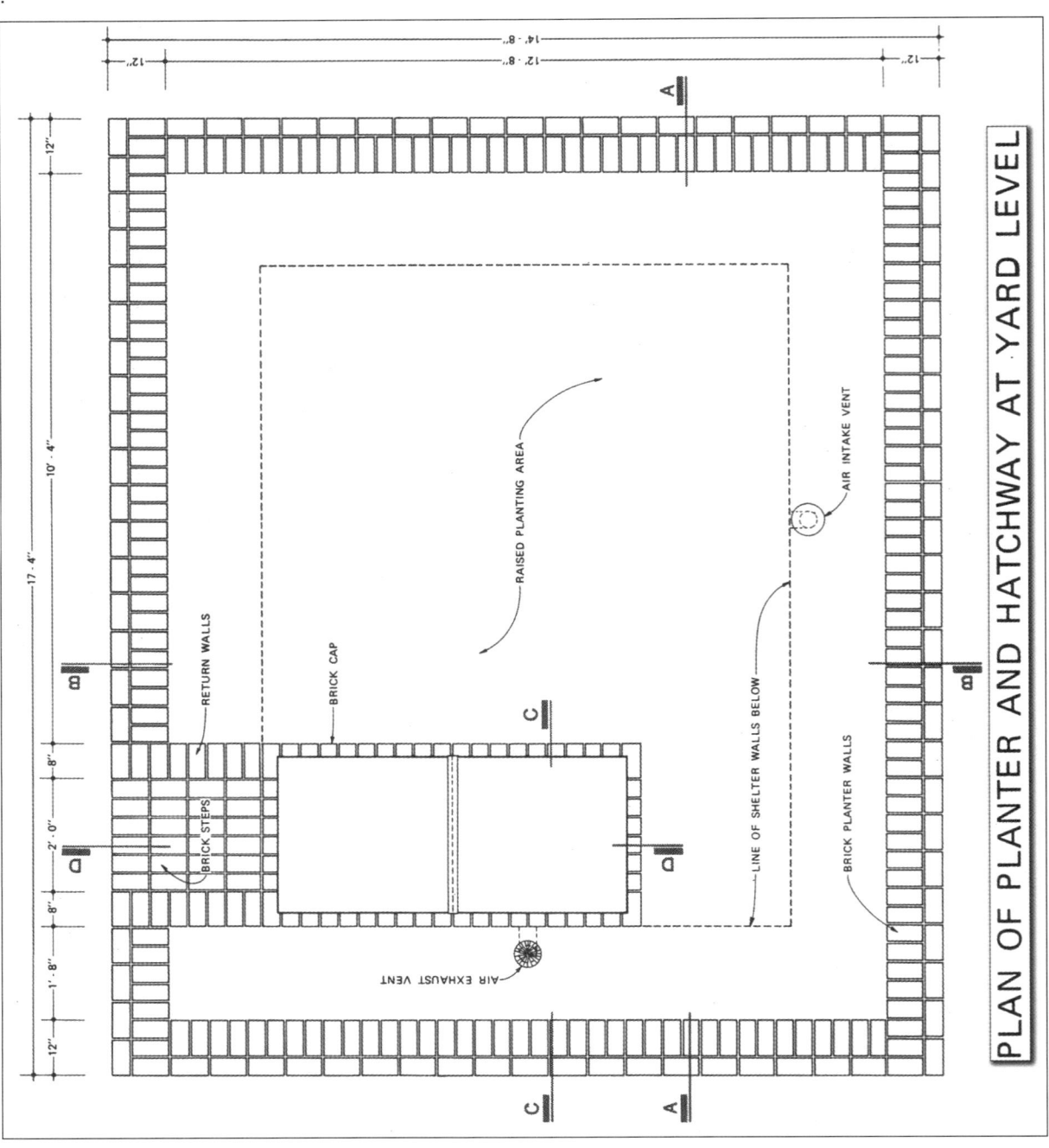

PLAN OF PLANTER AND HATCHWAY AT YARD LEVEL

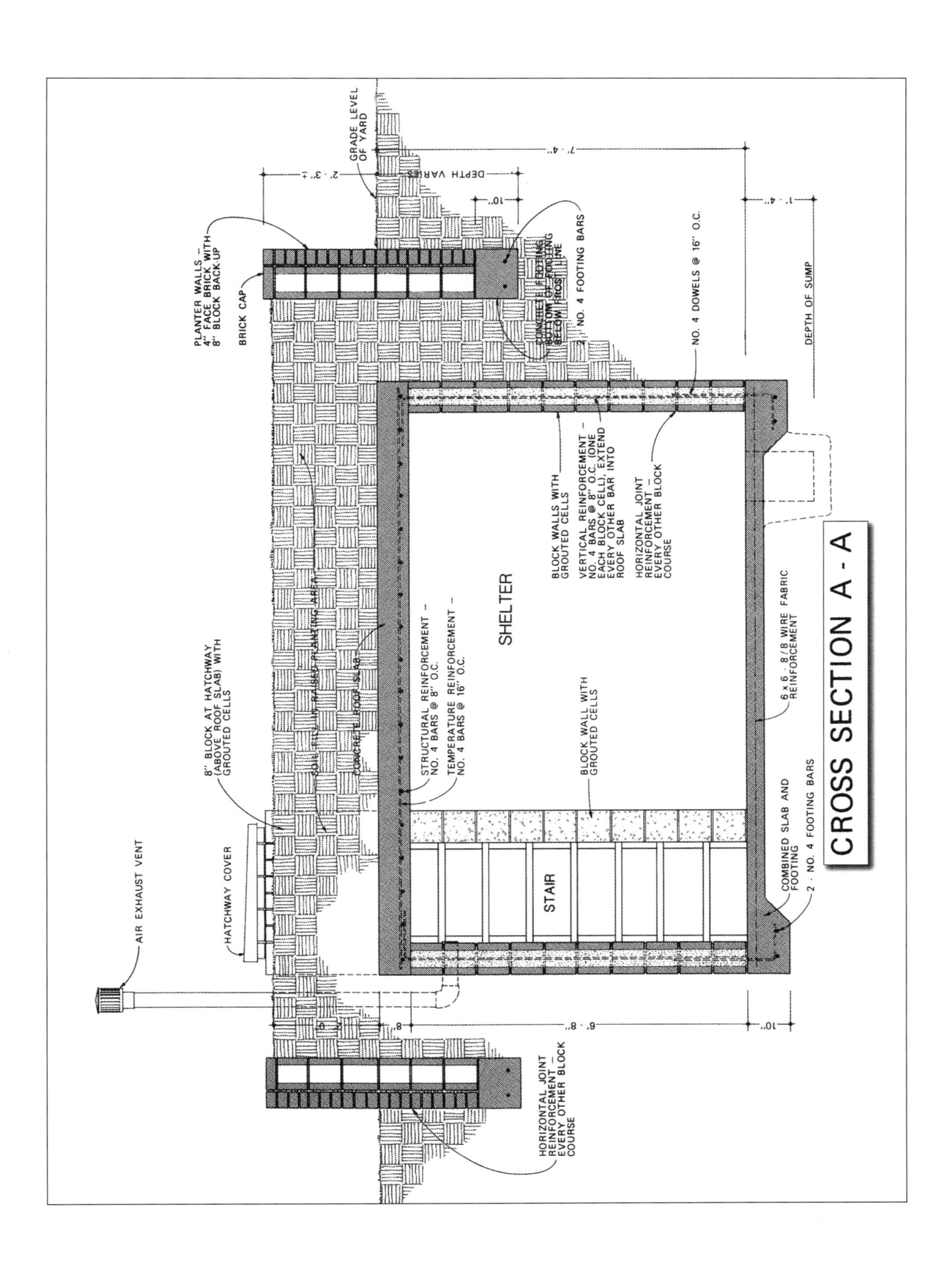

Dare To Prepare: Chapter 45: Shelter During Nuclear Emergencies

CROSS SECTION A - A

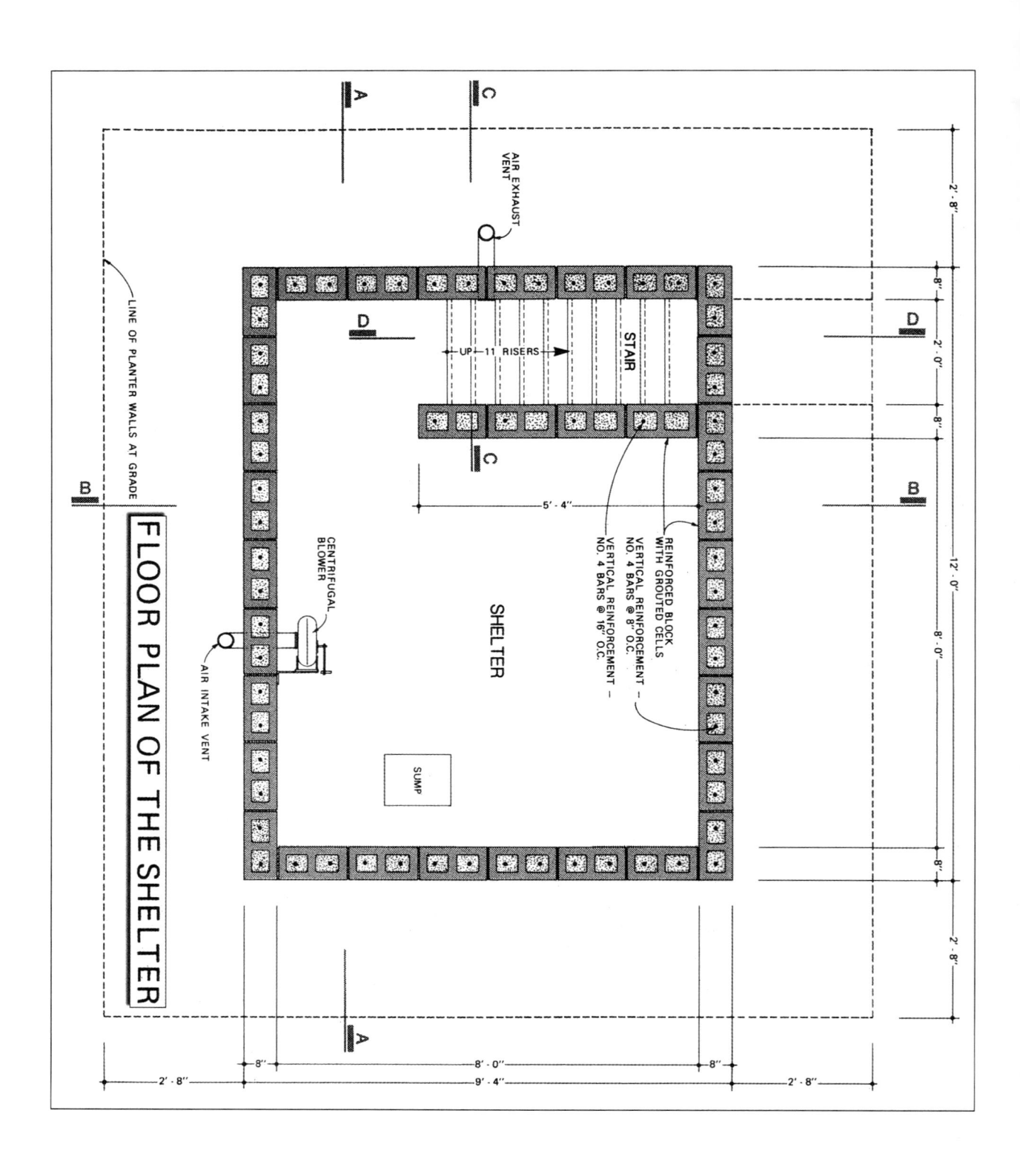

466 Dare To Prepare: Chapter 45: Shelter During Nuclear Emergencies

FLOOR PLAN OF THE SHELTER

- AIR EXHAUST VENT
- LINE OF PLANTER WALLS AT GRADE
- UP — 11 RISERS
- STAIR
- REINFORCED BLOCK WITH GROUTED CELLS
- VERTICAL REINFORCEMENT — NO. 4 BARS @ 8" O.C.
- VERTICAL REINFORCEMENT — NO. 4 BARS @ 16" O.C.
- CENTRIFUGAL BLOWER
- AIR INTAKE VENT
- SHELTER
- SUMP

Dimensions: 2'-8", 8", 2'-0", 8", 12'-0", 8'-0", 8", 2'-8", 8", 8'-0", 8", 2'-8", 9'-4", 5'-4"

CROSS SECTION B - B

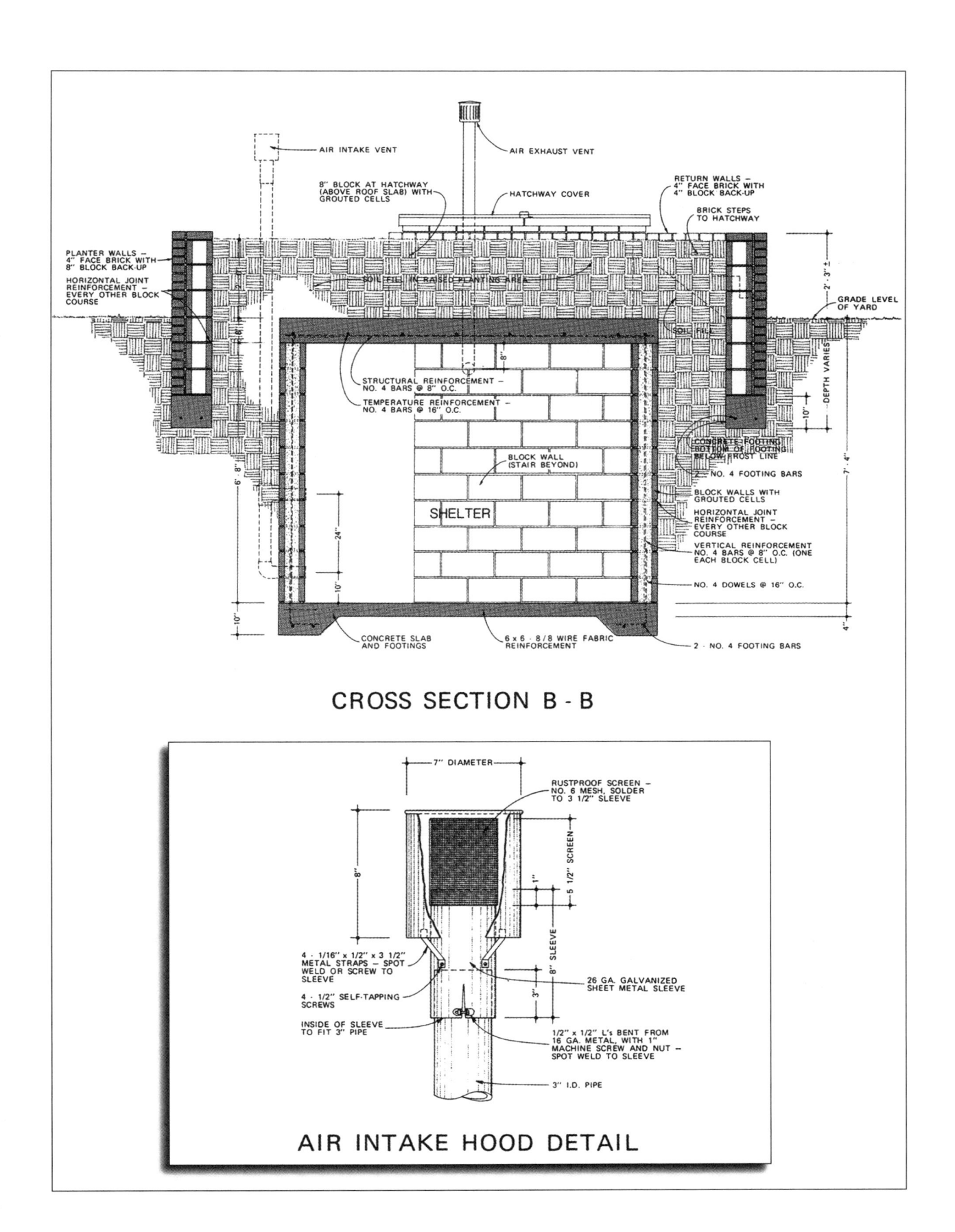

AIR INTAKE HOOD DETAIL

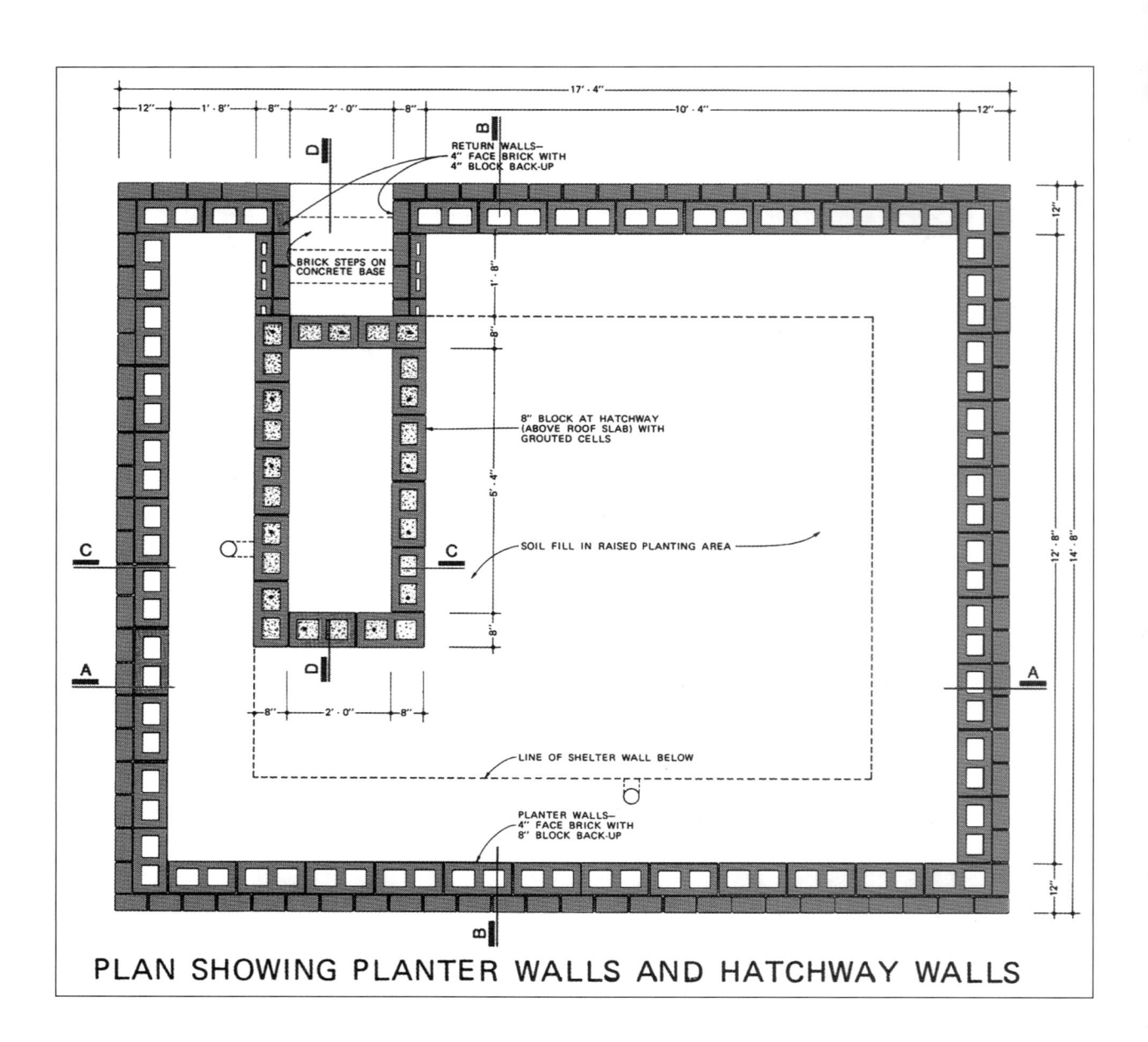

468   Dare To Prepare: Chapter 45: Shelter During Nuclear Emergencies

PLAN SHOWING PLANTER WALLS AND HATCHWAY WALLS

SECTION C-C AT HATCHWAY

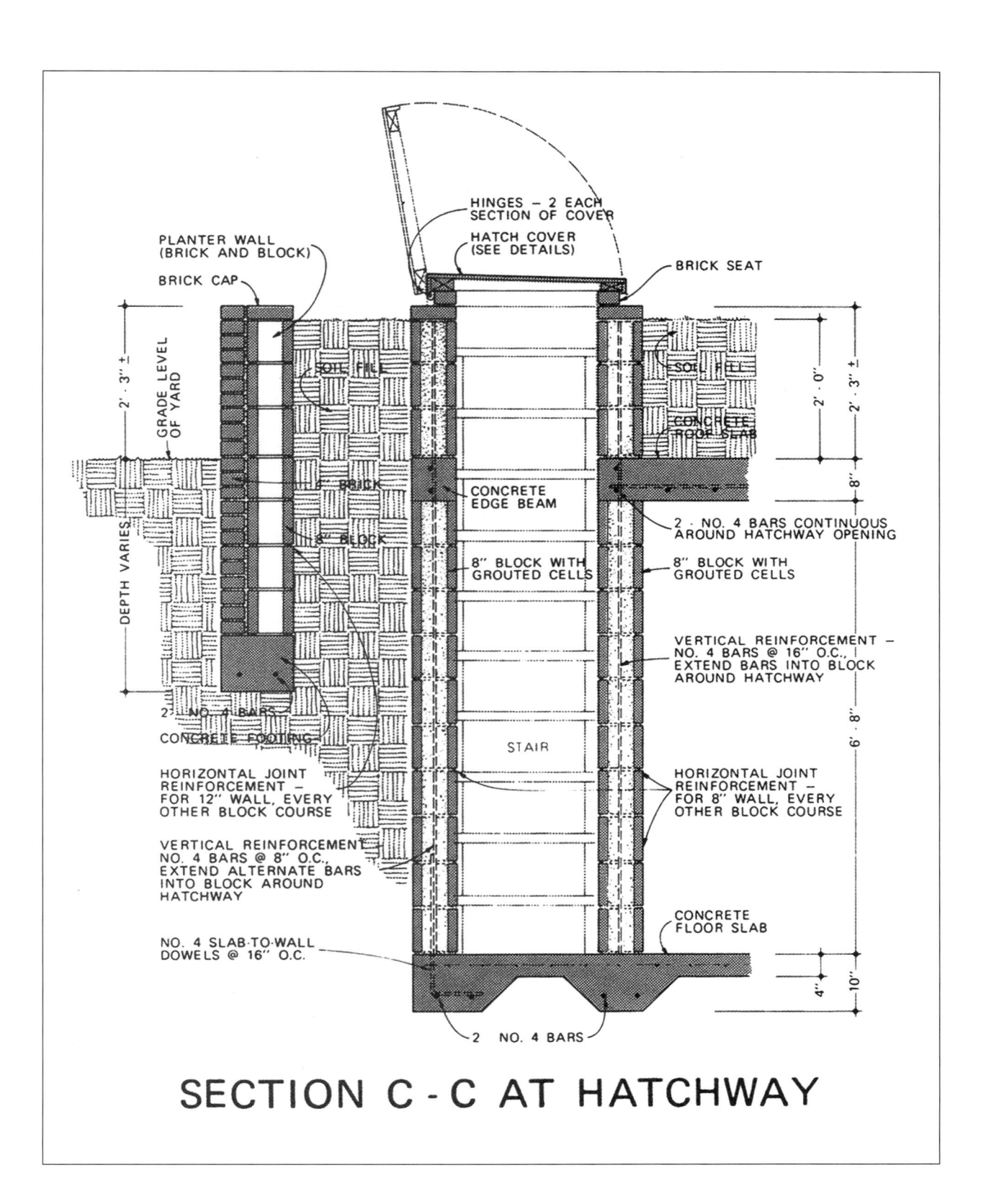

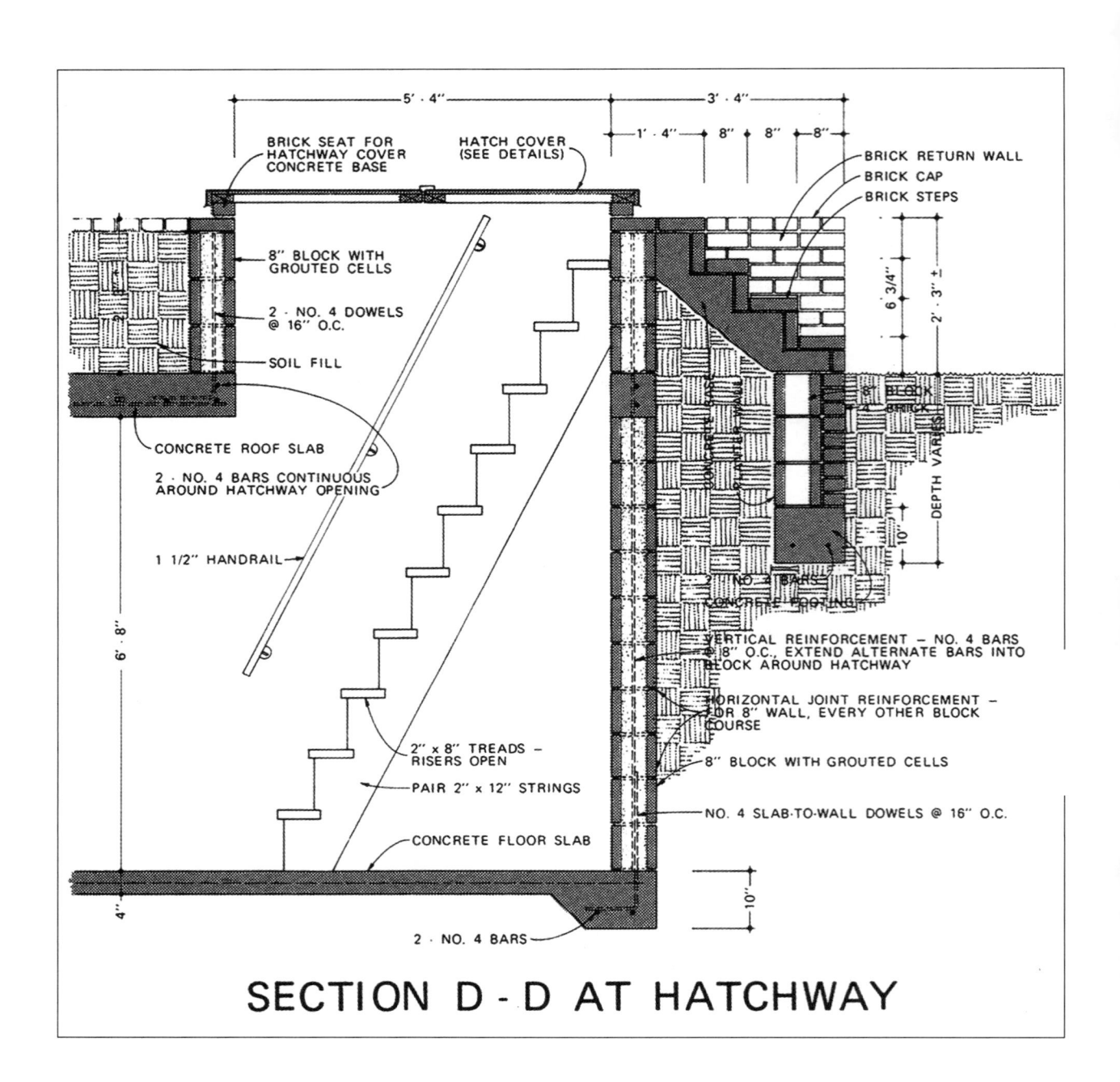

470 Dare To Prepare: Chapter 45: Shelter During Nuclear Emergencies

SECTION D-D AT HATCHWAY

Labels on drawing:
- BRICK SEAT FOR HATCHWAY COVER CONCRETE BASE
- HATCH COVER (SEE DETAILS)
- BRICK RETURN WALL
- BRICK CAP
- BRICK STEPS
- 8" BLOCK WITH GROUTED CELLS
- 2 - NO. 4 DOWELS @ 16" O.C.
- SOIL FILL
- CONCRETE ROOF SLAB
- 2 - NO. 4 BARS CONTINUOUS AROUND HATCHWAY OPENING
- 1 1/2" HANDRAIL
- 2" x 8" TREADS – RISERS OPEN
- PAIR 2" x 12" STRINGS
- CONCRETE FLOOR SLAB
- 2 - NO. 4 BARS
- NO. 2 BARS
- CONCRETE FOOTING
- VERTICAL REINFORCEMENT – NO. 4 BARS @ 8" O.C., EXTEND ALTERNATE BARS INTO BLOCK AROUND HATCHWAY
- HORIZONTAL JOINT REINFORCEMENT – FOR 8" WALL, EVERY OTHER BLOCK COURSE
- 8" BLOCK WITH GROUTED CELLS
- NO. 4 SLAB-TO-WALL DOWELS @ 16" O.C.

Dimensions: 5'-4", 3'-4", 1'-4", 8", 8", 8", 6 3/4", 2'-3"±, DEPTH VARIES, 10", 6'-8", 4", 10"

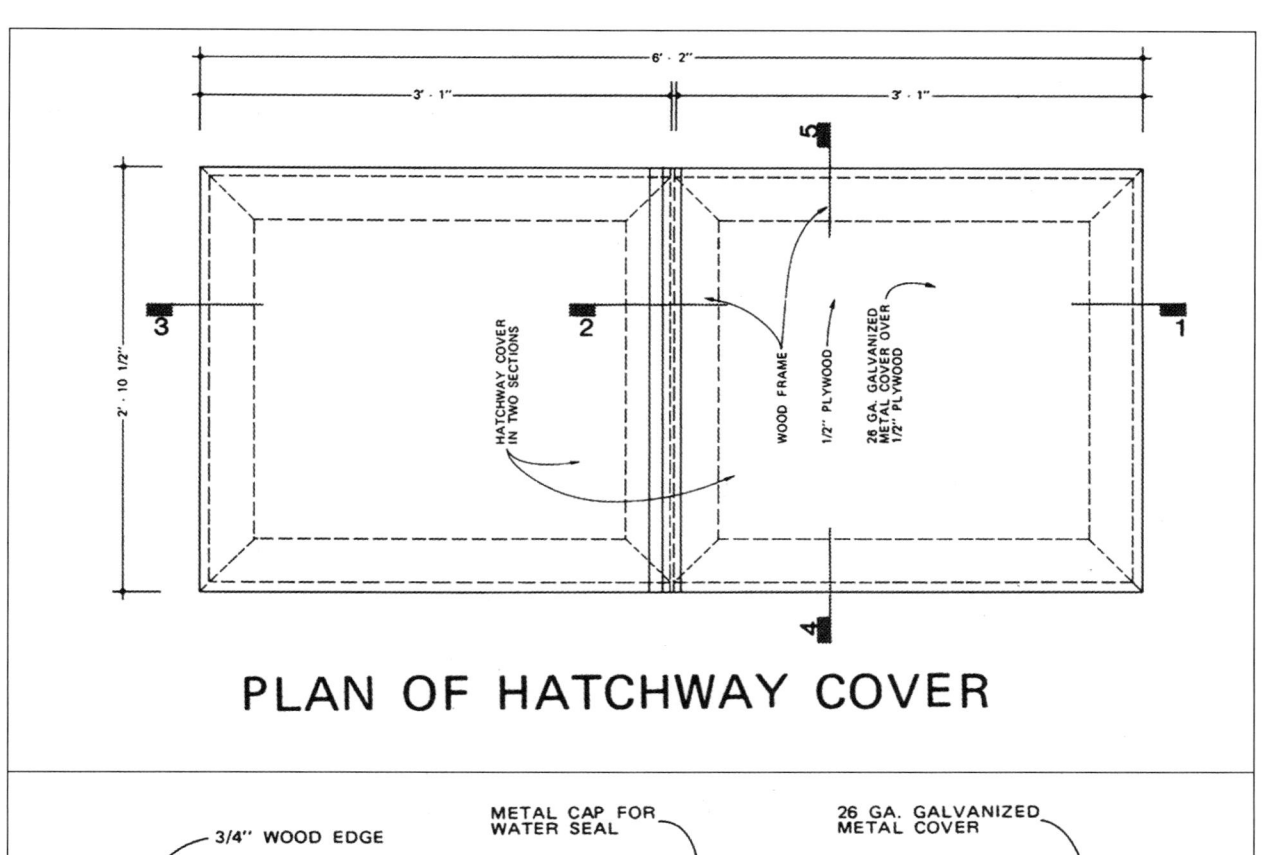

Dare To Prepare: Chapter 45: Shelter During Nuclear Emergencies

PLAN OF HATCHWAY COVER

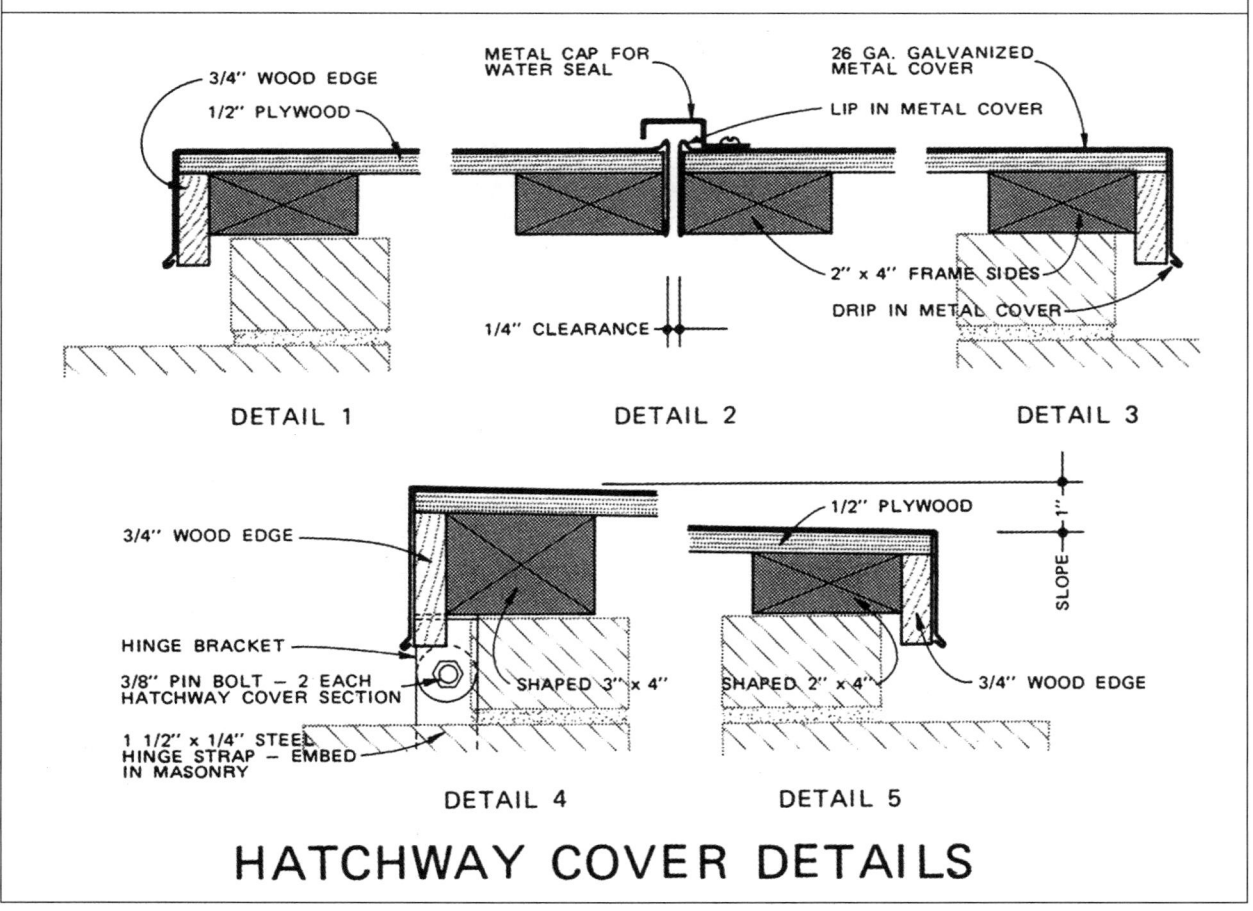

- 6' - 2"
- 3' - 1"
- 3' - 1"
- 2' - 10 1/2"
- HATCHWAY COVER IN TWO SECTIONS
- WOOD FRAME
- 1/2" PLYWOOD
- 26 GA. GALVANIZED METAL COVER OVER 1/2" PLYWOOD

HATCHWAY COVER DETAILS

DETAIL 1
- 3/4" WOOD EDGE
- 1/2" PLYWOOD

DETAIL 2
- METAL CAP FOR WATER SEAL
- 1/4" CLEARANCE

DETAIL 3
- 26 GA. GALVANIZED METAL COVER
- LIP IN METAL COVER
- 2" x 4" FRAME SIDES
- DRIP IN METAL COVER

DETAIL 4
- 3/4" WOOD EDGE
- HINGE BRACKET
- 3/8" PIN BOLT - 2 EACH HATCHWAY COVER SECTION
- 1 1/2" x 1/4" STEEL HINGE STRAP - EMBED IN MASONRY
- SHAPED 3" x 4"

DETAIL 5
- 1/2" PLYWOOD
- SLOPE 1"
- SHAPED 2" x 4"
- 3/4" WOOD EDGE

ROOF SLAB REINFORCEMENT PLAN

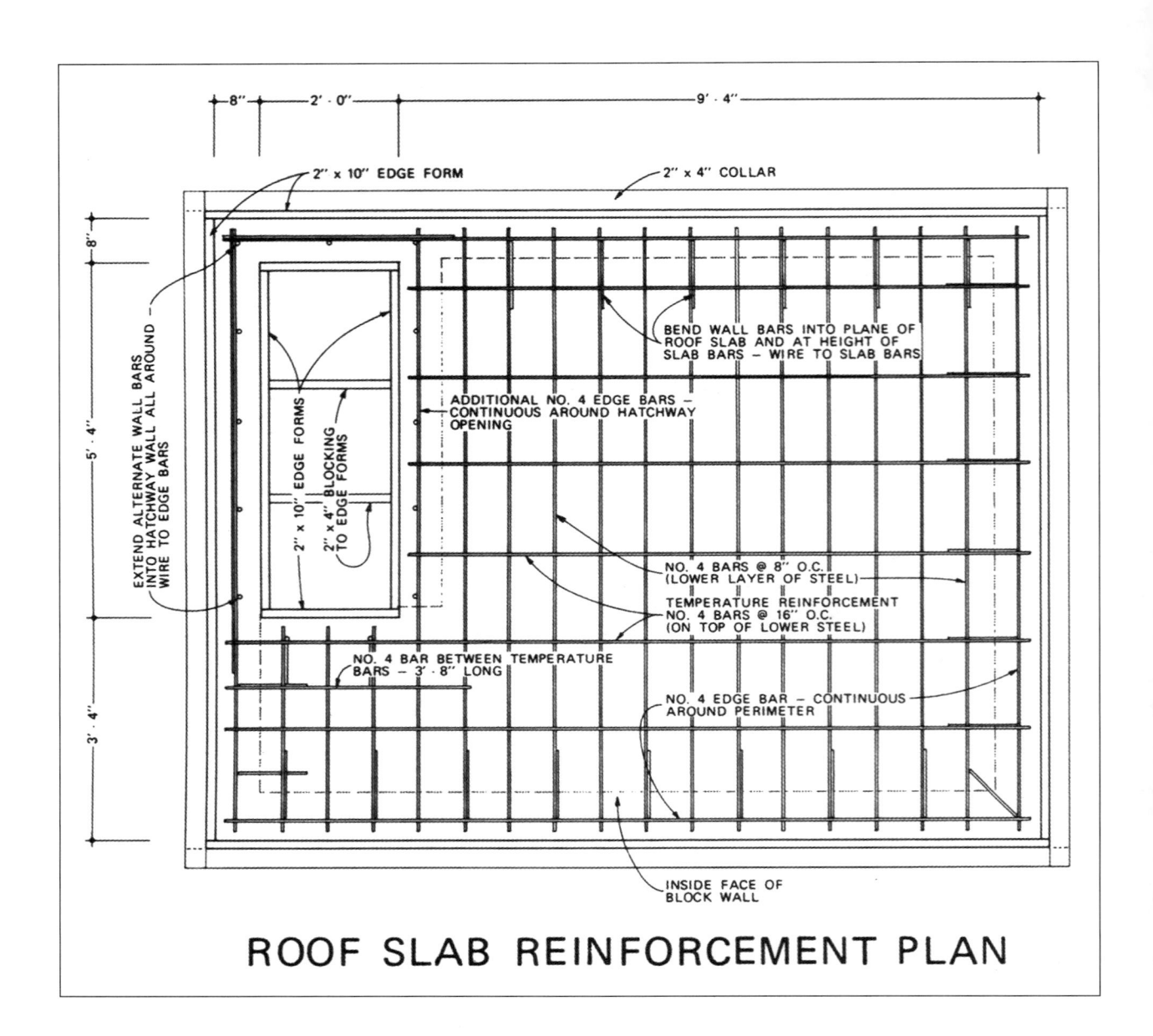

Labels:
- 2" x 10" EDGE FORM
- 2" x 4" COLLAR
- EXTEND ALTERNATE WALL BARS INTO HATCHWAY WALL ALL AROUND – WIRE TO EDGE BARS
- 2" x 10" EDGE FORMS
- 2" x 4" BLOCKING TO EDGE FORMS
- BEND WALL BARS INTO PLANE OF ROOF SLAB AND AT HEIGHT OF SLAB BARS – WIRE TO SLAB BARS
- ADDITIONAL NO. 4 EDGE BARS – CONTINUOUS AROUND HATCHWAY OPENING
- NO. 4 BARS @ 8" O.C. (LOWER LAYER OF STEEL)
- TEMPERATURE REINFORCEMENT NO. 4 BARS @ 16" O.C. (ON TOP OF LOWER STEEL)
- NO. 4 BAR BETWEEN TEMPERATURE BARS – 3' - 8" LONG
- NO. 4 EDGE BAR – CONTINUOUS AROUND PERIMETER
- INSIDE FACE OF BLOCK WALL

Dimensions: 8", 2'-0", 9'-4"; 8", 5'-4", 3'-4"

LIST OF MATERIALS

ITEM	MATERIAL	GRADE	QUANTITY	ITEM	MATERIAL	GRADE	QUANTITY
SLAB AND FOOTINGS				**PLANTER WALLS**			
Batter Boards	1" x 6"	Construction	8 @ 4'–0"	Footing Forms	2" x 10"	Construction	2 @ 17'–7"
Edge Forms	2" x 4"	Construction	2 @ 12'–0"		2" x 10"	Construction	2 @ 15'–4"
	2" x 4"	Construction	2 @ 9'–7"		2" x 10"	Construction	2 @ 14'–8"
Footing Reinf. Steel	No. 4 Bars	Grade 40	4 @ 11'-10"		2" x 10"	Construction	2 @ 12'–5"
	No. 4 Bars	Grade 40	4 @ 9'-2"	Footing Reinf.	No. 4 Bars	Grade 40	4 @ 17'–0"
	No. 4 Bars	Grade 40	2 @ 5'–ll"		No. 4 Bars	Grade 40	4 @ 14'–4"
Footing Dowels	No. 4 Bars	Grade 40	30 @ 2'–8"	Footing Bar Supports	No. 4 Bars	Grade 40	44 @ 1'–0"
Support Bars (Opt.)	No. 4 Bars	Grade 40	36 @ 1'–0"	Concrete	—	2,500 psi	2 cu. yd.
Wire Fabric	6x6 – 8/8	ASTM A185	108 sq. ft.	Block	8"	Concrete	258 units
Dowel Supports	2" x 4"	Construction	2 @ 12'–0"		4"	Concrete	10 units
	2" x 4"	Construction	2 @ 10'–0"	Brick	Standard	—	2,100 units
	2" x 4"	Construction	4 @ 3'–0"	Horizontal Joint Reinf.	12" Wall	Trussed Wire	130 lin. ft.
Sump Forms	2" x 4"	Construction	4 @ 1'–4"		8" Wall	Trussed Wire	16 lin. ft.
	½" Plywood	C – D	½ pc. 4' x 8'	Prefab. Corner Reinf.	12" Wall	Trussed Wire	8 pieces
Concrete	—	2,500 psi	2.75 cu. yd.	Mortar	—	Type S	40 cu. ft.
SHELTER WALLS (Perimeter, Partition, and Hatchway)				**HATCHWAY COVER**			
Block	8"	Concrete	380 units	Framing Lumber	3" x 4"	Construction	2 @ 3'–0"
Horiz. Joint Reinf.	8" Wall	Trussed Wire	212 lin. ft.		2" x 4"	Construction	2 @ 3'–0"
Prefab. Corner Reinf.	8" Wall	Trussed Wire	20 pieces		2" x 4"	Construction	4 @ 2'–9"
Vertical Reinf. Steel	No. 4 Bars	Grade 40	23 @ 8'–0"	Cover	½" Plywood	C – D	1 pc. 4' x 8'
	No. 4 Bars	Grade 40	30 @ 6'–8"	Trim	1" x 4"	No. 2 Pine	24 lin. ft.
Hatchway Vert. Steel	No. 4 Bars	Grade 40	11 @ 9'–4"	Sheet Metal	—	26 gauge	2 @ 14 sq.ft.
Hatchway Dowels	No. 4 Bars	Grade 40	2 @ 3'–4"	Hinges	—	—	4 pieces
Mortar	—	Type S	17 cu. ft.	**STAIR**			
Grout	—	Type S	94 cu. ft.	Strings	2" x 12"	No. 2 Fir	2 @ 12'–0"
ROOF SLAB				Treads	2" x 8"	No. 2 Fir	10 @ 2'–0"
Shoring Lumber	2" x 4"	Construction	27 @ 6'–7"	**VENTILATION**			
	2" x 6"	Construction	7 @ 8'–0"	Centrifugal Blower	—	—	1 unit
	2" x 6"	Construction	5 @ 2'–8"	Wall Sleeves	8" long	Steel or ABS	3 pieces
Deck Forms	½" Plywood	C.D	½" pieces	Piping	3" ID	Steel or ABS	22 lin. ft.
Edge Forms	2" x 10"	Construction	2 @ 12'–0"	90° Elbows	3" ID	Steel or ABS	2 pieces
	2" x 10"	Construction	2 @ 9'–7"	Tees	3" ID	Steel or ABS	1 piece
Hatchway Edges	2" x 10"	Construction	2 @ 5'–1"	Intake Filter	—	—	1 unit
	2" x 10"	Construction	2 @ 2'–0"	Exhaust Filter	—	—	1 unit
	2" x 4"	Construction	2 @ 1'–9"	**DAMPPROOFING**			
Collar Boards	2" x 4"	Construction	2 @ 12'–10"	All Surfaces	6 Mil	Polyethylene	760 sq. ft.
	2" x 4"	Construction	2 @ 10'–2"	**MISCELLANEOUS ITEMS**			
Collar Supports	2" x 4"	Construction	14 @ 7'–0"	Stakes, String, Nails, Wire, Other Fasteners			
Structural Reinf.	No. 4 Bars	Grade 40	18 @ 9'–2"	Plumbing Piping (Optional)			
	No. 4 Bars	Grade 40	1 @ 3'–8"	Electrical Wiring (Optional)			
	No. 4 Bars	Grade 40	3 @ 3'–2"				
Temp. Reinf.	No. 4 Bars	Grade 40	4 @ 11'–10"				
	No.4 Bars	Grade 40	4 @ 9'–2"				
Hatchway Edges	No. 4 Bars	Grade 40	2 @ 6'–8"				
	No. 4 Bars	Grade 40	2 @ 3'–4"				
Concrete	—	2,500 psi	2 ¾ cu. yd.				

* Materials quantities do not include allowances for waste.
** Some forming lumber may be reused during different phases of the construction work.

BURYING SHIPPING CONTAINERS

In lieu of constructing a fallout shelter, you may want to consider using shipping containers. They offer the solution to a number of problems. People often use them to inconspicuously store supplies. Properly built, they can be excellent protection as storm or fallout shelters.

An engineering friend in Montana designed the following layouts for various size plans. He preferred to donate the designs rather than have public acknowledgement so in keeping with his wishes, he quietly has our deep gratitude.

1) How much do shipping containers cost?

In quantity, used 20 foot shipping containers in Denver can be purchased for just over $1000 each, and used 40-foot containers run $1500-2000. New containers are roughly 50-80% above the used prices.

Costs vary depending upon location. The closer you live to a major shipping port, the cheaper they are likely to be. In Alaska, for example, they're almost dirt cheap, running $500-700 for a 40 footer, because once shippers get them there, there's no financial incentive to haul them back to the ships.

In Long Beach, CA; Oakland, CA; or Seattle, WA, as well as Houston and Miami, and many other major sea ports, containers can be quite inexpensive. In some non-port major cities like Dallas, a single 40 ft. container, delivered and rolled off onto the ground, costs about $1700. Prices vary, so check around.

2) Should I spend the extra money and buy new shipping containers?

Not necessarily. You never quite know what you're going to get unless you have the opportunity to inspect them first. Potential problems with used containers do exist, but most container dealers and brokers will have scrapped non-serviceable units. Most dealers or brokers emphatically state that all containers pass rigorous inspections. However, make your preferences, concerns, and intended use known to your supplier. If they know you won't accept rust, weatherproofing or sealing problems, dents, and potentially contaminated units, they'll be more inclined to help you find the highest quality used containers.

Dept. of Transportation-certified steel shipping containers are designed to take a tremendous amount of surface rust and discoloration before they are ever affected structurally. If you buy used containers, sort them according to structural defects and interior quality, and place them accordingly in your underground home. The ugly ones will do just fine as silos, workshops, or cold storage. Reserve the "pretty" ones for your living areas.

New shipping containers have recently become less expensive as many more end-users are electing to purchase their goods from China and elsewhere, buying the containers along with their goods. New units are built to the rigid DOT standards and certified for sea worthiness. Because they're only used one time, they are considered and sold as NEW. If you have the opportunity to buy new containers and don't have to pay a big premium, you'll likely have less to worry about in the long run.

3) What do I look for when I'm inspecting used shipping containers?

If practical, take a hammer, or geologist's pick, and bang on rusty spots, especially where there may have been damage or creasing due to impacts. If a fresh coat of paint has been applied, try to look beneath to see if rust and weak places have been covered. If you see damage to the outside, look to see how it affects the interior. Minor and sometimes major impacts are often self-healing and do not significantly affect the integrity of the overall structure.

Check the weather stripping around doors, the ease or difficulty in opening and closing the doors, as well as damage and wear to the hardwood floor.

Walk all the way to the end inside and check for any contamination or overpowering odors. Case in point. The engineer who designed these plans, saw a very inexpensive 40 footer and walked inside to tour the container. Once inside his eyes stung and watered profusely. After only a couple of minutes, he had difficulty breathing and had to go outside to fresh air. He asked, "What's up with this?" and was informed that it had been used to transport chilies from Mexico. The "burn" made it uninhabitable.

Look underneath for any damage. Last, close the doors while you're inside to look for light leaks. If you discover a small hole, call it to the dealer's attention and he'll likely reduce the price. Small holes are fairly easy to spot weld shut; medium size holes can be scabbed and welded. Give containers a miss that have major structural defects.

4) How much will delivery cost?

Delivery costs vary depending on the distance to destination. In general, you're probably going to spend about $1.50 per mile hauled by an independent trucker to your location, more if fuel costs remain elevated. If transporting them more than 400 or 500 miles, it might be more cost effective to ship by rail and then by truck. In most cases, shipping by rail may not be practical for hauls of less than 1,000 miles until your quantities are greater than five.

5) What size shipping containers should I buy?

Containers come in several sizes, though most will be the standard 40-foot steel cargo container with outside dimensions of 8'Wx8½'Hx40'L. The next most common size is 20' long with the same height and width as the standard 40 foot. Occasionally you'll see the high cube 40 footers, which are 1 foot taller, or 8'Wx9½'H.

Anything else is quite rare, like the 24', 44' or 48' standards used in rail shipments. Refrigerated containers are also available which can be the same price as the non-refrigerated units as long as the cooling systems aren't functional or have been removed. One might think these would be a good deal since they already come with insulation, however since it's located on the *inside*, which not only reduces living space, it reduces interior thermal mass. Insulation is always better located far enough away to acquire a reasonable amount of thermal mass within the structure of your underground living space.

6) Which are better, the 20 foot or the 40 foot containers?

When it comes to building underground structures, the 20' containers turn out to be a bit stronger and more versatile, but they'll also cost a bit more. The increased cost of the 20s versus the 40s varies with location and season.

At the start of the Iraq War in early 2003, 20' containers were in high demand for supplies headed to the Middle East. Availability of 20's on the East coast plummeted and prices jumped considerably. By the Fall 2003, supplies and prices had stabilized to pre-war rates.

7) Are shipping containers strong enough to be buried underground?

In fact, many open sea oil rigs utilize hundreds of shipping containers welded together to form the massive deck infrastructures on which the superstructure buildings are erected. Virtually any 20 or 40 foot shipping container can hold cargo in excess of 80,000 pounds, secured only by the 8 corner mounts located on each end. Many of the newer DOT certified containers are actually built and rated to hold cargo in excess of 100,000 pounds and some as much as 120,000 pounds.

While 100,000 pounds of soil on top of a container may seem like a lot, it's actually only a little more than three feet of soil covering a 40 footer, or a little more than 6 feet for a twenty. Shipping containers aren't designed with load-bearing roofs as are their floors.

So, what's the best way to bury these things and not have their roofs buckle or cave in? This is solved by is reinforcing the roofs in one of two ways, either with used railroad ties or, by a combination of railroad ties and rebar reinforced concrete. By distributing the load of the oversoil along the edges, and thereby to the walls, the load can be evenly transmitted down to the lengthwise beams that are designed to bear the weight of the container's cargo deck.

8) How do I reinforce the roof to withstand the weight of the soil?

Soil weighs about 100 pounds per cubic foot, or 2,700 pounds per cubic yard. Depending on how deep the container is buried, consider reinforcing your container's roof with either a course of used railroad ties or a combination of both railroad ties and rebar reinforced concrete. Without reinforcement, the container can't be buried deeper than about one or two feet. At minimum, stick with a course of #5 grade used railroad ties. The grade #5 railroad tie comes either with the edges rounded, or squared, and are always 7"Hx8"W across the flats by 8'L, plus or minus ½" on the width and height and 1" on the length. While other grades (#2 through #6) may work as well, the #5's seem to be the most commonly available and are quite able to take the loads of up to 5 or 6 feet of soil. Beyond this soil depth, however, you must employ rebar-reinforced, or pre-stressed concrete.

In practice, if you're not using a 6" thick rebar-reinforced concrete roof on top of your railroad ties, add rows of #5 railroad ties along the length of the containers' roof edges that will be bearing the soil's weight. These spacer rows are positioned so that the 7" dimension is vertical, and the 8" dimension is horizontal, and the 8' length is aligned with, and directly centered over, the edges of the roof. The edge spacers reinforce the actual roof supports to allow for both sagging and insulation.

If you're not planning on adding a rebar-reinforced concrete roof over the railroad ties, the spacer rows along the long edges of the container roof are optional. The reason these spacer rows aren't needed is that the reinforced rebar drastically reduces sagging potential under the load of the soil. Additionally, you definitely want to insulate on top of the concrete to maximize the interior thermal mass of your living space.

9) Why should I have to insulate my containers? Won't 4 or 5 feet of soil do that?

No, soil is not an effective insulator at any depth, especially when it's damp or moist. Even though soil is a terrible overall insulator, it does, of course, have some insulating properties. Factoid: the first 5 feet of soil over the roof will supply 90% of the insulating ability, if 10' of soil were over the roof. The only thing soil does well is act as a thermal capacitor, or thermal storage material. Soil may be a poor insulator, but it's great at storing and conducting heat.

Imagine a 5,000+ sq. ft. four story underground home is sitting on top of and surrounded by millions of tons of soil, rock, and water. All of this soil has a tremendous amount of thermal mass, or thermal potential, stored in it. In summer, heat from the sun is slowly conducted down into the first 10, or perhaps 20 feet of soil. Then in winter that residual summer heat radiates or is conducted out into air or outer space. By placing your home deep enough to penetrate into the temperature-stable soil depths, you've tapped into a tremendous storage medium of thermal capacity. And, through the strategic use of insulation and/or a modest internal heat source, you can keep the living area of your home cool, temperature-stable and comfortable all year long.

10) Should I insulate my containers before or after I bury them?

Before, and they must be insulated on the *outside*. Remember you're going to need all the thermal mass you can get in the living area to buffer and store heat or cool, so heating and ventilation systems won't have to work overtime to regulate the living environment.

At minimum, insulate the roof and walls of your uppermost containers. Depending upon latitude and altitude, soil temperature is going to vary throughout the year.

Soil temperature at a depth 10 or 20 feet will change very little seasonally. But living underground in southern Texas or Arizona is quite a bit different compared to northern Montana or Minnesota. On average, stable soil temperature is going to be slightly above the average yearly mean air temperature for your area over the past 30 years. The exception would be if you live in a geo-thermally active, which wouldn't be a good location for underground containers. (See *Prudent Places USA* by Holly Deyo for maps of geothermal activity in America.)

Rather than dig a hole and lower a thermometer inside, an easier way to determine your soil temperature 20' underground is to go to The Weather Channel's website **www.weather.com**. Once there, type in your zip code and it will bring up information relevant to your location. Check the monthly average temperatures by adding the monthly mean temperatures and divide by 12. This gives the average mean temperature, and thereby, an approximate soil temperature at a stable depth.

For example, the average yearly mean temperature for Laredo, Texas is 74.2°F and 69.2°F in Tucson, Arizona. Either way, you could live very comfortably in an underground home with a constant year round temperature of either 69.2 or 74.2°F. However, don't let this comfort zone entice you into thinking you won't need insulation. While you could, in theory, avoid insulation if your roof is covered by at least 10' of soil, it's more practical to insulate the roof and only have to bury the container 5' or so. In most areas of the southern States you'd likely need only to insulate the roof and walls down to about a depth of 10-12' feet from the surface. The need for heat in winter, or air conditioning in summer would be almost nonexistent.

One word of caution... If you're planning on living in Fargo, North Dakota, at 41.4°F, or coldest of all, International Falls, Minneapolis, at 37.5°F, you'd likely need heat *all year long*. In fact, most of the middle-to-northern latitudes will need both heat and complete insulation of roof, walls, and floor.

The most economical way to insulate is with fiberglass batting, however, this form of insulation would only be practical on the roof underneath the railroad ties in the area between the railroad tie spacers and the railroad tie roof. While this might be the least expensive, it's not practical because you'd have to sacrifice significant thermal mass in that the both the railroad ties and the concrete above the ties would be outside the envelope of the insulated living space.

11) What sort of skills, tools, and equipment will I need to build an underground container home?

In addition to the same type of skills, tools, and equipment required to build conventional housing, you must be able to weld and use a cutting torch. You'll also need to rent, borrow, or purchase a front-loader backhoe or excavator, a dump truck, and a crane to lift and place your containers in their proper assembled configuration. Large (½") penetrating welds are necessary to securely join the corner blocks of the shipping containers into a massive single assembly. Steel is very strong, and sufficiently flexible to withstand many of the stresses involved when the earth shifts and moves in earthquakes and ground slippages.

12) Are there building codes that would accommodate my building an underground container home?

Absolutely not. Building codes are written to accommodate virtually no alternative building methods or materials. Your best bet is to build your underground home in a county or parish of your state that doesn't have or doesn't enforce strict residential building codes. While this leaves out about 95% of America's prime underground real estate, you're likely safer away from the big cities more prone to enforcing building codes. Another approach is to treat underground containers as storage sheds only, i.e. not intended for anything more than underground storage shed or underground shelter. Building codes for these vary considerably and are less strict for storage.

Dare To Prepare: Chapter 45: Shelter During Nuclear Emergencies

RULES OF THUMB SUMMARY

1. Properly painted, assembled, positioned, welded, bolted, braced and insulated, a home constructed from shipping containers can be buried under 3-10' of soil (and perhaps a lot more) depending upon how the soil load is distributed over the roof of the uppermost containers.
2. One cubic foot of soil weighs about 100 pounds.
3. When the overhead soil load is properly distributed to the vertical edges and walls of the assembly, as well as with added vertical steel supports, the total practical load exceeds well over a half a million pounds per 20' container. That works out to over 30' of soil!
4. Five feet of soil achieves 90% of the thermal capacive benefit of 10' feet, so going deeper than 5' is likely unnecessary.
5. One of the most inexpensive ways to reinforce the roof structure (which allows more soil to be placed over the top of the container), is with a combination of used 8' railroad ties and a 6" thick over pour of rebar-reinforced concrete.
6. The benefit of living underground, especially in cooler climates, is a low requirement for either heating or air conditioning. Once the depth reaches 15-20', there is very little temperature variation between summer and winter. With sufficiently insulated roof, walls and floor, the cooling and thermal stabilizing effect of the soil surrounding the walls, and under the deepest floors of the house will reduce the energy for cooling or heating to almost zero (in the northern latitudes).

Why do steel shipping containers make the most efficient and inexpensive underground building material?

1. Shipping containers are relatively inexpensive, costing about $1000 per 20-foot container or just over $3 per square foot.
2. They are also extremely strong and durable when properly assembled.
3. Shipping containers are almost completely waterproof. If a leak occurs, it can be easily spot-welded and sealed.
4. They already come with a durable hardwood floor.
5. They can be easily welded together at the corner blocks, and ½ – ¾" steel plates and brackets can be welded along the lengths to increase their load bearing and assembly strength.
6. They can easily be reinforced with steel pipe, channel, or square stock, either for vertical loads, or for creating large interior rooms surrounded by containers on all sides, ceiling, and the floor.
7. Shipping containers come in many lengths, 20, 24, 40, 44, 48, and 53 are among the most common lengths, but all containers are 8'W wide, and most are 8½'H, except for the "high cube" which run 9½'H.
8. Any length of shipping container can be positioned vertically with a spiral staircase installed or used as a grain silo, lined or bagged for water storage, or used for a coal bin.

SHIPPING CONTAINER HOUSE PLANS

One Bedroom, One 40-foot Container: 320 sq ft 1-2 People with 5-person years cool food storage (see drawings next page)

The One Bedroom, Single 40-foot Container earth sheltered home is designed to hold 3 to 5 feet of overburden (soil) when a rebar (steel) reinforced 4" concrete roof slab is used to distribute the load of the earth placed over the top of the container. Ideally the roof, walls, and floor of the container should be insulated from the soil, and 4 inch (on walls) to 8 inch (on roof) high density extruded polystyrene foam is used (usually tinted blue). When insulating earth sheltered homes, it's important to place the insulation as far away from the interior living space as possible, i.e. to place it on the other side of the concrete roof and to capture a 6-12" layer of soil between the outer steel walls of the container and the insulation if practical. Without a rebar reinforced concrete roof you probably wouldn't want to trust an average steel container to hold more than 2 feet of soil.

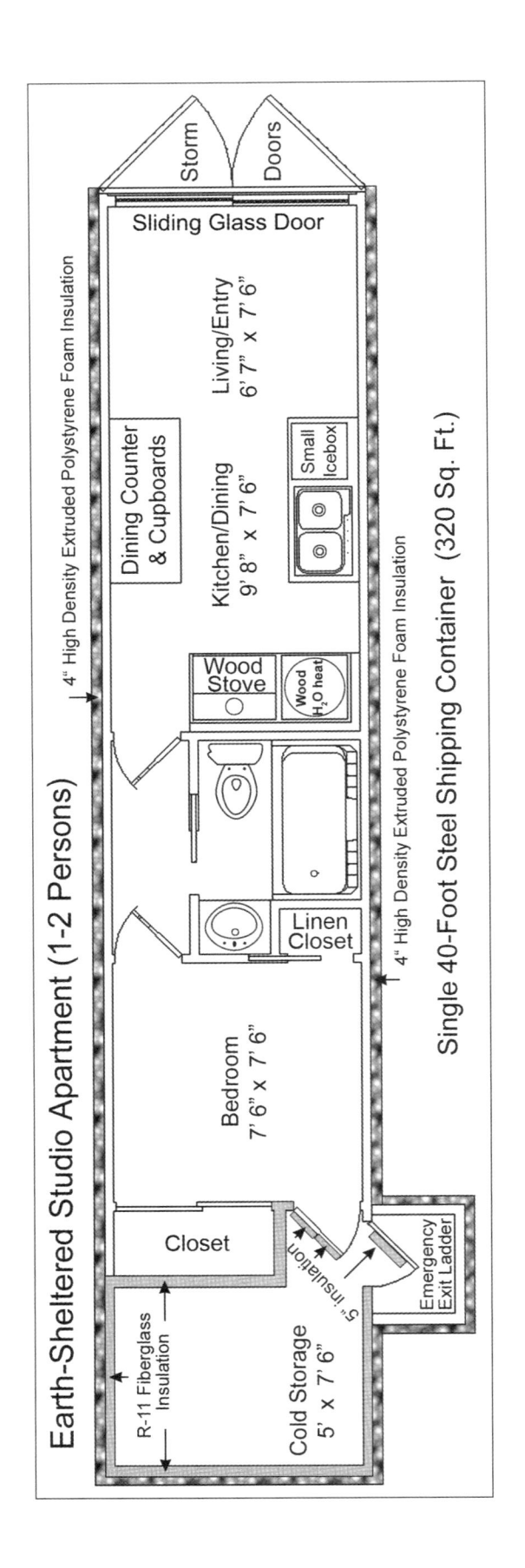

Four Bedrooms, Three 40-foot Containers: 960 sq ft 4-6 People, 20-person years cool food storage

The Four Bedroom, Three 40-foot Container earth sheltered home is designed to maintain the same economy of space as the two smaller structures above, i.e. the bedrooms are all very small, smaller than most conventional homes, and nothing about it would tend to give one the impression of spaciousness. There are just more of the same very small features that would make this design ideal for any family seeking to live with the superior economy, security, and efficiency that a wilderness earth sheltered home can offer versus the conveniences of modern city living. All three of these minimal designs are intended to be located off the electrical grid and far away from cities, towns, and structured society.

The two and three container designs have a solar panel retreat (illustrated and) located behind the container doors (storm doors) such that two solar panels could be stored on the inside of the doors between the sliding glass doors and the storm doors for safety when storms or concealment demands warrant their withdrawal from service. When hinged at the top of the panel to the top edge of the southerly positioned container opening, the panels can easily be swung up and adjusted to the optimal angle for maximal solar efficiency, depending upon season. This three container design, therefore, could accommodate up to 6 securable solar panels.

Three Bedroom, Six 40-foot Containers: 1,920 sq ft 4 to 6 People with 30-person years cool food storage

The Three Bedroom Deluxe, Six 40-foot Container earth sheltered home is designed with the optimal balance of economy and luxury with ample space in bedrooms and living areas. This home definitely gives one a feeling of roominess in a more generous way than the previous plans and tends to overcome the cramped feelings that some people occasionally experience in an underground home. There are glass front wood stoves or potbelly stoves in all bedrooms and living room for increased comfort control for northern latitude locations without the requirement for a central powered heating system. There are 15 small dual purpose ventilation and light pipes to provide day time sky-light as well as adjustable passive ventilation for maximum fresh air control.

The unique feature in this model is the 1,000-plus cu. ft. Ice House located in the deepest part of the rear of the cold/cool storage container. With the capacity of holding several tons of salted ice, this icy cold storage will keep meat and other frozen or semi-frozen food through the hot summer months. This plan also features recessed retreats for a maximum of 10 solar panels located behind the storm doors. There is a small side entrance/exit door for easy access in or out when the storm doors are secured and solar panels are securely nested inside. The outside of the storm doors would optimally be insulated with 4 to 6 inches of high density closed cell extruded polystyrene foam and fitted with either imitation rock or local vegetation camouflage.

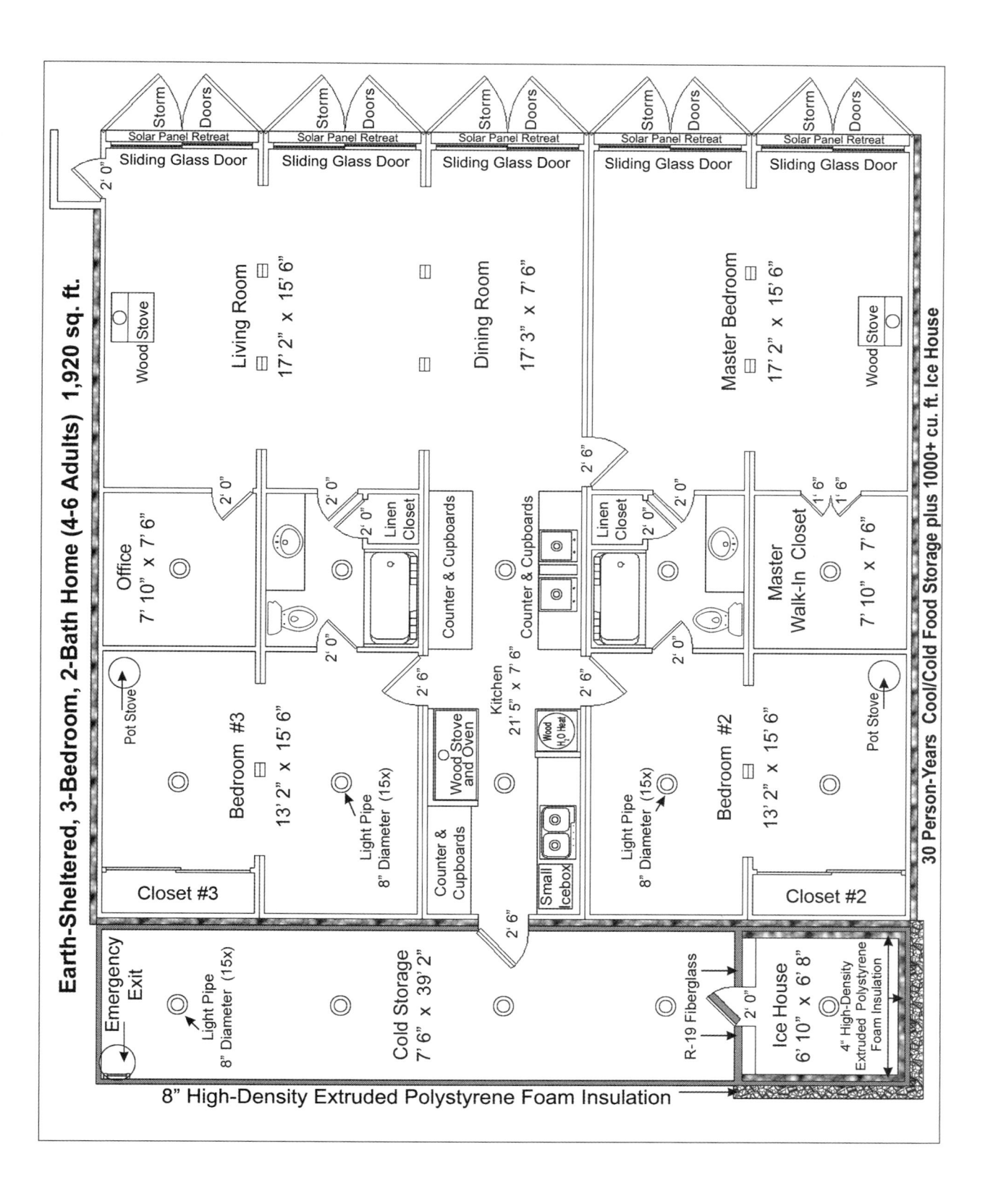

Dare To Prepare: Chapter 45: Shelter During Nuclear Emergencies

Earth-Sheltered, 3-Bedroom, 2-Bath Home (4-6 Adults) 1,920 sq. ft.

Storm Doors (×5)
Solar Panel Retreat (×5)
Sliding Glass Door (×5)

2' 0"

Wood Stove

Living Room
17' 2" x 15' 6"

Dining Room
17' 3" x 7' 6"

Master Bedroom
17' 2" x 15' 6"

Wood Stove

2' 6"

Office
7' 10" x 7' 6"

2' 0" 2' 0"

Linen Closet

Counter & Cupboards

Counter & Cupboards

Linen Closet

2' 0" 2' 0"

Master Walk-In Closet
7' 10" x 7' 6"

1' 6" 1' 6"

2' 0"

2' 6"   2' 6"   2' 0"

Pot Stove

Bedroom #3
13' 2" x 15' 6"

Light Pipe 8" Diameter (15x)

Wood Stove and Oven

Kitchen
21' 5" x 7' 6"

Wood H₂O Heat

Small Icebox

Light Pipe 8" Diameter (15x)

Bedroom #2
13' 2" x 15' 6"

Pot Stove

Counter & Cupboards

Closet #3

Closet #2

30 Person-Years Cool/Cold Food Storage plus 1000+ cu. ft. Ice House

Emergency Exit

Light Pipe 8" Diameter (15x)

Cold Storage
7' 6" x 39' 2"

R-19 Fiberglass

2' 0"

Ice House
6' 10" x 6' 8"

4" High-Density Extruded Polystyrene Foam Insulation

8" High-Density Extruded Polystyrene Foam Insulation

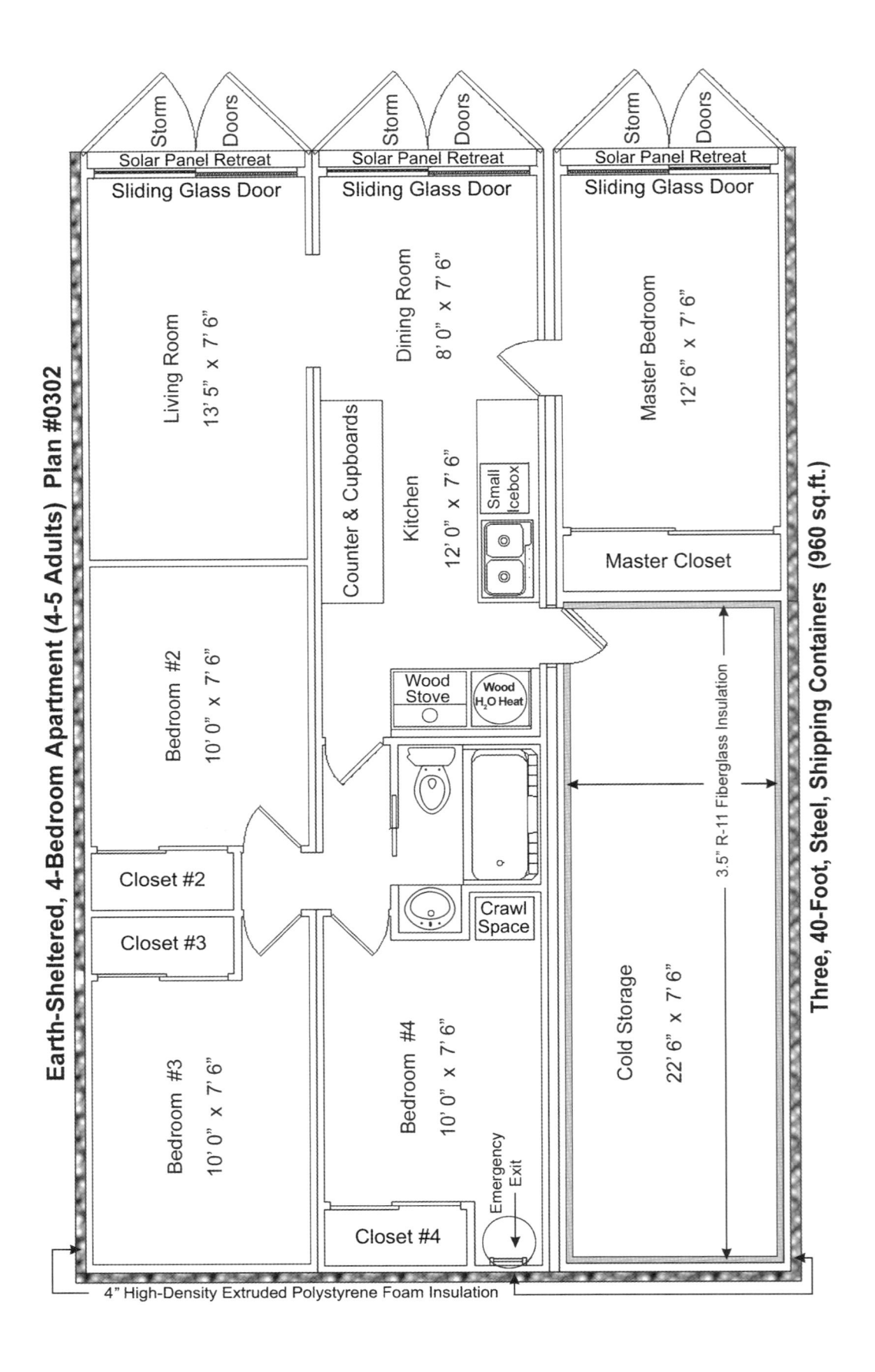

Earth-Sheltered, 4-Bedroom Apartment (4-5 Adults) Plan #0302 — **Three, 40-Foot, Steel, Shipping Containers (960 sq.ft.)**

Storm Doors (×3)

Solar Panel Retreat / Sliding Glass Door (×3)

- Living Room — 13' 5" x 7' 6"
- Dining Room — 8' 0" x 7' 6"
- Master Bedroom — 12' 6" x 7' 6"
- Counter & Cupboards
- Kitchen — 12' 0" x 7' 6"
- Small Icebox
- Master Closet
- Bedroom #2 — 10' 0" x 7' 6"
- Wood Stove
- Wood H₂O Heat
- Closet #2
- Closet #3
- Crawl Space
- Bedroom #3 — 10' 0" x 7' 6"
- Bedroom #4 — 10' 0" x 7' 6"
- Closet #4
- Emergency Exit
- Cold Storage — 22' 6" x 7' 6"

3.5" R-11 Fiberglass Insulation

4" High-Density Extruded Polystyrene Foam Insulation

Chapter 46: Nuclear and Radiological Attack

In addition to traditional nuclear devices, terrorists using a radiological dispersion device (RDD) – a "dirty nuke" or "dirty bomb" – is considered far more likely. Radiological weapons are a combination of conventional explosives, like dynamite, TNT or C4 packaged with radioactive material. They're designed to scatter radioactive particles over a general area rather than create blast damage. Such radiological weapons appeal to terrorists because they require very little technical knowledge to build and deploy compared to a nuclear device.

Terrorists using a nuke would probably be limited to smaller "suitcase" weapons. Their strength would be like the bombs used during World War II. Though the effect would be the same as a weapon delivered by an intercontinental missile, the area and severity would be greatly limited. That's the good news.

DIRTY BOMB ATTACK 'ALL BUT INEVITABLE'

On the downside, components for this type bomb are too readily available. Radioactive materials are widely used in medicine, agriculture, industry and research. With such heavy use, they would be much easier to obtain than weapons grade uranium or plutonium.

The Nuclear Regulatory Commission revealed that since 1996 some 1,500 pieces of radioactive material have gone missing or were stolen. Of that amount, half have never been recovered.

Additionally, 2 million places in the U.S. alone use radioactive material for medical procedures, food disinfection, medical equipment sterilization, oil drilling, and in research and industrial processes. That's a lot of potential theft targets.

Some of these materials have accidentally turned up in junkyards. The Internet is another avenue for obtaining them. One person who obviously wasn't thinking advertised an unwanted cancer treatment machine on the Net – free for carting it off.

Based on the abundance of radioactive material, its wide use throughout the world and subsequent poor tracking history, we're biding time till a dirty nuke explodes. Charles D. Ferguson, a science and technology fellow at the Council on Foreign Relations summed up things this way: "I don't want to fan hysteria but ... a dirty bomb attack is all but inevitable in the coming years."[128]

WHAT MIGHT HAPPEN

Experts agree the danger of a dirty nuke is not from the blast as with a massive nuclear weapon but from radioactive particles blown into the air. Some harm would come from radiation exposure but more problems could stem from panic and disruption. In order to put the RDD threat into proper context, consider the consequences proposed in this hypothetical New York City scenario:

> "At 8:30 a.m. on a Tuesday morning, as commuters converge on Manhattan, an al Qaeda operative explodes a dirty bomb outside the New York Stock Exchange. The device, while not especially powerful, contains a radioactive payload – in this case, cesium extracted from radiological equipment that was stolen from a New Jersey hospital by a sleeper working there as a lab tech.
>
> "The initial blast kills only a few dozen people, but radiation is quickly dispersed by the prevailing winds. Minutes after the explosion, New York City Police officers arrive – still unaware of the real nature of the blast. But when a radiation detector in one officer's car goes wild, it becomes clear that a dirty bomb has detonated in the financial center of America's biggest city.
>
> "Word of the explosion reverberates throughout New York. Many residents panic – despite assurances from the mayor and police chief that contamination levels would exceed government limits only in about 40 city blocks. And by 3 p.m., half of Manhattan has tried to leave, clogging trains, highways, and bridges.
>
> "Six months later, the financial district remains largely off-limits, and the local economy is limping along amid a cratering of business confidence, the collapse of the tourism industry, and a property market in free fall. Economists put the eventual economic losses at an astronomical $1 trillion."[129]

CESIUM-137 (CS-137) SCENARIO

Cs-137 is a by-product of nuclear energy in spent fuel rods. Since virtually all facilities store their nuclear waste on-site, they provide another avenue for acquisition. This unsettling thought became a bigger concern when video revealed nuke plant guards regularly sleeping while on duty in 2007. "The tape, eventually given to WCBS, a CBS television affiliate in New York City, showed the armed workers snoozing against walls, slumped on tabletops or with eyes closed and heads bobbing." [130]

Concern over transporting nuclear waste from the 104 existing reactors to a central storage site is a primary argument against Yucca Mountain. To reach the proposed destination in southern Nevada, most spent nuclear fuel (SNF) would travel hundreds of miles over interstates and highways. From the Wiscasset, Maine storage facility, that's nearly a 3,000-mile trek.

The Dept. of Energy expects more than 100,000 shipments will be trucked, railed or shipped to Yucca Mountain. That means 100,000 opportunities for interception. This only counts SNF for existing reactors. With a growing demand for electricity, another 35 to 40 nukers are being considered.

The current SNF travel routes slice through 703 counties. Since some of the proposed reactors would be in new areas, it adds to the number of counties exposed. Surely the spent fuel will be safely housed to the best of anyone's ability, but we must make allowances for "Murphy".

You have to wonder what presents the greater risk: nuclear reactor guards sleeping on the job or 77,000 tons of radioactive material on the move.

For dirty bomb plumes, both this and the next illustration assume:
1) the dirty bomb is released on a calm day with wind speed of 1 mph
2) material is distributed by an explosion causing a mist of fine particles to spread downwind in a cloud
3) 20% of the material is small enough to be inhaled.

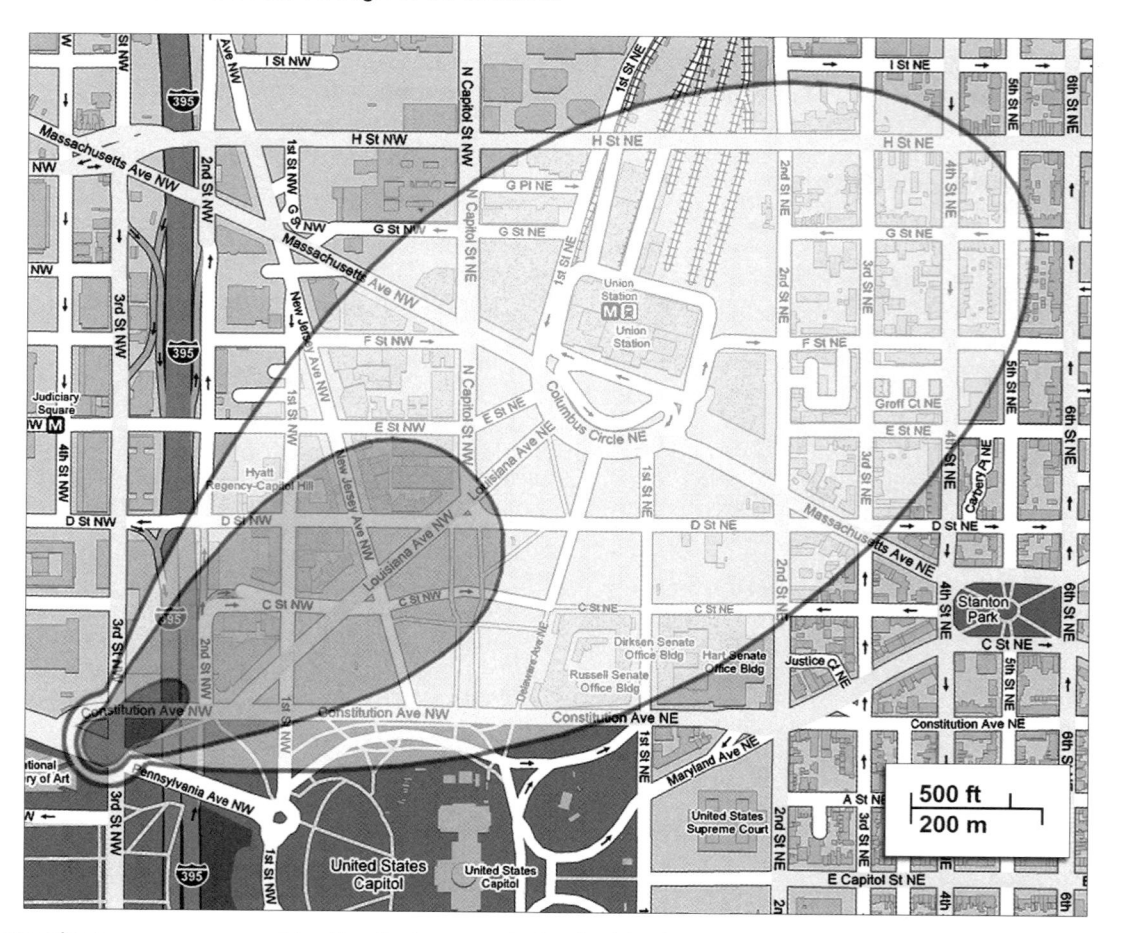

To contaminate an area roughly .8 mile long and .4 mi wide, it would take just 10 pounds of dynamite and a pea-size bit of cesium 137. That's about the amount found in a medical gauge.

Exposure to cesium 137 is deadly if ingested or inhaled in large enough amounts. Lesser quantities can cause acute radiation sickness and burns.

Though people wouldn't knowingly breathe or eat it, Cs 137 can be concentrated through the food chain and end up in both man's and animal's soft tissue and muscle. This brings a slower form of death.

If the blast area has not been thoroughly decontaminated, people would die from radiation-induced cancer. For each of the rings over a 30-year period, these are the odds for cancer death:
- **Inner ring**: one in every 100
- **Middle ring**: one in every 1,000
- **Outer ring**: one in 10,000.

Beyond the blast radius, there would be "hot spots" where survivors couldn't enter.

CLEANUP NIGHTMARE

Since most cesium is already in powder form dispersal would be fairly easy. Weaponized it would drift onto every exposed area and slide into minute pits and ridges. It would hide in naturally rough exteriors like tree bark and weathered wood and blow into every imaginable nook and crevice.

Adding to this, radioactive grains would "chemically bind to asphalt, concrete and glass," according to Jaime M. Yassif of the Federation of American Scientists. Cleanups might entail using extreme methods such as concrete-eating bacteria. Just locating all contaminants would be nearly impossible since they're easily absorbed by soil and disappear into cracks and pavement. People would always wonder, *did they get all of it?*

COBALT-60

Cobalt is used for the same things as Cesium 137, but it's far more lethal. Though it emits a higher amount of gamma particles, it's dangerous for a much shorter time with a half-life of 5.27 years.

This scenario below uses a 1 x 12" or "pencil" rod of cobalt-60, like the one pictured right. If exploded in the same area as the previous graphic, the result would be much more deadly. This is what it would look like.

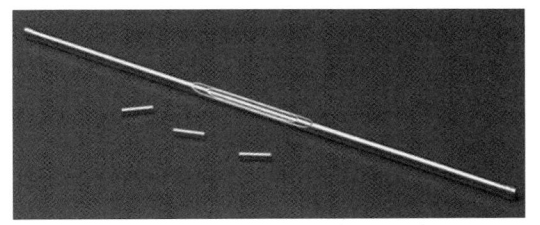

Compared to Cs 137, instead of poisoning less than a mile, radiation would cover over 50 miles and an area twice as wide. With its higher level of contamination, decades would pass before the city was inhabitable and demolition might be the only recourse. If such an event took place in New York City, it would bring trillion dollars losses. If it were detonated in Washington DC, the seat of government would have to permanently relocate.

The "rings" would experience the following:

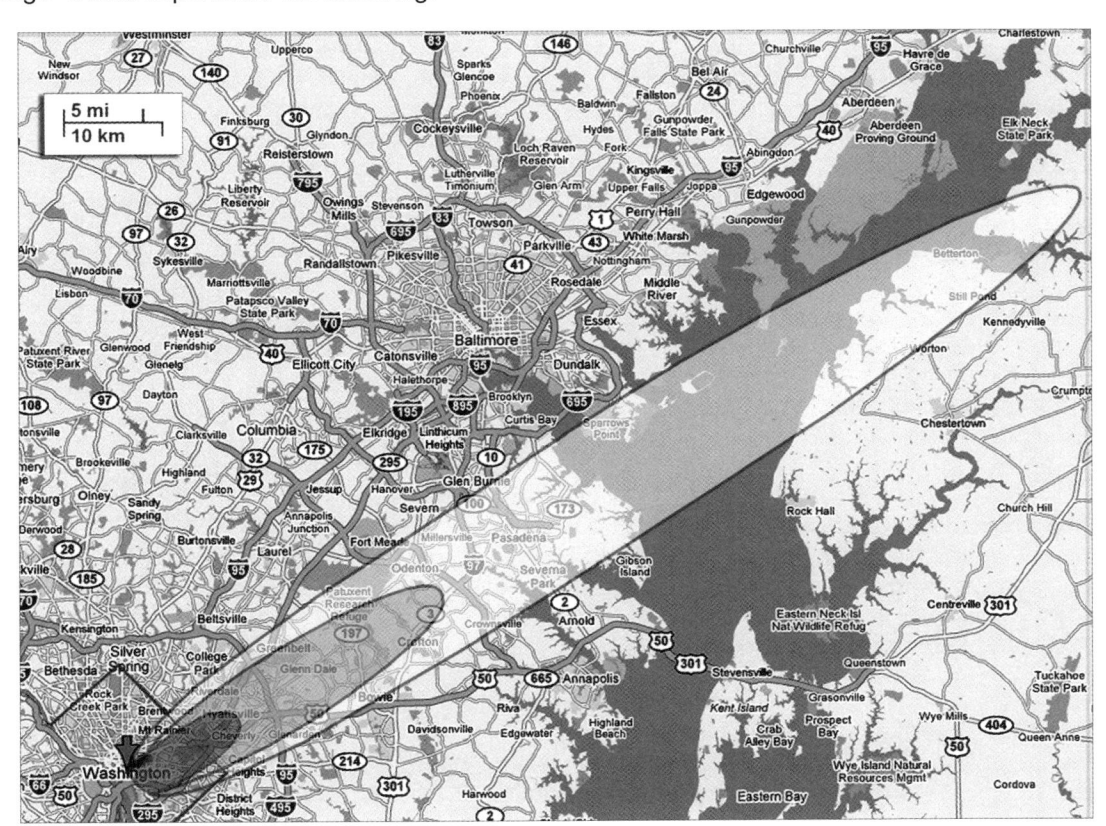

Inner ring: 1 cancer death per 100, but may be as high as 1 in 30.
Middle ring: 1 cancer death per 1000.
Outer ring: 1 cancer death per 10,000.
NOTE: Average cancer risk is 2,000 in 10,000 or 20%.

A terrorist using Cesium 137 or Cobalt 60 in a dirty bomb wouldn't likely create enough radiation to cause immediate serious illness except for those close to the blast. Since particles would be dust-size, the radiation concentration is relatively low. Consequences of a dirty bomb wouldn't be near the same as for a nuclear weapon. This is a *huge and important distinction* that people often confuse in the two events. Once people hear the word "nuclear", panic takes over, logic shuts down and they forget what to do.

Because of the big disparity in radiation exposure for the two events, protection is different. For a dirty bomb, defense is fairly straightforward.

PROTECTION

A dirty bomb's main danger is from the explosion itself, which can cause serious injury and property damage. However, radioactive dust spread in the plume could be harmful if it's inhaled.

If you are outside and close to the incident
1. Cover your nose and mouth with a cloth to reduce the risk of breathing in radioactive dust or smoke.
2. Don't touch anything thrown off by the explosion – it might be radioactive.
3. Quickly go into a building where the walls and windows have not been broken. This area will shield you from radiation that might be outside.
4. If possible, remove your shoes and outer layer of clothing first. This may get rid of up to 90% of the radioactive dust.
5. Once inside, shower or wash with soap and water. Be sure to wash your hair. Washing will remove any remaining dust.
6. Pets, too, will need to be brought inside and shampooed.
7. To keep radioactive dust from getting inside, shut all windows, outside doors and fireplace dampers. Turn off fans and heating and air-conditioning systems.
8. If your home leaks air, seal with duct tape and plastic to keep out radioactive dust particles.

If you are in a car when the incident happens
1. Close the windows and turn off the air conditioner, heater and vents.
2. Cover your nose and mouth with a cloth to avoid breathing radioactive dust or smoke.
3. If you are close to your home, office, or a public building, go there immediately and go inside quickly.
4. If you can't get home or to another building safely, drive perpendicularly to the plume and continue driving till you're out from under its path.
5. If this is impossible, pull over to the side of the road and stop under a bridge or overpass.
6. Turn off the engine and listen to the radio for instructions.
7. Stay in the car until you are told it is safe to get back on the road.

Will food and water supplies be safe?
1. Food and water supplies most likely will remain safe except for unpackaged items or water that was out in the open and close to the incident.
2. Food in cans and other sealed containers will be safe to eat. Wash the outside of the container before opening it.
3. Authorities will monitor food and water quality for safety and keep the public informed.

Should I take potassium iodide?

Potassium iodide (KI) and Potassium iodate (KIO$_3$) only protect a person's thyroid gland from exposure to radioactive iodine. It won't protect other parts of the body. One dose every 24 hours, and no more than that, should be taken as soon as possible after public health officials tell you.

These two products protect the thyroid by "filling up" the gland with iodine. Taking more than the gland can hold won't do more good and it could be harmful.

Who shouldn't take potassium iodide?

People who know they are allergic to iodide should avoid it. It is safe for children and pregnant women.

NUCLEAR POWER PLANTS

In America, 104 nuclear power plants are operational along 32 non-power reactors used at test and research facilities. Another 14 nuclear plants are in various stages of decommissioning.

"Many of these decommissioned plants, though, still store spent nuclear fuel on site. Federal regulations are intended to protect the public from harm caused by exposure to radioactive material released by sabotage of any US nuclear reactor. But Americans face undue risk because these security regulations are not consistently enforced and because regulations underestimate the terrorism threat. Practical measures must be taken to reduce the risk of sabotage.

"In fall 2001, the NRC identified 12 nuclear power plants as being highly susceptible to corrosion or cracking. The commission shut down all of these plants for inspection, except Davis-Besse. Davis-Besse started leaking boric acid in 1996. Between 1998 and 2000, the leakage began causing problems for other equipment.

"In 1999, FirstEnergy, the corporation that operates Davis-Besse, found traces of rust particles in the filters of radiation monitors. In August, FirstEnergy admitted to NRC investigators that it placed production before public safety by deferring inspections and corrective action programs. FirstEnergy is spending more than $400 million on repairs.

"A similar, but less severe discovery was made April 2003 at the South Texas 1 plant, about 90 miles southwest of Houston. In May 2002, 23 new cracks were discovered at the Oconee Nuclear Station's three reactors. The cracks were in the 'control rod nozzles', which enter the reactor core from the top and serve to stop the nuclear chain reaction. It is a concern when, as with the Davis-Besse plant, structural deterioration advances this far before it is detected and action is taken." [131]

TEMPTING TO TERRORISTS

Officials worry that terrorists will target nuclear facilities. Indian Point in New York is on everyone's short list as a potential target. It's only 24 miles from Manhattan and 20 million people live within a 50-mile radius of Indian Point reactors. A large radioactive release triggered by a terrorist attack or a facility accident could have devastating health and economic consequences. It could render much of the Hudson River Valley, including New York City, uninhabitable like Chernobyl. More than 20 years after history's worst nuclear disaster, this Ukrainian city is a ghost town. To this day, Chernobyl remains in the top 10 of Blacksmith Institute's worst polluted sites.

Nationwide 42 million Americans live within a 50-mile radius of a nuclear reactor.[132] That's 1 out of every 7 Americans. With a growing push to get off fossil fuels, 35-40 new units are being considered which will put millions more people in close proximity.

While a nuclear accident can affect a wider area, a 10-mile radius around each facility marks where direct radiation exposure could occur. Check with your state's Emergency Management Agency for information on Emergency Planning Zones (EPZ). Their maps show which routes should be taken for the quickest, least congested evacuation.

A second ring drawn around reactors – The Ingestion Pathway Zone (IPZ) – marks a 50-mile radius where food and water would be contaminated. What is considered a safe distance for people would be determined, in part, by the prevailing winds on the day and severity of the mishap.

WHAT TO DO BEFORE A NUCLEAR OR RADIOLOGICAL ATTACK

1. **Signals** Learn the warning signals and all sources of warning used in your community. Make sure you know what the signals are, what they mean, how they will be used, and what you should do if you hear them.
2. **Kit** Assemble and maintain a disaster supplies kit with food, water, medications, fuel and personal items adequate for at least 4 weeks – the more the better.

3. **Public Shelters** Find out what public buildings in your community may have been designated as fallout shelters. It may have been years since they were clearly marked as such. With the end of the Cold War, many of the signs have been removed altogether. Learn which buildings are still in use or could be designated as shelters again. To locate this information, call your local emergency management office. Look for yellow and black fallout shelter signs on public buildings.
4. **No Shelters** If no official designations have been made, make your own list of potential shelters near your home, workplace and school: basements, or the windowless center area of middle floors in high-rise buildings, as well as subways and tunnels.
5. **Family** Give your household clear instructions about where fallout shelters are located and what actions to take in case of attack.
6. **Apartments** If you live in an apartment building or high-rise, talk to the manager about the safest place in the building for sheltering, and about providing for building occupants until it is safe to go out.
7. **Home Shelters** There are few public shelters in many suburban and rural areas. If you are considering building a fallout shelter at home, keep the following in mind: A basement or any underground area is the best place to shelter from fallout. Often only few major changes are needed especially if the structure has two or more stories and its basement – or one corner of it – is below ground.

    TIP: You can improve this expedient basement shelter area by adding a strong table stocked with appropriate materials. (See Chapter 44) A hose could be brought from the water heater to the shelter for drinking water, and a toilet bucket with plastic bags (See Chapter 36) improvised for sanitation. Fallout shelters can be used for storage during non-emergency periods, but only keep things there that can be very quickly removed. (Use dense, heavy items for added shielding.)

8. **Evacuation** Learn about your community's evacuation plans. They should include evacuation routes, relocation sites, how the public will be notified and transportation options for people who don't own cars and those with special needs.

WHAT TO DO DURING A NUCLEAR OR RADIOLOGICAL ATTACK

1. **Flash** Do not look at the flash or fireball – it can blind you.
2. **Warning** If you hear an attack warning: Take cover as quickly as you can, BELOW GROUND IF POSSIBLE, and stay there unless instructed to do otherwise. If caught outside, unable to get inside immediately, take cover behind anything that might offer protection. A ditch or culvert is better. Lie flat and cover your head. If the explosion is some distance away, it could take 30 seconds or more for the blast wave to hit.
3. **Fallout** Protect yourself from radioactive fallout. If you are close enough to see the brilliant flash of a nuclear explosion, fallout will arrive in about 20 minutes. Take shelter, even if you are many miles from ground zero – radioactive fallout can be carried by the winds for hundreds of miles. Remember the three protective factors: shielding, distance and time.
4. **Getting info** Keep a battery-powered radio with you, and listen for official information. Follow the instructions given. Local instructions should always take precedence: officials on the ground know the local situation best.

WHAT TO DO AFTER A NUCLEAR OR RADIOLOGICAL ATTACK

In a public or home shelter:
1. **Wait for instructions** Do not leave the shelter until officials say it's safe. Follow their instructions when leaving. The length of your stay can range from a day or two up to four weeks. People in most of the areas that would be affected could be allowed to come out of shelter and, if necessary, evacuate to unaffected areas within a few days.
2. **Sanitation** Although it may be difficult, make every effort to maintain sanitary conditions in your shelter space.
3. **Water and food** may be scarce. Use them prudently but do not impose severe rationing, especially for children, the ill or elderly.
4. **Cooperate** with shelter managers. Appreciate you have some place to go. Living with many people in confined space can be difficult and unpleasant.

> *Learn how to build a Temporary fallout shelter to protect yourself from radioactive fallout even if you do not live near a potential nuclear target.* –
> FEMA's Are You Ready: A Guide to Citizen Preparedness, page 93.

RETURNING TO YOUR HOME

1. **Listen for news** Keep listening to the radio for news about what to do, where to go, and places to avoid. Listen to your radio for instructions and information about community services. Monitor the radio and your television for information on assistance that may be provided. Local, state and federal governments and other organizations will help meet emergency needs and help you recover from damage and losses.
2. **Check for damage** If your home was within the range of a bomb's shock wave, or you live in a high-rise or other apartment building that experienced a non-nuclear explosion, check first for any sign of collapse or damage, such as:
   - Toppling chimneys, falling bricks, collapsing walls, plaster falling from ceilings.
   - Fallen light fixtures, pictures and mirrors
   - Broken glass from windows
   - Overturned bookcases, wall units or other fixtures
   - Fires from broken chimneys
   - Ruptured gas and electric lines
   - Broken water mains and fallen power lines may add to the danger.
3. **Cleaning up** Immediately clean up spilled medicines, drugs, flammable liquids, and other potentially hazardous materials.
4. **Utilities** If you turned gas, water and electricity off at the main valves and switch before you went to shelter:
   - Don't turn the gas back on. The gas company will turn it on for you or you'll get other instructions.
   - Turn water on at main valve only after you know the water system is working and not contaminated.
   - Turn electricity back on at the main switch only after you know the wiring is undamaged in your home and the community electrical system is functioning.
   - Check to see that sewage lines are intact before using sanitary facilities.
5. **Safety** Stay away from damaged areas. Stay away from areas marked "radiation hazard" or "HAZMAT".

Chapter 47: Water and Food in Nuclear Emergencies

WATER

The good news is while it may contain radioactive particles, water itself does not become radioactive. Traditional methods of water purification don't make it drinkable; it needs to be filtered. For water containing fallout particles use these methods:

LIGHT FALLOUT REMOVAL

Filter the water through paper towels or several thicknesses of clean cloth to remove the majority of the fallout particles. Allow water to stand for several hours to let fallout particles settle to the bottom of the container. Be sure to take the water off the top.

HEAVY FALLOUT REMOVAL

To filter heavily contaminated water, use one of the filtering methods listed above, then filter the water further with one of the following methods:

Add clean soil to the water and allow it to settle until the water is clear. Remove the clear water from the top, being careful not to stir up the soil.

Use a flower pot or can with small drain holes punched in the bottom. Fill the container with clean, uncontaminated soil. Pour the water through the soil and collect it in a clean container. Let any soil that passes through with the water settle before using the water.

If water is in short supply, you will need to adjust your meal plans. Limit the number of foods that need water to prepare. Also reduce the amount of high-protein food such as meat or peanut butter. A person who eats high-protein food requires more water than does a person who takes in an equal number of calories from other kinds of food.

SOURCES OF WATER IN FALLOUT AREAS

Survivors of a nuclear attack should realize that neither fallout particles nor dissolved radioactive elements or compounds could be removed from water by chemical disinfection or boiling. Therefore, water should be obtained from the least radioactive sources available. Before a supply of stored drinking water has been exhausted, other sources should be located. The main water sources are given below, with the safest source listed first and the other sources listed in decreasing order of safety.

1. **Water from deep wells and from water tanks and covered reservoirs** into which no fallout particles or fallout-contaminated water has been introduced. (Caution: Although most would be safe, some spring water includes surface water that has flowed into and through underground channels without benefit of filtering.)
2. **Water from covered seepage pits or shallow, hand-dug wells.** This water is usually safe IF fallout or fallout-contaminated surface water has been prevented from entering by the use of waterproof coverings and by waterproofing the surrounding ground to keep water from running down outside the well casing. If the earth is not sandy, gravelly, or too porous, filtration through earth is very effective.
3. **Contaminated water from deep lakes.** Water from a deep lake would be much less contaminated by dissolved radioactive material and fallout particles than water from a shallow pond would be, if both had the same amount of fallout per square foot of surface area deposited in them. Furthermore, fallout particles settle to the bottom more rapidly in deep lakes than in shallow ponds, which are agitated more by wind.
4. **Contaminated water from shallow ponds** and other shallow, still water.
5. **Contaminated water from streams**, which would be especially dangerous if the stream is muddy from the first heavy rains after fallout is deposited.

Dare To Prepare: Chapter 47: Water and Food in Nuclear Emergencies

The first runoff will contain most of the radioactive material that can be dissolved from fallout particles deposited on the drainage area. Runoff after the first few heavy rains following the deposit of fallout is not likely to contain much dissolved radioactive material, or fallout.

6. **Water collected from fallout-contaminated roofs.** This would contain more fallout particles than would the runoff from the ground.
7. **Water obtained by melting snow that has fallen through air containing fallout particles**, or from snow lying on the ground onto which fallout has fallen. Avoid using such water for drinking or cooking, if possible.

WATER FROM WELLS

The wells of farms and rural homes would be the best sources of water for millions of survivors. Following a massive nuclear attack, the electric pumps and the pipes in wells usually would be useless. Electric power in most areas would be eliminated by the effects of electromagnetic pulse (EMP) from high-altitude bursts and by the effects of blast and fire on power stations, transformers, and transmission lines. However, enough people would know how to remove these pipes and pumps from wells so that bail-cans could be used to reach water and bring up enough for drinking and basic hygiene.

An ordinary large fruit juice can works well, if its diameter is at least 1" smaller than the diameter of the well-casing pipe. A hole 1" in diameter should be cut in the center of the can's bottom. Cut from the inside of the can: this keeps the inside of the bottom smooth, so it has a smooth seat for a practically watertight valve. To cut the hole, stand the can on a flat wood surface and press down repeatedly with the point of a sheath knife, a butcher knife, or a sharpened screwdriver.

The best material for the circular, unattached valve is soft rubber, smooth and thin, like an inner-tube. Alternately, the lid of a can about ¾" smaller in diameter than the bail-can may be used, with several thicknesses of plastic film taped to its smooth lower side. Plastic film about 4-mil thick is best. The bail (handle) of a bail-can should be made of wire, with a loop at the top to which a rope or strong cord should be attached.

Filling-time can be reduced by taping a half-pound of rocks or metal to the bottom of the bail-can.

REMOVING FALLOUT AND DISSOLVED RADIOACTIVE MATERIAL

The dangers from drinking fallout contaminated water could be greatly lessened by using expedient settling and filtration methods to remove fallout and most of the dissolved radioactive material. Fortunately, in areas of heavy fallout, less than 2% of the radioactivity from fallout particles contained in the water would become dissolved in water. If nearly all the radioactive fallout particles could be removed by filtering or settling methods, few casualties would be likely to result from drinking and cooking with most fallout-contaminated water.

FILTERING

Filtering through earth removes essentially all fallout particles and more of the dissolved radioactive material than boiling-water distillation, a generally impractical purification method that does not eliminate dangerous radioactive iodines. Earth filters are also more effective in removing radioactive iodines than are ordinary ion-exchange water softeners or charcoal filters. In areas of heavy fallout, about 99% of the radioactivity in water could be removed by filtering it through ordinary earth.

You can make a simple, effective filter with materials found in and around the home. An expedient filter can be built easily this way:

1. Perforate the bottom of a 5 gallon can, a large bucket, a watertight wastebasket, or a similar container with about a dozen nail holes. Punch the holes from the bottom upward, staying within about 2" of the center.
2. Place a layer 1" thick of washed pebbles or small stones on the bottom of the can. If pebbles aren't available, twisted coat-hanger wires or small sticks can be used.
3. Cover the pebbles with one thickness of terry cloth towel, burlap sackcloth, or other quite porous cloth. Cut the cloth in a circle 3" larger than the diameter of the can.
4. Take soil containing some clay (almost any soil will work) from at least 4" below the surface of the ground. (Nearly all fallout particles remain near the surface except after deposition on sand or gravel.)
5. Pulverize the soil, then gently press it in layers over the cloth that covers the pebbles so that the cloth is held snugly against the sides of the can. Do not use pure clay (not porous enough) or sand (too porous). The soil in the can should be 6-7" thick.
6. Completely cover the surface of the soil layer with one thickness of fabric as porous as a bath towel. This is to keep the soil from being eroded as water is poured into the filtering can. The cloth also will remove some of the particles from the water. A dozen small stones placed on the cloth near its edges will secure it adequately.
7. Support the filter can on rods or sticks placed across the top of a container that is larger in diameter than the filter can. (A dishpan will do.)

8. Pour contaminated water into the filter can, preferably after allowing it to settle as described below. The filtered water should be disinfected by one of the previously described methods.

If the 6-7" of filtering soil is a sandy clay loam, the filter will begin delivering about 6 quarts of clear water per hour. (If the filtration rate is faster than 1 quart in 10 minutes, remove the upper fabric and re-compress the soil.) After several hours, the rate will reduce to about 2 quarts per hour.

When the filtering rate becomes too slow, remove and rinse the surface fabric, remove about 1 inch of soil, and then replace the fabric. The life of a filter is extended and its efficiency increased if muddy water is first allowed to settle for several hours in a separate container, as described below. After about 50 quarts have been filtered, rebuild the filter by replacing the used soil with fresh soil.

SETTLING

Settling is one of the easiest methods to remove most fallout particles from water. Furthermore, if the water to be used is muddy or murky, settling it before filtering will extend the filter life. The procedure is as follows:
1. Fill a bucket or other deep container ¾ full with contaminated water.
2. Dig pulverized clay or clayey soil from a depth of four or more inches below ground surface, and stir it into the water. Use about a 1" depth of dry clay or dry clayey soil for every 4" depth of water. Stir until practically all the clay particles are suspended in the water.
3. Let the clay settle for at least 6 hours. The settling clay particles will carry most of the suspended fallout particles to the bottom and cover them.
4. Carefully dip out or siphon the clear water, and disinfect it.

SETTLING AND FILTERING

Although dissolved radioactive material usually is only a minor danger in fallout-contaminated water, it is safest to filter even the clear water produced by settling, if an earth filter is available. Then disinfect it.

POST-FALLOUT REPLENISHMENT OF STORED WATER

When fallout decays enough to permit shelter occupants to go out of their shelters for short periods, they should try to replenish their stored water. An enemy may make scattered nuclear strikes for weeks after an initial massive attack. Some survivors may be forced back into their shelters by the resultant fallout. Therefore, all available water containers should be used to store the least contaminated water within reach. Even without filtering, water collected and stored shortly after the occurrence of fallout will become increasingly safer with time, due particularly to the rapid decay of radioactive iodines. These would be the most dangerous contaminants of water during the first few weeks after an attack.

FOOD DURING AND IMMEDIATELY AFTER A NUCLEAR ATTACK

During the first few days, or even weeks after an attack, you may have to live on the food you brought with you. Adequate radiation protection and water are much more important than food for survival during this period. *Healthy adults can generally live for up to several weeks with little or no food, provided they have plenty of water and aren't physically active.*

FOOD PREPARATION AND MEAL PLANNING FOR SHELTERING

During the first days, when you cannot safely leave the shelter, keep food preparation to a minimum. Cooking adds heat to the shelter. If your shelter does not have adequate ventilation, you may need to avoid cooking as much as possible, especially in warm weather.

Use any perishable foods brought to the shelter first. If anyone brought coolers with ice, you can keep milk, butter, juice, and meat for several days. Check all meats and dairy products for spoilage before serving them, especially in warm weather.

Drink fruit juices instead of water.

Boiled eggs last longer than raw eggs.

If mold grows on hard cheeses such as cheddar or Swiss, you can remove the mold and safely eat the cheese. However, if mold grows on bread, do not eat any of the bread.

If the weather is cool, root vegetables such as potatoes and carrots and hard fruits such as apples will last for several weeks if they are kept cool and dry. If you suspect that any of these foods have been exposed to fallout, simply wash them off to remove fallout particles. The food itself will not become radioactive.

Dare To Prepare: Chapter 47: Water and Food in Nuclear Emergencies 491

Prepare small amounts of food to avoid waste and leftovers. You'll have a problem with waste storage and disposal and will want to keep garbage to a minimum. Waste can create unpleasant odors, attract rodents and insects, and cause disease. Take a sealable 5 gallon bucket into the shelter.

In stocking a fallout shelter, select dried, canned or instant foods. A supply of MREs, HeaterMeals or Inferno Meals would come in very handy. No refrigeration is required and they offer a hot meal without adding heat to the environment or wasting fuel. Don't forget a manual can opener.

EXPEDIENT COOK STOVE

You may run out of fuel or find firewood is very scarce, but you can conserve fuel by sharing cooking with others. Oak Ridge National Laboratories developed and field tested a number of expedient stoves and finds this one the most efficient. If operated properly, this stove burns only about ½ pound of dry wood or newspaper to heat 3 quarts of water from 60°F to boiling.

MATERIALS REQUIRED FOR THE STOVE:
- 1 metal bucket or can, 12-16 quart (11-15 liter) sizes work best
- 9 all-metal coat hangers (To secure the separate parts of the movable coat-hanger wire grate, 2' [61cm] of finer wire is helpful.)
- 1 – 6x10" (15-25.4 cm) piece of a large fruit-juice can, for a damper.

TO CONSTRUCT

With a chisel (or a sharpened screw driver) and a hammer, cut a 4½x4½" (11.5x11.5cm) hole in the side of the bucket about 1½" above its bottom. To avoid denting the side of the bucket when chiseling the hole, place the bucket over the end of a log or similar solid object.

To make the damper, cut a 6"-wide by 10"-high piece out of a large fruit juice can or from similar light metal. Fashion two springs from wire coat hangers. Attach them to the piece of metal by bending and hammering the outer 1" of the two 6"-long sides over and around the two spring wires. This damper can be slid up and down, to open and close the hole in the bucket. The springs hold it in any desired position. (If materials for making this damper aren't available, the air supply can be regulated fairly well by placing a brick, rock, or piece of metal so that it will block off part of the hole in the side of the bucket.)

To make a support for the pot, punch 4 holes in the sides of the bucket, equally spaced around it and bout 3½" (9cm) below the bucket's top. Run a coat-hanger wire through each of the two pairs of holes on opposite sides of the bucket. Bend these two wires over the top of the bucket, so their 4 ends form free-ended springs to hold the cooking pot centered in the bucket. Pressure on the pot from these four free-ended, sliding springs does not hinder putting it into the stove or taking it out.

Bend and twist 4 or 5 coat hangers to make the movable grate. For adjusting the burning pieces of fuel on the grate, make a pair of 12"-long (30.5cm) tongs of coat hanger wire.

To lessen heat losses through the sides and bottom of the bucket, cover the bottom with about 1" of dry sand or earth. Then line part of the inside and bottom with two thicknesses of heavy-duty aluminum foil, if available.

To make it easier to place the pot in the stove or take it out without spilling its contents, replace the original bucket handle with a longer piece of strong wire.

OPERATING THE EXPEDIENT STOVE

The expedient bucket stove burns only one-half pound of dry wood or paper to bring 3 quarts of water to a boil. It's efficient because the flame can be kept close to the pot, and hot exhaust gases pass close to the pot. You can adjust the flame by adjusting the air supply damper and the depth of the wood piled on the grate.

For safety, keep the stove near the ventilation opening in your shelter and keep the shelter vents open when the stove is operating. The vents should be fully open when you start the stove, but they can be closed partially (never closed completely), while cooking. Never use fire starter liquid, gasoline, or kerosene to start the stove.

Fuel for cooking can be either wood or paper. Wood should be cut into small pieces about ½"x5". Newspaper should be rolled and twisted into a 5" long "stick". Paper fires are easily started, but wood fires need kindling (twisted paper, wood shavings or splinters) and attention. Place the kindling under the grate and light it. Keep the damper open fully as you slowly add wood.

Adjust the damper when the wood itself starts to burn. Adjust the flame during cooking by opening and closing the damper. Keep the flame just below the pot; do not let it go up the sides of the pot.

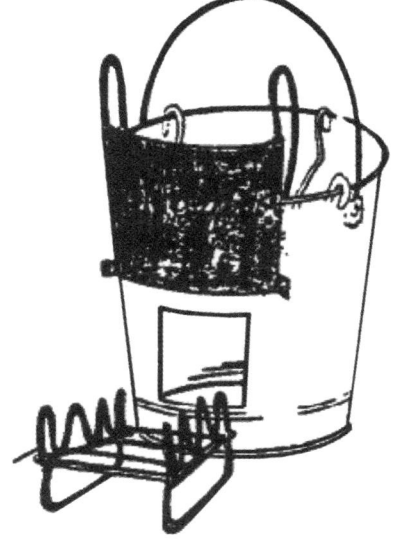

REPLENISHING FOOD SUPPLIES

After an attack, meat and milk will probably be scarce. Fallout radiation may have killed and injured many animals. However, grain should be plentiful. Stored grains may be the nation's main food source after a large-scale nuclear attack. However, with largely depleted global grain reserves, what you have stored may be your largest grain access. Before consuming stored grain, remove the uppermost several inches where fallout particles have fallen and the rest is safe to eat.

Most food in your house will not be harmed by the radiation, no matter how intense the radiation. Food and water in dust-tight containers or vacuum packed won't be contaminated. Wash all cans before opening.

Peeling fruits and vegetables removes essentially all fallout. Foods with their own jackets like eggs, bananas, potatoes, oranges, grapefruits are also safe.

Open packages of cereal, rice, flour, etc. may be contaminated. If other food options are available, give partially used packages a miss.

AVAILABILITY OF GRAINS

The yield of field crops will vary a great deal depending upon their resistance to radiation and the time of year the attack occurred.

Normal harvesting operations and rain will remove most of the fallout that initially contaminated crops. Furthermore, the radioactivity of the remaining fallout will be greatly reduced by the time the grain is consumed.

Most likely, your diet after an attack will consist mainly of grains plus whatever uncontaminated meat and milk you can find. A physically active person can survive quite well on a diet of about two pounds of ground grain per day, such as ground wheat and corn supplemented by soybeans for protein and some vitamins.

AVAILABILITY OF MEAT AND MILK

In major areas of the country, many farm animals may be dead within a few weeks from fallout radiation. Radiation will also prevent farmers from safely watering and feeding their animals. Grazing animals in the pasture can fend for themselves, but many may die because of their exposure to radiation.

In areas where stored grain is in short supply, there will be an immediate short term need for meat as a human food until grain is distributed to those areas. The meat of animals that don't show signs of radiation sickness will be safe to eat if cooked thoroughly. When grain is made available, healthy animals should be raised as breeding stock rather than as food sources.

If local authorities permit you to risk eating the animals in your area, you must take the following precautions:
- Do not eat an animal that appears to be sick. Look around to see if any deceased animals are in the area.
- Do not eat the internal organs (heart, liver, kidneys) from any animal.
- Do not eat meat next to the bones as well as the marrow in the bones.

Milk from cows that ate contaminated grass or feed may not be safe after an attack. Cows that were pastured outside in fallout areas may consume fallout particles with the grass they eat. Their milk will be contaminated. Unless otherwise advised by local authorities, the only safe milk is from cows that were protected in a shelter and fed uncontaminated food.

EMERGENCY FOOD FOR BABIES

Infants and very small children are more susceptible to starvation, and to vitamin and mineral deficiencies. Their bodies grow and develop rapidly, and they need proper nutrition. Special care must be taken to provide them with adequate diets, which would be a difficult task when food is scarce.

EMERGENCY BABY FOOD		
Ingredients	Per day	Weight
Instant non-fat dry milk powder	1 cup + 2 Tbsp (2¼ oz.)	8 grams
Vegetable cooking oil	3 Tbsp (1 oz.)	30 grams
Sugar	2 Tbsp (.7oz.)	20 grams
Daily multi-vitamin pills	⅓ pill	

Breast milk is the most complete food for infants and babies. Mothers should continue to nurse their babies for as long as possible. In some countries, mothers nurse for as long as two years with little or no supplements to their children. A nursing mother must eat an adequate diet in order to supply enough milk for her child. The grain diet with vitamin A, C, and D supplements is sufficient for a nursing mother. In addition, you do not need to worry about sterilizing of bottles and formula, carrying sterilizing and feeding utensils, or mixing formulas.

If babies are not nursed, they need special food. Babies over six months can eat grain, but infants require special formulas. If the mother runs out of foods and formula brought from home and cannot obtain more, three sources of emergency baby food are available: dry milk solids, safe cow's milk, and finely ground grain meal mush. These foods must be freshly prepared and the utensils sterilized for each serving.

A. DRY MILK SOLIDS

The best infant food under emergency circumstances is powdered milk with vitamins, sugar, and oil added. The formula for each feeding is listed in the following chart.

B. SAFE WHOLE COW'S MILK

Whole milk from safe cows will be scarce and should be allocated to infants under six months old. Healthy cows that are kept in a fallout-protected shelter and fed uncontaminated feed and water produce safe milk.

C. MIXED GRAIN PUREE

Finely pureed grains can be fed to infants under six months old if milk is not available. Use a mixture of 3 parts yellow corn or rice plus one part soybeans. Do not feed wheat to infants. Follow these steps to make the meal puree:
1. Finely grind and sieve the grain mixture.
2. Boil the mixture for 15 minutes in water, one part grain to three parts water until the water is absorbed.
3. Press the cooked meal through a fine sieve (cheesecloth or bed sheet} with a spoon.
4. Boil the sieved puree in a small amount of water until it reaches a consistency of pablum. It should be spoonable but thin. Store the puree in a sterilized covered container.
5. At each serving, add sugar and oil and boil again. Cool mixture before adding vitamins and feeding the infant.

Sterilized food and utensils are required for feeding infants under 6 months old. Boil the food before each serving. Clean the feeding utensils after each feeding and sterilize them by boiling for 5 minutes. If fuel is scarce, you can sterilize cleaned utensils by storing them in covered container with a solution of cold water and household bleach that lists hypochlorite as its only active ingredient. Use 1 teaspoon of bleach to one quart of water. Use the utensils without rinsing, and prepare a fresh solution daily.

MAINTAINING A BALANCED GRAIN DIET

A diet of two pounds of cooked grain per day and some vitamins will provide a healthy, hard-working person with an adequate diet. A balanced diet requires that four parts of ground wheat or corn grain be mixed with one part of ground soybeans. Soybeans are used to add protein to the diet. The grain must be ground because whole grains are not easily digested. Cooking also aids digestion by softening the ground grain. You need about ¾ teaspoon of salt per day, which can be added to the grain to improve the taste.

Soybeans have a strong flavor that many people find unpleasant. Mixing corn or wheat meal with soy beans improves the taste of the meal, as does salt and fat.

Rice, grain sorghum and barley are good substitutes for corn and wheat. Other dry legumes such as red beans or peanuts, which also provide needed protein, can replace soybeans. Meat or eggs could be added as the protein source if these are available. Since they are much higher in protein, you need only one part of these proteins to 20 parts dry grain.

MEETING VITAMIN AND FAT REQUIREMENTS

A mixed grain and soybean diet supplies adequate calories and protein, and most of the vitamins and minerals that you need to maintain a healthy body. However, it does lack a few essential vitamins, especially Vitamin C. Children are most sensitive to vitamin deficiencies. Vitamin deficiencies are avoided if children take half a multivitamin tablet each day. Adults should take a full tablet. If you do not have or have run out of vitamin tablets, you can add vitamins to your diet through the expedient methods described in this section.

Vitamin C is needed to prevent scurvy, a disease that results in softened, bleeding gums and loose teeth. You need 10mg of vitamin C daily to prevent scurvy. If no tablets are available, you can supply the necessary amount by eating 1/5 cup of sprouted wheat or bean grain per day.

Vitamin D is needed by children to prevent rickets, a disease that causes deformed bones. Adults do not get rickets. Although you can add it to your diet in a multivitamin pill or food supplement, Vitamin D is supplied naturally by exposure to sunlight. You will have to use caution even when radiation levels are safe for adults. Young children and infants cannot tolerate as much gamma radiation. Place them in the sunlight for only a few minutes a day to replenish their Vitamin D without being overexposed.

Vitamin A is required by children more than by adults for healthy skin and eyes. Your liver stores Vitamin A and adults usually have enough to last for several months. If vitamin supplements are not available, yellow corn grain and leafy vegetables (including dandelion greens) supply plenty Vitamin A. Shake out greens and wash carefully to remove any fallout. Cook them briefly. Cooking causes them to lose their vitamins. Cover the pot to retain any lost vitamins, and drink the liquid.

Vitamin B-12 is rapidly depleted during times of stress. It's essential for all cells to function correctly as well as for bone marrow and nervous tissue, and required for red blood cell formation. B-12 is also necessary for normal digestion, absorption of foods, proteins synthesis and carbohydrate and fat metabolism. Your body's ability to process and absorb nutrition after a nuclear event will help fight in its fight against radiation effects. Found in liver, kidney, meats, fish, dairy products and eggs.

Minerals such as **Calcium, Iron, Potassium** and **Zinc** help suppress the body the uptake of certain forms of radiation. This is not to be confused with a cure, preventative or fix.

Fat added to grain meal mush adds fat and improves the flavor of the food.

GARDENING AND FARMING AFTER A NUCLEAR ATTACK

People often ask, *is it possible to garden and farm after a nuclear attack?* Yes, you can, with a little patience and preparation.

As seen with the Rate of Decay rule, radioactive fallout becomes harmless relatively quickly. Though it might take 20-30 years for land to be *completely* radiation free, the remaining minuscule amount would be tolerable. Land would be pretty safe to use within a year's time. Setting aside at least a year's worth of food should see you safely through the interim.

For healthiest growing conditions, remove the top several inches of dirt with the fallout dust and radioactive particles. If the land was very contaminated or you plan to farm a large area, use a bobcat or heavy equipment to remove the soil. However, if the nuclear blast created an EMP effect and electronics are shot, you may have to do the dirt moving with a shovel. This is a scenario when square foot gardening is the best option. It allows you to grow the greatest amount of food in the smallest space and requires minimal weeding. See my newest book: *Garden Gold: Growing Maximum Veggies With Minimum Effort*. It's our favorite way to garden – any time!

Nuclear weapons don't just destroy things on earth, but above it as well. While earth rids itself of radioactivity, the ozone layer will be repairing itself. Until this mending is as complete as possible, you may notice stunted growth and plants burning in the Sun especially young tender starts. It's the same situation as on high UV days.

Shade cloth stretched over the top of growing areas filter strong rays. If you find materials to build a greenhouse, that is another option.

Colorado Sun is harder on plants because of higher elevation and thinner air. The day's UV intensity and slant of the Sun pack a double whammy. Factor in a damaged ozone layer and even plants at lower altitudes may experience the same burn.

We've had great success with SunBlocker 30% - 40% Shade Cloth. Farmtek **www.farmtek.com**, aka Grower's Supply, carries both these levels of protection plus lower and higher rated cloth. SunBlocker type fabrics are knitted from high-density polyethylene, which makes them very resistant to UV degradation and temperature extremes. It can be cut to size without unraveling and secured in place with these oversize plastic clips.

Since rabbits are an on-going battle, Stan and I surrounded the garden boxes with ½" hardware cloth. To this we snapped on the shade cloth. Reusable clips form a loop at the top where cord can be strung. This allows the fabric to be tied to anything in addition to the snap-on option. After the garden finished producing last fall, the cloth snapped off easily and rolled up waiting to be used next spring. Bulk rolls come in a variety of widths up to 20 feet. It's cheap insurance with 6' wide rolls running just a little over $1/ft.

SunBlocker works great as a wind barrier, hail protector and bird net in addition to a UV shield. In rural southern Colorado, we've given it a good test on all of the above and the shade cloth performed as advertised. Granted, it's not going to withstand baseball-size hail, but it's sufficient for normal size ice balls.

If covering large crops isn't practical, grow the most UV resistant grains: alfalfa, barley, corn, rye, soy and wheat.

WORST CASE GROWING SCENARIO

Should food supplies run short and you're forced to start a garden in under a year, it is doable. It's a pretty easy choice if it's between starving and *maybe* experiencing health problems down the road. Ingested radiation can cause leukemia, but symptoms likely wouldn't appear for 20-30 years IF they show up. It's not guaranteed.

For plants grown in contaminated soil, brush them off thoroughly to rid them of fallout, then wash. Most of the radioactivity will be in the dust on the plant's exterior. Wash potatoes and other root vegetables thoroughly and then peel the outer layer for added protection. Smooth skinned fruits and vegetables are safe to eat after washing and peeling.

Chapter 48: First Aid in Nuclear Emergencies

RADIATION SICKNESS

Recognizing the symptoms of radiation sickness will be difficult. The early symptoms are similar to the early stages of many contagious diseases. They are also similar to signs of fear and stress.

APPEARANCE OF SYMPTOMS		
Symptoms Appear	**Symptoms Disappear**	**Symptoms Reappear**
1-2 days	3-4 days	1-2 weeks

Keep the patient warm and resting. In addition to the treatments prescribed for early symptoms, give antibiotics, if available, to reduce the chance of infections.

Early Symptoms

Radiation sickness begins with headache, nausea, vomiting, diarrhea, and a general feeling of tiredness. So do many other illnesses.

Treating Early Symptoms

Whether the symptoms are from radiation sickness or another condition, the patient should be kept warm and as comfortable as possible.

SYMPTOM	TREATMENT
Headache	Give aspirin or aspirin substitute. Follow the recommended dosage given on the container.
Nausea	Dramamine or motion sickness tablets should be given according to directions on the container.
Sore mouth or bleeding gums	Give saline mouthwash made by mixing ½ teaspoon salt to one quart of water.
Vomiting or diarrhea	Have the person drink slowly several glasses each day a salt-and-soda solution (one teaspoonful of salt and ½ teaspoon baking soda to one quart cool water), plus bouillon or fruit juices. If available, give a mixture of (Kaopectate) for diarrhea.

Later Symptoms of Radiation Sickness

The early symptoms of radiation sickness will usually disappear in a day or two. In more serious cases, they will return within 2 weeks and be accompanied by symptoms such as:
- Hair loss
- Small hemorrhages under the skin
- Bloody diarrhea

> *Radiation Sickness is not contagious*

Radiation sickness is caused by radiation damage to cells of the body. A victim is not contagious. Other people can't "catch it." In fact, it's like sickness from poisoning. You can safely help a person with radiation sickness just as you can safely help a victim of poisoning.

POTASSIUM IODIDE AND IODATE

Potassium iodide (KI) or potassium iodate (KIO_3) is not a fix, preventative or cure. KI cannot protect the body's cells against radiation but it can protect the thyroid gland. It works by "saturating" the thyroid with stable iodide so it can't absorb radioactive iodine.

Under current dosing guidelines, a fully saturated thyroid is protected for up to one month, which is long enough for radioactive iodine (which has a half life of 8 days) to disappear from the environment. Without taking KI in advance of an attack, its protective effect lasts about 24 hours.

WHAT IS THE DAILY DOSAGE REQUIRED?

THRESHOLD THYROID RADIOACTIVE EXPOSURES AND RECOMMENDED DOSES OF KI FOR DIFFERENT RISK GROUPS[133]				
Age Range	Predicted Thyroid Exposure	KI Dose (mg)	# of 130mg Tablets	# of 65mg Tablets
Adults over 40 yrs	≥500	130	1	2
Adults over 18 – 40 yrs	≥10	130	1	2
Pregnant or nursing women	≥5	130	1	2
Adolescents over 12 – 18 yrs*	≥5	130	1	2
Children over 3 – 12 yrs	≥5	65	½	1
Over 1 month – 3 years	≥5	32	¼	½
Birth – 1 month	≥5	16	⅛	¼

**Adolescents approaching adult size (> 70 kg) should receive the full adult dose (130 mg).

WHAT IS THE SHELF LIFE OF POTASSIUM IODIDE?
Potassium Iodide is inherently stable. If kept dry in an unopened container at room temperature, it can be expected to last indefinitely.

PSYCHOLOGICAL FIRST AID
A nuclear attack crisis will produce emotional reactions in almost everyone. The events, the difficult living conditions, the uncertainty about the future, and the lack of communication with friends and relatives will test the strength and courage of the entire population.

Some people will cope better than others. Most everyone will show signs of fear, and some may panic. Some will overreact, and some will show signs of depression.

Treat serious emotional reactions with patience and reassurance. The following guidelines will help you recognize problems and handle the situation appropriately.

HELPING VICTIMS
Be aware of your own feelings and reactions. You, too, may be reacting to the strain of the situation. You may be tempted to use drastic measures. Restrain yourself. Remember that persons with severe emotional reactions are victims. Here are some of the actions to avoid:
- Do not show resentment.
- Do not over-sympathize.
- Do not blame, ridicule, or ignore the victim.
- Do not argue, suggest the victim is acting or tell him to "snap out of it".
- Never use brutal restraint. If you must restrain a victim, be gentle but firm. Do not strike or throw water in the face of the victim.
- Avoid giving sedatives unless a medical doctor trained to handle psychological problems prescribes them.
- In all actions, use common sense and treat the person as you would want to be treated. Show kindness and understanding during this difficult time.

SIGN OF PSYCHOLOGICAL DISTRESS		
If You See These Symptoms	**Diagnosis May Be**	**Treatment**
Trembling Muscular tension Perspiration Nausea Mild diarrhea Frequent urination Pounding heart Rapid breathing	Normal Fear	Give reassurance Provide group identification Motivate Talk with the person Observe to see that individual IS regaining composure
Unreasoning attempt to flee Loss of judgment Uncontrolled weeping Wild running about	Panic	Be empathetic Give something warm to eat or drink Get help to isolate, if necessary Encourage talk Be aware of your own limitations
Argumentative Talks rapidly Jokes inappropriately Makes endless suggestions Jumps from one activity to another	Overactive Reaction	Let the person talk about it Find the person jobs which require physical effort Give warm food, drink Supervision necessary Be aware of own feelings
Stands or silts without moving or talking Vacant expression Lack of emotional display	Depression	Make contact gently Secure rapport Get the person to tell you what happened Be empathetic Recognize feelings of resentment in the person and yourself Find simple routine jobs Give warm food, drink
Severe nausea and vomiting Can't use some part of the body	Physical Reaction	Show interest in the person Find small jobs for the person to do Make comfortable Get medical help if possible Be aware of own feelings

DEALING WITH DEATH

Persons may enter the shelter with serious injuries or exposure to radiation levels so high they may not survive. Dying is difficult to think about, but a plan by shelter occupants must be in place if death occurs.

For reasons of health and morale, the deceased must be removed from the shelter area. Members of the shelter may want to conduct a simple service. Wrap the body in a sheet, blanket, or other suitable materials, and, when possible, quickly remove it from the area, out of sight of the shelter occupants. Provide emotional support to the family of the deceased as well as to other shelter members.

The death should be recorded and some form of identification should be attached to the body. Consult local officials at the Emergency Operations Center (EOC) for guidance on burying the body, especially if the death occurs when outside radiation levels are high. If no guidance is available, carry the body outside. Bury the body in a marked grave as soon as radiation levels permit.[134]

This can be avoided by having adequate shelter.

Chapter 49: Electromagnetic Pulse – EMP

ELECTROMAGNETIC PULSE

In addition to the previously mentioned effects, a nuclear weapon detonated in or above the earth's atmosphere can create an electromagnetic pulse (EMP), a high-density electrical field. EMP acts like a stroke of lightning but is stronger, faster, briefer. EMP can seriously damage electronic devices connected to power sources or antennas. This includes communication systems, computers, electrical appliances, and automobile or aircraft ignition systems. The damage could range from a minor interruption to actual burnout of components. Most electronic equipment within 1,000 miles of a high-altitude nuclear detonation (HEMP) could be affected. Battery powered radios with short antennas generally would not be affected. Although EMP isn't likely to injure people, it could harm those with pacemakers or other implanted electronic devices.

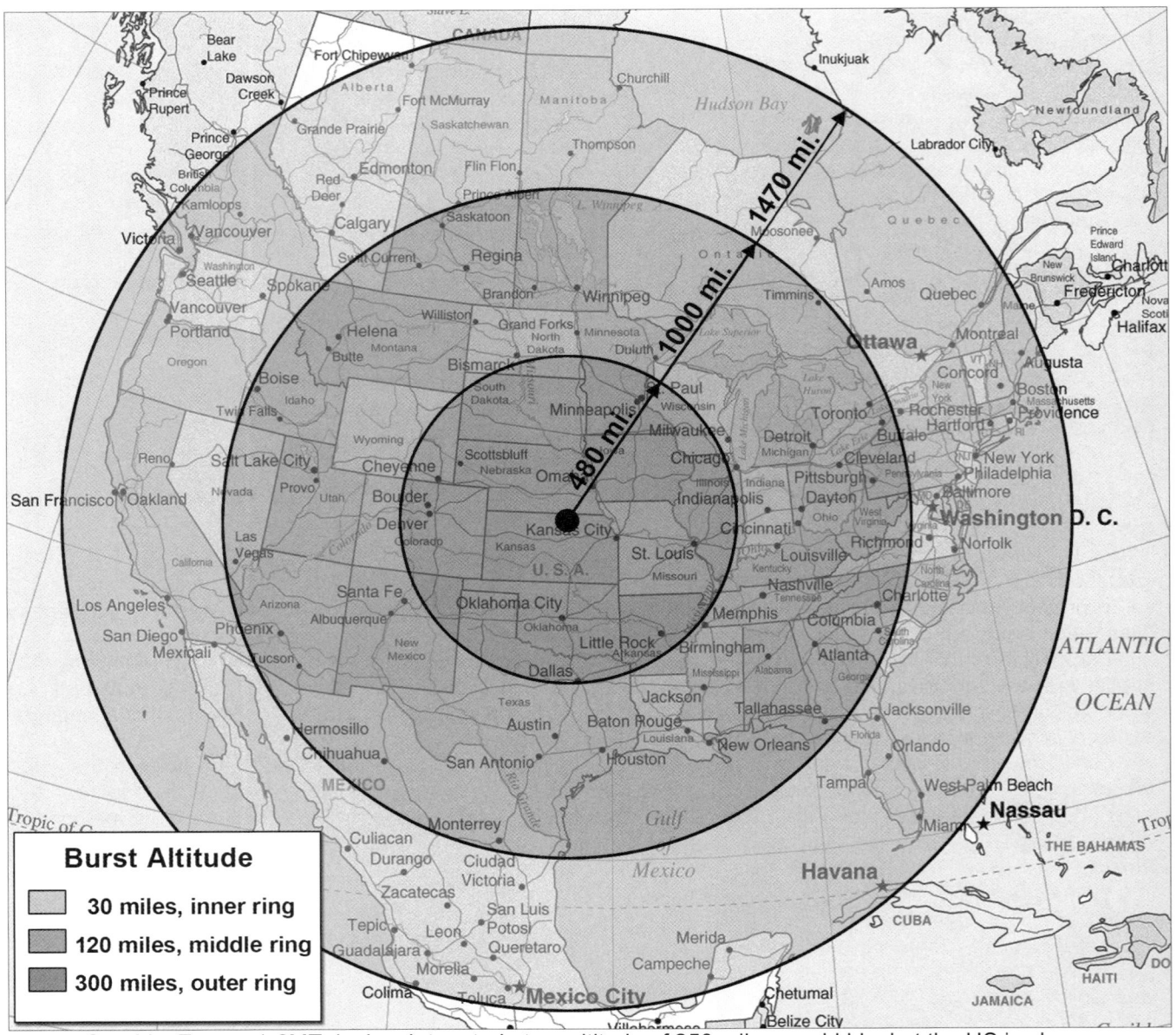

Burst Altitude
- 30 miles, inner ring
- 120 miles, middle ring
- 300 miles, outer ring

Graphic: Even a 1-2MT device detonated at an altitude of 250 miles would blanket the US in chaos.

The U.S. military first witnessed effects after a series of high-altitude nuclear tests on Johnston Atoll in 1962. Starfish Prime's EMP unexpectedly generated electronic systems disruptions in Hawaii over 1000 miles away. Electronic systems failed across the island, radio broadcasts were interrupted, streetlights burned out and burglar alarms sounded. The Soviets experienced similar damage to overhead and underground cables some 400 miles from ground zero. Its relatively low yield of 300 kiloton still brought significant damage due to high altitude detonation.[135]

> *Most electronic equipment within 1,000 miles of a high altitude nuclear detonation could by damaged by EMP.*
> Are You Ready: A Guide to Citizen Preparedness, page 90.

When a nuclear device is detonated, "initial gamma rays and resultant EMP move with the speed of light. The effects encompass an area along the line-of-sight from the detonation to the earth's horizon. Any system within view of the detonation will experience some level of EMP. For example, if a high-yield weapon were detonated 400 kilometers (250 miles) above the United States, nearly the entire contiguous 48 states would be within the line-of-sight.

The frequency range of the pulse is enormously wide – from below one hertz to one gigahertz. Peak electric fields can reach tens of thousands of volts per meter."[136] Simply stated, EMP damages components by overloading them and all modern electronics are potentially at risk.

While the Dept. of Defense has hardened some of its critical equipment, no such provision has been made for the public. This includes the power grid, telecommunications networks, banking systems, water and fuel supplies, and basically every electronic device we use daily.

There would be no waiting for government assistance, no FEMA knocking with bottled water, no public service announcements to tell you how recovery is progressing. If not back to the Stone Age, we would effectively be bombed back to the Amish way of life. It would be the single most effective way to cripple a nation economically and force people to become self-reliant.

To protect our equipment and vehicles, their components would need to surrounded in wire mesh like a Faraday cage and grounded. While it's too impractical to protect most things we use every day from EMP, critical back-up components would need to be kept in this type shielding.

Unfortunately, EMP-type damage isn't limited to nuclear weapons. There are High Power Microwave (HPM) bombs to consider.

Photo: Sandia National Laboratory researchers Willy Morse and James Pacheco fine-tune the small-sized Active Denial System (ADS). The new class of nonlethal weaponry uses 95 GHz-millimeter-wave directed energy. (Photo by Randy Montoya)

HIGH POWER MICROWAVE (HMP)

Since mid-1980, the US Air Force has funded programs to develop radio frequency and high power microwave weapons systems. These weapons operate at the 1 MHz to 20 GHz frequencies. Unlike HEMP that do wide-range damage, microwave weapons can be designed to target small geographic areas down to individual systems. In other words, they use "directed energy".

Microwave weapons are like HEMPs in that their impact is nearly instantaneous. They can locked up equipment or totally destroy it. To counter HMP damage, an entire system must be protected, not just individual components or circuits.[137] Fortunately, HMP weapons require more know-how to build than E-bombs, which is why only a handful of countries possess this technology.

WHAT WOULD HAPPEN IF AN EMP DETONATED?

Because most countries' infrastructure, including the United States, is largely unprotected from EMP, such a strike is our Achilles heel. Nothing has been protected at this point that the public depends upon. An EMP strike, while it would leave people unharmed, could render life very, very difficult within seconds. Consider this attack scenario presented by Major Colin R. Miller (US Air Force) in 2005.

"Background

On July 15, 1996, President Bill Clinton issued Executive Order No. 13010, in which he identified infrastructures critical to the nation's survival: telecommunications, electrical power systems, oil and gas storage, transportation, banking and finance, water supply systems, and emergency services. Unfortunately, these critical infrastructures were also singled out by a 2004 congressional report as being vulnerable to EMP attack. The report concluded that America's reliance on electronics makes "EMP one of a small number of threats that can hold [US] society at risk of catastrophic consequences." It went on to say that EMP damage to electric power systems, telecommunications, energy, and other infrastructures could seriously impact the nation's financial system, means of getting food, water, and medical care to the citizenry, trade, and the production of goods and services. This vulnerability will present an increasingly attractive target to America's enemies as US use of, and dependence on, electronics continues to grow, and nuclear weapons proliferate. In the context of theater operations, adversaries could use an EMP attack against the US homeland as either a deterrent to US involvement or as a preemptive strike to task saturate US leadership and focus US forces at home. Amazingly, Vladimir Lukin, a member of the Russian Duma, actually suggested such a course of action in 1999. Mr. Lukin told Rep. Bartlett, who was part of a delegation sent to ease tensions with Russia over US involvement in the Balkans, that if Russia really wanted to hurt the United States, they would launch a missile from a submarine, explode it high over the US, and shut down the US power grid for six months.

"Scenario

US-Russian relations cool dramatically by 2010 due to tensions over US military presence and action in the Caucuses. The Russians demand US expeditionary forces withdraw within 72 hours or face dire consequences. Seeing no significant Russian troop build up in concert with the threat, the US calls Russia's bluff, while attempting to negotiate a settlement. Twenty-four hours after the deadline, a Russian "spy satellite" explodes over the central United States, releasing a high altitude electromagnetic pulse that blankets the entire continent.

"**Consequences**

The effect of a HEMP attack on the continental US would be devastating, causing several trillions of dollars of damage (by conservative estimates) in cascading failures of interdependent infrastructures. The primary avenue for destruction would be through electrical power and telecommunications, on which all other infrastructures, including energy, transportation, banking and finance, water, and emergency services, depend. The cumulative effect of infrastructure failures would effectively send the country back in time. The majority of the US would be without electrical power. Telephones, televisions, and radios would be inoperative, and fuel/energy would be scarce. Most cars would not work, and public transportation – plane, rail, and bus, would be immobilized. Banking and financial services would become unavailable, and the amount in one's wallet or purse would define their liquid worth. At the same time, emergency services would have trouble functioning and responding to the disaster. The discussion below describes the most critical failures.

"**Electrical Power**

The US economy and functioning society is critically dependent on electricity. Fortunately, the electrical power system in North America is outstanding in its ability to deliver relatively cheap, high-quality power to end-users. At the same time however, the system has become increasingly fragile. While demand for electrical power has increased dramatically over the last decade, little has been done to upgrade power transmission systems. At the same time, the few power generation systems added to the grid have been built at considerable distances from load centers for environmental purposes. The result is a system operating near peak capacity to move power from generation to load. The August 14, 2003 blackout provides a clear example of system fragility. At approximately 4:10 pm, a power surge of approximately 3,500 MW entered the New York power system. Within seconds, 50 million North Americans found themselves without power, and thousands of businesses had to close operations. The blackout was a wake up call to American leadership on the fragility of the infrastructure. The effects of an HEMP-induced blackout would be far more severe for at least three reasons.

First, an HEMP attack would induce power surges simultaneously over the entire continent, degrading at least 70% of the Nation's electrical service in an instant. Second, the late-time EMP component (E3) would couple more efficiently to long power transmission lines than naturally occurring phenomenon do, and thus would produce far more damage than seen on August 14th. Third, the electrical power system requires proper functioning communications, financial systems, transportation, and fuel supply for operation, all of which would also suffer damage from HEMP, which would extend the recovery time to a period of months or a year.

"**Telecommunications**

Telecommunications are critical to modern society's function because they enable other key infrastructures such as financial markets, transportation, and energy distribution, facilitate business and commerce, provide personal convenience, and allow for coordinated emergency response. Fortunately, efforts have been underway since 1985 to harden critical parts of US telecommunications infrastructure from HEMP. The four major elements of the infrastructure: wireline, wireless, satellite, and radio, have overlapping capabilities and different vulnerabilities to EMP. After an attack, some portion of the system would still be intact, but would be overloaded by massive call volume, leading to significantly degraded service. In anticipation, the US government developed National Security and Emergency Preparedness (NS/EP) telecommunications services that guarantee government priority on surviving infrastructure. An unfortunate side effect of NS/EP, in the event of an HEMP attack, is that most civilian users would be locked out of the communications grid, making disaster response problematic. In many cases, authorities would have no way to contact citizens and provide instructions.

"**Fuel/Energy**

US fuel and energy production and distribution systems depend heavily on electronic control systems that use real-time data flows for operation, and use electronic sensors to monitor critical processes and react quickly to malfunctions. An EMP attack would fatally damage at least some of these electronics, causing ungraceful system shutdowns resulting in extensive damage, while providing an incomplete picture for troubleshooting and repair. Simultaneous failures in the electrical and communications sectors would also affect fuel and energy availability. Electrical power needed to operate valves, pumps, and other machinery required to deliver fuel wouldn't be available, and communications needed to coordinate activities at refineries and ensure safety of on-site personnel and the surrounding environment would be scarce. In the end, the fuel and energy shortage would probably persist for extended periods while interrelated infrastructures were repaired. Consequently, the US could experience many casualties due to exposure if the attack occurred in the winter.

"**Transportation**
The US transportation infrastructure includes freight and commuter railroads, roadways (auto and truck), water, and commercial air, all of which are increasingly reliant on information technology and public information networks. The push to achieve superior performance has led to tremendous reliance on electronics vulnerable to EMP. Examples include microprocessor-controlled internal combustion engines and electronic tracking of freight shipments outfitted with miniature radio frequency identification tags. The Commission to Assess the Threat to the United States from EMP Attack determined that significant degradation of US transportation infrastructure would result from EMP attack. In particular, municipal road traffic would experience gridlock, traffic lights would fail, and many autos would shut down permanently.

Railroad traffic would stop because of lost communications, and commercial air traffic would cease operations for safety reasons. Similarly, ports would stop loading and unloading ships until power and telecommunications infrastructures were restored.

"**Banking and Finance**
Almost all US economic activity depends on proper functioning of the financial industry, built on a foundation of electronic technologies. Most financial transactions involved in preserving and promoting National wealth, as well as the preponderance of personal and institutional transactions, are performed and recorded electronically. In addition, the financial system depends on reliable and robust telecommunications to coordinate interrelated business, and electrical power to sustain operations.

The attacks of September 11, 2001 illustrated that disruption of critical infrastructures has a direct effect on financial markets and increases liquidity risks for the United States financial system. In response to this, the Federal Reserve Board identified key functions that require same-day recovery after an attack to ensure viability of the US financial system. These functions included large-value inter-bank funds transfer capability, automated clearinghouse operations, key clearinghouse settlement utilities, and treasury automated auction and processing system operation. Each of these systems and their underlying infrastructures are potentially vulnerable to EMP. If they fail for greater than 24 hours, which they probably would in this scenario, the viability of the entire US economy would be at risk.

"**Emergency Services**
EMP attack would severely debilitate emergency services required for adequate response, primarily due to service reliance on computer and communications equipment, but also due to their reliance on electricity. Emergency services are also critically dependent on transportation, fuel for backup generators, and network equipment, all debilitated by EMP as previously discussed. Thus, emergency services represent another critical infrastructure in the chain of cascading failures that would contribute to the growing catastrophe".[138]

SHIELDING

Conflicting information for EMP protection is rampant because without an actual attack, solutions offered are unproven. Military conducted test results have not been released to the public. For example, protection with a wire mesh Faraday cage is adequate – to a point. It would protect against low frequency EMP, but not that in the gigahertz range.

Solid metal boxes like heavy duty filing cabinets and safes provide better protection because they'll shield against higher frequencies too. Containers constructed of thicker metal with good conductivity like copper or aluminum are better still. Protection would have to provide full metal-to-metal contact without gaps. Additionally whatever components are inside must not come in contact with the metal container. Grounding would need to be provided since EMP, like lightening, wants to take the path of least resistance. You do not want this path to dump into your electronics.

After an EMP, not everything will automatically shut down, but it would take out enough equipment and appliances we rely on daily to make life fairly challenging. Radios with antennas less than 30" should still function and certainly battery, solar and hand-crank types will be fine. One thing to definitely shield is a shortwave radio. If power has gone out all over, chances are your little radio won't be strong enough to pick up a working station.

Which cars will still run after EMP exposure is debatable. Cars built before 1975 when engines didn't rely on electronic ignition systems should be fine. Ones that depend *less heavily* on computer chips *may* survive. The common wisdom is that a few may be largely unaffected, but specifically which ones are hazy. It would depend on how much metal is in your car – more fiberglass, less shielding – and where it was when the blast detonated. You shouldn't expect it to run and if it does, that's the good news.

Anything considered being essential survival electronics must remain in the sealed metal box. As with an earthquake, there is no specific prior warning.

Chapter 50: Preparing for Challenges

TIME TO PREPARE

In the original edition of *Dare To Prepare*, many pages illustrated how natural disasters were escalating. This information was primarily intended for people whose spouse or family members refused to acknowledge the necessity for personal preparedness. This subject has caused many family rifts and left the "awake" person with hard choices. *Do I risk angering my family and spend money preparing? Or, do I let all of us stay vulnerable?*

That information armed the "awakened" person with all the ammo he or she needed to make their case. In the intervening years nothing has changed; weather is even more erratic and violent, the Sun is more unpredictable, the economy is sagging and terrorism is much more aggressive. Now the threat of a pandemic hovers.

Weather anomalies and freak storms are the norm. It's chronicled daily in mainstream press, as is terrorism. The evidence is all around us. No doubt can remain for even the most ardent naysayer. Presenting facts on global weather change, increasing natural disasters and continual crises is no longer needed. We are living it.

Every effort has been made to give you the most detailed, accurate information – help beyond the basics.

The following is based on the national *Are You Ready* guides. These have been bolstered with additional material to give you the most *complete* preparedness material.

THREE DAYS IS NOT ENOUGH

What's wrong with the majority of preparedness information is saying 3 days' food and water is enough. It's simply NOT TRUE for all instances. As events escalate and "the norm" deteriorates, more isn't just better; it's crucial.

If everyone knew they had sufficient supplies to see them through a crisis, tension and panic would lessen. People would be more inclined to trust government if they *knew* they were told the truth. They could relax because they knew facts and logic led them to be relatively self-sufficient. We have simply become too dependent, too needy and sometimes too greedy. People need to grasp what might lie ahead, instead of being feed pablum. It's part of being an adult; hopefully we don't need babysitting.

FINALLY, even the government changed its official tune.

> *"Assemble and maintain a disaster supplies kit with food, water, medications, fuel and personal items adequate for up to 2 weeks-the more the better."*
> – page 91, *Are You Ready: A Citizen's Guide to Preparedness*, 2002

How much plainer can it be said?

Every Emergency Management official I've spoken with, both on local and national levels privately state that three days supplies are not sufficient. I understand their thinking. Telling people they need to prepare for longer than 72 hours looks like they're *expecting* trouble. They don't want people to panic, feel afraid. Understandable. But we are now dealing with bigger disasters, escalating terrorism, possibilities of a nuclear incident and a pandemic. If they think warning people causes goosebumps, wait till they see millions of people stampeding for the last supplies.

This was evident in 2004's hurricanes Charley, Frances, Ivan and Jeanne. In these monster storms, some residents were without electricity for four weeks. The massive 2003 blackout in Canada and the U.S. lasted 15 days. Hurricane Katrina victims were without power for *months*. Hurricane Frances emptied shelves of food and water. ATMs ran out of cash. Gas stations ran out of fuel.

HURRICANE FRANCES – A VALUABLE LESSON FOR ALL

PREPARATIONS

By nightfall Thursday, scores of South Florida gas stations had run out of gas. Sheets of plywood were a scarce commodity.

Many stores were out of C and D batteries and water jugs. Cash machines had run dry.

Hurricanes always set off a run on gas, water and supplies. But Hurricane Frances poses a unique set of problems. It comes three weeks after Hurricane Charley, a storm that lowered inventories and raised fears across the state. And given the size of this storm, customers up and down Florida were looking for the same things.

The shortages left even hurricane-savvy residents startled.

"I feel like a scavenger, picking things off the floor and searching for anything," said Claudio Nino, 35, who spent the day at a Wal-Mart in West Dade. "There aren't even any potato chips left here."

Gas seemed the scarcest of all. Florida's two main gasoline ports were closed to tanker ships for safety reasons. Along U.S. 1 and U.S. 441 and other arteries in wide swaths of Miami-Dade and Broward, service stations wrapped yellow tape around dry pumps and shut down until further notice.

It could be Sunday or later before supplies are replenished, a prospect that might make Frances' aftermath that much more frustrating.

One of the few stations still open late Thursday was the Shell on Northwest 12th Street and 87th Avenue. Scores of cars waited for at least 45 minutes, backing up traffic for 20 blocks.

"I'm so nervous, because they might run out of gas before I get there," said Nery Ng, 22, of Doral.

SUPPLIES TRUCKED IN

Supermarkets, pharmacies and hardware superstores trucked in bottled water and plywood from upstate and out of state to their South Florida outlets. But supplies could not arrive quickly enough. Many never reached the stripped-bare shelves.

The Hallandale Beach Wal-Mart received a shipment of 28 pallets of water about 4 a.m. Thursday. It was gone in 20 minutes.

Publix workers didn't even bother to put new deliveries of water on the shelves. They dumped the pallets at the front of the store. Paying customers helped themselves.

Said spokeswoman Maria Rodamis: "It's going as quickly as we can open the case."

At one Hialeah Publix on Thursday afternoon, checkout lines stretched deep into the aisles. Tempers flared.

"I'm grabbing whatever I can get," said Revelda Harvin of Liberty City, a school security guard, who managed to snare one of the last cases of bottled water.

Across the street, two dozen people stood in line to use a Bank of America ATM; money, too, seemed in short supply. A security guard directed traffic in the clogged lot.

Bridgette Gaitor, a Miami-Dade schools employee, was there to withdraw $400 for post-storm emergencies. After that, it was on to Super Wal-Mart and Best Buy to hunt for a battery-operated television. Every Radio Shack in town was sold out.

"It's the price we pay," she said, "to live in Florida."

At the Seminole Smoke Shop at Davie Blvd. and U.S. 441 in Davie, the line for discount cigarettes snaked around the parking lot, 20 cars deep.

At Family's Bakery on Northwest Seventh Avenue in Miami, Joshua Joseph waited an hour for three loaves of Haitian bread.

'YOU HAVE TO WAIT'

"Everywhere, you have to wait in line. Wherever you go right now. It's life," he said.

At a Blockbuster in North Miami, John Rolon waited 20 minutes to rent a few comedies.

"You would think, at a moment like this, we'd get Passion of the Christ," Rolon said. "But we're thinking funny. We have a child. Keep it light."

All day, nervous drivers swerved on the roads and honked at the gas lines and cursed at the checkout lanes.

And, all day, there were poignant moments of human kindness.

Gloria Carter went to 84 Lumber in Davie for lumber to board up her aunt's house in Lauderhill. She knew she couldn't fit the boards in her Toyota Camry and hoped she would find a generous soul with some trunk space.

That would be James Williams, who was there picking up lumber for his home in unincorporated central Broward.

GOOD DEEDS

"This is a time where everybody comes together and helps one another," Williams said. "I figure if I do a good deed for her, someone will do a good deed for me."

The approaching storm put thousands of South Floridians in a sociable mood. Homeowners with shutters proffered Friday-night dinner invitations to neighbors without. Shoppers made friends in line. Restaurants did a bustling trade.

"This could be my last good meal for days," said Jeremy Martinez, 11, who begged his parents to take him to Chili's in Doral ahead of Frances.

The spiraling needs of South Florida consumers put particular pressure on grocery chains and home-improvement superstores; parking lots outside nearly every Publix, Winn-Dixie, Home Depot and Lowe's in the region were filled to capacity late into the night.

Both supermarket chains had been running their filtered-water plants 24/7 since Charley. The chains were trucking in canned food, batteries and other hurricane emergency items from stores well outside the hurricane strike zone.

At a Home Depot in Davie, in a typical scene, 100 customers waited for four hours Thursday morning for a delivery of plywood.

"This is the biggest resupply mission we have gone through in 25 years," spokesman Don Harrison said. "Fifteen-hundred trucks have gone in."

The company sent 40,000 generators to Florida's West Coast after Charley, leaving little to send to the East Coast before Frances.

The Atlanta-based retailer is already planning to stage hundreds of filled trucks north of the hurricane zone, ready to roll in as soon as the hurricane has passed.

"We're pulling products off shelves at almost every store in the country, even Seattle and California," Harrison said.

The company also plans to send at least 800 sales associates to Florida after the hurricane to relieve local staff.

An increasing number of ATMs were out of cash as the storm neared. Both Bank of America and Wachovia said they were restocking as soon as the machines are depleted, but people were drawing out cash at nearly a breathtaking pace; neither institution anticipated that they would run out of money altogether.

The shortages only complicated preparations for people still laboring to seal up their homes and clear their yards.[139]

Photo: Clean up begins following devastating 1993 Midwestern floods. A total of 534 counties in nine states were declared disaster areas. As a result of the floods, over 168,000 people registered for federal assistance. (FEMA News Photo)

The following chapters explain what to do before, during and after different disaster scenarios. Instead of duplicating information, check the food, water, first aid and general supplies chapters for specific lists.

Chapter 51: Preparing for Earthquakes

Photo: The 7.1 Loma Prieta earthquake shook Californians to the core. It's amazing that only 68 lives were lost during this rush hour event. Residences didn't fare as well. Over 23,000 homes sustained damage and more than 1,100 were completely demolished. Homes like this Boulder Creek residence in the Santa Cruz Mountains collapsed because it lacked adequate shear walls and was built on fill soil. (JK Nakata, USGS, October 17, 1989)

Earthquakes can cause buildings and bridges to collapse, telephone and power lines to fall, and create fires, explosions and landslides. Earthquakes also can generate huge ocean waves, called tsunamis, which travel long distances over water until they crash into coastal areas.

The following information includes general guidelines for earthquake preparedness and safety. Because injury prevention techniques may vary from state to state, it is recommended that you contact your local emergency management office, health department, or American Red Cross chapter.

WHAT TO DO BEFORE AN EARTHQUAKE

1. Know the terms associated with earthquakes.
   Earthquake – a sudden slipping or movement of a portion of the earth's crust, accompanied and followed by a series of vibrations.
   Aftershock – an earthquake of similar or lesser intensity that follows the main earthquake.

Fault – the earth's crust slips along a fault – an area of weakness where two sections of crust have separated. The crust may only move a few inches to a few feet in a severe earthquake.
Epicenter – the area of the earth's surface directly above the origin of an earthquake.
Seismic Waves – are vibrations that travel outward from the center of the earthquake at speeds of several miles per second. These vibrations can shake some buildings so rapidly that they collapse.
Magnitude – indicates how much energy was released. This energy can be measured on a recording device and graphically displayed through lines on a Richter scale. A magnitude of 7.0 on the Richter scale would indicate a very strong earthquake. Each whole number on the scale represents an increase of about 30 times the energy released. Therefore, an earthquake measuring 6.0 is about 30 times more powerful than one measuring 5.0.

2. Look for items in your home that could become a hazard in an earthquake:
   - Repair defective electrical wiring, leaky gas lines, and inflexible utility connections.
   - Bolt down water heaters and gas appliances (have an automatic gas shut-off device installed that is triggered by an earthquake).
   - Place large or heavy objects on lower shelves. Fasten shelves to walls. Brace high and top-heavy objects.
   - Store bottled foods, glass, china and other breakables on low shelves or in cabinets that can fasten shut.
   - Anchor overhead lighting fixtures.
   - Check and repair deep plaster cracks in ceilings and foundations. Get expert advice, especially if there are signs of structural defects.
   - Be sure the residence is firmly anchored to its foundation.
   - Install flexible pipe fittings to avoid gas or water leaks. Flexible fittings are more resistant to breakage.

3. Know where and how to shut off electricity, gas and water at main switches and valves. Check with your local utilities for instructions.
4. Hold earthquake drills with your household:
   - Locate safe spots in each room under a sturdy table or against an inside wall. Reinforce this information by physically placing yourself and your household in these locations.
   - Identify danger zones in each room – near windows where glass can shatter, bookcases or furniture that can fall over, or under ceiling fixtures that could fall down.
5. Develop a plan for reuniting your household after an earthquake. Establish an out-of-town telephone contact for household members to call to let others know that they are okay.
6. Review your insurance policies. Some damage may be covered even without specific earthquake insurance. Protect important home and business papers.
7. Prepare to survive on your own for at least three days. Assemble a disaster supply kit. Keep a stock of food and extra drinking water. See the "Emergency Planning and Disaster Supplies" and "Evacuation" chapters for more information.

> *Remain calm and stay inside during an earthquake. Most earthquake injuries occur when falling debris hit people entering or exiting buildings.*

WHAT TO DO DURING AN EARTHQUAKE

Stay inside until the shaking stops and it is safe to go outside. Most earthquake injuries occur when falling objects hit people entering or exiting buildings.

1. **Drop, Cover** and **Hold On**! Minimize your movements during an earthquake to a few steps to a nearby safe place. Stay indoors until the shaking has stopped and you are sure exiting is safe.
2. If you are **indoors**, take cover under a sturdy desk, table or bench, or against an inside wall, and hold on. Stay away from glass, windows, outside doors or walls and anything that could fall, such as lighting fixtures or furniture. If you are in bed, stay there, hold on and protect your head with a pillow, unless you are under a heavy light fixture that could fall.
3. If there isn't a table or desk near you, cover your face and head with your arms and crouch in an inside corner of the building. Doorways should only be used for shelter if they are in close proximity to you and if you know that it is a strongly supported load-bearing doorway.
4. If you are outdoors, stay there. Move away from buildings, streetlights and utility wires.

5. If you live in an **apartment building** or other multi-household structure with many levels, consider the following:
   - Get under a desk and stay away from windows and outside walls.
   - Stay in the building (many injuries occur as people flee a building and are struck by falling debris from above).
   - Be aware that the electricity may go out and sprinkler systems may come on.
   - DO NOT use the elevators.
6. If you are in a crowded indoor public location:
   - Stay where you are. Do not rush for the doorways.
   - Move away from tall shelves, cabinets and bookcases containing objects that may fall.
   - Take cover and grab something to shield your head and face from falling debris and glass.
   - Be aware that the electricity may go out or the sprinkler systems or fire alarms may turn on.
   - DO NOT use elevators.
7. In a moving **vehicle**, stop as quickly as safety permits, and stay in the vehicle. Avoid stopping near or under buildings, trees, overpasses or utility wires. Then, proceed cautiously, watching for road and bridge damage.
8. If you become trapped in debris:
   - Do not light a match.
   - Do not move about or kick up dust.
   - Cover your mouth with a handkerchief or clothing.
   - Tap on a pipe or wall so rescuers can locate you. Use a whistle if one is available. Shout only as a last resort – shouting can cause you to inhale dangerous amounts of dust.
9. Stay indoors until the shaking has stopped and you are sure exiting is safe.

> *If you must go out after an earthquake, watch for fallen objects, downed electrical wires, weakened walls, bridges, roads and sidewalks.*

WHAT TO DO AFTER AN EARTHQUAKE

1. Be prepared for aftershocks. These secondary shock waves are usually less violent than the main quake but can be strong enough to do additional damage to weakened structures.
   - Check for injuries. Do not attempt to move seriously injured persons unless they are in immediate danger of death or further injury. If you must move an unconscious person, first stabilize the neck and back, then immediately call for help.
   - If the victim is not breathing, carefully position the victim for artificial respiration, clear the airway and start mouth-to-mouth resuscitation.
   - Maintain body temperature with blankets. Be sure the victim does not become overheated.
   - Never try to feed liquids to an unconscious person.
3. If the electricity goes out, use flashlights or battery powered lanterns. Do not use candles, matches or open flames indoors after the earthquake because of possible gas leaks.
4. Wear sturdy shoes in areas covered with fallen debris and broken glass.
5. Check your home for structural damage. If you have any doubts about safety, have your home inspected by a professional before entering.
6. Check chimneys for visual damage; however, have a professional inspect the chimney for internal damage before lighting a fire.
7. Clean up spilled medicines, bleaches, gasoline and other flammable liquids. Evacuate the building if gasoline fumes are detected and the building is not well ventilated.
8. Visually inspect utility lines and appliances for damage.
   - If you smell gas or hear a hissing or blowing sound, open a window and leave. Shut off the main gas valve. Report the leak to the gas company from the nearest working phone or cell phone available. Stay out of the building. If you shut off the gas supply at the main valve, you will need a professional to turn it back on.
   - Switch off electrical power at the main fuse box or circuit breaker if electrical damage is suspected or known.
   - Shut off the water supply at the main valve if water pipes are damaged.
   - Do not flush toilets until you know that sewage lines are intact.

9. Open cabinets cautiously. Beware of objects that can fall off shelves.
10. Use the phone only to report life-threatening emergencies.
11. Listen to news reports for the latest emergency information.
12. Stay off the streets. If you must go out, watch for fallen objects, downed electrical wires, weakened walls, bridges, roads and sidewalks.

LIVING IN EARTHQUAKE COUNTRY

Because the global population continues to expand in shaker-prone areas and must be increasingly job-mobile, some of us may end up living in an earthquake zone. Unfortunately, earthquakes occur with alarming regularity in some of the more desirable living areas like all along the West Coast of the US. It's relatively cheap "insurance" to protect your home – existing or future against shakers.

Knowing you might be building or buying on shaky ground could convince you to locate elsewhere or at least take extra precautions to reinforce the cripple walls and bolt the foundation.

Since it's hard for buildings to move in response to earthquakes, they often end up with damage. Brick and masonry homes in particular weren't meant to shake, rattle and roll. Nor were they meant to do their variation of the hula as pictured to right.

The basic rectangular, single-story, wood-frame house is one of the safest, most stable types of structures during an earthquake. The amount of damage incurred should be minimal if the house is properly engineered and built. The key to a well-designed building is its ability to withstand an earthquake as a single unit.

HOUSE MOVEMENT IN AN EARTHQUAKE

Happy Times
Ground and house at rest

Uh-oh. . .
did you feel something?
You shake it to the left. . .

More —

You shake it to the right...

Ground stops, but nothing else does!

House does the shimmy shimmy shake. . .

With all of its might. . .

UH-OH!
Honey, do we have earthquake insurance?

Ground shaking has stopped, but house continues shaking due to inertia

BEFORE YOU BUY OR BUILD

There's an old saying about not borrowing trouble. For earthquake areas, keep these rules of thumb in mind before purchasing property. If you find these conditions in a seismically active area, you'll know it's already primed for trouble. Sometimes moving only a few miles one direction or another can improve the odds considerably. Avoid property if it includes one or more of these scenarios:
1. Too close to or is on the downside of dykes, reservoirs, dams, water towers, or poorly constructed buildings.
2. Too close to electrical wires, power lines (these aren't good for health reasons too) and old or leaning trees. These should be cut down.
3. Poor soil (discussed below)

GETTING THE DIRT

Soil conditions under and around your house play a part in how much damage it could sustain. Depending on soil type, it can either help or hinder during a shaker.

During earthquakes, these soils change from a solid to a liquid acting like quicksand. Liquefaction. The ground can crack or heave, causing uneven settling or buildings to collapse. You can take steps to minimize damage by reinforcing the foundation, floors, walls, and roof and by securing the contents of your house. More on this later.

Good Soil to Build on in EQ Prone Areas	Poor Soil to Build on in EQ Prone Areas
Bedrock (deep, unbroken rock formations) Stiff soils	Deep, loose sand and gravel Salty clays Soft, saturated granular soils

If you're unsure what type soil exists in your area, the local building authority and soil engineers can tell you by taking a few samples.

If you're considering building on poor soil, reinforce the foundation. My former home in northern Colorado had lousy soil; it was full of bentonite. When this clay is dry, it's comparable to cement. No kidding. Since this was a new housing division, the soil had been undisturbed for decades. Breaking through the cement, er, uh dirt, depending on where you dug, required a pick axe. However, a good rain saturated the surface and turned it slippery as snail slime. To compensate, the house foundation was built on caissons – long pillars of concrete about 12" in diameter sunk deep into the ground. Before filling the caisson hole with cement, rebar (metal reinforcing bars) was embedded for further strength. Depending on how many caissons are required, it can significantly add to the expense of a house, but saves grief in the long run.

While it would be nearly impossible to retrofit an existing house with caissons, many other things can be done to secure your home. Most you can do quite easily yourself while others may require the skill of a contractor or tradesman.

WHAT TO DO?[140]

Most one- or two-story wood-frame buildings aren't likely to collapse during earthquakes, but this doesn't mean they won't have problems. The most common damage is light cracking of interior walls and brick chimneys, and cracking or collapse of brick veneer on exterior walls. Have a qualified professional inspect cracked chimneys before using fireplaces.

MOBILE HOMES

One reason a mobile home can be so dangerous is that they are manufactured from lightweight metal or a combination of wood and steel. When combining wood and steel, the wood frame structure is erected on a steel frame chassis in aluminum or fiberglass. Mobile homes are often structurally linked to a second unit to form a "double-wide" living space called a "coach". Mobile homes are frequently seen on the freeway being pulled by semis to their new location. They are then leveled and supported in one of the following ways.

1. The coach can rest on the ground with only small metal devices called screwjack levels between it and the soil. The screwjack level consists of a metal triangle shaped base, similar to a tripod, with a screw and plate to connect it to the coach.

2. The coach can be supported above ground by resting on piers spaced about six feet apart. The undercarriage is leveled between these piers with screwjack levelers or wood blocks (called shims). Piers are made of concrete, steel, unreinforced concrete, or cinderblock. These piers can rest on either a concrete slab or on treated wood that sits directly on the ground.

Without reinforcing and bolting, it's easy to see how they can slide off their bases.

In an earthquake, the typical jacks the coach sits on will tip, allowing the coach to fall off of its supports. It's also common when this happens for the jacks to punch holes through the floors of the mobile home, but otherwise remain relatively undamaged. Even with relatively low damage, the mobile home becomes uninhabitable. It first must be returned to the foundation, re-leveled and reconnected to utilities. A corner foundation helps prevent the coach from falling off its base making the damage less severe.

The best solution is to support the mobile home with a reinforced foundation at the corners coupled with tie down connections to the frame.

WOOD FRAME HOMES

Some one- or two-story wood-frame buildings can be hazardous too. Those built before 1940 can fail at or near ground level if they aren't adequately bolted to the foundation or if the short "cripple" walls, (often found between the foundation and the first floor), aren't adequately braced. Correcting these two problems will drastically reduce earthquake risk for residents in older homes. Bracing chimneys may be required to prevent toppling during earthquakes.

- A   Replace unreinforced masonry or deteriorating concrete foundations with reinforced concrete.
- B   Add concrete foundations under walls that lack support.
- C   Add a steel frame or plywood panels to both sides of garage door and window openings. Secure frame to foundation with anchor bolts.
- D   Check exterior masonry periodically, especially brick or block veneer. Repair cracks to prevent toppling during an earthquake.
- E   Reinforce ceilings below chimneys with additional plywood sheathing to prevent bricks and mortar from falling through the ceiling.
- F   Add steel collar braces to chimneys.
- G   In new houses, use a lightweight flue system or a structural backup wall for chimney masonry.

H   Fix loose roof tiles and properly anchor heavy roofing material on a strongly braced roof frame. (Clay tiles are more vulnerable to earthquake pressures.)

I   Secure bookshelves to walls with screws or bolts.

J   Hang light fixtures and fans from electrical boxes that are securely fastened to ceiling joists. Add safety chains if necessary.

BOLT THE FOUNDATION

Bolting the wood frame of an older house to the concrete foundation can significantly reduce earthquake damage. Mobile homes, portable classrooms, and modular buildings can slide off their foundations during earthquakes. Their supports need to be braced to resist horizontal forces. If portable classrooms are used at your local school, you should ask school officials whether they are properly braced.

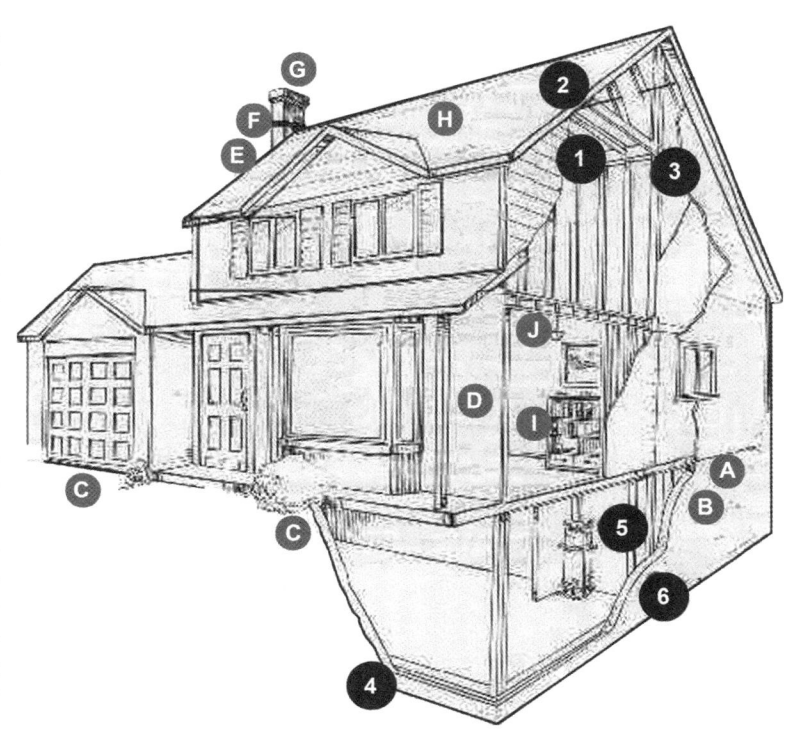

Bolting a structure to the foundation is a fairly easy 4-step task. For this project you'll need these materials: ½" or ⅝" diameter foundation bolts that are at least 7" long with nuts and square plate washers; rotary hammer drill with an appropriately-sized carbide tip drill bit; (right-angle drill if possible); short-handled sledge hammer for setting bolts; adjustable wrench; measuring tape and chalk line; dust mask and eye/ear protection and a torque wrench.

FOUR EASY STEPS

First, mark the places for each bolt on the mud sill. Make the first mark 9-12 inches from the corner, and then measure another four to the next bolt, and so on. Continue this pattern along all of the foundation walls. Place an extra bolt within 9 to 12 inches from any joint or step in the mudsill. Then follow the ABC's.

A. Drill the holes
Using the rotary hammer drill equipped with an appropriately sized carbide bit, drill down through the mudsill at least five inches (12.7cm) into the concrete.

B. Clean the holes
Use flexible tubing to gently blow the concrete dust out of the hole. (This is especially important if you are using chemical anchors.)

C. Install the bolts
Expansion bolts are designed to be hammered into place. This can be done without damaging the bolt's threads by turning the washer and nut past the end of the bolt and tapping on the end of the bolt shaft to hammer the assembly into place. Once the bolt is in place, tighten the nut down firmly using an adjustable wrench.

STEPPED FOUNDATION

If your house is built on a hill or even a slight grade, chances are you have some step-like offsets in your foundation to compensate. Every step must be bolted down even if it is adjacent to another bolted step.

FOUNDATION ANCHOR PLATE

If you don't have working room above the mudsill to drill straight down and can't find a right angle drill, you can secure the mudsill to the foundation with an anchor plate. This is a metal plate that is nailed or screwed to the top of the mudsill and bolted to the side of the foundation.

EXPANSION BOLTS

When you tighten the nut on an installed expansion bolt, the bolt's other end expands to grip the concrete. When the bolt is inserted properly, you will actually feel it "grab" the foundation as you tighten the nut. Test at least one out of every four new bolts for tightness with a torque wrench applying 40 foot-pounds of pressure.

CHEMICAL ANCHORS (epoxy bolts)

If you have an older foundation and worry about cracking it with the pressure of expansion bolts, consider using chemical anchors (also called epoxy bolts). Always follow the manufacturer's installation instructions. Measure, drill and clean the holes per the manufacturer's instructions. Be careful not to drill deeper than the bolt's length. Before you place the bolt in the hole, inject the epoxy mixture into the hole. Press the bolt into place and wait for the epoxy to harden (usually 24 hours). Once the epoxy has hardened, tighten the nut with an adjustable wrench until the washer just begins to indent the wood mudsill. Chemical anchors can be a bit more time-consuming to install. However, they are very effective, and are the preferred method.

CRIPPLES WALLS

Even though most modern homes are bolted down, they can fail because of another weak link called the "cripple wall." This is a short wall that connects the foundation to the floor of the house and encloses the home's "crawl space." The cripple wall is often not strong enough to survive the force of an earthquake and must be braced and strengthened. If not, an earthquake may damage the cripple wall and knock a home off its foundation, even if the house is properly bolted at the foundation.

ANCHORING

For this project you'll need these materials: 8d and 10d common nails, Simpson HD2A holddown or equivalent, Simpson A35 framing clips with N8 nails or equivalent and anchor bolts. Tools need to complete the work are circular saw, jigsaw, 1½" hole saw, framing square, hammer, plywood blade, tape measure chalk line and a pencil. This will give you an overview of what should be done and where.

REINFORCE CRIPPLE WALLS WITH PLYWOOD

Oftentimes bolts alone aren't sufficient to prevent damage from sideways shaking during an earthquake. Bracing cripple walls with plywood helps tremendously.

HOW MANY PANELS?

The number and length of panels needed depends on the height and length of each section of cripple wall and how many stories the cripple wall supports. For **all** houses, panels should be placed at both ends of each cripple wall section. For a single-story house, additional panels should be spaced evenly so no less than 50% of the total length of each cripple wall section is braced.

Two story houses, should have panels spaced to cover no less than 80% of each cripple wall section. For optimum strength, use the longest piece of plywood possible; instead of multiple pieces of plywood to make up the 4' – 8' panels. Distribution of the plywood panels should be "balanced'. Keep the panels equal in length and as evenly spaced conditions allow. For example, a cripple wall, which is 52' long and 12" in height in a single-story house, requires a minimum of 26' of braced panels. A typical solution would be a 4' plywood panel at each end and three 6' panels evenly spaced between the end panels.

MADE TO MEASURE

To provide adequate strength, each plywood sheet must be nailed along all edges, and along the interior studs. In most cases, the cripple wall studs are flush with the mudsill and with the "top plates" (located at the top of the cripple wall). This provides an even nailing surface for each plywood edge. However, if the cripple wall is set back from the edge of the mudsill, you will have to add blocking between the wall studs to create a nailing surface for the plywood.

Measure the height from the top of the double top plate to the bottom of the mudsill. If your condition requires blocking above the mudsill, then measure to the bottom of the cripple studs. Cut the plywood so that it covers this area and reaches from the center of one stud to the center of another. Mark the center of each stud on the foundation and above the top plates. These marks will provide a nailing guide. Remember, you must nail the plywood securely to all studs at the specified nail spacing. Also, note the location of any pipes so you can cut rounded notches in the plywood to fit around them.

BLOCKING

Often the mudsill is wider than the stud wall or embedded into the concrete foundation too deeply to allow nailing along its edge. If so, you will need to add a piece of wood 2x4 or 2x6 blocking on top of the mud sill, as shown above, to provide a nailing surface. Install blocking to fit over the anchor bolts per the city's plan set, and nail it to the mud sill using four 10-penny common nails. Blunt the tips of the nails and stagger them across the wood to prevent splitting. If the blocks still split, you may have to pre-drill the nail holes. To prevent dry rot or termite damage, it is a good idea to use foundation grade redwood or a pressure-treated wood for the blocking.

NAILING

When a job requires a lot of nailing, your arm will thank you for using a nail gun. Not only will the work go much faster, but it also cuts down on the wood splitting.

Make sure you get a gun that uses the right size and type nails for the task at hand.

VENTILATION HOLES

Each sheet of plywood must be nailed every 4" around the edges and every 12" along all interior studs and cross bracing in the "field" area. The edge nails provide most of the strength and the field nails prevent the center of the sheet from bowing outward during an earthquake.

With the plywood in place, drill 2½" to 3" diameter ventilation holes in each sheet. These holes should be centered between each set of studs and 2½" above the mudsill and 2½" below the bottom of the top plates.

The holes provide ventilation and allow inspection of the cripple wall and mudsill bolts. Drill only one hole if the plywood sheet is less than 18" tall. If the wall has an exterior ventilation screen, cut a hole in the plywood opposite the screen and similar in size. Add blocking around this vent hole and nail the plywood edges at 4" on center. With the first sheet of plywood nailed into place, repeat the process to brace the wall of plywood in sheets no shorter than 4' in length. Long continuous sheets provide maximum strength. When installing adjacent pieces of plywood, make sure they join at the center of a stud or that an additional stud has been added to provide for proper nailing. Check the cripple walls for termite and dry rot damage, and replace any damaged materials before installing the plywood shear panels.

Photo: Buildings, cars and personal property were all destroyed when the earthquake struck Northridge, CA, January 17, 1994. Approximately 114,000 residential and commercial structures were damaged and 72 deaths were attributed to the earthquake. Damage costs were estimated at $25 billion. (FEMA News Photo)

Chapter 52: Preparing for Drought and Water Shortage

EMERGENCY WATER SHORTAGE

Weather either dumps too much rain on already saturated areas or existing drought-prone regions are even drier. Such as is the case for much of the western U.S. and western Canada.

In 2002, Australia went through its worst drought in a century. Rainfall had declined nearly 20% in seven years over parts of Western Australia, and from Victoria through New South Wales and into Queensland.

Pictured left: Identical location photographs of Lake Powell taken at the confluence with the Dirty Devil River (entering from left). A. June 29, 2002. B. December 23, 2003. (Photographs by John C. Dohrenwend)

Today drought ensnares many parts of the world, but unless it affects your own backyard, people tend to ignore the problem. It's not headline grabbing like a massive earthquake or destructive hurricane. However, we see its effects in higher food prices, lost jobs, and severe water restrictions.

Drought also increases the risk of fire, flash flood, and possible landslides.

WATER WARS

Water wars are waged between states over who gets what share. Communities and businesses argue how much should be allotted to farmers and how much should be diverted for tourism.

It's harder to convince soggy parts of the nation that water is becoming increasingly scarcer. But the key need is *fresh* water. Maybe this will help.

LAKE POWELL

Though we boated this magnificent Utah lake for 11 years, parts of it remain a mystery. It glows like an emerald jewel among desert sage, red rocky cliffs and parched land. Against azure skies, such stark beauty sears the eye. More than a million people flock to Powell every year, but the lake is so vast that you may not bump into anyone for several days.

The portion of Powell pictured is not even a drop in the bucket, so to speak. The lake runs for 180 miles mostly through southern Utah and dumps into Page, Arizona – the site of America's third highest dam. Powell offers more than 2000 miles of shoreline jutting into magical finger canyons whose access rise and fall with water levels.

Dare To Prepare: Chapter 52: Preparing for Drought and Water Shortage

One summer the depth finder quit reading at 1000 feet, though officially, it's listed several hundred feet less. When full, Lake Powell holds 24 million acre-feet, but at the end of June 2004 there were only 10.4 million acre-feet, the lowest it'd been since 1980.

Look closely at the two photographs. In the top photo "A", cliffs are ringed by white where water left its mark. Though low in June of 2003, significant water still covers the bottom half of this image. Now look at "B". That large water area has shrunk to about one-fifth in six months. This is scary considering the mammoth size of this lake.

Concern is cropping up that should the drought persist another 18 months, water levels could sink below the dam's turbines, which supply part of the West's power. So there are more than just recreational concerns.

MORE THAN DROUGHT

In addition to drought, emergency water shortages can also be caused by water supply contamination. A major spill of a petroleum product or hazardous chemical on a major river can force communities to shut down water treatment plants. Although typically more localized, contamination of ground water or an aquifer can also disrupt the use of well water.

Conserving water is very important during emergency water shortages. Water saved by one person may be enough to protect the critical needs of others.

WATER CONSERVATION

Conserving water is very important during emergency water shortages. Water saved by one user may be enough to protect the critical needs of others. Irrigation practices can be changed to use less water or crops that use less water can be planted. Cities and towns can ration water, factories can change manufacturing methods, and individuals can practice water-saving measures to reduce consumption. If everyone reduces water use during a drought, more water will be available to share.

1.   *PRACTICE INDOOR WATER CONSERVATION:*
General
  Never pour water down the drain when there may be another use for it. Use it to water your indoor plants or garden.
  Repair dripping faucets by replacing washers. One drop per second wastes 2,700 gallons of water per year!
Bathroom
  Check all plumbing for leaks. Have leaks repaired by a plumber. Consider purchasing a low-volume toilet that uses less than half the water of older models. NOTE: Many areas require by law, low-volume units.
  Install a toilet displacement device to cut down on the amount of water needed to flush. Place a one-gallon plastic jug of water into the tank to displace toilet flow (do not use a brick, it may dissolve and loose pieces may cause damage to the internal parts). Be sure installation does not interfere with the operating parts.
  Don't flush the toilet unnecessarily. Dispose of tissues, insects, and other similar waste in the trash rather than the toilet.
  Replace your showerhead with an ultra-low-flow version.
  Do not take baths – take short showers – only turn on water to get wet and lather and then again to rinse off.
  Place a bucket in the shower to catch excess water for watering plants.
  Don't let the water run while brushing your teeth, washing your face or shaving.
Kitchen
  Operate automatic dishwashers only when they are fully loaded. Use the "light wash" feature if available to use less water.
  Hand wash dishes by filling two containers – one with soapy water and the other with rinse water containing a small amount of chlorine bleach.
  Most dishwashers can clean soiled dishes very well, so dishes do not have to be rinsed before washing. Just remove large particles of food, and put the soiled dishes in the dishwasher.
  Store drinking water in the refrigerator. Don't let the tap run while you are waiting for water to cool.
  Do not waste water waiting for it to get hot. Capture it for other uses such as plant watering or heat it on the stove or in a microwave.
  Do not use running water to thaw meat or other frozen foods. Defrost food overnight in the refrigerator, or use the defrost setting on your microwave.
  Clean vegetables in a pan filled with water rather than running water from the tap.
  Kitchen sink disposals require a lot of water to operate properly. Start a compost pile as an alternate method of disposing of food waste, or simply dispose of food in the garbage.

Laundry
>Operate automatic clothes washers only when they are fully loaded or set the water level for the size of your load.

Long-term indoor water conservation
>Retrofit all household faucets by installing aerators with flow restrictors.
>
>Consider installing an instant hot water heater on your sink.
>
>Insulate your water pipes to reduce heat loss and prevent them from breaking if you have a sudden and unexpected spell of freezing weather.
>
>If you are considering installing a new heat pump or air-conditioning system, the new air-to-air models are just as efficient as the water-to air type and do not waste water.
>
>Install a water-softening system only when the minerals in the water would damage your pipes. Turn the softener off while on vacation.
>
>When purchasing a new appliance, choose one that is more energy and water efficient.

2. PRACTICE OUTDOOR WATER CONSERVATION:

General
>If you have a well at home, check your pump periodically. If the automatic pump turns on and off while water is not being used, you have a leak.

Car washing
>Use a hose shut-off nozzle that can be adjusted down to a fine spray, so that water flows only as needed.
>
>Consider using a commercial car wash that recycles water. If you wash your own car, park on the grass so that you will be watering it at the same time.

Lawn Care
>Don't over water your lawn. A heavy rain eliminates the need for watering for up to two weeks. Most of the year, lawns only need one inch of water per week.
>
>Water in several short sessions rather than one long one in order for your lawn to better absorb moisture.
>
>Position sprinklers so water lands on the lawn and shrubs and not on paved areas.
>
>Avoid sprinklers that spray a fine mist. Mist can evaporate before it reaches the lawn. Check sprinkler systems and timing devices regularly to be sure they operate properly.
>
>Raise the lawn mower blade to at least three inches, or to its highest level. A higher cut encourages grass roots to grow deeper, shades the root system, and holds soil moisture.
>
>Plant drought-resistant lawn seed.
>
>Avoid over-fertilizing your lawn. Applying fertilizer increases the need for water. Apply fertilizers that contain slow-release, water-insoluble forms of nitrogen.
>
>Use a broom or blower instead of a hose to clean leaves and other debris from your driveway or sidewalk.
>
>Do not leave sprinklers or hoses unattended. A garden hose can pour out 600 gallons or more in only a few hours.

Pool
>Consider installing a new water-saving pool filter. A single back flushing with a traditional filter uses 180 to 250 gallons of water.
>
>Cover pools and spas to reduce evaporation of water.

Long term outdoor conservation
>Plant native and/or drought-tolerant grasses, ground covers, shrubs and trees. Once established, they do not need water as frequently and usually will survive a dry period without watering. Small plants require less water to become established. Group plants together based on similar water needs.
>
>Install irrigation devices that are the most water efficient for each use. Micro and drip irrigation and soaker hoses are examples of efficient devices.
>
>Use mulch to retain moisture in the soil. Mulch also helps control weeds that compete with landscape plants for water.
>
>Avoid purchasing recreational water toys that require a constant stream of water.
>
>Avoid installing ornamental water features (such as fountains) unless they use recycled water.

Participate in public water conservation programs of your local government, utility or water management district. Follow water conservation and water shortage rules in effect. Remember, you are included in the restrictions even if your water comes from a private well. Be sure to support community efforts that help develop and promote a water conservation ethic.

>Contact your local water authority, utility district, or local emergency management agency for information specific to your area.

Chapter 53: Preparing for Heat Waves and Heat Emergencies

OUR MERCURIAL STAR

Despite what we were taught in school several decades ago, it has long been known that our Sun is not a constant glowing ball of hydrogen. It's continually changing blowing off portions of itself, forming loops and holes in its outer layers, and by producing magnetic storms and wild plasma winds. All these things generate and use enormous amounts of energy.

On May 27, 1998, the Sun revealed it's prone to solar-quakes. Stanford and Glasgow scientists found that "sun-quakes" closely resemble earthquakes – except in size. Sun quakes are **huge** containing 40,000 times the energy released in the great 1906 San Francisco earthquake. That '98 sun-quake produced enough energy to power the United States for 20 years – equivalent to an 11.3 magnitude quake on Earth.[141]

But that's not all, 1998 brought yet another discovery. The Sun is plagued by tornadoes, making Earth's F5's seem irrelevant. Earth's strongest tornadoes blow around 320mph. The Sun's are 1000 times as violent[142].

In 1991, the Sun began emitting two new spectral bandwidths in the ultraviolet range. This means more radiation to pummel Earth and its inhabitants.

Around this same time, scientists discovered that the Sun doesn't emit neutrinos (neutral particles) at the rate physicists had predicted using their most advanced theoretical models. If this information were wrong, what else was? This discovery forced scientists to re-think their solar model. Until they can resolve the true nature of our Sun's nuclear physics and chemistry, they can't be certain of its stability and future behavior.

New research shows the Sun has increased its magnetic field by 40% since 1964. Solar magnetism is closely linked with sunspot activity and the strength of sunlight reaching Earth. Scientists at Rutherford Appleton Labs near Oxford, England, showed the Sun has definitely become more "energetic".[143]

Why is this important? This increased energy is, in great part, responsible for our erratic weather and climate extremes. Furthermore, unlike greenhouse gases, it is nothing we can correct.

Photo: SOHO (Solar & Heliospheric Observatory) image depicting the Nov. 4, 2003 X45 flare. NOTE: The dark ring outside the circle labeled "Sun" is a shield placed on the camera blocking its normal light. Without it, the Sun's activity would be an indistinguishable ball of fire. The brilliant lights are solar flares. In subsequent frames, the flare material traveled much, much further – all the way to Earth and beyond.

THE NEW "BIG BANG"

November 4, 2003, saw the largest solar flare EVER erupt from the Sun. Existing scientific instruments weren't even equipped to measure output this great. Currently scales only go to an X9. Initial estimates put this eruption at an X28[144] – way, way off the chart. Then came the upgrade.

"Researchers from the University of Otago in New Zealand used radio wave measurements of the x-rays' effects on the Earth's upper atmosphere to revise the flare's size from a merely huge X28 to a *"whopping"* X45, say researchers Neil Thomson, Craig Rodger, and Richard Dowden.

"X-class flares are major events that can trigger radio blackouts around the world and long-lasting radiation storms in the upper atmosphere that can damage or destroy satellites. The biggest previous solar flares on record were rated X20, on 2 April 2001 and 16 August 1989.

"This makes it more than twice as large as any previously recorded flare, and if the accompanying particle and magnetic storm had been aimed at the Earth, the damage to some satellites and electrical networks could have been considerable," says Thomson. Their calculations show that the flare's x-ray radiation bombarding the atmosphere was equivalent to that of 5,000 Suns"[145]. Whatever, it was massive.

HOPI PROPHECY

When Stan and I visited the Hopi in 1996 and 1997, they shared prophecy that foretold of the Sun getting so hot, people would have to live underground for several weeks. They have already equipped their kivas with food and water anticipating this event.

Perhaps it's not as farfetched as some might think. For these emergencies, you too will need to seek shelter, possibly in a cave if underground. For cave locations map, see *Prudent Places USA* by Holly Deyo.

HOT SHOTS

Heat kills by pushing the human body beyond its limits. Under normal conditions, the body's internal thermostat produces perspiration that evaporates and cools the body. However, in extreme heat and high humidity, evaporation is slowed and the body must work extra hard to maintain a normal temperature.

Most heat disorders occur because the victim has been overexposed to heat or has over-exercised for his or her age and physical condition. The elderly, young children, and those who are sick or overweight are more likely to succumb to extreme heat.

Conditions that can induce heat-related illnesses include stagnant atmospheric conditions and poor air quality. Consequently, people living in urban areas may be at greater risk from the effects of a prolonged heat wave than those living in rural areas. Also, asphalt and concrete store heat longer and gradually release heat at night, which can produce higher nighttime temperatures known as the "urban heat island effect."

The elderly, young children, and those who are ill or overweight are more likely to succumb to extreme heat.

WHAT TO DO BEFORE AN EXTREME HEAT EMERGENCY

1. Know the terms associated with extreme heat:
   Heat wave – Prolonged period of excessive heat, often combined with excessive humidity.
   Heat index – A number in degrees Fahrenheit (F) that tells how hot it feels when relative humidity is added to the air temperature. Exposure to full sunshine can increase the heat index by 15 degrees.
   Heat cramps – Muscular pains and spasms due to heavy exertion. Although heat cramps are the least severe, they are often the first signal that the body is having trouble with the heat.
   Heat exhaustion – Typically occurs when people exercise heavily or work in a hot, humid place where body fluids are lost through heavy sweating. Blood flow to the skin increases, causing blood flow to decrease to the vital organs. This results in a form of mild shock. If not treated, the victim's condition will worsen. Body temperature will keep rising and the victim may suffer heat stroke.
   Heat stroke – Heat stroke is life-threatening. The victim's temperature control system, which produces sweating to cool the body, stops working. The body temperature can elevate so high that brain damage and death may result if the body is not cooled quickly.
   Sun stroke – Another term for heat stroke.
2. Consider the following preparedness measures when faced with the possibility of extreme heat.
   Install window air conditioners snugly, insulate if necessary.
   Check air-conditioning ducts for proper insulation.
   Install temporary window reflectors (for use between windows and drapes), such as aluminum foil covered cardboard, to reflect heat back outside and be sure to weather-strip doors and sills to keep cool air in.
   Cover windows that receive morning or afternoon sun with drapes, shades, awnings or louvers. Outdoor awnings or louvers can reduce the heat that enters a home by up to 80%. Consider keeping storm windows up all year.

Conserve electricity as much as possible during heatwaves. In these conditions, we use so much extra power for air conditioning, it often leads to rolling brownouts or complete outages.

WHAT TO DO DURING EXTREME HEAT OR A HEAT WAVE EMERGENCY

1. Stay indoors as much as possible. If air conditioning is not available, stay on the lowest floor out of the sunshine. Circulating air can cool the body by increasing the perspiration rate of evaporation.
2. Eat well-balanced, light and regular meals. Avoid using salt tablets unless directed to do so by a physician.
3. Drink plenty of water regularly even if you do not feel thirsty. Persons who have epilepsy or heart, kidney, or liver disease, are on fluid-restrictive diets, or have a problem with fluid retention should consult a doctor before increasing liquid intake.
4. Limit intake of alcoholic beverages. Although beer and alcoholic beverages appear to satisfy thirst, they actually cause further body dehydration.
5. Never leave children or pets alone in closed vehicles.
6. Dress in loose fitting clothes that cover as much skin as possible. Lightweight, light-colored clothing reflects heat and sunlight; helps maintain normal body temp.
7. Protect face and head by wearing a wide-brimmed hat.
8. Avoid too much sunshine. Sunburn slows the skin's ability to cool itself. Use a sunscreen lotion with a high SPF (sun protection factor) rating (i.e., 30 or greater).
9. Avoid strenuous work during the warmest part of the day. Use a buddy system when working in extreme heat and take frequent breaks.
10. Spend at least two hours per day in an air-conditioned place. If your home is not air conditioned, consider spending the warmest part of the day in public buildings such as libraries, schools, movie theaters, shopping malls and other community facilities.
11. Check on family, friends, and neighbors who don't have air conditioning and spend much of their time alone.

FIRST-AID FOR HEAT-INDUCED ILLNESSES

SUNBURN
Symptoms: Skin redness and pain, possible swelling, blisters, fever, headaches.
First Aid: Take a shower, using soap, to remove oils that may block pores, preventing the body from cooling naturally. If blisters occur, apply dry, sterile dressings and get medical attention.

HEAT CRAMPS
Symptoms: Painful spasms, usually in leg and abdominal muscles. Heavy sweating.
First Aid: Get the victim out to a cooler location. Lightly stretch and gently massage affected muscles to relieve spasm. Give sips of up to a half glass of cool water every 15 minutes. Do not give liquids with caffeine or alcohol. If nauseous, discontinue liquids.

HEAT EXHAUSTION
Symptoms: Heavy sweating and skin may be cool, pale or flushed. Weak pulse. Normal body temperature is possible but temperature will likely rise. Fainting or dizziness, nausea or vomiting, exhaustion and headaches are possible.
First Aid: Get victim to lie down in a cool place. Loosen or remove clothing. Apply cool, wet cloths. Fan or move victim to air-conditioned place. Give sips of water if victim is conscious. Be sure water is consumed slowly. Give half glass of cool water every 15 minutes. If nausea occurs, discontinue. If vomiting occurs, seek immediate medical attention.

HEAT STROKE (SUN STROKE)
Symptoms: High body temperature (105°+F / 41+°C). Hot, red, dry skin. Rapid, weak pulse and rapid, shallow breathing. Possible unconsciousness. Victim will likely not sweat unless victim was sweating from recent strenuous activity.
First Aid: Heat stroke is a severe medical emergency. Call 911 or emergency medical services or get the victim to a hospital immediately. Delay can be fatal. Move victim to a cooler environment. Remove clothing. Try a cool bath, sponging or wet sheet to reduce body temperature. Watch for breathing problems. Use extreme caution. Use fans and air conditioners.

Chapter 54: Preparing for Fires

Photo: November 2003, San Bernardino, California. A few chairs and some fencing is all that remains after the area was ravaged by wildfire. (Michael Raphael/FEMA Photo)

Every year more than 4000 Americans die and 25,000+ are injured in fires, many of which could be prevented. Direct property losses peg an estimated at $8.6 billion.

To protect yourself, it's important to understand the basic characteristics of fire. Fire spreads quickly and there may be no time to gather valuables or make a phone call. In just two minutes a fire can become life threatening. In five minutes a residence can be engulfed in flames.

Heat and smoke from fire can be more dangerous than the flames. Inhaling the super-hot air can sear your lungs. Fire produces poisonous gases that make you disoriented and drowsy. Instead of being awakened by a fire, you may fall into a deeper sleep. Asphyxiation is the leading cause of fire deaths, exceeding burns, by a three-to-one ratio.

> *Working smoke alarms decrease your chances of dying in fire by half.*

WHAT TO DO BEFORE FIRE STRIKES
1. Install smoke alarms. Working smoke alarms decrease your chances of dying in a fire by half.
   Place smoke alarms on every level of your residence: outside bedrooms on the ceiling or high on the wall, at the top of open stairways or at the bottom of enclosed stairs and near (but not in) the kitchen.
   Test and clean smoke alarms once a month and replace batteries at least once a year. Replace smoke alarms once every 10 years.

2. With your household, plan two escape routes from every room in the residence. Practice with your household escaping from each room.
   Make sure windows are not nailed or painted shut. Make sure security gratings on windows have a fire safety-opening feature so that they can be easily opened from the inside.
   Consider escape ladders if your home has more than one level and ensure that burglar bars and other anti-theft mechanisms that block outside window entry are easily opened from inside.
   Teach household members to stay low to the floor (where the air is safer in a fire) when escaping from a fire.
   Pick a place outside your home for the household to meet after escaping from a fire.
3. Clean out storage areas. Don't let trash such as old newspapers and magazines accumulate.
4. Check the electrical wiring in your home.
   Inspect extension cords for frayed or exposed wires or loose plugs.
   Outlets should have cover plates and no exposed wiring.
   Make sure wiring does not run under rugs, over nails, or across high traffic areas.
   Do not overload extension cords or outlets. If you need to plug in two or three appliances, get a UL-approved unit with built-in circuit breakers to prevent sparks and short circuits.
   Make sure home insulation does not touch electrical wiring.
   Have an electrician check the electrical wiring in your home.
5. Never use gasoline, benzine, naptha or similar liquids indoors.
   Store flammable liquids in approved containers in well-ventilated storage areas.
   Never smoke near flammable liquids.
   After use, safely discard all rags or materials soaked in flammable material.
6. Check heating sources. Many home fires are started by faulty furnaces or stoves, cracked or rusted furnace parts and chimneys with creosote build-up. Have chimneys, wood stoves and all home heating systems inspected and cleaned annually by a certified specialist.
7. Insulate chimneys and place spark arresters on top. The chimney should be at least three feet higher than the roof. Remove branches hanging above and around the chimney.
8. Be careful when using alternative heating sources, such as wood, coal and kerosene heaters and electrical space heaters.
   Check with your local fire department on the legality of using kerosene heaters in your community. Be sure to fill kerosene heaters outside after they have cooled.
   Place heaters at least three feet away from flammable materials. Make sure the floor and nearby walls are properly insulated.
   Use only the type of fuel designated for your unit and follow manufacturer's instructions.
   Store ashes in a metal container outside and away from the residence.
   Keep open flames away from walls, furniture, drapery and flammable items. Keep a screen in front of the fireplace.
   Have chimneys and wood stoves inspected annually and cleaned if necessary.
   Use portable heaters only in well-ventilated rooms.
9. Keep matches and lighters up high, away from children, and if possible, in a locked cabinet.
10. Do not smoke in bed, or when drowsy or medicated. Provide smokers with deep, sturdy ashtrays. Douse cigarette and cigar butts with water before disposal.
11. Safety experts recommend that you sleep with your door closed.
12. Know the locations of the gas valve and electric fuse or circuit breaker box and how to turn them off in an emergency. If you shut off your main gas line for any reason, allow only a gas company representative to turn it on again.
13. Install A-B-C type fire extinguishers in the home and teach household members how to use them (*Type A* – wood or papers fires only; *Type B* – flammable liquid or grease fires; *Type C* – electrical fires; *Type A-B-C* – rated for all fires and recommended for the home).
14. Consider installing an automatic fire sprinkler system in your home.
15. Ask your local fire department to inspect your residence for fire safety and prevention.
16. Teach children how to report a fire and when to use 911.
17. To support insurance claims in case you do have a fire, conduct an inventory of your property and possessions and keep the list in a separate location. Photographs are also helpful.
18. See the "Emergency Planning and Disaster Supplies" chapter for additional information.

Install A-B-C fire extinguishers in the home; teach household members how to use them.

WHAT TO DO DURING A FIRE

1. Use water or a fire extinguisher to put out small fires. Do not try to put out a fire that is getting out of control. If you're not sure if you can control it, get everyone out of the residence and call the fire department from a neighbor's residence.
2. Never use water on an electrical fire. Use only a fire extinguisher approved for electrical fires.
3. Smother oil and grease fires in the kitchen with baking soda or salt, or put a lid over the flame if it is burning in a pan. Do not attempt to take the pan outside.
4. If your clothes catch on fire, **stop, drop** and **roll** until the fire is extinguished. Running only makes the fire burn faster.
5. If you are escaping through a closed door, use the back of your hand to feel the top of the door, the doorknob, and the crack between the door and door frame before you open it. **Never** use the palm of your hand or fingers to test for heat - burning those areas could impair your ability to escape a fire (i.e., ladders and crawling).
   If the door is cool, open slowly and ensure fire and/or smoke is not blocking your escape route. If your escape route is blocked, shut the door immediately and use an alternate escape route, such as a window. If it's clear, leave immediately through the door. Be prepared to crawl. Smoke and heat rise. The air is clearer and cooler near the floor.
   If the door is warm or hot, do not open. Escape through a window. If you cannot escape, hang a white or light-colored sheet outside the window, alerting fire fighters to your presence.
6. If you must exit through smoke, crawl low under the smoke to your exit – heavy smoke and poisonous gases collect first along the ceiling.
7. Close doors behind you as you escape to delay the spread of the fire.
8. Once you are safely out, stay out. Call 911.

If your clothes are on fire, STOP, DROP, and ROLL until the fire is extinguished.

WHAT TO DO AFTER A FIRE

1. Give first aid where needed. After calling 911 or your local emergency number, cool and cover burns to reduce chance of further injury or infection.
2. Do not enter a fire-damaged building unless authorities say it is okay.
3. If you must enter a fire-damaged building, be alert for heat and smoke. If you detect either, evacuate immediately.
4. Have an electrician check your household wiring before the current is turned on.
5. Do not attempt to reconnect any utilities yourself. Leave this to the fire department and other authorities.
6. Beware of structural damage. Roofs and floors may be weakened and need repair.
7. Contact your local disaster relief service, such as the American Red Cross or Salvation Army, if you need housing, food, or a place to stay.
8. Call your insurance agent.
   Make a list of damage and losses. Pictures are helpful.
   Keep records of clean up and repair costs. Receipts are important for both insurance and income tax claims. Do not throw away any damaged goods until an official inventory has been taken. Your insurance company takes all damages into consideration.
9. If you are a tenant, contact the landlord. It's the property owner's responsibility to prevent further loss or damage to the site.
10. Secure personal belongings or move them to another location.
11. Discard food, beverages and medicines that have been exposed to heat, smoke or soot. Refrigerators and freezers left closed hold their temperature for a short time. Do not attempt to refreeze food that has thawed.
12. If you have a safe or strong box, do not try to open it. It can hold intense heat for several hours. If the door is opened before the box has cooled, the contents could burst into flames.
13. If a building inspector says the building is unsafe and you must leave your home:

Ask local police to watch the property during your absence.
Pack identification, medicines, glasses, jewelry, credit cards, checkbooks, insurance policies and financial records if you can reach them safely.
Notify friends, relatives, police and fire departments, your insurance agent, the mortgage company, utility companies, delivery services, employers, schools and the post office of your whereabouts.

WILDFIRES

If you live on a remote hillside, or in a valley, prairie or forest where flammable vegetation is abundant, your residence could be vulnerable to wildland fire. These fires are usually triggered by lightning or accidents.

1. **Fire facts about rural living:**
   Once a fire starts outdoors in a rural area, it is often hard to control. Wildland firefighters are trained to protect natural resources, not homes and buildings.
   Many homes are located far from fire stations. The result is longer emergency response times. Within a matter of minutes, an entire home may be destroyed by fire.
   Limited water supply in rural areas can make fire suppression difficult.
   Homes may be secluded and surrounded by woods, dense brush and combustible vegetation that fuel fires.

2. **Ask fire authorities for information about wildland fires in your area. Request that they inspect your residence** and property for hazards.

3. **Be prepared and have a fire safety and evacuation plan:**
   Practice fire escape and evacuation plans.
   Mark the entrance to your property with address signs that are clearly visible from the road.
   Know which local emergency services are available and have those numbers posted near telephones.
   Provide emergency vehicle access through roads and driveways at least 12 feet wide with adequate turnaround space.

4. **Tips for making your property fire resistant:**
   Keep lawns trimmed, leaves raked, and the roof and rain-gutters free from debris such as dead limbs and leaves.
   Stack firewood at least 30 feet away from your home.
   Store flammable materials, liquids and solvents in metal containers outside the home at least 30 feet away from structures and wooden fences.
   Create defensible space by thinning trees and brush within 30 feet around your home. Beyond 30 feet, remove dead wood, debris and low tree branches.
   Landscape your property with fire resistant plants and vegetation to prevent fire from spreading quickly. For example, hardwood trees are more fire-resistant than pine, evergreen, eucalyptus, or fir trees.
   Make sure water sources, such as hydrants, ponds, swimming pools and wells, are accessible to the fire department.

5. **Protect your home:**
   Use fire resistant, protective roofing and materials like stone, brick and metal to protect your home. Avoid using wood materials. They offer the least fire protection.
   Cover all exterior vents, attics and eaves with metal mesh screens no larger than 6 millimeters or ¼" to prevent debris from collecting and to help keep sparks out.
   Install multi-pane windows, tempered safety glass or fireproof shutters to protect large windows from radiant heat.
   Use fire-resistant draperies for added window protection.
   Have chimneys, wood stoves and all home heating systems inspected and cleaned annually by a certified specialist.
   Insulate chimneys and place spark arresters on top. Chimney should be at least three feet above the roof.
   Remove branches hanging above and around the chimney.

6. **Follow local burning laws:**
   Do not burn trash or other debris without proper knowledge of local burning laws, techniques and the safest times of day and year to burn.
   Before burning debris in a wooded area, make sure you notify local authorities and obtain a burning permit.
   Use an approved incinerator with a safety lid or covering with holes no larger than ¾".
   Create at least a 10-foot clearing around the incinerator before burning debris.
   Have a fire extinguisher or garden hose on hand when burning debris.

7. **If wildfire threatens your home and time permits, consider the following:**

INSIDE

Shut off gas at the meter. Turn off pilot lights.
Open fireplace damper. Close fireplace screens.
Close windows, vents, doors, blinds or noncombustible window coverings, and heavy drapes. Remove flammable drapes and curtains.
Move flammable furniture into the center of the home away from windows and sliding-glass doors.
Close all interior doors and windows to prevent drafts.
Place valuables that won't be damaged by water in a pool or pond.
Gather pets into one room. Make plans to care for your pets if you must evacuate.
Back your car into the garage or park it in an open space facing the direction of escape. Shut doors and roll up windows. Leave the key in the ignition and the car doors unlocked. Close garage windows and doors, but leave them unlocked. Disconnect automatic garage door openers.

OUTSIDE

Seal attic and ground vents with precut plywood or commercial seals.
Turn off propane tanks.
Place combustible patio furniture inside.
Connect garden hose to outside taps. Place lawn sprinklers on the roof and near aboveground fuel tanks. Wet the roof.
Wet or remove shrubs within 15 feet of the home.
Gather fire tools such as a rake, axe, handsaw or chainsaw, bucket, and shovel.

8. **If advised to evacuate, do so immediately.** Choose a route away from the fire hazard. Watch for changes in the speed and direction of fire and smoke.

Photo: Forest fires ravaged Florida after extreme drought plagued the state. Some fires ignited after lightning strikes; others were the product of arson. (Liz Roll / FEMA News Photo)

Chapter 55: Preparing for Floods

Photo: Though not lightning fast after a massive Midwest flood, inflatables were the only option. Still on duty, law enforcement officers patrol the Sherlock Park area of East Grand Forks, Minnesota; April, 1997. (Photo by David Saville/FEMA)

THE BIG WET

Floods are one of the most common hazards in the U.S. However, all floods are not alike. Some floods develop slowly, sometimes over several days; however, flash floods can arrive quickly, sometimes in just a few minutes, and without any visible signs of rain. Flash floods often have a dangerous wall of roaring water that carries a deadly cargo of rocks, mud and other debris and can sweep away most things in its path. Overland flooding occurs outside a defined river or stream, such as when a levee is breached, but still can be destructive. Flooding can also occur from dam breaks, producing effects similar to flash floods.

Flood effects can be very local, impacting a neighborhood or community, or very large, affecting entire river basins and multiple states.

Be aware of flood hazards no matter where you live, but especially if you live in a low-lying area, near water or downstream from a dam. Even very small streams, gullies, creeks, culverts, dry streambeds or low-lying ground that appear harmless in dry weather can flood. Every state is at risk from this hazard.

Go to higher ground during floods. Moving water only 6 inches deep can knock you off your feet.

WHAT TO DO BEFORE A FLOOD

1. Know the terms used to describe flooding:
   - **Flood Watch** – Flooding is possible. Stay tuned to NOAA Weather Radio or commercial radio or television for information. Watches are issued 12 to 36 hours in advance of a possible flooding event.
   - **Flash Flood Watch** – Flash flooding is possible. Be prepared to move to higher ground. A flash flood could occur without any warning. Listen to NOAA Weather Radio or commercial radio or television for additional information.
   - **Flood Warning** – Flooding is occurring or will occur soon. If advised to evacuate, do so immediately.
   - **Flash Flood Warning** – A flash flood is occurring. Seek higher ground on foot immediately.
2. Ask local officials whether your property is in a flood-prone or high-risk area. (Remember that floods often occur outside high-risk areas.) Ask about official flood warning signals and what to do when you hear them. Also ask how you can protect your home from flooding.
3. Identify dams in your area and determine whether they pose a hazard to you.
4. Purchase a NOAA Weather Radio with battery backup and a tone-alert feature that automatically alerts you when a **Watch** or **Warning** is issued (tone alert not available in some areas). Purchase a battery-powered commercial radio and extra batteries.
5. Be prepared to evacuate. Learn your community's flood evacuation routes and where to find high ground
6. Talk to your household about flooding. Plan a place to meet your household in case you are separated from one another in a disaster and cannot return home. Choose an out-of-town contact for everyone to call to say they are okay. In some emergencies, calling out-of-state is possible even when local phone lines are down.
7. Determine how you would care for household members who may live elsewhere but might need your help in a flood. Determine any special needs your neighbors might have.
8. Prepare to survive on your own for at least three days. Assemble a disaster supply kit. Keep a stock of food and extra drinking water
9. Know how to shut off electricity, gas and water at main switches and valves. Know where gas pilot lights are located and how the heating system works.
10. Consider purchasing flood insurance.
    Flood losses are not covered under homeowners' insurance policies.
    FEMA manages the National Flood Insurance Program, which makes federally backed flood insurance available in communities that agree to adopt and enforce floodplain management ordinances to reduce future flood damage.
    Flood insurance is available in most communities through insurance agents.
    There is a 30-day waiting period before flood insurance goes into effect, so don't delay.
    Flood insurance is available whether the building is in or out of the identified flood-prone area.
11. Consider options for protecting your property.
    Make a record of your personal property. Take photographs or videotapes of your belongings. Store these documents in a safe place.
    Keep insurance policies, deeds, property records and other important papers in a safe place away from your home.
    Avoid building in a floodplain unless you elevate and reinforce your home.
    Elevate furnace, water heater, and electric panel to higher floors or the attic if they are susceptible to flooding.
    Install "check valves" in sewer traps to prevent floodwater from backing up into the drains of your home.
    Construct barriers such as levees, berms, and floodwalls to stop floodwater from entering the building.
    Seal walls in basements with waterproofing compounds to avoid seepage.
    Call your local building department or emergency management office for more information.

Keep supplies on hand for an emergency. Remember a battery operated NOAA Weather Radio with a tone alert feature and extra batteries.

WHAT TO DO DURING A FLOOD

1. Be aware of flash flood. If there is *any* possibility of a flash flood, move immediately to higher ground. Don't wait for instructions to move.
2. Listen to radio or television stations for local information.
3. Be aware of streams, drainage channels, canyons and other areas known to flood suddenly. Flash floods can occur in these areas with or without such typical warning signs as rain clouds or heavy rain.

4. If local authorities issue a flood watch, prepare to evacuate:
   Secure your home. *If you have time*, tie down or bring outdoor equipment and lawn furniture inside. Move essential items to the upper floors.
   If instructed, turn off utilities at the main switches or valves. Disconnect electrical appliances. *Do not touch electrical equipment if you are wet or standing in water.*
   Fill the bathtub with water in case water becomes contaminated or services cut off. Before filling the tub, sterilize it with a diluted bleach solution.
5. Don't walk through moving water. Six inches of moving water can knock you off your feet. If you must walk in a flooded area, walk where the water is not moving. Use a stick to check the firmness of the ground in front of you.
6. Don't drive into flooded areas. Six inches of water will reach the bottom of most passenger cars causing loss of control and possible stalling. A foot of water will float many vehicles. Two feet of water will wash away almost all vehicles. If floodwaters rise around your car, abandon the car and move to higher ground, if you can do so safely. You and your vehicle can be quickly swept away as floodwaters rise.

> *If there is any possibility of a flash flood, move immediately to higher ground.*
> *Do not wait for instructions to move.*

WHAT TO DO AFTER A FLOOD

1. Avoid floodwaters. The water may be contaminated by oil, gasoline or raw sewage. The water may also be electrically charged from underground or downed power lines.
2. Avoid moving water. Moving water only six inches deep can sweep you off your feet.
3. Be aware of areas where floodwaters have receded. Roads may have weakened and could collapse under the weight of a car.
4. Stay away from downed power lines and report them to the power company.
5. Stay away from designated disaster areas unless authorities ask for volunteers.
6. Return home only when authorities indicate it is safe. Stay out of buildings if surrounded by floodwaters. Use extreme caution when entering buildings. There may be hidden damage, particularly in foundations.
7. Consider your family's health and safety needs:
   If you come in contact with floodwaters, wash hands frequently with soap and clean water.
   Throw away food that has come in contact with floodwaters.
   Listen for news reports to learn whether the community's water supply is safe to drink.
   Listen to news reports for information about where to get assistance for housing, clothing and food.
   Seek necessary medical care at the nearest medical facility.
8. Service damaged septic tanks, cesspools, pits, and leaching systems as soon as possible. Damaged sewage systems are serious health hazards.
9. Contact your insurance agent. If your policy covers your situation, an adjuster will be assigned to visit your home. To prepare:
   Take photos of your belongings and your home or videotape them.
   Separate damaged and undamaged belongings.
   Locate your financial records.
   Keep detailed records of cleanup costs.

Chapter 56: Sanitation After a Flood

LIVING IN SOGGYVILLE

Especially during an emergency, we need to be **very careful** about sanitation. Regardless of the disaster, the one consistent rule is WASH YOUR HANDS OFTEN! Medical staff may already be inundated with injured people, and personnel available for non-life threatening conditions could be in short supply. During disasters there are enough problems without compounding matters. We don't need to add food poisoning or dysentery.

Good sanitation not only involves proper hygiene during a crisis, but also if sewer lines break or septic tanks are unusable, disposing of garbage and human waste can be a problem.

Because flooding brings its own set problems to the equation and because it's so prevalent, we'll look at this issue separately.

Photo: Santa Cruz River, Tucson, Arizona during El Niño flooding.
(Peter L. Kresan, Dept. of Geosciences, University of Arizona, Tucson, AZ)

SANITATION AND FLOODS

Floods accompany many disasters and are the #1 weather-related killer. Every year floods and flash floods cost billions in damages. Water problems are also experienced when sewer lines break during earthquakes adding disease to the chaos. During floods, sewers can back up with water overburden. Burgeoning creeks, spillways, arroyos, streams and rivers become living creatures snatching everything within grasp. These normally tame, beautiful waterways spread disease from sewage collected along their raging paths.

FUN FOR KIDS, MISERY FOR ADULTS

When I was 8, we lived in suburban Kansas City. Our street, situated at the bottom of a six-block hill, was terrific to skate down in summer and sled down in winter. The neighborhood was filled with lots of kids and hard-working parents. Most of these middle class families didn't have central air conditioning; it was a luxury most couldn't afford. To keep cool during Missouri's steamy summers, every patio was armed with BBQ grills, picnic tables, lawn furniture and kiddy pools. At the back of our property was a storm drain, but to a child, it was a bubbling stream to explore filled with crawdads and stepping stones.

Summer 1962, it rained non-stop for a week. All the kids were cranky from playing inside. Parents were exhausted dealing with us, but it was nothing compared to what they were about to face.

Clouds kept their angry gray faces and continued depositing more wet stuff. Looking out the dining room window, I could see the creek filling and roiling about.

Thirty minutes later, it popped over the two-foot embankment inching toward the peach trees. Another 15 minutes passed and the water had crept 30 feet closer – halfway to the house.

The rain showed no sign of stopping as water touched the patio. By now, since flood warnings had been issued, most parents were home from work. It was a good thing because storm drains throughout the neighborhood could no longer hold their watery burden. Flows that normally trickled through these three-foot cement tunnels cascaded down streets in massive torrents. The ground was completely saturated and by the time the flow hit our neighborhood, it was a roaring, angry mass.

The once green backyard swirled like a brown river colorfully dotted with passing lawn furniture. Squinting through the downpour, we could see floodwaters heading for our finished basement. It squirmed under the basement door and poured through window wells. Mopping became futile and Mom resorted to buckets and shovels when mud oozed under the door.

Dad worked frantically outside with the rest of the neighborhood men to corral floating cars, swing sets, barbecues and bikes. The kids? We thought it wonderfully exciting. Dad and the next door neighbor were in the midst of rescuing a wayward picnic table when he abruptly dropped his end and charged through knee-deep water.

Always wanting to be with the family, Zippy, our red dachshund had slipped quietly outside in the chaos. Unable to make those short legs work against such strong current, Zippy became another floating object. Barks and squeaks came from the terrified pooch before Dad scooped him to safety.

After the rain subsided, our neighborhood resembled a junkyard. The Ware's rock garden was now scattered through our backyard along with smashed pottery, 2x4's and a birdhouse. Verdant green grass had transformed into a slimy brown rug. Mud was everywhere. The worst hit homes were ranch styles where every carpet squished underfoot. It was great news for carpet cleaners, bad news for homeowners.

NOTHING IS WORTH THE RISK

AFTER A FLOOD... DISCARD
Meat, poultry, fish and eggs
Fresh fruit and vegetables
Jams/jellies sealed with paraffin
Home canned foods
Foods sold in glass jars or beverages including "never opened" jars sealed with waxed cardboard like mayonnaise and salad dressing. Containers with cork-lined, waxed cardboard, pop tops, peel-off tops, or paraffin (waxed) seals are nearly impossible to clean around the lid/opening
All foods in cardboard boxes, paper, foil, cellophane, cloth, or any other kind of flexible container.
Spices, seasonings and extracts
Opened containers and packages of any kind
Flour, sugar, grains, pasta, coffee and other staples stored in canisters
Canned goods that are dented (on lids or seams), leaking, or bulging
Canned goods that are rusted UNLESS the rust can be easily removed by light rubbing

While it's painful to see food go to waste, but it's better to toss anything that could be contaminated. Diseases that run rampant after flooding can be avoided by using the following guidelines for disinfection. You don't want "the trots" – or worse – on top of flood clean up.

Sometimes it's hard to know if these swirling waters have been in contact with sewage, so treat everything as though it has. What should you do?

After A Flood... certain foods must be tossed and a few may be kept safely though the list is pretty short.

KEEP undamaged commercial canned goods.

THROW AWAY any cans that may have come in contact with industrial or septic waste.
If you're unsure about the safety of any food... THROW IT OUT!

CANNED FOODS

Canned goods **must** be sterilized. To sanitize cans, first mark contents on can lids with indelible ink. Remove labels; paper can harbor dangerous bacteria. Use strong detergent solution and a scrub brush to wash cans. Immerse containers for 15 minutes in a mixture of 2 teaspoons chlorine bleach per quart (liter) of room temperature water. **Air dry** before opening.

FROZEN / REFRIGERATED FOODS AND POWER OUTAGES

If your refrigerator or freezer may be without power for a long period:
- Divide your frozen foods among friends' freezers if they have electricity and room to spare.
- Seek freezer space in a store, church, school, or commercial freezer that has electrical service
- Use dry ice. 25 pounds (11.3 kg) will keep a 10-cubic-foot freezer below freezing for 3-4 days. Use heavy gloves when handling dry ice.

REFRIGERATED FOOD – WHAT TO KEEP, WHAT TO TOSS	
Discard the Following	**Generally Safe Without Refrigeration for a Few Days**
Perishable Foods, if kept <u>above</u> refrigerator temperature (40°F or 4.4°C) for more than 2 hours	Double check each food and discard food if it turns moldy or has unusual odor or look. These foods spoil and lose quality much faster at warmer temperatures.
Raw or cooked meat, poultry or seafood	Butter, margarine
Cooked pasta, pasta salads	Dried fruits
Custard, chiffon, or cheese pies	Opened jars of peanut butter, jelly, relish, taco sauce, barbecue sauce, ketchup, mustard, olives
Fresh eggs, egg substitutes	Oil-based salad dressings
Meat or cheese-topped pizza, luncheon meats	Fruit juices
Casseroles, stew or soups	Hard or processed cheeses
Mayonnaise, tartar sauce, and creamy Dressings	
Refrigerated cookie dough	
Cream-filled pastries	

Thawed food can usually be eaten or refrozen if it still contains ice crystals. To be safe, "When in doubt, throw it out." Discard any food that has been at room temperature for two hours or more, and any food that has an unusual odor, color, or texture. Even if it looks and smells OK, if food has passed the 2-hour no refrigeration limit, toss it. It's not worth food poisoning and bacteria multiply rapidly. **Never refreeze foods that have completely thawed.**

Refrigerators will keep food cool for about 4 hours without power if the door is unopened. Room temperature and whether or not the refrigerator has a good seal also play a role in keeping the refrigerated foods cold. Now is a good time to see if the seal around the refrigerator door fits well and is still flexible. Food in a full, freestanding freezer will be safe for about 2 days, a half-full freezer for about 1 day.

TIP: Add block or dry ice wrapped in newspaper to your refrigerator if the electricity will be off longer than 4 hours.

KITCHEN CLEANUP

Clean and sanitize with warm soapy water any kitchen areas or items that have come in contact with flood waters including countertops, pantry shelves, refrigerators, stoves. Rinse and wipe with a solution of 2 teaspoons of chlorine bleach to one quart (liter) of water using a clean cloth. Sanitize dishes and glassware the same way.

To disinfect metal pans and utensils, boil them in water for 10 minutes. Discard wooden spoons, wooden cutting boards, plastic utensils, and baby bottle nipples and pacifiers. These items may absorb or hide bacteria making them difficult to clean and sanitize.

Wash all kitchen linens in detergent and hot water. Use chlorine bleach to sanitize the linens following directions on the bleach container.

Photo: Ascension Parish, Louisiana; June 28, 2001 – Interior of a home shows the effect of Tropical Storm Allison (Adam Dubrowa/FEMA)

GENERAL CLEANUP

Clean walls, hard-surfaced floors, and many other household surfaces with soap and water then disinfect with a solution of 1 cup (237 ml) bleach to five gallons (19 liters) water. Thoroughly disinfect surfaces that may come in contact with food, such as countertops, pantry shelves, refrigerators, etc. Carefully clean areas where small children play. Wash all linens and clothing in hot water, or dry-clean them.

For items that cannot be washed or dry-cleaned, such as mattresses and upholstered furniture, air dry them in the Sun and then spray them thoroughly with a disinfectant. Steam clean all carpeting. If there has been a backflow of sewage into the house, wear rubber boots and waterproof gloves during cleanup.

Remove and discard contaminated household materials that cannot be disinfected, such as wallcoverings, cloth, rugs, and drywall.

STANDING WATER

Large amounts of pooled water remaining after a flood will increase mosquito populations. Mosquitoes are most active at sunrise and sunset. The majority will be pests and not carry communicable diseases. To protect you from mosquitoes, use screens on dwellings, and wear long-sleeves and pants. Insect repellents containing DEET are very effective. Be sure to read all instructions before using DEET. Instead of using DEET on children's skin, spray their clothes. Products containing DEET are available from most grocery and camping supply stores. To control mosquito populations, drain all standing water left in containers around your home.

Photo: Clean up begins following devastating 1994 Midwestern floods. A total of 534 counties in nine states were declared disaster areas. As a result of the floods, 168,340 people registered for federal assistance. Look where the watermark hit – at the TOP of the window! The floors were covered in thick ooze and slime – and probably a snake or two. (FEMA News Photo)

WATER QUALITY

Listen for public announcements on the safety of the municipal water supply. There may be boil orders in effect. Flooded, private water wells will need to be tested and disinfected after floodwaters recede. Direct questions about testing to your local or state health departments. For information on disinfecting wells, see "Chlorinating Water Outside" in Chapter 5.

WATER FOR DRINKING AND COOKING

Safe drinking water includes bottled, boiled, or treated water. Here are some general rules concerning water for drinking and cooking.

Do not use questionable water to wash dishes, brush teeth, wash and prepare food or make ice.

If using bottled water, know where it came from. Otherwise, water should be boiled or treated before use. Drink only bottled, boiled, or treated water until your supply is tested and found safe. Refer to Chapter 4 for numerous ways to disinfect drinking water.

Containers for water should be rinsed with a bleach solution before using them. Use water storage tanks and other types of containers with caution.

Chapter 57: Preparing for Hurricanes

Photo: Hurricane Frances barreled straight for Florida (outlined) where it promptly stalled. This Texas-sized hurricane, dumped up to 20" of rain and knocked out power to more than 5 million residents. (NOAA satellite imagery, September 3, 2004)

Mix together a weather disturbance, warm tropical oceans, moisture and relatively light winds, and you might end up with Earth's most violent storm – the hurricane.

All Atlantic and Gulf of Mexico coastal areas are subject to hurricanes and tropical storms. Although less frequent, parts of the Southwest United States and the Pacific Coast experience heavy rains and floods each year from hurricanes spawned off Mexico. We have to watch for these beasts from June to November with peak season running from mid-August to late October.

Hurricanes can cause catastrophic damage to coastlines and several hundred miles inland. Winds can exceed 155 miles-per-hour. Hurricanes and tropical storms generally spawn tornadoes and microbursts, create surge along the coast, and cause extensive damage with inland flooding.

Tornadoes most often occur in thunderstorms embedded in rain bands well away from the center of the hurricane; however, they also occur near the eye-wall. Typically, tornadoes produced by tropical cyclones are relatively weak and short-lived but still pose a threat.

Storm surge is a huge dome of water pushed on-shore by hurricane and tropical storm winds. Storm surges can reach 25 feet high and be 50-100 miles wide.

Storm tide is a combination of the storm surge and the normal tide (i.e., a 15 foot storm surge combined with a 2 foot normal high tide over the mean sea level creates a 17 foot storm tide). These phenomena cause severe erosion and extensive damage to coastal areas.

Despite improved warnings and a decrease in the loss of life, property damage continues to rise because an increasing number of people are living or vacationing near coastlines. Those in hurricane-prone areas need to be prepared for hurricanes and tropical storms.

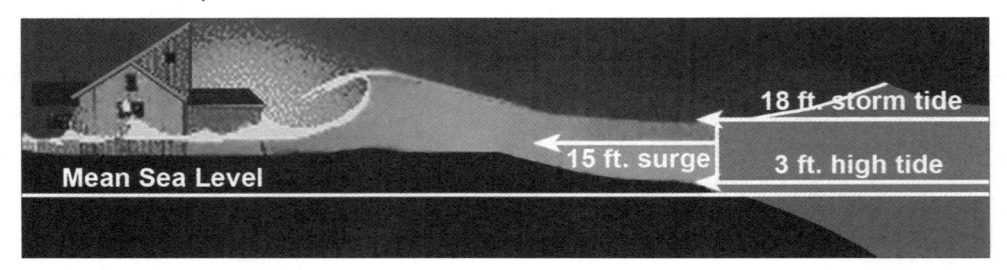

Hurricanes are classified into five categories based on their wind speed, central pressure and damage potential. Category Three and higher are considered major hurricanes, though Category One and Two are still extremely dangerous and warrant your full attention.

\multicolumn{4}{c}{SAFFIR-SIMPSON HURRICANE SCALE}
Category	Sustained Winds (mph)	Damage	Storm Surge
1	74-95	**Minimal:** Unanchored mobile homes, vegetation and signs.	4-5 feet
2	96-110	**Moderate:** All mobile homes, roofs, small crafts, flooding.	6-8 feet
3	111-130	**Extensive:** Small buildings, low-lying roads cut off.	9-12 feet
4	131-155	**Extreme:** Roofs destroyed, trees down, roads cut off, mobile homes destroyed. Beach homes flooded.	13-18 feet
5	>155	**Catastrophic:** Most buildings destroyed. Vegetation destroyed. Major roads cut off. Homes flooded.	>18 feet

INLAND / FRESHWATER FLOODING FROM HURRICANES

Hurricanes often produce widespread torrential rains resulting in deadly and destructive flooding. Excessive rain can also trigger land or mud slides, especially in mountainous regions. Flash flooding can occur unexpectedly. Flooding on rivers and streams may persist for several days or more after the storm. No place is exempt.

The speed of the storm and the geography beneath the storm are the primary factors regarding the amount of rain produced. Slow moving storms and tropical storms moving into mountainous regions tend to produce more rain.

Between 1970 and 1999, more people lost their lives from hurricanes' freshwater flooding than from any other weather hazard related to tropical cyclones.

See the "Floods" chapter for more specific information on flood related emergencies.

> *Create a household disaster plan. Plan to meet your family in case you are separated. Choose an out-of-town contact for everyone to call to say they are safe.*

WHAT TO DO BEFORE A HURRICANE

1. Learn the terns used by weather forecasters:
    - **Tropical Depression.** An organized system of clouds and thunderstorms with a defined surface circulation and maximum sustained winds of 38 mph (33 knots) or less. Sustained winds are defined as one-minute average wind measured at about 33 ft (10 meters) above the surface.
    - **Tropical Storm.** An organized system of strong thunderstorms with a defined surface circulation and maximum sustained winds of 39-73 mph (34-63 knots).
    - **Hurricane.** An intense tropical weather system of strong thunderstorms with a well-defined surface circulation and maximum sustained winds of 74 mph (64 knots) or higher.

- **Storm Surge.** A dome of water pushed on shore by hurricane and tropical storm winds.
- **Storm Tide.** A combination of storm surge and normal tide (e.g., 15-foot storm surge combined with a 2-foot normal tide over the mean sea level creates a 17-foot storm tide.)

2. Know the difference between "Watches" and "Warnings."
   - **Hurricane/Tropical Storm Watch** – Hurricane/tropical storm conditions are possible in the specified area, usually within 36 hours.
   - **Hurricane/Tropical Storm Warning** – Hurricane/tropical storm conditions are expected in the specified area, usually within 24 hours.
   - **Short Term Watches and Warnings** – These warnings provide detailed information on specific hurricane threats, such as flash floods and tornadoes.
3. Listen for local radio or television weather forecasts. Purchase a NOAA Weather Radio with battery backup and a tone-alert feature that automatically alerts you when a Watch or Warning is issued (tone alert is not available in some areas). Purchase a battery-powered commercial radio and extra batteries or crank radio.

Photo: October 2, 2002, bridges were closed going to Louisiana's coast due to evacuation orders issued in preparation for Hurricane Lili coming ashore. Have an alternate route planned. (Photo by Lauren Hobart/FEMA News Photo)

4. Ask your local emergency management office about community evacuation plans relating to your neighborhood. Learn evacuation routes. Determine where you would go and how you would get there if you needed to evacuate. Sometimes alternate routes are necessary.
5. Talk to your household about hurricane issues. Create a household disaster plan. Plan to meet at a place away from your residence in case you are separated. Choose an out-of-town contact for everyone to call to say they are safe.
6. Determine the needs of your household members who may live elsewhere but need your help in a hurricane. Consider the special needs of neighbors, such as people that are disabled or those with limited sight or vision problems.
7. Prepare to survive on your own for *at least* three days. Longer is better. Assemble a disaster supplies kit. Keep a stock of food and extra drinking water.
8. Make plans to secure your property. Permanent storm shutters offer the best protection for windows. A second option is to board up windows with ⅝" marine plywood, cut to fit and ready to install. Tape does not prevent windows from breaking.
9. Learn how to shut off utilities and where gas and water shutoffs are located. Don't actually shut off the gas to see how it works or to show others. Only the gas company can safely turn it back on.
10. Have your home inspected for compliance with local building codes. Many of the roofs destroyed by hurricanes were not constructed or retrofitted according to building codes. Installing straps or additional clips to securely fasten your roof to the frame structure will substantially reduce roof damage.
11. Be sure trees and shrubs around your home are well trimmed. Dead limbs or trees could cause personal injury or property damage. Clear loose and clogged rain gutters and downspouts.
12. If you have a boat, determine where to secure it in an emergency.
13. Consider flood insurance. Purchase insurance well in advance—there is a 30-day waiting period before flood insurance takes effect.
14. Make a record of your personal property. Take photographs or videotapes of the exterior and interior of your home, including personal belongings. Store these documents in a safe place, such as a safe deposit box.

> *Alcoholic beverages and weapons are prohibited within shelters.*
> *Also, pets are not allowed in public shelters for health reasons.*

WHAT TO DO DURING A HURRICANE THREAT

1. Listen to radio or television newscasts. If a hurricane "Watch" is issued, you typically have 24 to 36 hours before the hurricane hits land.
2. Talk with household members. Make sure everyone knows where to meet and who to call, in case you are separated. Consider the needs of relatives and neighbors with special needs.
3. Secure your home. Close storm shutters. Secure outdoor objects or bring them indoors. Moor your boat if time permits.
4. Gather several days' supply of water and food for each household member. Water systems may become contaminated or damaged. After sterilizing the bathtub and other containers with a diluted bleach solution of one part bleach to ten parts water, fill them with water to ensure a safe supply in case you are unable or told not to evacuate.
5. If evacuating, take your disaster supplies kit with you to the shelter. Remember that alcoholic beverages and weapons are prohibited within shelters. Also, pets are not allowed in a public shelter due to health reasons.

Photo: The threat of Cat. 4 Hurricane Bret, required Padre Island and Corpus Christi residents to evacuate. Cars jammed Hwy. 37 heading northwest toward San Antonio just ahead of winds and rains that lead the main storm. (Dave Gatley/FEMA News Photo)

6. Prepare to evacuate. Fuel your car – service stations may be closed after the storm. If you do not have a car, make arrangements for transportation with a friend or relative. Review evacuation routes. If instructed, turn off utilities at the main valves or switches.
7. Evacuate to an inland location, if:
   - Local authorities announce an evacuation and you live in an evacuation zone.
   - You live in a mobile home or temporary structure – they are particularly hazardous during hurricanes no matter how well fastened to the ground.
   - You live in a high-rise. Hurricane winds are stronger at higher elevations.
   - You live on the coast, on a floodplain near a river or inland waterway.
   - You feel you are in danger.
8. When authorities order an evacuation:
   - Leave immediately.
   - Follow evacuation routes announced by local officials.
   - Stay away from coastal areas, riverbanks and streams.
   - Tell others where you are going.

9. If you are not required or are unable to evacuate, stay indoors during the hurricane and away from windows and glass doors. Keep curtains and blinds closed. Do not be fooled if there is a lull, it could be the eye of the storm – winds will pick up again.
10. If not instructed to turn off, turn the refrigerator to its coldest setting and keep closed.
11. Turn off propane tanks.
12. In strong winds, follow these rules:
    - Take refuge in a small interior room, closet or hallway.
    - Close all interior doors. Secure and brace external doors.
    - In a two-story residence, go to an interior first-floor room, such as a bathroom or closet.
    - In a multiple-story building, go to the first or second floors and stay in interior rooms away from windows.
    - Lie on the floor under a table or another sturdy object.
13. Avoid using the phone except for serious emergencies. Local authorities need first priority on telephone lines.

> *Consider your household's health and safety needs and be aware of symptoms of stress and fatigue. Seek crisis counseling if you have need.*

WHAT TO DO AFTER A HURRICANE

1. Stay where you are if you are in a safe location until local authorities say it is safe to leave. If you evacuated the community, don't return to the area until authorities say it is safe.
2. Keep tuned to local radio or television stations for information about caring for your household, where to find medical help, how to apply for financial assistance, etc.
3. Drive only when necessary. Streets will be filled with debris and downed power lines. Roads will have weakened and could collapse. Don't drive on flooded or barricaded roads or bridges. Roads are closed for your protection. As little as six inches of water may cause you to lose control of your vehicle—two feet of water will carry most cars away.
4. Do not drink or prepare food with tap water until notified by officials that it is safe to do so.
5. Consider your family's health and safety needs. Be aware of symptoms of stress and fatigue. Keep your household together and seek crisis counseling if you have need.
6. Talk with your children about what has happened and how they can help during the recovery. Being involved will help them deal with the situation. Consider the needs of your neighbors. People often become isolated during hurricanes.
7. Stay away from disaster areas unless local authorities request volunteers. If you are needed, bring your own drinking water, food and sleeping gear.
8. Stay away from riverbanks and streams until potential flooding has passed. Do not allow children to play in flooded areas. There is a high risk of injury or drowning in areas that may appear safe.
9. Stay away from moving water. Moving water only six inches deep can sweep you off your feet. Standing water may be electrically charged from underground or downed power lines.
10. Stay away from downed power lines and report them to the power company. Report broken gas, sewer or water mains to local officials.
11. Don't use candles or other open flames indoors. Use a flashlight to inspect damage.
12. Set up a manageable schedule to repair property.
13. Contact your insurance agent. An adjuster will be assigned to visit your home. To prepare:
    - Take photos or videotapes of your damaged property.
    - Separate damaged and undamaged belongings.
    - Locate your financial records.
    - Keep detailed records of cleanup costs.
14. Consider building a "Safe Room or Shelter" to protect your household.

UTILITIES AND SERVICES

After a big storm, expect basic services to be disrupted. Here's what to do:

Electricity. For a power outage national directory, call 10-10-27-500. This is not a free call. Power is first restored to police and fire departments, hospitals, utility plants, Red Cross centers and government buildings, and then whole neighborhood blocks. If everyone else in your neighborhood has power and you don't, check all circuit breakers and fuses before calling the electric company.

Even if your power is off, it's a good idea to disconnect or unplug all but a few electrical appliances so that systems will not be overloaded when electricity is restored.

Use flashlights or kerosene lamps until power is restored. Don't leave candles unattended.

Gas. Avoid open flames and sparks. Call police or the gas company if you smell or suspect leaking gas.

Cables and Wires. Treat all inside and out, as if they were electrically charged – regardless of whether they are electrical, cable TV or telephone wires.

Downed Power Lines. Call the power company or police immediately if there are lines down or sparking in your yard or neighborhood.

Electrical Appliances. Don't touch any wires or equipment unless they're in a dry area or you're standing on dry wood while wearing rubber gloves and rubber footwear.

Standing water. Be careful of standing water and water flowing through damaged walls. If there is any question conditions are unsafe, call the power company or a licensed electrician.

Phones and Cable TV. Report problems and schedule repairs. Be patient; it may take a while. Cordless phones won't work if the electricity is off.

DEBRIS

Pile debris as neatly and as close to the street as you can. Keep clutter from around utility poles; crews won't be able to make repairs if pathways are blocked.

GARBAGE

Call your local trash hauler to find out when pickup will resume. Meanwhile, double-bag all garbage in plastic bags and keep the bags in covered containers.

Spray the inside of the containers with insect repellent to control pests.

Use Lysol or some other disinfectant spray to help control bacteria and odor.

If the smell becomes unbearable, find a neighbor with a pickup truck who can haul the garbage to a central collection point.

Ask a hurricane volunteer from outside the immediate area if he wouldn't mind taking a few sacks of trash back home.

ADDITIONAL GUIDES AND INFORMATION

FOR APARTMENTS OR CONDOS

Buy renters or condo insurance. The building may not be yours to lose, but you have valuables inside.

Get shutters or panels for your sliding glass doors and windows. Check to see if the condo association requires a specific style. If renting, check to see if your landlord provides them and who will put them up before the storm.

Bring indoors any patio or balcony items: BBQ grills, plants and furniture.

Name floor captains. A key duty for them is to check on residents with special needs before and after the hurricane.

Trace the route to the nearest exit stairs. That will be important if power is out and your building has an elevator.

Designate your safest room, probably an interior bedroom, bath or hall, and stay there when the wind's blowing. The safest place is the condo's inner hallways. Consider staying in a lower apartment if you live on a higher floor.

If you live in an evacuation zone, arrange for a storm refuge farther west. Make plans to stay in a hotel or with a friend or relative.

If you <u>must</u> stay in a high rise, choose a floor that is lower down, but above storm surge levels. Higher locations are subject to stronger winds.

SELECTING WINDOW SHUTTERS

Shielding your windows and doors can greatly reduce hurricane damage done to the interior of a home as well as protect the glass. Flying glass often cause injuries. Not only does this measure help minimize clean up from broken furnishings, it minimizes water and wind damage. Below is a comparison of various window shutter options.

WINDOW / DOOR PROTECTION OPTIONS

TYPE	PROS	CONS
Barrel-Bolt / Overlapping Plywood Shutters	Very inexpensive. One person could hang depending on window size. Materials readily available	Don't meet most building codes. Requires storage when not in use. Plywood disappears rapidly with news of approaching storm.
Storm Panels	Most inexpensive of permanent shutters. Removable. Strong, and can provide excellent protection for both doors and windows.	Require storage, but take up little space. Hanging requires more than one person. Sometimes don't line up properly. Have sharp edges.
Accordion Shutters	Permanently affix beside the windows. Can easily be storm-ready by one person. Some models can be locked.	Can look bulky and out-of-place. Glide on wheels, and have the potential to break more easily than other systems. Some require a storm bar or center rod to lock shutters, increasing installation time.
Colonial shutters	Permanently affix beside the windows. Can easily be storm-ready by one person. Are decorative; can beautify and protect.	Can't protect doors; must be used with another shutter system to ensure complete home protection.
Bahama Shutters	Permanently affix beside windows. Can be made storm-ready by one person. Provide permanent shade and privacy, even in open position.	Traditionally weaker than other systems, but the newest models protect well. May block too much light. Design limits use; can't protect doors.
Roll-Down Shutters	Permanently affix above windows. Can be made storm-ready by one person. Excellent storm protection & theft deterrent. Easy to operate.	Most expensive of popular systems. Push-button-operated roll-down shutters require battery backup system for lowering and raising during power outages.
Hurricane Glass	Eliminates need for shutters. Most practical type is similar to a car windshield, with a durable plastic-like layer sandwiched between glass. The outside layers break, but the center prevents a hole.	Must be installed by a window contractor. Frame must be replaced along with the panes to meet code. More costly if retrofitting windows.

COMPUTERS, ELECTRONICS

For all the advantages one has with personal computers or a high-tech home office setup, there are huge disadvantages to being plugged in during the approach of a serious storm. Lost data can be devastating. While it's simple enough to log off, shut down and unplug at the first warning signs, you might want to take a few extra steps to preserve information that is vital to a home-based business or the family archives.

Along with other valuable property, document what you own with a videotape or camera. Save copies of purchase receipts.
Be sure the electric wiring in your home or business is properly grounded and that all voltage-sensitive equipment is grounded.
Purchase electronic equipment with a back-up battery or capacitor to retain settings should a momentary power disturbance occur.
Protect computers from loss of information by copying data periodically

PROTECTIVE EQUIPMENT

Consider purchasing protective equipment that can help against lethal storm and electrical conditions. These include:
Surge suppressors designed to lower the momentary high voltage of a surge or spike.
Voltage regulators maintain voltage output within narrow limits.
Isolation transformers prevent noise on a circuit from being passed to your equipment.
Un-interruptible Power Supply (UPS) maintains power to critical loads during power outages.
Surge Protectors: Make sure the suppressor has 3-way protection and is listed for compliance with the 1449 TVSS (Transient Voltage Surge Suppressor) standard. Features of the plug-in type surge protector include multiple outlets, on/off switches, audible alarms, and indicator lights to let you know the suppressor is working, and

connections for telephone or data cable lines. Choose the correct voltage rating for the equipment you want to protect. A clamping level is the voltage level at which the suppressor will react. The lower the clamping level, the better the protection.

OTHER PREPARATIONS
Back up your computer's hard drive.
Make duplicate copies of files and store them in two separate locations such as your home office and a deposit box or home of a relative.
Make sure backup batteries are charged for cell phones and computers.
Assess storage options for software and hardware equipment.
Move electronics to a central location in the building or home – one with no windows. Seal in plastic.
Unplug all equipment including computers networked to other computers.

RELATED EQUIPMENT, PERIPHERALS
Take care of all related electronics by unplugging, storing and covering. These include:

- Cash registers
- Digital cameras
- Electronic clocks
- Fax machines
- Microphones
- Modems
- Printers
- Process controls
- Robotics and automation, copiers and laser printers
- Scanners
- Speakers

Don't forget more common appliances such as answering machines, cordless phones, microwave ovens, satellite receivers, security systems, TVs, VCRs, garage door openers, stereo systems.

POOL PREPARATION
There are several steps you can take to prepare and protect your swimming pool during hurricane season.

BEFORE THE STORM
1. Tropical storms and hurricanes can drop a lot of water onto your pool deck and out to your yard so make sure water drains from the deck as quickly as possible. Test deck drainage by squirting a garden hose on the deck and watch how quickly the water disappears.
2. Most pools have a plastic slotted deck drain which takes water from the slab to the yard. Make sure none of the slats have been painted over. Use a small flat-head screwdriver to carefully push paint through to open the slats. If the drain is dirty, flush with a garden hose.
3. During any test, make sure that the water runs unobstructed from the drain to low spots in the yard – away from the house and pool deck. Remove grass, mulch or dirt that may block drainage.
4. If you don't have a deck drain, make sure high grass, dirt, mulch or stones don't obstruct the deck's edge. These obstacles can prevent water from quickly moving off the edge and into the yard. TIP: For edges that don't drain quickly, dig a small trench directing the water to a low spot away from the house and pool deck.
5. Trim trees of extra limbs and branches that may become airborne during afternoon thunderstorms and high winds. This debris could cause damage to your house, pool equipment or screen enclosure.
6. Store toys and patio furniture so they don't become missiles.

WHAT TO DO WHEN A STORM APPROACHES
Keeping sufficient water levels in your pool provides the important weight to hold the sides and bottom in place, especially when heavy rains that accompany most storms raise the local water table.
Never empty your pool. Pools that have been emptied may experience serious structural problems and could even be lifted off their foundations.
If your pool is properly equipped with adequate drains and skimmers and the surrounding area is properly drained, the water level can be left as is. Clear around deck drains to allow maximum water flow off your deck.
It is recommended that you superchlorinate the pool water. You should shock the pool as you normally would.
All electric power should be turned off at the circuit breakers before the storm hits.
If you cannot store loose objects such as plastic or PVC chairs, tables, pool equipment and toys inside a building and your pool is concrete, gently place them in the pool to help shield them from the winds. Just dropping them in may scratch or damage the inside finish of your pool.

Never put any metal or glass items into your pool at any time. If glass were to shatter on the deck or in the pool, it would be almost impossible to locate and remove every small sliver.

If your pool is vinyl or fiberglass, don't ever put anything in the pool because the vinyl liner could tear and the fiberglass could be scratched.

BOAT PREPARATIONS

Practice in calm weather what measures you'd take to protect your boat.

NEVER ever ride out a storm in a boat. It may cost you your life. Hurricane winds, whether inland or near the beach, can haul a boat out of the water, hurl it or sink it – even when secured in a marina. 2004's Hurricane Frances in Florida lifted boats and stacked them like they were toys.

When a "hurricane watch" is first issued, implement whatever you worked out before the storm. The majority of people wait for the actual "hurricane warning" which may make saving your boat more complicated. In some areas, that's when flotilla plans, designed to move the largest number of boats in the shortest period of time, are invoked to coordinate the opening and closing of drawbridges with boat traffic.

If you're going to join a flotilla or head inland, make sure your ship is in shape to move by checking the fuel, fuel filters, batteries and bilges. Emergency authorities will announce over radio and TV when the flotilla plan will be invoked. Within a few hours, drawbridges will be locked in the down position.

If you plan to trailer your boat to another location, do so well in advance of a storm. Consider the time required to go to the new destination and whether your route will cross the storm's path. The challenges of trailering multiply many-fold when dealing with high wind, particularly on causeways, and other boaters in the same predicament.

GENERAL TIPS
- Check your insurance policy carefully to see if your boat is sufficiently protected from hurricane damage.
- Find someone to take care of your boat if you can't.
- Keep a list of boat registration numbers.
- Obtain in advance the line and other materials needed to secure your boat.
- Make sure fire extinguishers and lifesaving equipment are working and in good shape.
- Remove or secure all deck gear, radio antennas, outriggers, Bimini tops, side canvases, side curtains, rafts, sails, booms, dinghies, anything that could blow away or cause damage.

DRY DOCKING/MARINAS
Shop around and arrange for dry-dock space early. Many marinas require evacuation during a hurricane alert. If you plan to keep your boat at a marina, check your slip lease rules or consult the dockmaster.

MOVE INLAND, BY WATER
Arrange now for dock space. You must have the permission of the property owner in advance. Make a trial run to ensure the water is deep enough and overhead clearances are high enough. Take into account the higher water levels that can precede a storm. Keep in mind that cars will take priority, so drawbridges may be locked down for long periods of time.

MOVE INLAND, BY TRAILER
Make a trial run. Know how long it takes to get from the water to destination. Plan for lines at loading ramps.

LEAVING THE AREA
Consider the time required to go to the new destination and whether your route will cross the storm's path. Be prepared to deal with the difficulties of driving with a trailer in a stiff wind, particularly on causeways.

GARAGES, TYING DOWN
If your boat is small enough, consider keeping it in your garage. As a last resort, tie down your boat and trailer outside – SECURELY.

Chapter 58: Preparing for Meteor and Asteroid Strikes

In January of 1997, Major Wynn Greene invited Stan and me to the U.S. Air Force Space Command Headquarters in Colorado Springs, Colorado as his guests. Since we were on a fact-finding trip at the time, we wanted to see what interesting tidbits we could discover. He gave us a private tour of the Space Command – then just up the road from the U.S. Air Force Academy where Stan was a cadet in the early 1960s. Major Greene, affectionately known around headquarters as "Major Meteor," was primarily interested in the subject of NEOs (Near Earth Objects). He so thoroughly believed these NEOs were such a "major" cause for concern, that upon retirement in 1998, he planned to devote his time to public awareness campaigns.

Painting: Don Davis (NASA Series)

METEOR CRATER

Nestled in the desert near Winslow, Arizona, we pulled off I-40 for a firsthand look at Barringer Crater (pictured on the front cover). Though the impact occurred 49,000 years ago, the crater is surprisingly well defined. Little goosebumps can't help but crawl over your skin when you consider what the hit must have entailed.

Though the meteor was only 150 ft across, plowing into Earth at 45,000 mph (72,420km/hr) made up for size.

Over the centuries, many craters have been obliterated due to erosion. However, Meteor Crater stands out like an angry wound surrounded by smooth desert hills. Its cavernous 4,000 ft wide hole flaunts what a "small" meteor can do. Smashed boulders the size of small houses rim the crater.

Initially, explorers and researchers thought the meteor had buried itself under the crater. Later studies revealed the meteor had mostly melted and spread over Four Corners – the point where Utah, Colorado, Arizona and New Mexico all meet. Upon impact it released the equivalent of 15 million tons of TNT! An event this size occurs once or twice every 1,000 years.

TUNGUSKA, JUNE 30, 1908

Around 7:30 am, near the Stony Tunguska River, a huge airburst exploded over remote Siberia. The 15-40 megaton blast equaled an 8.0 earthquake or the force of Mt. St. Helens erupting or 2000 times the energy of Hiroshima's atomic bomb. Had this happened over a populated area, it would be one of the greatest natural disasters of all time. Since no crater exists and no meteor was found, scientists base its size on blast evidence. Best estimates put the meteor at 60-100 meters (197-328 ft.) in diameter and weighing 100,000 tons.

Eyewitnesses summarized the noisy event saying it was like "a strong wind followed immediately by a fearful crash accompanied by a subterranean shock which caused buildings to tremble. Two equally forceful blows followed. The interval between the first and third blows was accompanied by an extraordinary underground roar like the sound of a number of trains passing simultaneously over rails, and then for five or six minutes followed a sound like artillery fire. Between 50 and 60 bangs becoming gradually fainter followed at short and almost regular intervals. A minute or so later, six more distant but quite distinct bangs resounded and the ground trembled."[146]

Its seismic shock was detected all the way to London and nearly 40,000 trees were destroyed. Nearest the blast, trees were left standing stripped bare of branches and leaves, looking like forlorn telephone poles. Further

Dare To Prepare: Chapter 58: Preparing For Meteor and Asteroid Strikes

from the blast, trees were flattened radially from the center of the airblast. At the epicenter, the forest exploded into columns of fire visible several hundred kilometers away. "The fires burned for weeks, destroying 1,000 square kilometers. Ash and powdered tundra were sucked skyward by the fiery vortex and then carried around the world. Meanwhile, bursts of thunder echoed across the land 800 kilometers away."[147]

Intense heat incinerated herds of reindeer and charred tens of thousands of evergreens. Hunting dogs, furs, stores and teepees were reduced to ash. For days across thousands of miles, the sky bore a bright eerie orange glow, like an enormous jack-o-lantern. People in Western Europe could read newspapers at night without a lamp. Tunguska's effect was similar to a great volcanic eruption minus the lava. Yet the only indication of this extraordinary event was a quiver on seismographs in Irkutsk, Siberia indicating a moderate quake some 1,000 miles north in a remote region called Tunguska.[148]

ARE THESE ISOLATED EVENTS?

To date, there are about 160[149] known meteor craters on the Earth. More meteorites may have struck our planet, but many land in the ocean or in unpopulated regions, remaining undetected. Life extinguishing events like the meteor impact at Chicxulub occur once every 50-100 million years.

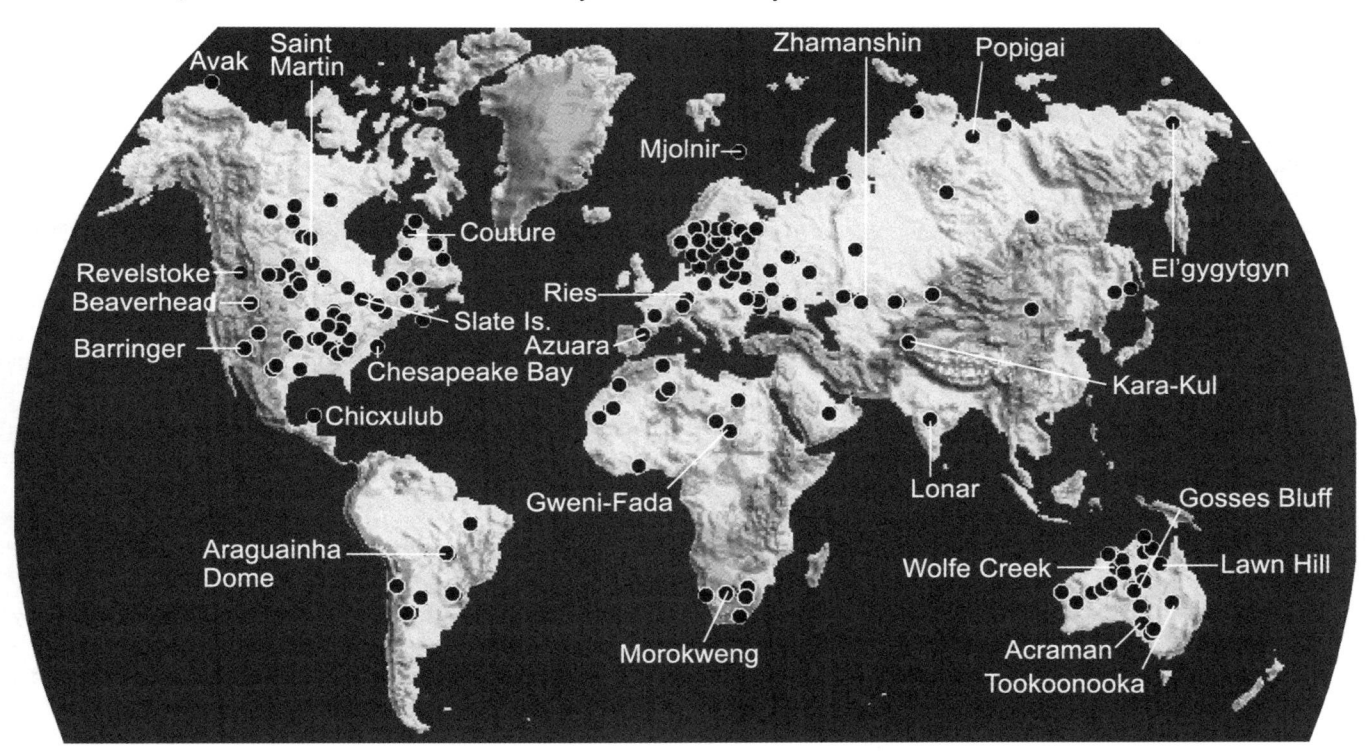

More recently, these meteors found their way to Earth.

DATE	LOCATION	COMMENTS[150]
1997	Texas	High airburst. No physical damage on ground.
1997	Greenland	Medium airburst. No apparent damage on ground.
1994	Micronesia	High airburst. No physical damage on ground.
1992	Peekskill, New York	Bolide witnessed across eastern USA. Minor damage on ground.
1990	Sterlitamak, Russia	5m crater produced
1972	Grand Teton, Wyoming	Object tracked 1500 miles through atmosphere before bouncing off.
1969	College, Alaska	High airburst. No physical damage on ground.
1966	Kincardine, Ontario	High airburst. No physical damage on ground.
1965	Revelstoke, British Columbia	High airburst. No physical damage on ground.
1947	Sikhote-Alin, Eastern Siberia	100 1-14m craters. Iron meteorite.
1937	Estonia	8.5m crater from fragment of ~50t body.
1930	Brazil	Tunguska like airburst, with significant ground damage

WATCH OUT!

However, it seems these space rocks are finding their way into our territory with increasing regularity. June 11, 2004 a fist-sized fragment exploded over Hawke's Bay, New Zealand. June 13, 2004, a grapefruit-size meteor crashed through the roof of a house in Auckland. The rock hit a sofa and then bounced back up to the ceiling, before coming to rest under a computer. Four days later numerous people in New South Wales reported a meteorite "the size of a house" crashing along their southern coast. August 19, 2004, while an elderly British woman hung out her wash, she felt a sharp pain in her arm. She looked down to find a 1-inch gash along her forearm. At first she thought her clothespin bag must have caused the nasty cut but the following day her husband spotted a walnut-shaped metallic rock on the garden path. Though the odds against being hit by a meteorite are billions to one in 2002, a 14-year-old in North Yorkshire, England had one land on her foot. She reported it was shiny and felt "quite hot".

One of the most striking tales again occurred in Australia December 1999, this time 250 miles north of Sydney. A meteorite slammed into the Guyra dam, leaving a large crater and attracting nationwide attention. The force of the impact left a 50 ft long, 20 ft wide crater in the dam. A meteorite the size of a golf ball accomplished all of this damage! It hit with such force that it penetrated the mud at the bottom of the dam and is now embedded in 13 feet of granite.

DEEP IMPACT: FACT OR FANTASY?

Bolides (exploding meteors and meteorites) don't need to be the size of the Chicxulub to pose a serious threat. A more serious problem, and one that we can do something about, is the chance that a smaller asteroid or comet, about a mile wide, might hit. The best calculations are that such an impact could threaten the future of modern civilization. It could literally kill billions and send us back into the Dark Ages. Such an impact would make a crater twenty times the size of Meteor Crater in Arizona.

The gaping hole in the ground would be bigger than all of Washington, D.C., and deeper than 20 Washington Monuments[151] stacked on top of each other.

It would loft so much debris into the stratosphere, spread worldwide, that agricultural production around our globe would come to a virtual halt: dust would dim the sunlight for months, perhaps a year. Especially if the asteroid struck without warning, there would be mass starvation. No nation would be unscathed, so no country could assist others, unlike the aftermath of World War II.

Such civilization-threatening impacts happen hundreds of times more often than Extinction Level Events, perhaps once every few hundred thousand years... or one chance in a few hundred thousand that one will impact next year...or one chance in a few thousand during the next century – during the lives of our grandchildren."[152]

ODDS OF DYING IN THE U.S. FROM SPECIFIC CAUSES	
Cause of Death	**Odds of Happening**
Motor vehicle accident	1 in 100
Homicide	1 in 300
Melanoma (skin cancer)	1 in 300
Fire	1 in 800
Firearms accident	1 in 2,500
Electrocution	1 in 5,000
Passenger airplane crash	1 in 20,000
Flood	1 in 30,000
Asteroid or Comet Impact	**1 in 20,000**[153]*
Tornado	1 in 60,000
Venomous bite or sting	1 in 100,000
Fireworks accident	1 in 1 million
Food poisoning by botulism	1 in 3 million

Actually, meteor impacts occur with more frequency than one might realize; but most burn up in the Earth's atmosphere before ever making impact.

If we had adequate notice, "at the very least, we could evacuate (the approximate) ground-zero, **and we could save up food supplies and try to weather the global environmental catastrophe.** We even have the military technology, provided we have a decade's warning time or more (which is likely), to study the threatening object, to launch a rocket with powerful bombs, and explode a bomb in just the right place to give the object a little kick, causing its path to change ever-so-slightly so that, years hence, it misses the Earth instead of bringing catastrophe to our planet."[154]

Scientists used to state that the odds of dying in the U.S. from a meteor impact was 1 in 20,000.

*Update Feb. 07: Despite its limitations, the Spaceguard Program has mostly eliminated a short-term threat from a large NEO impact (the un-surveyed proportion of large NEOs has gone from 100% to about 10%). Recent estimates put the current risk at 1 in 200,000. The long-term risk (over centuries) remains at about 1 in 20,000 due to the number of large NEOs in space.

WHAT'S BEING DONE – AND NOT?

Both progress and resistance have emerged. In November 2007, NASA met with heated accusations by the Committee on Science and Technology. They charged that NASA was ignoring the threat of smaller asteroids. NASA countered that they "cannot (read that 'will not') place a new NEO program above current scientific and exploration missions." Former astronaut Rusty Schweickart and head of asteroid research group, the B612 Foundation, accused NASA of "sacrificing public safety for science."[155]

Schweickart further warned the committee with NASA not taking on the task, "no one is in charge of protecting the Earth from impacts. Until NASA or someone else is given responsibility ... that job will not be done."[156] It's ironic that should we experience an "unfortunate impact", NASA's exploration focus would be moot. As with many government agencies, priorities are backwards. Money and prestige first, people second.

NASA also failed to heed an important Congressional directive passed in 2005. NASA was ordered to plan and budget a NEO-identifying program and figure out how to circumvent disaster. This directive was ignored.

However, on December 19, 2007 Congress introduced H. R. 4917, The NEO Preparedness Act. This bill requires NASA to set up "procedures and systems, for deflecting and mitigating potentially hazardous near-Earth objects."[157] Maybe this attempt will net action.

NEW "EYES"

On the plus side, a $100 million 4-telescope array, Pan-STARRS (Panoramic Survey Telescope And Rapid Response System), is being built in Hawaii. Instead of viewing only deep, narrow portions of space, Pan-STARRS is designed for wide-field imaging. It's hoped that by combining four relatively small mirrors with very large digital cameras they will be able to observe the entire available sky several times a month. This system will enable astronomers to detect objects as small as 330 yards in diameter and 100 times fainter than those observed by other telescopes. The best scopes now have a resolution of 300 million pixels.[158]

The first phase, PS1, built at the 10,000 ft summit of Haleakala, Maui is a single-mirror prototype. PS1's dome construction is complete and the telescope's "eyes" are snapping shots with the world's largest, most advanced digital camera. Image resolution of one gigapixel is about 200 times that of high-end consumer cameras.

PS1, a single mirror prototype telescope at Haleakala, Hawaii. (Photo by Brett Simison)

The favored location for the four-mirror telescope, PS4, is the site of the University of Hawaii's existing 2.2-meter scope on Mauna Kea. If permission were granted, they would remove the old equipment and building, and replace it with a structure that blends more into the background. The project, at this point, hit a snag. Some residents voice opposition to any telescope on Mauna Kea though the new scope would be slightly smaller than the current one. Suspicion of a hidden military agenda surfaced since the U.S. Air Force provided $50 million for the four scopes and NASA has only contributed $200,000.

On December 6, 2008 PS1 was activated and the Pan-STARRS Project will now focus on building PS4. When completed in 2012, scientists expect to detect about 100,000 asteroids a month. By 2022, Pan-STARRS should have found about 90% of potentially hazardous objects measuring 140 meters to a kilometer across.

NEW MISSIONS

The European Space Agency (ESA) is focusing on a different approach. Their current mission is to smash into a space rock to deflect it and study its structure. They feel they deflect or destroy data is so vital it's been given priority over five other potential asteroid projects. While no asteroids are currently known to be on track to hit the planet, experts say a regional catastrophe is inevitable in the very long run.[159]

WHAT'S BEEN FOUND SO FAR

As of July 14, 2008, 5,533 Near-Earth objects have been discovered. Of these NEOs, 746 are asteroids with a diameter of approximately 1 kilometer (about ⅔-mile) or larger. Also, 962 are classed as PHAs (potentially hazardous asteroids), which have the potential to travel threateningly close to Earth. These "potential threats" may never impact the Earth. It's estimated there are a total of 1000 (give or take 100) NEAs larger than 1 km (0.6 miles). At the close of 2003, 63% of these had been found.

Photo: Ida is the second asteroid ever encountered by a spacecraft. It's estimated to be about 32 miles in length, more than twice as large as Gaspra, the first asteroid observed by Galileo in October 1991. Ida is an irregularly shaped asteroid believed to be like a stony or stony iron meteorites. (NASA/JPL)

PREPAREDNESS

I wish there were an easy answer to this one, but endless variables make it impossible. Repercussions from such a scenario depend on where it impacts as well as size. Outcomes might range from an interesting tourist attraction to... "life altering". As for any disaster, keep supplies on hand. Some events are simply beyond our control.

Chapter 59: Preparing for Tornadoes

Tornadoes are nature's most violent storms. Spawned from powerful thunderstorms, twisters can uproot trees, destroy buildings and turn harmless objects into deadly missiles. They can devastate a neighborhood in seconds.

A tornado appears as a rotating, funnel-shaped cloud that extends to the ground with whirling winds that can reach 300 miles per hour. Damage paths can be in excess of one mile wide and 50 miles long. Every state is at some risk. Climate change encourages twisters pop up in areas that have never before experienced them. May 2007 brought a "rare" twister to Connecticut and in August that same year, the first-ever tornado hit Brooklyn, New York.

An average of 1,000 tornadoes[160] cause over $1 billion in property damages[161] in America every year. This figure doesn't include crop losses. Since 1998, tornadoes have significantly *exceeded* 1,200 every year except 1999 where it barely missed pegging the mark. In 2004, twister counts shot off the charts with a record-breaking 1,817 tornadoes. At the present rate, 2008 will likely come very close to that number.

Photo: This half-mile wide tornado touched down just south of Dimmit, Texas, June 2, 1995. (Harald Richter, NOAA Photo Library)

TORNADO FACTS
1. Tornadoes may strike quickly, with little or no warning.
2. Tornadoes may appear nearly transparent until dust and debris are picked up or a cloud forms in the funnel. The average tornado moves SW to NE but tornadoes have been known to move in any direction.
3. The average forward speed is 30 mph but may vary from stationary to 70 mph with rotating winds that can reach 300 miles per hour.
4. Tornadoes can accompany tropical storms and hurricanes as they move onto land.

5. Waterspouts are tornadoes that form over water.
6. Tornadoes are most frequently reported east of the Rocky Mountains during spring and summer months but can occur in any state at any time of year.
7. In the southern states, peak tornado season is March through May, while peak months in the northern states are during the late spring and early summer.
8. Tornadoes are most likely to occur between 3 p.m. and 9 p.m., but can occur at any time of the day or night.

WHAT TO DO BEFORE TORNADOES THREATEN

1. Know the terms used to describe tornado threats:
   Tornado Watch – Tornadoes are possible. Remain alert for approaching storms. Watch the sky and stay tuned to radio or television to know when warnings are issued.
   Tornado Warning – A tornado has been sighted or indicated by weather radar. Take shelter immediately.
2. Ask your local emergency management office or American Red Cross chapter about the tornado threat in your area. Ask about community warning signals.
3. Purchase a NOAA Weather Radio with a battery backup and tone-alert feature that automatically alerts you when a Watch or Warning is issued (tone alert not available in some areas). Purchase a battery-powered commercial radio and extra batteries as well.
4. Know the county or parish in which you live. Counties and parishes are used in Watches and Warnings to identify the location of tornadoes.
5. Determine places to seek shelter, such as a basement or storm cellar. If an underground shelter is not available, identify an interior room or hallway on the lowest floor.
6. Practice going to your shelter with your household.
7. Know the locations of designated shelters in places where you and your household spend time, such as public buildings, nursing homes and shopping centers. Ask local officials whether a registered engineer or architect has inspected your children's schools for shelter space.
8. Ask your local emergency manager or American Red Cross chapter if there are any public safe rooms or shelters nearby. See the "Safe Room and Shelter" section at the end of this chapter for more information.
9. Assemble a disaster supplies kit. Keep a stock of food and extra drinking water.
10. Make a record of your personal property. Take photographs or videotapes of the exterior and interior of your home, including personal belongings. Store these documents in a safe place, such as a safe deposit box.

WHAT TO DO DURING A TORNADO WATCH

1. Listen to NOAA Weather Radio or to commercial radio or television newscasts for the latest information.
2. Be alert for approaching storms. If you see any revolving funnel shaped clouds, report them immediately by telephone to your local police department or sheriff's office.
3. Watch for tornado danger signs:
   - Dark, often greenish sky
   - Large hail
   - A large, dark, low-lying cloud (particularly if rotating)
   - Loud roar, similar to a freight train

   CAUTION:
   - Some tornadoes are clearly visible, while rain or nearby low-hanging clouds obscure others.
   - Occasionally, tornadoes develop so rapidly that little, if any, advance warning is possible.
   - Before a tornado hits, the wind may die down and the air may become very still.
   - A cloud of debris can mark the location of a tornado even if a funnel is not visible.
   - Tornadoes generally occur near the trailing edge of a thunderstorm. It is not uncommon to see clear, sunlit skies behind a tornado.
4. Avoid places with wide-span roofs such as auditoriums, cafeterias, large hallways, supermarkets or shopping malls.
5. Be prepared to take shelter immediately. Gather household members and pets. Assemble supplies to take to the shelter such as flashlight, battery powered radio, water, and first aid kit.

With your household, determine where you would take shelter in case a Tornado Warning was issued. Storm cellars or basements provide the best protection. If underground shelter is not available seek shelter in an interior room or hallway on the lowest floor.

WHAT TO DO DURING A TORNADO WARNING

When a tornado has been sighted, go to your shelter immediately.

1. In a residence or small building, move to a pre-designated shelter, such as a basement, storm cellar or "Safe Room or Shelter."
2. If there is no basement, go to an interior room on the lower level (closets, interior hallways). Put as many walls as possible between you and the outside. Get under a sturdy table and use arms to protect head and neck. Stay there until the danger has passed.
3. Do not open windows. Use the time to seek shelter.
4. Stay away from windows, doors and outside walls. Go to the center of the room. Stay away from corners because they attract debris.
5. In a school, nursing home, hospital, factory or shopping center, go to predetermined shelter areas. Interior hallways on the lowest floor are usually safest. Stay away from windows and open spaces.
6. In a high-rise building, go to a small, interior room or hallway on the lowest floor possible.
7. Get out of vehicles, trailers and mobile homes immediately and go to the lowest floor of a sturdy nearby building or a storm shelter. Mobile homes, even if tied down, offer little protection from tornadoes.
8. If caught outside with no shelter, lie flat in a nearby ditch or depression and cover your head with your hands. Be aware of potential for flooding.
9. Do not get under an overpass or bridge. You are safer in a low, flat location.
10. Never try to outrun a tornado in urban or congested areas in a car or truck; instead, leave the vehicle immediately for safe shelter. Tornadoes are erratic and move swiftly.
11. Watch out for flying debris. Flying debris from tornadoes causes most fatalities and injuries.

If caught outside with no shelter when a tornado hits, lie flat in a nearby ditch or depression and cover your head with your hands. Be aware of potential for flooding.

WHAT TO DO AFTER A TORNADO

1. Look out for broken glass and downed power lines.
2. Check for injuries. Do not attempt to move seriously injured persons unless they are in immediate danger of death or further injury. If you must move an unconscious person, first stabilize the neck and back, and then call for help immediately.
   - If the victim is not breathing, carefully position the victim for artificial respiration, clear the airway and commence mouth-to-mouth resuscitation.
   - Maintain body temperature with blankets. Be sure the victim does not become overheated.
   - Never try to feed liquids to an unconscious person.
3. Be careful when entering a damaged building. Make sure that walls, ceiling and roof are in place and that the structure rests firmly on the foundation. Wear sturdy work boots and gloves.
4. Watch for washed out roads, contaminated buildings, contaminated water, gas leaks, broken glass, damaged electrical wiring, and slippery floors.

SAFE ROOM AND SHELTER

Extreme windstorms in many parts of the country pose a serious threat to buildings and their occupants. Your residence may be built "to code," but that doesn't mean that it can withstand winds from extreme events like tornadoes or major hurricanes.

The purpose of a "Safe Room" is to provide a space where you and your household can seek refuge that provides a high level of protection. You can build a shelter in one of the several places in your home:

- In your basement
- Beneath a concrete slab-on-grade foundation or garage floor
- In an interior room on the first floor

Photo: Norma Bartlett standing in front of the safe room in her daughter's home. She and her daughter were in the safe room during the tornado, along with two dogs and two cats. As you can see, the room outside their shelter did not fare as well. Not only was the room trashed, but also insulation from the ceiling indicates significant damage. (FEMA News Photo)

Shelters built below ground level provide the greatest protection, but a shelter built in a first-floor interior room can also provide the necessary protection. Below-ground shelters must be designed to avoid accumulating water during the heavy rains that often accompany severe windstorms.

To protect its occupants, an in-house shelter must be built to withstand high winds and flying debris, even if the rest of the residence is severely damaged or destroyed.

The shelter must be adequately anchored to resist overturning and uplift.

The walls, ceiling, and door of the shelter must withstand wind pressure and resist penetration by windborne objects and falling debris.

The connections between all parts of the shelter must be strong enough to resist the wind.

If sections of either interior or exterior residence walls are used as walls of the shelter, they must be separated from the structure of the residence, so that damage to the residence will not cause damage to the shelter.

AVERAGE COST TO BUILD A SAFE ROOM IN EXISTING HOME

FOUNDATION TYPE	SHELTER TYPE[1]	AVERAGE COST
Basement	Lean-To	$3,000
	AG – Reinforce Masonry	$3,500
	AG – Wood-Frame w/Plywood & Steel Sheathing	$5,000
	AG – Wood-Frame w/ Concrete Masonry Unit Infill	$4,500
	AG – Insulating Concrete Foam	$3,200
	In-Ground	NA
Slab-on-Grade	Lean-To	NA
	AG – Reinforce Masonry	$3,500
	AG – Wood-Frame w/Plywood & Steel Sheathing	$4,500[2]
	AG – Wood-Frame w/ Concrete Masonry Unit Infill	$4,000[2]
	AG – Insulating Concrete Foam	$3,700
	In-Ground	$2,000
Crawlspace	Lean-To	NA
	AG – Reinforce Masonry	$4,500
	AG – Wood-Frame w/Plywood & Steel Sheathing	$6,000
	AG – Wood-Frame w/ Concrete Masonry Unit Infill	$5,500
	AG – Insulating Concrete Foam	$4,200
	In-Ground	NA

NA = shelter type not applicable for the foundation type shown

[1] AG = aboveground shelter (which can also be built in a basement)

[2] A first-floor, wood-framed interior room, such as a bathroom or closet, would be a normal part of a new house; therefore, the dollar amount shown is the additional cost for building the room as a shelter rather than as a standard interior room.

NOTE: The cost of retrofitting an existing house to add a shelter will vary with the size of the house and its construction type. In general, shelter costs for existing house will be approximately 205 higher than those shown in previous chart.

FREE FEMA TORNADO SHELTER PLANS

If you live in high-risk areas, you should consider building a shelter. Publications are available from FEMA for FREE to assist in determining if you need a shelter and how to construct it. Contact the FEMA distribution center (1.888.565.3896) for a copy of *Taking Shelter From the Storm, Building a Safe Room Inside Your House* (L-233 for the brochure or, FEMA-320 for the booklet with complete construction plans).

TIP: In talking with the FEMA Preparedness Division Director, he stated that a number of plans in this booklet would serve as a good fallout shelter with a few modifications.

Photo: Carter County, Missouri, April 27, 2002 -- A mobile home near Ellsinore is left shattered and roofless after an April 24 tornado blew it 50 feet from its foundation and smashed it into the rear of a flatbed trailer. (Anita Westervelt/FEMA News Photo)

Chapter 60: Preparing for Tsunamis

THE BIG WAVE

Tsunamis (pronounced soo-ná-mees), also known as seismic sea waves, are a series of enormous waves created by an underwater disturbance such as an earthquake. Earthquake-induced movement of the ocean floor most often generates tsunamis. Landslides, volcanic eruptions, and even meteor impacts can generate seismic waves. A tsunami can move hundreds of miles per hour in the open ocean and smash into land with 100-foot waves, though most are less than 18 feet. And yes, mega-tsunami waves are much, much greater, but these events are rare.

Photo: Paul Sargeant (Queensland, Australia)

From where a tsunami originates, waves travel outward in all directions much like ripples on a pond. In deep water tsunami waves are invisible. People onshore may suspect nothing except a curious sucking away of all water in a harbor. As the wave approaches shore it multiplies in size and crashes onto land.

By the time people see a problem, it's often too late. Seismic waves are too large and too fast to outrun. If a major earthquake or landslide occurs close to shore, the first wave in a series could reach the beach in a few minutes, even before a warning is issued.

All tsunamis are potentially dangerous, even though they may not damage the coastline they flood. They can strike anywhere along most of the U.S. coast, but the most destructive waves have hit California, Oregon, Washington, Alaska and Hawaii.

THE REAL DEAL

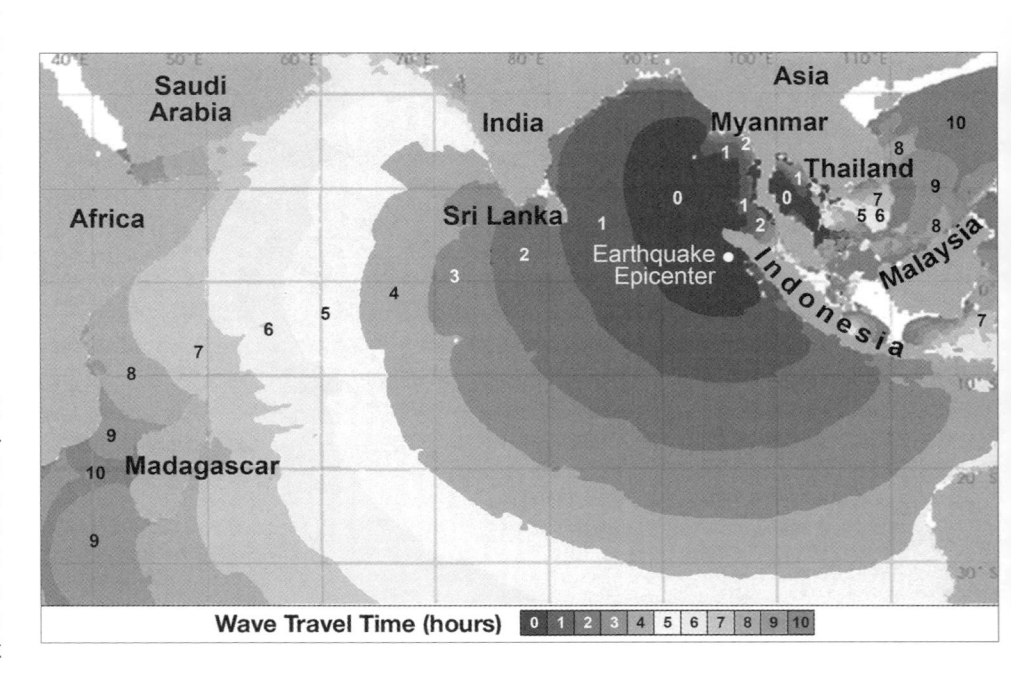

The largest tsunami wave ever recorded was initiated by a massive rock fall in Lituya Bay, Alaska in 1958. Triggered by an 8.3 earthquake, rain-saturated ground released its grip on land at the island's north end. Its tremendous weight gathered momentum as it dropped some 3,600 feet into the sea. In response, an unbelievable 1,722-foot wave belched forth from the depths. Entire forests were swept away as the tsunami rocketed around the Bay. Two boaters died when their craft smashed at sea. Though the tsunami struck 60 years ago, the land still bears ragged scars.

More recently, Indonesia experienced a horrific tsunami the day after Christmas, 2004. Spurred by a Richter 9.3 earthquake, 100-foot tsunamis inundated Indonesia and ploughed into surrounding countries. This tsunami caused more casualties than any other in recorded history. Though the epicenter occurred just off the coast of Sumatra, it claimed more than 225,000 lives in 14 countries. Nearly 48,000 people were missing and over 1.7 million were displaced in South Asia and East Africa. (See *Prudent Places USA* for next likely mega-tsunami event.)

> *Areas are at greater risk if less than 25 feet above sea level and within a mile of the shoreline.*

Drowning is the most common cause of death associated with a tsunami. Tsunami waves and the receding water are very destructive to structures in the run-up zone. Other hazards include flooding, contamination of drinking water and fires from gas lines or ruptured tanks.

Take tsunami warnings seriously.
Follow local instructions.

If you live in a region where hazard zone signs exist, it gives you a big heads up. This particular sign was installed in Alaska, the first state to post tsunami warnings in remote areas.

WHAT TO DO BEFORE A TSUNAMI

1. The terms used by the West Coast/Alaska Tsunami Warning Center (WC/ATWC – is responsible for tsunami warnings for California, Oregon, Washington, British Columbia, and Alaska) and the Pacific Tsunami Warning Center (PTWC – is responsible for tsunami warnings to international authorities, Hawaii, and the U.S. territories within the Pacific basin).
   - **Advisory** – An earthquake has occurred in the Pacific basin, which might generate a tsunami. WC/ATWC and PTWC will issue hourly bulletins advising of the situation.
   - **Watch** – A tsunami was or may have been generated, but is at least two hours travel time to the area in Watch status.
   - **Warning** – A tsunami was or may have been generated, which could cause damage; therefore, people in the warned area are strongly advised to evacuate.
2. Listen to radio or television for more information and follow the instructions of your local authorities.
3. Immediate warning of tsunamis sometimes comes in the form of a noticeable recession in water away from the shoreline. This is nature's tsunami warning. Heed it by moving inland to higher ground immediately.
4. If you feel an earthquake in a coastal area, leave the beach or low-lying areas. Then turn on your radio to learn if there is a tsunami warning.
5. Know that a small tsunami at one beach can be a larger wave a few miles away. The topography of the coastline and the ocean floor will influence the size of the wave.
6. A tsunami may generate more than one wave. Do not let the modest size of one wave allow you to forget how dangerous a tsunami is. The next wave may be bigger.
7. Prepare for possible evacuation. Learn evacuation routes. Determine where you would go and how you would get there if you needed to evacuate.

WHAT TO DO DURING A TSUNAMI

> *Do not let the modest size of one wave allow you to forget how dangerous tsunamis are. The next wave in the series may be much larger.*

1. If you are advised to evacuate, do so immediately.
2. Stay away from the area until local authorities say it is safe. Do not be fooled into thinking that the danger is over after a single wave – a tsunami is not a single wave but a series of waves that can vary in size.
3. Do not go to the shoreline to watch for a tsunami. When you can see the wave, it is too late to escape.

WHAT TO DO AFTER A TSUNAMI

1. Stay away from flooded and damaged areas until officials say it is safe to return.
2. Stay away from debris in the water, it may pose a safety hazard to boats and people.
3. Save yourself, not your possessions.

Photo: This rare photograph shows a tsunami in progress. Most images reveal the resulting devastation since people this close to the event are too panicked or too busy trying to escape its watery grip to take pictures. The majority of people cannot outrun a tsunami's speed and it is likely many of these did not. On December 26, 2004 more than 225,000 people died around the Indian Ocean when a magnitude 9.3 undersea earthquake shook the region. New research shows the great Indian Ocean earthquake set off tremors nearly 9,000 miles away in the San Andreas fault at Parkfield, Calif. The earthquake shot around the Ring of Fire sending tsunami waves to 14 countries in one of the deadliest disasters in modern history. The highest in the series of waves reached 100 feet. This photograph shows the tsunami as it struck Ao Nang, Thailand. (Photo by David Rydevik)

Chapter 61: Preparing for Volcanic Eruptions

Depending on the type of volcano, molten rock either pours quietly down its sides or erupts violently in magnificent fountains. Because its heat is so intense, lava poses great fire hazards. Molten rock consumes everything in its path, but most flows travel slowly enough that people and animals can move out of the way.

When an eruption occurs, sideways blasts can flatten trees for miles. Hot, poisonous gases flow down the sides of a volcano. Eruptions don't have to take place for these gasses to sicken or kill; noxious fumes can quietly seep from vents.

Fresh volcanic ash that is really pulverized rock. It's abrasive, acidic, gritty, glassy and smelly. While not immediately dangerous to most adults, the combination of acidic gas and ash can cause lung damage to small infants, very old people or those suffering from severe respiratory illnesses. Volcanic ash, or tephra, can also damage machinery, including engines and electrical equipment. Ash mixed with water becomes very heavy and cause roofs to collapse.

Volcanic eruptions can be accompanied by other natural hazards: earthquakes, mudflows, flash floods, rock and landslides, acid rain, fired, and under special conditions, tsunamis. Active volcanoes in the U.S. are found mainly in Hawaii, Alaska and the Pacific Northwest.

MOUNT ST. HELENS

It's hard to believe a 5.1 magnitude earthquake triggered such a mammoth eruption. "As the entire north side disappeared, destructive, lethal blasts of gas, steam, and rock shot northward across the landscape at nearly 700 mph. That's faster than commercial jets travel by nearly 100 mph!

Within minutes, a massive ash plume thrust 12 miles into the sky. Prevailing winds carried 520 million tons of ash across 22,000 square miles of western America. Spokane, Washington, 250 miles from the volcano, plunged into total darkness. Ash piled up 10 inches deep 10 miles away. Another 300 miles downwind ash covered everything ½ thick".

By day three, the eruptive cloud's murkiness had crossed the entire US. Two weeks later, it had encircled the planet.

The eruption killed 58 people and countless wildlife. Everything was incinerated that couldn't "burrow in" to escape the burning explosion. Another 7,000 big game animals perished as well. Hatcheries lost 12 million salmon fingerlings. The force of this 24 megaton thermal energy blast flattened enough trees to build 300,000 two-bedroom homes.[162]"

Photo: Mt. St. Helens, May 1980, (USGS)

The May 18, 1980 eruption of Mount St. Helens in Washington took the lives of 58 people and caused property damage in excess of $1.2 billion.

WHAT TO DO BEFORE AN ERUPTION

1. Make evacuation plans. If you live in a known volcanic hazard area, plan a main and alternate route out.
2. Develop a household disaster plan. In case household members are separated from one another during a volcanic eruption (a real possibility during the day when adults are at work and children are at school), have a plan for getting back together. Ask an out-of-town relative or friend to serve as the "household contact," because after a disaster, it's often easier to call long distance. Make sure everyone knows the name, address, and phone number of the contact person.
3. Assemble a disaster supplies kit.
4. Get a pair of goggles and a disposable dust mask for each member of the household in case of ashfall.
5. Do not visit an active volcano site unless officials designate a safe viewing area.

WHAT TO DO DURING AN ERUPTION

1. If close to the volcano evacuate immediately away from the volcano to avoid flying debris, hot gases, lateral blast, and lava flow.
2. Avoid areas downwind from the volcano to avoid volcanic ash.
3. Be aware of mudflows. The danger from a mudflow increases as you approach a stream channel and decreases as you move away from a stream channel toward higher ground. This danger increases with prolonged heavy rains. Mudflows can move faster than you can walk or run. Look upstream before crossing a bridge, and do not cross if the mudflow is approaching. Avoid river valleys and low-lying areas.
4. Stay indoors until the ash has settled unless there is danger of the roof collapsing.
5. During an ash fall, close doors, windows, and all ventilation in the house (chimney vents, furnaces, air conditioners, fans and other vents).
6. Do not drive in heavy ashfall unless absolutely required. If you do drive in dense ashfall, keep speed down to 35 mph or slower.
7. Remove heavy ash from flat or low-pitched roofs and rain gutters.
8. Volcanic ash is actually fine, glassy fragments and particles that can cause severe injury to breathing passages, eyes, and open wounds, and irritation to skin. Follow these precautions to keep yourself safe from ashfall:

- Wear long-sleeved shirts and long pants.
- Use goggles and wear eyeglasses instead of contact lenses.
- Use a dust mask or hold a damp cloth over your face to help breathing.
- Do not run car or truck engines. Driving can stir up volcanic ash that can clog engines and stall vehicles. Moving parts can be damaged from abrasion, including bearings, brakes, and transmissions.

WHAT TO DO AFTER THE ERUPTION

1. Stay away from ashfall areas if possible. If you are in an ashfall area cover your mouth and nose with a mask, keep skin covered, and wear goggles to protect the eyes.
2. Clear roofs of ashfall because it can be very heavy and may cause buildings to collapse. Exercise great caution when working on a roof.
3. Do not drive through ashfall, which is easily stirred up and can clog engine air filters, causing vehicles to stall.
4. If you have a respiratory ailment, avoid contact with any amount of ash. Stay indoors until local health officials advise it is safe to go outside.

Chapter 62: Preparing for Winter Storms, Extreme Cold

Photo: New York City blizzard 2006 (NYCnstar)

Heavy snowfall and extreme cold can immobilize an entire region. Even areas that normally experience mild winters can be hit with a major snowstorm or extreme cold. The impacts include flooding, storm surge, closed highways, blocked roads, downed power lines and hypothermia.

You can protect your household from the many hazards of winter by planning ahead.

WHAT TO DO BEFORE A WINTER STORM THREATENS

1. Know the terms used by weather forecasters:
   - **Freezing rain** – Rain that freezes when it hits the ground, creating a coating of ice on roads, walkways, trees and power lines.
   - **Sleet** – Rain that turns to ice pellets before reaching the ground. Sleet also causes moisture on roads to freeze and become slippery.
   - **Winter Storm Watch** – A winter storm is possible in your area.
   - **Winter Storm Warning** – A winter storm is occurring, or will soon occur in your area.
   - **Blizzard Warning** – Sustained winds or frequent gusts to 35mph or greater and considerable amounts of falling or blowing snow (reducing visibility to less than a quarter mile) are expected to prevail for a period of three hours or longer.
   - **Frost/Freeze Warning** – Below freezing temperatures are expected.
2. Prepare to survive on your own for at least six days. Assemble a disaster supplies kit. Be sure to include winter specific items such as rock salt to melt ice on walkways, sand to improve traction, snow shovels and other snow removal equipment. Keep a stock of food and extra drinking water.
3. Prepare for possible isolation in your home:
   - Have sufficient heating fuel; regular fuel sources may be cut off.
   - Have emergency heating equipment and fuel (a gas fireplace or a wood burning stove or fireplace) so you can keep at least one room of your residence at a livable temperature. (Be sure the room is well ventilated.) If a thermostat controls your furnace and your electricity is cut off by a storm, you will need emergency heat.

- Kerosene heaters like the Mr. Heater are another emergency heating option. Never use any fuel other than kerosene in a kerosene heater.
- Store a good supply of dry, seasoned wood for your fireplace or woodburning stove.
- Keep fire extinguishers on hand, and make sure your household knows how to use them.
- Never burn charcoal indoors.
4. Winterize your home to extend the life of your fuel supply.
   - Insulate walls and attics.
   - Caulk and weather-strip doors and windows.
   - Install storm windows or cover windows with plastic.
5. Maintain several days' supply of medicines, water, and food that needs no cooking or refrigeration.

> *Be careful when shoveling snow. Overexertion can bring on a heart attack. Stretch before going outside and don't overexert yourself.*

WHAT TO DO DURING A WINTER STORM

1. Listen to your radio, television, or NOAA Weather Radio for weather reports and emergency information.
2. Eat regularly and drink ample fluids, but avoid caffeine and alcohol.
3. **Dress for the season:**
   - Wear several layers of loose fitting, lightweight, warm clothing rather than one layer of heavy clothing. The outer garments should be tightly woven and water repellent.
   - Mittens are warmer than gloves.
   - Wear a hat; most body heat is lost through the top of the head.
   - Cover your mouth with a scarf to protect your lungs.
4. Be careful when shoveling snow. Over-exertion can bring on a heart attack – a major cause of death in the winter. If you must shovel snow, stretch before going outside and don't overexert yourself.
5. **Watch for signs of frostbite:** loss of feeling and white or pale appearance in extremities such as fingers, toes, ear lobes or the tip of the nose. If symptoms are detected, get medical help immediately
6. **Watch for signs of hypothermia:** uncontrollable shivering, memory loss, disorientation, incoherence, slurred speech, drowsiness and apparent exhaustion. If symptoms of hypothermia are detected, get the victim to a warm location, remove any wet clothing, warm the center of the body first, and give warm, non-alcoholic beverages if the victim is conscious. Get medical help as soon as possible.
7. **When at home:**
   - Conserve fuel by keeping your residence cooler than normal.
   - Temporarily "close off" heat to some rooms.
   - Check around doors and windows for cold air leaks. Block airflow with towels or rags.
   - Close blinds and curtails to help retain inside warmth.
   - When using kerosene heaters, maintain ventilation to avoid buildup of toxic fumes. Refuel kerosene heaters outside and keep them at least three feet from flammable objects.

> *About 70% of winter deaths related to snow and ice occur in automobiles. Travel by car in daylight, don't travel alone, keep others notified of your schedule and stay on main roads – avoid back-road short cuts.*

WINTER DRIVING (SEE CHAPTER 63 ON PREPARING YOUR VEHICLE)

About 70% of winter deaths related to snow and ice occur in automobiles. Consider public transportation if you must travel. If you travel by car, travel in the day, don't travel alone, and keep others informed of your schedule. Stay on main roads; avoid back-road shortcuts.

1. **Winterize your car.** This includes a battery check, antifreeze, wipers and windshield washer fluid, ignition system, thermostat, lights, flashing hazard lights, exhaust system, heater, brakes, defroster, oil level, and tires. Consider snow tires with studs or chains. Keep gas tank full; more weigh gives better traction.
2. **Carry a disaster supplies "winter car kit" in the trunk of your car.** The kit should include:

- Bag of road salt and sand
- Battery-powered or crank radio
- Blanket
- Cell telephone or two-way radio
- Emergency flares
- Extra batteries
- Flashlight
- Fluorescent distress flag
- Hat, mittens, heavy coat, boots
- Insulated socks
- Jumper/booster cables
- Road maps
- Shovel
- Snack food
- Tire chains
- Tow chain or rope
- Water
- Windshield scraper

3. **If a blizzard traps you in your car:**
   - Pull off the highway. Turn on hazard lights and hang a distress flag from the radio aerial or window.
   - Remain in your vehicle where rescuers are most likely to find you. Do not set out on foot unless you can see a building close by where you know you can take shelter. Be careful: distances are distorted by blowing snow. A building may seem close but be too far to walk to in deep snow.
   - Run the engine and heater about ten minutes each hour to keep warm. When the engine is running, open a window slightly for ventilation. This will protect you from possible carbon monoxide poisoning. Periodically clear snow from the exhaust pipe.
   - Exercise to maintain body heat, but avoid overexertion. In extreme cold, use road maps, seat covers and floor mats for insulation. Huddle with passengers and use your coat for a blanket.
   - Take turns sleeping. One person should be awake at all times to look for rescue crews.
   - Drink fluids to avoid dehydration.
   - Be careful not to waste battery power. Balance electrical energy needs – the use of lights, heat and radio – with supply.
   - At night, turn on the inside light so work crews or rescuers can see you.
   - If stranded in a remote area, stomp large block letters in an open area spelling out HELP or SOS and line with rocks or tree limbs to attract the attention of rescue personnel who may be surveying the area by airplane.
   - Once the blizzard passes, you may need to leave the car and proceed on foot.

Chapter 63: Preparing Your Vehicle

We spend so much time in our vehicles, it is very likely an emergency could occur while traveling. Some events are avoidable or at least can be expected, but others can catch us totally by surprise. In bad weather, anticipate getting caught in potential disasters like a winter storm, tornado, hurricane or a flood. Even when we know conditions may be right for these events, sometimes their reality hasn't sunk in.

Nasty surprises like earthquakes, solar storms, volcanic eruptions, tsunamis, flash floods and freak storms can catch us unaware AND unprepared. Other events that have nothing to do with natural disasters can also really crimp our plans. As climate continues its wild swings and extremes, formerly freak, unusual scenarios are the norm. So how else can we prepare?

Make sure all vehicles are maintained in good running condition. A checklist of the following should get the biggest problems out of the way. Statistics show winter brings more car trouble than any time of the year. Many problems can be avoided by regularly changing the fuel and air filters, but there are other areas to check.

NORMAL MAINTENANCE
ANTIFREEZE.
Most antifreeze requires changing every 24 months. Even if it's labeled "permanent", it does not mean forever. Dirty antifreeze has sediments that may plug the radiator and cause overheating.
BATTERY.
At 32°F (0°C), a battery may have only 50% of its summer output, but need twice the amount to start up. Check connections for a tight fit. Remove corrosion from posts and cable connections with a wire brush or fine sand paper. A little vinegar helps the process.
BELTS.
Check overall condition and tension on the belt. Too tight a belt can ruin an alternator; too loose can result in a dead battery. Look for cracks in serpentine type belts.
BRAKES.
Road contamination and moisture affects braking. This is especially true in winter due to salt and other materials used to battle snow and ice. Have the brakes inspected, especially the pads and shoes.
EXHAUST SYSTEM.
Have a qualified technician check the exhaust system lift for leaks, soft exhaust pipes, small holes in trunk and floorboards, and cracked rubber hangers or broken clamps. Failure to replace faulty components could be deadly.
FUEL.
Keep the fuel tank as full as possible. You never know when you might be waiting in a long line and run out. Pour fuel de-icer in the tank once a month during winter to prevent moisture from freezing in the fuel line. It also provides weight for traction in winter.
HEATER/DEFROSTER.
The heater and defroster provide warmth and comfort as well as good visibility for safe driving. A screeching sound when you turn on the heater or a stiff control lever can mean trouble. Check the radiator and hoses for

cracks and leaks. Make sure the radiator cap, water pump and thermostat work properly. Test the strength of the anti-freeze, the heater and defroster.

HOSES.
Hoses should be inspected every year and changed every three. They wear from the inside out, so defects are not always visible. Squeeze hoses to check for flexibility and look for cracked, bulging, brittle or limp hoses.

IGNITION SYSTEM.
Damaged ignition wires or a cracked distributor cap may cause a sudden breakdown.

LIGHTS.
Make sure they are clean, working and properly aligned.

OIL.
Oil changes should be more frequent in winter because oil thickens as the temperatures drop and provides less efficient lubrication. Using a lighter weight oil (5W-30 or 10W-40) or synthetic oil that flows better in extremely cold weather may help. Check the owner's manual for additional suggestions.

TIRES.
When the temperature drops so does air pressure in tires. Improper inflation causes premature wearing which, in turn, can cause an accident. Check tire pressure when the tires are cold, not after driving. Make sure all four tires have the same tread pattern for even traction. Check them periodically for cuts, abrasions and uneven wear. The law in Australia is if there is less than a match head of tread left, the tires are not roadworthy and must be changed.

WINDSHIELD/WINDSCREEN.
Invest in rubber-clad winter blades that can help prevent ice and snow build-up. Wipers work harder clearing snow, frost, ice and road salt. Replace blades when they start to leave places on the windshield uncleaned. Make sure windshield wiper fluid is full.

WINTER DRIVING

Winter driving presents the most challenges for the greatest number of motorists. Generally we'll know when driving conditions are hazardous. Good judgment while driving helps avoid the biggest mistakes, but what about the other guy who isn't paying attention?

Every single winter in Colorado it's the same story. I-25 and I-70 sees the inevitable multi-car pile-ups. The first several snows always bring accidents. It's like everyone goes brain dead from one winter to the next. We forget how slippery roads can be. Occasionally a deer scampers across the freeway causing accidents, but most often, it's simply unwise driving for the conditions at hand. Sounds pretty simple to correct doesn't it...

COMMON SENSE

1. If you must drive in bad weather, plan ahead and make sure you have a FULL tank of fuel. It adds weight for better traction.
2. See and be seen; clear all snow from the hood, roof, windows and lights. Clear all windows of fog. If visibility becomes poor, find a place to safely pull off the road as soon as possible. Scrape off all snow on windows, not just a plate-sized "peep hole".
3. Keep to main roads. They will be plowed and salted/sanded first.
4. Wear warm clothes that don't restrict movement. Take along boots.
5. Drive with caution. Match your speed to conditions.
6. Don't press on. If the going gets tough, turn back or find a place to stop.
7. Avoid passing when weather conditions and roads are bad.
8. Keep the radio tuned to a local station for weather advice.
9. Buckle up at all times. Properly secure small children in child restraints.
10. Don't drive after drinking alcohol and don't drive if you're feeling drowsy.
11. In bad weather, let someone know your route and intended arrival time, so you can be searched for if you don't turn up after a reasonable delay.
12. Take a cell phone if you have it.
13. Take food, water, a blanket, flashlight and a candle in a jar plus matches.
14. If you need extra weight, put sand bags over each wheel in your trunk. Should you get stuck, use the sand on ice or snow for traction.

TRAPPED IN A STORM OR SNOW BANK

1. Don't panic.
2. Avoid over-exertion and exposure. Shoveling and bitter cold can kill.
3. Stay in your car. You won't get lost and you'll have shelter.

4. Keep fresh air in your car. Open a window on the side sheltered from the wind. Run the motor sparingly. Beware of exhaust fumes and the possibility of carbon monoxide poisoning. Ensure the tailpipe is not blocked by snow.
5. Use the candle for heat instead of the car's heater, if possible.
6. Set out a warning light or flares. Put on the dome light. Overuse of headlights may run your battery down.
7. Exercise your limbs, hands and feet vigorously. Keep moving and don't fall asleep.
8. Keep watch for traffic or searchers.
9. Wear a hat. You can lose up to 60% of your body heat through your head.

WHAT TO DO IF YOUR CAR GETS STUCK IN THE SNOW

Turn your wheels from side to side a few times to push snow out of the way. Keep a light touch on the gas and ease forward. Don't spin the wheels—you'll just dig deeper.

Rocking the vehicle is another way to get unstuck. Check your owner's manual first—it can damage the transmission on some vehicles. Shift from forward to reverse, and back again. Each time you are in gear, give a light touch on the gas until the vehicle gets going.

Front-wheel drive vehicles: snow tires should be on the front, which is the driving axle, for better driving in mud or snow.

ICE AND SLEET

These conditions can totally eliminate traction. Ice is often not easy to see and can be found even when the temperature does not appear to be conducive to ice forming. When "black ice" forms, it's nearly invisible blending in with the road. You have to be alert and use foresight when temperatures hover around freezing.

Keep track of conditions. Ice is twice as slippery at 30°F (-1°C) than at 0°F (-17.8°C). When water is turning into ice is the most dangerous time to drive.

Know where to expect ice: bridges, overpasses, and shady areas. Bridges and overpasses have cold air circulating around the surfaces, not just on top or bottom. These road surfaces freeze sooner and thaw more slowly.

Look ahead; know what is going on in advance; watch other drivers who may be experiencing trouble and increase your following distance as much as possible. When driving on ice, there are two basic rules: slow down and do not make any sudden movements.

ON "SKID" ROW

REAR-WHEEL SKIDS

The most effective way to get a vehicle back under control during a skid is as follows:

Step 1 Take your foot off the brake or accelerator.
Step 2 De-clutch on a car with a manual transmission, or shift to neutral on a car with automatic transmission.
Step 3 Steer in the direction you want the front of the car to go.
Step 4 As the rear wheels stop skidding to the right or left, steer in the opposite direction until you are going in the desired direction.
Step 5 In a rear-wheel drive vehicle, if you over-correct the first skid (Step 4), be prepared for a rear-wheel skid in the opposite direction, called fishtailing. Gentle turning of the steering wheel will avoid this type of skid.
Step 6 Once the vehicle is straight, release the clutch or shift to drive, apply gentle accelerator pressure so that the engine speed matches the road speed, and accelerate smoothly to a safe speed.

Hard braking or acceleration cause front-wheel skids if your vehicle has front-wheel drive. When the front wheels lose traction, you can't steer the vehicle.

FOUR-WHEEL SKIDS

Sometimes all four wheels lose traction. This generally occurs when the vehicle is driven too fast for conditions. To get a vehicle under control when all four wheels skid:

Step 1 Ease foot off the accelerator or take your foot off the brake.
Step 2 Let the clutch out with manual transmission or shift to neutral with an automatic, if you can do so quickly.
Step 3 Steer in the direction you want the front of the car to go.
Step 4 Wait for the wheels to grip the road again. As soon as traction returns, the vehicle will travel in the desired direction.
Step 5 Release clutch or shift to drive; maintain a safe speed. **Avoid using overdrive on slippery surfaces.**

REGAINING CONTROL

Regardless of whether the vehicle has front-, rear- or four-wheel drive, the best way to regain control of a front wheel skid is:

Step 1 Take your foot off the brake or accelerator.
Step 2 Let the clutch out on a car with manual transmission, or shift to neutral with automatic transmission.
Step 3 If the front wheels were turned before the loss of traction, don't move the steering wheel. The wheels are skidding sideways so some braking force will be exerted. (Unwinding the steering wheel will result in regaining steering sooner, but the vehicle will be traveling faster because there is little sideways braking force. This technique should only be attempted in situations where limited space and sharp curves exist. However, in this case do not reduce pressure on the brakes, because the vehicle will shoot off in the direction the wheels are facing.)
Step 4 Wait for the front wheels to grip the road. As soon as traction returns, the vehicle will start to steer again.
Step 5 When the front wheels have regained their grip, steer the wheels gently in the desired direction of travel.
Step 6 Release the clutch or shift to drive and apply gentle accelerator pressure so the engine speed matches the road speed, and accelerate smoothly to a safe speed.

ANTI-LOCK BRAKING SYSTEM

When driving in poor weather conditions, whether it is wet, ice, snow or slush, braking can be tricky. Anti-lock brakes, which are standard in more than half of the cars sold today, detect when the wheel stops turning and starts to skip. As soon as a skid begins, anti-lock brakes open and close faster than you can pump the brakes to avoid a lock up. This lets you steer while you bring the car to a stop. Pumping the pedal, as you would with a traditional system, prevents the system from working. Your car is equipped with an anti-lock braking system (ABS) if you can feel the brake pedal pulse back against your foot.

If you feel your rear wheels begin to skid, take your foot off the brake or ease off the accelerator, shift to neutral and steer in the direction you want the front of the car to go.

These are all things we can be aware of, how to "steer" clear of certain hazards, anticipate the dangers of bad weather and make sure our vehicles are in tip-top running condition. Unless we have a crystal ball, there are some disasters, some nasty zappers we can't anticipate. For this reason, it's important to carry a 72-hour kit in your vehicle and not just during winter. As weather becomes more unpredictable, these supplies become a nice safety valve.

WHO WOULD HAVE THOUGHT THIS COULD HAPPEN?

Whether we are bricklayers or business execs, homemakers or hair stylists, all we want to do after a day's work is get home safely. After donating 8 to10 hours for "the buck" many of us are focused on relaxation, a good meal, a little TV or a night out clubbing. Rarely do we consider something might happen to prevent us from reaching our destination.

In winter we might be a little more conscious of this if home is in snow territory, but how many of us think about this on a brilliant blue summer day? Do we ever think an earthquake could block our path? Could a disaster ever strike on the way to work? During vacations? How about en route to the football game? Emergencies have an annoying way of catching us unaware, unprepared.

We generally have a clue if it's freezing and ominous black clouds lurk overhead that it'd be clever to tuck winter boots in the car. Do we think about including water, candles, blankets and a bar of chocolate? If the weather person warns that a hurricane is swirling off the coast, late preppers might purchase batteries, extra food and bottled water. Sometimes events happen that we just don't foresee.

Picture your drive home from work. Rush hour crawls by and cars play bumper tag while you mull over the day's meetings. Possibly you grouse about why you didn't make this or that brilliant remark to your boss or you mentally walk through the kitchen and plan dinner. You drive home on autopilot when a car lurches into the next lane. Concrete ripples under the tires and cars slide around like balls on a billiard table. Two miles ahead, the road has ruptured and traffic crunches to a halt.

In the background, a radio announcer breaks in with news of an earthquake fifteen miles from your home. That puts the epicenter five miles dead ahead. Police pull everyone over and explain that the roads are closed. No one is going anywhere.

How would you fare? Would you be warm enough? Do you have candles and matches? Is there food to nibble and water to drink? Where would you relieve yourself? Do you have an area map and compass? Circumstances vary, but every time we get in our cars, we leave the security of our home and supplies. As disasters mount and the world gets crazier, view your vehicles as mini-homes with survival supplies on board.

GO OR STAY... THE DILEMMA

If you're in winter conditions, the choice should nearly always be to stay with the vehicle. It is far too easy to get lost in a blizzard, become severely hypothermic and not know it, or slip on ice and break a leg.

However, if an earthquake has torn up the road and you know where you are, walking may be your best option. Chances are too many emergency vehicles will be tied up with other crises to look for you. If you live in an area where volcanic eruptions are possible, plan ahead. Wearing a face mask while outside in ashfall helps keep it from your nose and lungs. Masks are also important if you're walking through a lot of traffic and are particularly susceptible to pollution.

If a tornado is visible, *get out of the car*, find a ditch and lie in it. Outrunning it is not an option.

If the disaster is flooding, get out of the car and climb. Don't try to save the car. It's replaceable, you aren't. Remember, 80% of flood deaths occur in vehicles when drivers try to navigate through floodwaters.

For hail, hurricanes and damaging storms, find an underpass to wait out the storm. It may be minutes or hours till it is safe enough to continue.

STAYING

Should you opt to remain with your vehicle, mark it with a sign that you need help saying "Call Police". If someone stops these days, unless you know the person well, do NOT get in the car with him or her. Ask them to phone a service station or your spouse or friend for assistance. Too often bad endings occur when people crawl into a car with a stranger.

Be aware of carbon monoxide poisoning. If you run the engine, keep the window partially open.

When stranded, it's easy to run the car battery down. Listening to the radio, using the lights or heater can drain the battery. If you doze off with these things running, chances are you'll wake with a dead battery. Every single person should know how to jump-start a car when they learn to drive. It's so easy to do, but if you don't know how, it doesn't matter how simple it is.

This is such a simple skill, one that everyone should know how to perform.

Step 1 Bring both cars together nose to nose, about 18" apart. Make sure both cars have their parking brakes on and are turned off.

Step 2 Put automatic transmission cars in Park. Put manual transmission cars in Neutral. Set the parking brake firmly so the vehicle cannot move.

Caution: Once you begin the next steps, don't touch the metal portion of the jumper cable clamps to each other or any part of the car except the battery terminal.

Step 3 Connect one end of the positive cable (red handle) to the positive terminal of the dead battery.

Step 4 Attach the other end of the positive cable (red handle) to the positive battery terminal providing the jump.

Step 5 Connect one end of the negative cable (black handle) to the negative battery terminal providing the jump.

Step 6 Attach the other end of that cable to the engine block of the car with the dead battery. Look for unpainted metal surfaces and be sure it will clear anything moving when the car starts. Do not attach the negative cable to the dead battery itself.

Step 7 Start the healthy car's engine and let it run for several minutes before starting the car with the dead battery. If it doesn't start, stop trying and wait a few minutes longer. Try again for no more than thirty seconds. If the car still doesn't start, chances are it's not going to. Call a tow truck.

Dare To Prepare: Chapter 63: Preparing Your Vehicle

Step 8 If it does start, the needle should move toward the positive side on your battery indicator gauge. When it's in the positive zone, remove the cables in the reverse the order above.

Caution: Do not try to jump-start a frozen battery. The battery could explode! If the battery casing is cracked, don't try to jump-start it. The battery needs to be replaced.

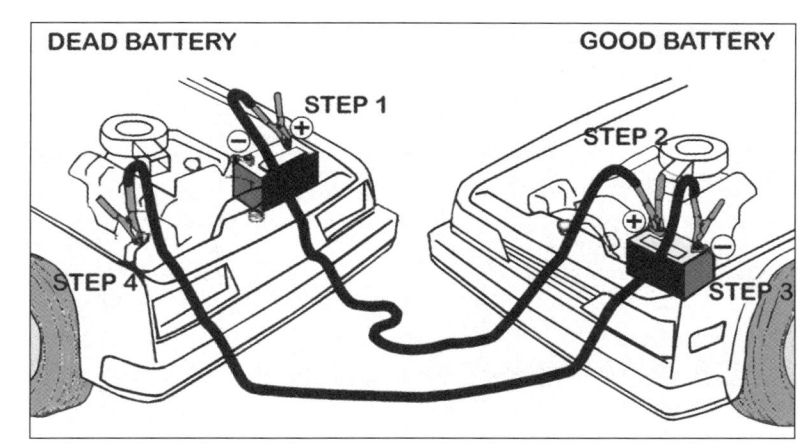

I'M OUTTA HERE!

This option can present just as many dilemmas as staying put. For the particularly antsy person, the choice is simple. Before you set out, know where you are and where you're going. For routes you take regularly, note which ones have bridges that might become unusable, note if you have to pass through any unsavory parts of town, where there might be police stations, phone booths, motels, hospitals, restaurants, churches or friends' homes. If you know you might normally drive through a high crime area, plan a different route on your map.

Pack what you anticipate needing in your backpack and dress for the weather in layers. Take the compass and street map to plot a "Plan B". Pay very close attention to your feet.

They are going to be your "wheels" till you arrive at the destination. Make sure you have supportive, comfortable shoes that do not rub your feet raw. If you even get a hint of a blister forming, put cushioning moleskin on this part of your foot. A blister, while not life threatening, can make walking painful beyond belief. When compensating for sore feet, it can force you into an unnatural gait resulting in pulled muscles.

If it's been a while since you've eaten, fuel the body before setting out. Depending on how far you are from your destination, pack some high-energy food and water. Leave a note with the time you left on your vehicle and where you're heading in case you miss connections with family and friends.

As you leave, pay attention to the cars and people around you. The number one reason muggers give for picking their victims is that people were oblivious to their surroundings. Many victims wore headphones, totally tuned out to everything around them. Walking with a purposeful stride, head up and obviously noticing your environment and the **people** around you will help keep you safe. If you feel particularly vulnerable, walk off the main path, unless people know your route and would be looking for you.

At every opportunity, phone to be picked up. Chances are if the disaster is widespread, phone service may be out. Carry cash for a motel room if your destination is a long way off. Your journey may be lengthy and people may stop to offer you a ride. To ride or not is your decision, but if in doubt, don't. You may be more tired hoofing it all the way, but statistically, it's safer.

Whether to go or stay sometimes becomes a larger issue than remaining with your car. In looking around your city, does it feel less-than-safe; should you move? This issue is discussed IN-DEPTH in *Prudent Places USA*.

CAR PREPAREDNESS (MAKE SEASONAL CHANGES)	
CAR ITEMS	
Belts, hoses, clamps	Sand, salt or kitty litter (traction under tires in mud, ice or snow and rear end weight)
Car key, spare	
Crow bar	Shovel, folding
De-icer	Siphoning hose
Duct tape (it has a thousand uses!)	Spare fuses
Fire extinguisher	Spare tire and jack
Ice scraper and brush	Tire pressure gauge
Instant tire repair kit, sealant and inflator	Tow chain
Jerry can	Warning light or road flares
Jumper cables	
TOOLS	
9-Piece socket wrench set	Slip joint pliers
Ax or hatchet	Socket driver
Phillips screwdriver	Straight screwdriver
Roll of electrical tape and emergency sign	

COMMUNICATION	
Book to pass time	Local map and compass
Cash: coins and small bills, enough for a motel room or tow service	Pencil/pen and paper
	Walkman type AM/FM radio & extra batteries
Flashlight/torch and batteries	Whistle
SANITATION & FIRST AID	
First-aid kit, including first aid book, plus any essential prescription medications	Pre-moistened towelettes
	Toilet paper, roll flattened
Moleskin, if you decide to walk, helps cushion against blisters	Tooth brush, tooth paste and deodorant
	Trash Bags for hygiene purposes, small-size
Paper towels	Ziploc or Click Zip bags
FOOD, CLOTHING, WARMTH	
Backpack	Knife, utility
Candle in a deep can (to warm hands, heat a drink or use as an emergency light)	Lighters, disposable or Matches
	Plastic collapsible cup
Clothing and footwear (1 set)	Rain poncho
Eating utensils, disposable	Sleeping bag, bedroll, heavy blanket
Face masks, disposable	Space blanket or space bag
Food "on the go": dried fruits, nuts, granola bars, crackers, seeds, jerky, MREs	Sunglasses
	Water
Heavy work gloves	

Chapter 64: Staying Warm Without Power

Photo: New Orleans, Louisiana; September 8, 2005: Many days after hurricane Katrina, areas still have not been cleared. Downed wires posed serious safety hazards and electricity was out of the question. (Liz Roll)

Power outages can and do happen year round, but arguably the worst occur in winter. Bitter cold adds to inconvenience making the experience doubly miserable. Take measures beforehand and transform a possibly life-threatening situation into a mere nuisance.

Hopefully your home is already winter-ready with doors and windows caulked and weatherstripped, walls and attic heavily insulated, and windows covered with plastic or storm windows installed. Even with these measures, should a prolonged power outage hit, room temperatures will plummet without heating.

STOVES

Due to high fuel prices, many people have purchased wood burning stoves if their homes didn't have fireplaces. Stan and I put in a stove similar to this one three winters ago. It's one of the best investments we've ever made. The stove works so efficiently – much more so than our past traditional fireplaces. The main floor actually becomes uncomfortably hot if too much wood is added. A freestanding stove like this can easily heat a 2,800 sq.ft room. It cuts heating bills considerably and adds ambience and value to the home.

One nice feature to consider is a built-in ash bucket, which is accessed by the door at the bottom. It minimizes cleanup since ash lands directly in the bucket. Wood is added either through the top, which doubles as a heating surface, or through the front door.

Since our floors are carpeted, we installed an over-the-carpet tile hearth. Between the heavy stove and hearth, it added about 500 pounds. Make sure your floor is equipped to handle this kind of weight without additional support. (See Chapter 21 for best wood choices.)

Pellet stoves are another option, but their hoppers require electricity to feed the fire and operate its blower. One of our neighbors who added a pellet stove, purchased a battery back-up pack, just in case...

Stoves have come a long way. Beside wood and pellets, manufacturers offer models that burn coal, gas, grain or oil.

KEROSENE HEATERS

Kerosene is one fuel that's safe to use indoors. This DuraHeat unit is rated to heat 930 sq.ft. at 23,000 BTU/hr. It holds just under 2 gallons of fuel, which is enough for a continuous 12-hour run. If you have kids or pets, you'll appreciate that newer models have an automatic switch-off that kicks in when they're knocked over. One important feature about this style is its ability to heat in all directions. Stan has this heater in his workshop and it keeps the area comfortably warm. A variety of manufacturers make similar-style heaters. Depending on manufacturer and source, expect to pay $110 - $180.

KEROSENE SAFETY

If you are using a kerosene heater, the U.S. Consumer Product Safety Commission and the National Kerosene Heater Association advise the following to minimize risk of fire and potential health effects from indoor air pollution.

- **Use only water-clear 1 K grade kerosene.** Never use gasoline. Gasoline is not the same as kerosene. Even small amounts of gasoline or other volatile fuels or solvents mixed with kerosene can substantially increase the risk of a fire or an explosion.
- **Always store kerosene in a separate container intended for kerosene,** not in a gas can or a can that has contained gasoline. This helps avoid using contaminated fuel or the wrong fuel by mistake. Kerosene containers are usually blue; gasoline containers are usually red.
- **When purchasing kerosene at the pump, make sure to use the kerosene pump, not the gasoline pump.** Some service stations have separate islands for kerosene. Some oil companies have also established quality control programs to minimize the chances of gasoline contamination of kerosene.
- **Purchase 1-K grade kerosene from a dealer who can certify that what is being sold is 1-K.** State operated and private sector certification programs that ensure the quality of kerosene are established in some states. Grades other than 1-K can lead to a release of more pollutants in your home, posing a possible health risk. Different grades of kerosene can look the same so it is important that the dealer certify that the product sold is 1-K grade kerosene.
- **Never refuel the heater inside the home.** Fill the tank outdoors, away from combustible materials, and only after the heater has been turned off and allowed to cool down. Do not refuel the heater when it is hot or is in operation. Do not fill the fuel tank above the "full" mark. The space above the "full" mark is to allow the fuel room to expand without causing leakage when the heater is operating.
- **In case of flare-up or if uncontrolled flaming occurs, do not attempt to move or carry the heater.** This can make the fire worse. If the heater is equipped with a manual shut-off switch, activate the switch to turn off the heater. If this does not extinguish the fire, leave the house immediately and call the fire department. As an added reminder and precaution, install at least one smoke detector near each sleeping area or on each level of the house.
- **Reduce your exposure to indoor air pollutants by properly operating and maintaining your portable kerosene heater.** Although portable kerosene heaters are very efficient in the burning of fuel to produce heat, low levels of certain pollutants such as carbon monoxide and nitrogen dioxide are produced. Exposure to low levels of these pollutants may be harmful, especially to individuals with chronic respiratory or circulatory health problems.

To assure that you and your family aren't exposed to significant levels of pollutants, follow these rules of safe operation:

- Operate your heater in a room with a door open to the rest of the house.
- If you must operate your heater in a room with the door closed to the rest of the house, open an outside window approximately an inch to permit fresh air to effectively dilute the pollutants below a level of concern.
- Always operate your heater according to the manufacturer's instructions, making sure that the wick is set at the proper level as instructed by your manufacturer.
- Keep the wick in your heater clean and in good operating condition by following the cleaning and maintenance procedures recommended by the manufacturer.
- Keep an outside window opened approximately an inch to insure adequate fresh air infiltration. This is true regardless of whether you use a kerosene heater or some other conventional method of heating, if your home is relatively new and tight, or if it is older but has been winterized to reduce air infiltration from the outside.[163]

PROPANE HEATERS

Propane heaters are another option. Certain styles – just a very few – are OK for indoor use; most are for strictly outside operation. Propane makes a lot of sense especially if your home already uses this fuel for its normal heating. Spare fuel is readily available.

HOUSEWARMER

Northern Tool & Equipment carries the HouseWarmer Slim-Profile series. A couple models use propane and several others use natural gas. HouseWarmer heaters are mounted next to exterior or outside walls thick so there's easy access to ventilation. Since provisions need to be made for venting and fuel hook-up, this isn't a unit you crank up immediately after a power outage without prior planning. While the heaters require no electricity, power of some descriptions is required for the .4 amp blower. The HouseWarmer Series make sense if you're in an area that experiences frequent power outages and you'd be motivated to have it already vented and fueled.

The 18,000 BTU propane or natural gas models run around $500 and measure 22¼W x 9⅜D x 25¼"H. The 8,000 BTU models are $400 measuring 18½W x 8 ⅞D x 21¾"H. Northern Tool's customer service stated that either the 8,000 or 18,000 BTU units will heat roughly 500 sq.ft. depending on the home's insulating factors.

Contact **www.northerntool.com** 1.800.221.0516; International Sales: 1.800.221.1589; UK Sales: (02392) 657600.

MR. HEATER

Mr. Heater is a terrific solution for emergency heating! The line currently offers two models suitable for the home. A third, wall-mount only style cannot be used in bathrooms, bedrooms or RVs. They sell two other super models without these caveats. The Buddies are safe to use in a variety of locations like barns, sheds, cabins, campers, patios, garages, hunting blinds and as well as in the home. Their dual heating system combines radiant heat comfort with convection heat airflow for maximum heating efficiency. Both models feature automatic low-oxygen shut off systems. While Mr. Heaters are freestanding, key-shaped holes on the back allow for wall mounting.

The smaller unit, **Portable Buddy**, has two settings – 4,000 & 9,000 BTUs – that heats up to 200 square feet. It operates 3-6 hours on a 1 lb. cylinder and 48-110 hours on a 20 lb. cylinder. Weighing just 8 pounds, Portable Buddy measures 14D x 7W x 14H. Depending on dealer, expect to pay $70-$100.

NOTE: This unit works best at altitudes *below* 5,000 ft. At higher altitudes, its oxygen depletion system cuts off operation. Because this important tidbit is left off many retailer sites, we had to exchange our Buddy heater.

Its brother, **Big Buddy**, heats up to 400 sq. ft. with settings of 4,000, 9,000 and 18,000BTUs. Heating gives a variety of options connecting directly to two, 1-lb disposable cylinders or a 20-lb cylinder with an optional hose. Fire up Big Buddy with an easy push-button piezo starter. Heating time is as follows: 1½-6 hours on one 1lb. cylinder; 3-12 hours on two 1lb. cylinders; 25-110 hours on one 20lb. cylinder; or 50-220 hours on two 20lb. cylinders. The blower fan uses an A/C adapter or 4 D-cell batteries for power. Big Buddy weighs 16 pounds and measures 17D x 10W x 17½H. NOTE: Big Buddy can be used at altitudes up to 7,000 feet. Various dealers price Big Buddy at $120-160. For this item too, Northern Tool & Equipment had the best pricing. Contact www.northerntool.com 1.800.221.0516; International Sales: 1.800.221.1589; UK Sales: (02392) 657600.

REFILLING PROPANE TANKS

Continually throwing away 1 pound propane cylinders becomes an expensive endeavor if you use a lot of fuel. MacCoupler easily solves this problem for less than the cost of 4 or 5 cylinders. For $20 purchase an adapter that lets you refill small cylinders. The MacCoupler E-Z Propane Filler allows you to easily refuel 1 lb. propane cylinders in less than a minute from any 20-40 lb. tank. These are the instructions from their .PDF file explaining how the refilling is accomplished. If your disposable tank has a composite collar hinders attachment of the E-Z Propane Filler, their extension circumvents this issue too. Look for the E-Z Propane Filler at **www.cabelas.com** and **www.harborfreight.com** NOTE: U.S. DOT prohibits transporting re-filled disposable bottles.

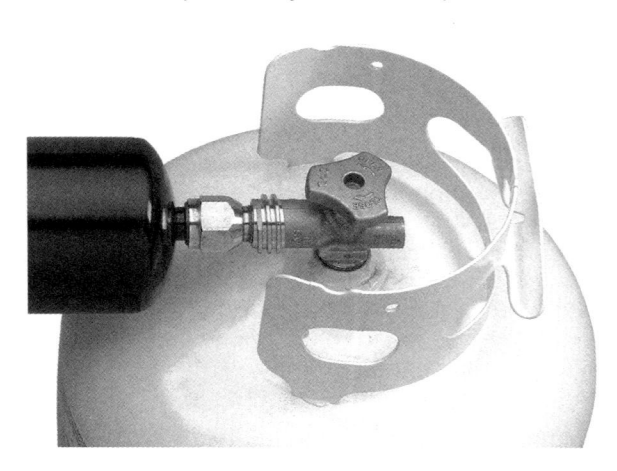

TO REFILL
Step 1 Before refilling, chill small cylinder for 15-20 minutes for the best refill. Have full tank at room temperature, never over 85°F (29.5°C)
Step 2 Connect left-hand threaded lug of E-Z Propane Filler to 20 lb. tank using a wrench.
Step 3 Connect right-hand threaded cap of E-Z Propane Filler to cylinder and hand tighten.
Step 4 Turn the 20 lb. tank on its die so the1 lb. cylinder's bottom points straight up.
Step 5 Open valve on tank for 1 minute, then shut valve.
Step 6 Right the 20 lb. tank so it sits on its base again with 1 lb. cylinder still attached.
Step 7 Disconnect the small cylinder FIRST.
Step 8 Check 1 lb. cylinder for leaks: Place small amount of ½ each soap and water on cylinder opening and on relief valve. If bubbles appear, discard small cylinder in safe area.

CAUTION IN REFILLING CYLINDERS
Don't refill a cylinder:
- If it's rusted or damaged.
- If it's not completely empty.
- If it doesn't have a pressure relief valve.
- In non-ventilated areas.
- Near fires or near smokers.
- With a different gas.

PROPANE CYLINDERS				
Bottle Size	**20#**	**30#**	**40#**	**100#**
Capacity (gallons)	4.7 gal	7.1 gal	9.4 gal	23.6 gal
Weight (empty)	18 lbs	24 lbs	29 lbs	68 lbs
Weight (full)	38 lbs	54 lbs	70 lbs	170 lbs
Overall Height	18 inches	24 inches	29 inches	48 inches
Diameter	12.5 inches	12.5 inches	12.5 inches	14.5 inches
BTU Capacity	4.7 gal	649,980	860,542	2,160,509

Dare To Prepare: Chapter 64: Staying Warm Without Power

IF YOU GET CAUGHT COMPLETELY BY SURPRISE...

Photo: Washington Park, Kansas City, Missouri; January 31, 2002: Many people were without electricity for two weeks when an ice storm swept through the region, bringing down trees, power and telephone lines. The heavy ice layer was more weight than this tree could withstand. (Heather Oliver / FEMA)

Once is a while we all get caught off-guard. More frequently weather surprises us with worse-than-expected storms. As a result, some people have endured three and four week power outages. If you are on a fixed income, experienced power failures that lasted longer than your supplies or you were caught unprepared, it can leave you very cold and completely vulnerable. If the outage is long enough, it can be life threatening.

In the case of a prolonged power failure, take these measures so you won't freeze to death. If you've done nothing at all toward preparing, the following will get you through – alive. Uncomfortable yes, but alive.

SETTING UP WITHOUT HEAT

Chances are you have candles. If you have candles and several space blankets, that's a good start. Here is your game plan.

Step 1: Close off all extra rooms. You don't have to heat the entire house. In a heating emergency, the fewer used, the better. Close doors to all exterior rooms; they will be the coldest – especially north facing rooms in the Northern Hemisphere. For homes south of the equator, the coldest rooms face south. Pack towels around windows that leak air and under doors to prevent cold air coming into your designated room of refuge.

Step 2: Set up a cubby. Use a couple of card tables, a dining room table, a camping tent, or anything that enables you to build an enclosure. Cover whatever you use as the frame with two layers of space blankets. Buy the heavy-duty Sportsman's variety, not the "emergency" mylar space blankets. When covered, the Sportsman returns 80% of your body's heat and these blankets are reusable. Emergency space blankets generally become brittle in 4 or 5 years. The Astrolar (a type of polyethylene) fabric used for the Sportsman's exterior should last about 20 years. The Sportsman also has grommeted corners, which makes setting up this shelter easier than taping or tying a space blanket in place. Unfolded, either type measures 5' x 7' (1.5 x 2.13m). Sportsman blankets run about $12 and they are well worth the $7 price difference over a mylar space blanket.

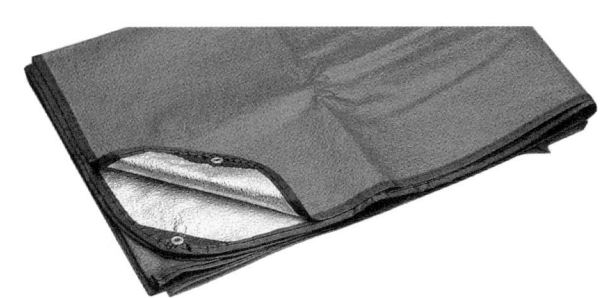

Step 3: Candles. Once the exterior is set up, if you have no other source of heat, even one candle can provide enough warmth to keep the cubby's air above freezing. A single candle can raise ambient temperature of this enclosure by 5-10°F. Two candles work even better. For candle suggestions, consider either NuWick 120 Hour Canned Candle or the 14-Day (yes, *14 day*) Emergency Candle.

EMERGENCY CANDLES

What's nice about the NuWick candle is that it transforms into a little cooker by adding 2-3 wicks. As a 120-hour candle, use only one wick. For heat, add more wicks as needed. Each lead-free, non-toxic wick burns more than 20 hours. Using more wicks cuts down hours of usage. Tweezers and 6 moveable wicks are included for about $10.

If you don't need to cook, the 14 Day Emergency Candle lasts longer. It's housed in a glass container and measures roughly 9" x 4". Product information says it is virtually smokeless and odorless while burning 24 hours a day for up to 14 days. Locate it at www.preparedness.com or www.safetycentral.com for $16.

Step 4: Sleeping Bag. You want the best-quality sleeping bag you can afford. Typically ones with the best insulating capacity have one bag slipped inside another. Former military personnel highly recommend Wiggy's as they are extremely warm, guaranteed for life and come in either the triangular "mummy" style or traditional rectangular dimensions. The mummies have a built-in hood to keep the head area warmer and their more confining style is designed to better warmth. Backpackers favor mummies since their design cuts out excess room making them lighter and easier to carry. Depending on your location and expected needs, Wiggy's sleeping bags are rated as low as -60°F and that is seriously cold!

Wiggy's even make a bag for babies for just $53. These "Baby Bunting" bags are 36" long and fit newborns up to 18 months.

Care for all Wiggy's sleeping bags is simple since they are machine washable and dryable. Expect to pay $200-$350 but they have been known to have terrific summer sales with up to 20% off. Wiggy's contact info: **www.wiggys.com** Grand Junction, Co (headquarters and factory location): 1.866.411.6465; Anchorage, AK: 907.336.1330; Whitehorse, NT, Canada: 867-668-4451.

PERSONAL NOTE: While many people appreciate and prefer the mummy style sleeping bag, I found it claustrophobic. If you like sleeping on your side with your knee bent or move around a lot at night, this is not the style of bag for you.

Another sleeping bag option is two that zip together, sometimes called Adam and Eve bags. There is an advantage in sharing body warmth to generate heat. Women will really appreciate these bags, especially in a power failure, as most say their husbands' bodies naturally throw off a lot heat. Cabelas has a nice line of Adam and Eve bags ranging from $130-$290. However, only their top-of-the-line product would be suitable for this frigid scenario. Their insulating power isn't as high as Wiggy's, but the best Adam and Eve bag protects in temperatures reaching -15°F. Check **www.cabelas.com**; they also have a line of mummy bags rated down to -40°F. Since you can pay nearly $700 for a Marmot bag, make sure you assess what rating is truly needed and what is overkill.

Step 5: Bring your candles and sleeping bag into the cubby. Set the candles a safe distance from flammables and take care not to knock them over. If you have a foam mat to place under the sleeping bag, it will improve comfort and add further insulation. Books and board games will pass the time till civilization returns.

CLOTHING

Keeping your feet and hands, and most importantly – your head – covered go a long way to staying warm. If hyperthermia sets it, about 55 percent of total body warmth leaves through our heads.[164] If your hands become too cold, it will be very difficult to perform even simple tasks. Severe cold makes people clumsier and instead of grasping a lighted candle, you could unintentionally knock it over or drop it.

In addition to ski parkas and regular winter gear, Thinsulate-lined clothing adds warmth without bulk. New fabrics and product lines come to the market every year. One such clothing line is the third generation (Gen III or G3) ECWCSs (Extended Cold Weather Clothing System). These feature seven layers of insulation including three Polartec fabrics: two layers of Polartec Power Dry and a layer of Polartec Thermal Pro High Loft. This clothing line's first field began in August 2007 with the 73rd Cavalry Regiment in Afghanistan. It shouldn't be long till it's produced for the general public.

In the meantime, a little known, but excellent choice is already available and at great prices. Samco has a terrific line that includes jackets, gloves and safety footwear. Some of their clothing is even rated down to -50°F. It has to offer serious cold protection as their products are specially designed for people working in the freezer industry. Their most expensive jacket is only $70. Buy them oversized so you can layer as needed. Sizes range from Small up through 5X. For the oversized pieces an additional fee is charged, but even so, you cannot beat the prices. Contact info: 3499 Lexington Ave. N.; Suit 205; St. Paul, MN 55126; 651.638.3888 or 800.726.2690; Fax: 651.638.3896 **www.freezerwear.com**.

Chapter 65: Preparing for a Pandemic

THE NEXT PANDEMIC

Most emergencies are local. Tornadoes, tsunamis, earthquakes, hurricanes, war, famine and even terrorists target specific areas. Pandemics are unique; they happen everywhere, more or less at the same time. Their capacity to overwhelm is extreme.

Not since 1969 has the world dealt with a worldwide epidemic – a pandemic. No one can predict when the next one will arrive, but based on the last three in this century, we're slightly overdue. Maybe this delay is due to medical improvements or global vigilance or maybe the conditions necessary for mass spreading haven't come together. If that's the case, we'd better pray they don't because a small though growing number of cases exist where H5N1 has passed human-to-human. Today H5N1 – avian flu – is the most likely next pandemic candidate.

The World Health Organization (WHO) views it as such for several reasons:
- Bird flu mutates rapidly and has a history of being able to acquire genes from viruses infecting other animal species.
- It's caused severe illness and death in humans.
- Lab studies show it's highly infectious.
- Birds that survive infection can excrete the virus for at least 10 days making it easier to spread at live poultry markets and by migratory birds.

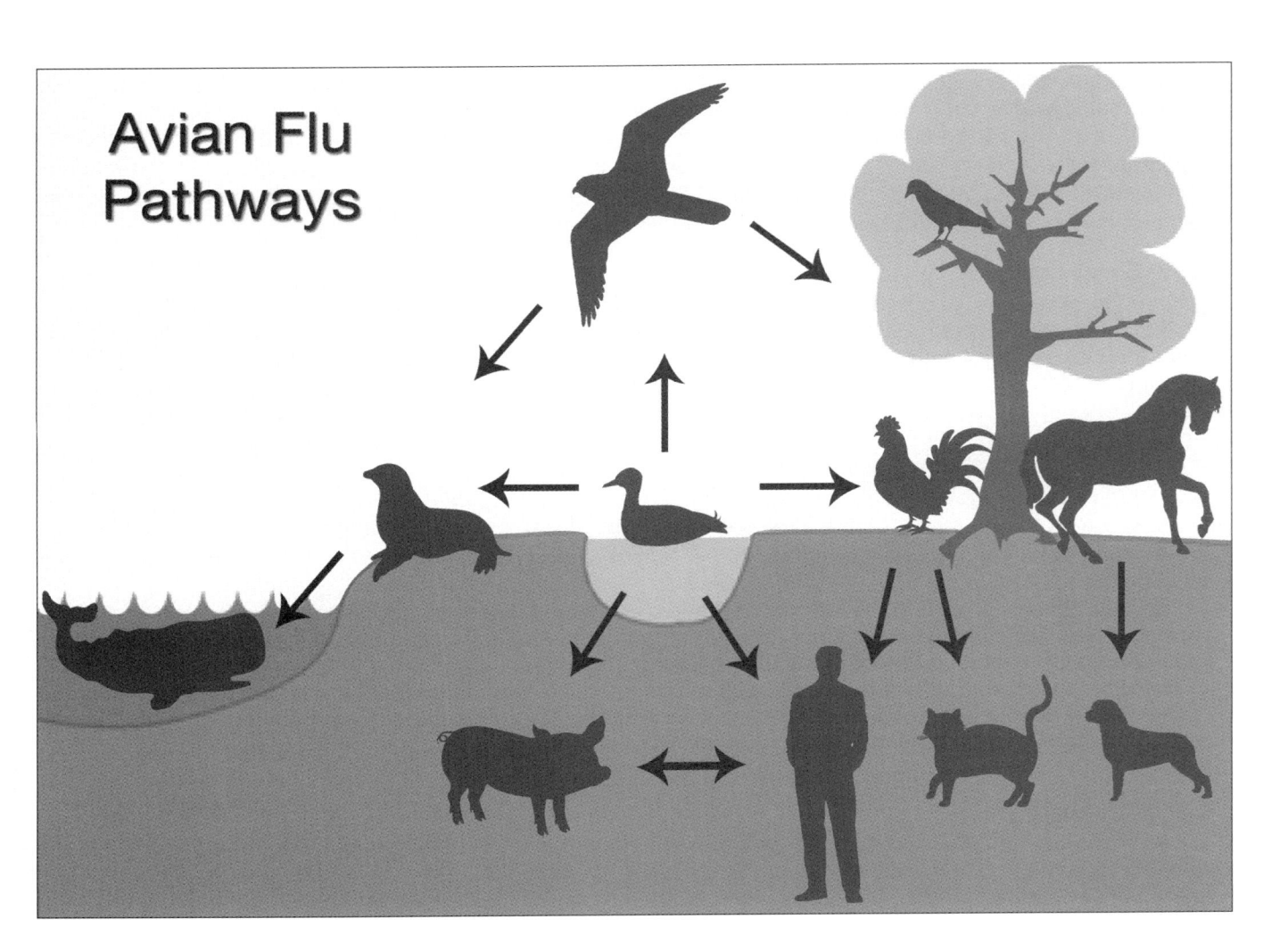

Avian Flu Pathways

NATURAL RESERVOIRS

Wild birds everywhere carry the viruses in their intestines, but most often they remain immune. When domesticated birds come in contact with infected birds, they usually become very ill and die. It is extremely infectious in chickens, ducks, and turkeys. Though transmission from animal to human is still difficult, cases do exist. As the virus mutates, it may make human infection much easier. Once it's easily transmitted person-to-person, the risk of a pandemic escalates dramatically.

BIRD FLU'S ENTRANCE

This influenza started in the Asian countries, as does most flu. H5N1 was first detected in Guangdong, China in 1996. By the next year, outbreaks hit Hong Kong's poultry farms and live animal markets. They saw the first human cases too, where 18 people sickened and six of them died.

Chickens in Asian countries are usually raised in very tight quarters – often in the space of a single sheet of paper. Sometimes the birds live in areas shared by humans. Since the virus is transmitted in birds' saliva, feces and nasal secretions, contamination is a given. Unsanitary conditions and this constant chicken-human interaction amplified the bird flu risk.

At the end of 2003, bird flu showed up in South Korea. By 2004, the virus had a toehold in Thailand, Japan, Indonesia, Viet Nam, Cambodia, Laos and Malaysia.

During 2004, two unsettling events transpired. The virus showed it could kill animals other than birds when two tigers and two leopards that ate fresh chicken carcasses died unexpectedly in a Thailand zoo. The other event held graver implications. The first family cluster appeared raising the likelihood of human-to-human transmission.

By 2007, bird flu had spread to 59 countries from Southeast Asia to China, Russia and Europe.

NORTH AMERICA

CANADA

In 2004, a different strain of bird flu, H7N3, showed up in British Columbia's densely populated Fraser Valley. While lethal to wild birds, it wasn't the strain killing humans. When two cullers experienced headaches and conjunctivitis, their tests showed positive for the mild strain and they made a full recovery. As a precaution, at least 17 million poultry were destroyed.[165] Two smaller outbreaks appeared the next year. One was on a commercial duck farm in Chilliwack, B.C and the other in 2006 on Prince Edward Island. In 2007, H7N3 popped up again in Saskatchewan where 50,000 birds at Pedigree Poultry were destroyed.[166]

UNITED STATES

In 2004 a strain of bird flu showed up on a San Antonio, Texas chicken farm. This was the first time since 1983 that highly infectious avian flu was detected in America. That year two other strains turned up in the northeast. One was found on a central Pennsylvania farm, and the other surfaced on two farms in Delaware and at live bird markets in New Jersey. None was the H5N1 virus that jumped to humans in Asia.[167]

In July 2007, turkeys at a Virginia farm had antibodies to a low pathogenic form of the H5N1. That strain was so mild it usually doesn't kill poultry. However, 54,000 birds were slaughtered as a precaution.[168]

ROUTE TO NORTH AMERICA

With several regions across Russia confirming the deadly H5N1, that's altogether too close to Alaska for comfort. It's theorized by a number of scientists that if – when – the human variety of bird flu hits North America, it will come by this route.

Russian Siberia is only 55 miles from Alaska just across the Bering Strait. The next map shows that birds in eastern Russia regularly travel the East Asia/Australian flyway that encompasses all of Alaska. The East Atlantic flyway also could bring bird flu into Canada's Northwest Territories.

Birds migrating from Asia, which are the most likely to bring avian flu, include Pacific Golden Plover, Northern Pintail, Bar-tailed Godwit, Emperor Goose, Dunlin and the Black Brant. Because birds travel great distances around the world and are natural reservoirs for this flu, a threat anywhere is a threat everywhere.

GRIM NUMBERS

As of November 2008, human avian flu had been confirmed in 15 countries with Indonesia and Viet Nam accounting for more than 60% of the disease. Since 2003, of 387 cases, 245 people have died. A 37% survivability rate is not particularly brilliant.

This disease goes against logic because the traditionally healthiest age groups succumb most readily. Roughly 88% of all fatalities occur in people under 40. From there, the death rate drops dramatically.

But because people are constantly traveling internationally, once this disease makes an easy transition to humans, a full-blown pandemic could ensue.

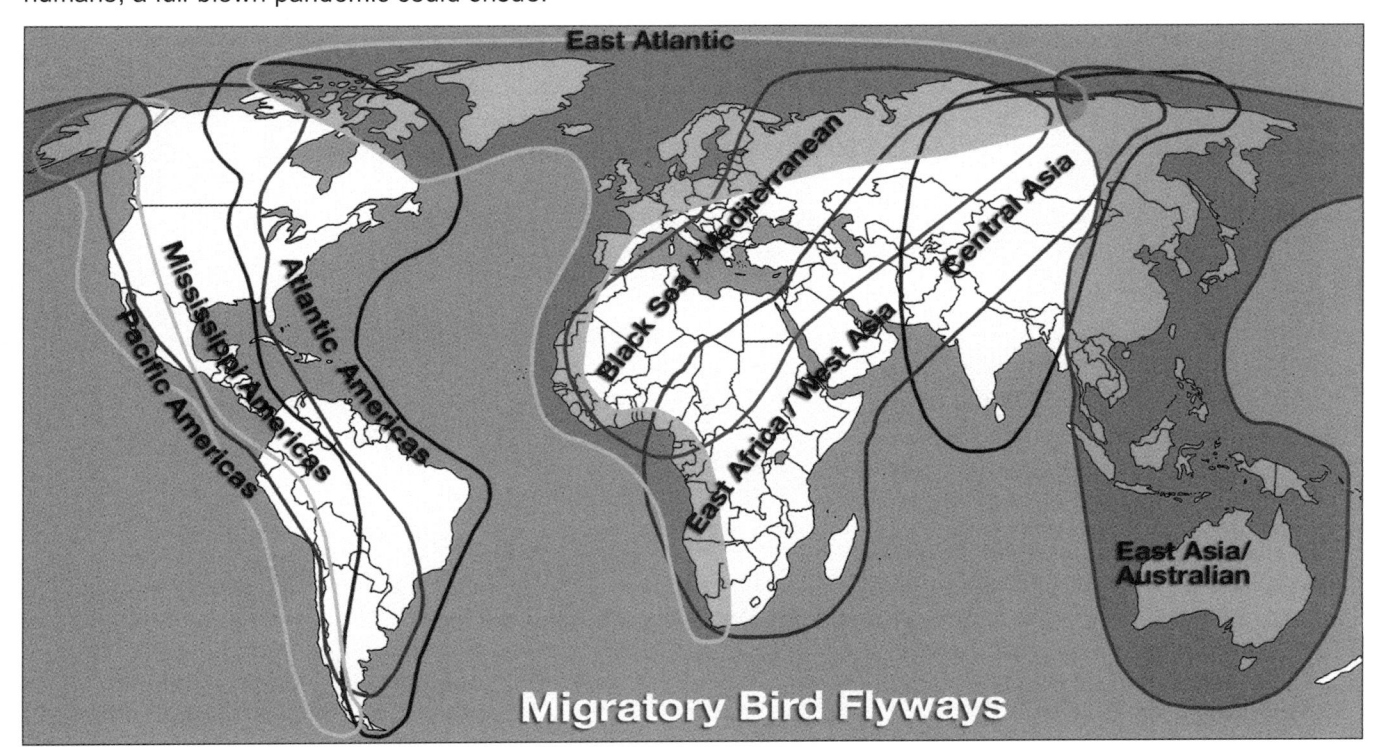

PANDEMIC IMPACTS
Scientists, doctors, academics and government planning agencies have all taken a stab at what the next pandemic might bring. Their numbers vary widely, but suffice it to say, none point to a pleasant picture. They agree on two things: the impact would be mighty and everyone needs to take protective measures both at home and at work. These are some of the scenarios experts fear will come to pass.

SIGNIFICANT DISRUPTION OF:
Health Care System
- Numbered sickened in the US: 90 million
- Hospitals overwhelmed: 10 million people needing admission and 1.5 million in ICU
- Extreme staffing shortages
    - Shortage of beds, facility space, supplies
    - Outpatient treatment: Another 45 million
- Coroner and mortuary services overwhelmed
    - Lack of coffins
- Deaths worldwide: 50 million or more

Infrastructure
- Transportation
- Commerce banking and finance
- Government and commercial facilities
- Defense industrial base (includes broad range from manufacturing, trade, weapons and Coast Guard)
- Public works and utilities
- Energy (dams and nuclear power plants)
- Chemical and hazardous materials management
- Communications
- Emergency response and services
- Postal and shipping
- Food and agriculture
- Water supplies and water treatment

Government and Businesses
- High absenteeism
- Significant threat to continuity of government
- Challenges getting to / from worksite
- Devastating impacts to small businesses
- Psychological impacts on workforce will be extreme
- Economic losses will be extreme and long term
    - US economy: serious recession with immediate costs up to $675 billion; permanent loss of $1.4 trillion.[169]
  - Economic losses globally: some countries may go completely broke

Law Enforcement
- 25% – 35% of officers absent due to illness, death, caring for family members
- 911 dispatch centers operating with reduced staff, higher call volumes
- Large numbers of people unable to purchase food, pay bills – high unemployment and schools closed
- Potential for civil unrest over weeks / months
- Hospitals may become high security areas
- No mutual aid available

Mass Transit / Transportation
- 25% – 35% of drivers, maintenance crews, leadership absent due to illness, death, caring for family
- Mechanics unavailable to affect repairs
- Fuel deliveries reduced in frequency or erratic
- Contractors normally relied upon also impacted

THE KATRINA OF MEDICINE

Pandemics are unique. They happen everywhere, more or less at once. "Avian flu could be the Katrina of medicine." —John Bartlett, chief of infectious diseases at Johns Hopkins University School of Medicine

Because relatively few cases have occurred, scientists don't have that much data to work from. Once the virus mutates and passes easily person-to-person, this disease description may change too. One of the greatest problems is that people may spread bird flu and not even know they themselves are sick.

HISTORICAL PANDEMICS				
Year	Flu Name	Deaths	Pandemic Severity**	Age Most Affected
1918-19	Spanish	50 million *	5	15-35, plus the very young, elderly and infirm
1957-58	Asian	1-4 million	2	Elderly
1968-69	Hong Kong	1 million	2	Over 65

*Newer estimates put death the toll at 50-100 million[170]
**Pandemic Severity Index (PSI) – proposed classification scale for reporting the severity of influenza pandemics in the U.S. See next page.

20TH CENTURY PANDEMICS

On average, about every 30 years disease drags up a global menace. It's ironic that even without as much international travel and before commercial airlines, the 1918 Spanish Flu spread across the world in 2 months.

During its 15-month impact, 30 % of the world's population was infected and about 50 million people died – many within 48 hours of becoming ill. Those who lived for more than a few days often later died of pneumonia. The bird flu, which many feel will be the next pandemic, seems to strike most similarly to the Spanish Flu except that the elderly are relatively unaffected.

PANDEMIC SEVERITY INDEX

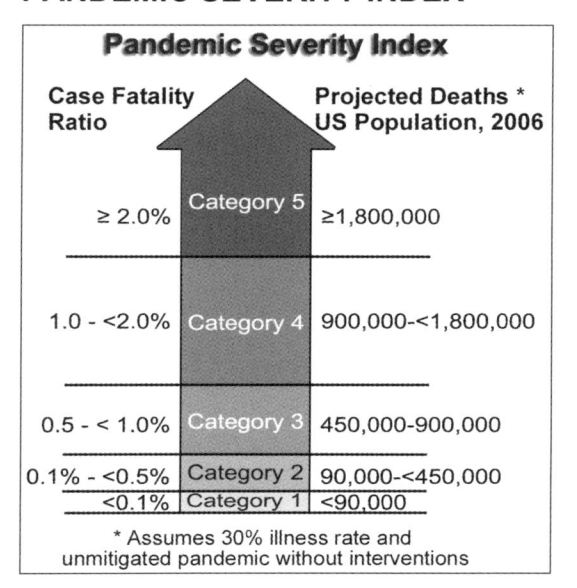

Case Fatality Ratio		Projected Deaths * US Population, 2006
≥ 2.0%	Category 5	≥1,800,000
1.0 - <2.0%	Category 4	900,000-<1,800,000
0.5 - < 1.0%	Category 3	450,000-900,000
0.1% - <0.5%	Category 2	90,000-<450,000
<0.1%	Category 1	<90,000

* Assumes 30% illness rate and unmitigated pandemic without interventions

Anticipating another outbreak, in 2007 the CDC created the Pandemic Severity Index – something akin to the Simpson-Saffir Hurricane scale. The chart is designed to indicate how severe a pandemic is. Once established, communities, businesses and schools would refer to the government's pandemic flu website, **www.pandemicflu.gov.** In a section called "Community Strategy for Pandemic Influenza Mitigation" they would find information how to best deal with the crisis. During the 1918 pandemic, of 44 cities studied, locales that acted quicker and had more protective layers in place fared better.

However, also based on the 1918 pandemic, the Index appears to fall short of the likely death rate – especially since no vaccine is in sight.

BIRD FLU DESCRIPTION
Incubation period:
2-17 days, but the current incubation period for H5N1 may be closer to 10 days[171]

Viral Shedding and Transmission:
- Greatest during the first 2 days of illness
- May be infectious 1-2 days BEFORE symptoms
- Infectious for about 10 days; children may shed virus longer
- On average, each person will transmit flu to two others
- The most common form of transmission is through sneeze, talk, wheeze or cough droplets.

Symptoms:
- Fever higher than 100°F (38 °C)
- Cough similar to regular flu
- Sore throat
- Muscle aches
- Shortness of Breath: Difficulties breathing and pneumonia
- Diarrhea and Abdominal Pain: Watery diarrhea and abdominal pain has been a symptom in some patients, but not all. It shows up before respiratory symptoms. Two young patients had encephalitis and diarrhea without any respiratory symptoms.
- Bleeding of nose and gums: in some patients.
- Vomiting: Nausea and vomiting in some patients.
- Conjunctivitis: common in people with other subtypes of avian flu, but not H5N1 avian flu[172]

Course of the Pandemic:
- In an affected community, a pandemic outbreak will last about 6 to 8 weeks
- Multiple waves (periods during which community outbreaks occur across the country) of illness could occur with each wave lasting 2-3 months.
- In the 1957 pandemic, the second wave began three months after the first wave, but in the 1968 pandemic, the second wave began 12 months after the first wave.
- Absenteeism may approach 40% in a severe pandemic

PREVENTION – THE BEST CURE

Because avian flu currently has at least 16 different strains and is still changing, there is no vaccine. It must mutate further to easy human transmission before doctors can proceed to this stage. When it does, scientists estimate it's still six months to a vaccine. Complicating matters, "American researchers now say the deadly H5N1 form of bird flu has split into two distinct strains, a development that could make it harder to develop vaccines to stop the spread of the disease".[173]

Right now there is no preventative treatment except Tamiflu and Relenza. Both must be taken within 48 hours of getting the flu. The "but" to this is that both of these antivirals are for *regular* influenza. Doctors don't know IF they will even work for bird flu. Tamiflu is showing resistance to the disease and this is the main defense governments have stockpiled.[174]

After receiving reports of patients experiencing delirium, psychosis and hallucinations, U.S. FDA staff recommend that flu drugs, Tamiflu and Relenza should carry warnings about possible side-effects.[175] However, if it's a life-saving choice between temporarily crazy or a 2-in-3 chance of dying, people will probably latch onto Relenza.

In a half ditch effort, doctors recommend people get a regular flu shot thinking it will beef up their overall immunity. For it to remotely work, scientists would have to "get it right" better than they did for the 2007-2008 flu season. That vaccine was pronounced only 40% effective.

HOW LONG CAN AVIAN FLU SURVIVE ON SURFACES?

The length of time varies with the surface ranging from 5 minutes to 48 hours. "Influenza viruses can survive for 24-48 hours on hard, nonporous surfaces such as stainless steel and plastic but survive for less than 8 hours on cloth, paper, and tissues. Influenza can be transferred from stainless steel surfaces to hands for 24 hours and from tissues to hands for up to 15 minutes. Virus survives on hands for up to 5 minutes after transfer from environmental surfaces. In order to prevent transfer and infection it is important to clean environmental surfaces and practice thorough hand hygiene regularly during the working day."[176]

HAND-WASHING: MEDICAL MARVEL

This simple little act is still the best prevention for bird flu and many other diseases. Because they spread in nasal, cough and sneeze droplets or when people talk, viruses have the potential to land everywhere. Large droplets can only travel a limited range and people should limit close contact with infected individuals to within 6 feet.

Everything we touch has the ability to feed those germs directly to us. Hands are the great germ transporters. Without washing, disease can get into your system just by touching your eyes, nose or mouth. That's why hand washing is vital.

A serious 20-second hand scrub is still the best defense. This doesn't mean a quick squirt of water and out the door. Work up lather with warm water, and then scrub palms, back of hands, between fingers and under nails. Rinse.

MASKS

Should bird flu come to your area, wearing a mask and personal protective equipment (PPE) is "good medicine" if you have to go out in public. Dust masks are NOT effective in this instance and gas masks are overkill. Bad pun not intended. So what is the right protection?

NIOSH-APPROVED N95, N99 AND N100 RESPIRATORS

Buy only NIOSH (National Institute for Occupational Safety and Health) and FDA-approved masks. In Europe, the equivalent is an FFP2 rating. NIOSH will printed on the facepiece, exhalation valve cover, or head straps, along with the manufacturer's name. If a respirator does not have these markings it hasn't been certified by NIOSH.

The right kind of mask for protecting against avian flu is also known as a "particulate respirator" or "air-purifying respirator" because they filter particles out of the air as you breathe. They protect *only* against particles – not gases or vapors. Since avian influenza is a virus particle, particulate respirators can filter it.

Respirators are given one of 9 different ratings based on their ability to filter out contaminants and how well they work around oil. The number refers to what percent of contaminants they filter and the letter pertains to the oil issue. The "P" (oil-Proof) rating is important because some industrial oils can degrade filter performance to the point that it doesn't work adequately. This generally isn't an issue for bird flu considerations. The ratings go like this: "N" if they are Not resistant to oil (N95, N99, N100); "R" if they are somewhat Resistant to oil (R95, R99, R100); and "P" if they are strongly resistant (P95, P99, P100). Masks earn their rating tested under "worst case" scenarios.

N95 Healthcare Particulate Respirator & Surgical Masks

1500N95

3200N95

N95 Particulate Respirators

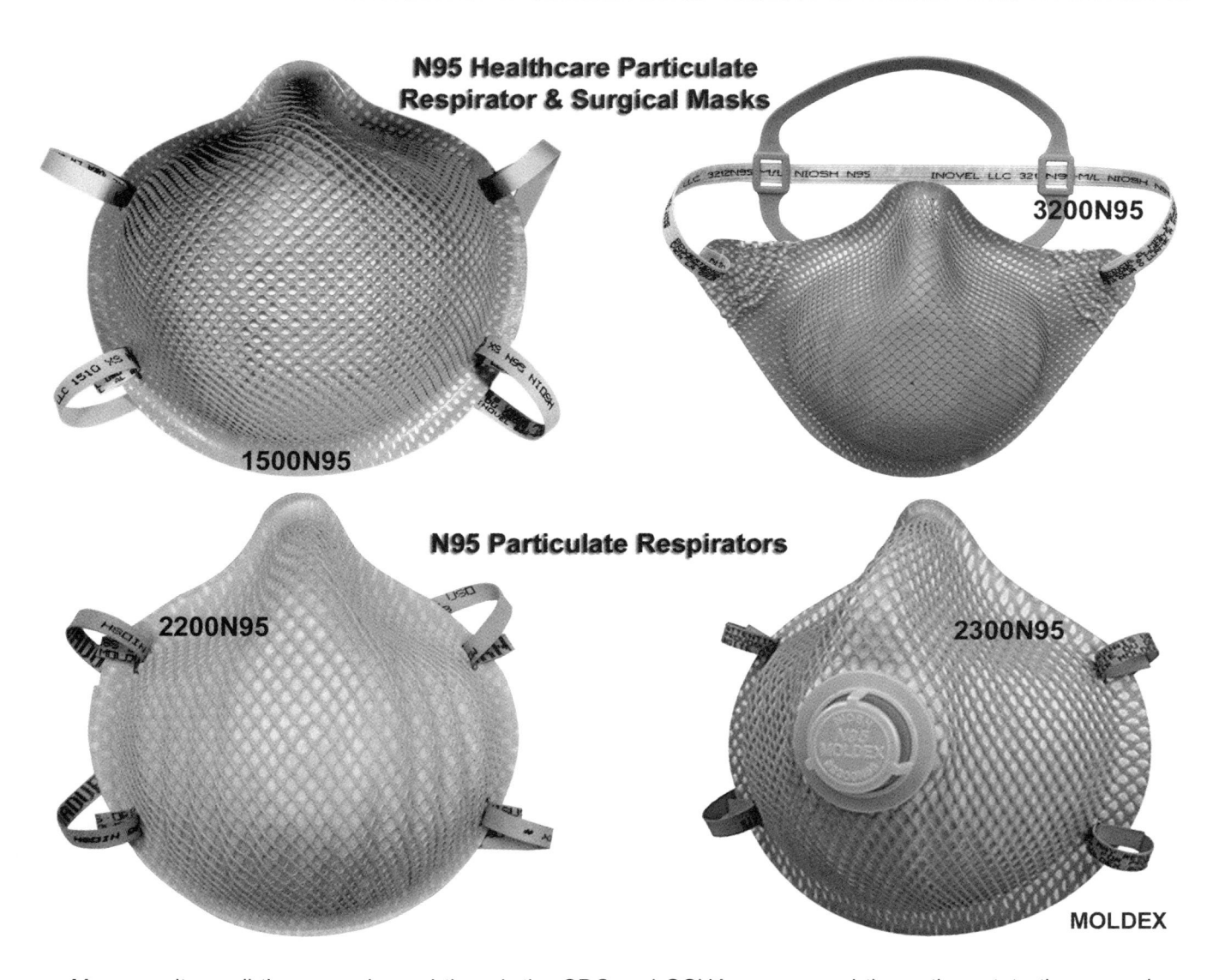

2200N95

2300N95

MOLDEX

Many wesites sell these masks and though the CDC and OSHA recommend them, they state these respirators are *minimum* protection. By calling them *minimum protection* gives the CDC an "out", because they don't protect unconditionally.

SIZE MATTERS

N95 respirators filter out 95% of harmful bacteria, viruses, etc. that you might breathe in. Respirators rated N99, filter out 99% of the same materials. N100 respirators remove 99.97% or essentially 100%, but there's a catch. None can filter out viruses by themselves. They're just too small.

N95 respirators are only capable of protecting against things that are .3 microns and larger. Viruses by nature are much smaller. If you look at Reverse Osmosis Filtering Spectrum in Chapter 5, you'll see viruses at their biggest, are just slightly over 0.1 microns.

Even highest rated N100 masks aren't capable of blocking them. It's still a matter of filtering size. These masks are efficient protection against meningitis, some smallpox, TB, pneumonia and anthrax. They are too porous to shield for hepatitis, herpes, SARS; influenzas A, B and C; hanta virus, AIDS, hepatitis B and others. The most telling comments come from major international respirator manufacturers. Both 3M and Aearo Technologies posted this comment. Cooper Safety Supply who sells 3M and North Safety also carries this warning on respirators protecting people from bacteria and viruses:

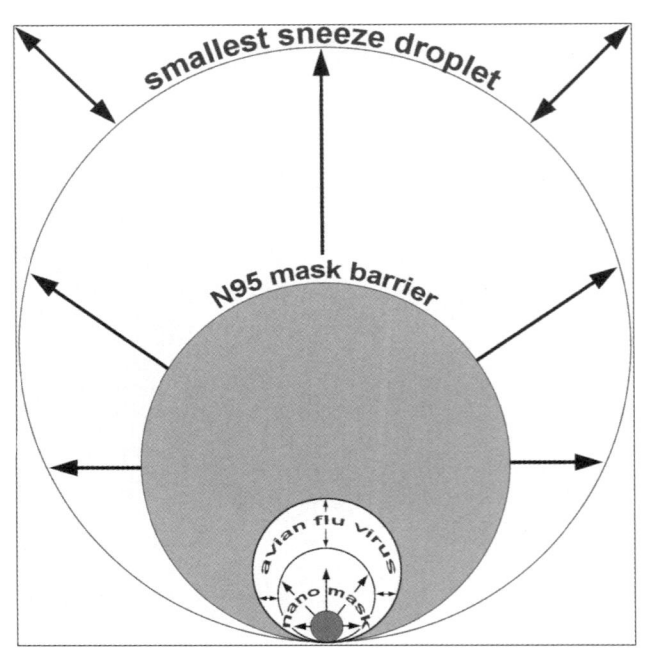

"Respirators are designed to reduce exposures of the wearer to airborne hazards. Biological agents, such as viruses, are particles and can be filtered by particulate filters with the same efficiency as non-biological particles having the same physical characteristics (size, shape, etc.). However, unlike most industrial particles there are no exposure limits established for biological agents. Therefore, while respirators will help reduce exposure to avian influenza viruses, there is no guarantee that the user will not contract avian flu. Respirators may help reduce exposures to airborne biological contaminants, but they don't eliminate the risk of exposure, infection, illness, or death."177

IMPORTANT NOTE: These respirators should be sufficient protection IF the disease doesn't mutate to airborne transmission. Airborne virus particles are much smaller than those carried by droplets and can travel much further than a sneeze's 6-foot spread.

THE SNEEZE FACTOR

Health officials count on the humble sneeze to keep us safe. When you sneeze, about 40,000 big droplets rocket out of the mouth at 90mph. Uncovered a mouth can spew germs up to 6 feet away. No wonder they're everywhere! Sneeze particles range in size from ½ to 5 microns – roughly 6 times the size of the avian flu virus. That's the key to keep us flu-free when using N95 – N100 masks. Since these masks block particles .3 microns and larger, they work simply by default. Virus-carrying sneeze drops are too big to pass through the mask.

So far they seem are the most reliable protection though not foolproof.

EXHALATION VALVES

Some filtering facepiece and all rubber-like respirators have an exhalation valve, which lowers the effort required to exhale. It also reduces the dampness and warmth that forms in the mask from breathing out. The valve opens to release exhaled breath and closes while breathing in so that inhaled air goes through the filter. These valves look like a button in the center of the mask. (See Moldex mask 2300N95 on previous page.)

People with infectious diseases whose germs can spread through exhalation droplets shouldn't use respirators with these valves. Also, healthcare givers shouldn't wear them around patients with open wounds.

If you are asthmatic or have emphysema, you might want to consider a PAPR – Powered Air-Purifying Respirator. This mask is a hood that fits loosely over the entire head. Not only is breathing nearly effortless, they are also helpful for people with claustrophobia. PAPRs use HEPA filters, which are as efficient as P100 filters for protection against airborne infectious agents. Powered air-purifying respirators provide a higher level of protection than disposable respirators. (See Chapter 40 on buying a Gas Mask and Filters.)

DISPOSABLE OR REUSABLE?

While disposable respirators may be more convenient and cheaper individually, a reusable respirator can be more economical in the long run. You'll need to assess how often you might have to go out into the public. If you are well prepared and plan to stay home during a pandemic, disposable respirators might work best. If you expect repeated possible exposure for whatever reason, your dollars would be best spent on a reusable mask. Reusable masks also sidestep respirator shortages. All it will take is a *hint* that avian flu has mutated to easy human transmission, and masks will be unavailable. If you opt for a disposable mask, make sure you've purchased plenty for all family members. For reusable respirators, be sure to buy replacement filters.

3M HALF FACEPIECE RESPIRATOR

3M's reusable Half Facepiece Respirator comes in three sizes: 6100 (small), 6200 (medium) and 6300 (large). Pictured here, the respirator is paired with a P100 filter and can be used in combination with NIOSH approved 3M 2091 Filters.

FIT TEST CHECK (WITH 2091 FILTERS)

Step 1 Place your thumbs on the center of the filters and restrict the airflow into the filters' breathing tube. Inhale gently. If you feel facepiece collapse slightly and pull closer to your face with no leaks between the face and facepiece, the mask fits properly.

Step 2 If the mask leaks air, reposition respirator on face and/or readjust tension of straps.

Step 3 Repeat above steps until the face seal is tight.

NOTE: If you can't achieve a proper seal, don't enter a contaminated area.

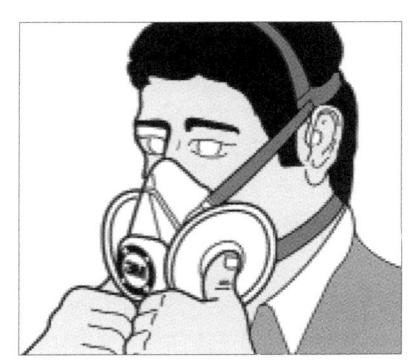

FILTERS

Replace the 2091 P100 filters if they are damaged, dirty or if it becomes harder to breathe. These filters should be replaced after 40 hours of use or 30 days, whichever is first.

As with filters for bio-chemical protection or gas masks, keep them sealed in the manufacturer's packaging, not exposed to the elements. You don't want them absorbing contaminants or moisture from the air, which will shorten the filter's service life.

INSPECT MASK AFTER USING AND CLEANING

- Check facepiece and inhalation valves for cracks, tears and dirt. Make sure facepiece, especially face seal area, isn't warped.
- Check the head straps to see that they are intact and have good elasticity.
- Examine all plastic parts for cracks or fatigue. Make sure filter gaskets are properly seated and in good condition.
- Remove exhalation valve cover and examine exhalation valve and valve seat for signs of dirt, distortion, cracking or tearing.
- Replace exhalation valve cover.

NOTE: For proper cleaning, see DISINFECTING MASKS AND PPE CLOTHING in this chapter.

SURGICAL MASKS

These loose fitting masks are less protection. They often form gaps around the face letting in all the things you want to keep at bay. A face-to-mask seal is vital. If it came to using these versus wearing nothing, they're a step up, but who'd want to bet their life on them when other choices available.

Even OSHA admits their limitations. "It should be noted that barrier protection, such as a surgical mask or face shield, will protect against droplet transmission of an infectious disease but will not protect against airborne transmission, to the extent that the disease may be spread in that manner."[178]

Further, "Surgical masks are not designed or certified to prevent the inhalation of small airborne contaminants. These small airborne contaminants are too little to see with the naked eye but may still be capable of causing infection."[179]

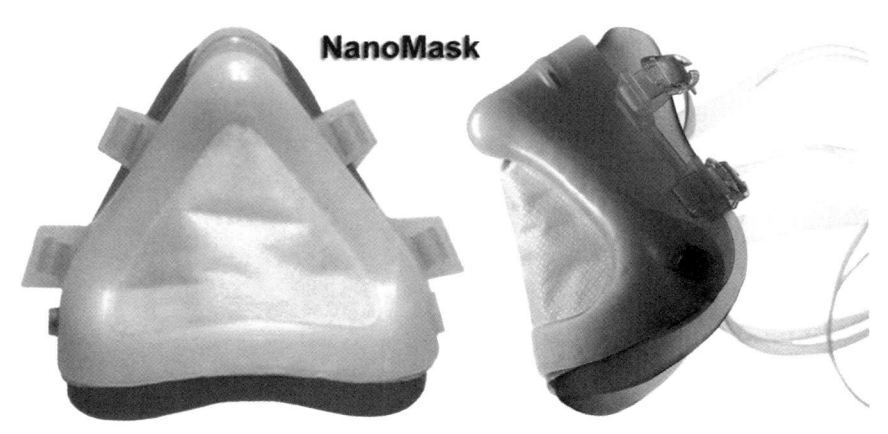

NANOMASKS

NanoMasks are one of the few products available that have tested well against avian flu. In addition to extensive testing by Nelson Laboratories in Salt Lake City, Utah, Turkey used these masks when they were hit by bird flu in 2006.[180]

NanoMasks use 2H Technology Plus™, a patented nanotech-enhanced filter media. Emergency Filtration Products, maker of the NanoMask, claims it removes viruses and bacteria and destroys them. Whether these claims are well founded remains to be seen. At press time, the company was still waiting on final clearance. Even without FDA approval NanoMasks are sold in other countries as well as on numerous Internet sites.

The simple two-piece facemask is reusable. Adjustable head straps provide a custom fit and good seal on the face. As in all instances where a good mask-to-face seal is vital, beards, stubble or moustaches should be shaved. NanoMasks are made to sit lower on the face, which makes them comfortable, and they won't interfere with glasses.

POSSIBLE DRAWBACKS

Because NanoMasks are chemically coated to destroy viruses and bacteria, this feature has a shelf life of only two years. The micron filtering size is good and not dependent on the germ-destroying feature.

One other aspect to keep in mind is filter surface area. NanoMask's filter is about one-third the size of N95-100 series. While it might be very comfortable, the length of time it can be worn before clogging could be considerably shorter.

USING YOUR NANOMASK

Handle the mask by using straps and don't wear it around the neck.

Keep the NanoMask dry. If the mask gets wet, it can't filter out microorganisms and then offers no protection.

When not in use, hang it by the straps where it won't contaminate anything. Don't place the mask in plastic or other types of bags as it will contaminate the interior and infect you when you remove it.

While putting on the NanoMask, wear gloves to position the mask. Remove the gloves and wash your hands before putting on the rest of the protective equipment.

When the NanoMask is no longer needed or the mask becomes wet or contaminated, it must be disposed of in the infectious waste bin for incineration.

NANOMASK FILTER REPLACEMENT

You should be able to wear the mask for 6-8 hours before filter replacement is necessary. They are individually wrapped with a shelf life of two years. IMPORTANT: Before purchasing replacements, verify with the retailer that the filters are not out of date. For supplies check **www.nanomask.co.uk**.

HOW MANY DISPOSABLE MASKS DO I NEED?

How many masks you'll need depends on your expected exposure. In the case of pandemic flu, a second round follows the first wave of the disease within a few months, so you may want to double mask quantities to be prepared for both events. These are *suggested* mask quantities for a pandemic lasting 12 weeks. It covers the first wave only. Based on the number of masks possibly needed, it may be more cost effective to purchase a reusable respirator or have a combination of both.

SUGGESTED NUMBER OF MASKS PER PERSON FOR 12 WEEKS PROTECTION		
Setting	Masks	Comment
Healthcare Workers	180	Constant use during shifts. Normally a worker needs at least 1 mask per shift. Using 3 masks per shift working 5 shifts a week for 12 weeks equals 180 per worker. Since healthcare workers historically have the highest exposure, stocking up on masks and respirators is a good investment. Some hospitals require a mask change between patients, but this would be impractical if many patients were placed in a single room.
Essential Public Service Workers	180	Based on 40-hour work week and following the possibility of the same mask use as healthcare personnel. See employer policy for mask use.
Family of Infected Patients	180	Wear a respirator type mask such as an N95, N99 or N100 rated mask when close to victim. Don't reuse the mask once it is taken off. Remember that respirator type masks are not made to fit children so children should be kept away from infected individuals and other sources of bird flu infection.
Patients In or Out of the Hospital	336	Stock up on surgical masks for victims. Do not use respirators with exhalation valves on patients. If hospitalized, see policy regulating mask use.
In Direct Contact With Live or Dead Poultry or Wild Birds	180	Wear while working. If working at a commercial poultry operation. See employer policy for mask use.
Funeral Service Personnel	180	Wear a mask when working with victims. Adjust amount depending upon time worked and use of mask. See employer policy for mask use.
At Home, Occasional Trips in Public During an Outbreak	36	Most people will choose to stay at home. However, circumstances may arise when possible exposure is unavoidable.

MASK OF LAST RESORT

This mask from the CDC is one you can make at home. HOWEVER, this should not be used in place of a NOISH/FDA-approved N95-or-higher-rated surgical respirator. It should be considered a last ditch effort at protection and better than nothing. Remember, it's better to bail a boat with a pump than a paper cup, but if a cup is all you have...

The CDC's website says the following about this reusable, cotton mask: "The World Health Organization recommends protective equipment including masks (if they are not available, a cloth to cover the mouth is recommended) for persons who must handle dead or ill chickens in regions affected by H5N1. Quality commercial masks are not always accessible, but anecdotal evidence has showed that handmade masks of cotton gauze were protective in military barracks and in healthcare workers during the Manchurian epidemic. A simple, locally made, washable mask may be a solution if commercial masks are not available."[181]

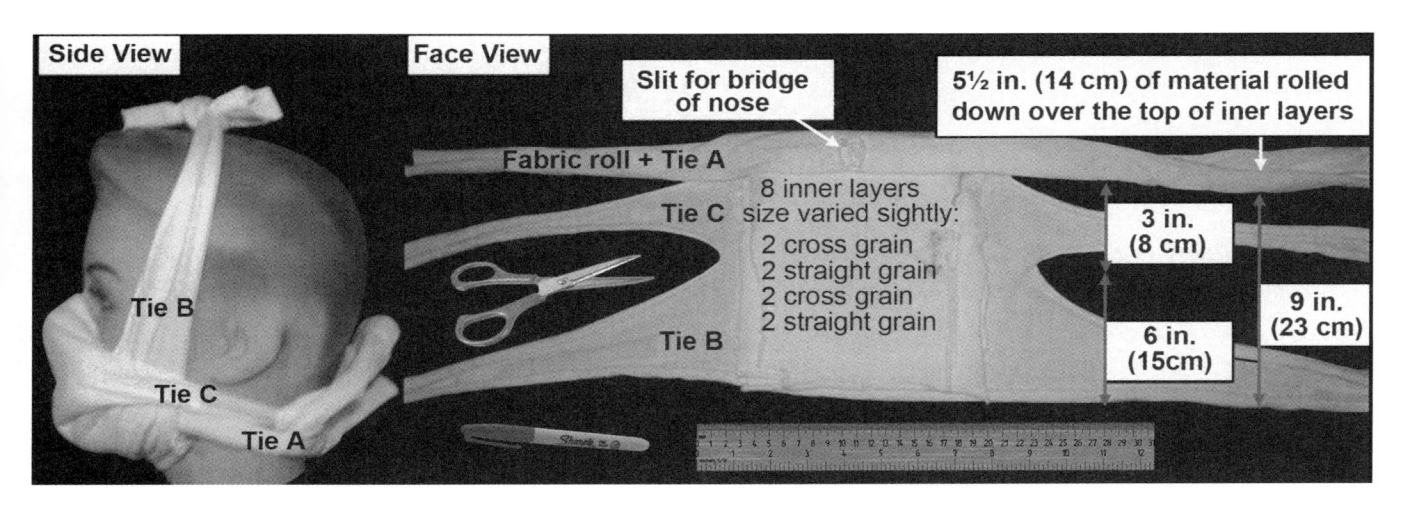

TO MAKE

Choose a heavy T-shirt like Hanes Heavyweight 100% preshrunk cotton. Make sure the T-shirt doesn't contain other fabrics like polyester that prevents shrinkage; use cotton-only.

Boil shirt for 10 minutes to maximize shrinkage. They air-dry. NOTE: Instructions didn't call for using a dryer. It might be that developing countries – for which these instructions were primarily written – don't have ready access to them.

With scissors, marker and ruler cut out one outer layer measuring 14½" x 37½" (37 × 72 cm) and 8 inner layers measuring 7 x 7" (18 x 18 cm). Assemble and fit the mask as shown.

TO WEAR

First, place the nose slit over the bridge of the nose and tie the roll below the back of the neck (Tie A). Adjust the area around the nose to eliminate leakage. If the seal isn't tight, adjust fit by adding extra material under the roll between the cheek and nose or by pushing the rolled fabric above or below the cheekbone. Fasten Tie B over the head. Add a cloth extension if Tie B is too short. Fasten Tie C behind the head. Test the mask for fit.

IMPORTANT REMINDER

This make-it-yourself mask was reviewed and tested by a Los Alamos National Laboratories panel. They found that though it was "insufficient (protection) for the workplace, this mask offered substantial protection from the challenge aerosol and showed good fit with minimal leakage.

"We do not advocate use of this respirator in place of a properly fitted commercial respirator. Although subjectively we did not find the work of breathing required with the prototype mask to be different from that required with a standard N95 filtering facepiece, persons with respiratory compromise of any type should not use this mask. While testers wore the mask for an hour without difficulty, we cannot comment on its utility during strenuous work or adverse environmental conditions."[182]

Translation: Use this mask as a <u>last</u> <u>ditch</u> <u>effort</u> for protection. It's better than nothing and will help fend off germs, but won't offer the protection of an N95 commercial respirator.

The same caveats apply as for other masks. Remove facial hair for the closest and best fit.

PPE (PERSONAL PROTECTIVE EQUIPMENT)

Whatever mask you choose, the eyes need protection. Any goggles that allow a good field of vision and snug up to the skin should work fine.

If you're going to walk through high exposure areas, a full protective suit is necessary, including gloves and boot or shoe covers.

SAFE DISPOSAL OF WORN PPE
- Always wear medical gloves
- Place used PPE into a tied plastic bag
- Carefully clean waste containers with disinfectant or diluted bleach (1 part bleach to 9 parts water)
- Wash hands thoroughly with soap and water or alcohol-based hand rub after handling.

DISINFECTING MASKS AND PPE CLOTHING

REUSABLE 3M MASKS
- **Step 1** Remove cartridges and filters.
- **Step 2** Clean facepiece (excluding filters and cartridges) by immersing in warm cleaning solution, water temperature not above 120°F (49°C), and scrub with soft brush until clean. Add neutral detergent if necessary. Don't use cleaners containing lanolin or oil. They can degrade the rubber and reduce the respirator's effectiveness.
- **Step 3** Disinfect the facepiece by soaking in a solution of 1-ounce (30ml) bleach to 2 gallons (7½L) of water, or in a solution of quaternary ammonia disinfectant.
- **Step 4** Rinse in fresh, warm water and air-dry in an uncontaminated atmosphere.

NANOMASK MASKS
Step 1 Wash the frame in warm (110°F/43°C maximum) water with a mild detergent, then rinse thoroughly in clean, warm (110°F/43°C max.), preferably running water.
Step 2 If the detergent doesn't contain a disinfecting agent, immerse the mask for two minutes in any of these:
- ½ tsp (2.5ml) laundry bleach to 1 quart of water at 110°F (43°C).
- ¼ tsp (1ml) tincture of iodine, like Lugol's solution, to 1 quart of water at 110°F (43°C).
- Quaternary ammonia disinfectant, one packet per 2 gallons or per manufacturer's recommendation.

Step 3 Rinse thoroughly as instructed above. Detergents or disinfectants that dry on the frame may result in dermatitis and may cause the frame's rubber to deteriorate.
Step 4 Allow the respirator to air dry in a non-contaminated environment out of sunlight.
Do not share respirators.

CLOTHING
For a 5 gallon bucket:
Step 1 Dilute Chlorine Bleach Solution: 1 part 5% bleach to 99 parts water. See bleach bottle for percentage of chlorine.
Step 2 Mix 3 ounces of chlorine bleach (about ⅓ cup) with 5 gallons water minus ⅓ cup of water.
Step 3 Allow clothing, shoes and other reusable equipment soak for 15 minutes. The solution can also be used to rinse gloves and boots after having contact with possible contaminate. Health care personnel working in basic conditions can use this solution after leaving a patient's room.
Step 4 After soaking, the water should still smell of bleach. If not, add more bleach and wait another 15 minutes.
Step 5 After disinfecting, wash clothing as usual with laundry detergent. Rubber shoes and aprons can be reused after disinfection.
Important Common Sense Note: Dispose of solution after 24 hours or before if solution no longer smells like chlorine. If the solution doesn't smell like chlorine, there is none left to kill any remaining germs.

DON'T WAIT TILL THE BOAT SINKS TO START BAILING
"We can predict now 12 to 18 months of stress of watching loved ones die, of wondering if you are going to have food on the table the next day. Those are all things that are going to mean that we are going to have to plan – unlike any other crisis that we have had in literally the last 80-some years in this country."[183]

With each pandemic influenza outbreak lasting from 6 to 8 weeks and waves continuing for a year or more, it is absolutely essential to have your family plan in place. If you are a business owner, ditto this statement.

Judging from impacts on infrastructure, nearly everything we depend on and expect to function either would be MIA – missing in action – or severely impaired. People should prepare as if they were going on a six-month camping trip with possibly miserable side effects.

In a 2005 interview, Tom Brokaw admitted he and his wife were stockpiling six months of supplies at their country home for a pandemic. Considering people who fluff off unpleasant possibilities, it must have been a sobering moment. When seemingly unflappable Brokaw revealed he gave the pandemic threat serious thought, it set a good example for the rest of the world. How many public figures ever admit preparing for anything? Moreover, how many other people acted?

The time to get ready is now, not when the first dead bird drops in your backyard.

FOOD SUPPLIES: JUST-IN-TIME SEVERELY IMPAIRED
During the 1918 Spanish flu pandemic, Americans lived a different lifestyle. More than half of the people lived rurally and produced their own food. They had their own water well. They were self-sufficient. By mid-century, only 43% of Americans lived on farms.[184]

Today, thanks to mechanized farming and years of young people migrating to cities, this number has shrunk to just 1%.[185] Instead of growing our own food, we depend on grocery stores. In many stances, women's careers have taken precedence over learning to cook and if it weren't for microwaveable food or take-out, families wouldn't eat.

Grocery stores' profiles, too, have changed over the years. Once fully stocked on-site warehouses have been whittled to shaky 3-day supplies. Replenishing trucks roll to and from stores with the precision of a marching band. What happens when the band stops playing?

If you have prepared your family for other possible emergencies, chances are your stored food is in good shape. Should this not be the case, once word is out that human bird flu is here, panic ensues – especially for those ill prepared. People would swoop to the stores and suck food and water off the shelves in a matter of hours.

Poultry of all varieties would experience mass culling making a huge dent in available protein. Eggs, another major protein source, would be scarce. People who had stocked up on dehydrated and freeze-dried yolks and whites would be very glad. As a result of massive culls, all egg-based vaccines would be very expensive and regular flu would have few impediments.

Once avian flu hits and people fall ill, truckers supplying food would likely refuse or may be unable to haul. Either they will have sickened or they'd be afraid of driving to areas where disease is raging. We often forget that truckers bring 70-80% of all food, equipment and goods to store shelves. If trucks don't roll, stores aren't restocked and restocking would not likely resume until the bird flu waves had passed.

Be sure to have a large supply of canned items on hand. If the public water system is functioning only intermittently, relying on dehydrated and freeze-dried foods will further deplete your stored supplies. While these foods are great choices in many circumstances, they carry obvious drawbacks if water supplies are at a premium.

Plan to have some shelf-stable foods like MREs or HeaterMeals that require no cooking. There may be times when you are too stressed or too tired and need a cook-free evening.

See Chapter 8 on long term stored food and use the Deyo Food Storage Planner to help with your selections.

WATER SUPPLIES

This area remains the most challenging for the greatest number of people. Water is heavy and it requires a lot of room to store. One of the most alarming impacts to infrastructure is that on water treatment plants. With only a 5-7 day supply of on-site chlorine, potable water would be a big question mark. Personnel are likely to fall ill at the same rate as the rest of the population. Should the power grid fail, water couldn't be transported to homes and businesses. Back-up generators may only be functional another few days and then we're on our own. With so many variables, how long the public water system would function is anyone's guess.

WELLS
This is another instance when living rurally is truly a blessing. People with this resource would become very popular! Be sure that any well openings are covered so the water is not contaminated.

WATER CATCHMENT
As you've read in Chapter 6, Stan and I used our rooftop rain for our main water source in Australia. With bird flu in country, it would be imperative to filter and disinfect this water in addition to concerns for giardia and cryptospordia. Remember birds can excrete the virus for up to 10 days after they have recovered from H5N1. See Chapter 6 for installing and using a rainwater catchment system.

WATER BODIES
It might be that people living in highly urbanized areas and unable to temporarily relocate will use their stored fuel for runs to haul water. People without adequate stored water or lacking out-of-sight storage space may need to rethink priorities. If it comes to cluttered living areas with filled rain barrels versus going thirsty, the question then becomes *how many barrels can I squeeze inside*. This wouldn't be recommended during normal times, but in an extreme emergency when water supplies could be at serious risk, it's any easy choice.

ENERGY

Avian flu would likely strike utility plant employees at the same rate as the general populace. Who then would man coal trains carrying this fuel to destination? In the county where Stan and I live, 100-plus car coal trains pass through several times each day. They supply a massive amount of coal to various plants. With these daily runs, you can bet there is virtually no extra coal stored on-site. Similarly, hydroelectric facilities and nuclear plants require supervision and personal attention.

In a worst-case scenario, significant portions of the power grid could go down. See Chapter 28 for a discussion of the fragile electrical grid and what is and isn't being done to fix the problem. It gives alternative power ideas.

PREPPING FOR PANDEMIC

In short, prepare for a possible pandemic, whether it is avian flu or some other strain, in much the same manner as you would any other emergency. You will need first aid supplies in addition to the masks and PPE clothing. Read Chapter 14 on first aid for thorough lists to build a complete kit.

Check the chapters on water purification and storage as well as your food supplies.

Communication, too, is vital. Undoubtedly emergency broadcasting would be in place with cable TV to fill in should local stations be unavailable.

Two-way radios are good for touching base with neighbors or family members. One of the best investments you can make would be a shortwave radio. During past emergencies ham operators have been invaluable. For more information communications, see Chapter 32.

Keep games and books on hand. Depending on strength, length and duration of the pandemic, quarantines in-house or otherwise are a given. These will serve to keep everyone's mind off the problem and occupied.

If the worst happens and trash pick-up ceases, you'll want a supply of heavy-duty garbage bags. *Lots* of them. In some instances you may need to double-bag to keep odor down till service is restored. Should it be safe to go outside, burying it is another option. In case sewer systems aren't operating, read Chapter 36 for toilet alternatives and hygiene information.

If power is out, see Chapters 28-31 and Chapter 63 for various solutions for heat, light and cooking.

Last, don't forget your pets. They will need food and water, kitty litter or any other specialty items suited to your pet. Check Chapter 37 on Pet Preparedness.

Chapter 66: Preparing for Financial Meltdown

Everyone knows that global economies are in meltdown and somebody is making tons of profit at our expense. It truly doesn't matter who is manipulating markets; it's beyond our control. Instead, we must deal with the fallout and focus on the big question, *how do I protect my assets?* It's an area where we still have input.

First, I am not a stock analyst, commodities expert or investment advisor. I am a hardworking citizen watching politicians slash our country's financial stability and in turn, our individual economic security. What Stan and I chose to do may not work for you, as it's a very conservative approach and not income-producing.

Saving accounts yield a miserable 1% interest. CDs require a 5-year commitment just to see less than 2% return. Today we wouldn't consider hedge funds or municipal bonds when entire cities and states are broke. These less-than-exciting income producers might make the stock exchange look tempting. In other times, we'd probably hop back into the market, but it's hard to have confidence in something that mimics a roller coaster. One of these days, the market will see another devastating crash and we want to avoid that ride.

THE COMING CRASH

At the time of this writing, mainstream news source, CBNC, published *Fear of 'Catastrophic' Crash Rising Despite Bull Market*. Most news agencies are busy propagating spin that the economy is in recovery, albeit minus jobs, but things are looking up. Those of us watching current events and are eyeball deep in news, know this is a weak attempt to keep sleepy citizens blind to the truth. Phrases describing the economy like "on the brink", "dire", "explosive" "catastrophic" don't reduce anxiety levels. Escalating foreclosures, declining world status, sickly economies, rising inflation, 20% underemployment, rising fuel, food and healthcare costs, disappointing job creation spell near-disastrous, exceptionally precarious scenarios. That's why the lead-in statements of this article is so timely:

"In an unprecedented move, the number of investors fearing a catastrophic stock market crash is rising even with the stock market at 2½ year highs. The unusual dislocation comes from two distinct reasons: a lack of trust in the U.S. financial markets following the so-called Flash Crash (the Dow Jones plunged about 900 points only to recover those losses within minutes) *last May and the collapse of Lehman Brothers in 2007. This means the Flash Crash Advisory Commission that met on Friday has a long way to go in restoring confidence to the point that will bring the individual investor back into a market still ruled by high frequency trading, exchange-traded funds and leveraged hedge funds. The Yale School of Management since 1989 has asked wealthy individual investors monthly to give the "probability of a catastrophic stock market crash in the U.S. in the next six months."*

"In the latest survey in December, almost 75 percent of respondents gave it at least a 10 percent chance of happening. That's up from 68 percent who gave it a 10 percent probability last April, just before the events of May 6, 2010.

"Even though the market is firing on all cylinders, that fear of big losses still looms large for investors in a way that it didn't prior to the last bear market," wrote analysts from Bespoke Investment Group in a report citing the Yale data. "Clearly, the financial crisis and the collapse it caused has impacted investor psyche in a big way."[186]

Financial advisors suggest that you should never risk more than you can afford to lose. That's sound advice, but it chews into principle. However, in this volatile market, *some of something is better than all of nothing*.

With that in mind, Stan and I look to the practical. What commodities or tangible items can we purchase *now* that will keep us functioning when times get *really* tough? Most of these goods fall into the category of storable foods, water and purifying measures, medicines, gardening supplies, alternative energy and other items people use every day.

Think of what you need to live comfortably if access to normal supplies is cut off. It's likely that others will need these same items too. They make great barterable goods.

Barterable Items That Disappear First in a Crisis

Honey, Syrups, White & Brown Sugars	Charcoal, Lighter Fluid	Tarps, Stakes, Twine, Nail, Rope, Spikes
Rice - Beans - Wheat	Lantern Hangers	Duct Tape
Salt Garlic, Spices, Vinegar	Propane Cylinders	Bow Saws, Axes, Hatchets, Wedges
Flour, Yeast, Baking Supplies	Propane Cylinder Handle-Holder	Knives, Sharpening Tools
Vegetable Oil	Mini Heater Head for propane	Glue, Nails, Nuts, Bolts, Screws
Tuna Fish in oil	Cook Stoves	Screen Patches
Soy Sauce, Bouillon, Gravy, Soup Base	Coleman's Pump Repair Kit	Roll-on Window Insulation Kit
Graham Crackers, Saltines, Pretzels, Trail Mix, Jerky	Lamp Oil, Wicks, Lamps	Lumber, all types
Popcorn, Peanut Butter, Nuts	Coleman Fuel	Bicycles, Tires, Tubes, Pump, Chains
Chewing Gum, Candies	Mantles: Aladdin, Coleman	Wagon, Cart
Canned Fruit, Veggies, Soup, Stew	Generator	Hand Pump, Siphon
Milk, Powdered and Condensed	Candles	Backpacks, Duffle Bag
Tea, Coffee	Matches	Sleeping Bag, Blanket, Pillow, Mat
Chocolate, Cocoa, Tang, Punch	Seasoned Firewood	Cots and Inflatable Mattress
Wine, Liquors	Flashlights, Light Sticks, Torches	Garbage Can, plastic
Grain Grinder	Baby Wipes and Baby Supplies	Garbage Bags
Manual Can Opener, Egg Beaters, Whisk	Reading Glasses	Gasoline Containers
Water Containers	Shaving Supplies	Batteries, all sizes
Paper Plates, Cups, Utensils	Feminine Hygiene, Hair and Skin Care	Fire Extinguishers
Writing Paper, Pads, Pencils, Solar Calculators	Men's Hygiene: Shampoo, Toothbrush, Paste, Mouthwash, Floss, Nail Clippers	Carbon Monoxide Alarm
Cast Iron Cookware	Portable Toilet	Guns, Ammunition, Pepper Spray, Knives, Clubs, Bats, Slingshots
Water Filters, Purifiers	Toilet Paper, Kleenex, Paper Towels	First Aid Kit
Fishing Supplies, Tools	Hats, Cotton Neckerchiefs	Insulated Ice Chests
Vitamins	Rain Gear, Rubberized Boots	Rat Poison, Roach Killer
Paraffin	Work Boots, Belts, Levis, Durable Shirts	Mousetraps, Ant Traps
Canning Supplies	Thermal Underwear Socks, Underwear, T-shirts	Mosquito Coils, Repellent Sprays, Creams
Aluminum Foil	Gloves: Work, Warming, Gardening	Laundry Detergent, liquid
Garden Tools, Supplies	Wool Clothing, Scarves, Ear Muffs, Mittens	Washboards, Mop Bucket w/wringer
Garden Seeds, Non-hybrid	Big Dogs, Dog Food	Clothespins, Line, Hangers
Board Games Cards, Dice	Goats, Chickens	Bleach, plain
Journals, Diaries, Scrapbooks	Cigarettes	Scissors, Fabrics, Sewing Supplies

PRACTICAL MONEY

Once you acquire the basic life necessities, consider a financial hedge in precious metals. Unless you invest massive dollars in this commodity, in which case it might require too much storage room, think precious metal coins high in intrinsic value, not high-end collectibles. If it comes down to financial survival through gold and silver, people aren't going to care how pretty or how rare a coin is. All that will matter is how much of that particular ore is actually in the coin and how much will it net you in a worst-case scenario. IF you feel there is time up your sleeve you might consider some semi-rare coins. In my opinion, I'd give collector's coins a miss.

For pure survival considerations, keep coins in small dollar amounts. If you invested thousands of dollars in a single gold bar, who would have the ability to "cash" it?

Take physical control of your purchase. Don't rely on certificates or shares. When things get *really* tough, if you don't possess it, it might be difficult to access it, if not impossible.

For those who are new to the idea of owning precious metals, here is a short outline of points to consider. The most basic question is *what should I purchase?*

For each person, his or her needs might be different. This overview should help you decide where to start. From that point on, it is strongly suggested you speak with a trusted metals advisor. Discuss with that person what your goals and concerns are and they will be best equipped to help with your choices.

	Summary of Gold Coin Classifications		
	Bullion / Bullion Coins	**Semi-rare** (Semi-Numismatic)	**Rare** (Twice the coin's value)
Spread *	7 - 10% of total purchase	13 - 15% of total purchase	20% of total purchase
Gold	Not as volatile as silver, better for long-term storage		
Examples	American Eagle Canadian Maple S. African Krugerrand	St. Gaudens $20 Liberty	
Pros	Easy to liquidate	Easy to liquidate Privately purchased, not dealer reported Not confiscatable	Privately purchased, not dealer reported Not confiscatable
Cons	Dealer reportable when sold back Confiscatable	None	Not as easy to liquidate
Who Buys	Short-term speculator not concerned with privacy	Hedge investors	Collectors only
Silver	Bags of 90% silver: quarters, dimes, dollars, 50-cent pieces (great for barter)		

   ***Spread**. This is your bottom line cost for the entire transaction. It covers dealer's commission and other fees. We've all heard commercials for '1% or 2% over dealer cost'. Sounds pretty good doesn't. Chances are hidden fees exist. They may not be disclosed unless you make the right inquiries. The bottom line question to ask a prospective dealer is *If I purchase (fill in what type of coin...), and you buy it back from me today, what will it cost - in total?* This is the 'spread'. There are different ways dealers 'massage' costs where it looks like you're getting a killer deal, but more than likely they haven't revealed the full cost.

   Most reputable dealers will charge close to the range listed above. If It is significantly above or below, get more comparison rates. If it's too low, they're not disclosing everything. Dealers have to stay in business and they're not going to cut their own throat for a sale. If it's several points higher than what's listed above, then you know they want to retire on your transaction.

   Just as vital as having the right hedge against financial chaos, it's important to find a broker you can trust. The vast majority of suppliers recommended in this book are ones Stan and I have personally patronized. Especially with something as necessary as financial security, it's important to recommend people we've dealt with employed by companies that have spotless reputations.

   Undoubtedly many companies deserve high marks, but chaotic times have spawned countless precious metals sellers. One company we recommend without hesitation is The McAlvany Financial Group **mcalvany.com**. Their precious metals wing, ICA, has been in business nearly 40 years. They are good about returning phone calls and patiently answer even the most basic questions. Though ICA has a team of highly qualified advisors, over the years we're primarily dealt with Kevin Orrick: **kevinorrick@mcalvany.com**. ICA, 166 Turner Drive, Durango, CO, 81303, 1.800.525.9556. In speaking with Kevin, he offered that if you mention Holly referred you, he will go 'above and beyond' to see your needs are met. Somehow I think he would do so regardless.

   At this point, it's important to underscore as stated on page 2 of *Dare To Prepare* that no remuneration of any description has been solicited or received by the author.

Chapter 67: Staying in a Shelter

Photo: San Bernardino, CA, October 31, 2003 -- Reverend Misael prays with shelteree Jeri Wilde in the evacuation shelter at Norton Air Force Base. Hanger 3 housed over 3,000 evacuees following the fires in Southern California. (Andrea Booher/FEMA News Photo)

> *Be sure everyone in your household knows where to find shelter from all hazards that affect your area.*

Long-term sheltering in your home and what you should have on hand for these times has already been addressed in the chapters on Food, Water, First Aid and General Supplies. These supplies constitute good household management and preparedness planning. But at some time it may be necessary to use public shelters.

It's certainly more advantageous to stay in your own home. You're in familiar, "safe" surroundings during a stressful time. You have access to personal items, food and water and not forced to "live out of a box". It's just easier on the nerves if you and family can stay in your own home.

Given the proper circumstances, though, availing yourself of pubic shelter may be critical.

REALITY CHECK

Public shelters can be loud, dispiriting and inconvenient and there is zero privacy. It's like camping with a ton of strangers minus the fun. Depending on length of stay and time of year, all those unwashed bodies may take on a (smelly) life of their own. Mix these ingredients with highly charged emotions, raw nerves and crying babies; it's not something to be envied. However, it may save your life.

If you've never had to avail yourself of public shelter, a "Disaster Hotel" requires that you supply certain items. It's understood residents agree to follow all shelter rules.

Photo: For nearly 2 weeks in October 2003, wildfires ravaged southern California. Huge blazes killed 20 people, destroyed more than 3,400 homes, and scorched 750,000+ acres. "I have cried and cried. I go through periods of incredible optimism and so much sadness that it goes right down and it hurts my toenails," said Kim Thurman, 55."[187] This evacuation shelter at Norton Air Force Base held over 3,000 evacuees following those fires.

(Andrea Booher, FEMA News Photo)

TIPS

- Tag or label everything you take to a shelter.
- Take a neck wallet or money belt to keep cash and credit cards safe.
- If possible, bath and eat a hearty meal before you leave home.
- Register immediately upon entering the shelter (family and friends may try to locate you).
- Shelters have no facilities to safeguard valuables, and they may not be safe in cars in a shelter parking lot.
- Put them in a safe place such as a safe deposit box before evacuating.
- Depending on time of year, a shelter could be extremely hot or cold. If power is out, there would be no way to regulate the heat or cold or, the shelter may not be equipped with these amenities at all.
- Sweaters, sweatshirts, socks and blankets may increase your comfort if the shelter is too cold.

Shelter Etiquette:
- Use an isolated part of the shelter to take or make cell phone calls, and keep your voice low to not disturb others. Turn your cell phone's ring volume as low as possible or put it on vibrate.
- Pack your shelter supplies in 5-gallon plastic buckets with lids. Handles make them easy to carry and they're strong enough to be used as seats.
- Restrict smoking to designated well-ventilated areas.

WHAT TO TAKE TO A SHELTER	
FOOD AND WATER	
Shelters may not always provide three meals a day. Sometimes only snacks and water are available. Depending on the situation, shelters may not be able to provide *any* food whatsoever. Plan to bring your own:	
Baby food and formula	MREs, HeaterMeals, no heating required foods
Fruit, Vegetables and Pudding, snack-size	Peanut butter and crackers
Granola bars, trail mix, other high-energy foods	Special dietary foods – diabetic, low salt, etc.
Meat or fish, snack-size portions	Water or other beverages – 1 gal. per person, per day

WHAT TO TAKE TO A SHELTER

FOOD AND WATER
- Eating and drinking utensils
- Manual can opener
- Paper plates, towels and napkins
- Portable ice chest with ice

HYGIENE
- Deodorant
- Feminine hygiene products
- Hand sanitizer or towelettes
- Razor
- Shampoo (no water required variety)
- Soap
- Teeth wipes, such as Oral-B's Brush-Ups, (requires no paste or water)
- Toilet paper (some shelters ran out during Hurricane Charley)
- Toothbrush and paste
- Washcloth and small towel

MEDICAL
- Mediations in their original containers – if there's a problem, shelter workers will know what you're taking and how much. You must be able to take all medications by yourself.
- First-Aid kit in a waterproof box
- Insect repellent (if appropriate to the season)
- Medical equipment and devices, such as dentures, crutches, prostheses, etc.

CHILDREN and INFANT NEEDS
- Bottles, nipples
- Baby food
- Blankets
- Changes of clothing
- Diapers, wipes
- Favorite toy or blanket that provides comfort
- Games, coloring books, story books, small hand-held computer games, and similar quiet activities

COMMUNICATION
- Cell phone and charger, a car charger adapter even better (electrical outlets in a shelter may be in high demand, or the shelter itself may lose power)
- Fully-charged extra cell-phone batteries

IMPORTANT HOUSEHOLD PAPERS
- Address book (nearest relative not living in area and your doctor)
- ATM card
- Cash (ATM's ran out during hurricane Frances
- Check book and credit cards (these may only be accepted if verification is possible)
- Computer back up files on CD
- Driver's license or personal ID; green card
- Food-stamp card
- Health-insurance card
- Household inventory
- Insurance policy
- Marriage and birth certificates
- Social Security card
- Stocks, bonds, and other negotiable certificates
- Wills, deeds, and copies of recent tax returns

SLEEPING GEAR
- Blanket
- Cot (especially for elderly or infirm)
- Sleeping bag, bedroll and pillow – 1 per family member

CLOTHES
You may be at the shelter for several days, so bring changes of clothes. Bring the clothes you will need when you are allowed to return home. Rain or snow gear, work gloves, closed-toe shoes or work boots, and boots or hip waders may be called for.

ENTERTAINMENT
- Stereos and radios, Battery-operated personal – use with headphones
- Battery-operated TV with a built-in VCR – use with headphones
- Books and magazines, cards, games, other diversions
- Extra batteries for anything battery-powered.

MISCELLANEOUS
- Eyeglasses (spare pair)
- Hearing-aid batteries
- Flashlight
- Keys (spare set)
- Map of the area

ITEMS NOT PERMITTED IN SHELTERS
- Alcohol
- Candles
- Grills
- Lanterns
- Matches or other fire-starters
- Pets, except for service animals (make plans before the storm hits for pet care)
- Weapons

Chapter 68: Dealing With Stress

The emotional toll that disaster brings can be more devastating than the financial strain of damages or loss of home, business and personal property. Children and the elderly are especially affected in the disaster's aftermath. Even individuals who experience trauma "second hand" through exposure to extensive media coverage can be affected.

Crisis counseling programs often include community outreach, consultation, and education. FEMA and state and local governments of the affected area may provide assistance to help people cope with and recover from disaster. If you feel you need assistance – get help.

COPING WITH DISASTER

You need to be aware of signs that indicate someone may need help in coping with the stress of a disaster.

1. THINGS TO CONSIDER WHEN TRYING TO UNDERSTAND DISASTER EVENTS.
- Everyone who sees or experiences a disaster is affected by it in some way.
- It is normal to feel anxious about your own safety and that of your family and close friends.
- Profound sadness, grief and anger are normal reactions to an abnormal event.
- Acknowledging your feelings helps you recover.
- Focusing on your strengths and abilities will help you to heal.
- Accepting help from community programs and resources is healthy.
- We each have different needs and different ways of coping.
- It's common to want to strike back at people who have caused great pain. However, nothing good is accomplished by hateful language or actions.

2. SIGNS THAT ADULTS NEED CRISIS COUNSELING/STRESS MANAGEMENT ASSISTANCE.
- Difficulty communicating thoughts.
- Difficulty sleeping.
- Difficulty maintaining balance in their life.
- Easily frustrated.
- Increased use of drugs/ alcohol.
- Limited attention span.
- Poor work performance.
- Headaches/stomach problems.
- Tunnel vision/muffled hearing.
- Colds or flu-like symptoms.
- Disorientation or confusion.
- Difficulty concentrating.
- Reluctance to leave home.
- Depression, sadness.
- Feelings of hopelessness.
- Mood-swings and crying easily.
- Overwhelming guilt and self-doubt.
- Fear of crowds, strangers, or being alone.

3. WAYS TO EASE DISASTER RELATED STRESS.
1. Talk with someone about your feelings – anger, sorrow, and other emotions – even though it may be difficult.
2. Seek help from professional counselors who deal with post-disaster stress.
3. Don't hold yourself responsible for the disastrous event or be frustrated because you feel that you cannot help directly in the rescue work.
4. Take steps to promote your own physical and emotional healing by staying active in your daily life patterns or by adjusting them. This healthy outlook will help you and your household (e.g., healthy eating, rest, exercise, relaxation, meditation).
5. Maintain a normal household and daily routine, limiting demanding responsibilities of you and your household.
6. Spend time with family and friends.
7. Participate in memorials.
8. Use existing support groups of family, friends, and church.
9. Establish a family disaster plan. Feeling there is something you can do is very comforting.

HELPING CHILDREN COPE WITH DISASTER

Disasters can leave children feeling frightened, confused and insecure. Whether a child has personally experienced trauma, has merely seen the event on television or heard it discussed by adults, it's important for parents and teachers to be informed and ready to help if reactions to stress begin to occur.

After a disaster, children are most afraid that:
- The event will happen again
- Someone will get hurt or injured
- They will be separated from the family or
- They will be left alone.

Keep them with you, even if it seems easier to look for housing or help on your own. At a time like this, it's important for the whole family to stay together. Children respond to trauma in many different ways. Some may have reactions very soon after the event; others may seem to be doing fine for weeks or months and then begin to show worrisome behavior. Knowing the signs that are common at different ages can help parents and teachers recognize problems and respond appropriately.

Reassurance is the key to helping children through a traumatic time. Very young children need a lot of cuddling, as well as verbal support. Answer questions about the disaster honestly, but don't dwell on frightening details or allow the subject to dominate family or classroom time indefinitely. Encourage children of all ages to express emotions through conversation, drawing or painting and to find a way to help others who were affected by the disaster. Also, limit the amount of disaster related material (television, etc.) your children are seeing or hearing and pay careful attention to how graphic it is.

Comfort and reassure them. Tell them what you know about the situation. Be honest but gentle. Encourage them to talk about the disaster. Encourage them to ask questions about the disaster. Give them a real task to do, something that gets the family back on its feet.

Try to maintain a normal household or classroom routine and encourage children to participate in recreational activity. Reduce your expectations temporarily about performance in school or at home, perhaps by substituting less demanding responsibilities for normal chores.

HELPING OTHERS

There is never anything quite so rewarding as helping someone else. It gets your mind off your own trials and helps someone in the process. It also underscores you're not alone. Seeing someone's smile of appreciation lifts your own load and helping is catching.

Photo: Virginia Rowell, whose home in Pine Island, FL was heavily damaged by hurricane Charley embraces Community Relations worker Ron Rios. Aug. 17, 2004.
(FEMA Photo/Andrea Booher)

Chapter 69: Hope and Encouragement

WHAT'S IN A NAME?
A lot of people ask why the name *Dare To Prepare*. They understand "prepare" but "dare" is puzzling. Some people think it's a catchy, rhyming title, but it's more. Those who choose to prepare have acknowledged on some level that things are changing all around us – rapidly. Sometimes it feels like it's more than we can deal with. We get overwhelmed thinking *how can I ever get it done?*

It doesn't help if one family member wants to be more self-sufficient and the other doesn't. This can lead to real frustration.

Truth be known, you probably already know how to do a lot of things that fall into the preparedness bucket. You may have started a pantry. It's likely you have many of these essentials on hand. All you needed was a little organization and some perspective. Small steps. With a little effort each week, pretty soon you will have accomplished a whole lot.

People at the other end of the spectrum – those who deny the world is any different from even five years ago – will have a doubly difficult time with challenges.

You have only to watch interviews with disaster victims to see how "to do it better". It was truly astounding with four back-to-back hurricanes hitting Florida that people didn't consider A) moving out of harm's way and B) getting the necessary preparedness items to see them through the next one.

For instance, building materials centers ran out of plywood. This item should be a required purchase for anyone living in a hurricane zone. It's such a simple precaution to take, yet lives are torn apart simply because people didn't plan ahead.

To do so, people must face reality. Disasters don't go away simply because we want them to. THAT'S daring to prepare – admitting there's a problem and doing something about it. You may not be able to fix the whole world or even your entire community, but you can help yourself and your loved ones.

YOU'RE NEVER ALONE
Nearly every day we are tested one way or another. Can we make the bills? Meet deadlines? People are out of work and stretched to the max. There's a lot to worry about if you want to, but all worry does is grow new ulcers and multiply gray hairs.

A lot of people are short on cash and long on challenges. Prayer lightens this load. The Lord never said life would be trouble-free, but He did promise to never abandon us. Faith has gotten us through a lot.

Life is scary at times, even for believers, if we are honest.

It was weird enough when weather became so unpredictable, and now there are nut-case terrorists to consider and nations who threaten nuclear swordplay. All this stuff could make us crazy IF we let it.

Wouldn't it be nice if we had a *real* crystal ball and could see the path ahead?

In a way you can. Scripture promises eternal life for all believers. What happens here – all the suffering and hardships – will be erased from our minds in the next life; "all tears will be wiped away."

Many more challenges lay ahead, possibly things that make the present look pretty quiet. If you're worried about not having enough of whatever, ask the Lord to show you the way. The Lord always gives you what you need, when asked, but not always what you want. He is the King of miracles and Creator of peaceful minds.

In the grand scheme of things, we're here but for a brief heartbeat, but the choices you make now last an eternity.

A MESSAGE TO CHRISTIANS
Frequently we are asked, *Why do I need to prepare? God will provide*, often citing Matthew 6:25. If we look at the preceding passages beginning with verse 20, we see God instructs us how to prioritize our life. It doesn't say anything about not preparing in the face of danger.

The most well known example of preparation is Noah. Everybody thought he was the neighborhood nut, but he followed God's instruction, which saved he and his family and all the "two by two's" (pairs of animals).

A second example of preparedness is in Genesis 41. It tells the story of Pharaoh's dream of a seven-year famine coming to Egypt. The dream shows him seven ugly, scrawny cows eating seven healthy, fat cows. Despite this, the scrawny cows remain skinny. Following this, Pharaoh dreams of seven heads of grain growing on

Dare To Prepare: Chapter 69: Hope and Encouragement

a single stalk. These thin, withered, scorched heads sprout and swallow up the healthy grain. Pharaoh is stumped to understand these warnings and calls on Joseph to interpret.

Joseph describes the coming trying times. Pharaoh is told there will be seven years of great abundance in Egypt followed by seven years of horrific famine. Joseph shares that God showed him the famine in two examples – the cows and the grain, because this event was cast in stone. It *would* occur.

Joseph advises Pharaoh to find a wise man and put him in charge of Egypt. Pharaoh heeds the warning and asks his officials if they know of any man *filled with the Spirit of God* for this job.

Pharaoh finally asks Joseph to take on this huge task and promises him the position of second-in-command of all Egypt. Because Joseph prepared for this famine, he was able to save the entire house of Israel ensuring the birth of Jesus.

Rev. 12:6 indicates that during Tribulation even though horrendous events will take place, the Lord will send *His people on Earth at that time* to a place of protection and provide for their needs. But a LOT of challenges and trying events will take place before the End of the Age (not the end of the world.) We are told both not to be slack and to "endure". In other words, be prepared and stick it out.

TAKING PERSONAL RESPONSIBILITY

We are to take **personal responsibility** as illustrated by this anecdote.

When Tom heard the emergency advisory on TV warning of the coming flood, he shrugged it off. "I'm staying put – God will provide!"

When the police cars drove through his neighborhood urging people over loudspeakers to evacuate, he thought, "Yep, God'll provide," and stayed put.

Water rose two feet up the walls of his house. The National Guard ordered Tom out, but he wouldn't budge. Water covered everything Tom could see including the first floor of his home. He leaned out of a second story window and waved off the rescue boat. He felt safe. God would provide.

He ignored the helicopter as he clung to the chimney. His house floated down-river yet Tom shouted into the wind, "Go away; I trust in God's Providence!"

After drowning, Tom stood before the Lord bitter and angry. God let him die despite trusting in Him. Tom demanded an explanation.

God replied, "Tom, I <u>did</u> help you. I spoke to you through the announcer and police. Who do you think sent the warnings, the truck, the boat and the helicopter?"

It's not a matter of trusting God. Instead of being a victim, it is choosing to take an active part in our survival and wellbeing. It is digesting information we have available and making the best possible choices. It is doing the best we can with what we have.

It's not waiting for our governments to bail us out of the next disaster. They may not be able to.

It *IS*......... **Daring to Prepare!**

Appendices

U.S. AND METRIC CONVERSION CHARTS

LIQUID OR VOLUME MEASURES				
U.S.			**METRIC**	
⅛ tsp	1 pinch	8 drops	0.5 ml	
¼ tsp		16 drops	1.0 ml	
½ tsp			2.5 ml	
¾ tsp	⅛ fluid oz		3.5 ml	
1 tsp	1/6 fluid oz	⅓ Tbsp	5.0 ml	.17 fluid oz (UK)
1½ tsp	¼ fluid oz	½ Tbsp	7.5 ml	1 dram
2 tsp	⅓ fluid oz		10.0 ml	
3 tsp = 1 Tbsp	½ fluid oz	1/16 cup	14.2 ml (U.S.) 15.0 ml (Canada) 17.7 ml (UK) 20.0 ml (Australia)	.52 fluid oz (UK)
⅛ cup	1 fluid oz	2 Tbsp = 6 tsp	30.0 ml	.96 fluid oz (UK)
¼ cup	2 fluid oz	4 Tbsp	60.0 ml	
⅓ cup	2.5 fluid oz	5⅓ Tbsp	80.0 ml	
⅜ cup	3 fluid oz		90.0 ml	
½ cup	4 fluid oz	1 gill	120.0 ml	
⅔ cup	5 fluid oz		140.0 ml	
¾ cup	6 fluid oz		180.0 ml	
⅞ cup	7 fluid oz		210.0 ml	
1 cup	8 fluid oz	16 Tbsp = 2 gills	240.0 ml	8.3 fluid oz (UK)
2 cups	1 pint	4 gills	475.0 ml	
3 cups	1½ pints	6 gills	720.0 ml	
4 cups	1 quart	2 pints	946.0 ml	
4¼ cups	34 fluid oz			
8 cups	2 quarts	½ gallon	1,893 ml 1.9 liters	
16 cups	4 quarts	1 gallon	3,784 ml 3.79 liters	
1 pint	16 fluid oz	2 cups	1,000 ml 1 liter	(U.S. and Canada)
1 imperial pint	20 fluid oz			(UK, Australia, Canada)
2 pints	32 fluid oz	1 quart		
4 quarts	128 fluid oz	1 gallon		
1 gallon		32 gills	3,784 ml 3.79 liters	

WEIGHT EQUIVALENTS

U.S. Ounces	Grams	U.S. Ounces	Grams	U.S. Ounces	Grams
½ oz	14	34 oz	964	70 oz	1984
1 oz	28	35 oz	992	71 oz	2013 = 2 kg
2 oz	57	35.3 oz	1000 =1 kg	72 oz = 4½ lb	2041
3 oz	85	36 oz = 2¼ lb	1021	73 oz	2070
4 oz = ¼ lb	113	37 oz	1049	74 oz	2098 = 1.1 kg
5 oz	142	38 oz	1077	75 oz	2126
6 oz	170	39 oz	1106	76 oz = 4¾ lb	2155
7 oz	198	40 oz = 2½ lb	1134 = 1.1kg	77 oz	2183
8 oz = ½ lb	227	41 oz	1162	78 oz	2211 = 1.2 kg
8.8 oz	250 = ¼ kg	42 oz	1191	79 oz	2240
9 oz	255	43 oz	1219 = 1.2kg	80 oz = 5 lb	2268
10 oz	283	44 oz = 2¾ lb	1247	81 oz	2297 = 1.3 kg
11 oz	312	45 oz	1276	82 oz	2325
12 oz = ¾ lb	340	46 oz	1304 = 1.3kg	83 oz	2353
13 oz	369	47 oz	1332	84 oz = 5¼ lb	2381
14 oz	397	48 oz = 3 lb	1361	85 oz	2410 = 1.4 kg
15 oz	425	49 oz	1389	86 oz	2438
16 oz = 1 lb	454	50 oz	1417 = 1.4kg	87 oz	2466
17 oz	482	51 oz	1446	88 oz = 5½ lb	2495 = 2.5 kg
17.6 oz	500 = ½ kg	52 oz = 3¼ lb	1474	89 oz	2523
18 oz	510	53 oz	1503 = 1.5kg	90 oz	2551
19 oz	539	54 oz	1531	91 oz	2580
20 oz = 1¼ lb	567	55 oz	1559	92 oz = 5¾ lb	2608 = 2.6 kg
21 oz	595	56 oz = 3½ lb	1588	93 oz	2636
22 oz	624	57 oz	1616 = 1.6kg	94 oz	2665
23 oz	652	58 oz	1644	95 oz	2693 = 2.7 kg
24 oz = 1½ lb	680	59 oz	1673	96 oz = 6 lb	2721
25 oz	709	60 oz = 3¾ lb	1701 = 1.7kg	97 oz	2750
26 oz	737	61 oz	1729	98 oz	2778
27 oz	765	62 oz	1758	99 oz	2807 = 2.8 kg
27.3 oz	775 = ¾ kg	63 oz	1786	100 oz = 6¼ lb	2835
28 oz = 1¾ lb	794	64 oz = 4 lb	1814 =1 .8kg	101 oz	2863
29 oz	822	65 oz	1843	102 oz	2892 = 2.9 kg
30 oz	850	66 oz	1871	103 oz	2920
31 oz	879	67 oz	1899 = 1.9kg	104 oz = 6½ lb	2948
32 oz = 2 lb	907	68 oz = 4¼ lb	1927	105 oz	2977
33 oz	935	69 oz	1956	106 oz	3005

LENGTH EQUIVALENTS

U.S.	Metric	U.S.	Metric	U.S.	Metric
1/16 in	1.59mm	10 in	25.40cm	27.00 in	68.58cm
⅛ in	3.18mm	11 in	27.94cm	28.00 in	71.12cm
3/16 in	4.76mm	12 in	30.48cm	29.00 in	73.66cm
¼ in	6.35mm	13 in	33.02cm	30.00 in	76.20cm
⅜ in	9.53mm	14 in	35.56cm	31.00 in	78.74cm
½ in	1.27cm	15 in	38.10cm	32.00 in	81.28cm
¾ in	1.91cm	16 in	40.64cm	33.00 in	83.82cm
1 in	2.54cm	17 in	43.18cm	34.00 in	86.36cm
1½ in	3.81cm	18 in	45.72cm	35.00 in	88.90cm
2 in	5.08cm	19 in	48.26cm	36.00 in	91.44cm
3 in	7.62cm	20 in	50.80cm	37.00 in	93.98cm
4 in	10.16cm	21 in	53.34cm	38.00 in	96.52cm
5 in	12.70cm	22 in	55.88cm	39.00 in	99.06cm
6 in	15.24cm	23 in	58.42cm	39.37 in	100.0cm
7 in	17.78cm	24 in	60.96cm	41.00 in	104.14cm
8 in	20.32cm	25 in	63.50cm	42.00 in	106.68cm
9 in	22.86cm	26 in	66.04cm	43.00 in	109.22cm

COOKING TEMPERATURE EQUIVALENTS (APPROXIMATE)

Description	Fahrenheit	Celsius	Gas	Description	Fahrenheit	Celsius	Gas
Very Slow	200°F	100°C	--	Moderate	350°F	180°C	4
Very Slow	225°F	110°C	¼	Moderately	375°F	190°C	5
Very Slow	250°F	120°C	½	Hot	400°F	200°C	6
Very Slow	275°F	135°C	1	Hot	425°F	220°C	7
Slow	300°F	150°C	2	Very Hot	450°F	230°C	8
Moderately Slow	325°F	165°C	3	Extremely Hot	475°F	250°C	9

CANDY TEMPERATURES

Candy Stage	Fahrenheit	Celsius	Candy Stage	Fahrenheit	Celsius
Syrup	230°	110°	Hard Ball	248° – 254°	120° -123°
Thread	230° – 234°	110° -112°	Very Hard Ball	254° – 265°	123° -129°
Soft Ball	234° – 238°	112° -114°	Light Crack	270° – 284°	132° -140°
Semi Firm Ball	238° – 244°	114° -118°	Hard Crack	290° – 300°	143° -149°
Firm Ball	244° – 248°	118° -120°	Caramelized	310° – 338°	154° -170°

To convert UTC (Coordinated Universal Time), add or subtract hours from your time zone. For persons west of the international date line (all North America), hours are subtracted from UTC. For persons east of the international date line, hours are added. Then in the next chart, find the UTC and match it with your local time zone.

HOURS DIFFERENT FROM UTC

Local Time	Subtract from UTC	Local Time	Subtract from UTC	Local Time	Subtract from UTC
Atlantic Standard	4 hours	Central Daylight	5 hours	Pacific Daylight	7 hours
Atlantic Daylight	3 hours	Mountain Standard	7 hours	Alaskan Standard	9 hours
Eastern Standard	5 hours	Mountain Daylight	6 hours	Alaskan Daylight	8 hours
Eastern Daylight	4 hours	Pacific Standard	8 hours	Hawaiian Standard	10 hours
Central Standard	6 hours				

CONVERTING UTC/GMT/ZULU TO LOCAL TIME

UTC GMT	EDT	EST	CDT	CST	MDT	MST	PDT	PST
0000	8 pm	7 pm	7 pm	6 pm	6 pm	5 pm	5 pm	4 pm
0100	9 pm	8 pm	8 pm	7 pm	7 pm	6 pm	6 pm	5 pm
0200	10 pm	9 pm	9 pm	8 pm	8 pm	7 pm	7 pm	6 pm
0300	11 pm	10 pm	10 pm	9 pm	9 pm	8 pm	8 pm	7 pm
0400	Midnight	11 pm	11 pm	10 pm	10 pm	9 pm	9 pm	8 pm
0500	1 am	Midnight	Midnight	11 pm	11 pm	10 pm	10 pm	9 pm
0600	2 am	1 am	1 am	Midnight	Midnight	11 pm	11 pm	10 pm
0700	3 am	2 am	2 am	1 am	1 am	Midnight	Midnight	11 pm
0800	4 am	3 am	3 am	2 am	2 am	1 am	1 am	Midnight
0900	5 am	4 am	4 am	3 am	3 am	2 am	2 am	1 am
1000	6 am	5 am	5 am	4 am	4 am	3 am	3 am	2 am
1100	7 am	6 am	6 am	5 am	5 am	4 am	4 am	3 am
1200	8 am	7 am	7 am	6 am	6 am	5 am	5 am	4 am
1300	9 am	8 am	8 am	7 am	7 am	6 am	6 am	5 am
1400	10 am	9 am	9 am	8 am	8 am	7 am	7 am	6 am
1500	11 am	10 am	10 am	9 am	9 am	8 am	8 am	7 am
1600	Noon	11 am	11 am	10 am	10 am	9 am	9 am	8 am
1700	1 pm	Noon	Noon	11 am	11 am	10 am	10 am	9 am
1800	2 pm	1 pm	1 pm	Noon	Noon	11 am	11 am	10 am
1900	3 pm	2 pm	2 pm	1 pm	1 pm	Noon	Noon	11 am
2000	4 pm	3 pm	3 pm	2 pm	2 pm	1 pm	1 pm	Noon
2100	5 pm	4 pm	4 pm	3 pm	3 pm	2 pm	2 pm	1 pm
2200	6 pm	5 pm	5 pm	4 pm	4 pm	3 pm	3 pm	2 pm
2300	7 pm	6 pm	6 pm	5 pm	5 pm	4 pm	4 pm	3 pm

To convert to UTC, find your local time in the first column and then locate your time zone.

CONVERTING LOCAL TIME TO UTC/GMT/ZULU TIME

LOCAL	EDT	EST	CDT	CST	MDT	MST	PDT	PST
Midnight	0400	0500	0500	0600	0600	0700	0700	0800
1 am	0500	0600	0600	0700	0700	0800	0800	0900
2 am	0600	0700	0700	0800	0800	0900	0900	1000
3 am	0700	0800	0800	0900	0900	1000	1000	1100
4 am	0800	0900	0900	1000	1000	1100	1100	1200
5 am	0900	1000	1000	1100	1100	1200	1200	1300
6 am	1000	1100	1100	1200	1200	1300	1300	1400
7 am	1100	1200	1200	1300	1300	1400	1400	1500
8 am	1200	1300	1300	1400	1400	1500	1500	1600
9 am	1300	1400	1400	1500	1500	1600	1600	1700
10 am	1400	1500	1500	1600	1600	1700	1700	1800
11 am	1500	1600	1600	1700	1700	1800	1800	1900
Noon	1600	1700	1700	1800	1800	1900	1900	2000
1 pm	1700	1800	1800	1900	1900	2000	2000	2100
2 pm	1800	1900	1900	2000	2000	2100	2100	2200
3 pm	1900	2000	2000	2100	2100	2200	2200	2300
4 pm	2000	2100	2100	2200	2200	2300	2300	2400
5 pm	2100	2200	2200	2300	2300	2400	2400	0100
6 pm	2200	2300	2300	2400	2400	0100	0100	0200
7 pm	2300	2400	2400	0100	0100	0200	0200	0300
8 pm	2400	0100	0100	0200	0200	0300	0300	0400
9 pm	0100	0200	0200	0300	0300	0400	0400	0500
10 pm	0200	0300	0300	0400	0400	0500	0500	0600
11 pm	0300	0400	0400	0500	0500	0600	0600	0700

AMERICAN CAN SIZES

CAN SIZE	VOLUME	CUPS approx.	CAN SIZE	VOLUME	CUPS approx.
4 ounce	4 oz	½	No. 3 squat	23 oz	2¾
5 ounce	5 oz	⅝	No. 3	33½	4¼
8 ounce	8 oz	1	No. 3 cylinder	46 oz	5¾
Picnic	10½ to 12 oz	1¼	No. 5	56 oz	7⅓
12 oz vacuum	12 oz	1½	No 10	6½ – 7 lbs. 5 oz. (104 -117 oz.)	12-13
No. 1	11 oz	1⅓	No. 211	12	1½
No. 1 juice	13 oz	1⅝	No. 300	14 – 16 oz	1¾
No. 1 tall	16 oz	2	No. 303	16 – 17 oz	2
No. 1 square	16 oz	2	Condensed milk	15 fl oz	1⅓
No. 2	1 lb. 4 oz or 1 pint 2 fl oz	2½	Evaporated milk (small)	6 fl oz	⅔
No. 2½	1 lb. 13 oz	3½	Evaporated milk (large)	14½ fl oz	1⅔
No. 2½ square	31 oz	scant 4	Frozen juice concentrate	6 oz	¾

TEMPERATURE EQUIVALENTS

FAHRENHEIT	CELSIUS	FAHRENHEIT	CELSIUS	FAHRENHEIT	CELSIUS
-20°F	-28.9°C	36°F	2.2°C	92°F	33.3°C
-18°F	-27.8°C	38°F	3.3°C	94°F	34.4°C
-16°F	-26.7°C	40°F	4.4°C	96°F	35.6°C
-14°F	-25.6°C	42°F	5.6°C	98°F	36.7°C
-12°F	-24.4°C	44°F	6.7°C	100°F	37.8°C
-10°F	-23.3°C	46°F	7.8°C	102°F	38.9°C
-8°F	-22.2°C	48°F	8.9°C	104°F	40.0°C
-6°F	-21.1°C	50°F	10.0°C	106°F	41.1°C
-4°F	-20.0°C	52°F	11.1°C	108°F	42.2°C
-2°F	-18.9°C	54°F	12.2°C	110°F	43.3°C
0°F	-17.8°C	56°F	13.3°C	112°F	44.4°C
2°F	-16.7°C	58°F	14.4°C	114°F	45.6°C
4°F	-15.6°C	60°F	15.6°C	116°F	46.7°C
6°F	-14.4°C	62°F	16.7°C	118°F	47.8°C
8°F	-13.3°C	64°F	17.8°C	120°F	48.9°C
10°F	-12.2°C	66°F	18.9°C	122°F	50.0°C
12°F	-11.1°C	68°F	20.0°C	124°F	51.1°C
14°F	-10.0°C	70°F	21.1°C	126°F	52.2°C
16°F	-8.9°C	72°F	22.2°C	128°F	53.3°C
18°F	-7.8°C	74°F	23.3°C	130°F	54.4°C
20°F	-6.7°C	76°F	24.4°C	132°F	55.6°C
22°F	-5.6°C	78°F	25.6°C	134°F	56.7°C
24°F	-4.4°C	80°F	26.7°C	136°F	57.8°C
26°F	-3.3°C	82°F	27.8°C	138°F	58.9°C
28°F	-2.2°C	84°F	28.9°C	140°F	60.0°C
30°F	-1.1°C	86°F	30.0°C	142°F	61.1°C
32°F	0.0°C	88°F	31.1°C	144°F	62.2°C
34°F	1.1°C	90°F	32.2°C	146°F	63.3°C

Index

2
2-liter bottles, 52, 74, 137

3
3G, 353

4
4-legged family member, 422

5
55-gallon container, 73

7
72-hour: 72-hour kits, 46
72-hour kits, 47, 51

A
above ground, 77, 206, 209, 363, 389, 437, 461, 510
absorbent, 35, 294, 390
absorbent material, 35
accelerator, 562, 563
accent, 154
accordion shutters, 539
Ace Model RFV75, 210
acetone, 201
acid, 72, 79, 114, 115, 131, 197, 240, 243, 247, 248, 283, 284, 285, 294, 381, 404, 555; (-s), 68, 229, 237; inorganic, 424; organic, 68; rain, 72, 79, 555
acidic gas, 555
acrylic, 245
Actifed, 51, 194
activated carbon, 56, 58, 82, 442; filters, 82
activated charcoal, 5, 9, 67, 68, 195, 261
adding oxygen to the room, 437
additives, 66, 73, 79, 83, 116, 204, 205, 213, 220, 227, 228, 232, 236, 238, 241, 242, 246, 247, 249, 250, 254, 285, 406
Aden Port, Yemen, 413
adequate diet, 492, 493
adequate radiation protection, 490
adequate ventilation, 400, 490
Admiral, 154
adsorption, 67
adult shares, 99
adults, 14, 16, 417, 529
advanced col. silver, 215
Advil, 51, 113, 194
aerate the waste, 393
aeration, 269
aerosol, 147, 200, 427, 429, 432, 433, 434, 584
aerosolized particles, 429
Africa, 87, 336, 553

African aid agencies, 53
after shave, 112, 184, 186, 203
aftershock, 24, 506, 508
AGSO (Geoscience Australia), 42
Ahmad Ajaj, 412
aim, 204, 205, 368, 456
air: filter, 189; safe, breathable, 440; supply, 436, 442, 491
air blast: waves, 448
air circulation, 144, 145, 253, 281, 288, 291, 310
air compressor, 308
air conditioner, 124, 127, 306, 438, 484, 518, 519, 556
air exchange, 436
air filtration system, 436
Air Power Sunshower, 384
air temperature,, 416, 476, 518
airborne and droplet precautions, 434
airborne transmission, 433, 580, 581
air-dried, 115, 281
airports, 459
airtight container, 65, 74, 133, 134, 135, 139, 140, 141, 143, 291, 293, 295, 297, 299, 323, 334; (-s), 74, 293, 334
Al Durtschi, 3, 133
Alaska, 31, 474, 543, 552, 553, 555, 574
Alberto Culver, 204
alcohol, 55, 62, 88, 98, 121, 192, 204, 220, 227, 233, 238, 244, 262, 264, 322, 323, 325, 326, 334, 345, 384, 391, 398, 404, 519, 558, 561, 593, 594; (-s), 68, 260; beverages, 519, 536; denatured, 327; isopropyl, 51, 193, 381, 382; rubbing, 37, 202
Alder, 252
algae, 59, 65, 67, 430
alkaline, 212, 428, 434
all known biological agents, 424
allen wrench, 211
allied signal, 412
alligator clips, 212, 213
Allspice, 107, 286
almond, 108, 222, 224, 228, 286
Almondettes, Mars, 120
aloe vera, 228
AlpineAire, 116
al-Qaeda, 412, 413
alternate escape route, 522
alternate sources for warmth, 43
alternator, 560
aluminum, 80, 130, 144, 218, 231, 242, 246, 248, 281, 286, 320, 325, 326, 328, 330, 333, 337,

339, 344, 345, 346, 348, 349, 373, 386, 452, 502, 510, 518; foil, 111, 185, 589
Amanda, 19, 20, 21, 22, 23, 24, 25, 26, 27
Amaranth, 280
America, 1, 3, 29, 52, 62, 120, 123, 131, 132, 196, 212, 306, 322, 336, 361, 371, 409, 411, 412, 413, 416, 425, 444, 445, 460, 476, 481, 485, 500, 501, 504, 505, 514, 547, 555, 574, 600
America the beautiful, 413
America the terrorized, 413
American, 19, 32, 56, 66, 97, 105, 109, 155, 170, 172, 192, 265, 282, 292, 297, 301, 333, 336, 360, 370, 371, 372, 410, 412, 417, 418, 422, 423, 438, 439, 440, 446, 483, 501, 506, 522, 548, 577, 590, 602; (-s), 97, 196, 411, 412, 413, 416, 444, 458, 485, 501, 520, 585; Native, 28
American can sizes, 602
American Architectural Manufacturers Association (AAMA), 438
American Beauty, 155, 170, 172
American C2, 422
American Harvest Gardenmaster, 282
American M-9, 422, 423
American M-95 filters, 423
American Red Cross, 32, 192, 370, 371, 506, 522, 548
American Safe Room, 440
amines, 68
ammonia, 112, 192, 200
amount on hand, 98
Anaheim, 290
analgesic cream, 51, 194
Anatoly Gribkov, 444
anchor plate, 511
ancient romans, 212
Andy Capp's, 159
angel food, 150
animal butchering, 410
animal droppings, 252
animal fat and ash, 216
animal that appears to be sick, 492
animals: 7,000 big game, 555
animals (outside), 398
annihilate ourselves... are we going to?, 444
antacid, 51, 194, 202
Antelope Valley, 26
antennas, 189, 361, 368

anthrax, 416, 429, 432; edpidemic, 432
anthrax spores, 430, 432; aerosolized, 427; kills, 426, 432; sunshine destroys, 432
antibacterial, 51, 191, 193, 425
anti-bacterial ointments, 37
anti-bacterial soap, 39, 427
antibiotic, 7, 62, 192, 194, 196, 205, 212, 373, 404, 405, 406, 433, 452, 495; triple ointment, 398
anti-diarrheal, 51, 194
antifreeze, 558, 560
anti-freeze, 561
antihistamine, 51, 113, 194, 202
anti-lock brakes, 563
anti-lock braking system (ABS), 563
antioxidants, 424; Vitamin E and B6, 424
antiseptic, 51, 194, 195, 202, 228
anti-viral effects, 425
ants, 89, 358, 388
Anusol, 51, 194
apartment, 22, 32, 137, 275, 322, 324, 332, 368, 389, 459, 486, 487, 508, 538; (-s), 23, 324, 333, 346, 364, 391, 451; dwellers, 368, 389
apartments or condos, 538
apothecary jars, 246
apple, 103, 104, 141, 163, 169, 228, 237, 252, 271, 352; cider, 141; juice & applesauce, 169
applesauce, 104, 286
appliances with motors, 306
apricot, 104, 220, 222, 224, 228
apricot kernel, 220, 222, 224
Aqua-Chem, 391
Aquamate, 72
Aquatabs, 56
aquifer, 515
Arab militant supporters, 414
Arachis, 222, 224
Argo cornstarch, 155
argyria, 215, 425
argyrosis, 62
Arizona, 91, 368, 476, 514, 528, 542, 544; Page, 514; Phoenix, 23, 64, 346, 393; Tucson, 64, 476, 528; , 542
Ark Institute, 276
Armour Star, 155
army disposal, 52
army surplus, 52
army surplus stores, 52
aroma, 19, 227, 229, 289, 334; (-s), 244, 273, 281

aromatherapy, 128; mixture, 128
Arrowroot, 139
arroyos, 528
arsenic, 72, 205, 406
arsine, 424
Art Bell, 369
artesian wells, 75
artichoke, 103, 278
ascorbic acid, 54, 283, 284, 285, 286
ash, 84, 136, 237, 336, 543, 555, 556, 567; ashes, 84, 136, 237, 254; removing ashes, 339
ashfall, 556, 564
Asian, 166, 220, 574, 576
asparagus, 103, 144, 278, 279, 287, 298, 352
aspartame, 286
aspen, 252
aspergillus niger, 431
Aspirin, 38, 196, 197, 402, 495
asteroid, 544, 545, 546
asteroids: potentially hazardous, 546
asthmatic, 282, 580
astronomically, 28
Atkins, 633
ATM: card, 593; machines, 45; ran out of cash, 503
atmospheric pressure, 71
attack warning, 445, 486
attic, 122, 127, 128, 137, 438, 524, 526, 567; (-s), 388, 523, 558
Aunt Nellie's vegetables, 155
Aussie, 306; (-s), 43, 206
Australia, 41-43, 48, 52, 56, 72, 76-78, 87, 94, 99, 122, 124, 125, 127, 128, 131, 132, 152-154, 156, 158, 162, 165, 175, 183, 189, 220, 231, 245, 251, 269, 270, 282, 292, 306, 312, 318, 320, 321, 322, 325, 326, 331, 333, 336, 337, 339, 346, 361, 372, 389, 396, 408, 411, 425, 441, 514, 544, 552, 561, 586, 598; Adelaide, 425; Ballarat, 72, 122, 124, 282; Guyra dam, 544; Melbourne, 43; New South Wales, 411, 514, 544; outback, 336; Perth, 64, 122, 128, 191, 282, 332, 346; Queensland, 279, 400, 514, 552; SAS (Special Air Service), 32; South Australia, 76; Sporting Shooters Association of, 411; Sydney, 544; Victoria, 43, 72, 76, 122, 128, 389, 514, 633; Western Australia Health Dept, 65
Australia:, 128, 306, 321
Australian: (-s), 52, 339, 372
autoclaving with steam, 429
automatic dishwashers, 515

automatic garage door openers, 524
automatic transfer switch, 311
autopsy, 432
available catchment area, 83
avocado, 219, 220, 236, 343
avocadoes, 143
avocados, 143
avoid skinning and eating meat, 434
avoid using overdrive on slippery surfaces, 562
ax or hatchet, 565
axe, 93, 188

B

B&G Foods, 155, 161
babies and toddlers, 418
Babies over six months, 492
baby, 20, 22, 34, 152, 377, 493, 531; bottle nipples and pacifiers, 531; clothes, 186; food, 152, 493, 592, 593
Baby Ben, 187
baby food and formula, 592
baby food jars, 245
baby powder, 186, 192, 194
baby wash, 186
bacillus anthracis, 430
bacillus bacteria, 431
back up your computer's hard drive., 540
backflow of sewage into the house, 531
backpack, 48, 183, 327, 566
backpack stoves, 327, 328
backup generator, 311, 502
backup power, 95, 301
Backwoods Home Magazine, 313
bacon, 19, 97, 267, 327, 341
bacteria, 49, 53, 55-57, 59, 61, 62, 64, 67, 72, 73, 79, 96, 116, 119, 121, 205, 212, 215, 266, 281, 287, 293, 294, 375, 378, 382, 405, 427- 430, 432, 483, 530, 531, 538, 579, 582; airborne, 53, 81
bacteria-free, 74
bacterial growth, 82, 127, 321
bacterial infections, 425; of the skin, 425
bacteriophage, 430
bag, 35, 36, 40, 48, 92, 94, 106, 121, 123, 131, 143, 144, 145, 192, 234, 258, 259, 260, 277, 289, 291, 292, 384, 385, 386, 395, 397, 403, 544, 566, 572, 593; brown paper, 111; bush, 385; holes in plastic, 299; ice, 193; liquid waste, 391; mylar, 6, 130, 131, 133; paper, 132, 143, 144, 276, 277, 291, 292, 323, 334; perforated, 143, 144,

145; perforated plastic, 144, 145; plastic, 34, 37, 40, 92, 143, 144, 145, 150, 151, 246, 289, 294, 295, 297, 299, 397, 398, 427, 486, 538, 584; plastic sealable, 46; sealed, 133, 143
bags: polymer-filled, 391; solid waste, 391; Ziploc, 37, 60, 131, 192, 194, 398, 457
bahama shutters, 539
bail wire, 245
baits, 128
bake chicken, 333
bake grain, 129
baking: cups, 111; ingredients, 123; mix, 164; powder, 106, 115, 117, 118, 139; sheets, 294, 295
baking soda, 106, 139, 237, 380, 381, 382, 383, 391, 442, 495, 522; test, 8, 237
balanced diet, 98, 493
balcony, 137, 322, 324, 332, 333, 344, 346, 368, 538
ball of fire, 517
balloon, 247
balsam fir, 252
balsam of Peru, 228
bamboo shoots, 103
banana boat, 204
bananas, 143, 284, 296
band saw, 309
bandage, 51, 183, 192, 194, 397, 398; (-s), 37, 38, 50, 113
band-aids, 50, 113, 192
bandanna, 35; (-s), 35, 36, 183
bank account numbers, 49, 187
bank statement, 187
bankruptcy, 31
banks, 38, 45, 76, 85, 87, 437
banquet, 159
baptism, 187
bar soaps, 221
Bardas / Shmartaf, 423
Barilla, 156
barley, 117, 118, 136, 352
barns, 34, 78, 378, 569
barrels, 319, 409, 586
bartering, 120, 130
basalt, 75, 77
basement, 127, 137, 206, 271, 314, 400, 412, 437, 455, 456, 458, 459, 461, 486, 529, 548, 549, 550
bases, 68, 87, 456, 510
bashful bodies, 441
basic four, 95
basic marinade, 294, 295
basic soap, 232
basil, 107, 280, 291; leaves, 107
bath, 83
bathroom cleaner, 187
bathroom fully taped, 436
bathtub, 137, 382, 441, 527, 536

batteries, 33, 43, 44, 45, 50, 183, 184, 194, 212, 213, 315, 354, 355, 368, 369, 385, 422, 457, 503, 505, 520, 526, 535, 540, 541, 548, 559, 563, 566, 570, 593
battery, 45, 48, 60, 183, 189, 212, 213, 259, 313, 314, 354-357, 368, 369, 385, 386, 419, 422, 435, 439-442, 502, 508, 526, 535, 539, 548, 558, 559, 560, 562, 564, 565, 568
battery cable cleaner, 189
battery charger, 308
battery cleaner, 189
battery indicator gauge, 565
battery-powered radio, 486
baxters, 156
Bay Bridge, 21, 22, 23, 25
bay leaf, 107, 291
BBQ: grill, 43, 46, 325, 331, 332, 334, 529, 538; grills, 46, 331, 332, 529, 538; sauce, 109, 141
bean: baked, 155, 157; Chinese, 222, 224; Cowpea (Kaffir), 278; Guada (Guada gourd), 278; Hyacinth, 278; pots, 337; runner, 279; soya, 279; winged, 280; yam, 280
beans: dried, 123; green, 157; red, 493; soybeans, 115, 493
beards (men with), 419
bed of sand, 67
bedding, 37
bedroll, 47, 182
Beech, 252
beef, 40, 100, 116, 149, 220, 221, 267, 292, 293, 340, 342, 343, 407, 578; corned, 146, 149; ground, 149; hamburger jerky, 293; hearty, 114; lean brisket, 295
beer, 21
bees, 89, 273, 388
beeswax, 223, 225, 241, 245
beetroot, 278
beets, 103, 104, 144, 287, 292, 296, 298, 352
belts and hoses, 189
Benadryl, 51, 113, 194, 402
bench grinder, 308
bentonite, 76, 509
benzine, 521
Benzoin powder, 228
berries, 143, 151, 296
Bertolli, 156
Best Buy, 170, 504
best-by date, 152, 153, 156-164, 166, 168- 172, 175-178
beta or alpha particles, 452
beta rays, 452
Betadine, 51, 54, 55, 113, 202
Betty Crocker, 102, 124, 162
beverage dealer, 73

Bible, 28, 42, 49, 62, 187, 443
Bible prophecy, 28
Biblical, 240
bicarbonate of soda, 50
bicycle, 44
Big Ben, 187
Big Berkey, 58, 60, 61, 72
Big G Cereals, 162
Big Jim, 290
big pharma, 196
Bigelow Teas, 156
bike, 33, 40, 348
Bikini Atoll, 453
billion, 29, 30, 31, 62, 196, 266, 359, 415, 513, 520, 547, 555, 576
billy can, 185
Bi-Lo, 52, 125
bin Laden, 415
bio-attack, 426
bio-chem attack, 424
biocide, 69, 321
biodegradable, 74, 263, 384, 393, 395
biodegradable plastics, 74
bioflavinoids, 424
biological, 67, 196, 370, 415, 416, 417, 418, 419, 422, 423, 424, 425, 426, 429, 432, 433, 452, 580
biological action, 67
biological agents, 416, 417, 419, 423, 424, 425, 429, 580
biologicals, 416, 425
biologist, 276
bio-warfare decontamination, 14, 426
birch bark, 252
bird, 72, 78, 80, 81, 252, 301, 399, 400, 409, 494, 574, 576, 577, 578, 582, 583, 585, 586; birds, 31, 87, 398, 399, 400, 573, 574, 583; cages, 400; droppings, 72, 78, 80; game, 149; perches, 80; seed, 205
Birds Eye, 156, 157, 161, 163, 169, 170
birth certificates, 593
birth control, 113, 202
birth of jesus, 597
births, 49, 187
biscuits, 148, 341
Bisquick, 100, 162
bitter apple spray, 398
Bivouac Buddy, 386
Black Ash (tree), 252
black currants, 284
black ice, 562
black olives, 156
bladder, 384, 386, 440, 441
blanching, 283, 287, 288
blanket, 37, 50, 193, 307, 398, 559, 589, 593
blankets, 186, 593
blast: explosive, 451; lateral, 556

BlastMatch, 256
blatant warnings, 445
blazo, 322
bleach, 38, 53, 54, 64, 65, 66, 73, 74, 116, 124, 138, 200, 209, 235, 294, 373, 374, 376, 377, 379, 380, 381, 382, 391, 426, 427, 428, 432, 493, 515, 527, 530, 531, 532, 536, 584, 585
bleeding gums, 493, 495
blended paraffin, 244
blended scents, 227
blender, 218, 307
blender soap, 218
blinding blue-white light, 448
blinding flash of light, 448
blistering, 403
blisters, 35, 519, 566
blistex, 51, 195
blizzard, 46, 325, 559, 564
blizzard warning, 557
blizzards, 32
Blockbuster, 504
blocked by snow, 562
blocks of magnesium, 255
blood, 88, 97, 98, 186, 191, 196, 375, 404, 405, 425, 452, 494, 518; circulation, 186; cleansers, 425
blood pressure medication, 50, 186
bloody stool, 404
blow dryer, 43, 212, 306, 404
blow dryers, 306
blower unit, 442
blue bonnet, 159
Blue Boy Vegetables, 155
blue gum, 252
blueberries, 284
bluefish, 148
bluestone, 257
blunt tipped scissors, 398
blush, 203
board games, 187, 589
boarding kennels, 396
boat, 41, 132, 332, 344, 358, 391, 413, 535, 536, 541, 583, 597; (-s), 20, 42, 68, 137, 378, 392, 395, 541, 554
body heat, 36, 47, 182, 558, 559, 562
body oils, 84
boil: food, 493; water, 71, 85, 330
boiled, 37, 53, 71, 84, 92, 233, 237, 405, 432, 433, 434, 532
boiler, 71, 228, 233, 241, 242, 246, 247, 249, 257, 258, 259; rooms, 459
boiling, 53, 429; or iodination, 432; point, 71; pool water, 84; water, 71, 84, 185, 233, 246, 283, 284, 285, 288, 289, 298, 382, 383

boils: water, 328, 329, 330
Bok Choy (Chinese Cabbage), 278
bolides, 544
bologna loaves, 146
bolt action rifle, 410
bomb, 413, 414, 415, 440, 446, 447, 448, 449, 451, 453, 454, 455, 481, 484, 487, 542, 544; ammonium nitrate, 412; cyanide dispersed with, 412
bombing: homicide, 413
bomb-making ingredients, 412
bonds, 49, 187
bone breaker, 37
bone marrow, 452, 494
bones, 205, 270, 272
boning knife, 185
Book of Revelation, 444
books, 34, 38, 44, 132, 137, 192, 361, 372, 389, 398, 443, 455, 457, 458, 587, 593
boosting the immune system, 424
boots, 35, 43, 48, 137, 183, 245, 398, 549, 559, 561, 585, 593
Borage, 222, 224, 278
borax, 233, 235, 380, 381
boric acid, 257; leaking, 485
borlotti, 101, 136
bottle opener, 185
botulinum toxin, 432; (-s), 431
botulism, 119, 432, 544
bouillon, 102, 139, 158, 589
Boulder Creek, 506
bountiful garden, 275
bowel discomfort, 95
bowels, 441
bowl, 200, 218
box oven cooking, 11, 345
boxelder, 252
boy scout training, 33
Brady model SFV75, 210
brain damage, 518
brake fluid, 189, 201
brakes, 560
bran, 96, 227, 229
brand electronics, 306
bras, 36
brass and copper cleaner, 382
Brazil, 222, 224, 543
brazil nut, 222, 224
bread, 19, 96, 115, 120, 121, 132, 138, 185, 268, 327, 333, 337, 490, 504; baking, 327, 341; brown, 155; crumbs, 139; garlic parmesan monkey, 342; loaf pan, 185; mixes, 100, 120; monkey, 342; nutritious recipe, 115; recipe, 115; sesame seed monkey, 342; yeast, 150
breakables, 123, 507
breast milk, 492

Brer Rabbit Molasses, 157
brick, 78, 254, 273, 274, 361, 394, 395, 462, 463, 491, 510, 515, 523
bricks, 184, 260, 273, 364, 390, 394, 455, 458, 510
Bridgette Gaitor, 504
Brillo, 39, 112, 187, 200
briquettes, 184, 323, 327, 340, 345
British Berkefeld, 58
British Columbia, 422, 543, 553, 574
British S-10 mask, 418
Britolite, 322
broccoli, 136, 144, 278, 288, 292, 296
broken bones, 23, 401
broken sewer mains, 44
bromine, 84
bromine chemistry, 84
brooks, 157
broom, 44, 516; and mop, 188
broth, 102, 141
brown rice, 96, 136, 352
brown spots on vegetables, 299
brown sugar, 295
brownies, 168, 333
brucella aerosols, 432
brucellosis, 14, 432
brushless, 310
brussel sprouts, 144, 278, 288
bubbles, 73, 75, 121, 220, 221, 226, 229, 230, 232, 238, 243, 245, 246, 248, 249, 570
bubonic plague, 433
Buck Tilton, 389
bucket, 75, 84, 91, 93, 129, 130, 131, 132, 133, 136, 237, 257, 384, 388, 389, 390, 391, 440, 441, 489, 490, 491, 514, 515, 524, 567, 585, 596; (-s), 76, 120, 122, 127, 130, 131, 132, 133, 134, 135, 136, 137, 266, 390, 529, 592; 5-gallon, 272, 440
buckwheat, 136
bud colors, 243
budget, 36, 37, 46, 52, 80, 83, 95, 98, 325, 415, 422, 459, 545; household water, 83
buffalo, 252, 324
buffered aspirin, 398
bug infestations, 397
bugs, 57, 64, 129, 271, 281, 358, 438
building codes, 476, 535, 539
bulging, 126, 138, 154, 155, 529, 561
bulk, 28, 37, 38, 39, 40, 52, 94, 122, 124, 125, 129, 331, 332, 341, 342, 572; buy in, 94, 227; food, 52; purchase, 52; purchasing power, 94
bung wrench, 188
bungee, 36; straps, 36

bungie: cord, 273
burlap, 258; sack, 258, 489
burn bans, 388
burners, 326, 331
burning restrictions, 388
burns, 194, 252, 256, 305, 322, 324; burn relief, 51
burrowing animals, 273
burying shipping containers, 15, 474
bush stove, 336
bushfires, 77
butane, 257, 325, 326, 327, 329; cylinders, 326; lighters, 257
butcher knife, 185
butter, 19, 97, 105, 108, 114, 116, 120, 125, 132, 141, 219, 226, 232, 267, 341, 342, 490, 592
butterfat, 223, 225
butterfly sutures, 50
buttermilk, 104, 147, 151, 174, 228
butternut squash (gramma), 278
BW aerosol, 426, 428

C

cabbage, 136, 144, 145, 150, 278, 288, 296, 298, 352
cabin, 33
cacti, 87, 245
Cadbury Confectionery, 158
caffeine, 519, 558
cajun seasoning, 295
cake, 100, 139, 148, 150; mix, 139; racks, 294
Calamine, 194
calcium, 65, 97, 195; chloride, 257; hypochlorite, 65
calendar days, 180
calendula, 228, 280
California, 26, 371, 415, 449, 505, 520, 552, 553, 591, 592; Long Beach, 474; Los Angeles, 64, 369, 416, 454; Oakland, 20, 22, 25, 474
Californians, 506
Camelbak, 183
camembert, 147, 151, 267
camp: fork, 185; heat, 323; oven, 333, 336; stove, 184, 185, 326; stoves, 326
Camp Filter, 58
campers, 42, 137, 325, 344, 355, 569
camphophenique, 51, 194
camping, 33, 36, 40, 41, 44, 46, 85, 119, 187, 241, 254, 281, 292, 323, 326, 333, 363, 384, 385, 386, 389, 391, 392, 393, 436, 440, 531, 571, 585, 591; gear, 46, 254; in home, 43; pillows, 36
Campmor, 328, 332, 386, 391, 392
campsite, 33, 386

can opener, 43, 47, 456, 491, 593
Canada, 124, 152, 160, 161, 162, 168, 173, 174, 179, 265, 301, 304, 310, 316, 321, 326, 333, 344, 346, 358, 360, 361, 372, 384, 396, 407, 411, 416, 418, 422, 425, 503, 514, 572, 574, 598, 633; Kincardine, Ontario, 543
Canadian, 310, 407, 418, 422, 590
Canadian M69 C3 and C4, 422
Canadian military, 418
Canadian supplier, 418
candle: for heat, 562; layered, 249
candle (injection molded), 240
candles, 32, 33, 43, 45, 46, 47, 184, 202, 240, 241, 242, 243, 244, 245, 246, 247, 248, 249, 257, 258, 443, 457, 508, 537, 538, 563, 571, 572, 589, 593; candlemaking, 8, 240, 243; cracks in, 248; dye, 230, 247; holder, 47, 184; (-s), 184; smokes, 249; stubs, 258
candy (hard), 47, 106
candy bars, 52
candy thermometer, 240
canister, 52, 61, 129, 256, 308, 322, 328, 331, 423
canned (tinned) butter, 120
canned food, 127, 325, 388, 505; (s), 40
canned goods, 32, 43, 94, 115, 119, 120, 137, 154, 432, 456, 529
canned items, 114
canning jars and lids, 185
cantaloupe (rockmelon), 278
canteen, 40
canteen bacteria-free, 40
capacitor start induction run, 309
Cape Gooseberry (Jam Fruit), 278
capers, 103
Capri Sun, 158
car, 22, 25, 33, 45, 46, 51, 58, 60, 61, 82, 95, 191, 195, 358, 392, 397, 398, 403, 405, 415, 425, 429, 439, 481, 484, 502, 511, 516, 524, 527, 536, 539, 549, 556, 558, 559, 560, 561, 562, 563, 564, 565, 593; carburetor, 305, 313; charger adapter, 593; clutch, 562, 563; damaged ignition wires, 561; motor oil, 201; radiator, 71, 560; radiator cap, 561; radiator fluid, 71; radiator sealer, 189; spare tire and rim, 189; spare tires, 44; spark plugs, 189; tire chains, 559; transmission fluid, 189; transmission lines, 303, 489, 501; two feet of water will carry away, 537

car gets stuck in the snow, 17, 562
car items, 565
car travel, 398
carabineer, 443
carbohydrates, 121
carbon, 58, 61, 62, 67, 68, 82, 84, 132, 265, 277, 302, 310, 313, 314, 321, 322, 323, 324, 366, 436, 559, 562, 564, 568
carbon core, 58
carbon monoxide, 310, 314; poisoning, 302, 310, 559, 562, 564
carcasses of animals, 432
carcinogenic, 324
cardboard, 51, 123, 128, 213, 219, 221, 231, 234, 246, 252, 254, 258, 269, 271, 277, 345, 346, 347, 348, 349, 351, 441, 456, 518, 529; boxes, 123, 128, 345, 456, 529
Cardoon, 278
cards, 589
careful hand-washing, 433
carriage bolts, 209, 211
carrot, 136, 278; (-s), 103, 144, 288, 292, 296, 298, 352
carry cart, 4, 41
cart, 38, 40, 41, 94, 125, 292, 392
carting waste, 395
cartridge, 58, 60, 61, 82, 429
carts, 33, 41
Cascade, 158
Cascadian Farm, 162
case pricing, 125
cash, 27, 31, 38, 45, 95, 124, 125, 457, 460, 505, 565, 589, 592, 596
Cashmere Bouquet, 204
casing, 66, 75, 209, 210, 373, 375, 565
cassava, 278
casserole mix, 139
casseroles, 150, 333
cast iron, 185, 320, 325, 336, 337, 339, 344
cast iron unit, 325
castor, 219, 236
casualties, 412, 489, 501, 553
cat, 33, 50, 53, 110, 120, 205, 397, 398, 401, 406; (-s) 397, 398, 400, 422, 550; food, 110, 205
catchment surface, 79, 80
catelli, 158
cauliflower, 144, 278, 288, 296
caulk, 188, 201, 558
caulking gun, 188
caustic, 216, 217, 219, 232, 237, 238, 264, 426, 428; soda, 216, 232, 237, 264
caves, 459
cayenne, 107, 290
CB, 308, 353

CD, 2, 183, 281, 593
Cedar, 252, 255
ceiling: drywall, 128; tiles, 259
Celeriac, 278
celery, 107, 108, 136, 144, 278, 288, 292, 296
cell phone and charger, 593
cellophane, 254, 529
celtuce (chinese lettuce), 278
central pressure, 534
Centre for Research on the Epidemiology of Disasters, 633
centrifugal, 309, 463, 473
Century-Primus, 330, 331
ceramic, 58, 59, 121, 221, 257
cereal bars, 139
chain saw, 308
chain with buckets, 75
chamomile, 228
chance of survival, 396
Chao Tan, 349
chapstick, 51, 112, 195, 204, 252
charcoal, 39, 56, 67, 68, 184, 260, 261, 322, 325, 327, 332, 334, 339, 343, 344, 345, 346, 489, 558; activated, 195; activated granulated, 68; briquettes, 327, 345; making, 9, 260; powdered, 68
charcoal filter: (-s) activated, 67
charcoal filters, 67
charge card account numbers, 49, 187
charge cards, 48, 183
charring process, 261
chat with the Lord, 32
check valve, 210, 526
check your household wiring, 522
checks, 38, 45, 48, 183, 411
cheddar, 105, 147, 151, 267
cheerios, 162
cheese, 97, 114, 120, 128, 132, 148, 150, 231, 245, 267, 268, 340, 341, 342, 343, 490, 530
cheese cake, 150
cheese spreads, 286
cheesecloth, 185
cheeses (hard), 490
chef boyardee, 159
chemical: (-s), 130, 391, 416; anchors, 512; heat, 37; products, 416; treatment, 53; warfare, 417, 422, 436
chemical agents, 415, 421, 424, 427, 433, 437
chemical and biological nasties, 423
chemical attack, 426
chemical contaminants, 71
chemical decontamination, 427
Chemical Defense Establishment, 436

cherries, 104, 143, 151, 284, 296; cherry, 252
chervil, 107, 280
chestnut, 252
chewing gum, 47, 106, 589
Chex, 162
chicken, 97, 101, 102, 114, 146, 149, 177, 190, 223, 225, 295, 352; fat, 223, 225; livers, 149
chicken tetrazzini, 114
chicken wire, 190
chicory (endive), 278
Chicxulub, 543, 544
chiffon, 148, 150, 267, 530
child, 41, 51, 353, 419, 441, 460, 492, 504, 529, 561, 595
children, 21, 23, 26, 32, 33, 35, 36, 43, 44, 46, 62, 119, 125, 128, 217, 227, 237, 326, 330, 401, 408, 409, 413, 418, 419, 425, 440, 441, 454, 484, 486, 492, 493, 518, 519, 521, 531, 537, 548, 556, 561, 577, 583, 595; respond to trauma, 595
children and infants masks, 14, 418
chile con carne, 114
chili, 101, 107, 109, 141, 155, 158, 163, 164, 279, 288, 289, 504; chilies, 107, 289; flakes, 107; pepper, 295
chimayo, 290
chimney, 43, 252, 334, 339, 344, 345, 346, 508, 510, 521, 523, 556, 597; (-s), 252, 487, 508, 510, 521, 523
China, 346, 354, 360, 445, 474, 574
Chinese Five-Spice Powder, 295
chiropractic, 37
chives, 107, 278
chloramines, 65, 84
Chlor-Floc, 56
chlorinated: hydrocarbons, 68; lime, 391
chlorination, 65
chlorine, 53, 54, 56, 57, 64, 65, 66, 67, 68, 69, 72, 73, 74, 75, 77, 82, 84, 116, 294, 373, 374, 375, 376, 377, 378, 379, 381, 382, 391, 428, 429, 432, 433, 515, 530, 531, 585, 586; free, 64, 74, 84; shoveling, 395; solid, 84; solution, 428; solutions, 428; test kit, 64; test kits, 64, 84
chocolate, 40, 105, 106, 114, 139, 141, 589; bar, 563; bars, 40, 106; chips, 106; hot cocoa, 47; hot mix, 40; melted, 286; melts, 106; syrup, 106, 141
choking, 406
choko (chayote, 278
cholera, 59, 84, 209, 389, 430
chopped dates, 286

chopped raisins, 286
chops, 146
Christmas scents, 227
Church of Jesus Christ of Latter Day Saints, 95
churches, 459, 565
cigar butts, 521
cigarette: douse, 521
cigarette lighter, 133, 255
cigarette lighters, 202
cigarettes, 51, 504
cinnamon, 107, 228, 257, 258, 286, 341; leaf, 236
circular saw, 308
cistern, 78, 79, 80, 81, 84
Citronella, 228, 245
citrus: fruit, 143, 151; rinds, 270, 272
civil defense, 444, 458
civil unrest, 32, 38, 206, 576
clams, 146
Claratyne, 51, 202
Claritin-D, 194, 196
clay, 75, 76, 77, 134, 135, 246, 252, 269, 489, 490, 509
clean rags, 189
clean vegetation, 35
cleaners, 12, 13, 381, 382
cleaning, 39, 41, 44, 79, 83, 124, 182, 191, 213, 338, 376, 377, 378, 381, 382, 391, 409, 429, 569, 581, 584
cleanser, 112, 200, 228
cleansers, 200, 203; 409, 112, 154, 158; Ajax, 200; Comet, 159; Exit Mould, 200; Glen 20, 112, 187, 200, 391; Lime Away, 167; Pine O Clean, 200, 391; Pine Sol, 112, 200
clear soap (faux neutrogena), 233
climate, 30, 31, 127, 416, 517, 560
clinique, 203
Clint Eastwood's movie, 409
clog remover, 112
Clorox, 12, 154, 158, 176, 200, 373, 375, 376, 426, 427, 428, 429, 432, 440; wash, 426
closed-cell foam pad, 36
clostridium bacteria, 431
clostridium botulinum, 431
cloth bandages, 37
clothes, 35, 38, 39, 48, 53, 84, 93, 110, 183, 187, 216, 336, 339, 381, 382, 427, 429, 441, 516, 519, 522, 531, 561, 593; change of, 48, 183, 593; freezer, 572; line, 182; pins, 182
clothing, 34, 35, 36, 43, 137, 183, 216, 217, 427, 428, 429, 434, 442, 457, 484, 508, 519, 527, 531, 558, 572, 585, 587, 593
cloud of debris, 548
cloves, 107, 228, 229, 238, 286, 425

CO_2, 131, 132, 277
coagulation, 431
coal, 324, 359; bin, 477
coat, 35, 252, 258, 282, 284, 285; hanger, 345, 491
cocoa, 106, 109, 139, 220, 222, 224, 228, 589; pods, 237
coconut, 87, 97, 106, 139, 220, 222, 224, 234, 296
cod, 148, 197
code, 41, 138, 152, 153, 154, 155, 157, 158, 162, 166, 168, 169, 170, 176, 178, 204, 205, 358, 360, 370, 476, 539, 549
coding systems, 152, 166, 168, 173, 178
Codral, 51, 202
coffee, 19, 20, 43, 53, 74, 120, 137, 241, 246, 270, 325, 392, 529; cans, 139, 245; filters, 111; maker, 185; pot, 39; seed, 222, 224; shops, 74; whiteners, 139
Coffee Mate, 105
coins, 52, 183, 566, 589
Coke, 73
colander, 217
cold compress, 403
Cold War, 459, 486
Coleman, 322, 328, 329, 330, 331, 333, 386, 589; Fuel, 322, 328, 589; Xpedition, 329
Coles Express, 52
Coles Supermarkets, 52
Coles-Myer, 52, 125; discount card, 52; stock, 52
colgin, 158
collapsing walls, 487
collar, 50, 473
collard, 278, 289
collection and storage, 5, 73
colloidal: silver, 62, 212, 213, 214, 425; solutions, 212
colonial shutters, 539
color blocks, 244
color changes in the fruit, 297
color code, 36
Colorado, 1, 2, 43, 76, 122, 123, 195, 277, 282, 294, 303, 311, 325, 359, 360, 373, 388, 404, 414, 448, 449, 450, 494, 509, 542, 561; Denver, 46, 359, 360, 448, 450, 451, 474; Fort Collins, 277
Colorado State University, 277, 294
colorant, 240; (-s), 8, 220, 227, 243
colorful burning pine cones, 257
colorful flames, 257
coloring soap, 229
Columbo, 162
Colza, 222, 224
comb and brush, 49, 184, 186
Combi Plus, 58

comet, 544
comfort foods, 119
commercial cleaning products, 380
commercial closet systems, 137
commercial drain opener, 382, 383
commercial dryer (cd), 281
commercial fuel suppliers, 318
commercial microfilters, 55
commode, 386
common appliances, 540
common sense, 32, 33, 37, 38, 46, 217, 240, 410, 496
communicable diseases, 531
communication, 7, 183, 566
communications: cell phone, 12, 38, 353, 354, 355, 540; shortwave, 12, 177, 358, 359, 360, 361, 368, 369, 370, 372, 443, 502, 587; shortwave antennas, 12, 361, 363, 368; shortwave antennas, expedient, 12, 364; shortwave classes, 360; shortwave emergency broadcasts, 12, 370; shortwave hurricane freq., 370; shortwave magazines, 372; shortwave organizations, 360, 370, 372; shortwave radios, 356, 368, 369; two-way radios, 12, 354, 355; walkie-talkie, 353, 354, 355, 356; walkie-talkie chart, 356
community, 43, 359, 459, 460, 485, 486, 487, 516, 519, 521, 525, 526, 527, 535, 537, 548, 577, 594, 596
comp checks, 425
compass, 46, 52, 355, 357, 563, 565, 566; (-es), 52, 182
complete lockdown, 459
compost: bench, 270; buckets, 190; pile, 271, 272, 273, 515; worm, 271, 272
composter, 270, 273, 393, 395
composting and burning, 388
compression bandage, 191
computer: (-s), 310
computers, 593
comstock fruit pie filling, 159
concrete, 28, 77, 78, 122, 123, 124, 201, 271, 314, 339, 361, 377, 378, 394, 455, 458, 459, 463, 475, 476, 477, 483, 510, 511, 512, 518, 540, 549; block, 81; tanks, 77, 78; walls, 122
conditioner, 112, 184, 186, 307
condo, 123, 275, 324, 459, 538; insurance, 538
conduits, 80
Congress, 445, 545

conspiracy, 412
constant storage, 127
constant temperature, 126, 151; (-s), 136
constipation, 51, 194
Contadina Products, 159
container: 40 ft. shipping, 474
container-grown veggies, 275
containers, 52, 56, 73, 74, 78, 85, 121-123, 125, 127, 128, 130, 131, 133, 134, 137, 150, 209, 212-214, 217, 231, 237, 245, 249, 257, 264, 269, 271, 277, 289, 297, 299, 318, 321, 334, 374, 377, 378, 393, 401, 428, 456, 474-476, 477, 484, 490, 492, 515, 521, 523, 529-532, 536, 538, 568, 584, 593; 55-gallon, 73, 80, 260, 261, 318, 319, 320, 388; food, 6, 130; fuel, 317, 318, 565
contaminants, 57, 60, 68, 69, 75, 79, 80, 261, 415, 423, 438, 440, 483, 490, 578, 580, 581
contaminate, 53, 79, 80, 317, 447, 453, 482, 582, 585; (-ed), 53, 55, 56, 71, 72, 74, 75, 79, 88, 121, 124, 194, 213, 265, 301, 374, 375, 418, 426, 428, 429, 432-434, 437, 439, 474, 485, 487-490, 492, 494, 527, 529, 531, 536, 549, 568, 581, 582, 586
contamination, 56, 57, 67, 74, 82, 84, 146, 293, 378, 406, 429, 432, 433, 434, 474, 481, 483, 515, 553, 568, 574
contracts, 187
controlling the temperature, 126
convection ovens, 281
convention centers, 459
conventional ovens, 281, 346
conversion charts, 18, 598
convert julian dating, 180
cookbook, 185
cooked grain per day, 493
cookie dough, 148
cookies, 47, 139, 148, 150, 352
cooking forks, 39
cooking power, 328, 331
Cooking Temperature Equivalents, 600
cooking without power, 11, 322
cool basement, 122
co-op, 52, 121, 125; (-s), 52
co-ops, 6, 125
copha, 105, 339
copper, 80, 257, 361
copper sulfate, 257
copper tubing, 71
coriander (cilantro), 107, 280, 286
corkscrew, 185
corn, 31, 97, 115, 119, 120, 136, 147, 168, 220, 262, 271, 276, 277, 283, 286, 288, 297, 492,

493, 494; Corn Meal, 117, 118; Corn Salad, 278; cornmeal, 96, 115, 119, 121, 268; on the cob, 288, 352
Corn Flakes, 101
Corn Syrup, 106, 117, 118
corrugated box, 345
corynebacterium diphtheriae, 430
cosmetics, 184, 186
cottage, 105, 147, 245, 267
cotton, 9, 37, 50, 112, 193, 259, 589; balls, 259; string, 258, 290
cough: drops, 194; syrup, 194
coughing, 65
country time, 159
couscous, 139
cover all exterior vents, 523
cover your mouth and nose, 556
covered container, 139, 147, 295, 493, 538
covered reservoirs, 488
cow, 223, 225, 252, 324, 406
coxiella burnetii, 433
coyotes, 270, 388
cracked skin, 39
crackers, 47, 100, 139, 589
craft glue, 201
cranberries, 143, 284
crane, 476
crater, 412, 413, 451, 542, 543, 544; (-s), 542, 543
crawlspace, 550; (-s), 137
crayons, 230
cream, 19, 147, 148, 150, 151, 231, 234, 245, 267, 268, 340, 341, 342, 343, 398
cream cheese, 148, 150
cream of: tartar, 107; wheat, 101
cream rinse, 112
creamette, 160
credit cards, 45, 48, 183, 523, 592, 593
creeks, 75, 525, 528
crescent wrenches, 211
Cresson H. Kearny, 114, 449
Crisco, 105, 141, 233, 337, 339
crops, 31, 262, 275, 276, 354, 492, 494, 515
cross-pollination, 276
crow bar, 565
crutches, 186
cryptosporidia, 56, 59, 61, 209
cryptosporidium, 429, 430
crystal ball, 314, 426, 563, 596
Crystal Lite, 109
crystallized, 142
Cuba, 371, 444
Cuban Missile Crisis, 444; revisited, 15, 444
cucumber, 144, 228, 278
culverts, 459
cumin, 107

cupboard storage charts, 7, 139
cupboards, 120, 137, 277
curdling, 219, 227, 238
cured soap, 238
curling iron, 43
cushioning moleskin, 565
custard, 148, 267, 268
cut into strips, 293
cuts from glass, 401
cutting boards, 39, 185
Cyalume, 184
cyanogen, 424
cyberspace, 44
cyclospora, 59
cylinders, 323, 331, 409, 460, 570, 588
Cypress, 26, 81
cysts, 55, 56, 59, 61, 81, 430

D

daily calories, 97
Daily Mfg. Col. Silver 20, 215
dairy: powders, 136; products, 132, 490, 494
dam, 5, 75, 76, 77, 514, 515, 525, 544; (-s), 75, 77, 509, 526, 575
damage potential, 534
damaged leaves, 144, 145
damper, 344, 491, 524
dandelion, 278
danger, 41, 87, 296, 312, 405, 406, 407, 433, 481, 484, 487, 490, 507, 508, 536, 548, 549, 554, 556, 596
dangerous radioactive iodines, 489
Daptex Plus, 438
Dare to Prepare, 2, 28, 32, 153, 182, 187, 460, 503, 590, 596
daring to prepare, 597
dark brown glass, 127, 213, 214
dark room, 73, 127, 291
date of manufacture (dom), 126
date of packing (dop), 154
date stamp, 99, 138, 152, 153, 159
davie, 504, 505
Davis-Besse, 485
dawdling can be expensive, 94
dawn, 160
De Arbol, 290
dead battery, 560, 564
dead date, 123, 126
dead leaves, 78
dead microbes, 57
dealing with: stress, 18, 594
death: certificates, 187; should be recorded, 497
debris, 53, 78, 79, 80, 82, 207, 208, 210, 217, 221, 253, 277, 313, 376, 377, 378, 379, 413, 448, 451, 462, 507, 508, 516, 523, 525, 537, 538, 540, 544, 547, 549, 550, 554, 556

Dec A Cake, 160
decayed fruit, 143
deceased animals, 492
dechlorination, 56
deck of cards, 187
deck screws, 207, 208
decompose, 271, 392
decomposing material, 271
decongestant, 51, 194
decontamination: and isolation, 432, 433, 434, 435; shower, 427
deep freezer, 307
deep well pumps, 75
deep wells, 65
deer, 87, 124, 294, 388, 409, 410, 561
Deet, 182
defroster, 558, 560
degradable, 81
degree, 203
dehumidifier, 124, 127
dehydrate, 92, 129, 281, 295; (-ing), 282, 287, 293
dehydrated: eggs, 120; foods, 281; fruits, 40; products, 116, 119; vegetables, 120, 287, 298
dehydrated food, 6, 114, 116, 456
dehydrating: foods, 9, 281
dehydrator, 281, 282, 283, 285, 286, 287, 292, 293, 294
dehyrdation: avoid, 559
de-icer, 565
Del Monte, 160, 174
delivery trucks, 94
Delta and Pine Land Company, 276
Demazin, 51, 202
dense fabrics, 429
densely populated city, 422
dental floss, 49, 50, 112, 184, 186, 193, 203
dented cans, 138
dentures, 593
dentures care, 50, 186
deodorant, 36, 49, 112, 184, 186, 203, 593
deodorizer, 187
deodorizing properties, 382
depression, 406, 497, 594
Derm-Aid, 51, 194
dermal exposure, 426, 428
dermally active, 432, 433, 434
desalinization plants (military), 71
desert, 42, 86, 87, 93, 127, 136, 281, 373, 409, 441, 514, 542
desiccant, 135; (-s), 120, 134; bag, 135; bags, 135
destroyer, 413, 414
destroys the retina, 448
detergent, 187, 200, 589; solution, 374, 378, 379, 530

detonation, 412, 446, 448, 449, 450, 451, 453, 455, 459, 499
Dettol, 51, 202
deviled ham, 177
Deyo, 1-3, 76, 95, 98, 119, 120, 123, 125, 126, 182, 185, 396, 586; dam, 76; food storage planner, 95, 98, 119, 120, 125, 126, 185, 586; Holly Drennan, 1, 2, 31, 42, 214, 422, 460, 476, 518, 633; Stan, 1-3, 57, 62, 65, 72, 75, 77, 94, 98, 114, 122, 123, 128, 129, 136, 191, 214, 245, 269, 306, 318, 320, 321, 331, 369, 373, 388, 393, 396, 397, 401, 404-406, 408, 414, 415, 430, 447, 449, 451, 494, 518, 542, 567, 568, 586, 588, 590
diaper rash ointment, 186
diapers, 50, 186, 394, 593
diarrhea, 64, 205, 209, 389, 397, 402, 403, 405, 406, 430, 435, 452, 495, 497, 577; medicine, 37
diasorb, 51, 194
diatomaceous earth (DE), 11, 62, 129, 195, 321
diatoms, 129
Dibucaine, 51
die-off, 67
diesel, 42, 44, 184, 188, 201, 262, 263, 264, 304, 305, 307, 313, 314, 316, 317, 318, 321, 325, 326, 328, 329, 330
diet scales, 217
dietary needs, 38
diethylene, 323
Difflan, 202
digestive tract, 397
digging fork, 190
digital scale, 244
dill, 107, 280
Dimetap, 194
Dimmit, 547
Dinty Moore, 101, 164
diphtheria, 430, 431
direct sunlight, 74, 145, 248, 271, 321, 386
dirt, 68, 80, 84, 129, 144, 206, 207, 208, 276, 376, 377, 378, 380, 388, 394, 395, 450, 456, 474, 494, 509, 540, 581
dirty bomb, 416, 481, 482, 484; Cesium 137, 482, 483, 484; Cobalt 60, 484; spent nuclear fuel, 482, 485
Dirty Devil River, 514
disaster, 24, 28-32, 37, 38, 42, 45, 46, 48, 53, 114, 116, 183, 265, 314, 354, 358, 388, 395-397, 399, 405, 415, 437, 450, 453, 459, 485, 501, 503, 505, 507, 522, 526-528, 532, 535-537, 545, 546, 548, 556-558, 563-565, 594-597; (-s), 28, 29, 30, 33, 44, 45, 114, 116, 191, 206, 226, 317, 395, 401, 402, 503, 528, 554, 560, 563; victims, 596
disaster plan (household), 534, 535, 556
discount stores, 35, 52, 131, 187, 229, 230, 254, 256, 276, 321, 393
disease, 31, 39, 40, 62, 88, 98, 214, 266, 377, 389, 392, 404, 416, 424, 425, 426, 433, 434, 491, 493, 519, 528, 574, 575, 576, 577, 578, 580, 581, 582, 586; waterborne, 430
disease-fighting capabilities, 425
dish, 38, 39, 114, 135, 147, 241, 283, 295, 347, 381; cloths, 185
dishes, 34, 35, 38, 110, 114, 119, 120, 123, 147, 267, 289, 397, 515, 530, 532
dishwasher, 83, 112, 217, 307
disinfect, 64, 79, 209, 376, 377, 392, 419, 490, 531, 532, 586; hands, 209
disinfectant, 32, 44, 57, 65, 69, 82, 124, 128, 338, 373, 375, 382, 397, 429, 457, 531, 538, 584, 585
disinfected, 53, 56, 65, 67, 123, 209, 377, 378, 405, 432, 490, 531, 532
disinfection, 53, 57, 65, 72, 81, 82, 84, 375, 391, 426, 481, 488, 529, 585
disorientation, 558
disposable cups, 46
Disprin, 202
dissolved minerals, 71
distillation, 71, 430, 489
distress reflector triangles, 189
divert surface runoff, 75
DNA, 276
doctors, 37, 575, 577, 578
Doctors for Disaster Preparedness, 458
dog, 110, 120, 205, 270, 272, 394, 589; (-s), 34, 76, 77, 120, 128, 129, 195, 205, 267, 373, 397, 400, 401, 402, 403, 404, 405, 406, 407, 422, 543, 550; droppings, 394; food, 110, 205, 589
dosimeter, 447
DOT certified containers, 475
double boiler, 240
double pole double throw (dpdt), 311
Douglas Fir, 81
downed power lines, 527, 537, 538, 549, 557
downspout, 80; (-s), 80
Dr. Arthur Robinson, 115
Dr. Jane Orient, 458
Dr. Marlene, 129
Dr. Ronald Gibbs, 214

dracunculus medinensis, 427
drainage and secretion precautions, 432
dramamine, 51, 113, 195, 202, 402, 495
Drano, 112, 174
dried: banana chips, 114; banana peels, 237; beef, 146, 155; food, 40, 115, 129, 296, 297; foods, 40, 115, 129, 137, 297; leaves, 271; meat, 292; palm branches, 237; soups, 123; vegetables, 114, 298
Dri-Kem, 391
drill, 188, 211, 271, 308, 511, 513
drill bits, 211
drink fruit juices, 490
drink tubes, 417
drinking system, 417, 418
dripless, 241
dromedary, 161
drop in usable power, 312
drop in voltage, 312
drought, 76, 128, 359, 514, 515, 524
drums, 54; 55 gallon, 80, 318, 320
dry: droppings, 252; granules, 66; ice, 131, 132, 134, 530; leaves, 273; legumes, 493; pine needles, 252; yeast, 117, 118
dry docking/marinas, 541
dryers, 306
drywall buckets, 390
dual heat, 323
dual-canister mount, 417
dual-fuels, 330
Dubon Petit Pois Peas, 157
duck, 146, 149, 200
duck and cover, 444, 458
duct tape, 50, 193, 201, 589
Dugway Proving Ground, 429
Dulcolax, 51, 194
dump truck, 476
durable white plastic seat, 389
Durkee, 161
Durolax, 51, 194
dust, 68, 78, 124, 129, 217, 281, 293, 424, 440, 447, 454, 460, 484, 494, 508, 511, 544, 547, 556
dust masks, 48, 113, 183
dutch oven, 11, 185, 336, 337, 338, 339, 340, 341, 342, 343, 344; (-s), 336, 337, 340, 342, 344; potatoes au gratin, 342; table, 339
dwarf varieties, 275
dye buds or chips, 243
dyes flakes, 244
dynamite, 76, 281, 481, 482
dynasty, 161
dysenteria, 59
dysentery, 209, 389, 430, 528

E

e.coli (Escherichia coli), 59
early symptoms, 495
Earth, 30, 32, 270, 456, 489, 517, 518, 533, 542, 543, 544, 545, 546, 597, 633
earthenware jar, 235
earthnut, 222, 224
earthquake, 21, 25, 26, 31, 33, 42, 45, 122, 123, 305, 449, 502, 506, 507, 508, 509, 510, 511, 512, 513, 514, 517, 542, 552, 553, 554, 555, 563, 564; (-s), 29, 30, 32, 33, 78, 370, 476, 506, 509, 510, 511, 517, 528, 555, 560, 573; Loma Prieta, 21, 25, 26, 31, 33, 42, 45, 122, 123, 305, 449, 502, 506, 507, 508, 509, 510, 511, 512, 513, 514, 517, 542, 552-555, 563, 564
East Grand Forks, Minnesota, 525
EasyFuel, 328
eat: more raw foods, 424
eating utensils, 35
eau de toilette, 204
echinacea, 113, 425
Echo Virus 29, 431
Eco-Fuel, 323
economically, 28, 389, 442, 499
Edam, 147, 151, 267
Edgar Cayce, 28
egg beater, 159, 185, 589; (-s), 159, 589
egg carton, 147, 257; (-s), 257
egg noodles, 140
eggplant, 278, 288, 296, 352
eggs, 19, 31, 56, 97, 125, 129, 147, 160, 266, 267, 268, 277, 327, 341, 342, 373, 378, 492, 493, 494, 529, 530; boiled, 490; raw, 490
eggshells, 270, 272
Egypt, 212, 596, 597
Egyptian fundamentalist, 412
ejector, 75
El Niño, 31, 528
elderly, 32, 50, 186, 304, 389, 440, 486, 518, 544, 576, 593, 594
electric, 19, 27, 43, 68, 119, 299, 301, 306, 313, 333, 487, 489, 499, 500, 521, 526, 537, 539, 540; blankets, 306; fence, 309; grinder, 119; power, 500, 540; razor, 43
electrical: fires, 521, 522; grid, 478, 586; spikes, 310; tape, 213, 565; wiring, 507, 521, 549
electricity, 34, 43, 44, 94, 121, 240, 251, 265, 302-304, 310, 320, 322, 325, 332, 353, 354, 358, 388, 457, 482, 487, 501-503, 507, 508, 518, 526, 530, 538, 557, 567-569, 571

electrodes, 213, 214
electromagnetic pulse (EMP), 489, 498
electronic equipment, 134, 310, 498, 499, 539
electronic ignition modules, 313
Elm, 252
EMA, 32, 358
emergency, 22, 25, 29, 32-34, 38, 39, 40, 42, 44-50, 52, 68, 71, 76, 79, 87, 94, 95, 130, 182, 192, 255, 262, 263, 302, 321, 325, 326, 332, 353, 354, 357-359, 361, 363, 368-370, 373, 384, 389, 393, 396, 397, 402, 437, 441, 442, 457, 459, 486, 487, 493, 500-502, 505, 506, 509, 515, 516, 519, 521-523, 526, 528, 535, 548, 557, 558, 560, 564-566, 569, 571, 586, 587, 597; prepared, 32, 46, 95, 130, 255, 325; preparedness centers, 130; preparedness supplies, 255; rations, 34, 38, 40; supplies, 46, 52, 332, 437, 442, 459
emergency candles, 33, 42, 571, 572
emergency flares, 559
emergency kits: 3 days, 45, 94; 72-Hour, 45, 46, 47, 51, 52, 129, 255, 435, 437, 443, 500, 503, 563
Emergency Management center, 459
emergency radio, 44, 315, 443, 457, 486, 526, 535, 548, 559, 593; NOAA Weather Radio, 357, 358, 369, 526, 535, 548, 558
emerging insects, 129
emotional toll, 594
EMP (electromagnetic pulse), 16, 304, 494, 498, 499, 500, 501, 502
EMU Oil, 223, 225
enamel pan, 233, 234
encephalomyocarditis virus, 431
enchilada: pie, 340, 343; sauce, 108
enchiladas, 342
End of the Age, 597
endive, 144, 278
energy, 31, 40, 46, 69, 71, 86, 210, 240, 281, 291, 302, 303, 324, 354, 363, 364, 366, 393, 424, 430, 448, 477, 482, 499, 500, 501, 507, 516, 517, 542, 559, 588; bars, 46
energy efficient, 281, 430
England: Oxford, 517
enter through the skin, 421
enteric coated, 402
enterovirus virus, 431
entertainment, 44, 446, 448
Envirolet, 393
environmental decontamination, 429, 432, 433, 434

EPA, 32, 55, 56, 62, 69
epicenter, 507
epileptics, 227
Epsom Salts, 193, 194, 202
eruption, 31, 517, 543, 555, 556
escape hoods, 419
Escherichia coli (e.coli), 431
Essential Oils (Eos), 114, 217, 220, 227, 244
Estee Lauder, 203
Esther Dickey, 114
esthetics, 75, 287, 303
Ethan Brand, 306
eucalyptus, 76, 523
Europe, 69, 124, 351, 360, 413, 543, 574, 578
evacuate your animals, 401
evacuation: routes, 42, 453, 486, 526, 535, 536, 553; zone, 536, 538
evaporated milk, 602
evaporation rate, 75
Evening Primrose Oil, 222, 224
Everest Expedition, 387
excavator, 206, 476; (-s), 76
excess air, 131, 150
exfoliating cream, 112, 203
exhaust: pipe, 310, 462, 463, 559, 560; pipes, 462, 560; system, 560
Ex-Lax, 51, 194
expansion bolts, 511
expiration date, 45, 51, 74, 99, 114, 123, 124, 126, 127, 138, 147, 152, 153, 154, 161, 165, 168, 172, 174, 188, 191, 196, 197, 199, 200, 205, 325, 418, 423; (-s), 45, 114, 123, 126, 191, 196
expire date, 99
explode, 65, 132, 253, 317, 323, 500, 544, 565; (-ed) 412, 413, 414, 483, 542, 543, 544
explosion, 320, 412, 413, 447, 448, 451, 462, 464, 481, 482, 484, 486, 487, 555, 568
explosive: yield (no) 451
explosives-filled van, 412
exposed skin decontaminated with soap, 434
exposure to sunlight, 433, 493
exposure to temperatures, 145
extension cord, 312, 313, 443, 521; (-s), 312, 521
extension poles, 184
extra blankets, 32, 46
extreme heat, 122, 354, 448, 518, 519
extremist groups, 412
eye: drops, 51, 113, 194, 202; shadow, 203; wash, 193
eyedropper, 51, 113, 187, 193, 398
eyeglasses, 34, 419, 556

eyes, 19, 20, 21, 22, 25, 27, 50, 55, 62, 90, 137, 207, 208, 227, 232, 263, 317, 358, 398, 404, 406, 409, 412, 414, 419, 424, 427, 428, 448, 474, 482, 493, 545, 556, 578, 584; flush with water, 427
eye-wall, 533

F

F. tularensis, 434
fabric: softener, 112, 187, 200
fabric dye, 229
face and body soap, 234
facial: scrub, 203; soap, 233
fajita sauce, 108
falling bricks, 487
fallout, 92, 415, 437, 440, 444, 445, 447, 449, 451, 453, 454, 455, 456, 457, 458, 459, 460, 461, 462, 474, 486, 488, 489, 490, 491, 492, 493, 494, 551, 588; arrival time, 486; distance from, 460; map, 449; walk away from, 15, 454
fallout areas: sources of water in, 15, 488
fallout particles settle to the bottom, 488
fallout shelter, 444, 455, 456, 457, 458, 459, 460, 462, 474, 486, 491, 551; (-s), 455, 486; (temporary), 445, 487; building shelter, 15, 460, 464; buying shelter, 15, 460; construction plans, 462; construction plans, download, 15, 461; expedient, 15, 455; protective materials, 456, 458; shipping containers, 15, 474
fallout shelters: existing sites, 15, 459
fallout-contaminated roofs, 489
family income, 94
family records, 34
fanny pack, 183
Fargo, North Dakota, 476
fast food, 52, 262
fat, 95, 97, 120, 217, 219, 220, 221, 223, 225, 226, 230, 232, 233, 234, 238, 292, 293, 294, 295, 343, 382, 405, 493, 494, 596; (-s), 40, 97, 217, 218, 219, 220, 221, 223, 225, 226, 230, 232, 234, 235, 236; deer, 223, 225; melted, 221, 236
fatty: acids, 221, 383; foods, 273, 274
faucet, 66, 74, 81, 386, 427; (-s), 66, 74, 515, 516
fault, 507
FDA, 43, 98, 116, 196, 197, 230, 406, 407, 578, 582

fear: of causing panic, 445; of crowds, 594
Federal Emergency Management Agency, 462
feed mill, 125
FEMA, 15, 17, 23, 30, 31, 32, 265, 266, 316, 359, 360, 370, 389, 398, 399, 401, 402, 445, 449, 460, 461, 462, 487, 499, 505, 513, 520, 524, 525, 526, 531, 532, 535, 536, 550, 551, 571, 591, 592, 594, 595, 633; Federal Emergency Management Agency, 15, 17, 23, 30, 31, 32, 265, 266, 316, 359, 360, 370, 389, 398, 399, 401, 402, 445, 449, 460, 461, 462, 487, 499, 505, 513, 520, 524, 525, 526, 531, 532, 535, 536, 550, 551, 571, 591, 592, 594, 595, 633; James Lee Witt, 15, 17, 23, 30-32, 265, 266, 316, 359, 360, 370, 389, 398, 399, 401, 402, 445, 449, 460-462, 487, 499, 505, 513, 520, 524-526, 531, 532, 535, 536, 550, 551, 571, 591, 592, 594, 595, 633; Preparedness Division Director, 551; publication, 461
FEMA FALLOUT AND TORNADO SHELTER, 15, 462
FEMA pamphlet H-12-4.0 (Oct 1987), 462, 463
FEMA pamphlet H-12-4.1, 462, 463
Fennel, 144, 280
ferrocement, 81
fertilizer, 190; (-s), 275, 516
fiber masks, 424
fiberglass, 78, 326, 367, 386, 476, 502, 510, 541
fiesta, 166
fifth wheels, 34, 137
fifty-five gallon, 73
fighting disease, 96
figs, 284, 296
film canister, 38, 52, 256, 277; (-s), 38, 52, 256, 277
filter, 21, 53, 55-62, 67-69, 72, 79, 80, 82, 84, 92, 212, 237, 262, 264, 270, 310, 313, 357, 418-421, 423-425, 427, 429, 438-440, 442, 443, 463, 464, 473, 488-490, 494, 516, 578-582, 586; degradation, 424; life, 58, 60
filtering, 53, 57, 58, 67, 72, 77, 78, 79, 427, 436, 437, 488, 489, 490, 579, 580, 582, 584; through earth, 489
filters: HEPA, 580; ratings, 578
filtration, 53, 61, 68, 81, 82, 84, 436, 440, 442, 462, 488, 489, 490; system, 84, 436, 442

fire, 23, 33, 42, 45, 47, 76, 85, 91, 136, 237, 240, 241, 246, 251, 252, 253, 254, 255, 257, 260, 261, 282, 304, 325, 330, 334, 336, 339, 347, 359, 360, 388, 410, 443, 448, 455, 491, 508, 514, 520, 521, 522, 523, 524, 537, 541, 542, 543, 555, 558, 568; building, 8, 251; departments, 459, 523, 537; extinguisher, 45, 240, 241, 325, 330, 521, 522, 523, 541, 558; hazard, 241, 246, 282, 347, 443, 524, 555; starters, 184
firearm-related injuries, 408
firearms, 408, 409, 410, 411; 10,000 rounds, 411; 125-grain hollow-point bullet, 409; 12-Gauge, 409; 177 air rifle, 410; 20-Gauge shotgun, 409; 22-Caliber, 409; 30,000 rounds, 411; 30-06, 410, 411; 38-Special, 409, 410; 44-Magnum, 409; AK47 or MAK-90, 409; ammo cheap to make, 410; ammo pouch, 41; ammo stockpile, 410; ammunition, 41, 187, 408, 409, 410, 411, 424, 503, 589; Colt AR-15, 409; Glock .40 caliber, 409; handgun, 41, 408, 409; high velocity of the bullet, 410; hollow point rounds, 409; larger game, 409; lever-action rifles in 30-30, 409; M1 Garand, 409; making your own ammunition, 410; military calibers, 410; practice with your weapons, 411; primer caps, 410; recoil of a shotgun, 409; reloading supplies, 410; Remington 12-Gauge, 409; revolver, 409; Ruger Mini-14, 409; S&W .357, 409, 411; semi-automatic, 409; Winchester Model 94, 409
fireball, 447, 448
fireplace, 24, 136, 322, 325, 384, 388, 438, 484, 521, 524, 557, 558; (-s), 53, 254, 255, 257, 510, 567
fireproof shutters, 523
fire-resistant draperies, 523
fires, 22, 31, 94, 237, 251, 254, 255, 302, 334, 359, 370, 491, 506, 520, 521, 522, 523, 524, 543, 553, 570, 591, 592
firestarters, 111, 202, 255, 344
first aid, 28, 32, 33, 37, 38, 45, 51, 153, 191, 192, 206, 397, 398, 402, 408, 457, 505, 522, 548, 566, 587; kit, 38, 46, 47, 52, 182, 566, 589, 593; tape, 51, 193

first runoff, 489
first time chlorination, 65
FirstEnergy, 301, 485
fish, 31, 101, 146, 148, 150, 153, 177, 195, 205, 267, 268, 270, 272, 295, 352, 589; aquariums, 397; food, 205
fishermen, 325
fishing: boats, 42; line, 37, 366, 367; poles, 182
five gallon pail, 48, 183
fixative: (-s), 228; for fragrances, 229
flammable: furniture, 524; liquids, 487, 508, 521; vegetation, 523
flanged lid, 336
flank steak, 295
flapper valve, 75
flares, 31, 189, 518, 562, 565
flash flood, 514, 525, 526, 527, 528, 535, 555, 560; (-s), 525, 528, 535, 555, 560
flash or fireball, 486
flashlight (, 45, 537, 548, 561
flat braid, 242
flea medications, 397
flea/tick/mosquito repellent, 398
flexible hose, 443
flexible metal snake, 383
flies, 88, 89, 274, 388, 395
flint, 184, 255, 256
floc together, 67
flocculation, 67
flood: (-s), 31, 33, 34, 39, 265, 370, 399, 505, 525, 526, 528, 532, 533; warning, 526; watch, 526; water pooled remaining, 531
flooding, 23, 27, 31, 32, 42, 266, 373, 400, 525, 526, 528, 529, 533, 534, 537, 549, 553, 557, 564
floodlight, 307
floodwaters, 359, 527, 529, 532, 564
floor and roof slabs, 462
floor captains, 538
Florida, 30, 56, 265, 304, 316, 371, 402, 444, 453, 503, 504, 505, 524, 533, 541, 596; gas stations, 503; Miami, 415, 453, 474, 504; Miami-Dade schools, 504; South Florida, 503, 504
flounder, 148
flour, 40, 100, 117, 118, 140, 185, 240, 268, 340, 342, 343, 352, 529, 589; (-s), 136
flow rate, 55, 62, 67, 68, 69, 83, 210
flower: oils, 220; petals, 258
flu, 51, 193, 194, 202, 576
flu-like symptoms, 124, 594
flush: first, 80
flushes, 80, 83, 393

fly larvae, 273
flying: glass, 448, 451; objects, 401
foam: caulk, 123, 128; mattress pads, 182; sealant, 436, 438
foil, 112, 127, 130, 144, 150, 245, 246, 248, 254, 258, 277, 281, 286, 293, 337, 339, 345, 346, 347, 348, 349, 518, 529
folding shovel, 50
fondue: cookbook, 325; pot, 43, 325
fondue pot, 43, 325
fondues from around the world, 325
food, 9, 33, 47, 50, 52, 73, 94, 95, 99, 114-116, 120, 123, 126, 130, 152, 162, 182, 185, 195, 205, 206, 230, 231, 245, 265, 272-274, 282, 296-299, 325, 334, 337, 346, 394, 405, 408, 409, 434, 447, 484, 492, 530, 544, 566, 575, 591, 592; bowl, 50; freshness, 152; planner, 123, 126, 182; processing plants, 130; processor, 226, 286, 298; removing moisture from, 281; scraps, 273
food containers, 6, 130
food grade containers, 130
food storage planner, 120; Deyo Food Storage Planner, 6, 95, 98, 99, 119, 120, 125, 126, 185, 586; Mormon 4, 95, 114, 115; Mormon Food Guides, 116, 117, 118; One Year Supply To Feed One Adult, 115, 119
foods: repackage, 94
foot: pump, 384; valve, 75, 209, 210, 211
forged Swedish passport, 412
formaldehyde, 429
formation of adhesions, 428
formula, 50, 186, 204, 365, 383
Fosseys, 52
foundation, 203, 545
Four Bedroom, 40 foot Containers (3 of), 478
four-wheel skids, 562
Fowlers Vacola, 282, 292
Fox Hill Corporation, 333
Fr. Lavender, 228
fragrance oils (FO), 217, 220, 227, 247
fragrances, 204, 220, 227, 228, 232, 235, 243, 244
France, 62, 346, 349
frankfurters, 146, 149
freak storm, 31, 503, 560
free-standing, 53
freeze, 141, 149, 151, 292
freeze seeds, 277
freeze-dried food, 6, 116

freezer, 38, 42, 43, 94, 116, 131, 132, 137, 148, 149, 150, 151, 226, 231, 234, 236, 246, 249, 266, 277, 286, 287, 297, 299, 308, 388, 398, 404, 530, 572
freezer bags: Click Zip, 131, 185, 398
freezer space, 530
freezing, 55, 129, 149, 150, 226, 557
freezing rain, 557
French/Belgian ANP M51, 422
frequency of cleaning, 67
frequent urination, 497
fresh produce, 94
freshlike, 161
fresh-looking packages, 138
Fresno, 290
fridge, 19, 24, 43, 141, 143, 144, 146, 277
friend in law enforcement, 408
frogs, 31
from USAMRIID (U.S. Army Medical Research Institute of Infectious Diseases), 426
front-loader backhoe, 476
frost/freeze warning, 557
frostbite, 39, 558
frosting, 106, 140
frozen: foods, 132, 177, 515, 530; items, 40; juice cans, 245; products, 177
fruit, 40, 77, 97, 114, 120, 125, 143, 148, 150, 152, 154, 170, 175, 227, 228, 231, 267, 269, 270, 271, 272, 273, 275, 276, 281, 282, 283, 285, 286, 287, 293, 294, 296, 297, 298, 299, 373, 399, 424, 489, 491, 495, 529; cake, 150; cocktail, 104; drink, 117, 118; drying chart, 296; flies, 271, 272, 273; juice, 47, 151, 283; leather, 10, 285, 286; snacks, 162
fruits, 97, 114, 119, 120, 123, 125, 134, 144, 267, 276, 280, 281, 282, 283, 287, 296, 297, 373, 490, 494, 530, 566; drying table, 282, 283, 284
fry pan, 299
frying pans, 39
fuel, 9, 10, 184, 201, 262, 305, 316, 321, 322, 326, 327, 328, 329, 343, 491, 501, 536, 560, 576; backpack stove, 11, 327; backpack stove fuel terms, 328; backpack stove fuel types, 11, 327; biodiesel ingredient comp., 9, 263; containers, 10, 73, 80, 260, 261, 317, 318, 319, 320, 388, 565; degradation, 317, 321; de-icer, 560; filter, 262, 313, 541;

handlers, 11, 73, 318, 319; making biodiesel, 9, 263; pump, 320; stabilizers, 11, 321; tank, 262, 263, 305, 316, 317, 326, 332, 524, 560, 568; types of, 11, 252, 322
fuelbiocide ft-400, 321
Fuelite, 322
Fueltreat Australia, 321
fungi, 252, 428
Fungi Cure, 194
funnels, 82
funnel-shaped cloud, 547
furnace: fan, 307; filter, 188
fuses, 189

G

gagging, 403
galvanized: buckets, 245; steel, 80
game meat, 292
gamma: radiation, 446, 452, 493; rays, 452, 499
garage, 52, 95, 122, 137, 246, 271, 277, 310, 314, 339, 389, 405, 406, 412, 427, 428, 438, 510, 524, 540, 541, 549; door operator, 307; sales, 52, 246
garbage: pits, 388
garbage bag, 35, 91, 339, 389, 390, 427, 441, 457, 587; (-s), 36; trash, 47, 49, 187, 194, 566
garbage cans, 81, 187, 374, 376, 377
garbage disposal, 44
garbanzo, 136
garden, 76, 80, 83, 120, 129, 145, 190, 211, 237, 270, 271, 272, 274, 275, 276, 280, 281, 383, 385, 427, 428, 462, 494, 515, 516, 523, 524, 529, 540, 544; harvests, 120; hose, 190, 383; label stakes, 190; mix, 270; soil, 272
garden tank sprayer, 427
gardening, 275, 276, 280, 494, 588
garland chrysanthemum, 278
garlic, 40, 107, 108, 278, 589; chives, 278; odors, 287; powder, 294, 295
gas, 27, 28, 42, 43, 45, 90, 94, 132, 184, 188, 189, 251, 277, 304, 305, 307, 313, 314, 316-318, 320, 321, 322, 325, 327, 328, 330, 331, 333, 358, 380, 385, 402, 414-419, 422, 423, 426, 427, 433, 438, 439, 442, 487, 500, 503, 504, 507, 508, 521, 524, 526, 535, 537, 538, 549, 553, 555, 557, 558, 562, 568-570, 578, 581; can, 189, 318, 328, 568; crunch, 94; leaks, 45, 508, 549; shutoff valve, 45; stations, 459

gas mask, 415, 417, 418, 419, 422, 423, 426, 438, 442, 578, 581; (-s), 417, 418, 419, 423, 442, 578, 581; and filters, 14, 417, 580
gas masks: on an animal, 422
Gas Match, 111, 202
gases, 127, 436, 555
gasket-sealing lids, 130
gasoline, 44, 125, 317, 320, 322, 325, 327, 328, 329, 330, 491, 504, 508, 521, 527, 568; fumes, 508
Gaspra (asteroid), 546
gastro-intestinal: problems, 39; tract, 424
gauze, 37, 193; bandages, 397
GDVII Virus, 431
gelatin, 106, 117, 118, 140, 164
General Ecology, 60
General Foods International Coffees, 162
General Mills, 162
general purpose soap, 8, 234
generator, 27, 42, 212, 262, 304, 305, 306, 310, 311, 312, 313, 314, 315, 316, 317, 325, 422; (perfect), 305; (-s), 215, 265, 302, 304, 305, 313, 314, 317, 321, 354, 358, 505, 586
Genesis 41, 596
gentle accelerator pressure, 562, 563
geodesic domes, 206
geophysically, 28, 31
geotextile layer, 67
geo-thermally active, 476
Geranium, 228
gerbils, 397, 399
Geri Guidetti, 276
germ, 96, 441, 578; (-s), 44
Germany, 346, 361
germicidal disinfection, 430
ghee, 105, 233
Ghirardelli, 162
giardia, 55, 56, 57, 69, 72, 209, 430; cysts, 429
giblets, 146, 149
Gigely Tree, 222, 224
Gillette, 203, 204
ginger, 107, 194, 228, 280, 286
Girl Scouts, 216
Glade, 162
glanders, 14, 433
glass, 24, 45, 55, 58, 61, 93, 96, 121, 122, 132, 143, 144, 145, 161, 212, 213, 231, 233, 246, 249, 269, 277, 281, 285, 291, 294, 299, 346, 347, 348, 349, 377, 378, 381, 382, 425, 451, 478, 483, 487, 507, 508, 519, 529, 537, 538, 539, 541, 549, 572
glass jars, 249, 277, 291, 294, 299, 347, 529

glasses, 34, 589
globes, 184
Gloria Carter, 504
gloves, 35, 36, 190, 193, 433, 589
glue gun, 188
glue sticks, 201
gluten making, 114
glycerin, 226, 233, 234, 264, 383
goat fat, 223, 225
God, 21, 23, 42, 412, 596, 597
goggles, 218, 419, 556, 584
Gold Bond, 194
Gold Metal, 162
Golden Circle, 162
Goldenseal, 425
good bacteria, 391
good diet, 95, 119
good sanitation, 528
goose, 146, 149, 223, 225, 574
Gordon-Michael Scallion, 28
gorilla, 123
gouda, 147, 151
gourd, 88, 278, 280
government, 30, 153, 301, 303, 314, 354, 413, 415, 444, 445, 446, 455, 460, 481, 483, 487, 499, 501, 503, 516, 537, 545, 575, 576, 577, 578, 594, 597
GPS, 353, 354, 355, 356, 357
Grace Brothers, 52
grain grinder, 43, 119
grain meal mush, 493, 494
grain sorghum, 493
grains, 15, 40, 89, 96, 99, 100, 136, 160, 272, 352, 492, 493
Grand Junction omelet, 341
grapefruit, 104, 143
grapes, 104, 143, 284, 296
grapeseed extract, 425
graph, 30
grass, 84, 87, 88, 89, 90, 252, 255, 270, 273, 274, 344, 388, 492, 516, 529, 540; clippings, 270, 273
grated soap, 218, 226, 227, 236
grater, 185, 218
gravel, 67, 88, 489, 509
Gravidyn Drip Filter, 58
gravity, 53, 57, 59, 60, 61, 79, 81, 326, 375, 384, 386; system, 81
gravy, 109, 141, 163, 267, 589
grease, 188, 233, 270, 272, 339; fires, 521, 522; gun, 188
Great Britain, 346, 372, 411
great catastrophes, 29
Greece, 346
Greek Villager's Diet, 633
green chili, 289
green flame, 257
Green Giant, 162, 167
green olives, 155
green onion (spring onion), 278

green pepper, 287, 298, 343; (-s), 287
Greene, Maj. Wynn, 542
greenwood, 163
gridlock, 33, 316, 453, 502
grilling steaks, 327
grits, 96, 168
grocery: shopping, 94; store, 27, 46, 49, 64, 65, 94, 114, 124, 132, 138, 220, 256, 275, 276, 281, 283, 285, 397, 407, 438, 585
gross contamination, 426, 428; biological, 426, 428
ground meat, 146, 292, 293
ground slippages, 476
ground squirrels, 270
grounds and filters, 270, 272
growing food, 9, 275
growing wheat grass, 114
gum boots, 36
gun: (-s), 408, 409, 410, 411
gun grab, 410
Gun Owners of America, 411
gutter, 80, 82; (-s), 78, 80, 535, 556; downspout, 80; sealant, 201
gutters and downspouts, 79

H

H2O, 69, 385
Haagen Dazs, 162
hackberry, 252
hacksaw, 213
hail, 494, 548, 564
hailstorms, 32
hair, 19, 21, 35, 38, 43, 130, 192, 195, 291, 382, 384, 398, 417, 419, 427, 452, 484, 563, 584; color, 112, 203, 204; conditioner, 204
half-and-half, 147, 151
hallandale beach, 504
ham, 101, 146, 149, 358, 372
Hamas, 412
hamburger, 148, 149, 292, 293, 342
hammer, 130, 207, 208, 474, 491, 511, 512
hammock, 37
hamsters, 399, 400
hand lotion, 49, 112, 184, 186, 204
hand pump, 75, 93, 209, 210; (-s), 75, 93; build it, 7, 209; priming, 93
hand sanitizer or towelettes, 593
hand trowel, 190
handicapped, 389, 440
hand-milled soap, 219, 220, 236; (-s), 218, 226, 238
Hanover Foods Corp, 163
hard copy, 44
hard rubber, 245

hardiest of biological agents, 426, 432
hardware cloth, 273, 494
harness, 397, 417, 419
Harvard-Sussex Program, 432
harvestable crops, 276
Hassock Toilet, 391
hat, 183, 559
hatchet, 41, 50, 188
hatchway cover, 473
Hawaii, 370, 372, 499, 545, 546, 552, 553, 555
HDPE, 73, 130
HDPE (High Density Polyethylene), 73, 130
head cover, 183
headache, 368, 495; (-s), 310, 519, 574
headband pad, 419
headphones, 565, 593
Headzyme Tablets, 391
health food stores, 214, 425
healthcare workers, 432, 433, 434, 583
health-insurance card, 593
Healthy Choice, 159, 163
healthy eating, 98, 594
hearing aids, 186
heart, 19, 21, 68, 97, 98, 146, 195, 268, 302, 452, 492, 519, 558; disease, 97, 195
heartworm, 397, 401
heat: cramps, 518; exhaustion, 518; index, 518; loss, 71, 347, 491, 516; reflector, 328; stroke, 39, 518; wave, 518
Heat it, 323
heat shrink insulation, 212
heater, 40, 264, 277, 308, 385, 386, 484, 486, 526, 558, 559, 560, 562, 564, 568, 569, 570
heaters: kerosene, 17, 568; propane, 17, 569
heating/cooling ducts, 441
heavy duty jack, 189
heavy fallout removal, 15, 488
heavy metals, 67, 68
heavy smoke and poisonous gases, 522
heavy-duty aluminum foil, 491
hedge trimmer, 308
Heinz, 142, 163
heirloom seed, 276
heirloom varieties of seed, 275
helicopter, 26, 597
Helper Dinner Mixes, 162
hemlock, 252
hemorrhage, 435
hemorrhoid, 51, 194, 202
hemostat, 193, 398
HEPA air filter, 425, 435, 439, 440, 442, 580
HEPA filters, 580

HEPA ventilation, 441
hepatitis, 59, 376, 430
herbal essence, 204
herbal healer col. silver 500, 215
herbicides, 275, 429
Herb-Ox Bouillon, 164
herbs, 38, 114, 169, 228, 229, 233, 268, 281, 291, 425
heroic acts, 412
herpes virus, 431
HEW standard, 69
hibiscus spinach, 278
hickory, 152, 294
hickory smoke-flavored salt, 294
high blood pressure, 227
high density extruded polystyrene foam, 477
high explosives, 413
high profile metropolitan city, 415
high voltage electric arc, 69
high-altitude bursts, 489
high-density electrical field, 498
high-density polyethylene, 440, 494
high-protein food requires more water, 488
hike, 35
hiking boots, 35, 36, 48
hip waders, 593
hiroshima, 448, 451, 542
Hirzel Canning, 163
hit by a car, 401
hobby stores, 220
holding tank, 67, 79, 392, 393, 441
holes in trunk and floorboards, 560
holiday, 94, 258, 406
home canned foods, 123, 529
Home Depot, 504, 505
home-based business, 216, 539
homegrown tomato, 275
Homeland Security, 412, 437, 439
hominy, 103
Honda 650, 312
Honda EG2500XK1, 317
Honduras, 343
honey, 19, 20, 21, 22, 26, 115, 119, 120, 121, 129, 229, 234, 235, 283, 286, 299
hope and encouragement, 18, 596
Hopi Indians, 136, 518
Hopi Prophecy, 16, 518
Hopi store food, 136
Hormel Products, 164
hornets, 273
horrific winds, 448
horror in the harbor, 414
horse troughs, 80
horseradish, 109, 142, 163, 288
horse-to-human transmission, 435

hoses, 75, 262, 516, 560, 561, 565
hospitals, 321, 375, 537, 565, 583
hot pads, 39, 185
hot water on demand, 386
hotdogs, 21, 185
house: keys, 187; paint, 201; plumbing, 74
house and life insurance policies, 49, 187
household appliances, 305, 324, 325
household bleach, 53, 64, 65, 124, 426, 429, 493
Houston, 474, 485
Hudson River, 485
human waste, 49, 187, 389, 528
humane societies, 396
humidity, 124, 127, 196, 277, 281, 282, 283, 340, 378, 518
hunting, 33, 35, 36, 41, 334, 409, 410, 411, 569
Hunting Knive, 41, 187
Hunting Knive(-s), 39
Hunting Knife, 31, 33, 206, 266, 358, 370, 397, 402, 453, 505, 514, 533, 534, 535, 536, 537, 538, 540, 541, 560, 563, 567, 593, 595, 596; (-s), 30, 32, 94, 503, 533, 534, 535, 536, 537, 540, 547, 549, 564, 573, 596; Charley, 30, 305, 402, 503, 505, 595; Dennis, 29; Frances, 30, 305, 503, 504, 505, 593; Jeanne, 30, 432, 503; Katrina, 29, 38, 44, 304, 314, 359, 370, 400, 503, 567, 576; match, 256; Rita, 29, 114; watch, 541; Wilma, 29, 304
Hurricane Andrew, 30
Hurricane Charley, 503, 593
Hurricane Frances, 316, 503, 533, 541
hurricane glass, 539
Hurricane Ivan, 265, 304
Hurricane Lili, 535
Hurricane/Tropical Storm Warning or Watch, 535
husks, 144
hybrid seeds, 275
hybrids, 275, 276
Hycar™ rubber, 417
hydraulic ram effect, 209
Hydro Photon, 60
hydrocortisone, 51, 194, 198, 398
hydrogen peroxide, 37, 57, 404
hydroponic tomatoes, 275
hygiene, 34, 47, 116, 182, 441, 457, 460, 489, 566, 578, 587, 593
hyperthyroidism, 56
hypochloride, 66
hypochlorite solution, 428, 429, 432, 433, 434
hypothermia, 304, 557, 558
hypothermic, 564

I

Ibuprofen, 51, 194
Ibuprophen, 202
ICBMs, 448
ice: chests, 40; cream, 74, 92, 93, 130, 132, 170, 175; house, 478; scraper, 189; storm, 32, 304, 310, 361, 571
ice and sleet, 17, 562
icy cold storage, 478
Idahoan Foods, 164
IDL Cover, 422
ignition system, 561
ill health, 96
illness, 28, 39, 42, 57, 86, 94, 119, 214, 265, 373, 400, 416, 425, 484, 573, 576, 577, 580
imitation bacon, 140
immune system, 96, 119, 424, 425
Imodium, 51, 113, 194, 202, 402
important documents: Certified copies of, 49, 187
impulse purchasing, 94
incoherence, 558
incorporate table scraps, 397
increasing natural disasters, 301, 503
indecipherable code, 153
India, 346, 451
indicators of dryness, 284
induce vomiting, 129
infant, 152, 418, 493
infant formula, 152
infected secretions, 433
infectious agent on a body surface, 426
infectious hepatitis, 389
infectious until all scabs separate, 434
Inferno Meals, 40, 47, 491
infiltration gallery, 67, 75
inflatable solar stills, 72
inflatable swimming pool, 441, 458
influenza, 376, 430, 431, 577, 578
infrared radiation, 135
ingestion pathway zone (ipz), 485
initial pulse, 448
in-line filters, 82
innovative natural prod. 500, 215
inorganic, 65, 67, 424
inorganic gases/vapors, 424
insect, 34, 35, 129, 194, 195, 204, 205, 252, 276, 277, 538; (-s), 35, 37, 42, 72, 79, 89, 129, 185, 277, 281, 293, 297, 389, 491, 515; killer, 203; repellent, 37, 51, 182, 202
insects hatched, 129
insects in jars, 299
inspections, 82, 474, 485
instant coffee, 47

Dare To Prepare: Index

insulated tin sheds, 127
insulating concrete foam, 550
insulin, 196
insurance, 29, 49, 593; claims, 521; companies, 29; policy, 541
inter-continental missile, 481
International Falls, 476
internet, 40, 44, 120, 214, 220, 231, 276, 325, 344, 353, 354, 369, 372, 392, 406, 419, 449, 450, 481, 582; resources, 40
interplanetary magnetic field, 31
invasive procedures, 432
inventory: official, 522
investments, 49, 187
iodine, 37, 54, 55, 56, 67, 633; allergic to, 56; Resin Filter, 55
ionic, 214, 215
Ipecac, 37, 195, 202
Iran, 445
Iraq War, 475
Iraqi passport (fake), 412
iron, 39, 57, 96, 131, 261, 320, 334, 336, 338, 344, 347, 546; cookware, 336, 338; meteorite, 543; tripod, 185
ironing board, 131
Islamic Jihad, 412
Isobutane, 322, 327
isolation and decontamination, 432, 433, 434, 435
Isolation transformers, 539
Isopropyl, 51, 193, 202, 382
Israel: (House of), 597
Israeli, 418, 420, 422, 442
Israeli Tent, 442
Italian food, 114
Italy, 346
itch, 37, 51, 194, 195
Ivarest, 195

J

jack hammer, 76
jack pine, 252
jacket, 35, 36
jalapeno: (-s), 245
jalapeño powder, 293
James Lee Witt, 31
James Williams, 504
jams, 117, 118, 178, 267, 529
Japanese subway, 416
jar, 51, 106, 120, 121, 123, 127, 142, 144, 213, 245, 246, 249, 267, 277, 285, 299, 342, 382, 561
jasmine, 228
jaws, 128
Jeanne Guillemin, 432
jeans, 35
jellies sealed with paraffin, 529
Jell-O, 94, 164, 231
Jeremy Martinez, 504
jerky, 40, 120, 281, 292, 293, 294, 295, 297, 407, 566; recipes, 293

Jerky Works, 292, 293; gun, 293
Jerry can, 317, 318, 565; (-s), 317, 318
jerusalem artichoke, 278
jet fixture, 75
Jet-A, 322
Jif Peanut Butter, 164
Jiffy: Mixes, 164; Pop, 159
JK Nakata, 506
Joan of Arc, 164
jock straps, 36
John C. Dohrenwend, 514
John Rolon, 504
John West, 165
joint garden, 275
Jojoba Oil, 222, 224
Jordan, 412, 413
Jose Canseco, 21
Joseph, 240, 597
Joseph Morgan, 240
Joshua Joseph, 504
juice cans, 245
juice of a lemon, 236
juices, 97, 114, 120, 266, 267, 294, 352, 424, 495, 530
Julian Date, 154
Julian dating, 152
jumper cables, 189
just in time supply, 18, 585

K

Kahn-Vassher solution, 55
Kale, 144, 279
Kansas City, 529, 571
Kaopectate tablets, 398
Kapok, 222, 224
Karo, 165
Katadyn, 56, 58, 60, 68, 69, 430
Katadyn Combi Water Filter, 430
katchung, 222, 224
Katies, 52
KC Masterpiece, 141, 142
Keebler, 165
keep to main roads, 561
keeping the dam healthy, 77
Keith Hendricks, 209
Kelly Col. Silver, 215
kelp, 228
Kenya, 346, 413
kernels, 100, 119, 120, 288, 297
kerosene, 111, 184, 201, 254, 262, 320, 321, 325, 326, 328, 330, 343, 491, 521, 538, 558, 568, 569; heaters, 521, 558, 568; kero, 262, 263, 322; lanterns, 184
Ketchup, 109, 142, 163
kettle, 185
keys, 453, 593
KI (potassium iodide and iodate), 484, 495, 496
kid cuisine, 159
kids, 14, 16, 441, 529

killing zone, 408
kindling, 252, 253, 254, 258, 261, 491
King Crab, 148
kitchen: scales, 218; thermometers, 218; trash, 270
kitty litter, 205
kivas, 136, 518
kiwi fruit, 143
Kleenex, 111, 123, 130, 193, 589
K-Mart, 52, 125, 256, 331
knife, 39, 188, 218, 307, 566; sharpener, 39, 188
knives, 38, 39
Knorr, 166, 167
knots, 75, 257, 534
KNOX gelatine, 166
KOH (potassium hydroxide), 8, 221, 224, 225
Kohlrabi, 144, 279
Kool-Aid, 55, 109, 166
Korila (Achoa), 279
Krusteaz, 166
Kukui Nut, 222, 224
Kwells, 51, 195
K-Y Jelly, 195

L

La Choy, 167
La Niña, 31
laboratory, 62, 81
lacquer thinner, 201
ladle, 219, 221
ladles, 39
Lady J, 392
Lake Powell, 131, 358, 514, 515
lakes, 39, 194, 328
lakeside foods, 167
lamb, 146, 149, 268, 352
Lamisil, 113, 194
Lanacane, 51, 202
Lancia, 167
lanolin, 223, 225, 228
lanterns, 184, 593
lard, 97, 220, 223, 225
large spoons, 39
Lassa fever, 435
laundry, 35, 44, 53, 66, 84, 182, 216, 220, 257, 271, 373, 382, 391, 441, 456, 585; chutes, 441; room, 271; soap, 8, 235; starch, 382
lava, 75, 88, 543, 555, 556; flow, 88, 556
lavender, 228, 244
law enforcement officers, 408, 525
lawn, 80, 83, 84, 516, 524, 527, 529
lawns trimmed, 523
LDS, 6, 95, 114, 115, 116, 117, 118
LDS canneries, 130
lead, 31, 65, 80, 85, 86, 125, 205, 212, 305, 324, 363, 366, 400,
406, 428, 429, 436, 446, 536, 568, 596
lead solder, 80
lead-based paint, 80
leaf screens, 79
leak detection, 317
leak-proof plastic bottle, 392
lean meat, 97, 292, 294, 295
lean times, 94
lean-tos, 38
leash, 50; (-es), 205
leather gloves, 339
leaves, 56, 66, 69, 72, 80, 87, 91, 92, 96, 107, 119, 129, 143, 144, 145, 219, 249, 252, 253, 254, 270, 271, 288, 291, 381, 388, 394, 415, 428, 450, 454, 476, 516, 523, 542, 572; raked, 523
LectraSan, 391
Leek, 279; (-s), 144
Legends of Claddah, 633
legionella pneumophilia, 430
lemon, 107, 108, 109, 128, 142, 228, 286, 291, 380, 381; (-s), 143; juice, 55, 114, 234, 239, 286, 287, 294, 341, 380, 381, 382; peel, 107, 228, 286
lemongrass, 280
length equivalents, 600
less temptation, 94
lethal gas, 412
lettuce, 144, 279
Leukostrips, 50, 113
Liberty City, 504
licensed electrician, 311, 538
lid lifter, 339
life extinguishing event, 543
life is scary at times, 596
life raft, 68
LifeSystems, 56
lift the water, 75
light, 23, 26, 27, 35-37, 40, 46, 54, 68, 69, 72-74, 82, 91, 93, 99, 106, 121, 123, 126-128, 140, 147, 151, 189, 196, 202, 213, 215, 216, 220, 234, 242, 246, 248, 253-257, 259, 261, 277, 283, 286, 291, 293, 297, 310, 313, 314, 322, 324, 327, 329, 332, 333, 338, 344, 351, 358, 385, 386, 392, 400, 429, 430, 434, 437, 438, 443, 446, 448, 452, 454, 457, 474, 478, 487, 491, 499, 504, 507, 508, 510, 511, 515, 517, 519, 529, 533, 539, 559, 562, 565, 566, 587
light bulb, 110, 184, 307
light fallout removal, 15, 488
light n' fluffy, 167
light sticks, 47
lighter fluid, 322, 589
lighting a fire, 257, 508
lights for all vehicle lights, 189

Dare To Prepare: Index

lightsticks, 184
lightweight, 35, 36, 38, 40, 42, 47, 69, 114, 130, 192, 244, 255, 281, 282, 290, 325, 328, 330, 347, 391, 418, 438, 510, 558
lilac, 228
lime: (-s), 143; juice, 109, 142, 286
Lindsay Olives, 167
line trimmer, 308
linseed oil, 201, 222, 224
lint, 184, 252, 257
lip balm, 51, 195
lip care, 204
Lip-Eze, 204
lipstick, 203
Lipton: sides, 167; teas, 168
liquefaction, 509
liquid, 39, 49, 53, 109, 112, 193, 194, 195, 198, 200, 229, 236, 244, 295, 322, 323, 402; dyes, 229, 244; gold, 317; smoke, 293, 295; soap, 39, 49, 236; soaps, 221
Liquorland, 52, 125
list of boat registration numbers, 541
Listerene, 204
Listermint, 204
liters, 47, 53, 65, 66, 72, 73, 86, 116, 130, 134, 218, 237, 264, 290, 321, 380, 393, 531, 598
lithium, 56, 60, 61, 355, 419; batteries, 419; battery, 60
Little Joh, 392
little rotter, 271
liver, 98, 146, 197, 268, 492, 493, 494, 519
liver sausage, 146
liverwurst and roast beef, 177
livestock supply centers, 130
lizards, 399
Lloyds Barbeque, 162
lobster tails, 148
local Emergency Management Division, 459
local precipitation, 83
location for underground containers, 476
Loccu, 222, 224
locked storage, 137
locking gas cap, 189
locking lids, 34
Lodge Manufacturing, 334
Logic Manufacturing, 338
logs, 246, 252, 323
Lohmann, 168
Loma Prieta earthquake, 23, 506
Lomotil, 51, 194
long range killing zone, 408
long-term storage, 116, 127, 281, 297, 321, 334, 590
Lord, 22, 596, 597
Lori Toye, 28

loss of income, 94
loss of judgment, 497
loss of traction, 563
lost her job, 94
lotion, 50, 186; (-s), 52, 216
Louisiana: Ascension Parish, 531
low humidity, 136, 429
low lathering soap, 220
low recoil, 409
low salt, 592
LPG, 305, 323
lubricant, 195
lucky charms, 162
Luffa, 279
lug wrench, 189
lumber, 188, 473, 504, 589
luster crystals, 243, 246, 247, 248
Lux, 204
lychees, 104
lye, 217, 218, 219, 221, 223, 225, 226, 231, 232, 233, 234, 235, 236, 237, 238, 239, 262, 263, 264, 339, 429
lye water, 8, 237
Lysol, 112, 187, 200, 391, 441, 538

M

M291 skin decontamination kit, 433
M9, 422, 424; filters, 424
M-95, 424; mask and filter, 417
M9A1, 422
mace, 286
machete, 41
Mackerel, 148
magnesium, 184, 255; block, 184
magnesium scraping/shavings, 255
magnetic antenna mount, 189
magnetic storm, 517, 518
magnifying glass, 42
magnitude, 507
Mahmud Abouhalima, 412
Mahogany, 252
Main Pack, 34, 35, 36, 37, 38, 40
maintenance schedule, 82
major destruction, 33
major sea ports, 474
make-up mirror, 43
mallee roots, 252
malt, 141
mantles, 184, 589
manual transfer switch, 311
manufacture or production date, 152
manure, 270, 273, 324
Manwich, 109, 159
map, 33, 42, 85, 86, 449, 450, 518, 563, 565, 566, 574; (-s), 42, 85, 358, 416, 449, 450, 476, 485, 559
map of your local area, 48, 183
maple, 106, 142, 252, 590
maple syrup, 106

margarine, 97, 136, 147, 222, 224
Marie Callender's, 159
marigold, 280
marinade, 294, 295
marinate, 295; (-ed), 293, 294; (-ing), 292
marine BBQ grills, 11, 332
marjoram, 107, 280
Mark McGwire, 21
marksman, 408
marriage, 49, 187, 593
marshmallow cream, 106, 140, 286
marshmallows, 40, 106, 140
Martha White, 168
Maruchan, 168
Mary Kitchen Hash, 164
mascara, 203
mask filters: 3M FR C2A1, 424; 3M FR-15 cbrn, 424; 3M FR-57, 424; 3M FR-64, 423, 424
masking tape, 188, 201
masks: East German, 422; GP-5, 422
masks and filters, 417
mason/canning, 245
masonry, 81
masonry eye-bolts, 123
massive leak, 76
matches, 41, 42, 46, 52, 111, 184, 203, 254, 255, 256, 257, 331, 508, 521, 561, 562, 563, 566, 589, 593; (NATO), 256
mats, 36, 457, 559
Maxim, 169
Maxwell House, 168, 169, 174, 179
mayonnaise, 105, 117, 118, 142, 530
McCormick Herbs and Spices, 169
McKenzie, 169
meals ready to eat, 38, 47
measuring cups, 39, 185
measuring spoons, 39
meat, 94, 97, 115, 132, 139, 146, 148, 149, 152, 154, 266, 267, 268, 274, 281, 292, 293, 294, 295, 340, 342, 343, 374, 388, 437, 478, 488, 490, 492, 515, 530; (-s), 39, 94, 114, 116, 120, 123, 149, 267, 268, 273, 297, 490, 494, 530
mechanical: filtering, 69; filtration, 53
mechanical decontamination, 427
meclizine, 51, 195
medical: advice, 425; aid, 29, 34; anthropologist, 432; grade, 429; kit, 34, 38; knowledge, 33; needs, 42; records, 49, 187

medical management of biological casualties handbook, 426
medical supplies, 41, 422, 445
medications, 34, 38, 45, 51, 182, 192, 195, 196, 197, 200, 397, 402, 485, 503, 566, 593
medicine, 123, 137, 191, 212, 398, 481, 576, 578
meeting place, 33
Mega Fresh, 52
Melamine Plates, 185
melanoma, 544
melioidosis, 14, 433
melons, 143, 284
melting pitcher, 240
membrane, 58, 59, 61, 68, 69, 429
memory loss, 558
mentholated spirits, 325
mercury bulb, 69
meringue, 148
Merle Norman, 203
Merthiolate, 113, 202
message to Christians, 18, 596
messmate common, 252
metal, 39, 185, 211, 242, 245, 377, 378, 473; bucket, 491; cup, 36; drum, 260, 319, 388; tank, 78
meteor: grapefruit-size, 544
meteor and asteroid strikes, 17, 542
Meteor Crater, 542, 544
meteor impact, 543, 544, 552; (-s), 544, 552
meteorite, 544
meteorologically, 28
meteorologist: Ed Greene, 46
methylated spirits (denatured alcohol), 330
Metric and U.S. Conversion Charts, 218
Mexican: foods, 123; restaurants, 74
Mexico, 303, 346, 474, 533
mice, 120, 122, 123, 124, 128, 202, 270, 273, 388, 399, 438
microbes, 55, 426, 430
microbial spoilage, 296
microbiology, 276
microcystin, 431
micro-organisms, 31, 69, 84, 271, 426, 430, 582
micro-strainer, 58, 61
microwave, 100, 135, 171, 217, 219, 240, 291, 500, 515, 540
microwave oven, 307
microwaveable dinners, 43
Middle East, 233, 413, 475
middle floors in high-rise buildings, 486
middle killing zone, 408
mighty gas explosion, 43
mildew, 35, 277, 382, 383

military, 36, 41, 54, 55, 69, 71, 151, 158, 162, 169, 172, 196, 329, 366, 408, 410, 416, 418, 419, 440, 442, 499, 500, 544, 546, 572, 583; surplus stores, 40
military type kits, 36
milk, 19, 40, 43, 74, 87, 93, 94, 97, 114, 115, 120, 121, 132, 133, 162, 170, 212, 231, 233, 234, 235, 266, 267, 268, 288, 320, 341, 437, 490, 492, 493, 602; cooler, 309; from cows, 492
milker (vacuum pump) 2 hp, 309
mill, 125, 220, 298
millions of degrees, 448
millipedes, 271, 274
mineral: spirits, 258, 330; supplements, 69, 95
Mineral Oil, 202, 402
mineral turps, 201
minerals, 79, 493, 516, 633
mines, 459
mini-kitchen, 38
minimum of 6 months provisions, 437
minimum shelf life, 99
mini-sewing kits, 52
MiniWorks EX, 58
mink, 222, 223, 224, 225
Minnesota, 476, 525
mint, 280, 286, 291
MIOX, 60
missiles, 444, 540, 547
Mississippi, 44, 276, 304, 358, 370, 371, 372
mixed grain puree, 493
mixing bowl, 185
Mizuna (Japanese Cabbage), 279
mobile home, 275, 322, 510, 534, 536, 549, 551; (-s), 510, 511, 549; dwellers, 275
Mobilite, 322
model FV75, 210
Mohammed Salameh, 412
moist paper towel, 144
moisture, 31, 34, 36, 37, 42, 47, 50, 86, 87, 89, 90, 91, 93, 99, 116, 123, 124, 126, 127, 131, 132, 134, 135, 137, 143-145, 150, 151, 207, 208, 219, 232, 254, 260, 270, 272, 274, 277, 281-285, 287, 289, 291-293, 296, 297, 299, 323, 324, 334, 339, 347, 382, 393, 419, 423, 463, 516, 533, 557, 560, 581; is absorbed, 127
moisture-permeable soil, 395
moisturizers, 203
molasses, 106, 117, 118, 140, 142
mold, 126, 127, 131, 154, 205, 219, 226, 230-232, 234, 235, 236, 238, 242-249, 268, 281, 284, 285, 291, 292, 296, 297, 377, 383, 490; (-s), 217- 219, 226, 227, 230-236,
238, 240, 241, 245-249, 430; killer, 13, 383; on: food, 299; prevention, 13, 383; release, 240
molecular biology, 276
molecules adsorbed, 68
Moleskin, 113, 193, 566
molten rock, 555
money, 20, 31, 37, 38, 52, 55, 74, 77, 94, 125, 126, 182, 191, 196, 206, 306, 314, 328, 329, 355, 380, 420, 474, 503, 504, 505, 592
money savers, 4, 6, 52, 124
Monopoly, 44
monosodium glutamate, 295
Montana, 474, 476
Moody Dunbar, 161
mop, 44, 88, 89, 374
more deadly, 410, 483
morgue, 459
Mormon 4, 95, 114, 115
Mormon food guidelines, 6, 116
mortality: 50%, 448
mortar, 394, 463, 510
Mortein, 203
mosquito, 42, 401, 435, 531; (-es), 245, 373, 435, 531; mozzy lights, 245; netting, 182; vector, 435
moss, 35, 91, 252, 255, 391
motion sickness, 51, 113, 202
motorists, 46, 561
Motrin, 51, 113, 194, 202
mottling, 248
Mount Sapo, 216
Mount St. Helens, 17, 555
Mountain House, 116
mountain lion: (-s), 270; tracks, 388
mountain springs, 84
mountains, 24, 46, 355
mouse, 122, 124, 128, 252, 277
mouse and rat traps, 188
Mouse Chaser, 128
mouse droppings, 128
mousetraps, 128, 397
moustaches, 427, 582
mouthwash, 112, 204, 589
move large animals, 399
mozzarella, 105, 147
MRE, 38, 40, 47, 102, 119, 120, 130, 151, 397, 456, 491, 566, 586, 592; Inferno Meals, 40, 47, 491; shelf life, 151
MREs, 38, 40, 47, 102, 119, 120, 130, 151, 397, 456, 491, 566, 586, 592
Mrs. Weiss, 170
MSA: Advantage 1000/3200, 423; CBRN, 424; ComfoFilter, 423; Millennium, 423; Optifilter GME-P100, 424; OptimAir PAPR, 423; Phalanx, 423
MSR, 11, 57, 58, 60, 72, 183, 328, 430
Mt. Pisgah, 75
mud buckets, 390
mudflow, 556; (-s), 556
mudslide, 42
muffin: (-s), 150, 268; cups, 258; mix, 100, 140, 166
muffler, 310, 314
Muir Glen Organic, 162
multi-car pile-ups, 561
MultiFuel, 328
multimineral supplement, 98
multi-purpose tool, 50
multi-vitamins, 38, 114; pills, 492
Munich Re, 29, 633
Munich Re annual disaster reports, 633
Murine, 51, 194, 202
Murrah Federal Building, 413
muscular tension, 497
mushroom cloud, 446, 447, 448, 453
mushrooms, 103, 144, 154, 162, 288, 296
musk, 228
Muslim extremists, 412
mustard, 107, 109, 142, 161, 163, 222, 224, 279; gas, 424; greens, 279
mutton, 220, 223, 225; fat, 223, 225
muzzle, 50; (-s), 205
mycobacterium tuberculosis, 430
Myer, 52, 125
Myer Direct, 52
Mylanta, 51, 113, 194, 202
mylar, 130, 131, 133, 571
myrrh, 228
myrtle wax, 222, 224

N

NaHOCl, 64
nail: clipper, 51, 193, 589; polish, 204; trimmer, 398
nails, 123, 207, 208, 438, 462, 512, 513, 521, 578
Nalley, 170
NaOH, 8, 216, 221, 223, 264, 434
Napoleon, 336
naptha, 322
NASA, 31, 439, 542, 545, 546
nasal decongestant, 51, 195
nasturtium, 279
National Center for Genetic Resources Preservation (NCGRP), 277
National Flood Insurance Program, 526
National Rifle Association, 411
national security, 415, 416
NATO, 256, 329, 410, 417, 418, 420, 423, 424, 438, 442
natural catastrophes in 2003, 633
natural disasters, 29, 30, 46, 122, 503, 542, 560
natural dyes, 230
natural fiber rope, 41
natural remedies, 38
Nature Valley, 162
naturopath, 425
nausea, 51, 195, 495, 497, 577
Navy, 20, 68, 244, 413, 439
NBC: (nuclear, biological and chemical) agents, 418; filtration system, 443
NCGRP, 277
Neats Foot Oil, 223, 225
nectarines, 284, 296
needle nose pliers, 50
needles, 37, 50, 193, 203
Neem, 222, 224
neighborhood, 23, 33, 270, 275, 336, 368, 385, 386, 388, 437, 525, 529, 535, 537, 538, 547, 596, 597
neighbors (needs of your), 537
Neosporin, 51, 113, 194
nerve gases, 424
nervous tissue, 494
Nestle Toll House, 170
Netherlands, 346, 361
Nevada, 446, 449, 482
New England, 206, 310
New Jersey, 301, 371, 372, 412, 416, 481, 574
New Mexicans, 289
New Mexico, 289, 302, 542
New Millennium Concepts, 60
New Skin, 51, 194
New South Wales, 301, 302, 371, 412, 415, 416, 425, 446, 448, 458, 481, 482, 483, 485, 501, 547, 633; Peekskill, 543
Vew Zealand, 127, 158, 279, 326, 411, 425, 517, 544
Newmart, 52
newspapers, 218, 259, 456
Nice N' Easy, 204
Nidal Ayyad, 412
Niger-seed, 222, 224
NIOSH, 417, 420, 423, 424, 578, 581
nitrogen, 95, 115, 120, 127, 131, 133, 134, 271, 274, 277, 516, 568
nitrogen flush, 131
nitroglycerin, 196
nitro-packing, 127
NOAA, 357, 358, 369, 439, 526, 533, 535, 547, 548, 558, 633; satellite imagery, 533; Weather Radio, 526, 535, 548, 558
Noah, 442, 596
No-Bake Desserts, 164
non-emergency periods, 486
non-potable, 81

Dare To Prepare: Index

Norma Bartlett, 550
North Korea, 445
North NBC-40, 424
Northridge earthquake, 26
Norton Air Force Base - Hanger 3, 591
Nostradamus, 28
notepad, 48, 183
notification numbers, 187
noxious gas, 348, 459
NP8000 NBC, 424
NRA, 408, 411
NRC, 485
nuclear: accident, 485; blast, 437, 446, 453, 455, 494; chain reaction, 485; Cuban Missile Crisis, 444; device, 447, 481, 499; Indian Point, 485; large fireball, 447; massive attack, 489; poisons, 422; potential target, 445, 487; radiation terms, 15, 372, 452, 456; traditional devices, 481; weapons, 444, 494; XX12 Grable test, 447
Nuclear and Radiological Attack, 15, 481
nuclear attack: large-scale, 492; survivors, 488
nuclear blast: 1 megaton surface, 451; 24 megaton thermal energy, 555; air, 448; and fire, 462, 489; and radiation protection, 459; shelter, 437, 455, 460, 461
nuclear bomb: 200mm artillery shell, 447; fission, 451; the A Bomb, 451
nuclear detonation, 448, 498, 499
nuclear emergencies, 15, 16, 444, 455, 495
nuclear power plant, 15, 485
nuclear power station: Oconee, 485
Nuclear War Survival Skills (book), 114, 115, 449
nuclear war survivalist, 115
nuke, 444, 445, 446, 451, 454, 460, 461, 481, 482; tactical, 444
NuMex, 290
Nurofen, 51, 194, 202
nursing mother, 492
nutmeg, 107, 222, 224, 228, 286
nutritional, 47, 98, 116, 120, 126, 136, 154
nutritious soil, 275
nuts, 102, 150, 188, 286, 352, 589
nylon: cord, 211; rope, 41; stocking, 246, 247, 249
Nyquil, 51, 194

O

O2, 69, 130
oak, 237, 442
Oak Ridge National Laboratories, 436, 491
oatmeal, 96, 220, 227, 229, 233, 234, 235
oats, 117, 118, 136, 352
obsolete masks, 422
Oca (New Zealand Yam), 279
Ocean Perch, 148
Ocean Spray, 171
ocean waves, 21, 506
odor, 39, 57, 66, 68, 129, 141, 143, 235, 243, 254, 266, 271, 273, 274, 322, 324, 384, 388, 391, 403, 440, 441, 530, 538, 587; (-s), 65, 272, 389, 390, 391, 430, 441, 474, 491
Officeworks, 52, 125
oil: almond, 222, 224, 228; avocado, 222, 224; Canola, 105, 222, 224; Carmellia, 222, 224; Castor, 222, 224; changes, 561; coconut, 222, 224; content, 115, 136, 164, 249; corn, 105, 222, 224; cottonseed, 222, 224; drum, 261; filter, 189; flax seed, 222, 224; grapeseed, 222, 224; hazelnut, 222, 224; hempseed, 222, 224; macadamia nut, 222, 224; meadowform, 222, 224; mink, 223, 225; olive, 220, 232, 233, 234, 235, 236, 337, 404; palm, 97, 222, 224, 233; peanut, 222, 224; pecan, 222, 224; pistachio nut, 222, 224; poppy seed, 222, 224; pumpkin seed, 222, 224; rapeseed, 222, 224; rice bran, 222, 224; safflower, 222, 224; shut-off, 314; soybean, 115, 223, 225; sunflower, 223, 225; sweet, 223, 225; synthetic, 561; thyme, 128; tung, 223, 225; walnut, 223, 225; wheat germ, 223, 225
oils, 8, 105, 220, 227, 228
oils known to be irritating, 227
Okie, 37, 188; Straps, 188
Oklahoma City bombing, 412, 413, 451
Oklahoma City's, 413
okra, 144, 279, 288, 298
Old El Paso, 101, 103, 108, 162
old stock, 138, 417
olium olivate, 222, 224
olive, 97, 105, 115, 140, 220, 222, 223, 224, 225, 233, 234
olive leaf extract, 425
olives, 109
OmniFuel, 328
One Bedroom, 40 foot Container, 477
one shot kills, 409
one year's food supply, 95, 115, 119
onion, 107, 108, 136, 279, 280, 296; (-s), 40, 103, 144, 161, 287, 288, 292, 298; powder, 294, 298
onset of symptoms, 435
opaque plastic containers, 127
open dating system, 152
open shelf areas, 123
open-pollinated, 275
optical inserts, 417
optimum nutritional value, 99
Oral-B, 204, 593
orange, 103, 104, 107, 108, 109, 228, 243, 244, 286; (-s), 143; juice, 103, 286; peel, 107, 228, 286
oregano, 107, 195
organic, 53, 54, 61, 64, 67, 68, 69, 129, 170, 389, 390, 424; fertilizer, 389; material, 53
organics, 65, 84
organisms, 57, 426, 432, 434
oriental cooking melon, 279
ornex, 51, 195
orris root, 228
ortega, 171
Orville Redenbacher's, 171
Osama bin Laden, 413, 414
OSHA, 579, 581
ostrich, 223, 225
other food storage programs, 6, 114
outbreak control, 432, 433, 434, 435
outdoor shops, 40, 384
outhouse, 386, 389, 395; dunny, 395; The, 395
oven, 111, 135, 240, 281, 295, 297, 307, 326, 336, 337, 338, 339, 342, 343, 344, 351, 381
over an open fire, 44, 185, 254, 334
over and under, 410
overlapping, 539
overpressure, 429, 436, 440, 442
overweight, 518
owens, 171
own at least 100 acres, 411
oxidation reaction, 56
oxygen, 69, 120, 126, 127, 130, 131, 132, 133, 134, 135, 260, 261, 277, 297, 322, 323, 325, 330, 345, 423, 437, 439, 443, 456, 457, 570; absorbers, 120, 131, 132, 133, 134, 135; barrier, 130, 131; flushing, 127; scavengers, 130, 131, 133
oysters, 146
ozone, 69, 431

P

Pacific basin, 553
Pacific Tsunami Warning Center, 553
pack, 32, 34, 35, 36, 38, 39, 42, 46, 51, 58, 91, 93, 134, 157, 158, 182, 183, 184, 186, 255, 259, 285, 296, 356, 357, 368, 403, 409, 494, 565, 568
packing food: dry ice, 6, 131, 132; mylar bags, 130, 131; nitrogen, 6, 132; oxygen aborbers, 134; removing moisture, 6, 120, 134, 135, 291; reusing desiccants, 135; using ash, 6, 136; vacuum, 6, 131
packing tape, 123
packs, 4, 33, 34
pad, 35, 59, 61, 192, 193, 314, 339, 399, 417
pad(-s), 36, 39, 192, 338, 339, 397, 560
paddocks, 75
Paha Que, 386
pail, 44, 130, 132, 133, 269, 376, 377, 391, 440, 441
pain reliever, 51
paint sprayer, 308
paint thinner, 201
Pakistan, 445
Palestinian, 412
palm, 97, 220, 222, 224, 233
Palmolive, 204
pam, 105, 231, 338
Panadol, 202
Panamax, 51, 202
pancake mix, 100, 140, 164
pandemic, 18, 416, 437, 573, 575, 576, 577, 587; avian flu on surfaces, 18, 578; bird flu, 301, 304, 573, 574, 576, 577, 578, 580, 581, 582, 583, 586, 587; bird flu origin, 574; bird flu statistics, 18, 574; bird flu symptoms, 18, 577; how masks protect, 18, 579; impacts, 18, 575; mask commercial, 580, 582; mask disinfection, 18, 581, 584; mask make it, 584; mask rating, 578; masks, 578; masks, how many, 582; past, 576
panic, 497
panic buying, 417
Pan-STARRS, 545, 546
Pansy, 279
Pantene, 204
pantry, 6, 122, 152
pantry items, 94, 126
panty liners, 112, 204
paper: bowls, 111; clips, 49, 187; core, 242; napkins, 111, 187; plates, 111, 589; towel, 49, 111, 187, 200, 270, 272, 589; towels, 111, 187, 200, 270, 272, 589
Paper Birch, 252

PAPR, 419, 424, 580
paprika, 107, 229
Paracetamol, 51, 194, 202
Paraderm, 51, 194
Paraderm Plus, 51, 194
paraffin, 241, 254, 259, 322, 589
paraffin treated, 184
parasites, 389, 430
paring knife, 185
parkay, 159
Parmesan, 105, 147, 267, 342
parsley, 107, 280, 288, 291, 296
parsnips, 144, 288
particle board, 128, 207, 208
particle surface area, 215
particles of silver, 212
Passion of the Christ, 504
Passport to Survival, 114
passports, 49, 187
pasta, 40, 94, 96, 114, 120, 123, 129, 138, 155, 267, 268, 352, 529, 530
pasteurized, 299, 432
pastries, 148, 267
Patchouli, 228
pathogens, 56, 62, 67, 68, 69, 72, 75, 416, 430; waterborne, 427
patio, 137, 271, 333, 344, 346, 524, 529, 538, 540
Paul Jackson, 389
Paul Revere, 336
pawing at eye, 403
Paxyl, 51, 195
pea (snow pea), 279
peach, 104, 228, 243, 244; (-es), 143, 151, 284, 296, 298
peanut, 47, 97, 102, 117, 118, 136, 140, 220, 222, 224, 267, 279, 286, 589, 592; (-s), 388, 493
peanut butter, 32, 46, 114, 175, 488, 530
pear, 104, 252; (-s), 143, 151, 285, 296, 298
peas, 101, 103, 117, 118, 145, 288, 292, 296, 298
peat moss, 252
peat pots, 258
pecan, 222, 224
pectin, 106, 140, 229
peeling fruits and vegetables, 492
Pegasol, 322
Pemmican, 159
pen, 48, 183
pencil, 48, 183, 240, 566
Pennsylvania Dutch, 336
Pennyroyal, 228
Penrose, 159
Pentagon, 44, 196, 415
people dying (millions of), 458
people in apartments, 137
pepper, 40, 107, 136, 342, 589
Pepperidge Farm, 158

peppermint (mentha piperata), 128, 228
peppers, 103, 140, 145, 155, 279, 288, 296
Pepsi, 73
Pepto-Bismol, 113, 196; tablets, 195, 398
perch, 19, 76
perennials, 276
perfume, 112, 204
Perilla, 222, 224
perishable foods, 530
permanent storm shutters, 535
persimmons, 285
personal: hygiene, 49, 52; identification, 34; items, 34, 485, 503, 591; killing zone, 408; protection, 408, 409; security in the home, 409
personal protective equipment, 18, 438, 578, 581, 584, 587
personalized plan, 32
person-to-person transmission, 432, 433
perspiration, 497
Peruvian Balsam, 228
Peruvian Parsnip, 279
pesticides, 68, 129, 424, 429
pests, 99, 120, 126, 128, 129, 137, 271, 273, 531, 538
pet: (-s), 32, 33, 45, 46, 47, 116, 128, 217, 363, 395, 396, 397, 398, 399, 400, 401, 406, 415, 423, 425, 427, 441, 454, 519, 524, 535, 536, 548, 568, 587; current photograph of the animal, 396; emergency help, 13, 402; feces, 274; first aid book, 398; food, 125, 126, 397; manure, 273; motels, 396; poster, 396; preparedness, 13, 205, 396, 587; protective devices, 419; slithery pets, 399
pet grooming scissors (straight blade), 398
Pet Safe, 422
Pet Shield, 422
pet supplies: doggy, 397
Peter Pan, 159
petrol, 201, 324
petroleum, 69, 233, 250, 255, 304, 328, 515; products, 69
petroleum jelly, 51, 195, 204
Petromax, 263, 329, 330; heater, 329
pets: 4-legged, 397, 399, 404
PetScape, 422
pH, 54, 64, 81, 84, 142, 158, 234, 236, 269, 428; test kits, 64
Pharmaceutical, 196
phenolic disinfectants, 435
phenols, 65, 68, 98, 260
phillips screwdriver, 565

phone numbers and addresses, 48, 183
phones and cable tv, 538
phosgene, 424
phosphates, 53, 64
photographs, 398, 514, 515, 526, 535, 548
photo-reactivation, 69
photos of your belongings, 527
Pick n Pay Hypermarket, 52
pickle relish, 109
pickles, 74, 267
pick-up, 43, 587
pie, 106, 107, 148, 150, 166, 268, 286
piecrust mix, 140
piezo ignition, 331
pigments, 230, 245
pillow, 37, 47, 182, 589
Pillsbury, 162
pine, 112, 200, 228, 252, 257, 391, 473, 595
pine cones, 257; with paraffin, 9, 257
pineapple, 103, 104, 143, 151, 285, 295, 296
pinecones, 257, 327
pins, 203
pinto, 101, 136, 157
pipe, 67, 72, 74, 75, 78, 80, 123, 209, 210, 211, 319, 320, 364, 383, 459, 463, 477, 489, 507, 508; (-s), 74, 75, 77, 79, 330, 460, 463, 478, 489, 508, 512, 516
pipe tape, 211
pipe wrenches, 211
pipinette, 392
pistachio, 102, 222, 224
pistol-caliber carbine, 409
pistols, 409
pit privy, 13, 395
pitchfork, 190, 271
pizza, 129, 168, 268, 333, 530
plague, 426, 433
plan, 32, 33, 34, 38, 39, 40, 43, 46, 73, 459, 526, 534, 535, 541, 565, 586, 592; for an emergency, 32, 43, 46
plant trimmings, 270, 272
Planters Peanuts, 172
plants, 31, 69, 71, 77, 87, 88, 89, 90, 92, 227, 269, 272, 273, 275, 276, 301, 304, 321, 374, 485, 494, 505, 515, 516, 523, 537, 538, 575, 586
plastic, 34, 36, 37, 39, 40, 46, 71, 73, 74, 78, 79, 91, 92, 116, 121, 128, 130, 131, 135, 143-146, 148-151, 185, 192, 207, 208, 210, 213, 214, 218, 221, 231, 232, 236, 237, 245, 246, 255, 257, 264, 269, 271, 282, 286, 289, 293-297, 299, 317, 318, 320, 334,

338, 349, 364, 378, 384, 386, 391, 394, 397, 398, 404, 409, 427, 428, 436-439, 441-443, 452, 456, 463, 484, 486, 489, 494, 515, 531, 538, 540, 558, 567, 578, 581, 582, 584, 589, 592; container, 143, 145, 231, 232, 237, 264, 294, 318; funnel, 189; garbage cans, 34; gloves, 217; liner, 78, 79; pails, 74; sheeting, 47, 182; sheeting permeability, 436; tarp, 36
plastic sheeting: 6 mil, 436, 441
Plastic Wrap, 111, 185, 231
plastics, 73, 74
plastics (hard), 74
plate, 307
playing cards, 49
pleasant odor, 391
pleated cartridge filters, 429
pleated glass, 58
Plexiglas, 245
pliers, 188, 213
plowed and salted/sanded, 561
plum, 104, 143, 416
plumbing, 473
plums, 285, 296
plywood, 188, 270, 272, 346, 438, 456, 473, 503, 504, 505, 510, 512, 513, 524, 535, 539, 550, 596
poblano, 290
pocket knife, 41
poison, 35, 37, 90, 128, 129, 205, 404, 406, 456; poison-control center, 35, 37, 90, 128, 129, 205, 404, 406, 456; syrup of Ipecac, 35, 37, 90, 128, 129, 205, 404, 406, 456
poison ivy, 35; Oak, 113, 195
poisoned bait, 128, 129
poisoning deaths, 310
poisons, 37, 72, 425
polaner all fruit, 172
Polar ice, 31
Polar Pure bottle, 55
poles, 38, 43, 332, 336, 368, 538, 542
police, 415, 418, 481, 523, 537, 538, 548, 565, 597
police stations, 565
Poliovirus (poliomyelitis), 430, 431
politically, 28
polluted, 39, 53, 62, 485
polyethylene, 81, 130, 264, 473
polystyrene foam, 310, 478
polyurethane foam, 438
pond, 71, 76, 77, 399, 524, 552
ponderosa pine, 252
pool, 30, 64, 65, 76, 84, 86, 248, 249, 250, 373, 441, 462, 524, 540, 541
poor weather conditions, 563

pop secret, 162
popcorn, 21, 100, 140, 297, 307, 589
poppy, 107, 222, 224, 279, 286
pork, 101, 146, 149, 268
porta potties, 391, 393
porta potty, 392, 441
portable, 38, 39, 40, 72, 131, 185, 304, 305, 327, 330, 331, 333, 351, 369, 384, 385, 386, 392, 430, 440, 441, 442, 511, 521, 568
portable grill, 39, 344
portable heater (kerosene, 307
portable kitchen, 38, 40
portable shower enclosures, 386
positive airflow (papr), 419
possums, 128, 388
post hole digger, 188
postage stamps, 183
pot marigold, 280
potable, 81, 84, 373, 374, 378, 586
Potable Aqua, 54, 55
potassium hydroxide (KOH), 221
potassium iodide and iodate (KI), 55, 484, 496
potassium permanganate, 72
potato, 136, 141, 268, 279, 296; flakes, 141
potatoes, 103, 145, 288, 337, 352
potholders, 240
potpourri, 258
pots, 39, 190, 245
potting soil, 190
potty, 187
pouch muffins, 168
poultry, 107, 146, 149, 150, 178, 268, 377, 574, 583, 586
pounding heart, 497
pourable candle wax, 347
poured concrete, 451
povidone iodine, 55
powder dyes, 244
powdered drink, 109
powdered milk, 40
power, 21, 23, 25, 27, 32, 33, 38, 42, 43, 45, 46, 48, 69, 75, 84, 95, 119, 134, 137, 182, 183, 207-209, 211, 235, 262, 263, 265, 266, 267, 281, 301-306, 310-314, 321, 322, 325, 331, 334, 342, 343, 353-355, 357, 363, 365, 366, 368, 399, 439, 440, 442, 443, 451, 463, 464, 485, 487, 490, 498-503, 508, 509, 515-518, 527, 530, 533, 537-539, 557, 559, 567, 569, 570, 571, 572, 575, 586, 587, 592, 593
power grid, 265, 303, 304, 499, 500, 586; collapse, 10, 304; EMP, 134, 310, 498, 499, 539; pandemic, 586
power outage, 32, 38, 46, 95, 119, 137, 183, 265, 267, 301, 302, 304, 305, 310, 311, 316, 322, 331, 334, 354, 501, 503, 537, 539, 567, 569, 571; (-s), 32, 38, 46, 95, 265, 302, 304, 322, 331, 354, 539, 569, 571
power stations, 489
power steering fluid, 189, 201
prairie dogs, 270
prayer, 596
precast concrete, 395
precautions, 65, 126, 129, 136, 217, 263, 264, 330, 363, 415, 416, 432, 433, 434, 435, 492, 509, 556
precious metals, 589, 590
pre-filter, 58, 69, 72, 82, 429, 438, 440, 442
pre-formed toxin, 432
Prego, 158
Premier Nikita Khrushchev, 444
prep gear, 325
Preparation H, 51, 194, 202
preparedness, 4, 17, 43, 46, 546, 565
preparedness gear, 408
preparing for: earthquakes, 16, 506; fires, 16, 520; floods, 16, 525; heat waves, 16, 517
preparing your vehicle, 17, 560
prescription glasses, 183
prescriptions, 50, 51, 186, 199
President John F. Kennedy, 444, 445
pressure, 53, 62, 66, 68, 69, 74, 81, 97, 98, 133, 143, 256, 296, 301, 303, 331, 367, 375, 404, 406, 419, 421, 422, 435, 440, 455, 504, 511, 512, 550, 561, 563, 565, 570
pressure canner, 185
pressure cooker, 185
pressure tank, 66, 81
pressure washer, 308, 309
prevailing winds, 450, 481, 485
PRI-D, 201, 321
PRI-G, 201, 321
Primus Expedition, 328
Primus unit, 328
prince, 172
privacy, 206, 386, 441, 539, 590
privacy screen, 386
privacy tent, 386, 387
processed carbohydrates, 97
procurement of food, 408
product date code, 152
progresso, 162, 172
propane, 39, 43, 184, 305, 322, 323, 325, 327, 329, 330, 331, 332, 334, 343, 344, 385, 386, 457, 524, 537, 569, 570, 589; refilling tanks, 570; tank sizes, 589
propane camp stoves, 322
propane lights, 332, 457
propane tanks, 43, 331, 524, 537
proper fit of masks, 14, 419
proper hygiene, 528
property losses, 520
prophecies, 136
prophecy, 136, 518
prophetically, 28
protect computers from loss of information, 539
protect your face and lungs, 425
protection, 49, 283, 408, 463, 502
protective goggles, 217
protective over-garments, 426
proteus bacteria, 431
protozoa, 56, 59, 61, 430
protozoan cysts, 62, 69, 72
provisions, 28, 33, 46, 395, 455, 459, 569
Prudent Places USA, 2, 42, 412, 422, 460, 476, 518, 553, 565
prunes, 285
pruning branches, 82
pruning shears, 190
prunings, 271
Prusik knot, 209
pseudomonal bacteria, 431
pseudomonas aeruginosa, 375, 430
public shelters, 400, 462, 486, 535, 591
public storage, 137
public transit, 422
pudding, 105, 141, 164, 174, 245, 592; (-s), 120, 267
puddles, 312
pulled muscles, 565
pulverized rock, 555
pumice, 228
pump, 57, 66, 68, 69, 75, 79, 81, 82, 93, 209, 210, 211, 262, 301, 309, 320, 328, 385, 386, 411, 439, 440, 516, 561, 563, 568, 583; (-s), 75, 81, 309, 317
pumpkin, 88, 103, 107, 222, 224, 279, 286, 292, 297, 298, 299
pumpkin leather, 299
pumps and meters, 317
pumps in wells, 75
PUR, 58, 68
purchase the freshest products, 129
pureed grains, 493
purification, 53, 55, 56, 57, 61, 62, 65, 68, 72, 78, 196, 209, 429, 430, 488, 489, 587
Puritabs, 56, 72
PVC: glue, 211; pipe, 80, 209, 210, 211, 231; solvent, 211
pyramid, 95, 96, 97, 253
Pyramid Fire, 253
Pyrex, 347
Pyromid, 327, 333, 334

Q

Q FEVER, 14, 433
Q-Tips, 112, 193
quake, 21, 25, 26, 31, 33, 42, 45, 122, 123, 305, 449, 502, 506, 507, 508, 509, 510, 511, 512, 513, 514, 517, 542, 552, 553, 554, 555, 563, 564
Quebec, 303, 304, 418
Queensland Arrowroot, 279
quiz for each family member, 44

R

rabbit, 149; (-s), 90, 400, 409, 434, 494
radiation, 31, 78, 195, 199, 366, 387, 415, 427, 429, 432, 437, 440, 445, 446, 447, 448, 449, 451, 452, 453, 455, 456, 457, 458, 459, 481, 482, 483, 484, 485, 487, 492, 493, 494, 495, 497, 517, 518; potassium iodate, dosage, 495; potassium iodate, shelf life, 16, 495; protection materials, 456, 458; safe dose, 452; sickness, 452, 456, 458, 482, 492, 495; thyroid protection, 199, 484, 495
radio, 21-23, 27, 33, 43-45, 48, 183, 212, 308, 353-356, 358-361, 363-366, 368-370, 372, 417, 425, 437, 439, 444, 447, 457, 484, 487, 499-502, 504, 517, 518, 526, 535-537, 541, 548, 553, 558, 559, 561, 563, 564, 566, 587; (-s), 306, 353, 354, 355, 358, 368, 369, 370, 372, 498, 501, 587, 593; AM/FM, 308
Radio Shack, 504
radio telephone handset, 417
radioactive: fallout, 445, 462, 486, 487, 489, 494; iodine, 484, 489, 490, 495, 496; material, 445, 447, 451, 481, 482, 485, 488, 489, 490; soil, 451
radiological dispersion device (RDD), 481
radish, 279; (-es), 145
radius of destructive circle, 451
Raid, 111, 174, 203
railroad ties, 475, 476, 477
rain, 24, 31, 35, 36, 38, 39, 72, 78, 79, 82, 83, 85, 90, 182, 216, 218, 232, 253, 346, 354, 358, 449, 492, 510, 514, 516, 525, 526, 529, 533, 534, 535, 548, 556, 586; pants, 48, 183; poncho, 48, 183
Rainbow 36A Protection System, 442
Rainbow Tent, 442, 443
raincoat, 35
rainfall, 79, 80, 84, 439

rainfall dependent, 79
rainwater, 72, 77, 78, 79, 80, 82, 83, 237, 586; harvesting, 82; roof catchment, 72; system, 82, 83
rake, 190
Ramic, 222, 224
Ramzi Yousef, 412
ranch style, 172
rancid, 136, 223, 225, 238, 292, 337
rancidity, 149
rapid breathing, 497
raspberries, 296
rat proof, 277
Raton Pass, 414
Ratsak, 111, 122, 128
raw, 55, 67, 100, 103, 106, 116, 147, 212, 235, 266, 268, 296, 301, 337, 412, 425, 490, 527, 565, 591
raw cherries, 296
raw food weight, 296
raw garlic, 425
raw nerves, 412, 591
razor blade, 51, 112, 184, 186; (-s), 51, 112
razors, 184, 186
RDA, 56
reactive loads, 306
Ready.gov, 437, 445, 446
rear-wheel skid, 562; (-s), 562
recent tax returns, 593
recession, 94, 303, 553, 576
recipe: books, 11, 325, 351
recipes, 121, 217, 221, 232, 233, 237, 243, 247, 273, 293, 294, 297, 351, 380; beef jerky, 10, 294; candles, 8, 247; cleaning supplies, 12, 380; Cornell Bread, 115; Dutch oven, 11, 340; laundry soap, 235; shampoo, 236; soap, 8, 221, 232; whole milk from powdered, 6, 120; yeast, 6, 121
recordkeeping, 241
recovery engineering, 68
rectal thermometer, 398
red chili pods, 289
Red Cross, 30, 358, 359, 372, 459, 537, 633
Red Cross chapter, 459
Red Devil, 232, 237
red flame, 257
Red Maple, 252
red meat, 374
Red Oak, 252
red pepper, 107
Red Rooster, 52
Red Wigglers, 272
reduce fogging, 417
reflective open box, 348, 349
refrigerate, 140, 141, 142, 143, 144, 145, 204, 221, 248

refrigerated items, 94
refrigerator, 34, 121, 137, 143, 144, 145, 146, 147, 148, 151, 196, 220, 221, 248, 266, 286, 290, 293, 297, 298, 299, 456, 515, 530, 537; (-s), 132, 277, 530, 531
refuge in a small interior room, 537
regenerate desiccants, 135
Regina, 173
rehydration, 40, 287, 298; time, 287
reinforced concrete, 78, 394, 462, 463, 475, 477, 510
re-insurer: Swiss Re, 31
relief organizations, 29
relocation sites, 486
remove the white foods, 424
rendered kitchen fats, 220
repair parts, 44
Repetabs, 51, 194
replacement, 58, 60, 110, 582
re-sealable plastic lids, 74
reservoirs, 75, 88, 89, 183, 433, 509, 574
residential homes, 459
resin oils, 227
resistance in the wire, 312
respirator, 416, 417, 419, 422, 435, 578, 579, 581, 582, 583, 584, 585; air purifying, 435
respiratory droplet precautions, 433
restaurants, 74, 130, 262, 301, 373, 565
restock, 94
Restop, 386, 387, 391
restroom, 386, 392
retards bacterial growth, 146
Revelation 12: 6, 597
Revelda Harvin, 504
reverse osmosis (RO), 68, 69, 173, 429, 430, 431, 579
Revlon, 203, 204
rhabdovirus virus, 431
rhubarb, 104, 143, 279, 285, 296
rice, 31, 40, 96, 119, 120, 124, 136, 267, 268, 405, 424, 447, 492, 493
Ricin, 431, 433
ricinus, 222, 224
ricotta, 147, 267
RID-X, 173
RID-X ULTRA 2 in 1, 173
rifle, 41, 408, 410, 411
rifle team, 408
rigid plastic, 75, 219, 245
ripening, 143, 289
ristra: (-s), 289, 290
Rit, 229
Ritz Crackers, 47, 100, 139, 589
rivers, 39, 75, 85, 88, 528, 534

road: (-s), 22, 24, 27, 33, 85, 94, 415, 429, 449, 504, 508, 509, 523, 534, 537, 549, 557, 558, 561, 563; contamination, 560; flares, 183; salt and sand, 559
roast coffee, 168
roasts, 146, 333
robbed, 38
robbery, 38
Robitussen, 194
robotics, 540
rock, 75, 76, 85, 88, 141, 227, 273, 274, 395, 476, 478, 491, 509, 529, 544, 546, 552, 555, 557; (-s), 85, 88, 91, 230, 251, 253, 273, 364, 395, 459, 489, 525, 559
Rocky Mountains, 548
rodent feces, 81
rodent-proof, 127, 137
rodents, 123, 124, 128, 205, 270, 271, 274, 299, 388, 433, 491
roentgen, 452
Roger Bernard, 348, 349
roll-down shutters, 539
rolling pin, 293, 295, 298
rolls, 148, 150, 268, 337
Roman, 216
romano, 147, 267
Ronzoni, 167, 173
roof catchment, 72, 78; rainwater, 5, 77; systems, 78, 79, 80
roof tiles, 128, 511
roof washers, 80
roofs, 128, 455, 475, 534, 535, 548, 555, 556
rooftops, 78, 366
room drying, 281
room temperature, 97, 121, 135, 140, 141, 143, 145, 248, 263, 272, 277, 287, 293, 294, 297, 298, 299, 496, 530, 567, 570
root cellar, 277; (-s), 137
roots, 87, 89, 90, 144, 145, 253, 269, 272, 288, 516
rope, 36, 41, 75, 363, 365, 366, 368, 427, 489
roquefort, 147, 151, 267
Rosarita, 173
rose, 228, 351
rosehips, 424
rosella (red sorrel), 279
rosemary, 107, 228, 280
Rosin, 229
Rota Loo, 394
rotate, 99, 114, 125, 126, 137, 195, 288, 321, 339, 340, 397
rotate effectively, 137
rotating stored goods, 42
rotating winds, 547
rotation, 42, 99, 120, 126, 321
rotors, 313
Rototiller, 190

rough terrain, 35, 41
routes, 33, 39, 42, 45, 85, 128, 316, 355, 357, 399, 482, 485, 521, 535, 565
rubber bands, 49, 187
rubber boots, 35, 531
rubber gloves, 187
Rubber Maid, 132, 231
rubber rafts, 42
rubber washers, 75, 209
rubberized parka, 48, 183
ruffled fur, 404
runoff, 459, 489
rural areas, 72, 518, 523
rural community, 415
russet spotting, 144
Russia: Sterlitamak, 543
Russian M-10, 422
Russian SMS Snorkel, 422
rust, 68, 81, 127, 154, 201, 246, 310, 328, 333, 338, 474, 485, 529
rust resistant, 333
rusted, 126, 138, 161, 521, 529, 570; cans, 138
Rust-Oleum, 127, 346
Rutgers University, 412
Rutherford Appleton Labs, 517
RV: (Recreational Vehicle), 34, 137, 323, 395, 569
rye, 136

S

S&W Fine Foods, 174
sacks, 40, 114, 120, 122, 132, 334, 389, 397, 438, 538
safe deposit box, 535, 548, 592
safe place, 32, 33, 363, 439, 507, 526, 535, 548, 592; (-s), 33
safe room, 51, 425, 436, 438, 439, 440, 441, 442, 443, 548, 550
safe room and shelter, 548
safe room or shelter, 537, 549
safe shelter, 427, 438, 439, 441, 549
safest treatment method, 53
safety deposit areas, 459
safety pins, 37, 49, 51, 187, 193, 203
safety shelters: commercial, 437
Saffir-Simpson Hurricane Scale, 534
safflower, 97, 220, 222, 224
sage, 107, 228, 233, 280, 291
salad burnet, 279
salad dressing, 105, 117, 118, 142
salad greens, 145
salami, 101, 146
saline irrigation, 434
saline solution, 51
salmon, 101, 148
salmonella, 59
salmonella typhosa, 430
salon selectives, 204

salsify (oyster plant), 279
salt, 38, 55, 62, 71, 85, 88, 90, 91, 108, 116, 119, 121, 147, 199, 213, 293, 294, 295, 297, 299, 340, 341, 342, 343, 381, 382, 383, 447, 493, 495, 519, 522, 557, 560, 561, 565; restrictions, 38
salted, 150, 478
saltines, 100, 589
salts, 68, 71, 192, 216, 238, 429
Salvation Army, 52, 359, 372, 522
San Bernardino, 520, 591
San Fernando earthquake, 26
San Francisco, CA, October 1989, 23
San Giorgio, 174
Sancor, 393
Sancor unit, 393
sand, 67, 90, 189, 228, 246, 565
Sandia, 290, 499
sandpaper, 201
sanitary, 35, 39, 45, 116, 125, 183, 209, 377, 378, 392, 394, 457, 486, 487
sanitary napkins, 35, 204
sanitary pad, 183, 394
sanitation, 29, 44, 91, 373, 389, 456, 486, 528
sanitation & first aid, 566
sanitation after a flood, 16, 528
Sanka, 174
Santa Cruz, 21, 22, 24, 506, 528; Mountains, 21, 22, 506
SAP Charts, 221
saponification, 217, 221, 227, 228
sardines, 177
sarin, 416, 424
sassafras, 235
SATELLITE PHONES, 12, 354
saturated fat, 97, 116, 238
sauces, 120, 141, 231, 267
sauerkraut, 156, 157, 167
sausage, 101, 146, 149, 155
save money, 28, 40, 42, 125
saving $$, 6, 122
sawdust, 258, 270, 272, 273, 394
saws, 309, 589
Saxitoxin, 431
SC JOHNSON, 162, 174
scale, 81, 85, 244, 264, 412, 414, 507, 576, 577
scallops, 146
scalpel, 193
scanners, 540
scenes of horror, 412
scents, 66, 220, 227, 228, 229, 235, 246, 257
schistosomes, 389
schools, 459
Schwarzkopf, 203, 204
science writer, 276
scissors, 37, 51, 188, 193, 213, 589

scoria, 75
Scott MPC Plus, 424
Scott NBC M95 Long Life, 424
Scott NTC-1 (2001 design), 424
screen mesh, 129, 277
screwdriver, 188
screw-on filters, 424
screws, 188, 589
sea: level, 53, 133, 534, 535, 553; |perch, 148; |salt, 212, 213; |trout, 148
seafood, 146, 148
SeaLand, 391
sealing surface, 131
sealing washers, 75
seamless aluminum, 80
seasonings, 109
secret coding, 154
securable solar panels, 478
sediment filter, 68, 82; |(-s), 82
seeds, 97, 107, 115, 120, 129, 136, 159, 169, 190, 196, 274, 275, 276, 277, 278, 280, 284, 286, 288, 289, 297, 342, 566, 589
seismic sea waves, 552
seismic waves, 507
seismically active area, 509
Seismo (one of our K9s), 76, 120, 123, 128, 129, 191, 205, 373, 396, 397, 398, 405, 406, 414, 422, 441
self-adhesive elastic wrap bandages (vetrap), 398
self-defense, 33, 411
self-pollinating, 276
self-sufficiency, 216, 275
sell-by or pull-by date, 152
semi-auto rifle, 409
Seminole Smoke Shop, 504
semi-permeable membrane, 68
SENECA, 174
sense of smell, 128, 388
September 11, 2001, 31, 170, 412, 414, 415, 426, 502
septic tank, 66, 393, 527, 528
septics, 84
serrated wheel, 255
Sesame, 108, 220, 223, 225, 286
sesame seed, 108, 223, 225, 286
severe injuries, 401
severe nausea and vomiting, 497
severe storm, 46, 399
sewage lines, 487, 508
sewer, 44, 49, 373, 389, 393, 526, 528, 537, 587
sewer lines break, 389, 528
sewers can back up, 528
shallot, 279
shallow pond, 488
shallow wells, 75
Shalon Chemical Industries, 418
shampoo, 39, 52, 204, 216, 236, 384

shampoo bar, 236
sharpened screw driver, 491
shattering, 76
shave cream, 112, 184, 186, 204
shaved face is best, 419
shed, 34, 122, 137, 277, 314, 412, 476, 577
sheep, 433
sheets, 21, 23, 37, 38, 112, 128, 219, 241, 246, 259, 272, 295, 339, 347, 457, 513
shelf life, 40, 47, 52, 55, 60, 65, 84, 95, 96, 98, 99, 114, 116, 119, 120, 122, 124, 126, 127, 129, 131, 132, 134, 136, 137, 141, 151, 152, 153, 154, 164, 169, 196, 197, 199, 200, 203, 204, 205, 254, 257, 275, 277, 294, 297, 321, 323, 391, 417, 422, 423, 496, 582
Shelf Life Extension, 196
Shelf Life of Medications, 7, 196, 197
shelf lives, 40, 99, 116, 126, 137, 151, 196, 197, 200
shellfish, 146
Shellite, 322
shelter, 29, 36, 38, 206, 207, 208, 395, 396, 399, 436, 437, 438, 439, 440, 442, 443, 444, 445, 446, 453, 455, 456, 457, 458, 459, 460, 461, 462, 463, 464, 486, 487, 490, 491, 492, 493, 497, 507, 518, 536, 548, 549, 550, 551, 559, 561, 571, 591, 592, 593; above ground, 437, 550; animals, 396; fallout and tornado, 461; home, 455, 461, 486; staying in, 18, 591; underground, 206, 476, 548
sheltering: long term, 591
sheltering in place, 14, 436
shelves, 26, 32, 94, 122, 123, 125, 136, 137, 138, 152, 162, 503, 504, 505, 507, 508, 509, 530, 531, 586
shelving, 122, 123, 137, 201
Sherlock Park, 525
shifting ground, 78
shigella, 59
shigella dysentariae, 430
shipping containers, 475, 477; cost, 206, 474
shipping crate, 271
shire, 269, 388
shirts, 35, 217, 556
shivers, 404
shock, 414, 449
shock waves, 448, 508
shoes, 35, 183
shortened shelf life, 127
shortness of breath, 124, 310
shortwave, 358, 360, 361, 368, 369, 370, 443, 502, 587
shovel: folding camp, 339

shower, 83, 216, 231, 236, 384, 385, 386, 427, 428, 484, 515, 519; bladders, 384; curtain, 427, 428; enclosures, 13, 386; facilities, 386
shredded coconut, 286
shrimp, 101, 108, 148
shrinkage, 35, 221, 243, 248, 584
shutters, 504, 536, 538, 539
sideboards, 122, 123
sieve, 82, 134, 221, 299, 493
sifter, 129
signal flares, 48, 183
silica, 129, 134, 135, 291
silica sand drying, 291
silicone, 255
Silicone Bakery Paper, 231
silt, 81
Siltstopper 5 micron, 58
silver, 56, 58, 62, 67, 199, 212, 213, 214, 215, 356, 373, 425, 590; dollar, 212; goblets, 212; ions, 56, 215; particles, 214, 215; plates, 212; protein, 214; vessels, 212; wire, 212
silver beet, 279
silver chloride, 213
Silver Gum, 252
Silver Ice, 214
Silver Wain Water, 215
Silverkaire, 214
Sinex, 51, 113, 195
siphon, 188, 320, 589
siphoning hose, 565
skidding sideways, 563
skillets, 306
skills, 28, 33, 94, 216, 230, 239, 408, 410, 476
skin: exposure, 426; flora, 428; irritation, 65, 229; lesions, 432; softener, 220, 229
skinner, 174
skip thomsen, 313
SKS, 409
skunk: (-s), 270, 388
slabs of dry ice, 132
sledgehammer, 188, 207, 208, 511
sleeping bag, 34, 36, 37, 42, 182, 422, 572; (-s), 34, 36, 42, 182, 422, 572
sleet, 557
SLEP, 196
Slim Jim, 159
slime, 65, 321, 375, 377, 378, 510, 532
slip joint pliers, 565
slivers, 42
slugs, 271, 274
slurred speech, 558
small animal, 50, 259
small bills, 38, 48, 183, 566
small dam, 75

small game, 409
small pillow, 37
small plastic bottles, 49
small plastic containers, 52
small town, 32
smallpox, 14, 434
smart ones, 174
Smart Sealer, 131
smoke, 45, 51, 242, 249, 260, 261, 287, 295, 326, 344, 401, 422, 424, 438, 448, 454, 484, 520, 521, 522, 524, 568; (-s), 333, 337; alarms, 45, 520; inhalation, 401, 422, 424; near flammable liquids, 521
smoked, 146, 148, 149, 407; meats, 146
smokeless fire, 252
smoker accessory, 327
smoker/oven, 333
smoking fish, 327
smoky odor, 382
Smuckers, 175
snack puddings, 47
snack-size portions, 592
snails, 271, 274
snake bath, 399
snake bite, 37, 182; kit, 37, 182
snakes, 27, 37, 190, 270
snare construction, 410
SNC Industrial Technologies, 418
sneakers, 35, 36
sneaky dating, 7, 152
sneezing, 18, 580
Snickers, 96, 114, 120
snow, 43, 46, 48, 85, 92, 93, 183, 253, 254, 266, 325, 361, 387, 489, 557, 558, 559, 560, 561, 562, 563, 565, 593; drifts, 43; melted, 39; plows, 43; territory, 563; tires, 558, 562; tires with studs, 558
soap, 38, 39, 53, 64, 73, 124, 216, 217, 218, 219, 220, 221, 223, 225, 226, 227, 228, 229, 230, 231, 232, 233, 234, 235, 236, 237, 238, 262, 264, 338, 378, 381, 382, 383, 407, 426, 428, 432, 433, 434, 438, 484, 519, 527, 531, 570, 584; balls, 221; faux ivory, 233
soapmaking, 7, 216, 217, 218, 381; techniques, 229
soapy water, 74, 294, 337, 428, 515, 530
social decline survivalist, 115
social security: card, 593; number, 49, 187
socket driver, 565
socket wrench set, 565
socks, 35, 36, 48, 183, 184, 589
soda, 47, 117, 118, 240, 341, 381
soda pop, 47, 341

soda pop biscuits, 341
sodium bisulfite, 283
sodium carbonate, 238
sodium count, 47
sodium hydroxide, 221
sodium hypochlorite, 53, 54, 64, 65, 373, 374, 426, 428, 432, 433, 434
sodium iodide, 55
sodium meta-bisulfite, 283
sodium sulfite, 283, 285
Sodium thiosulfate, 54, 199
soft drink, 52, 73, 74, 96, 234, 424; (-s), 52, 96, 234; bottles, 73, 74
soft food items, 388
soft rubber, 245
soft wash liquid soap, 112, 200
soft woods, 252
SOHO (Solar & Heliospheric Observatory), 517
soil (one cubic foot of weighs), 477
soil depth, 475, 476
soil fertility, 274
soil over the roof, 475
soil texture, 269
solar, 31, 33, 44, 45, 60, 71, 72, 183, 282, 304, 346, 347, 348, 349, 351, 354, 384, 385, 386, 429, 478, 502, 517, 518, 560; box cookers, 346; cookbooks, 11, 351; cooker, 351; cooking, 11, 345, 351; drying, 281; energy, 346, 354; shower, 182, 385; stills, 91
solar flare: megaflare, 31, 517, 518
solar ultraviolet (UV) radiation, 429
solarcaine, 51, 113, 195
soldering iron, 213, 309
sombreros, 245
sore mouth, 495
Sorrel, 279
SOS, 112, 200, 559
soup, 47, 102, 114, 117, 118, 141, 231, 240, 589; (-s), 114, 120, 123, 163, 268, 298, 325, 530
sour cream, 147, 342
sourdough cinnamon rolls, 341
South America, 77, 124
South Texas 1 plant, 485
Sovereign Silver, 215
Soviet General and Army Chief of Operations, 444
sow bugs, 274
soy, 31, 97, 115, 117, 118, 140, 147, 220, 267, 293, 294, 295, 493, 494
soy flour, 115
soy sauce, 293, 294, 295
space: bag, 566; blanket, 47, 182; heater, 43, 521; rocks, 544
spacecraft, 439, 546

spackling compound, 201
spade, 190
spaghetti, 26, 94, 100, 140; and macaroni, 117, 118
spaghetti sauce, 103, 142
spam, 101, 164
spare batteries, 419
spare fuses, 565
spark arresters, 521, 523
Spark-Lite, 255
sparks, 252, 255, 256, 259, 320, 334, 521, 523, 538
spasms, 518, 519
spatula, 339; (-s), 39
SPC Limited, 175
special dietary: foods, 592; items, 50, 186
special forces, 408, 409
speed: 300 mph, 547
sperm whale blubber, 223, 225
Spice Islands, 175
spices, 107, 286
spillage, 45
spillways, 528
spinach, 103, 145, 278, 279, 289, 296, 298
spinal cord injuries, 428
spiral staircase, 477
spirits, 201, 322
spiritual, 42
splint, 368, 403
splints, 37
split phase, 309, 310
sponge, 49, 382; (-s), 112, 187, 200, 374
spoons, 111, 185
sporicidal agent (hypochlorite)., 432
spray & wipe, 112, 200
spray nozzle, 190
spring, 31, 43, 75, 86, 88, 89, 210, 328, 389, 488, 491, 494, 548; (-s), 75, 88, 359, 404, 542
sprouting, 44, 114
sprouting garden, 44
spruce, 252
square braid, 242
square sterile pads, 397
squash, 145, 279, 289, 292, 296, 298, 352
squirrel, 149; (-s), 434
SSF filter, 67
STA-BIL, 321
stabilize the neck, 508, 549
stabilized oxygen, 4, 56, 74
stable iodide, 495
stack food, 137
stagg chili, 175
stainless steel, 78, 80, 123, 185, 217, 221, 234, 237, 264, 314, 320, 325, 327, 328, 331, 339, 344, 385, 578; ladle, 218; pots, 217

stamped postcards, 48, 183
stampeding into fences, 401
standard rate of decay, 447
staphylococcal enterotoxin, 431
staphylococcal enterotoxin b, 14, 434
staphylococci, 431
staphylococcus epidermidis, 430
staple gun, 188
starch, 297
Starkist Tuna, 175
starting fires, 42
start-up wattage, 306, 310
stated shelf life, 154
stay away from ashfall areas, 556
steak sauce, 109, 142, 295
steaks, 146
steam, 71, 85, 287, 288, 327, 338, 555
steam clean, 531
steaming rack, 339
stearic acid, 223, 225, 240
Stearine, 243, 244
Stearns Air Power Sunshower, 13, 384
Stearns Shower Enclosure, 386
steel drums, 81
steel pads, 39, 112
steel wool pads, 187, 200
Steelo, 39, 112, 187
Stephen King's movie, 415
sterile seed, 276
sterile waste product, 389
Steri-Pen, 60, 61
Steritabs, 56
Sterno, 43, 184, 322, 323, 325, 327
stethoscope, 194
stew meat, 146
stills, 71
stir-fry, 327
stitches, 37, 398, 588
stocked pantries, 94
stocking up, 94, 410, 583
stocks, 49, 187, 593
stokes, 176
stomach, 19, 37, 124, 194, 402, 406, 594
stomatitis virus, 431
stone, 81, 112, 499
storage, 2, 34, 42, 51, 58, 65, 69, 72, 74, 77-79, 81, 82, 95, 98, 99, 114, 115, 120, 122-124, 126-132, 134, 136-38, 140, 143, 145, 146, 148, 149, 151, 185, 196, 201, 206-209, 231, 277, 285, 286, 291, 297, 305, 308, 316-321, 323, 324, 327-329, 334, 349, 386, 441, 459, 462, 474, 476, 477, 478, 482, 486, 491, 500, 521, 539, 540, 586, 587, 589
storage bins, 34
storage life, 127, 136

Dare To Prepare: Index

storage tank, 80; (-s), 72, 78, 79, 82, 209, 318
Storax Oil, 228
store ashes in a metal container, 521
stored drinking water, 488
stored goods, 99, 122, 126, 415
stored grains, 492
stored tank water, 84
storing extra food, 94
storing foods, 126
storing seed, 276, 277
storing short term, 4, 46
storing tips, 139, 141, 143, 144, 146, 147, 148, 149, 150, 151
storm, 33, 402, 534, 535, 539, 548, 551; (-s), 29, 30, 31, 304, 358, 399, 478, 503, 518, 534, 540, 547, 548, 560, 564, 571; surge, 402, 534, 535, 538, 557; tide, 534, 535
stoves, 11, 17, 326, 567; backpack, 11, 327, 328, 329, 330; camp, 11, 330; fireplace, 567; kerosene, 11, 326; pellet, 385, 568
straddle the fire, 336
strainer boxes, 80
strange breath, 404
stratosphere, 544
straw, 270, 273
strawberries, 229, 285, 296
strawberry, 104, 228
streams, 39, 88, 525, 526, 528, 534, 536, 537
street map, 565
Strepsils, 202
streptococcus bacteria, 431
streptococcus faecaelis, 430
string, 50, 188, 258, 259, 288, 473
striped bass, 148
strips of meat, 294
stroke of lightning, 498
strong odors, 74
structural damage, 454, 508, 522
stuffing mix, 100, 141
styrofoam, 111, 347, 388; sheets, 123
submerged, 75, 209, 212, 213, 358
submersible, 75, 309; pumps, 75
sub-sonic rounds, 409
suburban and rural areas, 486
subways, 459; and tunnels, 486
Sudafed, 51, 113, 194, 202
Sudanese National Islamic Front, 412
suet, 217, 220, 221, 234
sufficient exposure, 69
sufficient heating fuel, 557
sugar, 40, 47, 95, 96, 106, 115, 117, 118, 119, 136, 141, 158, 195, 252, 286, 492, 600; (-s), 97, 120
Sugar Maple, 252

sulfa drugs, 212
sulfite dip, 283
sulfur, 283, 284, 285, 297; dioxide, 283; fumes, 297
sulfured fruit, 297
sulfuring, 282, 283, 284
sump pump, 309
Sun, 31, 37, 71, 74, 91, 127, 136, 183, 271, 275, 281, 284, 285, 289, 297, 349, 351, 354, 373, 494, 503, 517, 518, 531
sun block, 37
sun glare, 417
sun stroke, 518
sunburn, 51, 195, 519
sundown, 204, 205
sunflower, 97, 102, 223, 225, 279, 286, 297
sunglasses, 48, 183, 566
Sun-Mar, 393
sunny days: 300 annually, 346
sun-quakes, 517
sunscreen, 51, 195, 204, 205
Super Glue, 201
superfatted, 223, 225, 226
superfatting, 219
supplies, 28, 32-34, 39-41, 43, 45-48, 51, 74, 77, 94, 98, 115, 119, 120, 123, 124, 126, 127, 137, 182, 183, 192, 206, 231, 241, 246, 265, 301, 316, 321, 327, 358, 368, 384, 386, 396, 401, 434, 437, 457, 474, 475, 484, 485, 493, 494, 499, 503, 504, 505, 526, 535, 536, 544, 546, 548, 556-558, 563, 571, 575, 582, 585-588, 591, 592
suppositories, 51, 113
surface area, 67, 91, 214, 215, 271, 272, 374, 429, 488, 582
surface collection area, 82
surface decontamination, 433
surface water, 75, 316, 463, 488
surge suppressors, 539
surgical gloves, 37, 49, 187
surgical mask, 435, 581, 583
surplus filters, 423
survival, 32, 41, 43, 46, 48, 52, 84, 123, 187, 255, 358, 400, 408, 409, 410, 452, 453, 490, 500, 502, 563, 589, 597; knife, 408; manual, 49; situation, 84, 409, 410
survivalist, 41, 115, 369
Survivor 06, 68
Survivor 35, 69
survivors (millions of), 489
suspended particles, 68, 81
suspending pots, 185
swag, 36, 37
swamp cooler, 127, 438
Swanson, 158

sweat, 35, 84, 86, 88, 93, 219, 384, 519; (-s), 35, 88; heavy sweating, 519
sweatsuit set, 183
Swedish, 330
Sweet 'N Low, 286
sweet fennel, 227
sweet potato, 279, 298
Sweetwater, 55, 58, 60, 430
swelling, 403, 404, 519
swimming pool: (-s), 64, 82, 523; filter equipment, 464; filters, 62, 129
Swiss, 31, 50, 105, 145, 147, 151, 159, 188, 204, 256, 267, 279, 346, 361, 490
Swiss Army Knife, 50, 188
Swiss Chard, 145, 279
Swiss naturalist, 346
Swiss Re, 31
symptoms of stress and fatigue, 537
synthetic dyes, 429
syringe (plastic 20 ml), 398
syrup, 37, 113, 142, 202, 283, 284, 600
Syrup of Ipecac, 37, 113

T

T-2 mycotoxin, 431
Tabasco sauce, 176
table saws, 309
tablets, 37, 51, 113, 185, 194, 197, 198, 199, 496
Taco (one of our K9s), 76, 100, 108, 120, 123, 128, 129, 142, 171, 191, 205, 373, 396, 397, 398, 405, 406, 414, 422, 441
taco and tostada shells, 171
taco sauce, 94, 267, 530
take personal responsibility, 597
tallow, 219, 221, 223, 225
tallow based soaps, 219
Tamarack, 252
Tampons, 36, 49, 112, 184, 186, 194, 204, 394
Tang, 55, 109, 176, 589
tangerine, 143, 228
tank sprayer, 428
tanks and cistern capacity, 81
tanks and cisterns, 81; capacity, 81
tap water, 52, 64, 74, 212, 537
tape, 113, 201, 213, 277, 438, 441, 535
tapers, 241
tar, 260, 413
target, 52, 98, 100, 101, 102, 103, 104, 105, 106, 107, 108, 109, 110, 111, 112, 113, 125

tarragon, 108, 163, 280, 292
tax file number, 49, 187
tea, 40, 47, 109, 113, 141, 195, 202, 228, 242, 270, 272, 425, 589; bags, 47, 270, 272
Tea Tree, 227, 236, 383; oil, 113, 195, 202, 228
teal, 223, 225, 243, 244
teas, 55, 120
teel, 223, 225
Teepee Fire, 251
teething ring, 50, 186
telephone and power lines, 506
television, 308; stations, 526, 537
temperature, 55, 56, 85, 123, 124, 126, 127, 129, 131, 132, 135, 143, 148, 213, 218, 219, 226, 235, 236, 241, 243, 246, 248, 249, 261, 263, 264, 266, 273, 274, 277, 281, 293, 295, 296, 299, 313, 325, 333, 334, 338, 339, 340, 344, 347, 373, 385, 386, 404, 406, 430, 463, 476, 477, 494, 508, 518, 519, 522, 530, 549, 557, 561, 562, 571, 584; and moisture, 123; equivalents, 602
tempered safety glass, 523
template, 221
tenacious bacteria, 84
tenderizer, 294
tennis shoes, 35
tent, 182, 201, 386, 409
tent repair kit, 201
tents, 36, 42, 387, 406
terra cotta, 245, 246
terrain and wind conditions, 453
terrorism, 28, 31, 46, 94, 412, 413, 414, 437, 445, 485, 503; threat, 485; targets 3, 354, 412, 413, 415, 416, 481, 485, 573, 596
terrorist attack, 31, 415, 485
testing the water, 3
tetracycline, 199
Tetraglycine hydroperiodide, 54, 55
Tex/Mex, 287
Texas, 30, 303, 370, 371, 372, 449, 463, 476, 543, 547, 574, 633; Dallas, 414, 445, 463, 474; Laredo, 476
Texsport, 389
thawed food, 530
The Big One, 21
The Cosmic Conspiracy, 2
The Depression, 32
The Medical Management of Biological Casualties Handbook, 426
The People, 136
the seven/ten rule, 447
The Stand, 415
the terminator seed, 276

The Vindicator Scrolls, 2
The Volcano, 11, 343; stove, 322, 325, 334, 344
Theobroma, 223, 225
thermal: blanket, 36, 132; capacitor, 475; mass, 475, 476; storage material, 475
thermometer, 43, 218, 240, 266, 273, 333, 340, 351, 476
thermos bottles, 185
thermostat, 124, 282, 518, 557, 558, 561
thieves, 128, 314, 317
thinners, 204
thread, 37, 50, 203, 211, 600
Three Bedroom, 40 foot Containers(6 of), 478
throat lozenges, 113, 202
thunderstorms, 32, 533, 534, 540, 547
thyme (thymus vulgaris), 108, 128, 280, 292
Tide, 176
Til Oil, 223, 225
Tilex, 158, 200
Tim Hawcroft, 398
time saver, 94
tin tank, 79
tinder, 22, 252, 253, 254, 255, 256, 259
Tinker Air Force Base, 413
tinned can, 79
tire pressure gauge, 189
tire sealer/inflator, 189
tires, 189, 561, 589; air pressure, 561
toaster, 101, 141, 308
toilet: basic bucket, 440; bowl, 380, 389, 391, 393; bowl ring, 380; bucket, 389, 390, 391, 392, 440, 457, 486; camping, 440; chemical, 392; compost, 393, 394; composting, 13, 393; existing, 389; flush, 83; folding, 13, 389; homemade composting, 393, 395; makeshift, 389, 390, 441; makeshift proper height of, 390; paper, 49, 111, 187, 200, 589; paper biodegradable, 393, 395; seat spacers, 390; shower tent, 386; tanks, 74; temporary, 390, 440
Tom Sponheim, 349
tomato, 103, 142, 145, 161, 190, 280, 289, 292, 296, 299; (-es), 103, 145, 289, 292, 296; juice, 114, 404, 425; paste, 103; sauce, 142; stewed can of, 240
tomatoes: stewed, 114
Tombstone pizza, 176
tone, 102, 176, 177

tongue depressor, 242; (-s), 51, 194
tool belt, 4, 41
tools, 43, 45, 46, 85, 125, 306, 476, 524
toothbrush, 36, 49, 112, 184, 186, 204, 589, 593
toothpaste, 36, 49, 112, 184, 186, 204, 205
toothpicks, 111
topography of the coastline, 553
torch, 50, 184
tornadoes, 20, 44, 397, 400, 462, 464, 547, 548, 549, 550, 551, 560, 564; (-es), 32, 94, 206, 462, 517, 533, 535, 547, 548, 549; shelter plans, 17, 551
tortillas, 100
toughest military standards, 422
tow chain, 559, 565; or rope, 559
towel against the door, 436
towelettes, 49, 186, 187, 193
towels, 218, 398
toxic, 55, 65, 74, 80, 92, 213, 251, 254, 255, 323, 324, 325, 330, 334, 380, 381, 382, 392, 416, 426, 439, 558; chemicals, 251, 254, 255; fumes, 323, 324, 325, 330, 334, 558
toxicity, 382, 416
toxins, 289, 429, 431, 434, 440
Toyota Camry, 504
toys, 50, 186, 205, 397, 457
tracing, 219, 235
tracking by sight, 410
traffic jam, 42
traffic lights, 22, 44, 502
trailers, 34, 137, 378, 399, 549
trailing, 219, 548
Trangia stoves, 330
transfer switch, 311, 314
transformers, 304, 489
traps, 82, 123, 526, 559
trash, 48, 120, 182, 187, 192, 234, 251, 257, 269, 273, 388, 389, 390, 391, 395, 397, 440, 515, 521, 523, 538, 587
Travacalm, 51, 195
travois, 38, 40
treatments prescribed for early symptoms, 495
treats and toys, 397
tree branches, 80, 92, 367, 386, 523
tree onion, 280
tree saw, 188
trees, 42, 43, 76, 77, 87, 89, 90, 332, 355, 366, 367, 448, 454, 508, 509, 516, 523, 529, 534, 535, 540, 542, 547, 555, 557, 571
treet, 155
trellises, 190
trembling, 497

trial run, 35, 541
Tribulation, 597
trichinella parasite, 292
tricothecene mycotoxicosis, 14, 434
trihalomethanes, 65, 69
tripods, 336
Trix, 162
tropical cyclone, 533, 534
tropical depression, 534
tropical storm, 531, 534, 535; (-s), 533, 534, 547
troubleshooting, 219, 226, 248
truckers, 437, 586
trusting God, 597
tsunami, 29, 552, 553, 554; (-s), 29, 31, 94, 506, 552, 553, 555, 560, 573
Tsunami Warning Center, 553
tube tent, 47
tularemia, 14, 434
tumeric, 280
Tums, 51, 194, 195
tuna, 101, 102, 153, 589
tundra, 543
Tunguska, 542
tunnel vision, 594
tunnels, 301, 459
Tupperware, 132, 231, 285
turbidity, 62, 67, 75, 375
turbulent flow, 69
turkey, 101, 146, 149, 352, 582
turnip, 280, 296, 298; (-s), 145
TV, 26, 44, 302, 303, 354, 360, 368, 414, 443, 448, 538, 541, 563, 587, 593, 597
TVP, 136
tweezers, 37, 49, 51, 184, 186, 194, 398, 572
twigs, 252, 253, 270, 271, 273, 327, 388, 454
twine, 50, 188, 290, 589
twitching, 404
two-burner, 329, 385
Tylenol, 51, 113, 195, 197
Type 80 NATO, 424
typhoid, 209, 389, 430
Tyremaster, 52; (-s), 125
TYSON, 177

U

U. S. Air Force, 409
U. S. Department of Agriculture (USDA), 276
U.S. Air Force, 542, 546; Space Command Headquarters, 542
U.S. Air Force Academy, 408
U.S. Department of Agriculture, 95, 265, 267
U.S. embassies, 413
U.S. government, 151
U.S. Pharmacopeia, 98
U.S. sailors, 413

UBL, 415
UFOs Are Here, 2
UK, 162, 425, 569, 570, 598
Ultra Pure Col. Silver, 215
UltraClear, 214
ultraviolet light, 69, 82
Uncle Ben's, 177
unconscious person, 508, 549
underdeveloped countries, 75
undergarments, 35, 36
underground, 34, 77, 83, 86, 127, 136, 206, 270, 277, 302, 317, 455, 459, 461, 463, 474, 475, 476, 477, 478, 486, 488, 499, 518, 527, 537, 542, 548; home, 474, 476, 478; parking garages, 459; storage, 7, 206
underpasses, 459
underwear, 48, 183, 589
Underwood, 177
Underwood Sardines, 177
unemployment, 28, 32, 576
unexpected company, 94
unfamiliar foods, 114
United States, 1, 346, 409, 410, 444, 499, 500, 502, 517, 533
University of Delaware, 214
unleaded gas, 324
unraveling dating codes, 7, 152
unsalted, 149, 150
unvaccinated personnel, 432
unwashed bodies, 591
upper story escape ladder, 45
upwind rural area, 425
urban heat island effect, 518
urban survival, 4, 43
urine, 86, 88, 124, 128, 389, 391, 392, 393, 395, 441
US M1, 409
US patent number 5, 276
USDA, 95, 98, 119, 178
use by, 40, 153, 156, 159, 160, 176
use-by date, 152
used 20 foot shipping containers, 474
USGS, 25, 26, 32, 34, 42, 85, 506, 555
USP, 55, 98
USS Cole, 412, 414
USSR, 432
Utah, 132, 514, 542, 582
Utah-Arizona desert, 132
utensils, 36, 38, 46, 121, 294, 338, 339, 433, 456, 492, 493, 531, 566, 593
UV: band, 69; filter, 69; lamp, 430; penetration, 429; rays, 428; treatment, 56, 69

V

V8, 103, 158
vaccinated, 432

vacuum, 44, 75, 94, 116, 124, 127, 131, 187, 277, 296, 306, 403, 492, 602; cleaner, 44, 306; sealer, 131, 187
Vagisil, 194, 202
van camp's, 159
vanilla, 19, 229, 341; extract, 286
vapors, 381, 424, 578
variety meats, 146
variety of fuels, 327, 330
VariFuel, 328
varnish, 246
Vaseline, 51, 194, 195, 204, 231, 252, 259, 419
veal, 146, 149, 268
vector and rodent control, 433
vegetable, 77, 90, 97, 114, 145, 217, 219, 226, 227, 228, 229, 230, 231, 232, 233, 234, 236, 237, 238, 243, 247, 249, 250, 262, 263, 264, 269, 270, 272, 287, 289, 298, 299, 337, 338, 339, 407; (-s), 43, 44, 97, 114, 116, 119, 120, 123, 125, 144, 152, 227, 275, 281, 286, 287, 289, 291, 296, 298, 299, 327, 333, 343, 352, 373, 399, 424, 490, 493, 494, 515, 529; juice, 298; leather, 298, 299; oil, 115, 117, 118, 220, 264, 589
vegetarian dishes, 287
vegetation, 71, 85, 86, 91, 478, 523, 534
venezuelan equine encephalitis, 14, 435
venison, 292
venomous bite or sting, 544
ventilation, 75, 123, 128, 145, 207, 208, 218, 252, 270, 271, 289, 291, 292, 323, 393, 440, 460, 462, 463, 476, 478, 491, 513, 556, 558, 559, 569; pipe, 123
vermin, 34
vertically roasting poultry, 327
veterinarian, 402, 403, 404, 405, 406, 407
veterinary records, 397
Vetivert, 228
vibro commo, 430
Vicks, 113
victim, 495, 496, 508, 518, 519, 549, 558, 583, 597
victim of poisoning, 495
videotapes, 526, 535, 537, 548; of your belongings, 526
vine drying, 281
vinegar, 38, 39, 217, 239, 294, 338, 380, 381, 382, 383, 560
Vintage Cellars, 52
vinyl, 124, 231, 541
violet, 243, 244, 280
viral hemorrhagic fevers, 14, 435
viral organisms, 429

ViralStop, 55, 57, 60, 61
viruses, 55, 56, 57, 59, 61, 62, 72, 376, 428, 429, 430, 432, 573, 574, 578, 579, 580, 582
visas, 187
visible light, 69
visine, 51, 113, 194
vision correction, 417
Vitamin A, 424, 493
Vitamin B-12, 494
Vitamin C, 54, 114, 275, 283, 493
Vitamin D, 97, 493
Vitamin K, 129
vitamins, 52, 96, 119, 127, 283, 400, 424, 492, 493
voicemitter, 418; (-s), 417, 418
volatile, 68, 324, 568, 588, 590
volcanic, 31, 75, 543, 552, 555, 556, 560, 564; ash, 555, 556; eruptions, 31, 552, 560, 564; region, 75
volcano, 31, 48, 555, 556
volcanoes, 30, 94, 555
voltage drop, 312
voltage regulators, 539
vomit inducer, 195
vomiting, 37, 86, 402, 403, 404, 406, 435, 452, 495, 519, 577
votives, 242
Vybar, 243, 244, 248, 249, 250

W

wading pool, 427
wafer board, 207
waffles, 150
wagon, 38
walkers, 186
walkie talkie, 38
walking painful beyond belief, 565
Wall Street, 302, 413
Walls of Water, 190
Wal-Mart, 52, 393, 504
walnut, 223, 225, 252
war in the heavens, 444
warehouses, 94, 125, 153, 586
warheads, 416
wash, 35, 36, 44, 49, 66, 74, 84, 85, 124, 143, 144, 145, 183, 217, 219, 236, 272, 294, 338, 339, 373, 374, 378, 381, 382, 383, 384, 403, 404, 407, 484, 490, 493, 494, 515, 516, 527, 530, 532, 544, 582, 585; board, 182; cloth, 183, 585; cloth and towel, 49, 184, 186; tub, 182
wash your hands often, 528
washer fluid, 189
washers, 80, 81, 211, 306, 367, 374, 378, 511, 515, 516
washing, 35, 38, 39, 49, 53, 73, 80, 83, 84, 88, 110, 116, 233, 282,

338, 339, 374, 378, 381, 426, 428, 433, 494, 515, 516, 578
washing benzene, 322
washing machine, 308
Washington: Oregon, 449, 552, 553, 633; Seattle, 474, 505; Spokane, 304, 555
Washington Park, 571
wasps, 273
waste water, 209, 515, 516
wasted space, 137
wasting money, 94
water, 23, 27-29, 32-35, 39, 40, 42-58, 60, 62, 64-69, 71- 94, 110, 114-116, 119-121, 124, 127, 136, 137, 144, 182, 184, 185, 187, 196, 201-203, 206, 209-223, 225-227, 229, 232-241, 243, 244, 246-249, 254-258, 260-262, 264, 266, 269-272, 274, 277, 283, 284, 286, 287, 289, 294, 296-298, 301, 316-325, 329, 330, 332, 338-342, 352, 357, 358, 373-381, 383-386, 389, 391-395, 397-401, 403-405, 422, 425-430, 432-434, 436, 438, 441, 442, 445, 447, 452, 453, 455-459, 461, 463, 464, 476, 477, 484-495, 496, 499, 500-509, 514-516, 518, 519, 521-532, 535-538, 540, 541, 548-550, 552-555, 558, 561-563, 565, 570, 575, 578, 584-588, 591-593; 99% of radioactivity in, 489; accessing cistern, 5, 81; backup, 79; bath, 43, 382; bathing, 110, 433; bottled, 52, 94, 458, 499, 504, 532, 563; budget, 83; chlorinated, 84, 375; cold, 54, 55, 74, 144, 145, 232, 233, 235, 282, 283, 287, 289, 298, 338, 373, 377, 378, 382, 401, 403, 493; cold faucet, 401; collection, 5, 75; concrete tank, 122; condensed, 71, 124; conductivity of, 213; contaminated from deep lakes, 488; contaminated from fallout, 488, 489, 490; contaminated from shallow ponds, 488; contaminated from streams, 488; continuous supply of raw, 67; continuous treatment, 67; daily consumption, 83; directly from creek, 67; distilled, 69, 74, 213, 218; drinkable, 57, 68, 89, 91, 393; drinking, 39, 47, 55, 62, 72, 77, 84, 110, 261, 377, 378, 427, 486, 507, 515, 526, 532, 535, 537, 548, 553, 557; evaporate, 71; filtered, 56, 67, 490; fresh, 68, 85, 87, 89, 91, 93, 221, 405, 441, 514; freshwater supply, 79; have it tested, 79; hidden, 5, 74; hot, 42, 55, 74, 115, 128,

142, 219, 221, 229, 234, 249, 257, 306, 338, 352, 374, 378, 379, 380, 382, 383, 385, 386, 404, 407, 516, 531; hot water heater, 42, 74, 516; household demand, 83; household use, 83; huge dome of, 534; manmade resources, 39; mineral, 52; mineralized, 83; municipal supply, 81, 532; municipal system, 74, 75; polluted, 39; pool, 76, 84, 540; pump, 189; purification, 34; purify, 69, 71; purifying, 39, 64, 185; purifying methods, 74, 429; quality, 58, 69, 80, 430, 484; safe drinking, 532; saltwater, 71, 90, 91; samples, 72, 209, 375; sea water, 91; softened, 232; standing, 312, 382, 383, 531, 538; storage, 53, 56, 73, 75, 477, 532; storage container, 53, 73; stored, 47, 52, 53, 72, 73, 84, 137, 456, 490, 586; storing, 5, 73; testing, 82; underground sources, 83; wastewater, 68, 393, 427, 430; wells, 209, 375, 532
water and food in nuclear emergencies, 15, 488
water bags: solar heated, 13, 385
water bowl, 50
water chestnut, 103, 280
water conservation: long term indoor, 516
water consumption, 83
water decontamination, 426, 428
water FAQs, 633
water from snow, 489
water main, 45, 487, 537
water purification: dry chlorine, 5, 65; household bleach, 5, 53, 54, 64, 65, 124, 426, 429, 493; hydrogen peroxide, 4, 37, 57, 193, 398, 404; iodine, 37, 54, 55, 56, 67, 633; iodine, Betadine, 51, 54, 55, 113, 202; iodine, Polar Pure, 54, 55, 72; iodine, Potable Aqua, 54, 55; liquid chlorine bleach, 53, 54; ozone, 69, 431; silver, 62; slow sand filters, 67; solar still, 5, 71, 72; stabilized oxygen, 4, 56, 74; tablets, 4, 56; ultraviolet light, 69, 72, 82, 430; wine, 5, 62
water repellent, 35, 386, 558
Water Spinach, 280
water to wash, 427
Watercress, 280
waterfall, 77
watering can, 271
Watermelon, 104, 143, 280

WaterOz, 214
waterproof, 34, 35, 77, 187, 207, 208, 255, 256, 354, 355, 358, 397, 477, 488, 531, 593; containers, 187; matches, 47; waterproofed, 34, 40, 256, 347; waterproofing, 36, 207, 256, 463, 488, 526; wind and waterproof, 256
water-saving pool filter, 516
watershed, 75
waterspouts, 548
watertight pouches, 187
wattage, 306, 310, 355, 366
wattage for each appliance, 306
watts, 184, 304, 306, 307, 310, 312, 332, 355
wax, 103, 111, 144, 193, 240, 241, 242, 243, 249, 258, 280
wax (melted), 246, 247, 257, 258, 259
wax paper, 111, 146, 148, 149, 235, 240, 252, 258, 259, 293
wax-coated pine cones, 184
WD-40, 189, 201
weapon, 33, 41, 408, 409, 410, 411, 416, 432, 446, 447, 481, 484, 498, 499; (-s), 593
weapons of mass destruction, 445
weather, 28, 29, 35, 39, 40, 42, 48, 55, 87, 93, 122, 183, 210, 251, 254, 256, 263, 276, 281, 310, 318, 322, 325, 327, 329, 340, 348, 355, 357, 358, 359, 388, 398, 400, 416, 427, 449, 453, 474, 476, 490, 503, 516, 517, 525, 533, 534, 535, 541, 544, 548, 557, 558, 560, 561, 563, 565, 571, 596; anomalies, 503; stripping, 348, 474
weather-strip doors and windows, 558
webbing, 408
Weber, 334
weed seeds, 274
weep hole, 210, 211
weevils, 277
weight equivalents, 599
well: casing, 66, 75, 209, 211, 488; depth, 209; depth of, 65, 66; diameter, 66; drilled (metric), 66; drilled (U.S.), 66
wells, 5, 6, 15, 65, 75, 91, 489; bored, disinfection, 5, 65; drilled, dinsinfection, 5, 66; hand pump, 75, 93, 209, 210
wells of farms, 489
wench, 188
westerner, 414
wet, 35, 43, 46, 83, 86, 87, 89, 93, 124, 232, 249, 253, 254, 255, 256, 257, 259, 276, 277, 284, 325, 354, 373, 376, 377, 380, 401, 442, 515, 519, 527, 529, 558, 563, 582
Wet/Dry Vac, 309
wheat: (hard red winter), 119; (hard), 115; dishes, 95; flour, 115; germ, 115; mush, 95
wheelbarrow, 188
wheelchairs, 186
wheels lose traction, 562
whipped topping, 147
whippersnipper, 308
whisk broom, 339
whiskey barrels, 80
whistle, 40, 41, 508
white (refined) sugar, 424
White Ash, 252
white flour, 96, 121, 424
white gas, 322
white oak, 252
white pine, 252
white tape, 37
whole grains, 96, 119, 129, 493
whole milk from safe cows, 493
whole wheat, 121, 140, 168
why do I need to prepare?, 596
wick, 240, 241, 242, 245, 246, 247, 248, 249, 250, 254, 258, 326, 569, 572; metal core, 242, 247
widespread torrential rains, 534
wilderness fruit pie filling, 178
willow, 252
wills, 49, 187, 593
wind: direction, 450, 453, 454; power, 304; shield, 326; speed, 454, 482, 534
wind direction, 454; determining, 450
wind speed: determining, 454
windborne objects, 550
windex, 112, 174, 187, 200
window shutter options, 538
windowed room, 127
windowless secured pantry, 122
windscreen, 326, 328, 329, 561
windshield, 559, 561
windstorms, 549, 550
wine, 110, 163, 589
winter blades, 561
winter boots, 563
winter deaths, 558
winter storm, 557, 560; warning, 557; watch, 557
wintergreen, 227, 235
winterize your car, 558
wiper blades, 189
wire, 39, 188, 213, 218, 364, 473; basket, 80, 287; cutters, 188; mesh, 72, 80, 269, 274, 499, 502; racks, 39
Wolfgang Puck, 178; Soup, 178
womb of invincibility, 412
Wonder Water, 215
wood, 23, 53, 62, 121, 136, 207, 231, 237, 246, 251-256, 258-261, 269-271, 323, 327, 333, 334, 338, 339, 343, 346, 347, 364, 366, 382, 390, 391, 397, 438, 441, 462, 478, 483, 489, 491, 510-513, 521, 523, 538, 557, 558, 567, 568; apple tree, 237; ash, 136; basswood, 252; boxwood, 252; CCA treated, 251; cedarwood, 228; cottonwood, 252; firewood, 43, 491, 523; hardwoods, 53, 252; kapok tree, 237; oak, 237; painted, 251; redwood, 81; sandalwood, 228; shaving, 252, 255, 258, 259, 270, 391, 397, 491; shavings, 252, 255, 258, 259, 270, 391, 397, 491
wood chisel, 258
wood-burning fireplace, 43
wooden bridge, 75
wooden mallet, 298
wool, 35, 36, 123, 128, 255, 259, 337, 338, 339, 347, 381; blankets, 47, 182
Worcestershire sauce, 293, 294, 295
work gloves, 48, 183
world series, 20
World Trade Center, 412, 413, 415, 458; bombing, 413
worldwide unrest, 28
worm, 56, 270, 271, 272, 274, 397; (-s), 270, 271, 272, 274; bin, 270, 272; castings (excrement), 272
worm drive, 309
worms: red, 272
wrench, 188
WTC and Pentagon bombing (911), 14, 37, 302, 353, 359, 412, 414, 415, 417, 519, 521, 522, 576
WW2 surplus models, 72
Wyoming: Grand Teton, 543

X

x-ray, 452, 518

Y

ye ole dunny, 13, 395
yeast, 100, 114, 121, 276, 341, 342
Yellow Birch, 252
yellow corn, 115, 493
yellow orange flame, 257
yellow pages, 52, 130, 132
Ylang Ylang, 228
yogurt, 105, 147; containers, 245; laces, 74; shops, 130
yolks, 139, 147, 352, 586
Yoplait, 162
your vehicle, 46, 51, 192, 368, 409, 425, 527, 537, 559, 562, 563, 564, 565
Yousef, 412
yuban, 179
yummy biscuits, 343

Z

zero privacy, 591
Ziploc, 37, 46, 60, 111, 116, 131, 185, 192, 194, 388, 398, 457, 566
Zippo, 257
Zippy, 529
zucchini, 298, 352

Endnotes

[1] Excerpted from Legends of Claddah, Holly Drennan Deyo, 2004

[2] Natural Catastrophes in 2003, Munich Re, January 1, 2004; http://www.munichre.com/pdf/TOPICSgeo_2003_e.pdf

[3] "Billion Dollar U.S. Weather Disasters, 1980-2007", NOAA, National Climatic Data Center, January 31, 2008; http://www.ncdc.noaa.gov/oa/reports/billionz.html

[4] FEMA, Disaster Fact Sheet; January 22, 1998; http://www.fema.gov/pdf/library/stats

[5] Reduction of Risks for Natural and Technical Disasters as a Condition for Sustainable Development; Statement delivered by Raimond Duijsens, Adviser, International Federation of Red Cross and Red Crescent Societies representative, at the 58th UN General Assembly in New York; October 16 2003; http://www.ifrc.org/docs/news/speech03/rd161003.asp

[6] Compiled data from Munich Re annual disaster reports and Centre for Research on the Epidemiology of Disasters, http://www.cred.be/

[7] UN: Disasters on the Rise; The Drudge Report, September 17, 2004; http://www.drudgereport.com/flash.htm

[8] Top Ten Major Disasters Ranked by FEMA Relief Costs, FEMA Disaster Facts Library; http://www.fema.gov/library/df_8.shtm

[9] Insurer Warns of Global Warming Catastrophe, Thomas Atkins, March 3, 2004; http://sg.news.yahoo.com/040303/3/3ihff.html

[10] Lisa R. Thiesse P.O. Box 19, Yelm, WA 98597-0019, updated by Holly Deyo September 2004 and July 2008

[11] "Water FAQs", Patton Turner, copyright 1998, updated by Holly Deyo June 2004, p. 7

[12] "Water FAQs", Patton Turner, copyright 1998, updated by Holly Deyo June 2004, p. 19-22

[13] "Iodine", Victoria J. Drake, Ph.D.; Linus Pauling Institute, Oregon State University, July 2007, http://lpi.oregonstate.edu/infocenter/minerals/iodine/

[14] "Water FAQs", Patton Turner, copyright 1998, updated by Holly Deyo June 2004, pp. 23-24

[15] Robert Byrnes, degreed Chemist with Nalco Chemical Company and eight years as a Water Treatment Specialist with the US Army.

[16] "Water FAQs", Patton Turner, copyright 1998, updated by Holly Deyo June 2004, pp. 22-23

[17] Dr. Trichopoulos, British Medical Journal discussing the Greek Villager's Diet

[18] Lifewater Canada; http://www.lifewater.ca/

[19] A Safe Water Supply Depends on Location and Construction - Bored Well, Illinois Department of Public Health, August 1999, http://www.idph.state.il.us/envhealth/factsheets/boredwlsFS.htm

[20] A Safe Water Supply Depends on Location and Construction - Drilled Wells, Illinois Department of Public Health, August 1999, http://www.idph.state.il.us/envhealth/factsheets/drilledwlsFS.htm

[21] "Water FAQs", Patton Turner, copyright 1998, updated by Holly Deyo June 2004, p.15-16

[22] "Water FAQs", Patton Turner, copyright 1998, updated by Holly Deyo June 2004, pp.24-26

[23] "Water FAQs", Patton Turner, copyright 1998, updated by Holly Deyo June 2004, p.7-9

[24] "Water FAQs", Patton Turner, copyright 1998, updated by Holly Deyo June 2004, p.23

[25] "Water FAQs", Patton Turner, copyright 1998, updated by Holly Deyo June 2004, p.1

[26] "Water FAQs", Patton Turner, copyright 1998, updated by Holly Deyo June 2004, pp.2-4

[27] Sustainable Building Sourcebook; Harvested Rainwater Guidelines; http://www.greenbuilder.com/sourcebook/RainwaterGuide3.html

[28] Sustainable Building Sourcebook; Harvested Rainwater Guidelines; http://www.greenbuilder.com/sourcebook/RainwaterGuide1.html

[29] "Design & Construction of Small Earth Dams", KD Nelson, 1985, p.20

[30] Texas Guide to Rainwater Harvesting, Second Edition 1997, pp. 6-13

[31] Robert Byrnes, degreed Chemist with Nalco Chemical Company and eight years as a Water Treatment Specialist with the US Army.

[32] Adapted from Fats and Cholesterol - The Good, The Bad, and The Healthy Diet; Harvard School of Public Health Nutrition; April 26, 2007

[33] Alcohol: Is Wine Fine, Or Beer Better?; April 26, 2007; Harvard School of Public Health; http://www.hsph.harvard.edu/nutritionsource/alcohol.html

[34] For more information on Cornell bread read "The Cornell Bread Book"-McCAY from Dover, or can be ordered from Jeanette B. McCay, 30 Lakeview Lane, Englewood, FL 33533.

[35] Hantavirus Deaths Reported in Three More Colorado Counties: Coloradans Urged to Take Precautions; Colorado Department of Public Health and Environment; Mark W. Salley; July 17, 2007; http://www.cdphe.state.co.us/release/2007/071707.html

[36] All About Hantaviruses; National Center for Infectious Diseases; June 10, 2004; http://www.cdc.gov/ncidod/diseases/hanta/hps/noframes/prevent.htm

[37] "Storage Life of Dry Food" by Al Durtschi, http://waltonfeed.com/ E-mail: mark@lis.ab.ca; 1999

[38] "Storage Life of Dry Food" by Al Durtschi, http://waltonfeed.com/ E-mail: mark@lis.ab.ca; 1999

[39] Al Durtschi, "A Short Lesson on Oxygen Absorbers"; http://waltonfeed.com/; 4 November 1998.

[40] Storage Life of Dry Food" by Al Durtschi, http://waltonfeed.com/ E-mail: mark@lis.ab.ca; 1996

[41] Defense Supply Center Philadelphia (DSCP) Subsistence Operational Rations Business Unit, Frequently Asked Questions (FAQs), January 2007, page 5, http://www.dscp.dla.mil/subs/rations/faqs.pdf

[42] SOPAKCO, FAQ, MRE Shelf Life, http://www.sopakco.com/faq_mreshelflife.html

[43] Meal, Ready-to-Eat, Individual (MRE), June 29, 2007; NSRDEC; US Army Natick Soldier Research, Development & Engineering Center; OPSEC 02-026; http://nsc.natick.army.mil/media/fact/food/mre.htm

[44] USDA, Food Safety and Inspection Service, Food Product Dating, Food Labeling, February 8, 2007; http://www.fsis.usda.gov/fact_sheets/Food_Product_Dating/index.asp

[45] Durable Life Information On Food Products, Canadian Food Inspection Agency, April 8, 2002; http://www.inspection.gc.ca/english/fssa/concen/tipcon/lifee.shtml

[46] Facts, Figures, and Trends, Costs – and Co-Pays – for Prescription Drugs Soar in the U.S., SC (South Carolina) Budget and Control Board's Employee Insurance Program; http://www.eip.sc.gov/didyouknow/facts.aspx?id=9

[47] Drugs Frequently Potent Past Expiration; Laurie P. Cohen; March 29, 2000; Wall Street Journal

[48] Ibid

[49] Many Medicines Are Potent Years Past Expiration Dates; April 2, 2000; Dr. Joseph Mercola; http://www.mercola.com/2000/apr/2/drug_expiration.htm

[50] Drugs Frequently Potent Past Expiration; Laurie P. Cohen; March 29, 2000; Wall Street Journal

[51] Ibid

[52] Silver Colloids: Do They Work?; Dr. Ronald J. Gibbs; 1999

[53] Silver Colloids, Scientific Information on Colloidal Silver; http://www.silver-colloids.com/Reports/reports.html#CompTable

[54] The Skinny on Charcoal; The Discovery Channel; Hannah Holmes; January 23, 1998; http://www.discovery.com/area/skinnyon/skinnyon980123/skinnyon.html

[55] Fuel For the New Millennium; Joshua and Kaia Taikill; Home Power, August / September 1999

[56] Outside the Grid, August 18, 2003, by Jerry Taylor and Peter VanDoren; http://www.cato.org/research/articles/taylor-030818.html

[57] Keeping Food Safe During An Emergency; Food Safety and Inspection Service, USDA; Sept.6, 2006; http://www.fsis.usda.gov/Fact_Sheets/keeping_food_Safe_during_an_emergency/index.asp

[58] Keeping Food Safe During an Emergency, FSIS, USDA; September 6, 2006; http://www.fsis.usda.gov/Fact_Sheets/keeping_food_Safe_during_an_emergency/index.asp

[59] Geri Guidetti, "Seed Terminator and Mega-Merger Threaten Food and Freedom", Food Supply Update: June 5, 1998

[60] National Center for Genetic Resources Preservation; U.S. Department of Agriculture, Agricultural Research Service, University of Colorado; Frequently Asked Questions; http://www.ars-grin.gov/ncgrp/center_faq.htm

[61] New Recommendations For Drying Fruit Leather And Meat Jerky, Donna Liess, Colorado State University. Cooperative Extension, Weld County, August 26, 2004; http://www.ext.colostate.edu/pubs/columncc/cc031007.html

[62] USING CHILE: Making Ristras, Making Chile Sauce, Circular 533, Priscilla Grijalva, Extension Food and Nutrition Specialist, College of Agriculture and Home Economics, New Mexico State University

[63] Drying Foods at Home, Marjorie M. Philips, Cooperative Extension Service. University of Arkansas, Little Rock, Arkansas

[64] New Recommendations For Drying Fruit Leather And Meat Jerky, Donna Liess, Colorado State University. Cooperative Extension, Weld County, August 26, 2004; http://www.ext.colostate.edu/pubs/columncc/cc031007.html

[65] Home Drying of Food; Utah State University; Charlotte P. Brennand, Extension Food Science Specialist; FN-330, August 1994

[66] Bush: Blackouts A 'Wake-Up Call', CBS News, August 15, 2003; http://www.cbsnews.com/stories/2003/08/15/politics/main568596.shtml

[67] Ibid

[68] Will Anyone Pay for the 'Smart' Power Grid?, Martin LaMonica, May 16, 2007; CNet News, http://www.news.com/Will-anyone-pay-for-the-smart-power-grid/2100-11392_3-6184046.html

[69] Xcel Energy Announces First Smart Grid City in the Nation, Xcel Energy press release; March 18, 2008; http://www.xcelenergy.com/XLWEB/CDA/0,3080,1-1-1_15531_46991-45401-0_0_0-0,00.html

[70] U.S. Power Grid's Unreliability Enabled By Legislation, Diane M. Grassi, August 8, 2006; Renew America, http://www.renewamerica.us/columns/grassi/060808

[71] Diesel Generator Power Is A Sensible Choice Especially When Integrated Into The Total System, Backwoods Home Magazine, by Skip Thomsen, Issue 28, http://www.backwoodshome.com/articles/thomsen43.html

[72] Staff Review Of Portable Generator Safety ©2006, page 8, Janet Buyer, Project Manager Directorate for Engineering Sciences (301)504-7542, www.cpsc.gov/library/foia/foia07/brief/PortableGenerators.pdf

[73] "Fuel Degradation In Storage - Are You Prepared?", Yellowstone River Trading, http://www.y2ksurvivalfood.com/fueldegradation.html

[74] "Is your groundwater protected from your fuel handling and storage activities?" University of North Carolina Farm ASyst Program; #2- IMPROVING FUEL STORAGE; http://h2osparc.wq.ncsu.edu/info/farmassit/f_fuel.html

[75] Gas Thefts Climb Along With Prices; June 1, 2004; The Tampa Tribune; http://www.tampatrib.com/MGBUQPABXUD.html

[76] Suspect Allegedly Pilfered 20,000 Gallons of Gas; Scott Gutierrez, Seattle Post-Intelligencer; March 21, 2008; http://seattlepi.nwsource.com/local/356078_gastheft21.html

[77] State of the Barbecue Industry Report, 2007, Hearth, Patio & Barbecue Association, http://www.hpba.org/

[78] Louise Seeley, Founding member of Solar Box Cooking Northwest; http://www.accessone.com/~sbcn

[79] Cell Phone Drops Calls? Blame the Sun, Robert Roy Britt, March 6, 2002, http://www.space.com/scienceastronomy/solarsystem/cell_phone_020306.html

[80] Beijing Secretly Fires Lasers to Disable US Satellites, Francis Harris, Sept. 26, 2006; The Telegraph; http://www.telegraph.co.uk/news/worldnews/1529864/Beijing-secretly-fires-lasers-to-disable-US-satellites.html

[81] Chinese Missile Destroys Satellite in Space, Richard Spencer, Jan. 19, 2007, The Telegraph; http://www.telegraph.co.uk/news/worldnews/1539948/Chinese-missile-destroys-satellite-in-space.html

[82] Hurricane Katrina Amateur Radio Emergency Communications Relief Effort Operations Review Summary, Gregory Sarratt; March 7, 2006; American Radio Relay League, http://www.fcc.gov/pshs/docs/advisory/hkip/GSpeakers060306/ACT1045.pdf

[83] Amateur Radio and the Hayman Fire, Jeff Ryan, December 2002, QST Magazine

[84] Shortwave Radio FAQ, Stas Bekman May 8, 2008; http://stason.org/TULARC/radio/shortwave/07-Could-you-explain-the-frequencies-used-What-s-the-49-met.html

[85] Understanding SWR by Example, Darrin Walraven, K5DVW; QST Magazine, November 2006

[86] The Infantry Reconnaissance Platoon And Squad (Airborne, Air Assault, Light Infantry), FM 7-92; December 23, 1992, updated December 13, 2001; Appendix E Communications

[87] Ibid

[88] Radio Nets, June 24, 2010; http://www2.mmae.ucf.edu/wiki/Radio_nets#Hurricane_nets/

[89] "Camp Hygiene"; Buck Tilton, MS, WEMT, and director of the Wilderness Institute; http://www.gorp.com/nyoutdoors/articles/hygiene.htm

[90] Talking About Disasters, FEMA, February 11, 2003; http://www.fema.gov/rrr/talkdiz/kit.shtm

[91] "Camp Hygiene"; Buck Tilton, MS, WEMT, and director of the Wilderness Institute; http://www.gorp.com/nyoutdoors/articles/hygiene.htm

[92] "Camp Sanitation"; Back Country Horsemen Guidebook; Chapter 20; http://bchc.com/BCHEA6-20.htm

[93] Veterinary Q & A: Pancreatitis in Dogs and Cat; Janet Tobiassen Crosby, DVM, http://vetmedicine.about.com/library/weekly/aa111700a.htm

[94] The Dangers of Rawhide Chewies, http://nmnm.essortment.com/rawhidechew_rbzt.htm

[95] Chocolate & Other Dangerous Goodies; Dr. Lucy L. Pinkston, D.V.M., 2003, http://www.dog.com/vet/holidays/04.html#4

[96] Chemical Plant Security; CRS Report for Congress, Linda-Jo Schierow, Specialist in Environmental Policy Resources, Science, and Industry Division; Page 7, January 20, 2004; Library of Congress; http://64.233.167.104/search?q=cache:vwPPjh6AM5gJ:www.fas.org/irp/crs/RL31530.pdf+%22Nidal+Ayyad%22+%2B+Rutgers&hl=en&ie=UTF-8

[97] "The World Trade Center Bomb: Who is Ramzi Yousef? And Why It Matters"; Federation of American Scientists; Laurie Mylroie; http://www.fas.org/irp/world/iraq/956-tni.htm

[98] Terrorism Sneaks Ashore, Holly D. Deyo; Building Community newsletter; September 30, 2000; http://standeyo.com/News_Files/Newsletters/News000930_10f5NCB/News_NBC_Pt1.html

[99] To Her Doom: Bin Laden Reads Poem About USS Cole's Fate at Son's Wedding; March 1, 2001; http://abcnews.go.com/sections/world/DailyNews/afghanistan010301_binladen.html

[100] Report: City Will Take $83B Hit Due to Attacks; November 16, 2001; By Elizabeth Sanger, Newsday; http://www.nycp.org/Web_News/Impact_Study_Press/Newsday_com%20-%20Report%20City%20Will%20Take%20$83B%20Hit%20Due%20to%20Attacks.htm

[101] Bin Laden Hails September 11 Economic Losses; April 18, 2002; CNN; http://www.cnn.com/2002/WORLD/asiapcf/central/04/17/bin.laden.tape/?related

[102] MIT Grad with Links to Al Qaeda Plotted to Kill Former U.S. Presidents, Authorities Say, August 14, 2008; Jana Winter, Fox News, http://www.foxnews.com/story/0,2933,404164,00.html

[103] USAMRIID's Medical Management of Biological Casualties Handbook; Sixth Edition April 2005; p. 11; http://www.usamriid.army.mil/education/instruct.htm

[104] Ibid, p. 120

[105] Ibid, p. 120

[106] Methods of Water Purification; from "Pure Water Handbook"; March 1, 1992; Osmonics, Inc; http://www.osmonics.com/products/Page716.htm

[107] Ibid

[108] Treatment Systems for Household Water Supplies; Fred Bergsrud, Water Quality Coordinator, Minnesota Extension Service; Bruce Seelig, Water Quality Specialist, North Dakota Extension Service; Russell Derickson; Extension Associate in Water and Natural Resources, South Dakota Extension Service; June 1992; North Dakota State University; http://www.ext.nodak.edu/extpubs/h2oqual/watsys/ae1047w.htm

[109] Water Conditioning and Purifying Magazine; 1993; http://www.cetsolar.com/uvdisinfection.htm

[110] Breathe No Evil; Stephen Quayle and Duncan Long; 1996; Safe-Trek Publishing

[111] Wannemacher RW Jr, Dinterman RE, Thompson WL, Schmidt MO, Burrows WS. Treatment for Removal of Biotoxins From Drinking Water; Fort Detrick, Frederick, MD: US Army Biomedical Research and Development Laboratory; Sept. 1993. Technical Report 9120.

[112] Anthrax Risk and Prevention; Jeanne Guillemin; October 15, 2001; http://www.cnn.com/2001/COMMUNITY/10/15/guillemin/

[113] USAMRIID's Medical Management of Biological Casualties Handbook; Fourth Edition February 2001; http://usamriid.detrick.army.mil/education/bluebook/bluebook.pdf for information on Isolation and Decontamination and Outbreak Control; and Virtual Naval Hospital Information for Providers; http://www.vnh.org/Providers.html

[114] Will Duct Tape and Plastic Really Work? Issues Related To Expedient Shelter-In-Place; John H. Sorensen and Barbara M. Vogt; ORNL/TM-2001/154; Oak Ridge National Laboratory; August 2001, p. 2

[115] Fourteen Days in October: The Cuban Missile Crisis; Overview of the Crisis; ThinkQuest Team 11046, 1999, http://library.thinkquest.org/11046/days/index.html

[116] Preparing for Doomsday: A year before Cuban crisis, JFK urged protection from fallout, The White House, Sept. 7, 1961; http://www.cnn.com/SPECIALS/cold.war/experience/the.bomb/jfk.essay/

[117] Nuclear Attack on D.C. a Hypothetical Disaster, By Gary Emerling, Washington Times; April 16, 2008; http://www.washingtontimes.com/apps/pbcs.dll/article?AID=/20080416/METRO/556828862/1001

[118] Ready America: Nuclear Threat; http://www.ready.gov/america/beinformed/nuclear.html

[119] U.S. Called Unprepared For Nuclear Terrorism, Experts Critical of Evacuation Plans; John Mintz; May 3, 2005; The Washington Post

[120] DOE, National Nuclear Security Administration, Atmospheric Photo Library, http://www.nv.doe.gov/news&pubs/photos&films/atm.htm

[121] The U.S. Nuclear War Plan: A Time for Change, Matthew G. McKinzie, Thomas B. Cochran, Robert S. Norris, William M. Arkin, Natural Resources Defense Council; June 2001, p. 31

[122] Wikipedia, Nuclear Explosion, http://www.fact-index.com/n/nu/nuclear_explosion.html

[123] Nuclear Weapon Detonation, Fact Sheet #36, pp. 2-3, Washington State Department of Health, July 2002, http://www.doh.wa.gov/ehp/rp/factsheets/factsheets-pdf/fs36nucwpdet.pdf.

[124] The Effects of Nuclear War, Washington: Office of Technology Assessment, Congress of the United States, 1979

[125] Radiation Safety Manual Radioisotopes; 5.0 Radiation Measurement; Radford University; http://www.radford.edu/~facman/Safety/Radiation/chp5.htm

[126] Fallout Protection: What to Know and Do About Nuclear Attack; DOD, Office of Civil Defense, H-6, Dec. 1961, p. 6

[127] The Need for Civil Defense, Protecting Our People, Rod Martin, 2001, http://www.natreformassn.org/statesman/01/protect.html

[128] Dirty Bomb Called 'All but Inevitable', Keay Davidson, San Francisco Chronicle, September 5, 2004, http://www.sfgate.com/cgi-bin/article.cgi?file=/c/a/2004/09/05/MNGJE8KA5N1.DTL

[129] "New York Takes Another Hit," Spencer E. Ante, Amy Barrett, and Paul Magnusson, BusinessWeek Online, September 19, 2005; http://www.businessweek.com/magazine/content/05_38/b3951012.htm

[130] Video of Sleeping Guards Shakes Nuclear Industry, Steven Mufson, The Washington Post; January 4, 2008

[131] Prudent Places USA – 3rd Edition, Operational Nuclear Reactors, Holly Deyo, July 2005; ISBN: 0-9727688-1-5

[132] Unnecessary Risk: The Case for Retiring Oyster Creek Nuclear Power Plant; p. 11, NJPIRG Law & Policy Center; Spring, 2002; http://www.jerseyshorenuclearwatch.org/NJPIRG.htm

[133] Potassium Iodide as a Thyroid Blocking Agent in Radiation Emergencies; U.S. Department of Health and Human Services; Food and Drug Administration Center for Drug Evaluation and Research (CDER); December 2001; p. 6, http://www.fda.gov/cder/guidance/index.htm

[134] Nuclear War Survival Skills, by Cresson Kearny, Chapter 8; pp 71-74; http://oism.org/nwss/s73p919.htm

[135] Electromagnetic Pulse Threats to U.S. Expeditionary Operations in 2010; Major Colin R. Miller, USAF; April 2005; pp. 18-24.

[136] House Military Research and Development Subcommittee, Statement of Dr. George W. Ullrich, Deputy Director, Defense Special Weapons Agency, 16 July 1997.

[137] High Power Microwaves: Strategic and Operational Implications for Warfare, Colonel Eileen M. Walling, USAF, February 2000

[138] Electromagnetic Pulse Threats to U.S. Expeditionary Operations in 2010; Major Colin R. Miller, USAF; April 2005; p. 6.

[139] Empty Shelves, Long Lines Test S. Floridians' Patience, Oscar Corral, Daniel De Vise, Christina Hoag; The Miami Herald Sun, September 3, 2004; http://www.miami.com/mld/miamiherald/news/local/states/florida/counties/broward_county/9568660.htm

[140] Adapted from Natural Resources Canada; http://www.seismo.nrcan.gc.ca/

[141] Solar Flare Leaves Sun Quaking, W.W. Hansen Experimental Physics Laboratory of Stanford University and the Solar and Astrophysics Laboratory of the Lockheed-Martin Advanced Technology Center, May 27, 1998; http://soi.stanford.edu/press/agu05-98/

[142] Surprises From SOHO Include Tornadoes on the Sun, April 24, 1998, European Space Agency Press Release; http://solar-center.stanford.edu/news/tornadoes.html

[143] "Global warming - Is the Sun to Blame?"; BBC News Online; David Whitehouse; June 3, 1999; http://news.bbc.co.uk/2/hi/science/nature/358953.stm

[144] The Biggest Solar X-Ray Flare Ever Is Classified as X28, ESA Space Science, November 6, 2003 http://www.esa.int/export/esaSC/SEMNFTWLDMD_index_0.html)

[145] Biggest Ever Solar Flare Was Even Bigger Than Thought, March 16, 2004; American Geophysical Union and Science Daily; http://www.sciencedaily.com/releases/2004/03/040316072425.htm

[146] Krasnoyarets Newspaper; July 13, 1908; http://desires.com/1.6/Travel/Siberia/Docs/Siberia2.html

[147] TUNGUSKA: The Cosmic Mystery of the Century; by Planetarium Director, Roy A. Gallant; http://www.usm.maine.edu/~planet/tung.html

[148] "The Last Great Impact on Earth," Discover Magazine, September, 1996

[149] Impact Crater Discovery; European Space Agency; April 18, 2005; http://earth.esa.int/rtd/Projects/ICDY/

[150] Spaceguard UK, Impact Probabilities; http://www.spaceguarduk.com/impactprob.htm

[151] This height would be 11,100 feet or 3,380 meters or 2.1023 miles or 3.3833 kilometers.

[152] "Statement on The Threat of Impact by Near-Earth Asteroids" by Dr. Clark R. Chapman to Subcommittee on Space and Aeronautics of the Committee on Science of the U.S. House of Representatives; May 21, 1998

[153] Does Spaceguard Make Us Safer or Just More Comfortable?, David Morrison, January 15, 2004, NASA, http://128.102.38.40/impact/news_detail.cfm?ID=133

[154] "HAZARD FROM THE SKIES?"; by Clark R. Chapman, 5 April 1998 (updated April 22, 1998)

[155] NASA Blasted for Ignoring Smaller Asteroids, Jeff Hecht, New Scientist, November 9, 2007; http://space.newscientist.com/article/dn12900-nasa-blasted-for-ignoring-smaller-asteroids.html

[156] Ibid.

[157] NEO Preparedness Act (Introduced in House), H. R. 4917; December 19, 2007; Library of Congress, http://thomas.loc.gov/cgi-bin/query/z?c110:H.R.4917

[158] Spaceguard: Current Progress and Future Capabilities, May 28, 2004, NASA Ames Research Center, http://128.102.38.40/impact/news_detail.cfm?ID=143

[159] Don Quijote, Toutatis, and & Sagan, NASA, August 19, 2004, http://128.102.38.40/impact/news_detail.cfm?ID=144

[160] Tornado Climatology, NOAA, National Severe Storms Laboratory; http://www.nssl.noaa.gov/primer/tornado/tor_climatology.html

[161] U.S. Tornado Property Damage; Economic and Other Societal Impacts Related to Hurricanes, Floods, Tornadoes, Lightning, and Other U.S. Weather Phenomena; Extreme Weather Sourcebook 2001; University of Colorado; http://sciencepolicy.colorado.edu/sourcebook/tornadoes.html

[162] Prudent Places USA — 2nd Edition, Volatile Volcanoes, Holly Deyo, July 2004; ISBN: 0-9727688-1-5

[163] CPSC and NKHA Stress Kerosene Heater Safety, U.S. Consumer Product Safety Commission, February 2001, http://www.cpsc.gov/cpscpub/pubs/463.html

[164] *Why do we lose most of our heat through our heads when we exercise?* Barry S. Brown, PhD; Professor of Kinesiology at University of Arkansas; March 2008; http://researchfrontiers.uark.edu/12401.php

[165] The Next Pandemic?, March 1, 2007; Canadian Broadcasting Centre News, http://www.cbc.ca/news/background/avianflu/

[166] Quarantine Lifted For Bird Flu Farm, Benson McCulloch, News Talk Radio 650, http://www.newstalk650.com/incoming/20080205/quarantine-lifted-bird-flu-farm-0

[167] Bird Flu Found In Texas, February 23, 2004; AP, http://www.cbsnews.com/stories/2004/02/24/health/main601877.shtml

[168] U.S. Confirms Low-Risk Bird Flu in Virginia Turkeys, July 12, 2007; Reuters, http://www.enn.com/top_stories/article/6918

[169] The Global Economic and Financial Impact of an Avian Flu Pandemic and the Role of the IMF, Avian Flu Working Group (in consultation with Departments and the Joint Bank-Fund Health Services Department, February 28, 2006; p. 3

[170] "The Story of Influenza", in Knobler S, Mack A, Mahmoud A, Lemon S: The Threat of Pandemic Influenza: Are We Ready? Workshop Summary (2005). Washington, D.C.: The National Academies Press, pp. 60–61.

[171] Avian Influenza A (H5N1) Infection in Humans, The New England Journal of Medicine, Volume 353:1374-1385, September 29, 2005, pp. 4-5, http://content.nejm.org/cgi/content/full/353/13/1374

[172] Ibid.

[173] The Next Pandemic?, March 1, 2007; Canadian Broadcasting Centre News, http://www.cbc.ca/news/background/avianflu/

[174] Avian Flu Virus Showing Resistance to Tamiflu, By Katrina Woznicki, MedPage Today, September 30, 2005; http://www.medpagetoday.com/PublicHealthPolicy/PublicHealth/tb/1850

[175] Tamiflu And Relenza Should Have Psychiatric Side Effects Warning, Say Regulators, Medical News Today, November 24, 2007; http://www.medicalnewstoday.com/articles/89734.php

[176] PanFlu: Colorado Physician Preparedness, Pandemic Flu Preparedness Guide; December 18, 2006; http://www.pandemicflu.gov/plan/healthcare/maskguidancehc.html

[177] Respiratory Protection and Avian Influenza Viruses Frequently Asked Questions, October 6, 2005; http://www.3m.com/intl/NZ/english/Avian_Bird_Flu/index.htm

[178] Guidance on Preparing Workplaces for an Influenza Pandemic, U.S. Department of Labor, Occupational Safety and Health Administration, OSHA 3327-02N, 2007, pp. 31-32

[179] Ibid, p. 21

[180] Letter from Rıfat Coskun, Veterinary Surgeon, Animal Health Branch Manager, April 25, 2006; NanoMask and Bird Flu in Turkey, http://birdfluprotection.com/nanomasks/nanomask_turkey_bird_flu.htm

[181] Simple Respiratory Mask, Emerging Infectious Diseases; Virginia M. Dato, David Hostler, and Michael E. Hahn, University of Pittsburgh, Pittsburgh, Pennsylvania; Volume 12, Number 6, June 2006, pp. 1033; Centers for Disease Control; http://www.cdc.gov/ncidod/eid/vol12no06/05-1468-G.htm

[182] Ibid. p. 1034

[183] quoting Dr. Michael Osterholm, infectious disease expert; University of Minnesota, Americans Brace for Avian Flu Pandemic, By Rosanne Skirble, November 2005, Voice of America, http://www.voanews.com/english/archive/2005-11/2005-11-04-voa51.cfm?CFID=44217395&CFTOKEN=74598614

[184] Revival of U.S. Rural Areas Signals Heartland No Longer a Hinterland, by Allison Tarmann, Populatio Reference Bureau, January 2003, http://www.prb.org/Articles/2003/RevivalofUSRuralAreasSignalsHeartlandNoLongeraHinterland.aspx

[185] Ibid.

[186] Fear of 'Catastrophic' Crash Rising Despite Bull Market, John Melloy, CNBC; February 18, 2010; http://www.cnbc.com/id/41655262

[187] Evacuees Survey Fires' Wrath, November 3, 2003; CBS News, http://www.cbsnews.com/stories/2003/11/04/national/main581663.shtml